PRO Football WEEKLY
1994 ALMANAC

Pro Football Weekly
1994 ALMANAC

By Richard Whittingham
and the Editors of Pro Football Weekly

A Perigee Book

Perigee Books
are published by
The Berkley Publishing Group
200 Madison Avenue
New York, NY 10016

Copyright © 1994 Pro Football Weekly
First Perigee edition: August 1994

All rights reserved. This book, or parts thereof,
may not be reproduced in any form without permission.
Published simultaneously in Canada.

Cover photo ©1994 by Bruce L. Schwartzman

Printed in the United States of America
1   2   3   4   5   6   7   8   9   10

TABLE OF CONTENTS

1994 Preview

The 1994 season	8
Week-by-week schedule	13
PFW predictions	15
Arizona Cardinals	16
Atlanta Falcons	24
Buffalo Bills	32
Chicago Bears	40
Cincinnati Bengals	48
Cleveland Browns	56
Dallas Cowboys	64
Denver Broncos	72
Detroit Lions	80
Green Bay Packers	88
Houston Oilers	96
Indianapolis Colts	104
Kansas City Chiefs	112
Los Angeles Raiders	120
Los Angeles Rams	128
Miami Dolphins	136
Minnesota Vikings	144
New England Patriots	152
New Orleans Saints	160
New York Giants	168
New York Jets	176
Philadelphia Eagles	184
Pittsburgh Steelers	192
San Diego Chargers	200
San Francisco 49ers	208
Seattle Seahawks	216
Tampa Bay Buccaneers	224
Washington Redskins	232
Draft analysis	240
Free-agency analysis	248

All rosters and team previews are as of May 13.

PREVIEW '94: Jerry Rice will try to lead the 49ers back to the Super Bowl

1993 Review

Top 10 stories of 1993	256
Week-by-week reviews	258
Playoffs	312
Super Bowl XXVIII	318
Pro Bowl	321
Atlanta Falcons	322
Buffalo Bills	324
Chicago Bears	326
Cincinnati Bengals	328
Cleveland Browns	330
Dallas Cowboys	332
Denver Broncos	334
Detroit Lions	336
Green Bay Packers	338
Houston Oilers	340
Indianapolis Colts	342
Kansas City Chiefs	344

CON'T ON PAGE 6

REVIEW '93: The Dallas Cowboys won their second consecutive Super Bowl

CON'T FROM PAGE 5
Los Angeles Raiders 346
Los Angeles Rams 348
Miami Dolphins 350
Minnesota Vikings 352
New England Patriots 354
New Orleans Saints 356
New York Giants 358
New York Jets 360
Philadelphia Eagles 362
Phoenix Cardinals 364
Pittsburgh Steelers 366
San Diego Chargers 368
San Francisco 49ers 370
Seattle Seahawks 372
Tampa Bay Buccaneers 374
Washington Redskins 376
1993 standings 378
Individual statistics 379
Team statistics 394
Team rankings 396
Efficiency charts, turnover table .. 398
1993 awards 399
Golden Toe Award 402

Records, honors and history
Individual player records 404
Team records 410
Super Bowl records 414
Chronological records 418
Top 20 lists 420
Coaching records 423
Annual leaders 424
Hall of Fame 430
Past PFW awards 434
League champions 436
Super Bowl summaries 438
NFL historical highlights 442
NFL directory 446
Tie-breaking procedures 447

PRO FOOTBALL WEEKLY STAFF
Publisher/Editor	**Hub Arkush**	Contributing editor	**Joel Buchsbaum**
Editor-in-chief/Associate publisher	**Rick Korch**	Art director	**Bob Peters**
Managing editor	**Ron Pollack**	Newstand manager	**Jim McClevey**
Executive editor	**Neil Warner**	General manager	**Fred Arkush**
Senior editors	**Steve Silverman**	Sales manager	**Bob Sherman**
	Dan Arkush	Subscription manager	**Nelson Rodriguez**
Assistant editor	**Keith Schleiden**		

SECTION

I

1994 Preview

PRO FOOTBALL WEEKLY 1994 ALMANAC

PREVIEW: THE 1994 SEASON

The slowly evolving game of professional football has been moving at fast forward for the past year. The game our fathers and grandfathers grew up with has become dramatically different. Free-agency has changed it. A salary cap has squeezed it. Rule changes have altered it. A new TV network will provide a different image. Even the game's lifeblood, the annual draft of college players, has been visited by the plastic surgeon.

All of these changes are of the major-league variety. They affect players, coaches, fans, management, advertisers and the media. The face of the game, once as familiar as Abraham Lincoln's on Mount Rushmore, now is more like a chameleon, constantly reinventing itself to suit its own purposes.

Wanted: More touchdowns

The 1993 season was marked by a dearth of touchdowns and a plethora of field goals. Scores of 9-6, 15-9 and 12-10 became familiar. The ratio of touchdowns to field goals, which once was as high as 6-1 in the 1950's, had fallen to 4-3 in 1993. Quarterbacks couldn't get into the endzone, and placekickers began to dominate. Grumblings were heard from the fans in the far reaches of the upper decks and the owners in the luxury suites. "Something has to be done," was the cry. The NFL did not turn a deaf ear to its critics. Instead, it changed the rules and will penalize teams whose kickers are unsuccessful. Instead of returning the ball to the line of scrimmage on failed attempts, the defending team will get to put the ball in play from the spot where the kick was attempted.

The idea behind the change was to make coaches think twice before kicking the three-pointer on 4th-and-5 or less when in field goal territory. Instead of kicking a 37-yard field goal, coaches will more often decide to go for it.

"The field goal will still be a part of the game," said Giant coach Dan Reeves. "And, as a matter of fact, good kickers will be of greater importance than they were."

Pittsburgh PK Gary Anderson said the rule change might be designed at limiting the importance of kickers, but that it was not enough to affect their job security. "You're down by two points late in the fourth quarter, there's only one way to end a game. And that isn't changing."

Another startling change was the approval of the two-point conversion option, a throwback to the American Football League and a key strategic element of the college game. Its effect will likely be seen when teams are trailing by eight or 11 points, but it won't likely be used when a team is down by seven in the late going with a chance to win if a touchdown is scored and a two-point conversion is attempted.

"I don't think teams will try to win with a two-pointer," said George Young, co-chairman of the rule-making competition committee. "The time it will come into play is when you're behind by eight points or 11 points."

"I don't think you'll see the prevent defense when a team is up by eight in the fourth quarter," said Green Bay coach Mike Holmgren. "In the past, you'd be willing to let a team march down the field on you to use time. You'd even let them score and get within a point. Now, if you do that, you're facing overtime."

The league will try to put more pizazz in the return game by moving kickoffs back to the 30-yard line. Also, the kicks will come off a one-inch tee (previously three-inch tees were used by all kickers) that will assure lower kickoffs that are more easily returned.

In an effort to improve communication between the sidelines and the quarterback, teams will have the option of using a radio communication system. The system, which costs about $25,000 per unit, will allow a coach on the sideline to call a play that will be heard in a headset inside the quarterback's helmet. The system should be especially effective for visiting teams playing before loud and vociferous crowds.

The league will also strictly enforce the five-yard no-contact rule for defensive backs and the one-step rule for pass rushers. In addition, a defensive lineman will be penalized the first time he enters the neutral zone, causing the offensive lineman opposite him to move.

Changing channels

The rule changes impact the on-field product, but the Fox network's $1.58 billion payment to the NFL over the next four seasons for the rights to televise NFC games has affected the league's overall image and set the broadcasting world on its ear. By accepting Fox's huge bid, the NFL said goodbye to CBS after a 38-year relationship of broadcasting NFL games. It's difficult to overstate this changing of the guard, and some industry observers called it the single biggest change in television programming history.

Fox made its huge bid even though owner Rupert Murdoch is guaranteed to lose more than $600 million over the course of the contract. Fox wanted to lift its profile nationally by being associated with

---

Quick look

Major rule changes for the 1994 season:
1. Two-point conversion option is adopted.
2. Kickoffs moved back to 30-yard line.
3. Defending teams will be given the football at the spot where unsuccessful field-goal attempts were attempted.

8

1994 PREVIEW ■ INTRODUCTION

Free-agent QB Scott Mitchell (far left) struck it rich as a free agent, Steeler PK Gary Anderson (above) will feel the impact of a rule change and Fox Broadcasting's Rupert Murdoch changed the face of television.

NFL football, but it also wanted to defend its turf from the onslaught of the new networks that have been announced by media conglomerates Paramount and Time Warner.

While NFL owners and players were thrilled to receive a bid that was $380 million higher than CBS was willing to pay, Fox has only 139 affiliates, including 120 that broadcast on the UHF band. CBS has approximately 200 affiliates, and that means that there will be some areas of the country that are not yet wired for cable and thus will not be able to pick up Fox's NFC broadcasts.

CBS Sports officials went into shock when they learned that they no longer had NFL broadcast rights.

"It's a terrible disappointment," said former CBS Sports president Neil Pilson, who was out of a job less than six months after losing the rights. "Total sadness. It comes as something of a surprise.

"Obviously, we would have preferred to stay with NFL football, but that decision has been made. We must go on from here."

CBS did make a bid to wrest AFC telecasts away from NBC, but NFL owners stuck with NBC because they said they had come to a "verbal agreement" with that network several days prior to making its decision to sell NFC broadcast rights to Fox. And, with that decision, broadcasting giant CBS was out in the cold.

Murdoch originally wanted to get the AFC games because he didn't believe there was any way the NFL owners would allow him to take the more lucrative NFC package from CBS, but he soon found out differently.

The NFL owners were willing to make the seismic change because they were faced with the prospects of skyrocketing player salaries as a result of free-agency. With the new television deal behind them, owners like Jerry Jones of Dallas and Pat Bowlen of Denver wanted the security of the increased revenue that Fox was able to provide. They got exactly what they wanted.

Bull market

While free-agency had come to fruition more than a year earlier, it had a much larger effect in the 1994 offseason than it had the previous year. By early May, more than 80 players had changed teams.

Three of the more notable signings included QB Erik Kramer flying out of Detroit to play with the Bears after signing a three-year, $8.1 million contract, QB Scott Mitchell leaving the Dolphins to sign a three-year, $11 million deal with the Lions, and CB Albert Lewis leaving the Chiefs and moving on to the arch-rival Raiders for four years and $7 million. Also, OLB Seth Joyner and DE Clyde Simmons left the Eagles and joined their old buddy, head coach Buddy Ryan, in Arizona with the Cardinals.

Lion head coach Wayne Fontes looked like a man who held the winning $50 million Lotto ticket when the Lions signed Mitchell, who had been pursued by the division-rival Vikings and several other teams.

"We considered him the best quarterback available and we set our sights on him," said Fontes. "I feel very good about our QB situation."

After the Bears signed Kramer, they unceremoniously dumped Jim Harbaugh, who had signed a three-year, $13 million contract in 1993 and had been Chicago's first-round draft choice in 1987. Harbaugh believes that his release by the Bears is indicative of the new way of doing business in the NFL, especially where high-priced quarterbacks are concerned.

"The quarterback position has always had a lot of pressure to do well," Harbaugh said after signing with the Colts. "Now it's even worse. It's become so easy now for teams to just get another guy when theirs doesn't do well. But it sure doesn't do much for stability."

The signing of Simmons and Joyner with the newly renamed Arizona Cardinals was not a surprise because both had been huge boosters of Ryan during his tenure in Philadelphia. Simmons is coming off an average year in Philadelphia, but Joyner is considered one of the top three outside linebackers in the game.

"Buddy's the one who brought me into the game and schooled me in how the game is meant to be played," Simmons said. "This is an exciting time for me. I started to go sour on things in Philly, and finding a new place was the right thing."

While players like Mitchell, Kramer and Simmons received the financial benefits of free-agency, many veteran players around the league felt its sting. Because the league imposed a $34.6 million salary cap on each team, many productive, solid players who weren't superstars had to be cut so that clubs could stay under the cap. Players like the Bears' Steve McMichael, the Giants' Mark Jackson, the Patriots' Marv Cook, the Lions' Bill Fralic, the Redskins' Al Noga and the Colts' Jack Trudeau were among those sent packing due to salary-cap considerations.

A change at the top

From the category that truth is indeed stranger than fiction, it's difficult to believe the Cowboys will try to win their third-straight Super Bowl title ... with Barry Switzer as head coach. The partnership of former head coach Jimmy Johnson and owner Jerry Jones had always been a volatile one. Both men had all-consuming egos, and a bad scene at an NFL offseason party precipitated the incredible breakup of the two.

Five years earlier, Jones and Johnson had ridden into Dallas vowing to return the franchise to its days of glory. With a shrewd trading and drafting strategy as their base, Jones and Johnson more than lived up to their promise. Johnson's football acumen and coaching skills gave Jones back-to-back Super Bowl champions, and the owner wanted to be viewed as more than just the guy who wrote the checks. When he attempted to take some of the credit for the Cowboys' on-field success, Johnson bristled. When Jones would walk on to the sidelines late in the game to join celebrations, Johnson seethed. Bit by bit, the relationship crumbled until it was no longer workable.

Johnson decided in late March that he had had enough of Jones, and they announced their public divorce in front of a media horde. Jones brought in Switzer, the former Oklahoma coach who had won three national championships but had been out of the game for the past five years after numerous controversies left him in an untenable situation with the administration at Oklahoma. Switzer had been one of Jones' coaches when the owner played college football at Arkansas in the early 1960's, and he was the first name on Jones' list of replacement candidates for Johnson.

Switzer accepted the job with the enthusiasm of a man whose career had just been rescued from the scrapheap, which it had indeed been. While amitting he was not familiar with the Cowboy personnel, he said that his primary goal was to keep the team together so it could win that third-straight Super Bowl.

"We've got to keep this thing going in the same direction, keep it moving down the middle of the highway," Switzer said. "And keep it out of the ditch."

In addition to Switzer taking over for Johnson, June Jones replaced Jerry Glanville in Atlanta, Buddy Ryan took over for Joe Bugel in Arizona, Pete Carroll received the Jet head-coaching job after Bruce Coslet was fired, and Norv Turner replaced Richie Petitbon after Petitbon's one sea-

Jerry Jones (left) and Jimmy Johnson weren't always at each other's throats

1994 PREVIEW ■ INTRODUCTION

son on the job in Washington. While all of those coaching changes had stories worth telling, none could compare with the soap-opera-like breakup of those two good buddies, Jimmy and Jerry.

Future shock

Being drafted in the first round used to be a ticket to long-term financial security in the NFL. The collective-bargaining agreement between the league and the NFL Players Association changed that because, along with implementing a salary cap for each team, it also imposed salary restrictions for rookies.

The top players in the draft will still do well, as evidenced by the six-year, $14.4 million contract signed by No. 1 draft pick DT Dan "Big Daddy" Wilkinson of the Bengals. The former Ohio Stater left school with two years of eligibility remaining because he has the extremely rare combination of size, speed, power and strength that will almost certainly allow him to become a Pro Bowl performer by his third or fourth season — at the latest.

After Wilkinson was selected, nine of the next 12 draftees were defensive players. The exceptions: Indianapolis picked RB Marshall Faulk (2nd), Washington took QB Heath Shuler (3rd) and Tampa Bay chose QB Trent Dilfer (6th).

Faulk was not only the most productive runner in the draft, he also performed brilliantly in private workouts with scouts. Shuler demonstrated the athletic and QB skills to allow the Redskins to cut former Super Bowl MVP Mark Rypien. The Bucs were incredulous that Dilfer was still available when they selected, and Sam Wyche believes that his new quarterback has all the skills that top NFL quarterbacks must have.

Both the face and pace of the draft changed significantly. In 1994, due to pressure from cable TV network ESPN, the draft started at 3:30 p.m. (EDT) on April 24, and only the first two rounds were completed. In previous years, it had started at 12 noon, and teams continued to draft as long as no round started after 9 p.m. The last five rounds of the draft were held on April 25, after a 10 a.m. start. Several rounds were extremely lengthy because the league awarded compensatory picks to teams that had lost free agents each of the past two seasons.

Anniversary plans

On Sept. 17, 1920, representatives of 10 football teams came together at a Hupmobile showroom in Canton, Ohio, to launch what would become the National Football League. Three-quarters of a century later, the league is planning to celebrate its history and accomplishments.

In order to remember those early teams, NFL members will don replica uniforms of an earlier generation. Beginning in Week Three of the regular season, players will wear authentic-looking jerseys, pants and socks from years ago. Even coaches will wear jackets and hats that reflect the era's style, as the league attempts to "throw back" the clock to its origins.

For example, the Bears will wear uniforms from

The long and the short of it

Odds to win Super Bowl XXIX, Jan. 29, 1995 at Joe Robbie Stadium, Miami, Fla.

San Francisco	4-1
Dallas	5-1
Kansas City	7-1
Houston	8-1
Buffalo	8-1
Denver	10-1
N.Y. Giants	12-1
Green Bay	12-1
Miami	12-1
Pittsburgh	15-1
Minnesota	15-1
San Diego	15-1
L.A. Raiders	25-1
New England	25-1
New Orleans	25-1
Chicago	30-1
Detroit	30-1
Philadelphia	30-1
N.Y. Jets	30-1
Phoenix	30-1
Atlanta	40-1
Cleveland	40-1
Seattle	40-1
Washington	40-1
Indianapolis	75-1
L.A. Rams	75-1
Tampa Bay	75-1
Cincinnati	100-1

their 1923 season. Teams that play on the road that weekend will wear throwback uniforms in their next home game.

In addition to the old-style uniforms, all players will wear a 75th anniversary patch on their jerseys throughout the season. The same logo will be embossed on all footballs used in NFL regular-season and postseason games.

Off the field, plans for the 75th anniversary include a book, a movie and a television special. A 47-man all-time team also will be honored.

The book will feature contributions from many of the nation's top sportswriters and will be released in early September. NFL Films and Turner Broadcasting are producing a movie about the league's history, which will be broadcast on Sept. 18.

League officials say they will try to give NFL fans the opportunity to participate in the anniversary celebration. "We are trying to create as many opportunities as possible for fans," said NFL special-event director Jim Steeg. "The fans are the backbone of our game, and I think they will enjoy reliving the great history of the NFL."

"Seventy-five years ago the NFL was on the running board of a Hupmobile in Canton, Ohio," said New York Giant president Wellington Mara. "Today we are nationwide and soon we will be worldwide. It has been an amazing story."

11

1994 NFL milestones

■ Don Shula, celebrating his 25th season in Miami, enters his 32nd season as an NFL head coach. Shula, the all-time winningest coach in league history with 327 career wins, needs just 10 regular-season wins to record the most regular-season victories in history. That achievement would surpass George Halas, who amassed 318 victories in 40 years as head coach of the Bears.

■ San Francisco WR Jerry Rice needs three touchdowns to become the NFL's all-time TD scoring leader, surpassing Jim Brown, who tallied 126 in his nine-year NFL career, and Walter Payton, with 125 in 13 seasons. Rice has totaled 124 touchdowns (118 receiving, six rushing) during his nine-year career. Rice needs 224 yards to become the first 49er and fifth NFL receiver to top the 12,000-yard mark.

■ Dallas RB Emmitt Smith can become only the second player in league history to win four straight rushing titles. Smith, who led the league with 1,486 yards in 1993, 1,713 yards in 1992 and 1,563 yards in 1991, would join Jim Brown, who won five consecutive rushing titles from 1957 through '61.

■ Miami QB Dan Marino needs 2,321 yards to move past Dan Fouts (43,040) into second place on the NFL's all-time passing-yardage chart behind Fran Tarkenton (47,003). Marino has passed for 40,720 yards during his 11 NFL seasons. Marino (3,219 completions in 5,434 attempts) needs 79 completions and 171 attempts to surpass Fouts in both categories, which would move Marino into second place behind Tarkenton (3,686 completions in 6,467 attempts).

■ Marino (298) also needs two TD passes to become only the second player in NFL history to reach 300 TD passes during a career. Fran Tarkenton threw 342 during his 18-year NFL career.

■ Marino (17) needs just one more game with at least four TD passes to break a tie for the NFL lead with Johnny Unitas.

■ Kansas City QB Joe Montana needs 2,732 yards to become the fifth quarterback in league history to throw for 40,000 yards or more. He would join Fran Tarkenton (47,003), Dan Fouts (43,040), Dan Marino (40,720) and Johnny Unitas (40,239). Montana has thrown for 37,268 yards in 15 NFL seasons.

■ With 47 more receptions, Minnesota TE Steve Jordan will pass Kellen Winslow (541) and move into second place on the all-time receiving list for tight ends. Jordan has 495 caches in his 12-year career. Former Cleveland star Ozzie Newsome is the NFL's all-time leader among tight ends with 662 receptions.

■ Sterling Sharpe needs 31 receptions in 1994 to become the Packers' all-time leading receiver. James Lofton holds the club record with 531 catches, while Sharpe has 501 through his first six seasons in the league.

■ John Elway of the Broncos has passed for 3,000 or more yards in eight of his 11 years in the league. If he passes for 3,000 or more yards this year, he'll tie Dan Marino's record of nine seasons

Dan Marino is climbing the statistical ladder

with 3,000 or more yards. Elway also needs 17 TD passes to reach the 200 mark for scoring passes in his career.

■ Warren Moon of the Vikings needs four TD passes to reach 200 for his NFL career. He threw 196 for the Oilers over the past 10 seasons.

■ Phil Simms of the Giants needs just one TD pass to reach the 200 mark for his career. Simms has thrown 199 in 15 seasons, all of them spent with New York.

■ Detroit's Mel Gray needs 549 yards to surpass Ron Smith (6,922) as the NFL's all-time kickoff-return yardage leader. Gray has gained 6,374 kickoff-return yards in eight NFL seasons. Gray has returned 264 kickoffs in his career and will pass Smith (275) with 12 more returns.

■ Falcon WR Andre Rison needs 18 catches and 891 receiving yards to surpass Alfred Jenkins (359 receptions for 6,257 yards) as the club's all-time leader in those two categories. Rison has 342 catches for 4,547 yards in four seasons with Atlanta.

■ Kansas City's Marcus Allen has scored 113 touchdowns and is tied with Lenny Moore for fifth on the all-time list. Ahead of him on the list are Jim Brown (126), Walter Payton (125), Jerry Rice (124) and John Riggins (116).

■ San Francisco QB Steve Young can extend his NFL record of three consecutive seasons with a passer rating greater than 100. Young, who recorded passer ratings of 101.8 in 1991 and 107.0 in 1992, completed 314-of-462 passes for a team single-season record of 4,023 yards with 29 touchdowns and 16 interceptions for a passer rating of 101.5 in 1993.

■ Dallas QB Troy Aikman has thrown for at least 3,000 yards in each of the past two seasons (3,445 in 1992 and 3,100 in 1993). With another 3,000-yard season in 1994, Aikman would become the first QB in Cowboy history to throw for over 3,000 yards in three consecutive seasons.

■ Washington RB Reggie Brooks gained 1,063 yards in his rookie season. He can become the first Redskin running back in team history to gain 1,000 yards in each of his first two seasons if he does it again in 1994.

1994 PREVIEW ■ INTRODUCTION

1994 NFL WEEKLY SCHEDULE

(ALL TIMES LOCAL)

WEEK ONE
SUNDAY, SEPT. 4
ARIZONA AT LOS ANGELES RAMS	1:00
ATLANTA AT DETROIT	1:00
CLEVELAND AT CINCINNATI	1:00
DALLAS AT PITTSBURGH	4:00
HOUSTON AT INDIANAPOLIS	12:00
KANSAS CITY AT NEW ORLEANS	12:00
MINNESOTA AT GREEN BAY	12:00
NEW ENGLAND AT MIAMI	4:00
N.Y. JETS AT BUFFALO	4:00
PHILADELPHIA AT N.Y. GIANTS	1:00
SEATTLE AT WASHINGTON	1:00
TAMPA BAY AT CHICAGO	12:00
SAN DIEGO AT DENVER	6:00

MONDAY, SEPT. 5
L.A. RAIDERS AT SAN FRANCISCO	6:00

WEEK TWO
SUNDAY SEPT. 11
BUFFALO AT NEW ENGLAND	1:00
CINCINNATI AT SAN DIEGO	1:00
DENVER AT N.Y. JETS	4:00
DETROIT AT MINNESOTA	12:00
HOUSTON AT DALLAS	3:00
INDIANAPOLIS AT TAMPA BAY	1:00
LOS ANGELES RAMS AT ATLANTA	1:00
MIAMI VS. GREEN BAY (AT MILW.)	12:00
PITTSBURGH AT CLEVELAND	1:00
SAN FRANCISCO AT KANSAS CITY	12:00
SEATTLE AT L.A. RAIDERS	1:00
WASHINGTON AT NEW ORLEANS	3:00
NEW YORK GIANTS AT ARIZONA	5:00

MONDAY, SEPT. 12
CHICAGO AT PHILADELPHIA	

WEEK THREE
SUNDAY, SEPT. 18
ARIZONA AT CLEVELAND	1:00
BUFFALO AT HOUSTON	12:00
GREEN BAY AT PHILADELPHIA	1:00
INDIANAPOLIS AT PITTSBURGH	1:00
L.A. RAIDERS AT DENVER	2:00
MINNESOTA AT CHICAGO	12:00
NEW ENGLAND AT CINCINNATI	1:00
NEW ORLEANS AT TAMPA BAY	1:00
N.Y. JETS AT MIAMI	1:00
SAN DIEGO AT SEATTLE	1:00
SAN FRANCISCO AT L.A. RAMS	1:00
WASHINGTON AT N.Y. GIANTS	4:00
KANSAS CITY AT ATLANTA	8:00

MONDAY, SEPT. 19
DETROIT AT DALLAS	8:00

WEEK FOUR
SUNDAY, SEPT. 25
ATLANTA AT WASHINGTON	1:00
CINCINNATI AT HOUSTON	3:00
CLEVELAND AT INDIANAPOLIS	12:00
L.A. RAMS AT KANSAS CITY	12:00
MIAMI AT MINNESOTA	12:00
NEW ENGLAND AT DETROIT	4:00
NEW ORLEANS AT SAN FRANCISCO	1:00
PITTSBURGH AT SEATTLE	1:00
SAN DIEGO AT L.A. RAIDERS	1:00
TAMPA BAY AT GREEN BAY	12:00
CHICAGO AT N.Y. JETS	8:00

MONDAY, SEPT. 26
DENVER AT BUFFALO	9:00

(OPEN DATES: ARIZONA, DALLAS, N.Y. GIANTS, PHILADELPHIA)

WEEK FIVE
SUNDAY, OCT. 2
ATLANTA AT LOS ANGELES RAMS	1:00
BUFFALO AT CHICAGO	3:00
DALLAS AT WASHINGTON	1:00
DETROIT AT TAMPA BAY	1:00
GREEN BAY AT NEW ENGLAND	1:00
MINNESOTA AT ARIZONA	1:00
N.Y. GIANTS AT NEW ORLEANS	3:00
N.Y. JETS AT CLEVELAND	1:00
PHILADELPHIA AT SAN FRANCISCO	1:00
SEATTLE AT INDIANAPOLIS	12:00
MIAMI AT CINCINNATI	8:00

MONDAY, OCT. 3
HOUSTON AT PITTSBURGH	9:00

(OPEN DATES: DENVER, KANSAS CITY, L.A. RAIDERS, SAN DIEGO)

WEEK SIX
SUNDAY, OCT. 9
ARIZONA AT DALLAS	3:00
DENVER AT SEATTLE	1:00
INDIANAPOLIS AT N.Y. JETS	1:00
KANSAS CITY AT SAN DIEGO	1:00
L.A. RAIDERS AT NEW ENGLAND	4:00
L.A. RAMS AT GREEN BAY	12:00
MIAMI AT BUFFALO	1:00
NEW ORLEANS AT CHICAGO	12:00
SAN FRANCISCO AT DETROIT	1:00
TAMPA BAY AT ATLANTA	1:00
WASHINGTON AT PHILADELPHIA	8:00

MONDAY, OCTOBER 10
MINNESOTA AT N.Y. GIANTS	9:00

(OPEN DATES: CINCINNATI, CLEVELAND, HOUSTON, PITTSBURGH)

WEEK SEVEN
THURSDAY, OCT. 13
CLEVELAND AT HOUSTON	7:00

SUNDAY, OCT. 16
ARIZONA AT WASHINGTON	1:00
CINCINNATI AT PITTSBURGH	1:00
INDIANAPOLIS AT BUFFALO	1:00
LOS ANGELES RAIDERS AT MIAMI	1:00
NEW ENGLAND AT N.Y. JETS	1:00
N.Y. GIANTS AT L.A. RAMS	1:00
PHILADELPHIA AT DALLAS	3:00
SAN DIEGO AT NEW ORLEANS	3:00
SAN FRANCISCO AT ATLANTA	1:00

MONDAY, OCT. 17
KANSAS CITY AT DENVER	7:00

(OPEN DATES: CHICAGO, DETROIT, GREEN BAY, MINNESOTA, SEATTLE, TAMPA BAY)

WEEK EIGHT
THURSDAY, OCT. 20
GREEN BAY AT MINNESOTA	7:00

SUNDAY, OCT. 23
ATLANTA AT L.A. RAIDERS	1:00
CHICAGO AT DETROIT	1:00
CINCINNATI AT CLEVELAND	1:00
DALLAS AT ARIZONA	1:00
DENVER AT SAN DIEGO	1:00
L.A. RAMS AT NEW ORLEANS	12:00
PITTSBURGH AT N.Y. GIANTS	1:00
SEATTLE AT KANSAS CITY	12:00
TAMPA BAY AT SAN FRANCISCO	1:00
WASHINGTON AT INDIANAPOLIS	12:00

MONDAY, OCT. 24
HOUSTON AT PHILADELPHIA	9:00

(OPEN DATES: BUFFALO, MIAMI, NEW ENGLAND, N.Y. JETS)

WEEK NINE
SUNDAY, OCT. 30
CLEVELAND AT DENVER	2:00
DALLAS AT CINCINNATI	1:00
DETROIT AT NEW YORK GIANTS	1:00
HOUSTON AT L.A. RAIDERS	1:00
KANSAS CITY AT BUFFALO	1:00
MIAMI AT NEW ENGLAND	1:00
MINNESOTA AT TAMPA BAY	4:00
N.Y. JETS AT INDIANAPOLIS	4:00
PHILADELPHIA AT WASHINGTON	1:00
SEATTLE AT SAN DIEGO	1:00
PITTSBURGH AT ARIZONA	6:00

MONDAY, OCTOBER 31
GREEN BAY AT CHICAGO	8:00

(OPEN DATES: ATLANTA, L.A. RAMS, NEW ORLEANS, SAN FRANCISCO)

13

PRO FOOTBALL WEEKLY 1994 ALMANAC

1994 NFL WEEKLY SCHEDULE

WEEK 10
SUNDAY, NOV. 6
ARIZONA AT PHILADELPHIA	4:00
BUFFALO AT N.Y. JETS	4:00
CHICAGO AT TAMPA BAY	1:00
CINCINNATI AT SEATTLE	1:00
DENVER AT L.A. RAMS	1:00
DETROIT VS. GREEN BAY (AT MILW.)	12:00
INDIANAPOLIS AT MIAMI	1:00
NEW ENGLAND AT CLEVELAND	1:00
NEW ORLEANS AT MINNESOTA	12:00
PITTSBURGH AT HOUSTON	12:00
SAN DIEGO AT ATLANTA	1:00
SAN FRANCISCO AT WASHINGTON	1:00
L.A. RAIDERS AT KANSAS CITY	7:00

MONDAY, NOV. 7
N.Y. GIANTS AT DALLAS	8:00

WEEK 11
SUNDAY, NOV. 13
ARIZONA AT NEW YORK GIANTS	1:00
ATLANTA AT NEW ORLEANS	12:00
CHICAGO AT MIAMI	1:00
CLEVELAND AT PHILADELPHIA	1:00
DALLAS AT SAN FRANCISCO	1:00
HOUSTON AT CINCINNATI	1:00
L.A. RAIDERS AT L.A. RAMS	1:00
MINNESOTA AT NEW ENGLAND	1:00
N.Y. JETS AT GREEN BAY	3:00
SAN DIEGO AT KANSAS CITY	12:00
SEATTLE AT DENVER	2:00
TAMPA BAY AT DETROIT	8:00

MONDAY, NOV. 14
BUFFALO AT PITTSBURGH	9:00

(OPEN DATES: INDIANAPOLIS, WASHINGTON)

WEEK 12
SUNDAY, NOV. 20
ATLANTA AT DENVER	2:00
CLEVELAND AT KANSAS CITY	12:00
DETROIT AT CHICAGO	12:00
GREEN BAY AT BUFFALO	1:00
INDIANAPOLIS AT CINCINNATI	1:00
MIAMI AT PITTSBURGH	1:00
NEW ORLEANS AT L.A. RAIDERS	1:00
N.Y. JETS AT MINNESOTA	3:00
PHILADELPHIA AT ARIZONA	2:00
SAN DIEGO AT NEW ENGLAND	1:00
TAMPA BAY AT SEATTLE	1:00
WASHINGTON AT DALLAS	12:00
L.A. RAMS AT SAN FRANCISCO	5:00

MONDAY, NOV. 21
N.Y. GIANTS AT HOUSTON	8:00

WEEK 13
THURSDAY, NOV. 24
BUFFALO AT DETROIT	12:30
GREEN BAY AT DALLAS	3:00

SUNDAY, NOV. 27
CHICAGO AT ARIZONA	2:00
CINCINNATI AT DENVER	2:00
HOUSTON AT CLEVELAND	1:00
KANSAS CITY AT SEATTLE	1:00
L.A. RAMS AT SAN DIEGO	1:00
MIAMI AT N.Y. JETS	1:00
N.Y. GIANTS AT WASHINGTON	4:00
PHILADELPHIA AT ATLANTA	1:00
PITTSBURGH AT L.A. RAIDERS	1:00
TAMPA BAY AT MINNESOTA	12:00
NEW ENGLAND AT INDIANAPOLIS	8:00

MONDAY, NOV. 28
SAN FRANCISCO AT NEW ORLEANS	8:00

WEEK 14
THURSDAY, DEC. 1
CHICAGO AT MINNESOTA	7:00

SUNDAY, DEC. 4
ARIZONA AT HOUSTON	3:00
ATLANTA AT SAN FRANCISCO	1:00
DALLAS AT PHILADELPHIA	:00
DENVER AT KANSAS CITY	3:00
GREEN BAY AT DETROIT	1:00
INDIANAPOLIS AT SEATTLE	1:00
NEW ORLEANS AT L.A. RAMS	1:00
N.Y. GIANTS AT CLEVELAND	4:00
N.Y. JETS AT NEW ENGLAND	1:00
PITTSBURGH AT CINCINNATI	1:00
WASHINGTON AT TAMPA BAY	1:00
BUFFALO AT MIAMI	8:00

MONDAY, DEC. 5
L.A. RAIDERS AT SAN DIEGO	6:00

WEEK 15
SATURDAY, DEC. 10
CLEVELAND AT DALLAS	3:00
DETROIT AT N.Y. JETS	12:30

SUNDAY, DEC. 11
CHICAGO AT GREEN BAY	12:00
CINCINNATI AT N.Y. GIANTS	1:00
DENVER AT L.A. RAIDERS	1:00
INDIANAPOLIS AT NEW ENGLAND	1:00
L.A. RAMS AT TAMPA BAY	1:00
MINNESOTA AT BUFFALO	1:00
PHILADELPHIA AT PITTSBURGH	1:00
SAN FRANCISCO AT SAN DIEGO	1:00
SEATTLE AT HOUSTON	3:00
WASHINGTON AT ARIZONA	2:00
NEW ORLEANS AT ATLANTA	8:00

MONDAY, DEC. 12
KANSAS CITY AT MIAMI	9:00

WEEK 16
SATURDAY, DEC. 17
DENVER AT SAN FRANCISCO	1:00
MINNESOTA AT DETROIT	12:30

SUNDAY, DEC. 18
ATLANTA VS. GREEN BAY (AT MILW.)	12:00
CINCINNATI AT ARIZONA	2:00
CLEVELAND AT PITTSBURGH	12:00
HOUSTON AT KANSAS CITY	3:00
L.A. RAMS AT CHICAGO	12:00
MIAMI AT INDIANAPOLIS	1:00
NEW ENGLAND AT BUFFALO	1:00
N.Y. GIANTS AT PHILADELPHIA	4:00
SAN DIEGO AT N.Y. JETS	1:00
TAMPA BAY AT WASHINGTON	1:00
L.A. RAIDERS AT SEATTLE	5:00

MONDAY, DEC. 19
DALLAS AT NEW ORLEANS	8:00

WEEK 17
SATURDAY, DEC. 24
ARIZONA AT ATLANTA	1:00
BUFFALO AT INDIANAPOLIS	1:00
DALLAS AT N.Y. GIANTS	1:00
GREEN BAY AT TAMPA BAY	1:00
KANSAS CITY AT L.A. RAIDERS	1:00
NEW ENGLAND AT CHICAGO	12:00
NEW ORLEANS AT DENVER	2:00
N.Y. JETS AT HOUSTON	3:00
PHILADELPHIA AT CINCINNATI	1:00
PITTSBURGH AT SAN DIEGO	1:00
SEATTLE AT CLEVELAND	1:00
WASHINGTON AT L.A. RAMS	1:00

SUNDAY, DEC. 25
DETROIT AT MIAMI	8:00

MONDAY, DEC. 26
SAN FRANCISCO AT MINNESOTA	8:00

POSTSEASON
SATURDAY, DEC. 31
AFC AND NFC WILD-CARD PLAYOFFS
SUNDAY, JAN. 1
AFC AND NFC WILD-CARD PLAYOFFS
SATURDAY, JAN. 7
AFC AND NFC DIVISIONAL PLAYOFFS
SUNDAY, JAN. 8
AFC AND NFC DIVISIONAL PLAYOFFS
SUNDAY, JAN. 15
AFC AND NFC CHAMPIONSHIP GAMES
SUNDAY, JAN. 29
SUPER BOWL XXIX AT JOE ROBBIE STADIUM, MIAMI, FLA.
SUNDAY, FEB. 5
AFC-NFC PRO BOWL AT HONOLULU, HI

1994 PREVIEW ■ INTRODUCTION

PFW PREDICTIONS

AFC East
1. Buffalo (10-6)
2. Miami (9-7)
3. New England (8-8)
4. New York Jets (5-11)
5. Indianapolis (5-11)

AFC Central
1. Pittsburgh (10-6)
2. Houston (9-7)
3. Cleveland (7-9)
4. Cincinnati (4-12)

AFC West
1. Denver (11-5)
2. L.A. Raiders (10-6)
3. Kansas City (10-6)
4. Seattle (7-9)
5. San Diego (4-12)

NFC East
1. Dallas (11-5)
2. Arizona (10-6)
3. N.Y. Giants (9-7)
4. Philadelphia (7-9)
5. Washington (6-10)

NFC Central
1. Green Bay (10-6)
2. Minnesota (10-6)
3. Chicago (8-8)
4. Detroit (8-8)
5. Tampa Bay (5-11)

NFC West
1. San Francisco (13-3)
2. New Orleans (7-9)
3. L.A. Rams (7-9)
4. Atlanta (4-12)

POSTSEASON PREDICTIONS

AFC wild-card teams: L.A. Raiders, Kansas City, Houston
NFC wild-card teams: Arizona, N.Y. Giants, Minnesota

AFC champion: Denver
NFC champion: San Francisco

Super Bowl champion: San Francisco

PRO FOOTBALL WEEKLY 1994 ALMANAC

PREVIEW: ARIZONA CARDINALS

Could this be the year the Cardinal franchise turns around? After years of constantly taking two steps backward for every step forward, Bill Bidwill may have made one of his best moves ever when he hired Buddy Ryan to run his team. While Ryan is arrogant, abrasive, stubborn and egocentric, he is a strong motivator who is excellent at building loyalty among his players.

While others have criticized Bidwill, Ryan is solidly behind his new boss. "The man showed he knows football," Ryan said. "He hired me, so he knows what he's doing."

He also is a top-notch defensive coach who builds a hard-charging, ferocious, attacking unit no matter where he goes. Ryan already had two strong players to build around in DT Eric Swann and LB Eric Hill, and in the offseason he added former Eagles DE Clyde Simmons and OLB Seth Joyner. Despite a down year in 1993, Simmons can still be a top-notch pass rusher, and Joyner will give the rest of the Cardinal defense a strong example to follow on how to play with ferocity and determination.

Since Ryan is a defensive coach, expect him to build an offense that can control the clock, avoid turning the ball over and make some occasional big plays. He also likes to operate from a two-RB set and will never let his team use the run-and-shoot.

While the Cardinals finished with a 7-9 record last season, they outscored their opponents 326-269, controlled the ball an average of 31:54 per game and led the NFC in third-down conversions. Eight of their nine losses were by a touchdown or less.

Steve Beuerlein is a decent NFL quarterback who shows signs of developing into a very productive leader. In his first year with the Cardinals, he threw for 3,164 yards, with 18 touchdowns and 17 interceptions, and he showed a very strong arm, intelligence and leadership ability. Beuerlein often gets himself into trouble, since his footwork leaves a lot to be desired. He can be very streaky with his throwing, but he usually does not try to go outside the parameters of the offense.

"This is a team that has a chance to get better in a hurry," said Beuerlein. "We've got the weapons and we're going to be able to compete."

Will Furrer appears to be the backup quarterback, which does not give Ryan much insurance. Furrer is a very strong-armed left-hander who does not have much polish. The ex-Bear was a favorite of Mike Ditka, but he was waived by Dave Wannstedt. There were rumors Ryan would sign Jim McMahon.

If the Cardinals are going to challenge the Cowboys and Giants in the NFC East, their improving running game will have to continue to get better. Last year the Cards had a rookie running back who made a huge impact, and his name was not Garrison Hearst. Ron Moore, a fourth-round pick out of Pittsburg (Kan.) State, ran for 1,018 yards and gave the Cardinals a consistent effort. Moore is a hard-running, between-the-tackles runner who can explode out of arm tackles and get first-down yardage. However, Moore does not have the speed to break away. That's where Hearst comes into the equation this year. The former Georgia star is a breakaway runner who is coming off a season-ending knee injury. In 1993 he carried 76 times for 264 yards and one

Eric Swann

16

1994 PREVIEW ■ ARIZONA

touchdown and never got untracked after a long holdout. The '94 season is obviously a huge season for Hearst, who will be under tremendous pressure from Ryan to become a Pro Bowl-type back. The Cardinals added a rookie speedster to their backfield in former Arizona star Chuck Levy. Levy can run a 4.48 40, can cut well and is usually at his best in big games. He can be used to spell Hearst and in third-down situations. Dual-threat RB Larry Centers adds more depth.

Beuerlein has an underrated group of receivers who have the potential to cause a lot of trouble for opposing defensive backs. Gary Clark was a top receiver for the Redskins for eight years but was troubled by a groin injury last year, his first with the Cardinals. Clark was ineffective or inactive in nearly half of the Cardinals' games last year, but he still caught 63 passes for 818 yards and four TD's. Clark runs sharp routes, has great hands and is at his best in clutch situations.

"Last year was very frustrating for me," Clark explained. "I've never had to miss games before, and that's why it really bothered me. I'm not used to sitting. I think things went OK when I came back, but I'm looking forward to being healthy for a full season."

Ricky Proehl exceeded Clark's reception total by two. Proehl is a classic possession receiver who stepped in when Clark was hurt and proved he could get into the endzone (seven TD catches). Proehl has good concentration in a crowd and has the ability to run after the catch. Randal Hill is the team's mystery man. He has game-breaking speed and acceleration and will make some big catches. However, he is a selfish player who sulks if he does not get the ball enough to suit him. If Ryan can get Hill's attitude turned around, he may have a big-time play maker. Anthony Edwards also has game-breaking potential, as he averaged 25 yards per reception on 13 catches.

The offensive line may hold the key to the Cardinal season. Veteran Luis Sharpe still mans the OLT spot, and even though he's been playing since 1982, he still has quick feet and pass-protection skills. ORT Rick Cunningham is a former World League player who made solid progress last year. Two second-year players, Ernest Dye and Ben Coleman, should start at the two OG spots. Dye will be the starting left guard, while Coleman will be at right guard as long as he beats out Joe Wolf. Dye had knee and weight problems last year, but if he's healthy and has his weight down, he can crush people. Coleman is a good athlete for such a large man, but he also had knee problems. Mark Tucker, a former guard, starts at center.

Simmons is coming off a down year in Philadelphia, but Ryan believes he was slowed by injuries and that he will still be able to do a big pass-rushing job from the DRE slot. Simmons has extremely long arms that allow him to bat down or deflect passes even if he doesn't get to the quarterback. Eric Swann has a chance to be one of the most dominating players in the game because of his size and strength. He has games where he is truly unstoppable, yet he can be average as well. Another troubling aspect to Swann's makeup is his tendency to get injured. Michael Bankston, who has a lot of quickness, will probably start next to Swann. Keith Rucker, who checked in at 360 pounds a year ago, will have to lose quite a bit of weight and get quicker if he is to play for Ryan. Mike Jones looks like the starter at defensive left end, but he will have to play consistently and give a better effort if he wants a key role in Ryan's defense.

Hill and Joyner will both play vital roles in the Cardinal defense. Hill came on last year and proved to be the team's best linebacker. Joyner is one of the game's most valuable linebackers. He is the complete package, a guy who who can rush the passer, make big hits and cover receivers out of the backfield. Now that he's back with Ryan, don't be surprised if Joyner performs at an even higher level. Rookie Jamir Miller, the No. 1 pick, could be a very effective pass rusher because of his superior speed. He was a hot-and-cold player in college who, at times, showed a very poor attitude. Tyronne Stowe lacks speed but led the team in tackles last year.

In the secondary, Ryan will start talented Aeneas Williams and former Bill J.D. Williams at cornerback. Aeneas Williams has become one of the better cover men in the league and plays with a lot of intelligence. J.D. Williams has better than 4.4 speed and a 40-inch vertical leap, but he has never been able to transform that athleticism into football ability. Ryan looks at J.D. Williams as a personal challenge. Lorenzo Lynch has size and will get the first chance to win the job at strong safety. FS Mike Zordich is very smart but is limited athletically.

Jeff Feagles has been brought in to replace Pro Bowl P Rich Camarillo, who wanted too much money to suit Ryan. Feagles does not have a strong distance leg, but he is proficient at dropping the ball inside the 20. PK Greg Davis was perfect on 13 kicks inside the 40 and was successful on 4-of-5 from 50-plus yards, but he made only 4-of-10 from 40-49 yards. Kick coverage was not a problem for the Cardinals, but it wasn't special, either.

FAST FACTS

■ In 1993 the Cardinals held six opponents to 10 points or less. That's the first time the defense has been that stingy since 1936.

■ The Cardinals were one of only four teams to have three players with 60 receptions or more in 1993.

■ The Cardinals haven't finished over .500 since Jim Hanifan coached the St. Louis Cardinals to a 9-7 record in 1984. And they haven't won a playoff game since 1947.

17

PRO FOOTBALL WEEKLY 1994 ALMANAC

1994 PLAYER ROSTER

NO.	NAME	POS.	HT.	WT.	EXP.	COLLEGE	GP/GS
45	Alexander, Brent	FS	5-10	184	R	Tennessee State	—
63	Bankston, Michael	DL	6-3	280	3	Sam Houston State	16/12
7	Beuerlein, Steve	QB	6-3	210	7	Notre Dame	16/14
51	Blackwell, Todd	C	6-3	295	R	California	—
25	Blount, Eric	RB-KR	5-9	200	3	North Carolina	6/0
42	Booty, John	S	6-0	180	7	Texas Christian	12/12
54	Braxton, David	LB	6-2	240	6	Wake Forest	16/0
78	Brown, Chad	DE	6-7	265	2	Mississippi	6/0
47	Bruere, Carl	WR	6-2	185	R	N. Mex. Highlands	—
33	Brunson, Mario	FB	6-1	246	R	Tennessee	—
26	Cecil, Chuck	FS	6-0	185	7	Arizona	15/7
37	Centers, Larry	RB	5-11	215	5	Stephen F. Austin	16/8
15	Ciaccio, Tom	QB	6-1	190	R	Holy Cross	—
84	Clark, Gary	WR	5-9	175	10	James Madison	14/9
62	Coleman, Ben	OT	6-6	335	2	Wake Forest	12/0
59	Cunningham, Ed	C	6-3	285	3	Washington	16/15
64	Cunningham, Rick	OT	6-7	320	4	Texas A&M	16/16
5	Davis, Greg	PK	6-0	205	7	The Citadel	16/0
22	Duerson, Dave	SS	6-1	220	12	Notre Dame	16/4
65	Dye, Ernest	OT	6-6	325	2	South Carolina	7/1
83	Edwards, Anthony	WR	5-10	190	6	N. Mex. Highlands	16/0
80	Fann, Chad	TE	6-3	250	2	Florida A&M	0/0
69	Faulkner, Jeff	OT	6-4	305	R	Millersville (Pa.)	—
10	Feagles, Jeff	P	6-1	205	7	Miami (Fla.)	16/0
2	Furrer, Will	QB	6-3	210	3	Virginia Tech	0/0
73	Gardner, Jerome	DT	6-0	260	R	Tennessee State	—
19	Gonzalez, Eduardo	QB	5-11	198	R	National U. (Mexico City)	—
31	Harris, Odie	S	6-0	190	7	Sam Houston St.	16/0
23	Hearst, Garrison	RB	5-11	215	2	Georgia	6/5
34	Henesey, Brian	RB	5-10	215	R	Bucknell	—
58	Hill, Eric	LB	6-2	255	6	Louisiana State	13/12
81	Hill, Randal	WR	5-10	180	4	Miami (Fla.)	16/9
97	Hyche, Steve	LB	6-3	250	5	Livingston	2/0
53	Jax, Garth	LB	6-3	250	9	Florida State	16/0
61	Jenkins, Lennie	DL	6-2	257	R	NE Louisiana	—
72	Johnson, Chuckie	DT	6-4	310	2	Auburn	4/0
55	Jones, Jock	LB	6-3	240	5	Virginia Tech	7/0
75	Jones, Mike	DE	6-4	295	4	North Carolina St.	16/4
59	Joyner, Seth	LB	6-2	235	9	Texas-El Paso	16/16
57	Kirk, Randy	LB-LS	6-2	231	7	San Diego State	16/0
66	Kurinsky, York	OT	6-3	286	R	Valdosta (Ga.)State	—
28	Lofton, Steve	CB	5-9	185	4	Texas A&M	13/0
93	Lopez, Kenny	DL	6-2	275	R	Miami (Fla.)	—
29	Lynch, Lorenzo	CB	5-11	200	8	Cal St.-Sacramento	16/15
16	McLeod, David	WR	5-11	172	R	James Madison	—
94	Merritt, David	LB	6-1	237	2	North Carolina State	7/0
74	Moody, Mike	OT	6-7	305	1	Southern California	0/0
30	Moore, Ron	RB	5-10	220	2	Pittsburg (Kan.) St.	16/11
50	Nunn, Freddie Joe	DE	6-5	255	10	Mississippi	16/9
27	Oldham, Chris	CB	5-10	195	4	Oregon	16/6
36	Owens, Anthony	WR	6-0	194	1	Tennessee State	0/0
86	Pinckney, John	WR	6-0	189	1	Stanford	0/0
87	Proehl, Ricky	WR	6-0	190	5	Wake Forest	16/16
45	Reeves, Bryan	WR	5-11	195	R	Nevada-Reno	—
43	Richardson, Mose	CB	6-2	180	R	Indiana	—

1994 PREVIEW ■ ARIZONA

1994 PLAYER ROSTER

NO.	NAME	POS.	HT.	WT.	EXP.	COLLEGE	GP/GS
79	Rucker, Keith	DL	6-4	360	3	Ohio Wesleyan	16/15
91	Shadwick, Richard	DE	6-4	255	R	Morehead State	—
67	Sharpe, Luis	OT	6-5	280	13	UCLA	16/16
96	Simmons, Clyde	DE	6-6	280	9	Western Carolina	16/16
90	Stowe, Tyronne	LB	6-2	250	8	Rutgers	15/15
98	Swann, Eric	DL	6-5	295	4	None	9/9
22	Tate, Will	WR	5-10	170	R	San Diego State	—
71	Tucker, Mark	C-OG	6-3	290	2	Southern Cal	0/0
48	Wallace, Sean	SS	5-8	185	R	Southern	—
92	Wallerstedt, Brett	LB	6-1	240	2	Arizona State	7/0
85	Ware, Derek	H-b/TE	6-3	250	3	Central State (Okla.)	16/1
35	Williams, Aeneas	CB	5-10	192	4	Southern-B.R.	16/16
21	Williams, James	CB	5-10	185	5	Fresno State	15/11
68	Wolf, Joe	OL	6-6	296	6	Boston College	8/5
55	Wolford, Eric	C	6-1	280	R	Kansas State	—
82	Wright, Michael	TE	6-4	250	2	Wyoming	0/0
38	Zordich, Michael	S	6-1	201	8	Penn State	16/9

'94 DRAFT PICKS

RD.	NAME	POS.	HT.	WT.	COLLEGE
1.	Miller, Jamir	LB	6-4	234	UCLA
2.	Levy, Charles	RB	6-0	199	Arizona
3.	Braham, Rich	OG	6-4	290	West Virginia
3.	England, Eric	DE	6-2	264	Texas A&M
4.	Carter, Perry	DB	6-0	187	Southern Mississippi
4.	Reece, John	DB	6-0	200	Nebraska
4.	Irving, Terry	LB	6-0	216	McNeese State
5.	Redmon, Anthony	OG	6-4	308	Auburn
6.	Samuels, Terry	TE	6-2	254	Kentucky
7.	Harvey, Frank	FB	6-0	245	Georgia

PRO FOOTBALL WEEKLY 1994 ALMANAC

TEAM AT A GLANCE

TEAM DIRECTORY

Address	P.O. Box 888 Phoenix, Arizona 85001 (602) 379-0101
Stadium	Sun Devil Stadium Fifth Street Tempe, Arizona 85287 Capacity: 73,521 Playing surface: Grass
Training Camp	Northern Arizona University Flagstaff, Arizona 86011
Colors	Cardinal red, black and white
Television	KNXZ, Channel 15
Radio	KESZ, 99.9 FM

ADMINISTRATION
President: William V. Bidwill
Executive vice president: Joe Rhein
Vice president: Larry Wilson
General manager-head coach: Buddy Ryan
Assistant general manager: Bob Ackles
Director of college scouting: Bo Bolinger
Public relations director: Paul Jensen
Director of community relations: Adele Harris
Director of marketing: Joe Castor
Director of sales: Eric Gronning
Ticket manager: Steve Walsh
Trainer: John Omohundro

1994 SCHEDULE

Preseason
AUG. 5	SAN FRANCISCO	6:30
AUG. 13	CHICAGO	6:00
AUG. 19	at Detroit	7:30
AUG. 25	at Denver	7:00

Regular season
SEP. 4	at L.A. Rams	1:00
SEP. 11	N.Y. GIANTS	5:00
SEP. 18	at Cleveland	1:00
SEP. 25	OPEN DATE	
OCT. 2	MINNESOTA	1:00
OCT. 9	at Dallas	3:00
OCT. 16	at Washington	1:00
OCT. 23	DALLAS	1:00
OCT. 30	PITTSBURGH	6:00
NOV. 6	at Philadelphia	4:00
NOV. 13	at N.Y. Giants	1:00
NOV. 20	PHILADELPHIA	2:00
NOV. 27	CHICAGO	2:00
DEC. 4	at Houston	3:00
DEC. 11	WASHINGTON	2:00
DEC. 18	CINCINNATI	2:00
DEC. 24	at Atlanta	1:00

HEAD COACH
Buddy Ryan

Ryan will begin his second head-coaching job in 1994 with the Cardinals. He was hired after installing his famed "46" defense while serving as defensive coordinator with the Oilers in 1993. Prior to his stint in Houston, Ryan was head coach of the Eagles from 1986 to '90. Under Ryan the Eagles went 43-35-1, and went to the playoffs three times without a postseason victory. Known as one of the most innovative and effective defensive coaches in the game, Ryan has been on the staff of three Super Bowl teams (1968 Jets, 1976 Vikings and 1985 Bears). Born Feb. 17, 1934, Frederick, Okla.

Previous NFL: defensive coordinator, 1993 Houston; head coach, 1986-90 Philadelphia; defensive coordinator, 1978-85 Chicago; defensive line, 1976-77 Minnesota; defensive assistant, 1968-75 N.Y. Jets.

Previous college: assistant coach, 1967 Pacific; assistant coach, 1966 Vanderbilt; assistant coach, 1961-65 Buffalo.

Player: No NFL. College, guard, 1952-55 Oklahoma State.

ASSISTANT COACHES

Dave Atkins: offensive coordinator-running backs
Previous NFL: offensive backfield, 1993 New England; 1986-92 Philadelphia. Player: NFL, running back, 1973 San Francisco; 1975 San Diego. College: running back, 1970-72 Texas-El Paso.

Matt Cavanaugh: quarterbacks
Previous NFL: None. Player: NFL, quarterback, 1990-91 N.Y. Giants; 1986-89 Philadelphia; 1983-85 San Francisco; 1978-82 New England. College: quarterback, 1975-77 Pittsburgh.

Ted Cottrell: defensive line
Previous NFL: defensive line, 1990-93 Phoenix; 1986-89 Buffalo; 1981-82 Kansas City. Player: NFL, linebacker, 1969-70 Atlanta. College: linebacker, 1966-68 Delaware Valley College.

Ronnie Jones: defensive coordinator
Previous NFL: linebackers, 1993 Houston; 1992 L.A. Raiders; 1991 L.A. Rams. Player: No NFL. College: running back, 1974-77 Northeastern (Okla.).

George Martinez: quality control
Previous NFL: None. Player: No NFL. College: quarterback, Arizona; NW Oklahoma State.

Guy Morriss: offensive line assistant
Previous NFL: offensive line, 1988-89 New England. Player: NFL, center, 1984-87 New England; 1973-83 Philadelphia. College: offensive lineman, 1970-72 Texas Christian.

Dan Neal: offensive line
Previous NFL: offensive line, 1986-91 Philadelphia. Player: NFL, center, 1975-83 Chicago; 1973-74 Baltimore. College: center, 1971-72 Kentucky.

Ted Plumb: tight ends
Previous NFL: tight ends, 1990-93 Phoenix; 1986-89 Philadelphia; 1980-85 Chicago; 1977-79 Atlanta; 1974-76 N.Y. Giants. Player: NFL, wide receiver, 1962 Buffalo. College: wide receiver, 1960-61 Baylor.

Al Roberts: special teams
Previous NFL: running backs, 1991-93 N.Y.

1994 PREVIEW ■ ARIZONA

TEAM AT A GLANCE

Jets; 1988-90 Philadelphia; 1984-85 Houston. Player: No NFL. College: running back, 1964-65 Washington; 1967-68 Puget Sound.

Rex Ryan: defensive line
Previous NFL: None. Player: No NFL. College: Southwestern Oklahoma State.

Rob Ryan: defensive backs
Previous NFL: None. Player: No NFL. College: defensive end-linebacker, SW Oklahoma State.

Bob Rogucki: strength and conditioning
Previous NFL: strength and conditioning, 1990-93 Phoenix. Player: No NFL. College: None.

COACHING RECORDS
(includes postseason games)

Years	Coach	W	L	T
1920-22	John "Paddy" Driscoll	17	8	4
1923-24	Arnold Horween	13	8	1
1925-26	Norman Barry	16	8	2
1927	Guy Chamberlin	3	7	1
1928	Fred Gillies	1	5	0
1929	Dewey Scanlon	6	6	1
1930	Ernie Nevers	5	6	2
1931	LeRoy Andrews	0	1	0
1931	Ernie Nevers	5	3	0
1932	Jack Chevigny	2	6	2
1933-34	Paul Schissler	6	15	1
1935-38	Milan Creighton	16	26	4
1939	Ernie Nevers	1	10	0
1940-42	Jimmy Conzelman	8	22	3
1943-45	Phil Handler	1	29	0
1946-48	Jimmy Conzelman	27	10	0
1949	Phil Handler-Buddy Parker	2	4	0
1949	Buddy Parker	4	1	1
1950-51	Curly Lambeau	7	15	0
1951	Phil Handler-Cecil Isbell	1	1	0
1952	Joe Kuharich	4	8	0
1953-54	Joe Stydahar	3	20	1
1955-57	Ray Richards	14	21	1
1958-61	Frank "Pop" Ivy	17	29	2
1961	Chuck Drulis-Ray Willsey-Ray Prochaska	2	0	0
1962-65	Wally Lemm	27	26	3
1966-70	Charley Winner	35	30	5
1971-72	Bob Hollway	8	18	2
1973-77	Don Coryell	42	29	1
1978-79	Bud Wilkinson	9	20	0
1979	Larry Wilson	2	1	0
1980-85	Jim Hanifan	39	50	1
1986-89	Gene Stallings	23	34	1
1989	Hank Kuhlmann	0	5	0
1990-93	Joe Bugel	20	44	0

HISTORICAL HIGHLIGHTS

1920 The Chicago Cardinals, known as the Racine Cardinals (after a Chicago street) and who boast football roots that go back to 1899, are a charter member of the American Professional Football Association, which would become the NFL in 1922. ... The Cardinals move their home field to Comiskey Park.

1925 The Cardinals are awarded their first NFL title, with a record of 11-2-1, a shade better than the 10-2 Pottsville Maroons. But controversy swirls around the title because the last two Cardinal wins are over disbanded teams and owner Chris O'Brien declines to accept the championship.

1929 Ernie Nevers joins the Cardinal backfield. In a game against the Bears, he scores all the team's 40 points, (six TDs and 4 PAT's), which remains today the most points ever scored by a player in an NFL game.

1933 Charles W. Bidwill buys the Cardinal franchise from David Jones for $50,000.

1944 With World War II depleting the rosters of many teams, the NFL allows the Cardinals to join forces with the Steelers and compete as one team. They come in last in the NFL West with a record of 0-10.

1947 Charley Trippi is signed to round out the Dream Backfield, which already includes Paul Christman, Pat Harder and Elmer Angsman. Trippi's contract is the biggest, $100,000 over four years, to be offered since the Red Grange's deal with the Bears in 1925. ... The Cardinals win the NFL West by defeating their intracity rivals, the Bears, in the last game of the season. Then they defeat the Eagles at Comiskey Park to win their first NFL crown since the controversial title of 1925.

1948 With an 11-1 record, the Cardinals repeat as the NFL West champions when they defeat the Bears in the last game of the season, by a score of 24-21. But this year the Cardinals lose to the Eagles for the NFL championship, losing 7-0.

1950 End Bob Shaw catches five touchdown passes from Jim Hardy in a game against the Colts to set a single-game NFL record.

1956 The Cardinals post their first (and only) winning season, 7-4, of the 1950's, placing second in the Eastern Conference.

1960 The Cardinals relocate to St. Louis, playing their games in Busch Stadium. ... John David Crow becomes the first (and only) Cardinal runner to rush for more than 200 yards in a game, gaining 203 on 24 carries against Pittsburgh. He also is the first Cardinal to gain more than 1,000 yards in a season, 1,071 on 183 carries, an average of 5.9 yards per carry.

1967 PK Jim Bakken kicks seven field goals in a game against the Steelers, setting an NFL record that has yet to be equalled.

1974 The Cardinals win their most games in a season, 10, since 1948. It is also their first division title since the 1940's. ... In their first playoff appearance since 1948, the Cardinals lose to Minnesota.

1975 The Cardinals repeat as division champs with a record of 11-3, but fall to the Rams in the playoffs.

1975 Terry Metcalf sets an NFL record with 2,462 combined yards (rushing, receiving, and kick, punt, interception and fumble returns), a mark that would stand for more than a decade.

1982 In a strike-shortened season, the Cardinals make the playoffs with a 5-4 record but are annihilated by the Packers 41-16 in the postseason.

1984 Neil Lomax becomes the first Cardinal to complete more than 300 passes and pass for more than 4,000 yards in a season (4,614 on 345 completions).

1988 The Cardinals relocate in Phoenix, Arizona. Their first-year home attendance of 472, 937 is the largest in franchise history.

1994 Owner Bill Bidwill fires head coach Joe Bugel and general manager Larry Wilson and hires Buddy Ryan to fill both posts.

PRO FOOTBALL WEEKLY 1994 ALMANAC

TEAM AT A GLANCE

HALL OF FAME MEMBERS

	Yrs with Cardinals	Inducted
FB Ernie Nevers*	1929-31	1963
Coach Jimmy Conzelman	1940-42, 46-48	1964
QB Paddy Driscoll	1920-25	1965
G Walt Kiesling	1929-33	1966
Owner Charles Bidwill	1933-47	1967
HB Charley Trippi	1947-55	1968
HB Ollie Matson	1952, 54-58	1972
CB Dick "Night Train" Lane	1954-59	1974
S Larry Wilson	1960-72	1978
TE Jackie Smith	1963-77	1994

* Charter member

RETIRED JERSEY NUMBERS

- 8 S Larry Wilson
- 77 T Stan Mauldin
- 88 TE J.V. Cain
- 99 HB Marshall Goldberg

FIRST-ROUND DRAFT CHOICES
(since 1980)

Year	Selection	College
1980	DE Curtis Greer	Michigan
1981	LB E.J. Junior	Alabama
1982	OT Louis Sharpe	UCLA
1983	CB Leonard Smith	McNeese State
1984	WR Clyde Duncan	Tennessee
1985	LB Freddie Joe Nunn	Mississippi
1986	LB Anthony Bell	Michigan State
1987	QB Kelly Stouffer	Colorado State
1988	LB Ken Harvey	California
1989	LB Eric Hill	Louisiana State
1990	No choice	
1991	DL Eric Swann	No college
1992	No choice	
1993	RB Garrison Hearst	Georgia
1994	LB Jamir Miller	UCLA

RECORD VS. OTHER NFL TEAMS
(includes postseason games)

	Record
Atlanta Falcons	11-5-0
Buffalo Bills	3-3-0
Chicago Bears	25-51-6
Cincinnati Bengals	1-3-0
Cleveland Browns	10-31-3
Dallas Cowboys	22-40-1
Denver Broncos	0-3-1
Detroit Lions	16-27-5
Green Bay Packers	21-40-4
Houston Oilers	3-2-0
Indianapolis Colts	6-5-0
Kansas City Chiefs	1-3-1
Los Angeles Raiders	1-2-0
Los Angeles Rams	19-23-2
Miami Dolphins	0-6-0
Minnesota Vikings	7-5-0
New England Patriots	6-2-0
New Orleans Saints	10-9-0
New York Giants	35-65-2
New York Jets	2-1-0
Philadelphia Eagles	45-44-5
Pittsburgh Steelers	21-29-3
San Diego Chargers	1-5-0
San Francisco 49ers	9-10-0
Seattle Seahawks	4-0-0
Tampa Bay Buccaneers	6-6-0
Washington Redskins	36-61-2

YEAR-BY-YEAR RECORDS

Year	Won	Lost	Tied	Year	Won	Lost	Tied
1920	6	2	2	1958	2	9	1
1921	3	3	2	1959	2	10	0
1922	8	3	0	1960	6	5	1
1923	8	4	0	1961	7	7	0
1924	5	4	1	1962	4	9	1
1925*	11	2	1	1963	9	5	0
1926	5	6	1	1964	9	3	2
1927	3	7	1	1965	5	9	0
1928	1	5	0	1966	8	5	1
1929	6	6	1	1967	6	7	1
1930	5	6	2	1968	9	4	1
1931	5	4	0	1969	4	9	1
1932	2	6	2	1970	8	5	1
1933	1	9	1	1971	4	9	1
1934	5	6	0	1972	4	9	1
1935	6	4	2	1973	4	9	1
1936	3	8	1	1974**	10	4	0
1937	5	5	1	1975**	11	3	0
1938	2	9	0	1976	10	4	0
1939	1	10	0	1977	7	7	0
1940	2	7	2	1978	6	10	0
1941	3	7	1	1979	5	11	0
1942	3	8	0	1980	5	11	0
1943	0	10	0	1981	7	9	0
1945	1	9	0	1982**	5	4	0
1945	1	9	0	1983	8	7	1
1946	6	5	0	1984	9	7	0
1947*	9	3	0	1985	5	11	0
1948**	11	1	0	1986	4	11	1
1949	6	5	1	1987	7	8	0
1950	5	7	0	1988	7	9	0
1951	3	9	0	1989	5	11	0
1952	4	8	0	1990	5	11	0
1953	1	10	1	1991	4	12	0
1954	2	10	0	1992	4	12	0
1955	4	7	1	1993	7	9	0
1956	7	5	0	Total	376	505	39
1957	3	9	0				

Number of NFL championships 2
Number of years .500 or better 29
Number of years below .500 44

*NFL champions
**Playoff team

1994 PREVIEW ■ ARIZONA

RECORDS

INDIVIDUAL

Service
Seasons played	18	Jim Hart (1966-83)
Games played	234	Jim Bakken (1962-78)
Consecutive games	234	Jim Bakken (1962-78)

Scoring
Points, career	1,380	Jim Bakken (1962-78)
Points, season	117	Neil O'Donoghue (1984)
		Jim Bakken (1967)
Points, game	40	Ernie Nevers (11/28/29)
Touchdowns, career	69	Roy Green (1979-90)
Touchdowns, season	17	John David Crow (1966)
Touchdowns, game	6	Ernie Nevers (11/28/29)
Field goals, career	282	Jim Bakken (1962-78)
Field goals, season	27	Jim Bakken (1967)
Field goals, game	7	Jim Bakken (9/24/67)
Extra points, career	534	Jim Bakken (1962-78)
Extra points, season	53	Pat Harder (1948)
Extra points, game	9	Pat Harder (10/17/48)

Rushing
Yards, career	7,999	Ottis Anderson (1979-86)
Yards, season	1,605	Ottis Anderson (1979)
Yards, game	203	John David Crow (12/18/60)
Attempts, career	1,859	Ottis Anderson (1979-86)
Attempts, season	331	Ottis Anderson (1979)
Attempts, game	36	Johnny Johnson (12/12/92)
		Ron Moore (11/7/93)
Touchdowns, career	46	Ottis Anderson (1979-86)
Touchdowns, season	14	John David Crow (1962)
Touchdowns, game	6	Ernie Nevers (11/28/29)

Passing
Rating, season	92.5	Neil Lomax (1984)
Completions, career	2,590	Jim Hart (1966-83)
Completions, season	345	Neil Lomax (1984)
Completions, game	37	Neil Lomax (12/16/84)
Yards, career	34,639	Jim Hart (1966-83)
Yards, season	4,614	Neil Lomax (1984)
Yards, game	468	Neil Lomax (12/16/84)
Attempts, career	5,096	Jim Hart (1966-83)
Attempts, season	560	Neil Lomax (1984)
Attempts, game	61	Neil Lomax (9/20/87)
Touchdowns, career	209	Jim Hart (1966-83)
Touchdowns, season	28	Charley Johnson (1963)
		Neil Lomax (1984)
Touchdowns, game	6	Charley Johnson (11/2/69)
		Charley Johnson (9/26/85)
		Jim Hardy (10/2/50)

Receiving
Receptions, career	522	Roy Green (1979-90)
Receptions, season	91	J.T. Smith (1987)
Receptions, game	16	Sonny Randle (11/4/62)
Yards, career	8,497	Roy Green (1979-90)
Yards, season	1,555	Roy Green (1984)
Yards, game	256	Sonny Randle (11/4/62)
Touchdowns, career	66	Roy Green (1979-80)
Touchdowns, season	16	Sonny Randle (1960)
Touchdowns, game	5	Bob Shaw (10/2/50)

Interceptions
Career	52	Larry Wilson (1960-72)
Season	12	Bob Nussbaumer (1949)
Game	4	Jerry Norton (11/26/61)
		Jerry Norton (11/20/60)
		Bob Nussbaumer (11/13/49)

Longest plays
Run from scrimmage	83	John David Crow (TD, 10/4/58)
Pass play	98	Ogden Compton to Dick Lane (TD, 11/13/55)
Field goal	55	Greg Davis (12/19/93)
Interception return	96	Larry Wilson (TD, 12/19/65)
Kickoff return	106	Roy Green (TD, 10/21/79)
Punt return	95	Frank Bernardi (TD, 10/14/56)
Punt	84	Doug Russell (9/11/38)

Top scorers
	Points
Jim Bakken (1962-78)	1,380
Roy Green (1979-90)	414
Neil O'Donoghue (1980-85)	439
Pat Harder (1946-50)	389
Bobby Joe Conrad (1958-68)	389
Sonny Randle (1959-66)	360

Top rushers
	Yards
Ottis Anderson (1979-86)	7,999
Stump Mitchell (1981-89)	4,649
Jim Otis (1973-78)	3,863
John Roland (1966-72)	3,608
Charley Trippi (1947-55)	3,511
John David Crow (1958-64)	3,489

Top passers
	Completions
Jim Hart (1966-83)	2,590
Neil Lomax (1981-89)	1,818
Charley Johnson (1961-69)	1,030

Top passers
	Yards
Jim Hart (1966-83)	34,639
Neil Lomax (1981-89)	22,771
Charley Johnson (1961-69)	12,928
Paul Christman (1945-49)	6,751
Lamar McHan (1954-58)	6,578

Top receivers
	Receptions
Roy Green (1979-90)	522
Jackie Smith (1963-77)	480
Pat Tilley (1976-86)	469
Bobby Joe Conrad (1958-68)	418
J.T. Smith (1985-90)	377
Mel Gray (1971-82)	351

Top receivers
	Yards
Roy Green (1979-90)	8,497
Jackie Smith (1963-77)	7,918
Pat Tilley (1976-86)	7,005
Mel Gray (1971-82)	6,644
Bobby Joe Conrad (1958-68)	5,828

Most interceptions
	No.
Larry Wilson (1960-72)	52
Roger Wehrli (1969-82)	40
Dick "Night Train" Lane (1954-59)	30
Pat Fischer (1961-67)	29

PREVIEW: ATLANTA FALCONS

After two consecutive 6-10 seasons, a change was needed for the Falcons. A big change.

Head coach Jerry Glanville. Gone.

QB Chris Miller. Gone.

OG Chris Hinton. Gone.

WR's Michael Haynes and Mike Pritchard. Gone.

During Glanville's four years as Atlanta's leader, the Falcons usually were on an emotional roller coaster and rarely played to form. The result was three double-digit-loss seasons in those four years, despite the presence of above-average personnel.

Taking Glanville's place is June Jones, the team's popular former assistant head coach who was in charge of offense. Unlike Glanville, who always seemed to be making headlines, Jones lets the players get the credit, is a good motivator in a positive way and does not have a large doghouse. Given that the Falcon roster is filled with diverse personalities and at times has had its share of internal problems, hiring from within figures to be a positive.

"I feel like I can work with the people here," said Jones. "I have a real good handle on the situation, what needs to be done. I'm real excited about the opportunity to get that job done and put us back in the playoffs and make us a winner again.

"I promise the people of Atlanta that you'll be proud of me when my tenure here is long gone, and I'll do everything I can to build a championship team here in Atlanta."

Although Jones spent his days as an assistant on the offensive side of the ball for Falcon teams that often were explosive on offense but porous on defense, he quickly let it be known that there needs to be more of a balance for Atlanta to win.

"I have great confidence in my abilities on the offensive side of the football," said Jones. "I know we will move the football. I know we'll be exciting. I know we will give our players an opportunity to win. The thing that we have to do is get better on the other side, and we're committed to do that through free-agency. Managing our (salary) cap might mean that we're going to have to make some sacrifices on the offensive side of the ball to do that."

Jones proved to be a man of his word. Soon after he had taken over, Miller, Hinton and Haynes had left via free-agency. Furthermore, Pritchard was dealt to the Broncos, while Chris Doleman, a big-time pass-rushing defensive end, was acquired from the Vikings.

The Falcons filled the void left by Miller with a blockbuster offseason deal to acquire former Colt QB Jeff George in exchange for three high draft choices. George has the strongest arm in the NFL and a lightning-quick release, but he can also be a whiner and finger-pointer. After watching George's pre-draft workout in 1990, Jones called it the finest QB workout he had ever seen. Jones has wanted to work with George ever since.

"We've always thought Jeff is a real talented player," said Jones. "We felt ever since the day we worked him out, he's probably the finest passer physically throwing the football we've ever seen.

"The thing we've got to do now is take him to another level of play. In our scheme, we're going to feature his skills."

Falcon president Taylor Smith said, "If you could mold the prototype quarterback, he'd be it."

Atlanta vice president Ken Herock said, "Every quarterback June has worked with has moved up a notch. We felt Jeff was something special four years ago, and we still see that in him."

George won't be able to throw to Haynes or Pritchard, who together caught 146 passes for 1,514 yards last season, but he still has Andre Rison who caught 86 passes for 1,242 yards and 15 touchdowns and was deadlier than ever inside the red zone. Rison has superior separation quickness and always seems to work his way free in the endzone. He is also a great runner after the catch and a great competitor.

The Falcons also must replace Hinton and C Jamie Dukes on the offensive line, but this is a unit that has quite a bit of talent. When 38-year-old Mike Kenn is healthy, he is still one of the most effective pass-blocking left tackles in the NFL. A superb technician and true student of the game, Kenn struggled with injuries early last year, then played very well down the stretch when he was healthier. In his first year as a starter at right tackle, Bob Whitfield struggled in some games but looked like a very good player in others. Whitfield should only get better, and the same holds true for Lincoln Kennedy at guard, if he keeps his weight down. The Falcons will look to replace Dukes and Hinton with Roman Fortin; Robbie Tobeck, who was on injured reserve last season; No. 3 pick Alai Kalaniuvalu and free-agent acquisition Mike Zandofsky, previously with the Chargers.

Whereas the Falcons have undergone considerable change at quarterback, receiver and the offensive line, the status quo appears in order at running back with Erric Pegram, who burst out of nowhere last season to rush for 1,185 yards on 292 carries. Pegram is not very big — his longest run last year was only 29 yards and he scored just three times. Nonetheless, he has good vision and balance, and for the first time in his Falcon career, he was quick to hit the hole and ran decisively instead of dancing.

Jones kept his word when he said the team would make some sacrifices on offense in order to help out the defense. In particular, the Falcons have used the offseason to upgrade their defensive line, with Doleman, and their secondary.

Last season when CB Deion Sanders was

1994 PREVIEW ■ ATLANTA

playing major-league baseball, the Falcons were 0-5. When Sanders was playing football, they were 6-5. In 16 games, the rest of the Falcon defense had six interceptions, while Sanders picked off seven passes in 11 games.

"I think he's the best football player in the National Football League, bar none," said former Phoenix head coach Joe Bugel.

In order to avoid a repeat of last year's disastrous start while Sanders was playing baseball, the Falcons went out and spent some free-agent money on defensive backs. New acquisitions were former Steeler D.J. Johnson and ex-Chief Kevin Ross.

Johnson lacks great skills and speed, but he is a solid player who the Falcons hope steps up to a new level at cornerback with the change of scenery.

"He's always been overshadowed because of (perennial Steeler Pro Bowl CB Rod) Woodson's presence," said Falcon DB coach Greg Brown. "But we think he can do things we want to do. He's very tough mentally. We want to get up in peoples' faces here, and he's got that type of mentality."

Johnson will be the team's best cornerback until Sanders returns from baseball. Vinnie Clark has great speed and jumps well, but he is a not a very aware ball athlete. Darnell Walker got some starts as a rookie last season, but he lacks size and deep cover speed.

Ross is a very good tackler, a tough hitter, has better range than pure speed and is extremely competitive. He should get a good look at free safety.

Roger Harper moved into the starting lineup last year at strong safety as a rookie. He has good range, but free safety may be the position for which he is better-suited. Scott Case has just about reached the end of the line at free safety. Alton Montgomery, who spent last year in Glanville's doghouse, is a great hitter who runs well, but he goes for the hit instead of the ball and blows too many assignments.

Atlanta was hoping for big things from ex-49er Pierce Holt last year, but he was totally beaten up and worn down from playing on AstroTurf by the end of the season. As a result, he had one of his least productive seasons and was not used properly, as the Falcons often ran him into double teams. Nonetheless, he was still the team's best defensive lineman and, this year, the presence of Doleman should help immensely. James Geathers can't play full time because of bad knees, but he is a very good situational pass rusher. Moe Gardner is undersized but active and intense, Lester Archambeau was a nice surprise last year and

Andre Rison

Mel Agee has size but is a very average player. Chuck Smith does not have the size, but he is a very intense player who can rush the quarterback.

Under new defensive coordinator Jim Bates, the Falcons will use a 4-2-5 alignment as their base defense, and the linebackers figure to be Jessie Tuggle and Jesse Solomon. Tuggle is only about 5-10, but he always seems to be in a natural hitting position, plays with great leverage and makes a lot of tackles. Solomon is still mobile and active. At one point the Falcons thought Darion Conner could be a dominating player at outside linebacker, but, as yet, he has not lived up to those expectations.

An area of strength for the Falcons is their special teams. PK Norm Johnson has had three great years in a row. Last season Johnson missed one kick all year, making 26-of-27 field goals and all 34 extra point attempts. After a shaky start lin 1993, Harold Alexander punted at close to a Pro Bowl level. Alexander finished with a 43.3-yard average and a 37.6 net with just three touchbacks and 21 kicks inside the 20-yard line. Tony Smith had a great year returning kickoffs and was adequate on punt returns. Sanders doesn't return as many kicks, but he is by far the team's best return man.

FAST FACTS

■ Andre Rison holds the NFL record for the most catches in the first five years of a player's career with 394.

■ LB Jessie Tuggle has led the team in tackles five consecutive years, during which time he averaged 193.8 tackles per season.

■ The Falcon WR corps has produced the NFL's top scoring tandem in each of the last three seasons (Rison and Mike Pritchard in 1993; Rison and Michael Haynes in '91 and '92).

PRO FOOTBALL WEEKLY 1994 ALMANAC

1994 PLAYER ROSTER

NO.	NAME	POS.	HT.	WT.	EXP.	COLLEGE	GP/GS
24	Addison, Bryan	S	6-0	200	1	Hawaii	0/0
98	Age, Louis	OT	6-7	360	2	S.W. Louisiana	0/0
68	Agee, Mel	DL	6-5	298	3	Illinois	11/7
62	Alex, Keith	OG	6-4	307	1	Texas A&M	13/0
5	Alexander, Harold	P	6-2	224	2	Appalachian State	16/0
92	Archambeau, Lester	DE	6-5	275	5	Stanford	15/11
69	Barber, Rudy	OG	6-2	286	R	Miami (Fla.)	—
77	Bedofsky, Mike	OG	6-4	289	R	Missouri	—
25	Case, Scott	S	6-1	188	11	Oklahoma	16/16
	Clark, Robert	WR	5-11	173	6	N. Carolina Central	0/0
27	Clark, Vinnie	CB	6-0	194	4	Ohio State	15/9
56	Conner, Darion	LB	6-2	245	5	Jackson State	14/10
51	Dinkins, Howard	LB	6-1	230	3	Florida State	3/0
19	Dixon, Corey	WR	5-7	155	R	Nebraska	—
59	Doleman, Chris	DE	6-5	275	9	Pittsburgh	16/16
63	Earle, John	OG	6-4	290	1	Western Illinois	0/0
8	Ferguson, Reggie	WR	5-9	180	R	Louisville	—
	Figaro, Cedric	LB	6-3	257	7	Notre Dame	0/0
65	Fortin, Roman	OG-C	6-5	295	5	San Diego State	16/0
14	Gagliano, Bob	QB	6-3	205	7	Utah State	0/0
76	Gann, Mike	DE	6-5	270	10	Notre Dame	8/8
67	Gardner, Moe	NT	6-2	261	4	Illinois	16/16
97	Geathers, James	DT	6-7	290	11	Wichita State	14/0
11	George, Jeff	QB	6-4	218	5	Illinois	13/11
50	George, Ron	LB	6-2	225	2	Stanford	12/4
71	Goldberg, Bill	DT	6-2	266	2	Georgia	5/0
53	Gordon, Dwayne	LB	6-1	231	2	New Hampshire	5/0
63	Guiles, Jonathon	DE	6-4	270	R	S. Carolina State	—
47	Harper, Roger	S	6-2	223	2	Ohio State	16/12
83	Harris, Leonard	WR	5-8	162	9	Texas Tech	4/2
18	Harrison, Tony	WR	5-10	188	R	Texas A&M	—
29	Hatch, Lawrence	CB	5-11	194	1	Florida	0/0
3	Hebert, Bobby	QB	6-4	215	9	NW Louisiana	14/12
74	Heidenreich, Jon	OG	6-5	285	1	NE Louisiana	0/0
95	Holt, Pierce	DE	6-4	275	7	Angelo State	16/16
39	Jack, Eric	CB	5-10	177	R	New Mexico	—
17	Jack, Keith	WR	5-9	177	R	Houston	—
98	Jackson, Tyoka	DE	6-1	266	R	Penn State	—
99	James, John	OL	6-3	300	1	Mississippi State	0/0
85	Jones, Tony	WR	5-7	145	5	Texas	2/0
16	Johnson, Clint	WR	5-7	178	R	Notre Dame	—
44	Johnson, D.J.	CB	6-0	183	5	Kentucky	16/15
9	Johnson, Norm	PK	6-2	203	13	UCLA	16/0
41	Johnson, Pat	S	6-1	201	R	Purdue	—
78	Kenn, Mike	OT	6-7	286	17	Michigan	16/16
66	Kennedy, Lincoln	OT-OG	6-6	335	2	Washington	16/16
88	LeBel, Harper	TE	6-4	248	6	Colorado State	16/0
73	Logan, Ernie	DE	6-3	285	4	East Carolina	8/1
43	Lowery, Tim	RB	5-11	247	1	Clark Atlanta	0/0
86	Lyons, Mitch	TE	6-4	255	2	Michigan State	16/8
87	Mathis, Terance	WR	5-10	177	5	New Mexico	16/3
34	Mims, David	WR	5-8	191	1	Baylor	15/2
22	Montgomery, Alton	CB	6-0	202	5	Houston	8/0
	Noga, Niko	LB	6-1	235	9	Hawaii	0/0
91	Paulk, Tim	LB	6-0	232	1	Florida	0/0

26

1994 PREVIEW ■ ATLANTA

1994 PLAYER ROSTER

NO.	NAME	POS.	HT.	WT.	EXP.	COLLEGE	GP/GS
33	Pegram, Erric	RB	5-9	188	4	North Texas State	16/14
2	Peterson, Todd	PK	5-10	175	1	Georgia	0/0
82	Phillips, Jason	WR	5-7	166	6	Houston	6/0
96	Richardson, Huey	DE	6-4	243	2	Florida	0/0
80	Rison, Andre	WR	6-1	188	6	Michigan State	16/16
15	Rogers, Joe	WR	5-7	161	R	Texas Southern	—
36	Ross, Kevin	S	5-9	182	9	Temple	15/15
55	Ruether, Mike	C-OG	6-4	286	9	Texas	16/0
93	Sally, Lamar	DE	6-5	281	1	Central Michigan	0/0
21	Sanders, Deion	CB	6-1	185	6	Florida State	11/10
37	Shelley, Elbert	CB	5-11	185	8	Arkansas State	16/0
90	Smith, Chuck	LB-DE	6-2	254	3	Tennessee	15/1
28	Smith, Tony	RB	6-1	224	3	Southern Miss.	15/0
54	Solomon, Jess	LB	6-0	240	9	Florida State	16/16
84	Spencer, Darryl	WR	5-8	172	1	Miami (Fla.)	0/0
32	Stinson, Lemuel	CB	5-9	180	6	Texas Tech	0/0
52	Tippins, Ken	LB	6-1	235	6	Middle Tenn. State	14/1
61	Tobeck, Robbie	C	6-4	275	1	Washington State	0/0
11	Tolliver, Billy Joe	QB	6-1	218	6	Texas Tech	7/2
58	Tuggle, Jessie	LB	5-11	230	8	Valdosta State (Ga.)	16/16
4	Tyner, Scott	P-PK	6-1	189	R	Oklahoma State	—
45	Walker, Darnell	CB	5-8	164	2	Oklahoma	15/8
40	Wallace, Anthony	RB	6-0	191	1	California	0/0
20	Walton, Tim	CB	5-11	180	R	Ohio State	—
46	Washington, Charles	S	6-1	217	6	Cameron	6/0
6	White, Stan	QB	6-2	202	R	Auburn	—
70	Whitfield, Bob	OT	6-5	308	3	Stanford	16/16
94	Wilkins, David	DE-LB	6-4	240	2	Eastern Kentucky	0/0
69	Williams, Thomas	DT	6-3	274	R	Wyoming	—
72	Zandofsky, Mike	C-OG	6-2	305	5	Washington	16/16

'94 DRAFT PICKS

RD.	NAME	POS.	HT.	WT.	COLLEGE
2.	Emanuel, Bert	WR	5-10	176	Rice
3.	Phillips, Anthony	DB	6-2	217	Texas A&M-Kingsville
3.	Kalaniuvalu, Alai	OG	6-3	303	Oregon State
4.	Klein, Perry	QB	6-2	214	C.W. Post
4.	Davis, Mitch	LB	6-1	238	Georgia
5.	Houston, Harrison	WR	5-9	170	Florida
7.	Anderson, Jamal	RB	5-10	252	Utah

PRO FOOTBALL WEEKLY 1994 ALMANAC

TEAM AT A GLANCE

TEAM DIRECTORY

Address	2745 Burnette Road
Suwanee, Georgia 30174
(404) 945-1111
Stadium	Georgia Dome
One Georgia Dome Drive
Atlanta, Georgia 30313
Capacity: 71,594
Playing surface: Artifical turf
Training Camp	2745 Burnette Road
Suwanee, Georgia 30174
Colors	Black, red, silver and white
Television	WATL, Channel 36
Radio	WSB, 750 AM

ADMINISTRATION
Chairman of the board: Rankin M. Smith Sr.
President: Taylor Smith
Vice president-chief financial officer: Jim Hay
Vice president-player personnel: Ken Herock
Controller: Wallace Norman
Director of administration: Rob Jackson
Director of pro personnel: Chuck Connor
Director of player development: Tommy Nobis
Director of public relations: Charlie Taylor
Director of community relations: Carol Breeding
Director of ticket operations: Jack Ragsdale
Trainer: Ron Medlin

1994 SCHEDULE

Preseason
JULY 30	vs. San Diego (at Canton, Oh.)	12:00
AUG. 6	at Denver	7:00
AUG. 12	BUFFALO	7:00
AUG. 19	at Cleveland	7:30
AUG. 26	PHILADELPHIA	7:00

Regular season
SEP. 4	at Detroit	1:00
SEP. 11	L.A. RAMS	1:00
SEP. 18	KANSAS CITY	8:00
SEP. 25	at Washington	1:00
OCT. 2	at L.A. Rams	1:00
OCT. 9	TAMPA BAY	1:00
OCT. 16	SAN FRANCISCO	1:00
OCT. 23	at L.A. Raiders	1:00
OCT. 30	OPEN DATE	
NOV. 6	SAN DIEGO	1:00
NOV. 13	at New Orleans	12:00
NOV. 20	at Denver	2:00
NOV. 27	PHILADELPHIA	1:00
DEC. 4	at San Francisco	1:00
DEC. 11	NEW ORLEANS	8:00
DEC. 18	vs. Green Bay at Milw.	12:00
DEC. 24	ARIZONA	1:00

HEAD COACH
June Jones
After spending three years as an assistant coach under Jerry Glanville, Jones will get his first opportunity as an NFL head coach in 1994. Jones is the architect of the high-powered "Red Gun" offense that has broken team offensive records in recent seasons. A former Falcon quarterback who mainly spent time backing up club-record-holder Steve Bartkowski, Jones has professional experience in three leagues: the NFL, CFL and USFL. Born Feb. 19, 1953, Portland, Ore.
Previous NFL: assistant head coach-offense, Atlanta 1991-93; quarterbacks-receivers Detroit 1989-90; QB coach Houston 1987-88.
Previous college: assistant coach, Hawaii 1983.
Player: NFL, quarterback, Atlanta 1977-81. College, quarterback, Portland State 1975-76, Hawaii 1973-74.

ASSISTANT COACHES
Keith Armstrong: defense
Previous NFL: none. Player: No NFL. College: running back, defensive back, 1983-86 Temple.
Jim Bates: defensive coordinator
Previous NFL: defensive line, 1991-93 Cleveland. Player: No NFL. College: linebacker, 1964-67 Tennessee.
Greg Brown: secondary
Previous NFL: secondary, 1984-86 Tampa Bay. Player: No NFL. College: cornerback, Texas-El Paso.
Mouse Davis: quarterbacks
Previous NFL: offensive coordinator, 1989-90 Detroit. Player: No NFL. College: quarterback, running back, 1952-55 Western Oregon State.
Frank Gansz: assistant head coach
Previous NFL: special teams, 1989-93 Detroit; 1986-88 Kansas City (head coach 1987-88); 1983-85 Philadelphia; 1981-82, 1979-80 Cincinnati; 1978 San Francisco. Player: No NFL. College: center, linebacker, 1957-59 Navy.
Joe Haering: linebackers
Previous NFL: special teams-linebackers, 1978-79 N.Y. Jets. Player: No NFL. College: linebacker, Bucknell.
Milt Jackson: wide receivers
Previous NFL: wide receivers, 1992-93 L.A. Rams; 1989-91 Indianapolis; 1986-88 Houston; 1985 Philadelphia; 1983-84 Buffalo; 1980-82 San Francisco. Player: NFL, defensive back, 1967, San Francisco. College: defensive back, 1965-66 Tulsa.
Tim Jorgensen: strength and conditioning
Previous NFL: Atlanta 1987; 1984-86 Philadelphia. Player: No NFL. College: guard, 1974-76 Southwest Missouri State.
Bill Kollar: defensive line
Previous NFL: Atlanta 1990; 1984 Tampa Bay. Player: NFL, defensive end, 1974-76 Cincinnati; 1977-81 Tampa Bay. College: defensive end, 1971-74 Montana State.
Bob Palcic: offensive line
Previous NFL: None. Player: No NFL. College: linebacker, 1967-70 Dayton.
Ollie Wilson: running backs
Previous NFL: Atlanta 1991. Player: No NFL.

1994 PREVIEW ■ ATLANTA

TEAM AT A GLANCE

College: wide receiver, 1971-73 Springfield.

COACHING RECORDS
(includes postseason games)

Years	Coach	W	L	T
1966-68	Norb Hecker	4	26	1
1968-74	Norm Van Brocklin	37	49	3
1974-76	Marion Campbell	6	19	0
1976	Pat Peppler	3	6	0
1977-82	Leeman Bennett	47	44	0
1983-86	Dan Henning	22	41	1
1987-89	Marion Campbell	11	32	0
1989	Jim Hanifan	0	4	0
1990-93	Jerry Glanville	28	38	0

HISTORICAL HIGHLIGHTS

1965 Rankin Smith, a 41-year-old businessman, is awarded the NFL franchise for Atlanta for $8.5 million. ... LB Tommy Nobis of Texas and QB Randy Johnson from Texas A&I are the Falcons' two first-round draft choices.

1966 After 10 straight losses, the Falcons win their first game by defeating the Giants 27-16.

1971 The Falcons post their first winning season, going 7-6-1.

1972 RB Dave Hampton sets a club record by rushing for 161 yards against the Rams. And, for the first time in team history, two backs rush for more than 100 yards in a game, as Art Malone gained another 103.

1973 The most points ever scored by the Falcons are racked up in an Opening Day 62-7 win over the Saints. A total of 35 club records are broken.

1978 The construction of a new, year-round training facility is begun in Suwanee, Georgia. ... The Falcons clinch their first playoff berth ever, then edge the Eagles 14-13 in the NFC wild-card game before falling to the Cowboys 27-20.

1979 RB William Andrews sets a club rushing record with a 167-yard performance against the Saints in overtime. He also becomes the first Falcon to rush for more than 1,000 yards in a season (1,023). ... QB Steve Bartkowski establishes a club mark by passing for 326 yards against the Broncos. ... RB Lynn Cain becomes the first Falcon to score three touchdowns in one game, on two receptions and a run against the Oakland Raiders.

1980 A team passing record is set when Bartkowski throws for 378 yards against the Cardinals. ... Atlanta wins its first NFC Western Division title with a record of 12-4. In the playoffs, however, they lose to Dallas 30-27 before a record crowd of 60,022 at Atlanta-Fulton County Stadium.

1982 The Falcons reach the playoffs for the third time in five years. In the first round of the Super Bowl Tournament of the strike-shortened 1982 season, however, they lose to Minnesota 30-24.

1984 RB Gerald Riggs sets team rushing records by carrying the ball 35 times for 202 yards against New Orleans.

1985 A new career record for rushing touchdowns is set by Gerald Riggs when he surpasses the 29 scored by William Andrews.

1987 Gerald Riggs becomes the all-time Falcon rushing leader, moving ahead of William Andrews' 5,986.

1989 Rookie CB Deion Sanders returns a punt 68 yards for a touchdown and becomes the first athlete in history to score an NFL touchdown and hit a major league home run (for the New York Yankees) in the same week.

1990 The Falcons celebrate their 25th anniversary. ... WR Andre Rison sets a club record with 82 pass receptions for the year.

1991 The Falcons play their final game in Fulton County Stadium and defeat the Seattle Seahawks before a sell-out crowd 26-13. ... Atlanta makes it to the playoffs as a wild-card with a record of 10-6, then defeat the Saints 20-17 in the first round but then fall to the Redskins 24-7.

1992 Atlanta plays its first game in the new Georgia Dome, a preseason 20-10 win over the Eagles. ... The Falcons lead the NFL with 33 touchdown passes, a club record. Other team records: 336 pass completions, 194 passing first downs and WR Andre Rison's 93 pass receptions.

1994 After successive 6-10 seasons, Jerry Glanville, head coach since 1990, is fired and replaced by June Jones.

PRO FOOTBALL WEEKLY 1994 ALMANAC

TEAM AT A GLANCE

HALL OF FAME MEMBERS
None

RETIRED JERSEY NUMBERS
31 RB William Andrews
57 C Jeff Van Note
60 LB Tommy Nobis

FIRST-ROUND DRAFT CHOICES
(since 1980)

Year	Selection	College
1980	TE Junior Miller	Nebraska
1981	DB Bobby Butler	Florida State
1982	RB Gerald Riggs	Arizona State
1983	DE Mike Pitts	Alabama
1984	DT Rick Bryan	Oklahoma
1985	OT Bill Fralic	Pittsburgh
1986	DT Tony Casillas	Oklahoma
	LB Tim Green	Syracuse
1987	QB Chris Miller	Oregon
1988	LB Aundray Bruce	Auburn
1989	DB Deion Sanders	Florida State
	WR Shawn Collins	Northern Arizona
1990	RB Steve Broussard	Washington State
1991	CB Bruce Pickens	Nebraska
	WR Mike Pritchard	Colorado
1992	OT Bob Whitfield	Stanford
	RB Tony Smith	So. Mississippi
1993	OT Lincoln Kennedy	Washington
1994	No choice	

RECORD VS. OTHER NFL TEAMS
(includes postseason games)

	Record
Arizona Cardinals	5-11-0
Buffalo Bills	3-3-0
Chicago Bears	9-9-0
Cincinnati Bengals	2-6-0
Cleveland Browns	2-8-0
Dallas Cowboys	6-11-0
Denver Broncos	3-4-0
Detroit Lions	5-17-0
Green Bay Packers	9-9-0
Houston Oilers	5-3-0
Indianapolis Colts	0-10-0
Kansas City Chiefs	0-3-0
Los Angeles Raiders	3-4-0
Los Angeles Rams	16-36-2
Miami Dolphins	1-5-0
Minnesota Vikings	6-12-0
New England Patriots	4-3-0
New Orleans Saints	28-22-0
New York Giants	6-6-0
New York Jets	3-3-0
Philadelphia Eagles	7-8-1
Pittsburgh Steelers	1-9-0
San Diego Chargers	3-1-0
San Francisco 49ers	21-32-1
Seattle Seahawks	1-4-0
Tampa Bay Buccaneers	6-6-0
Washington Redskins	3-14-1

YEAR-BY-YEAR RECORDS

Year	Won	Lost	Tied	Year	Won	Lost	Tied
1966	3	11	0	1980**	12	4	0
1967	1	12	1	1981	7	9	0
1968	2	12	0	1982**	5	4	0
1969	6	8	0	1983	7	9	0
1970	4	8	2	1984	4	12	0
1971	7	6	1	1985	4	12	0
1972	7	7	0	1986	7	8	1
1973	9	5	0	1987	3	12	0
1974	3	11	0	1988	5	11	0
1975	4	10	0	1989	3	13	0
1976	4	10	0	1990	5	11	0
1977	7	7	0	1991**	10	6	0
1978**	9	7	0	1992	6	10	0
1979	6	10	0	1993	6	10	0
				Total	156	255	5

Number of NFL championships   0
Number of years .500 or better   8
Number of years below .500   20

*NFL champions
**Playoff team

1994 PREVIEW ■ ATLANTA

RECORDS

INDIVIDUAL

Service
Seasons played	18	Jeff Van Note (1969-86)
Games played	246	Jeff Van Note (1969-86)
Consecutive games	155	Jeff Van Note (1976-86)

Scoring
Points, career	558	Mick Luckhurst (1981-87)
Points, season	114	Mick Luckhurst (1981)
Points, game	18	By many players
Touchdowns, career	48	Gerald Riggs (1982-88)
		Andre Rison (1990-93)
Touchdowns, season	15	Andre Rison (1993)
Touchdowns, game	3	By many players
Field goals, career	115	Mick Luckhurst (1981-87)
Field goals, season	26	Nick Mike-Mayer (1973)
		Norm Johnson (1993)
Field goals, game	5	Nick Mike-Mayer (11/4/73)
		Tim Mazzetti (10/30/78)
Extra points, career	213	Mick Luckhurst (1981-87)
Exta points, season	51	Mick Luckhurst (1981)
Extra points, game	8	Nick Mike-Mayer (9/16/73)

Rushing
Yards, career	6,631	Gerald Riggs (1982-88)
Yards, season	1,719	Gerald Riggs (1985)
Yards, game	202	Gerald Riggs (9/2/84)
Attempts, career	1,587	Gerald Riggs (1982-88)
Attempts, season	397	Gerald Riggs (1985)
Attempts, game	41	Gerald Riggs (11/17/85)
Touchdowns, career	48	Gerald Riggs (1982-88)
Touchdowns, season	13	Gerald Riggs (1984)
Touchdowns, game	3	By many players

Passing
Rating, career	78.8	Bob Berry (1968-72)
Rating, season	110.2	Wade Wilson (1992)
Completions, career	1,870	Steve Bartkowski (1975-85)
Completions, season	297	Steve Bartkowski (1981)
Completions, game	37	Chris Miller (12/24/89)
Yards, career	23,468	Steve Bartkowski (1975-85)
Yards, season	3,830	Steve Bartkowski (1981)
Yards, game	416	Steve Bartkowski (11/15/81)
Attempts, career	3,329	Steve Bartkowski (1975-85)
Attempts, season	533	Steve Bartkowski (1981)
Attempts, game	66	Chris Miller (12/24/89)
Touchdowns, career	154	Steve Bartkowski (1975-85)
Touchdowns, season	31	Steve Bartkowski (1980)
Touchdowns, game	5	Wade Wilson (12/12/92)

Receiving
Receptions, career	359	Alfred Jenkins (1975-83)
Receptions, season	93	Andre Rison (1992)
Receptions, game	15	William Andrews (11/15/81)
Yards, career	6,257	Alfred Jenkins (1975-83)
Yards, season	1,358	Alfred Jenkins (1981)
Yards, game	193	Alfred Jackson (12/2/84)
Touchdowns, career	48	Andre Rison (1990-93)
Touchdowns, season	15	Andre Rison (1993)
Touchdowns, game	3	By four players

Interceptions
Career	39	Rolland Lawrence (1973-81)
Season	10	Scott Case (1988)
Game	2	By many players

Longest Plays
Run from scrimmage	67	Mike Rozier (12/30/90)
Pass play	98	Bobby Hebert to Michael Haynes (TD, 9/12/93)
Field goal	54	Paul McFadden (11/5/89)
		Norm Johnson (9/6/92, 11/29/92, 9/5/93)
Interception return	101	Tom Pridemore (TD, 9/20/81)
Kickoff return	100	Dennis Pearson (12/17/78)
		Deion Sanders (10/13/91)
Punt return	79	Deion Sanders (TD, 10/28/90)
Punt	75	John James (11/30/75)
		Harold Alexander (10/3/93)

Top scorers
	Points
Mick Luckhurst (1981-87)	558
Norm Johnson (1991-93)	300
Andre Rison (1990-93)	288
Gerald Riggs (1982-88)	288
Nick Mike-Mayer (1973-77)	282
William Andrews (1979-86)	246

Top rushers
	Yards
Gerald Riggs (1982-88)	6,631
William Andrews (1979-86)	5,986
Dave Hampton (1972-76)	3,490
Haskel Stanback (1974-79)	2,662
Lynn Cain (1979-84)	2,313
Jim Butler (1968-71)	2,250

Top passers
	Completions
Steve Bartkowski (1975-85)	1,870
Chris Miller (1987-93)	1,129
Bob Berry (1968-72)	598
Randy Johnson (1966-70)	435
David Archer (1984-87)	331

Top passers
	Yards
Steve Bartkowski (1975-85)	23,468
Chris Miller (1987-93)	14,066
Bob Berry (1968-72)	8,489
Randy Johnson (1966-70)	5,538
David Archer (1984-87)	4,275

Top receivers
	Receptions
Alfred Jenkins (1975-83)	359
Andre Rison (1990-93)	342
Jim Mitchell (1969-79)	305
William Andrews (1979-86)	276
Michael Haynes (1988-93)	254
Wallace Francis (1975-81)	244

Top receivers
	Yards
Alfred Jenkins (1975-83)	6,257
Andre Rison (1990-93)	4,547
Jim Mitchell (1969-79)	4,348
Michael Haynes (1988-93)	4,066
Wallace Francis (1975-81)	3,695
Stacey Bailey (1982-89)	3,378

Most interceptions
	No.
Rolland Lawrence (1973-81)	39
Ray Brown (1971-77)	31
Ken Reaves (1966-74)	29
Scott Case (1984-93)	28
Bobby Butler (1981-92)	27
Deion Sanders (1989-93)	24

Most Sacks
	No.
Claude Humphrey (1968-78)	62.5

PREVIEW: BUFFALO BILLS

The Buffalo Bills are used to the stares. They are used to the raised eyebrows. They are used to the sophomoric remarks made by late-night talk-show hosts. They know that derisive remarks are part of the territory after losing four straight Super Bowls.

Still they come back for more. What else can they do? The Bills are a football team, so they must play football. There is nothing heroic about coming back and getting beaten repeatedly with the championship on the line. But there is something very admirable about laughing in the face of your critics and persevering.

The Bills are not the offensive machine they were a few years ago. In 1990 the Buffalo no-huddle attack struck fear in their hearts of nearly every defensive coordinator throughout the AFC. But that once-devastating offensive unit isn't what it once was. After scoring 428 points in 1990, 458 in '91 and 381 in '92, the Bills only put 329 points on the board in '93.

There are at least two reasons for this slump. First, the Buffalo running game suffered dramatically. In 1992 the Bills averaged 4.4 yards per carry. In '93 that figure dropped to 3.5 yards per crack. RB Thurman Thomas is still a versatile, dependable back; but he may no longer be the explosive game-breaker who could dominate for three or four games. The Bills' passing game also lacks the big-time receiver who can burn a defense with his ability to get deep. Don Beebe is the lone burner, and he's not durable. As a result, defenses no longer respect the Bills' ability to make big plays.

One thing the Bills do have going for them is the play of QB Jim Kelly. While the 1993 season was not one of Kelly's best statistically, he appeared to make great strides from a team-leadership point of view. In the past, Kelly relied on his arm strength to make big plays for the Bills, and he often made huge mistakes because of it. But with more study and attention to detail, Kelly changed his personal game plan and stopped making big errors. There are questions about Kelly's arm. He was injured in an offseason QB competition last year, and for a good part of 1993, he was unable to throw the deep ball or demonstrate adequate velocity. However, by the second half of the season, Kelly was throwing the ball as well as ever. But the experience was not lost on Kelly.

"I can promise you one thing," he said. "There's no way I'm getting involved in one of those competitions again."

If Kelly does get injured, he probably has the league's best backup, Frank Reich, ready to jump in. While most backups can be classified as cerebral types, none can hold a candle to the well-studied Reich. The former Maryland quarterback, who has engineered perhaps the greatest comebacks in the history of college and professional football, spends all of his time in front of the projector studying upcoming opponents. This leaves him prepared in case he has to go in for Kelly, but it also allows him to pass on his findings to Kelly in crucial game situations. Physically, Reich is not imposing as a thrower or a runner, but he is adequate in both areas.

Thomas rebounded well after two previous Super Bowl disappointments, so it will be interesting to see how he comes back from his latest debacle. Thomas has carried a chip on his shoulder since his rookie season, because he was not a first-round selection. That resentment provides serious motivation for Thomas, who rushed for 1,315 yards and also caught 48 passes. Thomas is a great all-around threat, but his yards per carry dipped to 3.5 in '93, so this could be the year that opposing defenses catch up with him. Backup Kenneth Davis fits in at running back nearly as well as Reich does at quarterback. Davis is bigger, faster and stronger than Thomas, but he does not cut as well or make tacklers miss very often. FB Carwell Gardner does not fit Buffalo's offense. He has size, power and toughness but fumbles too often. Former WR-TE Nate Turner has a chance to

Bruce Smith

PHOTO BY HARRY SCULL JR

1994 PREVIEW ■ BUFFALO

move ahead of Gardner in training camp.

The Buffalo receivers do not pose the threat they once did during the heyday of the no-huddle offense. The biggest problem may be Andre Reed, who never was a deep threat and appears to have slowed down. Reed still has solid hands, is fearless crossing the middle and runs hard after the catch. However, his major problem is that he tends to sulk, and that tendency appears to have gotten worse. He gets upset when the Bills throw passes in the direction of other receivers or if an official's call goes against him. Former Colt Bill Brooks had a solid season for the Bills in 1993 but really is not a breakaway threat. One thing Brooks can do is break away from tacklers and get the extra few yards needed for crucial first downs. Brooks caught 60 passes last season, but none was for more than 32 yards. Beebe is a great favorite of Kelly's, but he is erratic. While he can make the most difficult catch at times, he will also drop catchable balls. However, Beebe is a great hustler, and his never-say-die attitude was apparent in Super Bowl XXVII, when he caught Dallas DT Leon Lett from behind and prevented yet another score. Second-year WR Russell Copeland had a good rookie year, but he's a size receiver, not a speed merchant. The Bills hope No. 2 pick WR Bucky Brooks adds the home-run speed that is sorely lacking. TE Pete Metzelaars led the Bills in receiving last year with 68 catches, but he's very slow. Metzelaars averaged only nine yards a reception in 1993. He is very effective when receiving tight coverage, because he's excellent at shielding defenders away from the ball with his huge body. No. 2 pick TE Lonnie Johnson can split the seam and go deep.

On the offensive line, John Fina took over left tackle from Will Wolford last year and showed good foot quickness. However, he needs to get stronger. He was beaten badly in the second half of the Super Bowl by Cowboy bull rusher Jim Jeffcoat. After losing Wolford to free-agency a year ago, Buffalo must cope with the loss of ORT Howard Ballard this year. "The House" was a superb run blocker for the Bills who got away with holding on his pass blocking. Jerry Crafts, a huge player, is his likely successor. If the Bills' line continues to play well, C Kent Hull will likely be the major reason. Hull makes all the line calls and adjustments and is very solid as a pass blocker. John Davis has size and strength at guard but is limited by his lack of agility. Glenn Parker has the size at the other OG slot, but he has even less athleticism than Davis.

Depending upon how you look at it, the Bills have either the worst good defense in football or the best bad defense. They forced a lot of turnovers last year and gave up only 242 points, but they gave up 5,554 yards and got pushed around on more than one occasion.

DE Bruce Smith is the best player on the Buffalo defense and often looks like the best defensive player in the league. Despite being double-teamed, Smith recorded 14 sacks and 24 QB hurries last year and showed explosive quickness and first-rate moves off the line. Smith is a bit undersized, and so are NT Jeff Wright and DLE Phil Hansen. But, unlike Smith, Wright and Hansen are just fairly good players, not the types who can dominate for long periods of time. When opposing offensive lines want to pound the ball on the ground, the Buffalo defensive line gets in major trouble.

Despite a new look last year after Shane Conlan and Carlton Bailey left via free-agency, the Bills got excellent play from their linebackers. Marvcus Patton and Mark Maddox stepped in at the ILB slots, and the results were good. Patton is somewhat better than Maddox, who is on the small side and struggles with bigger blockers. Outside, Darryl Talley was terrific once again, as he led the team with 136 tackles. Cornelius Bennett has nearly unlimited talent, but he is not put in a position to make big plays on a regular basis. The Bills like to line him up over a tight end, while he would put bigger numbers on the board if he were given more freedom. Keith Goganious is a solid backup at inside backer who is somewhat limited by his lack of speed.

The Bills lost Nate Odomes to Seattle in free-agency and traded J.D. Williams to Arizona, which means Thomas Smith, Mickey Washington and versatile No. 1 draft pick Jeff Burris will compete for starting jobs at cornerback. Smith is a tremendous athlete who can vertical jump over 40 inches. He is aggressive in coverage and enjoys mixing it up. Washington doesn't have great physical talent but is very well-prepared and a fighter. Henry Jones is a Pro Bowler at strong safety with great range and tremendous hitting impact. Matt Darby will probably replace Mark Kelso at free safety. Darby is a better athlete and has more size than Kelso, but he lacks Kelso's savvy and leadership ability.

The Bills probably have the league's best special-team player in Steve Tasker. He is joined by Mark Pike and Gardner, who are both aggressive on special teams. PK Steve Christie is solid but not among the league's elite. P Chris Mohr does not have a huge gross average, but he gets good hang time and is among the leaders in net punting.

FAST FACTS

■ The Bills allowed only 25 touchdowns last season, the fewest they've allowed in a 16-game schedule.

■ The Bills have won seven straight home playoff games since losing to the Chiefs in the AFL championship game in 1967.

■ In 1993 Thurman Thomas tied O.J. Simpson's team record for most consecutive 1,000-yard seasons (five).

PRO FOOTBALL WEEKLY 1994 ALMANAC

1994 PLAYER ROSTER

NO.	NAME	POS.	HT.	WT.	EXP.	COLLEGE	GP/GS
77	Barnett, Oliver	DE	6-3	292	5	Kentucky	16/6
82	Beebe, Don	WR	5-11	180	6	Chadron State	14/14
97	Bennett, Cornelius	LB	6-2	238	8	Alabama	16/16
61	Bock, John	OG	6-3	286	R	Indiana State	—
19	Branch, Darrick	WR	5-11	195	1	Hawaii	0/0
80	Brooks, Bill	WR	6-0	189	9	Boston U.	16/13
96	Brown, Monty	LB	6-0	228	2	Ferris State	13/0
29	Bryant, Phil	RB	5-10	208	1	Virginia Tech	0/0
2	Christie, Steve	PK	6-0	185	5	William & Mary	16/0
42	Collins, Mike	S	5-11	195	R	West Virginia	—
85	Copeland, Russell	WR	6-0	200	2	Memphis State	16/2
66	Crafts, Jerry	OT	6-6	351	3	Louisville	16/0
43	Darby, Matt	S	6-1	200	3	UCLA	16/3
65	Davis, John	OG	6-4	310	8	Georgia Tech	16/16
23	Davis, Kenneth	RB	5-10	208	9	Texas Christian	16/0
62	Devlin, Mike	C	6-1	293	2	Iowa	12/0
41	Evans, Greg	S	6-1	217	R	Texas Christian	—
5	Feexico, Sonny	P	6-2	240	R	E. Central Oklahoma	—
54	Fieldings, Anthony	LB	6-1	237	1	Morningside	0/0
70	Fina, John	OL	6-4	285	3	Arizona	16/16
33	Fuller, Eddie	RB	5-9	198	5	Louisiana State	7/0
35	Gardner, Carwell	FB	6-2	244	5	Louisville	13/2
50	Goganious, Keith	LB	6-2	239	3	Penn State	16/7
26	Gulledge, David	FS	6-1	203	2	Jacksonville State	0/0
90	Hansen, Phil	DE	6-5	278	4	North Dakota State	11/9
36	Henderson, Jerome	DB	5-10	189	4	Clemson	3/0
79	Hendrickson, Craig	OL	6-3	290	1	Minnesota	0/0
64	Herget, Todd	LB	6-2	226	R	Brigham Young	—
76	Hoyem, Steve	OT	6-7	287	R	Stanford	—
67	Hull, Kent	C	6-5	284	9	Mississippi State	14/13
30	Jourdain, Yonel	RB	5-11	204	1	Southern Illinois	0/0
12	Kelly, Jim	QB	6-3	226	9	Miami (Fla.)	16/16
68	Lacina, Corbin	OL	6-4	297	2	Augustana (SD)	0/0
31	Lawson, Shawn	CB	5-11	176	1	Baylor	0/0
63	Lingner, Adam	C	6-4	268	12	Illinois	16/0
73	Lodish, Mike	NT	6-3	280	5	UCLA	15/1
55	Maddox, Mark	LB	6-1	233	4	Northern Michigan	11/8
48	Marrow, Vince	TE	6-3	251	1	Toledo	0/0
15	McKay, Orlando	WR	5-10	176	1	Washington	0/0
88	Metzelaars, Pete	TE	6-7	254	13	Wabash (Ind.)	16/6
9	Mohr, Chris	P	6-5	215	5	Alabama	16/0
60	Ostroski, Jerry	G	6-4	310	2	Tulsa	0/0
74	Parker, Glenn	OG-OT	6-5	305	5	Arizona	16/9
92	Parrella, John	DL	6-3	296	2	Nebraska	10/0
44	Paterra, Greg	FB	5-11	224	2	Slippery Rock	0/0
99	Patton, James	DL	6-3	287	3	Texas	2/0
53	Patton, Marvcus	LB	6-2	243	5	UCLA	16/16
71	Philion, Ed	DT	6-2	273	R	Ferris State	—
94	Pike, Mark	DE	6-4	272	9	Georgia Tech	14/0
83	Reed, Andre	WR	6-2	190	10	Kutztown State	15/15
14	Reich, Frank	QB	6-4	205	10	Maryland	15/0
7	Rodgers, Matt	QB	6-3	205	2	Iowa	0/0
24	Schulz, Kurt	S	6-1	208	3	East. Washington	12/0
6	Silvestri, Don	PK	6-4	210	1	Pittsburgh	0/0
78	Smith, Bruce	DE	6-4	273	10	Virginia Tech	16/16

34

1994 PREVIEW ■ BUFFALO

1994 PLAYER ROSTER

NO.	NAME	POS.	HT.	WT.	EXP.	COLLEGE	GP/GS
28	Smith, Thomas	CB	5-11	188	2	North Carolina	16/1
11	Strom, Rick	QB	6-2	197	5	Georgia Tech	0/0
56	Talley, Darryl	LB	6-4	235	12	West Virginia	16/16
89	Tasker, Steve	WR	5-9	181	10	Northwestern	15/0
16	Thomas, Damon	WR	6-2	215	R	Wayne State	—
34	Thomas, Thurman	RB	5-10	198	7	Oklahoma State	16/16
40	Tindale, Tim	FB	5-10	220	R	Western Ontario	—
21	Turner, Nate	RB	6-1	255	3	Nebraska	13/0
25	Washington, Mickey	CB	5-9	191	4	Texas A&M	16/6
91	Wright, Jeff	NT	6-3	274	7	Central Missouri St.	15/15
57	Young, Glenn	LB	6-3	240	1	Syracuse	0/0

'94 DRAFT PICKS

RD.	NAME	POS.	HT.	WT.	COLLEGE
1.	Burris, Jeff	DB	6-0	204	Notre Dame
2.	Brooks, Bucky	WR	6-0	190	North Carolina
2.	Johnson, Lonnie	TE	6-3	230	Florida State
2.	Rogers, Sam	LB	6-3	245	Colorado
3.	Perry, Marlo	LB	6-4	250	Jackson State
3.	Louchiey, Corey	OT	6-7	305	South Carolina
4.	Crocker, Sean	DB	5-9	191	North Carolina
5.	Ofodile, A.J.	TE	6-7	260	Missouri
6.	Abrams, Anthony	DE	6-3	298	Clark Atlanta
6.	Knox, Kevin	WR	6-3	195	Florida State
7.	Johnson, Filmel	DB	5-10	186	Illinois

PRO FOOTBALL WEEKLY 1994 ALMANAC

TEAM AT A GLANCE

TEAM DIRECTORY

Address	One Bills Drive Orchard Park, New York 14127 (716) 648-1800
Stadium	Rich Stadium One Bills Drive Orchard Park, New York 14127 Capacity: 80,290 Playing surface: AstroTurf
Training Camp	Fredonia State University Fredonia, New York 14063
Colors	Royal blue, scarlet red and white
Television	WGRZ, Channel 2
Radio	WBEN, 930 AM

ADMINISTRATION

President: Ralph C. Wilson
Exec. vice president-general manager: John Butler
Vice president-administration: Jerry Foran
Corporate vice president: Linda Bogdan
Vice president-head coach: Marv Levy
Assistant GM-business operations: Bill Munson
Director of pro personnel: A.J. Smith
Director of player personnel: Dwight Adams
Director of marketing and sales: John Livsey
Director of public relations: Denny Lynch
Ticket director: June Foran
Trainer: Ed Abramoski

1994 SCHEDULE

Preseason

AUG. 8	WASHINGTON	8:00
AUG. 12	at Atlanta	7:00
AUG. 20	vs. Houston (at San Antonio)	7:00
AUG. 26	KANSAS CITY	8:00

Regular season

SEP. 4	N.Y. JETS	4:00
SEP. 11	at New England	1:00
SEP. 18	at Houston	12:00
SEP. 26	DENVER (Mon.)	9:00
OCT. 2	at Chicago	3:00
OCT. 9	MIAMI	1:00
OCT. 16	INDIANAPOLIS	1:00
OCT. 23	OPEN DATE	
OCT. 30	KANSAS CITY	1:00
NOV. 6	at N.Y. Jets	4:00
NOV. 14	at Pittsburgh (Mon.)	9:00
NOV. 20	GREEN BAY	1:00
NOV. 24	at Detroit (Thanks.)	12:30
DEC. 4	at Miami	8:00
DEC. 11	MINNESOTA	1:00
DEC. 18	NEW ENGLAND	1:00
DEC. 24	at Indianapolis	1:00

HEAD COACH

Marv Levy
The only coach to lead his team to four consecutive Super Bowls, Levy has been head coach of the Bills since midway through the 1986 season. He has amassed a record of 88-44, the best winning percentage (.667) of any coach in Buffalo history. Including his five-year stint as head coach in Kansas City, Levy has a career record of 106-87. Born Aug. 3, 1928, Chicago, Ill.

Previous NFL: head coach, Kansas City 1978-82; special teams, Washington 1971-72; assistant coach, L.A. Rams 1970; assistant coach, Philadelphia 1969.

Previous college: head coach, William & Mary 1964-68; head coach, California 1960-63; head coach, New Mexico 1958-59; assistant coach, New Mexico 1956-57; assistant coach, Coe College 1953-55.

Player: No NFL. College, running back, Coe College, 1948-50.

ASSISTANT COACHES

Tom Bresnahan: offensive coordinator-offensive line
Previous NFL: offensive coordinator, 1989-93 Buffalo; 1981-82 Kansas City; 1983-84 N.Y. Giants; 1986-88 St. Louis. Player: No NFL. College: tackle, 1953-55 Holy Cross.

Walt Corey: defensive coordinator-linebackers
Previous NFL: defensive coordinator-linebackers, 1987-93 Buffalo; 1978-86 Kansas City; 1975-77 Cleveland; 1971-74 Kansas City. Player: NFL: linebacker, 1960-66 Kansas City. College: defensive end, 1957-59 Miami (Fla.).

Bruce DeHaven: special teams
Previous NFL: special teams, 1987-93 Buffalo. Player: No NFL. College: None.

Charlie Joiner: receivers
Previous NFL: receivers, 1992-93 Buffalo; 1987-91 San Diego. Player: NFL, wide receiver, defensive back, 1969-72 Houston; 1972-75 Cincinnati; 1976-86 San Diego. College: wide receiver, 1965-68 Grambling.

Rusty Jones: strength and conditioning
Previous NFL: strength and conditioning, 1985-94 Buffalo. Player: No NFL. College: None.

Don Lawrence: offensive quality control-tight ends
Previous NFL: offensive quality control-tight ends, 1990-93 Buffalo; 1987-88 Kansas City; 1985-86 Tampa Bay; 1983-84 Buffalo; 1980-82 Kansas City. Player: NFL, offensive, defensive lineman, 1959-61 Washington. College: offensive/defensive lineman, 1957-59 Notre Dame.

Chuck Lester: admin. assistant-asst. linebackers
Previous NFL: assistant linebackers, 1987-93 Buffalo; 1984-86 Kansas City. Player: No NFL. College: linebacker, 1974 Oklahoma.

Elijah Pitts: assistant head coach-running backs
Previous NFL: running backs, 1985-93 Buffalo; 1981-83 Houston; 1978-80 Buffalo; 1974-77 L.A. Rams. Player: NFL, running back, 1961-69 Green Bay; 1970 L.A. Rams; 1970 Chicago; 1970 New Orleans; 1971 Green Bay. College: running back, 1957-60 Philander Smith.

36

1994 PREVIEW ■ BUFFALO

TEAM AT A GLANCE

Dick Roach: defensive backs
Previous NFL: defensive backs, 1987-93 Buffalo; 1985-86 Tampa Bay; 1981 New England; 1978-80 Kansas City. Player: No NFL. College: defensive back, 1953-55 Black Hills State.

Dan Sekanovich: defensive line
Previous NFL: defensive line 1992-93 Buffalo; 1986-91 Miami; 1983-85 Atlanta; 1977-82 N.Y. Jets. Player: No NFL. College: end, 1951-53 Tennessee.

Jim Shofner: quarterbacks
Previous NFL: quarterbacks, 1992-93 Buffalo; 1990-91 Cleveland (head coach for seven games in 1990); 1986-89 St. Louis/Phoenix; 1983-85 Dallas; 1981-82 Houston; 1978-80 Cleveland; 1977, 1967-73 San Francisco. Player: NFL, defensive back, 1958-63 Browns. College: running back, 1955-57 Texas Christian.

COACHING RECORDS
(including postseason games)

Years	Coach	W	L	T
1960-61	Buster Ramsey	11	16	1
1962-65	Lou Saban	38	18	3
1966-68	Joe Collier	13	17	1
1968	Harvey Johnson	1	10	1
1969-70	John Rauch	7	20	1
1971	Harvey Johnson	1	13	0
1972-76	Lou Saban	32	29	1
1976-77	Jim Ringo	3	20	0
1978-82	Chuck Knox	38	38	0
1983-85	Kay Stephenson	10	26	0
1985-86	Hank Bullough	4	17	0
1986-93	Marv Levy	89	45	0

HISTORICAL HIGHLIGHTS

1960 Ralph C. Wilson is granted a franchise for Buffalo by the AFL. The team will play in War Memorial Stadium, and the city agrees to enlarge the stadium to 36,500 seats.
1962 Cookie Gilchrist gains 1,099 yards during the season, the AFL's first 1,000-yard runner.
1963 Gilchrist gains 243 yards rushing and scores five touchdowns in a game against the Jets ... The Bills' season mark of 7-6-1 lands them in a tie for the Eastern Division title with the Boston Patriots, but Buffalo loses 26-8 in a playoff game.
1964 The Bills win the Eastern Division with a record of 12-2 (the best in their history), then go on to capture the AFL championship, beating San Diego 20-7 before a capacity crowd at War Memorial Stadium. Jack Kemp completes 10 passes and scores the Bills' final touchdown.
1965 Winning 10 of 14 games, the Bills take their second-straight Eastern Division title. The Bills shut out the Chargers 23-0 to win their second-consecutive AFL championship.
1966 The Bills claim their third-straight Eastern Division title posting a record of 9-4-1, but are stopped in the AFL title game by the Chiefs 31-7.
1969 The Bills draft Heisman Trophy winner O.J. Simpson.
1972 Simpson is named AFC Offensive Player of the Year.
1973 The Bills have their first winning season in six years (9-5) as they move into Rich Stadium in Orchard Park ... O.J. Simpson sets an NFL single-game rushing record of 250 yards against New England. Simpson finishes the season with 2,003 yards, a record that will last until 1984.
1974 Buffalo claims the AFC East title with a 9-5 record. In their first postseason playoff appearance since 1966, the Bills fall to Pittsburgh 32-14 in the first round.
1976 O.J. Simpson breaks his own single-game rushing mark when he gains 273 yards against the Lions. He also gains more than 1,000 yards rushing for the fifth season.
1979 Joe Ferguson becomes the first Bill to pass for more than 3,000 yards in a season (3,572 on 238 completions) ... Jerry Butler sets a club record by gaining 255 yards on pass receptions in a game against the Jets.
1980 After four losing seasons Buffalo goes 11-5 and wins the AFC East. The Bills, however, cannot get by the Chargers in the playoffs, losing 20-14.
1981 The 10-6 Bills make it to the playoffs for the second year in a row. They defeat the Jets 31-27 in a wild-card game, but fall to the Bengals 28-21 ... Frank Lewis sets two club marks by catching 70 passes for 1,244 yards.
1981 For the first time in team history, home attendance exceeds 600,000 (601,712).
1983 Joe Ferguson sets single-game records by completing 38 passes for 419 yards in a game against Miami.
1986 Jim Kelly sets a club passing mark when he completes 285 passes in a season.
1988 The Bills clinch the AFC East crown with a 9-6 overtime victory over the Jets ... Buffalo defeats the Oilers 17-10 in the first playoff contest but loses to the Bengals 21-10 in the AFC title game.
1989 Buffalo wins its second-straight AFC East title. In the playoffs they lose to the Browns 34-30.
1990-91 The Bills win their third-consecutive AFC East title ... Buffalo defeats the Dolphins 44-34 in their first playoff game, setting an NFL mark for the most combined points scored in a postseason game. Buffalo wins its first AFC title by demolishing the Raiders 51-3 ... The Bills represent the AFC in Super Bowl XXV but lose to the Giants 20-19.
1991-92 RB Thurman Thomas becomes the first Bill to gain 100 yards rushing and 100 yards receiving in a single game, doing so in the season opener against Miami. He is also named the league's MVP ... Buffalo again wins the AFC East. The Bills defeat Kansas City and Denver to win their second AFC title, then lose to Washington in Super Bowl XXVI 37-24.
1992-93 Once again the Bills triumph in the AFC East ... They defeat the Oilers in the greatest comeback game in NFL history, when they overcome a 32-point deficit in the third quarter to win 41-38 in OT. The Bills beat the Steelers and Dolphins to become become only the second team to appear in three-straight Super Bowls ... Then the Bills become the first team ever to lose three consecutive Super Bowls when the Cowboys whip them 52-17.
1993-94 With a record of 12-4, Buffalo again triumphs in the AFC East ... They defeat the Raiders and Chiefs to make it to Super Bowl XXVIII ... For the fourth-straight season, the Bills lose in the Super Bowl, again to the Cowboys, this time 30-13.

PRO FOOTBALL WEEKLY 1994 ALMANAC

TEAM AT A GLANCE

HALL OF FAME MEMBERS

	Yrs with Bills	Inducted
RB O. J. Simpson	1969-77	1985

RETIRED JERSEY NUMBERS
None

FIRST-ROUND DRAFT CHOICES
(since 1980)

Year	Selection (Pos.)	College
1980	C Jim Ritcher	North Carolina St.
1981	RB Booker Moore	Penn State
1982	WR Perry Tuttle	Clemson
1983	TE Tony Hunter	Notre Dame
	QB Jim Kelly	Miami (Fla.)
1984	RB Greg Bell	Notre Dame
1985	DE Bruce Smith	Virginia Tech
	CB Derrick Burroughs	Memphis State
1986	RB Ronnie Harmon	Iowa
	OG Will Woolford	Vanderbilt
1987	LB Shane Conlan	Penn State
1988	No choice	
1989	No choice	
1990	CB James Williams	Fresno State
1991	DB Henry Jones	Illinois
1992	OL John Fina	Arizona
1993	DB Thomas Smith	North Carolina
1994	S Jeff Burris	Notre Dame

RECORD VS. OTHER NFL TEAMS
(includes postseason games)

	Record
Arizona Cardinals	3-3-0
Atlanta Falcons	3-3-0
Chicago Bears	2-3-0
Cincinnati Bengals	7-11-0
Cleveland Browns	3-8-0
Dallas Cowboys	2-5-0
Denver Broncos	17-10-1
Detroit Lions	1-2-1
Green Bay Packers	4-1-0
Houston Oilers	14-20-0
Indianapolis Colts	26-20-1
Kansas City Chiefs	17-14-1
Los Angeles Raiders	16-15-0
Los Angeles Rams	3-3-0
Miami Dolphins	20-37-1
Minnesota Vikings	2-4-0
New England Patriots	33-34-1
New Orleans Saints	3-2-0
New York Giants	4-3-0
New York Jets	38-29-0
Philadelphia Eagles	3-4-0
Pittsburgh Steelers	8-7-0
San Diego Chargers	9-17-2
San Francisco 49ers	3-2-0
Seattle Seahawks	1-3-0
Tampa Bay Buccaneers	2-4-0
Washington Redskins	3-5-0

YEAR-BY-YEAR RECORDS

Year	Won	Lost	Tied	Year	Won	Lost	Tied
1960	5	8	1	1977	3	11	0
1961	6	8	0	1978	5	11	0
1962	7	6	1	1979	7	9	0
1963**	7	6	1	1980**	11	5	0
1964***	12	2	0	1981**	10	6	0
1965***	10	3	1	1982	4	5	0
1966**	9	4	1	1983	8	8	0
1967	4	10	0	1984	2	14	0
1968	1	12	1	1985	2	14	0
1969	4	10	0	1986	4	12	0
1970	3	10	1	1987	7	8	0
1971	1	13	0	1988**	12	4	0
1972	4	9	1	1989**	9	7	0
1973	9	5	0	1990**	13	3	0
1974**	9	5	0	1991**	13	3	0
1975	8	6	0	1992**	11	5	0
1976	2	12	0	1993**	12	4	0
				Total	234	258	8

Number of NFL championships 0
Number of years .500 or better 17
Number of years below .500 17

*NFL champions
**Playoff team
***AFL champions prior to merger

1994 PREVIEW ■ BUFFALO

RECORDS

INDIVIDUAL

Service
Seasons played	14	Jim Ritcher (1980-93)
Games played	222	Jim Ritcher (1980-93)
Consecutive games	188	Darryl Talley (1983-93)

Scoring
Points, career	670	Scott Norwood (1985-91)
Points, season	138	O.J. Simpson (1975)
Points, game	30	Cookie Gilchrist (12/8/63)
Touchdowns, career	70	O.J. Simpson (1969-77)
Touchdowns, season	23	O.J. Simpson (1975)
Touchdowns, game	5	Cookie Gilchrist (12/8/63)
Field goals, career	133	Scott Norwood (1985-91)
Field goals, season	32	Scott Norwood (1988)
Field goals, game	5	Pete Gogolak (12/5/65)
		Scott Norwood (9/25/88)
Extra points, career	271	Scott Norwood (1985-91)
Exta points, season	56	Scoot Norwood (1991)
Extra points, game	7	Booth Lustig (9/18/66)
		Scott Norwood (9/8/91)

Rushing
Yards, career	10,183	O.J. Simpson (1969-77)
Yards, season	2,003	O.J. Simpson (1973)
Yards, game	273	O.J. Simpson (11/25/76)
Attempts, career	2,123	O.J. Simpson (1969-77)
Attempts, season	355	Thurman Thomas (1993)
Attempts, game	39	O.J. Simpson (10/29/73)
Touchdowns, career	57	O.J. Simpson (1969-77)
Touchdowns, season	16	O.J. Simpson (1975)
Touchdowns, game	5	Cookie Gilchrist (12/8/63)

Passing
Completions, career	2,188	Joe Ferguson (1973-84)
Completions, season	304	Jim Kelly (1991)
Completions, game	38	Joe Ferguson (10/9/83)
Yards, career	27,590	Joe Ferguson (1973-84)
Yards, season	3,844	Jim Kelly (1991)
Yards, game	419	Joe Ferguson (10/9/83)
Attempts, career	4,166	Joe Ferguson (1973-84)
Attempts, season	508	Joe Ferguson (1983)
Attempts, game	55	Joe Ferguson (10/9/83)
Touchdowns, career	181	Joe Ferguson (1973-84)
Touchdowns, season	33	Jim Kelly (1991)
Touchdowns, game	6	Jim Kelly (9/8/91)

Receiving
Receptions, career	586	Andre Reed (1985-93)
Receptions, season	88	Andre Reed (1989)
Receptions, game	13	Thurman Thomas (9/15/91)
		Andre Reed (9/18/89)
		Greg Bell (9/8/85)
Yards, career	8,233	Andre Reed (1985-93)
Yards, season	1,312	Andre Reed (1989)
Yards, game	255	Jerry Butler (9/23/79)
Touchdowns, career	58	Andre Reed (1985-93)
Touchdowns, season	10	Andre Reed (1991)
		Bob Chandler (1976)
	10	Elbert Dubenion (1964)
Touchdowns, game	4	Don Beebe (9/9/91)
		Jerry Butler (9/23/79)

Interceptions
Career	40	George Byrd (1964-70)
Season	10	Tom Janik (1967)
Game	3	By many players

Sacks
Career	106	Bruce Smith (1985-93)
Season	19	Bruce Smith (1990)
Game	4	Bruce Smith (12/9/90)

Longest Plays
Run from scrimmage	94 O.J. Simpson (TD, 10/29/72)
Pass play	94 Jack Kemp to G. Bass (10/11/64)
Field goal	59 Steve Christie (9/26/93)
Interception return	101 Tony Greene (TD, 10/3/76)
Kickoff return	102 Curtis Brown (TD, 9/24/78)
	Charley Warner (TD, 11/7/65)
Punt return	91 Keith Moody (TD, 10/23/77)
Punt	78 Marv Bateman (9/19/76)
	Paul Maguire (9/21/69)

Top scorers
	Points
Scott Norwood (1985-91)	670
O.J. Simpson (1969-77)	420
John Leypoldt (1971-76)	369
Andre Reed (1985-93)	354
Thurman Thomas (1988-93)	342
Cookie Gilchrist (1962-64)	248

Top rushers
	Yards
O.J. Simpson (1969-77)	10,183
Thurman Thomas (1988-93)	7,631
Joe Cribbs (1980-83,1985)	4,445
Wray Carlton (1960-67)	3,368
Cookie Gilchrist (1962-64)	3,056
Jim Braxton (1971-78)	2,842

Top passers
	Completions
Joe Ferguson (1973-84)	2,188
Jim Kelly (1986-93)	2,112
Jack Kemp (1962-69)	1,040
Dennis Shaw (1970-73)	485
Frank Reich (1985-93)	166
Daryle Lamonica (1963-66)	150

Top passers
	Yards
Joe Ferguson (1973-84)	27,590
Jim Kelly (1986-93)	26,413
Jack Kemp (1962-69)	15,138
Dennis Shaw (1970-73)	6,286
Daryle Lamonica (1963-66)	2,499
John Green (1960-61)	2,170

Top receivers
	Receptions
Andre Reed (1985-93)	586
Elbert Dubenion (1960-67)	296
Bob Chandler (1971-78)	295
Thurman Thomas (1988-93)	295
Pete Metzelaars (1985-93)	280
Jerry Butler (1979-83, 85-86)	278

Top receivers
	Yards
Andre Reed (1985-93)	8,233
Elbert Dubenion (1960-67)	5,309
Frank Lewis (1978-83)	4,638
Jerry Butler (1979-83, 85-86)	4,301
Bob Chandler (1971-79)	3,999
Thurman Thomas (1988-93)	3,053

Most interceptions
	No.
George Byrd (1964-70)	40
Tony Greene (1971-79)	37
Mark Kelso (1986-93)	30
Charles Romes (1977-86)	28
Nate Odomes (1987-93)	26
Mario Clark (1976-83)	25

Most sacks
	No.
Bruce Smith (1985-93)	106
Ben Williams (1976-85)	45.5
Cornelius Bennett (1987-93)	42.5

PRO FOOTBALL WEEKLY 1994 ALMANAC

PREVIEW: CHICAGO BEARS

True to their word, the Bears were one of the more aggressive pursuers of free-agent talent this offseason. Predictably, the emphasis has been on reviving what turned out to be the league's lowest-ranked offense in 1993.

Shortly after the '93 season ended, team president Michael McCaskey spelled out the Bears' free-agency game plan. "We are trying to be well-organized, and we will see if the other side is willing to move quickly," he said.

After making relatively modest free-agent gains in 1993, the Bears swung into action quickly this offseason, signing three new offensive starters in the first three weeks of free-agency — QB Erik Kramer from Detroit, OT Andy Heck from Seattle and FB Merril Hoge from Pittsburgh.

For starters, the Bears lured Kramer away from division-rival Detroit with a three-year, $8.1 million contract. Kramer, who has made a habit out of playing well against teams with which Bear head coach Dave Wannstedt has been affiliated in Dallas and Chicago, emerged from a muddled QB situation in Detroit late last season to lead the Lions into the playoffs.

Last season the Bears' new coaching staff tried to implement a 49ers-style offense with quicker releases for QB Jim Harbaugh and timing routes for the receivers. For a number of reasons, though, Harbaugh, who has now moved on to Indianapolis, had problems adapting.

"Erik has been in the three- and five-step drop passing game longer than Harbaugh," said Bear offensive coordinator Ron Turner. "He has a better feel for it and makes decisions a bit quicker."

One of the biggest reasons Harbaugh had problems with the new system, however, was an extremely weak offensive line; a less durable quarterback wouldn't have made it through September, let alone the season.

With that in mind, the Bears tendered a four-year, $10 million offer sheet to Heck just one day after signing Kramer. The Seahawks, who had designated Heck as a transition player, failed to match the offer, and Heck became by far the highest-paid offensive lineman in Bear history. A sturdy performer during his five years in Seattle, Heck was quickly designated as the Bears' new right tackle, but, because he can play both guard and tackle effectively, it gives the Bear line the kind of flexibility that could have helped immensely at different times during the '93 season. His signing also created the kind of competition Wannstedt craves at virtually every OL position.

An earlier move geared toward fortifying the Bears' porous front wall was the re-signing of 11-year veteran Mark Bortz, a fixture at left guard since becoming a starter in 1984. "He's been a dependable, tough, hard-working guy for us a long time, and he's the kind of guy we can build on," McCaskey said.

A few weeks after obtaining Heck, they turned their attention to fullback by signing ex- Steeler Hoge. "We need a three-dimensional fullback, someone who can catch five or six balls a game, run with the ball and block," said Turner. "Merril is a great receiver. He's shown he can run the ball effectively, and yet he's also capable of being a lead blocker."

In early April, the Bears further upgraded their backfield by signing Lewis Tillman, who had performed admirably with the Giants in '93 as a backup to Rodney Hampton, to a three-year, $2.9 million contract. At the end of the month, they obtained WR Jeff Graham from Pittsburgh in a trade. The Bears hope Graham will provide the same big-play ability on crossing patterns as he did two years ago for the Steelers. In early May, Chicago added ex-Patriot TE Marv Cook, a former All-Pro, to the mix. Tim Worley, who looked impressive averaging four yards per crack in '93, also wasn't with the Bears at the beginning of last season, having been obtained from Pittsburgh shortly before the '93 trade deadline. He has already been suspended once by the league, though, for a drug offense, and he will be watched closely this season after another offseason run-in with the law.

Now, hardly a trace of the Bears' initial 1993 offense remains. Amazingly, by the time the '94 season opener arrives, it's quite possible the team will have changed starters at 10 of 11 offensive positions from the ones who started just a year ago.

While Kramer replaces Harbaugh, and Hoge and a combination of Tillman and Worley in effect replace Craig Heyward and Neal Anderson, re-

Donnell Woolford
PHOTO BY PETE J. GROH

1994 PREVIEW ■ CHICAGO

spectively, Heck is just one big part of what's expected to be a major overhaul on the offensive line. Jay Leeuwenburg will probably move from tackle, where he was out of position last year, to center. Jerry Fontenot, last year's man in the pivot, will probably switch to guard, where he will battle Bortz and up-and-coming Todd Perry for playing time. Troy Auzenne initially gets the nod at left tackle, but he had injury problems in '93, and he must show more toughness and willingness to hit the weights if he is to secure the position. No. 2 draft pick Marcus Spears will provide depth at guard and tackle.

Regarding the team's receiver corps, the major concern is outside, where Wendell Davis, the team's best wideout before suffering a season-ending double-kneecap injury on the Veteran Stadium AstroTurf in Philadelphia, is a major question mark. Due to the uncertainty with Davis, Curtis Conway, the Bears' No. 1 pick in '93, moves to the forefront. Conway is considered to have game-breaker potential in the Anthony Miller mold, but, after coming out as a junior, his lack of maturity and concentration was a big disappointment. The other WR slot appears to be in much surer hands, with reliable veteran Tom Waddle sharing the load with Graham and Terry Obee, who showed a knack for making plays last year as a first-year free-agent.

The Bears are also hoping for much more production from their tight ends, where it's hoped Cook will continue to be as durable and productive as he was with the Patriots. Second-year man Chris Gedney, a large target with soft hands and respectable speed who had shoulder and foot problems in '93, and Keith Jennings, a 265-pound former wide receiver who has improved as a blocker, will share the load.

While most of the changes on the Bears this season are on offense, free-agency has also significantly changed the face of one of the league's better overall defenses in '93.

The first big change was the decision to release fiery veteran DT Steve McMichael. After spending a lot of money on new offensive firepower, McMichael's age (37 this year), salary ($1.2 million) and the fact he was no longer an every-down player led directly to his exit. The Bears made a point of acknowledging McMichael's value as a leader and spiritual force, however, and left the door wide open for his possible return to the team at a lesser salary.

Age and payroll considerations also led to the departure of DRE Richard Dent, the NFL's third all-time sack leader, and an unrestricted free agent. When Dent failed to agree to Chicago's contract offer, Alcorn State's John Thierry was drafted in the first round as his heir apparent. Another unrestricted free agent whose future with the Bears was tinged with uncertainty was SS Shaun Gayle, who played well in '93.

No matter how dramatic the changes, Wannstedt's defense will once again emphasize speed, quickness and maximization of talent.

Holdovers on the defensive front expected to make sizable contributions in '94 include DLE Trace Armstrong, DT Chris Zorich and Alonzo Spellman. Both Armstrong (11.5 sacks) and Zorich are undersized overachievers who had their best seasons last year. Spellman, a former first-rounder with great pass-rushing potential, gets the inital nod at right end, with Thierry expected to offer a stern challenge. Combining to replace McMichael will be veterans Carl Simpson and Tim Ryan and rookie Jim Flanigan.

At linebacker, Dante Jones is the anchor in the middle after agreeing to a new contract the second week in May. He led the Bears in tackles in '93 and played at a Pro bowl level. Vinson Smith and Joe Cain appear set at strong and weakside linebacker, respectively. Smith is a sturdy pro who knows the defense as well as anyone on the team, since he played in Dallas during Wannstedt's stint as the Cowboys' defensive coordinator. Cain, a free-agent acquisition last year, is unspectacular but usually effective enough. Also figuring in the Bear LB picture are Ron Cox, who has been a decent player for the most part despite his share of blown assignments and knee problems, and Myron Baker, who displayed flashes as a rookie last year and could contend for a starting job.

In the secondary, the Bears' headline performer is CB Donnell Woolford, who had an outstanding season in '93 and was rewarded with a Pro Bowl invitation. At the other corner, rapidly improving Jeremy Lincoln challenges Anthony Blaylock, another '93 free agent who formerly played with San Diego.

Gayle, who gets the job done despite size and speed limitations, and Mark Carrier, who showed renewed enthusiasm at free safety, give the Bears a very solid pair of starters. Inexperienced John Mangum is waiting in the wings should Gayle move on.

On special teams, the Bears are in good shape. Despite hitting on just 3-of-7 FG's between 40 and 49 yards last year, PK Kevin Butler is above average. The same definitely can be said of P Chris Gardocki, whose coffin-corner punting ability (28 punts inside the 20-yard line in '93) should come in handy with new kicking rules on the horizon that emphasize that particular talent. Conway has the potential to be one of the best kick returners in the game, and Obee is no slouch.

FAST FACTS

■ The Bears were the first team in NFL history to win three straight road games (over the Chargers, Chiefs and Lions) in a 12-day span.

■ Last season Bear P Chris Gardocki had the NFL's best difference between net and gross (1.9) punting yards.

■ New Bear FB Merril Hoge leads all active NFL players in consecutive games played with 107.

PRO FOOTBALL WEEKLY 1994 ALMANAC

1994 PLAYER ROSTER

NO.	NAME	POS.	HT.	WT.	EXP.	COLLEGE	GP/GS
13	Alcorn, Daron	PK	6-2	235	1	Akron	0/0
93	Armstrong, Trace	DE	6-4	270	6	Florida	16/16
70	Auzenne, Troy	OT	6-7	300	3	California	11/11
91	Baker, Myron	LB	6-1	228	2	Louisiana Tech	16/0
63	Bass, Robert	LB	6-1	239	R	Miami (Fla.)	—
16	Bellamy, Mike	WR	6-0	195	2	Illinois	0/0
47	Blaylock, Anthony	CB	5-10	185	7	Winston-Salem St.	9/9
62	Bortz, Mark	OG	6-6	290	12	Iowa	16/16
10	Brooks, Anthony	WR	5-11	179	1	East Texas State	0/0
48	Brooks, Donny	CB	5-11	188	R	Texas Tech	—
63	Burger, Todd	OG	6-3	296	1	Penn State	0/0
69	Bussie, Arthur	DE	6-4	258	R	N.E. Louisiana	—
6	Butler, Kevin	PK	6-1	205	10	Georgia	16/0
59	Cain, Joe	LB	6-1	237	6	Oregon Tech	15/15
20	Carrier, Mark	S	6-1	190	5	Southern Cal	16/16
30	Carter, Antonio	FB	5-11	216	R	Minnesota	—
44	Christian, Bob	RB	5-10	225	2	Northwestern	14/1
80	Conway, Curtis	WR-KR	6-0	193	2	Southern Cal	16/7
86	Cook, Marv	TE	6-4	234	6	Iowa	16/12
54	Cox, Ron	LB	6-2	235	5	Fresno State	16/2
82	Davis, Wendell	WR	6-0	188	7	Louisiana State	5/4
37	Douglass, Maurice	DB	5-11	202	8	Kentucky	16/1
65	Dunning, Josh	OG	6-3	302	R	Washington State	—
31	Durgin, Marcus	CB	6-0	191	R	Samford (Ala.)	—
65	Epps, Tory	DT	6-1	280	5	Memphis State	4/0
96	Fontenot, Albert	DE	6-4	265	2	Baylor	16/0
67	Fontenot, Jerry	OG-C	6-3	285	6	Texas A&M	16/16
15	Frier, Matt	WR	5-11	190	R	Florida State	—
17	Gardocki, Chris	P-PK	6-1	196	4	Clemson	16/0
23	Gayle, Shaun	S	5-11	202	11	Ohio State	16/16
84	Gedney, Chris	TE	6-5	265	2	Syracuse	7/3
49	Givens, Reggie	LB	6-0	220	1	Penn State	0/0
81	Graham, Jeff	WR	6-2	196	4	Ohio State	15/12
22	Green, Robert	RB	5-8	212	3	William & Mary	16/0
72	Hawkins, Garland	DE	6-3	253	1	Syracuse	0/0
64	Heck, Andy	OT	6-6	296	6	Notre Dame	16/16
49	Hightower, Mike	RB	5-9	191	R	East Texas State	—
33	Hoge, Merril	FB	6-2	230	8	Idaho State	16/13
60	Ireland, Darwin	LB	5-11	240	R	Arkansas	—
85	Jennings, Keith	TE	6-4	270	5	Clemson	13/11
25	Johnson, Keshon	CB	5-10	183	2	Arizona	15/0
53	Jones, Dante	LB	6-2	235	7	Oklahoma	16/16
72	Kmet, Frank	OL-DL	6-3	294	1	Purdue	0/0
12	Kramer, Erik	QB	6-1	200	5	North Carolina State	5/4
58	Leeuwenburg, Jay	OT-C	6-2	290	3	Colorado	16/16
39	Lincoln, Jeremy	CB	5-10	180	3	Tennessee	16/7
26	Mangum, John	CB	5-10	192	5	Alabama	12/1
36	Marshall, Anthony	S	6-1	205	R	Louisiana State	—
43	Martin, John	RB	5-7	185	R	Memphis State	—
9	Matthews, Shane	QB	6-3	197	2	Florida	0/0
60	McGuire, Gene	C	6-2	300	3	Notre Dame	9/0
24	Miniefield, Kevin	CB	5-9	180	2	Arizona State	8/0
92	Minter, Barry	LB	6-2	239	2	Tulsa	2/0
69	Myslinski, Tom	OG	6-2	289	2	Tennessee	2/0
72	Norman, Todd	OT	6-5	300	R	Notre Dame	—

1994 PREVIEW — CHICAGO

1994 PLAYER ROSTER

NO.	NAME	POS.	HT.	WT.	EXP.	COLLEGE	GP/GS
83	Obee, Terry	WR	5-10	189	2	Oregon	16/5
75	Perry, Todd	OG	6-5	310	2	Kentucky	13/3
18	Primus, Greg	WR	5-11	190	1	Colorado State	0/0
99	Ryan, Tim	DT	6-4	275	5	Southern Cal	11/0
19	Sanders, Steven	WR	5-8	161	R	Virginia Tech	—
52	Schwantz, Jim	LB	6-2	232	1	Purdue	0/0
78	Shorten, Oscar	DT	6-3	285	R	Abilene Christian	—
98	Simpson, Carl	DT	6-2	285	2	Florida State	11/0
55	Smith, Vinson	LB	6-2	247	7	East Carilina	16/13
96	Snow, Percy	LB	6-2	240	5	Michigan State	10/0
90	Spellman, Alonzo	DE	6-4	285	3	Ohio State	16/0
88	Thompson, Aubrey	TE	6-1	230	R	Utah State	—
27	Tillman, Lewis	RB	6-0	204	6	Jackson State	16/7
87	Waddle, Tom	WR	6-0	190	5	Boston College	15/15
46	Walker, Cedric	S	6-0	205	R	Stephen F. Austin	—
4	Walsh, Steve	QB	6-3	200	6	Miami (Fla.)	2/1
89	Wetnight, Ryan	TE	6-2	235	2	Stanford	10/1
71	Williams, James	DT	6-7	335	4	Cheyney (Pa.)	3/0
21	Woolford, Donnell	DB	5-9	188	6	Clemson	16/16
38	Worley, Tim	RB	6-2	228	5	Georgia	15/3
97	Zorich, Chris	DT	6-1	277	4	Notre Dame	16/16

'94 DRAFT PICKS

RD.	NAME	POS.	HT.	WT.	COLLEGE
1.	Thierry, John	DE	6-4	260	Alcorn State
2.	Spears, Marcus	OT	6-4	300	Northwest Louisiana
3.	Flanigan, Jim	DT	6-2	281	Notre Dame
4.	Harris, Raymont	RB	6-0	225	Ohio State
6.	Hill, Lloyd	WR	6-1	189	Texas Tech
7.	Collier, Dennis	DB	5-9	188	Colorado

PRO FOOTBALL WEEKLY 1994 ALMANAC

TEAM AT A GLANCE

TEAM DIRECTORY

Address	250 N. Washington Road Lake Forest, Illinois 60045 (708) 295-6600
	(Ticket Office) 950 N. Western Avenue, Suite 1 Lake Forest, Illinois 60045 (708) 615-2327
Stadium	Soldier Field 425 East McFetridge Drive Chicago, IL 60605 Capacity: 66,950 Playing surface: Grass
Training Camp	U. of Wisconsin-Platteville Platteville, Wisconsin 53818
Colors	Navy blue, orange and white
Television	WFLD, Channel 32
Radio	WGN, 720 AM

ADMINISTRATION
Chairman of the board: Ed McCaskey
President-chief executive officer: Michael McCaskey
Vice president: Tim McCaskey
Vice president-operations: Ted Phillips
Director of administration: Tim LeFevour
Director of player personnel: Rod Graves
Director of community involvement: Pat McCaskey
Director of marketing: Ken Valdiserri
Director of public relations: Bryan Harlan
Ticket manager: George McCaskey
Trainer: Fred Caito

1994 SCHEDULE

Preseason
AUG. 5	PHILADELPHIA	7:00
AUG. 13	at Arizona	6:00
AUG. 22	at Kansas City	7:00
AUG. 27	N.Y. GIANTS	7:00

Regular season
SEP. 4	TAMPA BAY	12:00
SEP. 12	at Philadelphia (Mon.)	9:00
SEP. 18	MINNESOTA	12:00
SEP. 25	at N.Y. Jets	8:00
OCT. 2	BUFFALO	3:00
OCT. 9	NEW ORLEANS	12:00
OCT. 16	OPEN DATE	
OCT. 23	at Detroit	1:00
OCT. 31	GREEN BAY (Mon.)	8:00
NOV. 6	at Tampa Bay	1:00
NOV. 13	at Miami	1:00
NOV. 20	DETROIT	12:00
NOV. 27	at Arizona	2:00
DEC. 1	at Minnesota (Thurs.)	7:00
DEC. 11	at Green Bay	12:00
DEC. 18	L.A. RAMS	12:00
DEC. 24	NEW ENGLAND	12:00

HEAD COACH
Dave Wannstedt
In his first year as a head coach in the NFL in 1993, Wannstedt, who replaced Mike Ditka, led Chicago to a 7-9 season and a fourth-place finish in the NFC Central Division. He was hired by Bear president Michael McCaskey after Wannstedt, as defensive coordinator of the NFL's top-ranked unit in 1992, helped guide the Dallas Cowboys to a victory in Super Bowl XXVII. Born May 21, 1952, Pittsburgh, Pa.
Previous NFL: assistant head coach/defensive coordinator, Dallas 1992; defensive coordinator, Dallas 1989-91.
Previous college: defensive coordinator, Miami (Fla.) 1986-88; assistant coach, Southern Cal 1983-85; assistant coach, Oklahoma State 1979-82; assistant coach, Pittsburgh, 1975-78.
Player: No NFL. College, offensive tackle, Pittsburgh 1970-73.

ASSISTANT COACHES
Danny Abramowicz: special teams
Previous NFL: special teams, Chicago 1992-93. Player: NFL, wide receiver, New Orleans 1967-73, 49ers 73-74. College: wide receiver, Xavier 1964-66.
Clarence Brooks: defensive line
Previous NFL: defensive line, Chicago 1993. Player: No NFL. College: guard, Massachusetts 1970-73.
Ivan Fears: wide receivers
Previous NFL: wide receivers, Chicago 1993; New England 1991-92. Player: No NFL. College: running back, William & Mary 1973-75.
Carlos Mainord: defensive assistant
Previous NFL: defensive assistant, Chicago 1993. Player: No NFL. College: linebacker, McMurry College 1964-65; linebacker, Navarro Junior College 1962-63.
Dave McGinnis: linebackers
Previous NFL: linebackers, Chicago 1986-92. Player: No NFL. College: defensive back, Texas Christian 1970-72.
Joe Pendry: running backs
Previous NFL: running backs, Chicago 1993; Kansas City 1989-92; Cleveland 1985-88. Player: No NFL. College: tight end, West Virginia 1965-66.
Mike Shula: tight ends
Previous NFL: tight ends, Chicago 1993; Miami 1991-92; Tampa Bay 1988-90. Player: NFL, quarterback, Tampa Bay 1987. College: quarterback, Alabama 1983-86.
Bob Slowik: defensive coordinator
Previous NFL: defensive coordinator, Chicago 1993; Dallas 1992. Player: No NFL. College: cornerback, Delaware 1973-76.
Ron Turner: offensive coordinator
Previous NFL: offensive coordinator, Chicago 1993. Player: No NFL. College: running back, defensive back, Pacific 1973-76.
Tony Wise: offensive line
Previous NFL: offensive line, Chicago 1993; Dallas 1989-92. Player: No NFL. College: offensive lineman, Ithaca 1971-72.

1994 PREVIEW ■ CHICAGO

TEAM AT A GLANCE

COACHING RECORDS
(includes postseason games)

Years	Coach	W	L	T
1920-29	George Halas	84	31	19
1930-32	Ralph Jones	24	10	7
1933-42	George Halas	88	24	4
1942-45	Hunk Anderson	24	12	2
	Luke Johnsos			
1946-55	George Halas	76	43	2
1956-57	John "Paddy" Driscoll	14	10	1
1958-67	George Halas	76	53	6
1968-71	Jim Dooley	20	36	0
1972-74	Abe Gibron	11	30	1
1975-77	Jack Pardee	20	23	0
1978-81	Neil Armstrong	30	35	0
1982-92	Mike Ditka	112	68	0
1993	Dave Wannstedt	7	9	0

HISTORICAL HIGHLIGHTS

1920 George Halas and Dutch Sternaman organize a pro football team for corn products manufacturer A. E. Staley in Decatur, Ill., to play in the newly formed NFL, and name it the Decatur Staleys.

1921 Halas and Sternaman take over the franchise and move it to Chicago. The Chicago Staleys play at Wrigley Field, home of the Chicago Cubs baseball team.

1925-26 College superstar Red Grange signs with the Bears, and they go on a 16-game, coast-to-coast barnstorming tour.

1930 The Bears and Chicago Cardinals play football's first indoor game on an 80-yard field in Chicago Stadium.

1932 The Bears and Cardinals play football's first indoor game on an 80-yard field in Chicago Stadium. ... After the season, Halas buys out Sternaman's interest in the Bears' franchise.

1933 The Bears win the first official NFL championship game, defeating the New York Giants 32-21.

1934 Rookie Beattie Feathers becomes the first running back to rush for more than 1,000 yards in a season (1,004). His average carry of 9.9 yards is another NFL record. The Bears go undefeated during the regular season (13-0), but lose the NFL title to the Giants 30-13 in the famous "Sneakers Championship."

1935 The Bears rush 72 times in a single game (vs. the Brooklyn Dodgers), an NFL record, and gain 408 yards rushing, a club record.

1937 The Bears lose in the title game to the Washington Redskins 28-21.

1940 The Bears score the most points in any NFL game ever when they defeat the Redskins in the championship game 73-0. Ten different Bears score touchdowns in the game.

1941 The Bears lose to the Giants in title game 37-9.

1942 Chicago falls in the NFL championship game 14-6 to the Redskins.

1943 Sid Luckman becomes the first NFL player to pass for more than 400 yards in a game (433, against the Giants). His seven TD passes that game is another NFL mark. ... The Bears take the NFL championship with a 41-21 win over the Redskins.

1946 The Bears become NFL champs for the fourth time in seven years with a 24-14 victory over the Giants.

1949 Johnny Lujack sets an NFL record by passing for 468 yards in a game against the Chicago Cardinals.

1956 Chicago makes it to the championship game but loses to the Giants 47-7.

1963 The Bears win the NFL championship, defeating the Giants 14-10.

1964 Flanker Johnny Morris sets an NFL season record by catching 93 passes.

1965 Rookie Gale Sayers ties an NFL record by scoring six touchdowns in a game against the 49ers. Sayers sets two NFL season records with 22 touchdowns and 2,440 combined yards.

1968 George Halas retires as head coach after 40 seasons, an NFL record. His 324 overall and 318 regular season victories are, at the time, NFL standards.

1971 The Bears move from Wrigley Field to Soldier Field.

1977 Walter Payton sets an NFL record by rushing for 275 yards in a game against the Vikings. ... The Bears make the playoffs for the first time in more than a decade but lose to the Cowboys in the first round.

1979 The Bears move into their new headquarters/training facility in Lake Forest, Ill. ... They make the playoffs for the second time in three years.

1982 Mike Ditka, a former tight end for the Bears, is hired as head coach. ... The Bears draft QB Jim McMahon in the first round.

1985-86 The Bears win 15 games, a club season record, and go on to win Super Bowl XX, defeating the Patriots 46-10, then the largest margin of victory in Super Bowl history.

1987 Walter Payton retires as the NFL all-time leading rusher with 16,726 yards and a total of eight NFL and 26 club records.

1991 Mike Ditka becomes the only Bear head coach besides George Halas to win 100 games.

1992-93 Mike Ditka is fired and replaced by Dave Wannstedt, the defensive coordinator for the Super Bowl champion Dallas Cowboys.

1993 The Bears play their 1,000th NFL game, the first team ever to reach that mark.

PRO FOOTBALL WEEKLY 1994 ALMANAC

TEAM AT A GLANCE

HALL OF FAME MEMBERS

	Yrs with Bears	Inducted
HB Red Grange*	1925, 29-34	1963
E-Coach George Halas*	1920-83	1963
FB-T Bronko Nagurski*	1930-37, 43	1963
T Ed Healey	1922-27	1964
T Link Lyman	1926-34	1964
C George Trafton	1920-32	1964
QB Paddy Driscoll	1920, 26-29	1965
G Danny Fortmann	1936-43	1965
QB Sid Luckman	1939-50	1965
HB George McAfee	1940-41, 45-50	1966
C Bulldog Turner	1940-52	1966
T Joe Stydahar	1936-42, 45-46	1967
E Bill Hewitt	1932-36	1971
LB Bill George	1952-65	1974
T-LB George Connor	1948-55	1975
HB Gale Sayers	1965-71	1977
LB Dick Butkus	1965-73	1979
QB-PK George Blanda	1949-58	1981
DE Doug Atkins	1955-66	1982
T George Musso	1933-44	1982
TE Mike Ditka	1961-66	1988
OG-DT Stan Jones	1954-65	1991
RB Walter Payton	1975-87	1993

* Charter member

RETIRED JERSEY NUMBERS

3	FB-T Bronko Nagurski
5	HB George McAfee
7	E-Coach George Halas
28	HB Willie Galimore
34	RB Walter Payton
41	HB Brian Piccolo
42	QB Sid Luckman
56	E Bill Hewitt
61	LB Bill George
66	C Bulldog Turner
77	HB Red Grange

FIRST-ROUND DRAFT CHOICES
(since 1980)

Year	Selection (Pos.)	College
1980	LB Otis Wilson	Louisville
1981	OT Keith Van Horne	Southern Cal
1982	QB Jim McMahon	Brigham Young
1983	OT Jim Covert	Pittsburgh
	WR Willie Gault	Tennessee
1984	LB Wilber Marshall	Florida
1985	DT William Perry	Clemson
1986	RB Neal Anderson	Florida
1987	QB Jim Harbaugh	Michigan
1988	RB Brad Muster	Stanford
	WR Wendell Davis	Louisiana State
1989	CB Donnell Woolford	Clemson
	DE Trace Armstrong	Florida
1990	S Mark Carrier	Southern Cal
1991	OT Stan Thomas	Texas
1992	DE Alonzo Spellman	Ohio St.
1993	WR Curtis Conway	Southern Cal
1994	DE John Thierry	Alcorn State

RECORD VS. OTHER NFL TEAMS
(includes postseason games)

	Record
Arizona Cardinals	51-25-6
Atlanta Falcons	9-9-0
Buffalo Bills	3-2-0
Cincinnati Bengals	2-3-0
Cleveland Browns	3-8-0
Dallas Cowboys	6-10-0
Denver Broncos	5-5-0
Detroit Lions	74-49-5
Green Bay Packers	82-59-6
Houston Oilers	2-4-0
Indianapolis Colts	16-21-0
Kansas City Chiefs	4-2-0
Los Angeles Raiders	3-5-0
Los Angeles Rams	45-30-3
Miami Dolphins	1-5-0
Minnesota Vikings	29-34-2
New England Patriots	3-3-0
New Orleans Saints	9-6-0
New York Giants	29-19-2
New York Jets	3-1-0
Philadelphia Eagles	24-4-1
Pittsburgh Steelers	16-4-1
San Diego Chargers	2-4-0
San Francisco 49ers	25-27-1
Seattle Seahawks	2-4-0
Tampa Bay Buccaneers	24-8-0
Washington Redskins	21-16-1

YEAR-BY-YEAR RECORDS

Year	Won	Lost	Tied	Year	Won	Lost	Tied
1920	10	1	2	1957	5	7	0
1921*	9	1	1	1958	8	4	0
1922	9	3	0	1959	8	4	0
1923	9	2	1	1960	5	6	1
1924	6	1	4	1961	8	6	0
1925	9	5	3	1962	9	5	0
1926	12	1	3	1963*	11	1	2
1927	9	3	2	1964	5	9	0
1928	7	5	1	1965	9	5	0
1929	4	9	2	1966	5	7	2
1930	9	4	1	1967	7	6	1
1931	8	5	0	1968	7	7	0
1932*	7	1	6	1969	1	13	0
1933*	10	2	1	1970	6	8	0
1934**	13	0	0	1971	6	8	0
1935	6	4	2	1972	4	9	1
1936	9	3	0	1973	3	11	0
1937**	9	1	1	1974	4	10	0
1938	6	5	0	1975	4	10	0
1939	8	3	0	1976	7	7	0
1940*	8	3	0	1977**	9	5	0
1941*	10	1	0	1978	7	9	0
1942**	11	0	0	1979**	10	6	0
1943*	8	1	1	1980	7	9	0
1944	6	3	1	1981	6	10	0
1945	3	7	0	1982	3	6	0
1946*	8	2	1	1983	8	8	0
1947	8	4	0	1984**	10	6	0
1948	10	2	0	1985*	15	1	0
1949	9	3	0	1986**	14	2	0
1950	9	3	0	1987**	11	4	0
1951	7	5	0	1988**	12	4	0
1952	5	7	0	1989	6	10	0
1953	3	8	1	1990**	11	5	0
1954	8	4	0	1991**	11	5	0
1955	8	4	0	1992	5	11	0
1956**	9	2	1	1993	7	9	0
				Total	574	368	41

Number of NFL championships 9
Number of years .500 or better 52
Number of years below .500 22

*NFL champions
**Playoff team

1994 PREVIEW ■ CHICAGO

RECORDS

INDIVIDUAL

Service
Seasons played	14	Bill George (1952-65)
		Doug Buffone (1966-79)
Games played	191	Steve McMichael (1981-93)
Consecutive games	184	Walter Payton (1975-87)

Scoring
Points, career	915	Kevin Butler (1985-93)
Points, season	144	Kevin Butler (1985)
Points, game	36	Gale Sayers (12/12/65)
Touchdowns, career	125	Walter Payton (1975-87)
Touchdowns, season	22	Gale Sayers (1965)
Touchdowns, game	6	Gale Sayers (12/12/65)
Field goals, career	199	Kevin Butler (1985-93)
Field goals, season	31	Kevin Butler (1985)
Field goals, game	5	Roger Leclerc (12/3/61)
		Mac Percival (10/20/68)
Extra points, career	318	Kevin Butler (1985-93)
Exta points, season	52	Roger Leclerc (1965)
Extra points, game	8	Bob Snyder (11/14/43)

Rushing
Yards, career	16,726	Walter Payton (1975-87)
Yards, season	1,852	Walter Payton (1977)
Yards, game	275	Walter Payton (11/20/77)
Attempts, career	3,838	Walter Payton (1975-87)
Attempts, season	381	Walter Payton (1984)
Attempts, game	40	Walter Payton (11/20/77)
Touchdowns, career	110	Walter Payton (1975-87)
Touchdowns, season	14	Gale Sayers (1965)
		Walter Payton (1977, 1979)
Touchdowns, game	4	Rick Casares (10/28/56, 12/6/59)
		Gale Sayers (12/12/65)
		Bobby Douglass (11/4/73)

Passing
Rating, career	80.4	Jim McMahon (1982-88)
Rating, season	107.8	Sid Luckman (1943)
Completions, career	1,023	Jim Harbaugh (1987-93)
Completions, season	275	Jim Harbaugh (1991)
Completions, game	33	Bill Wade (10/25/64)
Yards, career	14,686	Sid Luckman (1939-50)
Yards, season	3,172	Bill Wade (1962)
Yards, game	468	Johnny Lujack (12/11/49)
Attempts, career	1,759	Jim Harbaugh (1987-93)
Attempts, season	478	Jim Harbaugh (1991)
Attempts, game	57	Bill Wade (10/25/64)
Touchdowns, career	137	Sid Luckman (1939-50)
Touchdowns, season	28	Sid Luckman (1943)
Touchdowns, game	7	Sid Luckman (11/14/43)
Receptions, career	492	Walter Payton (1975-87)
Receptions, season	93	Johnny Morris (1964)
Receptions, game	14	Jim Keane (10/23/49)
Yards, career	5,059	Johnny Morris (1958-67)
Yards, season	1,200	Johnny Morris (1964)
Yards, game	214	Harlon Hill (10/31/54)
Touchdowns, career	50	Ken Kavanaugh (1940-41, 45-50)
Touchdowns, season	13	Ken Kavanaugh (1947)
		Dick Gordon (1970)
Touchdowns, game	4	Harlon Hill (10/31/54)
		Mike Ditka (10/13/63)

Interceptions
Career	38	Gary Fencik (1976-87)
Season	10	Mark Carrier (1990)
Game	3	By many players

Sacks
Career	124.5	Richard Dent (1983-93)
Season	17.5	Richard Dent (1984)
Game	4.5	Richard Dent (11/4/84, 12/27/87)

Longest Plays
Run from scrimmage	86	Bill Osmanski (TD, 10/15/39)
Pass play	98	Bill Wade to Bo Farrington (TD, 10/8/61)
Field goal	55	Bob Thomas (11/23/75)
Interception return	101	Richie Petitbon (TD, 12/9/62)
Kickoff return	103	Gale Sayers (TD, 9/17/67)
Punt return	95	Johnny Bailey (TD, 12/29/90)
Punt	94	Joe Litzenich (11/16/31)

Top Scorers
	Points
Kevin Butler (1985-93)	915
Walter Payton (1975-87)	750
Bob Thomas (1975-84)	629
George Blanda (1948-58)	541
Mac Percival (1967-73)	456
Neal Anderson (1986-)	426

Top Rushers
	Yards
Walter Payton (1975-87)	16,726
Neal Anderson (1986-93)	6,166
Rick Casares (1955-64)	5,675
Gale Sayers (1965-71)	4,956
Roland Harper (1975-82)	3,044
Willie Galimore (1957-63)	2,985

Top Passers
	Completions
Jim Harbaugh (1987-93)	1,023
Sid Luckman (1939-50)	904
Jim McMahon (1982-88)	874
Bill Wade (1961-66)	767
Ed Brown (1954-61)	607
Bob Avellini (1975-82)	530

	Yards
Sid Luckman (1939-50)	14,686
Jim Harbaugh (1987-93)	11,567
Jim McMahon (1982-88)	11,203
Bill Wade (1961-66)	9,958
Ed Brown (1954-61)	9,698
Bob Avellini (175-82)	6,823

Top Receivers
	Receptions
Walter Payton (1975-87)	492
Johnny Morris (1958-67)	356
Mike Ditka (1961-66)	316
Neal Anderson (1986-93)	302
Matt Suhey (1980-89)	259
Dick Gordon (1965-71)	238

	Yards
Johnny Morris (1958-67)	5,059
Harlon Hill (1954-61)	4,616
Walter Payton (1975-87)	4,538
Mike Ditka (1961-66)	4,503
Willie Gault (1983-1987)	3,650
Ken Kavanaugh (1940-41, 45-50)	3,626

Top Interceptors
	Total
Gary Fencik (1976-87)	38
Richie Petitbon (1959-68)	37
Bennie McRae (1962-70)	27
Dave Whitsell (1961-66)	26
George McAfee (1940-41, 45-50)	25
J.C. Caroline (1956-65)	24
Doug Buffone (1966-79)	24

47

PREVIEW: CINCINNATI BENGALS

Last season the Bengals had big problems.

Now they have "Big Daddy."

They hope he helps them take a big step toward respectability.

As a result of their 3-13 record last season, the worst in the NFL, the Bengals got to pick first in this year's draft. With that choice, they took Ohio State DT Dan "Big Daddy" Wilkinson.

Although there is no chance that he will waste away to nothing, Wilkinson said he was trimming down a bit. The day of the draft, Wilkinson said he had slimmed down to 315 pounds and planned to lose another 10 pounds before the start of training camp.

"I plan to come in long and thin and ready to practice," said Wilkinson.

Wilkinson weighed 348 pounds when he started college in 1991 and was listed at 327 in the weeks leading up to the draft. But it was his strength and speed, more than his size, that impressed scouts during workouts.

Wilkinson, who played only two years at Ohio State, ran an impressive 4.79 in the 40. He also can bench-press 500 pounds and jump 30 inches vertically.

"I think I'll be the impact player they need," said Wilkinson.

Arizona coach Buddy Ryan, who supposedly tried to swing a deal to get the pick necessary to take Wilkinson, said, "A guy like him comes along once every 10 years or so, and you've got to go after him."

Look for the Bengals to switch from a 3-4 defense to a 4-3 scheme. The addition of Wilkinson to John Copeland, Alfred Williams and Tim Krumrie along the defensive line gives the team a very strong foundation.

"When we put him (Wilkinson) with Copeland and the other guys we have, we're going to have a front seven in short order that is going to rank with the better ones in the league," said Bengal GM Mike Brown.

Bengal defensive coordinator Larry Peccatiello said, "Defense starts with your front four. When you get a Dan Wilkinson, that's one step in that direction toward accomplishing what you want to do — have four dominant players."

Copeland, the Bengals' No. 1 pick last year, was very solid as a rookie despite coming in late and out of shape, and he should only get better as he improves his strength. Copeland can play the run and pass, has a real feel for the game and is a natural football player. Krumrie started every game last year and held his own, because he is so tough and has so much heart and dedication. Williams is a DE-OLB type whose strong point is the pass rush. Among the reserves, Mike Frier is big, strong and can play the run. Ty Parten is a very good athlete, but his durability is a major concern. George Hinkle is a journeyman.

Just as the Bengals have upgraded their defensive line, they now look very strong at safety. FS Darryl Williams is the star of the secondary and has done nothing but get better since joining the Bengals. Williams is a fearless hitter with excellent range and anticipation and very good hands.

The Bengals now have a dynamic 1-2 combination at safety after signing ex-Dolphin Louis Oliver as a free agent.

"This is a young team, and I think I can come in here and provide some leadership and get some guys fired up," said Oliver.

Oliver has a great size-speed ratio and hitting ability, but he is not very good on pass coverage and gets caught out of position more than he should.

At cornerback, two veteran journeymen who are not very highly regarded around the league, Michael Brim and Rod Jones, played better than most thought they could last year.

In the way of depth in the secondary, a pair of '93 draft picks, Marcello Simmons and Forey Duckett, are still relative unknowns. Lance Gunn started at strong safety before he injured his knee just after midseason, but he really struggled in pass coverage. Fernandus Vinson is a decent backup who took over after Gunn was injured. Leonard Wheeler doesn't look like an NFL cornerback, so now he will get a chance to show if he can play safety.

At linebacker the Bengals really liked what they saw of Steve Tovar at inside linebacker as a rookie and feel that, with a little more discipline, he can be a big-time player. Tovar is big, fast, aggressive and more instinctive than originally believed. However, he will overreact, does not always play under control and doesn't tackle very well in the open field. Ricardo McDonald, who started at inside linebacker his first two years, is coming off a very serious late-season knee injury, which makes him a question mark. McDonald is a sideline-to-sideline player who does not always make good reads. OLB James Francis can be as good as anyone in football if he will pay the price. He seems to lack a passion for the game, is not a good offseason worker and seems to get nicked a lot and heal very slowly. He is DE-sized and can cover backs, pick off passes and block kicks. If somebody can push the right buttons with him, he can be a Pro Bowl player.

The Bengals seem to think that they have enough talent on defense to make some noise if the offense will provide a little help.

"I've said all along that, if our offense is able to go out and get some things going, keep possession of the football and get some points on the board, we're going to be a hell of a football team," said Brim.

How good the offense can become will be decided in large part by whether or not QB David

1994 PREVIEW ■ CINCINNATI

Klingler is the real deal. It is very hard to judge Klingler, because he has been playing behind one of the worst offensive lines in football and always seems to be throwing on the run. Klingler's critics say he holds on to the ball too long, is very inaccurate throwing deep and on quick post and slant patterns, can't find secondary receivers, has not made the adjustment from the run-and-shoot to a conventional offense and is not much of a leader in the huddle. However, when you are constantly under siege, you have very little time to throw deep or find secondary receivers, and it *is* hard to lead.

"I feel I played well at times, and I attribute that to the offensive line," said Klingler. "When they played well, I played well."

On the plus side for Klingler, he has ideal size and stature, a bazooka arm and excellent mobility.

Jay Schroeder is the backup quarterback and still has a very strong but erratic arm. Donald Hollas gets the highest grades for leadership and spunk of the trio of quarterbacks, but he clearly has the weakest arm.

Klingler wasn't the only Bengal who was hurt by the poor play of the offensive line last year. The same held true for RB Harold Green. In '92 Green rushed for 1,170 yards and averaged 4.4 yards per carry. In '93 he rushed for 589 yards and averaged 2.7 yards per carry. Green's decline can be traced to the fact that he was unhappy after a bitter contract dispute and that the team's offensive line went from bad in 1992 to worse than awful in 1993. He is a big-time back with quickness in the hole, moves and exceptional balance. However, he does lack breakaway speed and had only two rushing touchdowns in the past two years.

One reason Green rarely scores is that the Bengals like to run Derrick Fenner near the goalline. Fenner is a tall, powerful, upright runner with impressive strength inside the tackles, but he lacks speed to the outside and gets hurt a lot. Last year he was the team's most effective back.

The Bengals have upgraded their offensive line a bit via free-agency. Former Giant Eric Moore and ex-Seahawk Darrick Brilz are almost certain to start. Moore has prototype size, speed, feet and athletic ability, but he is not mentally tough. The Bengals want to play him at left tackle, but he feels more comfortable at guard. Brilz is a smart, steady, efficient, overachieving guard who gets the job done. OT Joe Walter has just about reached the end of the line, but Bruce Kozerski still can be an effective guard in the Bengal scheme. Kozerski is a really good line leader who

PHOTO BY GEORGE GOJKOVICH

Carl Pickens

can make the adjustments and steady the troops. Of the youngsters, only Kevin Sargent has shown much promise.

Another area in which the Bengals need to improve is at receiver. The closest thing they have to a go-to receiver is Carl Pickens, who has good size and great jumping ability and body control but lacks explosive deep speed and has trouble separating. Jeff Query has good speed but is viewed more as a No. 3 or No. 4 receiver. The Bengals brought veterans Tim McGee and Reggie Rembert back into the organization. Cincinnati appears to have helped itself by drafting Darnay Scott early in the second round of this year's draft.

"We were looking for a speed receiver that can get down the field and get the ball into the endzone," said Bengal head coach Dave Shula. "Darnay gives us those qualities."

Tony McGee looks like he is going to be a fine NFL tight end. As a rookie McGee caught 44 passes and also did a solid job blocking.

PK Doug Pelfrey got off to a shaky start last year then settled down. He made 24-of-31 FG attempts but was good on only 13-of-16 extra points. P Lee Johnson had a career year, averaging 43.9 yards with a 36.6-yard net and 24 kicks inside the 20. He also does a fine job on kickoffs.

FAST FACTS

■ Last season the Bengals failed for the first time since 1980 to have a player selected for the Pro Bowl. They also have the NFL's worst record over the last three years (11-37).

■ In 1993 Harold Green became the first runner in NFL history to carry the ball at least 200 times and average less than three yards per attempt.

■ The Bengal defensive players averaged 22.7 yards per interception return last season, while opposing defenders averaged a mere 4.5 yards per interception return.

PRO FOOTBALL WEEKLY 1994 ALMANAC

1994 PLAYER ROSTER

NO.	NAME	POS.	HT.	WT.	EXP.	COLLEGE	GP/GS
42	Ball, Eric	RB	6-2	220	6	UCLA	15/1
60	Beckett, Andrew	DE	6-4	265	R	Rutgers	—
21	Benjamin, Ryan	RB	5-7	183	2	Pacific	1/0
60	Bradley, Chuck	OT	6-5	296	2	Kentucky	1/0
65	Brilz, Darrick	OG	6-3	287	8	Oregon State	16/16
43	Brim, Michael	CB	6-0	192	7	Virginia Union	16/16
33	Broussard, Steve	RB	5-7	201	5	Washington State	8/0
72	Brumfield, Scott	OT	6-8	320	2	Brigham Young	16/7
32	Carpenter, Ron	S	6-1	188	2	Miami (Ohio)	13/0
92	Copeland, John	DT	6-3	286	2	Alabama	14/14
17	Dickey, Troy	WR	6-3	226	R	Arizona	—
18	Drage, Eric	WR	6-1	180	R	Brigham Young	—
41	Duckett, Forey	CB	6-3	195	1	Nevada-Reno	0/0
20	English, Willie	RB	5-11	225	R	Central Florida	—
44	Fenner, Derrick	RB	6-3	228	6	North Carolina	15/14
70	Ford, Artis	DT	6-3	275	2	Mississippi	0/0
50	Francis, James	LB	6-5	252	5	Baylor	14/12
97	Frier, Mike	DE	6-5	299	3	Appalachian State	16/6
47	Frisch, David	TE	6-7	260	2	Colorado State	11/2
58	Gordon, Alex	LB	6-5	245	8	Cincinnati	16/3
24	Grant, Alan	CB	5-10	187	5	Stanford	12/1
28	Green, Harold	RB	6-2	222	5	South Carolina	15/15
27	Gunn, Lance	S	6-3	222	2	Texas	8/8
16	Harris, Lee	WR	6-2	195	R	Fresno State	—
19	Hill, Jeff	WR	5-11	178	R	Purdue	—
98	Hinkle, George	DT	6-5	288	7	Arizona	13/9
12	Hollas, Donald	QB	6-3	215	3	Rice	0/0
71	Howe, Garry	NT	6-1	298	3	Colorado	1/0
45	Jefferson, Kevin	LB	6-2	232	R	Lehigh	—
99	Johnson, Donnell	OT	6-7	310	2	Johnson C. Smith	7/0
55	Johnson, Lance	LS	6-1	265	R	Notre Dame	—
11	Johnson, Lee	P-PK	6-2	200	10	Brigham Young	16/0
78	Jones, Dan	OT	6-7	298	2	Maine	15/5
25	Jones, Rod	CB	6-0	185	9	Southern Methodist	16/16
7	Klingler, David	QB	6-2	205	3	Houston	14/13
64	Kozerski, Bruce	C-OG	6-4	287	11	Holy Cross	15/15
69	Krumrie, Tim	NT	6-2	274	12	Wisconsin	16/16
75	Linn, Jack	OG-OT	6-5	285	3	West Virginia	6/3
56	McDonald, Ricardo	LB	6-2	235	3	Pittsburgh	14/12
85	McGee, Tim	WR	5-10	183	9	Tennessee	13/12
82	McGee, Tony	TE	6-3	246	2	Michigan	15/15
59	McGill, Karmeeleyah	LB	6-3	224	2	Notre Dame	4/0
36	Miles, Ostell	RB	6-0	236	3	Houston	15/2
62	Moore, Eric	OG	6-5	290	7	Indiana	7/5
73	Moyer, Ken	OT	6-7	297	5	Toledo	16/14
95	Nix, Roosevelt	DE	6-6	292	3	Central State (Ohio)	10/0
29	Oliver, Louis	S	6-2	224	6	Florida	11/11
93	Parten, Ty	NT	6-4	272	2	Arizona	11/1
9	Pelfrey, Doug	PK	5-11	185	2	Kentucky	15/0
26	Phillips, Jey	CB	6-2	183	R	Arizona	—
80	Pickens, Carl	WR	6-2	206	3	Tennessee	13/12
89	Query, Jeff	WR	6-0	165	6	Millikin	16/16
88	Rembert, Reggie	WR	6-5	200	3	West Virginia	3/0
39	Richardson, Terry	RB	6-1	205	R	Syracuse	—
81	Robinson, Patrick	WR	5-8	176	2	Tennessee State	15/3

1994 PREVIEW ■ CINCINNATI

1994 PLAYER ROSTER

NO.	NAME	POS.	HT.	WT.	EXP.	COLLEGE	GP/GS
87	Sadowski, Troy	TE	6-5	250	5	Georgia	13/1
77	Sargent, Kevin	OT	6-6	284	3	Eastern Washington	1/1
10	Schroeder, Jay	QB	6-4	215	11	UCLA	9/3
74	Scott, Tom	OT	6-6	330	2	East Carolina	13/13
90	Shaw, Eric	LB	6-3	248	3	Louisiana Tech	14/9
22	Simmons, Marcello	CB	6-1	180	2	Southern Methodist	16/2
91	Smith, Brad	LB	6-2	228	2	Texas Christian	7/0
84	Stegall, Milt	WR	6-0	184	3	Miami (Ohio)	4/0
53	Stephens, Santo	LB	6-4	232	2	Temple	16/0
30	Stowers, Don	S	6-2	200	R	New Mexico State	—
96	Stubbs, Daniel	DE	6-4	264	7	Miami (Fla.)	16/0
49	Thomason, Jeff	TE	6-4	233	3	Oregon	3/0
48	Thompson, Craig	TE	6-2	244	3	North Carolina A&T	13/0
51	Tovar, Steve	LB	6-3	244	2	Ohio State	16/9
55	Truitt, Greg	LS	6-0	235	1	Penn State	0/0
86	Turner, Elbert	WR	5-11	165	1	Illinois	0/0
34	Vinson, Fernandus	S	5-10	197	4	North Carolina St.	16/7
63	Walter, Joe	OT	6-7	292	10	Texas Tech	16/16
37	Wheeler, Leonard	CB	5-11	189	3	Troy State	16/2
4	Wilhelm, Erik	QB	6-3	217	5	Oregon State	1/0
94	Williams, Alfred	LB	6-6	240	4	Colorado	16/16
31	Williams, Darryl	S	6-0	191	3	Miami (Fla.)	16/16
38	Williams, Ronald	RB	6-1	203	1	Clemson	0/0
67	Woodside, Ray	OG	6-4	280	R	Cincinnati	—

'94 DRAFT PICKS

RD.	NAME	POS.	HT.	WT.	COLLEGE
1.	Wilkinson, Dan	DT	6-4	327	Ohio State
2.	Scott, Darnay	WR	6-1	185	San Diego State
3.	Cothran, Jeff	RB	6-0	249	Ohio State
3.	Shine, Steve	LB	6-5	232	Northwestern
4.	Sawyer, Corey	DB	5-10	170	Florida State
5.	Pollard, Trent	OT	6-3	338	Eastern Washington
6.	Von Oelhoffen, Kimo	DT	6-3	290	Boise State
6.	Reynolds, Jerry	OT	6-5	324	Nevada-Las Vegas
7.	Stallings, Ramondo	DE	6-7	282	San Diego State

PRO FOOTBALL WEEKLY 1994 ALMANAC

TEAM AT A GLANCE

TEAM DIRECTORY

Address	200 Riverfront Stadium Cincinnati, Ohio 45202 (513) 621-3550
Stadium	Riverfront Stadium 200 Riverfront Stadium Cincinnati, Ohio 45202 Capacity: 60,389 Playing surface: AstroTurf
Training Camp	Wilmington College Wilmington, Ohio 45177
Colors	Black, orange and white
Television	WLWT, Channel 5
Radio	WLWA, 550 AM

ADMINISTRATION
Chairman of the board: Austin E. Knowlton
President-general manager: Michael Brown
Vice president: John Sawyer
Asst. GM-director of player personnel: Pete Brown
Scouting: Paul H. Brown
Asst. director of player personnel: Frank Smouse
Business manager: Bill Connelly
Director of public relations: Jack Brennan
Ticket manager: Paul Kelly
Trainer: Paul Sparling

1994 SCHEDULE

Preseason

AUG. 6	at Tampa Bay	7:30
AUG. 13	INDIANAPOLIS	7:30
AUG. 20	at Philadelphia	7:30
AUG. 26	DETROIT	7:30

Regular season

SEP. 4	CLEVELAND	1:00
SEP. 11	at San Diego	1:00
SEP. 18	NEW ENGLAND	1:00
SEP. 25	at Houston	3:00
OCT. 2	MIAMI	8:00
OCT. 9	OPEN DATE	
OCT. 16	at Pittsburgh	1:00
OCT. 23	at Cleveland	1:00
OCT. 30	DALLAS	1:00
NOV. 6	at Seattle	1:00
NOV. 13	HOUSTON	1:00
NOV. 20	INDIANAPOLIS	1:00
NOV. 27	at Denver	2:00
DEC. 4	PITTSBURGH	1:00
DEC. 11	at N.Y. Giants	1:00
DEC. 18	at Arizona	2:00
DEC. 24	PHILADELPHIA	1:00

HEAD COACH
Dave Shula

The youngest head coach in the NFL, Shula has been surrounded by football all of his life. He got his start in the professional ranks in Miami, where he worked under his father, Don, as the Dolphins' quarterback and receiver coach. At the age of 26, Shula was offered the head-coaching job in Philadelphia, but declined. He stayed with the Dolphins for seven seasons before moving on to Dallas, where he was offensive coordinator, and then Cincinnati. Born: May 28, 1959, Lexington, Ky.

Previous NFL: head coach, 1992-93 Cincinnati; wide receivers, 1991 Cincinnati; offensive coordinator-quarterbacks, 1989-90 Dallas; assistant head coach, 1988 Miami; quarterbacks-wide receivers, 1982-87 Miami.

Previous college: None.

Player: NFL, wide receiver, 1981 Baltimore. College, wide receiver, 1978-81 Dartmouth.

ASSISTANT COACHES

Paul Alexander: tight ends
Previous NFL: offensive assistant-tight ends, 1992-93 N.Y. Jets. Player: No NFL. College: tackle, 1978-81 Cortland State.

Jim Anderson: running backs
Previous NFL: running backs, 1984-93 Cincinnati. Player: No NFL. College: linebacker, defensive end, 1967-70 Cal-Western.

Ken Anderson: quarterbacks
Previous NFL: quarterbacks, 1992-93 Cincinnati. Player: NFL, quarterback, 1971-86 Cincinnati. College: quarterback, 1967-70 Augustana (Ill.).

Marv Braden: special teams
Previous NFL: special teams, 1990-93 Cincinnati; 1986-89 St. Louis/Phoenix; 1981-85 San Diego; 1977-80 Denver. Player: No NFL: College: linebacker, 1956-59 Southwest Missouri State.

Bruce Coslet: offensive coordinator
Previous NFL: head coach, 1990-93 N.Y. Jets; 1981-89 Cincinnati; 1980 San Francisco. Player: tight end, 1969-76 Cincinnati. College: tight end, 1965-67 Pacific.

Bobby DePaul: defensive assistant
Previous NFL: administrative assistant-defensive line, 1989-93 Washington. Player: No NFL. College: linebacker, 1982-83 Maryland.

Jim McNally: offensive line
Previous NFL: offensive line, 1980-93 Cincinnati. Player: No NFL. College: guard, 1961-65 Buffalo.

Ron Meeks: defensive backfield
Previous NFL: defensive backfield, 1992-93 Cincinnati; 1991 Dallas. Player: No NFL. College: defensive back, 1975-76 Arkansas State.

Joe Pascale: linebackers
Previous NFL: outside inebackers, 1986-93 St. Louis/Phoenix. Player: No NFL. College: linebacker, 1963-66 Connecticut.

Larry Peccatiello: defensive coordinator
Previous NFL: assistant head coach, 1981-93 Washington; 1976-80 Seattle; 1972-75 Houston. Player: No NFL. College: receiver, 1955-58 William & Mary.

1994 PREVIEW ■ CINCINNATI

TEAM AT A GLANCE

Joe Wessel: defensive line
Previous NFL: None. Player: No NFL. College: quarterback, safety, 1981-84 Florida State.

Richard Williamson: wide receivers
Previous NFL: wide receivers, 1992-93 Cincinnati; 1983-86 Kansas City; 1987-91 Tampa Bay (head coach 1990-91). Player: No NFL. College: receiver, 1961-62 Alabama.

Kim Wood: strength and conditioning
Previous NFL: strength and conditioning, 1975-93 Cincinnati. Player: No NFL. College: running back, 1965-68 Wisconsin.

COACHING RECORDS
(includes postseason records)

Years	Coach	W	L	T
1968-75	Paul Brown	55	59	1
1976-78	Bill Johnson	18	15	0
1978-79	Homer Rice	8	19	0
1980-83	Forrest Gregg	34	27	0
1984-91	Sam Wyche	64	68	0
1992-93	Dave Shula	8	24	0

HISTORICAL HIGHLIGHTS

1967 Headed by Paul Brown, famed former coach of the Cleveland Browns, a group of investors wins a franchise for Cincinnati. Brown names the team the Bengals.

1969 Rookie QB Greg Cook is the top-rated passer in the AFL, LB Bill Bergey is honored as the AFL Defensive Rookie of the Year and Paul Brown is named AFL Coach of the Year.

1970 With an 8-6 record, the Bengals become the first third-year expansion team to win a division title when they take the AFC Central. Their luck does not follow them to the playoffs, however, where they fall to Baltimore 17-0.

1973 The Bengals win their second AFC divisional title after splitting their first eight games and then sweeping their last six to finish the year with a 10-4 record. The club is again thwarted in the playoffs, losing this time to Miami 24-16 ... RB Boobie Clark is named AFC Rookie of the Year, finishing the season with 988 yards rushing and 45 pass receptions, while tandem back Essex Johnson gains 997 yards rushing ... Issac Curtis gains more yards receiving (843) and sports the best receiving average, 18.7 yards, in the AFC.

1974 QB Ken Anderson is the top passer in the NFL, completing 214 passes for 2,667 yards and 18 TD's. His 64.9 completion percentage is also a club record ... Lemar Parrish leads the NFL in punt returns, averaging 18.8 yards on 18 returns.

1975 Cincinnati posts a record of 11-3, its best regular-season showing to date, and qualifies as the AFC wild-card team in the playoffs. The Bengals fall a third time to Oakland 31-28.

1976 After 41 seasons of coaching, Paul Brown announces his retirement and names Bill Johnson, his OL coach, to replace him. Brown continues to serve as general manager and vice president.

1981 Wearing their new tiger-striped helmets, the Bengals triumph in the AFC Central under head coach Forrest Gregg, their 12-4 record the best in club history ... Ken Anderson once again leads the league in passing with a 98.5 rating, his highest career mark, completing 300 passes for 3,754 yards and 29 TD's, and is named AFC Offensive Player of the Year.

1981-82 In 1981 the Bengals snap their postseason losing streak by defeating the Buffalo Bills in the AFC divisional playoff game 28-21. Then, despite a howling wind and sub-zero temperatures at Riverfront Stadium in Cincinnati, the Bengals take the AFC crown, defeating San Diego 27-7 and earn a trip to Super Bowl XVI. At the Pontiac Silverdome in Super Bowl XVI, a halftime deficit of 20-0 overwhelms the Bengals, and they fall to the San Francisco 49ers 26-21.

1982 Finishing the strike-shortened season with a 7-2 mark, second only to the Raiders, the Bengals again make the playoffs but lose to the Jets 44-17.

1982 Ken Anderson again takes passing honors in the AFC with 218 completions for 2,495 yards and 12 TD's. His completion percentage of 70.6 is by far the best in the NFL.

1986 Cincinnati posts its first winning season since 1982 with a record of 10-6, but because of tiebreakers, the team loses out on a wild-card entry in the playoff ... James Brooks sets a club rushing record by gaining 1,087 yards.

1988 The Bengals post the biggest single-season turnaround in NFL history, going from 4-11 in 1987 to 12-4 in '88.

1988-89 After finishing in first place in the AFC Central, the Bengals go on to win the AFC championship game when they defeat the Buffalo Bills 21-10 at Riverfront Stadium ... Cincinnati goes to Super Bowl XXIII to face San Francisco, but loses 20-16 when the 49ers come from behind and score a touchdown with 34 seconds left in the game.

1990 The Bengals win the AFC Central with a record of 9-7 ... In the playoffs, Cincinnati overwhelms the Houston Oilers 41-14 but then loses to the L.A. Raiders 20-10.

1991 Bengal founder and Pro Football Hall of Fame enshrinee Paul Brown dies.

1992 Dave Shula, son of Dolphin legend and the game's winningest coach, Don Shula, replaces Sam Wyche as head coach of the Bengals.

PRO FOOTBALL WEEKLY 1994 ALMANAC

TEAM AT A GLANCE

HALL OF FAME MEMBERS
None

RETIRED JERSEY NUMBERS
54   C Bob Johnson

FIRST-ROUND DRAFT CHOICES
(since 1980)

Year	Selection	College
1980	OT Anthony Munoz	Southern Cal
1981	WR David Verser	Kansas
1982	DE Glen Collins	Mississippi State
1983	C Dave Rimington	Nebraska
1984	LB Ricky Hunley	Arizona
	DE Pete Koch	Maryland
	OT Brian Blados	North Carolina
1985	WR Eddie Brown	Miami (Fla.)
	LB Emanuel King	Alabama
1986	LB Joe Kelly	Washington
	WR Tim McGee	Tennessee
1987	DE Jason Buck	Brigham Young
1988	CB Rickey Dixon	Oklahoma
1989	No choice	
1990	LB James Francis	Baylor
1991	LB Alfred Williams	Colorado
1992	QB David Klingler	Houston
	DB Darryl Williams	Miami (Fla.)
1993	DE John Copeland	Alabama
1994	DT Dan Wilkinson	Ohio State

RECORD VS. OTHER NFL TEAMS
(includes postseason games)

	Record
Arizona Cardinals	3-1-0
Atlanta Falcons	6-2-0
Buffalo Bills	11-7-0
Chicago Bears	3-2-0
Cleveland Browns	24-23-0
Dallas Cowboys	2-3-0
Denver Broncos	6-10-0
Detroit Lions	3-3-0
Green Bay Packers	4-3-0
Houston Oilers	25-25-1
Indianapolis Colts	5-9-0
Kansas City Chiefs	9-11-0
Los Angeles Raiders	7-16-0
Los Angeles Rams	5-2-0
Miami Dolphins	3-10-0
Minnesota Vikings	3-4-0
New England Patriots	7-8-0
New Orleans Saints	3-5-0
New York Giants	4-0-0
New York Jets	6-10-0
Philadelphia Eagles	5-1-0
Pittsburgh Steelers	21-26-0
San Diego Chargers	9-12-0
San Francisco 49ers	1-8-0
Seattle Seahawks	6-6-0
Tampa Bay Buccaneers	3-1-0
Washington Redskins	2-4-0

YEAR-BY-YEAR RECORDS

Year	Won	Lost	Tied
1968	3	11	0
1969	4	9	1
1970**	8	6	0
1971	4	10	0
1972	8	6	0
1973**	10	4	0
1974	7	7	0
1975**	11	3	0
1976	10	4	0
1977	8	6	0
1978	4	12	0
1979	4	12	0
1980	6	10	0
1981**	12	4	0
1982**	7	2	0
1983	7	9	0
1984	8	8	0
1985	7	9	0
1986	10	6	0
1987	4	11	0
1988**	12	4	0
1989	8	8	0
1990**	9	7	0
1991	3	13	0
1992	5	11	0
1993	3	13	0
Total	182	205	1

Number of NFL championships   0
Number of years .500 or better   14
Number of years below .500   12

*NFL champions
**Playoff team

1994 PREVIEW ■ CINCINNATI

RECORDS

INDIVIDUAL

Service
Seasons played — 16 Ken Anderson (1971-76)

Scoring
Points, career	1,151	Jim Breech (1980-92)
Points, season	120	Jim Breech (1985)
Points, game	24	Larry Kinnebrew (10/28/84)
Touchdowns, career	70	Pete Johnson (1977-83)
Touchdowns, season	16	Pete Johnson (1981)
Touchdowns, game	4	Larry Kinnebrew (10/28/84)
Field goals, career	225	Jim Breech (1980-92)
Field goals, season	120	Jim Breech (1985)
Field goals, game	5	Horst Muhlmann (11/8/70)
		Horst Muhlmann (9/24/72)
		Jim Breech (11/1/87)
Extra points, career	476	Jim Breech (1980-92)
Exta points, season	56	Jim Breech (1988)
Extra points, game	8	Jim Breech (10/29/89)

Rushing
Yards, career	6,447	James Brooks (1984-91)
Yards, season	1,239	James Brooks (1989)
Yards, game	201	James Brooks (12/23/90)
Attempts, career	1,402	Pete Johnson (1977-83)
Attempts, season	274	Pete Johnson (1981)
Attempts, game	38	Pete Johnson (12/4/83)
Touchdowns, career	64	Pete Johnson (1977-83)
Touchdowns, season	15	Ickey Woods (1988)
Touchdowns, game	3	By many players

Passing
Rating, career	81.9	Ken Anderson (1971-86)
Rating, season	98.5	Ken Anderson (1981)
Completions, career	2,654	Ken Anderson (1971-86)
Completions, season	300	Ken Anderson (1981)
Completions, game	40	Ken Anderson (12/20/82)
Yards, career	32,838	Ken Anderson (1971-86)
Yards, season	3,959	Boomer Esaison (1986)
Yards, game	490	Boomer Esaison (11/7/90)
Attempts, career	4,475	Ken Anderson (1971-86)
Attempts, season	479	Ken Anderson (1981)
Attempts, game	56	Ken Anderson (12/20/82)
Touchdowns, career	197	Ken Anderson (1971-86)
Touchdowns, season	29	Ken Anderson (1981)
Touchdowns, game	5	Boomer Esaison (11/29/89)
		Boomer Esaison (12/21/86)

Receiving
Receptions, career	420	Isaac Curtis (1973-84)
Receptions, season	71	Dan Ross (1981)
Receptions, game	12	James Brooks (12/25/89)
Yards, career	7,106	Isaac Curtis (1973-84)
Yards, season	1,273	Eddie Brown (1988)
Yards, game	216	Eddie Brown (11/16/88)
Touchdowns, career	53	Isaac Curtis (1973-84)
Touchdowns, season	10	Isaac Curtis (1974)
		Cris Collinsworth (1986)
Touchdowns, game	3	Bob Trumpy (11/9/69)
		Isaac Curtis (12/9/73)
		Isaac Curtis (11/4/79)
		Cris Collinsworth (12/21/86)

Interceptions
Career	65	Ken Riley (1969-83)
Season	9	Ken Riley (1976)
Game	3	By many players

Longest plays
Run from scrimmage	87	Paul Robinson (TD, 10/27/68)
Pass play	94	Ken Anderson to Billy Brooks (TD, 11/13/77)
Field goal	55	Chris Bahr (9/23/79)
Interception return	102	Louis Breeden (1981)
Kickoff return	98	Stanford Jennings (TD, 11/13/88)
Punt return	95	Carl Pickens (TD, 9/20/92)
Punt	70	Lee Johnson (9/23/90)
		Lee Johnson (11/22/90)

Top scorers — Points
Jim Breech (1980-92)	1,151
Horst Muhlmann (1969-74)	549
Pete Johnson (1977-83)	420
James Brooks (1984-90)	384
Isaac Curtis (1973-84)	318
Chris Bahr (1976-79)	316

Top rushers — Yards
James Brooks (1984-91)	6,447
Pete Johnson (1977-83)	5,421
Essex Johnson (1968-75)	3,070
Boobie Clark (1973-78)	2,978
Harold Green (1990-93)	2,843
Archie Griffin (1976-83)	2,808

Top passers — Completions
Ken Anderson (1971-86)	2,654
Boomer Esaison (1984-92)	1,897
Virgil Carter (1970-73)	328
David Klingler (1992-93)	237
Turk Schonert (1981-89)	216
Jack Thompson (1979-82)	175

Top passers — Yards
Ken Anderson (1971-86)	32,838
Boomer Esaison (1984-92)	25,671
Virgil Carter (1970-73)	3,850
Turk Schonert (1981-89)	2,756
David Klingler (1992-93)	2,465
Jack Thompson (1979-82)	2,072

Top receivers — Receptions
Isaac Curtis (1973-84)	420
Cris Collinsworth (1981-87)	417
Eddie Brown (1985-91)	363
Rodney Holman (1982-92)	318
Bob Trumpy (1968-77)	298
James Brooks (1984-91)	290

Top receivers — Yards
Isaac Curtis (1973-84)	7,106
Cris Collinsworth (1981-87)	6,698
Eddie Brown (1985-91)	6,134
Bob Trumpy (1968-77)	4,630
Tim McGee (1986-92)	4,528
Rodney Holman (1982-92)	4,339

Most interceptions — No.
Ken Riley (1969-83)	65
Louis Breeden (1978-87)	34
David Fulcher (1986-92)	31
Lemar Parrish (1970-78)	25
Tommy Casanova (1972-77)	17
Eric Thomas (1987-92)	16
Reggie Williams (1976-89)	16

PREVIEW: CLEVELAND BROWNS

So close.

That's how near the Browns felt they were to being a quality team after finishing 7-9 for the second consecutive season in 1993.

"I think the talent is good enough," said LB Clay Matthews. "We just have to find whatever that magical thing is that makes you believe you're going to win those close games, rather than lose them."

All-purpose RB Eric Metcalf said, "We were so close in so many games. I think four or five games could have been saved if we had done what we needed to do on the field, regardless of what was happening off the field."

What was happening off the field last season will continue to have a direct bearing on how the Browns fare this season. The defining moment of Cleveland's '93 season came on Nov. 8, when head coach Bill Belichick shocked the team and the city by cutting QB Bernie Kosar, one of the most popular players in franchise history. The team was 5-3 and in first place in the AFC Central on the day Kosar was released. The Browns proceeded to lose six of their next eight games.

The backlash from Kosar's release was evident in more ways than just the standings. The boos in Cleveland Stadium hurt, according to WR Michael Jackson, even if they were directed at Belichick.

"It was terrible, really," said Jackson. "You know Bernie's gone, and that's what a lot of that was about. But I don't think he was going to come back, no matter what the fans did. How do you think that made the players feel? A team is more than one player."

The question now is how will the Browns do in '94 with Kosar's replacement, Vinny Testaverde?

If the Browns were just missing the boat by a little bit last season in the games referred to by Matthews and Metcalf, is there reason to believe anything will change this year with Testaverde firmly entrenched in the starter's role from Day One? Is Testaverde the man to silence the boos, or is he more likely to cause them?

From the neck down, Testaverde is as gifted as just about any quarterback in the NFL. Almost every team in the league had him rated as the best player in the 1987 draft. But doubts persist about Testaverde from the neck up. He isn't very tough mentally, and, when things go bad, he quickly loses his confidence. Last year Testaverde had his best NFL season, completing 130-of-230 passes for 1,797 yards, 14 touchdowns, nine interceptions and an 85.7 passer rating. However, last year Testaverde was brought in as a backup, where anything he did was viewed as a bonus. This season the pressure will be on from the start of training camp. If he should falter, ex-Redskin Mark Rypien, who has been reunited

Tommy Vardell

with Rod Dowhower, will be waiting in the wings.

Testaverde can count on very good support from the Cleveland running backs. Tommy Vardell can develop into a solid blocker-receiver. The Browns want to get the ball to Metcalf in the open field as much as possible in order to take full advantage of his lightning quickness, instant acceleration and magical moves. Last season Metcalf caught a team-high 63 passes, averaged 4.7 yards per carry and rushed for 611 yards while making the Pro Bowl as a return specialist. Leroy Hoard has the size, speed, power, running skills and hands to be a terrific back, but to date he has been an enigma, flashing greatness and then disappearing.

Veterans Kevin Mack and Earnest Byner, who each gained 1,000 yards with the Browns in 1985, add depth.

Testaverde won't get as much help from his receivers, who are mediocre at best. Jackson can stretch the defense deep. He has better speed than quickness. His hands are inconsistent, but

1994 PREVIEW ■ CLEVELAND

he is big, fast and always a threat if the quarterback can reach him. Mark Carrier is a pretty solid possession receiver who is fearless over the middle, but his 4.7 speed doesn't scare anyone. First-rounder Derrick Alexander has the tools to become a solid size-speed receiver. Patrick Rowe has had a full season to overcome the side effects of his knee surgery in '92, and this is the season for him to show what he can do. Rowe has size and speed but wasn't productive last year. Rico Smith is the fastest player on the roster, but he has been slow to develop. Keenan McCardell is an effective third or fourth receiver. The Browns finally have a big, blocking tight end in Walter Reeves, who they acquired via free-agency.

Along the offensive line, the Browns have two outstanding building blocks in OLT Tony Jones and C Steve Everitt. Jones is one of the NFL's best pass-blocking and most athletic left tackles. He played better in 1993 than two of the three AFC tackles in the Pro Bowl. As for Everitt, it is difficult to imagine a rookie center doing a better job than he did last season, and he should only improve with experience if he can avoid injury. As is the case with Jones, the Browns would like to see Everitt develop into a more dominating run blocker. Bob Dahl is a tough, physical, blue-collar guard. Houston Hoover, who started at the other OG spot, may be too old and beat up and could be replaced, perhaps by free-agent acquisition Mike Withycombe. Last year the Browns went with Eugene Williams and Ed King at right tackle, but both are probably better-suited for guard. Herman Arvie has quick feet and could get the nod at right tackle if he can keep his weight down.

The Browns' biggest problem on defense last year was their inability to force more turnovers. Since Cleveland's defensive strength has shifted from the linebackers to the defensive line, Belichick plans to allow his big men to rush the passer more and make more plays.

Along the defensive line, the Browns are very deep. Rob Burnett has developed into one of the NFL's better all-around left ends. He has notched nine sacks in each of the past two seasons and has also held his own against the run. DRE Anthony Pleasant came into his own last season, leading the team with 11 sacks. Pleasant is a speed rusher who has gained 35 pounds since coming into the NFL, and it is all good, solid weight. DT Michael Dean Perry is not as dominating as he once was, but he is still awfully good. Perry's strengths are quickness, explosiveness and power. After Jerry Ball ate his way out of the lineup last year, James Jones stepped in and had his usual solid season. Two backups who could really come on are oft-injured Bill Johnson and 1993's second-round draft choice, Dan Footman. No. 3 pick Romeo Bandison adds more depth.

At linebacker, the Browns slipped last year. After 16 years in the league, Matthews finally started to show his age, and, although Mike Johnson led the team in tackles, he was not nearly as effective as he was a year earlier and eventually signed with Detroit. After David Brandon was cut in '93, Pepper Johnson took over, but he struggled much of the time. The most glaring weakness displayed by this trio was a lack of speed, which is why '93 draft picks Mike Caldwell, Travis Hill and Rich McKenzie will get every chance to claim jobs. Caldwell, who is very athletic, played in nickel situations last season and did an excellent job. Hill spent the year rehabilitating from knee surgery, while McKenzie was attempting to make the move from college defensive end to pro linebacker. Richard Brown could get a shot at middle linebacker if he is healthy.

In the secondary, both safeties had excellent seasons. Eric Turner and Stevon Moore finished second and third on the team last season in tackles with 159 and 155, respectively. Turner also had a team-high five interceptions. Moore may not have intercepted any passes, but he was the team's best player in the secondary. He plays the run like a strong safety should, and he has the coverage skills of a cornerback. Turner is a devastating hitter, but at times he will miss tackles and overrun plays because he is so intent on delivering knockout blows. The Browns should be dramatically upgraded on the corners, with No. 1 pick Antonio Langham and free-agent Don Griffin entered into the mix. Langham's film grades in college were better than Deion Sanders', and Griffin is a heady veteran who should provide stability and leadership. CB Najee Mustafaa gets the job done in man-on-man coverage, but he is not as effective in a zone defense, and ball-hawking Selwyn Jones must show that he will hit and tackle as well as cover. But suddenly, a paper-thin weakness has turned into a strength.

The star of the special teams is Metcalf. He won the first Pittsburgh game last season, returning punts 91 and 75 yards for scores and bringing back memories of Gale Sayers in the process. He and Hoard were also reasonably successful on kickoff returns.

PK Matt Stover had his best year, making 16-of-22 field goals and 36-of-36 extra points. Nonetheless, the Browns still aren't completely comfortable with him. The Browns will also have to find a punter to replace Brian Hansen, who signed as an unrestricted free agent with the Jets.

FAST FACTS

■ Last season was the first time in Vinny Testaverde's seven-year pro career that he threw more TD passes (14) than interceptions (9).

■ Eric Metcalf has returned at least one punt or kickoff for a touchdown in three of the last four seasons.

■ DE Anthony Pleasant had more sacks last season (11) than he had recorded in the first three years of his pro career, when he had 10 from 1990 to '92.

PRO FOOTBALL WEEKLY 1994 ALMANAC

1994 PLAYER ROSTER

NO.	NAME	POS.	HT.	WT.	EXP.	COLLEGE	GP/GS
73	Arvie, Herman	OT	6-4	305	2	Grambling	16/0
93	Ball, Jerry	DT	6-1	315	8	Southern Methodist	16/6
91	Bomba, Matt	DL	6-5	275	1	Indiana	0/0
25	Briggs, Greg	S	6-3	210	2	Texas Southern	0/0
77	Brown, Orlando	OL	6-7	325	2	S. Carolina State	0/0
52	Brown, Richard	LB	6-3	240	7	San Diego State	0/0
90	Burnett, Rob	DE	6-4	280	5	Syracuse	16/16
23	Byner, Earnest	RB	5-10	215	11	East Carolina	16/3
56	Caldwell, Mike	LB	6-2	235	2	Middle Tenn. St.	15/11
83	Carrier, Mark	WR	6-0	185	8	Nicholls State	16/16
4	Cobb, Robert	QB	6-2	217	R	Northeast Louisiana	—
72	Dahl, Bob	OG-OT	6-5	300	3	Notre Dame	16/16
49	Derby, John	LB	6-0	232	1	Iowa	0/0
51	Dixon, Gerald	LB	6-3	250	3	South Carolina	11/10
2	Eichloff, Dan	K	6-0	215	R	Kansas	—
61	Everitt, Steve	C-OG	6-5	290	2	Michigan	16/16
25	Ferrell, Kerry	WR	5-11	173	1	Syracuse	0/0
78	Footman, Dan	DE	6-5	290	2	Florida State	8/0
37	Frank, Donald	CB	6-0	192	5	Winston-Salem	16/16
8	Goebel, Brad	QB	6-3	198	4	Baylor	0/0
79	Gray, Jim	DT	6-2	285	1	West Virginia	0/0
28	Griffin, Don	CB	6-0	176	9	Mid. Tennessee St.	12/12
31	Hairston, Stacey	CB	5-9	180	2	Ohio Northern	16/0
48	Hartley, Frank	TE	6-2	268	1	Illinois	0/0
55	Hill, Travis	LB	6-2	240	2	Nebraska	0/0
33	Hoard, Leroy	RB	5-11	225	5	Michigan	16/7
64	Hoover, Houston	OG-OT	6-2	300	7	Jackson State	16/16
81	Jackson, Michael	WR	6-4	195	4	Southern Mississippi	16/15
41	Jacobs, Tim	CB	5-10	185	2	Delaware	0/0
94	Johnson, Bill	DL	6-4	290	3	Michigan State	10/0
53	Johnson, Pepper	LB	6-3	248	9	Ohio State	16/11
47	Jones, David	TE	6-3	255	3	Delaware State	0/0
96	Jones, James	DT	6-2	290	4	Northern Iowa	16/12
22	Jones, Selwyn	CB	6-0	185	3	Colorado State	11/2
66	Jones, Tony	OT	6-5	295	7	Western Carolina	16/16
15	Kalal, Tim	P	6-3	205	1	Miami (Fla.)	0/0
59	Killian, P.J.	LB	6-2	242	R	Virginia	—
88	Kinchen, Brian	TE	6-2	240	7	Louisiana State	16/15
68	King, Ed	OT-OG	6-4	300	4	Auburn	6/2
22	Lee, Marcus	RB	5-10	227	R	Syracuse	—
74	Leomiti, Carlson	OL	6-3	384	R	San Diego St.	—
77	Lyle, Rick	DL	6-5	275	R	Missouri	—
34	Mack, Kevin	FB	6-0	225	9	Clemson	4/0
57	Matthews, Clay	LB	6-2	245	17	Southern Cal	16/15
87	McCardell, Keenan	WR	6-1	175	3	Nevada-Las Vegas	6/3
99	McKenzie, Rich	LB	6-2	240	1	Penn State	0/0
80	McLemore, Tom	TE	6-5	250	3	Southern-B.R.	0/0
21	Metcalf, Eric	RB	5-10	190	6	Texas	16/9
65	Milstead, Rod	OG	6-2	290	3	Delaware State	0/0
47	Montford, Joe	LB	6-0	210	R	South Carolina St.	—
27	Moore, Stevon	S	5-11	210	6	Mississippi	16/16
48	Mustafaa, Najee	CB	6-1	190	8	Georgia Tech	14/14
71	Myles, Tim	DDL	6-1	280	R	Vermillion J.C.	—
92	Perry, Michael Dean	DT	6-1	285	7	Clemson	16/13
17	Philcox, Todd	QB	6-4	225	5	Syracuse	5/4

58

1994 PREVIEW ■ CLEVELAND

1994 PLAYER ROSTER

NO.	NAME	POS.	HT.	WT.	EXP.	COLLEGE	GP/GS
98	Pleasant, Anthony	DE	6-5	280	5	Tennessee State	16/13
49	Reeves, Walter	TE	6-4	270	6	Auburn	16/15
42	Riddick, Louis	S	6-2	215	3	Pittsburgh	15/0
86	Rowe, Patrick	WR	6-1	195	3	San Diego State	5/0
11	Rypien, Mark	QB	6-4	234	8	Washington State	12/10
75	Sagapolutele, Pio	DL	6-6	297	4	San Diego State	8/0
84	Smith, Rico	WR	6-0	185	3	Colorado	10/1
43	Speer, Del	DB	6-0	200	2	Florida	16/2
20	Stacy, Siran	RB	5-11	205	2	Alabama	0/0
50	Stams, Frank	LB	6-2	230	6	Notre Dame	14/0
3	Stover, Matt	PK	5-11	178	5	Louisiana Tech	16/0
54	Sutter, Ed	LB	6-3	235	2	Northwestern	15/0
24	Taylor, Terry	CB	5-10	185	10	Southern Illinois	10/7
12	Testaverde, Vinny	QB	6-5	215	8	Miami (Fla.)	10/6
85	Tillman, Lawyer	WR	6-5	230	6	Auburn	7/0
30	Toney, Eudean	S	6-1	208	R	Grambling	—
18	Tremble, Greg	S	5-11	188	R	Georgia	—
7	Tupa, Tom	P-QB	6-4	230	6	Ohio State	0/0
29	Turner, Eric	S	6-1	207	4	UCLA	16/16
44	Vardell, Tommy	FB	6-2	230	3	Stanford	16/12
6	Werdel, John	P	6-2	205	R	Washington	—
62	Williams, Gene	OT-OG	6-2	305	4	Iowa State	16/14
67	Williams, Wally	C	6-2	300	2	Florida A&M	2/0
60	Withycombe, Mike	OL	6-5	300	7	Fresno State	0/0
26	Wolfley, Ron	RB	6-0	220	10	West Virginia	16/5

'94 DRAFT PICKS

RD.	NAME	POS.	HT.	WT.	COLLEGE
1.	Langham, Antonio	DB	6-0	179	Alabama
1.	Alexander, Derrick	WR	6-2	195	Michigan
3.	Bandison, Romeo	DT	6-5	290	Oregon
5.	Booth, Isaac	DB	6-3	190	California
6.	Strait, Robert	RB	6-1	255	Baylor
7.	Hewitt, Hamza	OT	6-6	286	Clemson

PRO FOOTBALL WEEKLY 1994 ALMANAC

TEAM AT A GLANCE

TEAM DIRECTORY

Address	80 First Avenue Berea, Ohio 44017 (216) 891-5000
Stadium	Cleveland Stadium West 3rd Street Cleveland, Ohio 44114 Capacity: 78,512 Playing surface: Grass
Training Camp	80 First Avenue Berea, Ohio 44017
Colors	Seal brown, orange and white
Television	WKYC, Channel 3
Radio	WKNR, 1220 AM WDOK, 102.1 FM

ADMINISTRATION
President and owner: Arthur B. Modell
Exec. vice president-legal, administration: Jim Bailey
Vice president-assistant to president: David Modell
Vice president-public relations: Kevin Byrne
Treasurer: Mike Srsen
Director of player personnel: Mike Lombardi
Director of pro personnel: Ozzie Newsome
Director of operations-information: Bob Eller
Director of marketing: Gary Gottfried
Ticket director: Bill Breit
Trainer: Bill Tessendorf

1994 SCHEDULE

Preseason

AUG. 6	at N.Y. Giants	8:00
AUG. 13	DETROIT	7:30
AUG. 19	ATLANTA	7:30
AUG. 25	at Indianapolis	7:30

Regular season

SEP. 4	at Cincinnati	1:00
SEP. 11	PITTSBURGH	1:00
SEP. 18	ARIZONA	1:00
SEP. 25	at Indianapolis	12:00
OCT. 2	N.Y. JETS	1:00
OCT. 9	OPEN DATE	
OCT. 13	at Houston (Thurs.)	7:00
OCT. 23	CINCINNATI	1:00
OCT. 30	at Denver	2:00
NOV. 6	NEW ENGLAND	1:00
NOV. 13	at Philadelphia	1:00
NOV. 20	at Kansas City	12:00
NOV. 27	HOUSTON	1:00
DEC. 4	N.Y. GIANTS	4:00
DEC. 10	at Dallas (Sat.)	3:00
DEC. 18	at Pittsburgh	1:00
DEC. 24	SEATTLE	1:00

HEAD COACH
Bill Belichick
Belichick became the 10th head coach in the history of the Browns following the 1990 season in which Cleveland went 3-13. With a career record of 20-28 in three years, Belichick has yet to lead his team to a winning season, though it has shown improvement. Before coming to Cleveland, Belichick served as defensive coordinator in New York, where he helped the Giants to Super Bowl victories in 1986 and 1990. Born April 16, 1952, Nashville, Tenn.

Previous NFL: head coach, 1991-93 Cleveland; defensive coordinator, 1983-90 N.Y. Giants; linebackers, 1981-82 N.Y. Giants; defensive assistant-special teams, 1979-80 N.Y. Giants; assistant coach, 1978 Denver; tight ends-receivers, 1976-77 Detroit; special assistant, 1975 Baltimore.

Previous college: None.
Player: No NFL. College, Wesleyan (Conn.)

ASSISTANT COACHES
Ernie Adams: special assignments
Previous NFL: 1991-93 Cleveland; 1979-85 N.Y. Giants; 1975-78 New England. Player: No NFL. College: None

Jacob Burney: defensive line
Previous NFL: None. Player: NFL, defensive lineman, 1981-82 Detroit. College: defensive tackle, 1976-80 Tennessee-Chattanooga.

Steve Crosby: offensive coordinator
Previous NFL: running backs, 1991-93 Cleveland; 1979-82 Miami; 1983-84 Atlanta; 1985 Cleveland; 1986-89 Atlanta; 1990 New England. Player: NFL, running back, 1974-76 N.Y. Giants. College: running back, 1969-72 Fort Hays State.

Rod Dowhower: quarterbacks
Previous NFL: offensive coordinator, 1990-93 Washington; 1987-89 Atlanta; 1985-86 Indianapolis (head coach); 1982-84 St. Louis; 1980-81 Denver; 1973 St. Louis. Player: No NFL. College: quarterback, 1963-65 San Diego State.

Kirk Ferentz: offensive line
Previous NFL: offensive line, 1993 Cleveland. Player: No NFL. College: linebacker, 1973-76 Connecticut.

Scott O'Brien: special teams
Previous NFL: special teams, 1991-93 Cleveland. Player: NFL, defensive end, 1979 Green Bay. College: defensive end, 1975-78 Wisconsin-Superior.

Nick Saban: defensive coordinator
Previous NFL: defensive coordinator, 1991-93 Cleveland; 1988-89 Houston. Player: No NFL. College: defensive back, 1969-72 Kent State.

Phil Savage: defensive assistant
Previous NFL: defensive assistant, 1991-93 Cleveland. Player: No NFL. College: quarterback, 1983-86 University of the South.

Mike Shepard: offensive assistant
Previous NFL: offensive assistant, 1993-93 Cleveland. Player: No NFL. College: wide receiver, 1969-72 Cal Lutheran.

Jerry Simmons: strength and conditioning
Previous NFL: strength and conditioning, 1991-

1994 PREVIEW ■ CLEVELAND

TEAM AT A GLANCE

93 Cleveland; 1988-90 New England. Player: No NFL. College: linebacker, 1976-77 Fort Hays State.

Kevin Spencer: offensive assistant
Previous NFL: offensive assistant, 1991-1993 Cleveland. Player: No NFL. College: None.

Rick Venturi: defensive backs
Previous NFL: defensive coordinator-linebackers, 1982-93 Indianapolis. Player: No NFL. College: quarterback-defensive back, 1965-67 Northwestern.

Woody Widenhofer: linebackers
Previous NFL: linebackers, 1993-93 Cleveland; 1973-83 Pittsburgh; 1989-92 Detroit. Player: No NFL. College: linebacker, 1961-64 Missouri.

COACHING RECORDS
(includes postseason games)

Years	Coach	W	L	T
1950-62	Paul Brown	115	49	5
1963-70	Blanton Collier	79	38	2
1971-74	Nick Skorich	30	26	2
1975-77	Forrest Gregg	18	23	0
1977	Dick Modzelewski	0	1	0
1978-84	Sam Rutigliano	47	52	0
1984-88	Marty Schottenheimer	46	31	0
1989-90	Bud Carson	12	14	1
1990	Jim Shofner	1	6	0
1991-93	Bill Belichick	20	28	0

HISTORICAL HIGHLIGHTS

1946 Cleveland is chosen as one of eight charter cities of the new All-America Football Conference, the franchise to be owned by Arthur "Mickey" McBride. Paul Brown is hired as coach and general manager. QB Otto Graham is the first player to be signed ... The Browns win their first AAFC Western Conference title with a record of 12-2, having outscored their opponents 423-137, and meet the New York Yankees for the league championship. The Browns defeat the Yankees 14-9 on a TD pass from Otto Graham to Dante Lavelli in the final period.
1950 The AAFC goes out of business, but the Browns merge into the NFL to play in the Eastern Conference along with the Giants, Eagles, Redskins, Steelers and Chicago Cardinals.
1950 With a 10-2 season mark, the Browns tie with the Giants for the Eastern title and win a playoff 8-3. Cleveland then defeats the Rams 30-28 and brings home its first NFL championship. Lou Groza kicks the game- and title-winning field goal with 28 seconds to go.
1951 The largest crowd ever to watch a Brown game, 92,180, fills Soldier Field in Chicago to watch Cleveland drub the College All-Stars 33-0.
1951 Dub Jones ties Ernie Nevers' NFL record of six touchdowns in one game when he runs for four and catches passes for two more against the Bears ... Cleveland wins 11 of its 12 games and its second conference title. But for the first time since the team was enfranchised in 1946, the Browns are not the league title holder, losing the championship to the Rams 24-17.
1952 Otto Graham, in a game against the Colts, sets a club record by passing for 401 yards, a

standard that would last until 1981 ... The Browns make it three NFL conference crowns in three years with an 8-4 record. They fall to the Lions, however, in the championship game 17-7.
1953 Mickey McBride sells the team to a syndicate headed by David Jones for $600,000, then the highest price ever paid for a pro football franchise.
1953 Cleveland takes its fourth consecutive conference title with a record of 11-1. But, just as they had the year before, the Browns lose to the Lions in the title game, this time 17-16.
1954 Making it five conference crowns in a row, Cleveland racks up a record of 9-3 and the right to face the Lions once again for the league championship. This time the Browns, with Otto Graham running for three touchdowns and passing for another three, devastate Detroit 56-10.
1955 The Browns repeat as NFL champs, taking their conference with a record of 9-2-1 and then destroying the Rams 38-14 in the championship game. Playing in his last game, Otto Graham runs for two touchdowns and throws two more against the Rams.
1958 Jim Brown sets an NFL record by rushing for 1,527 yards in a season and is the first Cleveland rusher ever to gain more than 1,000 yards in a year.
1961 Art Modell, a former television and advertising executive, buys the Browns.
1963 Jim Brown breaks his own league rushing record when he gains 1,863 yards (a 6.4-yard average per carry).
1964 Winning the division title over the Giants 52-40, the Browns advance to the championship game and capture the crown by defeating the Colts 27-0, their first title since 1955.
1965 Behind the running of Jim Brown, Cleveland again gets to the NFL title game. The Browns, however, are beaten by Green Bay 23-12.
1966 Jim Brown retires at the start of training camp.
1967 After the realignment of the NFL, the Browns are placed in the Century Division and win it with a record of 9-5. Cleveland falls to the Cowboys in the playoffs 52-10.
1968 The Browns take their division again with a 10-4 record. Although they defeat Dallas in the first playoff game, the Browns are eliminated by Baltimore 34-0 in the NFL title game.
1969 Cleveland wins its third consecutive division crown but loses to Minnesota in the championship game.
1972 The Browns qualify for the playoffs with a mark of 10-4, but lose to the eventual champion Dolphins 20-14.
1979 Brian Sipe, in his second year at quarterback, set two club records by completing 286 passes for 3,793 yards (the first Brown to surpass 3,000 yards).
1980 Cleveland posts an 11-5 season mark to win the AFC Central, but loses to the eventual Super Bowl champion Raiders in the first playoff game ... Brian Sipe sets three team records by completing 337 passes for 4,132 yards and 30 touchdowns and is chosen league MVP.
1985 Capturing their third Central Division title, the Browns face Miami in the playoffs and fall 24-21.
1986-87 Cleveland posts a record of 12-4, the best in the AFC. The Browns, who have not won a

PRO FOOTBALL WEEKLY 1994 ALMANAC

TEAM AT A GLANCE

playoff game since 1969, come from behind to tie the Jets in the divisional playoff game with just seven seconds left in the game, then win it 23-20 with a field goal from Mark Moseley in the second overtime period ... In the AFC title game, the Browns lose 23-20 to Denver in overtime.

1987-88 The Browns capture their third AFC Central title with a 10-5 record. In the first game of the playoffs they defeat the Colts, then fall to the Broncos in the AFC championship game 38-33, despite scoring 30 points in the second half. ... Bernie Kosar wins the AFC passing title with a passer rating of 95.4. An NFL-high eight Browns are invited to the Pro Bowl.

1988 Cleveland makes it to the playoffs as a wild-card but loses to the Oilers in the first playoff game.

1989-90 The Browns win their fourth division title in five years. In the playoffs they defeat the Bills but then lose to the Broncos in the AFC title game.

1991 Bill Belichick is hired as the eighth full-time head coach in Cleveland history.

1993 The Browns cut Bernie Kosar who had quarterbacked the team since 1985 ... Eric Metcalf, as running back, receiver and kick returner, leads the NFL with 1,932 all-purpose yards.

HALL OF FAME MEMBERS

	Yrs with Browns	Inducted
QB Otto Graham	1946-55	1965
Coach Paul Brown	1946-62	1967
FB Marion Motley	1946-53	1968
FB Jim Brown	1957-65	1971
T-PK Lou Groza	1946-59, 61-67	1974
E Dante Lavelli	1946-56	1975
E Len Ford	1950-57	1976
NG Bill Willis	1946-53	1977
HB Bobby Mitchell	1958-61	1983
WR Paul Warfield	1964-69, 76-77	1983
OT Mike McCormack	1954-62	1984
C Frank Gatski	1946-56	1985
RB Leroy Kelly	1964-73	1994

RETIRED JERSEY NUMBERS
- 14 QB Otto Graham
- 32 FB Jim Brown
- 45 RB Ernie Davis
- 46 DB Don Fleming
- 76 T-PK Lou Groza

FIRST-ROUND DRAFT CHOICES
(since 1980)

Year	Selection	College
1980	RB Charles White	Southern Cal
1981	CB Hanford Dixon	So. Mississippi
1982	LB Chip Banks	Southern Cal
1983	No choice	
1984	DB Don Rogers	UCLA
1985	QB Bernie Kosar	Miami (Fla.) (supplemental)
1986	No choice	
1987	LB Mike Junkin	Duke
1988	LB Clifford Charlton	Florida
1989	RB Eric Metcalf	Texas
1990	No choice	
1991	DB Eric Turner	UCLA
1992	RB Tommy Vardell	Stanford
1993	C Steve Everitt	Michigan
1994	CB Antonio Langham	Alabama
	WR Derrick Alexander	Michigan

RECORD VS. OTHER NFL TEAMS
(includes postseason games)

	Record
Arizona Cardinals	31-10-3
Atlanta Falcons	8-2-0
Buffalo Bills	8-3-0
Chicago Bears	8-3-0
Cincinnati Bengals	23-24-0
Dallas Cowboys	16-10-0
Denver Broncos	5-15-0
Detroit Lions	4-14-0
Green Bay Packers	6-8-0
Houston Oilers	27-21-0
Indianapolis Colts	14-9-0
Kansas City Chiefs	7-6-2
Los Angeles Raiders	4-10-0
Los Angeles Rams	10-8-0
Miami Dolphins	4-8-0
Minnesota Vikings	3-8-0
New England Patriots	9-3-0
New Orleans Saints	9-3-0
New York Giants	26-17-2
New York Jets	9-6-0
Philadelphia Eagles	30-12-1
Pittsburgh Steelers	52-36-0
San Diego Chargers	6-8-1
San Francisco 49ers	9-6-0
Seattle Seahawks	3-9-0
Tampa Bay Buccaneers	4-0-0
Washington Redskins	32-9-1

YEAR-BY-YEAR RECORDS

Year	Won	Lost	Tied	Year	Won	Lost	Tied
1950*	10	2	0	1972**	10	4	0
1951**	11	1	0	1973	7	5	2
1952**	8	4	0	1974	4	10	0
1953**	11	1	0	1975	3	11	0
1954*	9	3	0	1976	9	5	0
1955*	9	2	1	1977	6	8	0
1956	5	7	0	1978	8	8	0
1957**	9	2	1	1979	9	7	0
1958**	9	3	0	1980**	11	5	0
1959	7	5	0	1981	5	11	0
1960	8	3	1	1982**	4	5	0
1961	8	5	1	1983	9	7	0
1962	7	6	1	1984	5	11	0
1963	10	4	0	1985**	8	8	0
1964*	10	3	1	1986**	12	4	0
1965**	11	3	0	1987	10	5	0
1966	9	5	0	1988	10	6	0
1967**	9	5	0	1989	9	6	1
1968**	10	4	0	1990	3	13	0
1969**	10	3	1	1991	6	10	0
1970	7	7	0	1992	7	9	0
1971**	9	5	0	1993	7	9	0
				Total	358	250	10

Number of NFL championships 4
Number of years .500 or better 33
Number of years below .500 11

*NFL champions
**Playoff team

1994 PREVIEW ■ CLEVELAND

RECORDS

INDIVIDUAL

Service
Seasons played	17	Lou Groza (1950-59, 1961-67)
Games played	232	Clay Matthews (1978-93)
Consecutive games	203	Doug Dieken (1971-84)

Scoring
Points, career	1,349	Lou Groza (1950-59, 1961-67)
Points, season	126	Jim Brown (1965)
Points, game	36	Dub Jones (11/25/51)
Touchdowns, career	126	Jim Brown (1957-65)
Touchdowns, season	21	Jim Brown (1965)
Touchdowns, game	6	Dub Jones (11/25/51)
Field goals, career	234	Lou Groza (1950-59, 1961-67)
Field goals, season	24	Matt Bahr (1984)
		Matt Bahr (1988)
Field goals, game	5	Don Cockroft (10/19/75)
Extra points, career	641	Lou Groza (1950-59, 1961-67)
Extra points, season	51	Lou Groza (1966)
Extra points, game	8	Lou Groza (12/6/53)

Rushing
Yards, career	12,312	Jim Brown (1957-65)
Yards, season	1,863	Jim Brown (1963)
Yards, game	237	Jim Brown (11/24/57)
		Jim Brown (11/19/61)
Attempts, career	2,359	Jim Brown (1957-65)
Attempts, season	305	Jim Brown (1961)
Attempts, game	37	Jim Brown (10/4/59)
Touchdowns, career	106	Jim Brown (1957-65)
Touchdowns, season	17	Jim Brown (1958, 65)
Touchdowns, game	5	Jim Brown (11/1/59)

Passing
Rating, career	89.9	Milt Plum (1957-61)
Rating, season	110.4	Milt Plum (1961)
Completions, career	1,944	Brian Sipe (1974-83)
Completions, season	337	Brian Sipe (1980)
Completions, game	33	Brian Sipe (12/5/82)
Yards, career	23,713	Brian Sipe (1974-83)
Yards, season	4,132	Brian Sipe (1980)
Yards, game	444	Brian Sipe (10/25/81)
Attempts, career	3,439	Brian Sipe (1974-83))
Attempts, season	567	Brian Sipe (1981)
Attempts, game	57	Brian Sipe (9/7/81)
Touchdowns, career	154	Brian Sipe (1974-83)
Touchdowns, season	30	Brian Sipe (1980)
Touchdowns, game	5	Frank Ryan (12/12/64)
		Bill Nelsen (11/2/69)
		Brian Sipe (10/7/79)

Receiving
Receptions, career	662	Ozzie Newsome (1978-90)
Receptions, season	89	Ozzie Newsome (1984)
		Ozzie Newsome (1983)
Receptions, game	14	Ozzie Newsome (10/14/84)
Yards, career	7,980	Ozzie Newsome (1978-90)
Yards, season	1,236	Webster Slaughter (1989)
Yards, game	191	Ozzie Newsome (10/14/84)
Touchdowns, career	70	Gary Collins (1962-71)
Touchdowns, season	13	Gary Collins (1963)
Touchdowns, game	3	By many players

Interceptions
Career	45	Thom Darden (1972-74, 1976-81)
Season	10	Thom Darden (1978)
Game	3	By many players

Sacks
Career	76.5	Clay Matthews (1978-93)
Season	14.5	Bill Glass (1965)
Game	4	Jerry Sherk (11/14/76)
		Mack Mitchell (11/20/77)

Longest plays
Run from scrimmage	90	Bobby Mitchell (TD, 11/15/59)
Pass play	97	Bernie Kosar to Webster Slaughter (TD, 10/23/89)
Field goal	60	Steve Cox (10/21/84)
Interception return	92	Bernie Parrish (TD, 12/11/60)
		David Brandon (TD, 11/29/92)
Kickoff return	104	Carl Ward (11/26/67)
Punt return	84	Gerald McNeil (TD, 9/28/86)
Punt	80	Horace Gillom (11/28/54)

Top scorers	Points
Lou Groza (1950-59, 1961-67)	1,349
Don Cockroft (1968-80)	1,080
Jim Brown (1957-65)	756
Matt Bahr (1981-89)	677
Leroy Kelly (1964-73)	540
Gary Collins (1962-72)	420

Top rushers	Yards
Jim Brown (1957-65)	12,312
Leroy Kelly (1964-73)	7,274
Mike Pruitt (1976-84)	6,540
Greg Pruitt (1973-81)	5,496
Kevin Mack (1985-93)	5,123
Ernie Green (1962-68)	3,204

Top passers	Completions
Brian Sipe (1974-83)	1,944
Bernie Kosar (1985-93)	1,853
Frank Ryan (1962-68)	907
Otto Graham (1950-55)	872
Bill Nelson (1968-72)	689
Mike Phipps (1970-76)	633

Top passers	Yards
Brian Sipe (1974-83)	23,713
Bernie Kosar (1985-93)	21,904
Otto Graham (1950-55)	13,499
Frank Ryan (1962-68)	13,361
Bill Nelson (1968-72)	9,725
Milt Plum (1957-61)	8,917

Top receivers	Receptions
Ozzie Newsome (1978-90)	662
Gary Collins (1962-71)	331
Brian Brennan (1984-91)	315
Reggie Rucker (1975-81)	310
Webster Slaughter (1986-91)	305
Ray Renfro (1952-63)	281

Top receivers	Yards
Ozzie Newsome (1978-90)	7,980
Ray Renfro (1952-63)	5,508
Gary Collins (1962-71)	5,299
Paul Warfield (1964-69, 76-77)	5,210
Reggie Rucker (1975-81)	4,953
Webster Slaughter (1986-91)	4,834

Most interceptions	No.
Thom Darden (1972-74, 76-81)	45
Warren Lahr (1950-59)	40
Clarence Scott (1971-83)	39
Ken Konz (1953-59)	30
Bernie Parrish (1959-66)	29
Ross Fichtner (1960-67)	27
Mike Howell (1965-72)	27

Most sacks	No.
Clay Matthews (1978-93)	76.5
Jerry Sherk (1970-81)	69
Walter Johnson (1965-76)	58
Michael Dean Perry (1988-93)	47.5
Bill Glass (1962-68)	46
Jack Gregory (1967-71, 79)	34.5

PREVIEW: DALLAS COWBOYS

"All My Children." "The Young and the Restless." "One Life to Live." None of these daytime soaps has anything on the Dallas Cowboys.

The Cowboys, when we last checked in, were winning their second consecutive Super Bowl, pounding the Bills with a relentless second-half attack.

But a funny thing happened on the way to training camp. The delicate balance that existed between owner Jerry Jones and head coach Jimmy Johnson disintegrated over drinks one night in Florida. And like Humpty Dumpty, once the relationship fell apart, it could not be put back together again.

Jones, once vilified for firing Tom Landry, was again viewed as the heavy in his public divorce with Johnson. But Jones is nothing if not resilient, as shown by his hiring of former Oklahoma boss Barry Switzer, who had been out of coaching since 1989 and was looked on as Johnson's sworn enemy.

But the hire may have been more than a slap at Johnson. Much like Johnson, Switzer is viewed as a great motivator who works well with the athletes he coaches. Switzer will let Ernie Zampese handle the offense and Butch Davis coach the defense, so as not to upset a team that has won two straight Super Bowl titles. However, when it comes down to evaluating talent and making personnel decisions, the Cowboys are not going to have the same advantage they had now that Johnson has split.

Will the Cowboys fall apart? Certainly not. They still have outstanding offensive talent with QB Troy Aikman, RB Emmitt Smith, WR Michael Irvin and OT Erik Williams. The defense, even though it lost MLB Ken Norton and role players Jimmie Jones and Tony Casillas on the defensive line, is mostly intact. This will still be the team to beat in 1994, but it may be an even bumpier ride than it was last year.

Offensively, the Cowboys will no longer be under the leadership of Norv Turner, who has taken his act to the nation's capital, where he will lead the Redskins. Zampese, long known as one of the game's foremost offensive innovators, will get a chance to work with some of the most talented players in the game. Zampese should get along with those stars because he's not one to grab the limelight. He likes to stay in the background and let his players grab the glory.

Aikman is the prototype quarterback of the decade. He has the size, strength, accuracy, quickness of delivery, guts and leadership ability. Despite having nearly unlimited natural talent, Aikman does not have to be the star of every game. He's willing to put his ego aside for the good of the team. Aikman also knows when a play is too risky, and he will throw the ball away if he

Troy Aikman

thinks it might result in an interception. Aikman's game is a combination of well-developed talent and coolness in the pocket. That self-confidence has enabled him to come up huge in some of the biggest games in his career and bodes well for the future. It has also allowed him to maintain a sense of perspective about himself.

"You look around here, and there's no doubt we have the talent," Aikman said. "What it comes down to is we believe in ourselves, and we believe in this football team. I know that it's not going to come down to what I do. It's going to come down to what we all do. Yes, there's a lot of pressure. But that pressure is on all of us, not just the quarterback. That's the kind of pressure that makes everybody perform better."

Former Detroit starter Rodney Peete replaces Bernie Kosar as Aikman's backup.

The presence of Smith makes life much easier for Aikman and the rest of the Cowboys. Even though Smith has led the NFL in rushing for the last three seasons, numbers don't really tell the story. During his much-publicized holdout, the Cowboy offense was out of sync and clearly lacking in confidence. Smith is its rudder, and he holds his course even in the roughest waters. Detroit's Barry Sanders and Buffalo's Thurman Thomas are nearly Smith's equal, but they just don't measure up. The difference between the three is consistency and durability. When Smith took a big hit that separated his right shoulder early in the season finale vs. the Giants, he wasn't about to come out of the game and retire to the

1994 PREVIEW ■ DALLAS

lockerroom. Instead, Smith sucked it up and led the Cowboys to a victory that gave them the NFC East title and homefield advantage through the playoffs.

"If we lose that game, then we're playing the wild-card game with no week off," Smith explained. "I wanted the week off and the homefield advantage, and I was going to give everything I had to get it."

Smith's partner, FB Daryl Johnston, has great leg strength and is probably the best blocking fullback in the league. He is a solid receiver (50 catches in 1993) who knows how to adjust to the ball while it is in the air. However, he lacks quickness and footspeed as a runner. Second-year RB Derrick Lassic is a competent backup to Smith.

When the Cowboys go to the air, Aikman's first option is always the opportunistic Irvin, who knows how to make the big play at the right time. Irvin is coming off a great season in which he caught 88 passes for 1,330 yards and seven touchdowns. Irvin is a very strong, physical receiver who knows how to push off opposing defensive backs, yet rarely gets called for it. The Cowboys' No. 2 wideout, Alvin Harper, is a big-play specialist. However, he has never been as consistent as Irvin, despite having superb physical gifts. Harper is a tremendous leaper who has sprinter's speed. From time to time, Harper will appear disinterested when he doesn't think he's getting the ball enough. TE Jay Novacek is solid and dependable, but he's coming off a season in which he caught 44-445-1 and appeared to struggle a lot of the time. Novacek is more comfortable when he's playing in the H-back slot, but the fact of the matter is that he may be starting to slow down. The Cowboys have depth at the outside receiver slot with Kevin Williams and Jimmy Smith. Williams looked explosive last year but also showed questionable judgment. Smith has size and speed and is coming back from an illness that forced him out of action for the entire season.

At right tackle, Erik Williams is one of the league's emerging stars. He is simply terrific as a run blocker and he handles the best bull-rushing defensive left ends in the NFL, including Green Bay All-Pro Reggie White. Williams is joined by two Pro Bowlers, C Mark Stepnoski and OG Nate Newton, on the offensive line. Newton learned discipline under Johnson and found a way to get his weight problem under control. He's a superior run blocker with tremendous leg strength and explosion. Stepnoski is coming back from a knee injury that forced him out at the end of last season. Stepnoski is tough and mean and has quick hands. He uses them to gain leverage on opposing defensive linemen. OLT Mark Tuinei is getting up in years but is smart and tough. Ex-Saint Derek Kennard and draft picks Larry Allen and George Hegamin figure to go a long way toward replacing departed free-agent OL's Kevin Gogan and John Gesek.

While Dallas has superstars on offense, its defense depends on a team effort. Under Davis, the Cowboys don't mind giving up yardage, but they rarely let their opponents in the endzone. If there's one player who truly helped the Dallas defense rise to the championship level, it's DRE Charles Haley. Last year Haley played much of the season with a ruptured disc, but because he smelled another title within his grasp, he would not retire to the bench. Haley came up big in the playoffs, especially in the NFC championship game against the 49ers. DLE Tony Tolbert led the Cowboys in sacks with 7.5 and is a hard worker. Veteran Jim Jeffcoat has great strength and lives in the weightroom, and rookie No. 1 pick Shante Carver adds pass-rushing punch on the outside. DT's Leon Lett and Russell Maryland have the potential to form an awesome duo. Lett has had a couple of hugely embarrassing moments, but he is a multi-talented player who can dominate. Maryland is small and has two very painful feet, but he compensates with quickness, intelligence and tenacity.

OLB Dixon Edwards was a starter last year after the Cowboys traded Vinson Smith. He improved throughout the season because of tremendous speed and athleticism, but he is on the small side. On the weak side, Darrin Smith fit in very nicely and used his speed to great advantage. Godfrey Myles may have to step in as the middle linebacker since Ken Norton signed with San Francisco. Myles has size and strength, but unless he starts working harder, he'll never amount to anything in the NFL. Robert Jones has failed to this point in his career because he doesn't stick people as much as the Cowboy coaching staff would like.

In the secondary, CB Kevin Smith has become a premier cover corner with excellent hands. Larry Brown is better than average in coverage and very tough against the run. Darren Woodson, a former linebacker, led the team in tackles with 155 from his SS position. FS James Washington was one of the heroes of last season's Super Bowl win. However, he must improve on his consistency by eliminating silly mistakes.

John Jett is a decent punter who got better as the year progressed. The PK situation is murky, since Eddie Murray signed with Philadelphia.

FAST FACTS

■ Michael Irvin's 4,249 receiving yards from 1991 to '93 is the second-highest three-year total in NFL history behind Jerry Rice (4,291 from 1988 to '90).

■ Emmitt Smith broke the Cowboy single-game rushing record with 237 yards vs. the Eagles Oct. 31.

■ Troy Aikman's interception rate of 1.5 percent last year broke Roger Staubach's team record (1.9 percent), established in 1971.

1994 PLAYER ROSTER

NO.	NAME	POS.	HT.	WT.	EXP.	COLLEGE	GP/GS
34	Agee, Tommie	FB	6-0	235	8	Auburn	12/0
8	Aikman, Troy	QB	6-4	228	6	UCLA	14/14
40	Bates, Bill	S	6-1	205	12	Tennessee	16/0
97	Batiste, Michael	DT	6-3	301	R	Tulane	—
45	Bell, Coleman	TE	6-2	232	1	Miami (Fla.)	0/0
18	Bonlol, Chris	PK	5-11	159	R	Louisiana Tech	—
11	Bretz, Brad	QB	6-5	218	1	Cal State-Hayward	0/0
72	Brewer, George	DT	6-5	295	R	Georgia	—
24	Brown, Larry	CB	5-11	182	4	Texas Christian	16/16
27	Burch, Alfie	CB	6-0	196	R	Michigan	—
44	Coleman, Lincoln	RB	6-1	249	2	Baylor	7/0
56	Collins, Roosevelt	LB	6-4	244	2	Texas Christian	0/0
68	Cornish, Frank	OG-C	6-4	287	5	UCLA	11/3
6	Cunningham, Richie	PK	5-10	165	R	S.W. Louisiana	—
81	Daniel, Tim	WR	5-11	192	3	Florida A&M	0/0
58	Edwards, Dixon	LB	6-1	222	4	Michigan State	16/15
5	Fayak, Craig	PK	6-1	188	R	Penn State	—
46	Fishback, Joe	S	6-0	212	5	Carson-Newman	6/0
89	Galbraith, Scott	TE	6-2	255	5	Southern Cal	7/0
29	Gant, Kenneth	S	5-11	189	5	Albany State	12/1
17	Garrett, Jason	QB	6-2	195	2	Princeton	5/1
32	Garrett, Judd	RB	6-2	214	1	Princeton	0/0
94	Haley, Charles	DE	6-5	250	9	James Madison	14/11
80	Harper, Alvin	WR	6-3	208	4	Tennessee	16/15
70	Hellestrae, Dale	OG-C	6-5	275	10	Southern Methodist	16/0
95	Hennings, Chad	DT	6-6	286	3	Air Force	14/0
2	Hill, Shelby	WR	6-0	207	R	Syracuse	—
47	Holmes, Clayton	CB	5-10	181	3	Carson-Newman	0/0
88	Irvin, Michael	WR	6-2	205	7	Miami (Fla.)	16/16
77	Jeffcoat, Jim	DE	6-5	280	12	Arizona State	16/3
19	Jett, John	P	6-0	184	2	East Carolina	16/0
48	Johnston, Daryl	FB	6-2	238	6	Syracuse	16/16
55	Jones, Robert	LB	6-2	237	3	East Carolina	13/3
38	Jones, Tommy	CB	5-8	167	R	Fresno State	—
75	Joyce, Matt	OL	6-7	283	R	Richmond	—
60	Kennard, Derek	OG	6-3	300	9	Nevada-Reno	16/16
25	Lassic, Derrick	RB	5-10	188	2	Alabama	10/3
78	Lett, Leon	DL	6-6	285	4	Emporia State	11/6
31	Marion, Brock	CB	5-11	189	2	Nevada-Reno	15/0
67	Maryland, Russell	DT	6-1	279	4	Miami (Fla.)	16/12
21	Mason, Mark	RB	5-7	189	R	Maryland	—
64	Mays, Marvin	DE	6-3	262	R	S.E. Oklahoma	—
57	McClanahan, Anthony	LB	6-1	238	R	Washington State	—
99	McCormack, Hurvin	DT	6-5	271	R	Indiana	—
54	Mills, Toby	C	6-0	270	R	Arizona State	—
49	Mundy, Aaron	TE	6-5	252	R	Virginia	—
98	Miles, Godfrey	LB	6-1	242	4	Florida	10/0
61	Newton, Nate	OG	6-3	325	9	Florida A&M	16/16
84	Novacek, Jay	TE	6-4	232	10	Wyoming	16/16
62	Parrish, James	OT	6-6	310	1	Temple	0/0
43	Patterson, Elvis	DB	5-11	195	11	Kansas	14/0
9	Peete, Rodney	QB	6-0	193	6	Southern Cal	10/10
93	Powe, Keith	DE	6-4	265	1	Texas-El Paso	0/0
89	Price, Jim	TE	6-4	247	4	Stanford	3/0
63	Rentie, Caesar	OL	6-3	323	2	Oklahoma	0/0

1994 PREVIEW ■ DALLAS

1994 PLAYER ROSTER

NO.	NAME	POS.	HT.	WT.	EXP.	COLLEGE	GP/GS
35	Richardson, Tony	FB	6-1	224	R	Auburn	—
87	Schorp, Greg	TE	6-3	242	R	Texas A&M	—
59	Smith, Darrin	LB	6-1	227	2	Miami (Fla.)	16/13
22	Smith, Emmitt	RB	5-9	209	5	Florida	14/13
82	Smith, Jimmy	WR	6-1	205	3	Jackson State	0/0
26	Smith, Kevin	CB	5-11	180	3	Texas A&M	16/16
53	Stepnoski, Mark	C	6-2	264	6	Pittsburgh	13/13
65	Stone, Ron	OL	6-5	309	2	Boston College	1/0
41	Thomas, Dave	CB	6-2	208	2	Tennessee	12/0
92	Tolbert, Tony	DE	6-6	263	6	Texas-El Paso	16/16
71	Tuinei, Mark	OT	6-5	305	12	Hawaii	16/16
91	Vanderbeek, Matt	LB-DE	6-3	243	5	Michigan State	16/0
76	Wagner, Keith	OT	6-4	302	R	Abilene Christian	—
37	Washington, James	S	6-1	209	7	UCLA	14/1
14	Wilkins, Jeff	PK	6-1	180	R	Youngstown State	—
79	Williams, Erik	OT	6-6	324	4	Central State (Ohio)	16/16
85	Williams, Kevin	WR	5-9	192	2	Miami (Fla.)	16/1
86	Williams, Tyrone	WR	6-5	220	2	Western Ontario	5/0
42	Wilson, Robert	FB	6-0	258	2	Texas A&M	0/0
28	Woodson, Darren	S	6-1	215	3	Arizona State	16/15
52	Younger, Jermaine	LB	6-0	262	R	Utah State	—

'94 DRAFT PICKS

RD.	NAME	POS.	HT.	WT.	COLLEGE
1.	Carver, Shante	DE	6-5	240	Arizona State
2.	Allen, Larry	OG	6-3	325	Sonoma State (Calif.)
3.	Hegamin, George	OT	6-7	355	North Carolina State
4.	Jackson, Willie	WR	6-1	205	Florida
4.	Dotson, DeWayne	LB	6-1	250	Mississippi
6.	Studstill, Darren	QB	6-1	186	West Virginia
7.	McIntosh, Toddrick	DT	6-3	277	Florida State

PRO FOOTBALL WEEKLY 1994 ALMANAC

TEAM AT A GLANCE

TEAM DIRECTORY

Address	Cowboys Center
	One Cowboys Parkway
	Irving, Texas 75063
	(214) 556-9900
Stadium	Texas Stadium
	Irving, Texas 75062
	Capacity: 65,024
	Playing surface: AstroTurf
Training Camp	St. Edward's University
	Austin, Texas 78704
Colors	Royal blue, metallic silver blue and white
Television	KDAF, Channel 33
Radio	KVIL, 103.7 FM

ADMINISTRATION
President-general manager: Jerry Jones
Vice president: Mike McCoy
Vice president: Stephen Jones
Vice president-director of marketing: George Hays
Treasurer: Jack Dixon
Director of operations-facility: Bruce Mays
Director of college scouting: Larry Lacewell
Director of public relations: Rich Dalrymple
Director of sales and promotions: Joel Finglass
Ticket manager: Carol Padgett

1994 SCHEDULE
Preseason

July 31	MINNESOTA	8:00
Aug. 7	L.A. RAIDERS	8:00
Aug. 15	vs. Houston (Mexico City)	*9:00
Aug. 21	DENVER	7:00
Aug. 25	at New Orleans	7:00

*Eastern time

Regular season

SEP. 4	at Pittsburgh	4:00
SEP. 11	HOUSTON	3:00
SEP. 19	DETROIT (Mon.)	8:00
SEP. 25	OPEN DATE	
OCT. 2	at Washington	1:00
OCT. 9	ARIZONA	3:00
OCT. 16	PHILADELPHIA	3:00
OCT. 23	at Arizona	1:00
OCT. 30	at Cincinnati	1:00
NOV. 7	N.Y. GIANTS (Mon.)	8:00
NOV. 13	at San Francisco	1:00
NOV. 20	WASHINGTON	12:00
NOV. 24	GREEN BAY (Thanks.)	3:00
DEC. 4	at Philadelphia	1:00
DEC. 10	CLEVELAND (Sat.)	3:00
DEC. 19	at New Orleans (Mon.)	8:00
DEC. 24	at N.Y. Giants	1:00

HEAD COACH
Barry Switzer

Following the firing and/or resignation of Jimmy Johnson, Barry Switzer was hired as the third Cowboy head coach in franchise history. Switzer has never coached at the professional level and has not coached at all since resigning amid controversy from his post as head coach at the University of Oklahoma following the 1988 season. While leading the Sooners, Switzer coached his teams to three national championships and an overall record of 165-34-4 over 16 seasons.

Previous NFL: None.

Previous college: head coach, Oklahoma, 1973-88; assistant head coach-offensive coordinator, Oklahoma 1970-72; offensive coordinator, Oklahoma 1967-69; offensive line coach, Oklahoma 1966; offensive ends, Oklahoma 1964-65; assistant coach, Arkansas 1962-63.

Player: No NFL. College, offensive lineman-linebacker, Arkansas 1957-59.

ASSISTANT COACHES
Hubbard Alexander: wide receivers
Previous NFL: wide receivers, 1989-93 Dallas. Player: No NFL. College: center, 1958-61 Tennessee State.

Joe Avezzano: special teams
Previous NFL: special teams, 1990-93 Dallas. Player: NFL, center, 1966 Boston Patriots. College: guard, 1961-65 Florida State.

John Blake: defensive line
Previous NFL: defensive line, 1993-93 Dallas. Player: No NFL. College: nose tackle, 1980-83 Oklahoma.

Joe Brodsky: running backs
Previous NFL: running backs, 1989-93 Dallas. Player: No NFL. College: fullback, linebacker, 1953-56 Florida.

Dave Campo: defensive backs
Previous NFL: defensive backs, 1989-93, Dallas. Player: No NFL. College: defensive back, 1967-70 Central Connecticut State.

Butch Davis: defensive coordinator
Previous NFL: defensive coordinator-linebackers, 1993; Dallas defensive line, 1989-92 Dallas. Player: No NFL. College: defensive end, 1971-74 Arkansas.

Jim Eddy: linebackers
Previous NFL: defensive assistant, 1993-93 Dallas; 1990-92 Houston. Player: No NFL. College: defensive back, running back, 1956-59 New Mexico State.

Robert Ford: tight ends
Previous NFL: tight ends, 1991-93 Dallas. Player: No NFL. College: wide receiver, 1970-72 Houston.

Steve Hoffman: kickers-research/development
Previous NFL: kickers-research and development, 1989-93 Dallas. Player: No NFL. College: quarterback, running back, wide receiver, 1979-82 Dickinson.

Hudson Houck: offensive line
Previous NFL: offensive line, 1993 Dallas; 1992 Seattle; 1983-91 L.A. Rams. Player: No NFL. Col-

1994 PREVIEW ■ DALLAS

TEAM AT A GLANCE

lege: center, 1962-64 Southern Cal.
Mike Woicik: strength and conditioning
Previous NFL: strength and conditioning, 1990-93 Dallas. Player: No NFL. College: None.
Ernie Zampese: offensive coordinator
Previous NFL: offensive coordinator, 1987-93 L.A. Rams; 1976, 1979-86 San Diego; 1977-78 N.Y. Jets. Player: No NFL. College: halfback, 1956-58 Southern Cal.
Mike Zimmer: defensive aide
Previous NFL: None. Player: No NFL. College: quarterback-linebacker, 1974, 1976 Illinois State.

COACHING RECORDS
(including postseason games)

Years	Coach	W	L	T
1960-88	Tom Landry	270	178	6
1989-93	Jimmy Johnson	51	37	0

HISTORICAL HIGHLIGHTS

1960 The NFL awards Clint Murchison Jr. and Bedford Wynne an expansion franchise. ... Tom Landry becomes head coach, hired by newly appointed GM Tex Schramm.
1962 Amos Marsh returns a 101-yard kickoff and Mike Gaechter returns a 100-yard pass interception in a fourth-quarter 41-19 win over Philadelphia. It is the first time two 100-yard runs are made in the same game by the same team in the same quarter.
1963 Bill Howton breaks Don Hutson's all-time receiving mark with a 14-yard catch against the Redskins, giving Howton 8,000 career yards.
1964 The Cowboys sign Tom Landry to a 10-year extension of his original contract.
1965 Dallas defeats the Giants 38-20 in the season finale, winning five of their last seven games and earning a trip to the Playoff Bowl, where they fall to Baltimore 35-3.
1966 After capturing the Eastern Conference title with a 10-3-1 record, the Cowboys lose the NFL championship game to Green Bay 34-27.
1967 The Cowboys easily win the Capitol Division, defeating Cleveland 52-14, in the Cotton Bowl for the Eastern Conference Championship ... The Packers again stop the Cowboys in their second bid for the NFL title, defeating them 21-17 in 13-degree-below-zero weather at Green Bay.
1968 The Cowboys win the Capitol championship again but are upset by Cleveland 31-20 in their third bid for the Eastern championship.
1969 The Cowboys again take the division championship with an 11-2-1 season but fall to Cleveland 38-14 in the game for the Eastern Division title.
1970-71 The Cowboys claim the Eastern Division title with a 10-4 season record, making the playoffs for the fifth year in a row. The Cowboys triumph over San Francisco 17-10 for the NFC crown and earn the right to meet Baltimore in the Super Bowl. There Dallas loses to the Colts 16-13.
1971 The Cowboys again win the NFC Eastern Division, then defeat Minnesota in the opening round of the playoffs.
1971-72 The NFC showdown again features the Cowboys and 49ers in a 14-3 victory for Dallas that qualifies the team for its second straight Super Bowl appearance ... in 1972 The Cowboys win Super Bowl VI, handing the Dolphins a 24-3 defeat. Roger Staubach is named Most Valuable Player.
1972 Calvin Hill becomes the first Dallas player to rush for 100 yards in a game when he gains 111 against the Redskins. Hill's season record totals 1,036 yards on a record 245 carries ... A record of 10-4 earns the Cowboys a wild-card berth. Roger Staubach passes for two TD's in the final minute and a half giving the Cowboys a 30-28 victory in the frist round of the playoffs. But Dallas falls 26-3 to the Redskins in their bid for a third straight NFC title.
1973 With a 10-4 record the Cowboys regain the NFC Eastern Division title and reach theplayoffs for the eighth year in a row. The Cowboys defeat the Rams in the first round but bow to Minnesota 27-10 in the NFC championship game.
1975 Roger Staubach's "Hail Mary" pass to Drew Pearson results in a 17-14 victory over Minnesota. Staubach shines again a week later in the NFC championship, throwing four touchdown passes, three to Drew Pearson to defeat the Rams 37-7.
1976 The Cowboys fall to Pittsburgh 21-17 in Super Bowl X.
1976 Dallas wins the Eastern Division with an 11-3 record, achieving their 10th straight playoff berth. The season ends with a first-round loss to Los Angeles.
1977-78 The Cowboys win their fourth NFC crown, defeating Vikings 23-6 and earn the right to meet the Broncos in Super Bowl XII ... The Cowboys defeat Denver 27-10 winning their second Super Bowl and tying Minnesota for most Super Bowl appearances (four) and Green Bay, Miami, and Pittsburgh for most Super Bowl victories (two). DL's Harvey Martin and Randy White are named co-Most Valuable Players.
1978 Dallas shuts out the Rams 28-0 for the NFC title ... The Cowboys lose to Pittsburgh 35-31 in the Super Bowl, the first Super Bowl rematch ever.
1979 Winning their 11th division championship after rallying from a midseason slump, the Cowboys finish the season with an 11-5 record and their 13th trip to the playoffs, but lose to Los Angeles, 21-19.
1980 The Cowboys achieve their 15th straight winning season with a 12-4 record with Danny White replacing retired Roger Staubach at quarterback ... Entering the playoffs as a wild-card bid, they rally past Los Angeles and Atlanta but are defeated 20-7 by Philadelphia in the NFC title game.
1981 Dallas wins the Eastern Division title, their 12th since 1966, with a 12-4 record and tie Oakland's record of 16 consecutive winning seasons ... They advance to the conference title game, but are edged out by San Francisco's last minute touchdown, 28-27.
1982 Dallas achieves an NFL record of 17 consecutive winning seasons, enters the playoffs for the eighth straight year but comes up short in the NFC championship, losing 31-17 at Washington.
1983 A record of 12-4 extends the Cowboys' NFL record to 18 straight winning seasons and a league record is set with their ninth straight appearance in the playoffs. A 24-17 upset victory by the Rams eliminates the Cowboys from the playoffs.
1984 The Murchison family sells the Cowboys to

69

PRO FOOTBALL WEEKLY 1994 ALMANAC

TEAM AT A GLANCE

an 11-member limited partnership headed by Dallas businessman, H.R. "Bum" Bright.

1985-86 The Cowboys open their new headquarters and training facility at in Valley Ranch, Texas ... Dallas wins its 13th divisional championship, posting a 10-6 record, but are shutout 20-0 by the Rams in their first playoff game.

1989 Jerry Jones purchases the Cowboys and replaces Tom Landry with Jimmy Johnson ... President and GM Tex Schramm resigns.

1991-92 Dallas qualifies as a wild-card with an 11-5 record ... RB Emmitt Smith and WR Michael Irvin become the first two players from the same team to lead the NFL rushing and receiving yardage (Smith 1,563 yards rushing, Irvin 1,523 receiving) ... The Cowboys defeat the Bears 17-13 in the wild-card game, then fall 38-6 to the Lions in the next round.

1992-93 The Cowboys win the NFC East, their first divisional title since 1985, with a record of 11-5 ... Emmitt Smith wins the rushing title with 1,713 yards ... Dallas defeats Philadelphia 34-10 in the playoffs and takes the NFC crown by beating the 49ers 30-20 ... The Cowboys go to Super Bowl XXVII, their first since 1978, and beat the Bills 52-17.

1993-94 The Cowboys win the NFC East with a record of 12-4. They beat the Packers and 49ers to win the NFC championship ... Making a record-seventh appearance in the Super Bowl, Dallas again faces the Bills and wins 30-13 ... RB Emmitt Smith is named the NFL's MVP and the Super Bowl MVP.

HALL OF FAME MEMBERS

	Yrs with Cowboys	Inducted
DT Bob Lilly	1961-74	1980
QB Roger Staubach	1969-79	1985
Coach Tom Landry	1960-88	1990
GM Tex Schramm	1960-88	1991
RB Tony Dorsett	1977-85	1994
DT Randy White	1975-85	1994

RING OF HONOR

LB Chuck Howley
LB Lee Roy Jordan
Coach Tom Landry
DT Bob Lilly
QB Don Meredith
RB Don Perkins
DB Mel Renfro
QB Roger Staubach

FIRST-ROUND DRAFT CHOICES
(since 1980)

Year	Selection	College
1980	No choice	
1981	OT Howard Richards	Missouri
1982	CB Rod Hill	Kentucky State
1983	OT Jim Jeffcoat	Arizona State
1984	LB Billy Cannon	Texas A&M
1985	DE Kevin Brooks	Michigan
1986	WR Mike Sherrard	UCLA
1987	DT Danny Noonan	Nebraska
1988	WR Michael Irvin	Miami (Fla.)
1989	QB Troy Aikman	UCLA
1990	RB Emmitt Smith	Florida
1991	DT Russell Maryland	Miami (Fla.)
	WR Alvin Harper	Tennessee
1992	CB Kevin Smith	Texas A&M
	LB Robert Jones	East Carolina
1993	No choice	
1994	DE Shante Carver	Arizona State

RECORD VS. OTHER NFL TEAMS
(including postseason games)

	Record
Arizona Cardinals	40-22-1
Atlanta Falcons	11-6-0
Buffalo Bills	5-2-0
Chicago Bears	10-6-0
Cincinnati Bengals	3-2-0
Cleveland Browns	10-16-0
Denver Broncos	4-2-0
Detroit Lions	8-6-0
Green Bay Packers	8-10-0
Houston Oilers	4-3-0
Indianapolis Colts	7-3-0
Kansas City Chiefs	3-2-0
Los Angeles Raiders	2-3-0
Los Angeles Rams	12-13-0
Miami Dolphins	2-6-0
Minnesota Vikings	11-7-0
New England Patriots	6-0-0
New Orleans Saints	13-3-0
New York Giants	40-21-2
New York Jets	5-1-0
Philadelphia Eagles	41-27-0
Pittsburgh Steelers	12-13-0
San Diego Chargers	4-1-0
San Francisco 49ers	11-10-1
Seattle Seahawks	4-1-0
Tampa Bay Buccaneers	8-0-0
Washington Redskins	37-29-2

YEAR-BY-YEAR RECORDS

Year	Won	Lost	Tied
1960	0	11	1
1961	4	9	1
1962	5	8	1
1963	4	10	0
1964	5	8	1
1965	7	7	0
1966**	10	3	1
1967**	9	5	0
1968**	12	2	0
1969**	11	2	1
1970**	10	4	0
1971*	11	3	0
1972**	10	4	0
1973**	10	4	0
1974	8	6	0
1975**	10	4	0
1976**	11	3	0
1977*	12	2	0
1978**	12	4	0
1979**	11	5	0
1980**	12	4	0
1981**	12	4	0
1982**	6	3	0
1983**	12	4	0
1984	9	7	0
1985**	10	6	0
1986	7	9	0
1987	7	8	0
1988	3	13	0
1989	1	15	0
1990	7	9	0
1991**	11	5	0
1992*	13	3	0
1993*	12	4	0
Total	**282**	**194**	**6**

Number of NFL championships   4
Number of years .500 or better   24
Number of years below .500   10

*NFL champions
**Playoff team

1994 PREVIEW ■ DALLAS

RECORDS

INDIVIDUAL

Service
Seasons played	15	Ed Jones (1974-78, 1980-89)
Games played	224	Ed Jones (1974-78)
Consecutive games	196	Bob Lilly (1961-74)

Scoring
Points, career	874	Rafael Septien (1978-86)
Points, season	123	Rafael Septien (1981)
Points, game	24	By many players
Touchdowns, career	86	Tony Dorsett (1977-87)
Touchdowns, season	19	Emmitt Smith (1992)
Touchdowns, game	4	By many players
Field goals, career	162	Rafael Septien (1978-88)
Field goals, season	28	Eddie Murray (1993)
Field goals, game	5	Roger Ruzek (12/21/87)
		Eddie Murray (10/3/93)
Extra points, career	388	Rafael Septien (1978-86)
Exta points, season	59	Rafael Septien (1980)
Extra points, game	8	Rafael Septien (10/12/80)
		Mike Clark (9/15/68)
		Danny Villanueva (10/19/66)

Rushing
Yards, career	12,036	Tony Dorsett (1977-87)
Yards, season	1,713	Emmitt Smith (1992)
Yards, game	237	Emmitt Smith (10/31/93)
Attempts, career	2,755	Tony Dorsett (1977-87)
Attempts, season	373	Emmitt Smith (1992)
Attempts, game	34	Emmitt Smith (11/24/91)
Touchdowns, career	72	Tony Dorsett (1977-87)
Touchdowns, season	18	Emmitt Smith (1992)
Touchdowns, game	4	Calvin Hill (9/19/71)
		Emmitt Smith (12/16/90)

Passing
Rating, career	83.5	Roger Staubach (1969-79)
Rating, season	104.8	Roger Staubach (1971)
Completions, career	1,761	Danny White (1976-88)
Completions, season	334	Danny White (1983)
Completions, game	33	Gary Hogeboom (9/3/84))
Yards, career	22,700	Roger Staubach (1969-79))
Yards, season	3,980	Danny White (1983)
Yards, game	460	Dan Meredith (11/10/63)
Attempts, career	2,958	Roger Staubach (1969-79)
Attempts, season	533	Danny White (1983)
Attempts, game	49	Roger Staubach (10/26/75)
		Gary Hogeboom (12/22/85)
		Danny White (12/13/87)
		Steve Walsh (10/29/89)
Touchdowns, career	155	Danny White (1976-88)
Touchdowns, season	29	Danny White (1983)
Touchdowns, game	5	By many players

Receiving
Receptions, career	489	Drew Pearson (1973-83)
Receptions, season	93	Michael Irvin (1991)
Receptions, game	13	Lance Rentzel (11/19/67)
Yards, career	7,988	Tony Hill (1977-86)
Yards, season	1,523	Michael Irvin (1991)
Yards, game	246	Bob Hayes (11/13/66)
Touchdowns, career	71	Bob Hayes (1965-74)
Touchdowns, season	14	Frank Clarke (1962)
Touchdowns, game	4	Bob Hayes (12/20/70)

Interceptions
Career	52	Mel Renfro (1964-77)
Season	11	Everson Walls (1981)
Game	3	Herb Adderley (9/26/71)
		Lee Roy Jordan (11/4/73)
		Dennis Thurman (12/13/81)

Sacks
Career	113	Harvey Martin (1973-1983)
Season	20	Harvey Martin (1977)
Game	5	Bob Lilly (11/20/66)
		Jim Jeffcoat (11/10/85)

Longest Plays
Run from scrimmage	99	Tony Dorsett (TD, 1/3/83)
Pass play	95	Don Meredith to Hayes (11/13/66)
Field goal	54	Toni Fritsch (9/24/72)
		Ken Willis (9/1/91)
Interception return	100	Mike Gaechter (TD, 10/14/62)
Kickoff return	102	Alexander Wright (TD, 12/22/91)
Punt return	98	Dennis Morgan (10/13/74)
Punt	84	Ron Widby (11/3/68)

Top scorers — Points
Rafael Septein (1978-86)	874
Tony Dorsett (1977-87)	516
Bob Hayes (1965-74)	456
Mike Clark (1968-71, 73)	386
Emmitt Smith (1990-93)	318
Toni Fritsch (1971-73, 75)	317

Top rushers — Yards
Tony Dorsett (1977-87)	12,036
Don Perkins (1961-68)	6,217
Emmitt Smith (1990-93)	5,699
Calvin Hill (1969-74)	5,009
Robert Newhouse (1973-83)	4,784
Walt Garrison (1966-74)	3,886

Top passers — Completions
Danny White (1976-88)	1,761
Roger Staubach (1969-79)	1,685
Troy Aikman (1989-93)	1,191
Don Meredith (1960-68)	1,170

Top passers — Yards
Roger Staubach (1969-79)	22,700
Danny White (1976-88)	21,959
Don Meredith (1960-68)	17,199
Troy Aikman (1989-93)	13,627

Top receivers — Receptions
Drew Pearson (1973-73)	489
Tony Hill (1977-86)	479
Tony Dorsett (1977-87)	382
Bob Hayes (1965-74)	365
Michael Irvin (1988-93)	337
Jay Novacek (1985-93)	313

Top receivers — Yards
Tony Hill (1977-86)	7,988
Drew Pearson (1973-83)	7,822
Bob Hayes (1965-74)	7,295
Michael Irvin (1988-93)	5,694
Frank Clarke (1960-67)	5,214
Doug Cosbie (1979-88)	3,728

Most interceptions — No.
Mel Renfro (1964-77)	52
Everson Walls (1981-89)	44
Charlie Waters (1970-78, 80-81)	41
Dennis Thurman (1978-85)	36
Cornell Green (1962-74)	34
Michael Downs (1981-88)	34

Most sacks — No.
Harvey Martin (1973-83)	113
Randy White (1975-88)	111
Ed Jones (1974-78, 1980-89)	105
Jim Jeffcoat (1983-93)	86.5

PRO FOOTBALL WEEKLY 1994 ALMANAC

PREVIEW: DENVER BRONCOS

This year the smile on Denver head coach Wade Phillips' face may be a little less wide. Last year Phillips was a rookie head coach who was thrilled to get the opportunity to lead an NFL team. Phillips was successful, as the Broncos got back to the postseason by taking the wild-card route. Basically, the fans and management were happy with a return to competitive football and a chance to compete in the playoffs.

But beneath the surface, getting into the postseason as a wild-card team and getting humiliated in the first round is not good enough. In the old days under Dan Reeves, the Broncos didn't undergo their annual depression until the day after the Super Bowl.

Getting to the playoffs is not what life is about in Denver. This is a team that has had 12 winning seasons in the last 17 years. This is a team that has an overall record of 159-102-1 in that span, second-best in the AFC and third-best in the NFL. The Broncos have been to the playoffs 10 times in those 17 years, and expectations are high.

That's why there is a ton of pressure on Phillips and the Broncos to improve this year.

Offensively, the Broncos have the kind of weapons on their side that should make them one of the most exciting teams in the league. QB John Elway is, of course, the bombardier of this attack. Elway is coming off the best statistical year of his career. He completed 348-of-551 passes for 4,030 yards with 25 TD's and 10 interceptions. What makes those numbers even more amazing is that the only big-name receiver he had to work with over the length of the season was TE Shannon Sharpe. At age 33, Elway is still the kind of athlete who can run away from the pass rush and buy time with his quick feet. While not as lightning-like as he was in 1986, Elway still moves better than a large majority of the game's quarterbacks.

Why did Elway's game go through a renaissance at this point in his career? Because offensive coordinator Jim Fassel took the reins off Elway and made him the focal point of the offense.

"When it comes to QB play, Elway is absolutely amazing," said Fassell. "I'll admit I'm prejudiced, but the fact of the matter is that Elway can make every play we ask of him, and I don't think you can say that about too many other quarterbacks. In addition to all the measurables, Elway has the competitiveness and the instincts to make winning plays when you think he's going to get hammered. Those are things that you just can't teach."

There's every reason to think that the Bronco passing game will get better in 1994. Denver tried to sign Raider WR Tim Brown in the offseason, but instead settled for former Charger WR Anthony Miller and ex-Falcon Mike Pritchard. Miller will give Elway the big-play wideout that has been missing, but he is not as good a receiver as Brown. The two major complaints about Miller are his moodiness and his somewhat inconsistent hands. While Brown will catch anything in his neighborhood, Miller will drop a big pass every once in a while, which is likely to send him into a serious funk. Pritchard is a very productive receiver who catches the ball underneath in traffic.

The Broncos have one of the game's emerging stars in Sharpe, a big tight end with the ability to get open and break big plays. Sharpe has the added impetus of breaking free from the shadow of his brother, Green Bay WR Sterling Sharpe, so Phillips and Elway know they'll always get the maximum effort from their tight end.

With Vance Johnson off to San Diego, look for Cedric Tillman and free-agent acquisition Jeff Campbell from Detroit to emerge as Elway's secondary receivers.

The running game should be in capable hands with Rod Bernstine, Robert Delpino and second-year breakaway back Glyn Milburn. Bernstine is an unusual runner because he is an upright power back who sees the cutback lanes and uses them well. He started slowly last year before getting hurt. Delpino is one of the tougher runners in the game, but he will never be more than a journeyman. Milburn is the kind of back who can make big

PHOTO BY GEORGE GOJKOVICH

John Elway

72

1994 PREVIEW ■ DENVER

plays on third downs because of his great moves, but he has no power to break tackles.

The Bronco offensive line should improve in 1994. The Broncos added Gary Zimmerman, Don Maggs and Brian Habib last year, and they should all be more familiar with the Denver scheme in 1994 than they were last year. Zimmerman is probably the best left tackle the Broncos have ever had and one of the three best in the game. Maggs, who may move to guard this year, missed much of last season with a back injury. Habib is very strong and an aggressive run blocker. C Keith Kartz is a dependable player, but he will never be the kind of athlete who can dominate.

With strength at quarterback, running back and the offensive line and an improved situation at the WR slot, there's little doubt the Broncos should be a powerful offensive team next season. However, their defense was very shaky at the end of last season.

The biggest problem defensive coordinator Charlie Waters had was the team's definitive lack of overall speed. In the last two games of the season — both against the Raiders — receivers like Brown, James Jett and Alexander Wright made the Denver secondary their own personal playground. In those games, the Denver defensive front had a hard time putting pressure on QB Jeff Hostetler, and the secondary was left to fend for itself. That turned out to be disastrous for Waters and Phillips.

In order to turn up the pressure on opposing quarterbacks, the Broncos are likely to switch from a 3-4 defense to a 4-3 alignment this fall.

The Denver defensive line could come into its own this season. The most exciting player on the unit could be DRE Dan Williams, who injured a knee at the end of last season. Williams plays a rough, physical style and likes to punish opposing blockers. That could turn out to be a problem for Williams, since he sometimes acts like winning individual battles is more important than winning games. Williams had only one sack last year, but that total should improve dramatically if he develops an improved view of the bigger picture. On the other side, DLE Shane Dronett recorded seven sacks and two interceptions and showed good instincts and a relentless attitude when it came to making plays. Ex-49er Ted Washington will probably replace Greg Kragen, who was cut, at one tackle while the other DT spot appears murky. Quirky Darren Drozdov has potential because of his power and toughness, but he is not experienced.

In recent years, the strength of the Bronco defense has been its LB play. OLB Simon Fletcher is the team's sack specialist who comes in and gobbles up quarterbacks. Last year he recorded 13.5 sacks, and that figure probably would have been even higher had he not overrun so many plays. Despite his strength and speed, Fletcher does not have great agility, and that's why he misses so many plays. On the other side, Mike Croel has tremendous speed, and he really improved at the point of attack. However, when it comes to rushing the passer, Croel is missing something extra, and that factor may keep him from developing into an All-Pro player. If the Broncos do switch to a 4-3 setup, former Seahawk Dave Wyman will most likely be the starting middle linebacker. Wyman is a thinking man's football player who normally finds a way to put himself in the right position to make a play. While he is very intelligent, he has also shown a tendency to get injured in the past. Last year, playing on the natural turf of Mile High Stadium, was the first time in his career that he managed to stay healthy. Veteran Karl Mecklenburg is still a smart player, but at age 34, he has slowed down considerably and can't come close to dominating a game. However, if you need a big play at a key moment, Mecklenburg can still deliver. He registered nine sacks last season. No. 2 pick Allen Aldridge adds depth.

The secondary was Denver's undoing throughout the season. The Broncos signed former Detroit CB Ray Crockett and traded for Eagle CB Ben Smith during the offseason, and they should upgrade the unit. Crockett has decent man-on-man cover skills, and he is not afraid to gamble in order to make a big play. Smith hasn't been the same since ripping up a knee late in '91, but he still has great natural ability. Other corners the Broncos can choose from are Ronnie Bradford, a promising second-year player, and veteran Tyrone Braxton. Braxton is a solid hitter but a limited athlete. CB Charles Dimry is still around, but he's been burned throughout his career by receivers like Jerry Rice and Tim Brown. At free safety, Steve Atwater is a Pro Bowl performer, but the consensus on him is that he played better in 1991 than he did in '92 or '93. The Broncos have to replace free-agent Dennis Smith at strong safety. Smith was a great hitter, but he was beaten with increasing frequency on deep plays in his later years. Second-year S Rondell Jones and ex-CFL player Darryl Hall have the inside track for the job.

From a special-team point of view, the Broncos appear to be in a good position with highly rated second-year PK Jason Elam, as well as P Tom Rouen. Milburn is the team's most exciting punt returner since Rick Upchurch.

FAST FACTS

■ Shannon Sharpe's 81 receptions were the most by a Bronco receiver since Lionel Taylor caught 85 in 1965.

■ The 13th player to pass for 4,000 yards in one season, John Elway ranks seventh on the NFL's all-time passing-yardage list (34,246).

■ Special-teamer Reggie Rivers blocked two punts last season, the only NFL player to block that many in 1993.

PRO FOOTBALL WEEKLY 1994 ALMANAC

1994 PLAYER ROSTER

NO.	NAME	POS.	HT.	WT.	EXP.	COLLEGE	GP/GS
58	Alexander, Elijah	LB	6-2	230	3	Kansas State	16/0
27	Atwater, Steve	S	6-3	217	6	Arkansas	15/15
11	Ball, Michael	DB	6-1	215	6	Southern	0/0
46	Bell, Trumane	TE	6-3	235	R	Nebraska	—
33	Bernstine, Rod	RB	6-3	238	8	Texas A&M	9/1
83	Bonner, Melvin	WR	6-3	207	2	Baylor	3/0
23	Bradford, Ronnie	CB	5-10	188	2	Colorado	10/3
10	Campbell, Jeff	WR	5-8	167	5	Colorado	10/0
15	Carlson, Jeff	QB	6-3	212	5	Weber State	0/0
48	Carsell, Dwayne	TE	6-3	261	R	Liberty	—
20	Crockett, Ray	CB	5-10	185	6	Baylor	15/15
51	Croel, Mike	LB	6-3	231	4	Nebraska	16/16
39	Delpino, Robert	RB	6-0	205	7	Missouri	10/4
29	Dimry, Charles	CB	6-0	175	8	Nevada-Las Vegas	16/8
54	Donahue, Mitch	LB	6-2	254	4	Wyoming	13/0
99	Dronett, Shane	DE	6-6	260	3	Texas	16/2
97	Drozdov, Darren	DT	6-3	280	2	Maryland	6/2
60	Dyet, Brian	OL	6-4	257	R	Colorado	—
1	Elam, Jason	PK	5-11	192	2	Hawaii	0/0
7	Elway, John	QB	6-3	215	12	Stanford	12/12
88	Evans, Jerry	TE	6-4	250	2	Toledo	0/0
70	Farkas, Kevin	OT	6-9	360	R	Appalachian State	—
73	Fletcher, Simon	DE	6-5	240	10	Houston	16/16
68	Freeman, Russell	OT	6-7	274	3	Georgia Tech	16/16
63	Fowler, Carlos	DL	6-2	278	R	Wisconsin	—
24	Fuller, Randy	CB	5-9	173	R	Tennessee State	—
25	Geter, Eric	CB	5-11	190	R	Clemson	—
75	Habib, Brian	OT	6-7	292	6	Washington	16/15
40	Hall, Darryl	S	6-2	210	2	Washington	0/0
69	Hall, Kenny	OG-OT	6-4	315	R	Fresno State	—
65	Hampel, Olaf	OL	6-6	305	1	None	0/0
93	Harvey, Richard	LB	6-1	242	5	Tulane	15/0
96	Hasselbach, Harald	DL	6-6	280	R	Washington	—
50	Jacobs, Ray	LB	6-2	244	R	North Carolina	—
89	Johnson, Reggie	TE	6-2	256	4	Florida State	15/6
31	Jones, Rondell	S	6-2	210	2	North Carolina	0/0
72	Kartz, Keith	C	6-4	270	8	California	15/15
82	Kimbrough, Tony	WR	6-2	179	2	Jackson State	15/0
21	Lang, Le-Lo	DB	5-11	185	5	Washington	16/0
62	Lofton, Billy	DE	6-2	290	R	Kentucky	—
59	Lucas, Tim	LB	6-3	230	8	California	9/0
37	Lynn, Anthony	RB	6-3	230	2	Texas Tech	0/0
8	Maddox, Tommy	QB	6-4	195	3	UCLA	13/4
78	Maggs, Don	OT	6-5	290	9	Tulane	7/2
77	Mecklenburg, Karl	LB	6-3	235	12	Minnesota	16/16
61	Meeks, Bob	C	6-2	279	3	Auburn	0/0
64	Melander, Jon	OG-OT	6-7	280	4	Minnesota	14/7
22	Milburn, Glyn	RB	5-8	177	2	Stanford	0/0
83	Miller, Anthony	WR	5-11	190	7	Tennessee	16/16
52	Mills, Jeff	LB	6-3	238	5	Nebraska	14/0
12	Moore, Shawn	QB	6-2	214	4	Virginia	3/0
14	Mosley, Tim	WR	6-3	187	R	Northern Iowa	—
91	Oshodin, Willie	DE	6-4	260	3	Villanova	0/0
81	Pritchard, Mike	WR	5-10	190	4	Colorado	15/14
30	Redmond, Jamie	CB	5-9	185	R	Mid. Tennessee St.	—

74

1994 PREVIEW — DENVER

1994 PLAYER ROSTER

NO.	NAME	POS.	HT.	WT.	EXP.	COLLEGE	GP/GS
38	Rivers, Reggie	RB	6-1	215	4	SW Texas State	16/3
36	Robinson, Frank	CB	5-11	174	3	Boise State	12/0
94	Robinson, Jeff	DE	6-4	265	2	Idaho	0/0
81	Rose, Barry	WR	6-0	185	2	Wis.-Stevens Point	3/0
16	Rouen, Tom	P	6-3	215	2	Colorado	0/0
85	Russell, Derek	WR	6-0	179	4	Arkansas	12/7
55	Sanders, Glenell	LB	6-1	237	4	Louisiana Tech	0/0
32	Savage, Sebastian	CB	5-11	196	R	North Carolina St.	—
76	Scrafford, Kirk	OT	6-6	255	5	Montana	15/0
84	Sharpe, Shannon	TE	6-2	230	5	Savannah (Ga.) St.	16/9
26	Smith, Ben	CB	5-11	185	5	Georgia	13/3
49	Smith, Dennis	S	6-3	200	14	Southern Cal	16/16
19	Smith, Rod	WR	6-0	183	R	Missouri Southern	—
35	Snowden, Chuck	RB	6-0	209	R	Northern Colorado	—
41	Strother, Deon	RB	5-11	213	R	Southern Cal	—
17	Swann, Charles	WR	6-1	188	R	Indiana State	—
95	Taylor, Alphonso	DL	6-3	350	2	Temple	3/0
81	Taylor, Kitrick	WR	5-11	189	7	Washington State	1/0
87	Tillman, Cedric	WR	6-2	204	2	Alcorn State	9/1
67	Vaughn, Scott	OL	6-5	319	R	Rutgers	—
98	Washington, Ted	NT	6-4	295	4	Louisville	12/12
79	Widell, Dave	OL	6-6	292	7	Boston College	16/1
90	Williams, Dan	DE	6-4	290	2	Toledo	0/0
57	Wyman, Dave	LB	6-2	248	8	Stanford	11/1
65	Zimmerman, Gary	OT	6-6	294	9	Oregon	16/16

'94 DRAFT PICKS

RD.	NAME	POS.	HT.	WT.	COLLEGE
2.	Aldridge, Allen	LB	6-1	243	Houston
4.	Fuller, Randy	DB	5-9	173	Tennessee State
7.	Burns, Keith	LB	6-2	245	Oklahoma State
7.	By'Not'e, Butler	RB	5-9	188	Ohio State
7.	Nalen, Tom	C	6-2	279	Boston College

PRO FOOTBALL WEEKLY 1994 ALMANAC

TEAM AT A GLANCE

TEAM DIRECTORY

Address	13655 Broncos Parkway Englewood, Colorado 80112 (303) 649-9000
Stadium	Denver Mile High Stadium 1900 West Eliot Denver, Colorado 80204 Capacity: 76,273 Playing surface: Grass
Training Camp	University of Northern Colorado Greeley, Colorado 80639
Colors	Orange, royal blue and white
Television	KCNC, Channel 4
Radio	KOA, 850 AM

ADMINISTRATION
President-chief executive officer: Pat Bowlen
General manager: John Beake
Treasurer-chief financial officer: Robert Hurley
Assistant to GM-community relations: Fred Fleming
Director of operations-player personnel: Bob Ferguson
Assistant director of player personnel: Ronnie Hill
Director of college scouting: Jeff Smith
Director of media relations: Jim Saccomano
Director of tickets-operations: Gail Stuckey
Trainer: Steve Antonopulos

1994 SCHEDULE

Preseason
JULY 31	vs. L.A. Raiders (Barcelona)*	1:00
AUG. 6	ATLANTA	7:00
AUG. 12	at San Francisco	5:00
AUG. 21	at Dallas	7:00
AUG. 25	ARIZONA	7:00

*Eastern Time

Regular season
SEP. 4	SAN DIEGO	6:00
SEP. 11	at N.Y. Jets	4:00
SEP. 18	L.A. RAIDERS	2:00
SEP. 26	at Buffalo (Mon.)	9:00
OCT. 2	OPEN DATE	
OCT. 9	at Seattle	1:00
OCT. 17	KANSAS CITY (Mon.)	7:00
OCT. 23	at San Diego	1:00
OCT. 30	CLEVELAND	2:00
NOV. 6	at L.A. Rams	1:00
NOV. 13	SEATTLE	2:00
NOV. 20	ATLANTA	2:00
NOV. 27	CINCINNATI	2:00
DEC. 4	at Kansas City	3:00
DEC. 11	at L.A. Raiders	1:00
DEC. 17	at San Francisco (Sat.)	1:00
DEC. 24	NEW ORLEANS	2:00

HEAD COACH
Wade Phillips

Following the firing of Dan Reeves, Phillips was promoted from defensive coordinator to head coach in 1993. In his first season heading up the Broncos, he guided them to a 9-7 record and a wild-card playoff berth. The son of former NFL coach Bum Phillips, Wade replaced his father and served as the Saints' interim head coach for four games in 1985, going 1-3. Born June 21, 1947, Orange, Texas.

Previous NFL: defensive coordinator, 1989-92 Denver; defensive coordinator-linebackers, Philadelphia 1986-88; defensive coordinator, New Orleans 1981-85 (interim head coach in 1985); defensive line, Houston 1977-80; linebackers, Houston 1976.

Previous college: assistant coach, Kansas 1975; assistant coach, 1973-74 Oklahoma State; assistant coach, Houston 1969.

Player: No NFL. College, linebacker, Houston 1966-68.

ASSISTANT COACHES
Vernon Banks: strength and conditioning
Previous NFL: strength and conditioning, 1993 Denver. Player: No NFL. College: defensive back, running back, 1978-79 Texas A&M.

Barney Chavous: defensive assistant
Previous NFL: defensive assistant, 1989-93 Denver. Player: NFL, defensive end, 1973-85 Denver. College: defensive end, 1969-72 South Carolina State.

Jim Fassel: assistant head coach/offensive coordinator
Previous NFL: offensive coordinator-quarterbacks, 1993 Denver; 1990-92 N.Y. Giants. Player: NFL, quarterback, 1972 Chicago; 1972 Houston; 1972 San Diego. College: quarterback, 1969-70 Southern Cal; 1971 Long Beach State.

Mo Forte: wide receivers
Previous NFL: 1988-93 Denver. Player: No NFL. College: running back, 1965-68 Minnesota.

Leon Fuller: defensive backs
Previous NFL: None. Player: No NFL. College: Alabama.

Bishop Harris: running backs
Previous NFL: running backs, 1993 Denver. Player: No NFL. College: defensive back, 1960-64 North Carolina College.

John Levra: offensive line
Previous NFL: offensive line, 1993 Denver; 1986-92 Chicago; 1981-85 New Orleans. Player: No NFL. College: guard, linebacker, 1963-65 Pittsburg (Kan.) State.

Rex Norris: defensive line
Previous NFL: defensive line, 1985-87 Detroit. Player: No NFL. College: defensive lineman, 1962 East Texas State.

Alvin Reynolds: defensive assistant-quality control
Previous NFL: defensive assistant-quality control, 1993 Denver. Player: No NFL. College: safety, 1978-81 Indiana State.

Harold Richardson: quality control-administra-

1994 PREVIEW ■ DENVER

TEAM AT A GLANCE

tive assistant
 Previous NFL: 1989-93 Denver; 1981-85 Saints. Player: No NFL. College: tight end, 1964-67 Southern Methodist.
Richard Smith: special teams
 Previous NFL: special teams, 1993 Denver; 1988-92 Houston. Player: No NFL. College: offensive lineman, 1977-78 Fresno State.
Les Steckel: tight ends/H-backs
 Previous NFL: tight ends-H-backs, 1993 Denver; 1985-88 New England; 1979-84 Minnesota (head coach in 1984); 1978 San Francisco. Player: No NFL. College: running back, 1964-68 Kansas.
Charlie Waters: defensive coordinator
 Previous NFL: defensive coordinator, 1988-93 Denver. Player: NFL, safety, 1970-81 Dallas. College: safety, 1967-69 Clemson.
John Paul Young: linebackers
 Previous NFL: linebackers, 1993 Denver; 1986-88 Kansas City; 1981-85 New Orleans; 1978-80 Houston. Player: No NFL. College: linebacker, 1959-61 Texas El-Paso.

COACHING RECORDS
(includes postseason games)

Years	Coach	W	L	T
1960-61	Frank Filchock	7	20	1
1962-64	Jack Faulkner	9	22	1
1964-66	Mac Speedie	6	19	1
1966	Ray Malavasi	4	8	0
1967-71	Lou Saban	20	42	3
1971	Jerry Smith	2	3	0
1972-76	John Ralston	34	33	3
1977-80	Red Miller	42	25	0
1981-92	Dan Reeves	117	79	1
1993	Wade Phillips	9	8	0

HISTORICAL HIGHLIGHTS

1960 Denver is selected as the site for charter membership in the AFL, and the franchise is awarded to Bob Howsam and other investors. ... Frank Filchock is named the first head coach.
1960 QB Frank Tripucka completes 248 passes, a club record that will stand until John Elway breaks it in 1985.
1961 A new syndicate headed by Cal Kunz and Gerry Phipps purchases the Broncos.
1968 The Broncos' home field is officially named Mile High Stadium.
1973 The Broncos enjoy their first winning season ever, 7-5-2. John Ralston is AFC Coach of the Year.
1974 Otis Armstrong wins the NFL rushing title with 1,407 yards, joining only a half-dozen players to average more than 100 yards a game in NFL history and becoming the first Bronco to rush for more than 1,000 yards in a season.
1977-78 The Broncos clinch a playoff berth and the AFC Western Division championship, both firsts in club history, posting their best season record ever, 12-2, and tying the Dallas Cowboys for the best record in the NFL. The Broncos are victorious over the Pittsburgh Steelers 34-21 in the first round of playoff action, a game in which they draw the largest crowd ever to watch a sporting event in the state of Colorado, 75,011. Then the Broncos take on the NFL's defending champion Oakland Raiders and win 20-17 to earn a trip the the Super Bowl in New Orleans. But Denver falls to Dallas in Super Bowl XII 27-10.
1978 The Broncos win 10 of 16 games and their second straight division championship. But Denver loses to the eventual Super Bowl victors, the Pittsburgh Steelers, 33-10 in the playoffs.
1979 Setting an NFL record in a game against New England, Rick Upchurch becomes the all-time top punt returner, surpassing Emlen Tunnell's mark of 2,209 yards. ... The Broncos secure a playoff berth for the third year in a row, but lose to Houston 13-7 in the wild-card game.
1981 The Broncos are purchased by Edgar F. Kaiser Jr., from principal owners Gerald and Allan Phipps ... They sport a record of 10-6, but lose out on a wild-card entry on qualifiers.
1983 Behind the passing of rookie QB John Elway, the 9-7 Broncos clinch a playoff berth. But Denver loses to Seattle in 13-7 in the wild-card game.
1984 New Bronco owner Pat Bowlen assumes the title of president and chief executive officer of the club. ... The club sets a team record of 10 straight victories and captures the AFC West title with a record of 13-3. Denver, however, falls to Pittsburgh 24-17 in the divisional playoff game.
1985 John Elway sets team records by completing 327 passes for 3,891 yards.
1986-87 The Broncos win the AFC West with a record of 11-5. ... RB Sammy Winder leads the AFC in touchdowns, with 84 points on nine rushing and five receiving TD's. ... Denver defeats the Patriots, the AFC's representative in the previous Super Bowl 22-17, and then edges the Browns in overtime 23-20 to take the AFC crown and earn its second invitation to the Super Bowl ... The Broncos fall to the Giants in Super Bowl XXI at the Rose Bowl 39-20.
1987-88 Denver wins its third AFC West title in four years, becoming the only team to post eight 10-win seasons since 1977. ... QB John Elway is named the NFL's MVP ... The Broncos defeat Houston 34-10 and then take the conference crown for the second year in a row by eliminating Cleveland 38-33. ... The Broncos go to Super Bowl XXII but lose to the Washington Redskins 42-10.
1989-90 Denver regains the AFC title, making it three in four years. ... In the first playoff game, Denver edges the Steelers 24-23, then takes the conference championship by beating the Browns 37-21. ... In Super Bowl XXIV at the New Orleans Superdome, the Broncos lose to the 49ers 55-10.
1991-92 With a 12-4 record, Denver wins its fifth AFC West crown in eight years. ... Overcoming a 21-6 deficit, Denver defeats the Oilers 26-24 in the playoffs but loses to the Buffalo Bills 10-7 in the AFC title game.
1993-94 After the release of 12-year head coach Dan Reeves, Denver signs Wade Phillips as the 10th coach in Bronco history. ... Denver makes it to the playoffs as a wild-card team but loses to the Los Angeles Raiders 42-24.

PRO FOOTBALL WEEKLY 1994 ALMANAC

TEAM AT A GLANCE

HALL OF FAME MEMBERS
None

RETIRED JERSEY NUMBERS
18 QB Frank Tripucka
44 RB Floyd Little

FIRST-ROUND DRAFT CHOICES
(since 1980)

Year	Selection	College
1980	No choice	
1981	DB Dennis Smith	Southern Cal
1982	RB Gerald Willhite	San Jose State
1983	OG Chris Hinton	Northwestern
1984	DE Andre Townsend	Mississippi
1985	RB Steve Sewell	Oklahoma
1986	No choice	
1987	WR Ricky Nattiel	Florida
1988	NT Ted Gregory	Syracuse
1989	DB Steve Atwater	Arkansas
	RB Bobby Humphrey	Alabama
	(supplemental)	
1990	No choice	
1991	LB Mike Croel	Nebraska
1992	QB Tommy Maddox	UCLA
1993	DE Dan Williams	Toledo
1994	No choice	

RECORD VS. OTHER NFL TEAMS
(includes postseason games)

	Record
Arizona Cardinals	3-0-1
Atlanta Falcons	4-3-0
Buffalo Bills	10-17-1
Chicago Bears	5-5-0
Cincinnati Bengals	10-6-0
Cleveland Browns	15-5-0
Dallas Cowboys	2-4-0
Detroit Lions	4-3-0
Green Bay Packers	4-2-1
Houston Oilers	13-20-1
Indianapolis Colts	9-2-0
Kansas City Chiefs	29-38-0
Los Angeles Raiders	20-47-2
Los Angeles Rams	3-3-0
Miami Dolphins	2-5-1
Minnesota Vikings	3-5-0
New England Patriots	17-12-0
New Orleans Saints	4-1-0
New York Giants	3-4-0
New York Jets	12-11-1
Philadelphia Eagles	2-5-0
Pittsburgh Steelers	12-7-1
San Diego Chargers	35-32-1
San Francisco 49ers	4-3-0
Seattle Seahawks	20-14-0
Tampa Bay Buccaneers	2-1-0
Washington Redskins	3-4-0

YEAR-BY-YEAR RECORDS

Year	Won	Lost	Tied
1960	4	9	1
1961	3	11	0
1962	7	7	0
1963	2	11	1
1964	2	11	1
1965	4	10	0
1966	4	10	0
1967	3	11	0
1968	5	9	0
1969	5	8	1
1970	5	8	1
1971	4	9	1
1972	5	9	0
1973	7	5	2
1974	7	6	1
1975	6	8	0
1976	9	5	0
1977**	12	2	0
1978**	10	6	0
1979**	10	6	0
1980	8	8	0
1981	10	6	0
1982	2	7	0
1983**	9	7	0
1984**	13	3	0
1985	11	5	0
1986**	11	5	0
1987**	10	4	1
1988	8	8	0
1989**	11	5	0
1990	5	11	0
1991**	12	4	0
1992	8	8	0
1993**	9	7	0
Total	241	249	10

Number of NFL championships   0
Number of years .500 or better   19
Number of years below .500   15

*NFL champions
**Playoff team

1994 PREVIEW ■ DENVER

RECORDS

INDIVIDUAL

Service
Seasons played	14	Tom Jackson (1973-86)
Games played	191	Tom Jackson (1973-86)

Scoring
Points, career	742	Jim Turner (1971-79)
Points, season	137	Eugene Mingo (1960-64)
Points, game	21	Eugene Mingo (10/10/60)
Touchdowns, career	54	Floyd Little (1967-75)
Touchdowns, season	14	Sammy Winder (1986)
Touchdowns, game	3	By many players
Field goals, career	151	Jim Turner (1971-79)
Field goals, season	27	David Treadwell (1991, 1989)
		Eugene Mingo (1962)
Field goals, game	5	Rich Karlis (11/20/83)
		Eugene Mingo (10/6/63)
Extra points, career	283	Jim Turner (1971-79)
Exta points, season	44	Rich Karlis (1986)
Extra points, game	6	By many players

Rushing
Yards, career	6,323	Floyd Little (1967-75)
Yards, season	1,407	Otis Armstrong (1974)
Yards, game	183	Otis Armstrong (12/8/74)
Attempts, career	1,641	Floyd Little (1967-75)
Attempts, season	296	Sammy Winder (1984)
Attempts, game	34	Bobby Humphrey (9/30/90)
		Sammy Winder (10/28/84)
Touchdowns, career	43	Floyd Little (1967-75)
Touchdowns, season	12	Floyd Little (1973)
Touchdowns, game	3	Gaston Green (9/22/91)
		Otis Armstrong (12/8/74)
		Jon Keyworth (11/18/74)
		Floyd Little (9/16/73)

Passing
Rating, career	75.9	John Elway (1983-93)
Rating, season	92.7	John Elway (1993)
Completions, career	2,723	John Elway (1983-93)
Completions, season	348	John Elway (1993)
Completions, game	34	Milton Slaughter (12/20/64)
Yards, career	34,246	John Elway (1983-93)
Yards, season	4,030	John Elway (1993)
Yards, game	447	Frank Tripucka (9/15/62)
Attempts, career	4,890	John Elway (1983-93)
Attempts, season	605	John Elway (1985)
Attempts, game	56	Frank Tripucka (9/15/62)
Touchdowns, career	183	John Elway (1983-93)
Touchdowns, season	25	John Elway (1993)
Touchdowns, game	5	Frank Tripucka (10/28/62)
		John Elway (11/18/84)

Receiving
Receptions, career	543	Lionel Taylor (1960-66)
Receptions, season	100	Lionel Taylor (1961)
Receptions, game	13	Bobby Anderson (9/30/73)
		Lionel Taylor (11/29/64)
Yards, career	6,872	Lionel Taylor (1960-66)
Yards, season	1,244	Steve Watson (1981)
Yards, game	199	Lionel Taylor (11/27/60)
Touchdowns, career	44	Lionel Taylor (1960-66)
Touchdowns, season	13	Steve Watson (1981)
Touchdowns, game	3	By five players

Interceptions
Career	44	Steve Foley (1976-86)
Season	11	Austin Gonsoulin (1960)
Game	4	Willie Brown (11/15/64)
		Austin Gonsoulin (9/18/60)

Sacks
Career	85.5	Simon Fletcher (1985-93)
Season	16	Simon Fletcher (1992)

Game	4	Simon Fletcher (11/4/90)
		Karl Mecklenburg (9/15/85)
		Karl Mecklenburg (12/1/85)

Longest Plays
Run from scrimmage	82	Eugene Mingo (10/5/62)
Pass play	97	George Shaw to Jerry Tarr (9/21/62)
Field goal	57	Fred Steinfort (10/13/80)
Interception return	93	Randy Gradishar (10/5/80)
Kickoff return	100	Goldie Sellers (10/2/66)
		Nemiah Wilson (10/8/66)
Punt return	92	Rick Upchurch (10/3/76)
Punt	83	Chris Norman (9/23/84)

Top scorers — Points
Jim Turner (1971-79)	742
Rich Karlis (1982-88)	655
David Treadwell (1989-92)	429
Eugene Mingo (1960-64)	408
Floyd Little (1967-75)	324
Sammy Winder (1982-90)	288

Top rushers — Yards
Floyd Little (1967-75)	6,323
Sammy Winder (1982-90)	5,428
Otis Armstrong (1973-80)	4,453
Jon Keyworth (1974-80)	2,653
John Elway (1983-93)	2,435
Bobby Humphrey (1989-91)	2,386

Top passers — Completions
John Elway (1983-93)	2,723
Craig Morton (1977-82)	907
Frank Tripucka (1960-63)	662
Charley Johnson (1972-75)	517
Steve Ramsey (1971-76)	456
Steve Tensi (1967-70)	348

Top passers — Yards
John Elway (1983-93)	34,246
Craig Morton (1977-82)	11,895
Frank Tripucka (1960-63)	7,676
Charley Johnson (1972-75)	7,238
Steve Ramsey (1971-76)	6,437
Steve Tensi (1967-70)	5,153

Top receivers — Receptions
Lionel Taylor (1960-66)	543
Vance Johnson (1985-93)	403
Riley Odoms (1972-83)	396
Steve Watson (1979-87)	353
Haven Moses (1972-81)	302
Mark Jackson (1986-92)	276

Top receivers — Yards
Lionel Taylor (1960-66)	6,872
Steve Watson (1979-87)	6,112
Riley Odoms (1972-83)	5,755
Vance Johnson (1985-93)	5,525
Haven Moses (1972-81)	5,450
Mark Jackson (1986-92)	4,746

Most interceptions — No.
Steve Foley (1976-86)	44
Austin Gonsoulin (1960-66)	43
Bill Thompson (1969-81)	40
Mike Harden (180-88)	33
Dennis Smith (1981-93)	30
Louis Wright (1975-86)	26

Most sacks — No.
Simon Fletcher (1985-93)	85.5
Karl Mecklenburg (1983-93)	78
Rulon Jones (1980-88)	73.5

PRO FOOTBALL WEEKLY 1994 ALMANAC

PREVIEW: DETROIT LIONS

A little success can raise expectations. A lot.

After turning in an NFC Central Division-winning performance in 1993, the Lions have set their sights on football's biggest game — the Super Bowl.

Perhaps a bit prematurely, considering the staff has yet to see how some of the team's new faces will fit within the Detroit system. Then again, no one ever died from optimism.

"Simply making the playoffs is not enough anymore," said Wayne Fontes, entering his sixth full season as the head coach of the Lions.

"Our expectations should be higher, our schedule will be tougher, but for us to get to where we want to be, you have to play teams like that. The expectations are going to be high. I can handle it," Fontes said.

Fontes, who has suffered through some lowly seasons with the Lions, including last-place NFC Central finishes in 1990 and '92, may be talking it up because he has to.

These high expectations are not only coming from the fans and players, they are coming from Fontes' boss, team owner and president William Clay Ford.

"I told Wayne, and he agrees, that while we were pleased to have won the NFC Central Division championship, it's time to move to the next level. And I expect that to happen next season," Ford said. "When you are entering the sixth year of any program, you should be talking about getting to the Super Bowl, not simply winning your division. And Wayne feels the same way."

"If we can be satisfied with just winning our division every couple years, then we are cheating ourselves, and more importantly, cheating our fans."

In order to avoid cheating anyone this season, the Lions went out and spent a bundle on a quarterback. Spending a bundle on a signal-caller is nothing new in Detroit — just look at how much cash Andre Ware has been paid since becoming the team's first pick in 1990 — but designating the No. 1 quarterback before the start of the season is new.

Through the past few seasons, Fontes has created and prolonged the league's most notorious QB controversy. Rodney Peete, Ware and Erik Kramer have all been the No. 1 guy, as well as the No. 3 guy, at some point over the past couple years.

But Kramer signed with Chicago and Peete signed with Dallas in free-agent moves, while Ware's future is in doubt, especially with ex-Chief Dave Krieg now on the payroll.

So what about the new man running the offense? Scott Mitchell is being handed the reins with only seven NFL starts under his belt after serving as a backup for Dan Marino in Miami for

PHOTO BY DAVID NELSON

Barry Sanders

four seasons. While filling in for the injured Marino last year, Mitchell, who was the 93rd pick in the 1990 draft, completed 133-of-233 passes for 1,773 yards, 12 touchdowns and eight interceptions.

Those stats, coupled with lots of potential, earned Mitchell a contract worth $11 million over three seasons.

"We're very fortunate to get this young man," Fontes said. "He was the No. 1 free agent available.

"This guy is hopefully the missing piece of the puzzle that one day will put the Detroit Lions in the Super Bowl."

There's that Super Bowl reference again.

Mitchell clearly is happy to have a chance to prove he is worthy of being a playoff-contending team's starting quarterback.

"From the time I was a little kid, I've always dreamed of being a starting quarterback in the NFL," Mitchell said. "I came here to win. I came here to be with people who can win.

"You can't always be conservative. Sometimes you have to take chances. Sometimes you have to throw the big pass," Mitchell added. "I'm 26

1994 PREVIEW ■ DETROIT

years old, I'm big, I'm strong, I can move around. The thing I lack right now is experience."

One position at which the Lions are not lacking in experience is at running back, with one of the game's greatest in Barry Sanders. Last season he rushed for 1,115 yards despite missing the final five regular-season games due to a knee injury. He is only the third player in the history of the NFL to gain over 1,000 yards in each of his first five seasons.

While Sanders was out of commission, RB Derrick Moore filled in extremely well, as did Eric Lynch when Moore was injured.

On the whole, the Lions will use both the run-and-shoot and TE offense under relatively new offensive coordinator Dave Levy, who replaced Dan Henning, who was fired near the end of last season.

Mitchell's primary receivers will be Herman Moore, Brett Perriman and probably No. 1 pick Johnnie Morton. Moore is about to become a star in the league, thanks to his great size, deceptive speed and leaping ability. In '93 Moore caught 61 passes for 935 yards and six touchdowns. Perriman, a free agent re-signed by the Lions for a reported $3.75 million over three years, is effective in the right situations and is considered quicker than his average per catch indicates. And Morton was Detroit's No. 1 draft pick. TE Ron Hall is a new option to the team, having signed as a free agent after playing in Tampa Bay.

Guarding the new quarterback and blocking for Sanders will be an offensive line that was built from expensive free agents prior to the '93 season. The salary cap has already had an effect on keeping this talented group together for '94, with OG Bill Fralic having been cut. Also weighing against the Lions is the loss of offensive line coach Jerry Wampfler.

The Lions will also head into the '94 campaign with a new defensive coordinator, after Hank Bullough opted to leave the professional ranks in favor of a position at Michigan State. Replacing Bullough is former Lion LB coach Herb Paterra. Despite the change, much of the Lions' defensive strategies will remain the same.

Detroit's "D" improved dramatically in 1993 over a dismal showing in '92. The Lions blew several leads in '92, thanks in part to allowing 133 fourth-quarter points. In '93, though, the Lions allowed only 67 fourth-quarter points and did a good job of shutting down the run.

The only free-agent casualties on the defensive side of the ball were CB Ray Crockett and LB Dennis Gibson.

Crockett signed with the Broncos, and his skills will be missed. But the Lions promptly signed CB Robert Massey from the Cardinals as a replacement. In Massey, the Lions end up getting a cornerback on the same talent level as Crockett without having to spend as much cash. Also anchoring the defensive backfield is FS Bennie Blades, who is coming off a broken ankle, which forced him to miss all of last season except for the first four games. S William White will also likely begin the season as a starter, although hard-hitting rookie Van Malone offers solid competition.

LB Chris Spielman is among the league's best, but the departure of Gibson leaves a hole on the inside that the Lions hope ex-Brown Mike Johnson can fill. OLB's Pat Swilling and Tracy Scroggins are back to terrorize opposing quarterbacks with their potent pass rush.

Along the line, DE's Robert Porcher and Kelvin Prichett are effective whether the Lions line up in the 3-4 or the 4-3. NT Marc Spindler is capable and more big and strong than mobile and athletic. Dan Owens can step in and fill any spot along the defensive line when necessary.

One of the stronger areas for the Lions in recent years has been special teams. Although special-team coach Frank Gansz has left for Atlanta, two premier players remain — KR Mel Gray and PK Jason Hanson. But the two are on opposite ends of the NFL age spectrum. Hanson is entering his third NFL season and will only get better, while the 33-year-old Gray is nearing the age when his performance can begin to drop at any time. Hanson made 34-of-43 FG's in '93, and was good on all 25 attempts within 35 yards. As for the Lions' punter, Jim Arnold, who signed with Miami, will be replaced by ex-Oiler Greg Montgomery.

Other than having a new, multimillion-dollar quarterback and exchanging one cornerback for another, much of the personnel will be the same in the Lion camp.

One important note, though, is the make-up of the coaching staff. Despite winning their division twice in three years, three assistant coaches left in the offseason — Wampfler, Gansz and Bullough — which leads some to wonder about the stability of the organization. Also lending credence to the theory of instability under Fontes is the fact that the Lions are on their third defensive coordinator and there have been four offensive-coordinator changes.

It remains to be seen what effects these coaching departures and player changes will have on the Lions. But, as Fontes and Clay said, the time has passed for being happy about winning division titles.

FAST FACTS

■ Wayne Fontes needs 13 victories to become the Lions' all-time winningest head coach. He is currently tied with Joe Schmidt and Monte Clark with 43 wins, behind only Buddy Parker (50) and George Wilson (55).

■ Mel Gray is third on the all-time combined kick-return (kickoff and punt returns) list.

■ Barry Sanders joined Eric Dickerson and Tony Dorsett as the only players to rush for 1,000 yards in each of their first five seasons.

PRO FOOTBALL WEEKLY 1994 ALMANAC

1994 PLAYER ROSTER

NO.	NAME	POS.	HT.	WT.	EXP.	COLLEGE	GP/GS
43	Anderson, Gary	RB	6-1	190	9	Arkansas	10/1
72	Batiste, Raymond	OG	6-4	305	R	NE Louisiana	—
36	Blades, Bennie	S	6-1	221	7	Miami (Fla.)	4/4
66	Bouwens, Shawn	OG	6-4	290	4	Nebraska-Wesleyan	16/1
70	Brown, Ernie	DE	6-2	260	R	Syracuse	—
75	Brown, Lomas	OT	6-4	287	10	Florida	11/11
68	Burton, Leonard	C	6-3	275	9	South Carolina	0/0
50	Caston, Toby	LB	6-1	243	8	Louisiana State	9/0
32	Clay, Willie	CB	5-9	184	3	Georgia Tech	16/1
21	Colon, Harry	S	6-0	203	4	Missouri	15/11
74	Compton, Mike	C-OG	6-6	297	2	West Virginia	8/0
76	Conover, Scott	OG	6-4	285	4	Purdue	1/0
53	Glover, Kevin	C	6-2	282	10	Maryland	16/16
23	Gray, Mel	WR-KR	5-9	171	9	Purdue	11/0
18	Green, Eric	WR-KR	5-10	170	R	Illinois-Benedictine	—
86	Green, Willie	WR	6-2	181	5	Mississippi	16/6
89	Hall, Ron	TE	6-4	245	9	Hawaii	16/16
49	Hallock, Ty	TE	6-3	249	2	Michigan State	16/4
4	Hanson, Jason	PK	5-11	183	3	Washington State	16/0
99	Hayworth, Tracy	LB	6-3	260	5	Tennessee	11/2
82	Holman, Rodney	TE	6-3	238	13	Tulane	16/16
58	Jamison, George	LB	6-1	235	9	Cincinnati	16/16
25	Jeffries, Greg	CB	5-9	184	2	Virginia	7/0
51	Johnson, Mike	LB	6-1	230	9	Virginia Tech	16/16
61	Jones, Jason	OG	6-3	282	R	Hampton Institute	—
57	Jones, Victor	ILB	6-2	256	7	Virginia Tech	16/1
52	Kowalkowski, Scott	LB	6-2	228	3	Notre Dame	0/0
17	Krieg, Dave	QB	6-1	202	15	Milton	12/5
55	London, Antonio	LB	6-2	234	2	Alabama	14/0
16	Long, Chuck	QB	6-4	217	8	Iowa	0/0
73	Lutz, Dave	OG-OT	6-6	305	12	Georgia Tech	16/16
26	Lynch, Eric	RB	5-10	224	2	Grand Valley State	4/2
40	Massey, Robert	CB	5-11	195	7	North Carolina Central	10/10
83	Matthews, Aubrey	WR	5-7	165	9	Delta State	15/1
33	McKyer, Tim	CB	6-0	174	9	Texas-Arlington	15/3
47	McNeil, Ryan	CB	6-0	175	2	Miami (Fla.)	16/2
19	Mitchell, Scott	QB	6-6	230	5	Utah	13/7
31	Moore, Derrick	RB	6-1	227	3	NE Oklahoma St.	13/3
84	Moore, Herman	WR	6-3	210	4	Virginia	15/15
90	Owens, Dan	DE	6-3	280	5	Southern Cal	15/11
80	Perriman, Brett	WR	5-9	180	7	Miami (Fla.)	15/15
91	Porcher, Robert	DE	6-3	283	3	South Carolina St.	16/5
34	Powers, Ricky	RB	6-0	205	R	Michigan	—
94	Pritchett, Kelvin	DE	6-2	281	4	Mississippi	16/5
67	Richards, David	OG	6-5	310	7	UCLA	15/15
48	Roberts, Ray	TE	6-2	251	R	Northern Illinois	—
63	Rodenhauser, Mark	C	6-5	280	7	Illinois State	16/0
40	Ryans, Larry	WR	5-11	182	1	Clemson	0/0
20	Sanders, Barry	RB	5-8	203	6	Oklahoma State	11/11
38	Scott, Kevin	CB	5-9	175	4	Stanford	12/10
59	Scroggins, Tracy	LB	6-2	255	3	Tulsa	16/0
54	Spielman, Chris	ILB	6-0	247	7	Ohio State	16/16
92	Spindler, Marc	DL	6-5	290	5	Pittsburgh	16/16
56	Swilling, Pat	LB	6-3	242	9	Georgia Tech	14/14
71	Tharpe, Larry	OT	6-4	299	3	Tennessee State	5/3

1994 PREVIEW ■ DETROIT

1994 PLAYER ROSTER

NO.	NAME	POS.	HT.	WT.	EXP.	COLLEGE	GP/GS
81	Thompson, Marty	TE	6-3	243	2	Fresno State	7/2
92	Travis, Mack	NT	6-1	280	2	California	4/0
35	White, William	S	5-10	191	7	Ohio State	16/16
64	Wilson, James	DE	6-3	253	R	Tennessee	—
44	Woodley, Richard	WR	5-9	180	R	Texas Christian	—

'94 DRAFT PICKS

RD.	NAME	POS.	HT.	WT.	COLLEGE
1.	Morton, Johnnie	WR	6-0	190	Southern Cal
2.	Malone, Van	DB	5-11	190	Texas
3.	Bonham, Shane	DT	6-2	275	Tennessee
4.	Bryant, Vaughn	DB	5-9	178	Stanford
5.	Semple, Tony	OG	6-4	287	Memphis State
6.	Borgella, Jocelyn	DB	5-10	182	Cincinnati
7.	Beer, Thomas	LB	6-2	238	Wayne State (Mich.)

PRO FOOTBALL WEEKLY 1994 ALMANAC

TEAM AT A GLANCE

TEAM DIRECTORY

Address	Pontiac Silverdome 1200 Featherstone Road Pontiac, Michigan 48342 (313) 335-4131
Stadium	Pontiac Silverdome 1200 Featherstone Road Pontiac, Michigan 48342 Capacity: 80,500 Playing surface: AstroTurf
Training Camp	Pontiac Silverdome 1200 Featherstone Road Pontiac, Michigan 43842
Colors	Honolulu blue and silver
Television	WKBD, Channel 50
Radio	WWJ, 950 AM

ADMINISTRATION
President-owner: William Clay Ford
Executive vice president-COO: Chuck Schmidt
Vice president-administration: Bill Keenist
Treasurer: William Clay Ford Jr.
Controller: Tom Lesnau
Secretary-legal counsel: Frederick C. Nash
Director of player personnel: Ron Hughes
Director of pro personnel: Kevin Colbert
Media relations coordinator: Mike Murray
Director of marketing: Steve Harms
Director of marketing, sales, tickets: Fred Otto
Director of community relations: Tim Pendell
Trainer: Kent Falb

1994 SCHEDULE

Preseason
AUG. 5	N.Y. JETS	7:30
AUG. 13	at Cleveland	7:30
AUG. 19	ARIZONA	7:30
AUG. 26	at Cincinnati	7:30

Regular season
SEP. 4	ATLANTA	1:00
SEP. 11	at Minnesota	12:00
SEP. 19	at Dallas (Mon.)	8:00
SEP. 25	NEW ENGLAND	4:00
OCT. 2	at Tampa Bay	1:00
OCT. 9	SAN FRANCISCO	1:00
OCT. 16	OPEN DATE	
OCT. 23	CHICAGO	1:00
OCT. 30	at N.Y. Giants	1:00
NOV. 6	vs. Green Bay at Milw.	12:00
NOV. 13	TAMPA BAY	8:00
NOV. 20	at Chicago	12:00
NOV. 24	BUFFALO (Thanks.)	12:30
DEC. 4	GREEN BAY	1:00
DEC. 10	at N.Y. Jets (Sat.)	2:30
DEC. 17	MINNESOTA (Sat.)	12:30
DEC. 25	at Miami	8:00

HEAD COACH
Wayne Fontes
Following the 1988 season Fontes was awarded the Lions' head-coaching position after he led the team to a 2-3 record as interim head coach. In his tenure, Fontes has led the Lions to NFC Central Division championships in 1991 and '93, and accumulated an overall record of 43-45. In '91, the Lions went 12-4 in the regular season and advanced to the NFC championship game. The 12-win mark was a franchise record for most victories in a single season. Before going to Detroit, Fontes was an assistant coach at Tampa Bay, and had brief stays at three major universities.
Previous NFL: defensive coordinator, Detroit 1985-1988; defensive coordinator, Tampa Bay 1982-84; secondary, Tampa Bay 1976-81.
Previous college: defensive backfield, Southern Cal 1972-75; defensive backfield, Iowa 1969-71; defensive backfield, Dayton 1968.
Player: NFL, defensive back, N.Y. Jets, 1962. College, defensive back, Michigan State 1960-61.

ASSISTANT COACHES
Don Clemons: outside linebackers
Previous NFL: outside linebackers, 1985-93 Detroit. Player: No NFL. College: defensive end, 1973-76 Muehlenberg College.
Paul Boudreau: offensive line
Previous NFL: offensive line, 1987-93 New Orleans. Player: No NFL. College: guard, 1971-73 Boston College.
Steve Kazor: special teams
Previous NFL: special teams-tight ends, 1982-92 Chicago; 1979-81 Dallas. Player: No NFL. College: Nose tackle, Westminster.
Lamar Leachman: defensive line
Previous NFL: defensive line, 1990-93 Detroit; 1980-89 N.Y. Giants. Player: No NFL. College: center, linebacker, 1952-55 Tennessee.
Dave Levy: offensive coordinator
Previous NFL: offensive assistant, 1989-93 Detroit; 1980-88 San Diego. Player: No NFL. College: guard, 1952-53 UCLA.
Billie Matthews: running backs
Previous NFL: running backs, 1989-93 Detroit; 1987-88 Kansas City; 1985-85 Indianapolis, 1983-84 Philadelphia; 1979-82 San Francisco. Player: No NFL. College: quarterback, 1948-51 Southern U.
Tom Moore: quarterbacks
Previous NFL: wide receivers, 1990-93 Minnesota; 1977-89 Pittsburgh. Player: No NFL. College: quarterback, 1957-60 Iowa.
Herb Paterra: defensive coordinator
Previous NFL: inside linebackers, 1989-93 Detroit; 1987-88 Tampa Bay; 1986 Buffalo; 1984-85 Green Bay, 1980-82 L.A. Rams. Player: NFL, linebacker, 1963-64 Buffalo. College: offensive guard, linebacker, 1960-62 Michigan State.
Charlie Sanders: receivers
Previous NFL: receivers, 1989-93 Detroit. Player: NFL, tight end, 1968-77 Detroit. College: tight end, 1966-67 Minnesota.
Howard Tippett: inside linebackers
Previous NFL: special teams-tight ends, 1992-

1994 PREVIEW ■ DETROIT

TEAM AT A GLANCE

93 L.A. Rams; 1988-91 Green Bay; 1981-86 Tampa Bay. Player: No NFL. College: quarterback-safety, 1956-58 East Tennessee State.

COACHING RECORDS
(includes postseason games)

Years	Coach	W	L	T
1930	Hal "Tubby" Griffen	5	6	3
1931-36	Potsy Clark	49	20	6
1937-38	Dutch Clark	14	8	0
1939	Elmer "Gus" Henderson	6	5	0
1940	Potsy Clark	5	5	1
1941-42	Bill Edwards	4	9	1
1942	John Karcis	0	8	0
1943-47	Gus Dorais	20	31	2
1948-50	Alvin "Bo" McMillin	12	24	0
1951-56	Buddy Parker	50	24	2
1957-64	George Wilson	55	45	6
1965-66	Harry Gilmer	10	16	2
1967-72	Joe Schmidt	43	35	7
1973	Don McCafferty	6	7	1
1974-76	Rick Forzano	15	17	0
1976-77	Tommy Hudspeth	11	13	0
1978-84	Monte Clark	43	63	1
1985-88	Darryl Rogers	18	40	0
1988-93	Wayne Fontes	43	45	0

HISTORICAL HIGHLIGHTS

1930 The Portsmouth (Ohio) Spartans join the NFL.
1934 The team is moved to Detroit and the name is changed to the Lions. The Lions play their first NFL game before a crowd of 12,000 at the University of Detroit Stadium, beating the New York Giants 9-0.
1935 The Lions take the Western Division crown, then win their first championship, defeating the New York Giants 26-7.
1948 Lyle Fife and Edwin J. Anderson head a syndicate which purchases the Detroit franchise for $185,000. Alvin "Bo" McMillin is named general manager and head coach.
1952 Detroit wins a conference title by defeating Los Angeles 31-21. The Lions defeat the Browns, 17-7, before a Cleveland crowd of 50,934 to win their first NFL championship since 1935.
1953 A 17-16 decision over Cleveland in Detroit gives the Lions their second straight NFL title before a crowd of 54,577.
1957 Detroit stages a great come-from-behind win in a playoff game for the Western Conference title, scoring 24 points in the second half to beat the 49ers ... The Lions claim their fourth NFL championship, slaughtering Cleveland 59-14, in front of 55,263 fans.
1961 William Clay Ford is elected president of the Lions' organization. Ford purchases the franchise for $4.5 million and takes over as the sole owner.
1970 In their first playoff game since 1957, the Lions, 10-4 for the season, lose to Dallas 5-0.
1971 Steve Owens becomes the first Lion to rush for more than 1,000 yards in a season, (1,035 on 246 carries).
1975 Detroit plays the first game in its new home, the Pontiac Silverdome, before a record crowd of 79,784, but lose to the Cowboys 26-10.

1982-83 After making it to the special playoff tournament because of the strike-shortened season, Detroit falls to the Redskins 31-7.
1983 The Lions win the NFC Central Division with a 9-7 record. Then, in their second playoff appearance in two years, they lose to the San Francisco 49ers 24-23 when a last second field-goal attempt fails.
1988 Wayne Fontes is named head coach, the 17th in club history.
1991-92 The Lions win 12 regular-season games, the most in team history, and capture the NFC Central division title ... Detroit hosts its first playoff game ever in the Silverdome and its first home playoff game since 1957. The Lions defeat the Dallas Cowboys 38-6 ... The Lions meet the Redskins for the NFC title in Washington but lose 41-10.
1992 RB Barry Sanders becomes Detroit's all-time leading rusher when he surpasses Billy Sims' record of 5,106 yards.
1993-94 The Lions post a 10-6 record and capture the NFC Central title ... Barry Sanders becomes only the third running back in NFL history to rush for 1,000 or more yards in his first five seasons ... Detroit faces divisional rival Green Bay in the playoffs but loses 28-24.

85

PRO FOOTBALL WEEKLY 1994 ALMANAC

TEAM AT A GLANCE

HALL OF FAME MEMBERS

	Yrs with Lions	Inducted
QB Dutch Clark*	1931-32, 34-38	1963
RB Bill Dudley	1947-49	1966
QB Bobby Layne	1950-58	1967
C-LB Alex Wojciechowicz	1938-46	1968
DB Jack Christiansen	1951-58	1970
LB Joe Schmidt	1953-65	1973
CB Dick "Night Train" Lane	1960-65	1974
S-P Yale Lary	1952-53, 56-64	1979
RB Doak Walker	1950-55	1986
CB Lem Barney	1967-77	1992

* Charter member

RETIRED JERSEY NUMBERS

- 7 QB Dutch Clark
- 22 QB Bobby Layne
- 37 RB Doak Walker
- 56 LB Joe Schmidt
- 85 WR Chuck Hughes
- 88 TE Charlie Sanders

FIRST-ROUND DRAFT CHOICES
(since 1980)

Year	Selection	College
1980	RB Billy Sims	Oklahoma
1981	WR Mark Nichols	Southern Cal
1982	LB Jimmy Williams	Nebraska
1983	FB James Jones	Florida
1984	TE David Lewis	California
1985	OT Lomas Brown	Florida
1986	QB Chuck Long	Iowa
1987	DE Reggie Rogers	Washington
1988	DB Bennie Blades	Miami (Fla.)
1989	RB Barry Sanders	Oklahoma State
1990	QB Andre Ware	Southern Cal
1991	WR Herman Moore	Virginia
1992	DL Robert Porcher	South Carolina St.
1993	No choice	
1994	WR Johnnie Morton	UCLA

RECORD VS. OTHER NFL TEAMS
(includes postseason games)

	Record
Arizona Cardinals	27-16-5
Atlanta Falcons	17-5-0
Buffalo Bills	2-1-1
Chicago Bears	49-74-5
Cincinnati Bengals	3-3-0
Cleveland Browns	14-4-0
Dallas Cowboys	6-8-0
Denver Broncos	3-4-0
Green Bay Packers	56-65-7
Houston Oilers	2-4-0
Indianapolis Colts	17-17-2
Kansas City Chiefs	3-4-0
Los Angeles Raiders	2-5-0
Los Angeles Rams	36-39-1
Miami Dolphins	2-2-0
Minnesota Vikings	23-40-2
New England Patriots	3-2-0
New Orleans Saints	6-7-1
New York Giants	18-15-1
New York Jets	3-3-0
Philadelphia Eagles	12-9-2
Pittsburgh Steelers	13-11-1
San Diego Chargers	3-2-0
San Francisco 49ers	26-27-1
Seattle Seahawks	2-4-0
Tampa Bay Buccaneers	16-16-0
Washington Redskins	8-24-0

YEAR-BY-YEAR RECORDS

Year	Won	Lost	Tied
1930	5	6	3
1931	11	3	0
1932	6	2	4
1933	6	5	0
1934	10	3	0
1935*	7	3	2
1936	8	4	0
1937	7	4	0
1938	7	4	0
1939	6	5	0
1940	5	5	1
1941	4	6	1
1942	0	11	0
1943	3	6	1
1944	6	3	1
1945	7	3	0
1946	1	10	0
1947	3	9	0
1948	2	10	0
1949	4	8	0
1950	6	6	0
1951	7	4	1
1952*	9	3	0
1953*	10	2	0
1954**	9	2	1
1955	3	9	0
1956	9	3	0
1957*	8	4	0
1958	4	7	1
1959	3	8	1
1960	7	5	0
1961	8	5	1
1962	11	3	0
1963	5	8	1
1964	7	5	2
1965	6	7	1
1966	4	9	1
1967	5	7	2
1968	4	8	2
1969	9	4	1
1970	10	4	0
1971	7	6	1
1972	8	5	1
1973	6	7	1
1974	7	7	0
1975	7	7	0
1976	6	8	0
1977	6	8	0
1978	7	9	0
1979	2	14	0
1980	9	7	0
1981	8	8	0
1982**	4	5	0
1983**	9	7	0
1984	4	11	1
1985	7	9	0
1986	5	11	0
1987	4	11	0
1988	4	12	0
1989	7	9	0
1990	6	10	0
1991**	12	4	0
1992	5	11	0
1993**	10	6	0
Total	402	415	32

Number of NFL championships   4
Number of years .500 or better   34
Number of years below .500   30

*NFL champions
**Playoff team

1994 PREVIEW ■ DETROIT

RECORDS

INDIVIDUAL

Service
Seasons played	15	Wayne Walker (1958-72)
Games played	200	Wayne Walker (1958-72)

Scoring
Points, career	1,113	Eddie Murray (1980-91)
Points, season	130	Jason Hanson (1993)
Points, game	24	Doak Walker (11/19/50)
		Cloyce Box (12/3/50)
		Barry Sanders (11/24/91)
Touchdowns, career	60	Barry Sanders (1989-93)
Touchdowns, season	17	Barry Sanders (1991)
Touchdowns, game	4	Dutch Clark (10/22/34)
		Cloyce Box (12/3/50)
		Barry Sanders (11/24/91)
Field goals, career	244	Eddie Murray (1980-91)
Field goals, season	34	Jason Hanson (1993)
Field goals, game	6	Garo Yepremian (11/13/66)
Extra points, career	384	Eddie Murray (1980-91)
Exta points, season	46	Eddie Murray (1981)
Extra points, game	8	Jim Martin (12/29/57)

Rushing
Yards, career	6,789	Barry Sanders (1989-93)
Yards, season	1,548	Barry Sanders (1991)
Yards, game	220	Barry Sanders (11/24/91)
Attempts, career	1,432	Barry Sanders (1989-93)
Attempts, season	342	Barry Sanders (1991)
Attempts, game	36	Billy Sims (11/20/83)
		James Jones (10/27/85)
		James Jones (9/7/86)
Touchdowns, career	55	Barry Sanders (1989-93)
Touchdowns, season	16	Barry Sanders (1991)
Touchdowns, game	4	Barry Sanders (11/24/91)

Passing
Completions, career	1,074	Bobby Layne (1950-58)
Completions, season	252	Gary Danielson (1984))
Completions, game	33	Eric Hipple (9/28/86)
		Chuck Long (10/25/87)
Yards, career	15,710	Bobby Layne (1950-58)
Yards, season	3,223	Gary Danielson (1980)
Yards, game	374	Bobby Layne (11/5/50)
Attempts, career	2,193	Bobby Layne (1950-58)
Attempts, season	417	Gary Danielson (1980)
Attempts, game	50	Eric Hipple (10/19/86)
Touchdowns, career	118	Bobby Layne (1950-58)
Touchdowns, season	26	Bobby Layne (1951)
Touchdowns, game	5	Gary Danielson (12/9/78)

Receiving
Receptions, career	336	Charlie Sanders (1968-77)
Receptions, season	77	James Jones (1984)
Receptions, game	12	Cloyce Box (12/3/50)
		James Jones (9/28/86)
Yards, career	5,220	Gail Cogdill (1960-68)
Yards, season	1,266	Pat Studstill (1966)
Yards, game	302	Cloyce Box (12/3/50)
Touchdowns, career	35	Terry Barr (1957-65)
		Leonard Thompson (1975-86)
Touchdowns, season	15	Cloyce Box (1952)
Touchdowns, game	4	Cloyce Box (12/3/50)

Interceptions
Career	62	Dick LeBeau (1959-72)
Season	12	Don Doll (1950)
		Jack Christiansen (1953)
Game	4	Don Doll (10/23/49)

Longest plays
Run from scrimmage	96	Bob Hoernschemeyer (TD, 11/23/50)
Pass play	99	Karl Sweetan to Pat Studstill (TD, 10/16/66)
Field goal	54	Eddie Murray (12/11/83)
		Glenn Presnell (10/7/34)
Interception return	102	Bob Smith (TD, 11/24/49)
Kickoff return	104	Terry Barr (92) & Gene Gedman (12) (TD, 10/26/58)
Punt return	90	Tommy Watkins (TD, 10/6/63)
Punt	85	Bill Shepherd (11/15/36)

Top scorers
	Points
Eddie Murray (1980-91)	1,113
Errol Mann (1969-76)	636
Doak Walker (1950-55)	534
Barry Sanders (1989-93)	360
Wayne Walker (1958-72)	345
Billy Sims (1980-84)	282

Top rushers
	Yards
Barry Sanders (1989-93)	6,789
Billy Sims (1980-84)	5,106
Dexter Bussey (1974-84)	5,105
Altie Taylor (1969-76)	4,297
Nick Pietrosante (1959-65)	3,933
James Jones (1983-88)	3,452

Top passers
	Completions
Bobby Layne (1950-58)	1,074
Greg Landry (1968-78)	957
Gary Danielson (1976-84)	952
Eric Hipple (1980-89)	830
Bill Munson (1968-76)	716
Milt Plum (1962-67)	671

Top passers
	Yards
Bobby Layne (1950-58)	15,710
Greg Landry (1968-78)	12,457
Gary Danielson (1976-84)	11,885
Eric Hipple (1980-89)	8,787
Milt Plum (1962-67)	8,536
Bill Munson (1968-76)	8,451

Top receivers
	Receptions
Charlie Sanders (1968-77)	336
Gail Cogdill (1960-68)	325
Jim Gibbons (1958-68)	287
James Jones (1983-88)	285
Leonard Thompson (1975-86)	277
David Hill (1976-82)	245

Top receivers
	Yards
Gail Cogdill (1960-68)	5,220
Charlie Sanders (1968-77)	4,817
Leonard Thompson (1975-86)	4,682
Terry Barr (1957-65)	3,810
Fred Scott (1978-83)	3,651
Jim Gibbons (1958-68)	3,561

Most interceptions
	No.
Dick LeBeau (1959-72)	62
Lem Barney (1967-77)	56
Yale Lary (1952-53, 1956-64)	50
Jack Christiansen (1951-58)	46
Jim David (1952-59)	36
Bob Smith (1949-53)	29

87

PRO FOOTBALL WEEKLY 1994 ALMANAC

PREVIEW: GREEN BAY PACKERS

Whether or not the Packers can take it to the next level as a team would appear to be directly tied to whether Brett Favre can take it to the next level as a quarterback.

"I'm convinced he will," said Packer head coach Mike Holmgren.

If Favre does, the Packers should improve on last season's 9-7 record, when they made the playoffs for the first time since 1982. In fact, they won a playoff game, bounced back from some devastating defeats and overcame a seemingly endless string of injuries. However, the Packers still seem to be a few pieces shy of challenging for the top spot in the NFL, which makes Favre's progress all the more important.

Holmgren may be convinced that Favre is ready to take the next step, but that is anything but a certainty. In 1992 Favre was a phenom, completing 302-of-471 passes for 3,227 yards, with 18 touchdowns and 13 interceptions. However, last year he looked more like a first-year starter, leading the league in interceptions and turnovers.

"He took us to the playoffs," said Holmgren. "He played the whole season. He played hurt. He threw and completed more passes than anybody in football. He had 20 TD passes.

"The statistic that people will talk about, unfortunately, will be his interceptions. The only stat where he is not consistent, where you could even question his consistency, is his interceptions. To take his game to the next level, which he can do, he has got to deal with those decision-making problems which occurred on occasion."

Favre has ideal size and stature, a bazooka arm, great toughness and leadership qualities and the ability to turn a busted play into a big play. However, until he improves his decision making and stops getting sidetracked, he will continue to mix big plays with bad plays. Favre must learn when to throw the ball away.

There are some scouts who hold the viewpoint that five years from now Favre will be the same erratic player.

"He was a big disappointment," said one NFC personnel executive. "He didn't improve one bit. Come game time he is the same raw, crazy guy. He made some great plays on the run, but he still feels he has to make the play all the time. He's just so unconventional. He'll throw sidearm, almost underhanded at times. He releases the ball from anywhere. He's still a sandlot guy."

Once again, Favre's favorite receiver figures to be Sterling Sharpe. Despite playing hurt and usually being double-teamed last year, Sharpe had a phenomenal season. He caught 112 passes for 1,274 yards and 11 touchdowns. Over 80 percent of his catches come within 10-15 yards of the line of scrimmage, but he does a terrific job of gaining yardage after the reception. He has tremendous strength, and, while he will drop some easy catches, he makes the seemingly impossible grabs and takes great pride in his work. Finding a second receiver to go with Sharpe has been a problem. That is not a problem at tight end, however, where Jackie Harris is one of the league's best pass catchers at the position and has become a decent blocker. Harris has enough speed to get deep and can really cause problems for a defense, but he does have a few careless drops.

Running back has been a problem for the Packers. However, after signing ex-Buccaneer free-agent Reggie Cobb and drafting LeShon Johnson out of Northern Illinois, the picture looks much brighter. Cobb is expected to start at running back, and he's a powerful runner if he can stay healthy. Johnson is a tough, fast runner, but he's not very elusive and doesn't catch well. Last

Sterling Sharpe

1994 PREVIEW ■ GREEN BAY

year, after John Stephens failed to get the job done and Eric Dickerson failed his physical, Green Bay went with former first-round disappointment Darrell Thompson. Thompson's future as a Packer is now considered shaky. FB Edgar Bennett was acceptable but not extraordinary, though he did score 10 touchdowns. He is not as big or powerful as the Packers would like, but he does catch the ball well and can pick and slide inside.

Along the offensive line, once you get past OLT Ken Ruettgers and ORG Harry Galbreath, the questions begin. But No. 1 pick OT Aaron Taylor, considered the best offensive linemen available in the draft by many, should provide some quick answers. Ruettgers is a very solid and technically sound tackle who overcomes limited athletic ability with preparation and anticipation. Galbreath did a good job last year, but he is short, has a reputation as a holder and had trouble keeping his weight up last year. After James Campen got hurt, Frank Winters stepped in at center and had a very solid year. Former DL Joe Sims could start at right tackle or left guard if he can keep his weight under 320 pounds. A good athlete, Sims started six games last year after Tootie Robbins was injured. Powerful Earl Dotson has a lot of potential. If the Packers get in a bind, the 36-year-old Robbins may have another year left. Nonetheless, the Packers would prefer to go with a younger player.

The Packers made great strides on defense last season. The big question is whether they can repeat that performance without defensive coordinator Ray Rhodes. Under Rhodes last year, the Packers improved from 23rd to second in total defense. Rhodes has since left the team to rejoin the 49ers. Another question is: Just how good was the Packer defense last season? After all, it did give up 177 second-half points, and most of its games were against weak offensive teams like the Bears, Lions, Buccaneers and Vikings. The team's new coordinator is Fritz Shurmur, who has long been known for his innovative schemes.

The star of the defense is DE Reggie White. After a slow start in '93, he had a Pro Bowl year and led the team in sacks with 13. However, he seemed to wear down late in the season and was unable to put back-to-back games together down the stretch. White is still an awesome pass rusher and a force against the run. He is a team leader and makes the players around him better, but he is 32 years old, no longer runs a 4.8 in the 40 and no longer can dominate on a weekly basis. White will be helped by the offseason signing of former Oiler free-agent Sean Jones. From the DRE spot, Jones will force opponents to pay less attention to White. NT John Jurkovic is coming off a solid season in which he appeared to be much quicker after dropping weight. For a nose tackle, he was a very productive pass rusher last year. After moving from left end to right, Matt Brock saw his production slip, and he did not apply the pressure the Packers had hoped for. Nonetheless, Brock was a decent starter in '92 and could bounce back in a backup role.

At linebacker, the Packers suffered a major loss when Tony Bennett signed with the Colts as a free agent. His pass-rushing skills will be missed. By the end of last year, ILB Johnny Holland was almost all the way back from a severe neck injury that he suffered a season earlier. He is a pumped-up, undersized player who relies on speed, range and instincts. OLB Wayne Simmons missed valuable time because of injury but still had a solid season. He has 4.6 speed, superb athletic ability, can play the run at or away from him, rushes the passer and can drop into coverage. This year the Packers are going to be looking for more big plays from him. Bryce Paup may have only 5.0 speed, but he gets the job done. Last season he had 74 tackles and 11 sacks. Paup has excellent size and instincts and a knack for getting around blockers on the corner, but he gets swallowed up when he rushes from inside. Versatile George Koonce also gets the job done despite size limitations and some trouble shedding blocks. He is very active and aggressive, and the Packers were really hampered when he was injured late last year. Former second-round draft choice Mark D'Onofrio has repeatedly been slowed by injuries.

In the secondary, there is no question that Terrell Buckley has great talent, but he must start making more big plays and fewer bad ones. Buckley has exceptional quickness and speed and can still become a top cover man, but, in his first two seasons in the NFL, he has been burned badly because his technique is sloppy and he keeps putting himself in bad positions by gambling and guessing so much. Roland Mitchell would be a better nickel cornerback than a starter. Sammy Walker has the speed and toughness to be a big-time cornerback, but he must start making plays on the ball and show better instincts. SS LeRoy Butler is coming off a great season in which he intercepted six passes and did a nice job of covering tight ends and slot receivers. FS George Teague has superior range and a knack for the big play.

The Packer special teams are really helped by PK Chris Jacke. Green Bay can be a tough place to kick, but Jacke made all 35 of his PAT attempts and 31-of-37 field goals. P Bryan Wagner was not as consistent as the Packers would like, and he could be challenged by Craig Hentrich. The Packers excelled returning kickoffs last season, when Corey Harris averaged 30.1 yards on 16 returns and Robert Brooks averaged 26.6 on 23 returns. However, the team's kick coverage units were only average the second half of last season.

FAST FACTS

■ DE Reggie White has 137 sacks in 137 career games.

■ Sterling Sharpe became the first player in NFL history to catch 100 passes in two seasons. Sharpe caught 112 passes last season and had 108 receptions in 1992.

■ QB Brett Favre threw an NFL-high 24 interceptions in 1993.

1994 PLAYER ROSTER

NO.	NAME	POS.	HT.	WT.	EXP.	COLLEGE	GP/GS
51	Barker, Tony	LB	6-2	235	2	Rice	0/0
34	Bennett, Edgar	RB	6-0	216	3	Florida State	16/14
61	Bierman, Randy	OT	6-5	298	R	Illinois	—
62	Brock, Matt	DE-NT	6-6	280	6	Oregon	16/12
87	Brooks, Robert	WR	6-0	174	3	South Carolina	14/0
71	Brown, Gilbert	NT	6-2	330	2	Kansas	2/0
25	Brown, Victor	S	6-2	208	R	Tennessee	—
8	Brunell, Mark	QB	6-1	208	2	Washington	0/0
27	Buckley, Terrell	CB	5-9	174	3	Florida State	16/16
69	Burgess, Yuseff	LB	6-1	240	R	Wisconsin	—
36	Butler, LeRoy	DB	6-0	193	5	Florida State	16/16
63	Campen, James	C	6-3	280	8	Tulane	4/4
89	Chmura, Mark	TE	6-5	242	3	Boston College	14/0
32	Cobb, Reggie	RB	6-0	215	5	Tennessee	12/10
54	Coleman, Keo	LB	6-1	255	3	Mississippi State	12/2
21	Cotton, Curtis	S	6-0	212	1	Nebraska	0/0
10	Cox, Johnnie	WR	5-10	185	R	Fort Lewis (Colo.)	—
82	Crawford, Lionell	WR	5-10	185	1	Wisconsin	0/0
99	Davey, Don	DE	6-4	270	4	Wisconsin	9/0
40	Dean, Charlie	TE	6-3	246	R	Florida	—
11	Detmer, Ty	QB	6-0	190	3	Brigham Young	3/0
32	Dingle, Mike	FB	6-2	240	3	South Carolina	0/0
58	D'Onofrio, Mark	LB	6-2	235	3	Penn State	0/0
72	Dotson, Earl	OT	6-4	315	2	Texas A&I	13/0
98	Eller, Matt	DE	6-5	275	1	Bethel College (Minn)	0/0
33	Evans, Doug	CB	6-1	188	2	Louisiana Tech	16/0
93	Evans, Mike	DE	6-3	270	2	Michigan	—
4	Favre, Brett	QB	6-2	218	4	S. Mississippi	16/16
65	Fisher, John	C	6-3	270	1	Tennessee	0/0
16	Frazier, Daryl	WR	6-1	181	R	Florida	—
76	Galbreath, Harry	OG	6-1	275	7	Tennessee	16/16
30	Harris, Corey	DB	5-11	195	3	Vanderbilt	11/0
80	Harris, Jackie	TE	6-3	243	5	NE Louisiana	12/12
83	Harris, Willie	WR	6-2	194	1	Mississippi State	0/0
24	Hauck, Tim	S	5-11	185	5	Montana	13/0
17	Hentrich, Craig	P-PK	6-3	200	1	Notre Dame	0/0
26	Holt, Reggie	S	5-11	205	R	Wisconsin	—
70	Hope, Charles	OG-OT	6-3	308	1	Central (Ohio) State	0/0
67	Hutchins, Paul	OT	6-5	335	2	Western Michigan	1/0
13	Jacke, Chris	PK	6-0	200	6	Texas-El Paso	16/0
96	Jones, Sean	DE	6-7	268	11	Northeastern	16/16
64	Jurkovic, John	NT	6-2	285	3	Eastern Illinois	16/12
77	Jurkovic, Mirko	OG	6-4	290	2	Notre Dame	0/0
53	Koonce, George	LB	6-1	238	3	East Carolina	15/15
78	LaBounty, Matt	DE	6-4	254	2	Oregon	—
85	Lewis, Ron	WR	5-11	189	5	Florida State	9/0
22	McGill, Lenny	CB	6-2	194	R	Arizona State	—
44	McNabb, Dexter	FB	6-2	245	3	Florida	16/0
97	Merriweather, Mike	LB	6-2	228	12	Pacific	0/0
94	Mersereau, Scott	NT	6-3	275	8	Southern Conneticut	13/13
47	Mitchell, Roland	CB	5-11	195	7	Texas Tech	16/16
81	Morgan, Anthony	WR	6-1	195	4	Tennessee	2/0
95	Paup, Bryce	LB	6-5	247	5	Northern Iowa	15/14
69	Perez, Chris	OT	6-6	295	1	Kansas	0/0
45	Prior, Mike	S	6-0	215	9	Illinois State	16/4

1994 PREVIEW ■ GREEN BAY

1994 PLAYER ROSTER

NO.	NAME	POS.	HT.	WT.	EXP.	COLLEGE	GP/GS
73	Robbins, Tootie	OT	6-5	315	13	East Carilina	12/11
75	Ruettgers, Ken	OT	6-6	290	10	Southern Cal	16/16
65	Shackerford, Lamark	NT	6-0	255	R	Wisconsin	—
84	Sharpe, Sterling	WR	6-1	210	7	South Carolina	16/16
61	Showell, Malcolm	DE	6-6	275	1	Delaware State	0/0
59	Simmons, Wayne	LB	6-3	240	2	Clemson	14//8
68	Sims, Joe	OT	6-3	310	4	Nebraska	13/5
55	Smith, LeRoy	LB	6-0	230	1	Iowa	0/0
31	Teague, George	DB	6-1	187	2	Alabama	16/12
9	Wagner, Bryan	P	6-2	200	7	Northridge State	16/0
23	Walker, Sammy	CB	5-11	203	4	Texas Tech	8/1
12	Warner, Kurt	QB	6-2	204	R	Northern Iowa	—
86	West, Ed	TE	6-1	245	11	Auburn	16/7
92	White, Reggie	DE	6-5	290	10	Tennessee	16/16
74	Widell, Doug	OG	6-4	280	6	Boston College	16/9
20	Williams, Kevin	RB	6-1	215	2	UCLA	3/0
43	Williams, Mark	LB	6-3	236	R	Ohio State	—
56	Willis, James	LB	6-2	235	2	Auburn	13/0
41	Wilner, Jeff	TE	6-5	253	R	Wesleyan (Conn.)	—
29	Wilson, Marcus	RB	6-1	210	3	Virginia	16/0
52	Winters, Frank	C-OG	6-3	285	8	Western Illinois	16/16
60	Zeno, Lance	C	6-4	279	3	UCLA	6/0

'94 DRAFT PICKS

RD.	NAME	POS.	HT.	WT.	COLLEGE
1.	Taylor, Aaron	OT	6-4	307	Notre Dame
3.	Johnson, LeShon	RB	5-11	203	Northern Illinois
4.	Wilkins, Gabe	DE	6-5	294	Gardner-Webb (N.C.)
5.	Mickens, Terry	WR	6-1	203	Florida A&M
5.	Levens, Dorsey	RB	6-1	229	Georgia Tech
6.	Kearney, Jay	WR	6-1	191	West Virginia
6.	Hamilton, Ruffin	LB	6-0	229	Tulane
6.	Schroeder, Bill	WR	6-1	195	Wisconsin-LaCrosse
6.	Duckworth, Paul	LB	6-1	245	Connecticut

PRO FOOTBALL WEEKLY 1994 ALMANAC

TEAM AT A GLANCE

TEAM DIRECTORY

Address	1265 Lombardi Avenue Green Bay, Wisconsin 54307 (414) 496-5700
Stadium	Lambeau Field 1265 Lombardi Avenue Green Bay, Wisconsin 54307 Capacity: 59,543
	Milwaukee County Stadium Highway I-94 Milwaukee, Wisconsin 53214 Capacity: 56,051
	Playing surfaces: Grass
Training Camp	St. Norbert College West DePere, Wisconsin 54115
Colors	Dark green, gold and white
Television	WGBA, Channel 26
Radio	WTMJ, 620 AM

ADMINISTRATION
President-chief executive officer: Bob Harlan
Exec. vice president-general manager: Ron Wolf
Chief financial officer: Mike Reinfeldt
Director of pro personnel: Ted Thompson
Director of college scouting: John Math
Administrator of college scouting: Bryan Broaddus
Executive director of public relations: Lee Remmel
Director of marketing: Jeff Cieply
Director of community relations: Mark Schiefelbein
Green Bay ticket director: Mark Wagner
Milwaukee ticket director: Marge Paget
Trainer: Pepper Burruss

1994 SCHEDULE
Preseason
AUG. 6	L.A. RAMS (at Madison, Wis.)	12:00
AUG. 13	MIAMI (at Milwaukee)	7:00
AUG. 19	at New Orleans	7:00
AUG. 26	NEW ENGLAND	7:00

Regular season
SEP. 4	MINNESOTA	12:00
SEP. 11	MIAMI (at Milw.)	12:00
SEP. 18	at Philadelphia	1:00
SEP. 25	TAMPA BAY	12:00
OCT. 2	at New England	1:00
OCT. 9	L.A. RAMS	12:00
OCT. 16	OPEN DATE	
OCT. 20	at Minnesota (Thurs.)	7:00
OCT. 31	at Chicago (Mon.)	8:00
NOV. 6	DETROIT (at Milw.)	12:00
NOV. 13	N.Y. JETS	3:00
NOV. 20	at Buffalo	1:00
NOV. 27	at Dallas (Thanks.)	3:00
DEC. 4	at Detroit	1:00
DEC. 11	CHICAGO	12:00
DEC. 18	ATLANTA (at Milw.)	12:00
DEC. 24	at Tampa Bay	1:00

HEAD COACH
Mike Holmgren
Holmgren was named the 11th head coach of the Packers on Jan. 11, 1992. In two seasons, he has a record of 19-15, including playoffs. He has guided Green Bay to 9-7 regular-season records the past two seasons, the first back-to-back winning seasons for the Packers since 1966 and '67. In 1993, the Packers made it into the postseason for the first time since the 1982 Super Bowl Tournament, which followed the strike-shortened season. Born June 15, 1948, San Francisco, Calif.
Previous NFL: offensive coordinator, San Francisco 1989-91; quarterbacks, San Francisco 1986-88.
Previous college: quarterbacks, Brigham Young 1982-85; offensive coordinator-quarterbacks, San Francisco State 1981.
Player: No NFL. College, quarterback, 1966-69 Southern Cal.

ASSISTANT COACHES
Larry Brooks: defensive line
Previous NFL: defensive line, 1983-90 L.A. Rams. Player: NFL, defensive lineman, 1972-83 L.A. Rams. College: defensive lineman, 1968-72 Virginia State.

Nolan Cromwell: special teams
Previous NFL: special teams, 1992-93 Green Bay; 1991 L.A. Rams. Player: NFL, defensive back, 1977-87 L.A. Rams. College: quarterback, safety, 1973-76 Kansas.

Jon Gruden: wide receivers
Previous NFL: wide receivers, 1992-93 Green Bay. Player: No NFL. College: quarterback, 1983-85 Dayton.

Gil Haskell: running backs
Previous NFL: running backs, 1992-93 Green Bay; 1983-91 L.A. Rams. Player: No NFL. College: defensive back, 1961 San Francisco State.

Dick Jauron: defensive backs
Previous NFL: defensive backs, 1986-93 Green Bay; 1985 Buffalo. Player: NFL, defensive back, 1973-77 Detroit; 1978-80 Cincinnati. College: defensive back, 1970-72 Yale.

Kent Johnston: strength and conditioning
Previous NFL: strength and conditioning, 1992-93 Green Bay; 1987-91 Tampa Bay. Player: No NFL. College: defensive back, 1974-77 Stephen F. Austin.

Sherman Lewis: offensive coordinator-receivers
Previous NFL: offensive coordinator, 1992-93 Green Bay; 1983-91 San Francisco. Player: NFL, running back, 1966 N.Y. Jets. College: running back, 1961-63 Michigan State.

Jim Lind: defensive assistant-quality control
Previous NFL: defensive assistant, 1992-93 Green Bay. Player: No NFL. College: linebacker, 1965-66 Bethel College, defensive back, 1971-72 Bemidji (Minn.) State.

Tom Lovat: offensive line
Previous NFL: offensive line 1992-93 Green Bay; 1990-91 Phoenix; 1985-88 Indianapolis; 1981-84 St. Louis; 1980 Green Bay. Player: No NFL. College: guard, linebacker, 1958-60 Utah.

1994 PREVIEW ■ GREEN BAY

Steve Mariucci: quarterbacks
Previous NFL: quarterbacks 1992-93 Green Bay; 1985 L.A. Rams. Player: No NFL. College: quarterback, 1974-77 Northern Michigan.

Andy Reid: tight ends-offensive line assistant
Previous NFL: tight ends-offensive line, 1992-93 Green Bay. Player: No NFL. College: offensive tackle, guard, 1978-80 Brigham Young.

Fritz Shurmur: defensive coordinator
Previous NFL: defensive coordinator, 1991-93 Phoenix; 1982-90 L.A. Rams; 1978-81 New England; 1975-77 Detroit. Player: No NFL. College: center, 1951-53 Albion.

Harry Sydney: general assistant
Previous NFL: None. Player: NFL, running back, 1987-91 San Francisco; 1992 Green Bay. College: running back, 1983-86 Kansas.

Bob Valesente: linebackers
Previous NFL: linebackers, 1992-93 Green Bay; 1990-91 Pittsburgh; 1982-83 Indianapolis. Player: No NFL. College: halfback, 1958-61 Ithaca.

COACHING RECORDS
(includes postseason games)

Years	Coach	W	L	T
1921-49	Earl "Curly" Lambeau	212	106	21
1950-53	Gene Ronzani	14	31	1
1953	Hugh Devore-Ray "Scooter" McLean	0	2	0
1954-57	Lisle Blackbourn	17	31	0
1958	Ray "Scooter" McLean	1	10	1
1959-67	Vince Lombardi	98	30	4
1968-70	Phil Bengtson	20	21	1
1971-74	Dan Devine	25	28	4
1975-87	Bart Starr	53	77	3
1984-87	Forrest Gregg	25	37	1
1988-91	Lindy Infante	24	40	0
1992-93	Mike Holmgren	19	15	0

HISTORICAL HIGHLIGHTS

1921 A franchise in the American Professional Football Association is granted to John Clair of the Acme Packing Company in Green Bay, Wis. The team, organized under the name Packers two years earlier, is led by star back and coach Curly Lambeau.
1922 The franchise is turned back to the league by John Clair after his team is disciplined for allowing college players to play under assumed names. The franchise is awarded to Curly Lambeau. Local merchants raise $2,500 to fund a non-profit corporation to run the franchise.
1925 City Stadium is built for the Packers, with a seating capacity of 6,000.
1929 The Packers win their first NFL championship, posting a record of 13-0-1.
1930 With a season record of 10-3-1, Green Bay wins its second consecutive NFL title.
1931 With an unbeaten streak of 23 games, the Packers repeat as NFL champions.
1932 Despite a record of 10-3-1, the Packers lose out to the 6-1-6 Chicago Bears for the NFL crown.
1933 The Packers go into receivership after being sued by a fan who fell and was injured in City Stadium. A local businessman raises $15,000 and saves the franchise.
1935 End Don Hutson from Alabama is signed and becomes an instant superstar.
1936 The Packers win the Western Division with a record of 11-1-1 and then defeat the Eastern champion Boston Redskins 21-6 for the NFL title.
1939 Green Bay again triumphs in the Western Division, then routs the New York Giants in the title game played in Milwaukee 27-0.
1941 The Packers and Bears tie for the division title, but Green Bay loses in the playoff game 33-14.
1944 Green Bay wins its sixth NFL title, defeating the Giants at the Polo Grounds in New York by a score of 14-7.
1945 Don Hutson sets an NFL record by scoring 29 points in one quarter — four touchdown pass receptions and five extra points — as the Packers trounce the Detroit Lions 57-21.
1949 HB Tony Canadeo becomes the first Packer to rush for more than 1,000 yards in a season when he gains 1,052 on 208 carries.
1950 Curly Lambeau ends a Packer career that began in 1919 by resigning to join the Chicago Cardinal franchise.
1957 The new Lambeau Field is christened, with a capacity of 32,000.
1959 Vince Lombardi takes over as head coach.
1960 With Paul Hornung, Bart Starr and Jim Taylor in the backfield, the Packers win their first division title since 1944, but lose to the Philadelphia Eagles, 17-13 in the NFL championship game.
1960 Paul Hornung sets an NFL record by scoring 176 points, a single-season record that has never been surpassed.
1961 In the first NFL championship game ever played in Green Bay, the Packers shut out the Giants 37-0 for their seventh NFL crown.
1962 Green Bay makes it back-to-back NFL championships by defeating the Giants 16-7.
1965 The Packers win their their ninth NFL title by beating the Cleveland Browns 23-12.
1966-67 Green Bay wins the NFL title again, this time playing in the first Super Bowl, with the Packers defeating the AFL champion Kansas City Chiefs 35-10.
1967-68 In the famous "Ice Bowl," QB Bart Starr sneaks in to give the Packers a 21-17 come-from-behind whn over the Cowboys and earn the right to play in Super Bowl II, where they defeat the Oakland Raiders 33-14.
1972 Green Bay wins its first division title since 1967 but loses to Washington in the playoffs 16-3.
1982 The Packers make it to the playoffs for the first time in a decade. They defeat St. Louis in the first round 41-16 but lose to Dallas 37-26 in the next round.
1985 WR James Lofton breaks Don Hutson's record of 7,991 for career receiving yardage.
1989 The Packers, with a record of 10-6, post their first winning season since 1972. But they still lose out on a playoff berth.
1991-92 The Packers realign their front office, fire Lindy Infante as head coach and hire Mike Homgren to replace him.
1993-94 With a record of 9-7, the Packers make it to the playoffs for the first time since 1982. They defeat the Lions 28-24 but lose to the Cowboys in the next round.

93

PRO FOOTBALL WEEKLY 1994 ALMANAC

TEAM AT A GLANCE

HALL OF FAME MEMBERS

	Yrs with Packers	Inducted
E Don Hutson*	1935-45	1963
Coach Curly Lambeau*	1921-49	1963
HB Johnny Blood (McNally)	1929-33, 35-36	1963
FB Clarke Hinkle	1932-41	1964
G Mike Michalske	1929-35, 37	1964
QB Arnie Herber	1930-40	1966
Coach Vince Lombardi	1959-68	1971
HB Tony Canadeo	1941-44, 46-52	1974
FB Jim Taylor	1958-66	1976
OT Forrest Gregg	1956, 58-70	1976
QB Bart Starr	1956-71	1977
LB Ray Nitschke	1958-72	1978
CB Herb Adderley	1961-69	1980
DE Willie Davis	1960-69	1981
C Jim Ringo	1953-63	1981
RB-PK Paul Hornung	1957-62, 64-66	1986
S Willie Wood	1960-71	1989

*Charter member

RETIRED JERSEY NUMBERS

- 3 HB Tony Canadeo
- 14 E Don Hutson
- 15 QB Bart Starr
- 66 LB Ray Nitschke

FIRST-ROUND DRAFT CHOICES
(since 1980)

Year	Selection	College
1980	LB George Cumby	Oklahoma
1981	QB Rich Campbell	California
1982	OG Ron Hallstrom	Iowa
1983	CB Tim Lewis	Pittsburgh
1984	DE Alphonso Carreker	Florida State
1985	OT Ken Ruettgers	Southern Cal
1986	No choice	
1987	RB Brent Fullwood	Auburn
1988	WR Sterling Sharpe	South Carolina
1989	OT Tony Mandarich	Michigan State
1990	LB Tony Bennett	Mississippi
	RB Darrell Thompson	Minnesota
1991	CB Vinnie Clark	Ohio State
1992	CB Terrell Buckley	Florida State
1993	LB Wayne Simmons	Clemson
	DB George Teague	Alabama
1994	OG-OT Aaron Taylor	Notre Dame

RECORD VS. OTHER NFL TEAMS
(includes postseason games)

	Record
Arizona Cardinals	40-21-4
Atlanta Falcons	9-9-0
Buffalo Bills	1-4-0
Chicago Bears	59-81-6
Cincinnati Bengals	3-4-0
Cleveland Browns	8-6-0
Dallas Cowboys	10-8-0
Denver Broncos	2-4-1
Detroit Lions	65-56-7
Houston Oilers	3-3-0
Indianapolis Colts	19-18-1
Kansas City Chiefs	2-4-1
Los Angeles Raiders	3-5-0
Los Angeles Rams	37-42-2
Miami Dolphins	0-7-0
Minnesota Vikings	31-33-1
New England Patriots	2-2-0
New Orleans Saints	12-4-0
New York Giants	25-21-2
New York Jets	1-5-0
Philadelphia Eagles	19-8-0
Pittsburgh Steelers	17-11-0
San Diego Chargers	4-1-0
San Francisco 49ers	25-21-1
Seattle Seahawks	3-3-0
Tampa Bay Buccaneers	17-12-1
Washington Redskins	14-13-1

YEAR-BY-YEAR RECORDS

Year	Won	Lost	Tied
1921	3	2	1
1922	4	3	3
1923	7	2	1
1924	7	4	0
1925	8	5	0
1926	7	3	3
1927	7	2	1
1928	6	4	3
1929*	12	0	1
1930*	10	3	1
1931*	12	2	0
1932	10	3	1
1933	5	7	1
1934	7	6	0
1935	8	4	0
1936*	10	1	1
1937	7	4	0
1938**	8	3	0
1939*	9	2	0
1940	6	4	1
1941	10	1	0
1942	8	2	1
1943	7	2	1
1944*	8	2	0
1945	6	4	0
1946	6	5	0
1947	6	5	1
1948	3	9	0
1949	2	10	0
1950	3	9	0
1951	3	9	0
1952	6	6	0
1953	2	9	1
1954	4	8	0
1955	6	6	0
1956	4	8	0
1957	3	9	0
1958	1	10	1
1959	7	5	0
1960**	8	4	0
1961*	11	3	0
1962*	13	1	0
1963**	11	2	1
1964**	8	5	1
1965*	10	3	1
1966*	12	2	0
1967*	9	4	1
1968	6	7	1
1969	8	6	0
1970	6	8	0
1971	4	8	2
1972**	10	4	0
1973	5	7	2
1974	6	8	0
1975	4	10	0
1976	5	9	0
1977	4	10	0
1978	8	7	1
1979	5	11	0
1980	5	10	1
1981	8	8	0
1982**	5	3	1
1983	8	8	0
1984	8	8	0
1985	8	8	0
1986	4	12	0
1987	5	9	1
1988	4	12	0
1989	10	6	0
1990	6	10	0
1991	4	12	0
1992	9	7	0
1993**	9	7	0
Total	494	422	36

Number of NFL championships   11
Number of years .500 or better   48
Number of years below .500   25

*NFL champions
**Playoff team

1994 PREVIEW ■ GREEN BAY

RECORDS

INDIVIDUAL

Service
Seasons played	16	Bart Starr (1956-71)
Games played	198	Bart Starr (1956-71)
Consecutive games	187	Forrest Gregg (1956, 58-70)

Scoring
Points, career	823	Don Hutson (1935-45)
Points, season	176	Paul Hornung (1960)
Points, game	33	Paul Hornung (10/8/61)
Touchdowns, career	105	Don Hutson (1935-45)
Touchdowns, season	19	Jim Taylor (1962)
Touchdowns, game	5	Paul Hornung (12/12/65)
Field goals, career	120	Chester Marcol (1972-80)
Field goals, season	33	Chester Marcol (1972)
Field goals, game	5	Chris Jacke (11/11/90)
Extra points, career	200	Fred Cone (1951-57)
Exta points, season	52	Jan Stenerud (1983)
Extra points, game	8	Don Chandler (10/23/66)

Rushing
Yards, career	8,207	Jim Taylor (1958-66)
Yards, season	1,474	Jim Taylor (1962)
Yards, game	186	Jim Taylor (12/3/61)
Attempts, career	1,811	Jim Taylor (1958-66)
Attempts, season	284	Terdell Middleton (1978)
Attempts, game	39	Terdell Middleton (11/26/78)
Touchdowns, career	81	Jim Taylor (1958-66)
Touchdowns, season	19	Jim Taylor (1962)
Touchdowns, game	4	Jim Taylor (10/15/61, 11/4/62, 11/11/62)
		Terdell Middleton (10/15/78)

Passing
Rating, career	80.5	Bart Starr (1956-71)
Rating, season	105.1	Bart Starr (1966)
Completions, career	1,808	Bart Starr (1956-71)
Completions, season	353	Don Majkowski (1989)
Completions, game	36	Brett Favre (12/5/93)
Yards, career	23,718	Bart Starr (1956-71)
Yards, season	4,458	Lynn Dickey (1983)
Yards, game	418	Lynn Dickey (10/12/80)
Attempts, career	3,149	Bart Starr (1956-71)
Attempts, season	599	Don Majkowski (1989)
Attempts, game	59	Don Majkowski (11/12/89)
Touchdowns, career	152	Bart Starr (1956-71)
Touchdowns, season	32	Lynn Dickey (1983)
Touchdowns, game	5	Cecil Isbell (11/1/42)
		Don Horn (12/21/69)
		Lynn Dickey (12/13/81, 9/4/83)

Receiving
Receptions, career	530	James Lofton (1978-86)
Receptions, season	112	Sterling Sharpe (1993)
Receptions, game	14	Don Hutson (11/22/42)
Yards, career	9,656	James Lofton (1978-86)
Yards, season	1,461	Sterling Sharpe (1992)
Yards, game	257	Bill Howton (10/21/56)
Touchdowns, career	99	Don Hutson (1935-45)
Touchdowns, season	17	Don Hutson (1942)
Touchdowns, game	4	Don Hutson (10/7/45)
		Sterling Sharpe (10/24/93)

Interceptions
Career	52	Bobby Dillon (1952-59)
Season	10	Irv Comp (1943)
Game	4	Bobby Dillon (11/26/53)
		Willie Buchanon (9/24/78)

Sacks
Career	55	Tim Harris (1986-90)
Season	19.5	Tim Harris (1989)
Game	4.5	Bryce Paup (9/15/91)

Longest plays
Run from scrimmage	97	Andy Uram (TD, 10/8/39)
Pass play	96	Tobin Rote to Billy Grimes (TD, 12/10/50)
Field goal	54	Chris Jacke (1/2/94)
Interception return	99	Tim Lewis (TD, 11/18/84)
Kickoff return	106	Al Carmichael (TD, 10/7/56)
Punt return	95	Steve Odom (TD, 11/10/74)
Punt	90	Don Chandler (10/10/65)

Top scorers
	Points
Don Hutson (1935-45)	823
Paul Hornung (1957-62, 64-66)	760
Jim Taylor (1958-66)	546
Chester Marcol (1972-80)	521
Chris Jacke (1989-93)	514
Fred Cone (1951-57)	455

Top rushers
	Yards
Jim Taylor (1958-66)	8,207
John Brockington (1971-77)	5,024
Tony Canadeo (1941-44, 46-52)	4,197
Clarke Hinkle (1932-41)	3,860
Gerry Ellis (1980-86)	3,826
Paul Hornung (1957-62, 64-66)	3,711

Top passers
	Completions
Bart Starr (1956-71)	1,808
Lynn Dickey (1976-77, 79-85)	1,592
Don Majkowski (1987-92)	889
Tobin Rote (1950-56)	826
Brett Favre (1992-93)	620
Randy Wright (1984-88)	602

Top passers
	Yards
Bart Starr (1956-71)	23,718
Lynn Dickey (1976-77, 79-85)	21,369
Tobin Rote (1950-56)	11,535
Don Majkowski (1987-92)	10,870
Randy Wright (1984-88)	7,106
Arnie Herber (1930-41)	6,741

Top receivers
	Receptions
James Lofton (1978-86)	530
Sterling Sharpe (1988-93)	501
Don Hutson (1935-45)	488
Boyd Dowler (1959-69)	448
Max McGee (1954, 1957-67)	345
Paul Coffman (1978-85)	322

Top receivers
	Yards
James Lofton (1978-86)	9,656
Don Hutson (1935-45)	7,991
Sterling Sharpe (1988-93)	7,015
Boyd Dowler (1959-69)	6,918
Max McGee (1954, 1957-67)	6,346
Bill Howton (1952-58)	5,581

Most interceptions
	No.
Bobby Dillon (1952-59)	52
Willie Wood (1960-71)	48
Herb Adderley (1961-69)	39
Irv Comp (1943-49)	34
Mark Lee (1980-91)	31
Don Hutson (1935-45)	30

Most sacks
	No.
Tim Harris (1986-90)	55
Ezra Johnson (1977-87)	41.5
Tony Bennett (1990-93)	36

PRO FOOTBALL WEEKLY 1994 ALMANAC

PREVIEW: HOUSTON OILERS

Let's see now. A preview of the Oilers' 1994 campaign …

Well, of course, you can't write about the Oilers without starting with QB Warren Moon. Oh, wait a minute, Moon's not with the team anymore.

OK, then let's talk about last season's headline-maker in Houston. You can't write about the Oilers without talking about defensive coordinator Buddy Ryan. Oh, wait a minute, Ryan's not with the team anymore.

Fine, then let's talk about the defensive line. Even before Ryan arrived in Houston, there were great defensive linemen like William Fuller and Sean Jones. Oh, wait a minute, Fuller and Jones aren't with the team anymore.

The run-and-shoot. Yeah, that's it. You can count on the run-and-shoot as a subject when the team is the Oilers. Oh, wait a minute …

"I've never been married to any offense," said Oiler head coach Jack Pardee, whose club will use aspects of the run-and-shoot in '94 but will also incorporate the tight end more than in the past. "That's something we're going to have to look at and study to figure out again what we can do best."

This is getting really frustrating. Why don't we talk about what Oiler GM Mike Holovak's future plans are for the team? Oh, wait a minute, Holovak, who is 74, has moved to Florida where he will aid in the scouting of pro and college players. Floyd Reese is now the general manager.

Hmmm. It's been a busy offseason for the Oilers.

The biggest change of all is the fact that Moon is now a Viking, and Cody Carlson is the No. 1 guy at quarterback. Carlson has the size, arm, mobility and toughness to be a big-time quarterback. In '92, when Moon was out for six games, he played extremely well. However, it remains to be seen if Carlson, who tends to hold on to the ball longer than Moon did, can stay healthy for an entire season. Whereas Moon lived in the weightroom during the offseason so he would be able to stay healthy, Carlson has done very little in that area, causing some to question his commitment. Carlson's ball security is not good. He fumbles exchanges with center and can be stripped by the rusher. He also has a low release point, which leads to passes being tipped and picked off, and has too much confidence in his arm, which leads to forced throws and interceptions. If Carlson gets hurt or struggles, ex-Viking Sean Salisbury has the size and arm to be a big-time throwing quarterback, but, in Minnesota, the coaches felt he came up a little short too often at the end of close games. Reserve QB Bucky Richardson has versatility, running ability and toughness, but he may not throw well enough to be a second-string quarterback in the Oilers' offense.

The Oilers already underwent change at running back last year. In '92 Lorenzo White showed up in the best shape of his career, rushed for 1,226 yards and did not lose a fumble all season. Last year he went to the sidelines with two sprained ankles just before midseason. With White sidelined, Gary Brown exploded on the scene. Starting the last eight games, Brown rushed for 1,002 yards during the season and averaged an AFC-high 5.1 yards per carry. Brown has excellent run skills, quick feet, superb balance and is a sturdy back who catches the ball better than White did. Brown was not a marked man in '93, but he will be in '94.

The Oiler receiving corps will have a different look this season, since they have vowed to incorporate a tight end into their offense. Ex-Ram Pat Carter has been signed via free-agency, and Roderick Lewis was selected in the fifth round of this year's draft.

The team's best wideout is Ernest Givins, who

PHOTO BY HARRY SCULL JR.

Bruce Matthews

96

1994 PREVIEW ■ HOUSTON

is quick, gutty, courageous, tough and elusive. Givins still has the great shake and the great burst, but the Oilers have to move him around more so the opposition can't take him out of the game. Webster Slaughter was Moon's go-to receiver in '93 and had caught 77 passes for 904 yards before suffering a very serious knee injury that makes him a question mark for this year. Slaughter is more quick than fast, runs superb patterns and works very well with quarterbacks. Haywood Jeffires put up some big numbers for the Oilers over the years, had a prototype size-speed ratio and vertical jump and made some big plays, but his dropped passes, hot-dogging and tendency to short-arm balls over the middle rubbed people in the organization raw. Slaughter and Jeffires are free agents and could end up with other teams. Curtis Duncan may have gone to the Pro Bowl two years ago, but he is nothing more than a smart, hard-working journeyman with average ability. At the end of last season when Slaughter got hurt, Gary Wellman came on like gangbusters. Travis Hannah has superb speed and will get a chance to play a lot more. Malcolm Seabron was selected in the third round of the draft.

The star of the offensive line is Bruce Matthews. He is still the best center and quite possibly the premier offensive lineman in the NFL. The Oilers may move him to left tackle if they are not convinced Brad Hopkins can handle the heat at that position. The only knocks on Matthews are that he does not always mash people and is not overly agile in the open field. Nonetheless, he blocks as well as anyone in the NFL. For a stretch, Hopkins played very well last year, but, at the end of the year, he was put in some difficult situations and lost his confidence. Hopkins has quick feet and great lower-body athleticism. If he can't handle playing tackle, he may have to move to guard. ORT David Williams is a very solid performer. John Flannery, who missed all of last year after undergoing knee surgery, will either replace long-time Pro Bowler Mike Munchak at guard or Matthews at center. Munchak was playing on heart and guts last year, because his knees were shot. Doug Dawson, one of the league's smartest offensive linemen, can play guard or center. Kevin Donnalley has struggled at times but is big, strong and can play guard or tackle.

Defensively, the Oilers must do without DE's Fuller and Jones, who left via free-agency. Lee Williams was a terrific pass rusher during his days in San Diego, but, in Houston, he has had a lot of injuries and a less-than-ideal attitude. Former Buccaneer first-round draft choice Keith McCants will get one more chance to show that he is not a bust. DT Glenn Montgomery is coming off his best year and established himself as a big-league player. Although Ray Childress was named to the Pro Bowl for the fifth time, he had his worst year as an Oiler. Houston needs Childress to bounce back in a big way and play with the great intensity and awareness that made him so great in the past. Tim Roberts is big and strong, but he is slow.

The Oilers will get DL help from the draft, having selected Henry Ford in the first round.

"I'm awfully pleased that we got Henry in the first round," said Oiler head coach Jack Pardee. "With any rookie, there's the problem of coming in and learning the system. I hope he comes in with fire in his eyes and ready to play."

In Round Two the Oilers again drafted for the defensive line, taking Jeremy Nunley.

At linebacker, Al Smith is a solid run-down middle linebacker who makes a lot of tackles and does a solid job. As a rookie Micheal Barrow replaced Smith on passing downs. Barrow made more good plays than bad but is a little light to be a run-stuffer at this stage in his career. Eddie Robinson had an invisible year at outside linebacker because Ryan dropped him into coverage so much, but he was generally viewed as the Oilers' steadiest linebacker. Joe Bowden can run and hit. Lamar Lathon has tremendous ability, but he mixes big plays with bad ones and makes way too many mental errors.

In the secondary, FS Marcus Robertson was having an All-Pro year before he suffered a knee injury. He has great range, very good hands, awareness and anticipation. SS Bubba McDowell struggled with injuries and tendinitis all season and was not the same player he had been in the past. CB Cris Dishman has had his ups and downs, but, in '93, there were more ups than downs. Darryll Lewis was off to a great start at cornerback before he injured his knee. Steve Jackson, his replacement, really struggled at first but had some fine late-season outings. Bo Orlando replaced Robertson at free safety and did a nice job. He is too small, but Orlando makes plays. Mike Dumas missed the entire season with an injury and has been a disappointment to date. Blaine Bishop did a very fine job of filling in for McDowell at strong safety.

PK Al Del Greco is coming off of his best year, having made 29-of-34 field goals. When the Oilers couldn't reach contract terms with P Greg Montgomery, they went out and signed ex-Cardinal P Rich Camarillo, a five-time Pro Bowler. The Oilers did a good job of covering kicks last year but did not have a return man who scared anyone.

FAST FACTS

■ For the ninth time in his nine-year career, Ray Childress led all Oiler defensive linemen in tackles last season.

■ In 1993 the Oilers became the first team since the 1972 Dolphins to win their final 11 games. They also set a franchise record with 12 victories.

■ You never know what position versatile Bruce Matthews will line up at. During his NFL career, he has started 75 games at guard, 59 at center and 30 at tackle.

PRO FOOTBALL WEEKLY 1994 ALMANAC

1994 PLAYER ROSTER

NO.	NAME	POS.	HT.	WT.	EXP.	COLLEGE	GP/GS
36	Aldridge, Melvin	S	6-2	195	2	Murray State	1/0
17	Brown, Reggie	WR	6-1	195	2	Alabama State	4/0
51	Barrow, Micheal	LB	6-1	236	2	Miami (Fla.)	16/0
23	Bishop, Blaine	CB	5-8	197	2	Ball State	16/2
59	Bowden, Joe	LB	5-11	230	3	Oklahoma	16/6
33	Brown, Gary	RB	5-11	233	4	Penn State	16/8
22	Brown, Tony	CB	5-9	183	3	Fresno State	16/0
16	Camarillo, Rich	P	5-11	200	14	Washington	16/0
14	Carlson, Cody	QB	6-3	202	8	Baylor	8/2
46	Carter, Pat	TE	6-4	258	8	Florida State	11/10
79	Childress, Ray	DT-DE	6-6	272	10	Texas A&M	16/16
87	Coleman, Pat	WR	5-7	176	4	Mississippi	13/1
66	Dawson, Doug	OG-C	6-3	288	8	Texas	16/16
3	Del Greco, Al	PK	5-10	202	11	Auburn	16/0
28	Dishman, Cris	CB	6-0	188	7	Purdue	16/16
77	Donnalley, Kevin	OT	6-5	305	4	North Carolina	16/6
38	Dumas, Mike	S	5-11	181	4	Indiana	0/0
80	Duncan, Curtis	WR	5-11	184	8	Northwestern	12/12
55	Flannery, John	C-OG	6-3	304	4	Syracuse	0/0
81	Givins, Ernest	WR	5-9	178	9	Louisville	16/16
82	Hannah, Travis	WR	5-7	161	2	Southern Cal	12/0
27	Hoage, Terry	S	6-2	201	11	Georgia	7/0
72	Hopkins, Brad	OT	6-3	306	2	Illinois	16/11
24	Jackson, Steve	CB	5-8	182	4	Purdue	16/12
84	Jeffires, Haywood	WR	6-2	201	8	North Carolina St.	16/16
56	Kozak, Scott	LB	6-3	222	6	Oregon	16/0
57	Lathon, Lamar	LB	6-3	252	5	Houston	13/1
29	Lewis, Darryl	CB	5-9	183	4	Arizona	4/4
58	Marshall, Wilber	LB	6-1	240	11	Florida	10/10
47	Maston, Le'Shai	RB	6-1	215	2	Baylor	10/0
74	Matthews, Bruce	C-OG	6-5	298	12	Southern Cal	16/16
78	McCants, Keith	DE	6-3	265	5	Alabama	13/0
25	McDowell, Bubba	S	6-1	198	6	Miami (Fla.)	14/14
48	Mills, John Henry	TE	6-0	222	2	Wake Forest	16/0
94	Montgomery, Glenn	DT	6-0	282	6	Houston	16/11
63	Munchak, Mike	OG	6-3	284	13	Penn State	13/12
64	Norgard, Erik	C-OG	6-1	282	5	Colorado	16/4
26	Orlando, Bo	S	5-10	180	5	West Virginia	16/3
7	Richardson, Bucky	QB	6-1	228	3	Texas A&M	2/0
68	Roberts, Tim	DT	6-6	318	3	S. Mississippi	5/0
31	Robertson, Marcus	S	5-11	197	4	Iowa State	13/13
50	Robinson, Eddie	LB	6-1	245	3	Alabama State	16/15
12	Salisbury, Sean	QB	6-5	217	6	Southern Cal	11/4
89	Slaughter, Webster	WR	6-1	175	9	San Diego State	14/14
54	Smith, Al	LB	6-1	244	8	Utah State	16/16
71	Teeter, Mike	DE	6-2	260	3	Michigan	14/0
70	Thomas, Stan	OT	6-5	295	4	Texas	14/0
32	Tillman, Spencer	RB	5-11	206	8	Oklahoma	15/0
88	Wellman, Gary	WR	5-9	173	3	Southern Cal	11/3
44	White, Lorenzo	RB	5-11	222	7	Michigan State	8/8
73	Williams, David	OT	6-5	292	6	Florida	15/15
97	Williams, Lee	DT-DE	6-6	275	11	Bethune-Cookman	14/5

1994 PLAYER ROSTER

'94 DRAFT PICKS

RD.	NAME	POS.	HT.	WT.	COLLEGE
1.	Ford, Henry	DE	6-3	283	Arkansas
2.	Nunley, Jeremy	DE	6-5	278	Alabama
3.	Seabron, Malcolm	WR	6-0	194	Fresno State
4.	Davis, Michael	DB	6-1	192	Cincinnati
4.	Jackson, Sean	RB	6-1	222	Florida State
5.	Lewis, Roderick	TE	6-5	255	Arizona
5.	Reid, Jim	OT	6-6	306	Virginia
6.	Gissendaner, Lee	WR	5-9	175	Northwestern
6.	Wortham, Barron	LB	5-11	244	Texas-El Paso
7.	Hall, Lemanski	LB	6-0	229	Alabama

PRO FOOTBALL WEEKLY 1994 ALMANAC

TEAM AT A GLANCE

TEAM DIRECTORY

Address	6910 Fannin Street Houston, Texas 77030 (713) 797-9111
Stadium	Astrodome Loop 610, Kirby and Fannin Houston, Texas 77054 Capacity: 62,439 Playing surface: AstroTurf
Training Camp	Trinity University San Antonio, Texas 78212
Colors	Columbia blue, scarlet and white
Television	KPRC, Channel 2
Radio	KTRH, 740 AM

ADMINISTRATION

President: K.S. "Bud" Adams Jr.
Exec. vice president-general manager: Floyd Reese
Exec. vice president-administration: Mike McClure
Exec. vice president-finance: Scott Thompson
Vice president-personnel-scouting: Mike Holovak
Vice president-general counsel: Steve Underwood
Sr. vice president-marketing: Don MacLachlan
Director of business operations: Lewis Mangum
Director of media services: Chip Namias
Director of ticket administration: Mike Mullis
Trainer: Brad Brown

1994 SCHEDULE

Preseason
JULY 31	at Kansas City	8:00
AUG. 8	vs. San Diego (San Antonio)	7:00
AUG. 15	vs. Dallas (Mexico City)	*9:00
AUG. 20	vs. Buffalo	7:00
AUG. 27	L.A. RAIDERS	1:00

*Eastern Time

Regular Season
SEP. 4	at Indianapolis	12:00
SEP. 11	at Dallas	3:00
SEP. 18	BUFFALO	12:00
SEP. 25	CINCINNATI	3:00
OCT. 3	at Pittsburgh (Mon.)	9:00
OCT. 9	OPEN DATE	
OCT. 13	CLEVELAND (Thurs.)	7:00
OCT. 24	at Philadelphia (Mon.)	9:00
OCT. 30	at L.A. Raiders	1:00
NOV. 6	PITTSBURGH	12:00
NOV. 13	at Cincinnati	1:00
NOV. 21	N.Y. GIANTS (Mon.)	8:00
NOV. 27	at Cleveland	1:00
DEC. 4	ARIZONA	3:00
DEC. 11	SEATTLE	3:00
DEC. 18	at Kansas City	3:00
DEC. 24	N.Y. JETS	3:00

HEAD COACH

Jack Pardee
Pardee has taken the Oilers to the playoffs in each of his four seasons after being hired as head coach on Jan. 9, 1990. He has an overall record of 86-69 as a head coach with three NFL teams — the Oilers, Bears and Redskins. Pardee has also been a head coach in the World Football League, the USFL and in college football. Prior to joining the Oilers, he headed the football program at the University of Houston, where in a span of three years his Cougars set over 100 NCAA and Southwest Conference records. Born April 19, 1936, Exira, Iowa.

Previous NFL: scout, 1986 Green Bay; defensive coordinator, 1981 San Diego; head coach, 1978-80 Washington; head coach, 1975-77 Chicago; assistant coach, 1973 Washington.

Previous college: head coach, 1987-89 Houston.

Player: NFL, linebacker, 1957-64, 1966-70 L.A. Rams; 1971-72 Washington. College, linebacker-fullback, 1953-56 Texas A&M.

ASSISTANT COACHES

Charlie Baggett: receivers
Previous NFL: receivers, 1993 Houston. Player: No NFL. College: quarterback, 1972-75 Michigan State.

Tom Bettis: defensive backs
Previous NFL: defensive backs, 1993 Houston; 1991 L.A. Rams; 1989-90 Philadelphia; 1988 Kansas City; 1986-87 Houston; 1985 Cleveland; 1978-84 St. Louis; 1966-77 Kansas City; 1964-65 Chicago (scout). Player: NFL, linebacker, 1955-61 Green Bay, 1962 Pittsburgh, 1963 Chicago. College: linebacker, 1952-54 Purdue.

Frank Bush: quality control
Previous NFL: quality control, 1987-93 Houston. Player: NFL, linebacker, 1985-86 Houston. College: linebacker, 1981-84 North Carolina State.

Dick Coury: offensive coordinator
Previous NFL: tight ends, 1993 Minnesota; 1991-92 New England; 1986-90, 1976-81 Philadelphia; 1975 San Diego; 1971-73 Denver. Player: No NFL. College: None.

Jeff Fisher: defensive coordinator
Previous NFL: defensive backs, 1992-93 San Francisco; 1991 L.A. Rams; 1986-90 Philadelphia. Player: NFL, defensive back, 1981-84 Chicago. College: defensive back, 1977-80 Southern Cal.

Kevin Gilbride: assistant head coach/offense
Previous NFL: offensive coordinator, 1989-93 Houston. Player: No NFL. College: quarterback-tight end, 1970-73 Southern Connecticut State.

Frank Novak: special teams-running backs
Previous NFL: running backs, 1989-93 Houston. Player: No NFL. College: quarterback, 1959-61 Northern Michigan.

Jim Stanley: defensive line
Previous NFL: defensive line, 1990-93 Houston; 1986 Tampa Bay; 1980-82 Atlanta; 1979 N.Y. Giants. Player: No NFL. College: guard-defensive tackle, 1954-57 Texas A&M.

Steve Watterson: strength and rehabilitation

1994 PREVIEW ■ HOUSTON

TEAM AT A GLANCE

Previous NFL: strength and conditioning, 1986-93 Houston; 1984-85 Philadelphia. Player: No NFL. College: None.

Gregg Williams: linebackers
Previous NFL: special teams, 1990-93 Houston. Player: No NFL. College: quarterback, 1976-79 Northeast Missouri State.

Bob Young: offensive line
Previous NFL: offensive line, 1990-93 Houston. Player: NFL, guard, 1966-70 Denver; 1971, 1980 Houston; 1972-79 St. Louis; 1981 New Orleans. College: guard, 1960-61 Texas; 1962-63 Howard Payne.

COACHING RECORDS
(includes postseason games)

Years	Coach	W	L	T
1960-61	Lou Rymkus	12	7	1
1961	Wally Lemm	10	0	0
1962-63	Frank "Pop" Ivy	17	12	0
1964	Sammy Baugh	4	10	0
1965	Hugh Taylor	4	10	0
1966-70	Wally Lemm	28	40	4
1971	Ed Hughes	4	9	1
1972-73	Bill Peterson	1	18	0
1973-74	Sid Gillman	8	15	0
1975-80	Bum Phillips	59	38	0
1981-83	Ed Biles	8	23	0
1983	Chuck Studley	2	8	0
1984-85	Hugh Campbell	8	22	0
1985-89	Jerry Glanville	35	35	0
1990-93	Jack Pardee	43	26	0

HISTORICAL HIGHLIGHTS

1960 K. S. "Bud" Adams is awarded a franchise for Houston in the new American Football League. ... Houston wins the East Division and then defeats the Los Angeles Chargers 24-16 for the first AFL championship.
1961 QB George Blanda ties a pro football record by throwing seven touchdown passes in a 49-13 Oiler win over the New York Titans. ... Houston again wins the AFL East. The Oilers win their second league title by defeating San Diego 10-3.
1962 The Oilers take their third consecutive division title but lose 20-17 in double overtime in the AFL title game to the Dallas Texans.
1967 Houston wins the AFL East but loses 40-7 to the Oakland Raiders in the championship game.
1968 The Astrodome becomes the Oilers' new home field.
1971 S Ken Houston ties the all-time NFL career record of seven touchdowns on interceptions.
1978-79 Rookie Earl Campbell leads the NFL and sets club records by rushing for 1,450 yards and 13 touchdowns. ... Houston makes it to the playoffs as a wild-card team, where it defeats the Miami Dolphins 17-9. The Oilers then beat the New England Patriots 31-14 but fall to the Pittsburgh Steelers 34-5 in the AFC championship game.
1979-80 The Oilers again make the playoffs as a wild-card. They defeat the Broncos 13-7 and then the Chargers 17-14 but lose in the championship game to the Steelers 27-13.
1980 Earl Campbell ties O. J. Simpson for the NFL mark by rushing for more than 200 yards in two consecutive games. Campbell also sets an NFL record by rushing for 200 yards four times in one season. ... The Oilers lose 27-7 to the Oakland Raiders in the playoffs.
1982 The Oilers move into a new training facility two miles from the Astrodome.
1987-88 The Oilers make the playoffs and defeat the Seattle Seahawks 23-20 in overtime but lose 34-10 the following week to the Denver Broncos.
1988-89 Houston edges the Cleveland Browns in the wild-card playoff game, but the Oilers lose 17-10 to the Buffalo Bills a week later.
1989 The Oilers lose to the Steelers 26-23 in overtime in the AFC wild-card game.
1990-91 QB Warren Moon becomes the first player to pass for more than 20,000 yards in both the NFL and the Canadian Football League. ... Houston makes it to the playoffs but loses in the wild-card game 41-14 to the Bengals.
1991-92 The Oilers win the AFL wild-card game, beating the Jets 17-10, then lose 26-24 to the Broncos.
1993-94 Houston wins the AFC Central with a record of 12-4 but loses 28-20 to the Kansas City Chiefs in the divisional playoff game.

PRO FOOTBALL WEEKLY 1994 ALMANAC

TEAM AT A GLANCE

HALL OF FAME MEMBERS

	Yrs with Oilers	Inducted
QB George Blanda	1960-66	1981
S Ken Houston	1967-72	1986
RB Earl Campbell	1978-84	1991

RETIRED JERSEY NUMBERS

- 34 RB Earl Cambell
- 43 DB Jim Norton
- 66 DE Elvin Bethea

FIRST-ROUND DRAFT CHOICES
(since 1980)

Year	Selection	College
1980	No choice	
1981	No choice	
1982	OG Mike Munchak	Penn State
1983	OT Bruce Matthews	Southern Cal
1984	OT Dean Steinkuhler	Nebraska
1985	DE Ray Childress	Texas A&M
	CB Richard Johnson	Wisconsin
1986	QB Jim Everett	Purdue
1987	RB Alonzo Highsmith	Miami (Fla.)
	WR Haywood Jeffires	North Carolina St.
1988	RB Lorenzo White	Michigan State
1989	OT David Williams	Florida
1990	LB Lamar Lathon	Houston
1991	DB Mike Dumas	Indiana
1992	No choice	
1993	OT Brad Hopkins	Illinois
1994	DE Henry Ford	Arkansas

RECORD VS. OTHER NFL TEAMS
(includes postseason games)

	Record
Arizona Cardinals	2-3-0
Atlanta Falcons	3-5-0
Buffalo Bills	20-14-0
Chicago Bears	4-2-0
Cincinnati Bengals	25-25-1
Cleveland Browns	21-27-0
Dallas Cowboys	3-4-0
Denver Broncos	20-13-1
Detroit Lions	4-2-0
Green Bay	3-3-0
Indianapolis Colts	7-6-0
Kansas City Chiefs	17-23-0
Los Angeles Raiders	13-22-0
Los Angeles Rams	2-5-0
Miami Dolphins	12-11-0
Minnesota Vikings	3-3-0
New England Patriots	15-17-1
New Orleans Saints	3-4-1
New York Giants	0-4-0
New York Jets	18-12-1
Philadelphia Eagles	0-5-0
Pittsburgh Steelers	18-32-0
San Diego Chargers	16-18-1
San Francisco 49ers	3-5-0
Seattle Seahawks	5-4-0
Tampa Bay Buccaneers	3-1-0
Washington Redskins	3-3-0

YEAR-BY-YEAR RECORDS

Year	Won	Lost	Tied	Year	Won	Lost	Tied
1960*	10	4	0	1977	8	6	0
1961*	10	3	1	1978**	10	6	0
1962**	11	3	0	1979**	11	5	0
1963	6	8	0	1980**	11	5	0
1964	4	10	0	1981	7	9	0
1965	4	10	0	1982	1	8	0
1966	3	11	0	1983	2	14	0
1967**	9	4	1	1984	3	13	0
1968	7	7	0	1985	5	11	0
1969**	6	6	2	1986	5	11	0
1970	3	10	1	1987**	9	6	0
1971	4	9	1	1988**	10	6	0
1972	1	13	0	1989**	9	7	0
1973	1	13	0	1990**	9	7	0
1974	7	7	0	1991**	11	5	0
1975	10	4	0	1992	10	6	0
1976	5	9	0	1993**	12	4	0
				Total	234	260	6

Number of NFL championships 0
Number of years .500 or better 19
Number of years below .500 15

*AFL champions (before merger with NFL)
**Playoff team

1994 PREVIEW ■ HOUSTON

RECORDS

INDIVIDUAL

Service
Seasons played	16	Elvin Bethea (1968-83)
Games played	210	Elvin Bethea (1968-83)
Consecutive games	147	Robert Brazile (1975-84)

Scoring
Points, career	596	George Blanda (1960-66)
Points, season	126	Al Del Greco (1993)
Points, game	30	Billy Cannon (12/10/61)
Touchdowns, career	73	Earl Campbell (1978-84)
Touchdowns, season	19	Earl Campbell (1979)
Touchdowns, game	5	Billy Cannon (12/10/61)
Field goals, career	117	Tony Zendejas (1985-90)
Field goals, season	29	Al Del Greco (1993)
Field goals, game	6	Skip Butler (10/12/75)
Extra points, career	299	George Blanda (1960-66)
Exta points, season	64	George Blanda (1961)
Extra points, game	7	George Blanda (11/5/61)
		Teddy Garcia (12/9/90)

Rushing
Yards, career	8,574	Earl Campbell (1978-84)
Yards, season	1,934	Earl Campbell (1980)
Yards, game	216	Billy Cannon (12/10/61)
Attempts, career	1,979	Earl Campbell (1978-84)
Attempts, season	373	Earl Campbell (1980)
Attempts, game	39	Earl Campbell (10/11/81)
Touchdowns, career	73	Earl Campbell (1978-84)
Touchdowns, season	19	Earl Campbell (1979)
Touchdowns, game	4	Earl Campbell (11/20/78)
		Lorenzo White (12/9/90)

Passing
Completions, career	2,632	Warren Moon (1984-93)
Completions, season	404	Warren Moon (1991)
Completions, game	41	Warren Moon (11/10/91)
Yards, career	33,685	Warren Moon (1984-93)
Yards, season	4,690	Warren Moon (1991)
Yards, game	527	Warren Moon (12/16/90)
Attempts, career	4,546	Warren Moon (1984-93)
Attempts, season	655	Warren Moon (1991)
Attempts, game	68	George Blanda (11/1/64)
Touchdowns, career	196	Warren Moon (1984-93)
Touchdowns, season	36	George Blanda (1961)
Touchdowns, game	7	George Blanda (11/19/61)

Receiving
Receptions, career	506	Ernest Givins (1986-93)
Receptions, season	101	Charley Hennigan (1964)
Receptions, game	13	Charley Hennigan (10/13/61)
		Haywood Jeffires (10/13/91)
Yards, career	7,477	Drew Hill (1986-91)
Yards, season	1,746	Charley Hennigan (1961)
Yards, game	272	Charley Hennigan (10/13/61)
Touchdowns, career	51	Charley Hennigan (1960-66)
Touchdowns, season	17	Bill Groman (1961)
Touchdowns, game	3	By many players

Interceptions
Career	45	Jim Norton (1960-68)
Season	12	Freddy Glick (1963)
		Mike Reinfeldt (1979)
Game	3	By many players

Sacks
Season	15.5	Jesse Baker (1979)

Longest plays
Run from scrimmage	91	Sid Blanks (TD, 12/13/64)
Pass play	98	Jacky Lee to Willard Dewveall (TD, 1/25/62)
Field goal	55	George Blanda (12/3/61)
Interception return	98	Pete Jaquess (TD, 9/16/64)
Kickoff return	104	Ken Hall (TD, 10/23/60)
Punt return	87	Billy Johnson (TD, 10/16/77)
Punt	79	Jim Norton (11/22/64)

Top scorers — Points
George Blanda (1960-66)	596
Tony Zendejas (1985-90)	548
Earl Campbell (1978-84)	438
Toni Fritsch (1977-81)	392
Skip Butler (1972-77)	330
Charley Hennigan (1960-66)	306

Top rushers — Yards
Earl Campbell (1978-84)	8,574
Hoyle Granger (1966-70, 72)	3,514
Mike Rozier (1985-90)	3,426
Lorenzo White (1988-93)	3,322
Charlie Tolar (1960-66)	3,288
Ronnie Coleman (1974-81)	2,738

Top passers — Completions
Warren Moon (1984-93)	2,632
Dan Pastorini (1971-79)	1,426
George Blanda (1960-66)	1,347
Ken Stabler (1980-81)	458
Pete Beathard (1967-69)	379
Cody Carlson (1987-93)	311

Top passers — Yards
Warren Moon (1984-93)	33,685
George Blanda (1960-66)	19,149
Dan Pastorini (1971-79)	16,846
Ken Stabler (1980-81)	5,190
Pete Beathard (1967-69)	5,128
Cody Carlson (1987-93)	3,742

Top receivers — Receptions
Ernest Givins (1986-93)	506
Drew Hill (1986-91)	480
Charley Hennigan (1960-66)	410
Ken Burrough (1971-81)	408
Haywood Jeffires (1987-93)	386
Curtis Duncan (1987-93)	322

Top receivers — Yards
Drew Hill (1986-91)	7,477
Ernest Givins (1986-93)	7,414
Ken Burrough (1971-81)	6,907
Charley Hennigan (1960-66)	6,823
Haywood Jeffires (1987-93)	4,652
Curtis Duncan (1987-93)	3,935

Most interceptions — No.
Jim Norton (1960-68)	45
Freddy Glick (1961-66)	30
Tony Banfield (1960-65)	27
W.K. Hicks (1964-69)	27
Mike Reinfeldt (1976-83)	26
Ken Houston (1967-72)	25

PRO FOOTBALL WEEKLY 1994 ALMANAC

PREVIEW: INDIANAPOLIS COLTS

Simply put, the Colts have basically been a disastrous team under the ownership of Robert Irsay. In their last years in Baltimore and their tenure in Indianapolis, the Colts have taken one step backward for every step forward.

Irsay, tired of the terminal malaise, believes he may have finally learned how to solve the problem by bringing in former Bear personnel boss Bill Tobin to turn the team around. Tobin is a rigid man who likes to stick to a single philosophy, which is primarily building through the draft. However, in this era of free-agency, that philosophy may be too limiting to be effective. Time will tell if Tobin is capable of adapting. Tobin also likes to win with a running game and defense, avoid mistakes and force his opponent into making them. His head coach, Ted Marchibroda, is an offensive innovator who likes to throw the football and probe weaknesses in the defense. The marriage of Tobin and Marchibroda may be as successful as the union of Burt Reynolds and Loni Anderson, and far less interesting.

If the Colts stumble and bumble once again and find themselves with a 2-6 record at the midpoint of the season, don't be shocked if the misunderstood Marchibroda is given the gate in favor of Tobin's brother Vince, who will be running the defense in the interim. Vince Tobin had long been considered a leading candidate for a head-coaching job when he was running Mike Ditka's defense during the Bears' heyday, but he was never offered a No. 1 job.

Offensively, the Colts have been in a major funk in recent years. In six games during the 1992 season and seven games last year, the Colts failed to reach the endzone. Three of the Colts' four victories last year came as a result of scoring only on field goals. The team was last in rushing offense and scored only 16 offensive touchdowns. As a result, it finished 27th in scoring.

Marchibroda will try to jump-start that offense with some new faces. Tobin sent QB Jeff George and his rocket arm south to Atlanta and brought in former Bear QB Jim Harbaugh, who had been cut by Chicago head coach Dave Wannstedt. Tobin had drafted Harbaugh with his first-round pick in 1987, so he obviously admires the ex-Michigan star's abilities. However, Harbaugh is limited as a quarterback. He does not have a great arm in terms of accuracy, delivery or strength, and, even though he is the son of a coach, he is not the most instinctive signal-caller. What Harbaugh does have is heart, resiliency and toughness, characteristics that George can only read about. Harbaugh's attitude and desire marked a big reason why Tobin brought him to Indianapolis.

"We have to improve our quarterback situation," Tobin explained. "We got rid of one quarterback (George) that didn't want to be here. We bring this one in that wants to be here. The one we got rid of had a 14-35 record, which is one of the worst in the league. This individual is 35-30, and over a two-year period he was 21-10."

Harbaugh sees the Indianapolis situation as a chance to show what he can do in a more wide-open offense than he was used to seeing in Chicago. "I want to get started here," Harbaugh said. "I've seen what coach Marchibroda has done here and with the Buffalo Bills. I need to be in that style of offense to show what I can do."

While Harbaugh may not have the natural gifts of the top quarterbacks, he is among the best runners and scramblers at his position. One of his trademarks is to keep drives alive by turning sure sacks into successful downfield runs.

Many observers expected the Colts to draft a quarterback with one of their first-round choices. However, Tobin did not, and he is content to give Harbaugh a shot and allow Don Majkowski to stay on as backup. Aside from one magical season in 1989, Majkowski has been an ordinary quarterback with an accuracy problem. Like Harbaugh, his mobility is a strength.

Since the Colts were the worst rushing team in the league last year, they used their No. 2 pick in the draft to take San Diego State RB Marshall Faulk, who many observers believe has the talent to join the likes of Emmitt Smith, Barry Sanders and Thurman Thomas. Faulk is an incredibly productive back with superior speed. He was clocked at 4.33 in the 40 in a private workout before Draft Day. Faulk has the ability to outrun defenders and burst through holes. He has great hands and can be a tremendous receiver. Faulk was not always very durable in his college career, and how he handles an NFL level of pounding remains to be seen. Roosevelt Potts had an impressive rookie season with 711 yards and a 4.0 average. He also caught 26 passes, but he did not get into the endzone once and is not much of a blocker. Anthony Johnson is another fine receiver out of the backfield. He does not have breakaway speed, but he is a willing blocker.

During the past two seasons, Reggie Langhorne caught 150 passes for the Colts, while Jessie Hester hauled in 116 over that same span. Nevertheless, Tobin cut both receivers because he thought they were too old and making too much money. If they don't sign elsewhere, they might be brought back at reduced salaries. Sean Dawkins was the Colts' No. 1 draft choice in 1993 and he caught 26 passes for 430 yards and a score, but he was not as good as advertised. He dropped several key passes last year and is not a burner. Journeymen Wesley Carroll and Floyd Turner were signed as free agents and will compete for one of the starting jobs. Shannon Baker has

1994 PREVIEW ■ INDIANAPOLIS

game-breaking speed but needs to get more consistent. TE Kerry Cash underachieved last season. He can get deep and has the speed most tight ends can only dream about, but he drops an alarming number of passes and is not a good blocker. Charles Arbuckle is another pass-catching tight end, but he doesn't have Cash's speed to get down the field and make big plays. Both could get pushed by rookie TE Branford Banta, who was drafted out of Southern Cal.

The Colt offensive line is led by former Buffalo All-Pro Will Wolford. Indianapolis spent a ton of money to get him and former Viking C Kirk Lowdermilk before the 1993 season, and the initial results were uninspiring. Wolford injured his shoulder and had to undergo rotator-cuff surgery, while Lowdermilk merely played decent football. ORT Zefross Moss is the team's best run blocker, but he did not make progress in his pass blocking. The guard play was poor last year, and Randy Dixon has had two bad years in a row. The Colts drafted Eric Mahlum to replace Bill Schultz, who was released.

Defensively, the Colts should be able to give opposing quarterbacks nightmares with the addition of Packer free-agent Tony Bennett and first-round pick Trev Alberts. Both are expected to line up on the same side, with Bennett usually at right end and Alberts at right outside linebacker, although they'll reverse positions on occasion.

Two years ago, the Colts made Steve Emtman the No. 1 pick in the draft because of his size, strength, speed, talent, tenacity and athleticism. However, after two serious knee injuries in each of his first two NFL seasons, it's unlikely he will play in 1994. DRE Bennett is one of the top pass rushers in the league, but Jon Hand, who led the team with 5.5 sacks playing right end last year, is not as fast as he was earlier in his career. DT Tony Siragusa is a slugger and mauler who makes plays on effort and tenacity. Skip McClendon is an ordinary lineman, the kind of player the coaching staff is always looking to improve upon. Willis Peguese looks the part because of his top speed and athletic ability, but he is not instinctive and gets blown off the line at times.

The LB crew appears to have been upgraded dramatically with the addition of Alberts. Alberts will start on the right side and Quentin Coryatt on the left, with Jeff Herrod in the middle. Herrod was troubled by a dislocated ankle last season and he came back too soon from the injury. He is stocky, solid and hard-hitting and should do well on the inside. Coryatt has struggled as a middle linebacker, but he has incredible tools and could become a dominant player if he learns the nuances of the defense under Tobin. Alberts has

great pass-rushing skills, will play hurt and always hustles.

The Indianapolis secondary is mediocre at best. CB Eugene Daniel was never a burner and is on the downside of his career. Chris Goode has decent talent but is not a big hitter. Jason Belser played surprisingly well at strong safety, considering he is quite small. Ray Buchanan led the team in interceptions with four as a rookie and should get better. Buchanan has good instincts and can cover, but he's on the small side and is not a ferocious hitter.

Veteran PK Dean Biasucci was the Colts' most consistent offensive player last year. He connected on 26-of-31 field goal attempts in 1993 and was nearly perfect (22-of-23) inside the 40-yard line. Rohn Stark, a former decathlete, remains one of the NFL's best punters. Stark averaged 43.3 gross yards per kick last season. On the other hand, the Indianapolis kick-return game is just ordinary, and the kick coverage is not very good.

Jeff Herrod

FAST FACTS

■ The Colts haven't won a game at Buffalo since a 17-12 victory in 1980.

■ The Colts were minus-14 on the turnover/takeaway table, which tied the Browns for the worst mark in the AFC.

■ With 16 career 50-yard-plus field goals, Dean Biasucci ranks fourth on the all-time list.

PRO FOOTBALL WEEKLY 1994 ALMANAC

1994 PLAYER ROSTER

NO.	NAME	POS.	HT.	WT.	EXP.	COLLEGE	GP/GS
64	Allen, Russell	DE	6-6	296	R	Oklahoma	—
33	Ambrose, Ashley	DB	5-10	185	3	Miss. Valley St.	14/6
81	Arbuckle, Charles	TE	6-3	248	4	UCLA	16/2
6	Bailey, Aaron	WR	5-10	184	R	Louisville	—
86	Baker, Shannon	WR	5-9	185	2	Florida State	0/0
36	Baylor, John	S	6-0	208	6	S. Mississippi	16/11
29	Belser, Jason	DB	5-9	187	3	Oklahoma	16/16
56	Bennett, Tony	LB	6-2	243	5	Mississippi	10/7
53	Butcher, Paul	LB	6-0	230	8	Wayne State	16/0
4	Biasucci, Dean	PK	6-0	190	10	Western Carolina	16/0
60	Borrelli, Marc	OL	6-5	286	R	Boston College	—
34	Buchanan, Ray	DB	5-9	193	2	Louisville	16/5
53	Butcher, Paul	LB	6-0	230	8	Wayne State	16/0
43	Campbell, Darnell	RB	6-1	224	R	Boston College	—
9	Carroll, Wesley	WR	6-0	195	4	Miami (Fla.)	12/0
88	Cash, Kerry	TE	6-4	252	4	Texas	16/14
2	Cook, Mike	WR	6-4	205	1	Stanford	0/0
55	Coryatt, Quentin	LB	6-3	250	3	Texas A&M	16/16
31	Courtney, Marvin	RB	6-0	204	R	Mississippi	—
35	Culver, Rodney	RB	5-9	224	3	Notre Dame	16/1
38	Daniel, Eugene	DB	5-11	188	11	Louisiana State	16/16
87	Dawkins, Sean	WR	6-4	213	2	California	16/7
69	Dixon, Randy	OG	6-3	305	8	Pittsburgh	15/15
90	Emtman, Steve	DE-DT	6-4	300	3	Washington	5/5
40	Ericson, Todd	DB	6-3	205	R	Montana	—
48	Etheredge, Carlos	TE	6-5	259	1	Miami (Fla.)	0/0
37	Goode, Chris	DB	6-0	199	8	Alabama	14/10
59	Grant, Stephen	LB	6-0	242	3	West Virginia	16/0
75	Gray, Cecil	OT	6-4	305	5	North Carolina	6/2
30	Gray, Derwin	DB	5-11	198	2	Brigham Young	11/0
78	Hand, Jon	DE	6-7	310	9	Alabama	15/14
12	Harbaugh, Jim	QB	6-3	215	8	Michigan	15/15
54	Herrod, Jeff	LB	6-0	249	7	Mississippi	14/14
20	Houston, William	RB	6-1	260	R	Ohio State	—
25	Humphrey, Ronald	RB	5-10	211	1	Miss. Valley State	0/0
23	Johnson, Anthony	RB	6-0	222	5	Notre Dame	13/8
14	Jordan, Todd	QB-P	6-2	231	R	Mississippi State	—
11	Justin, Paul	QB	6-4	202	1	Arizona State	0/0
63	Lowdermilk, Kirk	C	6-4	280	10	Ohio State	16/16
7	Majkowski, Don	QB	6-3	203	8	Virginia	3/0
61	McCoy, Tony	NT	6-0	279	3	Florida	6/0
57	McDonald, Devon	LB	6-4	248	2	Notre Dame	16/0
27	McEntyre, Kenny	DB	5-9	181	R	Kansas Stae	—
73	Moss, Zefross	OT	6-6	338	6	Alabama State	16/16
32	O'Neil, Robert	DB	6-1	199	2	Clemson	0/0
41	Orton, Jason	DB	5-11	175	R	Indiana	—
96	Peguese, Willis	DE	6-4	273	5	Miami (Fla.)	13/4
8	Pointer, Deron	WR	5-11	174	R	Washington State	—
42	Potts, Roosevelt	RB	6-0	245	2	NE Louisiana	16/15
52	Ratigan, Brian	LB	6-4	241	1	Notre Dame	0/0
68	Ray, John	OT	6-8	350	2	West Virginia	2/0
60	Simon, Jose	DL	6-3	291	R	Texas A&I	—
92	Sims, Thomas	DL	6-2	308	5	Pittsburgh	5/3
98	Siragusa, Tony	NT	6-3	325	5	Pittsburgh	14/14
5	Smith, Terry	WR	6-0	200	R	Clemson	—
1	Stablein, Brian	WR	6-1	191	1	Ohio State	0/0

1994 PREVIEW ■ INDIANAPOLIS

1994 PLAYER ROSTER

NO.	NAME	POS.	HT.	WT.	EXP.	COLLEGE	GP/GS
3	Stark, Rohn	P	6-3	203	13	Florida State	16/0
26	Starks, Glenn	RB	6-1	205	R	Central Oklahoma St.	—
79	Staysniak, Joe	OT	6-4	302	4	Ohio State	14/1
94	Thomas, Marquise	LB	6-4	255	2	Mississippi	0/0
28	Toner, Ed	RB	6-0	240	3	Boston College	16/1
85	Turner, Floyd	WR	5-11	198	6	NW Louisiana	10/1
2	Vander Poel, Mark	OT	6-7	303	4	Colorado	0/0
62	Vickers, Kip	OL	6-2	288	1	Miami	0/0
58	Ware, Cassius	LB	5-11	243	R	Mississippi	—
95	Wittingham, Bernard	DE	6-6	257	R	Indiana	—
67	Wolford, Will	OT	6-5	300	9	Vanderbilt	12/12

'94 DRAFT PICKS

RD.	NAME	POS.	HT.	WT.	COLLEGE
1.	Faulk, Marshall	RB	5-10	207	San Diego State
1.	Alberts, Trev	LB	6-4	242	Nebraska
2.	Mahlum, Eric	OG	6-4	284	California
3.	Mathews, Jason	OT	6-6	274	Texas A&M
4.	Banta, Bradford	TE	6-5	250	Southern Cal
5.	Covington, John	DB	6-1	203	Notre Dame
6.	Warren, Lamont	RB	6-0	194	Colorado
7.	Teichelman, Lance	DT	6-4	274	Texas A&M

PRO FOOTBALL WEEKLY 1994 ALMANAC

TEAM AT A GLANCE

TEAM DIRECTORY

Address	P.O. Box 535000 Indianapolis, Indiana 46253 (317) 297-2658
Stadium	Hoosier Dome 100 South Capitol Avenue Indianapolis, Indiana 46225 Capacity: 60,129 Playing surface: AstroTurf
Training Camp	Anderson University Anderson, Indiana 46011
Colors	Royal blue and white
Television	WTHR, Channel 13
Radio	WNDE, 1260 AM WFBQ, 94.9 FM

ADMINISTRATION
President-treasurer: Robert Irsay
Vice president-general manager: James Irsay
Vice president-football operations: Bill Tobin
Vice president-general counsel: Michael Chernoff
Assistant general manager: Bob Terpening
Controller: Kurt Humphrey
Director of pro player personnel: Clyde Powers
Director of college player personnel: George Boone
Director of operations: Pete Ward
Director of public relations: Craig Kelley
Ticket manager: Larry Hall
Director of sales: Rene Longoria
Trainer: Hunter Smith

1994 SCHEDULE

Preseason
Aug. 5	SEATTLE	7:30
Aug. 13	at Cincinnati	7:30
Aug. 20	at Pittsburgh	6:00
Aug. 25	CLEVELAND	7:30

Regular season
SEP. 4	HOUSTON	12:00
SEP. 11	at Tampa Bay	1:00
SEP. 18	at Pittsburgh	1:00
SEP. 25	CLEVELAND	12:00
OCT. 2	SEATTLE	12:00
OCT. 9	at N.Y. Jets	1:00
OCT. 16	at Buffalo	1:00
OCT. 23	WASHINGTON	12:00
OCT. 30	N. Y. JETS	4:00
NOV. 6	at Miami	1:00
NOV. 13	OPEN DATE	
NOV. 20	at Cincinnati	1:00
NOV. 27	NEW ENGLAND	8:00
DEC. 4	at Seattle	1:00
DEC. 11	at New England	1:00
DEC. 18	MIAMI	1:00
DEC. 24	BUFFALO	1:00

HEAD COACH
Ted Marchibroda

With a head-coaching record of 54-55, Marchibroda is third on the Colts' career victories list behind Don Shula (73, 1963-69) and Weeb Ewbank (61, 1954-62). Marchibroda coached the Colts for the first time from 1975 to '79, and then spent time as an assistant coach with the Bears, Lions, Eagles and Bills. While serving in Buffalo as offensive coordinator, his no-huddle offense helped the Bills accomplish 13-3 seasons in 1990 and '91, along with AFC championships and berths in Super Bowls XXV and XXVI. On Jan. 28, 1992, Marchibroda was rehired to lead the Colts. In the second stint with Marchibroda at the helm, Indianapolis went 9-7 in 1992 and 4-12 in '93. Born March 15, 1931, Franklin, Pa.

Previous NFL: offensive coordinator, Buffalo 1989-91; assistant coach, Buffalo 1987-88; offensive coordinator, Philadelphia 1984-85; offensive coordinator, Detroit 1982-83; quarterback, Chicago 1981; head coach, Baltimore 1975-79; offensive coordinator, Washington 1971-74; assistant coach, L.A. Rams 1966-70; backfield, Washington 1961-65.

Previous college: None.

Player: NFL, quarterback, Pittsburgh 1953, 1955-56. College, quarterback, St. Bonaventure 1950-51; Detroit 1952.

ASSISTANT COACHES
Greg Blache: defensive line
Previous NFL: defensive line, 1988-93 Green Bay. Player: No NFL. College: None.

Ron Blackledge: offensive line
Previous NFL: offensive line, 1992-93 Indianapolis; 1982-91 Pittsburgh. Player: No NFL. College: tight end, defensive end, 1957-59 Bowling Green.

Fred Bruney: offensive assistant
Previous NFL: offensive assistant, 1993-93 Indianapolis; 1991-92 N.Y. Giants; 1990 Tampa Bay; 1986-89 Atlanta; 1977-85 Philadelphia;1969-76 Atlanta; 1964-68 Philadelphia; 1962-63 Boston. Player: NFL, defensive back, 1953-56 San Francisco; 1957 Pittsburgh; 1958 L.A. Rams; 1960-62 Boston. College: running back, defensive back, 1950-52 Ohio State.

Gene Huey: running backs
Previous NFL: running backs, 1992-93 Indianapolis. Player: No NFL. College: defensive back, wide receiver, 1966-69 Wyoming.

Jim Johnson: linebackers
Previous NFL: secondary, 1986-93 St. Louis/Phoenix. Player: tight end, 1963-64 Buffalo. College: quarterback, 1959-62 Missouri.

Hank Kuhlman: tight ends
Previous NFL: offensive coordinator-running backs, 1991 Tampa Bay; 1986-1990 St. Louis/Phoenix; 1978-82 Chicago; 1972-74 Green Bay. Player: No NFL. College: running back, 1956-59 Missouri.

Nick Nicolau: offensive coordinator
Previous NFL: offensive coordinator, 1992-93 Indianapolis; 1989-91 Buffalo; 1988 L.A. Raiders;

1994 PREVIEW ■ INDIANAPOLIS

TEAM AT A GLANCE

1981-87 Denver; 1980 New Orleans. Player: No NFL. College: running back, 1957-59 Southern Connecticut.

Jimmy Robinson: wide receivers
Previous NFL: wide receivers, 1991-93 Atlanta. Player: NFL, wide receiver, 1981 Denver; 1980 San Francisco; 1976-79 N.Y. Giants; 1975 Atlanta. College: wide receiver, 1971-75 Georgia Tech.

Pat Thomas: secondary
Previous NFL: secondary, 1990-92 Houston. Player: NFL, defensive back, 1976-82 L.A. Rams. College: defensive back, 1972-75 Texas A&M.

Vince Tobin: defensive coordinator
Previous NFL: defensive coordinator, 1986-92 Chicago. Player: No NFL. College: defensive back, 1961-64 Missouri.

COACHING RECORDS
(including postseason games)

Years	Coach	W	L	T
1953	Keith Molesworth	3	9	0
1954-62	Weeb Ewbank	61	52	1
1963-69	Don Shula	73	26	4
1970-72	Don McCafferty	26	11	1
1972	John Sandusky	4	5	0
1973-74	Howard Schnellenberger	4	13	0
1974	Joe Thomas	41	36	0
1975-79	Ted Marchibroda	41	36	0
1980-81	Mike McCormack	9	23	0
1982-84	Frank Kush	11	28	1
1984	Hal Hunter	0	1	0
1985-86	Rod Dowhower	5	24	0
1986-91	Ron Meyer	36	36	0
1991	Rick Venturi	1	10	0
1992-93	Ted Marchibroda	13	19	0

HISTORICAL HIGHLIGHTS

1946 Bud Rodenburg heads a group that purchases the bankrupt Miami Seahawks in the All-America Football Conference and moves the franchise to Baltimore.
1950 The Colts join the NFL after the AAFC goes out of business.
1951 The franchise is dissolved by the league due to its failing financial condition.
1953 Carroll Rosenbloom becomes the majority owner of the Colts and moves them from Dallas to Baltimore.
1955 Baltimore signs Johnny Unitas, Raymond Berry and Alan Ameche.
1958 The Colts set an all-time club record for margin of victory when they defeat the Packers 56-0. ... Baltimore wins the Western Conference title, then defeats the Giants 23-17 in a sudden death overtime game for the NFL title.
1959 Baltimore again prevails in the NFL West, then again defeats the Giants 31-16 for a second consecutive NFL title.
1964 NFL records are set by Raymond Berry, when he catches his 506th career pass, and by Lenny Moore, who scores 20 touchdowns in one season. ... Baltimore makes it to the NFL championship game but loses to the Cleveland Browns 27-0.
1965 The Colts lose to the Packers 13-10 in a sudden-death playoff for the Western Conference title.
1968 Baltimore plays for the conference title but loses to the Vikings 24-14.
1969 In the new NFL realignment, the Colts move to the American Football Conference.
1970-71 Baltimore wins the AFC East and then defeats the Bengals 17-0 in the playoffs. ... The Colts win the first AFC title by defeating the Oakland Raiders 27-17. ... Baltimore meets the Dallas Cowboys in Super Bowl V and wins 16-13 for the world championship.
1971-72 The Colts make the playoffs as a wild-card team, defeat the Browns 20-3, but lose to the Miami Dolphins in the AFC title game 21-0.
1972 Owner Carroll Rosenbloom trades the Colts to Bob Irsay for the Los Angeles Rams.
1974 QB Bert Jones sets an NFL record by completing 17 consecutive passes, and RB Lydell Mitchell sets another by carrying the ball 40 times in one game.
1975 Lydell Mitchell becomes the first Colt ever to rush for more than 1,000 yards in a season (1,193). The Colts win the AFC East but lose in the playoffs to the Steelers 28-10.
1976 Baltimore again wins the AFC East and again falls to the Steelers in the playoffs, this time by a score of 40-14.
1977 The Colts win their third straight AFC East title, but lose in double overtime 37-31 to the Oakland Raiders in the playoffs.
1984 The Colts move to Indianapolis to play in the Hoosier Dome.
1987-88 The Colts win the AFC East, but lose in the playoffs 38-21 to the Browns.
1992 Ted Marchibroda is hired as head coach, his second stint with the team.
1994 Bill Tobin takes over as vice president of football operations.

109

PRO FOOTBALL WEEKLY 1994 ALMANAC

TEAM AT A GLANCE

HALL OF FAME MEMBERS

	Yrs with Colts	Induction
DT Art Donovan	1953-61	1968
DE Gino Marchetti	1953-64, 66	1972
E Raymond Berry	1955-67	1973
OG-OT Jim Parker	1957-67	1973
HB-FL Lenny Moore	1956-67	1975
Coach Weeb Ewbank	1954-62	1978
QB Johnny Unitas	1956-72	1979
LB Ted Hendricks	1969-73	1990
TE John Mackey	1963-71	1992

RETIRED JERSEY NUMBERS

- 19 QB Johnny Unitas
- 22 HB Buddy Young
- 24 HB-FL Lenny Moore
- 70 DT Art Donovan
- 77 OG-OT Jim Parker
- 82 E Raymond Berry
- 89 DE Gino Marchetti

FIRST-ROUND DRAFT CHOICES
(since 1980)

Year	Selection	College
1980	HB Curtis Dickey	Texas A&M
1981	FB Randy McMillian	Pittsburgh
	DT Donnell Thompson	North Carolina
1982	LB Johnnie Cooks	Mississippi State
	QB Art Schlichter	Ohio State
1983	QB John Elway	Stanford
1984	CB Leonard Coleman	Vanderbilt
	OG Ron Solt	Maryland
1985	LB Duane Bickett	Southern Cal
1986	DE Jon Hand	Alabama
1987	LB Cornelius Bennett	Alabama
1988	No choice	
1989	WR Andre Rison	Michigan State
1990	QB Jeff George	Illinois
1991	No choice	
1992	DT Steve Emtman	Washington
	LB Quentin Coryatt	Texas A&M
1993	WR Sean Dawkins	California
1994	RB Marshall Faulk	San Diego State
	LB Trev Alberts	Nebraska

RECORD VS. OTHER NFL TEAMS
(including postseason games)

	Record
Arizona Cardinals	5-6-0
Atlanta Falcons	10-0-0
Buffalo Bills	20-26-1
Chicago Bears	21-16-0
Cincinnati Bengals	8-5-0
Cleveland Browns	9-14-0
Dallas Cowboys	3-7-0
Denver Broncos	2-9-0
Detroit Lions	17-17-2
Green Bay	18-18-1
Houston Oilers	6-7-0
Kansas City Chiefs	4-6-0
Los Angeles Raiders	3-5-0
Los Angeles Rams	20-16-2
Miami Dolphins	14-35-0
Minnesota Vikings	12-6-1
New England Patriots	20-27-0
New Orleans Saints	3-2-0
New York Giants	7-5-0
New York Jets	27-21-0
Philadelphia Eagles	6-6-0
Pittsburgh Steelers	4-12-0
San Diego Chargers	5-9-0
San Francisco 49ers	21-16-0
Seattle Seahawks	2-1-0
Tampa Bay Buccaneers	5-2-0
Washington Redskins	16-7-0

YEAR-BY-YEAR RECORDS

Year	Won	Lost	Tied
1953	3	9	0
1954	3	9	0
1955	5	6	1
1956	5	7	0
1957	7	5	0
1958*	9	3	0
1959*	9	3	0
1960	6	6	0
1961	8	6	0
1962	7	7	0
1963	8	6	0
1964**	12	2	0
1965**	10	3	1
1966	9	5	0
1967	11	1	2
1968**	13	1	0
1969	8	5	1
1970*	11	2	1
1971**	10	4	0
1972	5	9	0
1973	4	10	0
1974	2	12	0
1975**	10	4	0
1976**	11	3	0
1977**	10	4	0
1978	5	11	0
1979	5	11	0
1980	7	9	0
1981	2	14	0
1982	0	8	1
1983	7	9	0
1984	4	12	0
1985	5	11	0
1986	3	13	0
1987**	9	6	0
1988	9	7	0
1989	8	8	0
1990	7	9	0
1991	1	15	0
1992	9	7	0
1993	4	12	0
Total	281	294	7

Number of NFL championships 3
Number of years .500 or better 22
Number of years below .500 19

*NFL champions
**Playoff team

1994 PREVIEW ■ INDIANAPOLIS

RECORDS

INDIVIDUAL

Service
Seasons played	17	Johnny Unitas (1956-72)
Games played	221	Johnny Unitas (1956-72)
Consecutive games	155	Jerry Logan (1963-72)

Scoring
Points, career	698	Dean Biasucci (1984, 86-93)
Points, season	120	Lenny Moore (1964)
Points, game	24	Lenny Moore (10/4/58)
		Lenny Moore (10/16/60)
		Lenny Moore (10/1/61)
		Lydell Mitchell (10/12/75)
		Eric Dickerson (10/31/88)
Touchdowns, career	113	Lenny Moore (1956-67)
Touchdowns, season	20	Lenny Moore (1964)
Touchdowns, game	4	Lenny Moore (10/4/58)
		Lenny Moore (10/16/60)
		Lenny Moore (10/1/61)
		Lydell Mitchell (10/12/75)
		Eric Dickerson (10/31/88)
Field goals, career	160	Dean Biasucci (1984, 86-93)
Field goals, season	30	Raul Allegre (1983)
Field goals, game	5	Lou Michaels (9/25/66)
		Raul Allegre (10/30/83)
		Dean Biasucci (9/25/88)
Extra points, career	263	Lou Michaels (1964-69)
Exta points, season	53	Lou Michaels (1964)
Extra points, game	8	Tom Feamster (11/25/56)
		Steve Myrha (11/2/58)

Rushing
Yards, career	5,487	Lydell Mitchell (1972-77)
Yards, season	1,659	Eric Dickerson (1988)
Yards, game	198	Norm Bulaich (9/19/71)
Attempts, career	1,391	Lydell Mitchell (1972-77)
Attempts, season	388	Eric Dickerson (1988)
Attempts, game	40	Lydell Mitchell (10/20/74)
Touchdowns, career	63	Lenny Moore (1956-67)
Touchdowns, season	16	Lenny Moore (1964)
Touchdowns, game	4	Eric Dickerson (10/31/88)

Passing
Rating, career	79.1	Bert Jones (1973-81)
Rating, season	102.6	Bert Jones (1976)
Completions, career	2,796	Johnny Unitas (1956-72)
Completions, season	292	Jeff George (1991)
Completions, game	37	Jeff George (11/7/93)
Yards, career	39,768	Johnny Unitas (1956-72)
Yards, season	3,481	Johnny Unitas (1963)
Yards, game	401	Johnny Unitas (9/17/67)
Attempts, career	5,110	Johnny Unitas (1956-72)
Attempts, season	485	Jeff George (1991)
Attempts, game	59	Jeff George (11/7/93)
Touchdowns, career	287	Johnny Unitas (1956-72)
Touchdowns, season	32	Johnny Unitas (1959)
Touchdowns, game	5	Gary Cuozzo (11/14/65)
		Gary Hogeboom (10/4/87)

Receiving
Receptions, career	631	Raymond Berry (1955-67)
Receptions, season	85	Reggie Langhorne (1993)
Receptions, game	13	Joe Washington (9/2/79)
		Lydell Mitchell (12/15/74)
Yards, career	9,275	Raymond Berry (1955-67)
Yards, season	1,298	Raymond Berry (1960)
Yards, game	224	Raymond Berry (11/10/57)
Touchdowns, career	68	Raymond Berry (1955-67)
Touchdowns, season	14	Raymond Berry (1959)
Touchdowns, game	3	By many players

Interceptions
Career	57	Bobby Boyd (1960-68)
Season	11	Tom Keane (1953)
Game	3	By many players

Sacks
Career	56.5	Fred Cook (1974-80)
Season	11.5	Johnnie Cooks (1984)
Game	4.5	Johnnie Cooks (11/25/84)

Longest plays
Run from scrimmage	80	Tom Matte (TD, 10/12/64)
Pass play	90	Bert Jones to Roger Carr (TD, 11/16/75)
Field goal	58	Dan Miller (12/26/82)
Interception return	94	Rick Volk (TD, 10/8/67)
		Larry Burroughs (TD, 12/12/82)
Kickoff return	104	Buddy Young (TD, 11/15/53)
Punt return	90	Carl Taseff (TD, 10/14/56)
Punt	76	David Lee (10/17/71)

Top scorers
	Points
Dean Biasucci (1984, 86-93)	698
Lenny Moore (1956-67)	678
Lou Michaels (1964-69)	586
Raymond Berry (1955-67)	408
Toni Linhart (1974-79)	394
Don McCauley (1971-81)	348

Top rushers
	Yards
Lydell Mitchell (1972-77)	5,487
Eric Dickerson (1987-91)	5,194
Lenny Moore (1956-67)	5,174
Tom Matte (1961-72)	4,646
Alan Ameche (1955-60)	4,045
Randy McMillan (1981-86)	3,876

Top passers
	Completions
Johnny Unitas (1956-72)	2,796
Bert Jones (1973-81)	1,382
Jeff George (1990-93)	874
Jack Trudeau (1986-93)	812
Mike Pagel (1982-85)	587
Earl Morrall (1968-71)	363

Top passers
	Yards
Johnny Unitas (1956-72)	39,768
Bert Jones (1973-81)	17,663
Jack Trudeau (1986-93)	9,647
Jeff George (1990-93)	9,551
Mike Pagel (1982-85)	7,474
Earl Morrall (1968-71)	5,666

Top receivers
	Receptions
Raymond Berry (1955-67)	631
Bill Brooks (1986-92)	411
Lenny Moore (1956-67)	363
Don McCauley (1971-81)	333
John Mackey (1963-71)	320
Jimmy Orr (1961-70)	303

Top receivers
	Yards
Raymond Berry (1955-67)	9,275
Lenny Moore (1956-67)	6,039
Jimmy Orr (1961-70)	5,859
Bill Brooks (1986-92)	5,818
John Mackey (1963-71)	5,126
Roger Carr (1974-81)	4,690

Most interceptions
	No.
Bobby Boyd (1960-68)	57
Don Shinnick (1957-68)	37
Jerry Logan (1963-72)	34
Andy Nelson (1957-63)	32
Rick Volk (1967-75)	31

Most sacks
	No.
Fred Cook (1974-80)	56.5
Duane Bickett (1985-93)	50.0
John Dutton (1974-78)	47.0

111

PRO FOOTBALL WEEKLY 1994 ALMANAC

PREVIEW: KANSAS CITY CHIEFS

The Kansas City Chiefs have the miraculous Joe Montana. They have the gifted Marcus Allen. They also have dominant Neil Smith and quick-striking Derrick Thomas.

With four of the game's most unique players on their side, the Chiefs are preparing for a 1994 season that will not leave them frustrated and disappointed. Last year they managed come-from-behind playoff victories over the Steelers and Oilers. However, when they had to go to Buffalo to play the AFC championship game, the Chiefs were never able to find their rhythm and never had much of a chance in losing 30-13. That loss on the road points out how important it is for the Chiefs to post the AFC's best record in order to have homefield advantage throughout the conference playoffs.

But that's a lesson the Chiefs should have learned before and didn't. Why should 1994 be any different?

In order to have a shot at gaining the best overall record in the AFC, the Chiefs need to keep Joe Montana, 38, healthy, which is a lot easier said than done. Last season Montana was plagued by nagging injuries that gave the Chiefs the appearance of a revolving door at the QB slot. Since his last Super Bowl appearance with the 49ers at the conclusion of the 1989 season, Montana has been virtually imprisoned by his injuries and has given the appearance of being frail by NFL standards.

The Chiefs could be a better team offensively than they were a year ago because they've had one year of experience with Montana and offensive coordinator Paul Hackett. The Chiefs' offensive guru installed a 49ers-style passing offense to coincide with Montana's arrival, a move that took the Chiefs out of the NFL stone age. And the one thing that Chief fans don't have to worry about is Montana being satisfied with his past accomplishments.

"I don't live in the past," Montana said. "I live for exactly what is taking place at that moment. The future and the past take care of themselves. I left Notre Dame, and I left San Francisco. I've always been able to focus on what is happening at the moment and not concern myself with before and after."

Chief fans believe that the Montana they have is still one of the game's masters. Even though he no longer runs well and has one of the weaker arms in the NFL, he is still a great competitor who makes plays. Montana can't run downfield, but he can sidestep the rush. Even though he can't throw the ball 60 yards, he can complete deep passes because he knows the routes his receivers are taking and lets go of the ball early. Montana completed 181-of-298 passes for 2,144 yards with 13 TD's and seven interceptions last year. But while his stats are good, the full story on Montana is not only seen in the numbers. He makes everyone on his team better because of his presence, and that's why Hackett and head coach Marty Schottenheimer continue to start him in the lineup.

When Montana is not in the lineup, the Chiefs will turn to another quarterback familiar with Hackett's offensive scheme, ex-49er Steve Bono, who replaces departed free-agent Dave Krieg. Matt Blundin, the former Virginia star, is still the team's quarterback of the future.

At the RB slot, Allen showed his gratitude to the Chiefs for rescuing him from the Los Angeles Raider scrapheap by rushing for 794 yards, catching 31 passes and scoring 15 touchdowns. Allen is not the breakaway threat he was, but, at age 34, he makes up in guile and savvy what he has lost in footspeed.

"People have tried to write me off in the past, but that never affected me," Allen said. "I always knew I could play. It was just a matter of getting the chance to make a contribution."

Allen's presence allowed the Chiefs to dump power backs Christian Okoye and Barry Word. GM Carl Peterson hoped Allen's presence would rub off on speedy Harvey Williams, but that didn't happen, and the Chiefs released him. Todd McNair, the third-down back, was released. FB Kimble Anders was once considered an afterthought. While he is still not a special performer, he gives a tremendous effort as a blocker and can run fairly effectively between the tackles when he's given that assignment. Rookies Greg Hill and Donnell Bennett are expected to make key contributions.

With Montana at quarterback, the Chief receivers should be as productive as Jerry Rice and John Taylor, right? Montana might make people around him better, but remember what was said about a sow's ear — it can't be turned into a silk purse. Willie Davis and J.J. Birden are not bad, but they certainly can't be compared to the Niners' dynamic duo. Davis caught 52 passes last year for 909 yards and seven touchdowns and is a genuine deep threat who can run away from defenders. Birden is even faster than Davis, and has the potential to give Montana a breakaway threat on every possession. Both Davis and Birden are undersized, and that is a problem in the West-Coast offense because receivers are asked to run quite a few crossing patterns and they end up taking a pounding when they go over the middle. Tim Barnett has the size to run the over-the-middle patterns, but he does not have the speed to run away from defenders. Fred Jones has the willingness to contend with the bumps and bruises on crossing patterns, but he lacks speed and size. At the end of the season and throughout the playoffs, TE Keith Cash was starting to show improvement. He caught a big TD pass in the upset win at Houston and could develop into a

112

1994 PREVIEW ■ KANSAS CITY

solid goalline target.

The Kansas City offensive line doesn't have any superstars but performed admirably in 1993. Its performance against the Oilers' blitzing schemes in the playoffs was incredible, enabling Montana to have the time to find his receivers. The group is often downgraded for overall athletic ability, but it finds ways to get the job done. Its leader is underrated OLT John Alt, one of the league's best pass blockers. Alt is a 6-8, 300-pound mountain of a man who has proved throughout his career he can play with pain. Back and elbow injuries have hampered him but have not forced him out of the lineup. OLG Dave Szott is tough and tenacious but was never able to make it all the way back to his best form after hurting his knee early in the season. C Tim Grunhard is probably the Chiefs' most athletic offensive lineman. He is strong and aggressive on running plays and does a solid job in pass protection. ORG Will Shields started every game as a rookie last season and was effective on the move. Former 49er Ricky Siglar is big and strong and was adequate at right tackle, but he had some bad games as well.

Until Montana joined the Chiefs, defense was the trademark of Kansas City football. Turnovers and creating pressure on opposing quarterbacks are the keys to their defensive game. Thomas, who plays a position called rushbacker, is the unit's most dynamic player. However, last year was not his best season. If he gets a favorable matchup, Thomas can virtually live in the opposing backfield and ring up several sacks in a game. But if he has to face a huge blocker, Thomas can disappear.

Smith might be the top power rusher in the NFL. He usually lines up at left end, and he led the league last year with 15 sacks and also added 27 QB pressures to go with four forced fumbles. Smith has a tremendous wingspan and can block kicks.

The Chiefs get a solid boost from DT's Dan Saleaumua and Joe Phillips. Both are extremely strong and can dominate the middle. Saleaumua is the better athlete, while Phillips is extremely smart. Depth is provided by DE Darren Mickell and former Cowboy Tony Casillas.

The LB crew is much less gifted than the defensive line, especially if you consider Thomas a defensive end. The Chiefs lost OLB Lonnie Marts to the Bucs via free-agency, and they believe that Jaime Fields can replace him. Fields is less than 6-0, but he is a hustler with good speed. Tracy Simien and Tracy Rogers are also overachievers who are limited physically.

Kevin Ross (Atlanta) and Albert Lewis (L.A. Raiders) are now former Chiefs, which means talented but inconsistent Dale Carter must take up the slack along with free-agent acquisition Mark Collins and Atlanta castoff Bruce Pickens. Carter must grow up and stay out of trouble off the field and keep his concentration on it. Collins is one of the game's better corners, but he has had occasional concentration lapses. Pickens was the third pick in the 1991 draft, but he has been a total bust despite having great athletic ability. Dave Whitmore, Charles Mincy and Doug Terry will be at safety. Whitmore is a big hitter, Terry is talented but inexperienced and Mincy is a good ball athlete who is somewhat slow.

Special teams are still an attribute for Kansas City with PK Nick Lowery and Carter returning punts. Inconsistent former Jet Louis Aguiar replaces P Bryan Barker. The Chief kick-blocking units blocked five kicks last year, including one against the Steelers that keyed the playoff victory.

Derrick Thomas

PHOTO BY KEVIN REECE

FAST FACTS

■ The Chiefs have won 23 of their last 28 games against divisional opponents.

■ Since the 1990 season, the Chiefs are plus-65 on the turnover/takeaway table, which is far and away the best in the NFL in that time period. The Redskins are second at plus-33.

■ Marty Schottenheimer is the only coach in the NFL to have taken his team to the playoffs eight times since the start of the 1985 season. He has also never finished worse than second place in any of his nine full seasons.

PRO FOOTBALL WEEKLY 1994 ALMANAC

1994 PLAYER ROSTER

NO.	NAME	POS.	HT.	WT.	EXP.	COLLEGE	GP/GS
5	Aguiar, Louis	P	6-2	215	4	Utah State	16/16
56	Ale, Arnold	LB	6-2	230	1	UCLA	0/0
51	Alexander, Ken	LB	6-3	254	R	Florida State	—
32	Allen, Marcus	RB	6-2	210	13	Southern Cal	16/10
76	Alt, John	OT	6-8	307	11	Iowa	16/16
38	Anders, Kimble	RB	5-11	221	4	Houston	16/13
93	Anderson, Dunstan	DE	6-4	260	R	Tulsa	—
50	Anderson, Erick	LB	6-1	235	3	Michigan	8/1
82	Barnett, Tim	WR	6-1	201	4	Jackson State	16/0
87	Bartrum, Mike	TE	6-4	234	2	Marshall	3/0
30	Bayless, Martin	S	6-2	219	11	Bowling Green	16/10
88	Birden, J.J.	WR	5-9	165	6	Oregon	16/16
14	Blundin, Matt	QB	6-6	233	3	Virginia	1/0
13	Bono, Steve	QB	6-4	215	10	UCLA	8/0
69	Booker, Vaughn	DE	6-5	290	1	Cincinnati	0/0
67	Boyd, Larry	DE	6-2	285	R	Arizona State	—
34	Carter, Dale	CB	6-1	188	3	Tennessee	15/11
89	Cash, Keith	TE	6-4	240	3	Texas	15/0
99	Casillas, Tony	DT	6-3	273	9	Oklahoma	15/14
22	Cobb, Trevor	RB	5-9	190	2	Rice	0/0
24	Collins, Mark	CB	5-10	190	9	Cal State-Fullerton	16/16
84	Davis, Willie	WR	6-0	170	3	Central Arkansas	16/15
6	DeGraffenreid, Allen	WR	6-3	200	1	Ohio State	0/0
23	Dickerson, Ron	WR	6-0	206	R	Arkansas	0/0
2	Elliott, Lin	PK	6-0	182	3	Texas Tech	2/0
59	Fields, Jaime	LB	5-11	230	2	Washington	6/0
59	Frease, Jerry	LB	6-2	221	R	NE Oklahoma	—
60	Gaddy, Robert	OT	6-4	295	R	Alcorn State	—
49	Gay, Matt	S	5-11	180	1	Kansas	0/0
74	Graham, Derrick	OT	6-4	306	5	Appalachian State	11/2
22	Grow, Monty	S	6-3	214	R	Florida	—
61	Grunhard, Tim	C	6-2	299	5	Notre Dame	16/16
57	Harris, Bernardo	LB	6-2	238	R	North Carolina	—
83	Hughes, Danan	WR	6-1	201	2	Iowa	6/0
91	Johnson, Jimmie	TE	6-2	248	6	Howard	6/5
65	Knapp, Lindsay	OG-OT	6-6	280	2	Notre Dame	0/0
62	Kwarta, Bret	OG	6-2	290	R	Cal-Davis	—
8	Lowery, Nick	PK	6-4	205	15	Dartmouth	16/0
95	Malafala, Nick	DT	6-2	295	1	Hawaii	0/0
64	Martin, Emerson	OG	6-2	293	R	Hampton	—
71	McCullough, Russ	OT	6-10	315	1	Missouri	0/0
77	McDaniels, Pellom	DE	6-3	278	2	Oregon State	10/0
92	Mickell, Darren	DE	6-4	280	3	Florida	16/1
42	Mincy, Charles	S	5-11	197	4	Washington	16/4
9	Montgomery, Fred	WR	6-0	183	1	New Mexico State	0/0
19	Montana, Joe	QB	6-2	205	16	Notre Dame	11/11
96	Newton, Tim	DT	6-0	269	9	Florida	16/0
75	Phillips, Joe	DT	6-5	300	9	Southern Methodist	16/16
39	Pickens, Bruce	CB	5-11	190	4	Nebraska	9/4
31	Randall, Brian	CB	6-0	185	R	Delaware State	0/0
52	Rogers, Tracy	LB	6-2	247	5	Fresno State	14/14
97	Saleaumua, Dan	NT	6-0	300	8	Arizona State	16/16
68	Shields, Will	OG	6-2	296	2	Nebraska	16/15
55	Shufelt, Pete	LB	6-2	241	1	Texas-El Paso	0/0
66	Siglar, Ricky	OT	6-7	304	3	San Jose State	14/14

1994 PREVIEW ■ KANSAS CITY

1994 PLAYER ROSTER

NO.	NAME	POS.	HT.	WT.	EXP.	COLLEGE	GP/GS
54	Simien, Tracy	LB	6-1	250	4	Texas Christian	16/14
90	Smith, Neil	DE	6-4	273	7	Nebraska	16/15
21	Stephens, John	RB	6-1	215	7	NW Louisiana	12/5
53	Stephens, Michael	WR	6-1	195	R	Nevada	—
79	Szott, Dave	OG	6-4	290	5	Penn State	14/13
27	Taylor, Jay	CB	5-10	170	6	San Jose State	15/1
25	Terry, Doug	S	5-11	197	3	Kansas	15/8
58	Thomas, Derrick	DE-LB	6-3	242	6	Alabama	16/15
45	Thompson, Ernie	RB	5-11	257	2	Indiana	16/2
94	Traylor, Keith	DE	6-2	290	3	Central Oklahoma	5/0
73	Valerio, Joe	OL	6-5	295	4	Pennsylvania	13/0
10	Van Pelt, Alex	QB	6-1	219	1	Pittsburgh	0/0
72	Villa, Danny	OT-OG	6-5	300	8	Arizona State	13/3
26	Watson, Tim	S	6-1	213	2	Howard	4/0
41	Whitmore, David	S	6-0	232	5	Stephen F. Austin	6/6
47	Wilburn, Barry	CB	6-3	186	7	Mississippi	0/0

'94 DRAFT PICKS

RD.	NAME	POS.	HT.	WT.	COLLEGE
1.	Hill, Greg	RB	5-11	207	Texas A&M
2.	Bennett, Donnell	RB	5-11	241	Miami (Fla.)
3.	Dawson, Lake	WR	6-1	204	Notre Dame
3.	Penn, Chris	WR	6-0	196	Tulsa
4.	Walker, Bracey	DB	5-10	200	North Carolina
5.	Burton, James	DB	5-9	185	Fresno State
5.	Waldrop, Rob	DT	6-1	275	Arizona
6.	Daigle, Anthony	RB	5-10	198	Fresno State
7.	Matthews, Steve	QB	6-2	217	Memphis State
7.	Greene, Tracy	TE	6-4	275	Grambling

PRO FOOTBALL WEEKLY 1994 ALMANAC

TEAM AT A GLANCE

TEAM DIRECTORY

Address	One Arrowhead Drive Kansas City, Missouri 64129 (816) 924-9300
Stadium	Arrowhead Stadium One Arrowhead Drive Kansas City, Missouri 64129 Capacity: 78,067 Playing surface: AstroTurf
Training Camp	University of Wisconsin-River Falls River Falls, Wisconsin 54022
Colors	Red, gold and white
Television	WDAS, Channel 4
Radio	KCFX, 101.1 FM

ADMINISTRATION
Founder: Lamar Hunt
Chairman of the board: Jack Steadman
President-general manager-COO: Carl Peterson
Executive vice president: Tim Connolly
Assistant general manager: Dennis Thum
Treasurer-director of finance: Dale Young
Vice president-player personnel: Lynn Stiles
Director of pro personnel: Mark Hatley
Director of college scouting: Terry Bradway
Director of public relations: Bob Moore
Director of marketing and sales: Dennis Watley
Director of operations: Jeff Klein
Director of ticket sales: Phil Youtsey
Trainer: Dave Kendall

1994 SCHEDULE

Preseason

JULY 31	HOUSTON	8:00
AUG. 6	vs. Minnesota (Tokyo)	*10:00
AUG. 12	at Washington	8:00
AUG. 22	CHICAGO	7:00
AUG. 26	at Buffalo	8:00

*Eastern Time

Regular Season

SEP. 4	at New Orleans	12:00
SEP. 11	SAN FRANCISCO	12:00
SEP. 18	at Atlanta	8:00
SEP. 25	L.A. RAMS	12:00
OCT. 2	OPEN DATE	
OCT. 9	at San Diego	1:00
OCT. 17	at Denver (Mon.)	7:00
OCT. 23	SEATTLE	12:00
OCT. 30	at Buffalo	1:00
NOV. 6	L.A. RAIDERS	7:00
NOV. 13	SAN DIEGO	12:00
NOV. 20	CLEVELAND	12:00
NOV. 27	at Seattle	1:00
DEC. 4	DENVER	3:00
DEC. 12	at Miami (Mon.)	9:00
DEC. 18	HOUSTON	3:00
DEC. 24	at L.A. Raiders	1:00

HEAD COACH
Marty Schottenheimer
With a career won-lost record of 96-57-1 (.627) Schottenheimer is among the top three winningest active NFL coaches. He first became a head coach in Cleveland in 1984 and guided the Browns to first-place division finishes in three of his five seasons there. He was hired by Kansas City in 1989, and guided the Chiefs to second-place finishes in the AFC West from '89 to 1992. In 1993, an 11-5 record was good enough for a division championship. In the '93 playoffs, the Chiefs advanced to the AFC championship game before losing to Buffalo. Born Sept. 23, 1943, Canonsburg, Pa.
Previous NFL: head coach, 1984-88 Cleveland; defensive coordinator-linebackers-defensive backs, 1980-84 Cleveland; linebackers, 1978-79 Detroit; linebackers, 1975-76 N.Y. Giants.
Previous college: None.
Player: NFL, linebacker, 1965-70 Buffalo; 1969-70 Boston. College, linebacker, 1962-64 Pittsburgh.

ASSISTANT COACHES
Dave Adolph: defensive coordinator-linebackers
Previous NFL: defensive coordinator-linebackers, 1992-93 Kansas City; 1989-91 L.A. Raiders; 1986-88 Cleveland; 1979-81, 1985 San Diego. Player: No NFL. College: guard-linebacker, 1955-58 Akron.

Russ Bell: assistant strength and conditioning
Previous NFL: assistant strength and conditioning, 1989-93 Kansas City. Player: No NFL. College: center, 1977-80 Central Missouri State.

John Bunting: defensive assistant
Previous NFL: defensive assistant, 1993 Kansas City. Player: NFL, linebacker, 1972-82 Philadelphia. College: linebacker, 1968-71 North Carolina.

Herman Edwards: defensive backs
Previous NFL: defensive backs, 1992-93 Kansas City. Player: NFL, cornerback, 1977-85 Philadelphia; 1986 L.A. Rams; 1986 Atlanta. College: defensive back, 1972-75 California; 1976-77 San Diego State.

Alex Gibbs: offensive line
Previous NFL: offensive line, 1993 Kansas City; 1992 Indianapolis; 1990-91 San Diego; 1988-89 L.A. Raiders; 1984-87 Denver. Player: No NFL. College: running back, defensive back, 1959-63 Davidson College.

Paul Hackett: offensive coordinator-quarterbacks
Previous NFL: offensive coordinator-quarterbacks, 1993 Kansas City; 1986-88 Dallas; 1983-85 San Francisco; 1981-82 Cleveland. Player: No NFL. College: quarterback, 1965-68 California-Davis.

Mike McCarthy: offensive assistant-quality control
Previous NFL: offensive assistant-quality control, 1993 Kansas City. Player: No NFL. College: tight end, 1985-86 Baker University.

Tom Pratt: defensive line
Previous NFL: defensive line, 1989-93 Kansas City; 1981-88 Cleveland; 1978-80 New Orleans; 1963-77 Kansas City. Player: No NFL. College:

116

1994 PREVIEW ■ KANSAS CITY

TEAM AT A GLANCE

linebacker, 1953-56 Miami (Fla.).
Dave Redding: strength and conditioning
Previous NFL: strength and conditioning, 1989-93 Kansas City; 1982-88 Cleveland. Player: No NFL. College: defensive end, 1972-75 Nebraska.
Al Saunders: assistant head coach-receivers
Previous NFL: assistant head coach-receivers, 1989-93 Kansas City; 1983-88 (1986-88 head coach) San Diego. Player: No NFL. College: defensive back, 1966-69 San Jose State.
Kurt Schottenheimer: special teams
Previous NFL: special teams, 1989-93 Kansas City; 1987-88 Cleveland. Player: No NFL. College: defensive back, 1969-70 Miami (Fla.).
Darvin Wallis: special assistant-quality control
Previous NFL: quality control, 1989-93 Kansas City; 1982-88 Cleveland. Player: No NFL. College: defensive end, 1970-71 Arizona.

COACHING RECORDS
(includes postseason games)

Years	Coach	W	L	T
1960-74	Hank Stram	129	79	10
1975-77	Paul Wiggin	11	24	0
1977	Tom Bettis	1	6	0
1978-82	Marv Levy	31	42	0
1983-86	John Mackovic	30	35	0
1987-88	Frank Gansz	8	22	1
1989-93	Marty Schottenheimer	53	33	1

HISTORICAL HIGHLIGHTS

1960 AFL founder Lamar Hunt retains the Dallas franchise and names the team the Texans.
1962 The Texans win the AFL West, then defeat the Houston Oilers 20-17 to take the AFL crown.
1963 Hunt moves the team to Kansas City and renames it the Chiefs.
1966-67 The Chiefs make the playoffs and beat the Bills 31-7. ... In the first Super Bowl, Kansas City loses to the Green Bay Packers 35-10.
1968 The Chiefs make the playoffs but lose to the Los Angeles Raiders 41-6.
1969-70 In the playoffs, Kansas City defeats the defending NFL champion New York Jets 13-6 and the Oakland Raiders 17-7. ... The Chiefs go to Super Bowl IV and defeat the Minnesota Vikings 23-7 for their first world championship.
1971 Kansas City wins the AFC West but loses in double overtime 27-24 to the Dolphins.
1975 After 15 years as the only head coach in Chiefs' history, Hank Stram is fired.
1981 The Chiefs post their first record above .500 since 1973, going 9-7.
1985 WR Stephone Paige breaks the NFL record for yardage on pass receptions in a single game, when he gains 309 on eight catches against the San Diego Chargers. ... DB Deron Cherry ties an NFL mark by intercepting four passes in a game against the Seattle Seahawks.
1986 The Chiefs make the playoffs for the first time since 1971 but lose to the Jets 35-15.
1990-91 Kansas City earns a wild-card berth in the playoffs but loses to the Dolphins 17-16.
1991-92 The Chiefs again make the playoffs. They defeat the Los Angeles Raiders 10-6 but lose to the Buffalo Bills 37-14 in the divisional playoff game.
1992-93 Kansas City earns a playoff spot but loses to the San Diego Chargers 17-0 in the first round.
1993-94 The Chiefs acquire QB Joe Montana in a trde with San Francisco ... The Chiefs win the AFC West with a record of 11-5. They defeat the Steelers 27-24 in overtime in the first round, and the Oilers 28-20 in the divisional playoff game. ... Kansas City loses to Buffalo in the AFC championship game 30-13.

PRO FOOTBALL WEEKLY 1994 ALMANAC

TEAM AT A GLANCE

HALL OF FAME MEMBERS

	Yrs with Chiefs	Induction
Owner Lamar Hunt	1960-	1972
LB Bobby Bell	1963-74	1983
LB Willie Lanier	1967-77	1986
QB Len Dawson	1962-75	1987
DT Buck Buchanan	1963-75	1990
PK Jan Stenerud	1967-79	1991

RETIRED JERSEY NUMBERS

- 3 PK Jan Stenerud
- 16 QB Len Dawson
- 28 RB Abner Haynes
- 33 RB Stone Johnson
- 36 RB Mack Lee Hill
- 78 LB Bobby Bell
- 86 DT Buck Buchanan

FIRST-ROUND DRAFT CHOICES
(since 1980)

Year	Selection	College
1980	OG Brad Budde	Southern Cal
1981	TE Willie Scott	South Carolina
1982	WR Anthony Hancock	Tennessee
1983	QB Todd Blackledge	Penn State
1984	NT Bill Maas	Pittsburgh
	OT John Alt	Iowa
1985	RB Ethan Horton	North Carolina
1986	OT Brian Jozwiak	West Virginia
1987	RB Paul Palmer	Temple
1988	DE Neil Smith	Nebraska
1989	LB Derrick Thomas	Alabama
1990	LB Percy Snow	Michigan State
1991	RB Harvey Williams	Louisiana State
1992	DB Dale Carter	Tennessee
1993	No choice	
1994	RB Greg Hill	Texas A&M

RECORD VS. OTHER NFL TEAMS
(includes postseason games)

	Record
Arizona Cardinals	3-1-1
Atlanta Falcons	3-0-0
Buffalo Bills	14-17-1
Chicago Bears	2-4-0
Cincinnati Bengals	11-9-0
Cleveland Browns	6-7-2
Dallas Cowboys	2-3-0
Denver Broncos	38-29-0
Detroit Lions	4-3-0
Green Bay	4-2-1
Houston Oilers	23-17-0
Indianapolis Colts	6-4-0
Los Angeles Raiders	32-36-2
Los Angeles Rams	1-3-0
Miami Dolphins	10-9-0
Minnesota Vikings	3-3-0
New England Patriots	13-7-3
New Orleans Saints	2-3-0
New York Giants	1-6-0
New York Jets	15-13-1
Philadelphia Eagles	1-1-0
Pittsburgh Steelers	5-13-0
San Diego Chargers	35-32-1
San Francisco 49ers	1-4-0
Seattle Seahawks	19-12-0
Tampa Bay Buccaneers	5-2-0
Washington Redskins	3-1-0

YEAR-BY-YEAR RECORDS

Year	Won	Lost	Tied
1960	8	6	0
1961	6	8	0
1962***	11	3	0
1963	5	7	2
1964	7	7	0
1965	7	5	2
1966**	11	2	1
1967	9	5	0
1968	12	2	0
1969***	11	3	0
1970	7	5	2
1971**	10	3	1
1972	8	6	0
1973	7	5	2
1974	5	9	0
1975	5	9	0
1976	5	9	0
1977	2	12	0
1978	4	12	0
1979	7	9	0
1980	8	8	0
1981	9	7	0
1982	3	6	0
1983	6	10	0
1984	8	8	0
1985	6	10	0
1986**	10	6	0
1987	4	11	0
1988	4	11	1
1989	8	7	1
1990**	11	5	0
1991**	10	6	0
1992**	10	6	0
1993**	11	5	0
Total	255	233	12

Number of NFL championships 1
Number of years .500 or better 21
Number of years below .500 13

*NFL champions
**Playoff team
***AFL champion (before merger); also won Super Bowl in 1969

1994 PREVIEW ■ KANSAS CITY

RECORDS

INDIVIDUAL

Service
Seasons played	15	Jerrel Wilson (1963-77)
Games played	212	Nick Lowery (1980-93)
Consecutive games	188	Nick Lowery (1980-92)

Scoring
Points, career	1,466	Nick Lowery (1980-93)
Points, season	139	Nick Lowery (1990)
Points, game	30	Abner Haynes (11/26/61)
Touchdowns, career	60	Otis Taylor (1965-75)
Touchdowns, season	19	Abner Haynes (1962)
Touchdowns, game	5	Abner Haynes (11/26/61)
Field goals, career	329	Nick Lowery (1980-93)
Field goals, season	34	Nick Lowery (1990)
Field goals, game	5	By many players
Extra points, career	479	Nick Lowery (1980-93)
Extra points, season	46	Tommy Brooker (1964)
Extra points, game	8	Tommy Brooker (9/8/63)
		Mike Mercer (10/23/66)

Rushing
Yards, career	4,897	Christian Okoye (1987-92)
Yards, season	1,480	Christian Okoye (1989)
Yards, game	200	Barry Word (10/14/90)
Attempts, career	1,246	Christian Okoye (1987-92)
Attempts, season	370	Christian Okoye (1989)
Attempts, game	38	Christian Okoye (12/10/89)
Touchdowns, career	40	Christian Okoye (1987-92)
Touchdowns, season	13	Abner Haynes (1962)
Touchdowns, game	4	Abner Haynes (11/26/61)

Passing
Rating, career	83.2	Len Dawson (1962-75)
Rating, season	101.9	Len Dawson (1966)
Completions, career	2,115	Len Dawson (1962-75)
Completions, season	346	Bill Kenney (1983)
Completions, game	31	Bill Kenney (12/11/83)
Yards, career	28,507	Len Dawson (1962-75)
Yards, season	4,348	Bill Kenney (1983)
Yards, game	435	Len Dawson (11/1/64)
Attempts, career	3,696	Len Dawson (1962-75)
Attempts, season	603	Bill Kenney (1983)
Attempts, game	52	Bill Kenney (10/30/83)
Touchdowns, career	237	Len Dawson (1962-75)
Touchdowns, season	30	Len Dawson (1964)
Touchdowns, game	6	Len Dawson (11/1/64)

Receiving
Receptions, career	416	Henry Marshall (1976-87)
Receptions, season	80	Carlos Carson (1983)
Receptions, game	12	Ed Podolak (10/7/73)
Yards, career	7,306	Otis Taylor (1965-75)
Yards, season	1,351	Carlos Carson (1983)
Yards, game	309	Stephone Paige (12/22/85)
Touchdowns, career	57	Otis Taylor (1965-75)
Touchdowns, season	12	Chris Burford (1962)
Touchdowns, game	4	Frank Johnson (12/13/64)

Interceptions
Career	58	Emmitt Thomas (1966-78)
Season	12	Emmitt Thomas (1974)
Game	4	Bobby Ply (12/16/62)
		Bobby Hunt (10/4/64)
		Deron Cherry (9/29/85)

Sacks
Career	72.5	Art Still (1978-87)
Season	20	Derrick Thomas (1990)
Game	7	Derrick Thomas (11/11/90)

Longest plays
Run from scrimmage	84	Ted McKnight (TD, 9/30/79)
Pass play	93	Mike Livingston to Otis Taylor & Robert Holmes (TD, 10/19/69)
Field goal	58	Nick Lowery (9/18/83)
		Nick Lowery (9/12/85)
Interception return	102	Gary Barbaro (TD, 12/11/77)
Kickoff return	106	Noland Smith (TD, 12/17/67)
Punt return	88	J.T. Smith (TD, 9/23/79)
Punt	74	Bob Grupp (11/4/79)

Top scorers
	Points
Nick Lowery (1980-93)	1,466
Jan Stenerud (1967-79)	1,231
Otis Taylor (1965-75)	360
Abner Haynes (1960-64)	348
Chris Burford (1960-67)	332
Stephone Paige (1983-91)	294

Top rushers
	Yards
Christian Okoye (1987-92)	4,897
Ed Podolak (1969-77)	4,451
Abner Haynes (1960-64)	3,837
Mike Garrett (1966-70)	3,246
Curtis McClinton (1962-69)	3,124
Herman Heard (1984-89)	2,694

Top passers
	Completions
Len Dawson (1962-75)	2,115
Bill Kenney (1979-88)	1,330
Steve DeBerg (1988-91)	934
Mike Livingston (1968-79)	912
Steve Fuller (1979-82)	465
Todd Blackledge (1983-87)	364

Top passers
	Yards
Len Dawson (1962-75)	28,507
Bill Kenney (1979-88)	17,277
Steve DeBerg (1988-91)	11,873
Mike Livingston (1968-79)	11,295
Steve Fuller (1979-82)	5,333
Cotton Davidson (1960-61)	4,919

Top receivers
	Receptions
Henry Marshall (1976-87)	416
Otis Taylor (1965-75)	410
Chris Burford (1960-67)	391
Stephone Paige (1983-91)	377
Carlos Carson (1980-89)	351
Ed Podolak (1969-77)	288

Top receivers
	Yards
Otis Taylor (1965-75)	7,306
Henry Marshall (1976-87)	6,545
Carlos Carson (1980-89)	6,360
Stephone Paige (1983-91)	6,341
Chris Burford (1960-67)	5,525
Fred Arbanas (1962-70)	3,101

Most interceptions
	No.
Emmitt Thomas (1966-78)	58
Johnny Robinson (1960-71)	57
Deron Cherry (1981-91)	50
Gary Barbaro (1976-82)	39
Albert Lewis (1983-93)	38
Bobby Hunt (1962-67)	37

Most sacks
	No.
Art Still (1978-87)	72.5
Derrick Thomas (1989-93)	66
Neil Smith (1988-93)	57
Mike Bell (1979-85, 87-91)	51

119

PRO FOOTBALL WEEKLY 1994 ALMANAC

PREVIEW: LOS ANGELES RAIDERS

Fly the friendly skies.

That has been the motto of an airline, but it is also the calling card of the Raiders now, because, whether they are on offense or defense during the 1994 season, the skies should be very friendly.

On offense, the Raider passing game is frightening enough to send the blood pressure of opposing defensive backs and assistant coaches skyrocketing.

You'd be nervous, too, if you had to defend the Raider receivers. They say speed kills. If that is the case, then the Raider WR corps is a group of football assassins.

Tim Brown is the best of the bunch. He is also the slowest of the team's top four receivers. Slowest, but not slow. His 4.45 speed is nothing to sneeze at, it's just not in the league of the rest of the burners on the roster.

Brown's statistics, however, took a backseat to no one on the Raider roster last season, when he caught 80 passes for 1,180 yards and seven touchdowns. In particular, Brown does an excellent job of running crossing patterns and turning them into long gains.

"The big thing about Timmy, once he catches the ball, anything can happen," said Raider QB Jeff Hostetler.

Brown's three sidekicks — James Jett, Alexander Wright and Raghib Ismail — all have world-class speed. Jett was the most productive of the trio, which came as quite a surprise since he was an undrafted rookie. An Olympic sprinter, Jett looks like the second coming of Cliff Branch after catching 33 passes for 771 yards, an extraordinary 23.4 yards per catch, last season.

"You can see he knows how to adjust to the ball and is making a lot of big-time catches," said Raider CB Terry McDaniel. "Anytime you've got a guy with the speed he's got who can also catch like he can, it's something special."

Jett said, "I like to think of myself as a football player who was also a sprinter. I wouldn't be out here if I didn't think of myself as a football player."

Wright caught 25 passes for 462 yards last season, but he still needs to work on looking like a natural receiver. Ismail joined the team late during the '93 campaign because of protracted contract negotiations and was set back by his lack of knowledge of the offense and the league. The Raiders are looking for him to have a big season this year, however.

The man who really made this group of receiving talent click last season was Hostetler, who was one of the best free-agent pickups in the NFL in '93. He threw for 3,242 yards, had just 10 of his 419 passes intercepted and was the best Raider quarterback since Ken Stabler. Hostetler gave the Raiders the type of toughness at the position that they had been lacking and also provided a legitimate scrambling threat.

Just how important is Hostetler to the Raiders? Consider what Brown said about him last season: "We feel like we can make first downs now. In the past, we weren't able to do that. This whole thing is about Jeff Hostetler. You hate to put the whole thing on his shoulders, but, in a sense, you have to. As he goes, so goes the team. If he has a bad game, I don't think we could rebound from that."

The Raider passing game is impressive, but don't think for a second that the team's secondary shakes in its boots during practices. The Raiders appear to be loaded at cornerback.

Last season the Raider defense ranked fifth in the NFL in passing yards allowed with Terry McDaniel and Lionel Washington manning the CB spots. McDaniel has been named to the last two Pro Bowls because of his speed and coverage ability. Washington, who is 33, was effective in '93.

"All I can say is they have one of the best secondaries in the league," said Cleveland head

PHOTO BY HARRY SCULL JR.

Jeff Hostetler

1994 PREVIEW ■ L.A. RAIDERS

coach Bill Belichick last season. "They have excellent cover men."

The rich get even richer. Not only do the Raiders have McDaniel and Washington on the roster this season, but they added former Chief Albert Lewis during the offseason. Don't be shocked if Lewis beats out Washington for the starting spot opposite McDaniel.

"I came here to compete," said Lewis. "I have no preconceived ideas about playing time or anything else. But I don't see myself as a backup."

At safety, the Raiders have big hitters Derrick Hoskins and Eddie Anderson, along with '93 first-round draft choice Patrick Bates, who has terrific size, speed and athleticism but still must prove he can get the job done.

Making the job of the Raider secondary easier is a defensive line that can provide a big-time pass rush. Howie Long's decision to retire was a big blow, but the Raiders still have DE Anthony Smith, who has great pass-rush skills and recorded 12.5 sacks last season. With Long out of the picture, the Raiders hope Greg Townsend, who once was a great pass rusher, can bounce back from a two-year downward trend. The team's best player on defense last year was DT Chester McGlockton, who gave blockers fits with his speed and strength.

Although they were solid rushing the passer and in coverage, the Raiders had some problems defensively last season. They ranked 20th in the NFL in rushing yards allowed and 21st in points allowed. Their linebackers were only so-so, but they drafted LB's Rob Fredrickson and James Folston 1-2 in the draft in April, and they should upgrade the unit. Fredrickson's forte is coverage, whereas Folston's strength is rushing the passer. OLB Winston Moss was very solid last year, but he still must prove that he can string good seasons back-to-back. OLB Aaron Wallace is fast and blitzes well, but he can be suckered and gets caught out of position a lot in pass coverage.

The Raiders' problem with the running game was even worse on offense than defense. Last year the Raiders ranked 26th in the NFL in rushing yards (1,425) and 27th in average gain per attempt (3.3 yards). Furthermore, Hostetler rushed for 202 of those yards from the QB spot, had the team's longest run (19 yards) and half of the club's rushing touchdowns. As a result, the Raiders signed ex-Chief free-agent Harvey Williams and drafted Calvin Jones out of Nebraska during the offseason. Both will compete for a starting job. Williams was a first-round pick who never lived up to expectations with Kansas City. Greg Robinson, an eighth-round draft choice in '93, led the team in rushing with 591 yards, but, despite having sprinter's speed, his longest regular-season run was only 16 yards. He is a straight-line runner who must learn to read his blocks better. He underwent offseason knee surgery and isn't expected to play until midseason. Nick Bell has been a disappointment and may be phased out. FB Steve Smith is still a good blocker but no longer a running threat. Although only a journeyman, Napoleon McCallum was the club's most effective runner at season's end.

The Raider offensive line was very good at times last year and very average in other instances. OLT Gerald Perry may have had his best season in the NFL and should have gone to the Pro Bowl. "It's a disappointment that he didn't get in because everybody he played (in '93), including some of the top-notch defensive ends in the league, he shut down," said Shell. OG Steve Wisniewski did receive a Pro Bowl berth, but he may have had his worst season as a Raider and got caught out of position more than in previous years. C Don Mosebar was effective, but he is showing some signs of aging. ORG Max Montoya rebounded nicely last year after an injury ruined his '92 season, but how much does he have left at age 38? The Raiders signed ex-Dallas free-agent Kevin Gogan during the offseason, and he likely will start ahead of Montoya. ORT Bruce Wilkerson is talented but erratic.

One of the biggest strengths of the Raiders figures to once again be their special teams. This group was the best in the NFL in '91, not very good in '92 and very good again last year. PK Jeff Jaeger made 35-of-44 field goals last season and scored a whopping 132 points. P Jeff Gossett gets the ball away quickly, is tough to block and does not have many punts returned. Ismail is the most explosive kick returner in football, while Brown had a terrific '93 returning punts, averaging 11.6 yards per return. The Raider coverage units were very good last year and figure to only get better with the addition of Lewis, who is known as a great kick blocker.

The Raiders feel that they would have beaten the Bills in the playoffs last season if not for some questionable calls, and, had they been victorious, could have then made it all the way to the Super Bowl. That attitude, coupled with their improvement over the '93 season, is a good sign, but the fact is that they were not a Super Bowl-caliber team last season. After all, despite finishing the regular season 10-6, they were outscored by 20 points (306-326) in those games. They have considerable talent in certain areas of their roster but still have some holes that need to be patched if they are to make it to this season's Super Bowl.

FAST FACTS

■ RB Napoleon McCallum scored three touchdowns during the 1993 regular season and five more in two playoff games.

■ Jeff Hostetler's 3,242 passing yards last season were the most by a Raider quarterback since Ken Stabler threw for 3,615 in 1979.

■ The Raiders didn't have a single ballcarrier average 4.0 yards or better per carry last season.

PRO FOOTBALL WEEKLY 1994 ALMANAC

1994 PLAYER ROSTER

NO.	NAME	POS.	HT.	WT.	EXP.	COLLEGE	GP/GS
33	Anderson, Eddie	S	6-1	210	9	Fort Valley State	16/16
29	Bates, Patrick	S	6-3	220	2	Texas A&M	13/0
38	Bell, Nick	RB	6-2	250	4	Iowa	10/3
54	Biekert, Greg	LB	6-2	235	2	Colorado	16/0
97	Broughton, Willie	DT	6-5	285	8	Miami, Fla.	15/0
81	Brown, Tim	WR	6-0	195	7	Notre Dame	16/16
56	Bruce, Aundray	DE	6-5	260	7	Auburn	15/0
92	Collons, Ferric	DT	6-6	295	2	California	0/0
31	Dixon, Rickey	S	5-11	185	7	Oklahoma	9/0
46	Dorn, Torin	CB	6-0	190	5	North Carolina	15/0
11	Evans, Vince	QB	6-2	215	14	Southern Cal	8/1
45	Fulcher, David	LB	6-3	245	9	Arizona State	3/0
	Gainer, Derrick	RB	5-11	240	4	Florida A&M	11/0
83	Gault, Willie	WR	6-1	175	12	Tennessee	15/0
87	Glover, Andrew	TE	6-6	245	4	Grambling	15/0
66	Gogan, Kevin	OG	6-7	325	8	Washington	16/16
7	Gossett, Jeff	P	6-2	195	13	Eastern Illinois	16/0
74	Harrison, Nolan	DT-DE	6-5	285	4	Indiana	16/14
80	Hobbs, Daryl	WR	6-2	180	2	Pacific	3/0
12	Hobert, Billy Joe	QB	6-3	230	2	Washington	0/0
20	Hoskins, Derrick	S	6-2	205	3	S. Mississippi	16/16
15	Hostetler, Jeff	QB	6-3	220	11	West Virginia	15/15
86	Ismail, Raghib	WR	5-10	180	2	Notre Dame	13/0
18	Jaeger, Jeff	PK	5-11	190	8	Washington	16/0
82	Jett, James	WR	5-10	165	2	West Virginia	15/1
52	Jones, Mike	LB	6-1	230	4	Missouri	16/2
85	Jordan, Charles	WR	5-10	175	2	Long Beach City	0/0
23	Jordan, Randy	RB	5-10	205	2	North Carolina	10/2
25	Land, Dan	CB	6-0	195	7	Albany State	15/0
79	Lanier, Ken	OT	6-3	290	14	Florida State	2/2
24	Lewis, Albert	CB	6-2	195	12	Grambling	14/13
41	McCallum, Napoleon	RB	6-2	225	6	Navy	13/1
36	McDaniel, Terry	CB	5-10	180	7	Tennessee	16/16
91	McGlockton, Chester	DT	6-4	315	3	Clemson	16/16
21	Montgomery, Tyrone	RB	6-0	190	2	Mississippi	12/0
65	Montoya, Max	OG	6-5	295	16	UCLA	16/16
72	Mosebar, Don	C	6-6	300	11	Southern Cal	16/16
99	Moss, Winston	LB	6-3	240	8	Miami (Fla.)	16/16
64	Peat, Todd	OG	6-2	305	6	Northern Illinois	16/0
71	Perry, Gerald	OT	6-6	300	7	Southern-B.R.	15/15
96	Powers, Warren	DT	6-7	285	5	Maryland	0/0
28	Robinson, Greg	RB	5-10	200	2	N.E. Louisiana	12/12
78	Skrepenak, Greg	OT	6-6	305	3	Michigan	15/1
94	Smith, Anthony	DE	6-3	260	5	Arizona	16/2
39	Smith, Kevin	TE	6-4	255	2	UCLA	10/1
77	Stephens, Rich	OG	6-7	300	2	Tulsa	16/1
93	Townsend, Greg	DE	6-3	270	12	Texas Christian	16/16
37	Trapp, James	CB	6-0	180	2	Clemson	14/2
67	Turk, Dan	C	6-4	290	10	Wisconsin	16/0
51	Wallace, Aaron	LB	6-3	240	5	Texas A&M	16/14
48	Washington, Lionel	CB	6-0	185	12	Tulane	16/16
68	Wilkerson, Bruce	OT	6-5	295	8	Tennessee	14/14
22	Williams, Harvey	RB	6-2	225	3	Louisiana State	7/6
88	Williams, Jamie	TE	6-4	245	10	Nebraska	16/0
76	Wisniewski, Steve	OG	6-4	285	6	Penn State	16/16

1994 PREVIEW ■ L.A. RAIDERS

1994 PLAYER ROSTER

NO.	NAME	POS.	HT.	WT.	EXP.	COLLEGE	GP/GS
89	Wright, Alexander	WR	6-0	190	5	Auburn	15/15
66	Wright, Steve	OT	6-6	260	12	Northern Iowa	0/0

'94 DRAFT PICKS

RD.	NAME	POS.	HT.	WT.	COLLEGE
1.	Fredrickson, Rob	LB	6-3	242	Michigan State
2.	Folston, James	DE	6-2	235	Northeast Louisiana
3.	Jones, Calvin	RB	5-11	212	Nebraska
4.	Robbins, Austin	DT	6-5	293	North Carolina
5.	Patterson, Roosevelt	OG	6-4	313	Alabama
7.	Holmberg, Rob	LB	6-3	225	Penn State

PRO FOOTBALL WEEKLY 1994 ALMANAC

TEAM AT A GLANCE

TEAM DIRECTORY

Address 332 Center Street
El Segundo, California 90245
(310) 322-3451

Stadium L.A. Memorial Coliseum
3911 South Figueroa Street
Los Angeles, California 90037
Capacity: 68,000
Playing surface: Grass

Training Camp Radisson Hotel
Oxnard, California 93030

Colors Silver and black

Television KNBC, Channel 4
Radio KFI, 640 AM
KWKW, 1330 AM (Spanish)

ADMINISTRATION
President of the general partner: Al Davis
Executive assistant: Al LoCasale
Football operations: Steve Ortmayer
Legal affairs: Jeff Birren, Amy Trask
Senior executive: John Herrera
Senior administrator: Morris Bradshaw
Finance: Gary Huff
Business manager: John Novak
Pro football scouting director: George Karras
Administrative assistant: Mark Arteaga
Publications: Mike Taylor
Community relations: Gil Lafferty-Hernandez
Ticket operations: Peter Eiges
Trainer: George Anderson

1994 SCHEDULE

Preseason
JULY 31	vs. Denver (Barcelona)	*1:00
AUG. 7	at Dallas	8:00
AUG. 13	at Pittsburgh	6:00
AUG. 20	at L.A. Rams	7:00
AUG. 27	at Houston	1:00

*Eastern Time

Regular season
SEP. 5	at San Francisco (Mon.)	6:00
SEP. 11	SEATTLE	1:00
SEP. 18	at Denver	2:00
SEP. 25	SAN DIEGO	1:00
OCT. 2	OPEN DATE	
OCT. 9	at New England	4:00
OCT. 16	at Miami	1:00
OCT. 23	ATLANTA	1:00
OCT. 30	HOUSTON	1:00
NOV. 6	at Kansas City	7:00
NOV. 13	at L.A. Rams	1:00
NOV. 20	NEW ORLEANS	1:00
NOV. 27	PITTSBURGH	1:00
DEC. 5	at San Diego (Mon.)	6:00
DEC. 11	DENVER	1:00
DEC. 18	at Seattle	5:00
DEC. 24	KANSAS CITY	1:00

HEAD COACH
Art Shell

A member of the Pro Football Hall of Fame, Shell has been head coach of the Raiders since Oct. 3, 1989, having been hired after Mike Shanahan was fired early in the season. Shell thus became the first African-American head coach in the NFL's modern era. He played for the Raiders 15 seasons and was regarded as one of the best offensive tackles ever. After he retired, he joined the Raiders as an OL coach. In his first full season as head coach in 1990, the Raiders went 12-4 and won the AFC West, reaching the playoffs. For his efforts, Shell won Coach of the Year honors that season. Under Shell, the Raiders have failed to make the playoffs only once — in 1992 when the club posted a 7-9 record. Born Nov. 26, 1946, Charleston, S.C.

Previous NFL: offensive line, L.A. Raiders 1983-89.
Previous college: None.
Player: NFL, offensive tackle, 1968-82 Oakland/L.A. Raiders. College, offensive tackle, 1965-67 Maryland State.

ASSISTANT COACHES
Fred Biletnikoff: wide receivers
Previous NFL: wide receivers, 1989-93 L.A. Raiders. Player: NFL, wide receiver, 1965-78 Oakland. College: wide receiver, 1962-64 Florida State.

Gunther Cunningham: defense-linebackers
Previous NFL: defense-linebackers, 1991-93 L.A. Raiders; 1985-90 San Diego; 1982-84 Baltimore/Indianapolis. Player: No NFL. College: linebacker, 1965-67 Oregon.

John Fox: defensive coordinator
Previous NFL: defensive backs, 1992-93 San Diego; 1989-91 Pittsburgh. Player: No NFL. College: guard, 1967-68 Maryland.

Ray Hamilton: defensive line
Previous NFL: defensive line, 1993 L.A. Raiders; 1991 Tampa Bay; 1985-89 New England. Player: NFL, nose tackle, 1973-81 New England. College: nose tackle, 1969-72 Oklahoma.

Jim Haslett: linebackers
Previous NFL: linebackers, 1992-93 L.A. Raiders. Player: NFL, linebacker, 1979-86 Buffalo; 1987 N.Y. Jets. College: defensive end, 1975-78 Indiana University (Pa.).

Odis McKinney: defensive backs
Previous NFL: defensive backs, 1990-93 L.A. Raiders. Player: NFL, defensive back, 1978-79 N.Y. Giants; 1980-85 Oakland/L.A. Raiders; 1985 Kansas City; 1986 L.A. Raiders. College: defensive back, 1976-77 Colorado.

Bill Meyers: offensive line
Previous NFL: offensive line, 1993 L.A. Raiders; 1984 Pittsburgh; 1982-83 Green Bay. Player: No NFL. College: tackle, 1970-71 Stanford.

Steve Ortmayer: football operations-special teams
Previous NFL: football operations-special teams, 1990-93 L.A. Raiders; 1987-89 San Diego (general manager); 1978-86 Oakland/L.A. Raiders; 1975-77 Kansas City. Player: No NFL. College: None.

1994 PREVIEW ■ L.A. RAIDERS

TEAM AT A GLANCE

Jack Reilly: running backs
Previous NFL: quarterbacks/passing-game coordinator, 1990-93 San Diego. Player: No NFL. College: quarterback, 1963 Washington State; 1964, Santa Monica College; 1965-66 Long Beach State.

Jack Stanton: defensive backs
Previous NFL: defensive backs, 1989-93 L.A. Raiders; 1984-85 Atlanta. Player: NFL, running back, 1961 Pittsburgh. College: running back, 1959-60 North Carolina State.

Tom Walsh: offense
Previous NFL: 1982-93 L.A. Raiders. Player: No NFL. College: None.

Mike White: offensive line
Previous NFL: offensive line, 1990-93 L.A. Raiders; 1978-79 San Francisco. Player: No NFL. College: offensive end, 1955-57 California.

COACHING RECORDS
(includes postseason games)

Years	Coach	W	L	T
1960-61	Eddie Erdelatz	6	10	0
1961-62	Marty Feldman	2	15	0
1962	Red Conkright	1	8	0
1963-65	Al Davis	23	16	3
1966-68	John Rauch	35	10	1
1969-78	John Madden	112	39	7
1979-87	Tom Flores	91	56	0
1988-89	Mike Shanahan	8	12	0
1989-93	Art Shell	47	34	0

HISTORICAL HIGHLIGHTS

1960 A syndicate headed by Y.C. "Chet" Soda and including Wayne Valley establishes the Oakland Raiders as a charter member of the American Football League.
1963 Al Davis becomes head coach and general manager of the Raiders.
1967-68 Oakland posts a record of 13-1 and wins the AFL championship by defeating Houston 40-7. ... The Raiders go to Super Bowl II but lose to the Green Bay Packers 33-14.
1968 The Raiders again reach the AFL title game but lose to the New York Jets 27-23.
1969 QB Daryle Lamonica sets a pro football record with six touchdown passes in one half in a 50-21 win over Buffalo. ... The Raiders win their third straight AFL West title. They set a club scoring record in a 56-7 win over Houston in the playoffs but lose to Kansas City 17-7 in the AFL title game.
1970 The Raiders become the first team to win four consecutive division titles. ... They beat the Dolphins 21-14 but fall to the Colts in the AFC championship game 27-17.
1972 Oakland wins its fifth division title in six years but loses to the Steelers 13-7 in the playoffs.
1973 After its sixth divisional crown, the Raiders beat the Steelers 33-14 in the first round of the playoffs but then lose 27-10 to the Dolphins.
1974 Oakland makes it seven division championships, defeats the Dolphins 28-26 in the playoffs, but loses to the Steelers 24-13 in the AFC championship game.
1975 George Blanda becomes the first and only NFL player to score 2,000 points. ... The Raiders make it to the AFC title game again but fall to the Steelers 16-10.
1976-77 Oakland wins its ninth divisional title, defeats New England 24-21 and takes the AFC crown with a 24-7 win over the Steelers. ... The Raiders face the Vikings at the Rose Bowl in Super Bowl XI and win 32-14.
1977-78 The Raiders again play for the AFC championship but lose at Denver 20-17.
1980-81 The Raiders become the first team in NFL history to post 16 consecutive winning seasons. ... Oakland defeats Houston 27-7 in the wild-card game, Cleveland in the divisional playoff 14-12, and San Diego 34-27 for the AFC title. ... The Raiders defeat the Philadelphia Eagles in Super Bowl XV by a score of 27-10.
1982 The Raiders move to Los Angeles and play their games at the Coliseum. ... The L.A. Raiders win their division in a strike-shortened season but then lose to the Jets 17-14 in the playoffs.
1983-84 With their 18th winning season in 19 years, the Raiders go to the playoffs and defeat the Steelers 38-10 and the Seattle Seahawks 30-12. ... In Super Bowl XVIII, the Raiders demolish the Washington Redskins 38-9.
1984 Once again the Raiders make the playoffs, this time as a wild-card, but they cannot get by Seattle, losing 13-7.
1985 The Raiders celebrate their 20th winning season and take the division crown. But they lose to New England in the playoffs 27-20.
1987 The L.A. Raiders open their new training facilities at Oxnard, Calif.
1990-91 Raiders win their 14th division championship and earn their 16th trip to the playoffs. The Raiders defeat the Bengals for their 20th postseason victory but are annihilated by the Buffalo Bills 51-3 in the AFC title game.
1991 Raiders make the playoffs as a wild-card team but lose 10-6 to Kansas City.
1993-94 The Raiders win their 300th regular-season game. ... With a record of 10-6, they make the playoffs as a wild-card and defeat Denver 42-24. In the divisional playoff game, the Raiders fall to the Bills 29-23.

PRO FOOTBALL WEEKLY 1994 ALMANAC

TEAM AT A GLANCE

HALL OF FAME MEMBERS

	Yrs with Raiders	Inducted
C Jim Otto	1960-74	1980
QB-PK George Blanda	1967-75	1981
CB Willie Brown	1967-78	1984
OG Gene Upshaw	1967-81	1987
WR Fred Biletnikoff	1965-78	1988
OT Art Shell	1968-82	1989
LB Ted Hendricks	1975-83	1990
Owner Al Davis	1963-94	1992

RETIRED JERSEY NUMBERS
None

FIRST-ROUND DRAFT CHOICES
(since 1980)

Year	Selection	College
1980	QB Mark Wilson	Brigham Young
1981	DB Ted Watts	Texas Tech
	OT Curt Marsh	Washington
1982	RB Marcus Allen	Southern Cal
1983	OT Don Mosebar	Southern Cal
1984	No choice	
1985	WR Jessie Hester	Florida State
1986	DE Bob Buczkowski	Pittsburgh
1987	OT John Clay	Missouri
1988	WR Tim Brown	Notre Dame
	CB Terry McDaniel	Tennessee
	DE Scott Davis	Illinois
1989	No choice	
1990	DE Anthony Smith	Arizona
1991	QB Todd Marinovich	Southern Cal
1992	DL Chester McGlockton	Clemson
1993	DB Patrick Bates	Texas A&M
1994	LB Rob Fredrickson	Michigan State

RECORD VS. OTHER NFL TEAMS
(includes postseason games)

	Record
Arizona Cardinals	2-1-0
Atlanta Falcons	4-3-0
Buffalo Bills	15-16-0
Chicago Bears	5-3-0
Cincinnati Bengals	16-7-0
Cleveland Browns	8-4-0
Dallas Cowboys	3-2-0
Denver Broncos	48-19-2
Detroit Lions	5-2-0
Green Bay Packers	5-3-0
Houston Oilers	22-13-0
Indianapolis Colts	5-3-0
Kansas City Chiefs	36-32-2
Los Angeles Rams	5-2-0
Miami Dolphins	16-5-1
Minnesota Vikings	7-2-0
New England Patriots	13-13-1
New Orleans Saints	3-2-1
New York Giants	4-2-0
New York Jets	14-11-2
Philadelphia Eagles	3-4-0
Pittsburgh Steelers	10-6-0
San Diego Chargers	42-25-2
San Francisco 49ers	5-2-0
Seattle Seahawks	19-15-0
Tampa Bay Buccaneers	3-0-0
Washington Redskins	6-2-0

YEAR-BY-YEAR RECORDS

Year	Won	Lost	Tied
1960	6	8	0
1961	2	12	0
1962	1	13	0
1963	10	4	0
1964	5	7	2
1965	8	5	1
1966	8	5	1
1967***	13	1	0
1968**	12	2	0
1969**	12	1	1
1970**	8	4	2
1971	8	4	2
1972**	10	3	1
1973**	9	4	1
1974**	12	2	0
1975**	11	3	0
1976*	13	1	0
1977**	11	3	0
1978	9	7	0
1979	9	7	0
1980*	11	5	0
1981	7	9	0
1982**	8	1	0
1983*	12	4	0
1984**	11	5	0
1985**	12	4	0
1986	8	8	0
1987	5	10	0
1988	7	9	0
1989	8	8	0
1990**	12	4	0
1991**	9	7	0
1992	7	9	0
1993**	10	6	0
Total	**304**	**185**	**11**

Number of NFL championships 3
Number of years .500 or better 26
Number of years below .500 8

*NFL champions
**Playoff team
***AFL champions (before merger)

1994 PREVIEW ■ L.A. RAIDERS

RECORDS

INDIVIDUAL

Service
Seasons played	15	Jim Otto (1960-74)
		Art Shell (1968-82)
		Gene Upshaw (1967-81)
Games played	217	Gene Upshaw (1967-81)
Consecutive games	210	Jim Otto (1960-74)

Scoring
Points, career	863	George Blanda (1967-75)
Points, season	117	George Blanda (1968)
Points, game	24	Art Powell (12/22/63)
		Marcus Allen (9/24/84)
Touchdowns, career	95	Marcus Allen (1982-92)
Touchdowns, season	18	Marcus Allen (1984)
Touchdowns, game	4	Art Powell (12/22/63)
		Marcus Allen (9/24/84)
Field goals, career	162	Chris Bahr (1980-88)
Field goals, season	35	Jeff Jaeger (1993)
Field goals, game	4	By many players
Extra points, career	395	George Blanda (1967-75)
Extra points, season	56	George Blanda (1967)
Extra points, game	7	Mike Mercer (10/22/63)
		Mike Mercer (12/22/63)
		Errol Mann (11/28/76)

Rushing
Yards, career	8,545	Marcus Allen (1982-92)
Yards, season	1,759	Marcus Allen (1985)
Yards, game	221	Bo Jackson (11/30/87)
Attempts, career	2,090	Marcus Allen (1982-92)
Attempts, season	380	Marcus Allen (1985)
Attempts, game	36	Mark van Eeghen (10/23/77)
Touchdowns, career	79	Marcus Allen (1982-92)
Touchdowns, season	16	Pete Banaszak (1975)
Touchdowns, game	3	By many players

Passing
Completions, career	1,486	Ken Stabler (1970-79)
Completions, season	304	Ken Stabler (1979)
Completions, game	34	Jim Plunkett (9/12/85)
Yards, career	19,078	Ken Stabler (1970-79)
Yards, season	3,615	Ken Stabler (1979)
Yards, game	419	Cotton Davidson (10/25/64)
Attempts, career	2,481	Ken Stabler (1970-79)
Attempts, season	498	Ken Stabler (1979)
Attempts, game	59	Todd Marinovich (9/20/92)
Touchdowns, career	150	Ken Stabler (1970-79)
Touchdowns, season	34	Daryle Lamonica (1969)
Touchdowns, game	6	Tom Flores (12/22/63)
		Daryle Lamonica (10/19/69)

Receiving
Receptions, career	589	Fred Biletnikoff (1965-78)
Receptions, season	95	Todd Christensen (1986)
Receptions, game	12	Dave Casper (10/3/76)
Yards, career	8,974	Fred Biletnikoff (1965-78)
Yards, season	1,361	Art Powell (1964)
Yards, game	247	Art Powell (12/22/63)
Touchdowns, career	76	Fred Biletnikoff (1965-78)
Touchdowns, season	16	Art Powell (1964)
Touchdowns, game	4	Art Powell (12/2/63)

Interceptions
Career	39	Willie Brown (1967-78)
		Lester Hayes (1977-86)
Season	13	Lester Hayes (1980)
Game	3	By five players

Longest plays
Run from scrimmage	92	Bo Jackson (TD, 11/5/89)
Pass play	99	Jim Plunkett to Cliff Branch (TD, 10/2/83)
Field goal	54	Jeff Jaeger (10/4/92)
		George Fleming (10/1/61)
Interception return	102	Eddie Anderson (TD, 12/14/92)
Kickoff return	104	Ira Matthews (TD, 10/25/79)
Punt return	97	Greg Pruitt (TD, 10/2/83)
Punt	77	Wayne Crow (10/29/61)

Top scorers
	Points
George Blanda (1967-75)	863
Chris Bahr (1980-88)	817

Top rushers
	Yards
Marcus Allen (1982-92)	8,545
Mark van Eeghen (1974-81)	5,907
Clem Daniels (1961-67)	5,107

Top passers
	Completions
Ken Stabler (1970-79)	1,486
Daryle Lamonica (1967-74)	1,138
Jim Plunkett (1978-86)	960

Top passers
	Yards
Ken Stabler (1970-79)	19,078
Daryle Lamonica (1967-74)	16,655
Jim Plunkett (1978-86)	12,665

Top receivers
	Receptions
Fred Biletnikoff (1965-78)	589
Cliff Branch (1972-85)	501
Todd Christensen (1979-88)	461

Top receivers
	Yards
Fred Biletnikoff (1965-78)	8,974
Cliff Branch (1972-85)	8,685
Todd Christensen (1979-88)	5,874

Most interceptions
	No.
Willie Brown (1967-78)	39
Lester Hayes (1977-86)	39

PREVIEW: LOS ANGELES RAMS

You can't build a towering skyscraper without a good, strong foundation. The Rams' foundation is rock-solid, thanks to DT Sean Gilbert and RB Jerome Bettis, the team's first-round draft choices in 1992 and '93, respectively. The organization will try to build from there, hoping to improve upon records of 5-11 in 1993 and 6-10 in 1992.

In Bettis, the Rams unleashed one of the most exciting rookies of the '93 campaign. He reminded many observers of former Oiler RB Earl Campbell. The most impressive thing about Bettis is his powerful running ability. In addition to his battering-ram style, Bettis also showed that he could break long runs to the outside. As a rookie, he rushed for 1,429 yards, averaged a whopping 4.9 yards per carry and was clearly the cornerstone of the offense. Ram head coach Chuck Knox has always loved to have a strong running game, so there is every reason to believe Bettis will follow up on his strong rookie campaign with an impressive season this year. Rest assured that opposing defenses are losing sleep at that thought.

"That man is a load," said New Orleans LB Vaughan Johnson.

Quite simply, Bettis can intimidate the opposition.

"Nobody is strong enough to tackle him with his arms, not unless he wants a dislocated shoulder," said OT Irv Eatman, who blocked for Bettis in 1993 but was cut during the offseason. "Being a lineman, I don't get to see it very often, but I sure hear it. You hear guys going, 'Ughhh!' all over the field. That's Jerome punishing them."

Bettis said, "I like to have them suffering out there a little bit. It really throws a defense off. The guy's partners say, 'Oooh, he just smacked the mess out of that man. Let's rethink this.' "

Opponents would do well to think twice about directing plays toward Gilbert, who was clearly the bright spot of last season's defense. Despite being constantly double-teamed, Gilbert still had a team-high 10.5 sacks and was the club's No. 2 tackler. He has incredible physical talent, and, as his technique gets better, he should only get better this season and beyond. The key for Gilbert is to stay healthy and motivated. If he does, he is on the verge of becoming an NFL superstar.

But, while Bettis and Gilbert appear to be ready for huge seasons in 1994, there is much uncertainty for the rest of the Rams.

On offense, the question is, how much help will Bettis get from his friends?

The quarterback will be Chris Miller, who the Rams acquired via free-agency.

"Chris Miller's our man because we felt he's proven what he can do at this level," said Knox. "He's won a lot of big games, he's been to the Pro Bowl and we felt that he was the best man available."

Clearly, the Rams had to make a move at quarterback in light of the way things had deteriorated for previous starter Jim Everett. Clearly, Miller has the potential to do great things.

Nonetheless, Miller is more a question mark than an exclamation point. When healthy, he has been an outstanding NFL performer. The problem is that he has not been terribly durable as a pro. In 1992 Miller suffered a knee injury around midseason, and last year he lasted only three games before suffering another knee injury.

The Rams say they expect the knee to be healthy and are not concerned. Ex-Cardinal Chris Chandler will back him up. *If* healthy, Miller is an accurate passer who does a tremendous job throwing the long ball. *If* healthy, Miller provides a nice complement to Bettis. *If* healthy, Miller figures to improve the Rams on offense. Notice a pattern?

Assuming Miller is healthy, the people he'll be throwing to also appear to have their share of question marks. WR Henry Ellard looked washed up in '92 but rebounded last season to catch 61 passes for 945 yards and two touchdowns. But he signed with the Redskins as a free agent during the offseason and will have to be replaced. In his first three years in the NFL, WR Willie Anderson averaged 29.0, 26.0 and 21.5 yards per catch and twice went over 1,000 yards receiving. But his numbers have been mediocre for the past three seasons and he no longer puts fear into the hearts of opposing defenses. Sure-handed rookie Isaac Bruce could replace Ellard, but former Charger Nate Lewis and ex-Patriot Greg McMurtry figure in the picture, too. Losing starting TE Pat Carter via free-agency hurts, even though he did not play up to expectations last season. Troy Drayton was often bewildered by the complexities of playing H-back last season, although he did seem to be catching on by year's end.

Although Bettis had a magnificent rookie season, don't take this to mean the Rams are set along the offensive line this season. Eatman, whose knees were shot and was cut, will probably be replaced by No. 1 pick Wayne Gandy at left tackle if things go right. ORT Jackie Slater has had a fantastic career, but he is 40 years old. OLG Tom Newberry seems to have gotten old in a hurry and missed the last seven games in 1993 after hurting his knee. C Bern Brostek can dominate with strength and muscle, and some experts feel he should have gone to the Pro Bowl last season.

Defensively, the Rams also have problems, despite the fact that Gilbert shows so much promise. Last season the Ram defense allowed 367 points, was awful on third down and collapsed in the secondary after injuries took their toll.

If the Ram defense holds up in '94, the defensive line will have to be its pillar of strength, since

1994 PREVIEW ■ L.A. RAMS

Jerome Bettis

that appears to be the area at which the club is best-equipped.

In addition to the presence of Gilbert, the Rams now have Jimmie Jones to man the other DT spot. The Rams shelled out big bucks to sign Jones away from the Cowboys because of his amazing quickness and speed for a tackle. "This is the guy we identified from the beginning who could help us," said Knox. However, Jones was a career backup with the Cowboys because of a lack of consistency. If Knox can find a way to keep Gilbert and Jones hungry on every down, they could be an awesome tandem this season.

The Rams also have talent at defensive end. DRE Fred Stokes had 9.5 sacks last season and played the run better than he had during his days with the Redskins. DLE Robert Young was leading the league in sacks in '93 with seven in the first four games, but he hurt his knee in Game Five and was never a factor after that.

Durability could be a problem at linebacker in '94. Shane Conlan is past his prime and has a hard time staying healthy. Keeping him on the field is key, because Conlan is a better-than-average middle linebacker who possesses toughness, hustle and intelligence. OLB Henry Rolling was pretty solid playing over the tight end last year, but he also is not know for his durability. OLB Roman Phifer developed nicely last year and had a team-high 96 solo tackles and 117 total tackles while displaying sideline-to-sideline range and good awareness.

The secondary is where the Rams need a lot of improvement over last season. This unit collapsed after CB Todd Lyght hurt his knee, finishing the season 27th in the league in average gain per pass play allowed. Although Lyght had only two interceptions when he hurt his knee during warmups before the Redskin game, the Rams' 10th game of the season, he was playing at or near a Pro Bowl level. Lyght may not be the most physical cornerback in the NFL, but he is smart in coverage, has a lot of athletic ability and possesses good ball awareness. The Rams hope speedy Steve Israel will be their other cornerback in '94, but, despite having all the tools, he has yet to show he can get the job done.

Safety was a real problem last season for the Rams. Pat Terrell should be a star, but he can't even hold a starting job because he doesn't make enough plays when needed and has major lapses. Anthony Newman has shown flashes of ability, but he didn't do so often enough last year. All told, the Rams' ballhawking safeties picked off a mere three passes last season on a team that often had a pretty good pass rush. Newman didn't have a single interception, even though he started every game at free safety. It's conceivable that rookies Toby Wright and Keith Lyle could be the Rams' starting safeties before the '94 season is over.

If you're looking for reasons for optimism, don't look in the direction of the Ram special teams. PK Tony Zendejas set accuracy records for kicks of 50 yards or more, but that is misleading. He has a below-average NFL leg and really hurts the teams in terms of field position with his weak kickoffs. While he was 6-of-8 from 50 yards or more, he did not make a kick from 40 to 49 yards all of last season. P Sean Landeta fares well if you look at gross average, but he does not place the ball well and will outkick his coverage. His net average was very poor last season.

In '93 the Ram kick-return and kick-coverage teams killed them, and the team's overall special-team play was the worst in the NFL. The Rams returned opposing punts 102 yards all year, with a long return of only 13 yards. The opposition averaged 12.4 yards per return and ran back two punts for scores. The Rams averaged a mere 16.8 yards per kickoff return with a long of 35 yards, while the opposition averaged 20.9 yards per return, even though Zendejas' kickoffs rarely made it to the goalline and short kickoffs should cut down on kickoff-return yardage.

Yes, Bettis and Gilbert give the Rams one of the most dynamic, young one-two punches in the NFL, but, if the Rams are to start making a move in the standings, those two are going to have to get more help from their teammates in '94.

FAST FACTS

■ For his career, Ram PK Tony Zendejas is 17-of-23 from 50-plus yards (73.9 percent), which makes him the NFL's all-time percentage leader from 50-plus yards based on a minimum of 15 attempts.

■ Over the last seven weeks of last season, RB Jerome Bettis ran 36 sweeps for 318 yards, an average of 8.8 yards per carry.

■ OT Jackie Slater owns the Ram record for most games played (246). He is tied for sixth place on the NFL's all-time list with Fran Tarkenton.

PRO FOOTBALL WEEKLY 1994 ALMANAC

1994 PLAYER ROSTER

NO.	NAME	POS.	HT.	WT.	EXP.	COLLEGE	GP/GS
83	Anderson, Willie	WR	6-0	172	7	UCLA	15/15
77	Ashmore, Darryl	OT	6-7	300	3	Northwestern	9/7
28	Bailey, Robert	CB	5-9	176	4	Miami (Fla.)	9/2
71	Belin, Chuck	OG	6-2	312	2	Wisconsin	0/0
36	Bettis, Jerome	RB	5-11	243	2	Notre Dame	16/12
45	Blackwell, Kelly	TE	6-1	255	2	Texas Christian	2/0
96	Boutte, Marc	DT	6-4	298	3	Louisiana State	16/16
21	Boykin, Deral	S	5-11	196	2	Louisville	16/0
49	Brasher, Bob	TE	6-5	244	1	Arizona State	0/0
61	Brostek, Bern	C	6-3	300	5	Washington	16/16
39	Bryant, Beno	RB	5-9	170	R	Washington	—
89	Buchanan, Richard	WR	5-10	178	2	Northwestern	5/0
15	Buffaloe, Jeff	P	6-1	194	1	Memphis State	0/0
51	Bush, Blair	C	6-3	275	17	Washington	16/0
17	Chandler, Chris	QB	6-4	225	7	Washington	4/2
54	Collins, Brett	LB	6-1	234	3	Washington	14/0
56	Conlan, Shane	LB	6-3	235	8	Penn State	13/11
29	Davis, Dexter	CB	5-10	185	4	Clemson	12/4
84	Drayton, Troy	TE	6-3	255	2	Penn State	16/;2
93	Esters, Jeff	DT	6-4	285	2	Pittsburgh	0/0
9	Farmer, Willie	WR	6-2	190	1	Virginia Union	0/0
94	Farr, D'Marco	DT	6-1	270	R	Washington	—
68	Fichtel, Brad	C	6-2	285	2	Eastern Illinios	0/0
43	Gary, Cleveland	RB	6-0	226	6	Miami (Fla.)	15/4
90	Gilbert, Sean	DT	6-4	315	3	Pittsburgh	16/16
79	Goeas, Leo	OG-OT	6-4	292	5	Hawaii	16/16
42	Griffin, Courtney	CB	5-10	180	2	Fresno State	0/0
30	Griffith, Howard	RB	6-0	226	2	Illinois	15/0
24	Henderson, Wyman	CB	5-10	188	8	Nevada-Las Vegas	9/4
23	Hicks, Clifford	S-CB	5-10	187	8	Oregon	10/0
57	Homco, Thomas	LB	6-0	242	2	Northwestern	16/3
31	Israel, Steve	CB	5-11	186	3	Pittsburgh	16/12
86	Jones, Ernie	WR	6-0	200	7	Indiana	10/0
98	Jones, Jimmie	DT	6-4	276	5	Miami (Fla.)	15/2
18	Jones, Jeff	WR	5-10	185	1	California	0/0
81	Kinchen, Todd	WR	6-0	187	3	Louisiana State	6/1
4	Kirchoff, Jay	PK	6-4	198	1	Arizona	0/0
45	LaChapelle, Sean	WR	6-3	205	2	UCLA	10/0
5	Landeta, Sean	P	6-0	210	10	Towson (Md.) State	16/0
38	Lang, David	RB	5-11	213	4	Northern Arizona	6/0
34	Lester, Tim	RB	5-9	215	3	Eastern Kentucky	16/14
87	Lewis, Nate	WR	5-11	198	5	Oregon Tech	15/10
64	Loneker, Keith	OG	6-3	330	2	Kansas	4/2
41	Lyght, Todd	CB	6-0	186	4	Notre Dame	9/9
53	Martin, Chris	LB	6-2	241	12	Auburn	16/4
8	Martin, Jamie	QB	6-2	215	2	Weber State	0/0
52	Mason, Andy	LB	6-2	228	R	Washington	—
14	McDougal, Kevin	QB	6-2	182	R	Notre Dame	—
82	McNeal, Travis	TE	6-3	244	6	Tenn.-Chattanooga	16/6
13	Miller, Chris	QB	6-2	212	8	Oregon	3/2
66	Newberry, Tom	OG	6-2	285	9	Wis.-LaCrosse	9/9
26	Newman, Anthony	S	6-0	199	7	Oregon	16/16
19	O'Bannon, Turhon	WR	6-0	195	R	New Mexico	—
69	Pahukoa, Jeff	OG-OT	6-2	298	3	Washington	16/0
91	Patrick, Kevin	DE	6-3	255	R	Miami (Fla.)	—

1994 PREVIEW ■ L.A. RAMS

1994 PLAYER ROSTER

NO.	NAME	POS.	HT.	WT.	EXP.	COLLEGE	GP/GS
58	Phifer, Roman	LB	6-2	230	4	UCLA	16/5
22	Pope, Marquez	S-CB	5-10	193	3	Fresno State	16/1
27	Price, Mitchell	CB	5-9	181	5	Tulane	6/0
72	Robbins, Kevin	OT	6-4	286	4	Michigan State	1/0
97	Robinson, Gerald	DE	6-3	262	7	Auburn	16/3
92	Rocker, David	DT	6-4	267	4	Auburn	14/0
59	Rolling, Henry	LB	6-2	225	8	Nevada-Reno	12/10
16	Ross, Jermaine	WR	5-11	192	R	Purdue	—
12	Rubley, T.J.	QB	6-3	205	3	Tulsa	9/7
47	Setzer, Rusty	RB	5-7	184	R	Grand Valley State	—
78	Slater, Jackie	OT	6-4	285	19	Jackson State	8/8
73	Starck, Justin	OT	6-6	310	R	Oregon	—
60	Stokes, Fred	DE	6-3	274	8	Georgia Southern	16/14
99	Tanuvasa, Maa	DT	6-2	277	2	Hawaii	0/0
37	Terrell, Pat	S	6-0	195	5	Notre Dame	13/3
1	Turk, Matt	P	6-5	230	1	Wisconsin-Whitewater	0/0
55	White, Leon	LB	6-3	242	9	Brigham Young	14/0
44	White, Russell	RB	5-11	216	2	California	5/0
25	Wilson, David	S	5-10	192	1	California	0/0
76	Young, Robert	DE	6-6	273	4	Mississippi State	6/6
10	Zendejas, Tony	PK	5-8	165	10	Nevada-Reno	16/0

'94 DRAFT PICKS

RD.	NAME	POS.	HT.	WT.	COLLEGE
1.	Gandy, Wayne	OT	6-4	288	Auburn
2.	Bruce, Isaac	WR	5-11	171	Memphis State
2.	Wright, Toby	DB	6-0	203	Nebraska
2.	Ottis, Brad	DT	6-4	271	Wayne State (Neb)
3.	Lyle, Keith	DB	6-2	200	Virginia
3.	Bostic, James	RB	5-11	225	Auburn
3.	Jones, Ernest	LB	6-2	239	Oregon
4.	Brantley, Chris	WR	5-10	175	Rutgers
6.	Brady, Rickey	TE	6-4	242	Oklahoma
6.	Edwards, Ronald	OT	6-5	311	North Carolina A&T

PRO FOOTBALL WEEKLY 1994 ALMANAC

TEAM AT A GLANCE

TEAM DIRECTORY

Address 2327 West Lincoln Avenue
Anaheim, California 92801
(714) 535-7267

(Ticket Office)
Anaheim Stadium
1900 State College Boulevard
Anaheim, California 92806
(714) 937-6767

Stadium Anaheim Stadium
Anaheim, California 92806
Capacity: 69,008
Playing surface: Grass

Training Camp California State-Fullerton
Fullerton, California 92634

Colors Royal blue, gold and white

Television KTTV, Channel 11
Radio KMPC, 710 AM

ADMINISTRATION

Owner-president: Georgia Frontiere
Executive vice president: John Shaw
Senior vice president: Jay Zygmunt
Vice president-media relations: Marshall Klein
Vice president-head coach: Chuck Knox
Director of player personnel: John Becker
Administrator of pro personnel: Jack Faulkner
Director of player relations: Paul "Tank" Younger
Exec. director-administration: Mary Olson-Kromolowski
Controller: Jeff Brewer
Director of promotions-sales: Pete Donovan
Director of public relations: Rick Smith
Trainer: Jim Anderson

1994 SCHEDULE

Preseason
AUG. 6	at Green Bay (Madison, Wis.)	12:00
AUG. 13	NEW ENGLAND	7:00
AUG. 20	L.A. RAIDERS	7:00
AUG. 25	at San Diego	7:00

Regular season
SEP. 4	ARIZONA	1:00
SEP. 11	at Atlanta	1:00
SEP. 18	SAN FRANCISCO	1:00
SEP. 25	at Kansas City	12:00
OCT. 2	ATLANTA	1:00
OCT. 9	at Green Bay	12:00
OCT. 16	N.Y. GIANTS	1:00
OCT. 23	at New Orleans	12:00
OCT. 30	OPEN DATE	
NOV. 6	DENVER	1:00
NOV. 13	L.A. RAIDERS	1:00
NOV. 20	at San Francisco	5:00
NOV. 27	at San Diego	1:00
DEC. 4	NEW ORLEANS	1:00
DEC. 11	at Tampa Bay	1:00
DEC. 18	at Chicago	12:00
DEC. 24	WASHINGTON	1:00

HEAD COACH

Chuck Knox

After leading the Seahawks to four playoff appearances in his nine years as head coch in Seattle, Knox was hired by the Rams prior to the 1992 season. Knox spent five years as head coach of the Rams in the mid-1970's before taking jobs in Buffalo and then in Seattle. Before his first stint with the Rams, Knox was an offensive line coach for the Lions and Jets. In his 21 years as an NFL head coach, Knox has amassed a record of 182-135-1, which places him sixth on the all-time coaching list. Born April 27, 1932, Sewickley, Pa.

Previous NFL: head coach, Seattle 1983-91; head coach, Buffalo 1978-82; head coach, L.A. Rams 1973-77; offensive line, Detroit 1967-72; offensive line, N.Y. Jets 1963-66.

Previous college: assistant coach, Kentucky 1961-62; assistant coach, Wake Forest 1959-60; assistant coach, Juniata College 1954.

Player: No NFL. College, tackle, Juniata College 1950-53.

ASSISTANT COACHES

Chris Clausen: strength and conditioning
Previous NFL: strength and conditioning, 1992-93 L.A. Rams; 1989-91 Seattle. Player: No NFL. College: cornerback, 1976-79 Indiana.

George Dyer: defensive coordinator
Previous NFL: defensive coordinator, 1992-93 L.A. Rams; 1983-91 Seattle; 1982 Buffalo. Player: No NFL. College: center-linebacker, 1961-63 Cal-Santa Barbara.

Jim Erkenbeck: offensive line
Previous NFL: offensive line, 1992-93 L.A. Rams; 1989-91 Kansas City; 1987-88 Dallas; 1986 New Orleans. Player: No NFL. College: linebacker, end, 1949-52 San Diego State.

Greg Gaines: defensive assistant
Previous NFL: defensive assistant, 1992-93 L.A. Rams. Player: NFL, linebacker, 1981-88 Seattle; 1989 Kansas City. College: linebacker, 1976-80 Tennessee.

Chick Harris: offensive coordinator
Previous NFL: running backs, 1992-93 L.A. Rams; 1983-91 Seattle; 1981-82 Buffalo. Player: No NFL. College: running back, 1966-69 Northern Arizona.

Mike Martz: quarterbacks
Previous NFL: offensive assistant, 1992-93 L.A. Rams. Player: No NFL. College: tight end, 1971 California-Santa Barbara; 1972 Fresno State.

Steve Moore: wide receivers
Previous NFL: offensive coordinator-receivers, 1983-88 Seattle; 1978-82 Buffalo. Player: No NFL. College: wide receiver, Glendale College, 1966-67; California-Santa Barbara, 1968-69.

Rod Perry: defensive backs
Previous NFL: defensive backs, 1992-93 L.A. Rams; 1989-91 Seattle. Player: NFL, defensive back, 1975-82 L.A. Rams; 1983-84 Cleveland. College: defensive back, 1972-74 Colorado.

Wayne Siever: special teams
Previous NFL: special teams, 1989-93 Wash-

132

1994 PREVIEW ■ L.A. RAMS

TEAM AT A GLANCE

ington; 1987-88 San Diego; 1981-86 Washington; 1979-80 San Diego; 1976 Atlanta; St. Louis 1974-75. Player: No NFL. College: quarterback, 1961-62 San Diego State.

Rennie Simmons: tight ends
Previous NFL: wide receivers, 1981-93 Washington. Player: No NFL. College: center, 1961-63 San Diego St.

Joe Vitt: assistant head coach-safeties
Previous NFL: assistant head coach-safeties, 1992-93 L.A. Rams; 1982-91 Seattle. Player: No NFL. College: linebacker, 1973-75 Towson State.

COACHING RECORDS
(includes postseason games)

Years	Coach	W	L	T
1937-38	Hugo Bezdek	1	13	0
1938	Art Lewis	4	4	0
1939-42	Dutch Clark	16	26	2
1944	Aldo "Buff" Donelli	4	6	0
1945-46	Adam Walsh	16	5	1
1947	Bob Snyder	6	6	0
1948-49	Clark Shaughnessy	14	8	3
1950-52	Joe Stydahar	19	9	0
1952-54	Hampton Pool	23	11	2
1955-59	Sid Gillman	28	32	1
1960-62	Bob Waterfield	9	24	1
1962-65	Harland Svare	14	31	3
1966-70	George Allen	49	19	4
1971-72	Tommy Prothro	14	12	2
1973-77	Chuck Knox	57	20	1
1978-82	Ray Malavasi	43	36	0
1983-91	John Robinson	79	74	0
1992-93	Chuck Knox	11	21	0

HISTORICAL HIGHLIGHTS

1937 An NFL franchise for Cleveland is awarded to a syndicate headed by Homer Marshman, and the team is named the Rams.
1941 The Rams are sold for $100,000 to a partnership of Dan Reeves and Fred Levy.
1943 The Rams are granted permission by the league to suspend operations because of the war.
1944 The Rams return to the NFL.
1945 With a record of 9-1, the Rams win their first divisional title. ... In the NFL championship game the Rams defeat the Washington Redskins 15-14.
1946 Losing money in Cleveland, Dan Reeves moves the franchise to Los Angeles.
1949 Los Angeles wins the NFL West but loses in the league championship game to the Philadelphia Eagles 14-0.
1950 The Rams win a second straight Western Division title, but lose in the last seconds of the NFL title game 30-28 to the Cleveland Browns.
1951 Rams win their third consecutive division title. They face the Browns for the NFL championship and win 24-17. ... QB Norm Van Brocklin passes for 554 yards in one game against the New York Yanks.
1955 Los Angeles snares the division crown, but loses to the Browns 38-14 in the NFL championship game.
1957 Pete Rozelle is named general manager.
1963 The Fearsome Foursome is formed, a defensive front line that consists of Deacon Jones, Lamar Lundy, Merlin Olsen and Rosevelt Grier.
1967 Los Angeles wins the division title but falls to the Green Bay Packers 28-7 in the playoffs.
1969 The Rams win the NFL West but fall to the Vikings 23-20 in the first round of the playoffs.
1972 The franchise is purchased by Robert Irsay for $19 million, and he then trades it to Carroll Rosenbloom for the Baltimore Colts.
1973 Los Angeles wins its division with a record of 12-2, the most wins in franchise history, but loses in the playoffs to the Dallas Cowboys 27-16.
1974 The Rams repeat as division champs, then beat the Redskins in the playoffs 19-10. ... In the NFC championship game, Los Angeles loses to Minnesota 14-10.
1975 Winning their division again, the Rams beat St. Louis 35-23 but then fall to the Cowboys 37-7.
1976 The Rams win the NFC West for the fourth year in a row. They defeat the Cowboys in the playoffs 14-12 but lose to Minnesota 24-13.
1977 For the fifth consecutive year, the Rams win their division but are eliminated in the playoffs by the Vikings 14-7.
1978 After defeating the Vikings 34-10 in the first round of the playoffs, the Rams lose the NFC title game to Cowboys 28-0.
1979-80 Georgia Frontiere Rosenbloom inherits the ownership of the Rams after the death of her husband, Carroll. ... Los Angeles wins its seventh divisional crown. In the playoffs the Rams defeat the Cowboys 21-19 and Tampa Bay 9-0. ... The Rams appear in Super Bowl XIV, but lose to the Pittsburgh Steelers 31-19.
1980 The Rams move out of Los Angeles, from the L.A. Coliseum to Anaheim Stadium in Orange County. ... The Rams make it to the playoffs as a wild-card but loses to Dallas 34-13.
1983 RB Eric Dickerson sets an NFL rookie rushing record and is the league's leading ground-gainer with 1,808 yards.
1984 Eric Dickerson sets the all-time single-season rushing record with 2,105 yards. ... The Rams go to the playoffs as a wild-card but lose to the Giants 16-13.
1985 Los Angeles wins the the NFC West. It defeats the Cowboys 20-0 but are then shutout by the Chicago Bears 24-0.
1986 Rams are an NFC wild-card team but lose to the Redskins 19-7 in the first round of the playoffs.
1988 John Robinson becomes the winningest coach in club history when he posts his 58th victory. ... Los Angeles qualifies for the playoffs for the fifth time in six years, but lost in the wild-card game to the Vikings 28-17.
1989 QB Jim Everett becomes the first Ram to pass for more than 4,000 yards in a season (4,310) and WR's Henry Ellard and Flipper Anderson the first two to gain over 1,000 yards in the same season. ... The Rams again go to the playoffs and defeat the Eagles 21-7 and the Giants 19-13 in overtime. ... Los Angeles plays the 49ers for the NFC title but loses 30-3.
1992 Chuck Knox is hired as head coach to replace John Robinson.
1993 Rookie RB Jerome Bettis is the second leading rusher in the NFL with 1,429 yards.

PRO FOOTBALL WEEKLY 1994 ALMANAC

TEAM AT A GLANCE

HALL OF FAME MEMBERS

	Yrs with Rams	Inducted
QB Bob Waterfield	1945-52	1965
Owner Dan Reeves	1941-71	1967
E Elroy Hirsch	1949-57	1968
E Tom Fears	1948-56	1970
QB Norm Van Brocklin	1949-57	1971
HB Ollie Matson	1959-62	1972
DE Deacon Jones	1961-71	1980
DT Merlin Olsen	1962-76	1982

RETIRED JERSEY NUMBERS
7   QB Bob Waterfield
74   DT Merlin Olsen

FIRST-ROUND DRAFT CHOICES
(since 1980)

Year	Selection	College
1980	DB Johnnie Johnson	Texas
1981	LB Mel Owens	Michigan
1982	RB Barry Redden	Richmond
1983	RB Eric Dickerson	Southern Methodist
1984	No choice	
1985	DB Jerry Gray	Texas
1986	OT Mike Schad	Queen's U. (Can.)
1987	No choice	
1988	RB Gaston Green	UCLA
	WR Aaron Cox	Arizona State
1989	DE Bill Hawkins	Miami (Fla.)
	RB Cleveland Gary	Miami (Fla.)
1990	C Bern Brostek	Washington
1991	CB Todd Lyght	Notre Dame
1992	DE Sean Gilbert	Pittsburgh
1993	RB Jerome Bettis	Notre Dame
1994	OT Wayne Gandy	Auburn

RECORD VS. OTHER NFL TEAMS
(includes postseason games)

	Record
Arizona Cardinals	23-19-2
Atlanta Falcons	36-16-2
Buffalo Bills	3-3-0
Chicago Bears	30-45-3
Cincinnati Bengals	2-5-0
Cleveland Browns	8-10-0
Dallas Cowboys	13-12-0
Denver Broncos	3-3-0
Detroit Lions	39-36-1
Green Bay Packers	42-37-2
Houston Oilers	5-2-0
Indianapolis Colts	16-20-2
Kansas City Chiefs	3-1-0
Los Angeles Raiders	2-5-0
Miami Dolphins	1-5-0
Minnesota Vikings	12-20-2
New England Patriots	3-3-0
New Orleans Saints	27-21-0
New York Giants	21-10-0
New York Jets	5-2-0
Philadelphia Eagles	16-12-1
Pittsburgh Steelers	14-5-2
San Diego Chargers	3-2-0
San Francisco 49ers	48-39-2
Seattle Seahawks	4-1-0
Tampa Bay Buccaneers	9-2-0
Washington Redskins	7-16-1

YEAR-BY-YEAR RECORDS

Year	Won	Lost	Tied	Year	Won	Lost	Tied
1937	1	10	0	1966	8	6	0
1938	4	7	0	1967**	11	1	2
1939	5	5	1	1968	10	3	1
1940	4	6	1	1969**	11	3	0
1941	2	9	0	1970	9	4	1
1942	5	6	0	1971	8	5	1
1944	4	6	0	1972	6	7	1
1945*	9	1	0	1973**	12	2	0
1946	6	4	1	1974**	10	4	0
1947	6	6	0	1975**	12	2	0
1948	6	5	1	1976**	10	3	1
1949**	8	2	2	1977**	10	4	0
1950**	9	3	0	1978**	12	4	0
1951*	8	4	0	1979**	9	7	0
1952	9	3	0	1980**	11	5	0
1953	8	3	1	1981	6	10	0
1954	6	5	1	1982	2	7	0
1955**	8	3	1	1983**	9	7	0
1956	4	8	0	1984**	10	6	0
1957	6	6	0	1985**	11	5	0
1958	8	4	0	1986**	10	6	0
1959	2	10	0	1987	6	9	0
1960	4	7	1	1988**	10	6	0
1961	4	10	0	1989**	11	5	0
1962	1	12	1	1990	5	11	0
1963	5	9	0	1991	3	13	0
1964	5	7	2	1992	6	10	0
1965	4	10	0	1993	5	11	0
				Total	394	337	20

Number of NFL championships   2
Number of years .500 or better   34
Number of years below .500   22

*NFL champions
**Playoff team

1994 PREVIEW ■ L.A. RAMS

RECORDS

INDIVIDUAL

Service
Seasons played	18	Jackie Slater (1976-93)
Games played	246	Jackie Slater (1976-93)
Consecutive games	201	Jack Youngblood (1971-84)

Scoring
Points, career	789	Mike Lansford (1982-90)
Points, season	130	David Ray (1973)
Points, game	24	Bob Shaw (1949)
		Elroy Hirsch (1951)
		Harold Jackson (1973)
Touchdowns, career	58	Eric Dickerson (1983-87)
Touchdowns, season	20	Eric Dickerson (1983)
Touchdowns, game	4	Bob Shaw (1949)
		Elroy Hirsch (1951)
		Harold Jackson (1973)
Field goals, career	158	Mike Lansford (1982-90)
Field goals, season	30	David Ray (1973)
Field goals, game	5	Bob Waterfield (1951)
Extra points, career	315	Bob Waterfield (1945-52)
		Mike Lansford (1982-90)
Extra points, season	54	Bob Waterfield (1950)
Extra points, game	9	Bob Waterfield (1950)

Rushing
Yards, career	7,245	Eric Dickerson (1983-87)
Yards, season	2,105	Eric Dickerson (1984)
Yards, game	247	Willie Ellison (1971)
Attempts, career	1,525	Eric Dickerson (1983-87)
Attempts, season	404	Eric Dickerson (1986)
Attempts, game	39	Jerome Bettis (1993)
Touchdowns, career	56	Eric Dickerson (1983-87)
Touchdowns, season	18	Eric Dickerson (1983)

Passing
Rating, career	78.1	Jim Everett (1983-87)
Rating, season	90.6	Jim Everett (1989)
Completions, career	1,847	Jim Everett (1986-93)
Completions, season	308	Jim Everett (1988)
Completions, game	35	Dieter Brock (1985)
Yards, career	23,758	Jim Everett (1986-93)
Yards, season	4,310	Jim Everett (1989)
Yards, game	554	Norm Van Brocklin (1951)
Attempts, career	3,313	Roman Gabriel (1962-72)
Attempts, season	554	Jim Everett (1990)
Attempts, game	53	Jim Hardy (1948)
Touchdowns, career	154	Roman Gabriel (1962-72)
Touchdowns, season	31	Jim Everett (1988)
Touchdowns, game	5	By many players

Receiving
Receptions, career	593	Henry Ellard (1983-93)
Receptions, season	86	Henry Ellard (1988)
Receptions, game	18	Tom Fears (1950)
Yards, career	9,761	Henry Ellard (1983-93)
Yards, season	1,495	Elroy Hirsch (1951)
Yards, game	336	Willie Anderson (1989)
Touchdowns, career	53	Elroy Hirsch (1949-57)
Touchdowns, season	17	Elroy Hirsch (1951)
Touchdowns, game	4	Bob Shaw (1949)
		Elroy Hirsch (1951)
		Harold Jackson (1973)

Interceptions
Career	46	Ed Meador (1959-70)
Season	14	Dick (Night Train) Lane (1952)
Game	3	By many players

Sacks
Career	72.5	Kevin Greene (1985-92)
Season	16.5	Kevin Greene (1989)
Game	5	Gary Jeter (1988)

Longest plays
Run from scrimmage	92	Kenny Washington (TD, 1946)
Pass play	96	Frank Ryan to Ollie Matson (TD, 1961)
Field goal	52	Mike Lansford (two times, 1985)
Interception return	99	Johnnie Johnson (1980)
Kickoff return	105	Jon Arnett (TD, 1961)
		Travis Williams (TD, 1971)
Punt return	90	Dick Bass (TD, 1961)
Punt	88	Bob Waterfield (1948)

Top scorers
	Points
Mike Lansford (1982-90)	789
Bob Waterfield (1945-52)	573
Bruce Gossett (1964-69)	571
David Ray (1969-74)	497
Frank Corral (1978-81)	379

Top rushers
	Yards
Eric Dickerson (1983-87)	7,245
Lawrence McCutcheon (1973-79)	6,186
Dick Bass (1960-69)	5,417
Dan Towler (1950-55)	3,493
Les Josephson (1964-67, 69-74)	3,407
Paul "Tank" Younger (1949-57)	3,296

Top passers
	Completions
Jim Everett (1986-93)	1,847
Roman Gabriel (1962-72)	1,705
Norm Van Brocklin (1949-57)	1,011
Bob Waterfield (1945-52)	814
Pat Haden (1976-81)	731
Vince Ferragamo (1977-84)	730

Top passers
	Yards
Jim Everett (1986-93)	23,758
Roman Gabriel (1962-72)	22,223
Norm Van Brocklin (1949-57)	16,114
Bob Waterfield (1945-52)	11,893
Vince Ferragamo (1977-84)	9,376
Pat Haden (1976-81)	9,296

Top receivers
	Receptions
Henry Ellard (1983-93)	593
Tom Fears (1948-56)	400
Elroy Hirsch (1949-57)	343
Jack Snow (1965-75)	340
Jim Phillips (1958-64)	316
Jim Benton (1938-40, 42, 44-47)	275

Top receivers
	Yards
Henry Ellard (1983-93)	8,816
Elroy Hirsch (1949-57)	6,289
Jack Snow (1965-75)	6,012
Tom Fears (1948-56)	5,397
Jim Phillips (1958-64)	4,708
Jim Benton (1938-40, 42, 44-47)	4,566

Most interceptions
	No.
Ed Meador (1959-70)	46
Nolan Cromwell (1977-87)	37
LeRoy Irvin (1980-89)	34
Will Sherman (1954-60)	28
Clarence Williams (1965-70)	28
Rod Perry (1975-82)	28

Most sacks
	No.
Kevin Greene	72.5

PRO FOOTBALL WEEKLY 1994 ALMANAC

PREVIEW: MIAMI DOLPHINS

In 1994 Dolphin QB Dan Marino will attempt a comeback of an entirely different sort.

For years he has thrilled Dolphin fans and terrorized opponents with last-minute comebacks that have turned Miami deficits into victories. This season, however, his comeback attempt will be from injury.

After a career of setting records, Marino finally got knocked from his pedestal last October. After avoiding a major injury for more than 10 seasons, Marino ruptured his Achilles in the fifth game of the '93 season.

After two and a half games, the fans were saying that Marino should be traded in light of how well Scott Mitchell was performing as his replacement. By year's end, however, they wanted Marino back in the worst way, and Mitchell moved on to Detroit via free-agency, where big money awaited.

Marino may be the finest pure passer ever. He has the quickest release in the game, a very strong and extremely accurate arm and a great knack for sidestepping the rush. He has matured as a field general over the years and will sacrifice his personal glory for the good of the team. A healthy Marino should act as insurance against last season's collapse down the stretch, when Miami lost its last five games to finish at 9-7.

If that isn't insurance enough, the Dolphins have a very solid backup plan, having signed Bernie Kosar as an unrestricted free agent. Kosar, who joined the Dolphins after finishing last season with the Super Bowl champion Cowboys, said he chose to sign as a backup to Marino because he wanted to remain with a winner.

"I had some other options," said Kosar after signing with Miami. "I had the opportunities to play more regularly with other teams. But I didn't really think the teams were as talented as the Miami Dolphins."

The Dolphin quarterbacks will certainly see an abundance of talent when they look for receivers downfield. Although he was never in shape and never totally healthy last season, TE Keith Jackson has great hands, running ability and body control. The key, however, is for him to control his weight. He also has a bad habit of fumbling the ball. Irving Fryar had a terrific season in '93, catching 64 passes for 1,010 yards and five touchdowns, breaking tackles after receptions and blocking as well as any wide receiver in the game. Mark Ingram struggled early last season but closed well. Like Fryar, he is a very tough player who blocks well and is fearless going over the middle. The Dolphins' No. 1 pick in '93, O.J. McDuffie, lacks top speed, but he is a very gifted runner after the catch who can make the acrobatic grab.

If the Dolphins hope to be a contender in '94, one place they must improve is in their running game. Mark Higgs is probably the Dolphins' best pure runner, but he really is not a breakaway threat and is not a very good receiver or blocker at only 5-7. As a rookie, Terry Kirby was superb catching the ball, but he averaged only 3.3 yards per carry, did not always make good run decisions and was guilty of far too many fumbles. By the end of last season, the Dolphins were starting to realize that FB Keith Byars was more than just a great receiver and pretty good blocker. He was also a good runner, averaging 4.2 yards per carry, although he carried the ball only 64 times. If he stays healthy, look for Byars to get approximately 130 carries in '94.

The Dolphins need to get better play out of their offensive line this season. Last year QB's Marino and Mitchell got hurt, while the running game produced only 1,459 yards and 10 scores, averaging just 3.5 yards per carry. The offensive line was a big part of these problems.

Richmond Webb had a great rookie season at offensive left tackle in 1990, but he has been erratic ever since. There are times when he has All-Pro games, but he also plays at a very mediocre level in other outings. OLG Keith Sims had his best year last season and went to his first Pro Bowl. He is a massive powerhouse with a lot of athleticism, although his concentration is inconsistent. With C Jeff Uhlenhake having moved on to New Orleans, either Jeff Dellenbach, a big-bodied, confident journeyman, or No. 2 pick Tim Ruddy will replace him. Bert Weidner starts at right guard, and Ron Heller can hold his own at right tackle. Although he lacks a good lower body and has only limited athletic ability, Heller does a pretty good job. Eddie Blake has awesome power and athletic ability, but, if he doesn't learn to concentrate, the Dolphins may lose patience. It will be a big boost to the line if Blake comes through this year.

There seems to be little doubt that the Dolphins will put a lot of points on the board with a healthy Marino and his talented receivers. The big question is whether the defense can slow down the opposition. Last season the Dolphin defense allowed 351 points, ranking 24th in the NFL in that category, and none of its units look any better than mediocre going into '94.

After a very promising rookie year, DE Marco Coleman tailed off some last season. However, in fairness to Coleman, it should be pointed out that in '92, he was often lined up wide of the tackle, while in '93 he was lined up inside over the tackle most of the time and had to play the run first. Coleman is an undersized leverage player with great strength in his hands. The big question with DE Jeff Cross going into the '94 campaign is whether he is the player who had 10 sacks in the first nine games last season or the guy who had only half a sack the rest of the year and was a non-factor during the Dolphins' five-game losing streak

136

1994 PREVIEW ■ MIAMI

at season's end. NT Chuck Klingbeil does a pretty good job tying blockers up and playing the run, but he does not provide a strong pass rush. Larry Webster has the ability to be a dominating performer, but he has been very inconsistent. No. 1 pick DT Tim Bowens adds depth and great potential inside.

If MLB John Offerdahl was capable of staying healthy, the Dolphin LB unit would be a definite area of strength. The fact is, however, that injuries have been a major problem during Offerdahl's career. Offerdahl has great instincts and leadership qualities, but he has had one injury after another in recent years. Offerdahl's future is uncertain with the Dolphins. Not only was he a free agent this offseason, but he was mulling retirement. Offerdahl's plans were to work with a personal trainer during the spring and then make a decision during the summer on whether to continue his football career.

"In talking to him, it seemed like if everything worked out well and he was healthy, and he had good sessions with his personal trainer, he would be interested," said Dolphin head coach Don Shula. "If he does continue his career, we'd like very much for him to be with us."

If Offerdahl does not return, Dwight Hollier will replace him. Hollier is better playing inside linebacker than outside, but he is not going to be a standout at either position because of speed and athletic limitations.

OLB Bryan Cox is the star of the defense and led the team with 122 tackles last season. However, some of his limitations were exposed when the rest of the defense was hit by injuries in '93. Unless he starts to do a better job of controlling his emotions, he will never realize his full potential. Cox is a natural football player with a great feel for the game. He has not worked as hard as he should to improve his strength and speed, though. He is a gambler who does not always play the assigned defense, and, after he loses his cool, he tends to break defenses and can make very costly mistakes.

Chris Singleton, a former Patriot first-round draft pick, impressed Miami with his raw physical tools and should compete for the other starting OLB spot, with No. 2 pick Aubrey Beavers, a player the Dolphins feel could contribute quickly. Singleton has always had the size, speed and strength scouts and coaches look for, but he has been hurt too much in the past and always seemed reluctant to turn it loose. He could use some of Cox's aggressiveness and confidence.

In the secondary, the Dolphins have replaced

Bryan Cox

last year's starting safeties — Louis Oliver and Jarvis Williams — with free-agent signees Gene Atkins and Michael Stewart. Atkins is a big hitter with good instincts and above-average range. Stewart also is known for his heavy hitting and sure tackling. CB J.B. Brown generally provides good coverage, but he isn't going to win any awards for his play vs. the run. CB Troy Vincent was having a pretty good campaign last year before he suffered a season-ending injury on a punt return in Game 13. Vincent has All-Pro tools, but he still tends to think too much and dwell on his mistakes.

On special teams, the Dolphins had to pay big bucks to keep PK Pete Stoyanovich from signing with the Patriots, but he is one of the game's best kickers and has almost 60-yard range. Stoyanovich had something of an off year in '93, making 24-of-32 field goals, but there is every reason to think he can bounce back. The Dolphins will replace P Dale Hatcher, who had a superb preseason last year but struggled mightily once the games were for real, with reliable ex-Lion Jim Arnold. The Dolphins are in very good shape on punt and kickoff returns with O.J. McDuffie. Kick coverage was average last season and punt coverage was a problem to which Hatcher contributed.

FAST FACTS

■ Dan Marino has thrown more TD passes than interceptions in each of his 11 NFL seasons. Despite the fact Marino was lost for the year due to an injury in the fifth game of the regular season, the Dolphins still led the NFL in passing yardage.

■ FB Keith Byars has caught more than 55 passes in each of his last six seasons in Philadelphia and Miami.

■ TE Keith Jackson's 39 receptions in 1993 were the lowest total of his professional career.

PRO FOOTBALL WEEKLY 1994 ALMANAC

1994 PLAYER ROSTER

NO.	NAME	POS.	HT.	WT.	EXP.	COLLEGE	GP/GS
71	Albright, Ethan	OT	6-5	274	R	North Carolina	—
32	Alexander, Bruce	CB	5-8	178	6	Stephen F. Austin	14/0
2	Araguz, Leo	P	5-11	179	R	Stephen F. Austin	—
6	Arnold, Jim	P	6-3	211	12	Vanderbilt	16/0
28	Atkins, Gene	S	5-11	200	8	Florida A&M	16/16
9	Ballard, Jim	QB	6-3	223	R	Mount Union	—
59	Barnett, J'Karl	LB	6-0	235	R	Jacksonville State	—
84	Baty, Greg	TE	6-6	240	8	Stanford	16/1
66	Blake, Eddie	OG	6-3	315	2	Auburn	0/0
34	Braxton, Tyrone	CB	5-11	185	8	North Dakota State	16/16
64	Brothen, Kevin	C	6-1	287	1	Vanderbilt	0/0
37	Brown, J.B.	CB	6-0	190	6	Maryland	16/16
86	Brown, Reggie	WR	5-11	175	2	Mesa (Colo.)	4/0
54	Bullough, Chuck	LB	6-1	238	2	Michigan State	3/0
41	Byars, Keith	FB	6-1	255	9	Ohio State	16/16
98	Caesar, Mark	DT	6-2	295	2	Miami (Fla.)	0/0
25	Cartwright, Ricardo	CB	5-10	176	1	Florida A&M	0/0
90	Coleman, Marco	DE	6-3	263	3	Georgia Tech	15/15
83	Coons, Rob	TE	6-5	239	1	Pittsburgh	0/0
68	Covington, Leevary	LB	6-0	246	R	North Carolina A&T	—
51	Cox, Bryan	LB	6-4	241	4	Western Illinois	16/16
34	Craver, Aaron	RB	6-0	216	4	Fresno State	0/0
91	Cross, Jeff	DE	6-4	274	7	Missouri	16/16
38	Davis, Dwayne	S	6-1	203	R	Colorado	—
24	Davis, Robert	CB	5-9	188	R	Vanderbilt	—
17	DeBerg, Steve	QB	6-3	220	18	San Jose State	8/5
65	Dellenbach, Jeff	C	6-5	290	10	Wisconsin	16/16
74	Dennis, Mark	OT	6-6	298	8	Illinois	16/0
26	Dixon, Johnny	S	5-11	204	R	Mississippi	—
46	Foxx, Dion	LB	6-3	249	R	James Madison	—
48	Francisco, Paul	TE	6-6	240	R	Boston U.	—
80	Fryar, Irving	WR	6-0	200	11	Nebraska	16/16
62	Gray, Chris	OG-OT	6-4	286	1	Auburn	5/0
42	Green, Chris	S	5-11	189	4	Illinois	14/0
59	Grimsley, John	LB	6-2	236	11	Kentucky	13/9
45	Harden, Bobby	S	6-0	205	5	Miami (Fla.)	8/0
73	Heller, Ron	OT	6-6	293	11	Penn State	16/16
21	Higgs, Mark	RB	5-7	196	7	Kentucky	16/8
50	Hollier, Dwight	LB	6-2	250	3	North Carolina	16/5
76	Hopkins, Jimmie	DE	6-5	257	R	Arizona	—
97	Hunter, Jeff	DE	6-4	291	5	Albany (Ga.) State	5/1
1	Ingram, Mark	WR	5-11	188	8	Michigan State	16/16
88	Jackson, Keith	TE	6-2	254	7	Oklahoma	15/15
24	Jackson, Vestee	CB	6-0	186	9	Washington	16/5
89	Johnson, Demeris	WR	6-2	185	1	Western Illinois	0/0
43	Kirby, Terry	RB	6-1	221	2	Virginia	16/8
99	Klingbeil, Chuck	NT	6-1	289	4	Northern Michigan	16/16
19	Kosar, Bernie	QB	6-5	215	10	Miami (Fla.)	11/7
17	Letcher, Morris	WR	5-9	164	R	East Carolina	—
47	Malone, Darrell	CB	5-10	182	3	Jacksonville (Ala.) St.	16/1
13	Marino, Dan	QB	6-4	224	12	Pittsburgh	5/5
81	McDuffie, O.J.	WR-KR	5-10	191	2	Penn State	16/0
10	McGuire, Stephen	FB	5-11	215	1	Miami (Fla.)	0/0
27	Middleton, Mike	S	5-10	211	1	Indiana	0/0
15	Millen, Hugh	QB	6-5	216	10	Washington	0/0

1994 PREVIEW ■ MIAMI

1994 PLAYER ROSTER

NO.	NAME	POS.	HT.	WT.	EXP.	COLLEGE	GP/GS
67	Novak, Jeff	OG-OT	6-6	300	1	SW Texas State	0/0
93	Odom, Cliff	LB	6-2	236	15	Texas-Arlington	14/1
56	Offerdahl, John	LB	6-3	238	9	Western Michigan	9/8
20	Oliver, Muhammad	CB	5-11	170	3	Oregon	4/0
30	Parmalee, Bernie	RB	5-11	201	3	Ball State	16/0
14	Pederson, Doug	QB	6-3	209	2	NE Louisiana	7/0
45	Qualrles, Shelton	LB	6-1	228	R	Vanderbilt	—
49	Richardson, Sean	RB	5-10	243	R	Jacksonville State	—
92	Rooks, George	DT	6-3	298	1	Syracuse	0/0
77	Rowell, Tony	OG	6-4	289	1	Florida	0/0
18	Rowley, Bryan	WR	5-10	179	R	Utah	—
22	Saxon, James	FB	5-11	237	7	San Jose State	16/0
44	Schulte, Scott	RB	5-10	199	R	Hillsdale	—
33	Seigler, Dexter	CB	5-9	182	R	Miami (Fla.)	—
69	Sims, Keith	OG	6-3	303	5	Iowa State	16/16
55	Singleton, Chris	LB	6-2	242	5	Arizona	17/4
28	Smith, Frankie	CB	5-9	186	2	Baylor	5/1
40	Spikes, Irving	RB	5-8	207	R	NE Louisiana	—
63	Spralding, Melvin	LB	6-1	253	R	South Carolina State	—
35	Stewart, Michael	S	6-0	195	8	Fresno State	16/14
11	Stouffer, Kelly	QB	6-3	214	6	Colorado State	0/0
10	Stoyanovich, Pete	PK	5-11	195	6	Indiana	16/0
72	Sturdivant, Mark	DE	6-3	271	R	Maryland	—
57	Thayer, Tom	OG-C	6-4	284	10	Notre Dame	3/0
94	Veasey, Craig	DT	6-2	300	5	Houston	15/0
23	Vincent, Troy	CB	6-0	192	3	Wisconsin	13/13
78	Webb, Richmond	OT	6-6	298	5	Texas A&M	16/16
79	Webster, Larry	DT	6-5	288	3	Maryland	13/9
60	Weidner, Bert	OG-C	6-2	290	5	Kent State	16/3
26	Williams, Jarvis	S	5-11	200	7	Florida	16/14
75	Williams, Jay	DE	6-3	266	R	Wake Forest	—
87	Williams, Mike	WR	5-11	183	4	Northeastern	13/0
85	Williams, Ronnie	TE	6-3	259	2	Oklahoma State	11/0

'94 DRAFT PICKS

RD.	NAME	POS.	HT.	WT.	COLLEGE
1.	Bowens, Tim	DT	6-4	315	Mississippi
2.	Beavers, Aubrey	LB	6-3	233	Oklahoma
2.	Ruddy, Tim	C	6-2	270	Notre Dame
4.	Woolfork, Ronnie	LB	6-3	253	Colorado
5.	Gaines, William	DT	6-4	300	Florida
6.	Boyer, Brant	LB	6-1	230	Arizona
7.	Hill, Sean	DB	5-10	175	Montana State

PRO FOOTBALL WEEKLY 1994 ALMANAC

TEAM AT A GLANCE

TEAM DIRECTORY

Address	Joe Robbie Stadium 2269 N.W. 199th Street Miami, Florida 33056 (305) 620-5000
Stadium	Joe Robbie Stadium 2269 N.W. 199th Street Miami, Florida 33056 Capacity: 73,000 Playing surface: Grass
Training Camp	Nova University 7500 S.W. 30th Street Davie, Florida 33314
Colors	Aqua, coral and white
Television	WTVJ, Channel 4
Radio	WIOD, 620 AM

ADMINISTRATION

Owner: H. Wayne Huizenga
President: Timothy J. Robbie
Executive vice president: Daniel T. Robbie
Executive vice president: Janet Robbie
Exec. vice president-general manager: Eddie Jones
Director of player personnel: Tom Heckert
Director of college scouting: Tom Braatz
Director of media relations: Harvey Greene
Marketing director: David Evans
Community relations director: Fudge Browne
Trainer: Ryan Vermillion

1994 SCHEDULE

Preseason

JULY 30	at N.Y. Giants	8:00
AUG. 6	PITTSBURGH	8:00
AUG. 13	vs. Green Bay (at Milw.)	7:00
AUG. 20	TAMPA BAY	8:00
AUG. 26	at Minnesota	7:00

Regular season

SEP. 4	NEW ENGLAND	4:00
SEP. 11	vs. Green Bay (at Milw.)	12:00
SEP. 18	N.Y. JETS	1:00
SEP. 25	at Minnesota	12:00
OCT. 2	at Cincinnati	8:00
OCT. 9	at Buffalo	1:00
OCT. 16	L.A. RAIDERS	1:00
OCT. 23	OPEN DATE	
OCT. 30	at New England	1:00
NOV. 6	INDIANAPOLIS	1:00
NOV. 13	CHICAGO	1:00
NOV. 20	at Pittsburgh	1:00
NOV. 27	at N.Y. Jets	1:00
DEC. 4	BUFFALO	8:00
DEC. 12	KANSAS CITY (Mon.)	9:00
DEC. 18	at Indianapolis	1:00
DEC. 25	DETROIT	8:00

HEAD COACH

Don Shula

During the 1993 season, Shula passed George Halas to become the all-time winningest coach in NFL history. Through 31 seasons as a head coach, 24 with the Dolphins and seven with the Colts, Shula has a record of 327-158-6. He has taken the Dolphins to the Super Bowl five times. Shula led Miami to back-to-back Super Bowl victories, defeating Washington 14-7 in Super Bowl VII and Minnesota 24-7 in Super Bowl VIII. His 1972 Dolphin team went 17-0, the only NFL team to ever go undefeated through an entire regular season and postseason. Shula spent seven years in the NFL as a player. Born Jan. 4, 1930, Painesville, Ohio.

Previous NFL: head coach, 1963-69 Baltimore; defensive coach, 1960-62 Detroit.

Previous college: assistant coach, 1959 Kentucky; assistant coach, 1958 Virginia.

Player: NFL, defensive back, 1951-52 Cleveland; 1953-56 Baltimore; 1957 Washington. College, running back, 1950 John Carroll.

ASSISTANT COACHES

Joel Collier: staff assistant
Previous NFL: 1991-93 New England; 1990 Tampa Bay. Player: No NFL. College: linebacker, 1984-87 Northern Colorado.

John Gamble: strength coach
Previous NFL: None. Player: No NFL. College: linebacker, Hampton Institute.

Joe Greene: defensive line
Previous NFL: defensive line, 1992-93 Miami; 1987-91 Pittsburgh. Player: NFL, defensive tackle, 1969-81 Pittsburgh. College: defensive tackle, 1966-68 North Texas State.

Kim Helton: offensive line
Previous NFL: offensive line, 1993 Miami; 1990-92 L.A. Raiders; 1987-89 Houston; 1983-86 Tampa Bay. Player: No NFL. College: center, 1967-69 Florida.

George Hill: linebackers
Previous NFL: linebackers, 1989-93 Miami; 1985-88 Indianapolis; 1979-84 Philadelphia. Player: No NFL. College: tackle, fullback, 1954-57 Denison.

Tony Nathan: offensive backs
Previous NFL: offensive backs, 1989-93 Miami. Player: NFL, running back, 1979-87, Miami. College: running back, 1975-78 Alabama.

Tom Olivadotti: defense
Previous NFL: defense, 1987-93 Miami; 1985-86 Cleveland. Player: No NFL. College: defensive back, wide receiver, 1963-66 Upsala.

Mel Phillips: defensive backs
Previous NFL: defensive backs, 1985-93 Miami; 1980-84 Detroit. Player: NFL, defensive back, 1966-77 San Francisco. College: defensive back, running back, 1964-65 North Carolina A&T.

John Sandusky: assistant head coach-tight ends
Previous NFL: offensive line, 1976-93 Miami; 1973-75 Philadelphia; 1959-72 (interim head coach for nine games in '72) Baltimore. Player: NFL, tackle, 1950-55 Cleveland; 1956 Green Bay. College: tackle, 1946-49 Villanova.

1994 PREVIEW ■ MIAMI

TEAM AT A GLANCE

Larry Seiple: wide receivers
Previous NFL: wide receivers, 1988-93 Miami; 1985-86 Tampa Bay; 1980-84 Detroit. Player: NFL, punter, tight end, receiver, running back, 1967-77 Dolphins. College: running back, receiver, punter, 1964-66 Kentucky.

Gary Stevens: offense-quarterbacks
Previous NFL: offense-quarterbacks, 1989-93 Miami. Player: No NFL. College: running back, 1963-65 John Carroll.

Junior Wade: strength and conditioning
Previous NFL: strength and conditioning, 1975-93 Miami. Player: No NFL. College: None.

Mike Westhoff: special teams
Previous NFL: special teams, 1986-93 Miami; 1982-84 Baltimore. Player: No NFL. College: center, linebacker, 1967-69 Wichita State.

COACHING RECORDS

Years	Coach	W	L	T
1966-69	George Wilson	15	39	2
1970-93	Don Shula	254	132	2

HISTORICAL HIGHLIGHTS

1965 Joe Robbie and television star Danny Thomas are awarded the AFL's first expansion franchise for $7.5 million.
1970 Bob Griese becomes the first Dolphin to pass for 300 yards in a game (327 on 19 completions) against the Bengals.
1970 Don Shula, former coach of the Baltimore Colts, becomes head coach and vice president of the Dolphins. ... With a 10-4 record, the Dolphins earn their first playoff berth. But, in their first postseason appearance, the Dolphins lose to the Oakland Raiders 21-14.
1971-72 Larry Csonka becomes the club's first 1,000-yard rusher with a season mark of 1,051 yards. WR Paul Warfield sets a club record by gaining 996 yards on 43 pass receptions. ... Miami goes to the playoffs and defeats the Kansas City Chiefs 27-24 in the second overtime of the AFC semifinals in the longest game in NFL history. Then Miami captures its first AFC championship, shutting out Baltimore 21-0 at the Orange Bowl before a crowd of 78,939, the largest ever to attend a Miami home game, and earning the right to represent the AFC in the Super Bowl. The Dolphins fall to Dallas 24-3 in Super Bowl VI.
1972-73 Miami goes 14-0 in the regular season, the first team ever to win that many games in a season. ... Both Larry Csonka and Mercury Morris rush for more than 1,000 yards (1,117 and 1,000, respectively). ... The Dolphins repeat as AFC champions by beating Cleveland 20-14 and then Pittsburgh 21-17. The Dolphins finish their perfect season when they defeat Washington 14-7 in Super Bowl VII.
1973-74 The Dolphins compile the best two-year record in NFL history, 26-2, when their 12-2 record wins another AFC East title. ... Miami beats Cincinnati in the playoffs 34-16 and then clinches its third AFC title at the Orange Bowl by defeating Oakland 27-10. ... The Dolphins win their second consecutive Super Bowl, beating Minnesota 24-7.

1974 The Oakland Raiders thwart the Dolphins' attempt for a third consecutive NFL championship by defeating them 28-26 in the AFC playoffs.
1977 In a Thanksgiving Day annihilation of the Cardinals (55-14) at St. Louis, the Dolphins set team records of 55 points and 503 yards. QB Bob Griese throws six TD passes, a club record that still stands.
1978 With a record of 11-5, Miami makes it to the playoffs for the first time since 1974 as a wild-card team but are eliminated by the Oilers 17-9.
1979 Miami takes the AFC East title after winning 10 games. But eventual Super Bowl-champion Pittsburgh overwhelms the Dolphins in the playoffs with a 20-point first quarter and 43-14 final score.
1981 In a 30-27 win over New England, coach Don Shula picks up his 200th NFL coaching victory. ... Miami prevails in the AFC East with a record of 11-4-1. Then the Dolphins face San Diego in what becomes the highest-scoring game in playoff history. Fighting back from a 24-0 deficit, the Dolphins tie the game in regulation only to fall 41-38 in overtime. Both teams' quarterbacks, Miami's Don Strock and San Diego's Dan Fouts, pass for more than 400 yards, an NFL record.
1982-83 In a strike-shortened season, Miami wins 7-of-9 games and goes to the playoffs, first beating the Patriots 28-13. The Dolphins then defeat San Diego 34-13 and the Jets 14-0. ... In their fourth appearance in a Super Bowl, Miami falls to Washington 27-17.
1983 With a record of 12-4, Miami again wins the AFC East title for the 10th time in 14 years. But the Dolphins lose to the Seattle Seahawks 27-20 in the first round of the playoffs.
1984-85 Miami wins 11 consecutive games to clinch the AFC Eastern Division title with a final record of 12-4. ... QB Dan Marino, the NFL's MVP, breaks three all-time records: touchdown passes in a season, 48; completions, 362; and yards gained passing, 5,084. In a game against the Raiders, Marino also shatters Miami's single-game records for most yards passing, 470, and most completions, 35. ... The Dolphins end the regular season with the best record in the AFC, 14-2, and another division crown, the 11th they have won or shared. ... Miami defeats the Seahawks 31-10 and the Steelers 45-28 to win the AFC title and a trip to the Super Bowl. ... In its fifth Super Bowl appearance, Miami falls to the San Francisco 49ers 38-16.
1985-86 The Dolphins again win the AFC East, their 12th title in 16 years. Then, Miami defeats the Browns 24-21 in the AFC divisional playoff game. But Miami experiences its first loss in the AFC title game in six attempts when the Patriots prevail 31-14.
1987 The Dolphins take up residence in new Joe Robbie Stadium, built at a cost of over $100 million.
1990-91 Joe Robbie, founder and owner of the Dolphins, dies at age 73. ... Miami goes to the playoffs for the first time since the 1985 season. ... The Dolphins lose to Buffalo 44-34, the highest-scoring non-overtime game in playoff history.
1992-93 The Dolphins win the AFC East with a record of 11-5. They defeat the Chargers 31-0 in the playoffs but lose the AFC title game to the Bills 29-10.
1993 Don Shula becomes the winningest head coach in NFL history, surpassing the 324 victories recorded by Chicago Bear legend George Halas.

141

PRO FOOTBALL WEEKLY 1994 ALMANAC

TEAM AT A GLANCE

HALL OF FAME MEMBERS

	Yrs with Dolphins	Inducted
WR Paul Warfield	1970-74	1983
FB Larry Csonka	1968-74, 79	1987
C Jim Langer	1970-79	1987
QB Bob Griese	1967-80	1990
OG Larry Little	1969-80	1993

RETIRED JERSEY NUMBERS
12 QB Bob Griese

FIRST-ROUND DRAFT CHOICES
(since 1980)

Year	Selection	College
1980	CB Don McNeal	Alabama
1981	RB David Overstreet	Oklahoma
1982	OG Roy Foster	Southern Cal
1983	QB Dan Marino	Pittsburgh
1984	LB Jackie Shipp	Oklahoma
1985	RB Lorenzo Hampton	Florida
1986	No choice	
1987	DE John Bosa	Boston College
1988	DE Eric Kumerow	Ohio State
1989	RB Sammie Smith	Florida State
	S Louis Oliver	Florida
1990	OT Richmond Webb	Texas A&M
1991	WR Randal Hill	Miami (Fla.)
1992	CB Troy Vincent	Wisconsin
	LB Marco Coleman	Georgia Tech
1993	WR O.J. McDuffie	Penn State
1994	DT Tim Bowens	Mississippi

RECORD VS. OTHER NFL TEAMS

	Record
Arizona Cardinals	6-0
Atlanta Falcons	5-1
Buffalo Bills	37-20-1
Chicago Bears	5-1
Cincinnati Bengals	10-3
Cleveland Browns	8-4
Dallas Cowboys	6-2
Denver Broncos	5-2-1
Detroit Lions	2-2
Green Bay Packers	7-0
Houston Oilers	11-12
Indianapolis Colts	35-14
Kansas City Chiefs	9-10
Los Angeles Raiders	5-16-1
Los Angeles Rams	5-1
Minnesota Vikings	5-1
New England Patriots	34-22
New Orleans Saints	4-2
New York Giants	1-2
New York Jets	28-28-1
Philadelphia Eagles	6-2
Pittsburgh Steelers	9-6
San Diego Chargers	7-11
San Francisco 49ers	4-3
Seattle Seahawks	5-2
Tampa Bay Buccaneers	4-1
Washington Redskins	6-3

YEAR-BY-YEAR RECORDS

Year	Won	Lost	Tied	Year	Won	Lost	Tied
1966	3	11	0	1980	8	8	0
1967	4	10	0	1981**	11	4	1
1968	5	8	1	1982**	7	2	0
1969	3	10	1	1983**	12	4	0
1970**	10	4	0	1984**	14	2	0
1971**	10	3	1	1985**	12	4	0
1972*	14	0	0	1986	8	8	0
1973*	12	2	0	1987	8	7	0
1974**	11	3	0	1988	6	10	0
1975	10	4	0	1989	8	8	0
1976	6	8	0	1990**	12	4	0
1977	10	4	0	1991	8	8	0
1978**	11	5	0	1992**	11	5	0
1979**	10	6	0	1993	9	7	0
				Total	253	159	4

Number of NFL championships   2
Number of years .500 or better   22
Number of years below .500   6

*NFL champions
**Playoff team

142

1994 PREVIEW ■ MIAMI

RECORDS

INDIVIDUAL

Service
Seasons played	15	Bob Kuechenberg (1970-84)
Games played	190	Bob Kuechenberg (1970-84)
Consecutive games	128	Jim Langer (1970-79)

Scoring
Points, career	830	Garo Yepremian (1970-78)
Points, season	124	Pete Stoyanovich (1992)
Points, game	24	Paul Warfield (12/15/73)
Touchdowns, career	82	Mark Clayton (1983-92)
Touchdowns, season	18	Mark Clayton (1984)
Touchdowns, game	4	Paul Warfield (12/15/73)
Field goals, career	165	Garo Yepremian (1970-78)
Field goals, season	31	Pete Stoyanovich (1991)
Field goals, game	5	Garo Yepremian (9/26/71)
Extra points, career	335	Garo Yepremian (1970-78)
Extra points, season	66	Uwe von Schamann (1984)
Extra points, game	7	Garo Yepremian (11/12/72)
		Garo Yepremian (11/24/77)

Rushing
Yards, career	6,737	Larry Csonka (1968-74, 79)
Yards, season	1,258	Delvin Williams (1978)
Yards, game	197	Mercury Morris (9/30/73)
Attempts, career	1,506	Larry Csonka (1968-74, 1979)
Attempts, season	272	Delvin Williams (1978)
Attempts, game	33	Larry Csonka (1/13/74)
Touchdowns, career	53	Larry Csonka (1968-74, 1979)
Touchdowns, season	12	Mercury Morris (1972)
		Don Nottingham (1975)
		Larry Csonka (1979)
Touchdowns, game	3	By many players

Passing
Rating, career	88.1	Dan Marino (1983-93)
Rating, season	108.9	Dan Marino (1984)
Completions, career	3,219	Dan Marino (1983-93)
Completions, season	378	Dan Marino (1986)
Completions, game	39	Dan Marino (11/16/86)
Yards, career	40,720	Dan Marino (1983-93)
Yards, season	5,084	Dan Marino (1984)
Yards, game	521	Dan Marino (10/23/88)
Attempts, career	5,434	Dan Marino (1983-93)
Attempts, season	623	Dan Marino (1986)
Attempts, game	60	Dan Marino (10/23/88)
Touchdowns, career	298	Dan Marino (1983-93)
Touchdowns, season	48	Dan Marino (1984)
Touchdowns, game	6	Bob Griese (11/24/77)
		Dan Marino (9/21/86)

Receiving
Receptions, career	550	Mark Clayton (1983-92)
Receptions, season	86	Mark Clayton (1988)
Receptions, game	12	Jim Jensen (11/6/88)
Yards, career	8,869	Mark Duper (1982-92)
Yards, season	1,389	Mark Clayton (1984)
Yards, game	217	Mark Duper (11/10/85)
Touchdowns, career	81	Mark Clayton (1983-92)
Touchdowns, season	18	Mark Clayton (1984)
Touchdowns, game	4	Paul Warfield (12/15/73)

Interceptions
Career	35	Jake Scott (1970-75)
Season	10	Dick Westmoreland (1967)
Game	4	Dick Anderson (12/3/73)

Sacks
Career	67.5	Bill Stanfill (1969-76)
Season	18.5	Bill Stanfill (1973)
Game	5	Bill Stanfill (10/7/73)
		Vern Den Herder (10/21/73)
		Bill Stanfill (11/17/74)

Longest plays
Run from scrimmage	77	Leroy Harris (TD, 12/5/77)
		Keith Byars (TD, 11/25/93)
Pass play	86	Bob Griese to Paul Warfield (TD, 11/14/71)
Field goal	59	Pete Stoyanovich (11/12/89)
Interception return	103	Louis Oliver (TD, 10/4/92)
Kickoff return	105	Mercury Morris (TD, 9/14/69)
Punt return	87	Tom Vigorito (TD, 9/10/81)
Punt	77	Reggie Roby (11/29/87)

Top scorers
	Points
Garo Yepremian (1970-78)	830
Pete Stoyanovich (1989-93)	549
Uwe von Schamann (1979-84)	540
Mark Clayton (1983-92)	492
Nat Moore (1974-86)	450
Mark Duper (1982-92)	354

Top rushers
	Yards
Larry Csonka (1968-74, 1979)	6,737
Mercury Morris (1969-75)	3,877
Jim Kiick (1968-74)	3,644
Tony Nathan (1979-87)	3,543
Delvin Williams (1978-80)	2,632
Mark Higgs (1990-93)	2,580

Top passers
	Completions
Dan Marino (1983-93)	3,219
Bob Griese (1967-80)	1,926
David Woodley (1980-83)	508
Don Strock (1974-87)	388
Rick Norton (1966-69)	156
Earl Morrall (1972-76)	153

Top passers
	Yards
Dan Marino (1983-93)	40,720
Bob Griese (1967-80)	25,092
David Woodley (1980-83)	5,928
Don Strock (1974-87)	4,613
Earl Morrall (1972-76)	2,335
Scott Mitchell (1990-93)	1,805

Top receivers
	Receptions
Mark Clayton (1983-92)	550
Mark Duper (1982-92)	511
Nat Moore (1974-86)	510
Tony Nathan (1979-87)	383
Duriel Harris (1976-83, 85)	269
Bruce Hardy (1978-89)	256

Top receivers
	Yards
Mark Duper (1982-92)	8,869
Mark Clayton (1983-92)	8,643
Nat Moore (1974-86)	7,547
Duriel Harris (1976-83, 85)	4,534
Tony Nathan (1979-87)	3,592
Paul Warfield (1970-74)	3,355

Most interceptions
	No.
Jake Scott (1970-75)	35
Dick Anderson (1968-77)	34
Glenn Blackwood (1979-87)	29
William Judson (1982-89)	24
Gerald Small (1978-83)	23
Tim Foley (1970-80)	22
Curtis Johnson (1970-78)	22

Most sacks
	No.
Bill Stanfill (1969-76)	67.5
Doug Betters (1978-87)	65.5
Vern Den Herder (1971-81)	64

143

PRO FOOTBALL WEEKLY 1994 ALMANAC

PREVIEW: MINNESOTA VIKINGS

There is a segment of Viking fans sighing and saying, "Finally," now that a solid No. 1 quarterback has moved to Minnesota.

Without any one quarterback playing in his prime for the Vikings since Tommy Kramer, the team has been forced to rely on a host of mediocre signal-callers for most of the past decade.

Those days are now gone, since Minnesota traded for QB Warren Moon. The 37-year-old former Oiler still has a strong arm and deadly accuracy.

When Minnesota released QB Jim McMahon, who started 12 of the 16 regular-season games last year and the wild-card playoff game against the Giants, the writing was on the wall. The Vikings were interested in a legitimate starting quarterback, so they went after Scott Mitchell. When that option failed, with Mitchell choosing to play for NFC Central rival Detroit, rumors of Moon in Minnesota became more rampant.

When the deal was finalized, the Vikings had to give up a fourth-round draft pick in 1994 and a conditional third-round selection in '95.

"This is just another challenge in my career. I see this as a very positive challenge for me," said Moon. "They do have an excellent organization, a great head coach. They just need a couple of pieces. Hopefully, I'm one of those pieces."

With the starting quarterback already in place, the Vikings will have a battle between Gino Torretta and Brad Johnson for the No. 2 and 3 spots, unless the team signs an experienced backup. The possibility remains that McMahon could be re-signed at a lower salary.

No portion of the Minnesota squad suffered through last season like the offensive backfield. For starters, RB Terry Allen was lost for the whole season because of a knee injury suffered during training camp. Allen had rushed for 1,201 yards the previous season and was expected to play a huge role in the offense.

RB's Roger Craig and Barry Word were benched after suffering bouts of fumble-itis, which opened the door for RB Robert Smith, a first-round draft pick. However, Smith suffered a season-ending knee injury in December, which led to the emergence of free-agent RB Scottie Graham, who came off the practice squad to set some team rushing records near the end of the season.

In '94 Allen will be watched closely to see if he has made a complete recovery. Minnesota hopes he can be the same low-to-the-ground runner with quick upfield moves he was prior to the injury. Smith was drafted to be a third-down back and kick returner, but he did a decent job as the featured back for the few games he started before getting injured.

Graham, who had been cut by the Steelers and Jets, rushed for 342 yards in the final three regular-season games, and he could become a key player again this season. Charles Evans, a first-year free agent last season, has potential, but he is coming off a wrist injury, which forced him to miss all of last year.

Prior to the '93 season, Minnesota lost three starting offensive linemen — OLT Gary Zimmerman, C Kirk Lowdermilk and OG Brian Habib. The group that played on the line last season did an adequate job, but the Vikings made steps to upgrade the unit.

The first move in the free-agent signing period was to lure OG-OT Chris Hinton away from the Falcons. Hinton, who was coached by Dennis Green at Northwestern and has been to the Pro Bowl as both a guard and tackle, is a nice addition to an offensive line that already features OLG Randall McDaniel. McDaniel did not have his greatest season in '93, but he did earn his fifth-straight Pro Bowl trip. He may be among the most athletic offensive linemen in the game, thanks to his 4.7 speed and tremendous vertical leap. But he does have some problems when facing a powerhouse player on the other side of the line.

C Adam Schreiber did an acceptable job but could be challenged by OG John Gerak for the starting job at center. The 6-2, 292-pound Gerak was drafted as a guard out of Penn State in '93.

Everett Lindsay, a fifth-round draft selection in '93, found his way into the starting lineup last season at left tackle. Although he was decent at the position in his 12 starts, he is more suited to play guard and may get switched to that position. Lindsay was injured late in the season, and OT Bernard Dafney held his own in relief. Todd Steussie, the Vikings' second No. 1 pick, figures in the equation at tackle.

The two Carters, Cris and Anthony, will be on the receiving end of Moon's passes. WR Cris Carter was the most important member of the offense last season, as he caught 86 passes for 1,071 yards and nine touchdowns. His hand-eye coordination and body control are his biggest attributes, which overshadow his lack of speed and quickness.

Ten-year veteran Anthony Carter picked up 774 yards by pulling down 60 receptions in '93. But he is not as fast as he once was; his longest pass play last year covered just 39 yards.

WR Qadry Ismail is among the fastest of Minnesota's good receivers, but the second-year pro out of Syracuse needs to become a more consistent pass catcher. He is an excellent runner after he catches the ball, but he still needs to figure out when to turn on the jets or slow down when running pass patterns. Also figuring to fit into the passing game will be Jake Reed, a big strider who has had his development slowed by

1994 PREVIEW ■ MINNESOTA

injuries since being drafted by the Vikings out of Grambling in 1991, and all-purpose rookie David Palmer, a second-round pick this year.

TE Mike Tice retired and Steve Jordan is getting on in years at age 33, which is why the team snagged Adrian Cooper from the Steelers. While in Pittsburgh, Cooper was stuck in the shadow of Eric Green. Cooper is a big, physical blocker who moves well and can catch. The other tight end figuring to see some action is Derek Tennell, a big target with decent pass-catching abilities. But he is not a starter.

Defensively, the Vikings had a banner year in '93 — if you look solely at the statistics.

Despite struggling at times, the Minnesota defense finished the season atop the NFL rankings, giving up a mere 275.3 yards per game. However, it should also be noted the club gave up 290 points.

"That stat might have been deceptive," said defensive coordinator Tony Dungy. "I don't think the team played as well (in 1993) as it did last year (1992). We gave up so many big plays."

The strongest section of the defensive unit is the line. The DT tandem of Henry Thomas and John Randle can be as effective as any in the league. Thomas may just be the best nose tackle in the league, and Randle made his first Pro Bowl appearance after a 12.5-sack season. Playing a backup DT role will be Esera Tuaolo, who did a fine job subbing for Thomas after he went down with an injury near the end of the season.

The team will have a different look at the ends, however, with unhappy DRE Chris Doleman moving on to Atlanta. Robert Harris, who has yet to realize his potential, gets the first crack at Doleman's slot, but rookie Fernando Smith also could challenge there. At left end, Roy Barker is a strong, solid player.

Back to anchor the middle of the defense is MLB Jack Del Rio, who led the club in tackles last season with 169. The 10-year veteran also picked off four passes. Joining Del Rio will be OLB's Fred Strickland and Carlos Jenkins. Strickland racked up 137 tackles in 1993, but, because he is not really a flow-position athlete, he may get replaced by the smaller, smoother Ed McDaniel. Jenkins had a strong '92 season but followed it with an average performance in '93. He is more than capable of running and hitting, but he can be a liability because of the number of mistakes he makes.

CB's Anthony Parker and Carl Lee are returning. Parker, a quick nickel back with fine coverage

PHOTO BY JEFF FISHBEIN

Randall McDaniel

skills, and No. 1 pick Dewayne Washington will compete for the CB spot vacated by Audray McMillian, who was released. Lee is 33 but is still considered a solid player. On the inside, FS Vencie Glenn is coming off his best season ever and is expected to start again. On the other side, SS's Lamar McGriggs and Todd Scott will try and earn their way into the starting lineup. McGriggs, the team's biggest, most physical defensive back, replaced Scott last season after the latter was injured during an error-filled season.

In the special-team department, PK Fuad Reveiz was a perfect 24-of-24 on field goals inside 46 yards, but he was only 2-of-13 on longer kicks. He also is known for his weak kickoffs. P. Harry Newsome started hot and finished cool last season. Mike Morris may be the most accurate deep-snapper in the NFL.

Ismail and Palmer will probably handle returner duties. Ismail still needs to gain more experience, and, with time, he could develop into a top-notch kick returner, although his hands may not be steady enough to handle punt returns.

FAST FACTS

■ Cris Carter became only the third player in Viking history to have 70 or more receptions twice (1991, 1993) in his career. Rickey Young (1978, 1979) and Anthony Carter (1988, 1990) are the others.

■ Scottie Graham tied a team record with 33 carries vs. Kansas City Dec. 26. His 166 yards rushing were the fourth highest in team history.

■ Counting the Vikings' '93 postseason appearance, Roger Craig has now reached the playoffs all 11 years he has been in the NFL.

PRO FOOTBALL WEEKLY 1994 ALMANAC

1994 PLAYER ROSTER

NO.	NAME	POS.	HT.	WT.	EXP.	COLLEGE	GP/GS
50	Abrams, Bobby	LB	6-3	230	5	Michigan	9/0
72	Adams, Scott	OL	6-5	293	3	Georgia	15/9
21	Allen, Terry	RB	5-10	197	5	Clemson	0/0
	Barker, Bryan	P	6-1	187	5	Santa Clara	16/16
92	Barker, Roy	DT	6-4	280	3	North Carolina	16/16
96	Boudreaux, Frank	DT	6-5	273	1	Northwestern	0/0
36	Boyd, Malik	CB	5-10	175	R	Southern	—
67	Boyd, Tracy	OT	6-4	296	1	Elizabeth City State	0/0
40	Brown, Phil	FB	5-10	210	R	Texas	—
47	Buck, Edward	S	5-11	175	R	Alcorn State	—
81	Carter, Anthony	WR	5-11	168	10	Michigan	15/15
80	Carter, Cris	WR	6-3	198	8	Ohio State	16/16
62	Christy, Jeff	C	6-3	277	2	Pittsburgh	9/0
87	Cooper, Adrian	TE	6-5	263	4	Oklahoma	14/3
77	Culpepper, Brad	DT	6-1	260	3	Florida	15/0
75	Dafney, Bernard	OT	6-5	331	3	Tennessee	16/4
55	Del Rio, Jack	LB	6-4	243	10	Southern Cal	16/16
29	Evans, Charles	RB	6-1	226	2	Clark Atlanta	3/0
54	Garnett, Dave	LB	6-2	219	2	Stanford	16/0
66	Gerak, John	OG	6-3	285	2	Penn State	4/0
25	Glenn, Vencie	S	6-0	201	9	Indiana State	16/16
31	Graham, Scottie	RB	5-9	215	2	Ohio State	7/3
30	Gray, Lance	FB	6-1	200	R	Nebraska	—
24	Griffith, Robert	DB	5-11	200	1	San Diego State	0/0
84	Guliford, Eric	WR	5-8	165	2	Arizona State	10/0
99	Harris, James	DE	6-4	270	2	Temple	6/0
90	Harris, Robert	DE	6-4	290	3	Southern-B.R.	16/0
48	Harrison, Todd	TE	6-4	260	1	North Carolina State	0/0
78	Hinton, Chris	OT	6-4	305	12	Northwestern	16/16
82	Ismail, Qadry	WR	6-0	192	2	Syracuse	15/6
51	Jenkins, Carlos	LB	6-3	217	4	Michigan State	16/16
14	Johnson, Brad	QB	6-5	221	3	Florida State	0/0
52	Jones, Donald	LB	6-0	231	1	Washington	0/0
11	Jones, Richard	P	6-3	198	1	Arizona State	0/0
32	Jones, Shawn	S	6-1	200	2	Georgia Tech	1/0
83	Jordan, Steve	TE	6-3	240	13	Brown	14/13
69	Kalis, Todd	OG	6-5	289	7	Arizona State	16/7
49	Lasley, J.J.	FB	6-0	220	1	Stanford	0/0
39	Lee, Carl	CB	5-11	186	12	Marshall	16/16
45	Lenseigne, Tony	TE	6-4	235	1	Eastern Washington	0/0
61	Lindsay, Everett	OG	6-4	290	2	Mississippi	12/12
91	Manusky, Greg	LB	6-1	233	7	Colgate	16/0
58	McDaniel, Ed	LB	5-11	230	3	Clemson	7/1
64	McDaniel, Randall	OG	6-3	275	7	Arizona State	16/16
37	McGriggs, Lamar	S	6-3	210	4	Western Illinois	9/4
1	Moon, Warren	QB	6-3	212	11	Washington	15/14
68	Morris, Mike	C	6-5	284	8	NE Missouri State	16/0
18	Newsome, Harry	P	6-0	193	10	Wake Forest	16/0
85	Novoselsky, Brent	TE	6-2	237	7	Pennsylvania	15/0
27	Parker, Anthony	CB	5-10	181	5	Arizona State	14/0
28	Pool, David	CB	5-9	182	5	Carson-Newman	2/0
93	Randle, John	DT	6-1	275	5	Texas A&I	16/16
86	Reed, Jake	WR	6-3	212	4	Grambling	10/1
7	Reveiz, Fuad	PK	5-11	223	10	Tennessee	16/0
74	Riemer, Troy	OT	6-5	287	R	Texas	—

146

1994 PREVIEW ■ MINNESOTA

1994 PLAYER ROSTER

NO.	NAME	POS.	HT.	WT.	EXP.	COLLEGE	GP/GS
60	Schreiber, Adam	C-OG	6-4	290	11	Texas	16/16
38	Scott, Todd	S	5-10	207	4	SW Louisiana	13/12
59	Sheppard, Ashley	LB	6-3	243	2	Clemson	10/0
57	Simms, William	LB	6-3	265	1	SW Louisiana State	0/0
26	Smith, Robert	RB	6-0	195	2	Ohio State	10/2
41	Staten, Robert	RB	5-11	235	1	Jackson State	0/0
53	Strickland, Fred	LB	6-2	245	7	Purdue	16/15
46	Tennell, Derek	TE	6-2	251	7	UCLA	16/4
97	Thomas, Henry	DT	6-2	277	8	Louisiana State	13/13
94	Thornton, John	DT	6-3	303	2	Cincinnati	0/0
13	Torretta, Gino	QB	6-2	215	2	Miami (Fla.)	1/0
89	Truitt, Olanda	WR	6-0	186	2	Mississippi State	8/0
98	Tuaolo, Esera	DT	6-2	275	4	Oregon State	11/3
15	Walsh, Chris	WR	6-1	185	2	Stanford	3/0
11	Ware, Andre	QB	6-2	205	5	Houston	5/2
35	West, Ronnie	WR	6-1	215	3	Pittsburg State (Kan.)	0/0

'94 DRAFT PICKS

RD.	NAME	POS.	HT.	WT.	COLLEGE
1.	Washington, Dewayne	DB	5-11	192	North Carolina State
1.	Steussie, Todd	OT	6-6	315	California
2.	Palmer, David	WR	5-8	167	Alabama
2.	Smith, Fernando	DE	6-5	284	Jackson State
4.	Wells, Mike	DT	6-3	281	Iowa
5.	Hammonds, Shelly	DB	5-9	183	Penn State
6.	Jordan, Andrew	TE	6-4	268	Western Carolina
7.	Bercich, Pete	LB	6-1	243	Notre Dame

PRO FOOTBALL WEEKLY 1994 ALMANAC

TEAM AT A GLANCE

TEAM DIRECTORY

Address	9520 Viking Drive Eden Prairie, Minnesota 55344
Stadium	Hubert H. Humphrey Metrodome 500 11th Avenue South Minneapolis, Minnesota 55415 Capacity: 63,000 Playing surface: AstroTurf
Training Camp	Mankato State University Mankato, Minnesota 56001
Colors	Purple, gold and white
Television	KITN, Channel 29
Radio	KFAN, 1130 AM

ADMINISTRATION
Chairman of the board: John C. Skoglund
President-chief executive officer: Roger L. Headrick
Vice president-administration: Jeff Diamond
Director of finance: Nick Valentine
Director of team operations: Breck Spinner
Assistant GM-player personnel: Jerry Reichow
Assistant GM-player personnel: Paul Wiggin
Player personnel coordinator: Scott Studwell
Director of public relations: David Pelletier
Director of marketing: Kernal Buhler
Ticket manager: Harry Randolph
Trainer: Fred Zamberletti

1994 SCHEDULE

Preseason

JULY 31	at Dallas	8:00
AUG. 6	vs. Kansas City (at Tokyo)	*10:00
AUG. 13	NEW ORLEANS	7:00
AUG. 20	at Seattle	7:00
AUG. 26	MIAMI	7:00

*Eastern Time

Regular season

SEP. 4	at Green Bay	12:00
SEP. 11	DETROIT	12:00
SEP. 18	at Chicago	12:00
SEP. 25	MIAMI	12:00
OCT. 2	at Arizona	1:00
OCT. 10	at N.Y. Giants (Mon.)	9:00
OCT. 16	OPEN DATE	
OCT. 20	GREEN BAY (Thurs.)	7:00
OCT. 30	at Tampa Bay	4:00
NOV. 6	NEW ORLEANS	12:00
NOV. 13	at New England	1:00
NOV. 20	N.Y. JETS	3:00
NOV. 27	TAMPA BAY	12:00
DEC. 1	CHICAGO (Thurs.)	7:00
DEC. 11	at Buffalo	1:00
DEC. 17	at Detroit (Sat.)	12:30
DEC. 26	SAN FRANCISCO (Mon.)	8:00

HEAD COACH
Dennis Green

In each of his two seasons as head coach of the Vikings, Green has taken the team to the playoffs. In 1992, the Vikings finished the regular season with a mark of 11-5 and won the NFC Central Division. Minnesota earned a wild-card berth last year after going 9-7. Green came to Minnesota after three seasons as head coach at Stanford. He also was head coach at Northwestern for five years, and was named the Big Ten coach of the year in 1982. Green's other NFL experience was two stints covering four seasons with the 49ers. After concluding his collegiate playing career at Iowa in 1970, Green spent one season as a defensive back with British Columbia in the CFL.

Previous NFL: wide receivers, 1986-88 San Francisco; special teams-wide receivers, 1979 San Francisco.

Previous college: head coach, 1989-91 Stanford; head coach, 1981-85 Northwestern; offensive coordinator, 1980 Stanford; running backs, 1977-78 Stanford; wide receivers-quarterbacks, 1974-76 Iowa; running backs-wide receivers, 1973 Dayton; graduate assistant, 1972 Iowa.

Player: No NFL. College, running back, 1968-70 Iowa.

ASSISTANT COACHES
Brian Billick: offensive coordinator
Previous NFL: offensive coordinator, 1993 Minnesota; tight ends, 1992 Minnesota. Player: NFL, tight end, 1977 Dallas. College: tight end, 1974-76 Brigham Young.

Tony Dungy: defensive coordinator
Previous NFL: defensive coordinator, 1992-93 Minnesota; 1989-91 Kansas City; 1981-88 Pittsburgh. Player: NFL, safety, 1977-78 Pittsburgh; 1979 San Francisco. College: quarterback, 1973-76 Minnesota.

Carl Hargrave: offensive assistant
Previous NFL: None. Player: No NFL. College: safety, Upper Iowa.

Monte Kiffin: inside linebackers
Previous NFL: inside linebackers, 1991-93 Minnesota; 1990 N.Y. Jets; 1986-89 Minnesota; 1984-85 Buffalo; 1983 Green Bay. Player: No NFL. College: offensive, defensive tackle, 1958-61 Nebraska.

Keith Rowen: offensive line
Previous NFL: offensive line, 1990-93 Atlanta; 1989 New England; 1985-88 Indianapolis; 1984 Cleveland. Player: No NFL. College: offensive tackle, 1970-74 Stanford.

Richard Solomon: defensive backs
Previous NFL: outside linebackers, 1992-93 Minnesota; 1987-91 N.Y. Giants. Player: No NFL. College: running back, defensive back, 1970-73 Iowa.

John Teerlinck: defensive line
Previous NFL: defensive line, 1992-93 Minnesota; 1991 L.A. Rams; 1989-90 Cleveland. Player: NFL, defensive tackle, 1974-76 San Diego. College: defensive lineman, 1970-73 Western Illinois.

Trent Walters: outside linebackers
Previous NFL: defensive backs, 1984 Cincin-

1994 PREVIEW ■ MINNESOTA

TEAM AT A GLANCE

nati. Player: No NFL. College: Indiana, 1962-65.

Tyrone Willingham: running backs
Previous NFL: running backs, 1992-93 Minnesota. Player: No NFL. College: quarterback, 1974-77 Michigan State.

Steve Wetzel: strength and conditioning
Previous NFL: strength and conditioning, 1992-93 Minnesota; 1991 Washington. Player: No NFL. College: None.

Gary Zauner: special teams
Previous NFL: None. Player: No NFL. College: 1968-72, Wisconsin-La Crosse.

COACHING RECORDS
(includes postseason games)

Years	Coach	W	L	T
1961-66	Norm Van Brocklin	29	51	4
1967-83	Bud Grant	161	99	5
1984	Les Steckel	3	13	0
1985	Bud Grant	7	9	0
1986-91	Jerry Burns	55	46	0
1992-93	Dennis Green	20	14	0

HISTORICAL HIGHLIGHTS

1960-61 A new franchise is granted to a group of investors from the twin cities of Minneapolis and St. Paul. The team takes the name Minnesota Vikings and will begin playing in the NFL in 1961.

1964 Jim Finks is named general manager of the Vikings.

1968 Bud Grant, coach of the Winnipeg Blue Bombers in the Canadian Football League, takes over the head-coaching duties for the Vikings.

1968 The "Purple People Eaters" is formed, a defensive front four that consists of DE's Carl Eller and Jim Marshall and DT's Alan Page and Gary Larsen. ... Minnesota wins its first title, taking the Central Division, but losing its first playoff game to the Baltimore Colts 24-14.

1969-70 Viking QB Joe Kapp ties the NFL mark with seven touchdown passes in a game against the Colts. ... Minnesota wins the NFC Central, then defeats the Los Angeles Rams and the Cleveland Browns in the playoffs. ... The Vikings go to Super Bowl IV but lose to the Kansas City Chiefs 23-7.

1970 Minnesota wins its third consecutive divisional title but is beaten by the San Francisco 49ers 17-14 in the playoffs.

1971 The Vikings add another division crown but lose to the Dallas Cowboys 20-12 in the playoffs.

1973-74 Minnesota posts a record of 12-2 and easily captures the NFC Central Division. ... The Vikings defeat the Redskins 27-20 and the Cowboys 27-10, earning a second Super Bowl appearance. ... The Vikings meet the Miami Dolphins in Super Bowl VIII at Rice Stadium in Houston but lose 24-7.

1974-75 Minnesota repeats as conference champions by defeating the Cardinals and Rams in the playoffs. ... The Vikings meet the Pittsburgh Steelers in Super Bowl IX in New Orleans, but again come up short, losing 16-6.

1975 With a record of 12-2, the Vikings win their seventh division title in eight years but are eliminated from the playoffs by the Cowboys, 17-14.

1976-77 Fran Tarkenton achieves two career milestones, completing more than 3,000 passes and more than 300 for touchdowns. He also becomes only the second quarterback in NFL history to pass for more than 40,000 yards. Minnesota again wins the NFC Central Division, with a record of 11-2-1. ... The Vikings defeat the Redskins 35-20 and the Rams 24-13 to earn a fourth trip to the Super Bowl. ... At the Rose Bowl in Pasadena, Calif., before more than 100,000 spectators, the Vikings fall to the Oakland Raiders 32-14.

1977-78 The Vikings post a 9-5 record identical to that of the Chicago Bears but are awarded the divisional crown on the basis of point differential in head-to-head competition (29-26, having defeated them 22-16 and lost to them 10-7). ... Minnesota defeats the Rams in the playoffs 14-7 but is then eliminated by the Dallas Cowboys 23-6.

1978 The Vikings win their sixth consecutive division championship, but fall to the L.A. Rams 24-10 in the first playoff game.

1980 The Vikings return to the top in the NFC Central Division with a 9-7 record after a one-year hiatus. But the Super Bowl-bound Philadelphia Eagles defeat them 31-16 in the playoffs.

1982 With a record of 5-4, Minnesota makes it to a playoff tournament devised for the strike-shortened season. After beating the Atlanta Falcons 30-24, the Vikings lose to the Redskins 21-7.

1985 At the end of the season, head coach Bud Grant ends a career with the Vikings that began back in 1967. He had retired following the 1983 season, only to come back after one year.

1987-88 Minnesota makes it to the playoffffs for the first time since 1982. In the wild-card game the Vikings defeat the Saints 44-10, then the 49ers 36-24. ... In the NFC title game, the Vikings lose to the Redskins 17-10.

1988-89 The Vikings make the playoffs for the second year in a row as a wild-card. They defeat the L.A. Rams 28-17 but then lose to the 49ers 34-9.

1989-90 Minnesota wins the NFC Central with a record of 10-6 but loses in the playoff to San Francisco 41-13.

1992-93 Dennis Green is named head coach, replacing Jerry Burns. ... The Vikings win the NFC Central Division, winning 11 of their 16 games. They are defeated by the Redskins 24-7 in the playoffs.

1993-94 Minnesota, with a record of 9-7, makes the playoffs as a wild-card, but is defeated by the Giants 17-10.

149

PRO FOOTBALL WEEKLY 1994 ALMANAC

TEAM AT A GLANCE

HALL OF FAME MEMBERS

	Yrs with Vikings	Inducted
QB Fran Tarkenton	1961-66, 72-78	1986
DT Alan Page	1967-78	1988
Coach Bud Grant	1967-83, 85	1994

RETIRED JERSEY NUMBERS
- 10 QB Fran Tarkenton
- 88 DT Alan Page

FIRST-ROUND DRAFT CHOICES
(since 1980)

Year	Selection	College
1980	DT Doug Martin	Washington
1981	No choice	
1982	RB Darrin Nelson	Stanford
1983	DB Joey Browner	Southern Cal
1984	DE Keith Millard	Washington
1985	LB Chris Doleman	Pittsburgh
1986	No choice	
1987	RB D.J. Dozier	Penn State
1988	OG Randall McDaniel	Arizona State
1989	No choice	
1990	No choice	
1991	No choice	
1992	No choice	
1993	RB Robert Smith	Ohio State
1994	CB Dewayne Washington	North Carolina St.
	OT Todd Steussie	California

RECORD VS. OTHER NFL TEAMS
(including postseason games)

	Record
Arizona Cardinals	5-7-0
Atlanta Falcons	12-6-0
Buffalo Bills	4-2-0
Chicago Bears	34-29-2
Cincinnati Bengals	4-3-0
Cleveland Browns	8-3-0
Dallas Cowboys	7-11-0
Denver Broncos	5-3-0
Detroit Lions	40-23-2
Green Bay Packers	33-31-1
Houston Oilers	3-3-0
Indianapolis Colts	6-12-1
Kansas City Chiefs	3-3-0
Los Angeles Raiders	2-7-0
Los Angeles Rams	20-12-2
Miami Dolphins	1-5
New England Patriots	2-3-0
New Orleans Saints	12-6-0
New York Giants	6-5-0
New York Jets	1-3-0
Philadelphia Eagles	10-7-0
Pittsburgh Steelers	7-5-0
San Diego Chargers	3-4-0
San Francisco 49ers	16-19-2
Seattle Seahawks	2-3-0
Tampa Bay Buccaneers	23-9-0
Washington Redskins	6-9-0

YEAR-BY-YEAR RECORDS

Year	Won	Lost	Tied
1961	3	11	0
1962	2	11	1
1963	5	8	1
1964	8	5	1
1965	7	7	0
1966	4	9	1
1967	3	8	3
1968**	8	6	0
1969*	12	2	0
1970**	12	2	0
1971**	11	3	0
1972	7	7	0
1973**	12	2	0
1974**	10	4	0
1975**	12	2	0
1976**	11	2	1
1977**	9	5	0
1978**	8	7	1
1979	7	9	0
1980**	9	7	0
1981	7	9	0
1982**	5	4	0
1983	8	8	0
1984	3	13	0
1985	7	9	0
1986	9	7	0
1987**	8	7	0
1988**	11	5	0
1989**	10	6	0
1990	6	10	0
1991	8	8	0
1992**	11	5	0
1993**	9	7	0
Total	**262**	**215**	**9**

Number of NFL championships   1
Number of years .500 or better   23
Number of years below .500   10

*NFL champions (Minnesota lost to Kansas City in Super Bowl IV, one year before the merger)
**Playoff team

1994 PREVIEW ■ MINNESOTA

RECORDS

INDIVIDUAL

Service
Seasons played	19	Jim Marshall (1961-79)
Games played	270	Jim Marshall (1961-79)
Consecutive games	270	Jim Marshall (1961-79)

Scoring
Points, career	1,365	Fred Cox (1963-77)
Points, season	132	Chuck Foreman (1975)
Points, game	24	Chuck Foreman (12/20/75)
Touchdowns, career	76	Bill Brown (1962-74)
Touchdowns, season	22	Chuck Foreman (1975)
Touchdowns, game	4	Chuck Foreman (12/20/75)
		Ahmad Rashad (9/2/79)
Field goals, career	282	Fred Cox (1963-77)
Field goals, season	31	Rich Karlis (1989)
Field goals, game	7	Rich Karlis (11/5/89)
Extra points, career	519	Fred Cox (1963-77)
Extra points, season	48	Chuck Nelson (1988)
Extra points, game	7	Fred Cox (9/28/69)
		Fred Cox (11/23/69)
		Chuck Nelson (10/23/88)

Rushing
Yards, career	5,879	Chuck Foreman (1973-79)
Yards, season	1,201	Terry Allen (1992)
Yards, game	200	Chuck Foreman (10/24/76)
Attempts, career	1,627	Bill Brown (1962-74)
Attempts, season	280	Chuck Foreman (1975)
Attempts, game	33	Chuck Foreman (11/23/75)
		Chuck Foreman (12/18/77)
		Terry Allen (12/20/92)
Touchdowns, career	52	Chuck Foreman (1973-79)
Touchdowns, season	13	Chuck Foreman (1975 & 1976)
		Terry Allen (1992)
Touchdowns, game	3	By many players

Passing
Rating, career	80.2	Fran Tarkenton (1961-66, 72-78)
Rating, season	93.2	Fran Tarkenton (1973)
Completions, career	2,635	Fran Tarkenton (1961-66, 72-78)
Completions, season	345	Fran Tarkenton (1978)
Completions, game	38	Tommy Kramer (12/14/80)
		Tommy Kramer (11/29/81)
Yards, career	33,098	Fran Tarkenton (1961-66, 72-78)
Yards, season	3,912	Tommy Kramer (1981)
Yards, game	490	Tommy Kramer (11/2/86)
Attempts, career	4,569	Fran Tarkenton (1961-66, 72-78)
Attempts, season	593	Tommy Kramer (1981)
Attempts, game	63	Rich Gannon (10/20/91)
Touchdowns, career	239	Fran Tarkenton (1961-66, 1972-78)
Touchdowns, season	26	Tommy Kramer (1981)
Touchdowns, game	7	Joe Kapp (9/28/69)

Receiving
Receptions, career	495	Steve Jordan (1982-93)
Receptions, season	88	Rickey Young (1978)
Receptions, game	15	Rickey Young (12/16/79)
Yards, career	7,635	Anthony Carter (1985-93)
Yards, season	1,225	Anthony Carter (1988)
Yards, game	210	Sammy White (11/7/76)
Touchdowns, career	52	Anthony Carter (1985-93)
Touchdowns, season	11	Jerry Reichow (1961)
Touchdowns, game	4	Ahmad Rashad (9/2/79)

Interceptions
Career	53	Paul Krause (1968-79)
Season	10	Paul Krause (1975)
Game	3	By many players

Sacks
Career	130	Carl Eller (1964-78)
Season	21	Chris Doleman (1989)
Game	5	Randy Holloway (9/16/84)

Longest plays
Run from scrimmage	80	Clinton Jones (TD, 11/2/69)
Pass play	89	Fran Tarkenton to C. Ferguson (TD, 11/11/62)
Field goal	54	Jan Stenerud (9/16/84)
Interception return	97	Reggie Rutland (TD, 12/15/91)
Kickoff return	101	Lance Rentzel (TD, 11/14/65)
Punt return	98	Charlie West (TD, 11/3/68)
Punt	84	Harry Newsome (12/20/92)

Top scorers
	Points
Fred Cox (1963-77)	1,365
Bill Brown (1962-74)	456
Chuck Foreman (1973-79)	450
Rick Danmeier (1978-83)	364
Anthony Carter (1985-93)	324
Ted Brown (1979-86)	318

Top rushers
	Yards
Chuck Foreman (1973-79)	5,879
Bill Brown (1962-74)	5,757
Ted Brown (1979-86)	4,546
Dave Osborn (1965-75)	4,320
Darrin Nelson (1982-89, 91-92)	4,231
Tommy Mason (1961-66)	3,252

Top passers
	Completions
Fran Tarkenton (1961-66, 72-78)	2,635
Tommy Kramer (1977-89)	2,011
Wade Wilson (1981-91)	929
Rich Gannon (1987-92)	561
Joe Kapp (1967-69)	351
Steve Dils (1979-83)	336

Top passers
	Yards
Fran Tarkenton (1961-66, 72-78)	33,098
Tommy Kramer (1977-89)	24,775
Wade Wilson (1981-91)	12,135
Rich Gannon (1987-92)	6,278
Joe Kapp (1967-69)	4,807
Steve Dils (1979-83)	3,867

Top receivers
	Receptions
Steve Jordan (1982-93)	495
Anthony Carter (1985-93)	478
Ahmad Rashad (1976-82)	400
Sammy White (1976-86)	393
Ted Brown (1979-86)	339
Chuck Foreman (1973-79)	336

Top receivers
	Yards
Anthony Carter (1985-93)	7,635
Sammy White (1976-86)	6,400
Steve Jordan (1982-93)	6,284
Ahmad Rashad (1976-82)	5,489
Hassan Jones (1986-92)	3,733
Bill Brown (1962-74)	3,177

Most interceptions
	No.
Paul Krause (1968-79)	53
Bobby Bryant (1967-80)	51
Ed Sharockman (1962-72)	40
Joey Browner (1983-91)	37
Nate Wright (1971-80)	31
Carl Lee (1983-93)	29

Most sacks
	No.
Carl Eller (1964-78)	130
Jim Marshall (1961-79)	127
Alan Page (1967-78)	108

151

PRO FOOTBALL WEEKLY 1994 ALMANAC

PREVIEW: NEW ENGLAND PATRIOTS

At the end of the 1993 season, Bill Parcells had every reason to smile. First of all, his young team had gotten better each week. At first, they started playing close games against opponents with superior talent. Then, they had a few heartbreaking defeats in games they could have won against seemingly superior opponents. Finally, the breakthrough came. The Patriots put away Cincinnati, Cleveland, Indianapolis and Miami to close the season. That last victory, a 33-27 overtime thriller, kept the Dolphins from earning a playoff berth, and it also led Don Shula to give this assessment of the Patriots. "The Patriots, right now, are a good team," Shula said. "They took everything we had, and they came out on top."

So Parcells, who had come out of retirement to take over the NFL's version of Ringling Bros. Barnum and Bailey Circus, had brought respectability to this previously ragtag unit. But he was not happy. He was not contemplating the future success this team would have with a young star like Drew Bledsoe at quarterback. He was worried about the team's stability. Owner James Busch Orthwein was sick of the football business, sick of New England and sick of the Patriots. He wanted out.

Orthwein was not worried about keeping the locals happy. If he sold to someone who would keep the team in Foxboro, fine, but, if not, it wasn't his problem.

Luckily for Parcells, the Patriots and their fans, the team was sold shortly after that season finale. Orthwein found a local buyer in Robert Kraft, who happens to own Foxboro Stadium and had the $170 million Orthwein wanted. Because the sale happened so quickly, Parcells could go on with the business of building a winning football team, and he continued to do just that. During the offseason, the Patriots signed players such as OG Bob Kratch, S Myron Guyton, RB Blair Thomas and LB Steve DeOssie. Throw in former Tampa Bay CB Ricky Reynolds and San Diego RB Marion Butts, who were acquired in trades, and the Patriots have a fairly decent team.

Hopes are high in New England, higher than they've been at any time since the Patriots were coming off their Super Bowl year in 1985. By May, more than 46,000 season tickets had been sold.

While there are a lot of reasons for optimism, probably the biggest is Bledsoe, who may be the NFL's quarterback of the future. He has size, a strong arm and great intelligence. As a rookie last year, Bledsoe completed 214-of-429 passes for 2,494 yards with 15 touchdowns and 15 interceptions. The numbers aren't overly noteworthy, but his progress was. Bledsoe got better each week, and the Patriot coaching staff was impressed with his ability to adapt to the pro game and keep from getting too high or too low depending on his performance.

PHOTO BY GEORGE GOJKOVICH

Drew Bledsoe

"We got hammered by the Jets early in the season (45-7 in Week Four at Giants Stadium), and you should have seen Drew," said offensive coordinator Ray Perkins. "He refused to hang his head. He wasn't down at all. At that point, you got the idea that he knew how to handle it."

Bledsoe has all the tools. Tremendous arm strength. Quick release. Escapability. Intelligence. The desire to get better. That last factor will probably determine the Patriots' fate over the next few years more than any single factor. Scott Zolak is Bledsoe's backup, and he has good size and a strong arm.

The running game is another area of strength. Parcells loves a strong running game, and last year RB Leonard Russell gained 1,088 yards on 300 carries. Parcells loved Russell's determination, work ethic and ability to get crucial yards in key situations. But the one thing Parcells didn't

1994 PREVIEW ■ NEW ENGLAND

love was Russell's contract status. Russell turned down a $1.4 million-per-year offer from the Patriots, and Parcells could not be sure of Russell's future. As a result, he traded for Butts, a player he has admired from afar for several years. "If you give Butts 250 carries a year, he'll get you 1,000 yards," said Parcells. "If you get him 300 carries, he'll get you 1,200 yards." It could be out with the old and in with the new. Parcells also signed Thomas, who was the No. 2 overall selection in the 1990 draft. Thomas had great speed and talent coming out of Penn State, but he was haunted by a critical fumble in a 1992 Monday night loss to the Bears and was misused by the coaching staff. A change of scenery could help him dramatically. If it doesn't, Parcells won't hesitate to cut him. New England has two good blocking fullbacks in Kevin Turner and Sam Gash. Of the two, Turner is the better runner and he is also quite proficient at catching the ball out of the backfield.

The Patriots don't have any big-name receivers for Bledsoe at this point, but Vincent Brisby had an interesting rookie year, as he caught 45 passes for 626 yards and two touchdowns. Brisby showed very good hands and good speed. What he lacks is the explosiveness to separate from defenders. Ray Crittenden does have that kind of speed, but he is very inexperienced and is still learning the nuances of the game after having been a soccer star in his early years. Free-agent Timpson probably has the most overall talent of all the New England receivers, but his concentration is not always what it should be. No. 2 draft pick Kevin Lee adds neededc size and speed. TE Ben Coates is coming off a huge year in which he caught 53 passes for 659 yards and eight touchdowns. He is an excellent clutch receiver and very good as a runner once he makes the catch. He is also the kind of physical blocker that Parcells likes.

The key to any Parcells-coached offense is the line. Last year the New England offensive line protected its quarterbacks very well. Patriot passers were sacked only 23 times, and, breaking that number down further, only 13 came in the last 12 games. OLT Bruce Armstrong, ORT Pat Harlow and OLG Eugene Chung are the group's leaders. Armstrong was playing at a near-Pro Bowl level by season's end. Harlow is tough, aggressive and nasty, and Chung has great mobility and has become more physical. Kratch, the former Giant, fits in at right guard and is an excellent run blocker. C Mike Arthur is not overly strong or dependable. Todd Rucci can bench-press the weightroom and fits in as a backup guard.

The Patriots played fairly well from a defensive standpoint last year, giving up only 286 points. However, unlike Parcells' Giant teams, these Patriots were extremely vulnerable in the fourth quarter. New England drafted Southern Cal DE-OLB Willie McGinest in an effort to beef up the pass rush, and the additions of Guyton and Reynolds should help.

The Patriot defensive line is somewhat small. DE Ray Agnew has good speed and strength but has a hard time getting rid of his blocks. Aaron Jones probably moves better than any of the defensive linemen, but he's not a very productive all-around player. NT Tim Goad is a hard-working, run-down player who is very quick and quite proficient at tying up blockers. Mike Pitts is a journeyman who leaves everything on the field. Brent Williams is not an every-down player but still is a good pass rusher. The Patriots believe McGinest has the potential to become another Lawrence Taylor. He should dramatically upgrade the Patriot pass rush because of his great speed coming around the corner.

The LB crew is led by Vincent Brown, who goes by the nickname of "the Undertaker." Brown plays with great enthusiasm and is a major-league hitter. He led New England with 158 tackles last season, while fellow ILB Todd Collins added 92. Collins is not as strong as Brown, but he has the speed and range that are needed to make plays sideline-to-sideline. Chris Slade led the team with nine sacks, but he was constantly out of position vs. the run. Backup OLB Dwayne Sabb is not a pass-rushing threat but has the kind of size Parcells likes.

Free-agent acquisitions Reynolds and Guyton strengthen the secondary significantly. Reynolds is a top cover cornerback, but he was better in 1992 than he was last year. Guyton will move in at free safety. He is tough and aware and is usually in the right place at key moments. Maurice Hurst is a solid cover corner and is somewhat improved against the run. Harlon Barnett and Corwin Brown are both hard-hitting safeties who lack speed and cover skills.

Last year rookie PK Scott Sisson was a miserable 14-of-26 on FG attempts and probably cost the Patriots four games. Parcells finally saw enough of Sisson and brought in ex-Giant PK Matt Bahr, who didn't miss a kick in '93. P Mike Saxon recorded a 34.8-yard net average and had three kicks blocked. Gash and Sabb were both impressive on special teams.

FAST FACTS

■ The Patriots' four-game winning streak to end the season was their longest since 1988.

■ Drew Bledsoe's 15 TD passes were the most by a Patriot quarterback since Tony Eason threw 19 in 1986. In his first nine games, Bledsoe threw seven TD's and 13 interceptions; in his last four games, he threw eight TD's and only two interceptions.

■ WR Michael Timpson is the only active NFL player with more than one overtime touchdown. He beat the Colts with an overtime TD in 1991 and finished off the Dolphins in the last game of the 1993 season.

PRO FOOTBALL WEEKLY 1994 ALMANAC

1994 PLAYER ROSTER

NO.	NAME	POS.	HT.	WT.	EXP.	COLLEGE	GP/GS
92	Agnew, Ray	DE	6-3	272	5	North Carolina St.	16/1
78	Armstrong, Bruce	OT	6-4	284	8	Louisville	16/16
65	Arthur, Mike	C	6-3	280	4	Texas A&M	13/11
3	Bahr, Matt	PK	5-10	175	16	Penn State	14/0
18	Ballard, Gregory	WR	6-3	190	R	Kansas	—
42	Barnett, Harlan	DB	5-11	200	5	Michigan State	14/12
64	Barnett, Troy	DE	6-4	282	R	North Carolina	—
62	Basham, Bernard	DE	6-6	281	R	Virginia Tech	—
52	Bavaro, David	LB	6-1	228	4	Syracuse	12/0
11	Bledsoe, Drew	QB	6-5	233	2	Washington State	13/12
49	Botkin, Kirk	TE	6-2	233	R	Arkansas	—
38	Boyd, Jean	SS	5-11	185	R	Arizona State	—
82	Brisby, Vincent	WR	6-1	186	2	NE Louisiana	16/12
30	Brown, Corwin	SS	6-1	192	2	Michigan	15/12
80	Brown, Troy	WR-KR	5-9	183	2	Marshall	12/0
59	Brown, Vincent	LB	6-2	245	7	Mississippi Valley St.	16/16
44	Butts, Marion	RB	6-1	248	6	Florida State	16/16
99	Carthen, Jason	LB	6-3	255	2	Ohio U.	5/0
69	Chung, Eugene	OG	6-4	295	3	Virginia Tech	16/16
87	Coates, Ben	TE	6-5	245	4	Livingstone College	16/10
54	Collins, Todd	LB	6-2	242	3	Carson-Newman	16/12
81	Crittenden, Ray	WR	6-1	188	2	Virginia Tech	16/2
26	Croom, Corey	RB	5-11	212	2	Ball State	14/1
50	DeOssie, Steve	LB	6-2	248	11	Boston College	15/0
17	Dixon, Todd	WR	5-10	175	R	Wake Forest	—
33	Gash, Sam	FB	5-11	224	3	Penn State	15/4
67	Gisler, Mike	OG	6-4	300	2	Houston	12/0
15	Glenn, Kevin	WR	6-1	166	R	Illinois State	—
72	Goad, Tim	NT	6-3	280	7	North Carolina	16/15
36	Green, Damacio	CB	5-10	183	R	Virginia State	—
88	Griffith, Richard	TE	6-5	256	2	Arizona	3/0
29	Guyton, Myron	SS	6-1	205	7	Eastern Kentucky	16/16
77	Harlow, Pat	OT	6-6	290	4	Southern Cal	16/16
84	Harris, Ronnie	WR	5-10	170	2	Oregon	5/0
12	Henry, Mario	WR	6-1	184	R	Rutgers	—
90	Hooks, Bryan	DE	6-3	286	1	Arizona State	0/0
37	Hurst, Maurice	CB	5-10	185	6	Southern-B.R.	16/16
98	Johnson, Mario	NT	6-3	288	3	Missouri	6/0
97	Jones, Aaron	DE	6-5	267	7	Eastern Kentucky	11/1
55	Kerr, Mike	LB	6-5	236	1	Florida	0/0
61	Kratch, Bob	OG	6-3	288	6	Iowa	16/16
28	Lambert, Dion	FS	6-1	185	3	UCLA	14/4
35	Legette, Burnie	FB	6-1	243	2	Michigan	7/0
75	Lewis, Bill	C	6-6	290	9	Nebraska	7/5
43	Lewis, Vernon	CB	5-10	192	2	Pittsburgh	10/0
86	McMurtry, Greg	WR	6-2	207	5	Michigan	14/8
70	Moore, Brandon	OT	6-6	290	2	Duke	16/0
93	Pitts, Mike	DE	6-5	277	12	Alabama	16/15
23	Ray, Terry	S	6-1	205	3	Oklahoma	15/1
94	Reynolds, Don	DE	6-3	278	1	Virginia	0/0
21	Reynolds, Ricky	CB	5-11	190	8	Washington State	14/13
71	Rucci, Todd	OG	6-5	291	1	Penn State	2/1
32	Russell, Leonard	RB	6-2	235	4	Arizona State	16/15
95	Sabb, Dwayne	LB	6-4	248	3	New Hampshire	14/7
7	Saxon, Mike	P	6-3	200	10	San Diego State	16/0

1994 PREVIEW ■ NEW ENGLAND

1994 PLAYER ROSTER

NO.	NAME	POS.	HT.	WT.	EXP.	COLLEGE	GP/GS
9	Sisson, Scott	PK	6-1	197	2	Georgia Tech	13/0
74	Skene, Doug	OG	6-6	295	1	Michigan	0/0
53	Slade, Chris	LB	6-4	232	2	Virginia	16/5
22	Smith, Rod	CB	5-11	187	3	Notre Dame	16/9
63	Stanley, Sylvester	NT	6-2	283	R	Michigan	—
66	Staten, Mark	G	6-6	308	1	Miami (Ohio)	0/0
41	Stephens, Eric	CB	5-10	170	R	Jacksonville State	—
31	Thomas, Blair	RB	5-10	202	5	Penn State	11/5
83	Timpson, Michael	WR	5-10	175	6	Penn State	16/7
34	Turner, Kevin	FB	6-1	224	3	Alabama	16/9
62	Tylski, Rich	OG	6-4	287	R	Utah State	—
39	Washington, Jarrod	RB	6-1	205	R	Virginia	—
76	Washington, John	DE	6-4	290	9	Oklahoma State	16/3
51	White, David	LB	6-2	235	2	Nebraska	6/0
40	Witherspoon, Derrick	RB	5-10	198	R	Clemson	—
27	Wren, Darryl	CB	6-1	188	2	Pittsburg (Kan.) St.	12/5
16	Zolak, Scott	QB	6-5	222	4	Maryland	3/0

'94 DRAFT PICKS

RD.	NAME	POS.	HT.	WT.	COLLEGE
1.	McGinest, Willie	DE	6-4	255	Southern Cal
2.	Lee, Kevin	WR	6-0	189	Alabama
3.	Collier, Ervin	DT	6-3	287	Florida A&M
3.	Burch, Joe	C	6-0	194	Texas Southern
4.	Burke, John	TE	6-3	258	Virginia Tech
5.	O'Neill, Pat	P	6-1	195	Syracuse
6.	Hawkins, Steve	DB	6-5	207	Western Michigan
6.	Lane, Max	OT	6-6	286	Navy
7.	Walker, Jay	QB	6-3	230	Howard
7.	Moore, Marty	LB	6-0	242	Kentucky

PRO FOOTBALL WEEKLY 1994 ALMANAC

TEAM AT A GLANCE

TEAM DIRECTORY

Address	Foxboro Stadium Route 1 Foxboro, Massachusetts 02035 (508) 543-8200
Stadium	Foxboro Stadium Route 1 Foxboro, Massachusetts 02035 Capacity: 60,794 Playing surface: Grass
Training Camp	Bryant College Route 7 Smithfield, Rhode Island 02917
Colors	Blue, red, silver and white
Television	WBZ, Channel 4
Radio	WBZ, 1030 AM

ADMINISTRATION

President-chief executive officer: Robert K. Kraft
Vice president: Jonathan A. Kraft
Vice president-football operations: Patrick Forte
Vice president-business operations: Andrew Wasynczuk
Vice president-finance: James Hausmann
Vice president-event management: Brian O'Donovan
Controller: Virginia Widman
Director of pro scouting: Bobby Grier
Director of college scouting: Charles Armey
Director of public relations: Donald Lowery
Director of ticketing: Ken Sternfeld
Marketing manager: Mitch Hardin
Trainer: Ron O'Neil

1994 SCHEDULE

Preseason

AUG. 5	NEW ORLEANS	8:00
AUG. 13	at L.A. Rams	7:00
AUG. 18	WASHINGTON	7:00
AUG. 26	at Green Bay	7:00

Regular season

SEP. 4	at Miami	4:00
SEP. 11	BUFFALO	1:00
SEP. 18	at Cincinnati	1:00
SEP. 25	at Detroit	4:00
OCT. 2	GREEN BAY	1:00
OCT. 9	L.A. RAIDERS	4:00
OCT. 16	at N.Y. Jets	1:00
OCT. 23	OPEN DATE	
OCT. 30	MIAMI	1:00
NOV. 6	at Cleveland	1:00
NOV. 13	MINNESOTA	1:00
NOV. 20	SAN DIEGO	1:00
NOV. 27	at Indianapolis	8:00
DEC. 4	N.Y. JETS	1:00
DEC. 11	INDIANAPOLIS	1:00
DEC. 18	at Buffalo	1:00
DEC. 24	at Chicago	12:00

HEAD COACH

Bill Parcells

In 1993 after two years away from the sidelines, Parcells came back to New England, where he first got his start in professional coaching. During the two-year hiatus, Parcells worked as an analyst for NBC. As head coach of the Giants from 1983 to '90, he led his teams to two Super Bowl titles. Parcells is the second-winningest coach in the history of the Giants. In his first season with with the Patriots, he guided the team to a 5-11 record, which brings his overall coaching record to 90-63-1. Born Aug. 22, 1941, Englewood, N.J.

Previous NFL: head coach, N.Y. Giants 1983-90; defensive coordinator, N.Y. Giants 1981-82; linebackers, New England 1980.

Previous college: head coach, Air Force 1978; defensive coordinator, Texas Tech 1975-77; defensive coordinator, Vanderbilt 1973-74; linebackers, Florida St. 1970-72; linebackers, Army 1966-69; defensive line, Wichita State 1965; defensive assistant, Hastings College (Neb.) 1964.

Player: No NFL. College, linebacker, 1960 Colgate; 1961-63 Wichita State.

ASSISTANT COACHES

Maurice Carthon: offensive assistant
Previous NFL: None. Player: NFL, running back, 1985-91 N.Y. Giants; 1992 Indianapolis. College: running back, 1979-82 Arkansas State.

Romeo Crennel: defensive line
Previous NFL: offensive line, 1993-93 New England; 1981-92 N.Y. Giants. Player: No NFL. College: defensive tackle, linebacker, 1966-69 Western Kentucky.

Al Groh: defensive coordinator
Previous NFL: defensive coordinator, 1993 New England; 1987 Atlanta; 1989-91 N.Y. Giants. Player: No NFL. College: defensive end, 1964-67 Virginia.

Fred Hoaglin: offensive line
Previous NFL: offensive line, 1993 New England; 1985-92 N.Y. Giants; 1978-84 Detroit. Player: NFL, center, 1966-72 Cleveland; 1973 Baltimore; 1974-75 Houston; 1976 Seattle. College: center, 1962-65 Pittsburgh.

Chris Palmer: wide receivers
Previous NFL: wide receivers, 1993 New England; 1990-92 Houston. Player: No NFL. College: quarterback, 1968-71 Southern Connecticut State.

Johnny Parker: strength and conditioning
Previous NFL: strength and conditioning, 1993 New England; 1984-92 N.Y. Giants. Player: No NFL. College: None.

Ray Perkins: offensive coordinator
Previous NFL: offensive coordinator, 1993 New England; 1987-90 Tampa Bay (head coach); 1979-82 N.Y. Giants (head coach); 1978 San Diego; 1974-77 New England. Player: NFL, receiver, 1967-71 Baltimore. College: wide receiver, 1964-66 Alabama.

Michael Pope: running backs
Previous NFL: offensive coordinator, 1992-93 Cincinnati; 1983-91 N.Y. Giants. Player: No NFL. College: quarterback, 1962-64 Lenoir Rhyne.

1994 PREVIEW ■ NEW ENGLAND

TEAM AT A GLANCE

Dante Scarnecchia: special assistant
Previous NFL: special assistant, 1991-93 New England; 1982-88 New England; 1989-90 Indianapolis. Player: No NFL. College: center, guard, 1968-70 California Western.

Mike Sweatman: special teams
Previous NFL: special teams, 1993 New England; 1985-92 N.Y. Giants; 1984 Minnesota. Player: No NFL. College: linebacker, 1964-67 Kansas.

Bob Trott: defensive backs
Previous NFL: defensive backs, 1993 New England; 1990-92 N.Y. Giants. Player: No NFL. College: defensive back, 1973-75 North Carolina.

Charlie Weis: tight ends
Previous NFL: tight ends, 1993 New England 1990-92 N.Y. Giants. Player: No NFL. College: None.

COACHING RECORDS
(including postseason records)

Years	Coach	W	L	T
1960-61	Lou Saban	7	12	0
1961-68	Mike Holovak	53	47	9
1969-70	Clive Rush	5	16	0
1970-72	John Mazur	9	21	0
1972	Phil Bengtson	1	4	0
1973-78	Chuck Fairbanks	46	41	0
1978	Hank Bullough Ron Erhardt	0	1	0
1979-81	Ron Erhardt	21	27	0
1982-84	Ron Meyer	18	16	0
1984-89	Raymond Berry	51	41	0
1990	Rod Rust	1	15	0
1991-92	Dick MacPherson	8	24	0
1993	Bill Parcells	5	11	0

HISTORICAL HIGHLIGHTS

1960 An AFL franchise is awarded for Boston to a syndicate headed by William H. Sullivan Jr., and the team is named the Boston Patriots.
1963-64 In a special playoff game, the Patriots win the AFL's Eastern Division title with a 26-8 victory over Buffalo. ... The Patriots lose the AFL title game to the Chargers 51-10 at San Diego.
1966 Jim Nance becomes the first Patriot to gain more than 200 yards rushing in a game (208 on 38 carries). He is also the first to gain 1,000 yards in a season (1,458).
1971 The team is moved to Foxboro, Mass., and renamed the New England Patriots.
1976 With a record of 11-3, the Patriots qualify for their first NFL playoff appearance and their first playoff game since 1963. ... They lose the AFC wild-card playoff game to the Oakland Raiders 24-21.
1978 The Patriots win their first divisional championship with a record of 11-5 but lose to Houston 31-14 in the first playoff game ever played in Foxboro.
1979 Harold Jackson and Stanley Morgan become the first Patriots to exceed the 1,000-yard receiving mark, by gaining 1,013 and 1,002 yards, respectively.
1982 New England makes the playoff tournament in a strike-shortened season with a record of 5-4 but is defeated by the eventual AFC champion Miami Dolphins 28-13.
1985-86 Winning 11 of their 16 games, the Patriots go to the playoffs as a wild-card team. They defeat the New York Jets 26-14, then the Raiders 27-20. ... New England triumphs over the Miami Dolphins 31-14 to win the AFC championship. ... At the Louisiana Superdome, the Patriots lose to the Chicago Bears 46-10 in Super Bowl XX.
1986-87 The Patriots win the AFC Eastern Division, but fall to the Super Bowl-bound Denver Broncos 22-17 in the divisional playoffs.
1993 Bill Parcells, former head coach of the Super Bowl champion New York Giants, is hired as head coach. ... Robert K. Kraft buys the Patriots and vows to keep the team in New England and at Foxboro Stadium.

PRO FOOTBALL WEEKLY 1994 ALMANAC

TEAM AT A GLANCE

HALL OF FAME MEMBERS

	Yrs with Patriots	Inducted
OG John Hannah	1973-85	1991

RETIRED JERSEY NUMBERS

- 20 RB Gino Cappelletti
- 57 LB Steve Nelson
- 73 G John Hannah
- 79 DT Jim Lee Hunt
- 89 DE Bob Dee

FIRST-ROUND DRAFT CHOICES
(since 1980)

Year	Selection	College
1980	DB Roland James	Tennessee
	RB Vagas Ferguson	Notre Dame
1981	OT Brian Holloway	Stanford
1982	DE Ken Sims	Texas
	DT Lester Williams	Miami (Fla.)
1983	QB Tony Eason	Illinois
1984	WR Irving Fryar	Nebraska
1985	C Trevor Matich	Brigham Young
1986	RB Reggie Dupard	Southern Methodist
1987	OT Bruce Armstrong	Louisville
1988	RB John Stephens	Northwestern St. (La.)
1989	WR Hart Lee Dykes	Oklahoma State
1990	LB Chris Singleton	Arizona
	DE Ray Agnew	North Carolina St.
1991	OT Pat Harlow	Southern Cal
	RB Leonard Russell	Arizona State
1992	OL Eugene Chung	Virginia Tech
1993	QB Drew Bledsoe	Washington State
1994	DE Willie McGinest	Southern Cal

RECORD VS. OTHER NFL TEAMS
(including postseason games)

	Record
Arizona Cardinals	2-6-0
Atlanta Falcons	3-4-0
Buffalo Bills	34-33-1
Chicago Bears	3-3-0
Cincinnati Bengals	8-7-0
Cleveland Browns	3-9-0
Dallas Cowboys	0-6-0
Denver Broncos	12-17-0
Detroit Lions	2-3-0
Green Bay Packers	2-2-0
Houston Oilers	17-15-1
Indianapolis Colts	27-20-0
Kansas City Chiefs	7-13-3
Los Angeles Raiders	13-13-1
Los Angeles Rams	3-3-0
Miami Dolphins	22-34-0
Minnesota Vikings	3-2-0
New Orleans Saints	5-2-0
New York Giants	1-3-0
New York Jets	29-38-1
Philadelphia Eagles	2-5-0
Pittsburgh Steelers	3-9-0
San Diego Chargers	13-12-2
San Francisco 49ers	1-6-0
Seattle Seahawks	6-7-0
Tampa Bay Buccaneers	3-0-0
Washington Redskins	1-4-0

YEAR-BY-YEAR RECORDS

Year	Won	Lost	Tied	Year	Won	Lost	Tied
1960	5	9	0	1977	9	5	0
1961	9	4	1	1978**	11	5	0
1962	9	4	1	1979	9	7	0
1963**	7	6	1	1980	10	6	0
1964	10	3	1	1981	2	14	0
1965	4	8	2	1982**	5	4	0
1966	8	4	2	1983	8	8	0
1967	3	10	1	1984	9	7	0
1968	4	10	0	1985**	11	5	0
1969	4	10	0	1986**	11	5	0
1970	2	12	0	1987	8	7	0
1971	6	8	0	1988	9	7	0
1972	3	11	0	1989	5	11	0
1973	5	9	0	1990	1	15	0
1974	7	7	0	1991	6	10	0
1975	3	11	0	1992	2	14	0
1976**	11	3	0	1993	5	11	0
				Total	221	270	9

Number of NFL championships 0
Number of years .500 or better 18
Number of years below .500 16

*NFL champions
**Playoff team

1994 PREVIEW ■ NEW ENGLAND

RECORDS

INDIVIDUAL

Service
Seasons played	16	Steve Grogan (1975-90)
Games played	206	Julius Adams (1971-77, 79-85, 87)
Consecutive games	161	Raymond Clayborn (1977-87)

Scoring
Points, career	1,130	Gino Cappelletti (1960-70)
Points, season	155	Gino Cappelletti (1964)
Points, game	28	Gino Cappelletti (12/18/65)
Touchdowns, career	68	Stanley Morgan (1977-89)
Touchdowns, season	13	Stanley Morgan (1979)
		Steve Grogan (1976)
Touchdowns, game	3	By many players
Field goals, career	333	Gino Cappelletti (1960-70)
Field goals, season	41	Tony Franklin (1984-87)
Field goals, game	6	Gino Cappelletti (3 times)
Extra points, career	342	Gino Cappelletti (1960-70)
Extra points, season	51	John Smith (1980)
Extra points, game	8	John Smith (9/9/79)

Rushing
Yards, career	5,453	Sam Cunningham (1973-79, 81-82)
Yards, season	1,458	Jim Nance (1966)
Yards, game	212	Tony Collins (9/18/83)
Attempts, career	1,385	Sam Cunningham (1973-79, 81-82)
Attempts, season	299	Jim Nance (1966)
Attempts, game	38	Jim Nance (10/30/66)
Touchdowns, career	45	Jim Nance (1965-71)
Touchdowns, season	12	Steve Grogan (1976)
Touchdowns, game	3	Mosi Tatupu (12/11/83)
		Tony Collins (9/18/83)
		Sam Cunningham (10/20/74)

Passing
Completions, career	1,879	Steve Grogan (1975-90)
Completions, season	276	Tony Eason (1986)
Completions, game	36	Tony Eason (11/16/86)
Yards, career	26,886	Steve Grogan (1975-90)
Yards, season	3,465	Babe Parilli (1964)
Yards, game	414	Tony Eason (9/21/86)
Attempts, career	3,593	Steve Grogan (1975-90)
Attempts, season	473	Babe Parilli (1964)
Attempts, game	59	Steve Grogan (11/12/89)
Touchdowns, career	182	Steve Grogan (1975-90)
Touchdowns, season	31	Babe Parilli (1964)
Touchdowns, game	5	Steve Grogan (9/9/79)
		Babe Parilli (11/15/64)
		Babe Parilli (10/15/67)

Receiving
Receptions, career	534	Stanley Morgan (1977-89)
Receptions, season	84	Stanley Morgan (1986)
Receptions, game	11	Tony Collins (11/29/87)
		Art Graham (11/20/66)
Yards, career	10,352	Stanley Morgan (1977-89)
Yards, season	1,491	Stanley Morgan (1986)
Yards, game	182	Stanley Morgan (11/8/81)
Touchdowns, career	67	Stanley Morgan (1977-89)
Touchdowns, season	12	Stanley Morgan (1979)
Touchdowns, game	3	By many players

Interceptions
Career	36	Raymond Clayborn (1977-89)
Season	11	Ron Hall (1964)
Game	3	By many players

Sacks
Career	91.5	Andre Tippett (1982-93)
Season	18.5	Andre Tippett (1984)
Game	3.5	Andre Tippett (10/26/86)

Longest plays
Run from scrimmage	85	Larry Garron (TD, 10/22/61)
Pass play	90	Tony Eason to Craig James (TD, 9/15/85)
Field goal	53	Gino Cappelletti (11/28/65)
		Jason Staurovsky (10/7/90)
Interception return	99	Rick Sanford (TD, 12/5/82)
Kickoff return	101	Raymond Clayborn (TD, 12/18/77)
Punt return	89	Mike Haynes (TD, 11/7/76)
Punt	93	Shawn McCarthy (11/3/91)

Top scorers
	Points
Gino Cappelletti (1960-70)	1,130
John Smith (1974-83)	692
Tony Franklin (1984-87)	442
Stanley Morgan (1977-89)	408
Sam Cunningham (1973-79, 81-82)	294
Jim Nance (1965-71)	276

Top rushers
	Yards
Sam Cunningham (1973-79, 81-82)	5,453
Jim Nance (1965-71)	5,323
Tony Collins (1981-87)	4,647
Don Calhoun (1975-81)	3,391
John Stephens (1988-92)	3,249
Larry Garron (1960-68)	2,981

Top passers
	Completions
Steve Grogan (1975-90)	1,879
Babe Parilli (1961-67)	1,140
Tony Eason (1983-89)	876
Jim Plunkett (1971-75)	729
Hugh Millen (1991-92)	370
Mike Taliaferro (1968-70)	305

Top passers
	Yards
Steve Grogan (1975-90)	26,886
Babe Parilli (1961-67)	16,747
Tony Eason (1983-89)	10,732
Jim Plunkett (1971-75)	9,932
Hugh Millen (1991-92)	4,276
Mike Taliaferro (1968-70)	3,920

Top receivers
	Receptions
Stanley Morgan (1977-89)	534
Irving Fryar (1984-92)	363
Gino Cappelletti (1960-70)	292
Jim Colclough (1960-68)	283
Tony Collins (1981-87)	261
Sam Cunningham (1973-79, 81-82)	210
Marv Cook (1989-93)	210

Top receivers
	Yards
Stanley Morgan (1977-89)	10,352
Irving Fryar (1984-92)	5,726
Jim Colclough (1960-68)	5,001
Gino Cappelletti (1960-70)	4,589
Russ Francis (1973-80, 87-88)	3,157
Art Graham (1963-68)	3,107

Most interceptions
	No.
Raymond Clayborn (1977-89)	36
Ron Hall (1961-67)	29
Roland James (1980-90)	29
Fred Marion (1982-91)	29
Mike Haynes (1976-82)	28
Nick Buoniconti (1962-68)	24
Ronnie Lippett (1984-91)	24

Most sacks
	No.
Andre Tippett (1982-93)	100
Julius Adams (1971-77, 79, 85, 87)	75.5
Tony McGee (1974-81)	74.5

PRO FOOTBALL WEEKLY 1994 ALMANAC

PREVIEW: NEW ORLEANS SAINTS

Head coach Jim Mora makes it all sound so simple. Speaking after the conclusion of the 1993 campaign, he outlined what it would take for his .500 team to achieve a higher level of success in '94.

"For us to be a better football team, we have to do three things. One, we have to do a better job of coaching," said Mora. "Two, we have to upgrade our talent. And three, the guys that are with us now that are going to be with us next year have to get better."

As for an improved coaching job, it remains to be seen how the staff handles the team before and during the season. As for the returning players from last season's roster, again, it remains to be seen how they perform once they get into camp.

That leaves the second part of Mora's plan — upgrading talent. Sure as there will be Mardi Gras in New Orleans next February, the Saints have gone out and upgraded a couple of key areas.

In recent years the Saints have not exactly struck the fear of God into opposing defenses. Quarterback has been a concern, and so has the need for speed at wide receiver.

In response to these needs, the Saints became aggressive in the offseason.

They actively pursued several free-agent quarterbacks in advance of eventually trading for Jim Everett of the Rams.

At receiver, New Orleans was able to take transitional free-agent Michael Haynes away from the Falcons, who opted not to match the Saints' offer of $10.5 million over four years.

What the Saints are getting is a quarterback who, in the past, proved he could produce huge individual statistics. But he isn't a proven winner.

"In my opinion, he's one of the top quarterbacks in the league," said Mora. "Now, he's played on some teams in recent years that haven't won a lot of games. But as an individual quarterback, he's got stats that are right up there with the best over the last seven or eight seasons."

Everett feels he has developed a new sense of confidence, something his critics have said he lacked.

"I believe I can get things done," said Everett. "I think Coach Mora thinks that we can get things done. Now we just have to prove it."

Everett still has a lot to prove. In two seasons (1988 and '89) he passed for more than 8,000 yards and 60 touchdowns. But last season he completed less than 50 percent of his passes and was eventually benched in favor of T.J. Rubley.

The Saints also re-signed Wade Wilson to be Everett's primary backup. Wilson's performance in '93 was one of the reasons New Orleans tried so hard to secure a new starter. Mike Buck will return as another backup.

The other segment of the Saints' new battery, the part that will add explosive speed, is Haynes. In the Falcons' run-and-shoot offense last season, he caught 72 passes for 778 yards and four touchdowns.

Haynes, who will primarily be used to stretch the offense as a deep-threat receiver, is not putting pressure on himself to be the lone man to revitalize the New Orleans offense.

"I don't think they are going to try to revolve the offense around me," said Haynes. "I think I'm just going to come in and add to what they are doing.

"In Atlanta, my job was to draw some coverages away from Andre (Rison). Now we can use Quinn Early and myself and Eric Martin. If I can draw some coverages away from those guys, that'll only improve the receiving corps."

Martin is a very productive possession catcher, but he is entering his 10th season in the NFL and cannot afford to lose another step. Early had a quick start last year but fell off when opposing teams began to pay attention to him. Torrance Small, entering his third season, was not a big help to the club last year, but he is young.

At tight end, '93 first-rounder Irv Smith figures

PHOTO BY DAVID NELSON

Derek Brown

to get more involved in the passing game in '94 after starting in eight contests last season and catching 16 passes for 180 yards and a pair of TD's.

On the ground, the top running back last season was rookie Derek Brown, who picked up 705 yards, even though he missed four games with an ankle injury. Brown was the prominent rusher because Vaughn Dunbar, the team's top pick and leading rusher in '92, missed the whole season while recovering from knee repairs. Lorenzo Neal, a rookie fullback, rushed for 175 yards on 21 carries in less than two games but then broke his ankle. Figure to see Brown, Dunbar, Neal and No. 2 pick Mario Bates as the primary combatants in the battle for a starting slot.

FB Brad Muster is not the greatest runner, but he will provide solid blocking and pass catching. Derrick Ned was a useful backup running back last season but is not a candidate to start.

New Orleans drafted a star last season in ORT Willie Roaf. As a rookie, he played at a Pro Bowl level, and some folks are saying he is the best offensive tackle to enter the NFL since Anthony Munoz. Richard Cooper has good size and athleticism and is becoming a solid offensive lineman.

OG Jim Dombrowski was the top dog on the line in 1992 but found himself in the coaching staff's doghouse in '93 because of a holdout. He came back as the swing guard in a three-man rotation. Dombrowski's biggest assets are his size, awareness and heavy hands, but he isn't very quick or athletic. The other starting guard will probably be Chris Port, who replaced Dombrowski. Port is not that quick or athletic, but he is smart and a hard worker. The defection of the third guard, Derek Kennard to Dallas, leaves the Saints without a lot of depth. At center, the Saints will go with free-agent acquisition Jeff Uhlenhake from Miami. Uhlenhake is a steady player when he's healthy. Joel Hilgenberg is still available as a backup.

With the oldest starting defensive unit in the league in '93, the Saints started to see the effects of age. The team gave up only 202 points in 1992, but that number jumped to 343 in 1993.

"The last two years we were one of the top two or three defensive teams in the NFL," said Mora. "In the past, because we were such a dominant defensive team, we were able to win games on defense with an offense that had never really been special. This year we weren't able to do that."

Along the line, DE Wayne Martin was not as dominant as he was in '92, but he was still the club's best down lineman. DE Frank Warren is entering his 13th season and is coming off a foot injury that sidelined him for the second part of last season. NT's Les Miller and Robert Goff are the primary players at that position, but Ronnie Dixon may become more prominent if he gets better at coming off blocks. No. 1 draft pick Joe Johnson, a speed rusher with a lot of potential, could end up starting opposite Martin.

By far the strongest part of the defensive unit is the LB corps, headed up by Renaldo Turnbull, who tied for the NFC lead in sacks with 13. LOLB Rickey Jackson is coming off another Pro Bowl-caliber year in which he recorded 11.5 sacks to give him 123 for his career. However, Jackson will be playing in his 14th NFL season and may have lost a step.

Vaughan Johnson, Sam Mills and James Williams are the primary players on the inside at linebacker. Johnson is an excellent run stuffer who led the team in tackles in '93 with 110. Mills has been called the brains of the defense, but he is 35 and missed seven games last year due to a staph infection. DE-OLB Joel Smeenge saw more minutes last season, and he will be there to fill in for the aging Jackson, as will No. 3 pick Winfred Tubbs.

In the secondary, free-agent FS Gene Atkins bailed in favor of Miami, leaving the Saints without their best defensive back. Toi Cook or Vince Buck, both cornerbacks, are possible replacements for Atkins. Neither Cook nor Buck are as quick as desired for cornerback, but they do have good hands. SS Brett Maxie missed all of last season except Game One because of a knee injury, and he has to prove he is well enough to run like he did before. If he isn't as quick, the younger Othello Henderson could get a shot. Sean Lumpkin, who is a bargain salary-wise, may also get consideration. CB Jimmy Spencer is the speediest of the corners, and Tyrone Legette is also a possibility. Spencer and Legette have improved to the point where they could be considered potential starters.

Morten Andersen is still one of the best placekickers in the NFL, especially with his ability to hit long field goals and boom kickoffs. Andersen made 28-of-35 field-goal attempts in 1993, including 16-of-16 inside the 40. P Tommy Barnhardt had another strong season in '93, averaging 43.6 yards with a 37.5 net and 26 punts landing inside the 20. As for a return specialist, NFL rookie Tyrone Hughes ran back a pair of punts and one kickoff for TD's and earned a trip to the Pro Bowl. Hughes averaged 13.6 yards per punt return and 25.1 yards per kickoff return.

FAST FACTS

■ WR Eric Martin had his sixth consecutive 60-plus reception season in 1993. He has led the Saints in receiving for the past seven seasons.

■ P Tommy Barnhardt had a career-high 26 punts downed inside the opponent's 20-yard line, with only six touchbacks in '93.

■ The Saints have not had a losing season since 1987. During that span the club has averaged 10 wins (70-41, .631) per year.

PRO FOOTBALL WEEKLY 1994 ALMANAC

1994 PLAYER ROSTER

NO.	NAME	POS.	HT.	WT.	EXP.	COLLEGE	GP/GS
7	Andersen, Morten	PK	6-2	221	13	Michigan State	16/0
78	Backes, Tom	OG	6-4	273	1	Oklahoma	0/0
6	Barnhardt, Tommy	P	6-2	207	8	North Carolina	16/0
59	Bowden, Andre	LB	6-3	240	1	Fayetteville State	0/0
24	Brown, Derek	RB	5-9	186	2	Nebraska	13/12
50	Brown, Tim	LB	6-0	222	R	West Virginia	—
16	Buck, Mike	QB	6-3	227	5	Maine	4/1
26	Buck, Vince	CB	6-0	198	5	Central St. (Ohio)	16/16
45	Byrd, Israel	CB	5-11	184	1	Utah State	0/0
10	Caldwell, Mike	WR	6-0	200	R	California	—
49	Campbell, Matt	TE	6-5	256	R	South Carolina	—
40	Coghill, George	S	6-2	196	2	Wake Forest	0/0
41	Cook, Toi	CB	5-11	188	8	Stanford	16/16
19	Cooper, Hunkie	WR	5-8	185	1	Nevada-Las Vegas	0/0
71	Cooper, Richard	OT	6-5	290	5	Tennessee	16/16
38	Dawkins, Ralph	RB	5-8	195	R	Louisville	—
56	Dixon, Ernest	LB	6-1	250	R	South Carolina	—
95	Dixon, Ronnie	NT	6-2	292	2	Cincinnati	2/0
72	Dombrowski, Jim	OG-OT	6-5	300	9	Virginia	16/2
80	Dowdell, Marcus	WR	5-10	179	2	Tennessee State	9/1
63	Dunbar, Karl	DE	6-4	275	3	Louisiana State	13/1
32	Dunbar, Vaughn	RB	5-10	204	3	Indiana	0/0
89	Early, Quinn	WR	6-0	190	7	Iowa	16/15
17	Everett, Jim	QB	6-5	212	9	Purdue	10/9
55	Freeman, Reggie	LB	6-1	233	2	Florida State	10/0
66	Garten, Joe	C-OG	6-2	290	2	Colorado	0/0
91	Goff, Robert	DE-NT	6-3	270	7	Auburn	16/9
47	Hamilton, Brandon	CB	5-9	173	R	Tulane	—
79	Hanna, Jim	NT	6-4	255	R	Louisville	—
81	Haynes, Michael	WR	6-0	184	7	Northern Arizona	16/16
20	Henderson, Othello	S	6-0	192	2	UCLA	5/1
12	Henry, Adam	WR	6-1	184	R	McNeese State	—
61	Hilgenberg, Joel	C-OG	6-2	252	11	Iowa	9/9
21	Hilliard, Dalton	RB	5-8	204	9	Louisiana State	16/0
33	Hughes, Tyrone	CB	5-9	175	2	Nebraska	16/0
57	Jackson, Rickey	LB	6-2	243	14	Pittsburgh	16/16
98	Jeffcoat, Jerold	DE	6-2	285	1	Temple	0/0
14	Johnson, Tyrone	WR	5-11	171	R	Western State (Col.)	—
53	Johnson, Vaughan	LB	6-3	240	9	North Carolina St.	15/13
27	Jones, Reginald	CB	6-1	202	4	Memphis State	12/2
68	Kline, Alan	OT	6-5	277	R	Ohio State	—
44	Knight, Kelvin	S	6-0	203	R	Mississippi State	—
9	Lebo, Brad	QB	6-4	210	1	Montana	0/0
43	Legette, Tyrone	CB	5-9	177	3	Nebraska	14/1
46	Lumpkin, Sean	S	6-0	206	3	Minnesota	12/0
84	Martin, Eric	WR	6-1	207	10	Louisiana State	16/14
93	Martin, Wayne	DE	6-5	275	6	Arkansas	16/16
39	Maxie, Brett	S	6-2	194	10	Texas Southern	1/1
25	McAfee, Fred	RB	5-10	195	4	Mississippi College	15/4
96	Mayfield, Corey	NT	6-3	290	2	Oklahoma	0/0
86	McCleskey, J.J.	WR	5-7	177	1	Tennessee	0/0
76	McDaniels, Terry	OT	6-3	287	R	Southern Cal	—
58	Milburn, Darryl	LB	6-3	245	1	Grambling State	0/0
69	Miller, Les	DE-NT	6-7	285	8	Ft. Hays St. (Kan.)	13/11
51	Mills, Sam	LB	5-9	225	9	Montclair State	9/7

1994 PREVIEW ■ NEW ORLEANS

1994 PLAYER ROSTER

NO.	NAME	POS.	HT.	WT.	EXP.	COLLEGE	GP/GS
22	Muster, Brad	FB	6-4	235	7	Stanford	13/11
23	Neal, Lorenzo	FB	5-11	240	2	Fresno State	2/2
36	Ned, Derrick	FB	6-1	210	2	Grambling State	14/1
79	Nelson, Royce	OG	6-4	315	2	Nicholls State	0/0
25	Orr, Thomas	CB	5-10	197	R	West Virginia	—
35	Pahukoa, Shane	S	6-2	202	1	Washington	0/0
70	Port, Chris	OG-OT	6-5	295	4	Duke	15/15
15	Rhem, Steve	WR	6-2	212	R	Minnesota	—
64	Ricketts, Tom	OG-OT	6-5	305	5	Pittsburgh	3/0
77	Roaf, William	OT	6-5	300	2	Louisiana Tech	16/16
75	Rollins, Baron	OG	6-4	335	1	Louisiana Tech	0/0
52	Roth, Tom	OG	6-5	285	1	Southern Illinois	0/0
83	Small, Torrance	WR	6-3	201	3	Alcorn State	11/0
99	Smeenge, Joel	LB	6-5	250	5	Western Michigan	16/2
82	Smith, Irv	TE	6-3	246	2	Notre Dame	16/8
37	Spencer, Jimmy	CB	5-9	180	3	Florida	16/3
52	Stonebreaker, Mike	LB	6-0	235	2	Notre Dame	0/0
48	Thomas, Franklin	TE	6-3	262	1	Grambling State	0/0
5	Thomas, Tyrone	WR	6-0	175	R	Southwestern (Kan.)	—
34	Tillison, Ed	FB	5-10	229	2	NW Missouri	0/0
97	Turnbull, Renaldo	LB	6-4	250	5	West Virginia	15/14
62	Uhlenhake, Jeff	C	6-3	284	6	Ohio State	5/5
87	Wainright, Frank	TE	6-3	245	4	Northern Colorado	16/2
85	Walls, Wesley	TE	6-5	250	6	Mississippi	6/0
73	Warren, Frank	DE	6-4	290	13	Auburn	8/7
30	Washington, Sean	CB	5-10	182	R	Rice	—
90	Williams, James	LB	6-0	230	5	Mississippi State	16/9
65	Williams, Willie	OT	6-6	295	3	Louisiana State	0/0
34	Wilson, Ray	S	6-2	202	R	New Mexico	—
18	Wilson, Wade	QB	6-3	206	14	East Texas State	14/14
92	Winston, DeMond	LB	6-2	239	5	Vanderbilt	16/0
38	Young, Jim	CB	5-11	188	R	Purdue	—

'94 DRAFT PICKS

RD.	NAME	POS.	HT.	WT.	COLLEGE
1.	Johnson, Joe	DE	6-4	280	Louisville
2.	Bates, Mario	RB	6-1	217	Arizona State
3.	Tubbs, Winfred	LB	6-4	250	Texas
4.	Nussmeier, Doug	QB	6-3	212	Idaho
5.	Carroll, Herman	DE	6-3	267	Mississippi State
5.	Novitsky, Craig	OG	6-5	295	UCLA
6.	Mitchell, Derrell	WR	5-9	189	Texas Tech
7.	Lundberg, Lance	OT	6-3	302	Nebraska

PRO FOOTBALL WEEKLY 1994 ALMANAC

TEAM AT A GLANCE

TEAM DIRECTORY

Address　　1500 Poydras Street
　　　　　　New Orleans, Louisiana 70112
　　　　　　(504) 733-0255

Stadium　　Louisiana Superdome
　　　　　　1500 Poydras Street
　　　　　　New Orleans, Louisiana 70112
　　　　　　Capacity: 69,056
　　　　　　Playing surface: AstroTurf

Training　　University of Wisconsin-La Crosse
Camp　　　La Crosse, Wisconsin 54601

Colors　　　Old gold, black and white

Television　WNOL, Channel 38
Radio　　　WQUE, 1280 AM

ADMINISTRATION

Owner: Tom Benson
Exec. vice president-administration: Jim Miller
Vice president-football operations: Bill Kuharich
Vice president-head coach: Jim Mora
Vice president-marketing: Greg Suit
Treasurer: Bruce Broussard
Director of pro personnel: Chet Franklin
Director of media relations: Rusty Kasmiersky
Director of ticket sales: Sandy King
Trainer: Dean Kleinschmidt

1994 SCHEDULE

Preseason
AUG. 5	at New England	8:00
AUG. 13	at Minnesota	7:00
AUG. 19	GREEN BAY	7:00
AUG. 25	DALLAS	7:00

Regular season
SEP. 4	KANSAS CITY	12:00
SEP. 11	WASHINGTON	3:00
SEP. 18	at Tampa Bay	1:00
SEP. 25	at San Francisco	1:00
OCT. 2	N.Y. GIANTS	3:00
OCT. 9	at Chicago	12:00
OCT. 16	SAN DIEGO	3:00
OCT. 23	L.A. RAMS	12:00
OCT. 30	OPEN DATE	
NOV. 6	at Minnesota	12:00
NOV. 13	ATLANTA	12:00
NOV. 20	at L.A. Raiders	1:00
NOV. 28	SAN FRANCISCO (Mon.)	8:00
DEC. 4	at L.A. Rams	1:00
DEC. 11	at Atlanta	8:00
DEC. 19	DALLAS (Mon.)	8:00
DEC. 24	at Denver	2:00

HEAD COACH

Jim Mora
　The longest-tenured mentor in the NFC, Mora has been the Saints' head coach since 1986. With an overall record of 77-54 through eight seasons, Mora is the winningest coach in Saint history. New Orleans has gone to the playoffs four times under the guidance of Mora, though it has yet to win a game in the postseason. Since 1987, the Saints have been at or above the .500 mark each season. In 1991, the team won its first-ever NFC Western Division title with an 11-5 record. Before getting the Saints' head-coaching job, Mora spent 23 years coaching in the collegiate and professional ranks.
　Previous NFL: defensive coordinator, New England 1982; defensive line, Seattle 1978-81.
　Previous college: defensive coordinator, Washington 1975-77; linebackers, UCLA 1974; defensive assistant, Colorado 1968-73; linebackers, Stanford 1967; head coach, Occidental 1964-66; assistant coach, Occidental 1960-63.
　Player: No NFL. College, tight end, defensive end, 1953-56 Occidental.

ASSISTANT COACHES

Vic Fangio: outside linebackers
　Previous NFL: outside linebackers, 1986-93 New Orleans. Player: No NFL. College: defensive back, 1976-78 East Stroudsburg.

Joe Marciano: tight ends-special teams
　Previous NFL: tight ends-special teams, 1986-93 New Orleans. Player: No NFL. College: quarterback, 1972-75 Temple.

John Matsko: offensive line
　Previous NFL: offensive line, 1993 Phoenix; 1989-91 San Diego. Player: No NFL. College: guard, linebacker, 1962-65 Huron (S.D.) College.

Chip Meyers: offensive assistant
　Previous NFL: receivers, 1990-93 N.Y. Jets; 1985-88 Indianapolis; 1983-84 Tampa Bay. Player: NFL, wide receiver, 1967 San Francisco; 1969-76 Cincinnati. College: wide receiver, 1964-66 Northwestern Oklahoma.

Jim Mora: defensive backs
　Previous NFL: defensive backs, 1992-93 New Orleans 1985-91 San Diego. Player: No NFL. College: defensive back 1980-83 Washington.

Russell Paternostro: strength and conditioning
　Previous NFL: strength and conditioning, 1981-93 New Orleans. Player: No NFL. College: None.

John Pease: defensive line
　Previous NFL: defensive line, 1986-93 New Orleans. Player: No NFL. College: wingback, 1963-64 Utah.

Steve Sidwell: defensive coordinator-inside linebackers
　Previous NFL: defensive coordinator, 1986-93 New Orleans; 1985 Indianapolis; 1982-84 New England. Player: No NFL. College: linebacker, 1962-65 Colorado.

Jim Skipper: running backs
　Previous NFL: running backs, 1986-93 New Orleans. Player: No NFL. College: defensive back, 1971-72 Whittier College.

Carl Smith: offensive coordinator-quarterbacks

164

1994 PREVIEW ■ NEW ORLEANS

TEAM AT A GLANCE

Previous NFL: offensive coordinator-quarterbacks, 1986-93 New Orleans. Player: No NFL. College: defensive back, 1968-70 Cal Poly-San Luis Obispo.

Steve Walters: wide receivers
Previous NFL: wide receivers, 1986-93 New Orleans; 1982-84 New England. Player: No NFL. College: quarterback, defensive back, 1967-70 Arkansas.

COACHING RECORDS
(includes postseason games)

Years	Coach	W	L	T
1967-70	Tom Fears	13	34	2
1970-72	J.D. Roberts	7	25	3
1973-75	John North	11	23	0
1975	Ernie Hefferle	1	7	0
1976-77	Hank Stram	7	21	0
1978-80	Dick Nolan	15	29	0
1980	Dick Stanfel	1	3	0
1981-85	Bum Phillips	27	42	0
1985	Wade Phillips	1	3	0
1986-93	Jim Mora	77	54	0

HISTORICAL HIGHLIGHTS

1966 The NFL awards the 16th franchise to New Orleans with John W. Mecom Jr. the majority stockholder.
1969 Tom Dempsey sets a team record with four field goals against the Giants, booting the fourth one with only seconds remaining to give New Orleans a 25-24 victory.
1970 The National Football Conference is realigned and the Saints join the Rams, 49ers and Falcons in the Western Division. ... Tom Dempsey kicks the longest field goal in NFL history, 63 yards, on the final play of the Saints' 19-17 win over Detroit.
1975 The Louisiana Superdome is dedicated, and the Saints lose to Houston 13-7 in a preseason game before 72,434 fans, their first in the new stadium.
1978 Archie Manning becomes the first Saint to pass for more than 3,000 yards in a season (3,416 on 291 completions).
1979 Chuck Muncie becomes the first Saint to surpass the 1,000-yard milestone, rushing for 1,198 yards on 238 carries.
1983 In an Opening Day win over St. Louis at the Superdome, RB George Rogers sets a team single-game record by rushing for 206 yards on 24 carries.
1985 John Mecom sells the Saints to Tom Benson for $70.2 million. Benson is to hold the position of managing general partner.
1986 The Saints name a new president and general manager, Jim Finks, a former top administrator with the Minnesota Vikings and Chicago Bears. Finks hires Jim Mora as head coach.
1987-88 New Orleans posts the then-largest margin of victory in team history when it defeats the Atlanta Falcons 38-0. ... The Saints have their first winning season in franchise history, going 12-3. ... In their first playoff game ever, New Orleans loses to the Vikings 44-10 in the wild-card game.
1990 New Orleans, with a record of 8-8, makes it to the playoffs for the second time in club history. The Saints lose to the Bears 16-6 in the first round of the playoffs.
1991-92 The 11-5 Saints win their first NFC divisional title but lose to the Falcons 27-20 in the playoffs.
1992-93 New Orleans makes it to postseason play as a wild-card team but loses to the Eagles in the first round of the playoffs 36-20.
1993 Because of health problems, president and general manager Jim Finks steps down.

PRO FOOTBALL WEEKLY 1994 ALMANAC

TEAM AT A GLANCE

HALL OF FAME MEMBERS
None

RETIRED JERSEY NUMBERS
31 FB Jim Taylor
81 DE Doug Atkins

FIRST-ROUND DRAFT CHOICES
(since 1980)

Year	Selection	College
1980	OT Stan Brock	Colorado
1981	RB George Rogers	South Carolina
	QB Dave Wilson (supplemental)	Illinois
1982	WR Lindsay Scott	Georgia
1983	No choice	
1984	No choice	
1985	LB Alvin Toles	Tennessee
1986	OT Jim Dombrowski	Virginia
1987	DE Shawn Knight	Brigham Young
1988	FB Craig Heyward	Pittsburgh
1989	DE Wayne Martin	Arkansas
1990	LB Renaldo Turnbull	West Virginia
1991	No choice	
1992	RB Vaughn Dunbar	Indiana
1993	OT Willie Roaf	Louisiana Tech
	TE Irv Smith	Notre Dame
1994	DE Joe Johnson	Louisville

YEAR-BY-YEAR RECORDS

Year	Won	Lost	Tied
1967	3	11	0
1968	4	9	1
1969	5	9	0
1970	2	11	1
1971	4	8	2
1972	2	11	1
1973	5	9	0
1974	5	9	0
1975	2	12	0
1976	4	10	0
1977	3	11	0
1978	7	9	0
1979	8	8	0
1980	1	15	0
1981	4	12	0
1982	4	5	0
1983	8	8	0
1984	7	9	0
1985	5	11	0
1986	7	9	0
1987**	12	3	0
1988	10	6	0
1989	9	7	0
1990**	8	8	0
1991**	11	5	0
1992**	12	4	0
1993	8	8	0
Total	160	237	5

Number of NFL championships 0
Number of years .500 or better 9
Number of years below .500 18

*NFL champions
**Playoff team

RECORD VS. OTHER NFL TEAMS
(includes postseason games)

	Record
Arizona Cardinals	9-10-0
Atlanta Falcons	22-28-0
Buffalo Bills	2-3-0
Chicago Bears	9-6-0
Cincinnati Bengals	5-3-0
Cleveland Browns	3-9-0
Dallas Cowboys	3-13-0
Denver Broncos	1-4-0
Detroit Lions	7-6-1
Green Bay Packers	4-12-0
Houston Oilers	4-3-1
Indianapolis Colts	2-3-0
Kansas City Chiefs	3-2-0
Los Angeles Raiders	2-3-1
Los Angeles Rams	21-27-0
Miami Dolphins	2-4-0
Minnesota Vikings	6-12-0
New England Patriots	2-5-0
New York Giants	6-9-0
New York Jets	3-4-0
Philadelphia Eagles	8-12-0
Pittsburgh Steelers	5-6-0
San Diego Chargers	1-4-0
San Francisco 49ers	14-33-2
Seattle Seahawks	3-2-0
Tampa Bay Buccaneers	11-4-0
Washington Redskins	5-11-0

1994 PREVIEW ■ NEW ORLEANS

RECORDS

INDIVIDUAL

Service
Seasons played	13	By five players
Games played	195	Rickey Jackson (1981-93)
Consecutive games	143	Eric Martin (1985-93)

Scoring
Points, career	1,202	Morten Andersen (1982-93)
Points, season	121	Morten Andersen (1987)
Points, game	18	By many players
Touchdowns, career	53	Dalton Hilliard (1986-93)
Touchdowns, season	18	Dalton Hilliard (1989)
Touchdowns, game	3	By many players
Field goals, career	274	Morten Andersen (1982-93)
Field goals, season	31	Morten Andersen (1985)
Field goals, game	5	Charlie Durkee (11/28/71)
		Morten Andersen (12/1/85)
		Morten Andersen (10/25/87)
		Morten Andersen (12/3/92)
Extra points, career	380	Morten Andersen (1982-93)
Extra points, season	44	Morten Andersen (1989)
Extra points, game	6	By many players

Rushing
Yards, career	4,267	George Rogers (1981-84)
Yards, season	1,674	George Rogers (1981)
Yards, game	206	George Rogers (9/4/83)
Attempts, career	1,126	Dalton Hilliard (1986-93)
Attempts, season	378	George Rogers (1981)
Attempts, game	35	Earl Campbell (11/24/85)
		Dwight Beverly (10/11/87)
Touchdowns, career	39	Dalton Hilliard (1986-93)
Touchdowns, season	13	George Rogers (1981)
		Dalton Hilliard (1989)
Touchdowns, game	3	By many players

Passing
Rating, career	79.2	Bobby Hebert (1985-89, 91-92)
Rating, season	82.9	Bobby Hebert (1987, 1992)
Completions, career	1,849	Archie Manning (1971-75, 77-82)
Completions, season	309	Archie Manning (1980)
Completions, game	33	Archie Manning (9/10/78)
Yards, career	21,734	Archie Manning (1971-75, 77-82)
Yards, season	3,716	Archie Manning (1980)
Yards, game	377	Archie Manning (12/7/80)
Attempts, career	3,335	Archie Manning (1971-75, 77-82)
Attempts, season	509	Archie Manning (1980)
Attempts, game	53	Archie Manning (9/10/78)
Touchdowns, career	115	Archie Manning (1971-75, 77-82)
Touchdowns, season	23	Archie Manning (1980)
Touchdowns, game	6	Billy Kilmer (11/2/69)

Receiving
Receptions, career	532	Eric Martin (1985-93)
Receptions, season	85	Eric Martin (1988)
Receptions, game	14	Tony Galbreath (9/10/78)
Yards, career	7,854	Eric Martin (1985-93)
Yards, season	1,090	Eric Martin (1989)
Yards, game	205	Wes Chandler (9/2/79)
Touchdowns, career	48	Eric Martin (1985-93)
Touchdowns, season	9	Henry Childs (1977)
Touchdowns, game	3	Danny Abramowicz (9/26/71)

Interceptions
Career	37	Dave Waymer (1980-89)
Season	10	Dave Whitsell (1967)
Game	3	By four players

Sacks
Career	123	Rickey Jackson (1981-93)
Season	17	Pat Swilling (1991)
Game	4	Rickey Jackson (12/14/86)
		Rickey Jackson (9/18/88)
		Pat Swilling (11/11/90)
		Wayne Martin (12/3/92)

Longest plays
Run from scrimmage	79	George Rogers (TD, 10/18/81)
Pass play	96	Billy Kilmer to Walt Roberts (TD, 11/19/67)
Field goal	63	Tom Dempsey (11/8/70)
Interception return	97	Tommy Myers (TD, 9/3/78)
Kickoff return	101	Mel Gray (TD, 9/21/86)
Punt return	83	Tyrone Hughes (TD, 12/26/93)
Punt	81	Tom McNeill (9/28/69)

Top scorers
	Points
Morten Andersen (1982-93)	1,202
Dalton Hilliard (1986-93)	318
Eric Martin (1985-93)	288
Charlie Durkee (1967-68, 71-72)	243
Danny Abramowicz (1967-73)	222
Tony Galbreath (1976-80)	205

Top rushers
	Yards
George Rogers (1981-84)	4,267
Dalton Hilliard (1986-93)	4,164
Rueben Mayes (1986-88)	3,408
Chuck Muncie (1976-80)	3,386
Tony Galbreath (1976-80)	2,865
Wayne Wilson (1979-86)	2,462

Top passers
	Completions
Archie Manning (1971-75, 77-82)	1,849
Bobby Hebert (1985-89, 91-92)	1,202
Billy Kilmer (1967-70)	592
Dave Wilson (1981, 1983-89)	551
Steve Walsh (1990-93)	336
Ken Stabler (1983-84)	326

Top passers
	Yards
Archie Manning (1971-75, 77-82)	21,734
Bobby Hebert (1985-89, 91-92)	14,630
Billy Kilmer (1967-70)	7,490
Dave Wilson (1981, 83-89)	6,987
Steve Walsh (1990-93)	3,879
Ken Stabler (1983-84)	3,670

Top receivers
	Receptions
Eric Martin (1985-93)	532
Danny Abramowicz (1967-73)	309
Tony Galbreath (1976-80)	284
Hoby Brenner (1981-93)	267
Dalton Hilliard (1986-93)	240
Henry Childs (1974-80)	207

Top receivers
	Yards
Eric Martin (1985-93)	7,854
Danny Abramowicz (1967-73)	4,875
Hoby Brenner (1981-93)	3,849
Henry Childs (1974-80)	3,220
Wes Chandler (1978-81)	2,801
Dave Parks (1968-72)	2,264

Most interceptions
	No.
Dave Waymer (1980-89)	37
Tommy Myers (1972-81)	36
Gene Atkins (1987-93)	21
Dave Whitsell (1967-69)	19
Johnnie Poe (1981-87)	17
Toi Cook (1987-93)	16
Brett Maxie (1985-93)	16

Most sacks
	No.
Rickey Jackson (1981-93)	123
Pat Swilling (1986-92)	76.5
Frank Warren (1981-89, 91-93)	53

167

NEW YORK GIANTS

PREVIEW

After an almost storybook season in 1993, the Giants took a few punches in the offseason. New York was at its height when it battled the Cowboys even for four quarters in the season finale at Giants Stadium in a game that was to decide the NFC East title and see who would get homefield advantage in the NFC. But the Cowboys prevailed in overtime, winning the division and sending the Giants into the wild-card game.

While they opened the playoffs with a win over the Vikings, the Giants came up woefully short when they were pounded by the 49ers the following week. That loss ended their season, and the offseason provided no respite. The Giants lost five key players to free-agency, including four starters in OG Bob Kratch, S Myron Guyton, OT Eric Moore and CB Mark Collins.

Head coach Dan Reeves has to make the adjustments to these losses and will probably find his second year with the Giants much more difficult than his first. Despite his reputation as a rigid traditionalist when he coached the Broncos, Reeves made a great impression on the Giants and won over veterans like Phil Simms and Lawrence Taylor. This year he won't have Taylor on his side but will have to continue his adaptation as a coach who can make the necessary moves.

Offensively, the Giants are perceived as a team that likes nothing more than dominating the opposition with its rushing game as its huge offensive line pounds defenders into oblivion. Don't believe it for a minute. Like Bill Parcells before him, Reeves realizes no team can win consistently simply by pounding the ball. With Simms at quarterback, the Giants have a leader who can consistently deliver the ball on the money as long as he's getting decent protection. Last year Simms had one of his best seasons, as he completed 247-of-400 passes for 3,058 yards with 15 touchdowns and nine interceptions. His TD figure was hurt badly when the Giants lost WR Mike Sherrard midway through the season because of a hip injury. Simms may be 38 years old, but he plays the game with as much courage and intensity as any quarterback around. He is coming off surgery on his throwing arm and, if he's unable to recapture last year's form, the Giants have only two inexperienced quarterbacks in Dave Brown and Kent Graham backing him up. Brown has a beautiful throwing motion and is viewed as the team's quarterback of the future.

One of the reasons Simms was so effective last year was that the Giant running attack was the best in the league. Underrated Rodney Hampton is the key to the ground game. Despite missing nearly four games with knee and ankle problems, Hampton was a 230-pound workhorse, rushing for 1,077 yards on 292 carries. Reeves is not afraid to keep pounding away with Hamtpon until the defense cracks. That strategy worked out extremely well for New York in the wild-card win over the Vikings, when Hampton broke a long TD run in the third quarter that gave the Giants control of the game. Hampton is a power runner with quick feet, top strength, great vision and soft hands. He is not in the class of Emmitt Smith or Barry Sanders, but he has the desire to earn that kind of recognition. "I don't like being classified as a power back or a between-the-tackles back," Hampton said. "I'm the kind of player who will do anything to help this team win. Whether it's run inside, run outside or catch the ball, I'm ready to do it."

FB Jarrod Bunch was slowed by a knee injury and bronchitis last year and carried only 33 times for 128 yards. However, those numbers could improve this season. Bunch is a 250-pound powerhouse who is an excellent blocker. He is also a good pass catcher who is very tough to bring down once he gets a full head of steam. Dave Meggett is one of the NFL's best third-down players and kick returners. On 3rd-and-4 or more, Meggett is almost always one of Simms' options. Speaking of options, Meggett is talented at throwing the option pass. A quarterback in his early college days at Morgan State, he fired a couple of TD passes last year against the Redskins. The

Rodney Hampton

1994 PREVIEW ■ N.Y. GIANTS

Giants lost backup RB Lewis Tillman to free-agency (Chicago), but they drafted North Carolina State RB Gary Downs to take his spot.

The Giants will benefit greatly from the return of Sherrard, the talented, big-play receiver who has been haunted by injuries throughout his NFL career. Sherrard has game-breaking ability but is not at all durable. That's why, in the first round, the Giants drafted Indiana WR Thomas Lewis, who appears to be a player on the rise. Lewis caught 55 passes last year, and Giant GM George Young did not hesitate in selecting him.

"Nobody on the board had higher value when we picked," said Young. "It's all in front of him as a receiver. To get a receiver who can run back punts and kickoffs is a different thing. This guy can do both."

Mark Jackson, a former Bronco, is a solid receiver who got off to a good start for the Giants but dropped quite a few passes in the late going. He was cut in May but might be re-signed for less money. Chris Calloway caught 35 passes last season and is a good leaper but does not have any other special qualities. Ed McCaffrey is another role player among the receivers, and he can eat up a lot of ground once he catches the ball. Arthur Marshall was acquired from Denver in an offseason trade. TE Howard Cross is underrated. He caught 21 passes (five TD's) last year and blocked extremely well. TE Derek Brown, a former No. 1 draft choice, is going to have to improve significantly if he is to justify the huge salary he is earning.

The Giant offensive line was as good as any in the game when OLT Jumbo Elliott was not troubled by a bad back. Now, however, Elliott is coming off surgery, and the Giants have lost Kratch and Moore to free-agency. The Giants signed former Cardinal Lance Smith to take Kratch's spot, and Smith is a much better run blocker than he is a pass blocker. OLG William Roberts is a very good athlete and often plays at a Pro Bowl level. ORT Doug Riesenberg has gotten better each year. C Brian Williams is expected to start after splitting time last year with Bart Oates, who is heady and competitive. Williams has great size and is a physical player, but he has had problems with injuries in prior seasons.

Defensively, the Giants underwent a metamorphosis last year. Instead of playing read-and-react football, they became an aggressive, attacking unit under Mike Nolan. The Giants loved the game plan and gave up a league-low 205 points. It will be much more difficult to match that performance this year due to the losses in the secondary and the retirement of L.T.

On the defensive line, DLE Keith Hamilton showed great improvement last season. He held his own against the run and led the team in sacks with 11.5. The Giants are solid at nose tackle with Stacey Dillard and Erik Howard. The other DE slot will be manned by either Mike Fox or Mike Strahan. Fox started last year and is a bull rusher with power but not much finesse. Strahan's season was wiped out after he tore ligaments in his knee during the preseason, but he had great speed and athleticism for the pass-rushing job before the injury.

The Giants got great play from their LB crew last season, and many observers were surprised by that result since Reeves allowed Carl Banks to leave via free-agency and cut Pepper Johnson in training camp. Corey Miller replaced Banks at the LOLB spot and had a terrific all-around year. He had 6.5 sacks, two interceptions, two fumble recoveries and four forced fumbles. Inside, Carlton Bailey, a former Bill, replaced Johnson and led the team in tackles and improved as the year progressed. Ex-Bronco Michael Brooks was New York's best linebacker even though he missed three games with a late-season foot injury. Kanavis McGhee and Jessie Armstead will battle to take Taylor's old job. McGhee has been disappointing because he is stiff and not instinctive. Armstead has great speed and is active but does not have the size to play over the tight end on a regular basis.

Because of the losses in the secondary, the Giants selected Kansas State CB Thomas Randolph and Southern Cal S Jason Sehorn with their two second-round picks. Randolph has exceptional speed, quickness and a 41-inch vertical leap and is good in coverage. Sehorn is good play maker who recorded six interceptions last year but will miss tackles occasionally. Returning SS Greg Jackson is a physical player and has great hands. Phillippi Sparks appeared to be on his way at cornerback last season, but he tore ligaments in his right foot early in the season. Corey Raymond is solid at cornerback, but is not a great athlete. David Tate is a very big hitter at safety, but is not very consistent in his coverage.

David Treadwell is a solid and consistent placekicker who connected on 25-of-31 FG attempts. He was cut in May, though he might be re-signed at a lower salary, too. Mike Horan gave the Giants consistent punting, and 13 of his 44 kicks were downed inside the 20. Kickoff specialist Brad Daluiso probably has the strongest leg in the league. He knocked 40 of his 64 kickoffs into the endzone and beat the Cardinals with a long field goal in very windy conditions.

FAST FACTS

■ Last season's series sweep of the Redskins marked the fourth time in the last six years that the Giants had taken both games from Washington.

■ Rodney Hampton's 41 rushing attempts against the Rams last year was the second-most in team history.

■ With 1,077 yards in 1993, Rodney Hampton became the first Giant to rush for 1,000 yards in three consecutive seasons.

PRO FOOTBALL WEEKLY 1994 ALMANAC

1994 PLAYER ROSTER

NO.	NAME	POS.	HT.	WT.	EXP.	COLLEGE	GP/GS
73	Alexander, Mike	C	6-3	260	R	San Diego State	—
98	Armstead, Jesse	LB	6-1	238	2	Miami (Fla.)	16/0
54	Bailey, Carlton	LB	6-3	235	7	North Carolina	16/16
21	Beamon, Willie	CB	5-11	170	2	Northern Iowa	13/0
78	Bishop, Greg	OT	6-5	298	2	Pacific	8/0
5	Bloedorn, Kurt	P	6-5	207	1	Cal State-Fullerton	—
70	Brannon, Steve	DE	6-3	265	1	Hampton	—
94	Brooks, Michael	LB	6-1	235	8	Louisiana State	13/13
17	Brown, Dave	QB	6-5	215	3	Duke	1/0
86	Brown, Derek	TE	6-6	252	3	Notre Dame	16/0
38	Brown, John	DB	5-9	183	R	Houston	—
36	Brown, Leon	RB	5-10	190	R	Louisville	—
55	Buckley, Marcus	LB	6-3	235	2	Texas A&M	16/2
33	Bunch, Jarrod	FB	6-2	248	4	Michigan	13/8
80	Calloway, Chris	WR	5-10	185	5	Michigan	16/9
37	Campbell, Jesse	S	6-1	215	4	North Carolina St.	16/0
85	Crawford, Keith	WR	6-2	180	2	Howard Payne	7/0
87	Cross, Howard	TE	6-5	245	6	Alabama	16/16
3	Daluiso, Brad	PK	6-2	207	4	UCLA	15/0
62	Davis, Scott	OG	6-3	289	2	Iowa	4/0
58	Dent, Burnell	LB	6-2	235	8	Tulane	0/0
64	Dillard, Ivory	OG-OT	6-3	299	R	Florida A&M	—
71	Dillard, Stacey	NT	6-5	288	3	Oklahoma	16/16
24	Douglas, Donald	S	6-2	203	R	Houston	—
91	Douglas, Omar	WR	5-10	170	R	Minnesota	—
43	Elias, Keith	RB	5-9	191	R	Princeton	—
76	Elliot, John	OT	6-7	305	7	Michigan	11/11
95	Flythe, Mark	DE	6-7	290	2	Penn State	2/0
13	Fox, Brian	QB	6-4	214	1	Florida	0/0
93	Fox, Mike	DE	6-6	275	5	West Virginia	16/16
35	Gant, Eric	FB	6-2	245	R	Grambling	—
10	Graham, Kent	QB	6-5	220	3	Ohio State	9/0
75	Hamilton, Keith	DE	6-6	280	3	Pittsburgh	16/16
27	Hampton, Rodney	RB	5-11	215	5	Georgia	12/10
2	Horan, Mike	P	5-11	190	11	Long Beach State	8/0
74	Howard, Erik	NT	6-4	268	9	Washington State	16/0
47	Jackson, Greg	S	6-1	200	6	Louisiana State	16/16
24	Jenkins, Izel	CB	5-10	190	7	North Carolina State	9/0
69	Johnson, Chuck	OT	6-3	280	3	Texas	0/0
99	Jones, Milton	DE	6-5	270	R	Central State (Ohio)	—
46	Kozlowski, Brian	TE	6-3	245	1	Connecticut	—
53	Marks, Duane	LB	6-4	238	R	Duke	—
19	Marshall, Arthur	WR	5-11	174	3	Georgia	16/9
81	McCaffrey, Ed	WR	6-5	215	4	Stanford	16/1
30	Meggett, David	RB	5-7	180	6	Towson State	16/1
57	Miller, Corey	LB	6-2	255	4	South Carolina	16/14
65	Oates, Bart	C	6-3	265	10	Brigham Young	16/15
84	Pierce, Aaron	TE	6-5	246	3	Washington	13/6
51	Powell, Andre	LB	6-1	226	2	Penn State	15/1
71	Pyne, Dave	C	6-4	292	R	Lafayette	—
44	Rasheed, Kenyon	FB	5-10	245	2	Oklahoma	5/3
91	Ray, Leonard	DT	6-3	295	R	Louisville	—
39	Raymond, Corey	S	5-11	180	3	Louisiana State	16/8
63	Reese, Darren	OG	6-4	285	R	Ohio U.	—
72	Riesenberg, Doug	OT	6-5	275	8	California	16/16

1994 PLAYER ROSTER

NO.	NAME	POS.	HT.	WT.	EXP.	COLLEGE	GP/GS
66	Roberts, William	OT	6-5	280	10	Ohio State	16/16
88	Sherrard, Mike	WR	6-2	187	9	UCLA	6/5
11	Simms, Phil	QB	6-3	214	16	Morehead State	16/16
28	Smith, Joey	DB	5-10	190	2	Louisville	0/0
61	Smith, Lance	G	6-3	285	10	Louisiana State	16/16
52	Smith, Shawn	LB	6-2	236	R	San Diego State	—
22	Sparks, Phillippi	CB	5-11	186	3	Arizona State	5/3
92	Strahan, Michael	DE	6-4	253	2	Texas Southern	9/0
49	Tate, David	S	6-1	200	7	Colorado	14/1
97	Thigpen, Tommy	LB	6-2	242	1	North Carolina	0/0
73	Townes, William	DT	6-5	270	R	Nevada-Las Vegas	—
82	Weir, Eric	WR	6-2	175	1	Vanderbilt	0/0
90	Widmer, Corey	DE	6-3	276	3	Montana State	11/0
59	Williams, Brian	C	6-5	300	6	Minnesota	16/1
23	Williams, Perry	CB	6-2	203	12	North Carolina St.	8/6

'94 DRAFT PICKS

RD.	NAME	POS.	HT.	WT.	COLLEGE
1.	Lewis, Thomas	WR	6-1	185	Indiana
2.	Randolph, Thomas	DB	5-9	176	Kansas State
2.	Sehorn, Jason	DB	6-2	212	Southern Cal
3.	Downs, Gary	RB	6-0	212	North Carolina State
4.	Maumalanga, Chris	DT	6-2	288	Kansas
5.	Bratzke, Chad	DE	6-4	262	Eastern Kentucky
6.	Winrow, Jason	OG	6-4	321	Ohio State

PRO FOOTBALL WEEKLY 1994 ALMANAC

TEAM AT A GLANCE

TEAM DIRECTORY

Address	Giants Stadium East Rutherford, New Jersey 07073 (201) 935-8111
Stadium	Giants Stadium East Rutherford, New Jersey 07073 Capacity: 77,311 Playing surface: AstroTurf
Training Camp	Farleigh Dickinson-Madison Florham Park, N.J. 07932
Colors	Blue, red and white
Television	WNYW, Channel 5
Radio	WOR, 710 AM

ADMINISTRATION

President: Wellington T. Mara
Chairman: Preston Robert Tisch
Exec. vice president-general counsel: John K. Mara
Vice president-general manager: George Young
Treasurer: Jonathan Tisch
Controller: John Pasquali
Director of administration: Tom Power
Assistant general manager: Harry Hulmes
Director of player personnel: Tom Boisture
Director of pro personnel: Tim Rooney
Director of college scouting: Jerry Shay
Asst. director of player personnel: Rick Donohue
Director of public relations: Pat Hanlon
Director of marketing: Rusty N. Hawley
Director of community relations: Francis X. Mara
Ticket manager: John Gorman
Head trainer: Ronnie Barnes

1994 SCHEDULE

Preseason

JULY 30	MIAMI	8:00
AUG. 6	CLEVELAND	8:00
AUG. 13	vs. San Diego (at Berlin)	*1:30
AUG. 20	at N.Y. Jets	8:00
AUG. 27	at Chicago	7:00

*Eastern Time

Regular season

SEP. 4	PHILADELPHIA	1:00
SEP. 11	at Arizona	5:00
SEP. 18	WASHINGTON	4:00
SEP. 25	OPEN DATE	
OCT. 2	at New Orleans	3:00
OCT. 10	MINNESOTA (Mon.)	9:00
OCT. 16	at L.A. Rams	1:00
OCT. 23	PITTSBURGH	1:00
OCT. 30	DETROIT	1:00
NOV. 7	at Dallas (Mon.)	8:00
NOV. 13	ARIZONA	1:00
NOV. 21	at Houston (Mon.)	8:00
NOV. 27	at Washington	4:00
DEC. 4	at Cleveland	4:00
DEC. 11	CINCINNATI	1:00
DEC. 18	at Philadelphia	4:00
DEC. 24	DALLAS	1:00

HEAD COACH

Dan Reeves

In 1993 Reeves became the Giants' 14th head coach. he had previously served 12 years as head coach of the Broncos. In his first year in New York, Reeves helped the Giants rebound to a 11-5 record and a playoff appearance. In Denver, the Broncos under Reeves won the AFC championship in 1986, '87 and '88 but lost the Super Bowl each year. During his 12 years in Denver, Reeves took the Broncos to the playoffs six times and compiled a record of 117-79-1. He is the 15th-winningest coach in NFL history. As a coach or player, Reeves has participated in eight Super Bowls, the most by any person. Born Jan. 19, 1944, Rome, Ga.

Previous NFL: head coach, Denver 1981-92; offensive coordinator, Dallas 1977-80; offensive backfield, Dallas 1972, 1974-76.

Previous college: None.

Player: NFL, running back, Dallas 1965-72. College, quarterback, South Carolina 1962-64.

ASSISTANT COACHES

Dave Brazil: defensive quality control
Previous NFL: defensive quality control, 1992-93 N.Y. Giants; 1989-91 Pittsburgh; 1984-88 Kansas City. Player: No NFL. College: None.

Joe DeCamillis: special teams
Previous NFL: special teams, 1993 N.Y. Giants; 1989-92 Denver. Player: No NFL. College: None.

James Daniel: tight ends
Previous NFL: tight ends, 1993 N.Y. Giants. Player: No NFL. College: offensive guard, 1970-73 Alabama State.

George Henshaw: offensive coordinator/quarterbacks
Previous NFL: offensive coordinator-quarterbacks, 1993 N.Y. Giants; 1988-92 Denver. Player: No NFL. College: defensive tackle, 1967-69 West Virginia.

Earl Leggett: defensive line
Previous NFL: defensive line, 1993 N.Y. Giants; 1991-92 L.A. Raiders; 1989-90 Denver; 1980-88 L.A. Raiders; 1978 San Francisco; 1976-77 Seattle. Player: NFL, defensive tackle, 1957-65 Chicago, 1966 L.A. Rams, 1967-68 New Orleans. College: tackle, 1955-56 Louisiana State.

Pete Mangurian: offensive line
Previous NFL: offensive line, 1993 N.Y. Giants; 1988-92 Denver. Player: No NFL. College: defensive lineman, 1975-78 Louisiana State.

Mike Nolan: defensive coordinator
Previous NFL: defensive coordinator, 1993 N.Y. Giants; 1987-92 Denver. Player: No NFL. College: safety, 1977-80 Oregon.

Dick Rehbein: wide receivers
Previous NFL: wide receivers, 1992 N.Y. Giants; 1984-91 Minnesota; 1979-83 Green Bay. Player: No NFL. College: center, 1973-77 Ripon.

George Sefcik: running backs
Previous NFL: running backs, 1991 N.Y. Giants; 1989-90 Cincinnati; 1988 Kansas City; 1984-87 Green Bay; 1979-83 Cincinnati; 1975-77 Cincinnati; 1973-74 Baltimore. Player: No NFL. College: halfback, 1959-61 Notre Dame.

1994 PREVIEW ■ N.Y. GIANTS

TEAM AT A GLANCE

Zaven Yaralian: defensive backs
Previous NFL: defensive backs, 1993 N.Y. Giants; 1990-92 Chicago. Player: NFL, defensive back, 1974 Green Bay. College: defensive back, 1972-73 Nebraska.

COACHING RECORDS
(Includes postseason games)

Years	Coach	W	L	T
1925	Bob Folwell	8	4	0
1926	Joe Alexander	8	4	1
1927-28	Earl Potteiger	15	8	3
1929-30	LeRoy Andrews	24	5	1
1930	Benny Friedman	2	0	0
1931-53	Steve Owen	153	108	17
1954-60	Jim Lee Howell	54	29	4
1961-68	Allie Sherman	57	54	4
1969-73	Alex Webster	29	40	1
1974-76	Bill Arnsparger	7	28	0
1976-78	John McVay	14	23	0
1979-82	Ray Perkins	24	35	0
1983-90	Bill Parcells	85	52	1
1991-92	Ray Handley	14	18	0
1993	Dan Reeves	12	6	0

HISTORICAL HIGHLIGHTS

1925 Tim Mara purchases an NFL franchise for New York and signs Jim Thorpe, an all-time great but now an over-the-hill back. He names the team the Giants and selects the Polo Grounds for home games. ... A crowd of more than 70,000 fills the Polo Grounds at the end of the season to watch the Giants play the Bears and superstar Red Grange. The gate receipts save the Giant franchise from bankruptcy.
1930 Tim Mara turns the club ownership over to sons Jack and Wellington.
1931 Future Hall of Famers Steve Owen, a tackle, is named head coach, and C Mel Hein is acquired.
1933 The Giants easily win the Eastern Division title but fall to the Bears 23-21 in the NFL's first championship game.
1934 The Giants wear basketball sneakers to increase traction on the icy Polo Grounds turf in the second half of the NFL title game and score 27 unanswered points to win the championship over Chicago 30-13.
1935 New York makes it to its third straight NFL championship game but loses to the Lions 26-7.
1938 The Giants win their third NFL title, beating the Packers 23-17.
1939 The Giants, in their fifth NFL championship game in seven years, are trounced by the Packers 27-0.
1941 The Giants lose the NFL title to the Bears 37-9.
1944 The Giants rack up five shutouts and outscore their opponents 206-75 to capture the Eastern Division title. But they lose the title game to the Packers 14-7.
1946 The Giants win the the Eastern Conference crown for the ninth time. ... Tailback Frank Filchock and teammate Merle Hapes are suspended for alleged gambling involvement, but Filchock is allowed to play in the championship game. The Giants still lose to the Bears 24-14.
1950 In the newly realigned NFL, the Giants are assigned to the American Conference along with the Cardinals, Eagles, Steelers, Redskins and Browns.
1956 The Giants switch their home games from the Polo Grounds to Yankee Stadium ... They win their conference and rout the Bears 47-7 to produce New York's first NFL title since 1938.
1958 The Giants defeat the Browns in a playoff game to win the conference, with Pat Summerall's 49-yard field goal in a snowstorm, then lose in the first NFL sudden-death overtime title game to the Colts 23-17.
1959 The Giants again lose to the Colts in the NFL championship game, this time 31-16.
1961 For the conference title, the Giants (10-3-1) edge the Eagles (10-4-1) but lose to the Packers 37-0 in the NFL championship game.
1962 Again facing Green Bay in the NFL title game, the Giants once more fall to the Packers, this time 16-7.
1963 The Giants win their third consecutive conference title but lose for the third straight year in their quest for the world championship, this time 14-10 to the Bears.
1970 Ron Johnson becomes the first Giant to rush for more than 1,000 yards in a season, gaining 1,027 on 263 carries.
1976 Giants Stadium in the Meadowlands sports complex in East Rutherford, N.J., becomes the club's new home.
1979 George Young takes over as general manager, the first person outside the Mara family to run club operations.
1981-82 The Giants make the playoffs as a wild-card entry, their first postseason appearance since 1963. They defeat the Eagles 27-21, then fall to the 49ers 38-24.
1984 Phil Simms becomes the first Giant quarterback to pass for more than 4,000 yards (4,044 on 286 completions) ... The Giants make the playoffs as a wild-card, beat the Rams 16-13, but then lose to the 49ers 21-10.
1985-86 The wild-card-entry Giants defeat the NFL defending-champion 49ers 17-3 but are defeated by the Bears 21-0.
1986-87 With a record of 14-2, the Giants win the NFC East, then beat San Francisco 49-3 and Washington 17-0 in the playoffs ... The Giants win their first NFL championship since 1956 by defeating the Denver Broncos 39-20 in Super Bowl XXI.
1988 Joe Morris becomes the Giants' all-time leading rusher, surpassing Alex Webster, and the first to exceed the 5,000-yard mark (5,296).
1989-90 The Giants win the NFC East with a 12-4 record but lose to the Rams 19-13 in the playoffs.
1990-91 The Giants again triumph in the NFC East, winning 13 of 16 games ... They then defeat the Bears 31-3 and the 49ers 15-13 in the playoffs ... The Giants win their second world title in five years, edging the Buffalo Bills 20-19 in Super Bowl XXV.
1991 Robert Tisch buys a 50 percent interest in the franchise from Tim Mara and shares ownership and CEO duties with Wellington Mara.
1993-94 Dan Reeves takes over as head coach and leads the Giants to the playoffs with a record of 11-5 ... New York defeats the Minnesota Vikings 17-10 in the wild-card game, but then is defeated 44-3 by the 49ers in the divisional playoff game.

PRO FOOTBALL WEEKLY 1994 ALMANAC

TEAM AT A GLANCE

HALL OF FAME MEMBERS

	Yrs with Giants	Inducted
Owner Tim Mara*	1925-59	1963
C Mel Hein*	1931-45	1963
T-Coach Steve Owen	1931-53	1966
FB-PK-P Ken Strong	1933-35, 39-47	1967
S Emlen Tunnell	1948-58	1967
DE Andy Robustelli	1956-64	1971
QB Y.A. Tittle	1961-64	1971
OT Roosevelt Brown	1953-65	1975
E Ray Flaherty	1928-35	1976
HB-FL Frank Gifford	1952-60, 62-64	1977
HB Tuffy Leemans	1936-43	1978
E Red Badgro	1927-35	1981
LB Sam Huff	1956-63	1982
DT Arnie Weinmeister	1950-53	1984
QB Fran Tarkenton	1967-71	1986

*Charter member

RETIRED JERSEY NUMBERS

- 1 E Ray Flaherty
- 7 C Mel Hein
- 14 QB Y.A. Tittle
- 32 T Al Blozis
- 40 HB-FL Joe Morrison
- 42 QB Charlie Conerly
- 50 FB-PK-P Ken Strong

FIRST-ROUND DRAFT CHOICES
(since 1980)

Year	Selection	College
1980	DB Mark Haynes	Colorado
1981	LB Lawrence Taylor	North Carolina
1982	RB Butch Woolfolk	Michigan
1983	DB Terry Kinard	Clemson
1984	LB Carl Banks	Michigan State
	OT William Roberts	Ohio State
1985	HB George Adams	Kentucky
1986	DE Eric Dorsey	Notre Dame
1987	WR Mark Ingram	Michigan State
1988	OT Eric Moore	Indiana
1989	C Brian Williams	Minnesota
1990	RB Rodney Hampton	Georgia
1991	RB Jarrod Bunch	Michigan
1992	TE Derek Brown	Notre Dame
1993	No choice	
1994	WR Thomas Lewis	Indiana

RECORD VS. OTHER NFL TEAMS
(includes postseason games)

	Record
Arizona Cardinals	65-35-2
Atlanta Falcons	6-6-0
Buffalo Bills	3-4-0
Chicago Bears	19-29-2
Cincinnati Bengals	0-4-0
Cleveland Browns	17-26-2
Dallas Cowboys	21-40-2
Denver Broncos	4-3-0
Detroit Lions	15-18-1
Green Bay Packers	21-25-2
Houston Oilers	4-0-0
Indianapolis Colts	5-7-0
Kansas City Chiefs	6-1-0
Los Angeles Raiders	4-2-0
Los Angeles Rams	10-21-0
Miami Dolphins	2-1-0
Minnesota Vikings	5-6-0
New England Patriots	3-1-0
New Orleans Saints	9-6-0
New York Jets	3-4-0
Philadelphia Eagles	63-54-2
Pittsburgh Steelers	42-26-3
San Diego Chargers	4-2-0
San Francisco 49ers	14-13-0
Seattle Seahawks	5-2-0
Tampa Bay Buccaneers	8-3-0
Washington Redskins	70-51-3

YEAR-BY-YEAR RECORDS

Year	Won	Lost	Tied
1925	8	4	0
1926	8	4	1
1927*	11	1	1
1928	4	7	2
1929	13	1	1
1930	13	4	0
1931	7	6	1
1932	4	6	2
1933**	11	3	0
1934*	8	5	0
1935**	9	3	0
1936	5	6	1
1937	6	3	2
1938*	8	2	1
1939**	9	1	1
1940	6	4	1
1941**	8	3	0
1942	5	5	1
1943**	6	3	1
1944**	8	1	1
1945	3	6	1
1946**	7	3	1
1947	2	8	2
1948	4	8	0
1949	6	6	0
1950**	10	2	0
1951	9	2	1
1952	7	5	0
1953	3	9	0
1954	7	5	0
1955	6	5	1
1956*	8	3	1
1957	7	5	0
1958**	9	3	0
1959**	10	2	0
1960	6	4	2
1961**	10	3	1
1962**	12	2	0
1963**	11	3	0
1964	2	10	2
1965	7	7	0
1966	1	12	1
1967	7	7	0
1968	7	7	0
1969	6	8	0
1970	9	5	0
1971	4	10	0
1972	8	6	0
1973	2	11	1
1974	2	12	0
1975	5	9	0
1976	3	11	0
1977	5	9	0
1978	6	10	0
1979	6	10	0
1980	4	12	0
1981**	9	7	0
1982	4	5	0
1983	3	12	1
1984**	9	7	0
1985**	10	6	0
1986*	14	2	0
1987	6	9	0
1988	10	6	0
1989**	12	5	0
1990*	13	3	0
1991	8	8	0
1992	6	10	0
1993**	11	5	0
Total	482	391	32

Number of NFL championships 6
Number of years .500 or better 46
Number of years below .500 23

*NFL champions
**Playoff team

1994 PREVIEW ■ N.Y. GIANTS

RECORDS

INDIVIDUAL

Service
Seasons played	15	Mel Hein (1931-45)
		Phil Simms (1979-93)
Games played	172	Mel Hein (1931-45)
Consecutive games	172	Mel Hein (1931-45)

Scoring
Points, career	646	Pete Gogolak (1966-74)
Points, season	127	Ali Haji-Sheikh (1983)
Points, game	24	Earnest Gray (9/7/80)
		Ron Johnson (10/2/72)
Touchdowns, career	78	Frank Gifford (1952-60, 62-64)
Touchdowns, season	21	Joe Morris (1985)
Touchdowns, game	4	Ron Johnson (10/2/72)
		Earnest Gray (9/7/80)
Field goals, career	126	Pete Gogolak (1966-74)
Field goals, season	35	Ali Haji-Sheikh (1983)
Field goals, game	6	Joe Danelo (10/18/81)
Extra points, career	268	Pete Gogolak (1966-74)
Exta points, season	52	Don Chandler (1963)
Extra points, game	8	Pete Gogolak (11/26/72)

Rushing
Yards, career	5,296	Joe Morris (1982-88)
Yards, season	1,516	Joe Morris (1986)
Yards, game	218	Gene Roberts (11/12/50)
Attempts, career	1,318	Joe Morris (1982-88)
Attempts, season	341	Joe Morris (1986)
Attempts, game	43	Butch Woolfolk (11/20/83)
Touchdowns, career	48	Joe Morris (1982-88)
Touchdowns, season	21	Joe Morris (1985)
Touchdowns, game	3	By many players

Passing
Completions, career	2,576	Phil Simms (1979-93)
Completions, season	286	Phil Simms (1984)
Completions, game	40	Phil Simms (10/13/85)
Yards, career	33,462	Phil Simms (1979-93)
Yards, season	4,044	Phil Simms (1984)
Yards, game	513	Phil Simms (10/13/85)
Attempts, career	4,647	Phils Simms (1979-93)
Attempts, season	533	Phils Simms (1984)
Attempts, game	62	Phils Simms (10/13/85)
Touchdowns, career	199	Phil Simms (1979-93)
Touchdowns, season	36	Y.A. Tittle (1963)
Touchdowns, game	7	Y.A. Tittle (10/28/62)

Receiving
Receptions, career	395	Joe Morrison (1959-72)
Receptions, season	78	Earnest Gray (1983)
Receptions, game	12	Mark Bavaro (10/13/85)
Yads, career	5,434	Frank Gifford (1952-60, 62-64)
Yards, season	1,209	Homer Jones (1967)
Yards, game	269	Del Shofner (10/28/62)
Touchdowns, career	48	Kyle Rote (1951-61)
Touchdowns, season	13	Homer Jones (1967)
Touchdowns, game	4	Earnest Gray (9/7/80)

Interceptions
Career	74	Emlen Tunnell (1948-58)
Season	11	Otto Schnellbacher (1951)
		Jim Patton (1958)
Game	3	By many players

Sacks
Career	132.5	Lawrence Taylor (1982-93)
Season	20.5	Lawrence Taylor (1986)
Game	4.5	Pepper Johnson (11/4/91)

Longest plays
Run from scrimmage	91	Hap Moran (11/23/30)
Pass play	98	Earl Morrall to Homer Jones (9/11/66)
Field goal	56	Ali Haji-Sheikh (9/26/83, 11/7/83)
Interception return	102	Erich Barnes (10/15/61)
Kickoff return	100	Emlen Tunnell (11/4/51)
		Clarence Childs (12/6/64)
Punt return	83	Eddie Dove (9/29/63)
Punt	74	Len Younce (11/14/43)
		Don Chandler (10/11/64)

Top scorers — Points
Pete Gogolak (1966-74)	646
Frank Gifford (1952-60, 62-64)	484
Joe Danelo (1976-82)	482
Joe Morrison (1959-72)	390
Raul Allegre (1986-91)	340
Alex Webster (1955-64)	336

Top rushers — Yards
Joe Morris (1982-88)	5,296
Alex Webster (1955-64)	4,638
Ron Johnson (1970-75)	3,836
Rodney Hampton (1990-93)	3,732
Frank Gifford (1952-60, 62-64)	3,609
Doug Kotar (1974-81)	3,378

Top passers — Completions
Phil Simms (1979-93)	2,576
Charlie Conerly (1948-61)	1,418
Fran Tarkenton (1967-71)	1,051
Y. A. Tittle (1961-64)	731
Scott Brunner (1980-83)	482
Craig Morton (1974-75)	461

Top passers — Yards
Phil Simms (1979-93)	33,462
Charlie Conerly (1948-61)	19,488
Fran Tarkenton (1967-71)	13,905
Y. A. Tittle (1961-64)	10,439
Scott Brunner (1980-83)	6,121
Craig Morton (1974-75)	5,734

Top receivers — Receptions
Joe Morrison (1959-72)	395
Frank Gifford (1952-60, 62-64)	367
Bob Tucker (1970-77)	327
Kyle Rote (1951-61)	300
Mark Bavaro (1985-90)	266
Aaron Thomas (1962-70)	247

Top receivers — Yards
Frank Gifford (1952-60, 62-64)	5,434
Joe Morrison (1959-72)	4,993
Homer Jones (1964-69)	4,845
Kyle Rote (1951-61)	4,797
Bob Tucker (1970-77)	4,376
Del Shofner (1961-67)	4,315

Most Interceptions — No.
Emlen Tunnell (1949-58)	74
Jim Patton (1955-66)	52
Carl Lockhart (1965-75)	41
Dick Lynch (1959-66)	35
Willie Williams (1965, 67-73)	35
Tom Landry ((1950-55)	31

Most Sacks — No.
Lawrence Taylor (1982-93)	132.5
Leonard Marshall (1983-92)	79.5
George Martin (1982-88)	45.5

PREVIEW: NEW YORK JETS

The Jets will have a new look in 1994, as GM Dick Steinberg bit the bullet and fired Bruce Coslet, the man he hired as head coach four years ago. Coslet was supposed to be an offensive genius for the Jets, but his last year in New York was noted for its pitiful play-calling and unimaginative offense.

As a result of that discharge, Steinberg promoted defensive coordinator Pete Carroll to run the team and former 49er and Packer assistant Ray Sherman to run the offense. Carroll is an enthusiastic leader who has the respect of his players, while Sherman will bring some of the "in vogue" West Coast offense to the Jets.

The Jets are talented, certainly more talented than the team Coslet was given when he was hired. Yet, when they had a chance to earn a playoff berth in the last game of the season at Houston, they came up flat. The feeling remains that the Jets are a team that doesn't know how to win the key games. If Carroll can get the Jets to overcome this stigma, he will indeed be doing what the Jets asked of him.

Boomer Esiason remains the Jets' No. 1 quarterback, despite a wildly divergent year that was almost like two seasons. For a little more than half the year, Esiason was a confident, savvy quarterback who looked like he had a chance at getting back to the Pro Bowl. But later in the year, Esiason lost his rhythm and looked like he belonged on the bench because so many of his throws were high. Esiason is gutty, courageous and mature, but 11 years of physical abuse in the NFL may have taken its toll. Esiason may have good games from time to time, but it seems too much to expect him to be productive on a consistent basis. But he is nothing if not confident.

"I enjoyed a lot of what happened last season, but the last game left a bad taste," Esiason said. "I think it bothered a lot of people here, and we'll all remember it going into the season. Personally, I'm sure I'll be ready, and I know this team will be ready."

Esiason completed 288-of-473 passes last season for 3,421 yards with 16 TD's and 11 interceptions. He is a good leader who is popular with his offensive linemen — he takes them out for pizza and beer every Thursday night — and is one of the best ball-handlers in the history of the game. From time to time he loses his rhythm, and, when he does, his techniques get sloppy. The Jets signed former Colt Jack Trudeau as their backup, replacing the departed Browning Nagle. Trudeau is valuable because he knows what his abilities are and plays within them, and he doesn't complain about his reserve role. Moreover, his experience in the AFC East should prove useful. Seventh-round draft choice Glenn Foley will be the No. 3 quarterback.

The Jets solidified their ground game last year when they acquired Johnny Johnson from the Cardinals. Johnson was a solid, productive player and was a solid citizen in the lockerroom, which ran counter to his reputation while in Phoenix.

"He was nothing but a great guy," said Esiason. "He was not the type to cause problems or do anything disruptive. You couldn't ask for anything better."

Johnson ran for 821 yards on 198 carries and scored three touchdowns, and he also caught a team-high 67 passes. Johnson is a powerful runner who can pound the ball up the middle and cut back well if he gets through the hole. He also has the speed to be dangerous if he gets into the secondary.

The Jets' designated scorer is FB Brad Baxter, who got into the endzone seven times last season. Baxter gained 559 yards on 174 carries, and, while his 3.2 yards-per-carry average was not impressive, his ability to find the cracks when the Jets get into the red zone is. Baxter had problems with fumbling in the past, but that problem appeared to be solved last year. Baxter is also a solid blocker. Adrian Murrell gives the Jets a change-of-pace back with speed. If Murrell can get to the outside, he has a chance to break a play. Richie Anderson was not used very much last season, but he has the size of a fullback and can run like a scatback.

Rob Moore is the best of the Jet receivers. He is an awesome physical talent who knows how to use his size extremely well. At 6-3 and 205 pounds, he is a tremendous leaper. As a result, few receivers in the NFL can take advantage of their size any better than Moore, who is an expert at walling off the defender and then outleaping him for the ball. Moore played extremely well for the Jets early in the season but slowed down after he got banged up. Still, Moore finished with 64 catches for 843 yards. However, he got into the endzone only once time.

The Jets selected two wideouts in the draft, speedy Orlando Parker and sure-handed Ryan Yarborough. Parker needs development and route-running skills but has world-class explosion. Yarborough has great hands and is great at running patterns. Rob Carpenter has good talent but seemingly has never gotten untracked. Kenny Shedd, a speedster out of Northern Iowa, is the Jets' fastest receiver since Wesley Walker but is still a major developmental project because he's so unrefined.

The Jets have a ton of weapons at tight end, and none has more to offer than Johnny Mitchell. The former Nebraska star looks like the best tight end in the NFL when he is healthy and his concentration is good. He got off to a tremendous start that included a three-TD game against the Eagles, but he slowed down dramatically after he sprained his knee. In addition to his good hands and

1994 PREVIEW ■ N.Y. JETS

Johnny Mitchell

running ability after he makes the catch, Mitchell is a good blocker when he wants to be. James "Robocop" Thornton has one of the great nicknames in professional sports but has been troubled by injuries throughout his career. He has decent speed but inconsistent hands. The Jets' third weapon at tight end is Fred Baxter, who has size, mobility and can run, catch and block. However, he seemed to struggle after returning from an injury late last season.

The Jet offensive line got better each week of the season until the season finale at Houston. Siupeli Malamala has size and strength at right tackle. Dwayne White came back after a poor season in 1992 and was very solid against the run. C Jim Sweeney is the heart and soul of the line. Despite numerous injuries over the years, Sweeney will simply not come out of the starting lineup. OLT Jeff Criswell had his best season in 1993 and appeared to take more pride in his work. C Cal Dixon and OG-OT David Ware are good athletes with the potential to be solid linemen.

Defensively, the Jets appear to be in pretty good shape. Last year's team gave up only 15.4 points per game and added No. 1 pick CB Aaron Glenn and former Steeler DE Donald Evans. However, last year the Jets blew big leads to Eagle QB Bubby Brister and Raider QB Vince Evans. Those kind of letdowns have to be avoided.

DRE Jeff Lageman is one of the most courageous players in the NFL. He was burdened by a terrible knee injury and several other problems, last year, but he always managed to strap on his uniform and make his way into the lineup, where he served as an inspiration to his teammates. Lageman registered 8.5 sacks and provided good pressure on the quarterback all season. He simply will not be denied if he smells a chance to get a sack. DLE Marvin Washington came on in the second half of the year and probably had his best season. Former Giant Leonard Marshall was a major disappointment at tackle before breaking his arm in the second half of the season. Evans and rookie Lou Benfatti will rotate at the other DT slot, providing fine quickness but not much size.

All reports indicate that Marvin Jones should come back at full strength from the hip injury that prematurely ended his rookie season. He has tremendous power and 4.6 speed and can make plays sideline-to-sideline. Kyle Clifton backs up Jones and he relies on brains and toughness to get the job done. OLB Mo Lewis led the team in tackles with 158 and also had four sacks. Bobby Houston, the other outside linebacker, has tremendous 4.5 speed and may have been the team's most improved player last year. Tough Kurt Barber provides depth at the OLB and DRE positions.

After drafting Glenn, the Jets let veteran Eric Thomas go, primarily because he made too much money and he's not a top run-support player. James Hasty is very solid and physical at the other CB slot. SS Brian Washington had six interceptions. FS Ronnie Lott simply can't run anymore, but he is a teacher and coach on the field.

The Jets are hoping to see a big improvement from their special teams this season. That probably won't be too difficult because they were the worst in the league in 1993. New York replaced P Louis Aguiar, who was pitiful, with former Brown Brian Hansen. Hansen is a good directional kicker and is used to kicking in poor weather. Glenn and Parker could upgrade the Jets' long-dormant return games.

FAST FACTS

■ Brian Washington has led the Jets with six interceptions each of the last two seasons.

■ The Jets have lost seven of their last nine games against NFC opponents.

■ The Jets ranked last in the NFL in kickoff returns last year, averaging only 14.7 yards per return.

PRO FOOTBALL WEEKLY 1994 ALMANAC

1994 PLAYER ROSTER

NO.	NAME	POS.	HT.	WT.	EXP.	COLLEGE	GP/GS
64	Adams, Kyle	OG	6-4	290	R	Syracuse	—
41	Allpate, Tulneau	LB	6-1	245	1	Washington State	0/0
18	Allen, Alan	WR	6-1	186	R	Idaho	—
45	Anderson, Mike	LB	6-0	235	R	Nebraska	—
20	Anderson, Richie	RB	6-2	225	2	Penn State	7/0
17	Anderson, Steve	WR	6-5	215	1	Grambling	0/0
83	Ball, LaVar	TE	6-5	263	R	Cal State-L.A.	—
98	Barber, Kurt	LB	6-4	249	3	Southern Cal	13/0
6	Baumann, Charlie	K	6-1	205	4	West Virginia	0/0
30	Baxter, Brad	RB	6-1	235	5	Alabama State	16/13
84	Baxter, Fred	TE	6-3	260	2	Auburn	7/0
38	Beckford, Gary	DB	5-11	200	R	Bowie State	—
9	Blake, Jeff	QB	6-0	202	3	East Carolina	0/0
10	Blanchard, Cary	PK	6-1	225	3	Oklahoma State	16/0
76	Brown, James	OT	6-6	321	2	Virginia State	13/1
46	Burke, Paul	TE	6-3	244	R	Idaho	—
66	Cadigan, Dave	OG	6-4	285	7	Southern Cal	16/16
50	Cadrez, Glenn	LB	6-3	245	3	Houston	16/0
82	Carpenter, Rob	WR	6-2	190	4	Syracuse	16/0
28	Chaffey, Pat	RB	6-1	220	4	Oregon State	3/0
25	Chapman, Lindsey	RB	5-8	197	R	California	—
59	Clifton, Kyle	LB	6-4	236	11	Texas Christian	16/16
94	Cooke, Jeff	DT	6-1	271	R	East Carolina	—
79	Crisp, Jackie	OT	6-7	296	R	Colorado Mines	—
69	Criswell, Jeff	OT	6-7	291	8	Graceland (Iowa)	16/16
61	Davis, Rob	DT	6-3	275	1	Shippensburg (Pa.)	0/0
52	Dixon, Cal	C	6-4	292	3	Florida	16/0
44	Doggette, Cecil	DB	5-8	177	1	West Virginia	0/0
62	Duffy, Roger	C-OG	6-3	294	5	Penn State	16/1
7	Esiason, Boomer	QB	6-5	220	11	Maryland	16/16
60	Evans, Donald	DT-DE	6-2	282	7	Winston-Salem St.	16/16
95	Fisher, Bill	DT	6-2	278	R	Rowan	—
91	Frase, Paul	DT-DE	6-5	270	7	Syracuse	16/4
21	Green, Victor	CB	5-9	195	2	Akron	0/0
96	Gunn, Mark	DT-DE	6-5	279	4	Pittsburgh	12/0
47	Hales, Ross	TE	6-6	262	R	Indiana	—
11	Hansen, Brian	P	6-4	215	10	Sioux Falls	16/0
63	Harrison, Tyler	OG	6-3	275	R	Texas A&M	—
40	Hasty, James	CB	6-0	201	7	Wahington State	16/15
55	Houston, Bobby	LB	6-2	245	4	North Carolina St.	16/14
39	Johnson, Johnny	RB	6-3	220	5	San Jose State	15/9
49	Johnson, Troy	LB	6-2	236	6	Oklahoma	0/0
54	Jones, Marvin	LB	6-2	240	2	Florida State	9/0
56	Lageman, Jeff	DE	6-5	266	6	Virginia	16/16
57	Lewis, Mo	LB	6-3	250	4	Georgia	16/16
42	Lott, Ronnie	S	6-1	203	14	Southern Cal	16/16
75	Malamala, Siupeli	OT	6-5	315	3	Washington	15/15
70	Marshall, Leonard	DT	6-4	288	12	Louisiana State	12/12
74	McIver, Everett	OT	6-6	315	1	Elizabeth City State	0/0
86	Mitchell, Johnny	TE	6-3	237	3	Nebraska	14/14
36	Mitter, Craig	RB	5-8	200	1	Rutgers	0/0
85	Moore, Rob	WR	6-3	205	5	Syracuse	13/13
29	Murrell, Adrian	RB	5-11	212	2	West Virginia	16/0
43	Nelson, Chico	DB	6-0	202	R	Ohio State	—
99	Papasedero, Fran	DT	6-2	280	1	Springfield	0/0

1994 PREVIEW ■ N.Y. JETS

1994 PLAYER ROSTER

NO.	NAME	POS.	HT.	WT.	EXP.	COLLEGE	GP/GS
71	Pickel, Bill	DT	6-5	265	12	Rutgers	16/3
26	Pieri, Damon	FS	6-0	186	1	San Diego State	5/0
37	Prior, Anthony	CB-S	5-11	185	2	Washington State	16/0
92	Rudolph, Coleman	DE-DT	6-4	270	2	Georgia Tech	4/0
4	Shale, Cris	P	6-0	200	1	Bowlinbg Green	0/0
19	Shedd, Kenny	WR-KR	5-9	166	1	Northern Iowa	0/0
51	Solari, Steve	LB	6-0	244	R	Texas A&M	—
53	Sweeney, Jim	C-OG	6-4	286	11	Pittsburgh	16/16
80	Thornton, James	TE	6-2	242	7	Cal State-Fullerton	13/6
27	Trice, Robert	RB	5-10	209	R	Cal State-Northridge	—
16	Trudeau, Jack	QB	6-3	227	9	Illinois	5/5
23	Turner, Marcus	CB-S	6-0	190	6	UCLA	16/1
68	Ware, David	OG-OT	6-6	285	2	Virginia	0/0
48	Washington, Brian	SS	6-1	206	6	Nebraska	16/16
97	Washington, Marvin	DE	6-6	272	6	Idaho	16/16
67	White, Dwayne	OG	6-2	315	5	Alcorn State	15/15
77	Willig, Matt	OT	6-8	305	2	Southern Cal	3/0
72	Wisdom, Terrence	OG	6-4	305	1	Syracuse	0/0
93	Yatkowski, Paul	DT	6-2	265	R	Tennesee	—
31	Young, Lonnie	S-CB	6-1	196	10	Michigan State	9/2

'94 DRAFT PICKS

RD.	NAME	POS.	HT.	WT.	COLLEGE
1.	Glenn, Aaron	DB	5-9	181	Texas A&M
2.	Yarborough, Ryan	WR	6-1	196	Wyoming
3.	Benfatti, Lou	DT	6-3	277	Penn State
4.	Parker, Orlando	WR	5-11	182	Troy (Ala.) State
5.	Morris, Horace	LB	6-2	232	Tennessee
6.	Lester, Fred	RB	6-1	231	Alabama A&M
7.	Foley, Glenn	QB	6-1	212	Boston College

PRO FOOTBALL WEEKLY 1994 ALMANAC

TEAM AT A GLANCE

TEAM DIRECTORY

Address	1000 Fulton Avenue Hempstead, New York 11550 (516) 538-6600
Stadium	Giants Stadium East Rutherford, New Jersey 07073 Capacity: 76,891 Playing surface: AstroTurf
Training Camp	1000 Fulton Avenue Hempstead, New York 11550
Colors	Kelly green and white
Television	WNBC, Channel 4
Radio	WFAN, 660 AM

ADMINISTRATION

Chairman of the board: Leon Hess
President: Steve Gutman
Vice president-general manager: Dick Steinberg
Director of player personnel: Dick Haley
Assistant general manager: James Harris
Treasurer-chief financial officer: Michael Gerstle
Controller: Mike Minarczyk
Director of business operations: Bob Parente
Pro personnel director: Jim Royer
Assistant pro personnel director: Pat Kirwan
Coordinator of college scouting: John Griffin
Director of public relations: Frank Ramos
Director of operations: Mike Kensil
Ticket manager: Gerry Parravano
Trainer: Bob Reese

1994 SCHEDULE

Preseason

AUG. 5	at Detroit	7:30
AUG. 13	at Philadelphia	7:30
AUG. 20	N.Y. GIANTS	8:00
AUG. 26	at Tampa Bay	7:30

Regular season

SEP. 4	at Buffalo	4:00
SEP. 11	DENVER	4:00
SEP. 18	at Miami	1:00
SEP. 25	CHICAGO	8:00
OCT. 2	at Cleveland	1:00
OCT. 9	INDIANAPOLIS	1:00
OCT. 16	NEW ENGLAND	1:00
OCT. 23	OPEN DATE	
OCT. 30	at Indianapolis	4:00
NOV. 6	BUFFALO	4:00
NOV. 13	at Green Bay	3:00
NOV. 20	at Minnesota	3:00
NOV. 27	MIAMI	1:00
DEC. 4	at New England	1:00
DEC. 10	DETROIT (Sat.)	12:30
DEC. 18	SAN DIEGO	1:00
DEC. 24	at Houston	3:00

HEAD COACH

Pete Carroll
After heading up the Jet defense for four seasons, Carroll was named head coach following the firing of Bruce Coslet after last season. His ball-hawking defenses accounted for 113 takeaways in the past three seasons. Before joining the Jets in 1990, Carroll spent five seasons with the Vikings as the secondary coach and one year with the Bills. Carroll was a coach at the college level for seven seasons prior to making the jump to the NFL. Born Sept. 15, 1951, San Francisco, Calif.
    Previous NFL: defensive coordinator, 1990-93 N.Y. Jets; secondary, 1985-89 Minnesota; secondary, 1984 Buffalo.
    Previous college: assistant coach, 1983 Pacific; assistant coach, 1980-82 North Carolina State; assistant coach, 1979 Ohio State; assistant coach, 1978 Iowa State; assistant coach, 1977 Arkansas.
    Player: No NFL. College, defensive back, 1969-72 Pacific.

ASSISTANT COACHES

Larry Beightol: offensive line
    Previous NFL: offensive line, 1990-93 N.Y. Jets; 1989 San Diego; 1987-88 Tampa Bay; 1985-86 Atlanta. Player: No NFL. College: guard, linebacker, 1961-63 Catawba College.
Don Breaux: tight ends
    Previous NFL: running backs, 1981-93 Washington. Player: NFL, quarterback, 1963 Denver; 1964-65 San Diego. College: quarterback, 1959-61 McNeese State.
Larry Coyer: defensive line
    Previous NFL: None. Player: No NFL. College: quarterback, defensive back, 1961-65 Marshall.
Ed Donatell: secondary
    Previous NFL: defensive backs, 1990-93 N.Y. Jets. Player: No NFL. College: safety, 1975-78 Glenville State.
Foge Fazio: linebackers
    Previous NFL: linebackers, 1990-93 N.Y. Jets; 1988-89 Atlanta. Player: No NFL. College: linebacker, center, 1957-60 Pittsburgh.
Walt Harris: quarterbacks
    Previous NFL: quarterbacks, 1992-93 N.Y. Jets. Player: No NFL. College: defensive back, 1966-67 Pacific.
Greg Mackrides: strength and conditioning
    Previous NFL: strength and conditioning, 1990-93 N.Y. Jets. Player: No NFL. College: None.
Richard Mann: wide receivers
    Previous NFL: wide receivers, 1985-93 Cleveland; 1982-84 Baltimore-Indianapolis. Player: No NFL. College: receiver, 1966-68 Arizona State.
Greg Robinson: defensive coordinator
    Previous NFL: defensive line, 1990-93 N.Y. Jets. Player: No NFL. College: linebacker, tight end, 1972-73 Pacific.
Johnny Roland: running backs
    Previous NFL: running backs, 1993 N.Y. Jets; 1983-92 Chicago; 1976-78 Philadelphia; 1974 Green Bay. Player: NFL, 1966-72 St. Louis; 1973 N.Y. Giants. College: running back, 1963-65 Missouri.

180

1994 PREVIEW ■ N.Y. JETS

TEAM AT A GLANCE

Brad Seeley: special teams
Previous NFL: special teams-tight ends, 1989-93 Indianapolis. Player: No NFL. College: tackle, guard, 1974-77 South Dakota State.

Ray Sherman: offensive coordinator
Previous NFL: wide receivers, 1991-93 San Francisco; 1990 Atlanta; 1988-89 Houston. Player: NFL, defensive back, 1973 Green Bay. College: wide receiver, 1969-70 Laney, Calif. J.C.; 1971-72 Fresno State.

Steve Trimble: defensive assistant-quality control
Previous NFL: NFL coaching fellowship program, 1993 Chicago; 1992 N.Y. Giants. Player: NFL, defensive back, 1981-83 Denver; 1987 Chicago. College: defensive back, 1976-80 Maryland.

Spanky Woods: offensive assistant
Previous NFL: None. Player: No NFL. College: Defensive back, 1972-76 Carson-Newman (Tenn.).

COACHING RECORDS
(including postseason games)

Years	Coach	W	L	T
1960-61	Sammy Baugh	14	14	0
1962	Bulldog Turner	5	9	0
1963-73	Weeb Ewbank	73	78	6
1974-75	Charley Winner	9	14	0
1975	Ken Shipp	1	4	0
1976	Lou Holtz	3	10	0
1976	Mike Holovak	0	1	0
1977-82	Walt Michaels	41	49	1
1983-89	Joe Walton	54	59	1
1990-93	Bruce Coslet	26	39	0

HISTORICAL HIGHLIGHTS

1960 A charter AFL franchise for New York is awarded to Harry Wismer, a former sports broadcaster, and the team is named the Titans. Wismer obtains permission to use the Polo Grounds for the Titan home games.

1963 A five-man syndicate comprised of Sonny Werblin, Townsend Martin, Leon Hess, Donald Lillis and Philip Iselin purchase the New York franchise for $1 million and change the team's name to the Jets. Weeb Ewbank, former coach of Baltimore, is named head coach.

1964 The Jets move into Shea Stadium.

1965 With a season mark of 164-of-340 completions for 2,220 yards and 19 TD's and 15 interceptions, QB Joe Namath is named AFL Rookie of the Year.

1967 Joe Namath finishes the regular season with a total of 4,007 yards and becomes the first pro to top the 4,000-yard passing mark. Don Maynard sets a club mark by gaining 1,434 yards on his 71 pass receptions.

1968-69 Joe Namath passes for three touchdowns, as the Jets defeat Oakland 27-23 for their first AFL title. ... A 16-7 victory over the Baltimore Colts in Miami's Orange Bowl gives the Jets a victory in Super Bowl III, the first ever won by an AFL team.

1969 The Jets defeat Houston 34-26 to win their second Eastern Division title. However, they are defeated by Kansas City 13-6 in the divisional playoffs.

1972 In the best game of his career, Joe Namath throws for 496 yards and six touchdowns, as the Jets defeat Baltimore 44-34. Namath and the Colts' Johnny Unitas set an NFL combined record for passing yardage in the game, totaling 872 yards.

1972 With his 632nd career reception, Don Maynard breaks Raymond Berry's record to become pro football's all-time receiving leader.

1975 John Riggins becomes the first running back in team history to gain 1,000 yards, as he picks up 1,005 yards on 238 carries.

1980 Richard Todd sets an NFL record with 42 completions in a 37-27 loss to San Francisco. An AFC record is also set in the game by Clark Gaines, who catches 17 passes.

1981 The Jets finish the season with a 10-5-1 record and clinch their first playoff spot since 1969. However, they lose to Buffalo 31-27 in the wild-card playoff game.

1982-83 The Jets finish the strike-shortened season with a 6-3 record. The Jets upset the Cincinnati Bengals 44-17 to mark their first playoff victory since 1968. ... The Jets defeat the Los Angeles Raiders 17-14 to advance to the AFC championship game. ... In the AFC title game at the Orange Bowl the Jets are shut out by the Miami Dolphins 14-0.

1984 DE Mark Gastineau sets an NFL record with 22 sacks.

1985 Scoring the most points in club history, the Jets annihilate the Tampa Bay Buccaneers 62-28. While racking up 581 yards on offense, QB Ken O'Brien throws five touchdown passes, three to TE Mickey Shuler. ... In the wild-card playoff, the Jets lose 26-14 to the New England Patriots.

1986-87 The Jets end the regular season with a 10-6 record and gain a wild-card berth in the playoffs. They beat the Kansas City Chiefs 35-15 to advance to the divisional playoffs, but in a double-overtime heartbreaker, the Jets lose to the Cleveland Browns 23-20.

1991 PK Pat Leahy becomes the the NFL's third-leading scorer of all-time when he ends the season with 1,470 points (in 250 games). ... The Jets make the playoffs for the first time since 1986 but lose to the Houston Oilers 17-10 in the AFC wild-card game.

1994 Head coach Bruce Coslet is fired and Pete Carroll is hired as his replacement.

PRO FOOTBALL WEEKLY 1994 ALMANAC

TEAM AT A GLANCE

HALL OF FAME MEMBERS

	Yrs with Jets	Inducted
Coach Weeb Ewbank	1963-73	1978
QB Joe Namath	1965-76	1985
WR Don Maynard	1960-72	1987
RB John Riggins	1971-75	1992

RETIRED JERSEY NUMBERS
12 QB Joe Namath
13 WR Don Maynard

FIRST-ROUND DRAFT CHOICES
(since 1980)

Year	Selection	College
1980	WR Johnny "Lam" Jones	Texas
1981	RB Freeman McNeil	UCLA
1982	LB Bob Crable	Notre Dame
1983	QB Ken O'Brien	California-Davis
1984	DB Russell Carter	Southern Methodist
	DE-DT Ron Faurot	Arkansas
1985	WR Al Toon	Wisconsin
1986	OT-OG Mike Haight	Iowa
1987	RB Roger Vick	Texas A&M
1988	OT Dave Cadigan	Southern Cal
1989	LB Jeff Lageman	Virginia
1990	RB Blair Thomas	Penn State
	WR Rob Moore (supplemental)	Syracuse
1991	No choice	
1992	TE Johnny Mitchell	Nebraska
1993	LB Marvin Jones	Florida State
1994	CB Aaron Glenn	Texas A&M

RECORD VS. OTHER NFL TEAMS
(including postseason games)

	Record
Arizona Cardinals	1-2-0
Atlanta Falcons	3-3-0
Buffalo Bills	29-38-0
Chicago Bears	1-3-0
Cincinnati Bengals	10-6-0
Cleveland Browns	6-9-0
Dallas Cowboys	1-5-0
Denver Broncos	11-12-1
Detroit Lions	3-3-0
Green Bay Packers	5-1-0
Houston Oilers	12-18-1
Indianapolis Colts	21-27-0
Kansas City Chiefs	13-15-1
Los Angeles Raiders	11-14-2
Los Angeles Rams	2-5-0
Miami Dolphins	28-28-1
Minnesota Vikings	3-1-0
New England Patriots	38-29-1
New Orleans Saints	4-3-0
New York Giants	4-3-0
Philadelphia Eagles	0-5-0
Pittsburgh Steelers	1-12-0
San Diego Chargers	9-16-1
San Francisco 49ers	1-6-0
Seattle Seahawks	3-8-0
Tampa Bay Buccaneers	5-1-0
Washington Redskins	1-4-0

YEAR-BY-YEAR RECORDS

Year	Won	Lost	Tied
1960	7	7	0
1961	7	7	0
1962	5	9	0
1963	5	8	1
1964	5	8	1
1965	5	8	1
1966	6	6	2
1967	8	5	1
1968***	11	3	0
1969**	10	4	0
1970	4	10	0
1971	6	8	0
1972	7	7	0
1973	4	10	0
1974	7	7	0
1975	3	11	0
1976	3	11	0
1977	3	11	0
1978	8	8	0
1979	8	8	0
1980	4	12	0
1981**	10	5	1
1982**	6	3	0
1983	7	9	0
1984	7	9	0
1985**	11	5	0
1986**	10	6	0
1987	6	9	0
1988	8	7	1
1989	4	12	0
1990	6	10	0
1991**	8	8	0
1992	4	12	0
1993	8	8	0
Total	**221**	**271**	**8**

Number of NFL championships   1
Number of years .500 or better   17
Number of years below .500   17

* NFL champions
**Playoff team
***AFL champions (before merger); also won Super Bowl in 1968

1994 PREVIEW ■ N.Y. JETS

RECORDS

INDIVIDUAL

Service
Seasons played	18	Pat Leahy (1974-91)
Games played	250	Pat Leahy (1974-91)
Consecutive games	195	Winston Hill (1963-76)

Scoring
Points, career	1,470	Pat Leahy (1974-91)
Points, season	145	Jim Turner (1968)
Points, game	24	Wesley Walker (9/21/86)
Touchdowns, career	88	Don Maynard (1960-72)
Touchdowns, season	14	Art Powell (1960)
		Don Maynard (1965)
		Emerson Boozer (1972)
Touchdowns, game	4	Wesley Walker (9/21/86)
Field goals, career	304	Pat Leahy (1974-91)
Field goals, season	34	Jim Turner (1968)
Field goals, game	6	Jim Turner (11/3/68)
		Bobby Howfield (12/3/72)
Extra points, career	558	Pat Leahy (1974-91)
Extra points, season	47	Bill Shockley (1960)
Extra points, game	8	Pat Leahy (11/17/85)

Rushing
Yards, career	8,074	Freeman McNeil (1981-92)
Yards, season	1,131	Freeman McNeil (1985)
Yards, game	192	Freeman McNeil (9/15/85)
Attempts, career	1,798	Freeman McNeil (1981-92)
Attempts, season	294	Freeman McNeil (1985)
Attempts, game	40	Johnny Hector (10/12/86)
Touchdowns, career	52	Emerson Boozer (1966-75)
Touchdowns, season	11	Emerson Boozer (1972)
		Johnny Hector (1987)
		Brad Baxter (1991)
Touchdowns, game	3	By four players

Passing
Completions, career	2,039	Ken O'Brien (1983-92)
Completions, season	308	Richard Todd (1983)
Completions, game	42	Richard Todd (9/21/80)
Yards, career	27,057	Joe Namath (1965-76)
Yards, season	4,007	Joe Namath (1967)
Yards, game	496	Joe Namath (9/24/72)
Attempts, career	3,655	Joe Namath (1965-76)
Attempts, season	518	Richard Todd (1983)
Attempts, game	62	Joe Namath (10/18/70)
Touchdowns, career	170	Joe Namath (1965-76)
Touchdowns, season	26	Al Dorow (1960)
		Joe Namath (1967)
Touchdowns, game	6	Joe Namath (9/24/72)

Receiving
Receptions, career	627	Don Maynard (1960-72)
Receptions, season	93	Al Toon (1988)
Receptions, game	17	Clark Gaines (9/21/80)
Yards, career	11,732	Don Maynard (1960-72)
Yards, season	1,434	Don Maynard (1967)
Yards, game	228	Don Maynard (11/17/68)
Touchdowns, career	88	Don Maynard (1960-72)
Touchdowns, season	14	Art Powell (1960)
		Don Maynard (1965)
Touchdowns, game	4	Wesley Walker (9/21/86)

Interceptions
Career	34	Bill Baird (1963-69)
Season	12	Dainard Paulson (1964)
Game	3	By four players

Sacks
Career	107.5	Mark Gastineau (1979-88)
Season	22	Mark Gastineau (1984)

Longest plays
Run from scrimmage	79	Bill Mathis (11/21/65)
Pass play	96	Ken O'Brien to Wesley Walker (TD, 12/8/85)
Field goal	55	Pat Leahy (12/14/85)
Interception return	92	Erik McMillan (TD, 10/1/89)
Kickoff return	101	Leon Burton (TD, 10/28/60)
Punt return	98	Terance Mathis (TD, 11/4/90)
Punt	98	Steve O'Neal (9/21/69)

Top scorers
	Points
Pat Leahy (1974-91)	1,470
Jim Turner (1964-70)	697
Don Maynard (1960-72)	534
Wesley Walker (1977-89)	428
Emerson Boozer (1966-75)	384
Freeman McNeil (1981-92)	300

Top rushers
	Yards
Freeman McNeil (1981-92)	8,074
Emerson Boozer (1966-75)	5,135
Matt Snell (1964-72)	4,285
Johnny Hector (1983-92)	4,280
John Riggins (1971-75)	3,880
Bill Mathis (1960-69)	3,589

Top passers
	Completions
Ken O'Brien (1983-92)	2,039
Joe Namath (1965-76)	1,836
Richard Todd (1976-83)	1,433
Al Dorow (1960-61)	398
Pat Ryan (1978-89)	354
Dick Wood (1963-64)	328

Top passers
	Yards
Joe Namath (1965-76)	27,057
Ken O'Brien (1983-92)	24,386
Richard Todd (1976-83)	18,241
Al Dorow (1960-61)	5,399
Dick Wood (1963-64)	4,503
Pat Ryan (1978-89)	4,218

Top receivers
	Receptions
Don Maynard (1960-72)	627
Al Toon (1985-92)	517
Wesley Walker (1977-89)	438
Mickey Shuler (1978-89)	438
Jerome Barkum (1972-83)	326
George Sauer (1965-70)	309

Top receivers
	Yards
Don Maynard (1960-72)	11,732
Wesley Walker (1977-89)	8,306
Al Toon (1985-1992)	7,020
George Sauer (1965-70)	4,965
Mickey Shuler (1978-89)	4,819
Jerome Barkum (1972-83)	4,789

Most interceptions
	No.
Bill Baird (1963-69)	34
Dainard Paulson (1961-65)	29
Larry Grantham (1960-72)	24
Erik McMillan (1988-92)	22
Darrol Ray (1980-84)	21
Burgess Owens (1973-79)	21
Al Atkinson (1965-74)	21
Bobby Jackson (1978-85)	21

Most sacks
	No.
Mark Gastineau (1979-88)	107.5
Joe Klecko (1977-87)	77.5
Gerry Philbin (1964-72)	64.5

183

PREVIEW: PHILADELPHIA EAGLES

The Philadelphia story has not been a very happy one since Rich Kotite replaced Buddy Ryan following the 1990 season. It's not that the Eagles have been an awful team, because they haven't. But they have been somewhat rudderless, with seemingly no direction as they appear to get weaker. Yes, last year's team finished with an 8-8 record. But since the end of the season, they have lost OLB Seth Joyner, DE Clyde Simmons, P Jeff Feagles and S Ben Smith (through a trade to Denver). The image of a rollicking group of marauders who would knock an opposing back's head off as soon as look at him has virtually disappeared. In addition to this year's losses, the Eagles have lost DE Reggie White, RB Keith Byars and TE Keith Jackson in recent years.

While gloom and doom appear on the horizon, they are tempered with the knowledge that new blood (and new money) has entered the organization. Jeff Lurie, a Hollywood producer who's had a lifelong love affair with sports, bought the team from Norman Braman for a record $185 million. Lurie has promised the organization and its fans that it would return to a competitive status. In an effort to make that happen, the Eagles signed free-agents Ed Murray and William Fuller. Murray, the former Cowboy, should upgrade the PK position, while Fuller, the former Oiler end, is a first-class pass rusher and is solid against the run. With a return to full health of QB Randall Cunningham and WR Fred Barnett, the Eagles may cause problems for several foes this season.

Offensively, the Eagles may be similar to a fast-break basketball team because their defense appears unstable. Cunningham, who is coming back from a broken leg that forced him to the sidelines for the last 12 games of the season, is at his best when he is allowed to improvise. Cunningham has a strong arm and throws a very catchable pass, but, at times, his judgment is questionable. Cunningham often tries to force the ball into coverage, and that has often been the Eagles' undoing. He is also extremely stat-conscious. However, he may be the most dangerous quarterback in the league when it comes to making plays on his own. Because of his quickness and agility, Cunningham is adept at scrambling out of the pocket before making big plays downfield. While he is not the runner he was when he came out of Nevada-Las Vegas 10 years ago, he is still able to make solid gains while running the football. When he is in sync, there is not a quarterback in the NFL who can do more to frustrate a defense.

"I feel fine and don't think there will be any lasting effects from the injury," Cunningham said. "I'm anxious to start playing again."

Backup QB Bubby Brister played well after Cunningham was hurt. Brister is usually an emotional player who is somewhat streaky, but he finished last season with 14 touchdowns and only five interceptions and was very effective.

As usual, the Eagle running game does not appear very threatening. Herschel Walker was voted by his teammates as the offensive MVP in '93, though he has had better years. He rushed for 746 yards and caught 75 passes for 610 yards and three touchdowns. Despite those numbers, Walker is just a straight-line runner who can be easily stopped if forced to run laterally. He runs with power on straight-ahead plays, but he rarely displays any moves to make a tackler miss. RB Heath Sherman is a solid back who runs extremely low to the ground and has good balance. He has periods of productivity, but he has never been consistent enough to gain the coaching staff's confidence. Sherman is similar to Walker because he's primarily a straight-line runner. Vaughn Hebron is the Eagles' only back with moves. However, Hebron is not very fast and has shown a tendency to fumble. Rookies Charlie Garner and Mark Montgomery have a chance to improve the running game. Garner has good speed, while Montgomery is a tough runner who

Herschel Walker (PHOTO BY FOTOSPORTS INTERNATIONAL)

never stops trying.

Barnett was ready to move into the NFL's upper echelon of wide receivers before he tore the anterior cruciate ligament of his right knee last season. Barnett has good size and speed and tremendous leaping ability. Calvin Williams is a solid complementary receiver who is not a big-play maker. He is very effective finding the seams in zone coverage and is also quite competent inside the red zone. Williams had 60 catches for 725 yards and 10 touchdowns last year. The Eagles also received a solid contribution from rookie WR Victor Bailey last season. He caught 41 passes for 545 yards and showed great athletic ability. However, Bailey's concentration was lax, and he needs to improve his work ethic. That's something that will never be said about TE Mark Bavaro, who will be entering his third season since the medical staff of the Giants said he was at tremendous risk if he continued to play football because of the poor condition of his knees. Bavaro played respectable football for the Eagles last year and was very tough in some clutch situations, but he is not the blocker he once was.

Before the draft, the Eagles felt they were a left tackle away from having their best offensive line since Stan Walters and Jerry Sisemore blocked for Ron Jaworski and Wilbert Montgomery. Philadelphia selected huge Bernard Williams, a 6-8 tackle, with its first pick, and he should be the starting left tackle. David Alexander is smart, tough and consistent at center. He has overcome his lack of size and strength with the savvy that comes with experience. While he was ridiculed as a rookie for his impersonation of a turnstile and his propensity for taking penalties, Antone Davis has gotten significantly better at right tackle. He has size, strength and athleticism, and he could still develop into a Pro Bowl player. Lester Holmes is a strong run blocker with plenty of explosiveness but still needs plenty of work on his pass blocking as a guard. Broderick Thompson was a major liability at left tackle last season because he simply could not pass-block effectively. The Eagles would like to move him to left guard, where he will be much less of a liability. Mike Schad has a history of injuries, but he is a decent player when he's not hurt. Backup Tom McHale did a nice job last year filling in at left tackle. He held his own, despite lacking the physical talents coaches normally associate with that position.

Defensively, the Eagles were once the scourge of the league. That changed last year when they got pushed around and finished 27th against the run. They were pushed around from pillar to post until they signed ex-Bear William Perry, who managed to plug the leak despite having limited mobility. Bud Carson is one of the best defensive coordinators in the game, but he'll need to do one of his best coaching jobs to make this group productive.

Fuller will be the team's new starter at left end. He has a great motor, top pass-rush technique and good quickness. However, he is 32 years old and showed signs that he may be starting to decline. The Eagles also added ex-Charger Burt Grossman, who will see significant playing time. Grossman is fast and athletic, but injuries have hampered his development. Grossman could become a leading sacker if he's not hurt. But if injuries continue to plague him, expect the Eagles to dump him. Tim Harris will be the starter at right end if he is healthy. DT Andy Harmon is a former outside linebacker who continues to improve at his new position. Harmon lacks bulk, but when he lines up next to Perry, he can be effective. Perry no longer has mobility, but he is nearly impossible to move against the run. Leonard Renfro was a first-round pick last year, but he is incredibly weak in his upper-body development. Unless he gets dramatically stronger, he will have a very limited future in the league. No. 2 pick DT Bruce Walker is eventually expected to replace Perry.

With Joyner in a Cardinal uniform, it will be up to MLB Byron Evans, OLB William Thomas and newly acquired Bill Romanowski to pick up the slack at linebacker. Evans is one of the game's best at his position. He missed five games with a broken arm last year but still led the team in tackles. Thomas is undersized, but he is very active and tough. Romanowski, a former 49er, is a solid performer who can play both inside and outside. John Roper is a fine athlete who can rush the passer, but his attitude has not always been good, and he needs to develop better work habits. Derrick Oden is somewhat short, but he is a big hitter with good speed.

Eric Allen may be the best cornerback in the NFL. He had six interceptions in '93, returning four of them for touchdowns. His 94-yard interception return for a touchdown against the Jets was the decisive play in the game and one of the best returns ever. On the other side, Mark McMillian is one of the smallest players ever to start at cornerback. The 5-7 McMillian has speed, athleticism and jumping ability, but he often gets outmuscled by bigger receivers. Andre Waters and Wes Hopkins may be the two slowest safeties in the entire league. Third-round draft pick Eric Zomalt may move in as a starter. Intelligent backup Rich Miano is a career journeyman with a big heart.

Rookie Mitch Berger will probably replace Jeff Feagles as the Eagle punter.

FAST FACTS

■ Eric Allen returned four interceptions for scores last year to tie the all-time record for a season. He shares the record with Ken Houston (1971) and Jim Kearney (1972).

■ After going 0-4 on grass fields in 1992, the Eagles were 3-1 on natural grass in 1993.

■ Calvin Williams, Mike Quick and Harold Carmichael are the only Eagle receivers to record 10 TD catches in a season over the last 26 years.

PRO FOOTBALL WEEKLY 1994 ALMANAC

1994 PLAYER ROSTER

NO.	NAME	POS.	HT.	WT.	EXP.	COLLEGE	GP/GS
72	Alexander, David	C	6-3	275	8	Tulsa	16/16
21	Allen, Eric	CB	5-10	180	7	Arizona State	16/16
82	Bailey, Victor	WR	6-2	196	2	Missouri	16/10
62	Baldinger, Brian	OG-OT	6-4	278	13	Duke	12/4
24	Barlow, Corey	CB	5-9	182	2	Auburn	10/0
43	Barnett, Alonza	CB	6-2	210	R	North Carolina A&T	—
86	Barnett, Fred	WR	6-0	199	5	Arkansas State	4/4
84	Bavaro, Mark	TE	6-4	245	9	Notre Dame	16/16
6	Brister, Bubby	QB	6-3	207	9	NE Louisiana	10/8
39	Brooks, Tony	RB	6-0	230	3	Notre Dame	0/0
64	Brown, Curt	DT	6-5	260	1	North Carolina	0/0
71	Chalenski, Mike	DE	6-5	288	2	UCLA	15/0
69	Clapp, Darrell	C-OT	6-5	300	R	Houston	—
77	Cummins, Jeff	DE	6-6	270	1	Oregon	0/0
12	Cunningham, Randall	QB	6-4	205	10	Nevada-Las Vegas	4/4
67	Dausin, Chris	C	6-4	285	R	Texas A&M	—
78	Davis, Antone	OT	6-4	325	4	Tennessee	16/16
64	Dixon, Mark	OG	6-4	290	R	Virginia	—
56	Evans, Byron	LB	6-2	235	8	Arizona	11/10
9	Fielder, Jay	QB	6-1	215	R	Dartmouth	—
95	Flores, Mike	DE	6-3	256	4	Louisville	16/11
61	Floyd, Eric	OG	6-5	310	5	Auburn	3/3
37	Frazier, Derrick	CB	5-10	178	1	Texas A&M	0/0
33	Frizzell, William	S	6-3	206	11	N. Carolina Central	0/0
93	Fuller, William	DE	6-3	274	9	North Carolina	16/16
11	Gamble, David	WR	6-1	193	R	New Hampshire	—
80	Garlick, Tom	WR	5-11	180	1	Fordham	0/0
69	Grossman, Burt	DE	6-4	275	6	Pittsburgh	10/10
54	Hager, Britt	LB	6-1	225	6	Texas	16/7
96	Hall, Ray	DT	6-4	267	R	Washington State	—
65	Hallstrom, Ron	G	6-6	315	12	Iowa	12/8
91	Harmon, Andy	DE	6-4	265	4	Kent State	16/15
97	Harris, Tim	DE	6-6	258	9	Memphis State	4/3
45	Hebron, Vaughn	RB	5-8	196	2	Virginia Tech	16/4
73	Holmes, Lester	OG	6-3	301	2	Jackson State	12/6
48	Hopkins, Wes	S	6-1	215	12	Southern Methodist	15/8
66	Hudson, John	OG-C	6-2	275	5	Auburn	16/0
26	Jackson, Al	CB	6-0	182	R	Georgia	—
98	Jeter, Tommy	DT	6-5	282	3	Texas	7/0
87	Johnson, Maurice	TE	6-2	243	4	Temple	16/2
8	Jones, Preston	QB	6-3	223	2	Georgia	0/0
32	Joseph, James	RB	6-2	222	4	Auburn	16/5
5	Knight, Dewayne	SS	6-2	206	R	Virginia Tech	—
19	Lawrence, Reggie	WR	6-0	178	1	North Carolina State	1/0
16	Lewis, Darrell	SS	6-0	205	R	San Diego State	—
24	McGill, Jason	WR	6-0	192	1	Georgia Tech	0/0
68	McHale, Tom	OG	6-4	290	8	Cornell	8/4
88	McKenzie, Mike	TE	6-2	247	1	Baylor	0/0
29	McMillian, Mark	CB	5-7	162	3	Alabama	16/12
2	Mendez, Jaime	FS	5-11	194	R	Kansas State	—
38	Miano, Rich	S	6-1	200	10	Hawaii	16/14
13	Miller, Derrick	WR	5-10	170	R	Virginia State	—
67	Morrill, Matt	DL	6-3	261	R	Delaware	—
3	Murray, Eddie	PK	5-11	195	16	Tulane	14/0
58	Oden, Derrick	LB	5-11	230	2	Alabama	12/0

1994 PREVIEW ■ PHILADELPHIA

1994 PLAYER ROSTER

NO.	NAME	POS.	HT.	WT.	EXP.	COLLEGE	GP/GS
26	O'Neal, Brian	FB	6-0	233	R	Penn State	—
71	Pale, Peter	OG	6-3	279	R	Hawaii	—
90	Perry, William	DT	6-2	335	10	Clemson	15/8
42	Reid, Mike	S	6-1	218	2	North Carolina St.	9/0
94	Renfro, Leonard	DT	6-2	291	2	Colorado	14/2
81	Richardson, Paul	WR	6-3	204	1	UCLA	0/0
53	Romanowski, Bill	LB	6-4	231	7	Boston College	16/16
55	Rose, Ken	LB	6-1	215	8	Nevada-Las Vegas	5/0
79	Schad, Mike	OG	6-5	290	9	Queens (Canada)	13/13
3	Schrock, Chris	P	6-2	225	1	Boston University	0/0
75	Selby, Rob	OG	6-3	286	4	Auburn	1/0
14	Shankle, William	CB	5-10	195	R	Oklahoma	—
23	Sherman, Heath	RB	6-0	205	6	Texas A&I	15/7
47	Simien, Erik	LB	6-2	233	R	Nevada-Las Vegas	—
63	Smith, Herman	DE	6-5	242	R	Portland State	—
10	Smith, JeMome	WR	6-5	200	R	Indiana (Pa.)	—
30	Smith, Otis	CB	5-11	184	5	Missouri	15/0
1	Starcevich, Steve	PK	6-4	225	1	Philadelphia Text.	0/0
85	Sydner, Jeff	WR	5-6	170	3	Hawaii	4/0
42	Thomas, Markus	RB	5-10	192	2	Eastern Kentucky	0/0
51	Thomas, William	LB	6-2	218	4	Texas A&M	16/16
76	Thompson, Broderick	OT	6-5	295	9	Kansas	10/10
34	Walker, Herschel	RB	6-1	225	9	Georgia	16/16
20	Waters, Andre	SS	5-11	200	11	Cheyney	9/8
89	Williams, Calvin	WR	5-11	190	5	Purdue	16/14
57	Woodard, Mark	LB	6-0	234	1	Mississippi State	0/0
27	Wooten, Al	FB	5-11	232	R	Syracuse	—
83	Young, Michael	WR	6-1	183	10	UCLA	10/0

'94 DRAFT PICKS

RD.	NAME	POS.	HT.	WT.	COLLEGE
1.	Williams, Bernard	OT	6-8	317	Georgia
2.	Walker, Bruce	DT	6-3	326	UCLA
2.	Garner, Charlie	RB	5-9	183	Tennessee
3.	Panos, Joe	OG	6-3	294	Wisconsin
3.	Zomalt, Eric	DB	5-11	199	California
5.	Goodwin, Marvin	DB	6-0	200	UCLA
6.	McCoy, Ryan	LB	6-2	238	Houston
6.	Berger, Mitch	P	6-3	230	Colorado
7.	Montgomery, Mark	FB	6-0	220	Wisconsin

PRO FOOTBALL WEEKLY 1994 ALMANAC

TEAM AT A GLANCE

TEAM DIRECTORY

Address	Veterans Stadium
	Broad Street and Pattison Ave.
	Philadelphia, Pa. 19148
	(215) 463-2500
Stadium	Veterans Stadium
	3501 South Broad Street
	Philadelphia, Pa. 19148
	Capacity: 65,178
	Playing surface: AstroTurf
Training Camp	West Chester University
	West Chester, Pa. 19382
Colors	Kelly green, silver and white
Television	WTFX, Channel 29
Radio	WYSP, 94.1 FM

ADMINISTRATION
Owner: Jeffrey Lurie
President-chief operating officer: Harry Gamble
Assistant to the president: George Azar
Asst. to the president-general counsel: Robert Wallace
Vice president-financial officer: Mimi Box
Vice president-player personnel: John Wooten
Director of pro scouting: Tom Gamble
Vice president-sales and development: Decker Uhlhorn
Director of marketing: Leslie Stephenson-Matz
Director of administration: Vicki Chatley
Director of public relations: Ron Howard
Ticket manager: Leo Carlin
Trainer: Otho Davis

1994 SCHEDULE

Preseason

AUG. 5	at Chicago	7:00
AUG. 13	N.Y. JETS	7:30
AUG. 20	CINCINNATI	7:30
AUG. 26	at Atlanta	7:00

Regular season

SEP. 4	at N.Y. Giants	1:00
SEP. 12	CHICAGO (Mon.)	9:00
SEP. 18	GREEN BAY	1:00
SEP. 25	OPEN DATE	
OCT. 2	at San Francisco	1:00
OCT. 9	WASHINGTON	8:00
OCT. 16	at Dallas	3:00
OCT. 24	HOUSTON (Mon.)	9:00
OCT. 30	at Washington	1:00
NOV. 6	ARIZONA	4:00
NOV. 13	CLEVELAND	1:00
NOV. 20	at Arizona	2:00
NOV. 27	at Atlanta	1:00
DEC. 4	DALLAS	1:00
DEC. 11	at Pittsburgh	1:00
DEC. 18	N.Y. GIANTS	4:00
DEC. 24	at Cincinnati	4:00

HEAD COACH
Rich Kotite

Kotite was hired as head coach on Jan. 8, 1991 after Buddy Ryan's contract was not renewed. He had served under Ryan for one season (1990) as the Eagles' offensive coordinator. In three seasons, Kotite has guided the Eagles to a 30-20 record and one playoff berth. In 1991, after a 3-5 start and injuries to QB's Randall Cunningham and Jim McMahon, the Eagles won seven of their final eight games and barely missed the playoffs. The Eagles went 11-5 in '92, earning a playoff berth. Kotite was a boxer for a short while before turning all of his efforts to football. He was the heavyweight boxing champion at Miami (Fla.) and was once a sparring partner for Cassius Clay, later known as Muhammad Ali. Born Oct. 13, 1942, Brooklyn, N.Y.

Previous NFL: offensive coordinator-quarterbacks, 1990 Philadelphia; offensive coordinator-wide receivers, 1983-89 N.Y. Jets; wide receivers, 1978-82 Cleveland; assistant coach, 1977 New Orleans.

Previous college: None.

Player: NFL, tight end, 1967, 1969-72 N.Y. Giants; 1968 Pittsburgh. College, tight end, Wagner.

ASSISTANT COACHES

Zeke Bratkowski: offensive coordinator
Previous NFL: offensive coordinator, 1991-93 Philadelphia; 1990 Cleveland; 1985-89 N.Y. Jets; 1982-84 Baltimore/Indianapolis; 1975-81 Green Bay; 1972-74 Chicago; 1972-74 Green Bay. Player: NFL, quarterback, 1954, 1957-60 Chicago; 1961-63 L.A. Rams; 1963-68, 1971 Green Bay. College: quarterback, 1951-53 Georgia.

Lew Carpenter: receivers-tight ends
Previous NFL: receivers, 1990 Philadelphia; 1986-88 Detroit; 1975-85 Green Bay;1973-74 Houston; 1971-72 St. Louis; 1969-70 Washington; 1967-68 Atlanta; 1964-66 Minnesota. Player: NFL, running back, defensive back, end, 1953-55 Detroit; 1957-58 Cleveland; 1959-63 Green Bay. College: running back, end, 1950-52 Arkansas.

Bud Carson: defensive coordinator-secondary
Previous NFL: defensive coordinator-secondary, 1991-93 Philadelphia; 1989-90 Cleveland (head coach); 1985-88 N.Y. Jets; 1983 Kansas City; 1982 Baltimore; 1978-81 L.A. Rams; 1972-77 Pittsburgh. Player: No NFL. College: defensive back, 1950-52 North Carolina.

Peter Giunta: defensive assistant
Previous NFL: defensive assistant, 1991-93 Philadelphia. Player: No NFL. College: running back, defensive back, 1974-77 Northeastern.

Dale Haupt: defensive line
Previous NFL: defensive line, 1986-93 Philadelphia; 1978-85 Bears. Player: No NFL. College: defensive lineman, linebacker, 1950-53 Wyoming.

Bill Muir: offensive line
Previous NFL: offensive line, 1992-93 Philadelphia; 1989-91 Indianapolis; 1985-88 Detroit; 1982-84 New England. Player: No NFL. College: tackle, 1962-64 Susquehanna.

Larry Pasquale: special teams
Previous NFL: special teams, 1992-93 Philadelphia; 1990-91 San Diego; 1980-89 N.Y. Jets; 1979

TEAM AT A GLANCE

Detroit. Player: No NFL. College: quarterback, 1961-63 Bridgeport.
Jim Vechiarella: linebackers
Previous NFL: linebackers, 1991-93 Philadelphia; 1990 Cleveland; 1986-89 N.Y. Jets; 1983-85 Kansas City; 1981-82 L.A. Rams. Player: No NFL. College: linebacker, 1955-57 Youngstown State.
Jim Williams: strength and conditioning
Previous NFL: strength and conditioning, 1991-93 Philadelphia; 1982-89 N.Y. Jets; 1979-81 N.Y. Giants. Player: No NFL. College: None.
Richard Wood: running backs
Previous NFL: 1983, 1991-93 Philadelphia; 1986-90 New England; 1987-88 Kansas City; 1978-82 Atlanta; 1976-77 New Orleans; 1974 Cleveland; 1969-70 Oakland. Player: NFL, quarterback, 1960-61 Baltimore; 1962 San Diego; 1962 Cleveland; 1963-64 N.Y. Jets; 1965 Oakland; 1966 Miami. College: quarterback, 1956-59 Auburn.

COACHING RECORDS
(including postseason games)

Years	Coach	W	L	T
1933-35	Lud Wray	9	21	1
1936-40	Bert Bell	10	44	2
1941-50	Earle "Greasy" Neale	66	44	5
1951	Bo McMillin	2	0	0
1951	Wayne Millner	2	8	0
1952-55	Jim Trimble	25	20	3
1956-57	Huge Devore	7	16	1
1958-60	Buck Shaw	20	16	1
1961-63	Nick Skorich	15	24	3
1964-68	Joe Kuharich	28	41	1
1969-71	Jerry Williams	7	22	2
1971-72	Ed Khayat	8	15	2
1973-75	Mike McCormack	16	25	1
1976-82	Dick Vermeil	57	51	0
1983-85	Marion Campbell	17	29	1
1985	Fred Bruney	1	0	0
1986-90	Buddy Ryan	43	38	1
1991-93	Rich Kotite	30	20	0

HISTORICAL HIGHLIGHTS

1930s The NFL awards the franchise formerly held by the Frankford Yellow Jackets to a syndicate headed by Bert Bell and Lud Wray for $2,500. In honor of the symbol of the New Deal, the club is named the Eagles.
1940 Art Rooney of Pittsburgh buys half interest in the Eagles after selling the Steeler franchise to Alexis Thompson. The Eagles move from Municipal Stadium to Shibe Park.
1941 Rooney and Thompson switch franchises, Rooney returning to Pittsburgh and Thompson taking over the Eagles. Thompson hires Earl "Greasy" Neale as head coach.
1943 Because of the war, the Eagles are allowed to merge with the Steelers and are known as the Phil-Pitt "Steagles," and post a record of 5-4-1, their first winning season in club history. The merger is dissolved at the end of the season.
1945 With a 7-3 record, the Eagles finish in second place and lead the league in scoring with 272 points. Steve Van Buren leads the NFL with 832 rushing yards and 110 points scored and sets an NFL record with 15 TD's rushing.
1947 Pete Pihos and Steve Van Buren combine with an overpowering defense to lead the Eagles to the NFL championship game for the first time. The Cardinals, however, defeat them at Comiskey Park.
1947 Steve Van Buren sets an NFL rushing record by gaining 1,008 yards.
1948 The Eagles win their first NFL championship, downing the Cardinals 7-0 at Shibe Park.
1949 Alexis Thompson sells the Eagles for $250,000 to a syndicate headed by James P. Clark. ... Philadelphia posts a record of 11-1, the best in their history, and the Eagles win their third straight division title. Philadelphia wins its second straight championship with a 14-0 victory over the Rams at the L.A. Coliseum.
1960 The Eagles are led to their first Eastern Division title in 11 years by the passing of 34-year-old Norm Van Brocklin and the 60-minute-a-game play of 35-year-old Chuck Bednarik. Philadelphia wins its third NFL title with a come-from-behind 17-13 victory over Green Bay at Franklin Field.
1963 RB Timmy Brown sets an NFL record for total offense in a year, 2,428 yards. ... Real-estate developer Jerry Wolman purchases the team for $5.5 million.
1969 Leonard Tose purchases the franchise from Jerry Wolman for $16.1 million, at the time a record price for a professional sports team.
1971 The Eagles move to Veterans Stadium.
1978 The Eagles post a 9-7 record, their first winning season since 1966, and make the NFL playoffs for the first time since 1960. ... They lose to Atlanta 14-13 on two late TD's in a wild-card playoff game.
1979 Wilbert Montgomery sets a club record with 1,512 rushing yards and Harold Carmichael sets an NFL record by catching a pass in his 106th consecutive game. ... The Eagles tie Dallas for first place in the NFC East and go to the playoffs as a wild-card team. They beat the Bears, but then fall to Tampa Bay.
1980-81 The Eagles win 11 of their first 12 games and go on to a mark of 12-4 and the NFC East title. ... Philadelphia beats Minnesota in their first playoff game and then defeats Dallas to win the NFC title. In Super Bowl XV, the Eagles fall to the Raiders.
1981 Under Dick Vermeil, the Eagles post a 10-6 record and appear in the playoffs for the fourth straight year but are upset in the wild-card game by the Giants.
1985 Leonard Tose sells the Eagles to Florida automobile dealer Norman Braman for $65 million.
1988 Philadelphia wins the NFC East with a record of 10-6. In a playoff game at Chicago, in what became known as the "Fog Bowl," the Eagles lose 20-12.
1989 The Eagles make the playoffs as a wild-card, but, playing their first postseason game in Philadelphia since 1981, lose to the Rams.
1990-91 Philadelphia again makes it to the playoffs as a wild-card, but loses to the Redskins.
1992-93 The Eagles record the highest attendance in club history, 1,127,715. They make the playoffs as a wild-card and defeat the Saints. The next week Philadelphia loses to the Cowboys.
1993 CB Eric Allen tied an NFL record by returning four interceptions fo touchdowns. He scored two of them in one game, another NFL record.
1994 Jeffrey Lurie purchases the team from Norma Braman for $185 million, the highest amount ever paid for a professional sports franchise.

PRO FOOTBALL WEEKLY 1994 ALMANAC

TEAM AT A GLANCE

HALL OF FAME MEMBERS

	Yrs with Eagles	Inducted
Owner Bert Bell*	1933-40	1963
RB Steve Van Buren	1944-51	1965
C-LB Chuck Bednarik	1949-62	1967
C-LB Alex Wojciechowicz	1946-50	1968
Coach Earl "Greasy" Neale	1941-50	1969
E Pete Pihos	1947-55	1970
QB Sonny Jurgensen	1957-63	1983

* Charter member

RETIRED JERSEY NUMBERS

- 15 RB Steve Van Buren
- 40 DB Tom Brookshier
- 44 E Pete Retzlaff
- 60 C-LB Chuck Bednarik
- 70 T Al Wistert
- 99 DT Jerome Brown

FIRST-ROUND DRAFT CHOICES
(since 1980)

Year	Selection	College
1980	CB Roynell Young	Alcorn State
1981	DE Leonard Mitchell	Houston
1982	WR Mike Quick	North Carolina St.
1983	FB Michael Haddix	Mississippi State
1984	WR Kenny Jackson	Penn State
1985	OT Kevin Allen	Indiana
1986	RB Keith Byars	Ohio State
1987	DT Jerome Brown	Miami (Fla.)
1988	TE Keith Jackson	Oklahoma
1989	No choice	
1990	DB Ben Smith	Georgia
1991	OT Antone Davis	Tennessee
1992	No choice	
1993	OL Lester Holmes	Jackson State
1994	OT Bernard Williams	Georgia

RECORD VS. OTHER NFL TEAMS
(includes postseason games)

	Record
Arizona Cardinals	44-45-5
Atlanta Falcons	8-7-1
Buffalo Bills	4-3-0
Chicago Bears	4-24-1
Cincinnati Bengals	1-5-0
Cleveland Browns	12-30-1
Dallas Cowboys	27-41-0
Denver Broncos	5-2-0
Detroit Lions	9-12-2
Green Bay Packers	8-19-0
Houston Oilers	5-0-0
Indianapolis Colts	6-6-0
Kansas City Chiefs	1-1-0
Los Angeles Raiders	4-3
Los Angeles Rams	12-16-1
Miami Dolphins	2-6-0
Minnesota Vikings	7-10-0
New England Patriots	5-2-0
New Orleans Saints	12-8-0
New York Giants	54-62-2
New York Jets	5-0-0
Pittsburgh Steelers	44-25-3
San Diego Chargers	2-3-0
San Francisco 49ers	5-13-1
Seattle Seahawks	4-1-0
Tampa Bay Buccaneers	3-2-0
Washington Redskins	46-67-5

YEAR-BY-YEAR RECORDS

Year	Won	Lost	Tied
1933	3	5	1
1934	4	7	0
1935	2	9	0
1936	1	11	0
1937	2	8	1
1938	5	6	0
1939	1	9	1
1940	1	10	0
1941	2	8	1
1942	2	9	0
1944	7	1	2
1945	7	3	0
1946	6	5	0
1947**	8	4	0
1948*	9	2	1
1949*	11	1	0
1950	6	6	0
1951	4	8	0
1952	7	5	0
1953	7	4	1
1954	7	4	1
1955	4	7	1
1956	3	8	1
1957	4	8	0
1958	2	9	1
1959	6	5	0
1960*	10	2	0
1961	10	4	0
1962	3	10	1
1963	2	10	2
1964	6	8	0
1965	5	9	0
1966	9	5	0
1967	6	7	1
1968	2	12	0
1969	4	9	1
1970	3	10	1
1971	6	7	1
1972	2	11	1
1973	5	8	1
1974	7	7	0
1975	4	10	0
1976	4	10	0
1977	5	9	0
1978**	9	7	0
1979**	11	5	0
1980**	12	4	0
1981**	10	6	0
1982	3	6	0
1983	5	11	0
1984	6	9	1
1985	7	9	0
1986	5	10	1
1987	7	8	0
1988**	10	6	0
1989**	11	5	0
1990**	10	6	0
1991	10	6	0
1992**	11	5	0
1993	8	8	0
Total	**349**	**421**	**23**

Number of NFL championships 3
Number of years .500 or better 25
Number of years below .500 35

*NFL champions
**Playoff team

1994 PREVIEW ■ PHILADELPHIA

RECORDS

INDIVIDUAL

Service
Seasons played	14	Chuck Bednarik (1949-62)
Games played	180	Harold Carmichael (1971-83)
Consecutive games	162	Harold Carmichael (1971-83)

Scoring
Points, career	881	Bobby Walston (1951-62)
Points, season	116	Paul McFadden (1984)
Points, game	25	Bobby Walston (10/17/54)
Touchdowns, career	79	Harold Carmichael (1971-83)
Touchdowns, season	18	Steve Van Buren (1945)
Touchdowns, game	4	Wilbert Montgomery (10/15/78)
		Ben Hawkins (9/28/69)
		Tommy McDonald (10/4/59)
		Clarence Peaks (11/16/58)
Field goals, career	91	Paul McFadden (1984-87)
Field goals, season	30	Paul McFadden (1984)
Field goals, game	6	Tom Dempsey (11/12/72)
Extra points, career	365	Bobby Walston (1951-62)
Extra points, season	50	Cliff Patton (1948)

Rushing
Yards, career	6,538	Wilbert Montgomery (1977-84)
Yards, season	1,512	Wilbert Montgomery (1979)
Yards, game	205	Steve Van Buren (11/27/49)
Attempts, career	1,465	Wilbert Montgomery (1977-84)
Attempts, season	338	Wilbert Montgomery (1979)
Attempts, game	35	Heath Sherman (10/6/91)
		Steve Van Buren (11/20/49)
Touchdowns, career	69	Steve Van Buren (1944-51)
Touchdowns, season	15	Steve Van Buren (1945)
Touchdowns, game	3	By many players

Passing
Completions, career	2,088	Ron Jaworski (1977-86)
Completions, season	301	Randall Cunningham (1988)
Completions, game	34	Randall Cunningham (9/17/89)
Yards, career	26,963	Ron Jaworski (1977-86)
Yards, season	3,808	Randall Cunningham (1988)
Yards, game	447	Randall Cunningham (9/17/89)
Attempts, career	3,918	Ron Jaworski (1977-86)
Attempts, season	560	Randall Cunningham (1988)
Attempts, game	62	Randall Cunningham (10/2/89)
Touchdowns, career	175	Ron Jaworski (1977-86)
Touchdowns, season	32	Sonny Jurgensen (1961)
Touchdowns, game	7	Adrian Burk (10/17/54)

Receiving
Receptions, career	589	Harold Carmichael (1971-83)
Receptions, season	81	Keith Byars (1990)
		Keith Jackson (1988)
Receptions, game	14	Don Looney (12/1/40)
Yards, career	8,978	Harold Carmichael (1971-83)
Yards, season	1,409	Mike Quick (1983)
Yards, game	237	Tommy McDonald (12/10/61)
Touchdowns, career	79	Harold Carmichael (1971-83)
Touchdowns, season	13	Mike Quick (1983)
		Tommy McDonald (1960 & 1961)
Touchdowns, game	4	Ben Hawkins (9/28/69)
		Joe Carter (11/6/34)

Interceptions
Career	34	Bill Bradley (1969-76)
Season	11	Bill Bradley (1971)
Game	4	Russ Craft (9/24/50)

Sacks
Career	124	Reggie White (1985-92)
Season	21	Reggie White (1987)
Game	4.5	Clyde Simmons (9/15/91)

Longest plays
Run from scrimmage	90	Wilbert Montgomery (TD, 12/19/82)
Pass play	99	Ron Jaworski to Mike Quick (TD, 11/10/85)
Field goal	59	Tony Franklin (11/12/79)
Interception return	99	Jerry Norton (TD, 10/5/57)
Kickoff return	105	Timmy Brown (TD, 9/17/61)
Punt return	87	Vai Sikahema (TD, 11/22/92)
Punt	91	Randall Cunningham (12/3/89)

Top scorers
	Points
Bobby Watson (1951-62)	881
Sam Baker (1964-69)	475
Harold Carmichael (1971-83)	474
Steve Van Buren (1944-51)	464
Tony Franklin (1979-83)	412
Tommy McDonald (1957-63)	402

Top rushers
	Yards
Wilbert Montgomery (1977-84)	6,538
Steve Van Buren (1944-51)	5,860
Randall Cunningham (1985-93)	4,096
Timmy Brown (1960-67)	3,703
Tom Woodeshick (1963-71)	3,563
Tom Sullivan (1972-77)	3,135

Top passers
	Completions
Ron Jaworski (1977-86)	2,088
Randall Cunningham (1985-93)	1,540
Norman Snead (1964-70)	1,154
Tommy Thompson (1941-42, 45-50)	723
Roman Gabriel (1973-77)	661
Sonny Jurgensen (1957-63)	602

Top passers
	Yards
Ron Jaworski (1977-86)	26,963
Randall Cunningham (1985-93)	19,043
Norman Snead (1964-70)	15,672
Tommy Thompson (1941-42, 45-50)	10,255
Sonny Jurgensen (1957-63)	9,639
Bobby Thomason (1952-57)	8,124

Top receivers
	Receptions
Harold Carmichael (1971-83)	589
Pete Retzlaff (1956-66)	452
Pete Pihos (1947-55)	373
Keith Byars (1986-92)	371
Mike Quick (1982-90)	363
Bobby Watson (1951-62)	311

Top receivers
	Yards
Harold Carmichael (1971-83)	8,978
Pete Retzlaff (1956-66)	7,412
Mike Quick (1982-90)	6,464
Pete Pihos (1947-55)	5,619
Tommy McDonald (1957-63)	5,499
Bobby Watson (1951-62)	5,363

Most interceptions
	No.
Bill Bradley (1969-76)	34
Herman Edwards (1977-85)	33
Eric Allen (1988-93)	31
Wes Hopkins (1983-93)	30
Don Burroughs (1960-64)	29
Joe Scarpati (1964-69, 71)	24

Most sacks
	No.
Reggie White (1985-92)	124
Clyde Simmons (1986-93)	76.5
Greg Brown (1982-86)	50.5
Seth Joyner (1986-93)	37.5
Dennis Harrison (1982-84)	34
Ken Clarke (1982-87)	31

PRO FOOTBALL WEEKLY 1994 ALMANAC

PREVIEW: PITTSBURGH STEELERS

The up-and-down Steelers of 1993 are looking to take the "down" out of their performance in 1994. At times the team was the perfect example of an AFC powerhouse, and at other times the club appeared as if it didn't even want to play.

Pittsburgh looked to be poised for its second consecutive AFC Central title last year, but the team didn't come prepared for a few crucial games, and then the Oilers' hot streak ended those dreams. Finally the Chiefs dashed the Steelers' hopes of redeeming themselves in the postseason. Kansas City ousted Pittsburgh from the playoffs in a heartbreaking overtime game.

"You can't be anything but disappointed," said CB Rod Woodson following the playoff loss. But the words he spoke summed up the feelings about much of the season.

Tom Donahoe, the Steelers' director of football operations, tried to explain what led to the problems the team had in 1993.

"There were too many players this year who were worried about their individual situations," said Donahoe. "Maybe we need more people in the lockerroom who are tough-minded. I'm more convinced than ever that you have to have guys who have the right attitude in your lockerroom."

Now the Steelers are hoping they can capture that all-important winning attitude so they can win their second division championship in three years.

In order to earn that division title, RB Barry Foster must have a full recovery from the ankle injury that cut short his 1993 season. He will also have to lose the chip on his shoulder and sometimes-selfish attitude. If those two factors become non-factors, Pittsburgh will be in fine shape, seeing as how Foster is one of the most talented and productive running backs in the NFL. Just look back to 1992, when he rushed for 1,690 yards, and you can see what this fifth-year star is capable of. Foster's low center of gravity, quick feet and body balance make him one of the hardest backs in the league to tackle. He does a superb job of turning what should have been a two-yard gain into seven or eight yards.

The man who replaced the injured Foster last season was Leroy Thompson. Thompson put up Foster-like numbers, running for 763 yards and three TD's, but he still is not as special as the man he replaced. He does not have the same explosive quickness, but he is a threat to catch the ball coming out of the backfield with his 38 receptions in 1993.

Replacing the departed Merril Hoge at fullback will be a newcomer to the team, former Seahawk John L. Williams. Williams catches the ball extremely well and can be an effective blocker.

At quarterback will be Neil O'Donnell, a player who has started for only two full seasons and continues to improve.

"I think he's a young guy on the rise," said offensive coordinator Ron Erhardt.

O'Donnell posted some impressive numbers last season, despite a slow start due to a bout with tendinitis. The fifth-year pro threw for 3,208 yards and 14 touchdowns in '93. He's big and strong and plays well within the framework of the Steeler offense. O'Donnell has developed into a good ball-handler and play-action passer who doesn't toss many interceptions.

Returning to back up O'Donnell is veteran QB Mike Tomczak, a 10-year veteran now on his fourth team in five years. He actually started the 1993 season opener but performed so poorly the coaching staff rushed O'Donnell back. Tomczak's judgment in the red zone is considered questionable at best, and he is a streaky passer.

With their first pick in the draft, the Steelers selected WR Charles Johnson out of Colorado. Not a bad route to go considering the Steelers' receiving corps did the worst job of catching the football in 1993 of any group in the league. Johnson, who had 127 receptions for 2,447 yards in 1992 and '93 at Colorado, is expected to be able to contribute right away. He was the 17th player taken overall in the draft.

Returning to the receiving corps are Dwight Stone and Ernie Mills — two players who have great speed but lack soft hands. Yancey Thigpen is a popular target within the red zone, and Charles Davenport has very good size but lacks speed. Andre Hastings had a very disappointing rookie season and may fear for his job if he doesn't get it together soon.

The man who led the Steelers in receiving last season was not a wide receiver but a tight end. Eric Green had 63 receptions for 942 yards and five touchdowns. Green dropped a few easy passes, was a bit heavy and worried about how much money his next contract would be worth in 1993, but he also had the best year of any tight end in the game. Green has all the tools — the running skills of a fullback, the blocking ability of an All-Pro offensive tackle, and the hands of wide receiver. The Steelers like to play two-TE sets and are hoping either Tim Jorden or Craig Keith can fill that second TE spot.

On the offensive line, Dermontti Dawson is one of the top three centers in the NFL. He anchors the line and is capable of doing things no other center can do. Nevertheless, he is not always as consistent as his coaches would like and he was slowed by some injuries in 1993. The other Pro Bowl caliber player along the line is OLT John Jackson. He improved his intensity, attention to detail and overall performance last season. ORT Leon Searcy, a former first-round pick, specializes in run blocking. Carlton Haselrig, who was a Pro Bowl guard in 1992, started only four regular-season games because he began the season rehabbing. Haselrig is capable of returning to Pro

1994 PREVIEW ■ PITTSBURGH

Bowl status. On the other hand, OG Duval Love is not in the same boat. Although he started every game last year, he is a journeyman who does a decent job but lacks any special qualities. Justin Strzelczyk can play either guard or tackle and will certainly see action.

Defensively, the Steelers favor the 3-4 alignment when competing against a team with a conventional offense. But they shift into a 4-1-6 on passing downs against a passing team like the Oilers. When going with a four-man front, they like to line up their outside linebackers as defensive ends.

But, the best segment of the Pittsburgh defense is the secondary. Last year the club held opponents to a 16-to-24 TD-interception ratio.

The Steelers boast the NFL's best cornerback in Woodson. He has a huge impact on every game in which he plays, but, at times, he will get burned because he overreacts. CB Deon Figures will get even more action in his second professional season due to the departure of D.J. Johnson. Figures started some games last year and did pretty well because of his size and good hands, but he doesn't possess outstanding speed. Carnell Lake is a top-notch strong safety, and FS Darren Perry can play the ball well. The bigger and faster Gary Jones may challenge Perry for the starting job.

At linebacker, Greg Lloyd usually plays on the outside and is the key for the Steelers. He had a huge 1993, leading the team with 111 tackles. He hits as hard as anyone in the game and consistently makes the big plays. The other outside linebacker is Kevin Greene, a 32-year-old who specializes in pass rushing. He had a team-high 12.5 sacks last season. On the inside, Levon Kirkland and Chad Brown are probably going to return as starters, but Reggie Barnes may challenge for one of those slots. Jerry Olsavsky is returning from a knee injury.

The Steelers used their second and third picks in the draft to get some depth along the defensive line. Selected were DE's Brentson Buckner out of Clemson and Jason Gildon from Oklahoma State. Buckner is a good prospect but needs to improve his work ethic and attitude if he's going to make it at the NFL level. Gildon is a talented pass rusher but may not be big enough to be an every-down defensive lineman. Also new to Pittsburgh is DE Ray Seals. While with the Buccaneers, Seals showed pass-rush ability but didn't play very well against the run. DE Kenny Davidson put up some nice numbers but is not all very instinctive. Perhaps the most versatile defensive lineman the Steelers have is Gerald Williams. He can play anywhere along the line, but the knock on him is he has a hard time staying healthy. Joel Steed used 1993 to develop into a decent starting nose tackle. DE Kevin Henry and NT Jeff Zgonina contributed a bit as rookies but need to continue to improve if they want to have a future in the game.

Pittsburgh needs to improve in almost every aspect of its special-team play except maybe placekicking and kick returning. Veteran PK Gary Anderson connected on 28-of-30 field-goal attempts and made all of his extra-point attempts in 1993. Woodson returned 15 kickoffs for 294 yards and 41 punts for 338 yards in 1993. But Mark Royals' net-punting average was a disappointing 34.2 yards. To get the club's special teams back on track, the Steelers hired away Bobby April, a very respected special-team coach, from the Falcons.

Rod Woodson
PHOTO BY GEORGE GOJKOVICH

FAST FACTS

■ With 285 career field goals, PK Gary Anderson, moved from 10th to seventh on the NFL's all-time field goal list in 1993.

■ C Dermontti Dawson has started 84 consecutive games, more than anyone else on the team.

■ CB Rod Woodson had a career-high eight interceptions in 1993, more than any Pittsburgh player since Mel Blount had 11 in 1975.

1994 PLAYER ROSTER

NO.	NAME	POS.	HT.	WT.	EXP.	COLLEGE	GP/GS
47	Adams, Frank	CB	5-8	176	R	South Carolina	—
62	Allen, Andre	C-OG	6-0	310	R	Jacksonville State	—
1	Anderson, Gary	PK	5-11	179	13	Syracuse	16/0
43	Avery, Steve	FB	6-2	233	1	Northern Michigan	0/0
19	Baker, Mike	WR	6-0	188	R	West Virginia	—
50	Barnes, Reggie	LB	6-1	235	2	Oklahoma	0/0
94	Brown, Chad	LB	6-2	240	2	Colorado	16/9
45	Calloway, Dominic	CB	6-0	182	R	Memphis State	—
42	Cuthbert, Randy	RB	6-2	225	2	Duke	10/0
80	Davenport, Charles	WR	6-3	210	3	North Carolina St.	16/0
64	Davidson, Kenny	DE	6-5	275	5	Louisiana State	16/9
63	Dawson, Dermontti	C	6-2	286	7	Kentucky	16/16
23	Dukes, Chuckie	RB	5-9	202	1	Boston College	0/0
92	Edwards, Pheathur	DE	6-2	281	R	Jackson State	—
21	Figures, Deon	CB	6-0	200	2	Colorado	15/4
79	Finn, Mike	OT	6-4	3-3	2	Arkansas-Pine Bluff	0/0
36	Foggie, Fred	DB	6-0	212	1	Minnesota	0/0
29	Foster, Barry	RB	5-10	218	5	Arkansas	9/9
60	Gammon, Kendall	C	6-4	286	3	Pittsburg (Kan.) St.	16/0
86	Green, Eric	TE	6-5	280	5	Liberty	16/16
91	Greene, Kevin	LB	6-3	247	10	Auburn	16/16
28	Haller, Alan	CB	5-11	185	3	Michigan State	4/0
77	Haselrig, Carlton	OG	6-1	295	5	Pittsburgh-Johnstown	9/4
88	Hastings, Andre	WR-KR	6-0	188	2	Georgia	6/0
76	Henry, Kevin	DE	6-4	275	2	Mississippi State	12/1
54	Hoffman, Dave	LB	6-2	233	1	Washington	0/0
17	Holliday, Corey	WR	6-2	208	R	North Carolina	—
65	Jackson, John	OT	6-6	297	7	Eastern Kentucky	16/16
25	Jones, Gary	S	6-2	214	5	Texas A&M	13/2
30	Jones, Victor	FB	5-8	223	5	Louisiana State	16/0
84	Jorden, Tim	TE	6-3	240	5	Indiana	16/1
85	Keith, Craig	TE	6-3	262	2	Lenoir-Rhyne	1/0
8	Kelly, Andy	QB	6-3	212	1	Tennessee	0/0
41	Kinsler, Latish	S	6-2	193	R	Cincinnati	—
99	Kirkland, Levon	LB	6-1	252	3	Clemson	16/13
37	Lake, Carnell	SS	6-1	210	6	UCLA	14/14
95	Lloyd, Greg	LB	6-2	226	8	Fort Valley State	15/15
67	Love, Duval	OG	6-3	288	10	UCLA	16/16
56	Mack, Rico	LB	6-4	239	2	Appalachian State	8/0
89	Mills, Ernie	WR	5-11	192	4	Florida	14/5
14	O'Donnell, Neil	QB	6-3	230	5	Maryland	16/15
55	Olsavsky, Jerry	LB	6-1	224	6	Pittsburgh	7/7
66	Palelei, Siulagi	OG	6-3	320	2	Nevada-Las Vegas	3/0
71	Parker, Curtis	OT	6-3	312	R	North Carolina	—
39	Perry, Darren	S	5-11	196	3	Penn State	16/16
85	Rasby, Walter	TE	6-3	247	R	Wake Forest	—
48	Robinson, Ed	LB	6-0	228	R	Florida	—
3	Royals, Mark	P	6-5	215	5	Appalachian State	16/0
46	Scott, Patrick	LB	6-4	229	R	S. Carolina State	—
97	Seals, Ray	DE	6-3	309	7	None	16/16
72	Searcy, Leon	OT	6-3	304	3	Miami (Fla.)	15/0
24	Shelton, Richard	S	5-10	202	5	Liberty	9/2
83	Shepherd, Leslie	WR	5-11	179	1	Temple	0/0
61	Simpson, Tim	C-OG	6-2	296	1	Illinois	0/0
69	Solomon, Ariel	C-OG	6-5	290	4	Colorado	16/0

1994 PREVIEW ■ PITTSBURGH

1994 PLAYER ROSTER

NO.	NAME	POS.	HT.	WT.	EXP.	COLLEGE	GP/GS
93	Steed, Joel	NT	6-2	295	3	Colorado	14/12
20	Stone, Dwight	WR-RB	6-0	180	8	Middle Tenn. State	16/15
73	Strzelczyk, Justin	OG-OT	6-6	295	5	Maine	16/12
96	Sutton, Ricky	DE	6-2	281	2	Auburn	7/0
82	Thigpen, Yancey	WR	6-1	207	3	Winston-Salem St.	12/0
34	Thompson, Leroy	RB	5-11	217	4	Penn State	15/6
18	Tomczak, Mike	QB	6-1	207	10	Ohio State	7/1
35	Volpe, Jon	RB	5-7	201	1	Stanford	0/0
68	Williams, Chris	DE	6-3	281	R	Hampton	—
98	Williams, Gerald	NT-DE	6-3	288	9	Auburn	10/8
22	Williams, John L.	FB	5-11	231	9	Florida	16/9
27	Williams, Willie	CB	5-9	188	2	Western Carolina	16/0
26	Woodson, Rod	CB	6-0	200	8	Purdue	16/16
90	Zgonina, Jeff	DT	6-1	284	2	Purdue	5/0

'94 DRAFT PICKS

RD.	NAME	POS.	HT.	WT.	COLLEGE
1.	Johnson, Charles	WR	6-0	186	Colorado
2.	Buckner, Brentson	DE	6-2	310	Clemson
3.	Gildon, Jason	LB	6-3	235	Oklahoma State
3.	Morris, Byron "Bam"	RB	6-0	241	Texas Tech
4.	Faumui, Taase	DE	6-4	270	Hawaii
5.	Bell, Myron	DB	5-11	200	Michigan State
5.	Brown, Gary	OT	6-4	316	Georgia Tech
6.	Miller, Jim	QB	6-2	222	Michigan State
6.	Ravotti, Eric	LB	6-2	246	Penn State
7.	Abrams, Brice	FB	6-1	257	Michigan State

PRO FOOTBALL WEEKLY 1994 ALMANAC

TEAM AT A GLANCE

TEAM DIRECTORY

Address	Three Rivers Stadium 300 Stadium Circle Pittsburgh, Pa. 15212 (412) 323-1200
Stadium	Three Rivers Stadium 300 Stadium Circle Pittsburgh, Pa. 15212 Capacity: 59,600 Playing surface: AstroTurf
Training Camp	St. Vincent College Latrobe, Pennsylvania 15650
Colors	Black and gold
Television	WPXI, Channel 11
Radio	WTAE, 1250 AM WVTY, 96.1 FM

ADMINISTRATION
President: Daniel M. Rooney
Vice president: John R. McGinley
Vice president: Arthur J. Rooney Jr.
Administration advisor: Chuck Noll
Director of communications: Joe Gordon
Controller: Michael J. Hagen
Director of football operations: Tom Donahoe
College personnel coordinator: Tom Modrak
Pro personnel coordinator: Charles Bailey
Ticket sales manager: Geraldine Glenn
Trainer: John Norwig

1994 SCHEDULE
Preseason

AUG. 6	at Miami	8:00
AUG. 13	L.A. RAIDERS	6:00
AUG. 20	INDIANAPOLIS	6:00
AUG. 26	at Washington	8:00

Regular season

SEP. 4	DALLAS	4:00
SEP. 11	at Cleveland	1:00
SEP. 18	INDIANAPOLIS	1:00
SEP. 25	at Seattle	1:00
OCT. 3	HOUSTON (Mon.)	9:00
OCT. 9	OPEN DATE	
OCT. 16	CINCINNATI	1:00
OCT. 23	at N.Y. Giants	1:00
OCT. 30	at Arizona	6:00
NOV. 6	at Houston	12:00
NOV. 14	BUFFALO (Mon.)	9:00
NOV. 20	MIAMI	1:00
NOV. 27	at L.A. Raiders	1:00
DEC. 4	at Cincinnati	1:00
DEC. 11	PHILADELPHIA	1:00
DEC. 18	CLEVELAND	1:00
DEC. 24	at San Diego	1:00

HEAD COACH
Bill Cowher
Cowher debuted as a head coach in 1992 and took the Steelers into the playoffs with an 11-5 record. He is one of only 12 NFL coaches to win 11 or more games in their first season as head coach. For his efforts in '92, he was selected as the Coach of the Year. In his second season with the Steelers in 1993, his team went 9-7 and earned a spot in the postseason. Cowher began his coaching career at the age of 29 as special-team coach of the Browns under Marty Schottenheimer. He spent four seasons in Cleveland before following Schottenheimer to Kansas City. Cowher was a three-year starter at North Carolina State, and then he played five seasons in the NFL. Born May 8, 1957, Pittsburgh, Pa.
Previous NFL: defensive coordinator, 1989-91 Kansas City; secondary, 1987-88 Cleveland; special teams, 1985-86 Cleveland.
Previous college: None.
Player: NFL, linebacker, 1983-84 Philadelphia; 1980-82 Cleveland. College, linebacker, 1975-78 North Carolina State.

ASSISTANT COACHES
Bobby April: special teams
Previous NFL: special teams, 1991-93 Falcons. Player: No NFL. College: linebacker, 1972-75 Nicholls State.

Dom Capers: defensive coordinator
Previous NFL: defensive coordinator, 1992-93 Pittsburgh; 1986-91 New Orleans. Player: No NFL. College: defensive back, 1968-71 Mount Union College.

Ron Erhardt: offensive coordinator
Previous NFL: offensive coordinator, 1992-93 Pittsburgh; 1973-81 New England (head coach 1978-81); 1982-91 N.Y. Giants. Player: No NFL. College: quarterback, 1951-54, Jamestown (N.D.) College.

Chan Gailey: wide receivers
Previous NFL: assistant coach, 1985-90 Denver. Player: No NFL. College: quarterback, 1971-74 Florida.

Dick Hoak: running backs
Previous NFL: running backs, 1972-93 Pittsburgh. Player: NFL, running back, 1961-70 Pittsburgh. College: halfback, quarterback, 1958-60 Penn State.

Pat Hodgson: tight ends
Previous NFL: tight ends, 1992-93 Pittsburgh; 1978 San Diego; 1979-87 N.Y. Giants. Player: NFL, tight end, 1966 Washington, 1967 Minnesota. College: tight end, 1963-65 Georgia.

Dick LeBeau: defensive backs
Previous NFL: defensive backs, 1992-93 Pittsburgh; 1980-91 Cincinnati; 1976-79 Green Bay; 1972-75 Philadelphia. Player: NFL, cornerback, 1959-72 Detroit. College: defensive back, halfback, 1954-57 Ohio State.

Marvin Lewis: linebackers
Previous NFL: linebackers, 1992-93 Pittsburgh. Player: No NFL. College: linebacker, 1977-80 Idaho State.

196

1994 PREVIEW ■ PITTSBURGH

TEAM AT A GLANCE

John Mitchell: defensive line
Previous NFL: defensive line, 1991-93 Browns. Player: No NFL. College: defensive end, 1969-70 Eastern Arizona J.C.; 1971-72 Alabama.

Kent Stephenson: offensive line
Previous NFL: offensive line, 1992-93 Pittsburgh; 1985-91 Seattle. Player: No NFL. College: guard-nose tackle, 1962-64 Northern Iowa.

COACHING RECORDS
(including postseason games)

Years	Coach	W	L	T
1933	Forrest "Jap" Douds	3	6	2
1934	Luby DiMelio	2	10	0
1935-36	Joe Bach	10	14	0
1937-39	Johnny Blood (McNally)	6	19	0
1939-40	Walt Kiesling	3	13	3
1941	Bert Bell	0	2	0
	Aldo "Buff" Donelli	0	5	0
1941-44	Walt Kiesling	13	20	2
1945	Jim Leonard	2	8	0
1946-47	Jock Sutherland	13	10	1
1948-51	Johnny Michelosen	20	26	2
1952-53	Joe Bach	11	13	0
1954-56	Walt Kiesling	14	22	0
1957-64	Buddy Parker	51	47	6
1965	Mike Nixon	2	12	0
1966-68	Bill Austin	11	28	3
1969-91	Chuck Noll	209	156	1
1992-93	Bill Cowher	20	14	0

HISTORICAL HIGHLIGHTS

1933 Art Rooney purchases an NFL franchise for $2,500 and names the team the Pirates.
1941 Art Rooney sells the franchise to Alexis Thompson, then buys an interest in the Philadelphia Eagles, which he later swaps with Thompson to regain control of the Pittsburgh franchise. The team is renamed the Steelers.
1944 The Steelers merge with the Chicago Cardinals and are known as Card-Pitt, but around the league are called "Carpet" because they lose all 10 of their games.
1947 After a six-game winning streak, the Steelers finish the season tied with Philadelphia for first place in the Eastern Division, but Pittsburgh loses 21-0 to Philadelphia in a playoff game.
1952 Pittsburgh scores the most points and runs up the widest winning margin in club history when it defeats the New York Giants 63-7.
1958 Bobby Layne sets a club record by passing for 409 yards in a game.
1962 The Steelers finish second in the Eastern Conference and post the finest record thus far in their history, 9-5. ... Pittsburgh wins a spot in the playoffs, but the Steelers lose to the Lions 17-10.
1970 The Steelers join NFL clubs Baltimore and Cleveland in a move to the AFC following the AFL-NFL merger. QB Terry Bradshaw from Louisiana Tech is chosen by Pittsburgh in the first round of the draft, after winnning a coin toss with Chicago.
1972 The Steelers capture the first division title in the club's history, posting an 11-3 record. ... In their first playoff game since 1947, the Steelers defeat Oakland 13-7 in the final 22 seconds of the game on a touchdown by Franco Harris. Their season ends with a loss to Miami in the AFC title game.
1973 Pittsburgh, winning 10 of its 14 games, makes it to the playoffs as a wild-card entry but is eliminated by the Raiders 33-14.
1974-75 With their Steel Curtain defense, the passing of Terry Bradshaw, and the rushing of Franco Harris, the Steelers easily take the AFC Central Division crown with a record of 10-3-1. ... Pittsburgh knocks off the Bills 32-14 to advance to the AFC title game. The underdog Steelers defeat the Raiders at Oakland 24-13 and earn their first invitation to the Super Bowl. ... The Steelers capture their first championship ever by defeating the Vikings 16-6 in Super Bowl IX in New Orleans.
1975-76 The Steelers repeat as victors of the AFC Central. Franco Harris sets a team record by rushing for 1,246 yards, and CB Mel Blount sets another by intercepting 11 passes. ... In the playoff opener, the Steelers defeat the Colts. The Steelers then make it two AFC titles in a row, beating Oakland. ... Facing the Cowboys, Pittsburgh wins and becomes the third team to win consecutive Super Bowls.
1976 The Steelers repeat as division champs with a record of 10-4, then decimate the Colts in the first round of the playoffs 40-14. ... In the AFC title game, Oakland destroys Pittsburgh's hope for a third straight Super Bowl appearance 24-7.
1977 Dominating their division again with a 9-5 record, the Steelers meet the Super Bowl-bound Broncos in the playoffs and fall 34-21.
1978-79 Pittsburgh wins the most games ever in its history, 14, to win the division title for the fifth straight year. ... The Steelers defeat the Broncos and the Oilers, earning another trip to the Super Bowl. ... In Super Bowl XIII in Miami, the Steelers defeat the Cowboys 35-31. Pittsburgh becomes the first team in history to win three Super Bowls.
1979-80 Pittsburgh wins the AFC Central for the sixth year in a row. ... In the playoffs, it defeats the Dolphins 34-14 and Houston 27-13, becoming the second team ever to appear in four Super Bowls. ... Pittsburgh beats the Rams 31-19 in Super Bowl XIV, the first team to win four Super Bowls.
1982-83 After a two-year layoff, the Steelers make it back to postseason play in a strike-shortened season with a record of 6-3 but lose in the first round of the playoff tournament to the Chargers 31-28.
1983 For the first time since 1979, the Steelers win their division with a record of 10-6, but fall to the Raiders 38-10 in the playoffs.
1984-85 The Steelers make it two division crowns in a row, winning nine of their 16 games. A 24-17 win over Denver sends Pittsburgh to the AFC title game, where they lose to the Dolphins.
1989 A 9-7 wild-card team, Pittsburgh defeats Houston 26-23 in OT, then loses to Denver 24-23.
1990 Head coach Chuck Noll posts his 200th win when the Steelers defeat the Patriots 24-23.
1991 After the season, Chuck Noll retires following 23 seasons as head coach.
1992-93 The Steelers win the AFC Central with a record of 11-5. ... Playing at home, Pittsburgh loses to the Bills in the divisional playoff game 24-3.
1993-94 Pittsburgh makes the playoffs as a wild-card but loses in overtime to the Chiefs 27-24.

PRO FOOTBALL WEEKLY 1994 ALMANAC

TEAM AT A GLANCE

HALL OF FAME MEMBERS

	Yrs with Steelers	Inducted
Owner Art Rooney	1933-88	1964
HB Bill Dudley	1942, 45-46	1966
G/Coach Walt Kiesling	1937-44, 49-61	1966
QB Bobby Layne	1958-62	1967
DT Ernie Stautner	1950-63	1969
DT Joe Greene	1969-81	1987
FB John Henry Johnson	1960-65	1987
LB Jack Ham	1971-82	1988
CB Mel Blount	1970-83	1989
QB Terry Bradshaw	1970-83	1989
RB Franco Harris	1972-83	1990
LB Jack Lambert	1974-84	1990
Coach Chuck Noll	1969-91	1993

RETIRED JERSEY NUMBERS
None

FIRST-ROUND DRAFT CHOICES
(since 1980)

Year	Selection	College
1980	QB Mark Malone	Arizona State
1981	DE Keith Gary	Oklahoma
1982	RB Walter Abercrombie	Baylor
1983	NT-DE Gabriel Rivera	Texas Tech
1984	WR Louis Lipps	Southern Mississippi
1985	DE Darryl Sims	Wisconsin
1986	OG John Rienstra	Temple
1987	CB Rod Woodson	Purdue
1988	DE Aaron Jones	Eastern Kentucky
1989	RB Tim Worley	Georgia
	OT Tom Ricketts	Pittsburgh
1990	TE Eric Green	Liberty
1991	LB Huey Richardson	Florida
1992	OT Leon Searcy	Miami (Fla.)
1993	CB Deon Figures	Colorado
1994	WR Charles Johnson	Colorado

RECORD VS. OTHER NFL TEAMS
(including postseason games)

	Record
Arizona Cardinals	29-21-3
Atlanta Falcons	9-1-0
Buffalo Bills	7-8-0
Chicago Bears	4-16-1
Cincinnati Bengals	26-21-0
Cleveland Browns	36-52-0
Dallas Cowboys	13-12-0
Denver Broncos	7-12-1
Detroit Lions	11-13-1
Green Bay Packers	11-17-0
Houston Oilers	32-18-0
Indianapolis Colts	12-4-0
Kansas City Chiefs	13-6-0
Los Angeles Raiders	6-10-0
Los Angeles Rams	5-14-2
Miami Dolphins	6-9-0
Minnesota Vikings	5-7-0
New England Patriots	9-3-0
New Orleans Saints	6-5-0
New York Giants	26-42-3
New York Jets	12-1-0
Philadelphia Eagles	25-44-3
San Diego Chargers	14-5-0
San Francisco 49ers	7-8-0
Seattle Seahawks	5-5-0
Tampa Bay Buccaneers	4-0-0
Washington Redskins	27-42-3

YEAR-BY-YEAR RECORDS

Year	Won	Lost	Tied
1933	3	6	2
1934	2	10	0
1935	4	8	0
1936	6	6	0
1937	4	7	0
1938	2	9	0
1939	1	9	1
1940	2	7	2
1941	1	9	1
1942	7	4	0
1945	2	8	0
1946	5	5	1
1947	8	4	0
1948	4	8	0
1949	6	5	1
1950	6	6	0
1951	4	7	1
1952	5	7	0
1953	6	6	0
1954	5	7	0
1955	4	8	0
1956	5	7	0
1957	6	6	0
1958	7	4	1
1959	6	5	1
1960	5	6	1
1961	6	8	0
1962	9	5	0
1963	7	4	3
1964	5	9	0
1965	2	12	0
1966	5	8	1
1967	4	9	1
1968	2	11	1
1969	1	13	0
1970	5	9	0
1971	6	8	0
1972**	11	3	1
1973**	10	4	0
1974*	10	3	1
1975*	12	2	0
1976**	10	4	0
1977**	9	5	0
1978*	14	2	0
1979*	12	4	0
1980	9	7	0
1981	8	8	0
1982**	6	3	0
1983**	10	6	0
1984**	9	7	0
1985	7	9	0
1986	6	10	0
1987	8	7	0
1988	5	11	0
1989**	9	7	0
1990	9	7	0
1991	7	9	0
1992**	11	5	0
1993**	9	7	0
Total	360	393	19

Number of NFL championships   4
Number of years .500 or better   30
Number of years below .500   29

*NFL champions
**Playoff team

1994 PREVIEW ■ PITTSBURGH

RECORDS

INDIVIDUAL

Service
Seasons played	15	Mike Webster (1974-88)
Games played	220	Mike Webster (1974-88)
Consecutive games	182	Ray Mansfield (1964-76)

Scoring
Points, career	1,239	Gary Anderson (1982-93)
Points, season	139	Gary Anderson (1985)
Points, game	24	Roy Jefferson (11/3/68)
		Ray Mathews (10/17/54)
Touchdowns, career	100	Franco Harris (1972-83)
Touchdowns, season	15	Louis Lipps (1985)
Touchdowns, game	4	Roy Jefferson (11/3/68)
		Ray Mathews (10/17/54)
Field goals, career	285	Gary Anderson (1982-93)
Field goals, season	33	Gary Anderson (1985)
Field goals, game	6	Gary Anderson (10/23/88)
Extra points, career	384	Gary Anderson (1982-93)
Extra points, season	50	Matt Bahr (1979)
Extra points, game	8	Gary Kerkorian (11/30/52)

Rushing
Yards, career	11,950	Franco Harris (1972-83)
Yards, season	1,690	Barry Foster (1992)
Yards, game	218	John Fuqua (12/20/70)
Attempts, career	2,881	Franco Harris (1972-83)
Attempts, season	390	Barry Foster (1992)
Attempts, game	41	Franco Harris (10/17/76)
Touchdowns, career	91	Franco Harris (1972-83)
Touchdowns, season	14	Franco Harris (1976)
Touchdowns, game	3	Merril Hoge (11/26/89)
		Rocky Bleier (12/5/76)
		Earl Gros (12/21/69)
		John Henry Johnson (10/10/64)

Passing
Rating, career	71.1	Terry Bradshaw (1970-83)
Rating, season	87.8	Terry Bradshaw (1975)
Completions, career	2,025	Terry Bradshaw (1970-83)
Completions, season	270	Neil O'Donnell (1993)
Completions, game	31	Joe Gilliam (9/22/74)
Yards, career	27,989	Terry Bradshaw (1970-83)
Yards, season	3,724	Terry Bradshaw (1979)
Yards, game	409	Bobby Layne (12/13/58)
Attempts, career	3,901	Terry Bradshaw (1970-83)
Attempts, season	486	Neil O'Donnell (1993)
Attempts, game	50	Joe Gilliam (9/22/74)
Touchdowns, career	212	Terry Bradshaw (1970-83)
Touchdowns, season	28	Terry Bradshaw (1978)
Touchdowns, game	5	Mark Malone (9/8/85)
		Terry Bradshaw (11/15/81)

Receiving
Receptions, career	537	John Stallworth (1974-87)
Receptions, season	80	John Stallworth (1984)
Receptions, game	12	J.R. Wilburn (10/22/67)
Yards, career	8,723	John Stallworth (1974-87)
Yards, season	1,395	John Stallworth (1984)
Yards, game	235	Buddy Dial (10/22/61)
Touchdowns, career	63	John Stallworth (1974-87)
Touchdowns, season	12	Louis Lipps (1985)
		Buddy Dial (1961)
Touchdowns, game	4	Roy Jefferson (11/3/68)

Interceptions
Career	57	Mel Blount (1970-83)
Season	11	Mel Blount (1975)
Game	4	Jack Butler (12/13/53)

Sacks
Career	73.5	L.C. Greenwood (1969-81)
Season	15.0	Mike Merriweather (1984)
Game	5.0	Joe Greene (12/10/72)

Longest plays
Run from scrimmage	97	Bobby Gage (TD, 12/4/49)
Pass play	90	Bubby Brister (10/14/90)
		Terry Bradshaw (TD, 11/8/81)
Field goal	55	Gary Anderson (11/25/84)
Interception return	99	Martin Kottler (TD, 9/27/33)
Kickoff return	101	Don McCall (TD, 11/23/69)
Punt return	90	Brady Keys (9/20/64)
Punt	82	Joe Geri (10/20/49)

Top scorers
	Points
Gary Anderson (1982-93)	1,239
Roy Gerela (1971-78)	731
Franco Harris (1972-83)	600
John Stallworth (1974-87)	384
Lynn Swann (1974-81)	318
Mike Clark (1964-67)	287

Top rushers
	Yards
Franco Harris (1972-83)	11,950
John Henry Johnson (1960-65)	4,383
Frank Pollard (1980-88)	3,989
Dick Hoak (1961-70)	3,965
Rocky Bleier (1968, 1970-80)	3,865
Walter Abercrombie (1982-87)	3,343

Top passers
	Completions
Terry Bradshaw (1970-83)	2,025
Bubby Brister (1986-91)	713
Mark Malone (1980-87)	690
Jim Finks (1949-55)	661
Neil O'Donnell (1990-93)	611
Bobby Layne (1958-62)	569

Top passers
	Yards
Terry Bradshaw (1970-83)	27,989
Bubby Brister (1986-91)	9,385
Bobby Layne (1958-62)	8,983
Jim Finks (1949-55)	8,854
Mark Malone (1980-87)	8,582
Neil O'Donnell (1990-93)	7,454

Top receivers
	Receptions
John Stallworth (1974-87)	537
Louis Lipps (1984-91)	358
Lynn Swann (1974-82)	336
Elbie Nickel (1947-57)	329
Franco Harris (1972-83)	306
Ray Mathews (1951-59)	230

Top receivers
	Yards
John Stallworth (1974-87)	8,723
Louis Lipps (1984-91)	6,018
Lynn Swann (1974-82)	5,462
Elbie Nickel (1947-57)	5,133
Buddy Dial (1959-63)	4,723
Ray Mathews (1951-59)	3,919

Most interceptions
	No.
Mel Blount (1970-83)	57
Jack Butler (1951-59)	52
Donnie Shell (1974-87)	51
Dwayne Woodruff (1979-85, 87-90)	37
Mike Wagner (1971-80)	36
Jack Ham (1971-82)	32

Most sacks
	No.
L.C. Greenwood (1969-81)	73.5
Joe Greene (1969-81)	66.0
Keith Willis (1982-87, 89-91)	59.0

PREVIEW: SAN DIEGO CHARGERS

Charger QB Stan Humphries must be wondering if it was something he said.

After all, the San Diego offense truly has become a unit you can't tell without a program.

Anthony Miller and Nate Lewis, last season's starting receivers, are both gone.

Marion Butts, the team's leading rusher last year, is gone.

Backup QB John Friesz, who started six games last year, is gone.

And then there's the offensive line. Starting OG Mike Zandofsky and backup Mike Withycombe are gone. Eric Moten, the team's best offensive lineman, probably won't play this season because of a knee injury that may be career-ending. Joe Milinichik also is a major question mark due to a knee injury.

Free-agency. Trades. Injuries. A triple crown of disruption for the Charger offense.

The most significant loss came when the Chargers chose not to match the Broncos' offer sheet to Miller.

"This isn't going to be popular with everybody," said Charger GM Bobby Beathard.

Miller caught 84 passes for 1,162 yards and seven touchdowns last season.

"You never like to lose an Anthony Miller," said Beathard, who nonetheless felt that matching the Broncos' four-year, $10.5 million offer to Miller would handcuff the team in its ability to improve itself elsewhere.

Lewis, meanwhile, was traded to the Rams. The result is that Humphries will be throwing to a new pair of starting receivers. The Chargers are counting on former Dolphin Tony Martin and ex-Bronco Vance Johnson to fill the void.

Martin has great speed and athletic ability but kept getting in trouble in Miami because he was so inconsistent.

"I've always liked Tony," said Beathard. "He's a big-play maker. He's got Anthony's type of speed, the kind of speed we need."

Before leaving Miami to go to the Chargers, Martin had slipped on the Dolphin depth chart. He joins the Chargers with the belief that the change of scenery will do him good.

"It's like a load off of me," Martin said of leaving Miami. "It's what I've always wanted (an opportunity to start). It's relaxing to be able to go to a place and just show them what I can do."

Johnson was having a fine comeback year for the Broncos in '93 before he got hurt. He no longer has 4.3 speed but still is very quick and can get separation from the defender. San Diego has shown great patience with Shawn Jefferson, and this is the year the Chargers hope to be rewarded for babying him along. WR Andre Coleman was selected in the third round of this year's draft. Duane Young, who really is a third tackle, returns at tight end. Alfred Pupunu will probably remain at H-back. The Chargers added TE Aaron Laing in the fifth round of this year's draft.

With the WR position looking more uncertain than when Miller was on the roster and with Butts having been traded to the Patriots, much of the load on offense will shift to Humphries at quarterback and young RB Natrone Means.

Humphries is a tough, cocky, charismatic quarterback who loves to throw the deep ball. However, last year he had little zip on his ball and could not get the ball down the field consistently until the last two games because of a shoulder injury. Former Bill Gale Gilbert is the new backup behind Humphries.

Means shared time with Butts last season and will be the featured back this year. Means has surprising speed for his size and very quick and agile feet for a big back. He can make defenders miss or run over or away from them. However, he does have a weight-gain problem. Ronnie Harmon is an excellent third-down back who has amazing moves and has caught 152 passes in the past two years. Harmon will make tacklers miss after the catch but does not have blazing speed. He also will drop some passes when he looks to run before securing the ball.

Uncertainty along the offensive line does not figure to help Humphries and Means. The likely loss of Moten for the season, the questions surrounding Milinichik's knee and with the loss of Zandofsky via free-agency all will hurt.

There is still talent, however. The Chargers have a top-flight center in Courtney Hall, who also is a superb line leader. OLT Harry Swayne also has the tools to be a big-time player. With his long arms and quick feet, he should only get better after being slowed by injuries last season. Joe Cocozzo, who played well as a rookie, will be one starting guard.

The Chargers' first selection in this year's draft was in the second round, when they took OG Isaac Davis.

"He's a huge, huge player," said Beathard. "He can run. He's probably the strongest, best run blocker that we saw in the country and has that kind of agility to become a very good pass protector. ... He moves like a smaller person."

With their second pick in the second round, the Chargers drafted Vaughn Parker, who Beathard said will get work at both guard and tackle. Eric Jonassen will be given a chance to start at right tackle, but he was a disappointment last year. Depth could come from OT Stan Brock and C-OG Curtis Whitley.

Although the Chargers traded away DE Burt Grossman and lost LB Gary Plummer via free-agency, their situation on defense looks to be more stable than on offense.

The star of the defense is Junior Seau, who had another Pro Bowl year last season at inside line-

1994 PREVIEW ■ SAN DIEGO

Natrone Means

league's finest outside pass rushers. O'Neal, a natural right end, has sneaky speed, great technique and uses his hands as well as anyone in the league. He watches film and knows how to set up and beat the tackles he is opposing.

Last year the Chargers found out the hard way that, no matter how big Chris Mims got, he was still too long-legged to play tackle on running downs. However, after he replaced Grossman at left end, he played the best football of his career. Mims has the long arms and upfield burst needed to play end. He will now be an end on running downs since Grossman was traded to the Eagles.

Along the interior of the defensive line, ex-Cardinal Reuben Davis is a big, powerful run stopper who needs to keep his weight below 325 pounds to be at his best. Shawn Lee has enough strength but is not that athletic and has a hard time coming off blocks.

Raylee Johnson showed great upfield pass-rush potential during the preseason as a rookie and could see a lot more action at end on passing downs, with Mims moving inside to tackle on those plays.

In the secondary, look for last year's first-round pick, Darrien Gordon, to continue to get better at one CB spot as he matures and ex-Seahawk Dwayne Harper to start across from him. Gordon is the prototype NFL cornerback in terms of size, speed, hands and jumping ability. Harper is not very big or fast, but he has great reactions and instincts.

At safety the Chargers' best player last season was Darren Carrington, who made 79 tackles and picked off seven passes as a strong safety and nickel back. However, Carrington really is a free safety, and he is not as physical as desired at strong safety. FS Stanley Richard had a disappointing year in terms of making big plays and big hits, and, with his salary, he will have to start playing up to the expectations that made him a first-round pick in '91 if he is to remain in the lineup. James Fuller is the team's best fit for strong safety, but he has been set back by injuries in the past and must step forward this year. Sean Vanhorse is a decent third cornerback but doesn't look like a starter. Eric Castle is a big, rangy free safety. DB Willie Clark was drafted in the third round of this year's draft.

PK John Carney was on fire in '92 and at the start of the '93 season but then cooled down. P John Kidd missed two games with a bad back, averaged 42.6 yards per kick, but, at times, he may have been too reluctant to kick directionally instead of kicking deep down the middle. Gordon did a fine job returning punts, and rookie WR Coleman has the big-play return ability the Chargers covet.

backer but was not nearly as effective as he was in '92 because he tried to do too much himself. Seau is a great hitter who makes plays sideline-to-sideline. However, he is not an effective blitzer because he has not developed pass-rush moves and does not use his hands well on the rush. Seau did not have one sack among his team-high 129 tackles or 19 tackles for loss last year.

Former Lion Dennis Gibson will replace Plummer at middle linebacker, and ex-Dolphin David Griggs should have an impact at outside linebacker. Gibson is a very smart, heady player who lost weight and was a step quicker last year. Griggs played outside linebacker and defensive end for the Dolphins and is a power player who performs best across from the tight end. Steve Hendrickson is a jack-of-all-trades. Two youngsters who could figure into the equation are Lewis Bush and Doug Miller.

Along the defensive line the Chargers look strong, as well. Leslie O'Neal remains one of the

FAST FACTS

■ QB Stan Humphries has a 20-10 record as an NFL starter.
■ The Charger defense allowed a league-low 3.2 yards per rushing attempt last season.
■ The Chargers led the league in turnover-takeaway differential with a plus-15 last year.

PRO FOOTBALL WEEKLY 1994 ALMANAC

1994 PLAYER ROSTER

NO.	NAME	POS.	HT.	WT.	EXP.	COLLEGE	GP/GS
85	Barnes, Johnnie	WR	6-1	180	3	Hampton (Va.)	13/0
62	Beeching, Todd	OT	6-7	305	R	Southern Missisippi	—
2	Bennett, Darren	P	6-5	235	1	None	—
65	Berger, Blaine	DE	6-5	285	R	Utah	—
49	Binn, David	TE	6-3	234	R	California	—
15	Boles, Eric	TE	6-3	210	2	Central Washington	0/0
13	Breedlove, Brad	WR	5-10	175	R	Duke	—
67	Brock, Stan	OT	6-6	295	15	Colorado	16/16
11	Brohm, Jeff	QB	6-1	200	R	Louisville	—
58	Bush, Lewis	OLB	6-2	245	2	Washington State	16/0
22	Byrd, Gill	CB-S	5-11	198	12	San Jose State	—
48	Caldwell, Henry	RB	5-10	216	R	Central Missouri St.	—
3	Carney, John	PK	5-11	170	5	Notre Dame	16/0
29	Carrington, Darren	S	6-2	200	6	Northern Arizona	16/13
50	Carter, Grant	LB	6-2	222	R	Pacific	—
44	Castle, Eric	S	6-3	212	2	Oregon	5/0
68	Cocozzo, Joe	OG	6-4	300	2	Michigan	15/5
51	Crews, Terry	LB	6-2	245	3	Western Michigan	10/0
39	Currie, Herschel	CB	6-1	190	R	Oregon State	—
93	Davis, Reuben	DE	6-5	340	7	North Carolina	16/14
23	Dunson, Walter	RB-KR	5-9	173	2	Middle Tennessee St.	—
82	Dyal, Mike	TE	6-2	240	7	Texas A&I	10/0
75	Engel, Greg	C	6-3	293	R	Illinois	—
40	Fuller, James	SS	6-0	208	3	Portland State	10/0
56	Gibson, Dennis	LB	6-2	243	8	Iowa State	15/15
5	Gilbert, Gale	QB	6-3	209	9	California	—
21	Gordon, Darrien	CB	5-11	182	2	Stanford	0/0
7	Green, Trent	QB	6-3	211	2	Indiana	0/0
66	Greene, Ernest	OT	6-5	294	R	Savannah State	—
78	Gregory, James	DT	6-3	283	R	Alabama	—
92	Griggs, David	OLB	6-3	250	6	Virginia	16/15
53	Hall, Courtney	C-OG	6-2	281	6	Rice	16/16
33	Harmon, Ronnie	RB	5-11	207	9	Iowa	16/1
28	Harper, Dwayne	CB	5-11	174	7	S. Carolina State	14/14
76	Hocker, Shawn	OG	6-4	288	R	North Carolina	—
9	Hollis, Mike	PK	5-7	164	R	Idaho	—
12	Humphries, Stan	QB	6-2	223	6	Northeast Louisiana	12/10
80	Jefferson, Shawn	WR	5-11	172	4	Central Florida	16/4
42	Johnson, Chris	S	6-0	205	R	San Diego State	—
99	Johnson, Raylee	DE	6-3	245	2	Arkansas	9/0
60	Johnson, Tom	LB	6-4	245	R	Georgia Tech	—
89	Johnson, Vance	WR	5-11	180	10	Arizona	10/8
74	Jonassen, Eric	OT	6-5	310	3	Bloomsburg (Pa.)	16/2
38	Lane, Greg	CB	5-9	181	R	Notre Dame	—
98	Lee, Shawn	DT	6-2	300	7	North Alabama	16/15
36	Long, Juan	LB	6-2	254	R	Mississppi State	—
81	Martin, Tony	WR	6-0	181	5	Mesa (Colo.)	12/0
88	May, Deems	TE	6-4	263	3	North Carolina	15/1
6	McAlister, Scott	P	6-3	210	1	North Carolina	0/0
20	Means, Natrone	RB	5-10	245	2	North Carolina	16/0
71	Milinichik, Joe	OG	6-5	300	9	North Carolina St.	10/10
54	Miller, Doug	ILB	6-3	232	2	South Dakota St.	8/0
94	Mims, Chris	DE-DT	6-5	290	3	Tennessee	16/7
41	Mitchell, Shannon	TE	6-2	245	R	Georgia	—
77	Moten, Eric	OG-OT	6-2	306	4	Michigan State	4/4

1994 PREVIEW ■ SAN DIEGO

1994 PLAYER ROSTER

NO.	NAME	POS.	HT.	WT.	EXP.	COLLEGE	GP/GS
61	Munoz, Jose	OG	6-3	280	R	Ball State	—
91	O'Neal, Leslie	DE	6-4	265	9	Oklahoma State	16/16
86	Pupunu, Alfred	TE	6-2	252	3	Weber State	16/6
76	Ramaekers, Kevin	DT	6-4	278	R	Nebraska	—
24	Richard, Stanley	FS	6-2	197	4	Texas	16/16
43	Rivers, Ron	RB	5-8	200	R	Fresno State	—
65	Rodahaffer, Chris	OT	6-5	295	R	San Diego State	—
55	Seau, Junior	ILB	6-3	250	5	Southern Cal	16/16
84	Seay, Mark	WR	6-0	175	2	Long Beach State	1/0
63	Smoot, Raymond	OG-OT	6-4	305	1	Louisiana State	—
8	Snyder, Sean	P	6-2	187	1	Kansas State	0/0
59	Stanley, Isreal	DE	6-2	250	1	Arizona State	—
1	Sullivan, Kent	P	6-0	202	2	California-Lutheran	—
72	Swayne, Harry	OT	6-5	295	8	Rutgers	11/11
17	Thomas, Chris	WR	6-1	180	1	Cal Poly-SLO	0/0
79	Thomas, Cornell	DE	6-3	250	R	West Georgia State	—
26	Thomas, Sean	CB	6-1	189	R	Duke	—
47	Thompson, Chris	LB	6-0	253	R	Bowie State (Md.)	—
25	Vanhorse, Sean	CB	5-10	180	5	Howard	15/10
69	Ward, Jim	DT	6-3	288	R	Slippery Rock (Pa.)	—
30	Watson, Darrius	FS	6-0	193	R	Louisville	—
90	White, Reggie	DT	6-4	300	3	North Carolina A&T	8/0
64	Whitley, Curtis	C	6-1	288	3	Clemson	14/0
76	Wilbert, Patrick	DT	6-4	330	R	Angelo State	—
57	Williams, Jerrol	OLB	6-4	240	6	Purdue	6/5
27	Williams, Michael	CB-S	5-10	185	1	UCLA	0/0
4	Wyatt, Earnest	WR	5-8	175	R	Northeast Louisiana	—
87	Young, Duane	TE	6-1	270	4	Michigan State	16/15

'94 DRAFT PICKS

RD.	NAME	POS.	HT.	WT.	COLLEGE
2.	Davis, Isaac	OG	6-3	324	Arkansas
2.	Parker, Vaughn	OG	6-2	305	UCLA
3.	Coleman, Andre	WR	5-9	165	Kansas State
3.	Clark, Willie	DB	5-10	180	Notre Dame
5.	Laing, Aaron	TE	6-2	261	New Mexico State
5.	Harrison, Rodney	DB	6-0	195	Western Illinois
5.	Krein, Darren	DE	6-3	264	Miami (Fla.)
5.	Vinson, Tony	RB	6-2	225	Towson State (Md.)
7.	Beehn, Zane	LB	6-4	252	Kentucky

PRO FOOTBALL WEEKLY 1994 ALMANAC

TEAM AT A GLANCE

TEAM DIRECTORY

Address	San Diego Jack Murphy Stadium P.O. Box 609609 San Diego, California 92160 (619) 280-2111
Stadium	San Diego Jack Murphy Stadium 9449 Friars Road San Diego, California 92108 Capacity: 60,836 Playing surface: Grass
Training Camp	Univ. of California-San Diego La Jolla, California 92037
Colors	Navy blue, white and gold
Television	KNSD, Channel 39
Radio	XTRA, 690 AM

ADMINISTRATION
Chairman of the board-president: Alex G. Spanos
Vice chairman: Dean A. Spanos
Vice president-finance: Jeremiah T. Murphy
General manager: Bobby Beathard
Assistant general manager: Dick Daniels
Director of player personnel: Billy Devaney
Director of pro personnel: Rudy Feldman
Director of college scouting: John Hinek
Coordinator of football operations: Marty Hurney
Director of public relations: Bill Johnston
Business manager: Pat Curran
Director of marketing: Rich Israel
Director of ticket operations: Joe Scott
Trainer: Keoki Kamau

1994 SCHEDULE

Preseason
JULY 30	vs. Atlanta (at Canton, O.)	12:00
AUG. 6	vs. Houston (at San Antonio)	7:00
AUG. 13	vs. N.Y. Giants (at Berlin)	*1:30
AUG. 18	SAN FRANCISCO	5:00
AUG. 25	L.A. RAMS	7:00

*Eastern Time

Regular season
SEP. 4	at Denver	6:00
SEP. 11	CINCINNATI	1:00
SEP. 18	at Seattle	1:00
SEP. 25	at L.A. Raiders	1:00
OCT. 2	OPEN DATE	
OCT. 9	KANSAS CITY	1:00
OCT. 16	at New Orleans	3:00
OCT. 23	DENVER	1:00
OCT. 30	SEATTLE	1:00
NOV. 6	at Atlanta	1:00
NOV. 13	at Kansas City	12:00
NOV. 20	at New England	1:00
NOV. 27	L.A. RAMS	1:00
DEC. 5	L.A. RAIDERS (Mon.)	6:00
DEC. 11	SAN FRANCISCO	1:00
DEC. 18	at N.Y. Jets	1:00
DEC. 24	PITTSBURGH	1:00

HEAD COACH
Bobby Ross
In his rookie NFL head-coaching season of 1992, Ross orchestrated one of the biggest turnarounds in NFL history. After a slow start, the Chargers won 11 of their final 12 regular-season games to go 11-5 and capture the AFC Western Division title for the first time since 1981. In his second season, the Chargers finished with a mark of 8-8 and failed to make the playoffs. Ross spent 15 years as a head coach at the collegiate level, amassing a record of 94-76-2. In the college ranks his biggest success was the resurrection of the Georgia Tech program. He took over in 1987 and the team finished 2-9. By 1990, Georgia Tech had improved to 11-0-1 and captured a share of the national championship. Born Dec. 23, 1936, Richmond, Va.

Previous NFL: offensive backs, 1980-81 Kansas City; special teams-defense, 1978-79 Kansas City.

Previous college: head coach, 1987-91 Georgia Tech; head coach, 1982-87 Maryland; head coach, 1973-77 The Citadel; assistant coach, 1972 Maryland; assistant coach, 1971 Rice; assistant coach, 1967-70 William & Mary; assistant coach, 1965-66 Virginia Military Institute.

Player: No NFL. College, quarterback-defensive back, 1958-59 Virginia Military Institute.

ASSISTANT COACHES
Bill Arnsparger: defensive coordinator
Previous NFL: defensive coordinator, 1992-93 San Diego; 1974-76 N.Y. Giants (head coach); 1970-73, 1976-83 Miami; 1964-69 Baltimore. Player: No NFL. College: tackle, 1946-49 Miami (Ohio).

Sylvester Croom: offensive backs
Previous NFL: offensive backs, 1992-93 San Diego; 1991 Indianapolis; 1987-90 Tampa Bay. Player: NFL, center, 1975 New Orleans. College: center, 1971-74 Alabama.

John Dunn: strength and conditioning
Previous NFL: strength and conditioning, 1990-93 San Diego; 1987-89 L.A. Raiders; 1984-86 Washington. Player: No NFL. College: guard, 1974-77 Penn State.

Frank Falks: tight ends/H-backs
Previous NFL: None. Player: No NFL. College: None.

Ralph Friedgen: offensive coordinator
Previous NFL: tight ends/running-game coordinator, 1992-93 San Diego. Player: No NFL. College: guard, 1967-68 Maryland.

Dale Lindsey: linebackers
Previous NFL: linebackers, 1992-93 San Diego; 1991 Tampa Bay; 1990 New England; 1986-87 Green Bay; 1974 Cleveland. Player: NFL, linebacker, 1965-73 Cleveland. College: linebacker, 1961-64 Western Kentucky.

Carl Mauck: offensive line
Previous NFL: offensive line, 1992-93 San Diego; 1991 Tampa Bay; 1986-88 Kansas City; 1982-85 New Orleans. Player: NFL, center, 1969 Baltimore; 1970 Miami; 1971-74 San Diego; 1975-

204

1994 PREVIEW ■ SAN DIEGO

TEAM AT A GLANCE

81 Houston. College: center, 1966-68 Southern Illinois.

John Misciagna: quality control
Previous NFL: quality control, 1992-93 San Diego. Player: No NFL. College: guard, 1973-76 Dickinson College.

Dennis Murphy: defensive line
Previous NFL: None. Player: No NFL. College: defensive lineman, tight end, 1960-62 Notre Dame.

Kevin O'Dea: defensive assistant
Previous NFL: None. Player: No NFL. College: None.

Dwaine Painter: quarterbacks
Previous NFL: wide receivers, 1992-93 Indianapolis; 1988-91 Pittsburgh. Player: No NFL. College: quarterback, defensive back, 1961-64 Rutgers.

Chuck Priefer: special teams
Previous NFL: special teams, 1992-93 San Diego; 1984-85 Green Bay. Player: No NFL. College: None.

Willie Shaw: secondary
Previous NFL: defensive backs, 1992-93 Minnesota; 1985-88 Detroit. Player: No NFL. College: cornerback, 1966-68 New Mexico.

Jerry Sullivan: wide receivers
Previous NFL: wide receivers, 1992-93 San Diego. Player: No NFL. College: quarterback, 1963-64 Florida State.

COACHING RECORDS

Years	Coach	W	L	T
1960-69	Sid Gillman	83	51	6
1969-70	Charlie Waller	9	7	3
1971	Sid Gillman	4	6	0
1971-73	Harland Svare	7	17	2
1973	Ron Waller	1	5	0
1974-78	Tommy Prothro	21	39	0
1978-86	Don Coryell	72	60	0
1986-88	Al Saunders	17	22	0
1989-91	Dan Henning	16	32	0
1992-93	Bobby Ross	20	14	0

HISTORICAL HIGHLIGHTS

1960 Los Angeles is awarded a charter membership in the AFL, the franchise going to Barron Hilton. The team is named the Chargers. ... The Chargers take the AFL Western Division title with a record of 10-4. ... The Los Angeles Chargers fall to Houston 24-16 in the first AFL championship game before a crowd of 32,183 at Jeppesen Stadium in Houston.

1961 The Chargers move to San Diego and will play in Balboa Stadium. ... San Diego wins the AFL West with a record of 12-2 but lose again to Houston 10-3 in the AFL championship game in San Diego.

1963-64 San Diego clinches the AFL West by winning 11 of its 14 games. ... The Chargers win their first AFL championship, defeating Boston 51-10.

1964 The Chargers take their fourth AFL West title in five years, posting a record of 8-5-1, but they fall to the Bills in the AFL title game in Buffalo 20-7.

1965 The Chargers win their fifth AFC Western Division title in six years with a record of 9-2-3 but again are deprived of the title by Buffalo, who beats them 23-0 in San Diego.

1966 The Chargers are purchased for a record $10 million by a syndicate of 21 business executives headed by Eugene V. Klein and Sam Schulman.

1967 The Chargers move into new San Diego Stadium.

1969 Lance Alworth sets a pro football record with pass receptions in 96 consecutive games, bettering the mark held by Don Hutson.

1979 Dan Fouts sets an NFL record of four consecutive 300-yard passing games. ... The Chargers beat New Orleans 35-0 to secure their first playoff berth in 14 years. They win their first division title since 1965 with a record of 12-4. ... Dan Fouts breaks the record for passing yardage in a season by gaining 4,082. ... In the AFC divisional playoff San Diego loses to Houston 17-14.

1980-81 With a record of 11-5, San Diego again wins the AFC West. After a 20-14 win over Buffalo in the playoffs, the Chargers fall to Oakland 34-27. ... San Diego Stadium is renamed Jack Murphy Stadium after the late sports editor of the *San Diego Union*.

1981-82 For the third straight year the Chargers win the AFC West, this time with a record of 10-6. ... Dan Fouts breaks the NFL passing yardage record, with 4,802 yards. ... The Chargers take a dramatic 41-38 victory over Miami in one of the epic games in NFL playoff history; Rolf Benirschke kicked the game-winning, 27-yard field goal in overtime. But then, in what may have been the coldest game in NFL history, with a wind-chill factor of 59-below zero and temperature of minus-9, the Chargers lose to the Cincinnati Bengals 27-7.

1982-83 With a record of 6-3 in a strike-shortened season, San Diego earns its way to the playoffs for the fourth straight year. The Chargers take the first-round playoff game against Pittsburgh 31-28, but San Diego is defeated in the second round by Miami 34-13.

1984 In the fourth quarter of a game against Pittsburgh, WR Charlie Joiner sets an NFL record with his 650th pass reception.

1990 Former Washington Redskin executive Bobby Beathard is hired as general manager of the Chargers.

1992-93 The Chargers earn a place in the playoffs for the first time in a decade and then defeat Kansas City 17-0 in an AFC wild-card game. ... San Diego loses 31-0 to Miami in the divisional playoffs.

PRO FOOTBALL WEEKLY 1994 ALMANAC

TEAM AT A GLANCE

HALL OF FAME MEMBERS

	Yrs with Chargers	Inducted
WR Lance Alworth	1962-70	1978
OT Ron Mix	1960-69	1979
Coach Sid Gillman	1960-69, 71	1983
QB Dan Fouts	1973-87	1993

RETIRED JERSEY NUMBERS
14 QB Dan Fouts

FIRST-ROUND DRAFT CHOICES
(since 1980)

Year	Selection	College
1980	No choice	
1981	RB James Brooks	Auburn
1982	No choice	
1983	LB Billy Ray Smith	Arkansas
	RB Gary Anderson	Arkansas
	CB Gill Byrd	San Jose State
1984	CB Mossy Cade	Texas
1985	OT Jim Lachey	Ohio State
1986	DE Leslie O'Neal	Oklahoma State
	OT James FitzPatrick	Southern Cal
1987	TE Rod Bernstine	Texas A&M
1988	WR Anthony Miller	Tennessee
1989	DE Burt Grossman	Pittsburgh
1990	LB Junior Seau	Southern Cal
1991	DB Stanley Richard	Texas
1992	DE Chris Mims	Tennessee
1993	CB Darrien Gordon	Stanford
1994	No choice	

RECORD VS. OTHER NFL TEAMS
(including postseason games)

	Record
Arizona Cardinals	5-1-0
Atlanta Falcons	1-3-0
Buffalo Bills	17-9-2
Chicago Bears	4-2-0
Cincinnati Bengals	12-9-0
Cleveland Browns	8-6-1
Dallas Cowboys	1-4-0
Denver Broncos	32-35-1
Detroit Lions	2-3-0
Green Bay Packers	1-4-0
Houston Oilers	17-17-1
Indianapolis Colts	9-5-0
Kansas City Chiefs	32-35-1
Los Angeles Raiders	25-42-2
Los Angeles Rams	2-3-0
Miami Dolphins	11-7-0
Minnesota Vikings	4-3-0
New England Patriots	12-13-2
New Orleans Saints	4-1-0
New York Giants	2-4-0
New York Jets	16-9-1
Philadelphia Eagles	3-2-0
Pittsburgh Steelers	5-14-0
San Francisco 49ers	3-3-0
Seattle Seahawks	15-15-0
Tampa Bay Buccaneers	6-0-0
Washington Redskins	0-5-0

YEAR-BY-YEAR RECORDS

Year	Won	Lost	Tied	Year	Won	Lost	Tied
1960**	10	4	0	1977	7	7	0
1961**	12	2	0	1978	9	7	0
1962	4	10	0	1979**	12	4	0
1963***	11	3	0	1980**	11	5	0
1964**	8	5	1	1981**	10	6	0
1965**	9	2	3	1982**	6	3	0
1966	7	6	1	1983	6	10	0
1967	8	5	1	1984	7	9	0
1968	9	5	0	1985	8	8	0
1969	8	6	0	1986	4	12	0
1970	5	6	3	1987	8	7	0
1971	6	8	0	1988	6	10	0
1972	4	9	1	1989	6	10	0
1973	2	11	1	1990	6	10	0
1974	5	9	0	1991	4	12	0
1975	2	12	0	1992**	11	5	0
1976	6	8	0	1993	8	8	0
				Total	245	244	11

Number of NFL championships 0
Number of years .500 or better 19
Number of years below .500 15

*NFL champions
**Playoff team
*** AFL champions (before the merger)

1994 PREVIEW ■ SAN DIEGO

RECORDS

INDIVIDUAL

Service
Seasons played	15	Russ Washington (1968-82)
		Dan Fouts (1973-87)
Games played	200	Russ Washington (1968-82)
Consecutive games	178	Russ Washington (1968-82)

Scoring
Points, career	766	Rolf Benirschke (1977-86)
Points, season	119	Rolf Benirschke (1980)
Points, game	30	Kellen Winslow (11/22/81)
Touchdowns, career	83	Lance Alworth (1962-70)
Touchdowns, season	19	Chuck Muncie (1981)
Touchdowns, game	5	Kellen Winslow (11/22/81)
Field goals, career	146	Rolf Benirschke (1977-86)
Field goals, season	31	John Carney (1993)
Field goals, game	6	John Carney (9/5/93, 9/19/93)
Extra points, career	328	Rolf Benirschke (1977-86)
Extra points, season	55	Rolf Benirschke (1981)
Extra points, game	7	By many players

Rushing
Yards, career	4,963	Paul Lowe (1960-67)
Yards, season	1,225	Marion Butts (1990)
Yards, game	217	Gary Anderson (12/18/88)
Attempts, career	1,031	Marion Butts (1989-93)
Attempts, season	296	Earnest Jackson (1984)
Attempts, game	39	Marion Butts (12/17/89)
Touchdowns, career	43	Chuck Muncie (1980-84)
Touchdowns, season	19	Chuck Muncie (1981)
Touchdowns, game	4	Clarence Williams (9/16/79)
		Chuck Muncie (11/29/81)

Passing
Rating, career	80.2	Dan Fouts (1973-87)
Completions, career	3,297	Dan Fouts (1973-87)
Completions, season	360	Dan Fouts (1981)
Completions, game	37	Dan Fouts (11/18/84)
		Mark Herrmann (12/22/85)
Yards, career	43,040	Dan Fouts (1973-87)
Yards, season	4,802	Dan Fouts (1981)
Yards, game	444	Dan Fouts (10/19/80 & 12/11/82)
Attempts, career	5,604	Dan Fouts (1973-87)
Attempts, season	609	Dan Fouts (1981)
Attempts, game	58	Mark Herrmann (12/22/85)
Touchdowns, career	254	Dan Fouts (1973-87)
Touchdowns, season	33	Dan Fouts (1981)
Touchdowns, game	6	Dan Fouts (11/22/81)

Receiving
Receptions, career	586	Charlie Joiner (1976-86)
Receptions, season	89	Kellen Winslow (1980)
Receptions, game	15	Kellen Winslow (10/7/84)
Yards, career	9,585	Lance Alworth (1962-70)
Yards, season	1,602	Lance Alworth (1965)
Yards, game	260	Wes Chandler (12/20/82)
Touchdowns, career	81	Lance Alworth (1962-70)
Touchdowns, season	14	Lance Alworth (1965)
Touchdowns, game	5	Kellen Winslow (12/1/68)

Interceptions
Career	42	Gill Byrd (1983-92)
Season	9	Charlie McNeil (1961)
Game	3	By many players

Sacks
Career	80.5	Leslie O'Neal (1986-93)
Season	17.5	Gary Johnson (1980)
Game	5	Leslie O'Neal (11/16/86)

Longest plays
Run from scrimmage	87	Paul Lowe (TD, 9/10/61)
Pass play	91	Jack Kemp to Keith Lincoln (TD, 11/12/61)
Field goal	54	John Carney (11/10/91)
Interception return	103	Vencie Glenn (TD, 11/29/87)
Kickoff return	103	Keith Lincoln (TD, 9/16/62)
Punt return	95	Leslie Duncan (TD, 11/24/68)
Punt	82	Paul Maguire (11/19/61)

Top scorers
	Points
Rolf Benirschke (1977-86)	766
Lance Alworth (1962-70)	500
John Carney (1990-93)	409
Dennis Partee (1968-75)	380
Gary Garrison (1966-76)	348
Charlie Joiner (1976-86)	282

Top rushers
	Yards
Paul Lowe (1960-67)	4,963
Marion Butts (1989-93)	4,297
Chuck Muncie (1980-84)	3,309
Don Woods (1974-80)	2,858
Keith Lincoln (1960-66)	2,698
Dick Post (1967-70)	2,519

Top passers
	Completions
Dan Fouts (1973-87)	3,297
John Hadl (1962-72)	1,824
Stan Humphries (1992-93)	436
John Friesz (1990-93)	401
Jack Kemp (1960-62)	389
Billy Joe Tolliver (1989-90)	305

Top passers
	Yards
Dan Fouts (1973-87)	43,040
John Hadl (1962-72)	26,938
Jack Kemp (1960-62)	5,996
Stan Humphries (1992-93)	5,337
John Friesz (1990-93)	4,396
Billy Joe Tolliver (1989-90)	3,671

Top receivers
	Receptions
Charlie Joiner (1976-86)	586
Kellen Winslow (1979-87)	541
Lance Alworth (1962-70)	493
Gary Garrison (1966-76)	404
Anthony Miller (1988-93)	374
Wes Chandler (1981-87)	373

Top receivers
	Yards
Lance Alworth (1962-70)	9,585
Charlie Joiner (1976-86)	9,203
Gary Garrison (1966-76)	7,533
Kellen Winslow (1979-87)	6,741
Wes Chandler (1981-87)	6,132
Anthony Miller (1988-93)	5,582

Most interceptions
	No.
Gill Byrd (1983-93)	42
Dick Harris (1960-65)	29
Kenny Graham (1964-69)	25
Mike Williams (1975-82)	24
Joe Beauchamp (1966-74)	22
Woodrow Lowe (1976-86)	21

Most sacks
	No.
Leslie O'Neal (1986-93)	80.5
Gary Johnson (1975-84)	67
Lee Williams (1984-90)	66.5

207

PRO FOOTBALL WEEKLY 1994 ALMANAC

PREVIEW: SAN FRANCISCO 49ERS

All or nothing.

When a franchise is as successful as the 49ers have been, nothing short of a Super Bowl victory will do.

The past two seasons the 49ers have had campaigns that would be thrilling to most organizations, earning berths in the NFC championship game against the Cowboys both times. But losses to Dallas in both of those games, however, have left the 49ers with an unsatisfied feeling. With that as a backdrop, the 49ers have spent this offseason taking dead aim on the Super Bowl.

"We had a pretty good season last year," said 49er coach George Seifert. "We didn't wind up where we wanted to be, though. We didn't win the championship, and that's what we are supposed to do. So, now we're trying to do everything we can to get ourselves back in position."

To do that, the 49ers have spent a busy offseason trying to upgrade a defense that allowed a total of 68 points in the two NFC championship game losses to Dallas.

For starters, the 49ers made sweeping changes at linebacker, signing ex-Cowboy Ken Norton and former Charger Gary Plummer as free agents.

Norton earned a Pro Bowl berth last season and never missed a game, even though he suffered a biceps injury in October. He should add versatility and speed to a 49er defense in need of play makers. He is also known as a vocal team leader.

"One of the things he brings is that attitude," said Seifert. "He's got that football-playing ability to go along with that attitude."

San Francisco president Carmen Policy said, "He's not just a talent. He's a presence because of his personality and his reputation. He'll be great for us."

Plummer's primary responsibility will be to shore up a 49er run defense that ranked 28th last season in average gain per rush allowed.

"Basically, they feel that I'm going to be a guy they can count on to stop the run," said Plummer. "And that's fine. The expectations that they had for me aren't any more than I had for myself, so it's not like there's going to be added pressure."

The 49ers continued to upgrade the defense during the offseason when they traded up in the first round to take DT Bryant Young with the seventh overall pick.

"We think we got a football player that can help our defense, which is a concern of ours," said Seifert. "He's got very good size, and he does have excellent movement."

He'll also have an excellent sidekick in DT Dana Stubblefield, who had a team-high 10.5 sacks and proved to be a disruptive force to the opposition last season as a rookie. Stubblefield's strength is exploding through gaps into the backfield.

DE Dennis Brown is incredibly quick and mobile for his size, but he has been a hot-and-cold performer who excels in spurts but wears down quickly because he is out of shape. DE Todd Kelly was a bust as a rookie, but he was thrown in before he was ready, got hammered and lost his confidence. DE-OLB Martin Harrison can provide a solid pass rush. Artie Smith and Karl Wilson saw quite a bit of action last season and did a good job.

Joining Norton and Plummer at linebacker will be John Johnson, who is very active and has outstanding speed for the position. He is not very instinctive or physical, however. Mike Walter

Jerry Rice

PHOTO BY DAVID NELSON

1994 PREVIEW ■ SAN FRANCISCO

has provided the 49ers with many good seasons, but he is on the downside of his career. Troy Wilson is a situational pass rusher who is too small to be an every-down player. Help could also come from Kevin Mitchell, one of the 49ers' second-round draft choices this year.

Besides the addition of Norton, Plummer and Young, the 49ers hope to improve on defense because of a returning player. Tim McDonald started at strong safety and made the Pro Bowl last season, his first as a 49er, but he did not make nearly as many impact plays as he did the previous year, when he played for the Cardinals. The 49ers are not down on McDonald, but they hope he will play better this season, now that he has had a chance to learn their scheme.

Former first-round pick Dana Hall has not lived up to expectations at free safety, despite having excellent size and speed, while former CB Merton Hanks has looked a lot more natural and instinctive. Other than a couple of bad games, Eric Davis played some of the best cornerback in the NFL last season. He is the club's best coverage man. Michael McGruder led the team with five interceptions last year while playing in the team's dime scheme. Adrian Hardy is raw, but he could come on if he gets playing time. Second-round draft choice Tyronne Drakeford should help at cornerback.

While the 49ers are looking for a lot of improvement on defense, there may not be room for much improvement on offense. During the 1993 season, the 49er offense ranked first in the league in total yards, average gain per rush, average gain per pass play, average gain per offensive play, first downs, third-down efficiency and points per game.

Everywhere you look, there are stars.

At quarterback there is Steve Young, who has led the NFL in passing efficiency the past three years. In fact, he has become the first quarterback in league history to have a 100-plus passer rating three years in a row. Young continues to make the transition from a running quarterback who can throw to a passing quarterback who has the added dimension of being a terrific runner. He is showing the ability to stay in the pocket longer and distribute the ball better. Nonetheless, until Young and the 49ers win a Super Bowl, he will always live in the shadow of former 49er legend Joe Montana. When Steve Bono went to Kansas City, the 49ers found themselves without a backup who had a lot of experience and first-hand knowledge of the San Francisco offense.

Ricky Watters can be self-centered, temperamental and egotistical, but he is also a terrific running back. He runs very hard and has tremendous power, toughness and an ability to make people miss. Tom Rathman is not the fullback he once was, and Marc Logan does a good job of running but is not a pure fullback. The fullback of the future appears to be first-round draft choice William Floyd, a powerful, complementary-type back who catches well and does a pretty good job as a ballcarrier.

WR Jerry Rice had, by his standards, an average year in 1993. Of course, by anyone else's standards, he had a phenomenal season. Despite dropping a lot of passes in the first month of the season, Rice still caught 98 passes for 1,503 yards and 15 touchdowns. Quite simply, he is in a league of his own. Rice doesn't have eye-popping stopwatch speed, but he appears to have blazing speed when the ball is in the air. Both Rice and John Taylor do a terrific job of blocking and running after the catch. Taylor is not the receiver that Rice is, but, at one time, he was an even better runner after the catch. However, injuries seem to have taken a little something out of him. Third-round pick Cory Fleming could provide some depth at wide receiver, as could Nate Singleton. TE Brent Jones is a Pro Bowl possession receiver with superb hand-eye coordination and a great feel for the passing game.

The 49ers have an outstanding one-two punch along the offensive line at tackle. Harris Barton may be the best pass-blocking right tackle in football. OLT Steve Wallace is not quite as agile as Barton, but he may be a little more powerful and definitely has a broader blocking base. Guy McIntyre is one of the game's best pulling guards, but he is small, and the 49ers may have a hard time keeping him because of the salary cap. After a shaky start last season, Ralph Tamm developed into an adequate replacement for the injured Roy Foster. C Jesse Sapolu is a very solid performer who plays the game on his feet. Harry Boatswain has developed into the ranking reserve along the offensive line, and the 49ers are starting to grow more comfortable when he has to play. Alec Millen and Brian Bollinger both look like they have futures along the line.

Special teams are an area the 49ers need to improve this season. Mike Cofer has been one of the five worst placekickers in the NFL the past three years, and, with this in mind, San Francisco drafted Doug Brien in the third round. P Klaus Wilmsmeyer could also be on the bubble after averaging 40.9 yards with a 34.5 net, but the 49ers seemed to feel he did a decent job last year, since very few of his punts were returned. Dexter Carter can be a dangerous return man, but he also had a couple of costly fumbles in a late-season loss to the Falcons last year.

FAST FACTS

■ Steve Young passed for 4,023 yards in 1993, the first time a 49er quarterback ever surpassed 4,000. He is also the first player to lead the NFL in passing three straight years

■ Jerry Rice has had 80 or more catches and double-digit touchdowns in each of the last five seasons. His 124 career touchdowns is only two behind Jim Brown's record of 126.

■ The 49er defense ranked 28th in the NFL last season in average gain per rush allowed.

PRO FOOTBALL WEEKLY 1994 ALMANAC

1994 PLAYER ROSTER

NO.	NAME	POS.	HT.	WT.	EXP.	COLLEGE	GP/GS
48	Bernes, Tomur	CB	5-10	188	1	North Texas	0/0
79	Barton, Harris	OT	6-4	286	8	North Carolina	15/15
83	Beach, Sanjay	WR	6-1	194	4	Colorado State	9/0
65	Boatswain, Harry	OT	6-4	295	4	New Haven	16/2
71	Bollinger, Brian	OG	6-5	285	3	North Carolina	16/0
15	Bridewell, Jeff	QB	6-5	220	1	Cal-Davis	0/0
96	Brown, Dennis	DE	6-4	290	5	Washington	16/16
7	Browning, Alphonzo	WR	6-2	203	R	Kentucky	—
66	Bryant, Junior	DE	6-4	275	1	Notre Dame	0/0
90	Burnett, Bryce	TE	6-3	225	1	San Jose State	0/0
86	Carolan, Brett	TE	6-3	241	R	Washington State	—
35	Carter, Dexter	RB	5-9	174	5	Florida State	16/0
67	Collins, Ron	OG	6-5	289	R	Fresno State	—
50	Dalman, Chris	OG-C	6-3	285	2	Stanford	15/0
25	Davis, Eric	CB	5-11	178	5	Jacksonville State	16/16
63	Deese, Derrick	OG	6-3	270	3	Southern Cal	0/0
67	Foster, Roy	OG	6-4	290	13	Southern Cal	1/0
78	Fountaine, Jamal	DE	6-3	240	R	Washington	—
18	Grbac, Elvis	QB	6-5	232	1	Michigan	0/0
28	Hall, Dana	S	6-2	206	3	Washington	13/7
36	Hanks, Merton	S	6-2	185	4	Iowa	16/14
45	Hardy, Adrian	CB	5-11	194	2	NW State (La.)	10/0
49	Hillman, Jay	FB	6-0	230	1	Boston University	0/0
20	Ivlow, John	FB	5-11	226	2	Colorado State	2/0
23	Jefferson, Anthony	CB	5-11	197	R	Sonoma State	—
55	Johnson, John	LB	6-3	230	4	Clemson	15/12
84	Jones, Brent	TE	6-4	230	8	Santa Clara	16/16
30	Kellogg, Jackie	CB	6-1	188	R	Eastern Washington	—
58	Kelly, Todd	DE	6-2	259	2	Tennessee	14/5
43	Logan, Marc	FB	6-0	212	7	Kentucky	14/11
46	McDonald, Tim	S	6-2	215	8	Southern Cal	16/16
62	McIntyre, Guy	OG	6-3	276	11	Georgia	16/16
76	Millen, Alec	OT	6-7	285	1	Georgia	0/0
14	Musgrave, Bill	QB	6-2	205	4	Oregon	1/0
51	Norton, Jr., Ken	LB	6-2	241	7	UCLA	16/16
81	Owens, Darrick	WR	6-2	216	1	Mississippi	0/0
58	Pay, Garry	C	6-4	285	1	Brigham Young	0/0
50	Plummer, Gary	LB	6-2	247	9	California	16/15
49	Popson, Ted	TE	6-4	250	1	Portland State	0/0
57	Preston, P.J.	LB	6-2	221	R	Virginia Tech	—
44	Rathman, Tom	FB	6-1	232	9	Nebraska	8/4
80	Rice, Jerry	WR	6-2	200	10	Miss. Valley State	16/16
38	Russell, Damien	S	6-1	204	3	Virginia Tech	16/0
61	Sapolu, Jesse	C	6-4	278	12	Hawaii	16/16
88	Singleton, Nate	WR	5-11	190	3	Grambling	16/0
95	Smtih, Artie	DE	6-4	303	2	Louisiana Tech	16/5
94	Stubblefield, Dana	DE	6-2	302	2	Kansas	16/14
64	Tamm, Ralph	OG	6-4	280	7	West Chester	16/16
82	Taylor, John	WR	6-1	185	9	Delaware State	16/16
72	Thomas, Mark	DE	6-3	273	3	North Carolina St.	11/1
5	Thompson, Tom	P	5-10	192	R	Oregon	—
27	Walker, Adam	RB	6-1	210	2	Pittsburgh	1/0
74	Wallace, Steve	OT	6-5	280	9	Auburn	15/15
99	Walter, Mike	LB	6-3	246	12	Oregon	15/9
32	Watters, Ricky	RB	6-1	212	4	Notre Dame	13/13

210

1994 PREVIEW ■ SAN FRANCISCO

1994 PLAYER ROSTER

NO.	NAME	POS.	HT.	WT.	EXP.	COLLEGE	GP/GS
10	Wilmsmeyer, Klaus	P	6-1	210	3	Louisville	15/0
77	Wilson, Karl	DE	6-5	277	7	Louisiana State	5/2
92	Wilson, Troy	DE	6-4	235	2	Pittsburg St. (Kan.)	10/0
93	Young, Alan	DE	6-3	253	R	Vanderbilt	—
8	Young, Steve	QB	6-2	205	10	Brigham Young	16/16

'94 DRAFT PICKS

RD.	NAME	POS.	HT.	WT.	COLLEGE
1.	Young, Bryant	DT	6-3	276	Notre Dame
1.	Floyd, William	FB	6-1	242	Florida State
2.	Mitchell, Kevin	LB	6-1	260	Syracuse
2.	Drakeford, Tyronne	DB	5-9	187	Virginia Tech
3.	Brien, Doug	PK	5-11	179	California
3.	Fleming, Corey	WR	6-1	212	Tennessee
5.	Peterson, Anthony	LB	6-0	225	Notre Dame
6.	Woodall, Lee	LB	6-0	220	Westchester (Pa.)

PRO FOOTBALL WEEKLY 1994 ALMANAC

TEAM AT A GLANCE

TEAM DIRECTORY

Address	4949 Centennial Boulevard
	Santa Clara, California 95054
	(408) 562-4949
Stadium	Candlestick Park
	San Francisco, California 94124
	Capacity: 66,513
	Playing surface: Grass
Training Camp	Sierra Community College
	Rocklin, California 95677
Colors	Gold and scarlet
Television	KTVU, Channel 2
Radio	KGO, 810 AM

ADMINISTRATION
Owner: Edward J. DeBartolo Jr.
President: Carmen Policy
Vice president-football administration: John McVay
Vice president-business operations: Keith Simon
Coordinator of football operations: Dwight Clark
Director of pro personnel: Allan Webb
Director of college scouting: Vinny Cerrato
Director of marketing-promotions: Laurie Albrecht
Director of public relations: Rodney Knox
Executive assistant-alumni coordinator: R.C. Owens
Ticket manager: Lynn Carrozzi
Trainer: Lindsy McLean

1994 SCHEDULE

Preseason

AUG. 5	at Arizona	6:30
AUG. 12	DENVER	5:00
AUG. 18	at San Diego	5:00
AUG. 26	SEATTLE	6:00

Regular season

SEP. 5	L.A. RAIDERS (Mon.)	6:00
SEP. 11	at Kansas City	12:00
SEP. 18	at L.A. Rams	1:00
SEP. 25	NEW ORLEANS	1:00
OCT. 2	PHILADELPHIA	1:00
OCT. 9	at Detroit	1:00
OCT. 16	at Atlanta	1:00
OCT. 23	TAMPA BAY	1:00
OCT. 30	OPEN DATE	
NOV. 6	at Washington	1:00
NOV. 13	DALLAS	1:00
NOV. 20	L.A. RAMS	5:00
NOV. 28	at New Orleans (Mon.)	8:00
DEC. 4	ATLANTA	1:00
DEC. 11	at San Diego	1:00
DEC. 17	DENVER (Sat.)	1:00
DEC. 26	at Minnesota (Mon.)	8:00

HEAD COACH
George Seifert

After serving as an assistant coach in the 49er organization for nine seasons, Seifert was named the successor to Bill Walsh prior to the 1989 season. Before achieving his current position, Seifert was the 49ers' defensive coordinator for six years and a DB coach for three. He also spent several years in the college ranks. In his first year as head coach he guided the 49ers to 14-2 record and a Super Bowl championship, making him only the second coach to win a Super Bowl title in his rookie season. Through five seasons, Seifert has a record of 68-21. Born Jan. 22, 1940, San Francisco, Calif.

Previous NFL: defensive coordinator, 1983-88 San Francisco; secondary, 1980-82 San Francisco.

Previous college: secondary, 1977-79 Stanford; head coach, 1975-76 Cornell; secondary, 1972-74 Stanford; assistant coach, 1967-71 Oregon; assistant coach, 1966 Iowa; head coach, 1965 Westminster College; graduate assistant, 1964 Utah.

Player: No NFL. College, offensive guard, linebacker, 1960-62 Utah.

ASSISTANT COACHES
Jerry Attaway: physical development coordinator
Previous NFL: conditioning, 1983-93 San Francisco. Player: No NFL. College: defensive back, 1967 California-Davis.

Michael Barnes: physical development assistant
Previous NFL: None. Player: No NFL. College: None.

Dwaine Board: defensive line
Previous NFL: defensive assistant, 1991-93 San Francisco. Player: NFL, defensive lineman, 1979-87 San Francisco; 1988 New Orleans. College: defensive lineman, 1974-77 North Carolina A&T.

Tom Holmoe: defensive backs
Previous NFL: None. Player: NFL, defensive back, 1983-89 San Francisco. College: defensive back, 1979-82 Brigham Young.

Carl Jackson: running backs
Previous NFL: running backs, 1992-93 San Francisco. Player: No NFL. College: quarterback, 1959-62 Prairie View A&M.

Larry Kirksey: wide receivers
Previous NFL: None. Player: No NFL. College: wide receiver, 1969-1972 Eastern Kentucky.

Gary Kubiak: quarterbacks
Previous NFL: None. Player: NFL, quarterback, 1983-91 Denver. College: quarterback, 1979-82 Texas A&M.

Alan Lowry: special teams
Previous NFL: special teams, 1992-93 San Francisco; 1991 Tampa Bay; 1982-90 Dallas. Player: No NFL. College: defensive back, quarterback, 1970-72 Texas.

John Marshall: linebackers
Previous NFL: defensive line, 1989-93 San Francisco; 1986-88 Indianapolis; 1983-85 Atlanta; 1980-82 Green Bay. Player: No NFL. College: linebacker, 1964 Washington State.

Bobb McKittrick: offensive line
Previous NFL: offensive line, 1979-93 San Francisco; 1973-78 San Diego; 1971-72 L.A. Rams.

212

1994 PREVIEW ■ SAN FRANCISCO

TEAM AT A GLANCE

Player: No NFL. College: guard, 1955-57 Oregon State.

Bill McPherson: assistant head coach
Previous NFL: defensive coordinator, 1979-93 San Francisco; 1978 Philadelphia. Player: No NFL. College: tackle, 1950-52 Santa Clara.

Ray Rhodes: defensive coordinator
Previous NFL: defensive coordinator, 1992-93 Green Bay; 1981-91 San Francisco. Player: NFL, defensive back 1974-79 N.Y. Giants; 1980 San Francisco. College: running back, wide receiver, 1969-70 Texas Christian, 1972-73 Tulsa.

Mike Shanahan: offensive coordinator
Previous NFL: offensive coordinator-quarterbacks, 1992-93 San Francisco; 1989-91 Denver; 1988-89 L.A. Raiders (head coach); 1984-87 Denver. Player: No NFL. College: quarterback, 1970-73 Eastern Illinois.

Mike Solari: tight ends-offensive line assistant
Previous NFL: tight ends-offensive line assistant, 1992-93 San Francisco; 1989 Phoenix; 1987-88 Dallas. Player: No NFL. College: offensive lineman, 1975-76 San Diego State.

COACHING RECORDS
(including postseason games)

Years	Coach	W	L	T
1950-54	Buck Shaw	33	25	2
1955	Norman "Red" Strader	4	8	0
1956-58	Frankie Albert	19	17	1
1959-63	Red Hickey	27	27	1
1963-67	Jack Christiansen	26	38	3
1968-75	Dick Nolan	56	56	5
1976	Monte Clark	8	6	0
1977	Ken Meyer	5	9	0
1978	Pete McCulley	1	8	0
1978	Fred O'Connor	1	6	0
1979-88	Bill Walsh	102	63	1
1989-93	George Seifert	67	20	0

HISTORICAL HIGHLIGHTS

1946 The 49ers are a charter member of the All-American Football Conference, the franchise ownership going to Tony Morabito.

1948 The 49ers score 495 points in 12 games, an average of more than 41 a game and 106 more than the Browns, but still end up in second place in the AAFC West with a 12-2 record. Both losses were to the undefeated Browns.

1949 In a special playoff series at season's end, the 49ers defeat the Brooklyn/New York Yankees but then fall to the Browns in the AAFC title game 21-7, which is also the last AAFC game.

1950 The 49ers are one of three teams from the defunct AAFC to join the NFL.

1957 The 49ers, with a record of 8-4, end up in a tie with the Detroit Lions for the Western Conference title but lose in a playoff 31-27.

1970 Posting a 10-3 record, their best as an NFL club, the 49ers take the NFC Western Division championship. San Francisco gets to the NFC title game by beating the Vikings, then falls to the Dallas Cowboys 17-10.

1971 In the team's first season in Candlestick Park, the 49ers win their second NFC Western Division title, clinching the crown on the final day by beating Detroit 31-27. ... After whipping the Redskins, San Francisco again faces Dallas in the NFC title game, but the Cowboys again win, this time 14-3.

1972 The 49ers win the division title but are beaten again by the Cowboys in the divisional playoff.

1977 The 49ers are bought by Edward J. DeBartolo Jr.

1981-82 Behind the passing and leadership of Joe Montana, the 49ers post a 13-3 record, win the NFC West title and then the NFC championship by defeating the Cowboys 28-27. ... The 49ers triumph in Super Bowl XVI at the Silverdome in Pontiac, Mich., defeating the Bengals 26-21.

1983 For the second time in three seasons, the 49ers play in the NFC championship game. After a 10-6 season, they beat Detroit 24-23, then lose to Washington 24-21 in the NFC championship.

1984-85 The 49ers win an NFL-record 15 games. The club breaks 14 team records and becomes the first NFC team to sweep all of its conference games. ... San Francisco caps the 1984 season by routing the Miami Dolphins 38-16 in Super Bowl XIX.

1985 After getting off to a slow start, the 49ers qualify for postseason play with a 10-6 record. ... The 49ers lose in the wild-card game, however, to the New York Giants 17-3.

1986 The 49ers post a 10-5-1 record and win the NFC West by beating the 10-6 Rams 24-14 in the last game of the season. San Francisco loses to the eventual Super Bowl-champion Giants 49-3.

1987-88 WR Jerry Rice sets two NFL records with 22 touchdown catches and TD's in 13 consecutive games. ... The 49ers reach the playoffs but lose to Minnesota 36-24 at Candlestick Park.

1988-89 The 49ers march through the playoffs with wins over the Vikings and Bears. San Francisco goes to Super Bowl XXIII and defeats the Cincinnati Bengals 20-16 in the last minute.

1989-90 With a record of 14-2, the 49ers again take the NFC West crown, outscoring thier opponents 442 to 253. ... San Francisco breezes through the playoffs, defeating the Vikings 41-13 and the Rams 30-3. In Super Bowl XXIV, the 49ers run up the biggest margin of victory in the game's history when they defeat the Denver Broncos 55-10.

1990-91 San Francisco again posts a 14-2 record. ... In the playoffs it defeats the Redskins 28-10 but loses the NFC title game to the Giants 15-13.

1992-93 For the third season in a row, the 49ers are 14-2 in the regular season. Again they beat the Redskins in the playoffs 20-13 but lose the NFC championship game to the Cowboys 30-20.

1993-94 San Francisco wins the NFC West with a record of 10-6. It beats the Giants 44-3 in the divisional playoff, but loses to Dallas 38-21 in the NFC title game.

PRO FOOTBALL WEEKLY 1994 ALMANAC

TEAM AT A GLANCE

HALL OF FAME MEMBERS

	Yrs with 49ers	Inducted
DT Leo Nomellini	1950-63	1969
FB Joe Perry	1948-60, 63	1969
HB Hugh McElhenny	1952-60	1970
QB Y.A. Tittle	1951-60	1971
T Bob St. Clair	1953-63	1990
Coach Bill Walsh	1979-88	1993
CB Jimmy Johnson	1961-76	1994

RETIRED JERSEY NUMBERS

- 12 QB John Brodie
- 34 FB Joe Perry
- 37 CB Jimmy Johnson
- 39 HB Hugh McElhenny
- 70 DT Charlie Krueger
- 73 DT Leo Nomellini
- 87 WR Dwight Clark

FIRST-ROUND DRAFT CHOICES
(since 1980)

Year	Selection	College
1980	RB Earl Cooper	Rice
	DE Jim Stuckey	Clemson
1981	DB Ronnie Lott	Southern Cal
1982	No choice	
1983	No choice	
1984	LB Todd Shell	Brigham Young
1985	WR Jerry Rice	Mississippi Valley St.
1986	No choice	
1987	OT Harris Barton	North Carolina
	RB Terrence Flagler	Clemson
1988	No choice	
1989	LB Keith DeLong	Tennessee
1990	RB Dexter Carter	Florida State
1991	NT-DE Ted Washington	Louisville
	RB Ricky Watters	Notre Dame
1992	DB Dana Hall	Washington
1993	DE Dana Stubblefield	Kansas
	DE Todd Kelly	Tennessee
1994	DT Bryant Young	Notre Dame
	FB William Floyd	Florida State

RECORD VS. OTHER NFL TEAMS
(including postseason games)

	Record
Arizona Cardinals	10-9-0
Atlanta Falcons	32-21-1
Buffalo Bills	2-3-0
Chicago Bears	27-25-1
Cincinnati Bengals	8-1-0
Cleveland Browns	6-9-1
Dallas Cowboys	10-11-1
Denver Broncos	3-4-0
Detroit Lions	27-26-1
Green Bay Packers	25-21-1
Houston Oilers	5-3-0
Indianapolis Colts	16-21-0
Kansas City Chiefs	4-1-0
Los Angeles Raiders	2-5-0
Los Angeles Rams	39-48-2
Miami Dolphins	3-4-0
Minnesota Vikings	18-16-1
New England Patriots	6-1-0
New Orleans Saints	33-14-2
New York Giants	13-14-0
New York Jets	6-1-0
Philadelphia Eagles	13-5-1
Pittsburgh Steelers	8-7-0
San Diego Chargers	3-3-0
Seattle Seahawks	4-1-0
Tampa Bay Buccaneers	11-1-0
Washington Redskins	12-7-0

YEAR-BY-YEAR RECORDS

Year	Won	Lost	Tied
1950	3	9	0
1951	7	4	1
1952	7	5	0
1953	9	3	0
1954	7	4	1
1955	4	8	0
1956	5	6	1
1957	8	4	0
1958	6	6	0
1959	7	5	0
1960	7	5	0
1961	7	6	1
1962	6	8	0
1963	2	12	0
1964	4	10	0
1965	7	6	1
1966	6	6	2
1967	7	7	0
1968	7	6	1
1969	4	8	2
1970**	10	3	1
1971**	9	5	0
1972**	8	5	1
1973	5	9	0
1974	6	8	0
1975	5	9	0
1976	8	6	0
1977	5	9	0
1978	2	14	0
1979	2	14	0
1980	6	10	0
1981*	13	3	0
1982	3	6	0
1983**	10	6	0
1984*	15	1	0
1985**	10	6	0
1986**	10	5	1
1987**	13	2	0
1988*	10	6	0
1989*	14	2	0
1990**	14	2	0
1991	10	6	0
1992**	14	2	0
1993**	10	6	0
Total	332	273	13

Number of NFL championships 4
Number of years .500 or better 29
Number of years below .500 15

*NFL champions
**Playoff team

1994 PREVIEW ■ SAN FRANCISCO

RECORDS

INDIVIDUAL

Scoring
Points, career	979	Ray Wersching (1977-87)
Points, season	138	Jerry Rice (1987)
Points, game	30	Jerry Rice (10/14/90)
Touchdowns, career	124	Jerry Rice (1985-93)
Touchdowns, season	23	Jerry Rice (1987)
Touchdowns, game	5	Jerry Rice (10/14/90)
Field goals, career	190	Ray Wersching (1977-87)
Field goals, season	29	Mike Cofer (1989)
Field goals, game	6	Ray Wersching (10/16/83)
Extra points, career	409	Ray Wersching (1977-87)
Extra points, season	56	Ray Wersching (1984)
Extra points, game	8	Mike Cofer (10/18/92)

Rushing
Yards, career	7,344	Joe Perry (1950-60, 63)
Yards, season	1,502	Roger Craig (1988)
Yards, game	194	Delvin Williams (10/31/76)
Attempts, career	1,686	Roger Craig (1983-90)
Attempts, season	268	Delvin Williams (1977)
Attempts, game	34	Delvin Williams (10/31/76)
Touchdowns, career	50	Joe Perry (1950-60, 63)
		Roger Craig (1983-90)
Touchdowns, season	10	Bill Kilmer (1961)
Touchdowns, game	4	Bill Kilmer (10/15/61)

Passing
Rating, career	103.2	Steve Young (1987-93)
Rating, season	112.4	Joe Montana (1989)
Completions, career	2,929	Joe Montana (1979-92)
Completions, season	347	Steve DeBerg (1979)
Completions, game	37	Joe Montana (10/6/85)
Yards, career	35,124	Joe Montana (1979-92)
Yards, season	3,944	Joe Montana (1990)
Yards, game	476	Joe Montana (10/14/90)
Attempts, career	4,600	Joe Montana (1979-92)
Attempts, season	578	Steve DeBerg (1979)
Attempts, game	60	Joe Montana (11/17/86)
Touchdowns, career	244	Joe Montana (1979-92)
Touchdowns, season	31	Joe Montana (1987)
Touchdowns, game	6	Joe Montana (10/14/90)

Receiving
Receptions, career	708	Jerry Rice (1985-93)
Receptions, season	100	Jerry Rice (1990)
Receptions, game	13	Jerry Rice (10/14/90)
Yards, career	11,776	Jerry Rice (1985-93)
Yards, season	1,570	Jerry Rice (1986)
Yards, game	286	John Taylor (12/11/89)
Touchdowns, career	118	Jerry Rice (1985-93)
Touchdowns, season	22	Jerry Rice (1987)
Touchdowns, game	5	Jerry Rice (10/14/90)

Interceptions
Career	51	Ronnie Lott (1981-90)
Season	10	Dave Baker (1960)
		Ronnie Lott (1986)
Game	4	Dave Baker (12/4/60)

Sacks
Career	111.5	Cedric Hardman (1970-79)
Season	18	Tommy Hart (1971)

Longest plays
Run from scrimmage	89	Hugh McElhenny (TD, 10/5/52)
Pass play	97	Steve Young to John Taylor (TD, 11/3/91)
Field goal	56	Mike Cofer (10/14/90)
Interception return	83	Alvin Randolph (TD, 12/11/66)

Kickoff return	105	Abe Woodson (TD, 11/8/59)
Punt return	95	John Taylor (TD, 11/21/88)
Punt	86	Larry Barnes (9/29/57)

Top scorers — Points
Ray Wersching (1977-87)	979
Jerry Rice (1985-93)	744
Tommy Davis (1959-69)	738
Mike Cofer (1988-93)	681
Gordy Soltau (1950-58)	644
Bruce Gossett (1970-74)	460

Top rushers — Yards
Joe Perry (1950-60, 1963)	7,344
Roger Craig (1983-90)	7,064
Ken Willard (1965-73)	5,930
J.D. Smith (1956-64)	4,370
Hugh McElhenny (1952-60)	4,288
Wendell Tyler (1983-86)	3,112

Top passers — Completions
Joe Montana (1979-92)	2,929
John Brodie (1957-73)	2,469
Y.A. Tittle (1951-60)	1,226
Steve Young (1987-93)	955
Steve DeBerg (1977-80)	670
Steve Spurrier (1967-75)	441

Top passers — Yards
Joe Montana (1979-92)	35,124
John Brodie (1957-73)	31,548
Y.A. Tittle (1951-60)	16,016
Steve Young (1987-93)	12,683
Steve DeBerg (1977-80)	7,220
Steve Spurrier (1967-75)	5,250

Top receivers — Receptions
Jerry Rice (1985-93)	708
Roger Craig (1983-90)	508
Dwight Clark (1979-87)	506
Billy Wilson (1951-60)	407
Gene Washington (1969-77)	371
Freddie Solomon (1978-85)	310

Top receivers — Yards
Jerry Rice (1985-93)	11,776
Dwight Clark (1979-87)	6,750
Gene Washington (1969-77)	6,664
Billy Wilson (1951-60)	5,902
Freddie Solomon (1978-85)	4,873
John Taylor (1987-93)	4,680

Most interceptions — No.
Ronnie Lott (1981-90)	51
Jimmy Johnson (1961-76)	47
Kermit Alexander (1963-69)	36
Dwight Hicks (1979-85)	30
Lowell Wagner (1950-53, 55)	25
Rex Berry (1951-56)	22

Most sacks — No.
Cedric Hardman (1970-79)	111.5
Tommy Hart (1968-77)	106
Charles Haley (1986-91)	63

PREVIEW: SEATTLE SEAHAWKS

The sun is shining in Seattle again.
That wasn't the case a year ago when the Seahawks were coming off of a 1992 season filled with rain clouds. The 1992 Seahawks scored a paltry 140 points and sputtered to a 2-14 record.

Last season Seattle scored 280 points en route to a much-improved 6-10 mark.

The man responsible for the skies clearing and rays of hope invading Seattle is QB Rick Mirer. As a rookie last year, he gave plenty of reason to believe that the Seahawks have a future star on their hands.

Despite the fact that he was sacked 47 times, whacked, blitzed, bent, folded and nearly mutilated, Mirer completed 274-of-486 passes for 2,833 yards.

"One year doesn't put you in the Hall of Fame," said Seahawk head coach Tom Flores. "But he's had as good a start for a rookie quarterback as I've seen."

Mirer said, "It's not a bad start, but we've got to get moving. It's better than taking a step back. I feel like myself and other guys who came in this year made things better than they were a year (earlier). All you want to do is make a difference."

Although the Seahawk offense was shaded toward vanilla, the multidimensional Mirer showed that he can make things happen with his legs, head or arm. He is a strong passer with a very quick arm who generally throws a nice, tight ball. He can throw all the passes in the book. What makes him special are his great improvisational skills, field awareness, mobility and ability to think and react on his feet.

"You sit back and imagine what you have to look forward to when he learns the offense and really gets comfortable," said Seahawk WR Brian Blades late last season. "He's going to be something special."

Flores said, "It's kind of fun watching him grow up out there on the field."

Mirer's favorite target last year was Blades, who bounced back from injuries to catch 80 passes for 949 yards, despite not really being a big-play receiver.

"Brian does so many things to help this offense," said Mirer. "He makes my job a lot easier. He's been through so many more plays than I have, and that's been a big help to me."

WR Kelvin Martin is more quick than fast. He knows how to get open and operates very well if he has time to set up the defender. However, the Seahawks need speed at receiver. They had hoped to address this problem via free-agency or the draft but were not able to do so. Thus, they are now hoping that either Michael Bates or Terrence Warren, each of whom has the extra gear that Blades and Martin lack, can develop into a complete NFL receiver who can control his speed and run routes.

TE Ferrell Edmunds no longer is a top deep threat with 4.65 speed, but, while he has slowed down as a receiver, he has really improved as a blocker. Paul Green has softer hands than Edmunds and maneuvers better underneath, but he is not going to knock anyone off the ball as a blocker or make the running game go like Edmunds does.

The leader of that running game is Chris Warren, who rushed for over 1,000 for the second year in a row in '93. Warren is not a physical runner, but he is almost 230 pounds, runs just over 4.4 in the 40 and is a terrific athlete. He has become tougher, is making better run decisions and is showing more anticipation. He also catches the ball very well.

The Seahawks received improved play from their offensive line last season. The biggest change last year was at center, where Ray Donaldson stepped in and, at 35, had one of his best seasons. Donaldson didn't miss a snap all year and played at close to a Pro Bowl level after replacing oft-injured Joe Tofflemire. The Seahawks also added C Kevin Mawae in the second round of this

Chris Warren

1994 PREVIEW ■ SEATTLE

year's draft.

After getting destroyed as a rookie and leading the league in sacks given up and penalties by an offensive lineman, OLT Ray Roberts started to develop into a good player over the second half of his second season. Roberts has the size, long arms and ability to be a top player if he can avoid the ups and downs that have plagued him to this point.

"There's no question that he has improved dramatically over (1992)," said Flores. "(In '92) every game was one of those where you held your breath."

Ex-Bill Howard Ballard will replace Andy Heck at right tackle. Ballard has awesome size but did not play that well last year because of a bad ankle, which limited his mobility. Because of his size, he is a much more physical run blocker than Heck is, but he is not nearly as mobile or athletic when blocking down the field.

At guard, Seattle will go with Bill Hitchcock, who is limited athletically but very strong and physical, and journeyman Mitch Frerotte. Jeff Blackshear could also figure at guard if he does a better job of controlling his weight.

On defense, the Seahawks are looking to improve over last year's performance. In '92 the Seattle defense did its best to carry the team. However, last year, after playing well early, the defense collapsed down the stretch, when injuries took their toll and forced a dozen players to miss a total of 59 games. As a result, Seattle gave up 128 points in its last five games.

The star of the Seahawk defense is Cortez Kennedy, who was the best defensive tackle and defensive player in football in '92. Last season he was double- and triple-teamed to death and really seemed to get frustrated after a while.

"It goes with the territory," said Seahawk MLB Rod Stephens. "He's such a great player that he gets all their attention."

The result was that Kennedy went from 14 sacks and 28 tackles for loss in '92 to 6.5 sacks and 13.5 tackles for loss last year.

With this in mind, the Seahawks drafted DL Sam Adams in the first round of this year's draft in an effort to give Kennedy some help.

"I think Sam will occupy a little more attention from Cortez than last year," said Seahawk player personnel director Mike Allman. "Sam's got many of the qualities that Cortez has. I'm not going to tell you he jumps a guy with the same power that Cortez does, but it's close. He's explosive in his takeoff like Cortez is. They're similar in a lot of respects."

Other defensive linemen for the Seahawks are Mike Sinclair, Antonio Edwards, Jeff Bryant, Natu Tuatagaloa, Mike McCrary and Joe Nash. Sinclair had eight sacks last year before an injury sidelined him. Edwards shows some promise as a pass rusher. Bryant is adequate against the run and tough to throw over due to his long wingspan. Tuatagaloa played a lot and did an OK job last year. McCrary is too small to play the run but does put some heat on the quarterback.

At linebacker, the Seahawks need to talk to a doctor to know their outlook for this season. When Rod Stephens played the assigned defense, he was an adequate middle linebacker, but, when he started to guess, he left gaping holes in the defense. If Bobby Spitulski ever stays healthy, he could replace Stephens, but the Seahawks are starting to worry that Spitulski may be one of those promising players who can never stay healthy long enough to make an impact. OLB Rufus Porter, who was an outstanding blitzer and rusher off the corner, tore his Achilles, making him a big question mark for this season. If he can't come back, David Brandon will replace him. Dean Wells could be another possibility. Terry Wooden does a solid job at left outside linebacker.

In the secondary, FS Eugene Robinson had his second big year in a row. He is a real student of the game and anticipates very well. SS Robert Blackmon really isn't physical enough for the position, although his athletic ability is a big plus. Ex-Bill Nate Odomes will replace Dwayne Harper at left cornerback. Odomes is a gambler who makes big plays but also will give some up. He is much more physical vs. the pass than the run. CB Patrick Hunter is coming off a solid year and has become a much more consistent player than he was in his early years. If either cornerback slips a little, last year's second-round pick, Carlton Gray, is good enough to start. At the very least, Gray will be on the field on passing downs provided he can stay healthy. Gray missed seven games with an ankle injury as a rookie.

The Seahawk special teams figure to be very good. After slumping in '92, PK John Kasay bounced back to make 23-of-28 field goals, and he also kicked off well. P Rick Tuten averaged over 44 yards per punt for the second year in a row. Bates did a phenomenal job of covering kicks. He had 20 solo tackles, caused two fumbles, recovered two and downed three punts inside the five-yard line. He also started to develop into a dangerous kickoff returner by year's end. Martin handled punts, and, while he did not break many, he did generally make the first man miss.

FAST FACTS

■ Rick Mirer rewrote the NFL record book for a rookie quarterback in 1993, establishing marks for attempts (486), completions (274) and yards (2,833).

■ Michael Bates set Seahawk special-team records in 1993 with 22 tackles, 20 of which were solo.

■ Seattle had three players (Eugene Robinson, Terry Wooden and Rod Stephens) with 100 or more tackles, the first time in franchise history that many defenders reached the century mark.

PRO FOOTBALL WEEKLY 1994 ALMANAC

1994 PLAYER ROSTER

NO.	NAME	POS.	HT.	WT.	EXP.	COLLEGE	GP/GS
39	Allred, Brian	CB	5-10	175	2	Sacramento State	4/0
74	Atkins, James	OG	6-6	291	1	SW Louisiana	0/0
55	Atkinson, Jason	LB	6-3	230	R	Texas A&M	—
75	Ballard, Howard	OT	6-6	336	7	Alabama A&M	16/16
40	Barrett, Reggie	WR	6-3	215	4	Texas-El Paso	0/0
81	Bates, Michael	WR	5-10	189	2	Arizona	16/1
20	Bellamy, Jay	S	5-11	177	R	Rutgers	—
25	Blackmon, Robert	S	6-0	197	5	Baylor	16/16
69	Blackshear, Jeff	OG	6-6	315	2	NE Louisiana	15/2
89	Blades, Brian	WR	5-11	189	7	Miami (Fla.)	16/16
51	Brandon, David	LB	6-4	230	8	Memphis State	13/0
77	Bryant, Jeff	DE	6-5	281	13	Clemson	16/15
57	Bryant, Steve	LB	6-3	240	R	Nevada	—
49	Butler, Hillary	LB	6-2	240	R	Washington	—
8	Carter, Marcus	WR	5-11	205	R	SW Louisiana	—
79	Childs, Jason	OT	6-4	285	2	North Dakota	0/0
50	Davis, Anthony	LB	6-0	231	2	Utah	10/0
62	DeVries, Jed	OT	6-5	282	R	Utah State	—
53	Donaldson, Ray	C	6-3	300	15	Georgia	16/16
82	Edmunds, Ferrell	TE	6-6	254	7	Maryland	16/16
67	Edwards, Antonio	DE	6-3	270	2	Valdosta (Ga.) St.	9/0
59	Frerotte, Mitch	OG	6-3	286	6	Penn State	0/0
18	Gelbaugh, Stan	QB	6-3	207	7	Maryland	1/0
54	Gordon, Steve	C	6-3	279	2	California	0/0
7	Graham, Jeff	QB	6-5	220	4	Long Beach State	0/0
26	Gray, Carlton	CB	6-0	191	2	UCLA	10/2
87	Green, Paul	TE	6-3	230	3	Southern Cal	15/8
66	Hamilton, Bobby	DE	6-4	266	R	Southern Mississippi	—
76	Hitchcock, Bill	OG	6-6	291	4	Purdue	14/14
27	Hunter, Patrick	CB	5-11	186	9	Nevada-Reno	1515
43	Johnson, Tracy	FB	6-0	230	6	Clemson	16/0
93	Junior, E.J.	LB	6-3	242	14	Alabama	14/0
83	Junkin, Trey	TE	6-2	237	12	Louisiana Tech	16/0
4	Kasay, John	PK	5-10	189	4	Georgia	16/0
65	Kegarise, Mike	OT	6-5	310	R	Edinboro	—
78	Keim, Mike	OT	6-7	301	3	Brigham Young	3/0
96	Kennedy, Cortez	DT	6-3	293	5	Miami (Fla.)	16/16
30	Lockwood, Scott	RB	5-11	205	2	Southern Cal	2/0
84	Martin, Kelvin	WR	5-9	162	8	Boston College	16/15
44	McCloughan, Dave	S	6-1	185	4	Colorado	15/0
92	McCrary, Michael	DE	6-4	250	2	Wake Forest	15/0
63	McDaniel, Curtis	DT	6-3	283	R	Jacksonville State	—
10	McGwire, Dan	QB	6-8	243	4	San Diego State	2/0
9	McKnight, James	WR	6-0	181	R	Liberty	—
3	Mirer, Rick	QB	6-2	216	2	Notre Dame	16/16
98	Murphy, Kevin	LB	6-2	235	9	Oklahoma	14/10
72	Nash, Joe	DT	6-3	278	13	Boston College	16/16
37	Odomes, Nate	CB	5-10	188	8	Wisconsin	16/15
97	Porter, Rufus	LB	6-1	227	7	Southern-B.R.	7/6
73	Roberts, Ray	OT	6-6	304	3	Virginia	16/16
41	Robinson, Eugene	S	6-0	191	10	Colgate	16/16
37	Robinson, Rafael	S	5-11	200	3	Wisconsin	16/1
91	Rodgers, Tyrone	DT	6-3	266	3	Washington	16/0
60	Seegars, Stacy	OG	6-3	337	R	Clemson	—
24	Shamsid, Deen, M.	RB	5-11	200	1	Tenn.-Chattanooga	0/0

218

1994 PREVIEW ■ SEATTLE

1994 PLAYER ROSTER

NO.	NAME	POS.	HT.	WT.	EXP.	COLLEGE	GP/GS
71	Shaw, Rickie	OT	6-4	294	2	North Carolina	0/0
70	Sinclair, Michael	DE	6-4	271	3	E. New Mexico	9/1
58	Spitulski, Bob	LB	6-3	235	3	Central Florida	6/0
94	Stephens, Rod	LB	6-1	237	6	Georgia Tech	13/13
38	Strong, Mack	FB	6-0	211	1	Georgia	0/0
85	Thomas, Doug	WR	5-10	178	4	Clemson	16/0
86	Thomas, Robb	WR	5-11	175	6	Oregon State	16/0
64	Tinner, Glenn	OG	6-5	292	R	Temple	—
56	Tofflemire, Joe	C	6-3	273	6	Arizona	0/0
99	Tuatagaloa, Natu	DE	6-4	274	6	California	16/15
14	Tuten, Rick	P	6-2	218	6	Florida State	16/0
22	Vaughn, Jon	RB	5-9	203	4	Michigan	16/2
42	Warren, Chris	RB	6-2	225	5	Ferrum (Va.)	14/14
88	Warren, Terrence	WR	6-1	200	2	Hampton Institute	2/0
31	Waters, Orlando	CB	5-11	177	R	Arkansas	—
95	Wells, Dean	LB	6-3	238	2	Kentucky	14/1
61	Werner, Matt	DT	6-3	265	R	UCLA	—
	Williams, Brent	DE	6-4	275	9	Toledo	13/2
35	Wood, Rick	FB	6-2	242	R	Norfolk State	—
90	Wooden, Terry	LB	6-3	239	5	Syracuse	16/16

'94 DRAFT PICKS

RD.	NAME	POS.	HT.	WT.	COLLEGE
1.	Adams, Sam	DT	6-2	292	Texas A&M
2.	Mawae, Kevin	C-OG	6-4	286	Louisiana State
3.	Smith, Lamar	RB	5-11	225	Houston
4.	Whigham, Larry	DB	6-1	199	Northeast Louisiana
7.	Crumpler, Carlester	TE	6-6	253	East Carolina

PRO FOOTBALL WEEKLY 1994 ALMANAC

TEAM AT A GLANCE

TEAM DIRECTORY

Address	11220 N.E. 53rd Street Kirkland, Washington 98033 (206) 827-9777
Stadium	Kingdome 201 South King Street Seattle, Washington 98104 Capacity: 66,000 Playing surface: AstroTurf
Training Camp	11220 N.E. 53rd Street Kirkland, Washington 98033
Colors	Blue, green and silver
Television	KING, Channel 5
Radio	KIRO, 710 AM

ADMINISTRATION
Owner: Ken Behring
President: David Behring
General manager-head coach: Tom Flores
Executive vice president: Mickey Loomis
Vice president-football operations: Chuck Allen
Vice president-admin., public relations: Gary Wright
Player personnel director: Mike Allman
Assistant player personnel director: Rick Thompson
Pro personnel director: Randy Mueller
College scouting director: Phil Neri
Publicity director: Dave Neubert
Community services director: Sandy Gregory
Sales and marketing director: Reggie McKenzie
Ticket manager: James Nagaoka
Trainer: Jim Whitesel

1994 SCHEDULE

Preseason
AUG. 5	at Indianapolis	7:30
AUG. 13	TAMPA BAY	6:00
AUG. 20	MINNESOTA	7:00
AUG. 26	at San Francisco	6:00

Regular season
SEP. 4	at Washington	1:00
SEP. 11	at L.A. Raiders	1:00
SEP. 18	SAN DIEGO	1:00
SEP. 25	PITTSBURGH	1:00
OCT. 2	at Indianapolis	12:00
OCT. 9	DENVER	1:00
OCT. 16	OPEN DATE	
OCT. 23	at Kansas City	12:00
OCT. 30	at San Diego	1:00
NOV. 6	CINCINNATI	1:00
NOV. 13	at Denver	2:00
NOV. 20	TAMPA BAY	1:00
NOV. 27	KANSAS CITY	1:00
DEC. 4	INDIANAPOLIS	1:00
DEC. 11	at Houston	3:00
DEC. 18	L.A. RAIDERS	5:00
DEC. 24	at Cleveland	1:00

HEAD COACH
Tom Flores

Flores is one of only two people in NFL history to win Super Bowl rings as a player, an assistant coach and a head coach. As a reserve quarterback with the Chiefs, he got his first ring after Super Bowl IV. The other two rings came with the Raiders — in Super Bowl XI as an assistant coach, and as a head coach in Super Bowls XV and XVII. Flores spent the majority of his career in the Raider organization from 1972-87. He was also a Raider quarterback for five seasons. He was named head coach of the Seahawks in 1992 after serving as their president and general manager for three years. In his two years as head coach, the Seahawks have gone 2-14 (1992) and 6-10 (1993). Born March 21, 1937, Fresno, Calif.

Previous NFL: general manager, 1989-91 Seattle; head coach, 1979-87 L.A. Raiders; assistant coach, 1972-78 L.A. Raiders; assistant coach, 1971 Buffalo.

Previous college: None.

Player: NFL, quarterback, 1960-61, 1963-66, Oakland; 1967-68 Buffalo; 1969-70 Kansas City.

ASSISTANT COACHES
Tommy Brasher: defensive line
Previous NFL: defensive line, 1992-93 Seattle; 1990 Tampa Bay; 1986-89 Atlanta; 1985 Philadelphia; 1982-84 New England. Player: No NFL. College: linebacker, 1962-63 Arkansas.

Bob Bratkowski: wide receivers
Previous NFL: wide receivers, 1992-93 Seattle. Player: No NFL. College: wide receiver, 1974, 1976-77 Washington State.

Dave Brown: defensive assistant
Previous NFL: defensive assistant, 1992-93 Seattle. Player: NFL, defensive back, 1975 Pittsburgh; 1976-86 Seattle; 1987-90 Green Bay. College: defensive back, 1972-74 Michigan.

Tom Catlin: assistant head coach
Previous NFL: assistant head coach, 1983-93 Seattle; 1978-82 Buffalo; 1966-77 L.A. Rams; 1960-65 Dallas/Kansas City. Player: NFL, linebacker, 1953-54, 1957-58 Cleveland; 1959 Philadelphia. College: center, linebacker, 1950-52 Oklahoma.

Larry Kennan: offensive coordinator-quarterbacks
Previous NFL: offensive coordinator-quarterbacks, 1992-93 Seattle; 1989-90 Indianapolis; 1982-87 L.A. Raiders. Player: No NFL. College: quarterback, 1962-65 La Verne College.

Paul Moyer: defensive backfield
Previous NFL: defensive backfield, 1990-93 Seattle. Player: NFL, safety, 1983-89 Seattle. College: safety, 1981-82 Arizona State.

Howard Mudd: offensive line
Previous NFL: offensive line, 1993 Seattle; 1989-92 Kansas City; 1983-88 Cleveland; 1978-82 Seattle; 1977 San Francisco; 1974-76 San Diego. Player: NFL, guard, 1964-69 San Francisco; 1969-71 Chicago. College: guard, 1961-63 Hillsdale College.

Russ Purnell: special teams-tight ends
Previous NFL: special teams-tight ends, 1986-

1994 PREVIEW ■ SEATTLE

TEAM AT A GLANCE

93 Seattle. Player: No NFL. College: center, 1968-69 Whittier College.

Frank Raines: strength and conditioning
   Previous NFL: strength and conditioning, 1990-93 Seattle; 1986-89 Washington. Player: No NFL. College: None.

Clarence Shelmon: running backs
   Previous NFL: running backs, 1992-93 Seattle; 1991 L.A. Rams. Player: No NFL. College: running back, 1971-75 Houston.

Rusty Tillman: defensive coordinator-linebackers
   Previous NFL: defensive coordinator, 1979-93 Seattle. Player: NFL, linebacker, 1970-77 Washington. College: linebacker, 1967-69 Northern Arizona.

1987-88 The Seahawks go to the playoffs but lose in the first round to the Houston Oilers in overtime 23-20.
1988-89 Seattle again makes it to postseason play but loses in the first round to the Bengals 23-13.
1992 Tom Flores, president of the club, also becomes head coach.

COACHING RECORDS

Years	Coach	W	L	T
1976-82	Jack Patera	35	59	0
1982	Mike McCormack	4	3	0
1983-91	Chuck Knox	83	67	0
1992-93	Tom Flores	8	24	0

HISTORICAL HIGHLIGHTS

1976 The Seahawks join the NFL as an expansion franchise, ownership going to a syndicate headed by Lloyd W. Nordstrom. The team is assigned to the NFC Western Division along with the Rams, 49ers, Saints and Falcons, and will play its games at the Kingdome.
1977 The Seahawks are moved to the American Football Conference and placed in the Western Division, joining the Raiders, Broncos, Chargers and Chiefs.
1978 The Seahawks post their first winning season, going 9-7 to tie with Oakland for second place in the AFC West. ... Steve Largent leads the AFC in receptions with 71 and in yards gained receiving with 1,168, while RB David Sims leads the NFL with touchdowns scored, 15, a club record.
1983 Behind the rushing of Curt Warner, who leads the AFC with 1,449 yards on 335 carries, the Seahawks win 9-of-16 games and secure their first playoff berth as a wild-card team. ... Seattle defeats Denver in the AFC wild-card game 31-7, highlighted by three TD passes from Dave Krieg. A 27-20 win over Miami qualifies the Seahawks to face the Los Angeles Raiders for the AFC championship, but they lose the title game 30-14.
1984 CB Dave Brown ties an NFL record by returning two interceptions for touchdowns in a 45-0 rout of the Kansas City Chiefs, and the Seahawks set an NFL mark with a total of four interceptions returned for scores in that game. ... The largest crowd ever to attend a Seahawk game, 64,411, fills the Kingdome to watch the Seahawks fall to the Broncos 31-14 . ... Seattle again earns a place in the playoffs with the best record in its history, 12-4, but still is a game behind the Broncos in the AFC West. In the wild-card match-up, the Seahawks defeat the Raiders 13-7, but then lose to the Dolphins in the divisional playoff 31-10.
1985 The Seahawks break ground for a new practice and training facility and office complex at Northwest College in Kirkland, Wash.

TEAM AT A GLANCE

HALL OF FAME MEMBERS
None

RETIRED JERSEY NUMBERS
12   "Fans," the 12th Man

FIRST-ROUND DRAFT CHOICES
(since 1980)

Year	Selection	College
1980	DE Jacob Green	Texas A&M
1981	DB Kenny Easley	UCLA
1982	DE Jeff Bryant	Clemson
1983	RB Curt Warner	Penn State
1984	CB Terry Taylor	Southern Illinois
1985	No choice	
1986	RB John L. Williams	Florida
1987	LB Tony Woods	Pittsburgh
	LB Brian Bosworth (supplemental)	Oklahoma
1988	No choice	
1989	OT Andy Heck	Notre Dame
1990	DT Cortez Kennedy	Miami (Fla.)
1991	QB Dan McGwire	San Diego State
1992	OT Ray Roberts	Virginia
1993	QB Rick Mirer	Notre Dame
1994	DL Sam Adams	Texas A&M

RECORD VS. OTHER NFL TEAMS
(including postseason games)

	Record
Arizona Cardinals	0-4-0
Atlanta Falcons	4-1-0
Buffalo Bills	3-1-0
Chicago Bears	4-2-0
Cincinnati Bengals	6-7-0
Cleveland Browns	9-3-0
Dallas Cowboys	1-4-0
Denver Broncos	14-20-0
Detroit Lions	4-2-0
Green Bay Packers	3-3-0
Houston Oilers	4-5-0
Indianapolis Colts	1-2-0
Kansas City Chiefs	12-19-0
Los Angeles Raiders	15-19-0
Los Angeles Rams	1-4-0
Miami Dolphins	2-5-0
Minnesota Vikings	3-2-0
New England Patriots	7-6-0
New Orleans Saints	2-3-0
New York Giants	2-5-0
New York Jets	8-3-0
Philadelphia Eagles	1-4-0
Pittsburgh Steelers	5-5-0
San Diego Chargers	15-15-0
San Francisco 49ers	1-4-0
Tampa Bay Buccaneers	2-0-0
Washington Redskins	1-5-0

YEAR-BY-YEAR RECORDS

Year	Won	Lost	Tied	Year	Won	Lost	Tied
1976	2	12	0	1985	8	8	0
1977	5	9	0	1986	10	6	0
1978	9	7	0	1987**	9	6	0
1979	9	7	0	1988**	9	7	0
1980	4	12	0	1989	7	9	0
1981	6	10	0	1990	9	7	0
1982	4	5	0	1991	7	9	0
1983**	9	7	0	1992	2	14	0
1984**	12	4	0	1993	6	10	0
				Total	127	149	0

Number of NFL championships   0
Number of years .500 or better   9
Number of years below .500   9

*NFL champions
**Playoff team

1994 PREVIEW ■ SEATTLE

RECORDS

INDIVIDUAL

Service
Seasons played	14	Steve Largent (1976-89)
Games played	200	Steve Largent (1976-89)
Consecutive games	106	Eugene Robinson (1985-93)

Scoring
Points, career	810	Norm Johnson (1982-90)
Points, season	110	Norm Johnson (1984)
Points, game	24	Daryl Turner (9/15/85)
		Curt Warner (12/11/88)
Touchdowns, career	101	Steve Largent (1976-89)
Touchdowns, season	15	David Sims (1978)
		Sherman Smith (1979)
		Derrick Fenner (1990)
Touchdowns, game	4	Daryl Turner (9/15/85)
		Curt Warner (12/11/89)
Field goals, career	159	Norm Johnson (1982-90)
Field goals, season	25	John Kasay (1991)
Field goals, game	5	Norm Johnson (9/20/87)
		Norm Johnson (12/18/88)
Extra points, career	333	Norm Johnson (1982-90)
Extra points, season	50	Norm Johnson (1984)
Extra points, game	8	John Leypoldt (10/20/77)

Rushing
Yards, career	6,705	Curt Warner (1983-89)
Yards, season	1,481	Curt Warner (1986)
Yards, game	207	Curt Warner (11/27/83)
Attempts, career	1,649	Curt Warner (1983-89)
Attempts, season	335	Curt Warner (1983)
Attempts, game	36	Chris Warren (9/19/93)
Touchdowns, career	55	Curt Warner (1983-89)
Touchdowns, season	14	David Sims (1978)
		Derrick Fenner (1990)
Touchdowns, game	4	Curt Warner (12/11/88)

Passing
Rating, career	82.3	Dave Krieg (1980-91)
Rating, season	95.0	Dave Krieg (1983)
Completions, career	2,096	Dave Krieg (1980-91)
Completions, season	286	Dave Krieg (1989)
Completions, game	33	Dave Krieg (10/13/85)
Yards, career	26,132	Dave Krieg (1980-91)
Yards, season	3,671	Dave Krieg (1984)
Yards, game	418	Dave Krieg (11/20/83)
Attempts, career	3,576	Dave Krieg (1980-91)
Attempts, season	532	Dave Krieg (1985)
Attempts, game	51	Dave Krieg (10/13/85)
Touchdowns, career	195	Dave Krieg (1980-91)
Touchdowns, season	32	Dave Krieg (1984)
Touchdowns, game	5	Dave Krieg (12/2/84, 9/15/85, & 12/18/88)

Receiving
Receptions, career	819	Steve Largent (1976-89)
Receptions, season	80	Brian Blades (1993)
Receptions, game	15	Steve Largent (10/18/87)
Yards, career	13,089	Steve Largent (1976-89)
Yards, season	1,287	Steve Largent (1985)
Yards, game	261	Steve Largent (10/18/87)
Touchdowns, career	100	Steve Largent (1976-89)
Touchdowns, season	13	Daryl Turner (1985)
Touchdowns, game	4	Daryl Turner (9/15/85)

Interceptions
Career	50	Dave Brown (1976-86)
Season	10	John Harris (1981)
		Kenny Easley (1984)
Game	3	Kenny Easley (10/29/84)
		Eugene Robinson (12/6/92)

Sacks
Career	116.0	Jacob Green (1980-91)
Season	16.0	Jacob Green (1983)
Game	4.0	Jacob Green (10/19/86)

Longest plays
Run from scrimmage	67	Sherman Smith (11/5/78)
		Al Hunter (11/11/79)
Pass play	82	Jim Zorn to David Sims (TD, 9/25/77)
Field goal	55	John Kasay (1/2/94)
Interception return	91	Sammy Green (TD, 10/7/79)
Kickoff return	97	James Jefferson (TD, 10/8/89)
Punt return	75	Will Lewis (TD, 11/23/80)
		Paul Johns (TD, 10/16/83)
		Bobby Joe Edmonds (TD, 11/23/86)
Punt	68	Ruben Rodriguez (9/4/88)

Top scorers — Points
Norm Johnson (1982-90)	810
Steve Largent (1976-89)	608
Curt Warner (1983-89)	372
Efren Herrera (1978-81)	331
John Kasay (1991-93)	256
Sherman Smith (1976-82)	228

Top rushers — Yards
Curt Warner (1983-89)	6,705
John L. Williams (1986-93)	4,579
Sherman Smith (1976-82)	3,429
Chris Warren (1991-93)	2,113
Dan Doornink (1979-85)	1,530
Jim Zorn (1976-84)	1,494

Top passers — Completions
Dave Krieg (1980-91)	2,096
Jim Zorn (1976-84)	1,593
Rick Mirer (1993)	274
Kelly Stouffer (1988-92)	225
Jeff Kemp (1987-91)	130
Stan Gelbaugh (1992-93)	124

Top passers — Yards
Dave Krieg (1980-91)	26,132
Jim Zorn (1976-84)	20,122
Rick Mirer (1993)	2,833
Kelly Stouffer (1988-92)	2,333
Jeff Kemp (1987-91)	1,735
Stan Gelbaugh (1992-93)	1,346

Top receivers — Receptions
Steve Largent (1976-89)	819
John L. Williams (1986-93)	471
Brian Blades (1988-93)	335
Sam McCullum (1976-81)	232
Sherman Smith (1976-82)	211
Dan Doornink (1979-85)	197

Top receivers — Yards
Steve Largent (1976-89)	13,089
Brian Blades (1988-93)	4,474
John L. Williams (1986-93)	4,151
Sam McCullum (1976-81)	3,409
Sherman Smith (1976-82)	2,342
Tommy Kane (1988-92)	2,034

Most interceptions — No.
Dave Brown (1976-86)	50
John Harris (1978-85)	41
Eugene Robinson (1985-93)	38
Kenny Easley (1981-87)	32
Keith Simpson (1978-85)	19
Terry Taylor (1984-88)	15

Most sacks — No.
Jacob Green (1980-91)	116.0
Jeff Bryant (1982-93)	63.0
Joe Nash (1982-93)	44.5

223

PREVIEW: TAMPA BAY BUCCANEERS

The Buccaneers, 5-11 in 1993, are good enough to be in the playoffs in '94.

A very bold statement, yes. A common belief, no.

But Tampa Bay head coach Sam Wyche stated at the end of the '93 season that the Bucs are a legitimate playoff contender. Considering some of the moves made in the offseason, along with playing in the NFC Central, maybe this team does have a shot.

"I can't guarantee anything," said Wyche following the conclusion of last season. "But I think this team will be good enough to be in the playoffs."

That's happened only three times in the 18-year history of the franchise, and not since 1982, when the players' strike led to 16 teams being admitted to the playoffs.

"This team is not finished, but the foundation is laid," said Wyche. "There's no doubt this team knows that it can step on the field, in any stadium, and play with anybody in the league."

Yes, the Buccaneers can play with anybody in the league. But can they beat anybody in the league? That question remains unanswered.

If they are to contend for a playoff position, the team certainly must improve offensively. In 1993 the Buccaneers were ranked near the bottom of the league in every offensive category except extra-point percentage. They were dead-last in total rushing yards with a mere 1,280 (Emmitt Smith alone rushed for 1,429).

RB Reggie Cobb was the squad's leading rusher last season with 658 yards, a far cry from his '92 total of 1,171 yards. When he opted to sign with the Packers as a free-agent, the Bucs' need for help at this position became a priority.

To replace Cobb, the Bucs drafted Errict Rhett out of Florida with their second-round pick. Rhett has the potential to step right in and start, but he will likely begin the year as the No. 2 running back. Although he was very productive in college, he isn't a burner. As a senior he carried the ball 247 times for 1,289 yards and 11 touchdowns. He also caught 36 passes for 271 yards.

Vince Workman filled in at running back for Cobb, who was often injured in '93, and he also played some fullback. Workman rushed for 284 yards and two TD's on 78 carries last year, but his biggest contribution was his pass-catching. His good hands led to 54 receptions for 411 yards and two scores. Although Workman may start the season as the No. 1 running back, don't be surprised to see him become more of a third-down back as soon as Rhett shows he's ready to take over.

FB Rudy Harris is speedy and powerful but needs more development. Anthony McDowell is a big back with nice pass-catching skills but needs to improve his blocking.

The Bucs' most notable Draft Day acquisition with the sixth choice overall was QB Trent Dilfer. This confuses the QB picture in Tampa Bay, as Craig Erickson was said to have been progressing nicely.

"This is no reflection on Craig Erickson. We're still happy with his progress. We'll see what happens in training camp," said Wyche after the draft.

Erickson, a third-year pro, completed 233-of-457 passes for 3,054 yards and 18 touchdowns in '93, his first year as a starter. His greatest asset is his intelligence, which has helped him to learn Wyche's extremely complicated offensive system. He is a good play-action passer with a slightly above-average arm.

With Dilfer waiting in the wings, Erickson may not receive many second chances if he falters during the season.

Dilfer, who left Fresno State with one year of eligibility remaining, passed for 3,000 yards in both his sophomore and junior years. Some scouts say he is more advanced at this stage than was Drew Bledsoe as a rookie, but he is not as gifted physically as the New England

PHOTO BY DAVID GRAHAM

Eric Curry

1994 PREVIEW ■ TAMPA BAY

quarterback.

"There's no written rule that says a rookie quarterback can't have success," said Dilfer. "I just think it's difficult. I played against Drew his last year of college and think I'm capable of doing what he did, if not more."

Catching passes from either Erickson or Dilfer will be WR Courtney Hawkins, who was the team's leading receiver in '92 with 933 yards on 62 receptions. Horace Copeland is extremely quick and has excellent jumping ability. As a rookie he recorded 633 receiving yards. Lamar Thomas, also a rookie last year, struggled a bit but could develop into a quality receiver. Lawrence Dawsey totaled his knee in the fourth game of the season, but he is a tough and physical wide receiver.

TE Ron Hall signed with the Lions, so Tyji Armstrong will get an opportunity to battle for the starting spot. He is big at 250 pounds but has instant speed. His time in the 40-yard dash is an impressive 4.7. His biggest hangup, however, is his erratic receiving. TE Harold Bishop was selected with the team's third draft pick and may challenge Armstrong.

C Tony Mayberry is returning as probably the most reliable offensive lineman from last season. He has started every game for the past three seasons. OLT Paul Gruber had a disappointing 1993 with a contract holdout and then a groin injury, but he may get back to form this year. OG Ian Beckles is a powerful, low-to-the-ground blocker. OT Charles McRae has been a big disappointment and has found himself in trouble with Wyche at times, but he will get another shot at starting — either at guard or tackle. If he continues to be inconsistent and disappoint the staff, he will lose that spot. Scott Dill demonstrated his versatility last season, starting at left tackle, right tackle and guard. New to the Bucs, coming via free-agency from Minnesota, is ORT Tim Irwin, a veteran who relies on his smarts due to a lack of quickness. OG Bruce Reimers is much like Irwin, a smart veteran without much quickness. Shawn Love is a young prospect with a future at guard.

As for defense, no team that qualified for the playoffs in '93 gave up 376 points as the Bucs did last season. The defensive unit will certainly have to play better this year if it wants to improve its record.

Anchoring the defense is LB Hardy Nickerson, the best free-agent acquisition made by any team last year. Nickerson was the club's leading tackler with 214. The other starting linebacker in the Bucs' 4-2-5 scheme will probably be Lonnie Marts, who played for the Chiefs last year. LB Demetrius DuBose — a second-round draft pick in 1993 — struggled as a rookie last year, but he may get it together as a sophomore. Broderick Thomas struggled in '93 and does not seem to fit into the new defensive system. His problems began after LB coach Dale Lindsay departed Tampa Bay in favor of San Diego.

The acquisition of FS Thomas Everett from the Cowboys has the Bucs hoping he will be the play maker they need in the defensive backfield. SS Marty Carter is a force against the run but is not as strong in coverage. Joe King, who started at free safety early last season, may move to another slot in the secondary. King is versatile enough to play anywhere in the defensive backfield. Also expected to see time in the safety slots will be Barney Bussey and John Lynch. Bussey has experience and toughness, and Lynch has the size and toughness to be an ideal nickel back. CB Martin Mayhew is good in zone coverage and a tough competitor. Ex-Colt CB Tony Stargell is a big hitter but doesn't play the ball well. Veteran CB Milton Mack is burned too often.

Last year DT's Santana Dotson and Mark Wheeler did not live up to their sensational rookie seasons in 1992 but are expected to again be a force in '94. Wheeler, who lines up as a nose tackle, has been compared to a young Henry Thomas but was slowed by injuries last season. Dotson recorded 10.5 sacks in '92 but had only five in '93. As a rookie last year DE Eric Curry had five sacks and looked like a very promising pass rusher before suffering a season-ending ankle sprain. Along the left side of the line, DE's Shawn Price and Chidi Ahanotu are the potential replacements for the departed Ray Seals. Price made the team as an undrafted free agent and wound up starting. Ahanotu didn't have a spectacular rookie season and is an overachiever type.

Probably the area in which the Buccaneers improved most overall last year was in special-team play. PK Michael Husted, a '93 rookie who hooked up with the club as a free agent, made all of his extra-point attempts and was 16-of-22 on field goals. In addition, he did well on kickoffs. P Dan Stryzinski gets excellent hang time and places the ball well but does not exactly blow away anyone with his distance. DB Curtis Buckley was a demon on kick coverage as a rookie, as was backup LB Darrick Brownlow. The biggest source of concern on special teams is the lack of a dangerous kick returner.

FAST FACTS

■ LB Hardy Nickerson shattered the Buccaneers' single-season tackle record in 1993 by finishing with 214 takedowns.

■ Last season WR Courtney Hawkins turned in the most receiving yardage (933) by a Tampa Bay player since Mark Carrier's Pro Bowl season in 1989.

■ QB Craig Erickson became only the fourth quarterback in franchise history to record a 3,000-yard passing season.

PRO FOOTBALL WEEKLY 1994 ALMANAC

1994 PLAYER ROSTER

NO.	NAME	POS.	HT.	WT.	EXP.	COLLEGE	GP/GS
73	Adams, Theo	OL	6-4	300	3	Hawaii	7/0
72	Ahanotu, Chidi	DL	6-2	280	1	California	16/10
2	Allison, Joe	PK	6-0	185	R	Memphis State	—
44	Anderson, Darren	CB	5-10	180	2	Toledo	14/1
86	Armstrong, Tyji	TE	6-4	250	3	Mississippi	12/7
62	Beckles, Ian	OG	6-1	295	5	Indiana	14/14
53	Brady, Ed	LB	6-2	235	11	Illinois	16/0
57	Brady, Jeff	LB	6-1	235	4	Kentucky	0/0
28	Buckley, Curtis	DB	6-0	185	2	East Texas	10/2
27	Bussey, Barney	S	6-0	210	9	South Carolina St.	16/7
23	Carter, Marty	S	6-1	200	4	Mid. Tennessee St.	16/14
89	Collins, Shawn	WR	6-2	205	6	Northern Arizona	0/0
88	Copeland, Horace	WR	6-2	195	2	Miami (Fla.)	14/8
25	Covington, Tony	S	5-11	195	4	Virginia	0/0
68	Crisman, Joel	OG	6-5	290	R	Southern Cal	—
75	Curry, Eric	DE	6-5	270	2	Alabama	10/10
1	Davis, Tyree	WR	5-9	165	1	Central Arkansas	0/0
80	Dawsey, Lawrence	WR	6-0	195	4	Florida State	4/4
76	Dill, Scott	OL	6-5	290	7	Memphis St.	16/16
71	Dotson, Santana	DL	6-5	270	3	Baylor	16/13
49	DuBose, Demetrius	LB	6-1	240	2	Notre Dame	15/4
37	Ellison, Jerry	RB	5-10	190	R	Tenn.-Chattanooga	—
7	Erickson, Craig	QB	6-2	205	3	Miami (Fla.)	16/15
22	Everett, Thomas	S	5-9	185	8	Baylor	16/16
20	Gray, Jerry	S	6-0	195	10	Texas	14/5
26	Green, Rogerick	CB	6-0	185	3	Kansas State	0/0
74	Gruber, Paul	OT	6-5	290	7	Wisconsin	10/10
40	Hadnot, Butch	RB	6-1	230	1	Texas	0/0
91	Hall, Rhett	DL	6-2	270	4	California	1/0
43	Harris, Rudy	FB	6-1	255	2	Clemson	10/2
85	Hawkins, Courtney	WR	5-9	180	3	Michigan State	16/12
95	Hill, Tony	DE	6-6	255	3	Tenn.-Chattanooga	0/0
65	Holliday, Tommy	OG	6-3	280	R	Southern-B.R.	—
16	Holstein, Scott	P	6-5	210	R	Louisiana State	—
90	Hunter, Jeff	DE	6-4	290	5	Albany State	—
5	Husted, Michael	PK	6-0	190	2	Virginia	16/0
78	Irwin, Tim	OT	6-7	297	14	Tennessee	16/16
24	Jones, Roger	CB	5-9	175	4	Tennessee State	16/5
41	King, Joe	S	6-2	195	4	Oklahoma State	15/10
79	Love, Sean	OG	6-3	290	2	Penn State	2/0
47	Lynch, John	S	6-2	220	2	Stanford	15/4
21	Mack, Milton	CB	5-11	195	8	Alcorn State	12/3
97	Marts, Lonnie	LB	6-1	230	5	Tulane	16/15
61	Mayberry, Tony	C	6-4	290	5	Wake Forest	16/16
35	Mayhew, Martin	CB	5-8	175	7	Florida State	15/14
33	McDowell, Anthony	FB	5-11	235	3	Texas Tech	4/3
70	McRae, Charles	OT	6-7	300	4	Tennessee	13/4
19	Mills, Vidal	S	5-11	190	R	Bethune-Cookman	—
83	Moore, Dave	TE	6-2	245	2	Pittsburgh	15/1
56	Nickerson, Hardy	LB	6-2	230	9	California	16/16
36	Paul, Marcus	S	6-2	200	6	Syracuse	9/0
92	Price, Shawn	DL	6-5	260	2	Pacific	9/6
66	Reimers, Bruce	OG	6-7	300	11	Iowa State	11/10
31	Royster, Mazio	RB	6-1	200	3	Southern Cal	14/0
64	Ryan, Tim	OG	6-2	280	4	Notre Dame	6/0

1994 PREVIEW ■ TAMPA BAY

1994 PLAYER ROSTER

NO.	NAME	POS.	HT.	WT.	EXP.	COLLEGE	GP/GS
48	Saunders, Cedric	TE	6-3	240	R	Ohio State	—
17	Small, Eddie	WR	6-1	200	R	Misissippi	—
10	Smith, Dedric	WR	5-7	170	R	Savannah State	—
45	Stargell, Tony	CB	5-11	189	5	Tennessee State	16/1
4	Stryzinski, Dan	P	6-1	195	5	Indiana	16/0
67	Sullivan, Mike	OG	6-3	290	3	Miami (Fla.)	11/3
51	Thomas, Broderick	LB	6-4	250	6	Nebraska	16/8
87	Thomas, Lamar	WR	6-1	170	2	Miami (Fla.)	14/2
94	Trumbull, Rick	OL	6-6	300	2	Missouri	0/0
30	Turner, Vernon	KR-WR	5-8	185	5	Carson-Newman	8/0
13	Vlasic, Mark	QB	6-3	205	6	Iowa	0/0
9	Warren, Corey	WR	5-10	195	R	Oklahoma	—
11	Weldon, Casey	QB	6-1	200	3	Florida State	3/0
77	Wheeler, Mark	NT	6-2	280	3	Texas A&M	10/10
18	White, Paul	DB	5-9	185	R	Miami (Fla.)	—
34	Williams, Germaine	FB	5-10	230	R	Louisiana State	—
54	Williams, Jimmy	LB	6-3	230	13	Nebraska	11/8
96	Wilson, Bernard	DL	6-2	295	2	Tennessee State	13/2
84	Wilson, Charles	WR	5-10	185	4	Memphis State	15/1
99	Winter, Blaise	DL	6-4	295	10	Syracuse	16/16
46	Workman, Vince	WR	5-10	205	6	Ohio State	16/11

'94 DRAFT PICKS

RD.	NAME	POS.	HT.	WT.	COLLEGE
1.	Dilfer, Trent	QB	6-3	228	Fresno State
2.	Rhett, Errict	RB	5-10	211	Florida
3.	Bishop, Harold	TE	6-4	252	Louisiana State
5.	Pierson, Pete	OT	6-5	287	Washington
6.	Carter, Bernard	LB	6-2	238	East Carolina
7.	Pyne, Jim	C	6-2	282	Virginia Tech

PRO FOOTBALL WEEKLY 1994 ALMANAC

TEAM AT A GLANCE

TEAM DIRECTORY
Address	One Buccaneer Place
	Tampa, Florida 33607
	(813) 870-2700
Stadium	Tampa Stadium
	Tampa, Florida 33607
	Capacity: 74,296
	Playing surface: Grass
Training Camp	University of Tampa
	Tampa, Florida 33606
Colors	Florida orange, white and red
Television	WFTS, Channel 28
Radio	WQYK, 99.5 FM
	WQYK, 1010 AM

ADMINISTRATION
Owner: Hugh F. Culverhouse
Vice president-football administration: Rich McKay
Asst. to president-ticket operations: Terry Wooten
Controller: Patrick Smith
Director of player personnel: Jerry Angelo
Director of college scouting: Tim Ruskell
Director of public relations: Rick Odioso
Director of corporate sales: Jim Overton
Director of advertising and sales: Paul Sickmon
Trainer: Chris Smith

1994 SCHEDULE
Preseason
AUG. 6	CINCINNATI	7:30
AUG. 13	at Seattle	6:00
AUG. 20	at Miami	8:00
AUG. 26	N.Y. JETS	7:30

Regular season
SEP. 4	at Chicago	12:00
SEP. 11	INDIANAPOLIS	1:00
SEP. 18	NEW ORLEANS	1:00
SEP. 25	at Green Bay	12:00
OCT. 2	DETROIT	1:00
OCT. 9	at Atlanta	1:00
OCT. 16	OPEN DATE	
OCT. 23	at San Francisco	1:00
OCT. 30	MINNESOTA	4:00
NOV. 6	CHICAGO	1:00
NOV. 13	at Detroit	8:00
NOV. 20	at Seattle	1:00
NOV. 27	at Minnesota	12:00
DEC. 4	WASHINGTON	1:00
DEC. 11	L.A. RAMS	1:00
DEC. 18	at Washington	1:00
DEC. 24	GREEN BAY	1:00

HEAD COACH
Sam Wyche

One of only three active head coaches in the NFL to participate in a Super Bowl as a player, assistant coach and head coach, Wyche joined the Buccaneers as head coach in 1992. In his first two seasons, the team posted records of 5-11 (1992) and 5-11 (1993). Prior to taking the job in Tampa Bay, Wyche was head coach of the Bengals for eight seasons. He led Cincinnati into the playoffs twice, in 1988 and '90. The Bengals went to the Super Bowl following the '88 season and lost 20-16 to the 49ers. Wyche is considered one of the best offensive thinkers in the game, having devised such innovations as the highly successful no-huddle offense. Born Jan. 5, 1945, Atlanta, Ga.

Previous NFL: head coach, 1992-93 Tampa Bay; 1984-91 Cincinnati; quarterbacks-passing game, 1979-82 San Francisco.

Previous college: head coach, 1983 Indiana; graduate assistant, 1967 South Carolina.

Player: NFL, quarterback, 1968-70 Cincinnati; 1971-73 Washington; 1974 Detroit; 1976 St. Louis; 1976 Buffalo. College, quarterback, 1963-65 Furman.

ASSISTANT COACHES
Maxie Baughan: linebackers

Previous NFL: linebackers, 1992-93 Tampa Bay; 1990-91 Minnesota; 1980-82 Detroit; 1975-79 Baltimore. Player: NFL, linebacker, 1960-65 Philadelphia; 1966-70 L.A. Rams; 1971, 1974 Washington. College: center, linebacker, 1956-60 Georgia Tech.

Ken Clarke: defensive line

Previous NFL: None. Player: NFL, nose tackle, 1978-87 Philadelphia; 1988 Seattle; 1989-91 Minnesota. College: defensive lineman, 1975-77 Syracuse.

David Culley: wide receivers

Previous NFL: None. Player: No NFL. College: 1973, 1975-77 Vanderbilt.

Johnnie Lynn: defensive backs

Previous NFL: None. Player: NFL, defensive back 1979-86 Jets. College: defensive back, 1975-78 UCLA.

Mike Mularkey: offensive assistant

Previous NFL: None. Player: NFL, tight end, 1983-88 Minnesota; 1989-91 Pittsburgh. College: tight end, 1981-83 Florida.

Willie Peete: running backs

Previous NFL: running backs, 1992-93 Tampa Bay; 1987-91 Green Bay; 1983-86 Kansas City. Player: No NFL. College: fullback, 1956-59 Arizona.

Floyd Peters: defensive coordinator

Previous NFL: defensive coordinator, 1991-93 Tampa Bay; 1986-90 Minnesota; 1982-85 St. Louis; 1978-81 Detroit; 1976-77 San Francisco; 1974-75 N.Y. Giants; 1971-73 Miami. Player: NFL, defensive tackle, 1958 Baltimore; 1959-62 Cleveland; 1963 Detroit; 1964-69 Philadelphia; 1970 Washington. College: defensive lineman, 1954-57 San Francisco State.

Turk Schonert: quarterbacks

1994 PREVIEW ■ TAMPA BAY

TEAM AT A GLANCE

Previous NFL: quarterbacks, 1992-93 Tampa Bay. Player: NFL, quarterback, 1981-85 Cincinnati; 1986 Atlanta, 1988-89 Cincinnati. College: quarterback, 1976-79 Stanford.

George Stewart: special teams
Previous NFL: special teams, 1991-93 Tampa Bay; 1989-91 Pittsburgh. Player: No NFL. College: guard, 1977-80 Arkansas.

Bob Wylie: offensive line
Previous NFL: offensive line, 1992-93 Tampa Bay; 1990-91 N.Y. Jets. Player: No NFL. College: linebacker, 1969-71 Colorado.

COACHING RECORDS
(including postseason games)

Years	Coach	W	L	T
1976-84	John McKay	45	91	1
1985-86	Leeman Bennett	4	28	0
1987-90	Ray Perkins	19	41	0
1990-91	Richard Williamson	4	15	0
1992-93	Sam Wyche	10	22	0

HISTORICAL HIGHLIGHTS

1974 The NFL's 27th franchise is awarded to Tampa Bay. Tampa Stadium is to be enlarged to 72,000 seats to accommodate the new team and its fans. ... Ownership is awarded to Hugh F. Culverhouse.

1975 As a result of a local contest, the club is named the Buccaneers. ... The Tampa Sports Authority approves a 30-year lease agreement with Buccaneer officials for Tampa Stadium.

1976 In their first season, the Bucs have the unfortunate distinction of becoming the first NFL team to lose all 14 games in one season.

1977 Aftrer 26 consecutive losses, the Bucs win their first game, defeating New Orleans 33-14.

1979 Ricky Bell becomes the first Buccaneer to rush for more than 1,000 yards in a season, gaining 1,263 on 283 carries. ... Tampa Bay defeats Philadelphia 24-17 in its first-ever postseason game, with Ricky Bell rushing for 142 yards and two TD's. But Tampa Bay's Super Bowl aspirations are soon crushed, as Los Angeles defeats the Bucs 9-0 at Tampa Stadium in the NFC championship game.

1981 In a winner-take-all showdown with the Detroit Lions in the last game of the season, Tampa Bay wins the NFC Central Division title by a score of 20-17 but is eliminated from the playoffs two weeks later by the Dallas Cowboys 38-0.

1982-83 The Buccaneers qualify for postseason play for the third time in four years after a 26-23 win over the Bears in the last game of a strike-shortened season gives them a record of 5-4. In the playoff tournament, however, Tampa Bay loses to Dallas 30-17.

1984 In a 17-12 Buccaneer victory over Minnesota, James Wilder gains 219 yards rushing, the most in club history and the most by an NFL running back since 1977. Wilder also sets the Tampa Bay season-rushing mark by gaining 1,544 yards. His 407 carries is an NFL record.

1987 Tampa Bay chooses Heisman Trophy-winning QB Vinny Testaverde with the first overall pick in the draft.

1991 The team opens its Krewe of Honor with charter members coach John McKay, RB Ricky Bell and DE Lee Roy Selmon.

1992 Sam Wyche is named head coach, the fifth in in franchise history.

229

PRO FOOTBALL WEEKLY 1994 ALMANAC

TEAM AT A GLANCE

HALL OF FAME MEMBERS
None

RETIRED JERSEY NUMBERS
63   DE Lee Roy Selmon

FIRST-ROUND DRAFT CHOICES
(since 1980)

Year	Selection	College
1980	OT-OG Ray Snell	Wisconsin
1981	LB Hugh Green	Pittsburgh
1982	OG Sean Farrell	Penn State
1983	No choice	
1984	No Choice	
1985	DE Ron Holmes	Washington
1986	RB Bo Jackson	Auburn
	DB Rod Jones	Southern Methodist
1987	QB Vinny Testaverde	Miami (Fla.)
1988	OT Paul Gruber	Wisconsin
1989	LB Broderick Thomas	Nebraska
1990	LB Keith McCants	Alabama
1991	OT Charles McRae	Tennessee
1992	No choice	
1993	DE Eric Curry	Alabama
1994	QB Trent Dilfer	Fresno State

RECORD VS. OTHER NFL TEAMS
(including postseason games)

	Record
Arizona Cardinals	6-6-0
Atlanta Falcons	6-6-0
Buffalo Bills	4-2-0
Chicago Bears	8-24-0
Cincinnati Bengals	1-3-0
Cleveland Browns	0-4-0
Dallas Cowboys	0-8-0
Denver Broncos	1-2-0
Detroit Lions	16-16-0
Green Bay Packers	12-17-1
Houston Oilers	1-3-0
Indianapolis Colts	2-5-0
Kansas City Chiefs	2-5-0
Los Angeles Raiders	0-3-0
Los Angeles Rams	2-9-0
Miami Dolphins	1-4-0
Minnesota Vikings	9-23-0
New England Patriots	0-3-0
New Orleans Saints	4-11-0
New York Giants	3-8-0
New York Jets	1-5-0
Philadelphia Eagles	1-3-0
Pittsburgh Steelers	0-4-0
San Diego Chargers	0-6-0
San Francisco 49ers	1-11-0
Seattle Seahawks	0-2-0
Washington Redskins	0-4-0

YEAR-BY-YEAR RECORDS

Year	Won	Lost	Tied	Year	Won	Lost	Tied
1976	0	14	0	1985	2	14	0
1977	2	12	0	1986	2	14	0
1978	5	11	0	1987	4	11	0
1979**	10	6	0	1988	5	11	0
1980	5	10	1	1989	5	11	0
1981**	9	7	0	1990	6	10	0
1982**	5	4	0	1991	3	13	0
1983	2	14	0	1992	5	11	0
1984	6	10	0	1993	5	11	0
				Total	81	194	1

Number of NFL championships   0
Number of years .500 or better   3
Number of years below .500   15

*NFL champions
**Playoff team

1994 PREVIEW ■ TAMPA BAY

RECORDS

INDIVIDUAL

Service
Seasons played	10	Steve Wilson (1976-85)
Games played	132	Richard Wood (1976-84)
Consecutive games	132	Richard Wood (1976-84)

Scoring
Points, career	416	Donald Igwebuike (1985-89)
Points, season	99	Donald Igwebuike (1989)
Points, game	24	Jimmie Giles (10/20/85)
Touchdowns, career	46	James Wilder (1981-89)
Touchdowns, season	13	James Wilder (1984)
Touchdowns, game	4	Jimmie Giles (10/20/85)
Field goals, career	94	Donald Igwebuike (1985-89)
Field goals, season	23	Steve Christie (1990)
Field goals, game	5	By many players
Extra points, career	134	Donald Igwebuike (1985-89)
Extra points, season	38	Obed Ariri (1984)
Extra points, game	6	Donald Igwebuike (9/13/87)

Rushing
Yards, career	5,957	James Wilder (1981-89)
Yards, season	1,544	James Wilder (1984)
Yards, game	219	James Wilder (11/6/83)
Attempts, career	1,575	James Wilder (1981-89)
Attempts, season	407	James Wilder (1984)
Attempts, game	43	James Wilder (9/30/84)
Touchdowns, career	37	James Wilder (1981-89)
Touchdowns, season	13	James Wilder (1984)
Touchdowns, game	3	Reggie Cobb (11/20/91)

Passing
Rating, career	73.9	Steve DeBerg (1984-87, 92-93)
Rating, season	85.3	Steve DeBerg (1987)
Completions, career	1,126	Vinny Testaverde (1987-92)
Completions, season	308	Steve DeBerg (1984)
Completions, game	31	Vinny Testaverde (12/10/89)
Yards, career	14,820	Vinny Testaverde (1987-92)
Yards, season	3,563	Doug Williams (1981)
Yards, game	486	Doug Williams (11/16/80)
Attempts, career	2,160	Vinny Testaverde (1987-92)
Attempts, season	521	Doug Williams (1980)
Attempts, game	56	Doug Williams (9/28/80)
Touchdowns, career	77	Vinny Testaverde (1987-92)
Touchdowns, season	20	Vinny Testaverde (1989)
		Doug Williams (1980)
Touchdowns, game	5	Steve DeBerg (9/13/87)

Receiving
Receptions, career	430	James Wilder (1981-89)
Receptions, season	86	Mark Carrier (1989)
Receptions, game	13	James Wilder (9/15/85)
Yards, career	4,928	Kevin House (1980-86)
Yards, season	1,422	Mark Carrier (1989)
Yards, game	212	Mark Carrier (12/6/87)
Touchdowns, career	34	Jimmie Giles (1978-86)
Touchdowns, season	9	Mark Carrier (1989)
		Bruce Hill (1988)
		Kevin House (1981)
Touchdowns, game	4	Jimmie Giles (10/20/85)

Interceptions
Career	29	Cedric Brown (1976-84)
Season	9	Cedric Brown (1981)
Game	2	By many players

Sacks
Career	78.5	Lee Roy Selmon (1976-84)
Season	13	Lee Roy Selmon (1977)
Game	3	By many players

Longest plays
Run from scrimmage	75	James Wilder (TD, 11/6/83)
Pass play	89	Vinny Testaverde to Willie Drewrey (TD, 12/2/90)
Field goal	57	Michael Husted (12/19/93)
Interception return	82	Neal Colzie (TD, 9/5/81)
Kickoff return	58	Phil Freeman (9/8/85)
Punt return	56	John Holt (11/22/81)
Punt	70	Dave Green (11/20/77)

Top scorers
	Points
Donald Igwebuike (1985-89)	416
James Wilder (1981-89)	276
Jimmie Giles (1978-86)	204
Bill Capece (1981-83)	196
Kevin House (1980-86)	186
Steve Christie (1990-91)	163

Top rushers
	Yards
James Wilder (1981-89)	5,957
Reggie Cobb (1990-93)	3,061
Ricky Bell (1977-81)	3,057
Jerry Eckwood (1979-81)	1,845
Gary Anderson (1990-93)	1,159
Lars Tate (1988-89)	1,056

Top passers
	Completions
Vinny Testaverde (1987-92)	1,126
Doug Williams (1978-82)	895
Steve DeBerg (1984-87, 92-93)	813
Jack Thompson (1983-84)	274
Steve Young (1985-86)	267
Craig Erickson (1992-93)	248

Top passers
	Yards
Vinny Testaverde (1987-92)	14,820
Doug Williams (1978-82)	12,648
Steve DeBerg (1984-87, 92-93)	9,439
Jack Thompson (1983-84)	3,243
Steve Young (1985-86)	3,217
Craig Erickson (1992-93)	3,175

Top receivers
	Receptions
James Wilder (1981-89)	430
Mark Carrier (1987-92)	321
Kevin House (1980-86)	286
Jimmie Giles (1978-86)	279
Gerald Carter (1981-87)	239
Ron Hall (1987-93)	209

Top receivers
	Yards
Mark Carrier (1987-92)	5,018
Kevin House (1980-86)	4,928
Jimmie Giles (1978-86)	4,300
James Wilder (1981-89)	3,492
Gerald Carter (1981-87)	3,443
Bruce Hill (1987-91)	2,942

Most interceptions
	No.
Cedric Brown (1976-84)	29
Mike Washington (1976-84)	28
Harry Hamilton (1988-91)	17
Mark Cotney (1976-80, 82-84)	17
Ricky Reynolds (1987-93)	17
Mark Robinson (1988-90)	12
Jeris White (1977-79)	12

Most sacks
	No.
Lee Roy Selmon (1976-84)	78.5
David Logan (1979-86)	29
Broderick Thomas (1989-93)	26.5

231

PREVIEW WASHINGTON REDSKINS

It was a disaster from start to finish. Check that. The Redskins actually opened the season with a convincing, one-sided win over the defending Super Bowl champion Cowboys. But, after that, it was all downhill. Losses to the Eagles, Cardinals, Giants, Rams and Jets. Underdogs to the Bucs. A very un-Redskin-like season, to say the least.

After a tremendously successful 19-year career as an assistant coach in the NFL, including 15 seasons with the Redskins, Richie Petitbon was given the Redskin head-coaching job after Joe Gibbs retired. But instead of picking up where Gibbs left off, the season was an unmitigated disaster for the Redskins, and owner Jack Kent Cooke dumped Petitbon after it ended.

Cooke, who took each of his team's 12 losses personally, reached into the pool of NFL assistants and came up with this year's hottest name, Norv Turner. Turner had been the offensive coordinator of the Cowboys, and their back-to-back Super Bowl titles told Cooke that Turner was the man for the job. The pressure is on Turner, because Cooke has already told the world that he expects the Redskins to have a winning record this season and return to the playoffs in 1995.

But rebuilding the Redskins will not be easy. They go into the 1994 season with a new head coach, a new coaching staff, a new quarterback, a new WR corps and new names on defense. To expect this group to show dramatic improvement may be Cooke's folly, but Turner knows what is expected. The pressure of being the Redskins' head coach is great, but with it come great rewards. If he's successful, he'll almost certainly be more popular than the president or any other politician in town. However, if he can't bring the Redskins out of their doldrums, he won't have a chance to get elected as dog-catcher.

"I know what is expected here, and I couldn't be more prepared," said Turner. "The Redskin tradition means something very important, and I'm intent on making sure this team plays as well as it possibly can."

The Redskins have seemingly always been a one-RB offense that allowed maximum protection for the quarterback. They tried to change that briefly last year and go to a quick-passing attack, but that turned out to be a disaster after QB Mark Rypien went down with a knee injury. With Turner at the controls, the Redskins will use a two-RB set and have the quarterback get rid of the ball quickly.

John Friesz is the Redskins' No. 1 quarterback at this point, but the job is his on a temporary basis only. The Redskins drafted former Tennessee QB Heath Shuler with their No. 1 pick, and he is clearly the team's quarterback of the future. Friesz was the Chargers' No. 1 quarterback and showed promise, but he fell out of favor in 1992 after he was injured and Stan Humphries took over. When healthy, Friesz is a fine touch passer with good accuracy and a moderately quick release. Friesz has the guts to hang in against a strong rush, but he has very little mobility. If the Redskins decide to give Shuler a crash course and get him in the lineup, they will get a very mobile quarterback who has an exceptionally quick release. Shuler is a fine ball-handler and a great faker, but he may have trouble adjusting to the complicated defensive fronts he'll see in the NFL.

If the Redskins are to make a run at respectability, the running game will likely lead the way. As a rookie, Reggie Brooks broke the 1,000-yard barrier and showed signs of becoming a great back. Brooks has exceptional speed and the ability to break long runs at any given moment. What makes his rookie achievement even more noteworthy is the fact that he did it behind a relatively ineffective offensive line. The Redskins were beaten up and hurt in that area throughout the season. Brooks is short and stocky, but he has explosive quickness, tremendous balance and

PHOTO BY HARRY SCULL JR.

Darrell Green

1994 PREVIEW ■ WASHINGTON

the ability to spin out of tackles. Brooks is not an all-around back. He is a limited receiver and even worse as a blocker.

Brian Mitchell is an excellent pass-catching back, a good return man and can even play quarterback in emergency situations. He's also a surprisingly tough runner between the tackles. Ricky Ervins has not done much since his rookie year of 1991, although he is a quick, tough runner in the mold of Brooks.

The Redskin receivers will have a completely new look. Former Ram Henry Ellard was once a potent deep threat, but he can no longer run by defenders. Nevertheless, he may be the Redskins' top receiver because he is an effective, intermediate-range wideout who works hard and has always developed a good rapport with his quarterback. When the Redskins drafted former Michigan Heisman Trophy winner Desmond Howard, they expected him to be a big-time receiver. Howard has been a bust in his first two seasons in Washington. While he has quickness and agility, he is not a speed receiver. He also needs to regain his confidence. Art Monk is undoubtedly a Hall of Famer-in-waiting, but he won't be back in Washington unless he takes a pay cut.

Washington picked up former Raider Ethan Horton, and he fills the role of pass-catching tight end. Horton is a big target who still runs well, but not as well as he once did. Ron Middleton is a third tackle who is not a pass-catching threat. Frank Wycheck is a solid receiver who can fill the role of H-back or fullback.

Washington's offensive line was devastated by injuries a year ago. None was bigger than the knee injury suffered by All-Pro OLT Jim Lachey, who was forced to the sidelines for the entire year. Lachey's rehabilitation is reportedly going very well, and, if he is able to play the entire season, the Redskin offensive line will be much better.

Injury-prone Ed Simmons is the right tackle, and he is backed up by Mo Elewonibi, another injury-prone player. Ex-Cowboy John Gesek will start at center, and that will send Raleigh McKenzie to guard, which is his best position. McKenzie is a solid pass protector, and Gesek performed very well for the Cowboys after Mark Stepnoski was injured. Former Pro Bowler Mark Schlereth is trying to come back from a mysterious injury that affected the nerves in his legs. If he can't play consistently, Ray Brown will likely be the other starting guard. Ex-Colt Trevor Matich and No. 2 pick Tré Johnson add depth.

Turner brought in Ron Lynn from Cincinnati to run his defense. Much like Arizona head coach Buddy Ryan, Lynn likes to bring as much pressure on opposing quarterbacks as possible. That means the cornerbacks will often be left in man-on-man coverage.

Former Michigan State DT Bobby Wilson is the key to the Redskin defensive line. Wilson is quick and powerful but has been troubled by injuries. Second-year DRE Sterling Palmer has the tools to develop into a solid pass rusher. He is tall and fast with extremely long arms and has a non-stop motor. Tim Johnson has been a good defensive tackle the last two years and will start next to Wilson. He is solid against the run and the pass. Former Seahawk Tony Woods has a good shot at starting at left end. Shane Collins is good against the run but can't rush the passer.

The key player on the Redskin defense may be former Cardinal Ken Harvey. He has great speed coming off the corner and is a solid pass rusher, but he has never shown all-around ability. Harvey does not have much coverage ability, unlike fellow OLB Andre Collins. Collins lacks size; thus, when he lines up over a big tight end, he has problems. MLB Kurt Gouveia is an easy player to discount because he isn't big, strong or fast, but he has tremendous instincts and never quits. Gouveia was hampered by an ankle injury a year ago, but, when healthy, he makes plays. Monte Coleman is now a nickel linebacker, and he still runs and pursues well. Rick Hamilton has the size and moxie to play well at inside linebacker.

Darrell Green is still wickedly fast and a tremendous leaper, even if he is 34 years old. The Redskins always leave him in one-on-one coverage, and, while he gets burned at times due to concentration lapses, he is still a top cover man. Tom Carter started opposite Green as a rookie, and he has very similar tools. Carter runs a sub-4.4 40, has a 40-inch vertical jump and he picked off six passes as a rookie. However, at this point in his career, he is more of a zone corner than a one-on-one cover guy. A.J. Johnson is a very fast third cornerback, but he is too slight to be a fulltimer. With SS Danny Copeland retiring, either Todd Bowles or ex-Saint Keith Taylor has an excellent shot at taking over the No. 1 job. FS Brad Edwards is anything but consistent. He played tremendous football at the end of the 1991 Super Bowl season, but he has usually been out of position since then.

PK Chip Lohmiller is coming off a poor season. He connected on only 16-of-28 FG attempts and needs to regain his best form if he wants to remain on the payroll. Lohmiller has one of the strongest legs in the game, as does P Reggie Roby. Roby has great distance but is not the kind of punter who kicks away from a returner. Mitchell and Howard are good returners, but both were less than stellar in 1993.

FAST FACTS

■ The Redskins' 4-12 record last season was their worst since going 3-11 in 1963.

■ Reggie Brooks' 85-yard TD run against the Eagles last year was the second-longest in team history. In fact, he had the two longest runs in the NFL in 1993.

■ No Redskin quarterback has led the league in passing since Sonny Jurgensen did it in 1969.

1994 PLAYER ROSTER

NO.	NAME	POS.	HT.	WT.	EXP.	COLLEGE	GP/GS
29	Bell, William	FB	5-11	203	R	Georgia Tech	—
40	Brooks, Reggie	RB	5-8	202	2	Notre Dame	16/11
67	Brown, Ray	OT	6-5	312	9	Arkansas State	16/14
99	Buck, Jason	DE	6-4	274	8	Brigham Young	13/3
25	Carter, Tom	CB	5-11	181	2	Notre Dame	14/11
81	Clifton, Gregory	WR	5-11	175	2	Johnson C. Smith	2/0
51	Coleman, Monte	LB	6-2	242	16	Central Arkansas	14/4
55	Collins, Andre	LB	6-1	231	5	Penn State	13/13
91	Collins, Shane	DE	6-3	267	3	Arizona State	8/5
58	Dingle, Nate	LB	6-3	254	R	Cincinnati	—
35	Duckett, Tico	RB	5-10	195	1	Michigan State	0/0
27	Edwards, Brad	FS	6-2	207	7	South Carolina	16/16
73	Earle, Guy	OT	6-4	290	1	Chadron State	0/0
24	Eilers, Pat	FS	5-11	197	4	Notre Dame	11/0
64	Elewonibi, Moe	OT	6-4	286	5	Brigham Young	15/15
85	Ellard, Henry	WR	5-11	182	12	Fresno State	16/16
52	Elliott, Matt	C	6-1	265	3	Michigan	0/0
32	Ervins, Ricky	RB	5-7	195	4	Southern Cal	15/1
93	Faulkner, Jeff	DE	6-4	305	4	Southern	6/3
50	Floyd, Gonzalo	LB	6-3	233	R	Texas-El Paso	—
19	Friesz, John	QB	6-4	218	4	Idaho	12/6
75	Gesak, John	C	6-5	282	8	Cal-Sacramento	14/0
54	Gouveia, Kurt	LB	6-1	233	8	Brigham Young	16/16
90	Graf, Rick	DE	6-5	244	8	Wisconsin	5/0
28	Green, Darrell	CB	5-8	170	12	Texas A&I	16/16
23	Hall, Chris	S	6-2	184	1	East Carolina	—
56	Hamilton, Rick	LB	6-2	241	2	Central Florida	16/0
57	Harvey, Ken	LB	6-2	245	7	California	16/6
6	Hinchcliff, Willie	WR	6-0	195	1	Aukland Institute	0/0
86	Hobbs, Stephen	WR	5-11	200	7	North Alabama	0/0
95	Hochertz, Martin	DE	6-5	269	2	Southern Illinois	0/0
96	Hollinquest, Lamont	LB	6-3	245	2	Southern Cal	16/0
89	Horton, Ethan	TE	6-4	240	8	North Carolina	16/16
80	Howard, Desmond	WR	5-9	180	3	Michigan	16/6
50	Huntington, Greg	C	6-3	287	2	Penn State	9/0
88	Jenkins, James	TE	6-2	241	4	Rutgers	15/5
47	Johnson, A.J.	CB	5-8	175	6	SW Texas State	13/3
78	Johnson, Tim	DT	6-3	275	8	Penn State	15/15
79	Lachey, Jim	OT	6-6	294	10	Ohio State	0/0
52	Lawrence, Tyler	LB	6-4	248	R	North Carolina St.	—
8	Lohmiller, Chip	PK	6-3	215	7	Minnesota	16/0
59	Matich, Trevor	C	6-4	297	10	Brigham young	16/4
20	Mays, Alvoid	CB	5-9	172	5	West Virginia	15/2
63	McKenzie, Raleigh	C-OG	6-2	277	10	Tennessee	16/16
87	Middleton, Ron	TE	6-2	262	9	Auburn	16/16
73	Mills, Lamar	DE	6-5	270	R	Indiana	—
30	Mitchell, Brian	RB	5-10	203	5	SW Louisiana	16/4
62	Moore, Darryl	OG	6-2	292	3	Texas-El Paso	12/0
37	Morrison, Darryl	CB	5-11	185	2	Arizona	4/0
4	O'Hara, Pat	QB	6-3	205	3	Southern Cal	0/0
10	Olobia, Austin	WR	5-11	195	1	Washington State	0/0
45	Owens, Dondro	CB	5-9	170	R	Howard	—
97	Palmer, Sterling	DE	6-5	256	2	Florida State	14/10
1	Roby, Reggie	P	6-2	258	12	Iowa	9/0
82	Rowe, Ray	TE	6-2	256	3	San Diego State	1/0

1994 PREVIEW ■ WASHINGTON

1994 PLAYER ROSTER

NO.	NAME	POS.	HT.	WT.	EXP.	COLLEGE	GP/GS
39	Rush, Tyrone	RB	5-11	196	R	North Alabama	—
46	Satterfield, Brian	FB	6-0	204	R	North Alabama	—
69	Schlereth, Mark	OG	6-3	278	6	Idaho	9/8
74	Siever, Paul	OT	6-6	294	3	Penn State	0/0
76	Simmons, Ed	OT	6-5	300	8	Eastern Washington	13/13
60	Simmons, Jason	DE	6-5	250	R	Ohio State	—
37	Smith, Cedric	FB	5-10	222	4	Florida	0/0
61	Smith, Vernice	OG	6-3	298	6	Florida A&M	14/8
84	Stock, Mark	WR	6-0	180	8	Virginia Military Inst.	3/0
29	Taylor, Keith	S	5-11	206	6	Illinois	16/14
41	Thomas, Johnny	CB	5-9	191	6	Baylor	16/0
18	Williams, Keith	WR	5-10	177	R	San Diego State	—
94	Wilson, Bobby	DT	6-2	297	4	Michigan State	12/9
98	Woods, Tony	DE	6-4	269	8	Pitttsburgh	14/8
36	Wycheck, Frank	FB	6-3	235	2	Maryland	9/7

'94 DRAFT PICKS

RD.	NAME	POS.	HT.	WT.	COLLEGE
1.	Shuler, Heath	QB	6-2	221	Tennessee
2.	Johnson, Tré	OT	6-3	304	Temple
3.	Winans, Tydus	WR	5-10	182	Fresno State
3.	Patton, Joe	OG	6-4	286	Alabama A&M
4.	Haws, Kurt	TE	6-4	248	Utah
6.	Nottage, Dexter	DE	6-4	273	Florida A&M
7.	Frerotte, Gus	QB	6-3	231	Tulsa

PRO FOOTBALL WEEKLY 1994 ALMANAC

TEAM AT A GLANCE

TEAM DIRECTORY

Address	Redskin Park, P.O. Box 17247
	Washington, D.C. 20041
	(703) 478-8900
Stadium	RFK Stadium
	Washington, D.C. 20003
	Capacity: 56,454
	Playing surface: Grass
Training Camp	Dickinson College
	Carlisle, Pennsylvania 17013
Colors	Burgundy and gold
Television	WTTG, Channel 5
Radio	WTEM, 570 AM

ADMINISTRATION

Chairman of the board: Jack Kent Cooke
Executive vice president: John Kent Cooke Sr.
Controller: Greg Dillon
General manager: Charley Casserly
Assistant general manager: Bobby Mitchell
Director of player contracts: Joe Mendes
Director of player personnel: Kirk Mee
Director of communications: Rick Vaughn
Ticket manager: Jeff Ritter
Trainer: Bubba Tyer

1994 SCHEDULE

Preseason

AUG. 8	at Buffalo	8:00
AUG. 12	KANSAS CITY	8:00
AUG. 18	at New England	7:00
AUG. 26	PITTSBURGH	8:00

Regular season

SEP. 4	SEATTLE	1:00
SEP. 11	at New Orleans	3:00
SEP. 18	at N. Y. Giants	4:00
SEP. 25	ATLANTA	1:00
OCT. 2	DALLAS	1:00
OCT. 9	at Philadelphia	8:00
OCT. 16	ARIZONA	1:00
OCT. 23	at Indianapolis	12:00
OCT. 30	PHILADELPHIA	1:00
NOV. 6	SAN FRANCISCO	1:00
NOV. 13	OPEN DATE	
NOV. 20	at Dallas	12:00
NOV. 27	N.Y. GIANTS	4:00
DEC. 4	at Tampa Bay	1:00
DEC. 11	at Arizona	2:00
DEC. 18	TAMPA BAY	1:00
DEC. 24	at L.A. Rams	1:00

HEAD COACH

Norv Turner

After spending three seasons as offensive coordinator of the Cowboys — two of which ended in Super Bowl victories — Turner was selected to replace the fired Richie Petitbon as head coach of the Redskins. Under the guidance of Turner and Dallas head coach Jimmy Johnson, the Cowboys boasted one of the most balanced offensive attacks in the NFL the last three years. Before working for the Cowboys, Turner spent five years with the Rams. Born May 17, 1952, LeJeune, N.C.

Previous NFL: assistant head coach-offensive coordinator-quarterbacks, 1991-93 Dallas; wide receivers, 1985-90 L.A. Rams.

Previous college: offensive coordinator, 1984 Southern Cal; quarterbacks, 1981-83 Southern Cal; defensive backs, 1980 Southern Cal; wide receivers, 1976-79 Southern Cal; graduate assistant, 1975 Oregon.

Player: No NFL. College, quarterback, 1972-74 Oregon.

ASSISTANT COACHES

Cam Cameron: quarterbacks
Previous NFL: None. Player: No NFL. College: 1982-83 Indiana.

Russ Grimm: tight ends
Previous NFL: tight ends, 1992-93 Washington. Player: NFL, guard, 1981-91 Washington. College: guard, 1978-80 Pittsburgh.

Mike Haluchak: linebackers
Previous NFL: linebackers, 1992-93 Cincinnati; 1986-91 San Diego. Player: No NFL. College: linebacker, 1967-70 Southern Cal.

Jim Hanifan: offensive line
Previous NFL: offensive line, 1990-93 Washington. 1987-89 Atlanta (interim head coach four games in 1989); 1974-85 St. Louis (head coach 1980-85). Player: No NFL. College: tight end, 1952-54 California.

Ray Horton: defensive assistant
Previous NFL: None. Player: NFL, safety, 1989-91 Dallas; 1983-88 Cincinnati. College: safety, 1979-82 Washington.

Bobby Jackson: running backs
Previous NFL: running backs, 1992-93 Phoenix; 1987-91 San Diego; 1983-86 Atlanta. Player: No NFL. College: linebacker, running backs 1959-62 Samford.

Bob Karmelowicz: defensive line
Previous NFL: defensive line, 1992-93 Cincinnati. Player: No NFL. College: nose tackle, 1972 Bridgeport.

Ron Lynn: defensive coordinator
Previous NFL: defensive coordinator, 1992-93 Cincinnati; 1986-91 San Diego. Player: No NFL. College: quarterback, defensive back, 1963-65 Mount Union (Ohio).

Terry Robiskie: wide receivers
Previous NFL: tight ends, 1982-93 L.A. Raiders. Player: NFL, running back, 1977-79 L.A. Raiders; 1980-81 Miami. College: running back, 1973-76 Louisiana State.

Pete Rodriguez: special teams

236

1994 PREVIEW ■ WASHINGTON

TEAM AT A GLANCE

Previous NFL: special teams, 1990-93 Phoenix; 1988-89 L.A. Raiders. Player: No NFL. College: guard, linebacker, 1959-60 Denver; 1961-63 Western State (Colo.).

Emmitt Thomas: defensive backs
Previous NFL: defensive coordinator, 1986-93 Washington. 1981-85 St. Louis. Player: NFL, defensive back, 1966-78 Kansas City. College: quarterback, wide receiver, 1963-65 Bishop (Tex.) College.

COACHING RECORDS
(including postseason games)

Years	Coach	W	L	T
1932	Lud Wray	4	4	2
1933-34	William "Lone Star" Dietz	11	11	2
1935	Eddie Casey	2	8	1
1936-42	Ray Flaherty	56	23	3
1943	Arthur "Dutch" Bergman	7	4	1
1944-45	Dudley DeGroot	14	6	1
1946-48	Glen "Turk" Edwards	16	18	1
1949	John Whelchel	3	3	1
1949-51	Herman Ball	4	16	0
1951	Dick Todd	5	4	0
1952-53	Curly Lambeau	10	13	1
1954-58	Joe Kuharich	26	32	2
1959-60	Mike Nixon	4	18	2
1961-65	Bill McPeak	21	46	3
1966-68	Otto Graham	17	22	3
1969	Vince Lombardi	7	5	2
1970	Bill Austin	6	8	0
1971-77	George Allen	69	35	1
1978-80	Jack Pardee	24	24	0
1981-1992	Joe Gibbs	140	65	0
1993	Richie Petitbon	4	12	0

HISTORICAL HIGHLIGHTS

1932 George Preston Marshall heads a syndicate that buys an NFL franchise for Boston. ... Playing in the home park of baseball's Boston Braves, the team is called the "Braves."
1936 The Redskins win the Eastern Division with a record of 7-5. ... The Redskins lose the NFL championship game to the Packers 21-6.
1937 The Redskins move to Washington, D.C. ... Washington selects Sammy Baugh of Texas Christian as its first-round draft choice. He leads the Redskins to an NFL championship, defeating the Bears 28-21.
1940 The Redskins win the NFL Eastern Division with a 9-2 record. ... Washington faces the Chicago Bears in the league title game at Griffith Stadium and loses 73-0, the most one-sided defeat in NFL history.
1942 The Redskins suffer only one loss during the season and advance to the NFL title game, where Sammy Baugh's 85-yard quick kick sets the Bears back and the Redskins win 14-6.
1943 The Redskins win the Eastern Division in a playoff, defeating the Giants 29-0. ... In the championship, Sammy Baugh suffers a concussion early in the game, and the Redskins lose 41-21 to Chicago.
1944 The Redskins abandon their single-wing formation and adopt the T-formation, and Sammy Baugh switches from tailback to a T-formation quarterback.
1945 In sub-zero weather the Redskins lose the title to the Rams 15-14 on two freakish plays.
1961 The first game in the new D.C. Stadium draws 27,767 fans, but the Redskins fail to hold a 21-0 lead and fall to the Giants 24-21.
1966 The Redskins and the Giants score the most points in NFL history in Washington's 72-41 rout.
1967 Sonny Jurgensen sets new Redskin and NFL passing records for most attempts (508), completions (288), and yards gained (3,747). Receivers Charlie Taylor, Jerry Smith and Bobby Mitchell finish 1, 2 and 4 in the league.
1969 Vince Lombardi, the fabled Packer coach, becomes head coach of the Washington Redskins.
1972-73 Head coach George Allen guides the Redskins to 11 wins, the most in 30 years. ... With an 11-3 record, the Redskins earn their way to the conference championship. ... Then, with a convincing 26-3 win over the Cowboys at RFK Stadium (formerly D.C. Stadium), the Redskins win a trip to Super Bowl VII. ... At the L.A. Coliseum, the Redskins lose the Super Bowl to the Dolphins 14-7.
1974 The Redskins have the best record in the NFC East, 10-4, and the second best in the NFL, and for the fourth consecutive year make the NFL playoffs.
1975 WR Charley Taylor becomes the all-time leading pass receiver in NFL history with his 634th career catch against the Eagles in the season's final game.
1976 The Redskins make the playoffs for the fifth time in six years by winning their final four games and turning in a record of 10-4 but then are defeated by the Vikings 35-20.
1982-83 John Riggins rushes for 185 yards in leading the Redskins to a 21-7 win over Minnesota and a spot in the NFC title game. ... The Redskins defeat the Cowboys 31-17 to reach the Super Bowl. Washington earns its first world championship in 40 years by defeating the Dolphins 27-17 in Super Bowl XVII.
1983 John Riggins breaks an NFL record with 24 rushing touchdowns and sets a Redskin mark with 1,347 yards rushing. ... PK Mark Moseley scores 161 points, second in NFL history to Paul Hornung's 176 registered in 1960.
1983-84 For the second year in a row, the Redskins finish with the best record in the NFL, 14-2. They also set an NFL record by scoring 541 points. ... In the most lopsided playoff game in 26 years, the Redskins defeat the LA Rams 51-7 in the NFC title game. ... The Redskins meet the Los Angeles Raiders at Tampa Stadium in Super Bowl XVIII but lose 38-9.
1984 The Redskins finish as Eastern Division champions for the 11th time in the club's history and for the third straight season but lose to the Chicago Bears 23-19 in the playoffs.
1985 Club owner Jack Kent Cooke purchases the team's remaining stock interest and becomes 100 percent owner of the Redskins.
1986 The Redskins win 12-of-16 games and qualify for the playoffs as a wild-card. After defeating the Rams 19-7, Washington surprises the Super Bowl defending-champion Chicago Bears 27-13. ... The Redskins fall in the NFC title game to the Giants 17-0.
1987-88 Washington makes the playoffs and defeat the Bears again 21-17. The Redskins then beat the Vikings 17-10 to win the NFC. ... In Super Bowl XXII, the Redskins defeat Denver 42-10 in a game in which 20 Super Bowl records are broken.
1990-91 The Redskins make it to the playoffs and beat the Eagles 20-6, but then fall to the 49ers 28-10.

237

PRO FOOTBALL WEEKLY 1994 ALMANAC

TEAM AT A GLANCE

1991-92 Washington wins the NFC East with a 14-2 record. ... In the playoffs, it defeats Atlanta 24-7 and Detroit 41-10. ... In Super Bowl XXVII, the Redskins defeat the Buffalo Bills 37-24.
1992-93 Washington makes the playoffs, beating Minnesota 24-7 but losing to San Francisco 20-13.
1993 Head coach Joe Gibbs leaves and assistant coach Richie Petitbon replaces him.
1994 Richie Petitbon is fired after a 4-12 season and is replaced by Dallas offensive coordinator Norv Turner.

HALL OF FAME MEMBERS

	Yrs with Redskins	Inducted
QB Sammy Baugh*	1937-52	1963
Owner George P. Marshall*	1932-69	1963
HB Bill Dudley	1950-51, 53	1966
HB Cliff Battles	1932-37	1968
E Wayne Millner	1936-41, 45	1968
T Turk Edwards	1932-40	1969
Coach Ray Flaherty	1936-42	1976
LB Sam Huff	1964-67, 69	1982
QB Sonny Jurgensen	1964-74	1983
WR Bobby Mitchell	1962-68	1983
WR Charley Taylor	1964-75, 77	1984
S Ken Houston	1973-80	1986
RB John Riggins	1976-79, 81-85	1992

* Charter member

RETIRED JERSEY NUMBERS
33   QB Sammy Baugh

FIRST-ROUND DRAFT CHOICES
(since 1980)

Year	Selection	College
1980	WR Art Monk	Syracuse
1981	OT Mark May	Pittsburgh
1982	No choice	
1983	CB Darrell Green	Texas A&I
1984	No choice	
1985	No choice	
1986	No choice	
1987	No choice	
1988	No choice	
1989	No choice	
1990	No choice	
1991	DT Bobby Wilson	Michigan State
1992	WR Desmond Howard	Michigan
1993	CB Tom Carter	Notre Dame
1994	QB Heath Shuler	Tennessee

RECORD VS. OTHER NFL TEAMS
(including postseason games)

	Record
Arizona Cardinals	61-36-2
Atlanta Falcons	14-3-1
Buffalo Bills	5-3-0
Chicago Bears	16-22-1
Cincinnati Bengals	4-2-0
Cleveland Browns	9-32-1
Dallas Cowboys	29-37-2
Denver Broncos	4-3-0
Detroit Lions	24-8-0
Green Bay Packers	13-14-1
Houston Oilers	3-3-0
Indianapolis Colts	7-16-0
Kansas City Chiefs	1-3-0
Los Angeles Raiders	2-6-0
Los Angeles Rams	16-7-1
Miami Dolphins	3-6-0
Minnesota Vikings	8-6-0
New England Patriots	4-1-0
New Orleans Saints	11-5-0
New York Giants	51-70-3
New York Jets	4-1-0
Philadelphia Eagles	77-46-5
Pittsburgh Steelers	42-27-3
San Diego Chargers	5-0-0
San Francisco 49ers	6-12-1
Seattle Seahawks	5-1-0
Tampa Bay Buccaneers	4-0-0

YEAR-BY-YEAR RECORDS

Year	Won	Lost	Tied	Year	Won	Lost	Tied
1932	4	4	2	1963	3	11	0
1933	5	5	2	1964	6	8	0
1934	6	6	0	1965	6	8	0
1935	2	8	1	1966	7	7	0
1936**	7	5	0	1967	5	6	3
1937*	8	3	0	1968	5	9	0
1938	6	3	2	1969	7	5	2
1939	8	2	1	1970	6	8	0
1940**	9	2	0	1971**	9	4	1
1941	6	5	0	1972**	11	3	0
1942*	10	1	0	1973**	10	4	0
1943**	6	3	1	1974**	10	4	0
1944	6	3	1	1975	8	6	0
1945**	8	2	0	1976**	10	4	0
1946	5	5	1	1977	9	5	0
1947	4	8	0	1978	8	8	0
1948	7	5	0	1979	10	6	0
1949	4	7	1	1980	6	10	0
1950	3	9	0	1981	8	8	0
1951	5	7	0	1982*	8	1	0
1952	4	8	0	1983**	14	2	0
1953	6	5	1	1984**	11	5	0
1954	3	9	0	1985	10	6	0
1955	8	4	0	1986**	12	4	0
1956	6	6	0	1987*	11	4	0
1957	5	6	1	1988	7	9	0
1958	4	7	1	1989	10	6	0
1959	4	8	0	1990**	10	6	0
1960	1	9	2	1991*	14	2	0
1961	1	12	1	1992**	9	7	0
1962	5	7	2	1993	4	12	0
				Total	430	362	26

Number of NFL championships 5
Number of years .500 or better 40
Number of years below .500 22

*NFL champions
**Playoff team

238

1994 PREVIEW ■ WASHINGTON

RECORDS

INDIVIDUAL

Service
Seasons played	16	Sammy Baugh (1937-52)
Games played	203	Dave Butz (1975-88)
Consecutive games	196	Len Hauss (1964-77)

Scoring
Points, career	1,207	Mark Moseley (1974-86)
Points, season	161	Mark Moseley (1983)
Points, game	24	Dick James (12/17/61)
		Larry Brown (12/16/73)
Touchdowns, career	90	Charley Taylor (1964-77)
Touchdowns, season	24	John Riggins (1983)
Touchdowns, game	4	Dick James (12/17/61)
		Larry Brown (12/16/73)
Field goals, career	263	Mark Moseley (1974-86)
Field goals, season	33	Mark Moseley (1983)
Field goals, game	5	By many players
Extra points, career	417	Mark Moseley (1974-86)
Extra points, season	62	Mark Moseley (1983)
Extra points, game	9	Charlie Gogolak (11/27/66)

Rushing
Yards, career	7,472	John Riggins (1976-79, 81-85)
Yards, season	1,347	John Riggins (1983)
Yards, game	221	Gerald Riggs (9/17/89)
Attempts, career	1,988	John Riggins (1976-79, 81-85)
Attempts, season	374	John Riggins (1983)
Attempts, game	45	Jamie Morris (12/17/88)
Touchdowns, career	79	John Riggins (1976-79, 81-85)
Touchdowns, season	24	John Riggins (1983)
Touchdowns, game	4	Dick James (12/17/61)
		Larry Brown (12/16/73)

Passing
Rating, career	85	Sonny Jurgensen (1964-74)
Rating, season	109.7	Sammy Baugh (1945)
Completions, career	2,044	Joe Theismann (1974-85)
Completions, season	293	Joe Theismann (1981)
Completions, game	32	Sonny Jurgensen (11/26/67)
Yards, career	25,206	Joe Theismann (1974-85)
Yards, season	4,109	Jay Schroeder (1986)
Yards, game	446	Sammy Baugh (10/31/48)
Attempts, career	3,602	Joe Theismann (1974-85)
Attempts, season	541	Jay Schroeder (1986)
Attempts, game	58	Jay Schroeder (12/1/85)
Touchdowns, career	187	Sammy Baugh (1937-52)
Touchdowns, season	31	Sonny Jurgensen (1967)
Touchdowns, game	6	Mark Rypien (11/10/91)
		Sammy Baugh (11/23/47)
		Sammy Baugh (10/31/43)

Receiving
Receptions, career	888	Art Monk (1980-93)
Receptions, season	106	Art Monk (1984)
Receptions, game	13	Art Monk (11/4/90)
		Art Monk (12/15/85)
		Kelvin Bryant (12/7/86)
Yards, career	12,026	Art Monk (1980-93)
Yards, season	1,436	Bobby Mitchell (1963)
Yards, game	255	Anthony Allen (10/4/87)
Touchdowns, career	79	Charley Taylor (1964-77)
Touchdowns, season	12	Ricky Sanders (1988)
		Charley Taylor (1966)
		Hugh Taylor (1952)
		Jerry Smith (1967)
Touchdowns, game	3	By many players

Interceptions
Career	36	Brig Owens (1966-77)
Season	13	Dan Sandifer (1948)
Game	4	Sammy Baugh (11/14/43)
		Dan Sandifer (10/31/48)

Sacks
Career	97.5	Dexter Manley (1981-89)
Season	18	Dexter Manley (1986)
Game	4	Diron Talbert (9/28/75)
		Dexter Manley (10/2/88)

Longest plays
Run from scrimmage	88	Billy Wells (TD, 11/21/54)
Pass play	99	Frank Filchock to Andy Farkas (TD, 10/15/39)
		George Izo to Bobby Mitchell (TD, 9/15/63)
		Sonny Jurgensen to Gerry Allen (TD, 9/15/68)
Field goal	57	Steve Cox (9/28/86)
Interception return	100	Barry Wilburn (TD, 12/26/87)
Kickoff return	102	Larry Jones (TD, 11/24/74)
Punt return	96	Bill Dudley (TD, 12/3/50)
Punt	85	Sammy Baugh (12/1/40)

Top scorers
	Points
Mark Moseley (1974-86)	1,207
Chip Lohmiller (1988-92)	697
Charley Taylor (1964-77)	540
John Riggins (1976-79, 81-85)	510
Curt Knight (1969-73)	475
Art Monk (1980-93)	390

Top rushers
	Yards
John Riggins (1976-79, 81-85)	7,472
Larry Brown (1969-76)	5,875
Earnes Byner (1989-93)	3,950
Mike Thomas (1975-78)	3,360
Don Bosseler (1957-64)	3,112
George Rogers (1985-87)	2,909

Top passers
	Completions
Joe Theismann (1974-85)	2,044
Sonny Jurgensen (1964-74)	1,831
Sammy Baugh (1937-52)	1,709
Mark Rypien (1987-93)	1,244
Billy Kilmer (1971-78)	953
Eddie LeBaron (1952-53, 55-59)	538

Top passers
	Yards
Joe Theismann (1974-85)	25,206
Sonny Jurgensen (1964-74)	22,585
Sammy Baugh (1937-52)	22,085
Mark Rypien (1987-93)	15,928
Billy Kilmer (1971-78)	12,352
Norm Snead (1961-63)	5,306

Top receivers
	Receptions
Art Monk (1980-93)	888
Charley Taylor (1964-77)	649
Gary Clark (1985-92)	549
Jerry Smith (1965-77)	421
Ricky Sanders (1986-93)	414
Bobby Mitchell (1962-68)	393

Top receivers
	Yards
Art Monk (1980-93)	12,026
Charley Taylor (1964-77)	9,140
Gary Clark (1985-92)	8,742
Bobby Mitchell (1962-68)	6,491
Ricky Sanders (1986-93)	5,854
Jerry Smith (1965-77)	5,496

Most interceptions
	No.
Brig Owens (1966-77)	36
Darrell Green (1983-93)	34
Sammy Baugh (1937-52)	31
Mike Bass (1969-75)	30
Joe Lavender (1976-82)	29
Paul Krause (1964-67)	28

Most sacks
	No.
Dexter Manley (1981-89)	97.5
Charles Mann (1983-92)	81.5
Dave Butz (1975-88)	59.5
Monte Coleman (1979-93)	54.5

239

PRO FOOTBALL WEEKLY 1994 ALMANAC

1994 DRAFT ANALYSIS
PREVIEW

Underclassmen, trades and pass rushers dominated the early going at this year's NFL draft. The first three picks, four of the first six and six of the first 10 players selected were underclassmen. Eight of the first 13 picks were defensive linemen or hybrid defensive ends-outside linebackers.

However, the underlying theme of this year's draft was the salary cap. Teams were often forced to fill needs created by free-agency or weaken one area in order to aid another.

The Falcons are a classic example. To get DE Chris Doleman and pay him the money he wanted, they had to unload WR Mike Pritchard. To fill the void left by Pritchard's departure, they used their top draft pick to select WR Bert Emanuel.

Because this was not a very deep draft, no club just flat-out dominated. But the Rams, Redskins, Vikings, Bucs, 49ers, Colts, Bills, Bengals and Eagles all appear to have drafted a handful of players who can be very helpful quickly. The 49ers, in fact, appear to have moved into a position where they could dethrone the Cowboys.

Here is a team-by-team analysis.

AFC EAST

BUFFALO BILLS

The Bills had to have a cornerback after losing Nate Odomes and trading J.D. Williams. S Jeff Burris was one of the most versatile athletes in the draft, having played running back, all four DB spots and return specialist, and he has the quick feet needed to play cornerback in the NFL. Lack of speed was a problem for Buffalo at wide receiver, and Bucky Brooks has the deep speed to stretch the defense and is a player on the rise. The Bills needed a tight end who could split the seam and get deep, and Lonnie Johnson fits the bill. Lack of size and depth were concerns at linebacker, and both Sam Rogers and Marlo Perry are 245 to 250 pound linebackers. Rogers is more of an outside rusher, while Perry, who is a cerebral player, can be a swingman. With Howard Ballard moving to Seattle, the Bills were very thin at tackle, but 300-pound-plus Corey Louchiey has a chance to develop if he turns some baby fat into muscle and learns to play a little lower.

Grade: B-plus.

INDIANAPOLIS COLTS

Over the past 10 years, no team in the NFL has done a worse job of running the football than the Colts. However, that should change in a hurry with Marshall Faulk in the backfield and Eric Mahlum joining Will Wolford, Kirk Lowdermilk, Zefross Moss and Randy Dixon blocking. Faulk has Curtis Dickey-type speed and the run skills and instant quickness that Dickey lacked. He also catches the ball well, blocks and doesn't fumble much. Mahlum is a C-OG swingman who tested out as the best athlete among the offensive linemen who did all the drills at the combine. Two other blocking possibilities are OT Jason Mathews, a former defensive lineman and tight end who runs well, and big TE Bradford Banta, who also doubles as a deep-snapper. Although Lamont Warren was drafted as a running back, he could move to wide receiver, where the Colts would welcome his speed and hands. Banta will push underachieving TE Kerry Cash. Cash is faster and more athletic, but Banta may be a better blocker. The Colts added a bookend outside linebacker-defensive end to go with Tony Bennett in Nebraska's Trev Alberts, who many scouts felt was the second-best defender in the draft and an impact player. Alberts and Bennett will be outside rushers, and, when Steve Emtman gets back, he and Jon Hand will put on the inside pressure.

Grade: B-plus.

MIAMI DOLPHINS

The Dolphins geared their draft to getting bigger, stronger and better on defense. The only offensive player selected was Tim Ruddy, who is projected to replace Jeff Uhlenhake at center. DT Tim Bowens was this year's Eric Swann-type pick. He played only nine games of major-college ball and is inexperienced and overweight. But he has awesome size and the ability to dominate on the inside. Another defensive lineman who could help is William Gaines. He has size and ability but dropped from a high second-round pick to the fifth round once doctors examined his surgically repaired knee and shoulder. The Dolphins were very close to taking athletic, pass-rushing OLB Aubrey Beavers in Round One instead of Bowens, and they pinched themselves when he was still there in Round Two. Don Shula was very impressed with Beavers at the Senior Bowl and feels he can step right in and start across from Bryan Cox at outside linebacker. OLB Ronnie Woolfork showed top initial quickness, but, as his body changed, he went from a sleek pass rusher to a much slower player. If Woolfork can bounce back, he could challenge Beavers.

Grade: B-minus.

NEW ENGLAND PATRIOTS

Knowing that Dallas was going to trade up with the Rams to grab DE Willie McGinest with the fifth

240

1994 PREVIEW ■ DRAFT ANALYSIS

Willie McGinest

pick, Bill Parcells had to stay put at No. 4 to claim the top outside speed rusher in the draft. McGinest can play up like a blitzing linebacker or down like a defensive end, and he has great speed and potential as an outside pass rusher. Although he played hard in college, he was not consistently productive. While some blame the scheme and say McGinest is a young Chris Doleman, others call him a workout warrior and feel he should have gone much later in the first round. WR Kevin Lee went ahead of David Palmer for three reasons. He is bigger, faster and a much more stable individual. The Patriots felt they needed a speed receiver with size, and Lee fits the mold. If things break right, quick-but-not-fast DL Ervin Collier will join McGinest on the defensive line. Scouts really liked how quickly Collier came off the ball and his initial surge. Joe Burch is viewed as the team's center of the future, and the future could be very soon. Parcells wanted a blocking tight end to replace Marv Cook and got the best one in the draft in John Burke. He also got a punter who kicks off very well in Pat O'Neill and two interesting developmental-type picks in OT Max Lane, who needs to get stronger, and Jay Walker, a big, strong-armed quarterback who reminds some of his godfather, James Harris.

Grade: B.

Dan Wilkinson

Marshall Faulk

NEW YORK JETS

Trading up one spot in Round One allowed the Jets to get one of the handful of impact players in the draft in CB-return specialist Aaron Glenn, a player who has the potential to be another Darrell Green. Glenn closes on the ball as well as Green and Deion Sanders, and he led the nation in punt returns. The Jet KR game was the worst in the NFL last year. While Glenn will be used on punts, WR Orlando Parker has put his world-class speed to good use returning kickoffs. Parker does not have the receiving skills of another Jet pick, WR Ryan Yarborough. Yarborough and Southern Cal's Johnnie Morton were the most productive and polished wideouts in the draft, but neither had blazing speed. DL Lou Benfatti will rotate with Donald Evans at nose tackle. Since the Jets are small up front, they like to rotate their players, and Benfatti is a warrior with fine initial quickness and good hand use. QB Glenn Foley was a steal for Round Seven who gives the Jets a low-priced third-stringer.

Grade: B.

AFC CENTRAL

CINCINNATI BENGALS

Many scouts feel Dan Wilkinson can be the NFL's next great defensive lineman. "Big Daddy" runs about 4.85 at 315 pounds. With Wilkinson and Tim Krumrie inside, John Copeland at left end and Alfred Williams at right end, the Bengals will definitely be much stronger up front on defense. Darnay Scott has the physical tools to be the big-time speed wide receiver Cincinnati has needed to go with Carl Pickens, but he must improve his concentration and clear up some off-field problems. Jeff Cothran is a tough, hard-nosed fullback who catches the ball well and fits coordinator Bruce Coslet's offense. Steve Shine will get a chance to start at weak outside linebacker across from James Francis, with Steve Tovar in the middle. Corey Sawyer will probably be a nickel corner and return specialist as a rookie. He lacks stopwatch speed, but he is very quick, agile and cocky. Trent Pollard could be a sleeper on the offensive line if he can keep his weight down to about 310 pounds. Bengal OL coach Jim McNally worked him out extensively and was very impressed.

Grade: B.

CLEVELAND BROWNS

If you forget about stopwatch times and just look at tapes of games, you would say Antonio Langham is as good a cornerback as you are going to see. His film grades in college were even better than Deion Sanders', and the Browns have a void at cornerback. Now, with Langham and free-agent Don Griffin joining Najee Mustafaa, a weak area becomes a strength, and the Cleveland secondary has five quality players when you throw in the starting safeties, Eric Turner and Stevon Moore. WR Derrick Alexander can develop into the big-time size-speed receiver the Browns hoped Patrick Rowe was going to be before Rowe hurt his knee as a rookie. The addition of DL Romeo Bandison will make Cleveland the deepest team in the league on the defensive line and allow it to rotate fresh players in and out like Dallas did the past two years. Bandison would have gone in the first round, if not for the fact most clubs flunked him on his physical because his knees lack cartilage and have bone rubbing on bone. However, many of those teams flunked Michael Dean Perry for a similar reason.

Grade: B.

HOUSTON OILERS

The Oilers' well was dry at defensive end after Sean Jones and William Fuller took the money and ran. However, the team hopes it struck it rich again by taking DE's Henry Ford and Jeremy Nunley 1-2. Ford has the quickness and speed to be a big-time rusher, while Nunley has the tenacity, toughness, non-stop motor and work ethic that Ford must develop if he is to realize his potential. Malcolm Seabron may be fast and polished enough to step right in and contribute as one of the Oilers' four wide receivers when they play the run-and-shoot. Since the Oilers may use some two-TE sets, Roderick Lewis could make a place for himself behind Pat Carter if he busts his butt and shows he is tough enough. Mike Davis has the speed and athletic skills to be a big-time corner, and the Oilers have a lot of defensive backs coming off injuries. Depth at running back is a problem Sean Jackson could solve. He also may be able to play fullback if he improves his blocking. While Lee Gissendaner does not make stopwatch gears, he was one of the best return men in the country, and the Oilers have been looking for one.

Grade: B.

PITTSBURGH STEELERS

The Steelers have been looking for a sure-handed, big-play wide receiver since Louis Lipps, and they appear to have their man in Charles Johnson. Almost everyone rated Johnson as the best catch of the receivers, and he should be an instant starter. The Steelers felt they had to get bigger, better and deeper on the defensive line, and Brentson Buckner is a 300-pounder who can move. He came on late in the season and has a background similar to the Raiders' Chester McGlockton. Jason Gildon is an outside speed rusher who can get upfield and sack the quarterback. DL Taase Faumui has the speed and strength the Steelers are looking for, but he did not make as many plays as he should have as a senior. King-sized tailback Bam Morris can spell Barry Foster and has the size to move to fullback if he will learn to block. Morris broke many of Earl Campbell's conference rushing records. S Myron Bell is a good football player, and his teammate, QB Jim Miller, was a steal in Round Six who should be the No. 3 signal-caller with a chance to move up to No. 2 in a year.

Grade: B.

AFC WEST

DENVER BRONCOS

The Broncos had only two picks before the seventh round this year, and, the way things are going, they may not have another meaningful pick before 1996. However, those picks went in trades for players such as Gary Zimmerman, Mike Pritchard and Ben Smith and put the team in a position to make a run at the Super Bowl this year. The Bronco scouting staff has a reputation for finding hidden gems. DE-deep-snapper-turned-LB Allen Aldridge can also play some tight end and has a very impressive blend of speed, power and athletic ability. DB Randy Fuller may not be a starter, but he is a quick, tough, feisty, undersized, aware player who could help in the nickel. While seventh-round picks are generally afterthoughts, C Tom Nalen was a very efficient player on film, and ILB Keith Burns looked like he was going to develop into a fine player after his junior season. Both Nalen, who may need further knee repairs, and Burns play positions where the Broncos need depth from players who make the minimum salary. RB Butler By'Not'e will be tried at cornerback, where his 4.4 speed will be an important asset. He will also return kickoffs.

Grade: Incomplete.

KANSAS CITY CHIEFS

Harvey Williams was a bust, Marcus Allen is 34 years old and FB Kimble Anders is really a pumped-up halfback, so Greg Hill and FB Donnell Bennett fill major voids. Hill is a fine artificial-turf runner who can cut on a dime and accelerate. He also catches the ball and is extremely athletic. Bennett is a true fullback with size, speed, power and pass-catching skills. Lake Dawson and Chris Penn are the type of big, physical catch-over-the-middle-and-break-tackles-after-the-catch receivers who fit the Chiefs' offense. They are good, solid football players who have the size Willie Davis, Fred Jones and J.J. Birden lack. Dawson also is a terrific blocker. DT-NT Rob Waldrop could offer a nice change of pace to Dan Saleaumua, and the rotation should make both players more effective, provided Waldrop stays healthy. DB Bracey Walker is a tough, undersized safety who excels on special teams, and CB James Burton has some cover skills.

Grade: B.

LOS ANGELES RAIDERS

Al Davis filled needs at linebacker in the first

and second rounds, figuring he could get a good runner in the third round. Rob Fredrickson is a large, fast, very athletic linebacker who can play any position. While the sure-handed Fredrickson's strength is coverage, James Folston is a blitz-backer who played defensive end in college. Both linebackers had great workouts with speed in the 4.6 area. I-back Calvin Jones was projected as a No. 2 selection, but, because of the way the draft played out, the Raiders got him by trading up in Round Three. Jones has good size, speed and hands, but some question his instincts. Austin Robbins adds size and speed to the defensive line, but many scouts feel he lacks instincts and the ability to come off blocks on defense and thus could wind up at offensive tackle.
Grade: B.

SAN DIEGO CHARGERS

Bobby Beathard needed blockers, catchers and money with which to operate, and he got all three by drafting OG Isaac Davis, OL Vaughn Parker, WR Andre Coleman and TE Aaron Laing and trading RB Marion Butts. With Eric Moten out for 1994 and Joe Milinichik a huge question mark with a seven-figure contract and a bad knee, Beathard had to get guards. Davis can be another Moten or Nate Newton if he continues to work hard, and he may have to play right away. He is an awesome physical talent. Parker is not overpowering like Davis is, but he knows how to pass-block pretty well and can also play tackle. Coleman was the fastest receiver in the Big Eight and, most important, is the big-play return man the Chargers have been wanting. Laing is a former quarterback and running back who will replace Derrick Walker. Depth at cornerback was a concern, and speedy Willie Clark has the raw tools to fill that void. Plus, he can return kickoffs. The Chargers were looking for a pure strong safety who would intimidate people, and that is where Rodney Harrison fits in. Darren Krein provides quality depth at defensive end and can also play on special teams. Tony Vinson is a big, productive tailback who can play behind Natrone Means, who replaces Butts as the Chargers' No. 1 running back.
Grade: B.

SEATTLE SEAHAWKS

The addition of DL Sam Adams means it will not be as easy to double- and triple-team Cortez Kennedy anymore. Like Kennedy, Adams is a terrific player with a bad body. Unlike Kennedy, Adams can be hard to handle and needs stroking. C Kevin Mawae also can start at guard, and he could fill in at either tackle and make the deep snap. Thus, his versatility will really help Seattle, and, since Ray Donaldson is 36 and Joe Tofflemire can't stay healthy, they needed a young center. Lamar Smith is a good, tough runner who may be able to make the move to fullback, where Seattle lost John L. Williams. Smith catches the ball very well. While Larry Whigham played cornerback in

Sam Adams

college, the Seahawks are looking at him more as a strong safety who can challenge Robert Blackmon. TE Carlester Crumpler slid until Round Seven because of medical problems, but he has ability and could help.
Grade: B-minus.

NFC EAST

ARIZONA CARDINALS

Buddy Ryan is convinced Jamir Miller will be a great blitzing weak-outside linebacker who will make a dramatic impact on his defense as a rookie. At UCLA they said, when Miller was up, the quarterback was going down, but Miller was not up all the time. But they said the same thing about Jerome Brown before Ryan got ahold of him. Chuck Levy can be a third-down back, return specialist and option quarterback. Knowing Ryan, he will use Levy all three ways. Rich Braham, an all-time tough guy, provides depth on an offensive line that needs it and also adds the toughness Ryan likes. Both Perry Carter and John Reece have the speed to run with the fliers in man-on-man coverage, but neither defensive back had an outstanding senior season. Eric England was Texas A&M's "other" defensive end with Sam Adams, and now he hopes to be the Cards' other defensive end with Clyde Simmons.
Grade: B.

DALLAS COWBOYS

The Cowboys think Shante Carver can be a big-time outside rusher in the Charles Haley mold. He is as quick as anyone off the ball and a natural

rusher. The marriage of Cowboy OL coach Hudson Houck and Larry Allen could work beautifully, since Allen is a super OL talent, and Houck is a great teacher who loves size and speed. Houck also has an even bigger project in George Hegamin, a 350-pound-plus offensive tackle with decent feet but a questionable work ethic and maturity. Houck is being asked to get a two-year project and a three-year project ready overnight, and both players have weight-gain problems which could make things more difficult. Willie Jackson is not a speed receiver, but he can jump, has very good hands and fits the Cowboy mold of big receivers who will go over the middle. Dewayne Dotson could be a key pick at the MLB spot. Since Ken Norton signed with San Francisco, the Cowboys want somebody to compete with Robert Jones for that key spot on their defense.
Grade: C.

NEW YORK GIANTS

The Giants needed a big-time speed receiver, and Thomas Lewis should fit the bill. Lewis was underscouted because he came out as a junior and then ran only in the low 4.6's at the combine. However, in later workouts he was running in the 4.4 area, and he also got high grades as a return man and blocker. By Draft Day, half the teams in the league were hoping to get him in Round Two, which is why the Giants took him in the first round. Speedy CB Thomas Randolph and big, athletic S Jason Sehorn were drafted to replace Mark Collins and Myron Guyton in a secondary that was wiped out by free-agency. Gary Downs will back up Rodney Hampton at running back, now that Lewis Tillman is gone. Downs is not as quick to the hole as Tillman, but he catches the ball better and is a more under-control runner. The addition of DT Chris Maumalanga and DE Chad Bratzke, along with the fact the Giants didn't draft any linebackers, indicates the team may be going to a 4-3 defense. Maumalanga played much better as a junior, while Bratzke was a more productive player than ex-Eastern Kentucky DE Aaron Jones. Jason Winrow adds depth to the offensive line.
Grade: B.

PHILADELPHIA EAGLES

The Eagles continued to upgrade their offensive line with the selection of OLT Bernard Williams, the fourth first-round pick Philadelphia has invested in the offensive line in the last four years. He joins former first-rounders Antone Davis (who cost two No. 1's) and Lester Holmes, C David Alexander and, most likely, Broderick Thompson to give the Eagles their best offensive line since the Stan Walter, Jerry Sisemore, Guy Morris days. DT Bruce Walker could replace William Perry if he has his head screwed on right. Walker was suspended last year, but, coming out of high school, he was one of the premier prospects in the country. Now he is a 300-pound-plus defensive tackle. Charlie Garner may have been the best pure runner in the draft, but, like Walker, he has a checkered background. He also is undersized. However, he could be the skillful, elusive, make-you-miss runner the Eagles have desperately needed. Joe Panos could start at guard and provide depth at center and right tackle. He is very tough and plays above his athletic ability. The Eagles were very unhappy with the play of their safeties last year, so SS Eric Zomalt and FS Marvin Goodwin will get every chance to prove they can play. MLB Ryan McCoy could provide quality depth behind Byron Evans. And Mitch Berger will get every chance to win the punting job.
Grade: B-plus.

WASHINGTON REDSKINS

Norv Turner feels he can develop Heath Shuler into a Troy Aikman-type quarterback. Shuler and Aikman are built along the same lines, and they have the same kind of strong, quick arms and powerful wrists. Shuler is a better foot athlete and scrambler, while Aikman is a more accurate passer who can learn quicker. If Tré Johnson can play up to his ability on a consistent basis, he can be a tremendous offensive lineman. He had a first-round workout and was a super practice player at the all-star games, but he did not play like it in many games. Many suspect he loses his concentration. WR Tydus Winans can run in the low 4.4's and had very good workouts, and the Redskins need speed on the outside. Joe Patton is a down-the-road guard with potential. The same can be said for DE Dexter Nottage, who last played at Florida A&M in 1991. Nottage runs a 4.78 40 at 276 pounds and works out very well. TE Kurt Haws was a late bloomer who could surprise if he continues to get better. QB Gus Frerotte has the size and arm, but he was erratic in college.
Grade: B-plus.

NFC CENTRAL

CHICAGO BEARS

The Bears wanted a speed pass rusher to replace Richard Dent at right end and believe John Thierry is their man. He is a Charles Haley-type athlete who can run the 40 in less than 4.6 at over 250 pounds, and he is also very agile and athletic. The offensive line was a problem last year, and Marcus Spears can provide size, speed and help down the road if he can be toughened up and improve his technique. Spears has the feet to play left tackle and the speed to be a pulling guard. If Alonzo Spellman can't replace Steve McMichael at defensive tackle, Jim Flanigan might. Flanigan was called a poor man's McMichael by many scouts who loved his work ethic, toughness and hustle. RB Raymont Harris is big, tough and productive, and he could turn out to be a fourth-round steal. WR Lloyd Hill may run about 4.65-4.7 in the 40. But he was very productive and is a big

DETROIT LIONS

target with soft hands and top instincts, and the Bears can use a possession catcher across from Curtis Conway.

Grade: B-minus.

DETROIT LIONS

The Lions feel Johnnie Morton can be a big-time contributor right away, and, because he is such a polished wide receiver, he could work beautifully with touch passer Scott Mitchell. S Van Malone will tear your head off and adds speed and toughness to an average secondary. He will start out in the nickel and could be starting at safety if anyone gets hurt. Last year the Lions struggled after Bennie Blades was injured because his replacement lacked speed. Shane Bonham is a slightly undersized defensive lineman with excellent speed and a non-stop motor. Like most of the Lion defensive linemen, he can play end or tackle. CB Vaughn Bryant played a lot of man-on-man and bump-and-run in college, but he lacks great recovery speed, which is something the Lions really need in the secondary.

Grade: B-minus.

GREEN BAY PACKERS

Aaron Taylor can step right in and upgrade the Green Bay offensive line at either guard or tackle. Right now he is penciled in at left guard. LeShon Johnson is a tough north-south runner with very good speed who led the nation in rushing last year. He lasted until the third round because he is not very elusive and does not catch the ball well. But he is a good, solid back who will spell Reggie Cobb and keep him on his toes. Dorsey Levens is another back who can contribute. He has size, speed and hands, but he never really put it all together in college. WR Terry Mickens has the size and hands the Packers look for and is fast enough to get separation on defensive backs. He will battle Robert Brooks for the starting spot across from Sterling Sharpe. Gabe Wilkins adds size, speed and athleticism to the defensive line. But he is a diamond-in-the-rough who will need a lot of polishing before he can challenge for a starting position.

Grade: B.

MINNESOTA VIKINGS

Since Audray McMillian is gone, Dewayne Washington is an instant starter at cornerback. He is a good, solid, all-around player. If things break right, Todd Steussie will step right in and start at one OT spot, and free-agent Chris Hinton will man the other. QB Warren Moon will also have an excellent weapon at his disposal in Alabama's great all-purpose football player David Palmer, who can catch, run, return and throw. Both Fernando Smith and Mike Wells add size, youth and depth to a defensive line that will be minus Chris Doleman. Doleman was a speed-rushing right end, so neither youngster is a good fit for his job. But if slow-developing Robert Harris comes on, he could claim that spot, allowing the Vikings to work Smith at left end and Wells at tackle.

Grade: B-plus.

TAMPA BAY BUCCANEERS

The Buccaneers almost traded up for Trent Dilfer, and then their top-rated quarterback fell right into their lap. Dilfer has all the tools to play quarterback in Sam Wyche's system, and he will give Craig Erickson a run for the starting job. Dilfer is as big as Roman Gabriel and hard to knock down. He has great touch on his long ball and can throw every pass in the book. He is very well-coordinated and runs about 4.8 in the 40, but he is no scrambler. With the departure of Reggie Cobb, Errict Rhett may be able to step right in and start at running back. He is a tough, hard-nosed runner with fine vision, terrific balance, great leg strength and fine hands. However, like Cobb, he is not going to break the long ones. Since the Bucs can't trust Tyji Armstrong's hands and Ron Hall left via free-agency, they took TE Harold Bishop to battle for the job. He has prototype size, adequate speed and soft but somewhat inconsistent hands. Pete Pierson and C Jim Pyne are the type of offensive linemen who play above their ability, and OLB Bernard Carter could surprise if he turns ability into plays and toughens up a bit.

Grade: B-plus.

NFC WEST

ATLANTA FALCONS

When June Jones said he was willing to sacrifice offense for defense, he wasn't kidding. Basically, the Falcons traded WR Mike Pritchard for

Aaron Taylor

1994 PREVIEW ■ DRAFT ANALYSIS

Chris Doleman, the big-time pass-rushing defensive end the Falcons haven't had since Claude Humphrey was around. Bert Emanuel has the great quickness, speed and athleticism the Falcons love at receiver, but he was a 170-pound option quarterback in college and has a lot to learn about his new position. Many scouts said, if Emanuel had listened to the coaches at UCLA and moved to wide receiver in college instead of transferring to Rice, he would have been one of the top two receivers in the draft. DB Anthony Phillips looks a lot like Lester Hayes in the computer. But it remains to be seen if he can go from being a mistake-prone collegiate player to a premier pro as Hayes did. Perry Klein played quarterback in a run-and-shoot offense as a senior and then had a great workout for Falcon coaches after looking so-so at the Senior Bowl. He will be the No. 3 quarterback. WR Harrison Houston could be a run-and-shoot sleeper.
Grade: C.

LOS ANGELES RAMS

By trading down after deciding he was not going to invest in a quarterback (Trent Dilfer) who probably would not help him win games this year, Chuck Knox was able to get three extra picks in the first three rounds and still draft high enough to select the most athletic offensive tackle in the draft, Wayne Gandy. If things go right, Gandy will replace Irv Eatman at left tackle, and Eatman will become a swing tackle. WR Isaac Bruce, a Webster Slaughter-type with great hands, is projected as the replacement for Henry Ellard. DB coach Rod Perry expects hard-hitting Toby Wright to be one of his starting safeties this year and wouldn't be shocked if Keith Lyle is the other. DE Brad Ottis and FB-RB James Bostic may not start, but they will play enough to keep the starters fresh. OLB Ernest Jones can be used as an outside rusher in certain defenses, while speedy Chris Brantley might be the third wide receiver.
Grade: B-plus.

NEW ORLEANS SAINTS

The Saints felt they had to have a big-time defensive lineman to go with Wayne Martin and traded down one spot in Round One and probably reached a little for Joe Johnson. He is a speed rusher who had a lot of sacks as a junior, but he had very quiet games against Tennessee and Texas A&M. However, those games were late in the year when he may have been beaten up. RB Mario Bates has an awesome size-speed ratio and could have been a first-round pick if he had gone back to school for one more year. The Saints have not had a back with his size and speed since the Chuck Muncie days, and they do not feel very secure with little Derek Brown as their starting running back. With Sam Mills getting old and Vaughan Johnson talking about leaving after next year, ILB Winfred Tubbs made sense in Round Three. Tubbs' speed and durability are questionable, but he has flashed big-time ability. Left-

Trent Dilfer

handed QB Doug Nussmeier could be a great fourth-round pick and the Saints' starting quarterback of the future. Two poor bowl games and a bad combine workout made people erase the first-round grades they had put on him. While Nussmeier is a developmental prospect at this stage, he has a lot going for him, and he can run the option on goalline and two-point situations.
Grade: B.

SAN FRANCISCO 49ERS

Bryant Young should be an instant starter on the 49er defensive line. He has the quickness, leveraged strength, intangibles and work ethic of a Russell Maryland and is almost two inches taller. He can play inside or outside in a 4-3 set and end in a 3-4. William Floyd is the ideal fullback for the 49er offense. He is an excellent pass blocker and lead run blocker, catches the ball well and is a powerful runner who can make a quick cut to daylight. He will make players around him better and is every bit as tough as Tom Rathman. DL Kevin Mitchell is a projection to linebacker, but, while he learns, he can be used as a rusher. He also is a fine special-team player who adds great toughness and intensity to the mix. With Don Griffin moving on, Tyronne Drakeford will get a chance to start at cornerback. He was a notch below Antonio Langham and Aaron Glenn but better than most. For years, the 49ers put up with PK Mike Cofer, and now they may have a viable alternative in Doug Brien, a very consistent college kicker with a compact kicking motion. WR Cory Fleming is not a stopwatch 40 guy, but watch how well he snatches the ball and runs after the catch. He should be a good fit for the 49er offense, provided he is quick enough to get separation.
Grade: B-plus.

PRO FOOTBALL WEEKLY 1994 ALMANAC

PREVIEW: FREE-AGENCY ANALYSIS

Let's see ... Bernie Kosar is a Dolphin ... Scott Mitchell is a Lion ... Erik Kramer is a Bear ... Jim Harbaugh is a Colt ... Jeff George is a Falcon ... Chris Miller is a Ram and Jim Everett is a Saint.

That's not to mention Warren Moon now lives in Minnesota, John Friesz is the starter in Washington and Rodney Peete is the backup in Dallas.

And Mark Rypien and Jim McMahon — Super Bowl-winning quarterbacks — were both looking for jobs in spring before Rypien signed with the Browns.

Free-agency, Year Two ... the QB shuffle.

No Reggie Whites changed teams in 1994, as that superstar did in '93. But, when quarterbacks move from city to city at a rate never before seen in the NFL, something is obviously different.

Teams such as the Cardinals, Seahawks, Patriots, 49ers and Bears seemed to help themselves enormously with the addition of new players.

The new factor in free-agency this year was the advent of a salary cap in pro football. Teams spent the offseason juggling their rosters and payrolls to keep under the cap, which is set at an average of $34.6 million per team.

One thing is certain: Fans won't be able to tell the players without a program.

In 1993 Jim Harbaugh was a coveted NFL quarterback. His contract having expired with the Bears, Harbaugh generated interest from the Vikings and Raiders.

Not wanting to start completely over barely one month into his new job, Bear coach Dave Wannstedt approved the signing of Harbaugh to a three-year, $13 million contract. Nine losses and countless boos later, Harbaugh was simply cut by the Bears after they signed Erik Kramer from the Lions.

"The quarterback position has always had a lot of pressure to do well," Harbaugh was saying after signing with the Colts. "Now, it's even worse. It's become so easy now for teams to just get another guy when theirs doesn't do well. But it sure doesn't do much for stability."

It sure doesn't. Only seven teams had their quarterback start all 16 games last season. Confident backups are at a premium. Yet, the second year of free-agency in the NFL, this one with a salary cap, created an atmosphere of change. And quarterbacks headed the list.

"We are all seeing how long it takes quarterbacks to get used to the system," New Orleans coach Jim Mora said. "Wade Wilson came in early last year and worked hard, and he still wasn't completely comfortable at the start of the season."

So what did the Saints do this year? They traded for Everett, meaning another learning experience. Of course, Everett won't be alone. Former San Diego QB Dan Fouts said he was recently playing a game with his son, where they tried to match the team with the quarterback.

"We started in the NFC Central," Fouts said. "After a few minutes, we quit. We couldn't do it. I mean, this is crazy."

By May, seven quarterbacks had changed addresses as unrestricted free agents, four were traded and another two signed with new teams after being terminated. Five re-signed with their own clubs, three were looking for jobs after being cut and 18 were unsigned as either restricted or unrestricted free agents.

Two quarterbacks who were cut before last season — Kelly Stouffer and Chuck Long — had even found spots to try to win a job.

The shuffle prompted Hall of Fame coach Sid Gillman to say: "I am tickled to death I'm not coaching anymore. I would not want to wake up every day and wonder who my quarterback is."

Friesz, a marginal backup the last two years in San Diego, figures he has a chance to start in Washington because he doesn't believe first-round pick Heath Shuler will be ready. Friesz signed a one-year contract worth $900,000 that includes a $200,000 signing bonus.

"I'm at the crossroad in my career where it's important to continue to be thought of as a starter and not be talked of as a backup and never be able to recover that," he said.

The offseason was filled with speculation that Green Bay's Brett Favre would receive an offer from another team, but nothing materialized and the deadline for offer sheets came and went.

Favre was not happy. Said his agent, Bus Cook,

Scott Mitchell shows off his new Detroit jersey

248

1994 PREVIEW ■ FREE-AGENCY

Howard "the House" Ballard hopes to provide a solid foundation for the Seattle offensive line

"Brett doesn't understand being told all the time, 'We're going to get your deal done. You're going to be taken care of, and you'll be a wealthy young man.' And then they never, ever, ever, ever, ever budged from or even talked about the number they offered way back when. (That figure was a reported $2.5 million a year.) We asked for money comparable to Reggie White (four years, $17 million). They didn't want to talk about it. They said, 'There's absolutely no way we're going to do that.'"

In Cleveland, personnel chief Mike Lombardi came closer than ever to admitting that Kosar was released last season for economic reasons. Even though Kosar is no longer in Cleveland, about $1.5 million from his last contract counts against the Browns' salary cap this year. Said Lombardi, "Bernie is gone, but his money is still here. Lombardi also said that, had the team not released Kosar when it did last November, other contract items would have kicked in. "We would be in worse shape than we are now," he said.

After trading Moon to Minnesota, the Oilers raided the Vikings' roster for Sean Salisbury, who will be the No. 2 man behind Cody Carlson. Houston also re-signed Bucky Richardson, who almost departed for the Canadian Football League. Richardson's two-year deal includes a $100,000 signing bonus, plus yearly salaries of $300,000 that could increase by another $300,000 if certain incentives are reached. One of those is a bonus for every time Richardson engineers a successful two-point conversion. Originally, the Oilers tendered the minimum offer of $162,000. But their strategy changed when Richardson received a two-year offer from the Hamilton Tiger-Cats for $1 million. "It always makes you feel good when another team wants you to play for them," Richardson said. "Obviously, the offer from Hamilton came along at a good time for me. But it didn't take a genius to know I wanted to stay in Houston, and (the offer) sped up the process of being able to do that."

Free-agency and its accompanying salary cap are at least having the expected effect.

"It's fairly early to tell, but we're seeing what I thought we would see," said Denver owner Pat Bowlen.

The best players are going to get the big money, veterans are going to get cut, young players are going to make the minimum, and there's going to be an enormous chasm between the salaries of the stars and the subs.

Charley Casserly, the Redskins' general manager, said, "There's no question you're going to have a corps of players who aren't going to cost much who are going to have to play for you."

A lot of veterans were expected to be cut as Opening Day approached.

"I think, as it goes along, players are going to realize they are going to be out there in the cold," said Bronco head coach Wade Phillips.

Chicago coach Dave Wannstedt said, "One of the realities of the salary cap is the 'what have you done for me yesterday' is really eliminated from the equation. There's not enough to go around to take care of guys because they've been loyal to you for X amount of years."

Washington TE Terry Orr saw teammates Charles Mann and Tim McGee cut by the Redskins. "I think definitely the quality of the game is going to go down," Orr said.

And Mike Kenn, the president of the NFL Players Association and a 17-year veteran offensive tackle with the Falcons, said, "It's a fact of life with the cap: Some players are simply going to have to be sacrificed because of the new economics of the game. That's just the reality of the situation."

If players want to hold their jobs, many will have to take huge salary cuts. "As a player, I'd take it, but I don't like it," said Terry Bradshaw, the Steeler Hall of Famer and Fox network studio host.

Pittsburgh CB Rod Woodson doesn't like the new system. "The owners love it and they should love it. Now they can say, 'Hey, we can't pay you because the salary cap you agreed to says we can't.' The cap screws the players."

Big contracts will have big ramifications for some teams. The Bills didn't match Seattle's four-year, $10.5 million offer for OT Howard Ballard because GM John Butler said he would have had to cut 10 players who make $250,000 apiece to match the offer to Ballard, a transitional free agent. Butler would rather have the 10 bodies than the one All-Pro — quantity over quality. Seattle saw it differently.

In other words, it's an exercise in budget balancing. When the Jets re-signed OL Roger Duffy, they terminated their rights to P Louie Aguiar to stay within the cap. Then S Ronnie Lott agreed to take a salary cut from $1.4 million to $1 million to open up some more money.

The Broncos damaged the Raiders' salary structure when they made a four-year, $10 million offer to WR Tim Brown that Al Davis reluctantly matched. Then Denver made the same offer to San Diego's Anthony Miller. Charger GM Bobby Beathard didn't match the offer because he didn't want to spend so much of his payroll on a wide receiver. So now the Broncos have one of the best receivers in the NFL on their roster for John Elway to throw to, but Bowlen and personnel director Bob Ferguson now face the same problem with their team's salary cap.

At one point, the Dolphins, after signing S Gene Atkins from New Orleans and re-signing PK Pete Stoyanovich, were only $250,000 under the cap. So, to be able to sign S Michael Stewart from the Rams, Miami removed the transition-player designation from S Louis Oliver. That made Oliver an unrestricted free agent, meaning he wouldn't count against the cap until he signed. However, restricted free agents, transition players and franchise players must be tendered minimum offers, so that figure counts. Oliver later signed with Cincinnati.

Indianapolis was forced to pare $7.96 million in contracts by Feb. 17 so it would be under the cap. Any team over the cap at any time is subject to a $2 million fine. So the Colts cut LB Duane Bickett ($2.1 million) and WR's Reggie Langhorne ($1.1 million), Clarence Verdin ($1.15 million) and Jessie Hester ($1 million). Langhorne set a club record last year with 85 receptions and combined with Hester for 149 catches. Later, the Colts temporarily cut another wide receiver, Aaron Cox, leaving them with only Sean Dawkins, a second-year player, as an experienced wideout.

1994 PREVIEW ■ FREE-AGENCY

DOIN' THE QB SHUFFLE

Abbreviations: UFA-unrestricted free agent; RFA-restricted free agent; EFA-exclusive rights free agent.

As of May 13

Player	1993 Team	1994 Team	Current Status	Transaction
STEVE BONO	49ers	Chiefs	Signed	Traded
BUBBY BRISTER	Eagles	Eagles	Signed	Re-signed UFA
CHRIS CHANDLER	Cardinals	Rams	Signed	UFA.....
CARY CONKLIN	Redskins	?????	Unsigned UFA	......
STEVE DeBERG	Dolphins	?????	Unsigned UFA	......
JIM EVERETT	Rams	Saints	Signed	Traded
BRETT FAVRE	Packers	Packers	Unsigned RFA	......
JOHN FRIESZ	Redskins	Chargers	Signed	UFA
BOB GAGLIANO	Falcons	?????	Unsigned UFA	......
RICH GANNON	Redskins	?????	Unsigned UFA	......
STAN GELBAUGH	Seahawks	?????	Unsigned UFA	......
JEFF GEORGE	Colts	Falcons	Signed	Traded
GALE GILBERT	Bills	Chargers	Signed	UFA
JIM HARBAUGH	Bears	Colts	Signed	Cut, signed
BOBBY HEBERT	Falcons	Falcons	Signed	Cut, re-signed
BERNIE KOSAR	Cowboys	Dolphins	Signed	UFA
ERIK KRAMER	Lions	Bears	Signed	UFA
DAVE KRIEG	Chiefs	Lions	Signed	UFA
CHUCK LONG	None	Lions	Signed	Cut, signed
DAN McGWIRE	Seahawks	Seahawks	Unsigned RFA	......
JIM McMAHON	Vikings	?????	Unsigned	Cut
CHRIS MILLER	Falcons	Rams	Signed	UFA
HUGH MILLEN	Dolphins	?????	Unsigned UFA	......
SCOTT MITCHELL	Dolphins	Lions	Signed	UFA
WARREN MOON	Oilers	Vikings	Signed	Traded
BROWNING NAGLE	Jets	?????	Unsigned	Cut
KEN O'BRIEN	Eagles	?????	Unsigned UFA	......
RODNEY PEETE	Lions	Cowboys	Signed	UFA
TODD PHILCOX	Browns	?????	Unsigned UFA	......
BUCKY RICHARDSON	Oilers	Oilers	Signed	Re-signed EFA
MARK RYPIEN	Redskins	Browns	Signed	Cut, signed
TONY SACCA	Cardinals	?????	Unsigned	Cut
SEAN SALISBURY	Vikings	Oilers	Signed	UFA
SCOTT SECULES	Patriots	?????	Unsigned	Cut
KELLY STOUFFER	None	Dolphins	Signed	Cut, signed
RICK STROM	Steelers	Bills	Signed	UFA
BILLY JOE TOLLIVER	Falcons	?????	Unsigned UFA	......
JACK TRUDEAU	Colts	Jets	Signed	Cut, signed
MARK VLASIC	Buccaneers	Buccaneers	Signed	UFA
STEVE WALSH	Saints	Bears	Signed	Cut, signed
ANDRE WARE	Lions	?????	Unsigned UFA	......
WADE WILSON	Saints	Saints	Signed	Cut, re-signed
SCOTT ZOLAK	Patriots	Patriots	Signed	Re-signed

PRO FOOTBALL WEEKLY 1994 ALMANAC

After signing LB Gary Plummer and cutting LB Keith DeLong, San Francisco was all of $456 under the cap before the figure was increased by $400,000 on March 24 following a leaguewide audit. The 49ers postponed the start of their offseason workout program because of their proximity to the cap. That's because money paid in offseason programs counts toward the cap.

But, if you think the problems now are difficult to handle, think what might occur when the season starts. Clubs will be forced to leave money available under the cap for injuries. The salaries of players who go on injured reserve will still count against the cap, so a team hit with several injuries could be in trouble.

"Last year we had 15 players injured, many of them top players," said Philadelphia coach Rich Kotite. "If that happened again, we'd be lucky to field a team. I mean it. If you need replacements (for injured players), we are going to have to let players go, a lot of players. I think you might see a situation where your third-string tight end has to go in and play left guard some game because the money just won't be there under the cap to get a replacement."

Some of the contracts signed by this year's free agents are good deals for the clubs.

The Bears think they got a good quarterback in Kramer, who led Detroit to two division titles in three years, for $2.7 million a year. Kramer isn't great, but neither is his salary by recent NFL standards.

And the Rams think they got a pretty good deal with Miller — $9 million for three years — if he's healthy. Miller could be one of the league's best quarterbacks, but he could also be a $3 million-a-year, injury-prone bust.

But some of the contracts signed by this year's free agents are ridiculous deals, too.

Mitchell left Miami for Detroit, signing a three-year, $11 million contract that included a $5 million bonus, the third-highest in NFL history. Minnesota was close to Detroit in the bidding for a quarterback who has started only seven NFL games. Said Viking vice president Jeff Diamond, "Our offer was crazy; theirs was insane."

Ray Crockett, an average cornerback with Detroit last year, signed with Denver for $6.4 million over four years. An *average* cornerback, that is.

And Jimmie Jones signed a four-year, $7.5 million contract with the Rams after having played for the Super Bowl-champion Cowboys the last two years. Some NFL general managers were laughing out loud at the amount of money the Rams paid a part-time defensive tackle. Jones' new contract includes a $2 million bonus — and he's a *part-time* defensive tackle.

The Dolphins had to let Louis Oliver go because of the salary cap

Teams such as the Bengals and Patriots were going to be successful in free-agency this year because they were so far under the salary cap and had millions of dollars to spend.

Agent Tom Condon, who represented three of the first six signees and who seemed to have the quickest grasp of the new system, said, "A lot of teams won't be able to compete with Cincinnati and New England. They're so far under the cap that they can put a lot of money into the first year of a contract, and others can't."

The Patriots quickly signed OG Bob Kratch and S Myron Guyton away from the Giants.

The Bengals, on the other hand, didn't make much of a splash in free-agency. In the first two months, Cincinnati had signed only Oliver and journeyman OG Darrick Brilz.

Mike Brown, the Bengals' general manager, admitted, "We're willing to pay a lot of money for what we think is a top-notch player. But we only have so much. And we have more money in this than anyone else. ... We're willing to pay the money. If you play well enough, you'll get the money. We don't want to guarantee it."

That is, however, what Brown had to do with Dan Wilkinson, the team's top draft pick, who received $14.4 million over six years.

Yes, the times they are a-changin'.

252

1994 PREVIEW ■ FREE-AGENCY
1994 FREE AGENTS

Here is a list of free agents who had signed as of May 9.

Abbreviations: UFA — unrestricted free agent, RFA — restricted free agent, TFA — transition free agent, EFA — exclusive-rights free agent.

Arizona Cardinals
Signed: P Jeff Feagles (Philadelphia), LB Seth Joyner (Philadelphia), LB Randy Kirk (Cincinnati), DE Clyde Simmons (Philadelphia).
Lost: P Rich Camarillo, QB Chris Chandler, DT Reuben Davis, LB Ken Harvey, CB Robert Massey, TE Walter Reeves, OG Lance Smith.
Re-signed: RB Larry Centers, WR Anthony Edwards, LB Eric Hill.

Atlanta Falcons
Signed: CB D.J. Johnson (Pittsburgh), WR Terance Mathis (N.Y. Jets), CB Kevin Ross (Kansas City), OG Mike Zandofsky (San Diego).
Lost: WR Michael Haynes, OT Chris Hinton, QB Chris Miller.
Re-signed: DT Mel Agee, DE Lester Archambeau, OG Roman Fortin, DT Mike Goldberg, OT Mike Kenn, TE Harper LeBel, DE Ernie Logan; WR Mike Pritchard (subsequently traded to Denver), DB Charles Washington.

Buffalo Bills
Signed: QB Rick Strom (Pittsburgh).
Lost: OT Howard Ballard, QB Gale Gilbert, LB Richard Harvey, CB Nate Odomes.
Re-signed: S Matt Darby, OG John Davis, RB Eddie Fuller, DE Phil Hansen, P Chris Mohr, WR Steve Tasker, RB Nate Turner.

Chicago Bears
Signed: TE Marv Cook (New England), OT Andy Heck (Seattle), FB Merril Hoge (Pittsburgh), QB Erik Kramer (Detroit), RB Lewis Tillman (N.Y. Giants).
Lost: None.
Re-signed: OG Mark Bortz, RB Robert Green, TE Keith Jennings, LB Dante Jones, DT Tim Ryan.

Cincinnati Bengals
Signed: OG Darrick Brilz (Seattle), OT Eric Moore (N.Y. Giants), S Louis Oliver (Miami), TE Troy Sadowski (N.Y. Jets).
Lost: LB Randy Kirk.
Re-signed: WR Milt Stegall, S Fernandus Vinson.

Cleveland Browns
Signed: CB Don Griffin (San Francisco), TE Walter Reeves (Arizona), QB Mark Rypien (Washington), OG Mike Withycombe (San Diego).
Lost: P Brian Hansen, LB Mike Johnson.
Re-signed: OT Orlando Brown, TE Brian Kinchen, LB Frank Stams, PK Matt Stover, DB Del Speer.

Dallas Cowboys
Signed: OG Derek Kennard (New Orleans), QB Rodney Peete (Detroit).
Lost: DT Tony Casillas, OG John Gesek, OG Kevin Gogan, DT Jimmie Jones, QB Bernie Kosar, PK Eddie Murray, LB Ken Norton.
Re-signed: S Joe Fishback, RB Derrick Gainer (subsequently traded to Raiders), FB Daryl Johnston, OG Nate Newton.

Denver Broncos
Signed: WR Jeff Campbell (Detroit), CB Ray Crockett (Detroit), LB Richard Harvey (Buffalo), WR Anthony Miller (San Diego did not match offer).
Lost: WR Vance Johnson, CB David Pool.
Re-signed: None.

Detroit Lions
Signed: TE Ron Hall (Tampa Bay), LB Mike Johnson (Cleveland), QB Dave Krieg (Kansas City), CB Robert Massey (Arizona), QB Scott Mitchell (Miami), P Greg Montgomery (Houston).
Lost: P Jim Arnold, WR Jeff Campbell, CB Ray Crockett, LB Dennis Gibson, QB Erik Kramer, QB Rodney Peete.
Re-signed: WR Reggie Barrett (subsequently traded to Seattle), KR Mel Gray, WR Brett Perriman.

Green Bay Packers
Signed: RB Reggie Cobb (Tampa Bay), DE Sean Jones (Houston).
Lost: LB Tony Bennett.
Re-signed: DE Don Davey, P Bryan Wagner, C Frank Winters.

Houston Oilers
Signed: P Rich Camarillo (Arizona), TE Pat Carter (L.A. Rams), QB Sean Salisbury (Minnesota).
Lost: WR Reggie Brown, DE William Fuller, DE Sean Jones, P Greg Montgomery.
Re-signed: OT Kevin Donnalley (matched L.A. Rams offer), OG Erik Norgard, QB Bucky Richardson.

Indianapolis Colts
Signed: LB Tony Bennett (Green Bay), WR Floyd Turner (Indianapolis).
Lost: C Trevor Matich, CB Tony Stargell, S Keith Taylor.
Re-signed: TE Charles Arbuckle, CB Eugene Daniel, DE Jon Hand, OT Mark Vander Poel.

Kansas City Chiefs
Signed: P Louis Aguiar (N.Y. Jets), DT Tony Casillas (Dallas), CB Mark Collins (N.Y. Giants).
Lost: WB Dave Krieg, CB Albert Lewis, LB Lonnie Marts, CB Kevin Ross.
Re-signed: WR Tim Barnett, RB Trevor Cobb, DT Joe Phillips.

Los Angeles Raiders
Signed: OG Kevin Gogan (Dallas), CB Albert Lewis (Kansas City), TE Jamie Williams (San Francisco).
Lost: TE Ethan Horton.
Re-signed: WR Tim Brown (matched Denver

253

PRO FOOTBALL WEEKLY 1994 ALMANAC

1994 FREE AGENTS

offer), OL Dan Turk.

Los Angeles Rams
Signed: QB Chris Chandler (Arizona), DT Jimmie Jones (Dallas), WR Greg McMurtry, QB Chris Miller (Atlanta).
Lost: TE Pat Carter, WR Henry Ellard, S Michael Stewart, DE Tony Woods.
Re-signed: P Sean Landeta, OG Jeff Pahukoa.

Miami Dolphins
Signed: P Jim Arnold (Detroit), S Gene Atkins (New Orleans), WR Reggie Brown (Houston), QB Bernie Kosar (Dallas), S Michael Stewart (L.A. Rams).
Lost: LB David Griggs, DE Jeff Hunter, QB Scott Mitchell, S Louis Oliver, C Jeff Uhlenhake.
Re-signed: RB Bernie Parmalee, FB James Saxon, PK Pete Stoyanovich.

Minnesota Vikings
Signed: OT Chris Hinton (Atlanta), CB David Pool (Denver).
Lost: OT Tim Irwin, QB Sean Salisbury.
Re-signed: RB Charles Evans, S Vencie Glenn, OG Randall McDaniel, CB Anthony Parker, WR Jake Reed.

New England Patriots
Signed: LB Steve DeOssie (N.Y. Jets), S Myron Guyton (N.Y. Giants), OG Bob Kratch (N.Y. Giants), CB Ricky Reynolds (Tampa Bay), RB Blair Thomas (N.Y. Jets).
Lost: WR Greg McMurtry, DE Brent Williams.
Re-signed: C Mike Arthur, LB David Bavaro, WR Vincent Brisby, TE Ben Coates, RB Sam Gash, OT Pat Harlow, DT Bryan Hooks, CB Maurice Hurst, DT Mario Johnson, OT Brandon Moore, DT Mike Pitts, S Terry Ray, OT Doug Skene, DT Mark Staten, DB Darryl Wren, QB Scott Zolak.

New Orleans Saints
Signed: WR Michael Haynes (transition player; Atlanta did not match offer), C Jeff Uhlenhake (Miami), TE Wesley Walls (San Francisco).
Lost: S Gene Atkins, OG Derek Kennard, WR Floyd Turner.
Re-signed: OT Chris Port, LB James Williams, QB Wade Wilson.

New York Giants
Signed: OG Lance Smith (Arizona).
Lost: CB Mark Collins, S Myron Guyton, OG Bob Kratch, OT Eric Moore, RB Lewis Tillman.
Re-signed: OT Doug Riesenberg, OG Brian Williams.

New York Jets
Signed: DE Donald Evans (Pittsburgh), P Brian Hansen (Cleveland).
Lost: P Louis Aguiar, LB Steve DeOssie, WR Terance Mathis, TE Troy Sadowski, RB Blair Thomas.
Re-signed: LB Glenn Cadrez, WR Rob Carpenter, OL Roger Duffy, DT Paul Frase, CB Victor Green, QB Browning Nagle (subsequently

cut), C Jim Sweeney.

Philadelphia Eagles
Signed: DE William Fuller (Houston), PK Eddie Murray (Dallas).
Lost: P Jeff Feagles, LB Seth Joyner, DE Clyde Simmons.
Re-signed: QB Bubby Brister, DT Mike Chalenski, OL John Hudson, TE Maurice Johnson, DT William Perry, S Otis Smith, WR Jeff Sydner.

Pittsburgh Steelers
Signed: DE Ray Seals (Tampa Bay), FB John L. Williams (Seattle).
Lost: DE Donald Evans, FB Merril Hoge, CB D.J. Johnson, QB Rick Strom.
Re-signed: LB Reggie Barnes, TE Adrian Cooper (subsequently traded to Minnesota); WR Jeff Graham (subsequently traded to Chicago).

San Diego Chargers
Signed: DT Reuben Davis (Arizona), LB Dennis Gibson (Detroit), QB Gale Gilbert (Buffalo), LB David Griggs (Miami), CB Dwayne Harper (Seattle), WR Vance Johnson (Denver).
Lost: QB John Friesz, WR Anthony Miller, LB Gary Plummer, OT Mike Withycombe, OL Mike Zandofsky.
Re-signed: OT Stan Brock, PK John Carney, CB Victor Green, WR Walter Dunson, TE Mike Dyal, C Courtney Hall, WR Shawn Jefferson, FS Stanley Richard, TE Duane Young.

San Francisco 49ers
Signed: LB Ken Norton (Dallas), LB Gary Plummer (San Diego).
Lost: CB Don Griffin, TE Wesley Walls, TE Jamie Williams.
Re-signed: RB Dexter Carter.

Seattle Seahawks
Signed: OT Howard Ballard (Buffalo), CB Nate Odomes (Buffalo), DE Brent Williams (New England).
Lost: OG Darrick Brilz, CB Dwayne Harper, OT Andy Heck, FB John L. Williams.
Re-signed: LB David Brandon, OT Mike Keim.

Tampa Bay Buccaneers
Signed: DE Jeff Hunter (Miami), OT Tim Irwin (Minnesota), LB Lonnie Marts (Kansas City), CB Tony Stargell (Indianapolis).
Lost: RB Reggie Cobb, TE Ron Hall, CB Ricky Reynolds, DE Ray Seals.
Re-signed: OG Ian Beckles, DB Curtis Buckley, DE Shawn Price, QB Mark Vlasic.

Washington Redskins
Signed: WR Henry Ellard (L.A. Rams), QB John Friesz (San Diego), OG John Gesek (Dallas), LB Ken Harvey (Arizona), TE Ethan Horton (L.A. Raiders), C Trevor Matich (Indianapolis), S Keith Taylor (Indianapolis) DE Tony Woods (L.A. Rams).
Lost: None.
Re-signed: DE Jeff Faulkner, WR Stephen Hobbs.

254

SECTION
II

1993 in Review

THE Top 10 Stories OF '93

Order in the courts. Finally. Just six days into 1993, a new, seven-year collective-bargaining agreement was officially agreed upon, thus setting the stage for a season in which fans could set their sights solely on the game again.

Well, almost. There's no doubt the primary focus was on a product that was changed significantly by full-scale free-agency player movement, as a lot of old faces in new places kept devoted pro football followers everywhere on their toes.

But there was also a lot of stuff off the field that demanded our attention. Like a bombshell TV contract, courtesy of the upstart network that gives us Bart Simpson and Al Bundy. And a pair of new franchises in the nation's fastest-growing region. And a pair of teams from Texas that entertainingly combined top-of-the-line football with spicy, soap-opera sideshows.

What were the top stories of 1993, according to PFW editors? Try these 10 on for size:

1. The free-agent factor

It was the biggest by-product of the new CBA, as a total of 120 players switched teams. In addition, overall player salaries rose 51 percent in '93, to an average of $737,850 per player.

Reggie White led the big-name caravan, fleeing Philadelphia and ending up in Green Bay, of all places, after signing a $17 million contract. The Packers, as you know, ended up in the playoffs, as did the Chiefs, who got a major-league contribution from free-agent RB Marcus Allen, and the Giants, who benefited greatly from the presence of free-agent WR's Mark Jackson and Mike Sherrard. Old faces in new places, adding badly needed new life to the NFL.

Free-agency, the Fox television deal and expansion were among the top NFL stories in 1993

2. CBS gets outfoxed

The story of the NFC's new TV contract was both interesting and bittersweet. Interesting because of the Fox Network, the upset winner in the battle for the senior circuit's TV rights, and the whopping price it paid — $1.58 billion, which pushed the overall TV package to $4.35 billion in addition to upping the ante in the salary-cap department.

Bittersweet because the CBS network's 38-year relationship with the NFL was terminated — at least for the next four years.

3. 'Team Turmoil' in Houston

"It's by far the strangest year I've been involved with," said Houston WR Ernest Givins of a crazy seesaw season both on and off the field punctuated in memorable fashion by irascible defensive coordinator Buddy Ryan's Sunday-night sucker punch in the general direction of offensive coordinator Kevin Gilbride in the team's regular-season finale.

While Ryan and Gilbride battled all year, there was also the "Babygate" incident involving OT David Williams, who was docked one game check for choosing to stay with his wife and newborn son instead of playing against the Patriots. Then there was the tragic suicide of DT Jeff Alm, none of which kept the Oilers from steamrolling into the playoffs on an 11-game winning streak. A guy named Montana put an end to Houston's season, but we'll get to him a bit later.

4. Enter Carolina and Jacksonville

When the Carolina Panthers were named the NFL's 29th franchise in October, it wasn't very surprising. The Carolina market was hot, and the ownership group, headed by former Colt Jerry Richardson, was rock-solid.

But, when the Jacksonville Jaguars became the NFL's 30th franchise on the last day of November, eyebrows were raised everywhere, as a group headed by shoe-magnate Wayne Weaver ended up doing a better of job of persuading NFL owners than bidders from Baltimore and St. Louis, two former NFL locales that were considered a lot more likely to receive new teams by most onlookers.

The Jacksonville area wasted no time saying thanks, selling in excess of 50,000 season tickets in what seemed like a blink of an eyelash.

5. Cowboys repeat, Bills 'Four-Beat'

After starting out the season 0-2, a record in great part caused by the absence of holdout RB Emmitt Smith, the Cowboys ended up just where most of the experts said they would be — in the Georgia Dome on Super Sunday, once again beating the Bills, who failed for a record fourth straight time to win a Super title.

The Cowboys strutted and swaggered, and the team's owner, Jerry Jones, and head coach, Jimmy Johnson, mastered the art of creative tension, NFL style. The Bills were much more of a blue-collar bunch, once again dominating all comers on their home turf in December and January before self-destructing in the Big One.

6. Shula passes 'Papa Bear'

Here's another story that ended up being bittersweet. Three weeks after Miami's Don Shula won his 325th game as a head coach Nov. 14 in Philadelphia and surpassed the legendary George Halas as the NFL's all-time winningest coach, the Dolphins hit the skids, losing their last five games and failing to make the playoffs after a blazing 9-2 start.

7. The Cleveland calamity

"Diminishing skills." For a few weeks right around the season's midpoint, those words became part of the NFL lexicon after they were used by Bill Belichick, the Browns' Napoleonic head coach, to explain why he was cutting QB Bernie Kosar, one of the most popular players ever to play in Cleveland.

The Browns were 5-3 at the time and right in the thick of things. To no one's surprise, they steadily sunk out of contention in the AFC Central, even though Belichick feebly tried to con the Cleveland faithful into believing the team was actually showing dramatic improvement. Pity the poor Dawg Pound.

8. The Year of the Kicker

For better or worse, kicking excellence was in vogue in '93, as placekickers such as PFW's Golden Toe recipient Norm Johnson in Atlanta, Chris Jacke in Green Bay, Jason Hanson in Detroit, Jeff Jaeger in Los Angeles, Gary Anderson in Pittsburgh, Morten Andersen in New Orleans and John Carney in San Diego provided a lion's share of the league's scoring.

Their success coincided with a marked increase in offensive failures inside the red zone, as well as a growing number of complaints among fans who had their fill of 15-13 and 9-6 affairs in '93.

9. The Emmitt Smith saga

Without PFW's Offensive MVP in the lineup, the Cowboys were an ordinary team. With him, they ended up being by far the league's *creme de la creme*, as he captured his third straight NFL rushing title despite missing the first two games because of his aforementioned contract holdout.

10. The ups and downs of Joe Montana

After missing five games with assorted aches and pains that made his playing status questionable on pretty much a weekly basis, we were all treated to the Joe Montana of old in Kansas City's thrilling, 27-24 overtime victory in the playoffs over Pittsburgh.

After rallying his team from a 17-7 halftime deficit in that game, fans across the nation were turned on by the prospect of seeing Montana play in his fifth Super Bowl.

Of course, reality set in a few weeks later. In Rich Stadium ... in January ...

Some stories never change.

PRO FOOTBALL WEEKLY 1994 ALMANAC

REVIEW: WEEK ONE

WEEK ONE STANDINGS

AMERICAN FOOTBALL CONFERENCE

AFC EAST	W	L	T	Pct.	PF	PA
Buffalo	1	0	0	1.000	38	14
Miami	1	0	0	1.000	24	20
Indianapolis	0	1	0	.000	20	24
N.Y. Jets	0	1	0	.000	20	26
New England	0	1	0	.000	14	38

AFC CENTRAL	W	L	T	Pct.	PF	PA
Cleveland	1	0	0	1.000	27	14
Houston	0	1	0	.000	14	27
Cincinnati	0	1	0	.000	14	27
Pittsburgh	0	1	0	.000	13	24

AFC WEST	W	L	T	Pct.	PF	PA
Kansas City	1	0	0	1.000	27	3
Denver	1	0	0	1.000	26	20
L.A. Raiders	1	0	0	1.000	24	7
San Diego	1	0	0	1.000	18	12
Sseattle	0	1	0	.000	12	18

NATIONAL FOOTBALL CONFERENCE

NFC EAST	W	L	T	Pct.	PF	PA
N.Y. Giants	1	0	0	1.000	26	20
Philadelphia	1	0	0	1.000	23	17
Washington	1	0	0	1.000	35	16
Dallas	0	1	0	.000	16	35
Phoenix	0	1	0	.000	17	23

NFC CENTRAL	W	L	T	Pct.	PF	PA
Green Bay	1	0	0	1.000	36	6
Detroit	1	0	0	1.000	30	13
Chicago	0	1	0	.000	20	26
Minnesota	0	1	0	.000	7	24
Tampa Bay	0	1	0	.000	3	27

NFC WEST	W	L	T	Pct.	PF	PA
New Orleans	1	0	0	1.000	33	21
San Francisco	1	0	0	1.000	24	13
Atlanta	0	1	0	.000	13	30
L.A. Rams	0	1	0	.000	6	36

WEEK 1 RESULTS / LINE

Result	Line
DETROIT 30, Atlanta 13	LIONS by 5.5
CLEVELAND 27, Cincinnati 14	BROWNS by 7.5
Denver 26, N.Y. JETS 20	Broncos by 1.5
N.Y. Giants 26, CHICAGO 20	BEARS by 1
Kansas City 27, TAMPA BAY 3	Chiefs by 7
GREEN BAY 36, L.A. Rams 6	PACKERS by 7
Miami 24, INDIANAPOLIS 20	Dolphins by 6.5
BUFFALO 38, New England 14	BILLS by 14.5
PHILADELPHIA 23, Phoenix 17	EAGLES by 6.5
San Francisco 24, PITTSBURGH 13	49ers by 6.5
L.A. RAIDERS 24, Minnesota 7	Vikings by 2.5
SAN DIEGO 18, Seattle 12	CHARGERS by 11
NEW ORLEANS 33, Houston 21	SAINTS by 2.5
WASHINGTON 35, Dallas 16	REDSKINS by 2.5

Home team in CAPS

The NFL's 1993 season jump-started with only a few surprises.

The world champion Cowboys, without holdout RB Emmitt Smith, the league's leading ground gainer in 1992, fell to the rival Redskins on Monday night, and, the day before, the NFC Central champion Vikings were drubbed by an underdog Raider team. The rest was relatively predictable.

The spotlight in Week One, however, was on quarterbacks.

The Dolphins' Dan Marino showed that he could still lead his team to a fourth-quarter comeback as well as anyone in the game, and the 49ers' Steve Young proved he could play despite having broken a thumb during the preseason. The Bills' Jim Kelly put the previous Super Bowl embarrassment behind him, and the Broncos' John Elway showed that he was adapting well to his team's new offensive style. Jeff Hostetler made the cross-country move from the Giants' camp to the Raiders' with ease, and the Redskins' Mark Rypien showed that he could bounce back from an off year in the nation's capital.

GAME OF THE WEEK: It had to be Dallas-Washington, not from the standpoint of excitement, but surprise. How often does the reigning world champion get blown out in its first game since triumphing in the Super Bowl? But the Redskins, under new head coach Richie Petitbon and behind

PHOTO BY STEVEN MURPHY

Washington shocked the Cowboys in Week One

the arm of Rypien, put the Cowboys in their place with a 19-point margin of victory.

OLD-HAND: Old-hand, hot-hand Joe Montana debuted with Kansas City and clearly showed he

258

1993 REVIEW ■ WEEK ONE

still had it. The three-time Super Bowl MVP for the 49ers led the Chiefs to an easy 27-3 win over Tampa Bay, throwing three TD passes and completing 14-of-21 passes for 246 yards.

OLD-HAND NO. 2: QB Jeff Hostetler, signed as a free agent by the Raiders after nine years with the Giants, sparked a major 24-7 upset over the Vikings by completing 23-of-27 passes for 150 yards and one touchdown.

IMPRESSIVE: The NFC Central Packers and Lions won big over non-division opponents; the Saints, Browns and Bills also looked mighty good on Opening Day.

PFW NOTES: Ram QB Jim Everett passed Roman Gabriel's club career passing-yardage record of 22,223 yards. LB Clay Matthews set a new games-played mark for the Browns, surpassing Hall of Fame OT/PK Lou Groza's 216. Marino moved into second place on the NFL's all-time list for touchdown passes when he threw his 251st. Green Bay PK Chris Jacke's four extra points gave him 90 straight, and WR Sterling Sharpe extended his streak of catching at least one pass in 72 consecutive games. The 49ers won their ninth straight regular-season game, currently the longest in the NFL. The Bears' streak of nine straight opening-day victories came to an end. RB Barry Sanders eclipsed Dexter Bussey's all-time rushing-attempt record of 1,203 for Detroit. New Orleans PK Morten Andersen kicked his 24th consecutive field goal, tying him for the NFL record with Kevin Butler of the Bears.

OFFENSIVE MVP: WR Andre Reed, Buffalo. Reed had three TD receptions in all of 1992. He matched that total in the first afternoon of the 1993 season.

DEFENSIVE MVP: CB Tyrone Braxton, Denver. Turnovers made the Broncos' day. Braxton had one interception and forced two fumbles while also logging nine solo tackles and two assists. The interception was the 16th of his career.

GOLDEN TOE: PK John Carney, San Diego. No debate here. Carney kicked six consecutive field goals to account for all of the Chargers' 18 points. Two were from 50-plus yards.

TOP PERFORMANCES
PASSING

Player, team	Comp.	Att.	Yds.	TD	Int.
Boomer Esiason, Jets	29	40	371	2	1
Phil Simms, Giants	24	34	277	2	0
John Elway, Broncos	20	29	269	0	0
Troy Aikman, Cowboys	17	29	267	2	0
Brett Favre, Packers	19	29	264	2	1
Chris Miller, Falcons	26	50	260	1	2

RUSHING

Player, team	Att.	Yds.	TD
Brian Mitchell, Redskins	21	116	2
Thurman Thomas, Bills	24	114	0
Barry Sanders, Lions	26	90	1
Marion Butts, Chargers	15	87	0
Leonard Russell, Patriots	23	81	0
Lorenzo Neal, Saints	13	89	0

RECEIVING

Player, team	Rec.	Yds.	TD
Rob Moore, Jets	9	140	1
Alvin Harper, Cowboys	5	140	2
Sterling Sharpe, Packers	7	120	1
Herman Moore, Lions	4	113	1
Eric Martin, Saints	7	111	0
Andre Reed, Bills	6	110	3
Andre Rison, Falcons	6	106	1

SCORING

Player, team	TD	XP	FG	Pts.
John Carney, Chargers	0	0/0	6/6	18
Andre Reed, Bills	3	0	0	18
Morten Andersen, Saints	0	3/3	4/4	15

GAME SUMMARIES
49ERS 24, STEELERS 13
Pittsburgh, Pa., Sept. 5, 1993

San Francisco	10	7	0	7	— 24
Pittsburgh	0	3	10	0	— 13

Scoring:
San Francisco: Cofer, 37 FG
San Francisco: Rice, 5 pass from Young (Cofer kick)
San Francisco: Rice, 6 pass from Young (Cofer kick)
Pittsburgh: Anderson, 29 FG
Pittsburgh: Foster, 5 run (Anderson kick)
Pittsburgh: Anderson, 39 FG
San Francisco: B. Jones, 5 pass from Young (Cofer kick)

BILLS 38, PATRIOTS 14
Orchard Park, N.Y., Sept. 5, 1993

New England	0	7	7	0	— 14
Buffalo	0	17	0	21	— 38

Scoring:
Buffalo: Christie, 28 FG
Buffalo: Brooks, 4 pass from Kelly (Christie kick)
New England: Coates, 54 pass from Bledsoe (Sisson kick)
Buffalo: Reed, 41 pass from Kelly (Christie kick)
New England: McMurtry, 2 pass from Bledsoe (Sisson kick)
Buffalo: Reed, 22 pass from Kelly (Christie kick)
Buffalo: Reed, 14 pass from Kelly (Christie kick)
Buffalo: Copeland, 47 punt return (Christie kick)

BRONCOS 26, JETS 20
East Rutherford, N.J., Sept. 5, 1993

Denver	6	7	13	0	— 26
N.Y. Jets	0	6	0	14	— 20

Scoring:
Denver: Elam, 28 FG
Denver: Elam, 30 FG
N.Y. Jets: Blanchard, 22 FG
N.Y. Jets: Blanchard, 43 FG
Denver: Tillman, 3 pass from Elway (Elam kick)
Denver: Milburn, 25 pass from Elway (Elam kick)
Denver: Elam, 41 FG
Denver: Elam, 41 FG
N.Y. Jets: Mitchell, 5 pass from Esiason (Blanchard kick)
N.Y. Jets: Moore, 6 pass from Esiason (Blanchard kick)

DOLPHINS 24, COLTS 20
Indianapolis, Ind., Sept. 5, 1993

Miami	7	3	7	7	— 24
Indianapolis	7	0	3	10	— 20

Scoring:
Indianapolis: Culver, 56 fumble return on punt (Biasucci kick)
Miami: K. Jackson, 40 pass from Marino (Stoyanovich kick)
Miami: Stoyanovich, 20 FG
Indianapolis: Biasucci, 26 FG
Miami: K. Jackson, 27 pass from Marino (Stoyanovich kick)
Indianapolis: Dawkins, 25 pass from Trudeau (Biasucci kick)
Indianapolis: Biasucci, 33 FG
Miami: Baty, 1 pass from Marino (Stoyanovich kick)

PRO FOOTBALL WEEKLY 1994 ALMANAC

BROWNS 27, BENGALS 14
Cleveland, Ohio, Sept. 5, 1993

Cincinnati	14	0	0	0	—	14
Cleveland	0	14	6	7	—	27

Scoring:
- Cincinnati: Miles, 4 run (Pelfrey kick)
- Cincinnati: Pickens, 5 pass from Klingler (Pelfrey kick)
- Cleveland: Jackson, 13 pass from Kosar (Stover kick)
- Cleveland: Vardell, 1 run (Stover kick)
- Cleveland: Stover, 28 FG
- Cleveland: Stover, 34 FG
- Cleveland: Moore, 22 fumble return (Stover kick)

GIANTS 26, BEARS 20
Chicago, Ill., Sept. 5, 1993

N.Y. Giants	3	6	7	10	—	26
Chicago	0	7	10	3	—	20

Scoring:
- N.Y. Giants: Treadwell, 19 FG
- N.Y. Giants: Treadwell, 35 FG
- N.Y. Giants: Treadwell, 23 FG
- Chicago: Obee, 2 pass from Harbaugh (Butler kick)
- Chicago: Baker, 5 blocked-punt return (Butler kick)
- Chicago: Butler, 20 FG
- N.Y. Giants: M. Jackson, 40 pass from Simms (Treadwell kick)
- N.Y. Giants: Treadwell, 36 FG
- Chicago: Butler, 34 FG
- N.Y. Giants: Bunch, 1 pass from Simms (Treadwell kick)

SAINTS 33, OILERS 21
New Orleans, La., Sept. 5, 1993

Houston	7	0	0	14	—	21
New Orleans	3	10	6	14	—	33

Scoring:
- Houston: Jeffires, 6 pass from Moon (Del Greco kick)
- New Orleans: Andersen, 28 FG
- New Orleans: Hilliard, 2 run (Andersen kick)
- New Orleans: Andersen, 37 FG
- New Orleans: Andersen, 18 FG
- New Orleans: Andersen, 47 FG
- New Orleans: Warren, 47 fumble return (Andersen kick)
- New Orleans: Brown, 2 run (Andersen kick)
- Houston: Carlson, 1 run (Del Greco kick)
- Houston: Robertson, 80 fumble return (Del Greco kick)

RAIDERS 24, VIKINGS 7
Los Angeles, Calif., Sept. 5, 1993

Minnesota	0	0	0	7	—	7
L.A. Raiders	7	14	0	3	—	24

Scoring:
- L.A. Raiders: Brown, 17 pass from Hostetler (Jaeger kick)
- L.A. Raiders: Robinson, 1 run (Jaeger kick)
- L.A. Raiders: McDaniel, 36 interception return (Jaeger kick)
- L.A. Raiders: Jaeger, 21 FG
- Minnesota: Craig, 1 run (Reveiz kick)

PACKERS 36, RAMS 6
Milwaukee, Wis., Sept. 5, 1993

L.A. Rams	3	3	0	0	—	6
Green Bay	9	10	14	3	—	36

Scoring:
- Green Bay: Safety, Paup and Koonce tackled Gary in endzone
- L.A. Rams: Zendejas, 31 FG
- Green Bay: Sharpe, 50 pass from Favre (Jacke kick)
- Green Bay: Jacke, 51 FG
- L.A. Rams: Zendejas, 32 FG
- Green Bay: Clayton, 4 pass from Favre (Jacke kick)
- Green Bay: Bennett, 11 run (Jacke kick)
- Green Bay: Bennett, 1 run (Jacke kick)
- Green Bay: Jacke, 33 FG

CHARGERS 18, SEAHAWKS 12
San Diego, Calif., Sept. 5, 1993

Seattle	7	3	0	2	—	12
San Diego	6	6	0	6	—	18

Scoring:
- Seattle: Nash, 13 interception return (Kasay kick)
- San Diego: Carney, 26 FG
- San Diego: Carney, 44 FG
- Seattle: Kasay, 27 FG
- San Diego: Carney, 50 FG
- San Diego: Carney, 32 FG
- San Diego: Carney, 51 FG
- San Diego: Carney, 19 FG
- Seattle: Safety, Kidd forced out of endzone

CHIEFS 27, BUCCANEERS 3
Tampa, Fla., Sept. 5, 1993

Kansas City	0	17	7	3	—	27
Tampa Bay	3	0	0	0	—	3

Scoring:
- Tampa Bay: Husted, 35 FG
- Kansas City: Davis, 19 pass from Montana (Lowery kick)
- Kansas City: Lowery, 20 FG
- Kansas City: Birden, 50 pass from Montana (Lowery kick)
- Kansas City: Allen, 12 pass from Montana (Lowery kick)
- Kansas City: Lowery, 23 FG

LIONS 30, FALCONS 13
Pontiac, Mich., Sept. 5, 1993

Atlanta	0	3	3	7	—	13
Detroit	14	10	3	3	—	30

Scoring:
- Detroit: Sanders, 26 run (Hanson kick)
- Detroit: Jamison, 35 interception return (Hanson kick)
- Detroit: Hanson, 44 FG
- Detroit: H. Moore, 21 pass from Peete (Hanson kick)
- Atlanta: Johnson, 54 FG
- Atlanta: Johnson, 20 FG
- Detroit: Hanson, 37 FG
- Atlanta: Rison, 32 pass from Miller (Johnson kick)
- Detroit: Hanson, 37 FG

EAGLES 23, CARDINALS 17
Philadelphia, Pa., Sept. 5, 1993

Phoenix	0	3	7	7	—	17
Philadelphia	7	7	2	7	—	23

Scoring:
- Philadelphia: Sherman, 1 run (Ruzek kick)
- Philadelphia: Cunningham, 9 run (Ruzek kick)
- Phoenix: G. Davis, 24 FG
- Philadelphia: Safety, team tackled Camarillo in endzone
- Phoenix: Centers, 27 pass from Chandler (G. Davis kick)
- Philadelphia: Hebron, 5 run (Ruzek kick)
- Phoenix: Lynch, 55 fumble return (G. Davis kick)

REDSKINS 35, COWBOYS 16
Washington, D.C., Monday night, Sept. 6, 1993

Dallas	6	0	7	3	—	16
Washington	0	14	14	7	—	35

Scoring:
- Dallas: Harper, 80 pass from Aikman (Elliott kick failed)
- Washington: Sanders, 15 pass from Rypien (Lohmiller kick)
- Washington: Mitchell, 1 run (Lohmiller kick)
- Washington: Middleton, 1 pass from Rypien (Lohmiller kick)
- Dallas: Harper, 32 pass from Aikman (Elliott kick)
- Washington: Monk, 15 pass from Rypien (Lohmiller kick)
- Dallas: Elliott, 22 FG
- Washington: Mitchell, 29 run (Lohmiller kick)

1993 REVIEW ■ WEEK TWO

WEEK TWO

WEEK TWO STANDINGS

AMERICAN FOOTBALL CONFERENCE

AFC EAST	W	L	T	Pct.	PF	PA
Buffalo	2	0	0	1.000	51	24
N.Y. Jets	1	1	0	.500	44	40
Miami	1	1	0	.500	38	44
Indianapolis	1	1	0	.500	29	30
New England	0	2	0	.000	30	57

AFC CENTRAL	W	L	T	Pct.	PF	PA
Cleveland	2	0	0	1.000	50	27
Houston	1	1	0	.500	51	33
Cincinnati	0	2	0	.000	20	36
Pittsburgh	0	2	0	.000	13	51

AFC WEST	W	L	T	Pct.	PF	PA
Denver	2	0	0	1.000	60	37
L.A. Raiders	2	0	0	1.000	41	20
San Diego	1	1	0	.500	35	46
Kansas City	1	1	0	.500	27	33
Seattle	0	2	0	.000	25	35

NATIONAL FOOTBALL CONFERENCE

NFC EAST	W	L	T	Pct.	PF	PA
N.Y. Giants	2	0	0	1.000	49	27
Philadelphia	2	0	0	1.000	43	34
Washington	1	1	0	.500	45	33
Phoenix	1	1	0	.500	34	33
Dallas	0	2	0	.000	26	48

NFC CENTRAL	W	L	T	Pct.	PF	PA
Detroit	2	0	0	1.000	49	29
Green Bay	1	1	0	.500	53	26
Minnesota	1	1	0	.500	17	31
Chicago	0	2	0	.000	27	36
Tampa Bay	0	2	0	.000	10	50

NFC WEST	W	L	T	Pct.	PF	PA
New Orleans	2	0	0	1.000	67	52
San Francisco	1	1	0	.500	37	36
L.A. Rams	1	1	0	.500	33	36
Atlanta	0	2	0	.000	44	64

WEEK 2 RESULTS / LINE

Result	Line
MINNESOTA 10, Bears 7	VIKINGS by 7
Detroit 19, NEW ENGLAND 16 (OT)	Lions by 7
Indianapolis 9, CINCINNATI, 6	Colts by 2.5
HOUSTON 30, Kansas City 0	OILERS by 3.5
New Orleans 34, ATLANTA 31	Saints by 3.5
Philadelphia 20, GREEN BAY 17	PACKERS by 3.5
Phoenix 17, WASHINGTON 10	REDSKINS by 10
N.Y. GIANTS 23, Tampa Bay 7	GIANTS by 10
L.A. RAMS 27, Pittsburgh 0	Steelers by 3.5
Buffalo 13, DALLAS 10	COWBOYS by 5
N.Y. Jets 24, MIAMI 14	DOLPHINS by 9
DENVER 34, San Diego 17	BRONCOS by 3
L.A. Raiders 17, SEATTLE 13	Raiders by 3
CLEVELAND 23, San Francisco 13	49ers by 7

Home team in CAPS

It was a week for exciting finishes — four certified last-second thrillers.

The heavily favored Lions had to do it in overtime, squeaking out a 19-16 win on Jason Hanson's fourth field goal of the day, a 38-yarder with less than four minutes remaining in the overtime period.

The Eagles, who came up with 13 unanswered points in the fourth quarter, did it with five seconds left when Roger Ruzek booted a 30-yard field goal for a 20-17 victory. A few minutes earlier, the Eagles had tied it on a Randall Cunningham TD pass and Ruzek's extra point.

PK Morten Andersen bailed out the Saints, who had blown a 31-10, fourth-quarter lead, with a 44-yard field goal as time expired, giving New Orleans a 34-31 win.

An interception by Indianapolis LB Quentin Coryatt and a 42-yard field goal by PK Dean Biasucci with four seconds remaining allowed Indianapolis to triumph 9-6 in an otherwise lackluster contest with the Bengals.

GAME OF THE WEEK: For tension, all of the above. For frustration, the Cowboys' 13-10 loss to the Bills, the team they had annihilated 52-17 eight months earlier in Super Bowl XXVII. This time, however, Dallas superstar RB Emmitt Smith was unsigned and out of uniform. For shock, the Oilers' 30-0 clock-cleaning of Kansas City, but then Chief QB Joe Montana sat this one out with an injured wrist.

SURPRISE: The 49ers, always a Monday-night drawing card for national television audiences and a solid favorite, were beaten at their own game — high-powered offense — by the Browns and the steady arm of QB Bernie Kosar and sure foot of PK Matt Stover.

RECORD-BREAKING TOE: New Orleans PK Morten Andersen went to the top of the list when he

Morten Andersen made his 25th consecutive field goal in Week Two for an NFL record

261

kicked his 25th consecutive field goal, breaking the NFL mark of 24 set by Chicago's Kevin Butler in 1988-89.

QUOTABLE: Dallas coach Jimmy Johnson after the second defeat in a row of his Super Bowl champion Cowboys: "Everything is going bad, from the hotel where we stayed (in Buffalo) to our field-goal kicker (Lin Elliott) to our running backs. You name it, and it has gone bad."

PFW NOTES: Miami's Dan Marino surpassed the 40,000-yard mark in career passing, only the fourth quarterback ever to achieve that feat. Green Bay WR Sterling Sharpe caught his 400th career pass. Bobby Hebert came off the bench to replace Chris Miller for the Falcons and threw three TD passes in the fourth quarter, but Atlanta still lost by three to the Saints. The Saints set a club record by racking up 557 total yards in that same game. Washington QB Mark Rypien suffered the most publicized injury of the week when we went down with a sprained ligament in his right knee. Ram PK Tony Zendejas kicked a club-record 54-yard field goal. Cowboy QB Troy Aikman, after 165 passes without an interception, finally had one picked off, two in fact, by Buffalo S Matt Darby and later CB Nate Odomes. Stingy: The Jets held the Dolphins to 27 yards rushing, and the Colts limited the Bengals to 141 passing.

OFFENSIVE MVP: QB Boomer Esiason, N.Y. Jets. New in New York City, the former Bengal registered his second straight 300-yard-plus passing performance in the Jets' 24-14 upset of the Dolphins. He completed 22-of-33 for 323 yards and two touchdowns and scored another on a four-yard run.

DEFENSIVE MVP: DT Sean Gilbert, L.A. Rams. The Rams' top draft choice in 1992, Gilbert logged four sacks and nine tackles in helping the Rams hold the Steelers scoreless in a surprising 27-0 rout.

GOLDEN TOE: P Harry Newsome, Minnesota. A nine-year veteran, Newsome boomed six punts for an average of 49 yards to keep the Bears in trouble all day and help the Vikings register a 10-7 intradivision win.

TOP PERFORMANCES

PASSING

Player, team	Comp.	Att.	Yds.	TD	Int.
Wade Wilson, Saints	22	34	341	3	1
Boomer Esiason, Jets	23	33	323	2	1
Stan Humphries, Chargers	28	49	298	2	1
Troy Aikman, Cowboys	28	45	297	0	2
John Elway, Broncos	24	34	294	2	1
Dan Marino, Dolphins	28	49	286	2	0

RUSHING

Player, team	Att.	Yds.	TD
Barry Sanders, Lions	32	148	0
Rodney Hampton, Giants	29	134	1
Barry Word, Vikings	24	94	0
Lorenzo Neal, Saints	8	86	1
Ricky Watters, 49ers	13	83	0
Derek Brown, Saints	18	82	0

RECEIVING

Player, team	Rec.	Yds.	TD
Michael Haynes, Falcons	7	182	2
Henry Ellard, Rams	9	127	0
Rob Moore, Jets	6	124	0
Nate Lewis, Chargers	10	119	1
Michael Irvin, Cowboys	8	115	0
Jay Novacek, Cowboys	8	106	0

SCORING

Player, team	TD	XP	FG	Pts.
Jason Hanson, Lions	0	1/1	4/5	13
Al Del Greco, Oilers	0	3/3	3/3	12
Quinn Early, Saints	2	0	0	12
Michael Haynes, Falcons	2	0	0	12

GAME SUMMARIES

SAINTS 34, FALCONS 31
Atlanta, Ga., Sept. 12, 1993

New Orleans	10	14	7	3	—	34
Atlanta	0	10	0	21	—	31

Scoring:
New Orleans: Neal, 74 run (Andersen kick)
New Orleans: Andersen, 27 FG
Atlanta: Pegram, 1 run (Johnson kick)
New Orleans: Early, 42 pass from Wilson (Andersen kick)
New Orleans: Early, 18 pass from Wilson (Andersen kick)
Atlanta: Johnson, 20 FG
New Orleans: Smith, 1 pass from Wilson (Andersen kick)
Atlanta: Haynes, 4 pass from Hebert (Johnson kick)
Atlanta: Haynes, 98 pass from Hebert (Johnson kick)
Atlanta: Pritchard, 3 pass from Hebert (Johnson kick)
New Orleans: Andersen, 44 FG

JETS 24, DOLPHINS 14
Miami, Fla., Sept. 12, 1993

N.Y. Jets	0	14	3	7	—	24
Miami	7	7	0	0	—	14

Scoring:
Miami: K. Jackson, 57 pass from Marino (Stoyanovich kick)
N.Y. Jets: Esiason, 4 run (Blanchard kick)
N.Y. Jets: F. Baxter, 3 pass from Esiason (Blanchard kick)
Miami: Ingram, 25 pass from Marino (Stoyanovich kick)
N.Y. Jets: Blanchard, 39 FG
N.Y. Jets: Chaffey, 20 pass from Esiason (Blanchard kick)

VIKINGS 10, BEARS 7
Minneapolis, Minn., Sept. 12, 1993

Chicago	7	0	0	0	—	7
Minnesota	0	3	0	7	—	10

Scoring:
Chicago: Harbaugh, 1 run (Butler kick)
Minnesota: Reveiz, 22 FG
Minnesota: C. Carter, 16 pass from McMahon (Reveiz kick)

RAMS 27, STEELERS 0
Anaheim, Calif., Sept. 12, 1993

Pittsburgh	0	0	0	0	—	0
L.A. Rams	0	14	3	10	—	27

Scoring:
L.A. Rams: Drayton, 22 pass from Everett (Zendejas kick)
L.A. Rams: Gary, 6 run (Zendejas kick)
L.A. Rams: Zendejas, 54 FG
L.A. Rams: Zendejas, 50 FG
L.A. Rams: Bettis, 29 run (Zendejas kick)

OILERS 30, CHIEFS 0
Houston, Texas, Sept. 12, 1993

Kansas City	0	0	0	0	—	0
Houston	0	7	6	17	—	30

Scoring:
Houston: Duncan, 3 pass from Moon (Del Greco kick)
Houston: Del Greco, 25 FG
Houston: Del Greco, 22 FG
Houston: Del Greco, 50 FG
Houston: Dishman, 58 fumble return (Del Greco kick)
Houston: White, 1 run (Del Greco kick)

1993 REVIEW ■ WEEK TWO

BILLS 13, COWBOYS 10
Irving, Texas, Sept. 12, 1993

Buffalo	7	3	0	3	—	13
Dallas	0	3	0	7	—	10

Scoring:
Buffalo: Gardner, 10 pass from Kelly (Christie kick)
Buffalo: Christie, 48 FG
Dallas: Elliott, 43 FG
Dallas: K. Williams, 5 run (Elliott kick)
Buffalo: Christie, 35 FG

CARDINALS 17, REDSKINS 10
Washington, D.C., Sept. 12, 1993

Phoenix	10	7	0	0	—	17
Washington	0	0	7	3	—	10

Scoring:
Phoenix: Bailey, 58 punt return (G. Davis kick)
Phoenix: G. Davis, 53 FG
Phoenix: Moore, 18 run (G. Davis kick)
Washington: Sanders, 9 pass from Conklin (Lohmiller kick)
Washington: Lohmiller, 23 FG

GIANTS 23, BUCCANEERS 7
East Rutherford, N.J., Sept. 12, 1993

Tampa Bay	0	7	0	0	—	7
N.Y. Giants	7	10	3	3	—	23

Scoring:
N.Y. Giants: Cross, 18 pass from Simms (Treadwell kick)
N.Y. Giants: Hampton, 2 run (Treadwell kick)
Tampa Bay: Armstrong, 17 pass from Erickson (Husted kick)
N.Y. Giants: Treadwell, 33 FG
N.Y. Giants: Treadwell, 22 FG
N.Y. Giants: Treadwell, 46 FG

RAIDERS 17, SEAHAWKS 13
Seattle, Wash., Sept. 12, 1993

L.A. Raiders	7	10	0	0	—	17
Seattle	0	10	0	3	—	13

Scoring:
L.A. Raiders: Hostetler, 2 run (Jaeger kick)
Seattle: Warren, 6 run (Kasay kick)
Seattle: Kasay, 39 FG
L.A. Raiders: Jaeger, 36 FG
L.A. Raiders: Brown, 33 pass from Hostetler (Jaeger kick)
Seattle: Kasay, 53 FG

EAGLES 20, PACKERS 17
Green Bay, Wis., Sept. 12, 1993

Philadelphia	0	7	0	13	—	20
Green Bay	7	3	7	0	—	17

Scoring:
Green Bay: Sharpe, 2 pass from Favre (Jacke kick)
Green Bay: Jacke, 23 FG
Philadelphia: Bavaro, 2 pass from Cunningham (Ruzek kick)
Green Bay: J. Harris, 15 pass from Favre (Jacke kick)
Philadelphia: Ruzek, 27 FG
Philadelphia: Bailey, 40 pass from Cunningham (Ruzek kick)
Philadelphia: Ruzek, 30 FG

BRONCOS 34, CHARGERS 17
Denver, Colo., Sept. 12, 1993

San Diego	0	0	14	3	—	17
Denver	0	17	7	10	—	34

Scoring:
Denver: Marshall, 34 pass from Elway (Elam kick)
Denver: Rivers, 12 pass from Elway (Elam kick)
Denver: Elam, 20 FG
San Diego: Walker, 25 pass from Humphries (Carney kick)
San Diego: Lewis, 24 pass from Humphries (Carney kick)
Denver: Bernstine, 1 run (Elam kick)
San Diego: Carney 30 FG
Denver: Elam, 54 FG
Denver: Delpino, 1 run (Elam kick)

LIONS 19, PATRIOTS 16 (OT)
Foxboro, Mass., Sept. 12, 1993

Detroit	7	3	6	3	—	19
New England	6	3	0	7	—	16

Scoring:
Detroit: Clay, 15 fumble return (Hanson kick)
New England: Sisson, 26 FG
New England: Sisson, 21 FG
New England: Sisson, 32 FG
Detroit: Hanson, 22 FG
Detroit: Hanson, 26 FG
Detroit: Hanson, 23 FG
New England: Brisby, 2 pass from Bledsoe (Sisson kick)
Detroit: Hanson, 38 FG

COLTS 9, BENGALS 6
Cincinnati, Ohio, Sept. 12, 1993

Indianapolis	0	3	3	3	—	9
Cincinnati	3	0	3	0	—	6

Scoring:
Cincinnati: Pelfrey, 35 FG
Indianapolis: Biasucci, 53 FG
Cincinnati: Pelfrey, 23 FG
Indianapolis: Biasucci, 31 FG
Indianapolis: Biasucci, 42 FG

BROWNS 23, 49ERS 13
Cleveland, Ohio, Monday night, Sept. 13, 1993

San Francisco	6	7	0	0	—	13
Cleveland	3	17	3	0	—	23

Scoring:
San Francisco: Cofer, 46 FG
Cleveland: Stover, 47 FG
San Francisco: Cofer, 28 FG
Cleveland: J. Jones, 1 run (Stover kick)
Cleveland: Stover, 41 FG
San Francisco: Logan, 4 run (Cofer kick)
Cleveland: Jackson, 30 pass from Kosar (Stover kick)
Cleveland: Stover, 33 FG

PRO FOOTBALL WEEKLY 1994 ALMANAC

REVIEW: WEEK THREE

WEEK THREE STANDINGS

AMERICAN FOOTBALL CONFERENCE

AFC EAST	W	L	T	Pct.	PF	PA
Buffalo	2	0	0	1.000	51	24
N.Y. Jets	1	1	0	.500	44	40
Miami	1	1	0	.500	38	44
Indianapolis	1	1	0	.500	29	30
New England	0	3	0	.000	44	74

AFC CENTRAL	W	L	T	Pct.	PF	PA
Cleveland	3	0	0	1.000	69	43
Houston	1	2	0	.333	68	51
Pittsburgh	1	2	0	.333	47	58
Cincinnati	0	3	0	.000	27	70

AFC WEST	W	L	T	Pct.	PF	PA
Denver	2	1	0	.667	67	52
Kansas City	2	1	0	.667	42	40
L.A. Raiders	2	1	0	.667	57	39
San Diego	2	1	0	.667	53	63
Seattle	1	2	0	.333	42	49

NATIONAL FOOTBALL CONFERENCE

NFC EAST	W	L	T	Pct.	PF	PA
Philadelphia	3	0	0	1.000	77	65
N.Y. Giants	3	0	0	1.000	69	37
Washington	1	2	0	.333	76	67
Phoenix	1	2	0	.333	44	50
Dallas	1	2	0	.333	43	58

NFC CENTRAL	W	L	T	Pct.	PF	PA
Detroit	2	1	0	.667	52	43
Green Bay	1	1	0	.500	53	26
Minnesota	1	1	0	.500	17	31
Chicago	0	2	0	.000	27	36
Tampa Bay	0	2	0	.000	10	50

NFC WEST	W	L	T	Pct.	PF	PA
New Orleans	3	0	0	1.000	81	55
San Francisco	2	1	0	.667	74	66
L.A. Rams	1	2	0	.333	43	56
Atlanta	0	3	0	.000	74	101

WEEK 3 RESULTS / LINE

Pittsburgh 34, CINCINNATI 7 — Steelers by 9
NEW ORLEANS 14, Detroit 3 — SAINTS by 6
N.Y. GIANTS 20, L.A. Rams 10 — GIANTS by 6.5
Seattle 17, NEW ENGLAND 14 — PATRIOTS by 2.5
PHILADELPHIA 34, Washington 31 — EAGLES by 6.5
SAN FRANCISCO 37, Atlanta 30 — 49ERS by 13
Cleveland 19, L.A. RAIDERS 16 — RAIDERS by 4.5
SAN DIEGO 18, Houston 17 — CHARGERS by 2.5
Dallas 17, PHOENIX 10 — Cowboys by 6.5
KANSAS CITY 15, Denver 7 — CHIEFS by 7
Home team in CAPS

After three weeks, the best word to describe the 1993 NFL season was "unpredictable."

Undefeated were the New York Giants, led by 36-year-old QB Phil Simms on offense, 34-year-old LB Lawrence Taylor on defense and new head coach Dan Reeves. The Giants, 6-10 in 1992, were a team thought to be merely concerned with rebuilding in '93. Also at 3-0 were the Cleveland Browns, who ended the previous season with a 7-9 record. And where were the world champs, the Cowboys of Dallas? Tied for last place in the NFC East with a record of 1-2.

The New Orleans Saints, expected to be a strong contender, remained undefeated after three games, as did the Eagles. Also untarnished were the Bills, but they were among the eight teams with a bye in Week Three, posting a 2-0 record.

Placekickers, however, proved predictable. After three weeks (38 games), NFL field-goal kickers had made 123-of-153 field goals (80.3%); after the first three weeks of the previous season (41 games), kickers had made only 98-of-152 (64.5%).

GAME OF THE WEEK: Cleveland chose to ignore the odds — it was a 4.5-point underdog — after going scoreless for three quarters in its meeting with the Raiders. Losing 13-0 at the start of the fourth quarter and 16-3 with less than five minutes to play in the game, former Tampa Bay QB Vinny Testaverde came off the bench to replace an ineffective Bernie Kosar and passed for 159 yards on two touchdown drives. That and a safety were enough to give the Browns a 19-16 victory. The last score, a one-yard run by Eric Metcalf, came with two seconds left to play.

ROOKIE QB'S DUEL: The two premium-ticket items in the 1993 draft, selected first and second, respectively, QB's Drew Bledsoe of Washington State and Rick Mirer of Notre Dame, went head-to-head for the first time. Mirer and the Seahawks prevailed over Bledsoe and his Patriots 17-14. Mirer was 12-of-16 for 117 yards and Bledsoe 20-of-44 for 240 yards; neither passed for a touchdown.

TOES: John Carney did it again for the Chargers, 6-of-6 field goals to account for all of their points in an 18-17 triumph over the Oilers. In so doing, he extended his streak to 29 consecutive field goals, breaking the NFL record of 25 set by New Orleans' Morten Andersen the week before. Veteran Nick Lowery followed suit with 5-of-5 on Monday night to give the Chiefs all the points they needed to defeat the Broncos 15-7.

LOWS: After three games, the 0-3 Bengals had exhibited the least-productive offense, scoring only 27 points, and the 0-3 Falcons the worst defense, giving up 101 points.

PFW NOTES: Ram PK Tony Zendejas kicked a 52-yard FG against the Giants, his eighth straight of 50 yards or longer. Redskin WR Art Monk extended his consecutive-game pass-reception streak through 150 games (the record is 177 by

1993 REVIEW ■ WEEK THREE

Steve Largent of Seattle, 1977-89). The Chargers had not scored a touchdown in either of their two wins, all 36 of their points coming from Carney field goals. Falcon RB Erric Pegram's 192 yards rushing were the most ever allowed by the 49ers, surpassing the 181 Willie Galimore of the Bears gained against them in 1962. It was also the first time in 28 games that any back had rushed for more than 100 yards against the 49er defense. The Broncos were charged with 12 penalties and the Chiefs six in the first half of their Monday-night game (seven of the Bronco infractions were false starts), and by game's end 25 penalties had been assessed.

OFFENSIVE MVP: WR Calvin Williams, Eagles. In his fourth season, Williams had his best game ever against the Redskins, catching eight passes for 181 yards, three of them for touchdowns, including the game-winner with only four seconds remaining.

DEFENSIVE MVP: Renaldo Turnbull, Saints. The replacement for departed All-Pro Pat Swilling, Turnbull proved worthy in the 14-3 New Orleans win over the Lions. He had three sacks, two of which forced fumbles.

GOLDEN TOE: PK John Carney, Chargers.

John Carney was 6-of-6 on field-goal attempts

Carney connected on 6-of-6 field goals and again contributed all of San Diego's points in its 18-17 win over Houston.

TOP PERFORMANCES

PASSING

Player, team	Comp.	Att.	Yds.	TD	Int.
Randall Cunningham, Eagles	25	39	360	3	2
John Elway, Broncos	28	45	300	1	1
Troy Aikman, Cowboys	21	27	281	0	0
Joe Montana, Chiefs	21	36	273	0	0
Drew Bledsoe, Patriots	20	44	240	1	2
Steve Beuerlein, Cardinals	20	27	218	1	1
Cary Conklin, Redskins	17	36	218	3	2

RUSHING

Player, team	Att.	Yds.	TD
Erric Pegram, Falcons	27	192	0
Chris Warren, Seahawks	36	174	1
Reggie Brooks, Redskins	22	154	1
Rodney Hampton, Giants	41	134	1
Derek Brown, Saints	25	121	0
Ricky Watters, 49ers	19	112	1

RECEIVING

Player, team	Rec.	Yds.	TD
Calvin Williams, Eagles	8	181	3
Willie Davis, Chiefs	6	139	0
Alvin Harper, Cowboys	6	136	0
Derek Russell, Broncos	6	104	0
Tim McGee, Redskins	6	93	1
Herschel Walker, Eagles	5	87	0

SCORING

Player, team	TD	XP	FG	Pts.
John Carney, Chargers	0	0	6/6	18
Andre Rison, Falcons	3	0	0	18
Calvin Williams, Eagles	3	0	0	18
Nick Lowery, Chiefs	0	0	5/5	15

GAME SUMMARIES

SEAHAWKS 17, PATRIOTS 14

Foxboro, Mass., Sept. 19, 1993

Seattle	7	0	10	0	— 17
New England	0	0	0	14	— 14

Scoring:
Seattle: Blades, 4 pass from Mirer (Kasay kick)
Seattle: Kasay, 24 FG
Seattle: C. Warren, 15 run (Kasay kick)
New England: Coates, 25 pass from Bledsoe (Sisson kick)
New England: Gash, 4 run (Sisson kick)

GIANTS 20, RAMS 10

East Rutherford, N.J., Sept. 19, 1993

L.A. Rams	0	3	0	7	— 10
N.Y. Giants	7	6	7	0	— 20

Scoring:
N.Y. Giants: Hampton, 1 run (Treadwell kick)
N.Y. Giants: Treadwell, 34 FG
L.A. Rams: Zendejas, 52 FG
N.Y. Giants: Treadwell, 19 FG
N.Y. Giants: Collins, 50 interception return (Treadwell kick)
L.A. Rams: Anderson, 51 pass from Everett (Zendejas kick)

CHARGERS 18, OILERS 17

San Diego, Calif., Sept. 19, 1993

Houston	0	14	0	3	— 17
San Diego	3	6	3	6	— 18

Scoring:
San Diego: Carney, 34 FG
San Diego: Carney, 34 FG
San Diego: Carney, 27 FG
Houston: Slaughter, 2 pass from Moon (Del Greco kick)
Houston: Lewis, 47 interception return (Del Greco kick)
San Diego: Carney, 27 FG
San Diego: Carney, 36 FG
Houston: Del Greco, 27 FG
San Diego: Carney, 27 FG

SAINTS 14, LIONS 3

New Orleans, La., Sept. 19, 1993

Detroit	0	3	0	0	— 3
New Orleans	0	7	7	0	— 14

Scoring:
Detroit: Hanson, 41 FG
New Orleans: Brenner, 17 pass from Wilson (Andersen kick)
New Orleans: E. Martin, 12 pass from Wilson (Andersen kick)

BROWNS 19, RAIDERS 16
Los Angeles, Calif., Sept. 19, 1993

Cleveland	0	0	0	19	—	19
L.A. Raiders	10	3	0	3	—	16

Scoring:
L.A. Raiders: Glover, 2 pass from Hostetler (Jaeger kick)
L.A. Raiders: Jaeger, 24 FG
L.A. Raiders: Jaeger, 27 FG
Cleveland: Stover, 32 FG
L.A. Raiders: Jaeger, 53 FG
Cleveland: Tillman, 12 pass from Testaverde (Stover kick)
Cleveland: Safety, Gossett ran out of endzone
Cleveland: Metcalf 1 run (Stover kick)

COWBOYS 17, CARDINALS 10
Phoenix, Ariz., Sept. 19, 1993

Dallas	7	3	7	0	—	17
Phoenix	0	0	7	3	—	10

Scoring:
Dallas: Lassic, 8 run (Murray kick)
Dallas: Murray, 23 FG
Dallas: Lassic, 2 run (Murray kick)
Phoenix: Proehl, 12 pass from Beuerlein (G. Davis kick)
Phoenix: G. Davis, 20 FG

EAGLES 34, REDSKINS 31
Philadelphia, Pa., Sept. 19, 1993

Washington	0	14	7	10	—	31
Philadelphia	3	7	7	17	—	34

Scoring:
Philadelphia: Bahr, 27 FG
Washington: McGee, 11 pass from Conklin (Lohmiller kick)
Washington: Sanders, 34 pass from Conklin (Lohmiller kick)
Philadelphia: Williams, 80 pass from Cunningham (Bahr kick)
Washington: Middleton, 1 run (Conklin kick)
Philadelphia: Allen, 29 interception return (Bahr kick)
Washington: Lohmiller, 38 FG
Philadelphia: Williams, 9 pass from Cunningham (Bahr kick)
Washington: Brooks, 85 run (Lohmiller kick)
Philadelphia: Bahr, 42 FG
Philadelphia: Williams, 10 pass from Cunningham (Bahr kick)

STEELERS 34, BENGALS 7
Pittsburgh, Pa., Sept. 19, 1993

Cincinnati	0	7	0	0	—	7
Pittsburgh	7	10	10	7	—	34

Scoring:
Pittsburgh: Mills, 3 pass from O'Donnell (Anderson kick)
Pittsburgh: Anderson, 33 FG
Cincinnati: Pickens, 15 pass from Klingler (Pelfrey kick)
Pittsburgh: Thigpen 15 pass from O'Donnell (Anderson kick)
Pittsburgh: Anderson, 34 FG
Pittsburgh: Stone, 9 pass from O'Donnell (Anderson kick)
Pittsburgh: Stone, 38 run (Anderson kick)

49ERS 37, FALCONS 30
San Francisco, Calif., Sept. 19, 1993

Atlanta	3	10	7	10	—	30
San Francisco	3	6	14	14	—	37

Scoring:
Atlanta: Johnson 42 FG
San Francisco: Cofer, 46 FG
Atlanta: Rison, 13 pass from Hebert (Johnson kick)
San Francisco: Williams, 9 pass from Young (Cofer kick failed)
Atlanta: Johnson, 38 FG
San Francisco: Jones 20 pass from Young (Cofer kick)
Atlanta: Rison, 3 pass from Hebert (Johnson kick)
San Francisco: Watters, 2 run (Cofer kick)
San Francisco: Singleton, 6 pass from Young (Cofer kick)
Atlanta: Johnson 27 FG
San Francisco: Rice, 43 run (Cofer kick)
Atlanta: Rison, 16 pass from Hebert (Johnson kick)

CHIEFS 15, BRONCOS 7
Kansas City, Mo., Monday night, Sept. 20, 1993

Denver	0	0	0	7	—	7
Kansas City	6	6	0	3	—	15

Scoring:
Kansas City: Lowery, 34 FG
Kansas City: Lowery, 41 FG
Kansas City: Lowery, 52 FG
Kansas City: Lowery, 44 FG
Kansas City: Lowery, 20 FG
Denver: R. Johnson, 2 pass from Elway (Elam kick)

1993 REVIEW ■ WEEK FOUR

WEEK FOUR

WEEK FOUR STANDINGS

AMERICAN FOOTBALL CONFERENCE

AFC EAST	W	L	T	Pct.	PF	PA
Miami	2	1	0	.667	60	57
Buffalo	2	1	0	.667	64	46
N.Y. Jets	2	1	0	.667	89	47
Indianapolis	2	1	0	.667	52	40
New England	0	4	0	.000	51	119

AFC CENTRAL	W	L	T	Pct.	PF	PA
Cleveland	3	1	0	.750	79	66
Pittsburgh	2	2	0	.500	92	75
Houston	1	3	0	.250	81	79
Cincinnati	0	4	0	.000	37	89

AFC WEST	W	L	T	Pct.	PF	PA
Denver	2	1	0	.667	67	52
L.A. Raiders	2	1	0	.667	57	39
San Diego	2	1	0	.667	53	63
Kansas City	2	1	0	.667	42	40
Seattle	2	2	0	.500	61	59

NATIONAL FOOTBALL CONFERENCE

NFC EAST	W	L	T	Pct.	PF	PA
Philadelphia	3	0	0	1.000	77	65
N.Y. Giants	3	0	0	1.000	69	37
Washington	1	2	0	.333	76	67
Dallas	1	2	0	.333	43	58
Phoenix	1	3	0	.250	64	76

NFC CENTRAL	W	L	T	Pct.	PF	PA
Detroit	3	1	0	.750	78	63
Minnesota	2	1	0	.667	32	44
Chicago	1	2	0	.333	74	53
Green Bay	1	2	0	.333	66	41
Tampa Bay	0	3	0	.000	27	97

NFC WEST	W	L	T	Pct.	PF	PA
New Orleans	4	0	0	1.000	97	68
San Francisco	2	2	0	.500	87	82
L.A. Rams	2	2	0	.500	71	69
Atlanta	0	4	0	.000	91	146

WEEK 4 RESULTS
INDIANAPOLIS 23, Cleveland 10
MINNESOTA 15, Green Bay 13
L.A. Rams 28, HOUSTON 13
Miami 22, BUFFALO 13
CHICAGO 47, Tampa Bay 17
DETROIT 26, Phoenix 20
NEW ORLEANS 16, San Francisco 13
Seattle 19, CINCINNATI 10
N.Y. JETS 45, New England 7
Pittsburgh 45, ATLANTA 17

LINE
Browns by 2.5
VIKINGS by 3
OILERS by 10.5
BILLS by 6
BEARS by 7
LIONS by 5
49ers by 1
Seahawks by 3
JETS by 9.5
FALCONS by 3

Home team in CAPS

Through four weeks, only three teams remained undefeated, and two of them, because of the open dates, had just three victories, the Eagles and the Giants. The Saints were the only team able to claim four.

Week Four cumulative stats had Houston QB Warren Moon passing for the most yards, 954, and 49er Steve Young completing the most passes, 83. Young's favorite target, WR Jerry Rice, claimed the most receptions, 24, while Ram WR Henry Ellard had gained the most yards on pass catches, 313.

Detroit All-Pro RB Barry Sanders stood as the most productive rusher with 404 yards and also carried the ball the most often, 97 times. The Lions also sported the league's leading scorer, PK Jason Hanson, with 42 points (12-of-15 FG's, 6-of-6 XP's).

On defense, New Orleans LB Renaldo Turnbull and Ram DE Robert Young shared sack honors with seven apiece, and Steeler CB Rod Woodson led the NFL with five interceptions.

The 2-2 49ers averaged the most yards per game on offense, 384.8, and the 3-0 Giants allowed the fewest per game, 213.0.

GAME OF THE WEEK: A toss-up. In the NFC, the Saints preserved their perfect record when PK Morten Andersen kicked a 49-yard field goal with five seconds on the clock to beat the favored 49ers 16-13. In this nail-biter, the 49ers had tied it on a Mike Cofer field goal a little over a minute earlier. In the AFC, the Dolphins upset the Bills in Buffalo by the low score of 22-13 to gain a share of the lead in the AFC East.

KICK POWER: The toe remained a powerful weapon in Week Four. Viking PK Fuad Reveiz accounted for all 15 of his team's points with five field goals. Seattle's John Kasay booted four for the Seahawks, as did Hanson of the Lions and Kevin Butler for the Bears. All three of their teams won.

PICKS: Woodson picked off two of Falcon QB Bobby Hebert's passes Monday night to bring his 1993 total to five interceptions in four games. The NFL record is 14 in one season, set by Ram DB Dick "Night Train" Lane his rookie year, 1952 (12 games).

DAZZLER: Second-year return man Tony Smith gave Falcon fans one of the few things they had to cheer about in their 45-17 Monday-night rout by the Steelers when he ran back a kickoff 97 yards for a touchdown in the first quarter.

PFW NOTES: Buffalo PK Steve Christie kicked a 59-yard field goal, tying him for the third-longest in NFL history (Tom Dempsey's 63-yarder for the Saints in 1970 remains the longest). Miami QB Dan Marino moved into third place on the NFL all-time passing-yardage list, edging ahead of Johnny Unitas' 40,239 but still trailing Fran Tarkenton (47,003) and Dan Fouts (43,040). Neal Anderson became the Bears' No. 2 all-time rusher, second only to NFL record-holder Walter Payton. Greg Davis' 54-yard FG was the longest in Cardinal history. Sanders passed the 6,000-yard career

PRO FOOTBALL WEEKLY 1994 ALMANAC

rushing barrier by 78 yards in Detroit's win over Phoenix. Moon connected with WR Ernest Givins for an 80-yard touchdown. Colt LB Duane Bickett and Saint LB Rickey Jackson were credited with three sacks each.

Offensive MVP: QB Jim Everett, Rams. After a poor performance the week before in a loss to the Giants, Everett led the Rams to a major upset of the Oilers 28-13 by completing 19-of-28 passes for 316 yards and three touchdowns.

Defensive MVP: Vaughan Johnson, Saints. A Pro Bowl participant the last four years, Johnson lived up to his reputation, as he was credited with an eye-popping 22 combined tackles, a sack and a forced fumble in New Orleans' 16-13 victory over the 49ers.

Golden Toe: PK Fuad Reveiz, Vikings. His one-man offensive attack, 5-of-6 field goals, accounted for all 15 points in Minnesota's win over Green Bay.

Jim Everett threw for 316 yards and three TD's

TOP PERFORMANCES

PASSING

Player, team	Comp.	Att.	Yds.	TD	Int.
Jim Everett, Rams	19	28	316	3	0
Warren Moon, Oilers	19	42	310	1	2
Steve Beuerlein, Cardinals	23	31	288	2	0
Dan Marino, Dolphins	20	32	282	1	1
Jack Trudeau, Colts	22	38	260	0	0
Neil O'Donnell, Steelers	19	25	259	2	0

RUSHING

Player, team	Att.	Yds.	TD
Ricky Watters, 49ers	25	135	0
Neal Anderson, Bears	23	104	1
Barry Sanders, Lions	23	90	0
Derek Brown, Saints	21	88	1
Mark Higgs, Dolphins	22	77	0
Chris Warren, Seahawks	19	75	0

RECEIVING

Player, team	Rec.	Yds.	TD
Henry Ellard, Rams	6	132	1
Jessie Hester, Colts	7	110	0
Ernest Givins, Oilers	3	107	1
Irving Fryar, Dolphins	7	103	1
Willie Green, Lions	3	102	0
Tony McGee, Bengals	7	102	0

SCORING

Player, team	TD	XP	FG	Pts.
Barry Foster, Steelers	3	0	0	18
Kevin Butler, Bears	0	5/5	4/4	17
Fuad Reveiz, Vikings	0	0	5/6	15

GAME SUMMARIES

RAMS 28, OILERS 13
Houston, Texas, Sept. 26, 1993

L.A. Rams	7	7	7	7	— 28
Houston	0	3	10	0	— 13

Scoring:
L.A. Rams: Anderson, 4 pass from Everett (Zendejas kick)
L.A. Rams: Bettis, 1 run (Zendejas kick)
Houston: Del Greco, 52 FG
Houston: Del Greco, 25 FG
Houston: Givins, 80 pass from Moon (Del Greco kick)
L.A. Rams: McNeal, 22 pass from Everett (Zendejas kick)
L.A. Rams: Ellard, 48 pass from Everett (Zendejas kick)

VIKINGS 15, PACKERS 13
Minneapolis, Minn., Sept. 26, 1993

Green Bay	7	3	0	3	— 13
Minnesota	3	3	6	3	— 15

Scoring:
Green Bay: Favre, 2 run (Jacke kick)
Minnesota: Reveiz, 35 FG
Minnesota: Reveiz, 19 FG
Green Bay: Jacke, 49 FG
Minnesota: Reveiz, 29 FG
Minnesota: Reveiz, 51 FG
Green Bay: Jacke, 20 FG
Minnesota: Reveiz, 22 FG

COLTS 23, BROWNS 10
Indianapolis, Ind., Sept. 26, 1993

Cleveland	0	0	7	3	— 10
Indianapolis	0	6	3	14	— 23

Scoring:
Indianapolis: Biasucci, 27 FG
Indianapolis: Biasucci, 19 FG
Cleveland: Kinchen, 10 pass from Testaverde (Stover kick)
Indianapolis: Biasucci, 26 FG
Cleveland: Stover, 32 FG
Indianapolis: Johnson, 6 run (Biasucci kick)
Indianapolis: Herrod, fumble recovery in endzone (Biasucci kick)

DOLPHINS 22, BILLS 13
Orchard Park, N.Y., Sept. 26, 1993

Miami	16	3	3	0	— 22
Buffalo	0	6	0	7	— 13

Scoring:
Miami: Stoyanovich, 30 FG
Miami: Fryar, 36 pass from Marino (no attempt)
Miami: Marino, 4 run (Stoyanovich kick)
Miami: Stoyanovich, 23 FG
Buffalo: Christie, 40 FG
Buffalo: Christie, 59 FG
Miami: Stoyanovich, 24 FG
Buffalo: Brooks, 27 pass from Kelly (Christie kick)

JETS 45, PATRIOTS 7
East Rutherford, N.J., Sept. 26, 1993

New England	0	0	0	7	— 7
N.Y. Jets	14	21	0	10	— 45

Scoring:
N.Y. Jets: B. Baxter, 1 run (Blanchard kick)
N.Y. Jets: J. Johnson, 6 run (Blanchard kick)
N.Y. Jets: B. Baxter, 4 run (Blanchard kick)
N.Y. Jets: Thornton, 13 pass from Esiason (Blanchard kick)
N.Y. Jets: Mathis, 17 run (Blanchard kick)
N.Y. Jets: Blanchard, 42 FG

1993 REVIEW ■ WEEK FOUR

N.Y. Jets: Murrell, 37 run (Blanchard kick)
New England: Russell, 5 run (Sisson kick)

SAINTS 16, 49ERS 13

New Orleans, La., Sept. 26, 1993

San Francisco	0	3	7	3	—	13
New Orleans	3	7	3	3	—	16

Scoring:
New Orleans: Andersen, 33 FG
New Orleans: Brown, 1 run (Andersen kick)
San Francisco: Cofer, 34 FG
San Francisco: Logan, 23 run (Cofer kick)
New Orleans: Andersen, 39 FG
San Francisco: Cofer, 30 FG
New Orleans: Andersen, 49 FG

SEAHAWKS 19, BENGALS 10

Cincinnati, Ohio, Sept. 26, 1993

Seattle	0	6	3	10	—	19
Cincinnati	0	0	0	10	—	10

Scoring:
Seattle: Kasay, 32 FG
Seattle: Kasay, 35 FG
Seattle: Kasay, 23 FG
Cincinnati: Pelfrey, 23 FG
Cincinnati: Pickens, 21 pass from Schroeder (Pelfrey kick)
Seattle: Stephens, fumble recovery in endzone (Kasay kick)
Seattle: Kasay, 35 FG

LIONS 26, CARDINALS 20

Pontiac, Mich., Sept. 26, 1993

Phoenix	0	17	0	3	—	20
Detroit	6	10	7	3	—	26

Scoring:
Detroit: Hanson, 44 FG
Detroit: Hanson, 22 FG
Phoenix: Proehl, 51 pass from Beuerlein (G. Davis kick)
Detroit: Hanson, 33 FG
Detroit: D. Moore, 1 run (Hanson kick)

Phoenix: Reeves, 2 pass from Beuerlein (G. Davis kick)
Phoenix: G. Davis, 54 FG
Detroit: Perriman, 9 pass from Ware (Hanson kick)
Phoenix: G. Davis, 30 FG
Detroit: Hanson, 38 FG

BEARS 47, BUCCANEERS 17

Chicago, Ill., Sept. 26, 1993

Tampa Bay	3	7	0	7	—	17
Chicago	0	28	3	16	—	47

Scoring:
Tampa Bay: Husted, 20 FG
Chicago: Anderson, 1 run (Butler kick)
Chicago: Harbaugh, 1 run (Butler kick)
Chicago: Wetnight, 25 pass from Harbaugh (Butler kick)
Chicago: Waddle, 17 pass from Harbaugh (Butler kick)
Tampa Bay: L. Thomas, 62 pass from Erickson (Husted kick)
Chicago: Butler, 33 FG
Chicago: Butler, 40 FG
Chicago: Baker, 8 fumble return (Butler kick)
Chicago: Butler, 32 FG
Tampa Bay: McDowell, 3 pass from DeBerg (Husted kick)
Chicago: Butler, 31 FG

STEELERS 45, FALCONS 17

Atlanta, Ga., Monday night, Sept. 27, 1993

Pittsburgh	7	17	7	14	—	45
Atlanta	14	3	0	0	—	17

Scoring:
Pittsburgh: Foster, 30 run (Anderson kick)
Atlanta: T. Smith, 97 kickoff return (Johnson kick)
Atlanta: Clark, 46 fumble return (Johnson kick)
Pittsburgh: Anderson, 21 FG
Atlanta: Johnson, 49 FG
Pittsburgh: Foster, 7 run (Anderson kick)
Pittsburgh: Stone, 4 pass from O'Donnell (Anderson kick)
Pittsburgh: Thigpen, 7 pass from O'Donnell (Anderson kick)
Pittsburgh: Foster, 1 run (Anderson kick)
Pittsburgh: Davidson, 18 fumble return (Anderson kick)

PRO FOOTBALL WEEKLY 1994 ALMANAC

REVIEW: WEEK FIVE

WEEK FIVE STANDINGS

AMERICAN FOOTBALL CONFERENCE

AFC EAST	W	L	T	Pct.	PF	PA
Miami	3	1	0	.750	77	67
Buffalo	3	1	0	.750	81	60
N.Y. Jets	2	2	0	.500	119	82
Indianapolis	2	2	0	.500	65	75
New England	0	4	0	.000	51	119

AFC CENTRAL	W	L	T	Pct.	PF	PA
Cleveland	3	1	0	.750	79	66
Pittsburgh	2	2	0	.500	92	75
Houston	1	3	0	.250	81	79
Cincinnati	0	4	0	.000	37	89

AFC WEST	W	L	T	Pct.	PF	PA
Denver	3	1	0	.750	102	65
Kansas City	3	1	0	.750	66	49
Seattle	3	2	0	.600	92	73
L.A. Raiders	2	2	0	.500	66	63
San Diego	2	2	0	.500	67	94

NATIONAL FOOTBALL CONFERENCE

NFC EAST	W	L	T	Pct.	PF	PA
Philadelphia	4	0	0	1.000	112	95
N.Y. Giants	3	1	0	.750	83	54
Dallas	2	2	0	.500	79	72
Washington	1	3	0	.250	86	84
Phoenix	1	3	0	.250	64	76

NFC CENTRAL	W	L	T	Pct.	PF	PA
Detroit	3	2	0	.600	88	90
Minnesota	2	2	0	.500	51	82
Chicago	2	2	0	.500	80	53
Green Bay	1	3	0	.250	80	77
Tampa Bay	1	3	0	.250	54	107

NFC WEST	W	L	T	Pct.	PF	PA
New Orleans	5	0	0	1.000	134	74
San Francisco	3	2	0	.600	125	101
L.A. Rams	2	3	0	.400	77	106
Atlanta	0	5	0	.000	91	152

WEEK 5 RESULTS

Result	Line
CHICAGO 6, Atlanta 0	BEARS by 6
TAMPA BAY 27, Detroit 10	Lions by 6
DALLAS 36, Green Bay 14	COWBOYS by 11
KANSAS CITY 24, L.A. Raiders 9	CHIEFS by 9
DENVER 35, Indianapolis 13	BRONCOS by 8.5
SAN FRANCISCO 38, Minnesota 19	49ERS by 10
New Orleans 37, L.A. RAMS 6	Saints by 4
Philadelphia 35, N.Y. JETS 30	JETS by 1
SEATTLE 31, San Diego 14	Chargers by 3.5
BUFFALO 17, N.Y. Giants 14	BILLS by 5.5
MIAMI 17, Washington 10	DOLPHINS by 5.5

Home team in CAPS

Had they been asked before the season which would be the only two teams to stand undefeated at the end of the fifth week, few would have picked either the Eagles or the Saints.

But New Orleans did it easily by routing the Rams 37-6 for its fifth win in a row, and Philadelphia did it spectacularly with a fourth-quarter comeback to nip the Jets 35-30 and post a 4-0 record.

There were three upsets in Week Five, the Eagles' win, Seattle's 31-14 triumph over San Diego and the astonishing, 27-10 victory in the NFC Central by the last-place Buccaneers over the first-place Lions.

The hapless Falcons, who had given up a league-high average of 38 points a game in the first four weeks, allowed their fifth-week opponent, the Bears, only six points and still came up a loser, when a shutout was added to their 0-5 record.

After five weeks, the league's top scorer was New Orleans PK Morten Andersen with 50 points (12-of-16 FG's, 14-of-14 XP's). Jet QB Boomer Esiason had thrown the most touchdown passes, nine, and Steeler RB Barry Foster, Falcon WR Andre Rison and Jet TE Johnny Mitchell had scored the most touchdowns, four apiece.

GAME OF THE WEEK: The Eagles were down 21-7 in the second quarter. Then their superbly athletic QB Randall Cunningham went down with a broken leg. It would have seemed that mercy at the hands of the volatile Jets and the NFL's top-rated passer, Esiason, would be all Philadelphia could have hoped for. Off the bench came backup QB Bubby Brister, and out of nowhere came CB Eric Allen to pick off an Esiason pass and run it back 94 yards for a game-winning, fourth-quarter touch-

PHOTO BY TOM BERG

Eric Allen returned an interception 94 yards for the game-winning touchdown vs. the Jets

1993 REVIEW ■ WEEK FIVE

down. Eagles 35, Jets 30!

MONTANA STORY: The aging legend Joe Montana, 37 years old, went down again, this time with a strained hamstring. In the opener he injured a wrist and missed the next week's game. As Chief DE Neil Smith said, "You get fired up when you see your quarterback on the ground." The Chiefs did, rallying to a 24-9 win over the Raiders and a share of the lead in the AFC West.

LOSS LEADERS: At the end of the fifth week, the 0-5 Falcons led the league in one category — turnovers, with 15 (six fumbles, nine interceptions). The Oilers, however, were breathing down Atlanta's neck with 14 (one fewer interception).

TD-MAKER: Kansas City RB Marcus Allen scored his 100th touchdown on a four-yard run, moving him into an eighth-place tie with Franco Harris on the NFL's all-time TD list. Only one current player, WR Jerry Rice of the 49ers, has more than Allen.

PFW NOTES: The Eagles became the first team in NFL history to overcome 10-point, second-half deficits in three consecutive games. The Bears' 6-0 win over the Falcons on two Kevin Butler field goals marked the sixth time in the season that a team won a game without scoring a touchdown. Charger PK John Carney's NFL-record 29 straight field goals ended when he missed a 48-yarder against Seattle. Bronco LB Simon Fletcher's league record for consecutive-game sacks ended at 10. Jet S Ronnie Lott's interception was his 61st, most among active players and seventh on the all-time NFL chart. Troy Aikman completed his 1,000th pass, reaching that milestone in fewer games than any quarterback in Cowboy history. The Bears did not allow a single rushing touchdown in their first four games. The longest run of the week was Packer Robert Brooks' 95-yard kickoff return for a touchdown against the Cowboys.

OFFENSIVE MVP: TE Johnny Mitchell, Jets. The Jets' top pick in the 1992 draft, Mitchell hauled in seven passes for 146 yards, three of them for touchdowns (one a 65-yarder). It wasn't his fault the Jets lost to the Eagles.

DEFENSIVE MVP: DE Neil Smith, Chiefs. Enraged at the sight of Montana being knocked out of the game on a late hit, Smith retaliated with four sacks and five tackles, one forcing a fumble, and inspired his team to a 24-9 romp over the division-rival Raiders.

GOLDEN TOE: PK Eddie Murray, Cowboys. Brought in to replace Lin Elliott two weeks earlier for Dallas, Murray, who had been kicking around the NFL since 1980, booted 5-of-5 field goals, tying the club record and contributing handsomely to the Cowboy win over Green Bay.

TOP PERFORMANCES

PASSING

Player, team	Comp.	Att.	Yds.	TD	Int.
Troy Aikman, Cowboys	18	23	317	1	0
Boomer Esiason, Jets	19	33	297	4	2
Rick Mirer, Seahawks	25	40	282	1	0
Dan Marino, Dolphins	16	30	253	1	1
John Elway, Broncos	20	30	230	2	0
Steve Young, 49ers	17	24	224	1	1

RUSHING

Player, team	Att.	Yds.	TD
Barry Sanders, Lions	22	130	1
Thurman Thomas, Bills	26	122	0
Reggie Cobb, Buccaneers	25	113	1
Jerome Bettis, Rams	22	102	0
Terry Kirby, Dolphins	16	94	0
Rodney Hampton, Giants	32	86	0

RECEIVING

Player, team	Rec.	Yds.	TD
Michael Irvin, Cowboys	7	155	1
Johnny Mitchell, Jets	7	146	3
Brian Blades, Seahawks	10	132	1
Anthony Miller, Chargers	10	123	1
Tony Martin, Dolphins	4	110	1
Chris Burkett, Jets	4	103	0

SCORING

Player, team	TD	XP	FG	Pts.
Johnny Mitchell, Jets	3	0	0	18
Eddie Murray, Cowboys	0	3/3	5/5	18
Morten Andersen, Saints	0	4/4	3/3	13

GAME SUMMARIES

BRONCOS 35, COLTS 13
Denver, Colo., Oct. 3, 1993

Indianapolis	0	10	3	0	—	13
Denver	21	7	7	0	—	35

Scoring:
Denver: Delpino, 2 run (Elam kick)
Denver: Bernstine, 9 run (Elam kick)
Denver: Milburn, 3 pass from Elway (Elam kick)
Denver: Sharpe, 22 pass from Elway (Elam kick)
Indianapolis: Biasucci, 28 FG
Indianapolis: Cash, 4 pass from Trudeau (Biasucci kick)
Indianapolis: Biasucci, 28 FG
Denver: Russell, 30 pass from Marshall (Elam kick)

BILLS 17, GIANTS 14
Orchard Park, N.Y., Oct. 3, 1993

N.Y. Giants	0	14	0	0	—	14
Buffalo	10	0	0	7	—	17

Scoring:
Buffalo: Christie, 24 FG
Buffalo: Jones, 85 interception return (Christie kick)
N.Y. Giants: Calloway, 5 pass from Simms (Treadwell kick)
N.Y. Giants: M. Jackson, 2 pass from Simms (Treadwell kick)
Buffalo: Metzelaars, 8 pass from Kelly (Christie kick)

SAINTS 37, RAMS 6
Anaheim, Calif., Oct. 3, 1993

New Orleans	10	3	3	21	—	37
L.A. Rams	3	0	3	0	—	6

Scoring:
New Orleans: Brown, 15 pass from Wilson (Andersen kick)
New Orleans: Andersen, 48 FG
L.A. Rams: Zendejas, 53 FG
New Orleans: Andersen, 25 FG
L.A. Rams: Zendejas, 37 FG
New Orleans: Andersen, 43 FG
New Orleans: Newman, 30 pass from Wilson (Andersen kick)
New Orleans: Hughes, 74 punt return (Andersen kick)
New Orleans: Ned, 35 run (Andersen kick)

49ERS 38, VIKINGS 19
San Francisco, Calif., Oct. 3, 1993

Minnesota	7	2	3	7	—	19
San Francisco	7	14	3	14	—	38

Scoring:
Minnesota: Tice, 3 pass from McMahon (Reveiz kick)

San Francisco: Rice, 39 pass from Young (Cofer kick)
San Francisco: Logan, 1 run (Cofer kick)
San Francisco: Davis, 41 interception return (Cofer kick)
Minnesota: Safety, Thomas tackled Young in endzone
San Francisco: Cofer, 22 FG
Minnesota: Reveiz, 21 FG
Minnesota: C. Carter, 9 pass from McMahon (Reveiz kick)
San Francisco: Watters, 3 run (Cofer kick)
San Francisco: Carter, 72 punt return (Cofer kick)

EAGLES 35, JETS 30
East Rutherford, N.J., Oct. 3, 1993

Philadelphia	0	14	7	14	— 35
N.Y. Jets	14	7	7	2	— 30

Scoring:
N.Y. Jets: Thornton, 7 pass from Esiason (Blanchard kick)
N.Y. Jets: Mitchell, 14 pass from Esiason (Blanchard kick)
N.Y. Jets: Mitchell, 12 pass from Esiason (Blanchard kick)
Philadelphia: Walker, 8 run (Bahr kick)
Philadelphia: Bavaro, 10 pass from Brister (Bahr kick)
N.Y. Jets: Mitchell, 65 pass from Esiason (Blanchard kick)
Philadelphia: Williams, 11 pass from Brister (Bahr kick)
Philadelphia: Hebron, 1 run (Bahr kick)
N.Y. Jets: Safety, M. Washington sacked Brister in endzone
Philadelphia: Allen, 94 interception return (Bahr kick)

SEAHAWKS 31, CHARGERS 14
Seattle, Wash., Oct. 3, 1993

San Diego	7	0	0	7	— 14
Seattle	7	10	7	7	— 31

Scoring:
Seattle: Mirer, 2 run (Kasay kick)
San Diego: Butts, 2 run (Carney kick)
Seattle: Kasay, 33 FG
Seattle: Blades, 17 pass from McGwire (Kasay kick)
Seattle: C. Warren, 1 run (Kasay kick)
Seattle: Martin, 18 pass from Mirer (Kasay kick)
San Diego: Miller, 11 pass from Friesz (Carney kick)

COWBOYS 36, PACKERS 14
Irving, Texas, Oct. 3, 1993

Green Bay	7	0	7	0	— 14
Dallas	10	6	13	7	— 36

Scoring:
Green Bay: E. Bennett, 1 run (Jacke kick)
Dallas: Irvin, 61 pass from Aikman (Murray kick)
Dallas: Murray, 33 FG
Dallas: Murray, 19 FG
Dallas: Murray, 19 FG
Dallas: Murray, 50 FG
Dallas: E. Smith, 22 run (Murray kick)
Green Bay: Brooks, 95 kickoff return (Jacke kick)
Dallas: Murray, 48 FG
Dallas: Lassic, 1 run (Murray kick)

BEARS 6, FALCONS 0
Chicago, Ill., Oct. 3, 1993

Atlanta	0	0	0	0	— 0
Chicago	0	3	3	0	— 6

Scoring:
Chicago: Butler, 48 FG
Chicago: Butler, 52 FG

CHIEFS 24, RAIDERS 9
Kansas City, Mo., Oct. 3, 1993

L.A. Raiders	0	3	0	6	— 9
Kansas City	14	7	3	0	— 24

Scoring:
Kansas City: Valerio, 1 pass from Montana (Lowery kick)
Kansas City: Davis, 15 pass from Montana (Lowery kick)
L.A. Raiders: Jaeger, 27 FG
Kansas City: Allen, 4 run (Lowery kick)
Kansas City: Lowery, 29 FG
L.A. Raiders: Ismail, 43 pass from Evans (kick blocked)

BUCCANEERS 27, LIONS 10
Tampa, Fla., Oct. 3, 1993

Detroit	7	3	0	0	— 10
Tampa Bay	0	3	21	3	— 27

Scoring:
Detroit: Sanders, 20 run (Hanson kick)
Detroit: Hanson, 30 FG
Tampa Bay: Husted, 50 FG
Tampa Bay: Hawkins, 15 pass from Erickson (Husted kick)
Tampa Bay: Cobb, 3 run (Husted kick)
Tampa Bay: Ro. Hall, 37 pass from Erickson (Husted kick)
Tampa Bay: Husted, 46 FG

DOLPHINS 17, REDSKINS 10
Miami, Fla., Monday night, Oct. 4, 1993

Washington	0	3	0	7	— 10
Miami	14	0	0	3	— 17

Scoring:
Miami: Martin, 80 pass from Marino (Stoyanovich kick)
Miami: Higgs, 1 run (Stoyanovich kick)
Washington: Lohmiller, 28 FG
Washington: Sanders, 12 pass from Gannon (Lohmiller kick)
Miami: Stoyanovich, 37 FG

1993 REVIEW — WEEK SIX

WEEK SIX

WEEK SIX STANDINGS

AMERICAN FOOTBALL CONFERENCE

AFC EAST	W	L	T	Pct.	PF	PA
Miami	4	1	0	.800	101	81
Buffalo	4	1	0	.800	116	67
Indianapolis	2	3	0	.400	68	102
N.Y. Jets	2	3	0	.400	139	106
New England	1	4	0	.200	74	140

AFC CENTRAL	W	L	T	Pct.	PF	PA
Cleveland	3	2	0	.600	93	90
Pittsburgh	3	2	0	.600	108	78
Houston	1	4	0	.200	88	114
Cincinnati	0	5	0	.000	52	106

AFC WEST	W	L	T	Pct.	PF	PA
Kansas City	4	1	0	.800	83	64
Denver	3	2	0	.600	129	95
L.A. Raiders	3	2	0	.600	90	83
Seattle	3	2	0	.600	92	73
San Diego	2	3	0	.400	70	110

NATIONAL FOOTBALL CONFERENCE

NFC EAST	W	L	T	Pct.	PF	PA
N.Y. Giants	4	1	0	.800	124	61
Philadelphia	4	1	0	.800	118	112
Dallas	3	2	0	.600	106	75
Washington	1	4	0	.200	93	125
Phoenix	1	4	0	.200	85	99

NFC CENTRAL	W	L	T	Pct.	PF	PA
Chicago	3	2	0	.600	97	59
Detroit	3	2	0	.600	88	90
Minnesota	3	2	0	.600	66	82
Green Bay	2	3	0	.400	110	104
Tampa Bay	1	4	0	.200	54	122

NFC WEST	W	L	T	Pct.	PF	PA
New Orleans	5	0	0	1.000	134	74
San Francisco	3	2	0	.600	125	101
L.A. Rams	2	3	0	.400	77	106
Atlanta	0	5	0	.000	91	152

WEEK 6 RESULTS / LINE

Chicago 17, PHILADELPHIA 6 — EAGLES by 7
KANSAS CITY 17, Cincinnati 15 — CHIEFS by 14
Dallas 27, INDIANAPOLIS 3 — Cowboys by 12
Miami 24, CLEVELAND 14 — Dolphins by 2
N.Y. Giants 41, WASHINGTON 7 — REDSKINS by 3.5
MINNESOTA 15, Tampa Bay 0 — VIKINGS by 11
PITTSBURGH 16, San Diego 3 — STEELERS by 6
New England 23, PHOENIX 21 — CARDINALS by 10
L.A. RAIDERS 24, N.Y. Jets 20 — RAIDERS by 2
GREEN BAY 30, Denver 27 — PACKERS by 3
BUFFALO 35, Houston 7 — BILLS by 3.5

Home team in CAPS

With the end of Week Six, the 18-week 1994 season was a third over, although, with the new bye system, each team had only played five of its 16 regular-season games.

At this juncture, there were some major surprises. What happened to such highly regarded preseason teams as Houston (1-4), Green Bay (2-3) and San Diego (2-3)? And how do you explain the previously unheralded Giants and Eagles (4-1 each) and the said-to-be pushover Seahawks and Bears (3-2)? And where was Dallas, the previous Super Bowl champion? Mired in the middle (3-2).

The NFC Central, often noted for defensive fortresses, was living up to its reputation, with the Bears having allowed the fewest points in the NFL, 59 (11.8 per game), and the Vikings the fewest yards, 1,131 (226.2 per game).

The Jets had racked up the most points, 139, while the Cowboys had earned the most yardage, 1,917.

According to Pro Football Weekly's Efficiency Ratings, the top five teams on offense were: Dallas, New Orleans, San Francisco, N.Y. Jets and Denver; the top defenses: Pittsburgh, L.A. Raiders, Kansas City, Minnesota and N.Y. Giants.

GAME OF THE WEEK: The Packers went into the second half, staring down at the Broncos 30-7, only to be outscored 20-0 in the next two quarters. But the defense finally held off a Denver drive in the waning minutes to eke out a 30-27 win. A runner-up game of the week was the Bears' 17-6 upset of the previously undefeated Eagles.

DEVASTATIONS: The ordinarily ultradurable Miami QB Dan Marino went down with a torn Achilles tendon and was lost for the season. The Colts' franchise DE Steve Emtman, the No. 1 pick of the 1992 draft, ended his season when he tore ligaments and a tendon in his right knee.

QB SWITCHES: In the Cleveland camp, Bernie Kosar lost his QB job to free-agent acquisition

Dan Marino suffered a season-ending injury

PRO FOOTBALL WEEKLY 1994 ALMANAC

Vinny Testaverde. At Houston, veteran Warren Moon was pulled in favor of Cody Carlson during the Oilers' Monday night disaster and was informed the next day that he was the second-string quarterback.

INTERCEPTIONS: Cleveland CB Najee Mustafaa snatched one of Miami QB Scott Mitchell's passes and returned it 97 yards for a touchdown, the longest in Browns' history. Two Bear defensive linemen registered interceptions in their win over the Eagles, DE Richard Dent and DT Steve McMichael.

PFW NOTES: The Redskins' 41-7 loss to the Giants was their worst defeat at home in 41 years since the Eagles trimmed them 45-0 in 1948. In this week's game the Giants scored on every first-half possession except one (when QB Phil Simms fell on the ball to let time run out). Lost for the season due to injuries were Bear WR Wendell Davis and Eagle LB Ken Rose. With his game-winning field goal for the Chiefs, Nick Lowery became only the fifth player to score more than 1,400 points. Despite losing, Denver's John Elway set single-game career highs in pass completions with 33 and pass attempts with 59. Steeler PK Gary Anderson kicked his 256th field goal and moved ahead of Hall of Famer Lou Groza as the ninth all-time NFL field goal kicker. In the same game, Packer Sterling Sharpe and Bronco Vance Johnson each caught 10 passes, more than any other receiver in Week Six. Until this week, the Patriots had not beaten the Cardinals since 1978.

OFFENSIVE MVP: QB Vince Evans, Raiders. Coming off the bench to replace an ineffective Jeff Hostetler, Evans, 38 years old and in the league since 1977, rallied the Raiders by completing 14-of-22 passes for 247 yards and two TD's. His last-gasp, 72-yard, 11-play drive resulted in a touchdown and a come-from-behind, 24-20 win.

DEFENSIVE MVP: DE Reggie White, Packers. 1993's foremost free agent, White logged three sacks and five tackles for Green Bay in its 30-27 triumph over the Broncos. Two of the sacks were back-to-back in the final 1:50 of the game to thwart a John Elway-led, last-ditch drive.

GOLDEN TOE: PK Doug Pelfrey, Bengals. The rookie's job was on the line in this game against Kansas City, and Pelfrey responded by successfully kicking 5-of-5 field goals for all of Cincinnati's points — but the Bengals still lost 17-15.

TOP PERFORMANCES

PASSING

Player, team	Comp.	Att.	Yds.	TD	Int.
John Elway, Broncos	33	59	367	1	1
Jim Kelly, Bills	15	25	247	3	0
Vince Evans, Raiders	14	22	247	2	1
Troy Aikman, Cowboys	21	28	245	1	0
Brett Favre, Packers	20	32	235	1	3
Mark Rypien, Redskins	21	35	220	1	1

RUSHING

Player, team	Att.	Yds.	TD
Leonard Russell, Patriots	28	116	0
Roosevelt Potts, Colts	18	113	0
Barry Foster, Steelers	23	110	0
Emmitt Smith, Cowboys	25	104	1
Lewis Tillman, Giants	29	104	0
Thurman Thomas, Bills	24	92	1

RECEIVING

Player, team	Rec.	Yds.	TD
Vance Johnson, Broncos	10	148	1
Sean Dawkins, Colts	8	144	0
Jackie Harris, Packers	5	128	1
Mike Sherrard, Giants	4	124	2
Michael Irvin, Cowboys	7	112	0
Victor Bailey, Eagles	4	94	0

SCORING

Player, team	TD	XP	FG	Pts.
Barry Foster, Steelers	3	0	0	18
Doug Pelfrey, Bengals	0	0	5/5	15

GAME SUMMARIES

GIANTS 41, REDSKINS 7
Washington, D.C., Oct. 10, 1993

N.Y. Giants	7	20	0	14	—	41
Washington	0	7	0	0	—	7

Scoring:
N.Y. Giants: Tillman, 3 run (Treadwell kick)
N.Y. Giants: Cross, 7 pass from Simms (Treadwell kick failed)
N.Y. Giants: Sherrard, 42 pass from Simms (Treadwell kick)
N.Y. Giants: Cross, 17 pass from Simms (Treadwell kick)
Washington: McGee, 12 pass from Rypien (Lohmiller kick)
N.Y. Giants: Sherrard, 55 pass from Simms (Treadwell kick)
N.Y. Giants: Rasheed, 23 run (Treadwell kick)

VIKINGS 15, BUCCANEERS 0
Minneapolis, Minn., Oct. 10, 1993

Tampa Bay	0	0	0	0	—	0
Minnesota	0	12	0	3	—	15

Scoring:
Minnesota: Reveiz, 26 FG
Minnesota: Safety, Erickson intentional grounding in endzone
Minnesota: Word, 1 run (Reveiz kick)
Minnesota: Reveiz, 25 FG

CHIEFS 17, BENGALS 15
Kansas City, Mo., Oct. 10, 1993

Cincinnati	3	9	0	3	—	15
Kansas City	0	7	7	3	—	17

Scoring:
Cincinnati: Pelfrey, 23 FG
Cincinnati: Pelfrey, 24 FG
Cincinnati: Pelfrey, 42 FG
Kansas City: Barnett, 8 pass from Krieg (Lowery kick)
Cincinnati: Pelfrey, 47 FG
Kansas City: Allen, 9 run (Lowery kick)
Cincinnati: Pelfrey, 34 FG
Kansas City: Lowery, 37 FG

STEELERS 16, CHARGERS 3
Pittsburgh, Pa., Oct. 10, 1993

San Diego	0	3	0	0	—	3
Pittsburgh	3	3	7	3	—	16

Scoring:
Pittsburgh: Anderson, 37 FG
Pittsburgh: Anderson, 34 FG
San Diego: Carney, 33 FG
Pittsburgh: Kirkland, 16 fumble return (Anderson kick)
Pittsburgh: Anderson, 35 FG

1993 REVIEW ■ WEEK SIX

COWBOYS 27, COLTS 3
Indianapolis, Ind., Oct. 10, 1993

Dallas	14	0	7	6	—	27
Indianapolis	0	3	0	0	—	3

Scoring:
- Dallas: Johnston, 1 pass from Aikman (Murray kick)
- Dallas: E. Smith, 20 run (Murray kick)
- Indianapolis: Biasucci, 27 FG
- Dallas: Novacek, 2 pass from Aikman (Murray kick)
- Dallas: Murray, 30 FG
- Dallas: Murray, 32 FG

DOLPHINS 24, BROWNS 14
Cleveland, Ohio, Oct. 10, 1993

Miami	0	10	14	0	—	24
Cleveland	7	7	0	0	—	14

Scoring:
- Cleveland: Jackson, 15 pass from Kosar (Stover kick)
- Miami: Stoyanovich, 52 FG
- Miami: Ingram, 13 pass from Marino (Stoyanovich kick)
- Cleveland: Mustafaa, 97 interception return (Stover kick)
- Miami: Martin, 19 pass from Mitchell (Stoyanovich kick)
- Miami: K. Jackson, 3 pass from Mitchell (Stoyanovich kick)

RAIDERS 24, JETS 20
Los Angeles, Calif., Oct. 10, 1993

N.Y. Jets	0	17	0	3	—	20
L.A. Raiders	0	7	10	7	—	24

Scoring:
- N.Y. Jets: B. Thomas, 6 run (Blanchard kick)
- N.Y. Jets: B. Washington, 62 interception return (Blanchard kick)
- N.Y. Jets: Blanchard, 25 FG
- L.A. Raiders: Jett, 42 pass from Evans (Jaeger kick)
- L.A. Raiders: Wright, 68 pass from Evans (Jaeger kick)
- L.A. Raiders: Jaeger, 42 FG
- N.Y. Jets: Blanchard, 20 FG
- L.A. Raiders: Bell, 1 run (Jaeger kick)

BEARS 17, EAGLES 6
Philadelphia, Pa., Oct. 10, 1993

Chicago	10	7	0	0	—	17
Philadelphia	0	0	0	6	—	6

Scoring:
- Chicago: Butler, 37 FG
- Chicago: Conway, 32 pass from Harbaugh (Butler kick)
- Chicago: Harbaugh, 1 run (Butler kick)
- Philadelphia: Williams, 9 pass from Brister (Bahr kick blocked)

PATRIOTS 23, CARDINALS 21
Phoenix, Ariz., Oct. 10, 1993

New England	0	13	3	7	—	23
Phoenix	0	14	0	7	—	21

Scoring:
- New England: Coates, 4 pass from Bledsoe (Sisson kick)
- Phoenix: Proehl, 6 pass from Beuerlein (G. Davis kick)
- Phoenix: Proehl, 15 pass from Beuerlein (G. Davis kick)
- New England: Sisson, 29 FG
- New England: Sisson, 23 FG
- New England: Sisson, 31 FG
- Phoenix: R. Hill, 30 pass from Beuerlein (G. Davis kick)
- New England: Coates, 2 pass from Secules (Sisson kick)

PACKERS 30, BRONCOS 27
Green Bay, Wis., Oct. 10, 1993

Denver	0	7	14	6	—	27
Green Bay	17	13	0	0	—	30

Scoring:
- Green Bay: Jacke, 28 FG
- Green Bay: Stephens, 1 run (Jacke kick)
- Green Bay: E. Bennett, 1 run (Jacke kick)
- Denver: V. Johnson, 14 pass from Elway (Elam kick)
- Green Bay: J. Harris, 66 pass from Favre (Jacke kick)
- Green Bay: Jacke, 32 FG
- Green Bay: Jacke, 21 FG
- Denver: Croel, 22 interception return (Elam kick)
- Denver: Bernstine, 2 run (Elam kick)
- Denver: Elam, 47 FG
- Denver: Elam, 37 FG

BILLS 35, OILERS 7
Orchard Park, N.Y., Monday night, Oct. 11, 1993

Houston	7	0	0	0	—	7
Buffalo	7	21	0	7	—	35

Scoring:
- Buffalo: Beebe, 34 pass from Kelly (Christie kick)
- Houston: L. Harris, 17 pass from Moon (Del Greco kick)
- Buffalo: Reed, 24 pass from Kelly (Christie kick)
- Buffalo: Reed, 39 pass from Kelly (Christie kick)
- Buffalo: Thomas, 7 run (Christie kick)
- Buffalo: K. Davis, 3 run (Christie kick)

PRO FOOTBALL WEEKLY 1994 ALMANAC

REVIEW: WEEK SEVEN

WEEK SEVEN STANDINGS

AMERICAN FOOTBALL CONFERENCE

AFC EAST

	W	L	T	Pct.	PF	PA
Buffalo	4	1	0	.800	116	67
Miami	4	1	0	.800	101	81
Indianapolis	2	3	0	.400	68	102
N.Y. Jets	2	3	0	.400	139	106
New England	1	5	0	.167	88	168

AFC CENTRAL

	W	L	T	Pct.	PF	PA
Cleveland	4	2	0	.667	121	107
Pittsburgh	4	2	0	.667	145	92
Houston	2	4	0	.333	116	128
Cincinnati	0	6	0	.000	69	134

AFC WEST

	W	L	T	Pct.	PF	PA
Kansas City	5	1	0	.833	100	78
L.A. Raiders	4	2	0	.667	113	103
Denver	3	3	0	.500	149	118
Seattle	3	3	0	.500	102	103
San Diego	2	4	0	.333	84	127

NATIONAL FOOTBALL CONFERENCE

NFC EAST

	W	L	T	Pct.	PF	PA
N.Y. Giants	5	1	0	.833	145	71
Dallas	4	2	0	.667	132	92
Philadelphia	4	2	0	.667	128	133
Phoenix	2	4	0	.333	121	105
Washington	1	5	0	.167	99	161

NFC CENTRAL

	W	L	T	Pct.	PF	PA
Detroit	4	2	0	.667	118	100
Chicago	3	2	0	.600	97	59
Minnesota	3	2	0	.600	66	82
Green Bay	2	3	0	.400	110	104
Tampa Bay	1	4	0	.200	54	122

NFC WEST

	W	L	T	Pct.	PF	PA
New Orleans	5	1	0	.833	148	111
San Francisco	3	3	0	.500	142	127
L.A. Rams	2	4	0	.333	101	136
Atlanta	1	5	0	.167	121	176

WEEK 7 RESULTS

Result	Line	
ATLANTA 30, L.A. Rams 24	Rams by 2	
Cleveland 28, CINCINNATI 17	Browns by 5	
Houston 28, NEW ENGLAND 14	Oilers by 6.5	
PITTSBURGH 37, New Orleans 14	Saints by 2.5	
N.Y. GIANTS 21, Philadelphia 10	GIANTS by 7.5	
DETROIT 30, Seattle 10	LIONS by 5	
PHOENIX 36, Washington 6	Redskins by 1.5	
Kansas City 17, SAN DIEGO 14	Chiefs by 4	
DALLAS 26, San Francisco 17	COWBOYS by 6.5	
L.A. Raiders 23, DENVER 20	BRONCOS by 6.5	

Home team in CAPS

The division races began to come into sharper perspective as Week Seven in the NFL ended.

The Cowboys, with Emmitt Smith back in the backfield and Eddie Murray straightening out their kicking game, were surging in the NFC East. But the Giants continued to surprise and, with five victories in six games, were making believers out of preseason non-believers and building a lot of interest in the matchup with Dallas looming in Week 10.

In the AFC, the Steelers were stealing the spotlight, and the talk there was of their impending confrontation with the defending AFC champion Bills in Week 11. And, of course, the overriding question: How would the highly touted Dolphins fare without QB Dan Marino?

The NFC Central, with the Bears on track and the Packers off track, appeared to be a division that was up for grabs for any team but the Buccaneers.

And hanging around with valid sights on division titles or playoff berths were Denver, Cleveland and the Raiders in the AFC and New Orleans, San Francisco and Philadelphia in the NFC.

GAME OF THE WEEK: In a rematch of last season's NFC title game between the Cowboys and 49ers, both teams needed a win. The Cowboys were trailing the Giants and the Eagles in the NFC East, and the 49ers were a pair of games behind the Saints. In this game, the lead went back and forth until the last 15:03, when the defending Super Bowl champion Cowboys took control and won it 26-17. San Francisco coach George Seifert summed it up best: "We made some big mistakes, but I'll say Dallas is all it's publicized to be."

MORTALITY: The last of the unbeatens, the Saints, were reduced to ordinary mortals when their perfect 5-0 record was besmirched by the raging Steelers. Not only did they lose, New Orleans was humiliated 37-14, and its 14 points did not come until the fourth quarter and after Pittsburgh had finished scoring for the day and cleared its bench.

DALLAS TALK: In Texas they always talk big, especially after a big win. WR Michael Irvin on QB Troy Aikman: "When Troy is on, it's like pitch and catch." Owner Jerry Jones on Irvin: "Michael is the kind of guy you want with you in a back alley."

DICKERSON RETIRES: The second all-time leading rusher, Eric Dickerson, traded by Atlanta to Green Bay during the week, failed his physical in Packerland because of a bulging disk in his neck. It signaled the end of the 33-year-old running back's NFL career, his career 13,259 yards rushing falling 3,467 shy of Walter Payton's record 16,726.

PFW NOTES: The Lions' 30-10 victory over the Seahawks was the franchise's 800th game since the Portsmouth (Ohio) Spartans moved to Detroit in 1934 and changed their name to Lions. The 5-1 Chiefs registered their best start in 22 years. Through six games, the Steelers had not allowed an opponent to rush for more than 100 yards. Astounding fact of the week: Denver and QB John Elway were held to minus passing yardage until

1993 REVIEW ■ WEEK SEVEN

Eric Swann recorded 12 tackles, a pair of sacks, a safety and forced a fumble in Week Seven

late in the third quarter of their 20-17 loss to the Raiders. Joe Montana threw his 250th career touchdown pass, only the sixth NFL player to reach that mark. Ram PK Tony Zendejas extended his consecutive streak of 50-yard-plus field goals to 10, an NFL record (as is his career total of 16 50-yarders in 20 attempts). QB Warren Moon, benched the week before in Houston, came on in relief to lead the Oilers to victory over the Patriots. Steeler Rod Woodson picked off two New Orleans passes to bring his 1993 interception total to seven (no one else in the NFL had more than three as of Week Seven). Mel Gray's 95-yard kickoff return for a TD was his longest as a Lion — as a Saint he ran one back 101 yards.

OFFENSIVE MVP: WR Michael Irvin, Cowboys. In Dallas, Irvin had a most productive day catching the football, 12 receptions for 168 yards. His juggling, 36-yard TD catch at the close of the third quarter gave Dallas a lead it would not relinquish in its much-needed 26-17 win over the 49ers.

DEFENSIVE MVP: DT Eric Swann, Cardinals: Swann, who never played college ball and before joining Phoenix three years ago was earning $5 an hour working for a landscaper, contributed 12 tackles, two sacks, a safety and a forced fumble to the Cardinals' 36-6 win over the Redskins.

GOLDEN TOE: PK Norm Johnson, Falcons. On Thursday night, Johnson was instrumental in Atlanta's first win of the year, kicking 3-of-3 field goals, two in the fourth quarter, as the Falcons topped the Rams 30-24.

TOP PERFORMANCES

PASSING

Player, team	Comp.	Att.	Yds.	TD	Int.
Jim Everett, Rams	17	35	294	2	2
Joe Montana, Chiefs	21	39	284	1	1
Scott Secules, Patriots	23	40	280	1	3
Steve Young, 49ers	24	33	267	1	0
Jeff Hostetler, Raiders	15	24	264	2	0
Steve Beuerlein, Cardinals	12	25	250	1	1

RUSHING

Player, team	Att.	Yds.	TD
Lewis Tillman, Giants	20	169	2
Rod Bernstine, Broncos	23	101	0
Barry Sanders, Lions	22	101	0
Leroy Thompson, Steelers	16	101	0
Ricky Ervins, Redskins	17	98	0
Tommy Vardell, Browns	25	98	0

RECEIVING

Player, team	Rec.	Yds.	TD
Michael Irvin, Cowboys	12	168	1
Tim Brown, Raiders	6	116	0
Ricky Proehl, Cardinals	5	115	1
Derek Russell, Broncos	5	111	0
Anthony Miller, Chargers	6	105	1
Herman Moore, Lions	8	98	2

SCORING

Player, team	TD	XP	FG	Pts.
Eddie Murray, Cowboys	0	2/2	4/5	14
Gary Anderson, Steelers	0	4/4	3/3	13

GAME SUMMARIES

FALCONS 30, RAMS 24

Atlanta, Ga., Thursday night, Oct. 14, 1993

L.A. Rams	10	7	7	0	—	24
Atlanta	3	7	7	13	—	30

Scoring:
L.A. Rams: Anderson, 56 pass from Everett (Zendejas kick)
Atlanta: Johnson, 28 FG
L.A. Rams: Zendejas, 52 FG
L.A. Rams: Bettis, 2 run (Zendejas kick)
Atlanta: Rison, 21 pass from Tolliver (Johnson kick)
Atlanta: Mims, 3 pass from Tolliver (Johnson kick)
L.A. Rams: Gary, 60 pass from Everett (Zendejas kick)
Atlanta: Johnson, 32 FG
Atlanta: Rison, 42 pass from Tolliver (Johnson kick)
Atlanta: Johnson, 34 FG

CHIEFS 17, CHARGERS 14

San Diego, Calif., Oct. 17, 1993

Kansas City	7	3	0	7	—	17
San Diego	0	7	0	7	—	14

Scoring:
Kansas City: Allen, 15 pass from Montana (Lowery kick)
San Diego: Means, 7 run (Carney kick)
Kansas City: Lowery, 37 FG
San Diego: A. Miller, 4 pass from Friesz (Carney kick)
Kansas City: Allen, 1 run (Lowery kick)

GIANTS 21, EAGLES 10

East Rutherford, N.J., Oct. 17, 1993

Philadelphia	0	3	0	7	—	10
N.Y. Giants	0	14	0	7	—	21

Scoring:
Philadelphia: Bahr, 47 FG
N.Y. Giants: McCaffrey, 17 pass from Simms (Treadwell kick)
N.Y. Giants: Tillman, 1 run (Treadwell kick)
N.Y. Giants: Tillman, 10 run, (Treadwell kick)
Philadelphia: Bavaro, 13 pass from O'Brien (Bahr kick)

OILERS 28, PATRIOTS 14

Foxboro, Mass., Oct. 17, 1993

Houston	0	14	7	7	—	28
New England	0	0	7	7	—	14

Scoring:
Houston: Carlson, 10 run (Del Greco kick)
Houston: Slaughter, 7 pass from Moon (Del Greco kick)
New England: Turner, 7 pass from Secules (Sisson kick)
Houston: Slaughter, 2 pass from Moon (Del Greco kick)
Houston: Jackson, 22 interception return (Del Greco kick)
New England: Russell, 1 run (Sisson kick)

PRO FOOTBALL WEEKLY 1994 ALMANAC

BROWNS 28, BENGALS 17
Cincinnati, Ohio, Oct. 17, 1993

Cleveland	7	14	0	7	— 28
Cincinnati	0	7	3	7	— 17

Scoring:
Cleveland: Vardell, 28 pass from Testaverde (Stover kick)
Cleveland: Baldwin, 5 pass from Testaverde (Stover kick)
Cleveland: Kinchen, 1 pass from Testaverde (Stover kick)
Cincinnati: Query, 11 pass from Schroeder (Pelfrey kick)
Cincinnati: Pelfrey, 49 FG
Cleveland: Carrier, 15 run (Stover kick)
Cincinnati: Pickens, 24 pass from Schroeder (Pelfrey kick)

CARDINALS 36, REDSKINS 6
Phoenix, Ariz., Oct. 17, 1993

Washington	3	0	3	0	— 6
Phoenix	0	13	7	16	— 36

Scoring:
Washington: Lohmiller, 43 FG
Phoenix: G. Davis, 23 FG
Phoenix: G. Davis, 45 FG
Phoenix: Hearst, 1 run (G. Davis kick)
Phoenix: Proehl, 42 pass from Beuerlein (G. Davis kick)
Washington: Lohmiller, 38 FG
Phoenix: Safety, Swann tackled Brooks in endzone
Phoenix: Bailey, 14 run (G. Davis kick)
Phoenix: Moore, 1 run (G. Davis kick)

COWBOYS 26, 49ERS 17
Irving, Texas, Oct. 17, 1993

San Francisco	10	0	7	0	— 17
Dallas	3	13	7	3	— 26

Scoring:
San Francisco: Davis, 47 fumble return (Cofer kick)
Dallas: Murray, 48 FG
San Francisco: Cofer, 25 FG
Dallas: Murray, 39 FG
Dallas: E. Smith, 1 run (Murray kick)
Dallas: Murray, 29 FG
San Francisco: Jones, 12 pass from Young (Cofer kick)
Dallas: Irvin, 36 pass from Aikman (Murray kick)
Dallas: Murray, 18 FG

LIONS 30, SEAHAWKS 10
Pontiac, Mich., Oct. 17, 1993

Seattle	7	0	3	0	— 10
Detroit	0	14	13	3	— 30

Scoring:
Seattle: Martin, 6 pass from Mirer (Kasay kick)
Detroit: H. Moore, 13 pass from Peete (Hanson kick)
Detroit: H. Moore, 11 pass from Peete (Hanson kick)
Seattle: Kasay, 19 FG
Detroit: Gray, 95 kickoff return (Hanson kick)
Detroit: Hanson, 34 FG
Detroit: Hanson, 32 FG
Detroit: Hanson, 35 FG

STEELERS 37, SAINTS 14
Pittsburgh, Pa., Oct. 17, 1993

New Orleans	0	0	0	14	— 14
Pittsburgh	14	10	6	7	— 37

Scoring:
Pittsburgh: Woodson, 63 interception return (Anderson kick)
Pittsburgh: Foster, 20 pass from O'Donnell (Anderson kick)
Pittsburgh: Anderson, 40 FG
Pittsburgh: Foster, 1 run (Anderson kick)
Pittsburgh: Anderson, 22 FG
Pittsburgh: Anderson, 29 FG
Pittsburgh: Green, 26 pass from Tomczak (Anderson kick)
New Orleans: Small, 3 pass from M. Buck (Andersen kick)
New Orleans: Early, 63 pass from M. Buck (Andersen kick)

RAIDERS 23, BRONCOS 20
Denver, Colo., Monday night, Oct. 18, 1993

L.A. Raiders	10	3	0	10	— 23
Denver	0	0	3	17	— 20

Scoring:
L.A. Raiders: Wright, 11 pass from Hostetler (Jaeger kick)
L.A. Raiders: Jaeger, 32 FG
L.A. Raiders: Jaeger, 49 FG
Denver: Elam, 40 FG
Denver: Marshall, 27 pass from Elway (Elam kick)
Denver: R. Johnson, 2 pass from Elway (Elam kick)
L.A. Raiders: Jett, 74 pass from Hostetler (Jaeger kick)
Denver: Elam, 37 FG
L.A. Raiders: Jaeger, 53 FG

1993 REVIEW — WEEK EIGHT

WEEK EIGHT

WEEK EIGHT STANDINGS

AMERICAN FOOTBALL CONFERENCE

AFC EAST	W	L	T	Pct.	PF	PA
Miami	5	1	0	.833	142	108
Buffalo	5	1	0	.833	137	77
N.Y. Jets	2	4	0	.333	149	125
Indianapolis	2	4	0	.333	95	143
New England	1	6	0	.143	97	178

AFC CENTRAL	W	L	T	Pct.	PF	PA
Cleveland	5	2	0	.714	149	130
Pittsburgh	4	3	0	.571	168	120
Houston	3	4	0	.429	144	140
Cincinnati	0	7	0	.000	81	162

AFC WEST	W	L	T	Pct.	PF	PA
Kansas City	5	1	0	.833	100	78
L.A. Raiders	4	2	0	.667	113	103
Seattle	4	3	0	.571	112	112
Denver	3	3	0	.500	149	118
San Diego	2	4	0	.333	84	127

NATIONAL FOOTBALL CONFERENCE

NFC EAST	W	L	T	Pct.	PF	PA
N.Y. Giants	5	1	0	.833	145	71
Dallas	4	2	0	.667	132	92
Philadelphia	4	2	0	.667	128	133
Phoenix	2	5	0	.286	135	133
Washington	1	5	0	.167	99	161

NFC CENTRAL	W	L	T	Pct.	PF	PA
Detroit	5	2	0	.714	134	113
Minnesota	4	2	0	.667	85	94
Chicago	3	3	0	.500	109	78
Green Bay	3	3	0	.500	147	118
Tampa Bay	1	5	0	.167	68	159

NFC WEST	W	L	T	Pct.	PF	PA
New Orleans	5	2	0	.714	163	137
San Francisco	4	3	0	.571	170	141
Atlanta	2	5	0	.286	147	191
L.A. Rams	2	5	0	.286	114	152

WEEK 8 RESULTS / LINE

Result	Line
Atlanta 26, NEW ORLEANS 15	SAINTS by 10.5
Buffalo 19, N.Y. JETS 10	Bills by 2.5
HOUSTON 28, Cincinnati 12	OILERS by 14
Green Bay 37, TAMPA BAY 14	Packers by 5
CLEVELAND 28, Pittsburgh 23	Steelers by 2.5
Detroit 16, L.A. RAMS 13	RAMS by 2.5
SEATTLE 10, New England 9	SEAHAWKS by 9.5
SAN FRANCISCO 28, Phoenix 14	49ERS by 10.5
MIAMI 41, Indianapolis 27	DOLPHINS by 6.5
Minnesota 19, CHICAGO 12	BEARS by 3.5

Home team in CAPS

In the AFC, there were a pair of surprises. First, the Dolphins gave no indication they missed the injured Dan Marino, running up the most points of the week, 41, behind the quarterbacking of Marino's replacement Scott Mitchell. By beating the Colts, Miami hung on to a tie for first place with the Bills in the AFC East. Second, the surging Steelers were stung by divisional-rival Cleveland, dropping them to second place behind the Browns in the AFC Central.

In the NFC, Detroit solidified its lead in the Central Division with its fifth win in seven games. While in the West the Saints dropped their second straight but managed to maintain a tenuous hold on the division lead by a game over the threatening 49ers.

The other two divisional leaders, Kansas City in the AFC West and the Giants in the NFC East, rested by way of Week Eight open dates.

After eight weeks, the highest Pro Football Weekly offensive efficiency rating went to the 49ers, and the top defensive efficiency rating was claimed by the Raiders. In terms of total yards gained, Dallas was the leader with 2,270, or 378.3 a game. Allowing the fewest yards was the Minnesota Vikings.

GAME OF THE WEEK: First place in the AFC Central was at stake, and the Steelers, even though they were playing in unfriendly Cleveland, were 2.5-point favorites. But Eric Metcalf won the game for the Browns with the second of his two punt-return touchdowns of the day; the 75-yarder with just over two minutes left in the game gave the Browns a 28-23 victory. The Steelers outgained the Browns 444 yards to 245, and Pittsburgh QB Neil O'Donnell had a career-high 355 yards passing, but special-team play won this one for Cleveland.

SHARPE SHARP: WR Sterling Sharpe was indeed sharp in Green Bay's 37-14 demolition of the Buccaneers, hauling in four touchdown passes, which tied the Packer record held by Don Hutson since 1945. His 10 catches in the game netted 147 yards, the 21st 100-yard receiving game of his career.

HOMECOMING: Revisiting the Superdome where he quarterbacked the Saints for seven years and once enjoyed a kind of folk-hero status around New Orleans, Bobby Hebert came off the bench where he had been nursing a wounded shoulder and completed 13-of-16 passes for two touchdowns to lead the Falcons to a stunning 26-15 upset over his former club.

TOUCHDOWNS: With his two TD receptions in Week Eight, 49er WR Jerry Rice slipped past Lenny Moore to take fourth place on the NFL's all-time touchdown list. With 114, Rice was now only two shy of John Riggins and 11 behind Walter Payton. Jim Brown holds the record with 126.

PFW NOTES: Vinny Testaverde, after having wrested the starting QB job from Bernie Kosar in Cleveland and throwing two TD passes in the Browns' 28-23 upset of the Steelers, went down with a separated shoulder and was lost for a few weeks. The Bears, defeated in their last four Monday-night TV appearances, extended the streak to five by losing to the Vikings 19-12, a game in which they tied a club record by allowing QB Jim Harbaugh to be sacked nine times. Buffalo, despite scoring 19 points and gaining 413 yards in beating the Jets, did not score a touchdown on offense ... the first time that had happened to the Bills in 73 games. Green Bay PK Chris Jacke extended his consecutive extra-point total to 102, breaking the club record held by Paul Hornung. Packer WR Sterling Sharpe played two downs at quarterback for Green Bay, running up the middle for five yards on one and then passing to Mark Clayton for a one-yard gain. Ram veteran QB Jim Everett was benched in favor of T.J. Rubley, who threw two fourth-quarter TD passes to tie the game with the Lions, only to see it lost on a Detroit field goal with four seconds left. Buffalo DE Bruce Smith logged his first NFL interception, his first ever, he later confided, including college and high-school play. The Colts' four touchdowns in Week Eight were one more than they scored in the previous five games.

OFFENSIVE MVP: RB Eric Metcalf, Browns. Metcalf's two punt-return touchdowns for the Browns against the Steelers tied the league mark, which is shared now by seven players. His game-winning 75-yard scamper came with just 2:05 left and his earlier one, for 91 yards, was the longest in Browns' history. Metcalf ended up the day with 237 total yards against the Steelers, which included 53 yards rushing and 18 yards on three pass receptions.

DEFENSIVE MVP: LB Darryl Talley, Bills. In a 19-10 triumph over the Jets, Talley contributed the Bills' only touchdown of the day on a 61-yard interception return. Talley was also credited with nine tackles, one sack and a fumble recovery.

GOLDEN TOE: PK Steve Christie, Bills. The only offensive player to put points on the board for the Bills was Christie, 4-of-4 field goals and one extra point. His 30-yarder late in the fourth quarter iced the victory over the Jets.

Eric Metcalf scored on two punt returns

TOP PERFORMANCES

PASSING

Player, team	Comp.	Att.	Yds.	TD	Int.
Neil O'Donnell, Steelers	25	39	355	0	1
Steve Beuerlein, Cardinals	26	50	334	2	3
Wade Wilson, Saints	27	45	277	1	2
Brett Favre, Packers	20	35	268	4	1
Jeff George, Colts	27	44	260	2	3
Warren Moon, Oilers	24	34	253	2	1

RUSHING

Player, team	Att.	Yds.	TD
Erric Pegram, Falcons	34	132	0
Thurman Thomas, Bills	27	117	0
Mark Higgs, Dolphins	17	114	0
Jerome Bettis, Rams	23	113	0
Darrell Thompson, Packers	21	105	0
Leonard Russell, Patriots	21	97	0

RECEIVING

Player, team	Rec.	Yds.	TD
Jerry Rice, 49ers	9	155	2
Sterling Sharpe, Packers	10	147	4
Carl Pickens, Bengals	7	127	0
Herman Moore, Lions	6	120	0
Anthony Edwards, Cardinals	4	112	1
Eric Green, Steelers	6	108	0

SCORING

Player, team	TD	XP	FG	Pts.
Sterling Sharpe, Packers	4	0	0	24
Rodney Culver, Colts	3	0	0	18
Norm Johnson, Falcons	0	2/2	4/4	14

GAME SUMMARIES

PACKERS 37, BUCCANEERS 14
Tampa, Fla., Oct. 24, 1993

Green Bay	7	17	6	7	— 37
Tampa Bay	0	0	7	7	— 14

Scoring:
Green Bay: Sharpe, 7 pass from Favre (Jacke kick)
Green Bay: Sharpe, 30 pass from Favre (Jacke kick)
Green Bay: Sharpe, 10 pass from Favre (Jacke kick)
Green Bay: Jacke, 50 FG
Green Bay: Jacke, 44 FG
Green Bay: Jacke, 24 FG
Tampa Bay: Copeland, 26 pass from Erickson (Husted kick)
Green Bay: Sharpe, 32 pass from Favre (Jacke kick)
Tampa Bay: Copeland, 67 pass from Erickson (Husted kick)

OILERS 28, BENGALS 12
Houston, Texas, Oct. 24, 1993

Cincinnati	0	9	0	3	— 12
Houston	7	0	7	14	— 28

Scoring:
Houston: Wellman, 9 pass from Moon (Del Greco kick)
Cincinnati: Query, 8 pass from Rchroeder (Pelfrey kick failed)
Cincinnati: Pelfrey, 53 FG
Cincinnati: Pelfrey, 50 FG
Houston: White, 4 run (Del Greco kick)
Houston: Jeffires, 11 pass from Moon (Del Greco kick)
Houston: G. Brown, 25 run (Del Greco kick)

BILLS 19, JETS 10
East Rutherford, N.J., Oct. 24, 1993

Buffalo	0	6	7	6	— 19
N.Y. Jets	7	0	0	3	— 10

Scoring:
N.Y. Jets: B. Baxter, 1 run (Blanchard kick)
Buffalo: Christie, 36 FG

1993 REVIEW ■ WEEK EIGHT

Buffalo: Christie, 33 FG
Buffalo: Talley, 61 interception return (Christie kick)
Buffalo: Christie, 22 FG
N.Y. Jets: Blanchard, 33 FG
Buffalo: Christie, 30 FG

49ERS 28, CARDINALS 14

San Francisco, Calif., Oct. 24, 1993

Phoenix	0	0	0	14	— 14
San Francisco	0	14	0	14	— 28

Scoring:
San Francisco: Logan, 1 run (Cofer kick)
San Francisco: Rice, 8 pass from Young (Cofer kick)
San Francisco: Rice, 7 pass from Young (Cofer kick)
San Francisco: Watters, 19 run (Cofer kick)
Phoenix: Edwards, 65 pass from Beuerlein (G. Davis kick)
Phoenix: Proehl, 4 pass from Beuerlein (G. Davis kick)

SEAHAWKS 10, PATRIOTS 9

Seattle, Wash., Oct. 24, 1993

New England	0	0	3	6	— 9
Seattle	0	3	0	7	— 10

Scoring:
Seattle: Kasay, 30 FG
New England: Sisson, 36 FG
New England: Sisson, 25 FG
New England: Sisson, 19 FG
Seattle: Blades, 1 pass from Mirer (Kasay kick)

LIONS 16, RAMS 13

Anaheim, Calif., Oct. 24, 1993

Detroit	0	3	3	10	— 16
L.A. Rams	0	0	0	13	— 13

Scoring:
Detroit: Hanson, 25 FG
Detroit: Hanson, 24 FG
Detroit: Sanders, 5 run (Hanson kick)
L.A. Rams: Jones, 4 pass from Rubley (Zendejas kick)
L.A. Rams: Jones, 21 pass from Rubley (Zendejas kick failed)
Detroit: Hanson, 18 FG

BROWNS 28, STEELERS 23

Cleveland, Ohio, Oct. 24, 1993

Pittsburgh	0	14	6	3	— 23
Cleveland	0	14	7	7	— 28

Scoring:
Cleveland: Jackson, 62 pass from Testaverde (Stover kick)
Cleveland: Metcalf, 91 punt return (Stover kick)
Pittsburgh: Foster, 4 run (Anderson kick)
Pittsburgh: Foster, 1 run (Anderson kick)
Pittsburgh: Anderson, 30 FG
Cleveland: Wolfley, 4 pass from Testaverde (Stover kick)
Pittsburgh: Anderson, 46 FG
Pittsburgh: Anderson, 29 FG
Cleveland: Metcalf, 75 punt return (Stover kick)

FALCONS 26, SAINTS 15

New Orleans, La., Oct. 24, 1993

Atlanta	0	17	3	6	— 26
New Orleans	3	3	7	2	— 15

Scoring:
New Orleans: Andersen, 40 FG
Atlanta: Johnson, 19 FG
Atlanta: Rison, 5 pass from Hebert (Johnson kick)
Atlanta: Haynes, 9 pass from Hebert (Johnson kick)
New Orleans: Andersen, 27 FG
Atlanta: Johnson, 32 FG
New Orleans: Early, 23 pass from Wilson (Andersen kick)
Atlanta: Johnson, 38 FG
Atlanta: Johnson, 30 FG
New Orleans: Safety, Stowers tackled Alexander in endzone

DOLPHINS 41, COLTS 27

Miami, Fla., Oct. 24, 1993

Indianapolis	0	6	7	14	— 27
Miami	17	3	14	7	— 41

Scoring:
Miami: Stoyanovich, 23 FG
Miami: McDuffie, 71 punt return (Stoyanovich kick)
Miami: Kirby, 44 pass from Mitchell (Stoyanovich kick)
Indianapolis: Culver, 3 pass from George (Biasucci kick failed)
Miami: Stoyanovich, 39 FG
Indianapolis: Culver, 1 run (Biasucci kick)
Miami: Fryar, 11 pass from Byars (Stoyanovich kick)
Miami: Kirby, 14 run (Stoyanovich kick)
Indianapolis: Langhorne, 6 pass from George (Biasucci kick)
Miami: Oliver, 56 interception return (Stoyanovich kick)
Indianapolis: Culver, 3 pass from George (Biasucci kick)

VIKINGS 19, BEARS 12

Chicago, Ill., Monday night, Oct. 25, 1993

Minnesota	10	3	6	0	— 19
Chicago	3	6	0	3	— 12

Scoring:
Chicago: Butler, 37 FG
Minnesota: Reveiz, 39 FG
Minnesota: R. Smith, 26 run (Reveiz kick)
Chicago: Butler, 39 FG
Chicago: Butler, 55 FG
Minnesota: Reveiz, 25 FG
Minnesota: McMillian, 22 interception return (Reveiz kick failed)
Chicago: Butler, 35 FG

PRO FOOTBALL WEEKLY 1994 ALMANAC

REVIEW: WEEK NINE

WEEK NINE STANDINGS

AMERICAN FOOTBALL CONFERENCE

AFC EAST	W	L	T	Pct.	PF	PA
Buffalo	6	1	0	.857	159	87
Miami	6	1	0	.857	172	118
N.Y. Jets	3	4	0	.429	159	131
Indianapolis	3	4	0	.429	104	149
New England	1	7	0	.125	103	187

AFC CENTRAL	W	L	T	Pct.	PF	PA
Cleveland	5	2	0	.714	149	130
Pittsburgh	4	3	0	.571	168	120
Houston	3	4	0	.429	144	140
Cincinnati	0	7	0	.000	81	162

AFC WEST	W	L	T	Pct.	PF	PA
Kansas City	5	2	0	.714	110	108
Denver	4	3	0	.571	177	135
L.A. Raiders	4	3	0	.571	136	133
Seattle	4	4	0	.500	129	140
San Diego	3	4	0	.429	114	150

NATIONAL FOOTBALL CONFERENCE

NFC EAST	W	L	T	Pct.	PF	PA
Dallas	5	2	0	.714	155	102
N.Y. Giants	5	2	0	.714	151	81
Philadelphia	4	3	0	.571	138	156
Phoenix	2	6	0	.250	152	153
Washington	1	6	0	.143	109	185

NFC CENTRAL	W	L	T	Pct.	PF	PA
Detroit	6	2	0	.750	164	140
Minnesota	4	3	0	.571	112	124
Green Bay	4	3	0	.571	164	121
Chicago	3	4	0	.429	112	95
Tampa Bay	2	5	0	.286	99	183

NFC WEST	W	L	T	Pct.	PF	PA
New Orleans	6	2	0	.750	183	154
San Francisco	5	3	0	.625	210	158
Atlanta	2	6	0	.250	171	222
L.A. Rams	2	6	0	.250	131	192

WEEK 9 RESULTS / LINE

Result	Line
GREEN BAY 17, Chicago 3	PACKERS by 5.5
MIAMI 30, Kansas City 10	Even
INDIANAPOLIS 9, New England 6	COLTS by 6.5
Tampa Bay 31, ATLANTA 24	FALCONS by 9.5
N.Y Jets 10, N.Y. GIANTS 6	GIANTS by 6
Dallas 23, PHILADELPHIA 10	Cowboys by 10
New Orleans 20, PHOENIX 17	Saints by 3
San Diego 30, L.A. RAIDERS 23	RAIDERS by 2.5
SAN FRANCISCO 40, L.A. Rams 17	49ERS by 13
DENVER 28, Seattle 17	BRONCOS by 9
Detroit 30, MINNESOTA 27	VIKINGS by 4
BUFFALO 24, Washington 10	BILLS by 9

Home team in CAPS

Halfway through the 18-week regular season, Pro Football Weekly selected its Midseason All-Pro team.

OFFENSE
WR Michael Irvin, Cowboys
WR Sterling Sharpe, Packers
TE Brent Jones, 49ers
OT Erik Williams, Cowboys
OT Jumbo Elliott, Giants
OG Randall McDaniel, Vikings
OG Steve Wisniewski, Raiders
C Bruce Matthews, Oilers
QB Troy Aikman, Cowboys
RB Barry Sanders, Lions
RB Barry Foster, Steelers

DEFENSE
DE Bruce Smith, Bills
DE Richard Dent, Bears
DT Cortez Kennedy, Seahawks
DT Sean Gilbert, Rams
OLB Seth Joyner, Eagles
OLB Rickey Jackson, Saints
ILB Junior Seau, Chargers
ILB Vaughan Johnson, Saints
CB Rod Woodson, Steelers
CB Mark Collins, Giants
S Henry Jones, Bills
S Dennis Smith, Broncos

SPECIAL TEAMS
PK Jason Hanson, Lions
P Greg Montgomery, Oilers
KR Eric Metcalf, Browns
ST Michael Bates, Seahawks

COACH
Dan Reeves, Giants

GAME OF THE WEEK: A toss-up. Both the Dolphins' decisive victory over the Chiefs and the Lions' come-from-behind win over the Vikings were significant. The Dolphins, with Scott Mitchell quarterbacking for the injured Dan Marino, a job the team hoped he would fill for the rest of the season, proved they could still do it by trouncing the AFC West front-running Chiefs 30-10. In a most important intradivision battle, the Lions went to Minnesota and pulled out a last-minute nail-biter 30-27 over the 1992 NFC Central champs to keep secure their division lead.

VENGEANCE: With the Bills' 24-10 trouncing of the Redskins on Monday night, they completed a round robin in the first nine weeks of the season. It gave them victories in 1993 over each of the teams that defeated them in the previous three Super Bowls. The other two: 13-10 in Week Two over Dallas, by whom they were humiliated 52-17 in Super Bowl XXVII, and 17-14 in Week Five over the Giants, who edged them 20-19 in Super Bowl XXV. Washington beat the Bills 37-24 in Super Bowl XXVI.

WINNING COACH: Miami head coach Don Shula chalked up his 324th win when the Dolphins crushed the Chiefs, tying him with Bear legend George Halas as the NFL's all-time winningest coach. Over 40 seasons, beginning with the charter year 1920, Halas amassed a record of 324-151-31 (.671). At the end of Week Nine 1993, Shula's totals were 324-152-6 (.678).

TOP PASSER: Kansas City's Joe Montana became the fourth quarterback in history to complete 3,000 passes, a mark he reached in the Chiefs'

282

1993 REVIEW ■ WEEK NINE

Emmitt Smith rushed for 237 yards, setting a Cowboy record for yards gained in a single game

otherwise doleful game with the Dolphins. The other three in that select club are Fran Tarkenton (3,686), Dan Fouts (3,297) and Dan Marino (3,219).

PFW NOTES: Packer DE Reggie White went to the head of the list in all-time sacks, his 130.5 one better than LB Lawrence Taylor's total with the Giants. With Emmitt Smith's big day rushing for Dallas, the Cowboys can claim a record of 32-1 when Smith carries the ball 20 or more times. Bear QB Jim Harbaugh gained the ignoble distinction of having been sacked 16 times in his last two games. Andre Rison's 42nd career touchdown catch for the Falcons set a club record. Ram QB Jim Everett's string of 87 starts ended when he was benched in favor of T.J. Rubley. San Diego CB Donald Frank set a Charger record by returning an interception 102 yards for a touchdown. Emmitt Smith's 237 yards rushing for the Cowboys was the sixth-highest single-game total in NFL history (Chicago's Walter Payton holds the record with 275). Jet S Ronnie Lott snagged his 62nd interception, tying him for fifth place in the NFL all-time chart. Ram PK Tony Zendejas extended his record of consecutive 50-yard-plus field goals to 11.

OFFENSIVE MVP: RB Emmitt Smith, Cowboys. Smith did it all for the Cowboys in their 23-10 win at Philadelphia. His 237 yards rushing, including a 62-yard touchdown run, was more than the Eagles gained running and passing all day. It was also a club record, eclipsing the 206 yards Tony Dorsett rushed for in 1977.

DEFENSIVE MVP: CB Aeneas Williams, Cardinals. Turning defense into offense for Phoenix, Williams contributed two touchdowns, returning a fumble recovery 20 yards for a touchdown and an interception 46 yards for another score against the Saints. He also was credited with six tackles. Despite his inspired play, the Cardinals still fell to New Orleans 20-17.

GOLDEN TOE: P Rich Camarillo, Cardinals. Another highlight on a losing day, Camarillo boomed seven punts for an average of 48.9 yards, including two that came to rest within the Saints' 20-yard line.

TOP PERFORMANCES

PASSING

Player, team	Comp.	Att.	Yds.	TD	Int.
Jeff Hostetler, Raiders	20	32	424	2	2
Scott Mitchell, Dolphins	22	33	344	3	0
Craig Erickson, Buccaneers	18	28	318	4	2
Scott Secules, Patriots	23	37	279	0	2
Bobby Hebert, Falcons	25	47	277	3	1
Rodney Peete, Lions	20	28	273	1	2

RUSHING

Player, team	Att.	Yds.	TD
Emmitt Smith, Cowboys	30	237	1
Thurman Thomas, Bills	28	129	1
Reggie Brooks, Redskins	24	117	1
Robert Smith, Vikings	23	115	1
Roosevelt Potts, Colts	23	86	0
Reggie Cobb, Buccaneers	18	75	0

RECEIVING

Player, team	Rec.	Yds.	TD
Andre Reed, Bills	7	159	1
Tim Brown, Raiders	5	156	2
Andre Rison, Falcons	11	147	2
Herman Moore, Lions	3	113	1
Ben Coates, Patriots	6	108	0
Horace Copeland, Buccaneers	2	104	2

SCORING

Player, team	TD	XP	FG	Pts.
(many)	—	—	—	12

GAME SUMMARIES

COWBOYS 23, EAGLES 10
Philadelphia, Pa., Oct. 31, 1993

Dallas	3	7	3	10	—	23
Philadelphia	0	7	0	3	—	10

Scoring:
Dallas: Murray, 35 FG
Dallas: K. Williams, 11 run (Murray kick)
Philadelphia: Walker, 3 pass from O'Brien (Bahr kick)
Dallas: Murray, 23 FG
Philadelphia: Bahr, 33 FG
Dallas: Murray, 40 FG
Dallas: E. Smith, 62 run (Murray kick)

BRONCOS 28, SEAHAWKS 17
Denver, Colo., Oct. 31, 1993

Seattle	7	0	3	7	—	17
Denver	0	21	7	0	—	28

Scoring:
Seattle: Williams, 10 run (Kasay kick)
Denver: V. Johnson, 20 pass from Elway (Elam kick)
Denver: Delpino, 2 run (Elam kick)
Denver: Sharpe, 5 pass from Elway (Elam kick)
Seattle: Kasay, 53 FG
Denver: Delpino, 1 run (Elam kick)
Seattle: Williams, 2 run (Kasay kick)

LIONS 30, VIKINGS 27
Minneapolis, Minn., Oct. 31, 1993

Detroit	7	6	0	17	—	30
Minnesota	7	10	10	0	—	27

Scoring:
Minnesota: A. Carter, 10 pass from Salisbury (Reveiz kick)
Detroit: Clay, 39 fumble return (Hanson kick)

PRO FOOTBALL WEEKLY 1994 ALMANAC

Detroit: Hanson, 34 FG
Minnesota: C. Carter, 5 pass from Salisbury (Reveiz kick)
Detroit: Hanson, 44 FG
Minnesota: Reveiz, 48 FG
Minnesota: Smith, 1 run (Reveiz kick)
Minnesota: Reveiz, 37 FG
Detroit: H. Moore, 93 pass from Peete (Hanson kick)
Detroit: Hanson, 32 FG
Detroit: D. Moore, 1 run (Hanson kick)

PACKERS 17, BEARS 3
Green Bay, Wis., Oct. 31, 1993

Chicago	0	3	0	0	—	3
Green Bay	3	7	0	7	—	17

Scoring:
Green Bay: Jacke, 40 FG
Green Bay: Sharpe, 21 pass from Favre (Jacke kick)
Chicago: Butler, 33 FG
Green Bay: Thompson, 17 run (Jacke kick)

JETS 10, GIANTS 6
East Rutherford, N.J., Oct. 31, 1993

N.Y. Jets	0	3	7	0	—	10
N.Y. Giants	3	3	0	0	—	6

Scoring:
N.Y. Giants: Treadwell, 28 FG
N.Y. Jets: Blanchard, 21 FG
N.Y. Giants: Treadwell, 23 FG
N.Y. Jets: B. Baxter, 2 run (Blanchard kick)

BUCCANEERS 31, FALCONS 24
Atlanta, Ga., Oct. 31, 1993

Tampa Bay	7	10	14	0	—	31
Atlanta	0	0	10	14	—	24

Scoring:
Tampa Bay: Workman, 42 pass from Erickson (Husted kick)
Tampa Bay: Cobb, 5 pass from Erickson (Husted kick)
Tampa Bay: Husted, 34 FG
Atlanta: Johnson, 34 FG
Tampa Bay: Copeland, 60 pass from Erickson (Husted kick)
Tampa Bay: Copeland, 44 pass from Erickson (Husted kick)
Atlanta: Rison, 53 pass from Hebert (Johnson kick)
Atlanta: Rison 9 pass from Hebert (Johnson kick)
Atlanta: Pritchard, 5 pass from Hebert (Johnson kick)

CHARGERS 30, RAIDERS 23
Los Angeles, Calif., Oct. 31, 1993

San Diego	7	3	14	6	—	30
L.A. Raiders	10	0	7	6	—	23

Scoring:
L.A. Raiders: Brown, 71 pass from Hostetler (Jaeger kick)
San Diego: A. Miller, 29 pass from Friesz (Carney kick)
L.A. Raiders: Jaeger, 38 FG
San Diego: Carney, 45 FG
L.A. Raiders: Brown, 38 pass from Hostetler (Jaeger kick)
San Diego: Butts, 12 run (Carney kick)
San Diego: Frank, 102 interception return (Carney kick)
San Diego: Carney, 36 FG
L.A. Raiders: Jaeger, 21 FG
San Diego: Carney, 38 FG
L.A. Raiders: Jaeger, 31 FG

49ERS 40, RAMS 17
San Francisco, Calif., Oct. 31, 1993

L.A. Rams	3	0	7	7	—	17
San Francisco	6	17	7	10	—	40

Scoring:
L.A. Rams: Zendejas, 50 FG
San Francisco: Watters, 1 run (Cofer kick failed)
San Francisco: Taylor, 15 pass from Young (Cofer kick)
San Francisco: Logan, 1 run (Cofer kick)
San Francisco: Cofer, 25 FG
L.A. Rams: Kinchen, 35 pass from Rubley (Zendejas kick)
San Francisco: Logan, 1 run (Cofer kick)
L.A. Rams: Bettis, 1 run (Zendejas kick)
San Francisco: Cofer, 28 FG
San Francisco: McGruder, 32 interception return (Cofer kick)

SAINTS 20, CARDINALS 17
Phoenix, Ariz., Oct. 31, 1993

New Orleans	7	0	3	10	—	20
Phoenix	10	7	0	0	—	17

Scoring:
New Orleans: Muster, 1 run (Andersen kick)
Phoenix: G. Davis, 28 FG
Phoenix: Williams, 20 fumble return (G. Davis kick)
Phoenix: Williams, 46 interception return (G. Davis kick)
New Orleans: Andersen, 48 FG
New Orleans: Early, 25 pass from Wilson (Andersen kick)
New Orleans: Andersen, 38 FG

DOLPHINS 30, CHIEFS 10
Miami, Fla., Oct. 31, 1993

Kansas City	0	3	0	7	—	10
Miami	6	7	14	3	—	30

Scoring:
Miami: Fryar, 27 pass from Mitchell (no attempt)
Miami: Byars, 8 pass from Mitchell (Stoyanovich kick)
Kansas City: Lowery, 47 FG
Miami: Ingram, 77 pass from Mitchell (Stoyanovich kick)
Miami: Kirby, 1 run (Stoyanovich kick)
Miami: Stoyanovich, 34 FG
Kansas City: Cash, 6 pass from Krieg (Lowery kick)

COLTS 9, PATRIOTS 6
Indianapolis, Ind., Oct. 31, 1993

New England	0	3	0	3	—	6
Indianapolis	3	0	0	6	—	9

Scoring:
Indianapolis: Biasucci, 27 FG
New England: Sisson, 40 FG
Indianapolis: Biasucci, 38 FG
New England: Sisson, 26 FG
Indianapolis: Biasucci, 37 FG

BILLS 24, REDSKINS 10
Orchard Park, N.Y., Monday night, Nov. 1, 1993

Washington	7	3	0	0	—	10
Buffalo	14	0	7	3	—	24

Scoring:
Buffalo: Reed, 65 pass from Kelly (Christie kick)
Washington: Brooks, 7 run (Lohmiller kick)
Buffalo: Brooks, 11 pass from Kelly (Christie kick)
Washington: Lohmiller, 19 FG
Buffalo: Thomas, 1 run (Christie kick)
Buffalo: Christie, 45 FG

1993 REVIEW ■ WEEK 10

WEEK 10

WEEK 10 STANDINGS

AMERICAN FOOTBALL CONFERENCE

AFC EAST	W	L	T	Pct.	PF	PA
Buffalo	7	1	0	.875	172	97
Miami	6	2	0	.750	182	145
N.Y. Jets	4	4	0	.500	186	141
Indianapolis	3	5	0	.375	128	179
New England	1	8	0	.111	113	200

AFC CENTRAL	W	L	T	Pct.	PF	PA
Cleveland	5	3	0	.625	163	159
Pittsburgh	5	3	0	.625	192	136
Houston	4	4	0	.500	168	154
Cincinnati	0	8	0	.000	97	186

AFC WEST	W	L	T	Pct.	PF	PA
Kansas City	6	2	0	.750	133	124
Denver	5	3	0	.625	206	149
L.A. Raiders	5	3	0	.625	152	147
San Diego	4	4	0	.500	144	167
Seattle	4	5	0	.444	143	164

NATIONAL FOOTBALL CONFERENCE

NFC EAST	W	L	T	Pct.	PF	PA
Dallas	6	2	0	.750	186	111
N.Y. Giants	5	3	0	.625	160	112
Philadelphia	4	4	0	.500	141	172
Phoenix	3	6	0	.333	168	156
Washington	2	6	0	.250	139	209

NFC CENTRAL	W	L	T	Pct.	PF	PA
Detroit	7	2	0	.778	187	140
Minnesota	4	4	0	.500	129	154
Green Bay	4	4	0	.500	180	144
Chicago	3	5	0	.375	126	111
Tampa Bay	2	6	0	.250	99	206

NFC WEST	W	L	T	Pct.	PF	PA
New Orleans	6	2	0	.750	183	154
San Francisco	5	3	0	.625	210	158
Atlanta	2	6	0	.250	171	222
L.A. Rams	2	6	0	.250	131	192

WEEK 10 RESULTS / LINE

L.A. Raiders 16, CHICAGO 14 — Raiders by 2.5
Buffalo 13, NEW ENGLAND 10 (OT) — Bills by 10
Denver 29, CLEVELAND 16 — BROWNS by 2.5
DALLAS 32, N.Y. Giants 9 — COWBOYS by 10.5
Pittsburgh 24, CINCINNATI 16 — Steelers by 9.5
San Diego 30, MINNESOTA 17 — VIKINGS by 3.5
HOUSTON 24, Seattle 14 — OILERS by 9.5
DETROIT 23, Tampa Bay 0 — LIONS by 12.5
N.Y. JETS 27, Miami 10 — Dolphins by 1.5
PHOENIX 16, Philadelphia 3 — CARDINALS by 2.5
WASHINGTON 30, Indianapolis 24 — REDSKINS by 6.5
KANSAS CITY 23, Green Bay 16 — CHIEFS by 3

Home team in CAPS

As the season moved into its latter half, it appeared the two teams to beat remained the same two that showed up at the Super Bowl a little more than nine months earlier, Dallas and Buffalo.

The 6-2 Cowboys were coming on like true rangebusters, winning six straight since RB Emmitt Smith rejoined the team and now claiming sole rights to the lead in the NFC East with their impressive 31-9 victory over the Giants.

The Bills did not have nearly as easy a day, but they prevailed 13-10 over the Patriots in overtime to preserve the best record in the NFL, 7-1.

Through Week 10 Dallas QB Troy Aikman headed the list of NFL passers with a rating of 100.8, and Boomer Esiason of the Jets was second at 97.1. Detroit RB Barry Sanders led in rushing, the only player approaching the 1,000-yard mark, with 977 yards, while the Bills' Thurman Thomas, with 806 yards, was the only other rusher to have gained more than 800. Leading receivers in terms of yardage gained were Cowboy Michael Irvin with 822 and 49er Jerry Rice with 648, but Packer Sterling Sharpe's 57 receptions were the most in the league. Far and away the top scorer was Lion PK Jason Hanson with 91 points on 25-of-30 field goals and a perfect 16-of-16 extra points.

GAME OF THE WEEK: It was not close, but it sent out a message as to who was rightfully in first place in the NFC East. Both the Giants and the Cowboys were 5-2 going into the confrontation in Irving, Texas, but Dallas came away with an impressive 31-9 triumph. Emmitt Smith rushed for 117 yards and two touchdowns and Troy Aikman threw a pair of touchdown passes, while the Dallas defense limited the New Yorkers to three field goals.

ULTIMATE SACK: Cleveland QB Bernie Kosar was sacked six times in the Browns' 29-16 loss to Denver. After the game, his own team delivered the ultimate sack when the nine-year veteran was abruptly released. Kosar joined the Browns in 1985 and threw for 21,904 yards and 116 touchdowns and made four playoff appearances as the Cleveland starter before management sacked him.

SACKS II and III: A Bear folk legend, 300-pound-plus DT William "Refrigerator" Perry was also given his walking papers after nine years in Chicago. And Sean Landeta, who had handled the punting chores for the Giants during the last nine years, was also cut despite his 42.1-yard average at the time.

BAD FEET: In a year when kickers had been routinely winning games with their educated feet, the reverse took hold in Week 10: Bear Kevin Butler missed two chip-shot field goals in the fourth quarter, either of which would have given Chicago a win over the Raiders; and New England's Scott Sisson missed a 28-yarder in regulation time that would have given the Patriots an upset victory over the Bills. The Bills' Steve Christie flubbed a 40-yarder in regulation time, too, but he redeemed himself with a 32-yarder in overtime.

PFW NOTES: Legendary Cowboy coach Tom Landry (270 total victories, third-most in NFL history, 1966-88) was added to the Ring of Honor at Texas Stadium in a special halftime ceremony. Bronco QB John Elway threw his 15th touchdown pass of 1993, only seven away from his season high of 22 in 1985. Minnesota's Steve Jordan became only the fourth tight end in NFL history to surpass 6,000 yards receiving. Jet LB Kurt Barber was a marvel on special teams, credited with four tackles on kickoff returns in the Jets' upset win over the Dolphins. The Bengals became the first team to rush for 100 yards against the Steelers thus far in the season. Redskin WR Art Monk extended his consecutive-game receiving streak to 156, second only to former Seahawk Steve Largent's 177 in NFL annals. Oiler PK Al Del Greco set a club record with his 76th consecutive extra point but then missed on his next attempt. The Lions allowed only two rushing touchdowns in their first nine games of the season, and the Cowboy defense has gone seven games without allowing a fourth-quarter touchdown.

OFFENSIVE MVP: QB John Elway, Broncos. Elway was the picture of offense efficiency in Week 10, guiding Denver to an important and decisive 29-14 victory over Cleveland. He completed 17-of-23 passes, three for touchdowns with no interceptions, and thus became the first quarterback to surpass 2,000 yards passing during the 1993 season.

DEFENSIVE MVP: DT Dan Saleaumua, Chiefs. On a Monday night, Saleaumua scooped up a fumble and ran it 16 yards for a touchdown in the third quarter to give the Chiefs a lead over the Packers they would not relinquish. He also forced a Packer fumble on the Kansas City three-yard line in the fourth quarter to save a score and was credited with six tackles in the Chiefs' 23-16 win over Green Bay.

GOLDEN TOE: P Dan Stryzinski, Buccaneers. Tampa Bay, with little to crow about thus far in the 1993 season, lost to the Lions 23-0, but Stryzinski put on an impressive show, averaging 44.8 yards on eight punts, four of which ended up inside the Lions' 20-yard line.

TOP PERFORMANCES

PASSING

Player, team	Comp.	Att.	Yds.	TD	Int.
Jeff George, Colts	37	59	376	3	1
Warren Moon, Oilers	36	55	369	2	2
Sean Salisbury, Vikings	29	47	347	1	1
Jim Kelly, Bills	29	46	317	1	0
Scott Mitchell, Dolphins	23	44	297	1	1
John Friesz, Chargers	20	32	268	2	0

RUSHING

Player, team	Att.	Yds.	TD
Barry Sanders, Lions	29	187	0
Ron Moore, Cardinals	36	160	0
Barry Foster, Steelers	25	120	1
Emmitt Smith, Cowboys	24	117	2
Thurman Thomas, Bills	30	111	0
Natrone Means, Chargers	17	105	1

RECEIVING

Player, team	Rec.	Yds.	TD
Reggie Langhorne, Colts	12	203	1
Anthony Carter, Vikings	10	164	1
Anthony Miller, Chargers	7	142	1
Webster Slaughter, Oilers	9	135	1
Irving Fryar, Dolphins	7	111	1
Eric Green, Steelers	3	91	1

SCORING

Player, team	TD	XP	FG	Pts.
(many)	—	—	—	12

GAME SUMMARIES

BRONCOS 29, BROWNS 14

Cleveland, Ohio, Nov. 7, 1993

Denver	0	16	7	6	—	29
Cleveland	0	0	7	7	—	14

Scoring:
Denver: Milburn, 2 pass from Elway (Elam kick)
Denver: Safety, Rivers blocked punt out of endzone
Denver: Russell, 38 pass from Elway (Elam kick)
Cleveland: Jackson, 8 pass from Kosar (Stover kick)
Denver: Sharpe, 33 pass from Elway (Elam kick)
Denver: Elam, 22 FG
Denver: Elam, 38 FG
Cleveland: Jackson, 38 pass from Kosar (Stover kick)

BILLS 13, PATRIOTS 10 (OT)

Foxboro, Mass., Nov. 7, 1993

Buffalo	0	0	0	10	3	—	13
New England	0	0	7	3	0	—	10

Scoring:
New England: Russell, 2 run (Sisson kick)
New England: Sisson, 27 FG
Buffalo: Metzelaars, 9 pass from Kelly (Christie kick)
Buffalo: Christie, 27 FG
Buffalo: Christie, 32 FG

CHARGERS 30, VIKINGS 17

Minneapolis, Minn., Nov. 7, 1993

San Diego	7	3	6	14	—	30
Minnesota	0	3	14	0	—	17

Scoring:
San Diego: Butts, 3 run (Carney kick)
San Diego: Carney, 36 FG
Minnesota: Reveiz, 20 FG
San Diego: A. Miller, 66 pass from Friesz (Carney kick failed)
Minnesota: A. Carter, 9 pass from Salisbury (Reveiz kick)
Minnesota: Word, 1 run (Reveiz kick)
San Diego: Means, 7 run (Carney kick)
San Diego: Jefferson, 18 pass from Friesz (Carney kick)

REDSKINS 30, COLTS 24

Washington, D.C., Nov. 7, 1993

Indianapolis	0	10	0	14	—	24
Washington	0	14	6	10	—	30

Scoring:
Washington: Green, 78 fumble return (Lohmiller kick)
Washington: Rypien, 1 run (Lohmiller kick)
Indianapolis: Langhorne, 72 pass from George (Biasucci kick)
Indianapolis: Biasucci, 22 FG
Washington: Rypien, 1 run (Lohmiller kick failed)
Washington: Lohmiller, 24 FG
Washington: Mitchell, 1 run (Lohmiller kick)
Indianapolis: Cash, 9 pass from George (Biasucci kick)
Indianapolis: Verdin, 1 pass from George (Biasucci kick)

1993 REVIEW ■ WEEK 10

CARDINALS 16, EAGLES 3
Phoenix, Ariz., Nov. 7, 1993

Philadelphia	3	0	0	0	—	3
Phoenix	3	13	0	0	—	16

Scoring:
- Philadelphia: Bahr, 27 FG
- Phoenix: G. Davis, 23 FG
- Phoenix: G. Davis, 20 FG
- Phoenix: Clark, 10 pass from Chandler (G. Davis kick)
- Phoenix: G. Davis, 29 FG

RAIDERS 16, BEARS 14
Chicago, Ill., Nov. 7, 1993

L.A. Raiders	3	10	0	3	—	16
Chicago	0	0	7	7	—	14

Scoring:
- L.A. Raiders: Jaeger, 31 FG
- L.A. Raiders: McCallum, 1 run (Jaeger kick)
- L.A. Raiders: Jaeger, 21 FG
- Chicago: Anderson, 3 run (Butler kick)
- L.A. Raiders: Jaeger, 20 FG
- Chicago: Obee, 13 pass from Harbaugh (Butler kick)

COWBOYS 31, GIANTS 9
Irving, Texas, Nov. 7, 1993

N.Y. Giants	0	6	0	3	—	9
Dallas	10	7	0	14	—	31

Scoring:
- Dallas: Murray, 34 FG
- Dallas: Harper, 28 pass from Aikman (Murray kick)
- N.Y. Giants: Treadwell, 21 FG
- Dallas: Harper, 50 pass from Aikman (Murray kick)
- N.Y. Giants: Treadwell, 45 FG
- Dallas: E. Smith, 1 run (Murray kick)
- Dallas: E. Smith, 2 run (Murray kick)
- N.Y. Giants: Treadwell, 29 FG

JETS 27, DOLPHINS 10
East Rutherford, N.J., Nov. 7, 1993

Miami	0	3	7	0	—	10
N.Y. Jets	10	7	3	7	—	27

Scoring:
- N.Y. Jets: Mitchell, 17 pass from Esiason (Blanchard kick)
- N.Y. Jets: Blanchard, 37 FG
- Miami: Stoyanovich, 48 FG
- N.Y. Jets: Mitchell, 2 pass from Esiason (Blanchard kick)
- N.Y. Jets: Blanchard, 43 FG
- Miami: Fryar, 65 pass from Mitchell (Stoyanovich kick)
- N.Y. Jets: Burkett, 12 pass from Esiason (Blanchard kick)

OILERS 24, SEAHAWKS 14
Houston, Texas, Nov. 7, 1993

Seattle	7	0	0	7	—	14
Houston	13	9	2	0	—	24

Scoring:
- Houston: Slaughter, 3 pass from Moon (Del Greco kick)
- Seattle: Martin, 53 pass from Mirer (Kasay kick)
- Houston: Givins, 14 pass from Moon (Del Greco kick failed)
- Houston: Del Greco, 33 FG
- Houston: Del Greco, 51 FG
- Houston: Del Greco, 39 FG
- Houston: Safety, Lathon sacked Mirer in endzone
- Seattle: C. Warren, 10 run (Kasay kick)

STEELERS 24, BENGALS 16
Cincinnati, Ohio, Nov. 7, 1993

Pittsburgh	0	14	0	10	—	24
Cincinnati	3	13	0	0	—	16

Scoring:
- Cincinnati: Pelfrey, 32 FG
- Cincinnati: D. Williams, 97 interception return (Pelfrey kick failed)
- Cincinnati: Query, 7 pass from Schroeder (Pelfrey kick)
- Pittsburgh: Green, 71 pass from O'Donnell (Anderson kick)
- Pittsburgh: Hoge, 9 pass from O'Donnell (Anderson kick)
- Pittsburgh: Foster, 1 run (Anderson kick)
- Pittsburgh: Anderson, 23 FG

LIONS 23, BUCCANEERS 0
Pontiac, Mich., Nov. 7, 1993

Tampa Bay	0	0	0	0	—	0
Detroit	3	3	7	10	—	23

Scoring:
- Detroit: Hanson, 29 FG
- Detroit: Hanson, 49 FG
- Detroit: Peete, 9 run (Hanson kick)
- Detroit: D. Moore, 1 run (Hanson kick)
- Detroit: Hanson, 37 FG

CHIEFS 23, PACKERS 16
Kansas City, Mo., Monday night, Nov. 8, 1993

Green Bay	3	6	0	7	—	16
Kansas City	3	0	10	10	—	23

Scoring:
- Kansas City: Lowery, 23 FG
- Green Bay: Jacke, 23 FG
- Green Bay: Jacke, 51 FG
- Green Bay: Jacke, 19 FG
- Kansas City: Saleaumua, 16 fumble return (Lowery kick)
- Kansas City: Lowery, 34 FG
- Kansas City: Allen, 1 run (Lowery kick)
- Green Bay: J. Harris, 35 pass from Favre (Jacke kick)
- Kansas City: Lowery, 40 FG

PRO FOOTBALL WEEKLY 1994 ALMANAC

REVIEW: WEEK 11

WEEK 11 STANDINGS

AMERICAN FOOTBALL CONFERENCE

AFC EAST	W	L	T	Pct.	PF	PA
Buffalo	7	2	0	.778	172	120
Miami	7	2	0	.778	201	159
N.Y. Jets	5	4	0	.556	217	158
Indianapolis	3	6	0	.333	145	210
New England	1	8	0	.111	113	200

AFC CENTRAL	W	L	T	Pct.	PF	PA
Pittsburgh	6	3	0	.667	215	136
Cleveland	5	4	0	.556	168	181
Houston	5	4	0	.556	206	157
Cincinnati	0	9	0	.000	100	224

AFC WEST	W	L	T	Pct.	PF	PA
Kansas City	7	2	0	.778	164	144
Denver	5	4	0	.556	229	175
L.A. Raiders	5	4	0	.556	172	178
Seattle	5	5	0	.500	165	169
San Diego	4	5	0	.444	157	183

NATIONAL FOOTBALL CONFERENCE

NFC EAST	W	L	T	Pct.	PF	PA
Dallas	7	2	0	.778	206	126
N.Y. Giants	6	3	0	.667	180	118
Philadelphia	4	5	0	.444	155	191
Phoenix	3	7	0	.300	183	176
Washington	2	7	0	.222	145	229

NFC CENTRAL	W	L	T	Pct.	PF	PA
Detroit	7	2	0	.778	187	140
Green Bay	5	4	0	.556	199	161
Minnesota	5	4	0	.556	155	177
Chicago	4	5	0	.444	142	124
Tampa Bay	2	7	0	.222	120	251

NFC WEST	W	L	T	Pct.	PF	PA
New Orleans	6	3	0	.667	200	173
San Francisco	6	3	0	.667	255	179
Atlanta	3	6	0	.333	184	222
L.A. Rams	2	7	0	.222	131	205

WEEK 11 RESULTS

Result	Line
Green Bay 19, NEW ORLEANS 17	SAINTS by 6.5
Houston 38, CINCINNATI 3	Oilers by 8.5
San Francisco 45, TAMPA BAY 21	49ers by 16.5
Miami 19, PHILADELPHIA 14	Dolphins by 4.5
N.Y. GIANTS 20, Washington 6	GIANTS by 8
DALLAS 20, Phoenix 15	COWBOYS by 13
Kansas City 31, L.A. RAIDERS 20	RAIDERS by 4
Atlanta 13, L.A. RAMS 0	RAMS by 4
SEATTLE 22, Cleveland 5	SEAHAWKS by 4
Minnesota 26, DENVER 23	BRONCOS by 6.5
N.Y. Jets 31, INDIANAPOLIS 17	Jets by 3.5
Chicago 16, SAN DIEGO 13	CHARGERS by 9
PITTSBURGH 23, Buffalo 0	STEELERS by 3.5

Home team in CAPS

This was the week when the sometimes overlooked and often underrated NFC Central asserted itself. The .500 Vikings rose up in Mile High Stadium in Denver and bumped the Broncos 26-23, and the .500 Packers surprised the leader in the always-feared NFC West, the Saints, by upsetting them 19-17. And the Bears, who had won only three of their eight games thus far, went out to San Diego and stiffed the favored Chargers 16-13. The 7-2 Lions, the unquestioned leader at this point in the NFC Central, rested with an open date.

Buffalo no longer sported the NFL's best record, having been put in its place by the Steelers, and now had to share that honor with four other 7-2 teams: Miami, Kansas City, Detroit and Dallas.

At the other end of the standings, Cincinnati reached a franchise low by dropping its ninth consecutive game and remained the only winless team in the NFL. New England, with a bye week, held steady at 1-8, the second-worst record.

With the week's wrap-up, 17 of the 28 teams had records of .500 or better, and no team, except perhaps the Cowboys, who had extended their winning streak to seven, seemed to be dominant in its division.

GAME OF THE WEEK: Monday night under the lights at Three Rivers Stadium in Pittsburgh. The Bills arrived, basking in the glow of having beaten the Steelers in their last five encounters. They left in the darkness of a 23-0 drubbing. For Pittsburgh, QB Neil O'Donnell was 16-of-27 for 212 yards and one touchdown, and Leroy Thompson gained 108 yards rushing and scored another TD. The result: The Bills now had to share the lead in the AFC East, and the Steelers gained sole possession of the lead in the AFC Central.

TOP COACH: Miami's Don Shula did it with a certain panache, winning his 325th NFL game to surpass the long-held head-coaching record of George Halas. Shula did it with a third-string quarterback, Doug Pederson, coming on in the second half for injured Scott Mitchell, who had been playing for sidelined Dan Marino. And Shula had to overcome a 14-13 halftime deficit to post the 19-14, record-breaking victory over the Eagles.

COWBOY KOSAR: Cut earlier in the week by the Browns, who felt his skills had "diminished," QB Bernie Kosar filled in ably for the injured Troy Aikman, leading the Cowboys on three scoring drives and completing 13-of-21 passes for 199 yards as Dallas defeated Phoenix 20-15. Meanwhile, the Kosar-less Browns lost to Seattle 22-5.

SACK MAN: Green Bay's famous free agent of '93, DE Reggie White, added two sacks to bring his career total to 133.5, the all-time NFL high. White, who has now played in 130 NFL games, is the only player to be able to claim more sacks than games played.

1993 REVIEW ■ WEEK 11

PFW NOTES: San Francisco WR Jerry Rice became the sixth player to pass the 11,000-yard mark in receptions and extended his career 100-yard receiving games to 41 (the NFL record of 50 is held by Don Maynard). Philadelphia's Vai Sikahema joined Rick Upchurch and Billy "White Shoes" Johnson as the only players in NFL history to have gained 3,000 yards on punt returns. For Dallas, Bernie Kosar's 86-yard pass play to Emmitt Smith was the second-longest of Kosar's career and the longest of Smith's, as well as the fifth-longest in Cowboy history. Viking Sean Salisbury, former backup to Jim McMahon, became the first Minnesota quarterback to post back-to-back 300-yard passing games since Tommy Kramer in 1985. Kansas City QB Dave Krieg became the 17th NFL quarterback to surpass the 30,000-yard mark in passing; he is also 10th on the all-time TD-pass list with 215. One safety in a game is a rarity, but there were two in the Cleveland at Seattle battle: Cleveland sacked Rick Mirer in the endzone in the first quarter, and Seattle tackled Todd Philcox in the endzone in the final period.

OFFENSIVE MVP: WR Jerry Rice, 49ers. Rice, a Pro Bowler in each of the last seven years, was a one-man wrecking crew in the 49ers' 45-21 demolition of the Buccaneers. He caught four touchdown passes and gained 172 yards on eight catches.

DEFENSIVE MVP: S Eugene Robinson, Seahawks. With Seattle minus several starting defensive players, Robinson picked up the slack and led the Seahawks to a 22-5 win over the Browns. Robinson was credited with two interceptions, one forced fumble, a fumble recovery and 10 tackles.

GOLDEN TOE: PK Chris Jacke, Packers. Jacke was an instrumental factor in Green Bay's 19-17 upset of the Saints. He booted 4-of-4 field goals, the last a 36-yarder to win the game with three seconds left.

TOP PERFORMANCES

PASSING
Player, team	Comp.	Att.	Yds.	TD	Int.
Sean Salisbury, Vikings	19	37	366	2	1
Steve Young, 49ers	23	29	311	4	0
John Elway, Broncos	30	40	290	2	1
Boomer Esiason, Jets	21	31	256	2	1
Craig Erickson, Buccaneers	17	27	239	2	1
Mark Rypien, Redskins	22	49	239	0	1

RUSHING
Player, team	Att.	Yds.	TD
Gary Brown, Oilers	26	166	1
Johnny Johnson, Jets	21	141	1
Erric Pegram, Falcons	27	128	0
Chris Warren, Seahawks	24	112	0
Leroy Thompson, Steelers	30	108	1
Derek Brown, Saints	21	106	0

RECEIVING
Player, team	Rec.	Yds.	TD
Jerry Rice, 49ers	8	172	4
Cris Carter, Vikings	6	134	1
Andre Rison, Falcons	5	120	1
Willie Davis, Chiefs	5	115	1
Reggie Langhorne, Colts	8	112	0
Anthony Carter, Vikings	4	111	0

SCORING
Player, team	TD	XP	FG	Pts.
Jerry Rice, 49ers	4	—	—	24
Haywood Jeffires, Oilers	3	—	—	18
Fuad Reveiz, Vikings	—	2/2	4/4	14

GAME SUMMARIES

DOLPHINS 19, EAGLES 14
Philadelphia, Pa., Nov. 14, 1993

Miami	6	7	3	3	— 19
Philadelphia	0	14	0	0	— 14

Scoring:
  Miami: Kirby, 8 pass from Mitchell (no kick attempted)
  Philadelphia: Williams, 11 pass from O'Brien (Bahr kick)
  Miami: Higgs, 1 run (Stoyanovich kick)
  Philadelphia: Williams, 8 pass from O'Brien (Bahr kick)
  Miami: Stoyanovich, 46 FG
  Miami: Stoyanovich, 45 FG

PACKERS 19, SAINTS 17
New Orleans, La., Nov. 14, 1993

Green Bay	3	7	3	6	— 19
New Orleans	0	14	0	3	— 17

Scoring:
  Green Bay: Jacke, 38 FG
  New Orleans: Early, 24 pass from Wilson (Andersen kick)
  Green Bay: J. Harris, 1 pass from Favre (Jacke kick)
  New Orleans: Dowdell, 11 pass from Wilson (Andersen kick)
  Green Bay: Jacke, 20 FG
  Green Bay: Jacke, 44 FG
  New Orleans: Andersen, 27 FG
  Green Bay: Jacke, 36 FG

49ERS 45, BUCCANEERS 21
Tampa, Fla., Nov. 14, 1993

San Francisco	10	21	7	7	— 45
Tampa Bay	0	14	7	0	— 21

Scoring:
  San Francisco: Rice, 12 pass from Young (Cofer kick)
  San Francisco: Cofer, 44 FG
  San Francisco: Tamm, 1 fumble recovery (Cofer kick)
  Tampa Bay: G. Anderson, 14 pass from Erickson (Husted kick)
  Tampa Bay: Workman, 18 pass from Erickson (Husted kick)
  San Francisco: Rice, 51 pass from Young (Cofer kick)
  San Francisco: Rice, 9 pass from Young (Cofer kick)
  Tampa Bay: Workman, 3 run (Husted kick)
  San Francisco: Rice, 26 pass from Young (Cofer kick)
  San Francisco: Watters, 1 run (Cofer kick)

FALCONS 13, RAMS 0
Anaheim, Calif., Nov. 14, 1993

Atlanta	3	3	7	0	— 13
L.A. Rams	0	0	0	0	— 0

Scoring:
  Atlanta: Johnson, 46 FG
  Atlanta: Johnson, 44 FG
  Atlanta: Rison, 31 pass from Hebert (Johnson kick)

OILERS 38, BENGALS 3
Cincinnati, Ohio, Nov. 3, 1993

Houston	7	21	10	0	— 38
Cincinnati	0	0	3	0	— 3

Scoring:
  Houston: Duncan, 3 pass from Moon (Del Greco kick)
  Houston: Brown, 4 run (Del Greco kick)
  Houston: Jeffires, 21 pass from Moon (Del Greco kick)

PRO FOOTBALL WEEKLY 1994 ALMANAC

Houston: Jeffires, 6 pass from Moon (Del Greco kick)
Houston: Jeffires, 12 pass from Moon (Del Greco kick)
Houston: Del Greco, 39 FG
Cincinnati: Pelfrey, 46 FG

JETS 31, COLTS 17
Indianapolis, Ind., Nov. 14, 1993

N.Y. Jets	7	10	7	7	— 31
Indianapolis	3	7	7	0	— 17

Scoring:
Indianapolis: Biasucci, 41 FG
N.Y. Jets: B. Baxter, 1 run (Blanchard kick)
N.Y. Jets: Burkett, 15 pass from Esiason (Blanchard kick)
Indianapolis: Cash, 3 pass from George (Biasucci kick)
N.Y. Jets: Blanchard, 22 FG
N.Y. Jets: Burkett, 4 pass from Esiason (Blanchard kick)
Indianapolis: Culver, 1 run (Biasucci kick)
N.Y. Jets: J. Johnson, 57 run (Blanchard kick)

VIKINGS 26, BRONCOS 23
Denver, Colo., Nov. 14, 1993

Minnesota	3	14	3	6	— 26
Denver	6	14	0	3	— 23

Scoring:
Denver: Russell, 4 pass from Elway (Elam kick blocked)
Minnesota: Reveiz, 25 FG
Denver: Delpino, 3 run (Elam kick)
Denver: V. Johnson, 15 pass from Elway (Elam kick)
Minnesota: C. Carter, 9 pass from Salisbury (Reveiz kick)
Minnesota: Craig, 17 pass from Salisbury (Reveiz kick)
Minnesota: Reveiz, 19 FG
Minnesota: Reveiz, 35 FG
Denver: Elam, 53 FG
Minnesota: Reveiz, 43 FG

SEAHAWKS 22, BROWNS 5
Seattle, Wash., Nov. 14, 1993

Cleveland	2	3	0	0	— 5
Seattle	7	0	7	8	— 22

Scoring:
Seattle: Blackmon, 5 fumble return (Kasay kick)
Cleveland: Safety, Pleasant sacked Mirer in endzone
Cleveland: Stover, 25 FG
Seattle: Williams, 23 pass from Mirer (Kasay kick)
Seattle: Kasay, 42 FG
Seattle: Kasay, 47 FG
Seattle: Safety, Edwards sacked Philcox in endzone

BEARS 16, CHARGERS 13
San Diego, Calif., Nov. 14, 1993

Chicago	0	6	10	0	— 16
San Diego	3	7	0	3	— 13

Scoring:
San Diego: Carney, 28 FG
San Diego: Kidd, 2 run (Carney kick)
Chicago: Butler, 33 FG
Chicago: Butler, 54 FG

Chicago: Butler, 20 FG
Chicago: Conway, 38 pass from Harbaugh (Butler kick)
San Diego: Carney, 26 FG

CHIEFS 31, RAIDERS 20
Los Angeles, Calif., Nov. 14, 1993

Kansas City	0	7	14	10	— 31
L.A. Raiders	7	10	0	3	— 20

Scoring:
L.A. Raiders: McCallum, 4 run (Jaeger kick)
L.A. Raiders: Horton, 8 pass from Hostetler (Jaeger kick)
Kansas City: Anders, 15 pass from Krieg (Lowery kick)
L.A. Raiders: Jaeger, 35 FG
Kansas City: Allen, 4 run (Lowery kick)
Kansas City: Davis, 66 pass from Krieg (Lowery kick)
L.A. Raiders: Jaeger, 30 FG
Kansas City: Lowery, 29 FG
Kansas City: Cash, 4 pass from Krieg (Lowery kick)

COWBOYS 20, CARDINALS 15
Irving, Texas, Nov. 14, 1993

Phoenix	0	0	10	5	— 15
Dallas	3	14	0	3	— 20

Scoring:
Dallas: Murray, 44 FG
Dallas: E. Smith, 4 run (Murray kick)
Dallas: Novacek, 1 pass from Kosar (Murray kick)
Phoenix: G. Davis, 19 FG
Phoenix: Centers, 17 pass from Chandler (G. Davis kick)
Dallas: Murray, 43 FG
Phoenix: Safety, Oldham tackled Kosar in endzone
Phoenix: G. Davis, 47 FG

GIANTS 20, REDSKINS 6
East Rutherford, N.J., Nov. 14, 1993

Washington	0	0	3	3	— 6
N.Y. Giants	7	7	3	3	— 20

Scoring
N.Y. Giants: Hampton, 1 run (Treadwell kick)
N.Y. Giants: Calloway, 21 pass from Meggett (Treadwell kick)
N.Y. Giants: Treadwell, 43 FG
Washington: Lohmiller, 27 FG
N.Y. Giants: Treadwell, 39 FG
Washington: Lohmiller, 33 FG

STEELERS 23, BILLS 0
Pittsburgh, Pa., Monday night, Nov. 15, 1993

Buffalo	0	0	0	0	— 0
Pittsburgh	7	3	10	3	— 23

Scoring:
Pittsburgh: Thompson, 2 run (Anderson kick)
Pittsburgh: Anderson, 37 FG
Pittsburgh: Green, 1 pass from O'Donnell (Anderson kick)
Pittsburgh: Anderson, 19 FG
Pittsburgh: Anderson, 31 FG

1993 REVIEW ■ WEEK 12

WEEK 12

WEEK 12 STANDINGS

AMERICAN FOOTBALL CONFERENCE

AFC EAST	W	L	T	Pct.	PF	PA
Buffalo	8	2	0	.800	195	129
Miami	8	2	0	.800	218	172
N.Y. Jets	6	4	0	.600	234	170
Indianapolis	3	7	0	.300	154	233
New England	1	9	0	.100	126	217

AFC CENTRAL	W	L	T	Pct.	PF	PA
Houston	6	4	0	.600	233	177
Pittsburgh	6	4	0	.600	228	173
Cleveland	5	5	0	.500	188	208
Cincinnati	0	10	0	.000	112	241

AFC WEST	W	L	T	Pct.	PF	PA
Kansas City	7	3	0	.700	181	163
Denver	6	4	0	.600	266	188
L.A. Raiders	6	4	0	.600	184	185
Seattle	5	5	0	.500	165	169
San Diego	4	6	0	.400	164	195

NATIONAL FOOTBALL CONFERENCE

NFC EAST	W	L	T	Pct.	PF	PA
Dallas	7	3	0	.700	220	153
N.Y. Giants	7	3	0	.700	187	121
Philadelphia	4	6	0	.400	158	198
Phoenix	3	7	0	.300	183	176
Washington	2	8	0	.200	151	239

NFC CENTRAL	W	L	T	Pct.	PF	PA
Detroit	7	3	0	.700	204	166
Green Bay	6	4	0	.600	225	178
Chicago	5	5	0	.500	161	141
Minnesota	5	5	0	.500	165	200
Tampa Bay	3	7	0	.300	143	261

NFC WEST	W	L	T	Pct.	PF	PA
San Francisco	7	3	0	.700	297	186
New Orleans	6	4	0	.600	207	215
Atlanta	4	6	0	.400	211	236
L.A. Rams	3	7	0	.300	141	211

WEEK 12 RESULTS | **LINE**
Chicago 19, KANSAS CITY 17 | CHIEFS by 10
N.Y. JETS 17, Cincinnati 12 | JETS by 16.5
ATLANTA 27, Dallas 14 | Cowboys by 9.5
GREEN BAY 26, Detroit 17 | PACKERS by 3.5
Houston 27, CLEVELAND 20 | Oilers by 5.5
BUFFALO 23, Indianapolis 9 | BILLS by 13
MIAMI 17, New England 13 | DOLPHINS by 8

N.Y. Giants 7, PHILADELPHIA 3 — Giants by 5
L.A. Raiders 12, SAN DIEGO 7 — CHARGERS by 3.5
DENVER 37, Pittsburgh 13 — BRONCOS by 3
L.A. RAMS 10, Washington 6 — RAMS by 2
TAMPA BAY 23, Minnesota 10 — Vikings by 8
SAN FRANCISCO 42, New Orleans 7 — 49ERS by 9
Home team in CAPS

This was not the week for division leaders. Five of them lost, and two won. One had to win in the NFC West because San Francisco and New Orleans were sharing the lead going into their game Monday night; the 49ers took the honors. Buffalo won, too, defeating the Colts. But the Chiefs were surprised by the Bears in Kansas City, Dallas was stunned by the Falcons, Pittsburgh was whipped by the Broncos, and Detroit fell to intradivisional challenger Green Bay. The result: All six divisional races tightened up considerably.

With 12 of the 18 weeks of the regular season over, the following stood out as the most spectacular plays:

Longest run from scrimmage: Reggie Brooks, Redskins, 85 yards.

Longest pass play: Bobby Hebert to Michael Haynes, Falcons, 98 yards.

Longest field goal: Steve Christie, Bills, 59 yards.

Longest interception return: Darryl Williams, Bengals, 97 yards.

Longest kickoff return: Tony Smith, Falcons, 97 yards.

Longest punt return: Eric Metcalf, Browns, 91 yards.

Longest punt: Greg Montgomery, Oilers, 77 yards.

GAME OF THE WEEK: There were two of significance. Dallas illustrated again it couldn't win without RB Emmitt Smith — the Cowboys lost their first two without him, won seven straight with him, then lost this week to Atlanta when he was injured before the end of the first half. San Francisco showed football fans it was for real, exploding ahead of the Saints to gain sole possession of the lead in the NFC West with a 42-7 victory.

OFF THE BENCH: Third-year RB Gary Brown of Houston, subbing for injured Lorenzo White, rushed for 194 yards, the best of the week. The previous week he gained 166 rushing. The 360 yards he gained in those two games were more than he rushed for in his first two years with the Oilers.

AGE AND EXPERIENCE: Steve DeBerg, the oldest starter in the NFL at age 39, was picked up two weeks earlier by the Dolphins as a free agent, the fifth team he has quarterbacked since his pro career began in 1978. Starting in place of the injured Dan Marino and Scott Mitchell, the grizzled veteran threw two touchdown passes in the fourth quarter to give Miami a 17-13, come-from-behind win over New England. DeBerg was 16-of-27 for 252 yards for the day.

TOP SOUTHPAW: Boomer Esiason of the Jets, who had played the previous nine seasons for Cincinnati, became the NFL's career-leading left-handed quarterback when he extended his passing yardage to 28,130, slipping ahead of Ken Stabler.

PRO FOOTBALL WEEKLY 1994 ALMANAC

PFW NOTES: Chief RB Marcus Allen became the 10th player in NFL history to surpass 9,000 yards rushing, and his two touchdowns brought his career total to 107, fifth on the all-time list. Detroit RB Barry Sanders became the third rusher in NFL history to gain 1,000 yards in each of his first five seasons (the others are Tony Dorsett and Eric Dickerson). The 49ers earned the distinction of having scored more than 40 points in each of their last three games. The Jets won their fourth in a row for the first time since 1986. The Eagles lost their sixth game in a row, the worst streak since they had lost seven straight in 1983. The Saints, who had three passes intercepted in the first half, staved off their first shutout since 1983 when they scored with just under two minutes left in a 42-7 rout at the hands of the 49ers. The extra point also enabled PK Morten Andersen to extend his scoring streak to 152 games. Ram PK Tony Zendejas missed a 50-yard field goal to end his NFL-record string of 50-yarders at 11. Green Bay PK Chris Jacke kicked four consecutive field goals for the second week in a row but then missed one to end his club record of 17 straight. Jet S Ronnie Lott logged his 64th career interception, the fifth-best total in NFL history.

OFFENSIVE MVP: QB Bobby Hebert, Falcons. Behind Hebert, the Falcons have suddenly become one of the hottest teams in the NFL. Completing 24-of-32 passes for 315 yards and three touchdowns, he led Atlanta to a 27-14 upset victory over the Cowboys.

DEFENSIVE MVP: S Marcus Robertson, Oilers. In his third year with Houston, Robertson had his best day, intercepting three passes in Houston's 27-20 win at Cleveland. Two of the grabs stopped fourth-quarter drives by the Browns. He also defensed four other passes and made six tackles. The three interceptions tied the club mark.

GOLDEN TOE: PK Jeff Jaeger, Raiders. Jaeger was the entire Raider offense in a 12-7 triumph over the Chargers. The six-year vet connected on four field goals, missing only on a 56-yarder just before halftime.

TOP PERFORMANCES

PASSING

Player, team	Comp.	Att.	Yds.	TD	Int.
Todd Philcox, Browns	22	47	316	2	4
Bobby Hebert, Falcons	24	32	315	3	0
John Elway, Broncos	18	25	276	1	0
Drew Bledsoe, Patriots	23	42	275	1	1
Jim Kelly, Bills	19	27	274	2	1
Jeff Hostetler, Raiders	19	31	270	0	1

RUSHING

Player, team	Att.	Yds.	TD
Gary Brown, Oilers	34	194	1
Thurman Thomas, Bills	27	116	0
Ricky Watters, 49ers	16	116	0
Mark Higgs, Dolphins	19	108	0
Rodney Hampton, Giants	24	101	0
Greg Robinson, Raiders	21	89	0

RECEIVING

Player, team	Rec.	Yds.	TD
James Jett, Raiders	7	138	0
Mark Carrier, Browns	7	123	1
Anthony Carter, Vikings	9	104	1
Eric Green, Steelers	7	99	0
Keith Jackson, Dolphins	5	99	0
Johnny Johnson, Jets	6	99	0

SCORING

Player, team	TD	XP	FG	Pts.
Chris Jacke, Packers	0	2/2	4/5	14
Jason Elam, Broncos	0	4/4	3/3	13

GAME SUMMARIES

OILERS 27, BROWNS 20
Cleveland, Ohio, Nov. 21, 1993

Houston	0	14	3	10	—	27
Cleveland	3	7	0	10	—	20

Scoring:
- Cleveland: Stover, 21 FG
- Houston: G. Brown, 11 run (Del Greco kick)
- Houston: Duncan, 4 pass from Moon (Del Greco kick)
- Cleveland: Metcalf, 13 pass from Philcox (Stover kick)
- Houston: Del Greco, 28 FG
- Houston: Moon, 4 run (Del Greco kick)
- Houston: Del Greco, 30 FG
- Cleveland: Carrier, 24 pass from Philcox (Stover kick)
- Cleveland: Stover, 44 FG

RAMS 10, REDSKINS 6
Anaheim, Calif., Nov. 21, 1993

Washington	3	0	3	0	—	6
L.A. Rams	0	0	0	10	—	10

Scoring:
- Washington: Lohmiller, 19 FG
- Washington: Lohmiller, 34 FG
- L.A. Rams: Drayton, 25 pass from Rubley (Zendejas kick)
- L.A. Rams: Zendejas, 23 FG

BRONCOS 37, STEELERS 13
Denver, Colo., Nov. 21, 1993

Pittsburgh	0	0	6	7	—	13
Denver	10	10	14	3	—	37

Scoring:
- Denver: Elam, 48 FG
- Denver: Delpino, 1 run (Elam kick)
- Denver: Russell, fumble recovery in endzone (Elam kick)
- Denver: Elam, 27 FG
- Pittsburgh: Anderson, 37 FG
- Denver: Delpino, 1 run (Elam kick)
- Denver: V. Johnson, 13 pass from Elway (Elam kick)
- Pittsburgh: Anderson, 38 FG
- Denver: Elam, 28 FG
- Pittsburgh: Thigpen, 39 pass from Tomczak (Anderson kick)

GIANTS 7, EAGLES 3
Philadelphia, Pa., Nov. 21, 1993

N.Y. Giants	0	0	0	7	—	7
Philadelphia	0	0	3	0	—	3

Scoring:
- Philadelphia: Bahr, 35 FG
- N.Y. Giants: M. Jackson, 26 pass from Simms (Treadwell kick)

RAIDERS 12, CHARGERS 7
San Diego, Calif., Nov. 21, 1993

L.A. Raiders	3	3	3	3	—	12
San Diego	0	0	0	7	—	7

Scoring:
- L.A. Raiders: Jaeger, 20 FG
- L.A. Raiders: Jaeger, 20 FG
- L.A. Raiders: Jaeger, 37 FG
- L.A. Raiders: Jaeger, 27 FG
- San Diego: Lewis, 9 pass from Humphries (Carney kick)

1993 REVIEW ■ WEEK 12

BEARS 19, CHIEFS 17
Kansas City, Mo., Nov. 21, 1993

Chicago	0	6	6	7	—	19
Kansas City	7	7	3	0	—	17

Scoring:
Kansas City: Allen, 2 run (Lowery kick)
Kansas City: Allen, 8 run (Lowery kick)
Chicago: Butler, 32 FG
Chicago: Butler, 45 FG
Chicago: Worley, 25 run (Butler kick blocked)
Kansas City: Lowery, 20 FG
Chicago: Anderson, 1 run (Butler kick)

BILLS 23, COLTS 9
Orchard Park, N.Y., Nov. 21, 1993

Indianapolis	3	3	3	0	—	9
Buffalo	0	16	7	0	—	23

Scoring:
Indianapolis: Biasucci, 26 FG
Indianapolis: Biasucci, 22 FG
Buffalo: Safety, Jones sacked George in endzone
Buffalo: K. Davis, 1 run (Christie kick)
Buffalo: Brooks, 23 pass from Kelly (Christie kick)
Indianapolis: Biasucci, 37 FG
Buffalo: McKeller, 13 pass from Kelly (Christie kick)

JETS 17, BENGALS 12
East Rutherford, N.J., Nov. 21, 1993

Cincinnati	3	0	0	9	—	12
N.Y. Jets	0	14	0	3	—	17

Scoring:
Cincinnati: Pelfrey, 28 FG
N.Y. Jets: B. Baxter, 5 run (Blanchard kick)
N.Y. Jets: J. Johnson, 6 run (Blanchard kick)
N.Y. Jets: Blanchard, 42 FG
Cincinnati: Query, 4 pass from Klingler (Pelfrey kick)
Cincinnati: Safety, Aguiar threw ball out of endzone

FALCONS 27, COWBOYS 14
Atlanta, Ga., Nov. 21, 1993

Dallas	0	0	7	7	—	14
Atlanta	3	10	7	7	—	27

Scoring:
Atlanta: Johnson, 26 FG
Atlanta: Johnson, 24 FG
Atlanta: Pritchard, 13 pass from Hebert (Johnson kick)
Atlanta: Pritchard, 10 pass from Hebert (Johnson kick)
Dallas: Galbraith, 1 pass from Kosar (Murray kick)
Atlanta: Sanders, 70 pass from Hebert (Johnson kick)
Dallas: K. Williams, 28 pass from Kosar (Murray kick)

DOLPHINS 17, PATRIOTS 13
Miami, Fla., Nov. 21, 1993

New England	3	0	3	7	—	13
Miami	0	0	3	14	—	17

Scoring:
New England: Sisson, 28 FG
Miami: Stoyanovich, 23 FG
New England: Sisson, 40 FG
Miami: Byars, 11 pass from DeBerg (Stoyanovich kick)
Miami: Fryar, 44 pass from DeBerg (Stoyanovich kick)
New England: Crittenden, 40 pass from Bledsoe (Sisson kick)

BUCCANEERS 23, VIKINGS 10
Tampa Bay, Fla., Nov. 21, 1993

Minnesota	0	7	3	0	—	10
Tampa Bay	3	3	10	7	—	23

Scoring
Tampa Bay: Husted, 26 FG
Tampa Bay: Husted, 54 FG
Minnesota: A. Carter, 2 pass from Salisbury (Reveiz kick)
Tampa Bay: Mack, 27 interception return (Husted kick)
Tampa Bay: Husted, 21 FG
Minnesota: Reveiz, 43 FG
Tampa Bay: Workman, 1 run (Husted kick)

PACKERS 26, LIONS 17
Milwaukee, Wisc., Nov. 21, 1993

Detroit	0	10	7	0	—	17
Green Bay	10	3	3	10	—	26

Scoring
Green Bay: E. Bennett, 1 run (Jacke kick)
Green Bay: Jacke, 27 FG
Detroit: Green, 17 pass from Peete (Hanson kick)
Detroit: Hanson, 50 FG
Green Bay: Jacke, 52 FG
Detroit: Hallock, 1 pass from Peete (Hanson kick)
Green Bay: Jacke, 20 FG
Green Bay: Jacke, 34 FG
Green Bay: E. Bennett, 2 run (Jacke kick)

SAN FRANCISCO 42, NEW ORLEANS 7
San Francisco, Calif., Monday night, Nov. 22, 1993

New Orleans	0	0	0	7	—	7
San Francisco	7	21	14	0	—	42

Scoring:
San Francisco: Hanks, 67 interception return (Cofer kick)
San Francisco: J. Taylor, 22 pass from Young (Cofer kick)
San Francisco: Rice, 11 pass from Young (Cofer kick)
San Francisco: Young, 7 run (Cofer kick)
San Francisco: Logan, 5 run (Cofer kick)
San Francisco: Rice, 14 pass from Young (Cofer kick)
New Orleans: F. Turner, 6 pass from M. Buck (Andersen kick)

PRO FOOTBALL WEEKLY 1994 ALMANAC

REVIEW WEEK 13

WEEK 13 STANDINGS

AMERICAN FOOTBALL CONFERENCE

AFC EAST	W	L	T	Pct.	PF	PA
Miami	9	2	0	.818	234	186
Buffalo	8	3	0	.727	202	152
N.Y. Jets	7	4	0	.636	240	170
Indianapolis	3	8	0	.273	154	264
New England	1	10	0	.091	126	223

AFC CENTRAL	W	L	T	Pct.	PF	PA
Houston	7	4	0	.636	256	180
Pittsburgh	6	5	0	.545	231	196
Cleveland	5	6	0	.455	202	225
Cincinnati	1	10	0	.091	128	251

AFC WEST	W	L	T	Pct.	PF	PA
Kansas City	8	3	0	.727	204	170
Denver	7	4	0	.636	283	197
L.A. Raiders	6	5	0	.545	194	201
Seattle	5	6	0	.455	174	186
San Diego	5	6	0	.455	195	195

NATIONAL FOOTBALL CONFERENCE

NFC EAST	W	L	T	PCt.	PF	PA
N.Y. Giants	8	3	0	.727	206	138
Dallas	7	4	0	.636	234	169
Philadelphia	5	6	0	.455	175	212
Phoenix	3	8	0	.273	200	195
Washington	2	9	0	.182	165	256

NFC CENTRAL	W	L	T	Pct.	PF	PA
Detroit	7	4	0	.636	210	176
Green Bay	7	4	0	.636	238	188
Chicago	6	5	0	.545	171	147
Minnesota	5	6	0	.455	179	217
Tampa Bay	3	8	0	.273	153	274

NFC WEST	W	L	T	Pct.	PF	PA
San Francisco	8	3	0	.727	332	196
New Orleans	7	4	0	.636	224	229
Atlanta	5	6	0	.455	228	250
L.A. Rams	3	8	0	.273	151	246

WEEK 13 RESULTS / LINE

Result	Line
Chicago 10, DETROIT 6	LIONS by 7
Miami 16, DALLAS 14	COWBOYS by 10
ATLANTA 17, Cleveland	FALCONS by 6.5
CINCINNATI 16, L.A. Raiders 10	Raiders by 9
New Orleans 17, MINNESOTA 14	VIKINGS by 1
N.Y. Jets 6, NEW ENGLAND 0	Jets by 4
GREEN BAY 13, Tampa Bay 10	PACKERS by 12
Philadelphia 17, WASHINGTON 14	REDSKINS by 3
Denver 17, SEATTLE 9	Broncos by 3
KANSAS CITY 23, Buffalo 7	CHIEFS by 3
N.Y. GIANTS 19, Phoenix 17	GIANTS by 6.5
San Francisco 35, L.A. RAMS 10	49ers by 14
HOUSTON 23, Pittsburgh 3	OILERS by 3
San Diego 31, INDIANAPOLIS 0	Even

Home team in CAPS

The race to the playoffs heated up. The 49ers did not make it four games in a row scoring 40 or more points, which would have been a league record, but they posted 35 in trouncing the Rams. That got a lot of people talking about a Super Bowl around the Golden Gate City.

Across the country, the perennial Super Bowl-contending Bills fell from grace and first place in the AFC East, and the growing feeling around the AFC was that maybe '93 might be somebody else's turn to represent the conference.

The NFC Central provided the biggest surprise of all with the Bears' emergence as a contender and the fact four teams were now in close contention for the division title, although Minnesota, a preseason favorite to some, appeared to be heading in the wrong direction.

The hottest tickets in the race at this point: the 49ers, Giants and Cowboys in the NFC and the Dolphins, Chiefs and Oilers in the AFC.

Cincinnati won its first game of the season, while New England lost its 10th to allow the two teams an equal share of the league's worst record, 1-10, and jump-start the race for the 1994 No. 1 draft pick.

GAME OF THE WEEK: It spiced up Thanksgiving Day celebrations: Miami 16, Dallas 13, with the Cowboys a 9.5-point favorite down in Texas Stadium. The Cowboys needed a win to stay in a first-place tie with the Giants in the NFC East; Miami wanted to pull ahead of the Bills atop the AFC East. Dallas had the victory in its grasp with 15 seconds left, leading 14-13, when it blocked a Dolphin field goal ... but the ball squibbed down to the one-yard line, where Cowboy Leon Lett touched it, making it a free ball. Miami gobbled it up and got another chance for a field goal, this one from one yard less than an extra point. And this one from Pete Stoyanovich's foot was not blocked.

MONTANA'S RETURN: Kansas City had been missing him, and QB Joe Montana was happy his hamstring miseries had abated. In his first start in a month, the Super Bowl veteran obtained from San Francisco led the Chiefs to a decisive 23-7 victory over the Bills. Montana threw for two touchdowns and completed 18-of-32 passes for a total of 208 yards.

THANK-YOU NOTE DUE: In winning their first game of the year, the Bengals should have sent a thank-you note to the Raiders afterward. The Raiders missed four field goals, dropped several critical passes and turned the ball over twice in scoring range. And they allowed Cincinnati to control the ball for almost 39 of the game's 60 minutes.

BONERS PLUS: Lett's blunder cost Dallas the game on Thursday. But, so Lett would not feel alone in the embarrassment department, Viking Fred Strickland on Sunday managed to incur a

294

1993 REVIEW ■ WEEK 13

holding penalty when Fuad Reveiz kicked what appeared to be a 41-yard, game-tying field goal with 48 seconds left. On his second try from 51 yards, Reveiz missed and Minnesota lost 17-14.

PFW NOTES: San Francisco WR Jerry Rice exceeded 1,000 yards in receiving for an NFL-record eighth consecutive year. Buffalo QB Jim Kelly threw his 2,000th career completion, becoming the 30th NFL quarterback to claim that honor. Kansas City PK Nick Lowery's three field goals moved him past Jim Turner to No. 4 on the league's all-time scoring list with 1,442 points (still a long way from George Blanda's NFL mark of 2,002). Atlanta WR Andre Rison broke the career 5,000-yard mark on pass receptions. Trivia: Tampa Bay, losing in Green Bay, where the temperature was 29 degrees at game time, moved its record to 0-14 in games that begin when the temperature is below 40. 49er QB Steve Young ended his club-record streak of 183 passes without an interception. Falcon PK Norm Johnson extended his field goal streak to 25 consecutive (including seven from 50 yards or more). Ram OT Jackie Slater, 39, played in his 246th NFL game, a record for offensive linemen. Cardinal WR Gary Clark surpassed 9,000 career receiving yards, most of them gained for his previous employer, the Redskins.

OFFENSIVE MVP: Steve Young, 49ers. Coming up with the finest performance of his career, Young threw four touchdown passes in San Francisco's 35-10 rout of the Rams. He was 26-of-32 for 462 yards, the most passing yardage racked up to that point in the '93 season.

DEFENSIVE MVP: DE William Fuller, Oilers. The standout in Houston's best defensive performance of the season when it whipped the Steelers 23-3, Fuller accounted for four of the team's six sacks. It brought his season total to eight sacks, tying him for sixth most in the AFC.

GOLDEN TOE: PK Brad Daluiso, Giants. A single field goal earned the Golden Toe when New York's Daluiso, ordinarily used only on kickoffs, booted a 54-yarder with 32 seconds left to give the Giants an important 19-17 victory over Phoenix. It was the third-longest field goal in the history of the Giants.

TOP PERFORMANCES

PASSING

Player, team	Comp.	Att.	Yds.	TD	Int.
Steve Young, 49ers	26	32	462	4	1
Phil Simms, Giants	22	41	337	1	0
Warren Moon, Oilers	21	34	295	1	1
Steve DeBerg, Dolphins	24	41	287	0	2
Rich Gannon, Redskins	20	31	279	2	2
John Elway, Broncos	20	37	226	1	1

RUSHING

Player, team	Att.	Yds.	TD
Leonard Russell, Patriots	27	147	0
Jerome Bettis, Rams	18	133	0
Chris Warren, Seahawks	19	95	0
Robert Smith, Vikings	24	94	0
Marion Butts, Chargers	13	80	1
Gary Brown, Oilers	19	79	1

RECEIVING

Player, team	Rec.	Yds.	TD
Jerry Rice, 49ers	8	166	2
John Taylor, 49ers	6	150	1
Haywood Jeffires, Oilers	7	139	1
James Jett, Raiders	4	117	0
Mark Jackson, Giants	7	113	0
Herschel Walker, Eagles	10	103	0

SCORING

Player, team	TD	XP	FG	Pts.
Jerry Rice, 49ers	2	0	0	12
Ricky Watters, 49ers	2	0	0	12
Kevin Williams, Cowboys	2	0	0	12

GAME SUMMARIES

BEARS 10, LIONS 6
Detroit, Mich., Thursday, Nov. 25, 1993

Chicago	0	10	0	0	—	10
Detroit	0	3	3	0	—	6

Scoring:
Chicago: Butler, 27 FG
Detroit: Hanson, 39 FG
Chicago: Obee, 42 pass from Harbaugh (Butler kick)
Detroit: Hanson, 27 FG

DOLPHINS 16, COWBOYS 14
Irving, Texas, Thursday, Nov. 25, 1993

Miami	7	0	3	6	—	16
Dallas	0	14	0	0	—	14

Scoring:
Miami: Byars, 77 run (Stoyanovich kick)
Dallas: K. Williams, 4 pass from Aikman (Murray kick)
Dallas: K. Williams, 64 punt return (Murray kick)
Miami: Stoyanovich, 20 FG
Miami: Stoyanovich, 31 FG
Miami: Stoyanovich, 19 FG

BRONCOS 17, SEAHAWKS 9
Seattle, Wash., Nov. 28, 1993

Denver	0	7	3	7	—	17
Seattle	0	0	2	7	—	9

Scoring:
Denver: Sharpe, 50 pass from Elway
Seattle: Safety, Stephens tackled Elway in endzone
Denver: Elam, 25 FG
Seattle: Martin 10 pass from Mirer (Kasay kick)
Denver: Bernstine, 2 run (Elam kick)

GIANTS 19, CARDINALS 17
East Rutherford, N.J., Nov., 28, 1993

Phoenix	10	0	7	0	—	17
N.Y. Giants	3	3	7	6	—	19

Scoring:
Phoenix: G. Davis, 47 FG
Phoenix: Rolle, 1 pass from Beuerlein (G. Davis kick)
N.Y. Giants: Treadwell, 22 FG
N.Y. Giants: Treadwell, 37 FG
N.Y. Giants: McCaffrey, 20 pass from Simms (Treadwell kick)
Phoenix: Proehl, 17 pass from Beuerlein (G. Davis kick)
N.Y. Giants: Treadwell, 22 FG
N.Y. Giants: Daluiso, 54 FG

OILERS 23, STEELERS 3
Houston, Texas, Nov. 28, 1993

Pittsburgh	0	3	0	0	—	3
Houston	0	10	10	3	—	23

Scoring:
Houston: Del Greco, 43 FG
Pittsburgh: Anderson, 42 FG
Houston: G. Brown, 3 run (Del Greco kick)
Houston: Jeffires, 66 pass from Moon (Del Greco kick)
Houston: Del Greco, 21 FG
Houston: Del Greco, 28 FG

JETS 6, PATRIOTS 0
Foxboro, Mass., Nov. 28, 1993

N.Y. Jets	3	3	0	0	— 6
New England	0	0	0	0	— 0

Scoring:
N.Y. Jets: Blanchard, 33 FG
N.Y. Jets: Blanchard, 23 FG

PACKERS 13, BUCCANEERS 10
Green Bay, Wisc., Nov. 28, 1993

Tampa Bay	0	0	3	7	— 10
Green Bay	0	3	3	7	— 13

Scoring:
Green Bay: Jacke, 24 FG
Tampa Bay: Husted, 30 FG
Green Bay: Jacke, 36 FG
Tampa Bay: Hawkins, 9 pass from Erickson (Husted kick)
Green Bay: Sharpe, 2 pass from Favre (Jacke kick)

FALCONS 17, BROWNS 14
Atlanta, Ga., Nov. 28, 1993

Cleveland	0	0	7	7	— 14
Atlanta	10	7	0	0	— 17

Scoring:
Atlanta: Johnson, 51 FG
Atlanta: Rison, 14 pass from Hebert (Johnson kick)
Atlanta: Pritchard, 8 pass from Hebert (Johnson kick)
Cleveland: Carrier, 35 pass from Philcox (Stover kick)
Cleveland: Philcox, 3 run (Stover kick)

BENGALS 16, RAIDERS 10
Cincinnati, Ohio, Nov. 28, 1993

L.A. Raiders	0	0	0	10	— 10
Cincinnati	3	7	3	3	— 16

Scoring:
Cincinnati: Pelfrey, 45 FG
Cincinnati: Ball, 1 run (Pelfrey kick)
Cincinnati: Pelfrey, 34 FG
L.A. Raiders: Hostetler, 4 run (Jaeger kick)
L.A. Raiders: Jaeger, 34 FG

CHIEFS 23, BILLS 7
Kansas City, Mo., Nov. 28, 1993

Buffalo	7	0	0	0	— 7
Kansas City	7	3	10	3	— 23

Scoring
Buffalo: K. Davis, 9 run (Christie kick)
Kansas City: Allen, 18 pass from Montana (Lowery kick)
Kansas City: Lowery, 30 FG
Kansas City: Cash, 1 pass from Montana (Lowery kick)
Kansas City: Lowery, 22 FG
Kansas City: Lowery, 34 FG

SAINTS 17, VIKINGS 14
Minneapolis, Minn., Nov. 28, 1993

New Orleans	7	0	7	3	— 17
Minnesota	7	0	7	0	— 14

Scoring
New Orleans: McAfee, 3 run (Andersen kick)
Minnesota: Jordan, 14 pass from Salisbury (Reveiz kick)
Minnesota: C. Carter, 7 pass from Salisbury (Reveiz kick)
New Orleans: Hughes, 99 kickoff return (Andersen kick)
New Orleans: Andersen, 24 FG

49ERS 35, RAMS 10
Anaheim, Calif., Nov. 28, 1993

San Francisco	7	14	7	7	— 35
L.A. Rams	3	0	0	7	— 10

Scoring
San Francisco: Watters, 6 run (Cofer kick)
L.A. Rams: Zendejas, 25 FG
San Francisco: Rice, 39 pass from Young (Cofer kick)
San Francisco: Watters, 48 pass from Young (Cofer kick)
San Francisco: Taylor, 76 pass from Young (Cofer kick)
San Francisco: Rice, 7 pass from Young (Cofer kick)
L.A. Rams: Ellard, 14 pass from Rubley (Zendejas kick)

EAGLES 17, REDSKINS 14
Washington, D.C., Nov. 28, 1993

Philadelphia	3	7	0	7	— 17
Washington	0	0	0	14	— 14

Scoring
Philadelphia: Bahr, 22 FG
Philadelphia: Hebron, 1 run (Bahr kick)
Washington: McGee, 17 pass from Gannon (Lohmiller kick)
Washington: Monk, 6 pass from Gannon (Lohmiller kick)
Philadelphia: Joseph, 2 pass from Brister (Bahr kick)

CHARGERS 31, COLTS 0
Indianapolis, Ind., Monday night, Nov. 29, 1993

San Diego	0	14	3	14	— 31
Indianapolis	0	0	0	0	— 0

Scoring:
San Diego: Jefferson, 39 pass from Humphries (Carney kick)
San Diego: Lewis, 8 pass from Humphries (Carney kick)
San Diego: Carney, 36 FG
San Diego: Butts, 1 run (Carney kick)
San Diego: Bieniemy, 4 run (Carney kick)

1993 REVIEW ■ WEEK 14

WEEK 14

WEEK 14 STANDINGS

AMERICAN FOOTBALL CONFERENCE

AFC EAST	W	L	T	Pct.	PF	PA
Miami	9	3	0	.750	248	205
Buffalo	8	4	0	.667	226	177
N.Y. Jets	7	5	0	.583	246	179
Indianapolis	4	8	0	.333	163	270
New England	1	11	0	.083	140	240

AFC CENTRAL	W	L	T	Pct.	PF	PA
Houston	8	4	0	.667	289	197
Pittsburgh	7	5	0	.583	248	210
Cleveland	6	6	0	.500	219	238
Cincinnati	1	11	0	.083	136	272

AFC WEST	W	L	T	Pct.	PF	PA
Kansas City	9	3	0	.750	235	186
Denver	7	5	0	.583	293	210
L.A. Raiders	7	5	0	.583	219	225
San Diego	6	6	0	.500	208	205
Seattle	5	7	0	.417	190	217

NATIONAL FOOTBALL CONFERENCE

NFC EAST	W	L	T	Pct.	PF	PA
N.Y. Giants	9	3	0	.750	225	152
Dallas	8	4	0	.667	257	186
Philadelphia	5	7	0	.417	192	235
Phoenix	4	8	0	.333	238	205
Washington	3	9	0	.250	188	273

NFC CENTRAL	W	L	T	Pct.	PF	PA
Chicago	7	5	0	.583	201	164
Detroit	7	5	0	.583	210	189
Green Bay	7	5	0	.583	255	218
Minnesota	6	6	0	.500	192	217
Tampa Bay	3	9	0	.250	170	297

NFC WEST	W	L	T	Pct.	PF	PA
San Francisco	9	3	0	.750	353	204
New Orleans	7	5	0	.583	237	246
Atlanta	5	7	0	.417	245	283
L.A. Rams	3	9	0	.250	161	284

WEEK 14 RESULTS / LINE

Result	Line
HOUSTON 33, Atlanta 17	Oilers by 7
CHICAGO 30, Green Bay 17	Bears by 2
Indianapolis 9, N.Y. JETS 6	Jets by 11
L.A. Raiders 25, BUFFALO 24	Bills by 6.5
Minnesota 13, DETROIT 0	Lions by 3
PITTSBURGH 17, New England 14	Steelers by 12
CLEVELAND 17, New Orleans 13	Saints by 3.5
Washington 23, TAMPA BAY 17	Bucs by 2.5
PHOENIX 38, L.A. Rams 10	Cardinals by 7
SAN DIEGO 13, Denver 10	Chargers by 3
N.Y. Giants 19, MIAMI 14	Dolphins by 3.5
Kansas City 31, SEATTLE 16	Chiefs by 6.5
SAN FRANCISCO 21, Cincinnati 8	49ers by 23.5
DALLAS 23, Philadelphia 17	Cowboys by 16.5

Home team in CAPS

With three-quarters of the regular season officially over, there were no runaways in the pursuit of division titles. The closest — and perhaps most unpredictable — race was in the NFC Central, where the Bears, Packers and Lions shared the lead, with the Vikings only a game behind.

Through 12 games, San Francisco claimed *Pro Football Weekly's* top offensive efficiency rating with an average of 6.31 yards, and the Bears and Steelers led in defensive efficiency with a low of 4.49 each. The 49ers were tops in total yards gained, 4,726, an average of 393.8 per game. The fewest yards allowed were the 3,137 given up by Pittsburgh, an average of only 261.4 a game. San Diego had the fewest turnovers, a mere 13, while the Oilers had the unwelcome distinction of turning the ball over the most times, 37.

The top passer rating in the AFC belonged to the often-injured Joe Montana of Kansas City, 94.2, and in the NFC, 49er Steve Young was well ahead of the pack at 102.5. Two rushers had exceeded 1,000 yards, Barry Sanders of the Lions with 1,115 and Buffalo's Thurman Thomas at 1,061. The top receiver in terms of yards gained was 49er Jerry Rice, the only player to stand above 1,000 yards (1,130), but the most receptions belonged to Green Bay's Sterling Sharpe with 86. Nate Odomes of Buffalo had the most interceptions, eight, and Raider DE Anthony Smith and Saint LB Renaldo Turnbull logged the most sacks, 12 apiece.

GAME OF THE WEEK: No one expected the Giants to be doing as well as they were at this point in the season, leading the always-rugged NFC East, and Miami to be thriving without QB Dan Marino on the field. But they both were playing well, and they met down in Miami in a brutal contest that the Giants trudged away from with a 19-14 win. New York forced three turnovers, earned a safety on a sack, turned back three scoring threats and left Dolphin QB Steve DeBerg bloodied with seven stitches in his face. Both teams now had records of 9-3 and led their respective divisions.

DEFENSE, DEFENSE: The defense of the Bears defeated the Packers 18-17, scoring three touchdowns, the first on an 80-yard interception and lateral, the second on a fumble recovery return and the third on a simple interception. The Bear offense added 12 unneeded points in the 30-17 defeat of the Packers.

ON THE AFC SEA: Both the Oilers and Bills claimed records of 8-4 and were looking for playoff ports but, like two ships passing in the night, they were cruising in different directions. By the end of Week 14, Houston had won seven straight games and Buffalo had lost three of its last four.

BAD DAY FOR QB'S: Besides DeBerg's seven

stitches, Bobby Hebert of the Falcons was intercepted six times by the Oilers, Patriot Drew Bledsoe had five picked off by the Steelers and Detroit's Rodney Peete threw four times into Viking hands. The Saints' Wade Wilson was sacked nine times by Cleveland pass rushers.

PFW NOTES: Buffalo RB Thomas made it five straight seasons with more than 1,000 yards rushing. Chicago DT Steve McMichael played in his 187th consecutive game, taking the club record away from Walter Payton. Redskin Art Monk upped his total of consecutive games in which he had caught at least one pass to 160, 17 behind NFL record-holder Steve Largent. Denver QB John Elway exceeded 3,000 yards passing for 1993, making it eight straight years he has topped that mark. Redskin rookie RB Reggie Brooks could now claim the two longest touchdown runs from scrimmage in 1993, 78 yards against Tampa Bay and 85 in an earlier game with the Eagles. Three of the Colts' four wins thus far were by the score of 9-6. The Giants' victory over the Dolphins gave them a 3-2 edge over teams coached by Don Shula, a rarity against the NFL's all-time winningest coach.

OFFENSIVE MVP: RB Ron Moore, Cardinals. Moore, a fourth-round draft pick in '93 out of Pittsburg (Kan.) State, became the first Cardinal in 16 years to run for four touchdowns in a game as Phoenix defeated the Rams 38-10. Moore rushed for 126 yards on 29 carries.

DEFENSIVE MVP: LB Jack Del Rio, Vikings. Picked up as a Plan B free agent from Dallas in 1992, Del Rio grabbed three interceptions and led Minnesota in tackles with eight in a 13-0 win over Detroit. Behind his defensive lead, the Vikings not only upset the Lions but held them scoreless.

GOLDEN TOE: PK Dean Biasucci, Colts. For the third time in 1993, Biasucci accounted for all the points posted by the Colts' offense. His three field goals were enough to give Indianapolis a 9-6 victory over the Jets. It also gave him the all-time Colt scoring record, 684 points, to top Hall of Famer Lenny Moore's 678.

TOP PERFORMANCES
PASSING

Player, team	Comp.	Att.	Yds.	TD	Int.
Brett Favre, Packers	36	54	402	2	3
Steve DeBerg, Dolphins	26	41	365	1	2
Warren Moon, Oilers	24	42	342	1	0
Bobby Hebert, Falcons	30	52	317	2	6
Drew Bledsoe, Patriots	18	48	296	1	5
Jeff Hostetler, Raiders	18	31	289	1	0

RUSHING

Player, team	Att.	Yds.	TD
Emmitt Smith, Cowboys	23	172	0
Reggie Brooks, Redskins	20	128	1
Ron Moore, Cardinals	29	126	4
Jerome Bettis, Rams	16	115	0
Derrick Moore, Lions	22	86	0
Leroy Thompson, Steelers	22	82	0

RECEIVING

Player, team	Rec.	Yds.	TD
Tim Brown, Raiders	10	183	1
Gary Clark, Cardinals	8	159	1
Brian Blades, Seahawks	7	134	0
Don Beebe, Bills	4	115	1
Sterling Sharpe, Packers	10	114	1
Courtney Hawkins, Bucs	8	112	1

SCORING

Player, team	TD	XP	FG	Pts.
Ron Moore, Cardinals	4	0	0	24
Marcus Allen, Chiefs	3	0	0	18
Ricky Watters, 49ers	3	0	0	18
Al Del Greco, Oilers	0	3/3	4/6	15

GAME SUMMARIES

CHIEFS 31, SEAHAWKS 16
Seattle, Wash., Dec. 5, 1993

Kansas City	10	7	14	0	—	31
Seattle	3	3	7	3	—	16

Scoring:
- Seattle: Kasay, 22 FG
- Kansas City: Allen, 1 run (Lowery kick)
- Kansas City: Lowery, 47 FG
- Kansas City: Thomas, 86 fumble return (Lowery kick)
- Seattle: Kasay, 26 FG
- Kansas City: Allen, 1 run (Lowery kick)
- Kansas City: Allen, 30 run (Lowery kick)
- Seattle: C. Warren, 1 run (Kasay kick)
- Seattle: Kasay, 37 FG

CHARGERS 13, BRONCOS 10
San Diego, Calif., Dec. 5, 1993

Denver	3	7	0	0	—	10
San Diego	0	0	3	10	—	13

Scoring:
- Denver: Elam, 30 FG
- Denver: Wyman, 1 pass from Maddox (Elam kick)
- San Diego: Carney, 27 FG
- San Diego: Means, 1 run (Carney kick)
- San Diego: Carney, 34 FG

49ERS 21, BENGALS 8
San Francisco, Calif., Dec. 5, 1993

Cincinnati	2	6	0	0	—	8
San Francisco	7	0	7	7	—	21

Scoring:
- San Francisco: Watters, 2 run (Cofer kick)
- Cincinnati: Safety, A. Williams sacked Young in endzone
- Cincinnati: Pelfrey, 48 FG
- Cincinnati: Pelfrey, 39 FG
- San Francisco: Watters, 2 run (Cofer kick)
- San Francisco: Watters, 4 run, (Cofer kick)

OILERS 33, FALCONS 17
Houston, Texas, Dec. 5, 1993

Atlanta	0	7	7	3	—	17
Houston	3	3	14	13	—	33

Scoring:
- Houston: Del Greco, 52 FG
- Houston: Del Greco, 43 FG
- Atlanta: Pritchard, 9 pass from Hebert (Johnson kick)
- Atlanta: Rison, 6 pass from Hebert (Johnson kick)
- Houston: Slaughter, 25 pass from Moon (Del Greco kick)
- Houston: Childress, recovered fumble in endzone (Del Greco kick)
- Houston: Del Greco, 21 FG
- Houston: G. Brown, 1 run (Del Greco kick)
- Atlanta: Johnson, 30 FG
- Houston: Del Greco, 36 FG

COLTS 9, JETS 6
East Rutherford, N.J., Dec. 5, 1993

Indianapolis	0	3	0	6	—	9
N.Y. Jets	0	3	3	0	—	6

Scoring:
- N.Y. Jets: Blanchard, 28 FG

Indianapolis: Biasucci, 40 FG
N.Y. Jets: Blanchard, 19 FG
Indianapolis: Biasucci, 24 FG
Indianapolis: Biasucci, 38 FG

GIANTS 19, DOLPHINS 14
Miami, Fla., Dec. 5, 1993

N.Y. Giants	7	7	3	2	—	19
Miami	7	0	0	7	—	14

Scoring:
N.Y. Giants: Hampton, 14 run (Treadwell kick)
Miami: Byars, 6 run (Stoyanovich kick)
N.Y. Giants: Cross, 20 pass from Simms (Treadwell kick)
N.Y. Giants: Treadwell, 42 FG
N.Y. Giants: Safety, Hamilton sacked DeBerg in endzone
Miami: Martin, 25 pass from DeBerg (Stoyanovich kick)

CARDINALS 38, RAMS 10
Phoenix, Ariz., Dec. 5, 1993

L.A. Rams	3	0	0	7	—	10
Phoenix	7	7	14	10	—	38

Scoring:
Phoenix: Moore, 1 run (G. Davis kick)
L.A. Rams: Zendejas, 22 FG
Phoenix: Clark, 22 pass from Beuerlein (G. Davis kick)
Phoenix: Moore, 19 run (G. Davis kick)
Phoenix: Moore, 1 run (G. Davis kick)
Phoenix: G. Davis, 27 FG
Phoenix: Moore, 1 run (G. Davis kick)
L.A. Rams: Drayton, 4 pass from Everett (Zendejas kick)

RAIDERS 25, BILLS 24
Orchard Park, N.Y., Dec. 5, 1993

L.A. Raiders	3	7	6	9	—	25
Buffalo	0	14	3	7	—	24

Scoring:
L.A. Raiders: Jaeger, 37 FG
Buffalo: Thomas, 3 run (Christie kick)
L.A. Raiders: Hostetler, 11 run (Jaeger kick)
Buffalo: Beebe, 65 pass from Kelly (Christie kick)
L.A. Raiders: Jaeger, 34 FG
Buffalo: Christie, 36 FG
L.A. Raiders: Jaeger, 26 FG
Buffalo: Thomas, 1 run (Christie kick)
L.A. Raiders: Jaeger, 47 FG
L.A. Raiders: Brown, 29 pass from Hostetler (Jaeger kick blocked)

REDSKINS 23, BUCCANEERS 17
Tampa, Fla., Dec. 5, 1993

Washington	7	3	13	0	—	23
Tampa Bay	0	0	10	7	—	17

Scoring:
Washington: Gannon, 1 run (Lohmiller kick)
Washington: Lohmiller, 51 FG
Washington: Brooks, 78 run (Lohmiller kick)
Tampa Bay: Husted, 31 FG
Tampa Bay: Seals, 8 interception return (Husted kick)
Washington: Gouveia, 59 interception return (Lohmiller kick failed)
Tampa Bay: Hawkins, 4 pass from Erickson (Husted kick)

1993 REVIEW ■ WEEK 14

BROWNS 17, SAINTS 13
Cleveland, Ohio, Dec. 5, 1993

New Orleans	7	0	3	3	—	13
Cleveland	10	0	7	0	—	17

Scoring:
Cleveland: Jackson, 8 pass from Philcox (Stover kick)
New Orleans: E. Martin, 10 pass from Wilson (Andersen kick)
Cleveland: Stover, 43 FG
New Orleans: Andersen, 41 FG
Cleveland: Jackson, 4 pass from Testaverde (Stover kick)
New Orleans: Andersen, 27 FG

VIKINGS 13, LIONS 0
Pontiac, Mich., Dec. 5, 1993

Minnesota	3	3	0	7	—	13
Detroit	0	0	0	0	—	0

Scoring:
Minnesota: Reveiz, 37 FG
Minnesota: Reveiz, 29 FG
Minnesota: McGriggs, 63 interception return (Reveiz kick)

BEARS 30, PACKERS 17
Chicago, Ill., Dec. 5, 1993

Green Bay	7	0	10	0	—	17
Chicago	7	3	10	10	—	30

Scoring:
Chicago: Lincoln, 80 return with lateral following interception (Butler kick)
Green Bay: Sharpe, 18 pass from Favre (Jacke kick)
Chicago: Butler, 29 FG
Chicago: Jones, 32 fumble return (Butler kick)
Green Bay: Jacke, 26 FG
Green Bay: Clayton, 22 pass from Favre (Jacke kick)
Chicago: Butler, 24 FG
Chicago: Butler, 29 FG
Chicago: Carrier, 34 interception return (Butler kick)

STEELERS 17, PATRIOTS 14
Pittsburgh, Pa., Dec. 5, 1993

New England	14	0	0	0	—	14
Pittsburgh	0	17	0	0	—	17

Scoring:
New England: Coates, 3 pass from Bledsoe (Sisson kick)
New England: Russell, 3 run (Sisson kick)
Pittsburgh: Hoge, 5 pass from O'Donnell (Anderson kick)
Pittsburgh: Anderson, 35 FG
Pittsburgh: Hoge, 1 pass from O'Donnell (Anderson kick)

COWBOYS 23, EAGLES 17
Irving, Texas, Monday night, Dec. 6, 1993

Philadelphia	0	3	7	7	—	17
Dallas	7	9	0	7	—	23

Scoring:
Dallas: Irvin, 11 pass from Aikman (Murray kick)
Dallas: Murray, 23 FG
Dallas: Murray, 19 FG
Dallas: Murray, 47 FG
Philadelphia: Bahr, 25 FG
Philadelphia: Bavaro, 2 pass from Brister (Bahr kick)
Dallas: Johnston, 2 run (Murray kick)
Philadelphia: Bavaro, 8 pass from Brister (Bahr kick)

PRO FOOTBALL WEEKLY 1994 ALMANAC

REVIEW: WEEK 15

WEEK 15 STANDINGS

AMERICAN FOOTBALL CONFERENCE

AFC EAST	W	L	T	Pct.	PF	PA
Buffalo	9	4	0	.692	236	184
Miami	9	4	0	.692	268	226
N.Y. Jets	8	5	0	.615	249	179
Indianapolis	4	9	0	.308	169	290
New England	2	11	0	.154	147	242

AFC CENTRAL	W	L	T	Pct.	PF	PA
Houston	9	4	0	.692	311	214
Pittsburgh	8	5	0	.615	269	230
Cleveland	6	7	0	.462	236	257
Cincinnati	1	12	0	.077	138	279

AFC WEST	W	L	T	Pct.	PF	PA
Kansas City	9	4	0	.692	256	213
L.A. Raiders	8	5	0	.615	246	248
Denver	8	5	0	.615	320	231
San Diego	6	7	0	.462	221	225
Seattle	5	8	0	.385	213	244

NATIONAL FOOTBALL CONFERENCE

NFC EAST	W	L	T	Pct.	PF	PA
N.Y. Giants	10	3	0	.769	245	158
Dallas	9	4	0	.692	294	206
Philadelphia	5	8	0	.385	199	245
Phoenix	4	9	0	.308	252	226
Washington	3	10	0	.231	188	276

NFC CENTRAL	W	L	T	Pct.	PF	PA
Green Bay	8	5	0	.615	275	231
Detroit	8	5	0	.615	231	203
Chicago	7	6	0	.538	211	177
Minnesota	6	7	0	.462	212	254
Tampa Bay	4	9	0	.308	183	307

NFC WEST	W	L	T	Pct.	PF	PA
San Francisco	9	4	0	.692	377	231
New Orleans	7	6	0	.538	257	269
Atlanta	6	7	0	.462	272	307
L.A. Rams	4	9	0	.308	184	304

WEEK 15 RESULTS / LINE

N.Y. Jets 3, WASHINGTON 0 — Jets by 3
ATLANTA 27, San Francisco 24 — 49ers by 8
Buffalo 10, PHILADELPHIA 7 — Bills by 3.5
TAMPA BAY 13, Chicago 10 — Bears by 4.5
NEW ENGLAND 7, Cincinnati 2 — Patriots by 6
HOUSTON 19, Cleveland 17 — Oilers by 10
N.Y. GIANTS 20, Indianapolis 6 — Giants by 12
L.A. Rams 23, NEW ORLEANS 20 — Saints by 14
Dallas 37, MINNESOTA 20 — Cowboys by 7
DENVER 27, Kansas City 21 — Broncos by 2.5
Detroit 21, PHOENIX 14 — Cardinals by 7.5
L.A. RAIDERS 27, Seattle 23 — Raiders by 8
Green Bay 20, SAN DIEGO 13 — Chargers by 3
Pittsburgh 21 MIAMI 20 — Dolphins by 3.5

Home team in CAPS

The Giants, under new head coach Dan Reeves and one of the year's most surprising success stories, became the first team to secure a playoff berth, and also the first team to register 10 wins when they defeated the Colts 20-7. The defending Super Bowl-champion Cowboys, however, were just a game behind in the NFC East, and in the words of their coach Jimmy Johnson, "We are not thinking wild-card."

While the battles for division titles and playoff spots heated up, offenses were noticeably cool. This complaint, voiced often earlier in the season, was especially noticeable in Week 15. Examples: The Jets, who had not scored a touchdown in 14 quarters, still managed to beat the Redskins 3-0. The Eagles, with a 7-0 lead in the fourth quarter, turned the ball over twice to enable two Buffalo scores and a 10-7 win for the Bills. Tampa Bay eked out a 13-10 victory over Chicago when the Bears failed on a fourth-quarter, 4th-and-1 at the Buccaneers' 36-yard line. And the meeting of the two teams with the fewest points and the worst records in the NFL ended in a baseball-like-score 7-2 win by New England over Cincinnati.

By this point in the season, only three teams had scored more than 300 points: the 49ers, 377; Broncos, 320; and Oilers, 311. And only four had allowed less than 200: the Giants, 158; Bears, 177; Jets, 179; and the Bills, 184.

GAME OF THE WEEK: At Mile-High Stadium in Denver, it was John Elway vs. Joe Montana in a real wild-west shootout. Elway's Broncos walked away from it with a 27-21 victory over Kansas City to draw them within a game of the division-leading Chiefs. They did it by scoring 10 unanswered points in the fourth quarter. Elway threw three touchdown passes to Shannon Sharpe, and Montana connected on two for the Chiefs.

COMEBACK OR GIVEAWAY? The 49ers held what appeared to be a comfortable 24-7 lead over the Falcons late in the third quarter. But the Falcons rallied behind the passing of Bobby Hebert, who threw two touchdowns in the fourth quarter. And San Francisco gave it away with two crucial turnovers in the same period, both by Dexter Carter, one on a muffed punt and the other on a kickoff-return fumble.

IRISH GIFTS TO THE NFL: In 1993, Notre Dame sent eight players on the NFL in the draft. Ram RB Jerome Bettis, the 10th pick, became the first 200-yard rusher of the year in Week 13 and one of only four to go over 1,000 yards up to that point. Former backfield mate Reggie Brooks, a second-round pick by the Redskins, had the two longest TD runs from scrimmage, 85 and 78 yards, while the No. 2 selection overall, QB Rick Mirer of Seattle,

1993 REVIEW ■ WEEK 15

had completed 228-of-397 passes for 2,411 yards through 13 games.

AMERICA'S TEAM: The Cowboys once again were laying claim to the title "America's Team." At Minnesota, they trounced the Vikings and recorded their 41st consecutive sellout game. Said Viking CB Carl Lee: "As disappointed as I was with our play, I was even more disappointed that the Cowboy fans were louder than ours."

PFW NOTES: Houston, which began the season with a 1-4 record, racked up its eighth straight win, the club's longest winning streak since 1961. Seattle tied an NFL record by scoring its fourth safety of the season. WR Anthony Carter broke Sammy White's Viking record for career touchdown receptions with his 51st. Falcon WR Andre Rison brought his season total of TD catches to 14, an Atlanta record. New Orleans PK Morten Andersen extended his scoring streak to 155 straight games, second only in NFL annals to Jim Breech's 186. Eddie Murray booted two field goals from more than 50 yards out, as well as a 46-yarder for Dallas. Redskin WR Art Monk could now claim receptions in 161 consecutive games, second most in the NFL and 16 shy of Steve Largent's record. The NFL's two lowliest teams, the Bengals and the Patriots, drew a season-low crowd of only 29,794 in Foxboro, Mass.

OFFENSIVE MVP: RB Jerome Bettis, Rams. The Rams' No. 1 draft pick became the first rookie in six years to rush for more than 200 yards in a game. His 212 yards and a touchdown were enough to spark the Rams to a 23-20 upset win over the Saints. It also put him over the 1,000-yard mark for the season (1,103).

DEFENSIVE MVP: CB Deion Sanders, Falcons. Two key interceptions by Sanders on San Francisco's first and last possessions turned one of the most exciting games of the year into a 27-24 Atlanta upset victory. Sanders was also credited with six tackles and a forced fumble while defensing 49er superstar WR Jerry Rice.

GOLDEN TOE: PK Al Del Greco, Oilers. Connecting on four-of-four field goals, Del Greco gave Houston just enough points to get past the Browns, 19-17. His last, a 25-yarder, was the game-winner and put him over the 100-point mark for the season.

TOP PERFORMANCES

PASSING

Player, team	Comp.	Att.	Yds.	TD	Int.
Steve DeBerg, Dolphins	27	44	344	1	2
Vinny Testaverde, Browns	19	37	319	2	2
Bubby Brister, Eagles	28	48	299	1	0
Bobby Hebert, Falcons	24	39	290	3	0
Jeff Hostetler, Raiders	18	25	278	1	0
Steve Young, 49ers	24	39	268	1	2

RUSHING

Player, team	Att.	Yds.	TD
Jerome Bettis, Rams	28	212	1
Rodney Hampton, Giants	33	173	1
Johnny Johnson, Jets	32	155	0
Gary Brown, Oilers	23	109	0
Derrick Moore, Lions	20	107	0
Emmitt Smith, Cowboys	19	104	1

RECEIVING

Player, team	Rec.	Yds.	TD
Michael Irvin, Cowboys	8	125	1
Herschel Walker, Eagles	11	109	0
Andre Rison, Falcons	6	107	2
Terry Kirby, Dolphins	7	107	0
Jerry Rice, 49ers	6	105	0
Anthony Miller, Chargers	8	103	0

SCORING

Player, team	TD	XP	FG	Pts.
Shannon Sharpe, Broncos	3	0	0	18
Al Del Greco, Oilers	0	1/1	4/4	13
Eddie Murray, Cowboys	0	4/4	3/3	13

GAME SUMMARIES

JETS 3, REDSKINS 0
Washington, D.C., Saturday, Dec. 11, 1993
N.Y. Jets   3   0   0   0   —   3
Washington   0   0   0   0   —   0
Scoring:
N.Y. Jets: Blanchard, 45 FG

FALCONS 27, 49ERS 24
Atlanta, Ga., Saturday, Dec. 11, 1993
San Francisco   7   10   7   0   —   24
Atlanta   7   0   0   20   —   27
Scoring:
San Francisco: Lee, 6 pass from Young (Cofer kick)
Atlanta: Rison, 5 pass from Hebert (Johnson kick)
San Francisco: Rathman, 2 run (Cofer kick)
San Francisco: Cofer, 32 FG
San Francisco: Young, 10 run (Cofer kick)
Atlanta: Haynes, 1 pass from Hebert (Johnson kick)
Atlanta: Rison, 6 pass from Hebert (Johnson kick)
Atlanta: Johnson, 47 FG
Atlanta: Johnson, 37 FG

BRONCOS 27, CHIEFS 21
Denver, Colo., Dec. 12, 1993
Kansas City   7   7   7   0   —   21
Denver   3   7   7   10   —   27
Scoring:
Kansas City: Hayes, 11 pass from Montana (Lowery kick)
Denver: Elam, 36 FG
Kansas City: Allen, 4 run (Lowery kick)
Denver: Sharpe, 9 pass from Elway (Elam kick)
Denver: Sharpe, 14 pass from Elway (Elam kick)
Kansas City: Davis, 29 pass from Montana (Lowery kick)
Denver: Sharpe, 6 pass from Elway (Elam kick)
Denver: Elam, 53 FG

COWBOYS 37, VIKINGS 20
Minneapolis, Minn., Dec. 12, 1993
Dallas   3   17   7   10   —   37
Minnesota   6   0   7   7   —   20
Scoring:
Minnesota: Reveiz, 19 FG
Dallas: Murray, 51 FG
Minnesota: Reveiz, 21 FG
Dallas: Irvin, 10 pass from Aikman (Murray kick)
Dallas: E. Smith, 4 run (Murray kick)
Dallas: Murray, 52 FG
Dallas: Johnston, 1 run (Murray kick)
Minnesota: Graham, 1 run (Reveiz kick)
Dallas: Murray, 46 FG
Dallas: Coleman, 1 run (Murray kick)
Minnesota: A. Carter, 9 pass from Salisbury (Reveiz kick)

RAIDERS 27, SEAHAWKS 23
Los Angeles, Calif., Dec. 12, 1993

Seattle	0	9	0	14	—	23
L.A. Raiders	3	7	17	0	—	27

Scoring:
- L.A. Raiders: Jaeger, 24 FG
- Seattle: C. Warren, 1 run (Kasay kick)
- Seattle: Safety, Stephens tackled Bell in endzone
- L.A. Raiders: Hostetler, 4 run (Jaeger kick)
- L.A. Raiders: Brown, 74 punt return (Jaeger kick)
- L.A. Raiders: Jaeger, 48 FG
- L.A. Raiders: Jett, 56 passs from Hostetler (Jaeger kick)
- Seattle: Mirer, 2 run (Kasay kick)
- Seattle: Martin, 7 pass from Mirer (Kasay kick)

BUCCANEERS 13, BEARS 10
Tampa Bay, Fla., Dec. 12, 1993

Chicago	0	3	7	0	—	10
Tampa Bay	3	7	3	0	—	13

Scoring:
- Tampa Bay: Husted, 38 FG
- Tampa Bay: Royster, 4 run (Husted kick)
- Chicago: Butler, 55 FG
- Chicago: Anderson, 1 run (Butler kick)
- Tampa Bay: Husted, 42 FG

LIONS 21, CARDINALS 14
Phoenix, Ariz., Dec. 12, 1993

Detroit	0	7	7	7	—	21
Phoenix	0	7	7	0	—	14

Scoring:
- Phoenix: Blount, 6 run (G. Davis kick)
- Detroit: H. Moore, 6 pass from Kramer (Hanson kick)
- Phoenix: Moore, 1 run (G. Davis kick)
- Detroit: Holman, 28 pass from Kramer (Hanson kick)
- Detroit: Green, 43 pass from Kramer (Hanson kick)

PACKERS 20, CHARGERS 13
San Diego, Calif., Dec. 12, 1993

Green Bay	7	6	7	0	—	20
San Diego	3	3	7	0	—	13

Scoring:
- Green Bay: E. Bennett, 3 run (Jacke kick)
- San Diego: Carney, 47 FG
- Green Bay: Jacke, 51 FG
- Green Bay: Jacke, 42 FG
- San Diego: Carney, 43 FG
- Green Bay: Thompson, 5 run (Jacke kick)
- San Diego: Lewis, 10 pass from Humphries (Carney kick)

RAMS 23, SAINTS 20
New Orleans, La., Dec. 12, 1993

L.A. Rams	10	0	13	0	—	23
New Orleans	7	6	0	7	—	20

Scoring:
- New Orleans: Mills, 30 fumble return (Andersen kick)
- L.A. Rams: Zendejas, 22 FG
- L.A. Rams: Bettis, 71 run (Zendejas kick)
- New Orleans: Andersen, 18 FG
- New Orleans: Andersen, 32 FG
- L.A. Rams: Boykin, 6 fumble return (Zendejas kick)
- L.A. Rams: Carter, 11 pass from Rubley (Zendejas kick blocked)
- New Orleans: Hilliard, 2 run (Andersen kick)

OILERS 19, BROWNS 17
Houston, Texas, Dec. 12, 1993

Cleveland	10	0	7	0	—	17
Houston	3	13	0	3	—	19

Scoring:
- Cleveland: Metcalf, 49 pass from Testaverde (Stover kick)
- Cleveland: Stover, 53 FG
- Houston: Del Greco, 27 FG
- Houston: Del Greco, 48 FG
- Houston: Tillman, 4 pass from Moon (Del Greco kick)
- Houston: Del Greco, 49 FG
- Cleveland: Carrier, 28 pass from Testaverde (Stover kick)
- Houston: Del Greco, 25 FG

GIANTS 20, COLTS 6
East Rutherford, N.J., Dec. 12, 1993

Indianapolis	0	6	0	0	—	6
N.Y. Giants	7	6	0	7	—	20

Scoring
- N.Y. Giants: Hampton, 1 run (Treadwell kick)
- N.Y. Giants: Calloway, 17 pass from Simms (Treadwell kick failed)
- Indianapolis: Biasucci, 21 FG
- Indianapolis: Biasucci, 26 FG
- N.Y. Giants: Bunch, 2 run (Treadwell kick)

BILLS 10, EAGLES 7
Philadelphia, Pa., Dec. 12, 1993

Buffalo	0	0	0	10	—	10
Philadelphia	0	0	7	0	—	7

Scoring
- Philadelphia: Williams, 10 pass from Brister (Bahr kick)
- Buffalo: Metzelaars, 2 pass from Reich (Christie kick)
- Buffalo: Christie, 34 FG

PATRIOTS 7, BENGALS 2
Foxboro, Mass., Dec. 12, 1993

Cincinnati	0	0	0	2	—	2
New England	0	7	0	0	—	7

Scoring
- New England: Coates, 8 pass from Bledsoe (Sisson kick)
- Cincinnati: Safety, ball snapped out of endzone

STEELERS 21, DOLPHINS 20
Miami, Fla., Monday night, Dec. 13, 1993

Pittsburgh	0	7	7	7	—	21
Miami	3	3	0	14	—	20

Scoring
- Miami: Stoyanovich, 31 FG
- Pittsburgh: Thompson, 1 run (Anderson kick)
- Miami: Stoyanovich, 22 FG
- Pittsburgh: Thompson, 3 run (Anderson kick)
- Pittsburgh: Hoge, 2 pass from O'Donnell (Anderson kick)
- Miami: K. Jackson, 3 pass from DeBerg (Stoyanovich kick)
- Miami: McDuffie, 72 punt return (Stoyanovich kick)

1993 REVIEW ■ WEEK 16

WEEK 16

WEEK 16 STANDINGS

AMERICAN FOOTBALL CONFERENCE

AFC EAST	W	L	T	Pct.	PF	PA
Buffalo	10	4	0	.714	283	218
Miami	9	5	0	.643	302	273
N.Y. Jets	8	6	0	.571	256	207
Indianapolis	4	10	0	.286	179	310
New England	3	11	0	.214	167	259

AFC CENTRAL	W	L	T	Pct.	PF	PA
Houston	10	4	0	.714	334	231
Pittsburgh	8	6	0	.571	286	256
Cleveland	6	8	0	.429	253	277
Cincinnati	2	12	0	.143	153	282

AFC WEST	W	L	T	Pct.	PF	PA
Kansas City	10	4	0	.714	284	237
L.A. Raiders	9	5	0	.643	273	268
Denver	9	5	0	.643	333	234
San Diego	6	8	0	.429	245	253
Seattle	5	9	0	.357	240	274

NATIONAL FOOTBALL CONFERENCE

NFC EAST	W	L	T	Pct.	PF	PA
N.Y. Giants	11	3	0	.786	269	172
Dallas	10	4	0	.714	322	213
Philadelphia	6	8	0	.429	219	255
Phoenix	5	9	0	.357	282	253
Washington	4	10	0	.286	218	293

NFC CENTRAL	W	L	T	Pct.	PF	PA
Green Bay	8	6	0	.571	292	252
Detroit	8	6	0	.571	248	248
Chicago	7	7	0	.500	214	190
Minnesota	7	7	0	.500	233	271
Tampa Bay	4	10	0	.286	203	334

NFC WEST	W	L	T	Pct.	PF	PA
San Francisco	10	4	0	.714	432	272
New Orleans	7	7	0	.500	271	293
Atlanta	6	8	0	.429	289	337
L.A. Rams	4	10	0	.286	187	319

WEEK 16 RESULTS | LINE
Denver 13, CHICAGO 3 — Broncos by 2
Dallas 28, N.Y. JETS 7 — Cowboys by 7
WASHINGTON 30, Atlanta 17 — Falcons by 3.5
Buffalo 47, MIAMI 34 — Dolphins by 2.5
Houston 26, PITTSBURGH 17 — Steelers by 4
CINCINNATI 15, L.A. Rams 3 — Rams by 2
Minnesota 21, GREEN BAY 17 — Packers by 6.5

New England 20, CLEVELAND 17 — Browns by 6
Phoenix 30, SEATTLE 27, OT — Seahawks by 2.5
KANSAS CITY 28, San Diego 24 — Chiefs by 8.5
San Francisco 55, DETROIT 17 — 49ers by 9
L.A. RAIDERS 27, Tampa Bay 20 — Raiders by 3
Philadelphia 20, INDIANAPOLIS 10 — Eagles by 1.5
N.Y. Giants 24, NEW ORLEANS 14 — Saints by 2

Home team in CAPS

The first two teams to clinch division titles did it in Week 16, the NFC West 49ers with a devastating 55-17 victory over the Lions and the Oilers by trouncing the Steelers 26-17 for the AFC Central crown.

The Cowboys ensured a playoff berth with their 28-7 win over the Jets. Their intradivisional rival Giants had secured a place in the postseason the week before. The remaining eight playoff invitations were still awaiting delivery. Buffalo and Kansas City were closest with 10 wins, and the Dolphins, Raiders and Broncos were hot on the trail with nine apiece. In the NFC Central, four teams maintained a legitimate shot at the division title, Green Bay and Detroit at 8-6 and Chicago and Minnesota with 7-7 records.

In all, 14 teams had a chance to join the four clinchers in postseason play, making for a dramatic final two weeks of the 1993 regular season.

After all the talk of the invisible offenses and low-scoring games that had come to typify 1993 in the NFL, the season took an explosive turn. The 49ers scored the most points of the year, and in the contest between the Bills and the Dolphins, the two teams amassed a total of 81 points. In only two games did the winner score less than 20 points, Denver defeating the Bears' stingy defense 13-3 and the Bengals, the league's lowest-scoring team, winning 15-3 over the Rams.

GAME OF THE WEEK: The wild showdown in the AFC East enabled Buffalo to claim sole possession of the division lead when it whipped the Dolphins 47-34 in the year's highest-scoring game. During a 13-minute span, Buffalo outscored Miami 38-3, helped by four Dolphin turnovers. "All of a sudden," Miami coach Don Shula said, "we started to play like Santa Claus."

CLEAN SWEEP: The Oilers won their ninth straight game of 1993, their longest win streak since 1961, and they also became only the 10th team since the NFL-AFL merger to sweep all eight of its division games. Of the other nine teams, five went on to win the Super Bowl in the year in which they swept their division.

SURNAME SACKS: Something in a name! With 14 games played, three defensive ends named Smith were among the top four in sacks in the AFC: Neil Smith of the Chiefs, 15; Anthony Smith of the Raiders, 12.5; and Bruce Smith of the Bills, 12.5. Another lineman with another common surname, Sean Jones of the Oilers, was the other member of the AFC's top-sack quartet with 13.

WHAT A DAY: In racking up the highest team score of the season, the Niners not only put 55 points on the scoreboard, they did not turn the ball over once, nor did they have to punt even once. They also scored on every possession in the first half and totaled 565 yards on offense for the game.

303

PRO FOOTBALL WEEKLY 1994 ALMANAC

PFW NOTES: Chief QB Joe Montana moved ahead of Sonny Jurgensen and into fourth place on the NFL's all-time touchdown pass list, as his total rose to 256 (still behind Fran Tarkenton, 342; Dan Marino, 298; and Johnny Unitas, 290). Cardinal WR Gary Clark moved up to 50 receptions for the season, becoming the first player in NFL history to accomplish that feat in nine consecutive seasons. Michael Husted's 57-yard field goal was the longest in Tampa Bay history. PK Matt Bahr, cut by the Browns a week earlier, kicked 2-of-2 field goals for the Patriots to provide the winning edge over favored Cleveland. QB Steve Beuerlein's 431 yards passing for the Cardinals has only been exceeded twice in club annals, both times by Neil Lomax. San Francisco WR Jerry Rice posted his 44th career 100-yard receiving game, second only in the NFL record book to Don Maynard, who claims 50. Dave Meggett's 75-yard punt return for a touchdown for the Giants was the longest in the NFC in 1993 and second in the league to Cleveland's Eric Metcalf, who returned one earlier for 91 yards. The Falcons turned the ball over six times to Washington, extending their ignoble NFL-high mark to 37.

OFFENSIVE MVP: QB Steve Young, 49ers. Playing less than three quarters, Young, the NFC's leading passer, tossed four passes for touchdowns and completed 17-of-23 for 354 yards. His TD passes included an 80-yarder to Jerry Rice and a 68-yarder to John Taylor.

DEFENSIVE MVP: LB Monte Coleman, Redskins. In his 16th year with Washington, the well-seasoned veteran Coleman gathered up a fumble and returned it 29 yards for a touchdown, forced another fumble, intercepted a pass and was credited with two sacks and nine tackles. Not a bad day for a 36-year-old linebacker called on to sub for the injured Carl Banks.

GOLDEN TOE: PK Greg Davis, Cardinals. In an overtime thriller, Davis provided the thrill and the kill, kicking a 55-yard field goal to tie the game as time expired and adding a 41-yarder in the extra period to give Phoenix a 30-27 victory over Seattle. He also kicked a 50-yarder during regulation.

TOP PERFORMANCES

PASSING

Player, team	Comp.	Att.	Yds.	TD	Int.
Steve Beuerlein, Cardinals	34	53	431	3	2
Steve Young, 49ers	17	23	354	4	0
Vinny Testaverde, Browns	21	31	297	2	2
Craig Erickson, Bucs	21	34	295	0	0
Steve DeBerg, Dolphins	20	35	273	2	1
Warren Moon, Oilers	19	38	268	1	0

RUSHING

Player, team	Att.	Yds.	TD
Chris Warren, Seahawks	27	168	1
Steve Broussard, Falcons	26	162	1
Scottie Graham, Vikings	30	139	0
Jerome Bettis, Rams	24	124	0
Rod Bernstine, Broncos	20	103	0
Gary Brown, Oilers	20	100	0

RECEIVING

Player, team	Rec.	Yds.	TD
Jeff Graham, Steelers	7	192	0
Gary Clark, Cardinals	12	152	1
Terry Kirby, Dolphins	9	148	1
Jerry Rice, 49ers	4	132	1
John Taylor, 49ers	4	115	1
Cris Carter, Vikings	6	106	0
Sterling Sharpe, Packers	6	106	1

SCORING

Player, team	TD	XP	FG	Pts.
Kenneth Davis, Bills	3	0	0	18
Al Del Greco, Oilers	0	2/2	4/5	14
Mike Cofer, 49ers	0	7/7	2/2	13

GAME SUMMARIES

BRONCOS 13, BEARS 3
Chicago, Ill., Saturday, Dec. 18, 1993

Denver	0	10	3	0	—	13
Chicago	3	0	0	0	—	3

Scoring:
Chicago: Butler, 31 FG
Denver: Elam, 29 FG
Denver: Delpino, 1 run (Elam, kick)
Denver: Elam, 24 FG

COWBOYS 28, JETS 7
East Rutherford, N.J., Saturday, Dec. 18, 1993

Dallas	0	7	14	7	—	28
N.Y. Jets	0	0	0	7	—	7

Scoring:
Dallas: Irvin, 42 pass from Aikman (Murray kick)
Dallas: Irvin, 3 pass from Aikman (Murray kick)
Dallas: K. Smith, 32 interception return (Murray kick)
N.Y. Jets: B. Baxter, 1 run (Blanchard kick)
Dallas: Johnston, 4 run (Murray kick)

CARDINALS 30, SEAHAWKS 27 (OT)
Seattle, Wash., Dec. 19, 1993

Phoenix	7	0	7	13	3	— 30
Seattle	10	10	0	7	0	— 27

Scoring:
Seattle: C. Warren, 45 run (Kasay kick)
Seattle: Kasay, 37 FG
Phoenix: R. Hill, 58 pass from Beuerlein (G. Davis kick)
Seattle: Kasay, 47 FG
Seattle: Edmunds, 1 pass from Mirer (Kasay kick)
Phoenix: Clark, 20 pass from Beuerlein (G. Davis kick)
Phoenix: Centers, 16 pass from Beuerlein (G. Davis kick)
Phoenix: G. Davis, 50 FG
Seattle: Mirer, 1 run (Kasay kick)
Phoenix: G. Davis, 55 FG
Phoenix: G. Davis, 41 FG

CHIEFS 28, CHARGERS 24
Kansas City, Mo., Dec. 19, 1993

San Diego	10	7	0	7	—	24
Kansas City	0	14	7	7	—	28

Scoring:
San Diego: Harmon, 28 pass from Humphries (Carney kick)
San Diego: Carney, 38 FG
San Diego: Young, 3 pass from Friesz (Carney kick)
Kansas City: Allen, 1 run (Lowery kick)
Kansas City: Davis, 9 pass from Montana (Lowery kick)
Kansas City: Birden, 4 pass from Montana (Lowery kick)
Kansas City: Davis, 28 pass from Krieg (Lowery kick)
San Diego: Means, 2 run (Carney kick)

EAGLES 20, COLTS 10
Indianapolis, Ind., Dec. 19, 1993

Philadelphia	10	0	7	3	—	20
Indianapolis	3	0	0	7	—	10

Scoring:
Philadelphia: Ruzek, 21 FG

1993 REVIEW ■ WEEK 16

Philadelphia: Sherman, 1 run (Ruzek kick)
Indianapolis: Biasucci, 39 FG
Philadelphia: Williams, 14 pass from Brister (Ruzek kick)
Philadelphia: Ruzek, 25 FG
Indianapolis: Langhorne, 24 pass from George (Biasucci kick)

RAIDERS 27, BUCCANEERS 20
Los Angeles, Calif., Dec. 19, 1993

Tampa Bay	0	10	0	10	—	20
L.A. Raiders	14	3	0	10	—	27

Scoring:
L.A. Raiders: Wright, 27 pass from Hostetler (Jaeger kick)
L.A. Raiders: McCallum, 5 run (Jaeger kick)
Tampa Bay: Cobb, 5 run (Husted kick)
L.A. Raiders: Jaeger, 50 FG
Tampa Bay: Husted, 57 FG
L.A. Raiders: Jaeger, 33 FG
L.A. Raiders: Hostetler, 1 run (Jaeger kick)
Tampa Bay: Cobb, 2 run (Husted kick)
Tampa Bay: Husted, 31 FG

49ERS 55, LIONS 17
Pontiac, Mich., Dec. 19, 1993

San Francisco	14	17	14	10	—	55
Detroit	0	10	0	7	—	17

Scoring:
San Francisco: Taylor, 68 pass from Young (Cofer kick)
San Francisco: Beach, 20 pass from Young (Cofer kick)
Detroit: Hanson, 51 FG
San Francisco: Rice, 80 pass from Young (Cofer kick)
San Francisco: Rathman, 2 run (Cofer kick)
San Francisco: Cofer, 43 FG
Detroit: D. Moore, 12 pass from Kramer (Hanson kick)
San Francisco: Rathman, 1 run (Cofer kick)
San Francisco: Lee, 12 pass from Young (Cofer kick)
San Francisco: Cofer, 21 FG
Detroit: H. Moore, 31 pass from Kramer (Hanson kick)
San Francisco: Carter, 50 run (Cofer kick)

PATRIOTS 20, BROWNS 17
Cleveland, Ohio, Dec. 19, 1993

New England	0	10	3	7	—	20
Cleveland	7	7	0	3	—	17

Scoring:
Cleveland: McCardell, 10 pass from Testaverde (Stover kick)
New England: Bahr, 23 FG
Cleveland: McCardell, 10 pass from Testaverde (Stover kick)
New England: Turner, 6 pass from Bledsoe (Bahr kick)
New England: Bahr, 34 FG
Cleveland: Stover, 23 FG
New England: Russell, 4 run (Bahr kick)

OILERS 26, STEELERS 17
Pittsburgh, Pa., Dec. 19, 1993

Houston	14	6	3	3	—	26
Pittsburgh	0	3	7	7	—	17

Scoring:
Houston: G. Brown, 38 pass from Moon (Del Greco kick)
Houston: Orlando, 38 interception return (Del Greco kick)
Houston: Del Greco, 34 FG
Houston: Del Greco, 22 FG
Pittsburgh: Anderson, 26 FG
Houston: Del Greco, 33 FG
Pittsburgh: Green, 36 pass from O'Donnell (Anderson kick)
Houston: Del Greco, 21 FG
Pittsburgh: Hoge, 5 run (Anderson kick)

BENGALS 15, RAMS 3
Cincinnati, Ohio, Dec. 19, 1993

L.A. Rams	0	3	0	0	—	3
Cincinnati	3	6	3	3	—	15

Scoring:
Cincinnati: Pelfrey, 43 FG
Cincinnati: Fenner, 1 run (Pelfrey kick failed)
L.A. Rams: Zendejas, 32 FG
Cincinnati: Pelfrey, 28 FG
Cincinnati: Pelfrey, 25 FG

REDSKINS 30, FALCONS 17
Washington, D.C., Dec. 19, 1993

Atlanta	7	0	7	3	—	17
Washington	0	16	0	14	—	30

Scoring:
Atlanta: Pritchard, 29 pass from Hebert (Johnson kick)
Washington: Safety, Coleman tackled Alexander in endzone
Washington: Rypien, 1 run (Lohmiller kick)
Washington: A. Johnson, 69 interception return (Lohmiller kick)
Atlanta: Broussard, 2 run (Johnson kick)
Atlanta: N. Johnson, 41 FG
Washington: Byner, 8 run (Lohmiller kick)
Washington: Coleman, 29 fumble return (Lohmiller kick)

VIKINGS 21, PACKERS 17
Milwaukee, Wis., Dec. 19, 1993

Minnesota	0	7	7	7	—	21
Green Bay	3	7	0	7	—	17

Scoring:
Green Bay: Jacke, 20 FG
Minnesota: Ismail, 6 pass from McMahon (Reveiz kick)
Green Bay: Sharpe, 37 pass from Favre (Jacke kick)
Minnesota: C. Carter, 6 pass from McMahon (Reveiz kick)
Minnesota: C. Carter, 25 pass from McMahon (Reveiz kick)
Green Bay: Clayton, 11 pass from Favre (Jacke kick)

BILLS 47, DOLPHINS 34
Miami, Fla., Dec. 19, 1993

Buffalo	9	17	21	0	—	47
Miami	7	13	7	7	—	34

Scoring:
Buffalo: K. Davis, 1 run (Christie kick)
Miami: Ingram, 14 pass from Mitchell (Stoyanovich kick)
Buffalo: Christie, 38 FG
Miami: Stoyanovich, 41 FG
Miami: K. Jackson, 16 pass from Mitchell (Stoyanovich kick)
Buffalo: K. Davis, 12 run (Christie kick)
Buffalo: Christie, 32 FG
Buffalo: Washington, 27 interception return (Christie kick)
Miami: Stoyanovich, 18 FG
Buffalo: Odomes, 25 fumble return (Christie kick)
Buffalo: K. Davis, 1 run (Christie kick)
Buffalo: Beebe, 27 pass from Kelly (Christie kick)
Miami: Kirby, 30 pass from DeBerg (Stoyanovich kick)
Miami: Ingram, 7 pass from DeBerg (Stoyanovich kick)

GIANTS 24, SAINTS 14
New Orleans, La., Monday night, Dec. 20, 1993

N.Y. Giants	7	7	3	7	—	24
New Orleans	0	7	0	7	—	14

Scoring:
N.Y. Giants: M. Jackson, 9 pass from Simms (Treadwell kick)
N.Y. Giants: Cross, 17 pass from Simms (Treadwell kick)
New Orleans: Muster, 1 run (Andersen kick)
N.Y. Giants: Treadwell, 22 FG
N.Y. Giants: Meggett, 75 punt return (Treadwell kick)
New Orleans: Hilliard, 5 pass from Buck (Andersen kick)

REVIEW: WEEK 17

PRO FOOTBALL WEEKLY 1994 ALMANAC

WEEK 17 STANDINGS

AMERICAN FOOTBALL CONFERENCE

AFC EAST	W	L	T	Pct.	PF	PA
Buffalo	11	4	0	.733	299	232
Miami	9	6	0	.600	322	318
N.Y. Jets	8	7	0	.533	270	223
Indianapolis	4	11	0	.267	179	348
New England	4	11	0	.267	205	259

AFC CENTRAL	W	L	T	Pct.	PF	PA
Houston	11	4	0	.733	344	238
Pittsburgh	8	7	0	.533	292	272
Cleveland	7	8	0	.467	295	291
Cincinnati	3	12	0	.200	174	299

AFC WEST	W	L	T	Pct.	PF	PA
Kansas City	10	5	0	.667	294	267
Denver	9	6	0	.600	343	251
L.A. Raiders	9	6	0	.600	273	296
San Diego	7	8	0	.467	290	273
Seattle	6	9	0	.400	256	280

NATIONAL FOOTBALL CONFERENCE

NFC EAST	W	L	T	Pct.	PF	PA
N.Y. Giants	11	4	0	.733	275	189
Dallas	11	4	0	.733	360	216
Philadelphia	7	8	0	.467	256	281
Phoenix	6	9	0	.400	299	259
Washington	4	11	0	.267	221	331

NFC CENTRAL	W	L	T	Pct.	PF	PA
Green Bay	9	6	0	.600	320	252
Detroit	9	6	0	.600	268	272
Minnesota	8	7	0	.533	263	281
Chicago	7	8	0	.467	228	210
Tampa Bay	5	10	0	.333	220	344

NFC WEST	W	L	T	Pct.	PF	PA
San Francisco	10	5	0	.667	439	258
New Orleans	7	8	0	.467	297	330
Atlanta	6	9	0	.400	306	358
L.A. Rams	4	11	0	.267	201	361

WEEK 17 RESULTS / LINE

Result	Line
Houston 10, SAN FRANCISCO 7	49ers by 9
CINCINNATI 21, Atlanta 17	Falcons by 3.5
Detroit 20, CHICAGO 14	Bears by 3
NEW ENGLAND 38, Indianapolis 0	Patriots by 6
GREEN BAY 28, L.A. Raiders 0	Packers by 3
PHILADELPHIA 37, New Orleans 26	Eagles by 3
BUFFALO 16, N.Y. Jets 14	Bills by 7
SEATTLE 16, Pittsburgh 6	Steelers by 3
Cleveland 42, L.A. RAMS 14	Browns by 2
PHOENIX 17, N.Y. Giants 6	Giants by 3
Tampa Bay 17, DENVER 10	Broncos by 13.5
DALLAS 38, Washington 3	Cowboys by 17
MINNESOTA 30, Kansas City 10	Chiefs by 2.5
SAN DIEGO 45, Miami 20	Chargers by 1

Home team in CAPS

The playoff picture became much clearer with nine of the 12 berths filled with one week remaining. Four teams could claim the best record in the NFL at 11-4, the Giants and Cowboys in the NFC and the Oilers and Bills in the AFC.

Adding drama to the upcoming final week, two clashes were destined to decide the divisional champions in both the NFC East and the NFC Central.

The Giants, who had led their division all the way through Week 16, lost to the Cardinals and were now forced to host the Cowboys, who defeated the Redskins, to see which team would emerge with 12 victories and the NFC East crown.

In the NFC Central, Both the Packers and Lions were victorious in Week 17 and now would meet in Detroit with identical 9-6 records to determine that division title.

Two spots remained open in the AFC, with Denver, Miami, Pittsburgh, the Raiders and the Jets all with a shot at them. Vying for the one open slot in the NFC would be the Vikings, Saints and Eagles.

GAME OF THE WEEK: The red-hot offenses of the 49ers, ranked No. 1 in the league, and the Oilers, third-ranked, met on Christmas Day in San Francisco, but the day belonged to the defenses. Houston shut down the 49er scoring machine, forcing the NFC's top quarterback, Steve Young,

PHOTO BY FLASH GORDON BAILA

Steve Young and the 49er offense, ranked No. 1 in the NFL, couldn't overcome the Oiler defense

306

1993 REVIEW ■ WEEK 17

into two endzone interceptions and a fumble and holding San Francisco to a single touchdown all day. The touchdown and field goal by Houston were enough to give the Oilers a 10-7 victory.

UNDERDOG DAYS: The 11-3 Giants did not expect to lose to the 5-9 Cardinals. And the Falcons, Steelers and Broncos, all with playoff hopes and the nod from the oddsmakers, did not figure to go down to defeat to the weakling Bengals, Seahawks and Buccaneers in this crucial week. But all four favorites came out on the wrong end of their respective final scores.

WIND-CHILL FACTORS: It was the coldest day of the season in many NFL cities. At game time, the wind-chill factor was minus-28 in Buffalo, minus-22 at Green Bay, minus -20 at Foxboro, Mass., minus-12 in Philadelphia and minus-11 in Chicago. All the home-town teams won, except for the Bears, who ordinarily delight in sub-zero temperatures.

BIG SCORES: Where were they the rest of the year? Dallas, with the second-highest point total for the year, was no surprise, scoring 38 points. But what about these otherwise listless offenses: San Diego scored 45 points, Cleveland 42, New England 38, Philadelphia 37 and Minnesota 30!

PFW NOTES: Packer WR Sterling Sharpe, with seven catches, brought his year's total to 106 and became the first receiver in NFL history to snare 100 passes in two seasons (he caught 108 in 1992, which set an NFL record.) Cleveland QB Vinny Testaverde set an NFL single-game completion-percentage record by connecting on 21-of-23 passes (91.3 percent); the previous record, 90.91 percent (20 of 22), had been held by Ken Anderson since 1974. Eric Allen's four interception returns for touchdowns matched a league record shared with Ken Houston of the Oilers (1971) and Kansas City's Jim Kearney (1972). RB Natrone Means' 65-yard touchdown run on Monday night was the longest run from scrimmage by a Charger in 12 years. The Patriots won in Week 17, but it was only their 13th victory in the 1990's with five of them coming at the expense of the Colts. New England also had the unwanted distinction of turning out the lowest crowd of the season, 26,571. RB Reggie Brooks became Washington's all-time leading rookie rusher when he moved to 995 yards, breaking Mike Thomas' mark of 919 set back in 1975. Giant QB Phil Simms moved ahead of Hall of Famer Y. A. Tittle to the 11th spot on the all-time NFL passing-yardage list (Tittle had 33,070, while Simms moved to 33,255).

OFFENSIVE MVP: RB Scottie Graham, Vikings. A free-agent pickup who was working in a pharmacy in Ohio two months earlier, Graham came on like an old pro by gaining 166 yards on 33 carries, which enabled Minnesota to control the clock in its 30-10 upset victory over Kansas City. The week before, he rushed for 139 yards against the Packers.

DEFENSIVE MVP: CB Eric Allen, Eagles. A three-time Pro Bowler, Allen picked off two passes and returned them for touchdowns in Philadelphia's impressive 37-26 win over the Saints. The two scores gave him an NFL-record-tying four interception touchdown returns in a single season.

GOLDEN TOE: PK Morten Andersen, Saints. Earning his keep as the highest-paid kicker in the NFL, Andersen booted 4-of-4 field goals for New Orleans in sub-zero, wind-swept Philadelphia, including a 56-yarder, the longest ever kicked at Veterans Stadium.

TOP PERFORMANCES

PASSING

Player, team	Comp.	Att.	Yds.	TD	Int.
T.J. Rubley, Rams	24	32	294	1	2
Neil O'Donnell, Steelers	20	43	285	0	1
Scott Mitchell, Dolphins	24	40	260	1	3
Jim Kelly, Bills	20	31	256	0	2
Stan Humphries, Chargers	19	29	248	3	0
Boomer Esiason, Jets	22	31	232	2	0

RUSHING

Player, team	Att.	Yds.	TD
Erric Pegram, Falcons	37	180	1
Scottie Graham, Vikings	33	166	1
Emmitt Smith, Cowboys	21	153	1
Leonard Russell, Patriots	26	138	2
Ron Moore, Cardinals	23	135	2
Jon Vaughn, Seahawks	26	131	0

RECEIVING

Player, team	Rec.	Yds.	TD
Sterling Sharpe, Packers	7	119	1
Eric Green, Steelers	7	119	0
Henry Ellard, Rams	8	114	0
Anthony Miller, Chargers	7	110	2
Courtney Hawkins, Bucs	8	105	1
Dwight Stone, Steelers	4	100	0

SCORING

Player, team	TD	XP	FG	Pts.
Natrone Means, Chargers	3	0	0	18
Morten Andersen, Saints	0	2/2	4/4	14

GAME SUMMARIES

OILERS 10, 49ERS 7

San Francisco, Calif., Saturday, Dec. 25, 1993

Houston	0	10	0	0	—	10
San Francisco	0	0	0	7	—	7

Scoring:
Houston: Del Greco, 24 FG
Houston: Givins, 7 pass from Moon (Del Greco kick)
San Francisco: Lee, 8 run (Cofer kick)

BROWNS 42, RAMS 14

Anaheim, Calif., Dec. 26, 1993

Cleveland	7	7	7	21	—	42
L.A. Rams	7	0	0	7	—	14

Scoring:
L.A. Rams: Bettis, 1 run (Zendejas kick)
Cleveland: Vardell, 1 run (Stover kick)
Cleveland: McCardell, 8 pass from Testaverde (Stover kick)
Cleveland: McCardell, 28 pass from Testaverde (Stover kick)
Cleveland: Carrier, 56 punt return (Stover kick)
Cleveland: Vardell, 1 run (Stover kick)
Cleveland: Mack, 1 run (Stover kick)
L.A. Rams: Anderson, 23 pass from Rubley (Zendejas kick)

LIONS 20, BEARS 14

Chicago, Ill., Dec. 26, 1993

Detroit	0	10	3	7	—	20
Chicago	7	0	0	7	—	14

Scoring:
Chicago: Worley, 1 run (Butler kick)
Detroit: Perriman, 20 pass from Kramer (Hanson kick)

Detroit: Hanson, 40 FG
Detroit: Hanson, 37 FG
Chicago: Harbaugh, 1 run (Butler kick)
Detroit: Hallock, 1 pass from Kramer (Hanson kick)

VIKINGS 30, CHIEFS 10
Minneapolis, Minn., Dec. 26, 1993

Kansas City	0	3	0	7	—	10
Minnesota	3	7	10	10	—	30

Scoring:
Minnesota: Reveiz, 22 FG
Minnesota: C. Carter, 31 pass from McMahon (Reveiz kick)
Kansas City: Lowery, 42 FG
Minnesota: C. Carter, 29 pass from McMahon (Reveiz kick)
Minnesota: Reveiz, 19 FG
Minnesota: Graham, 6 run (Reveiz kick)
Minnesota: Reveiz 34 FG
Kansas City: Cash, 2 pass from Krieg (Lowery kick)

COWBOYS 38, REDSKINS 3
Irving, Texas, Dec. 26, 1993

Washington	3	0	0	0	—	3
Dallas	7	14	14	3	—	38

Scoring:
Washington: Lohmiller, 32 FG
Dallas: E. Smith, 1 run (Murray kick)
Dallas: Irvin, 8 pass from Aikman (Murray kick)
Dallas: Harper, 15 pass from Aikman (Murray kick)
Dallas: Coleman, 1 run (Murray kick)
Dallas: K. Williams, 62 punt return (Murray kick)
Dallas: Murray, 38 FG

CARDINALS 17, GIANTS 6
Phoenix, Ariz., Dec. 26, 1993

N.Y. Giants	3	3	0	0	—	6
Phoenix	0	0	10	7	—	17

Scoring:
N.Y. Giants: Treadwell, 19 FG
N.Y. Giants: Treadwell, 22 FG
Phoenix: G. Davis, 20 FG
Phoenix: Moore, 19 run (G. Davis kick)
Phoenix: Moore, 1 run (G. Davis kick)

BUCCANEERS 17, BRONCOS 10
Denver, Colo., Dec. 26, 1993

Tampa Bay	0	10	7	0	—	17
Denver	7	0	3	0	—	10

Scoring:
Denver: Rivers, 5 run (Elam kick)
Tampa Bay: Moore, 19 pass from Erickson (Husted kick)
Tampa Bay: Husted, 48 FG
Tampa Bay: Hawkins, 14 pass from Erickson (Husted kick)
Denver: Elam, 24 FG

SEAHAWKS 16, STEELERS 6
Seattle, Wash., Dec. 26, 1993

Pittsburgh	0	3	0	3	—	6
Seattle	7	3	3	3	—	16

Scoring:
Seattle: Green, 2 pass from Mirer (Kasay kick)
Seattle: Kasay, 32 FG
Pittsburgh: Anderson, 42 FG
Seattle: Kasay, 48 FG
Pittsburgh: Anderson, 43 FG
Seattle: Kasay, 35 FG

BILLS 16, JETS 14
Orchard Park, N.Y., Dec. 26, 1993

N.Y. Jets	7	0	7	0	—	14
Buffalo	7	6	0	3	—	16

Scoring:
Buffalo: Thomas, 2 run (Christie kick)
N.Y. Jets: J. Johnson, 24 pass from Esiason (Blanchard kick)
Buffalo: Christie, 38 FG
Buffalo: Christie, 36 FG
N.Y. Jets: Burkett, 6 pass from Esiason (Blanchard kick)
Buffalo: Christie, 40 FG

PATRIOTS 38, COLTS 0
Foxboro, Mass., Dec. 26, 1993

Indianapolis	0	0	0	0	—	0
New England	7	10	14	7	—	38

Scoring:
New England: Russell, 2 run (Bahr kick)
New England: Bahr, 19 FG
New England: Cook, 1 pass from Bledsoe (Bahr kick)
New England: Timpson, 30 pass from Bledsoe (Bahr kick)
New England: Russell, 3 run (Bahr kick)
New England: Croom, 5 run (Bahr kick)

BENGALS 21, FALCONS 17
Cincinnati, Ohio, Dec. 26, 1993

Atlanta	7	0	3	7	—	17
Cincinnati	7	7	0	7	—	21

Scoring:
Cincinnati: Thompson, 3 pass from Klingler (Pelfrey kick)
Atlanta: Rison, 21 pass from Hebert (Johnson kick)
Cincinnati: Pickens, 24 pass from Klingler (Pelfrey kick)
Atlanta: Johnson, 49 FG
Atlanta: Pegram, 1 run (Johnson kick)
Cincinnati: Pickens, 6 pass from Klingler (Pelfrey kick)

PACKERS 28, RAIDERS 0
Green Bay, Wisc., Dec. 26, 1993

L.A. Raiders	0	0	0	0	—	0
Green Bay	0	7	7	14	—	28

Scoring:
Green Bay: E. Bennett, 1 run (Jacke kick)
Green Bay: Sharpe, 23 pass from Favre (Jacke kick)
Green Bay: Butler, 25 fumble return (Jacke kick)
Green Bay: Thompson, 60 run (Jacke kick)

CHARGERS 45, DOLPHINS 20
San Diego, Calif., Monday night, Dec. 27, 1993

Miami	3	10	7	0	—	20
San Diego	10	14	14	7	—	45

Scoring:
San Diego: Carney, 32 FG
Miami: Stoyanovich, 31 FG
San Diego: Means, 1 run (Carney kick)
Miami: Stoyanovich, 50 FG
San Diego: Means, 65 run (Carney kick)
Miami: Byars, 1 run (Stoyanovich kick)
San Diego: A. Miller, 41 pass from Humphries (Carney kick)
San Diego: Harmon, 21 pass from Humphries (Carney kick)
San Diego: A. Miller, 14 pass from Humphries (Carney kick)
Miami: Byars, 13 pass from Mitchell (Stoyanovich kick)
San Diego: Means, 1 run (Carney kick)

1993 REVIEW ■ WEEK 18

WEEK 18

WEEK 18 STANDINGS

AMERICAN FOOTBALL CONFERENCE

AFC EAST	W	L	T	Pct.	PF	PA
Buffalo	12	4	0	.750	329	242
Miami	9	7	0	.563	349	351
N.Y. Jets	8	8	0	.500	270	247
New England	5	11	0	.313	238	286
Indianapolis	4	12	0	.250	189	378

AFC CENTRAL	W	L	T	Pct.	PF	PA
Houston	12	4	0	.750	368	238
Pittsburgh	9	7	0	.563	308	281
Cleveland	7	9	0	.438	304	307
Cincinnati	3	13	0	.188	187	319

AFC WEST	W	L	T	Pct.	PF	PA
Kansas City	11	5	0	.688	328	291
L.A. Raiders	10	6	0	.625	306	326
Denver	9	7	0	.563	373	284
San Diego	8	8	0	.500	322	290
Seattle	6	10	0	.375	280	314

NATIONAL FOOTBALL CONFERENCE

NFC EAST	W	L	T	Pct.	PF	PA
Dallas	12	4	0	.750	376	229
N.Y. Giants	11	5	0	.688	288	205
Philadelphia	8	8	0	.500	293	315
Phoenix	7	9	0	.438	326	269
Washington	4	12	0	.250	230	345

NFC CENTRAL	W	L	T	Pct.	PF	PA
Detroit	10	6	0	.625	298	292
Minnesota	9	7	0	.563	277	290
Green Bay	9	7	0	.563	340	282
Chicago	7	9	0	.438	234	230
Tampa Bay	5	11	0	.313	237	376

NFC WEST	W	L	T	Pct.	PF	PA
San Francisco	10	6	0	.625	473	295
New Orleans	8	8	0	.500	317	343
Atlanta	6	10	0	.375	316	385
L.A. Rams	5	11	0	.313	221	367

WEEK 18 RESULTS	LINE
Minnesota 14, WASHINGTON 9	Vikings by 7
Buffalo 30, INDIANAPOLIS 10	Bills by 11
PITTSBURGH 16, Cleveland 9	Steelers by 5.5
Dallas 16, N.Y. GIANTS 13, OT	Cowboys by 6.5
DETROIT 30, Green Bay 20	Packers by 1
NEW ENGLAND 33, Miami 27, OT	Patriots by 1
Phoenix 27, ATLANTA 10	Falcons by 1.5
KANSAS CITY 34, Seattle 24	Chiefs by 7.5
L.A. RAIDERS 33, Denver 30, OT	Raiders by 3
San Diego 32, TAMPA BAY 17	Even
L.A. RAMS 20, Chicago 6	Bears by 3
NEW ORLEANS 20, Cincinnati 13	Saints by 5.5
HOUSTON 24, N.Y. Jets 0	Oilers by 4
Philadelphia 37, SAN FRANCISCO 34, OT	49ers by 12.5

Home team in CAPS

The 1993 finale: 16 teams close down shop for the year, 12 think about postseason play and maybe that lustrous silver Vince Lombardi trophy that comes at the end of each Super Bowl Sunday ... still several games down the road.

Minnesota secured the last playoff vacancy in the NFC when it slipped by the Redskins on New Year's Eve. The Steelers and Raiders earned postseason appearances in the AFC by defeating the Browns and the Broncos, respectively.

The Cowboys and 49ers proved to be repeat divisional champs in the NFL, although neither posted as good a record as they had in 1992 when Dallas won 13 games and San Francisco 14. The Bills also won their division again. Five teams that missed the playoffs in 1992 earned berths in '93: the Raiders, Broncos, Giants, Lions, and Packers.

At season's end, only six NFC teams could claim winning seasons; the AFC boasted seven. Only one team scored over 400 points, the 49ers with 473. The next closest was Dallas, far behind with 376. The Giants were the stingiest, allowing only 205 points, and Dallas was second in this department as well, giving up a mere 229.

GAME OF THE WEEK: Had to be two, both overtime thrillers. The Cowboys held off a Giant comeback in the second half and won the NFC East title with a field goal in the extra period, 16-13. The Raiders, who almost saw their playoff hopes dashed when the Broncos tried a field goal in overtime but missed, rallied with a kick of their own, a 47-yarder to win 33-30.

OVERTIME: To round out the regular season on a dramatic note, four games were decided in overtime. Three were of crucial consequence. The Cowboys and Giants fought for the NFC East crown. The Raiders and Broncos had a playoff berth for Los Angeles at stake. The Patriots, stepping out of the doldrums with their fifth win of the season, doused Miami's playoffs hopes with an overtime touchdown pass from rookie Drew Bledsoe. And the Eagles surprised the favored 49ers with an OT field goal on Monday night.

TOP TURNAROUNDS: Detroit went from 5-11 and last place in the NFC Central the year before to 10-6 and the division crown in 1993. The Giants, who were 6-10 and next to last in the NFC East, came back to post an 11-5 record and almost win the division title from the NFL's reigning champion Cowboys on the last day of the season. The Raiders improved from 7-9 to 10-6 and earned a playoff slot, and the Jets went from 4-12 to 8-8.

DISAPPOINTMENTS: The Redskins, 9-7 and a wild card in '92, dropped to 4-12 and the cellar of the NFC East in 1993. The Saints, another '92 wild card with a 12-4 record, dropped to 8-8 and no postseason play. San Diego, the AFC West

PRO FOOTBALL WEEKLY 1994 ALMANAC

champs of 1992 at 11-5, sunk to fourth place with an 8-8 record. And the Eagles, another 11-5 team and playoff participant the previous year, also fell to 8-8 in '93.

PFW NOTES: Packer WR Sterling Sharpe proved sharper than ever. In 1992 he set the all-time NFL record by catching 108 passes in a season; in 1993 he broke it by hauling in 112. To illustrate that offense and defense, even on the same team, do not necessarily get along, Oiler defensive coordinator Buddy Ryan threw a punch at offensive coordinator Kevin Gilbride on the sideline shortly before halftime of the Oiler-Jet game. It was hard to tell what the beef was about, since Gilbride's offense produced 24 points and Ryan's defense held the Jets scoreless. Kansas City PK Nick Lowery extended his NFL record for 100-point seasons to 11. Ram rookie RB Jerome Bettis set a club record when he carried the ball 39 times against the Bears. His 146 yards for the day gave him a season rushing total of 1,429 yards, second only to Emmitt Smith of the Cowboys in the NFL (only Eric Dickerson, George Rogers, Earl Campbell, Ottis Anderson and Barry Sanders gained more yards rushing as a rookie than Bettis in NFL history). Buffalo coach Marv Levy tied George Allen for 15th place on the NFL's all-time coaching victory list with his 118th victory (against 86 defeats over 12 seasons).

OFFENSIVE MVP: QB Drew Bledsoe, Patriots. The rookie capped off the finest day of his young career by tossing a 36-yard touchdown pass in overtime to give New England a 33-27 victory over the Dolphins. It was his fourth touchdown pass of the game, one in which he completed 27-of-43 passes for 329 yards.

DEFENSIVE MVP: DT Ray Childress, Oilers. A Pro Bowl electee, Childress anchored the Oiler front line, recording eight tackles, 2.5 sacks and a forced fumble, as Houston held the Jets scoreless. Childress and his defensive-unit teammates allowed only 11.3 points a game during Houston's 11-game winning streak to close out the season.

GOLDEN TOE: PK Jeff Jaeger, Raiders. With a 47-yard field goal in overtime, Jaeger gave the Raiders a 33-30 win over the Broncos and a place in the playoffs with home-field advantage. It was his last of four field goals during the day.

TOP PERFORMANCES

PASSING

Player, team	Comp.	Att.	Yds.	TD	Int.
John Elway, Broncos	25	36	361	3	0
Bubby Brister, Eagles	26	43	350	3	1
Jeff George, Colts	30	48	330	1	0
Drew Bledsoe, Patriots	27	43	329	4	1
Jeff Hostetler, Raiders	25	41	310	3	0
Steve Beuerlein, Cardinals	27	33	278	3	0

RUSHING

Player, team	Att.	Yds.	TD
Emmitt Smith, Cowboys	32	168	0
Jerome Bettis, Rams	39	146	1
Rodney Hampton, Giants	30	114	0
Eric Lynch, Lions	30	115	2
Thurman Thomas, Bills	26	110	1
John L. Williams, Seahawks	16	102	1

RECEIVING

Player, team	Rec.	Yds.	TD
Tim Brown, Raiders	11	173	2
Gary Clark, Cardinals	9	121	1
Eric Martin, Saints	5	120	1
Anthony Miller, Chargers	7	119	1
Mark Carrier, Browns	4	118	0
Shannon Sharpe, Broncos	6	115	2

SCORING

Player, team	TD	XP	FG	Pts.
Jeff Jaeger, Raiders	0	3/3	4/4	15
John Carney, Chargers	0	2/3	4/4	14
Roger Ruzek, Eagles	0	4/4	3/3	13

GAME SUMMARIES

VIKINGS 14, REDSKINS 9
Washington, D.C., Friday, Dec. 31, 1993

Minnesota	0	7	7	0	— 14
Washington	0	3	3	3	— 9

Scoring:
Minnesota: Graham, 1 run (Reveiz kick)
Washington: Lohmiller, 37 FG
Washington: Lohmiller, 35 FG
Minnesota: A. Carter, 11 pass from McMahon (Reveiz kick)
Washington: Lohmiller, 34 FG

RAIDERS 33, BRONCOS 30 (OT)
Los Angeles, Calif., Jan. 2, 1994

Denver	10	17	3	0	0 — 30
L.A. Raiders	0	13	7	10	3 — 33

Scoring:
Denver: Elam, 52 FG
Denver: Tillman, 27 pass from Elway (Elam kick)
Denver: Elam, 24 FG
L.A. Raiders: Brown, 4 pass from Hostetler (Jaeger kick)
Denver: Sharpe, 54 pass from Elway (Elam kick)
L.A. Raiders: Jaeger, 43 FG
Denver: Sharpe, 1 pass from Elway (Elam kick)
L.A. Raiders: Jaeger, 50 FG
Denver: Elam, 27 FG
L.A. Raiders: Brown, 24 pass from Hostetler (Jaeger kick)
L.A. Raiders: Jaeger, 39 FG
L.A. Raiders: Wright, 4 pass from Hostetler (Jaeger kick)
L.A. Raiders: Jaeger, 47 FG

CHIEFS 34, SEAHAWKS 24
Kansas City, Mo., Jan. 2, 1994

Seattle	3	7	0	14	— 24
Kansas City	10	17	0	7	— 34

Scoring:
Seattle: Kasay, 55 FG
Kansas City: Davis, 14 pass from Montana (Lowery kick)
Kansas City: Lowery, 23 FG
Kansas City: McNair, 3 run (Lowery kick)
Kansas City: Lewis, recovered blocked punt in endzone (Lowery kick)
Seattle: Johnson, 2 pass from Mirer (Kasay kick)
Kansas City: Lowery, 47 FG
Seattle: Williams, 23 run (Kasay kick)
Seattle: Edmunds, 4 pass from Mirer (Kasay kick)
Kansas City: McNair, 2 run (Lowery kick)

RAMS 20, BEARS 6
Anaheim, Calif., Jan. 2, 1994

Chicago	0	3	0	3	— 6
L.A. Rams	3	3	0	14	— 20

Scoring:
L.A. Rams: Zendejas, 29 FG
L.A. Rams: Zendejas, 29 FG
Chicago: Butler, 27 FG

1993 REVIEW ■ WEEK 18

L.A. Rams: Drayton, 11 pass from Rubley (Zendejas kick)
Chicago: Butler, 53 FG
L.A. Rams: Bettis, 4 run (Zendejas kick)

BILLS 30, COLTS 10
Indianapolis, Ind., Jan. 2, 1994

Buffalo	3	7	6	14	— 30
Indianapolis	0	3	0	7	— 10

Scoring:
Buffalo: Christie, 39 FG
Indianapolis: Biasucci, 22 FG
Buffalo: Thomas, 3 run (Christie kick)
Buffalo: Christie, 49 FG
Buffalo: Christie, 40 FG
Buffalo: Metzelaars, 1 pass from Kelly (Christie kick)
Buffalo: Brooks, 30 pass from Reich (Christie kick)
Indianapolis: Hester, 10 pass from George (Biasucci kick)

LIONS 30, PACKERS 20
Pontiac, Mich., Jan. 2, 1994

Green Bay	7	3	10	0	— 20
Detroit	0	10	6	14	— 30

Scoring:
Green Bay: E. Bennett, 39 pass from Favre (Jacke kick)
Detroit: Lynch, 5 run (Hanson kick)
Green Bay: Jacke, 54 FG
Detroit: Hanson, 37 FG
Detroit: Hanson, 53 FG
Green Bay: E. Bennett, 2 run (Jacke kick)
Detroit: Hanson, 48 FG
Green Bay: Jacke, 47 FG
Detroit: Lynch, 1 run (Hanson kick)
Detroit: Holman, 8 pass from Kramer (Hanson kick)

COWBOYS 16, GIANTS 13 (OT)
East Rutherford, N.J., Jan. 2, 1994

Dallas	3	10	0	0	3	— 16
N.Y. Giants	0	0	10	3	0	— 13

Scoring:
Dallas: Murray, 32 FG
Dallas: E. Smith, 5 pass from Aikman (Murray kick)
Dallas: Murray, 38 FG
N.Y. Giants: Bunch, 1 run (Treadwell kick)
N.Y. Giants: Treadwell, 29 FG
N.Y. Giants: Treadwell, 31 FG
Dallas: Murray, 41 FG

CHARGERS 32, BUCCANEERS 17
Tampa, Fla., Jan. 2, 1994

San Diego	10	3	3	16	— 32
Tampa Bay	0	3	7	7	— 17

Scoring:
San Diego: Carney, 48 FG
San Diego: A. Miller, 48 pass from Humphries (Carney kick)
Tampa Bay: Husted, 21 FG
San Diego: Carney, 38 FG
Tampa Bay: L. Thomas, 20 pass from Erickson (Husted kick)
San Diego: Carney, 43 FG
Tampa Bay: Hawkins, 42 pass from Erickson (Husted kick)
San Diego: Carney, 45 FG
San Diego: Young, 12 pass from Humphries (Carney kick failed)
San Diego: Means, 15 run (Carney kick)

CARDINALS 27, FALCONS 10
Atlanta, Ga., Jan. 2, 1994

Phoenix	7	10	3	7	— 27
Atlanta	3	0	7	0	— 10

Scoring:
Phoenix: R. Hill, 7 pass from Beuerlein (G. Davis kick)
Atlanta: Johnson, 24 FG
Phoenix: R. Hill, 9 pass from Beuerlein (G. Davis kick)
Phoenix: G. Davis, 29 FG
Atlanta: Pegram, 19 run (Johnson kick)
Phoenix: G. Davis, 20 FG
Phoenix: Clark, 20 pass from Beuerlein (G. Davis kick)

PATRIOTS 33, DOLPHINS 27 (OT)
Foxboro, Mass., Jan. 2, 1994

Miami	0	7	3	17	0 — 27
New England	3	7	7	10	6 — 33

Scoring:
New England: Bahr, 31 FG
New England: Coates, 11 pass from Bledsoe (Bahr kick)
Miami: Higgs, 5 run (Stoyanovich kick)
Miami: Stoyanovich, 29 FG
New England: Brisby, 11 pass from Bledsoe (Bahr kick)
Miami: Ingram, 9 pass from Mitchell (Stoyanovich kick)
New England: Bahr, 37 FG
Miami: Kirby, 15 run (Stoyanovich kick)
New England: Coates, 11 pass from Bledsoe (Bahr kick)
Miami: Stoyanovich, 24 FG
New England, Timpson, 36 pass from Bledsoe

OILERS 24, JETS 0
Houston, Texas, Jan. 2, 1994

N.Y. Jets	0	0	0	0	— 0
Houston	7	7	3	7	— 24

Scoring:
Houston: Givins, 22 pass from Carlson (Del Greco kick)
Houston: G. Brown, 8 pass from Carlson (Del Greco kick)
Houston: Del Greco, 38 FG
Houston: G. Brown, 16 run (Del Greco kick)

SAINTS 20, BENGALS 13
New Orleans, La., Jan. 2, 1994

Cincinnati	0	3	0	10	— 13
New Orleans	0	6	7	7	— 20

Scoring:
New Orleans: Andersen, 43 FG
New Orleans: Andersen, 49 FG
Cincinnati: Pelfrey, 22 FG
New Orleans: Smith, 9 pass from Walsh (Andersen kick)
Cincinnati: Pelfrey, 31 FG
Cincinnati: Brim, 23 interception return (Pelfrey kick)
New Orleans: E. Martin, 54 pass from Walsh (Andersen kick)

STEELERS 16, BROWNS 9
Pittsburgh, Pa., Jan. 2, 1994

Cleveland	0	9	0	0	— 9
Pittsburgh	0	3	3	10	— 16

Scoring:
Pittsburgh: Anderson, 36 FG
Cleveland: Stover, 36 FG
Cleveland: Stover, 47 FG
Cleveland: Stover, 44 FG
Pittsburgh: Anderson, 38 FG
Pittsburgh: Green, 14 pass from O'Donnell (Anderson kick)
Pittsburgh: Anderson 26 FG

EAGLES 37, 49ERS 34 (OT)
San Francisco, Calif., Monday night, Jan. 3, 1994

Philadelphia	10	14	10	0	3 — 37
San Francisco	3	7	14	10	0 — 34

Scoring:
Philadelphia: Ruzek, 34 FG
Philadelphia: Evans, 30 fumble return (Ruzek kick)
San Francisco: Cofer, 30 FG
Philadelphia: C. Williams, 13 pass from Brister (Ruzek kick)
Philadelphia: M. Young, 8 pass from Brister (Ruzek kick)
San Francisco: Rice, 3 pass from Young (Cofer kick)
San Francisco: Watters, 11 run (Cofer kick)
San Francisco: Taylor, 38 pass from Young (Cofer kick)
Philadelphia: Walker, 21 pass from Brister (Ruzek kick)
Philadelphia: Ruzek, 32 FG
San Francisco: Bono, 1 run (Cofer kick)
San Francisco: Cofer, 29 FG
Philadelphia: Ruzek, 28 FG

WILD-CARD PLAYOFFS

CHIEFS 27, STEELERS 24 (OT)

It took overtime, but the Chiefs managed to oust the Steelers with a Nick Lowery field goal at 11:03 in the extra period in an AFC wild-card game.

Kansas City benefited from some of Joe Montana's magic when he threw a seven-yard touchdown pass to Tim Barnett on fourth down to tie the score with 1:43 left in regulation.

But Montana couldn't have done it without the Chiefs' special teams, as Keith Cash blocked a punt and Fred Jones returned it 31 yards to the Pittsburgh nine-yard line just before the two-minute warning.

The Steelers led 17-7 at halftime, but the Chiefs began to take over in the third quarter, a period in which Montana was 17-of-21. A field goal from Lowery and a touchdown from Marcus Allen tied the score.

Trailing by seven in the fourth quarter, Kansas City went for a blocked punt and succeeded. Montana took over, tying the score and then moving the Chiefs into position on their second overtime possession for the game-winning field goal.

PFW NOTES: This was the 13th postseason game to go into overtime in NFL history and the seventh longest at 71:03.

SCORING SUMMARY
Kansas City, Mo., Jan. 8, 1994

Pittsburgh	7	10	0	7	0	— 24
Kansas City	7	0	3	14	3	— 27

Scoring:
Pittsburgh: Cooper, 10 pass from O'Donnell (Anderson kick)
Kansas City: Birden, 23 pass from Krieg (Lowery kick)
Pittsburgh: Anderson, 30 FG
Pittsburgh: Mills, 26 pass from O'Donnell (Anderson kick)
Kansas City: Lowery, 23 FG
Kansas City: Allen, 2 run (Lowery kick)
Pittsburgh: Green, 22 pass from O'Donnell (Anderson kick)
Kansas City: Barnett, 7 pass from Montana (Lowery kick)
Kansas City: Lowery, 32 FG

INDIVIDUAL STATS
PASSING
Steelers — O'Donnell 23-42-286, 35L, 3TD
Chiefs — Montana 28-43-276, 25L, 1TD; Krieg 1-1-23, 1TD
RUSHING
Steelers — Thompson 25-60, 10L; Hoge 6-27, 9L; Stone 3-11, 9L; O'Donnell 1-minus 1
Chiefs — Allen 21-67, 17L, 1TD; Anders 5-27, 15L; Montana 4-13, 7L; McNair 2-9, 8L; F. Jones 1-9
RECEIVING
Steelers — Graham 7-96, 35L; Mills 4-60, 26L, 1TD; Hoge 3-43, 32L; Stone 3-36, 26L; Thompson 3-4, 5L; Green 2-37, 22L, 1 TD; Cooper 1-10, 1TD
Chiefs —Cash 7-56, 18L; Birden 6-72, 23L, 1TD; Allen 4-29, 14L; Anders 3-30, 12L; Barnett 3-30, 15L, 1TD; Davis 2-47, 25L; Hayes 2-11, 6L; Hughes 1-15; McNair 1-9

PACKERS 28, LIONS 24

Green Bay QB Brett Favre, ridiculed after throwing four interceptions against the Lions a week earlier in the regular-season finale, hooked up with Sterling Sharpe for three TD passes, the last a game-winning 40-yarder with 55 seconds left.

The Lions led 17-14 late in the third quarter and appeared ready to punch in another score with the ball at the Packer five-yard line. S George Teague, however, intercepted a pass by Detroit QB Erik Kramer and returned it 101 yards for a touchdown, the longest TD in NFL playoff history (the old mark was 98 yards by the Jets' Darrol Ray against the Bengals in 1982).

The Lions regained the lead 24-21 with 8:27 left in the fourth quarter when Derrick Moore ran it in from five yards out. But in the closing minute, Favre found Sharpe all alone in blown coverage behind Detroit CB Kevin Scott.

PFW NOTES: Each team scored a touchdown on an interception return, which had not happened in an NFL postseason game since the Rams and St. Louis Cardinals met in 1975.

SCORING SUMMARY
Pontiac, Mich., Jan. 8, 1994

Green Bay	0	7	14	7	— 28
Detroit	3	7	7	7	— 24

Scoring:
Detroit: Hanson, 47 FG
Green Bay: Sharpe, 12 pass from Favre (Jacke kick)
Detroit: Perriman, 1 pass from Kramer (Hanson kick)
Detroit: Jenkins, 15 interception return (Hanson kick)
Green Bay: Sharpe, 28 pass from Favre (Jacke kick)
Green Bay: Teague, 101 interception return (Jacke kick)
Detroit: D. Moore, 5 run (Hanson kick)
Green Bay: Sharpe, 40 pass from Favre (Jacke kick)

INDIVIDUAL STATS
PASSING
Packers — Favre 15-26-204, 40L, 1I, 3TD
Lions — Kramer 22-31-248, 31L, 2I, 1TD
RUSHING
Packers — Thompson 12-41, 12L; E. Bennett 9-30, 10L; Favre 4-18, 10L
Lions — Sanders 27-169, 44L; D. Moore 1-5, 1TD; Kramer 1-1
RECEIVING
Packers — Sharpe 5-101, 40L, 3TD; West 3-40, 23L; Thompson 3-32, 12L; E. Bennett 2-21, 12L; Clayton 1-9; Brooks 1-1
Lions — Perriman 10-150, 31L, 1TD; D. Moore 4-14, 10L; Holman 3-31, 16L; Green 2-33, 21L; Sanders 2-0, 3L; H. Moore 1-20

GIANTS 17, VIKINGS 10

The Giants went into the lockerroom trailing 10-3 at halftime and came back out with some offensive adjustments. The most significant was a sweep toward the motion, which RB Rodney Hampton executed to perfection. Early in the third quarter, he circled the right side, stiff-armed Carlos Jenkins at about the Minnesota 35, got a crucial block from WR Chris Calloway and went 51 yards for a touchdown. It was the longest TD run from scrimmage in Giant playoff history.

The Vikings shanked a punt from their own five later in the third quarter and the Giants took advantage, moving 26 yards for another touchdown to give them a 17-10 lead. The New York defense, the stingiest in the NFL in terms of points allowed during the regular season, took over and held Minnesota scoreless in the final period.

QUOTABLE: Giant LB Lawrence Taylor, in re-

1993 REVIEW ■ WILD CARDS

The Raiders shut down John Elway and the Broncos in the second half of a wild-card playoff game

sponse to the 75,000-plus fans chanting, "L.T.! L.T.!" as a tribute: "If it is my last game at Giants Stadium, I enjoyed it. I've been treated well by everybody for 13 years." Taylor had one tackle, two assists and one pass defensed.

SCORING SUMMARY
East Rutherford, N.J., Jan. 9, 1994

Minnesota	0	10	0	0	—	10
N.Y. Giants	3	0	14	0	—	17

Scoring:
N.Y. Giants: Treadwell, 26 FG
Minnesota: C. Carter, 40 pass from McMahon (Reveiz kick)
Minnesota: Reveiz, 52 FG
N.Y. Giants: Hampton, 51 run (Treadwell kick)
N.Y. Giants: Hampton, 2 run (Treadwell kick)

INDIVIDUAL STATS
PASSING
Vikings — McMahon 12-25-145, 40L, 1TD; Salisbury 3-9-47, 30L
Giants — Simms 17-26-94, 18L

RUSHING
Vikings — Graham 19-29, 16L; McMahon 1-5; A. Carter 1-4; Craig 1-1
Giants — Hampton 33-161, 51L, 2TD; Simms 4-14, 7L; Bunch 1-1; M. Jackson 1-1; Tillman 2-minus 1, 1L

RECEIVING
Vikings — C. Carter 4-83, 40L, 1TD; Jordan 4-31, 15L; A. Carter 2-37, 24L; Graham 2-19, 17L; Reed 2-16, 12L; Ismail 1-6
Giants — Hampton 6-24, 7L; Meggett 4-12, 9L; Calloway 2-30, 18L; Cross 2-11, 6L; M. Jackson 2-9, 6L; Pierce 1-8

RAIDERS 42, BRONCOS 24

The first half was a shootout, and it looked like anybody's ballgame with the score tied at 21 apiece. But behind the passing of Jeff Hostetler, the running of Napoleon McCallum and a rejuvenated Raider defense, L.A. took total control of the game in the second half and walked off with an easy victory.

It was, in fact, the second week in a row the Raider defense shut down John Elway and the Denver offense in the second half. The week before, with the Raiders trailing 30-13 in the third quarter, they came back to win 33-30 in overtime to earn a berth in the playoffs.

QUOTABLE: Raider LB Aaron Wallace: "We made a few mistakes in the first half, but we came out in the second half and put out their fire." Raider QB Jeff Hostetler: "I thought the last team to score would win, but our defense came up big in the second half."

PFW NOTES: The only turnover of the game was an interception thrown by Elway which was picked off by Raider CB Torin Dorn. It was Elway's first interception in 141 passes.

SCORING SUMMARY
Los Angeles, Calif., Jan. 8, 1994

Denver	7	14	0	3	—	24
L.A. Raiders	14	7	14	7	—	42

Scoring:
L.A. Raiders: Horton, 9 pass from Hostetler (Jaeger kick)
Denver: Sharpe, 23 pass from Elway (Elam kick)
L.A. Raiders: Brown, 65 pass from Hostetler (Jaeger kick)
Denver: R. Johnson, 16 pass from Elway (Elam kick)
L.A. Raiders: Jett, 54 pass from Hostetler (Jaeger kick)
Denver: Russell, 6 pass from Elway (Elam kick)
L.A. Raiders: McCallum, 26 run (Jaeger kick)
L.A. Raiders: McCallum, 2 run (Jaeger kick)
Denver: Elam, 33 FG
L.A. Raiders: McCallum, 1 run (Jaeger kick)

INDIVIDUAL STATS
PASSING
Broncos — Elway 29-47-302, 25L, 1I, 3TD; Maddox 3-7-34, 13L
Raiders — Hostetler 13-19-294, 65L, 3TD

RUSHING
Broncos — Delpino 9-32, 16L; Elway 5-23, 6L; Rivers 1-2; Maddox 1-1; Milburn 2-minus 2, -2L
Raiders — McCallum 13-81, 26L, 3TD; Montgomery 15-50, 15L; Hostetler 4-5, 4L

RECEIVING
Broncos — Sharpe 13-156, 23L, 1TD; Marshall 5-69, 20L; Milburn 5-8, 6L; Russell 2-31, 25L, 1TD; Tillman 2-25, 16L; R. Johnson 2-19, 16L, 1TD; Taylor 1-13; Rivers 1-8; Evans 1-7
Raiders — Jett 3-111, 54L, 1 TD; Brown 3-86, 65L, 1TD; Horton 3-45, 33L, 1TD; Montgomery 3-29, 18L; Wright 1-23

PRO FOOTBALL WEEKLY 1994 ALMANAC

REVIEW: DIVISIONAL PLAYOFFS

Torin Dorn interfered with Andre Reed, which gave the Bills the ball on the eight-yard line

PHOTO BY TOM CROKE

BILLS 29, RAIDERS 23

The Raiders had their chance to take away Buffalo's AFC title belt but never unleashed the knockout punch. All game long, the Raiders seemed to have the Bills staggering, but Buffalo refused to go down for the count.

The Raiders took a 3-0 lead and were ahead 17-6 with 1:57 left in the first half. But Buffalo and QB Jim Kelly came back — Kelly to Thurman Thomas, Kelly to Andre Reed, Kelly to Don Beebe, a 37-yard pass-interference penalty and an eight-yard run by Thomas — and the halftime deficit was cut to four points.

The lead shifted in the second half to the Bills and then back to Los Angeles, but again Kelly took over, completing 5-of-5, the last a touchdown with less than three minutes remaining, enough to keep the Bills in contention for a fourth straight AFC title.

TURNING POINT: The pass-interference call on Raider Torin Dorn which gave the Bills the ball on the L.A. eight-yard line and led to a touchdown moments later.

OFFENSIVE MVP: Buffalo QB Jim Kelly, 27-of-37 for 287 yards, no interceptions and two touchdowns; his audibles led to big plays, and his staggered counts cost the Raiders five offside penal-ties.

DEFENSIVE MVP: Buffalo DE Bruce Smith, a very disruptive force credited with two sacks, four tackles, two assists and one forced fumble.

SCORING SUMMARY
Orchard Park, N.Y., Jan. 15, 1994

L.A. Raiders	0	17	6	0	—	23
Buffalo	0	13	9	7	—	29

Scoring:
 L.A. Raiders: Jaeger, 30 FG
 Buffalo: K. Davis, 1 run (Christie kick failed)
 L.A. Raiders: McCallum, 1 run (Jaeger kick)
 L.A. Raiders: McCallum, 1 run (Jaeger kick)
 Buffalo: Thomas, 8 run (Christie kick)
 Buffalo: Brooks, 25 pass from Kelly (Christie kick blocked)
 Buffalo: Christie, 29 FG
 L.A. Raiders: Brown, 86 pass from Hostetler (Jaeger kick failed)
 Buffalo: Brooks, 22 pass from Kelly (Christie kick)

INDIVIDUAL STATS
PASSING
 Raiders — Hostetler 14-20-230, 86L, 1TD
 Bills — Kelly 27-37-287, 25L, 2TD
RUSHING
 Raiders — McCallum 19-56, 9L, 2TD; Hostetler 5-29, 12L; Montgomery 9-22, 7L; Bell 2-3, 3L
 Bills — Thomas 14-44, 8L, 1TD; K. Davis 11-36, 6L, 1TD; Kelly 5-minus-5, -1L
RECEIVING
 Raiders — Brown 5-127, 86L, 1TD; Montgomery 3-26, 19L; Horton 2-42, 36L; McCallum 1-15; Bell 1-12; Duff 1-5; Jett 1-3
 Bills — Brooks 6-96, 25L, 2TD; Thomas 6-48, 18L; Metzelaars 5-43, 17L; Reed 4-53, 20L; McKeller 3-21, 8L; K. Davis 1-16; Beebe 1-9; Gardner 1-1

49ERS 44, GIANTS 3

San Francisco was out to prove why it held the mark for the most productive offense in the 1993 regular season and had little trouble illustrating it. In the annihilation, RB Ricky Watters set an NFL playoff record by rushing for five touchdowns, the previous record being three.

The 49er defense played with as much inspiration, holding the Giants to a mere 41 yards rushing and 153 passing and sacking New York QB Phil Simms four times. The Giants recorded only nine first downs on their own but picked up another three on penalties.

The Giants entered the game with the distinction of having allowed the fewest points in the league during the regular season, but the postseason was a different ballgame.

TURNING POINT: The coin toss, which the 49ers won and elected to receive.

OFFENSIVE MVP: San Francisco RB Ricky Watters, an NFL-playoff-record five touchdowns, 118 yards rushing and 46 more from pass receptions.

DEFENSIVE MVP: The entire 49er unit, but in particular, OLB Bill Romanowski, who tipped a pass for an interception and had a team-high five tackles.

SCORING SUMMARY
San Francisco, Calif., Jan. 15, 1994

N.Y. Giants	0	3	0	0	—	3
San Francisco	9	14	14	7	—	44

1993 REVIEW ■ DIVISION PLAYOFFS

Scoring:
San Francisco: Watters, 1 run (Cofer kick failed)
San Francisco: Cofer, 29 FG
San Francisco: Watters, 1 run (Cofer kick)
San Francisco: Watters, 2 run (Cofer kick)
N.Y. Giants: Treadwell, 25 FG
San Francisco: Watters, 6 run (Cofer kick)
San Francisco: Watters, 2 run (Cofer kick)
San Francisco: Logan, 2 run (Cofer kick)

INDIVIDUAL STATS
PASSING
Giants — Simms 12-25-124, 23L, 2I, 0TD
49ers — Young 17-22-226, 43 L; Bono 2-2-15, 10L
RUSHING
Giants — Hampton 7-12, 6L; Tillman 4-8, 3L; Da. Brown 1-8; Bunch 2-5, 3L; Meggett 2-5, 5L; Simms 2-3, 2L; M. Jackson 1-0
49ers — Watters 29-118, 20L, 5TD; Logan 9-40, 15L, 1TD; Young 3-17, 9L; Rathman 2-7, 6L; Lee 1-5; Rice 1-minus-9
RECEIVING
Giants — McCaffrey 5-59, 14L; Meggett 3-17, 10L; Cross 2-32, 23L; Calloway 2-24, 15L; M. Jackson 2-16; 12L; Hampton 2-11, 7L; Tillman 1-14; Pierce 1-7
49ers — Watters 5-46, 13L; L. Jones 4-39, 11L; Rice 3-43, 18L; Taylor 2-74, 43L; Rathman 2-16, 9L; Lee 2-15, 10L; Logan 1-8

COWBOYS 27, PACKERS 17

After stumbling most of the first 30 minutes, the Cowboys turned a tenuous 7-3 edge into a 17-3 lead in a period of 18 seconds at the end of the first half, the result of a field goal by Eddie Murray, a Packer fumble by Corey Harris on the ensuing kickoff and a Troy Aikman-to-Jay Novacek touchdown pass.

Aikman came back to extend the lead to 24-3 with a pump-fake touchdown pass to WR Michael Irvin.

The Packers came back with a touchdown in the same period, and were again threatening after a 43-yard punt return by Robert Brooks, but that was thwarted by an interception by Cowboy DE Charles Haley. Green Bay was never back in the game after that.

The fearsome Cowboy defense held the Packers to 31 yards rushing.

TURNING POINT: The kickoff fumble by Green Bay's Harris, which turned what would have been a 10-3 deficit at the half to a much more intimidating 17-3 score.

OFFENSIVE MVP: Cowboy OT Erik Williams, who has always had success against Packer DE Reggie White, limited the All-Pro to one tackle, one assist and no sacks.

DEFENSIVE MVP: Cowboy DT Leon Lett, who was perhaps remembered more for his gaffes in the previous Super Bowl and a play that cost Dallas a game against Miami earlier in the year, changed images and contributed five tackles, one fumble recovery and a tipped pass that resulted in an interception.

SCORING SUMMARY
Irving, Texas, Jan. 16, 1994

Green Bay	3	0	7	7	—	17
Dallas	0	17	7	3	—	27

Scoring:
Green Bay: Jacke, 30 FG
Dallas: Harper, 25 pass from Aikman (Murray kick)
Dallas: Murray, 41 FG
Dallas: Novacek, 6 pass from Aikman (Murray kick)
Dallas: Irvin, 19 pass from Aikman (Murray kick)
Green Bay: Brooks, 13 pass from Favre (Jacke kick)
Dallas: Murray, 38 FG
Green Bay: Sharpe, 29 pass from Favre (Jacke kick)

INDIVIDUAL STATS
PASSING
Packers — Favre 28-45-331, 48L, 2I, 2TD
Cowboys — Aikman 28-37-302, 27L, 2I, 3TD
RUSHING
Packers — Thompson 7-28, 10L; E. Bennett 6-3, 6L
Cowboys — E. Smith 13-60, 14L; Coleman 5-19, 9L; Johnston 3-12, 5L; Lassic 2-6, 7L; Aikman 3-0, 1L; Bates 1-0
RECEIVING
Packers — E. Bennett 9-53, 13L; Sharpe 6-128, 48L, 1TD; West 4-41, 20L; Thompson 3-54, 30L; Brooks 3-39, 17L, 1TD; Ingram 2-9, 7L; Lewis 1-7
Cowboys — Irvin 9-126, 27L, 1TD; Novacek 6-59, 14L, 1TD; Johnston 6-43, 12L; Harper 2-33, 25L, 1TD; E. Smith 2-27, 22L; Coleman 2-6, 6L; Lassic 1-8

CHIEFS 28, OILERS 20

The game was hyped as a battle between Chief QB and superstar Joe Montana vs. outspoken Oiler defensive coach Buddy Ryan. Montana was victorious.

Houston had bounced back from an eight-point deficit to pull within one in the fourth quarter. There was 3:27 left, and the onus was on Ryan's defense to hold and get the ball back. But, on 3rd-and-1 at the Kansas City 30-yard line, Montana found TE Keith Cash, who broke into Oiler territory. On a subsequent 3rd-and-1, RB Marcus Allen burst through Ryan's defense and ran 21 yards for a touchdown to ensure the victory.

All the Chiefs' 28 points came in the second half with 21 in the fourth quarter. And, as it turned out, it was the Kansas City defense which made the day, sacking Oiler QB Warren Moon nine times and causing seven Houston fumbles.

TURNING POINT: With Houston ahead 13-7 in the fourth quarter, Oiler CB Cris Dishman interfered with Chief WR Wilie Davis, which gave Kansas City a first down at the Oiler 11 and the opportunity for Montana to follow up with a touchdown pass.

OFFENSIVE MVP: Kansas City QB Joe Montana, performing under great pressure, threw three second-half touchdown passes, and was 22-of-38 for 299 yards for the day.

DEFENSIVE MVP: Chief DE Derrick Thomas had the biggest impact, racking up two sacks, forcing two fumbles and defensing one pass.

SCORING SUMMARY
Houston, Texas, Jan. 16, 1994

Kansas City	0	0	7	21	—	28
Houston	10	0	0	10	—	20

Scoring:
Houston: Del Greco, 49 FG
Houston: G. Brown, 2 run (Del Greco kick)
Kansas City: Cash, 7 pass from Montana (Lowery kick)
Houston: Del Greco, 43 FG
Kansas City: Birden, 11 pass from Montana (Lowery kick)
Kansas City: Davis, 18 pass from Montana (Lowery kick)
Houston: Givins, 7 pass from Moon (Del Greco kick)
Kansas City: Allen, 21 run (Lowery kick)

INDIVIDUAL STATS
PASSING
Chiefs — Montana 22-38-299, 41L, 2I, 3TD
Oilers — Moon 32-43-306, 30L, 1I, 1TD
RUSHING
Chiefs — Allen 14-74, 21 L, 1TD; Anders 1-0; Montana 1-minus-1; Krieg 2-minus-2, -1L
Oilers — Moon 3-22, 17L; G. Brown 11-17, 6L, 1 TD
RECEIVING
Chiefs — Birden 6-60, 14L, 1TD; Davis 5-96, 36L, 1TD; Cash 4-80, 41L, 1TD; Barnett 2-24, 14L; McNair 2-9, 9L; Allen 1-12; Hayes 1-9; F. Jones 1-9
Oilers — Jeffires 9-88, 28L; Givins 7-63, 15L, 1TD; Wellman 6-80, 30L; Duncan 6-49, 14L; G. Brown 4-26, 12L

315

PRO FOOTBALL WEEKLY 1994 ALMANAC

REVIEW: CONFERENCE CHAMPIONSHIPS

BILLS 30, CHIEFS 13

Over and over, Buffalo QB Jim Kelly stuck the ball in Thurman Thomas' stomach and shouted, "Go!"

"He must have said that 15-16 times today," Thomas said. "He sees a lot of things that I see. He knows that on certain plays, I'm going to get a lot of yardage."

And "go!" he did, as Thomas rushed for 186 yards and three touchdowns. As a result, Thomas, Kelly and the rest of the Bills ended up going to the Super Bowl, representing the AFC for the fourth consecutive year.

A Kansas City defense that held Thomas to 44 yards in a 23-7 victory during the regular season was, for the most part, at a loss to explain how it let him quadruple his total when it counted most. Except DT Dan Saleaumua, who said, "I don't think they did anything different. They just did everything better."

Beyond the Bills' dominance running the football, it was just two plays when Kansas City had the ball that knocked the Chiefs out of the Super Bowl hunt — QB Joe Montana's last pass of the first half and his first pass of the second.

What appeared to be a short touchdown pass to RB Kimble Anders at the end of the first half bounced out of his hands and was intercepted by S Henry Jones. The Bills ended up with a 20-6 halftime lead instead of 20-13. Then came the killer in the third quarter. A trio of Buffalo defenders collapsed on Montana as he threw a 17-yard completion at the start of the second half. The collision sent Montana to the sidelines for the remainder of the game.

The Go-Go Bills just kept going through the last half.

TURNING POINT: The apparent touchdown pass from Montana to Anders as the first half was coming to a close which ended up instead as a Buffalo interception.

OFFENSIVE MVP: Buffalo RB Thurman Thomas was unstoppable, gaining 186 yards on 33 carries, three for touchdowns. His running enabled the Bills to control the clock.

DEFENSIVE MVP: Buffalo LB Darryl Talley was very productive, making 10 tackles, one sack and defensing one pass.

SCORING SUMMARY
Orchard Park, N.Y., Jan. 23, 1994

Kansas City	6	0	7	0	—	13
Buffalo	7	13	0	10	—	30

Scoring:
- Buffalo: Thomas, 12 run (Christie kick)
- Kansas City: Lowery, 31 FG
- Kansas City: Lowery, 31 FG
- Buffalo: Thomas, 3 run (Christie kick)
- Buffalo: Christie, 23 FG
- Buffalo: Christie, 25 FG
- Kansas City: Allen, 1 run (Lowery kick)
- Buffalo: Christie, 18 FG
- Buffalo: Thomas, 3 run (Christie kick)

INDIVIDUAL STATS

PASSING
Chiefs — Krieg 16-29-198, 27L, 1I, 1TD; Montana 9-23-125, 31L, 1I
Bills — Kelly 17-27-160, 28L

RUSHING
Chiefs — Allen 18-50, 24L, 1 TD; Anders 2-1, 3L; Montana 1-1
Bills — Thomas 33-186, 33L, 3 TD; K. Davis 10-32, 15L; Reed 1-8; Kelly 2-3, 4L

RECEIVING
Chiefs — Cash 6-87, 19L; Davis 5-57, 17L; Birden 4-60, 26L; Allen 2-36, 27L; McNair 2-33, 31L; Hayes 2-14, 10L; E. Thompson 1-12; Hughes 1-11; Anders 1-7; Szott 1-6
Bills — Reed 4-49, 28L; Brooks 4-34, 11L; Metzelaars 4-29, 12 L; Thomas 2-22, 15L; Beebe 2-19, 11L; McKeller 1-7

PHOTO BY ROBERT L. SMITH

Cornelius Bennett let it be known the Bills earned their fourth-straight trip to the Super Bowl

1993 REVIEW ■ CONFERENCE CHAMPIONSHIP

Jay Novacek scored one touchdown as the Cowboys topped the 49ers in the NFC title game

COWBOYS 38, 49ERS 21

"We will win the ballgame," Cowboy coach Jimmy Johnson proclaimed earlier in the week. He was right, and he would have been equally correct if he had added his team would totally dominate the game.

It was, in fact, the third time in the last 13 months that Dallas defeated the 49ers. The first was in the NFC title game a year earlier when the Cowboys won 30-20 at San Francisco. The second was at Dallas during Week Seven of the regular season when the Cowboys won 26-17.

In this conference title game, Dallas scored touchdowns on four of its first five possessions to jump to a 28-7 lead. RB Emmitt Smith shouldered the load for Dallas, which outgained the 49ers 177-74 yards in the first half. The Cowboys also controlled the ball for 20:20 during those first two quarters.

The 49ers tried to threaten in the third quarter. First, Dallas QB Troy Aikman was knocked out of the game with a concussion. Then, San Francisco RB Ricky Watters scored a touchdown. The score was 28-14, and it appeared the 49ers were rolling.

Dallas backup QB Bernie Kosar came on, however, and turned things back around. On 3rd-and-8 back on their own 29-yard line, Kosar hit Michael Irvin for 12. Four plays later, he rifled a quick slant to WR Alvin Harper, who made a leaping grab and raced 42 yards for a Dallas touchdown.

The Cowboy defense dug in. Smith continued to rack up yards rushing and gather in passes. The 49ers never came close to getting back into the game.

TURNING POINT: The 49ers, cutting the lead to two touchdowns in the third quarter and with momentum going, faced off with the Dallas offense, 3rd-and-8, and Kosar stung them with a first-down pass to Irvin, which started a drive that resulted in a touchdown.

OFFENSIVE MVP: Emmitt Smith, despite an injured shoulder, carried 23 times for 88 yards, caught seven passes for another 85 yards and scored two of the Cowboys' first three touchdowns.

DEFENSIVE MVP: Dallas DE Charles Haley led the assault on 49er QB Steve Young. He was all over the field and contributed one sack, one forced fumble and a deflected pass.

SCORING SUMMARY
Irving, Texas, Jan. 23, 1994

San Francisco	0	7	7	7	—	21
Dallas	7	21	7	3	—	38

Scoring:
Dallas: E. Smith, 5 run (Murray kick)
San Francisco: Rathman, 7 pass from Young (Cofer kick)
Dallas: Johnston, 7 run (Murray kick)
Dallas: E. Smith, 11 pass from Aikman (Murray kick)
Dallas: Novacek, 19 pass from Aikman (Murray kick)
San Francisco: Watters, 4 run (Cofer kick)
Dallas: Harper, 42 pass from Kosar (Murray kick)
Dallas: Murray, 50 FG
San Francisco: Young, 1 run (Cofer kick)

INDIVIDUAL STATS
PASSING
49ers — Young 27-45-287, 25L, 1TD
Cowboys — Aikman 14-18-177, 28L, 2TD; Kosar 5-9-83, 42L, 1TD; Harper 0-1

RUSHING
49ers — Young 7-38, 18L, 1TD; Watters 12-37, 8L, 1TD; Rathman 2-9, 6L
Cowboys — E. Smith 23-88, 9L, 1TD; Aikman 3-25, 12L; Johnston 4-13, 4L, 1TD; Lassic 1-1; Kosar 2-minus 3, -1L

RECEIVING
49ers — Watters 7-33, 9L; Rice 6-83, 23L; Taylor 3-61, 22L; Williams 3-44, 25L; Jones 3-26, 13L; Logan 3-21, 8L; Turner 1-12; Rathman 1-7, 1TD
Cowboys — E. Smith 7-85, 28L, 1TD; Harper 4-78, 42L, 1TD; Novacek 4-57, 20L, 1 TD; Irvin 2-23, 12L; Johnston 2-17, 9L

PRO FOOTBALL WEEKLY 1994 ALMANAC

SUPER BOWL XXVIII

REVIEW

PHOTO BY MIKE LASSITER

Emmitt Smith scored two touchdowns and earned MVP honors as Dallas beat up on Buffalo again

COWBOYS 30, BILLS 13

It was Tuesday, Jan. 25, still five long days before Super Bowl XXVIII, when Cowboy S James Washington described his club before a milling throng of the nation's sporting press, each scribe searching for a nugget of truth from which to spawn his very own super hype.

"We're coming downhill on the run, and we're running through people on the pass, and people are thinking about us," Washington said. "We work hard when it's time to work hard, and we have fun when it's time to have fun."

Washington, it turned out, was quite the pre-Super Bowl prophet. Consider his response to this query: "What single factor most makes your team successful?"

"Emmitt Smith, Emmitt Smith, Emmitt Smith. He's the best running back, the greatest running back there is," answered Washington.

Washington was describing Super Bowl XXVIII, the Cowboys' 30-13 victory over the Buffalo Bills, with remarkable accuracy for anybody who wanted to listen, almost a week before it was played. Still, it seemed nobody wanted to hear. For all the marvelous accomplishments of the Dallas defense, when the 'Boys come to town, Smith, Troy Aikman, Michael Irvin and Alvin Harper are all anybody seems able to talk about.

In the end, it was Smith who was given the trip to Disney World that comes with the Super Bowl Most Valuable Player honor, even though Washington deserved it just as much.

Dallas rolled up 341 yards of offense while earning a nine-minute time-of-possession advantage over the Bills. But the difference in the game was a Cowboy defense that limited Buffalo to 87 yards on the ground and 5-of-17 efficiency on third downs. It also sacked Jim Kelly three times for 33 yards in losses and created three takeaways, with Washington the key figure in all of them.

What did Smith think was the key to the Cowboys becoming back-to-back champions, given the advantage of 20-20 hindsight immediately follow-

318

ing the game in the tumult of a jubilant lockerroom celebration?

"I think Washington's fumble recovery for a touchdown was a big, big plus in this game," he said. "Before every game I always talk about the touchdowns and turnovers, and James Washington came up big with turnovers today. I think he was the big motivating factor for us to go back on the field as an offense and get things going (in the second half), because we were kind of in a slump. After that, it just picked up our momentum from then on."

The game looked like it could get out of hand fast, as Cowboy WR Kevin Williams returned the game's opening kickoff 50 yards to the Bills' 48-yard line. Aikman hit Irvin for 20 yards and Jay Novacek for four more, but, after Smith was stopped for no gain on his first rush of the game, Aikman tried to force the ball into a well-covered Williams, throwing incomplete and forcing Dallas to settle for a 41-yard field goal by Eddie Murray and a 3-0 lead.

The Bills came right back. Jim Kelly used just seven plays to march his team 43 yards, a big chunk of them coming on a 24-yard catch-and-run by Thurman Thomas. But Buffalo's drive stalled when Kelly threw high and behind an open Bill Brooks on 3rd-and-7 at the Dallas 36. Still, a Super Bowl-record 54-yard field goal by Steve Christie tied the score at 3-3 and clearly energized the Bills.

The Buffalo defense stormed out and stuffed Dallas on a three-and-out, thanks in part to a holding penalty by Dallas OG John Gesek, and Buffalo got the ball back at its own 41 with 8:01 left in the first period.

On first down, Kelly tossed Thomas a shovel pass, and the running back carried the ball for seven yards, where he met Washington, who created the first of his three takeaways.

"The shovel play was a read that was given real simple," Washington said. "I had an opportunity to read it. Watching film, you get the chance to key in on certain things, and I got a jump on it and caused a fumble."

Buffalo DE Bruce Smith wondered after the game if that wasn't the beginning of the end right there. "Turnovers will kill you every time," he said. "That is what happened today. I am not one to point the finger or anything like that, but turnovers pretty much decided the outcome of this ballgame."

Certainly, the game didn't end there. Dallas marched 40 yards in four plays to the Buffalo 10. Murray's 24-yard field goal gave the Cowboys a 6-3 lead but seemed to inspire Buffalo a great deal more than Dallas.

The Bills dominated the remaining 18:55 of the first half, putting up 10 unanswered points and controlling both sides of the line of scrimmage. Following Murray's kickoff, the Bills marched 80 yards in 17 plays, eating 6:29 off the clock, to score the game's first touchdown on a run by Thomas. Buffalo CB Nate Odomes later intercepted a Dallas pass which led to another Christie field goal, giving the Bills a 13-6 halftime advantage.

The Bills returned the opening kickoff of the third period to their own 28-yard line. Thomas rushed for six yards on the first play, and then Kelly passed for nine yards to Brooks.

But, on the third play of the half, Thomas took a handoff up the middle, gained about three yards and then was met in the pile by Dallas DT Leon Lett. The ball squirted out, and Washington picked it up in stride and danced 46 yards around some rather feeble tackle attempts by Kelly and Don Beebe to a touchdown and a 13-13 tie.

The Bills immediately went three downs and out on the ensuing kickoff, the key play being a 13-yard sack of Kelly by Jim Jeffcoat on 3rd-and-8.

Now it was time for Smith to take charge.

Dallas marched 42 yards on six straight Smith runs. Then, following a three-yard Aikman-to-Daryl Johnston pass, Smith provided what was probably the final turning point play of the game. On 3rd-and-3 at the Bills' 15, Buffalo NT Jeff Wright broke through the line clean and got both arms around Smith three yards deep into the backfield. But Smith broke through Wright's tackle for a 15-yard touchdown. Instead of a morale-boosting stop that would have led to a field-goal attempt and a three-point deficit, the Bills trailed 20-13 with just 6:18 gone in the half.

After the game, Levy said, "They just went to the run more than I believed they had in the first half. They pounded it out pretty well on us. I don't know if they ran that well on us the rest of the game. That was certainly a key drive for them."

Still, the Bills wouldn't quit, or so it seemed. While the defense forced the Cowboys to punt on their next two possessions, the Buffalo offense managed drives of only 17 and seven yards, punting twice. Thomas remained on the bench with cramps through both possessions. The Bills' third possession following the Cowboys' go-ahead score ended in disaster on the first play of the fourth quarter when Kelly was picked off by, of course, Washington at the Buffalo 46, from where he returned it 12 yards to the 34.

It was time for Dallas to put the game away, but not without one last piece of drama. The Cowboys moved from the 34 to the one in eight plays. But, on 3rd-and-goal, Smith was stuffed for no gain by Darryl Talley.

With 4th-and-1 at the goalline with a seven-point lead in the Super Bowl and 10 minutes left, the Cowboys chose to go for seven points. On a pitch off left tackle, Smith went into the endzone for his second touchdown of the game and a 27-13 lead.

The Bills would punt once more, which the Cowboys answered with a 10-play, 49-yard drive and a 20-yard field goal by Murray for the final margin of victory.

Then the Bills came up empty again, moving 51 yards over the last 2:39 of the game but unable to dent the scoreboard. All that remained was a Bernie Kosar kneel-down, and a hot time in "Hotlanta" for the tens of thousands of Cowboy fans who came to cheer their 'Boys.

And for the inevitable talk of three-peats and dynasties, Jeffcoat, the senior citizen of the Cowboys, said, "If we can keep this team together, if free-agency doesn't destroy it, this team is going to be one of the best teams that has ever come into the NFL. I guarantee you."

It's funny, but it's hard to doubt that anybody who watched Super Bowl XXVIII is arguing now. Especially not in Buffalo.

COWBOYS 30, BILLS 13

SCORING
Atlanta, Ga., Jan. 30, 1994

Dallas	6	0	14	10	—	30
Buffalo	3	10	0	0	—	13

SCORING:

FIRST QUARTER
Dallas: Murray 41 field goal, 12:41. Drive: 24 yards in 5 plays, 2:19. Dallas 3, Buffalo 0.

Buffalo: Christie 54 field goal, 10:19. Drive: 43 yards in 8 plays, 2:22. Dallas 3, Buffalo 3.

Dallas: Murray 24 field goal, 3:55. Drive: 43 yards in 7 plays, 4:02. Dallas 6, Buffalo 3.

SECOND QUARTER
Buffalo: Thomas 4 run (Christie kick), 12:26. Drive: 80 yards in 17 plays, 6:29. Buffalo 10, Dallas 6.

Buffalo: Christie 28 field goal, 0:00. Drive: 38 yards in 7 plays, 1:03. Buffalo 13, Dallas 6.

THIRD QUARTER
Dallas: Washington 46 fumble return (Murray kick), 14:05. Dallas 13, Buffalo 13.

Dallas: E. Smith 15 run (Murray kick), 8:42. Drive: 64 yards in 8 plays, 4:32. Dallas 20, Buffalo 13.

FOURTH QUARTER
Dallas: E. Smith 1 run (Murray kick), 9:50. Drive: 34 yards in 9 plays, 5:03. Dallas 27, Buffalo 13.

Dallas: Murray 20 field goal, 2:50. Drive: 49 yards in 10 plays, 4:10. Dallas 30, Buffalo 13.

ATTENDANCE: 72,817

STATISTICS

TEAM STATISTICS

	Dall.	Buff.
FIRST DOWNS	20	22
Rushing	6	6
Passing	14	15
Penalty	0	1
TOTAL YARDS	341	314
Rushing	137	87
Passing	204	227
PASSES ATTEMPTED	27	50
Completed	19	31
Had Intercepted	1	1
Tackled Attempting to Pass	2	3
Yards Lost Att. to Pass	3	33
PUNTS	4	5
Average	43.8	37.6
Returned	1	1
Yards returned	5	5
KICKOFFS RETURNED	2	6
Yards Returned	72	144
PENALTIES	6	1
Yards penalized	50	10
RUSHING PLAYS	35	27
Average Gain	3.9	3.2
TOTAL PLAYS	64	80
Average Gain	5.3	3.9
FUMBLES	0	3
Lost	0	2
FIELD GOALS ATTEMPTED	3	2
Made	3	2
THIRD-DOWN PLAYS	13	17
Converted to First Down	5	5
TIME OF POSSESSION	34:29	25:31

INDIVIDUAL STATISTICS

RUSHING
COWBOYS — E. Smith 30-132, 15L, 2TD; K. Williams 1-6; Aikman 1-3; Johnston 1-0; Kosar 1-(-1); Coleman 1-(-3).
BILLS — K. Davis 9-38, 11L; Thomas 16-37, 6L, 1TD; Kelly 2-12, 8L.

PASSING
COWBOYS — Aikman 19-27-207, 1I, 35L.
BILLS — Kelly 31-50-260, 1I, 24L.

RECEIVING
COWBOYS — Irvin 5-66, 20L; Novacek 5-26, 9L; E. Smith 4-26, 10L; Harper 3-75, 35L; Johnston 2-14, 11L.
BILLS — Brooks 7-63, 15L; Thomas 7-52, 24L; Reed 6-75, 22L; Beebe 6-60, 18L; K. Davis 3-(-5), 7L; Metzelaars 1-8; McKeller 1-7.

PUNTS
COWBOYS — Jett 4 for 43.8 avg, 47L, 2 in 20.
BILLS — Mohr 5 for 37.6 avg, 52L, 1 in 20.

PUNT RETURNS
COWBOYS — K. Williams 1-5, 1fc.
BILLS — Copeland 1-5, 1fc.

KICKOFF RETURNS
COWBOYS — K. Williams 1-50; Gant 1-22.
BILLS — Copeland 4-82, 22L; Beebe 2-62, 34L.

INTERCEPTIONS
COWBOYS — Washington 1-12.
BILLS — Odomes 1-41.

SACKS
COWBOYS — Jeffcoat 1.5 for 19.5 yds; Casillas 0.5 for 3.5 yds; Haley 0.5 for 6.5 yds; Tolbert 0.5 for 3.5 yds.
BILLS — Wright 2 for 3 yds.

FUMBLES
BILLS — Thomas 2, K. Davis 1.

FUMBLE RECOVERIES
COWBOYS — Washington 1, Woodson 1.
BILLS — K. Davis.

BUFFALO BILLS

WR 82	Don Beebe	DLE 90	Phil Hansen
OLT 70	John Fina	NT 91	Jeff Wright
OLG 74	Glenn Parker	DRE 78	Bruce Smith
C 67	Kent Hull	LOLB 53	Marvcus Patton
ORG 65	John Davis	LILB 97	Cornelius Bennett
ORT 75	Howard Ballard	RILB 55	Mark Maddox
TE 88	Pete Metzelaars	ROLB 56	Darryl Talley
WR 83	Andre Reed	LCB 47	Mickey Washington
WR 80	Bill Brooks	RCB 37	Nate Odomes
QB 12	Jim Kelly	SS 20	Henry Jones
RB 34	Thurman Thomas	FS 38	Mark Kelso

SUBSTITUTIONS
2 Steve Christie, 9 Chris Mohr, 14 Frank Reich, 23 Kenneth Davis, 24 Kurt Schulz, 28 Thomas Smith, 35 Carwell Gardner, 36 Jerome Henderson, 43 Matt Darby, 50 Keith Goganious, 51 Jim Ritcher, 52 Richard Harvey, 62 Mike Devlin, 63 Adam Lingner, 66 Jerry Crafts, 73 Mike Lodish, 77 Oliver Barnett, 84 Keith McKeller, 85 Russell Copeland, 89 Steve Tasker, 94 Mark Pike, 96 Monty Brown. **Not active:** 21 Nate Turner. **Did not play:** 7 Gale Gilbert, 29 James Williams, 33 Eddie Fuller, 68 Corbin Lacina, 81 Brad Lamb, 87 Chris Walsh, 92 John Parrella, 99 James Patton.

DALLAS COWBOYS

WR 80	Alvin Harper	DLE 92	Tony Tolbert
OLT 71	Mark Tuinei	DLT 75	Tony Casillas
OLG 61	Nate Newton	DRT 78	Leon Lett
C 63	John Gesek	DRE 94	Charles Haley
ORG 66	Kevin Gogan	MLB 51	Ken Norton
ORT 79	Erik Williams	RLB 59	Darrin Smith
TE 84	Jay Novacek	DB 20	Darren Woodson
WR 88	Michael Irvin	LCB 26	Kevin Smith
QB 8	Troy Aikman	RCB 24	Larry Brown
RB 22	Emmitt Smith	SS 27	Thomas Everett
RB 48	Daryl Johnston	FS 37	James Washington

SUBSTITUTIONS
3 Eddie Murray, 18 Bernie Kosar, 19 John Jett, 29 Kenneth Gant, 39 Derrick Gainer, 40 Bill Bates, 41 Dave Thomas, 43 Elvis Patterson, 44 Lincoln Coleman, 46 Joe Fishback, 55 Robert Jones, 58 Dixon Edwards, 67 Russell Maryland, 68 Frank Cornish, 70 Dale Hellestrae, 77 Jim Jeffcoat, 85 Kevin Williams, 89 Scott Galbraith, 91 Mark Vanderbeek, 95 Chad Hennings, 97 Jimmie Jones, 98 Godfrey Myles. **Not active:** 25 Derrick Lassic. **Did not play:** 17 Jason Garrett, 31 Brock Marion, 34 Tommie Agee, 62 James Parrish, 65 Ron Stone, 81 Tim Daniel, 83 Joey Mickey, 86 Tyrone Williams.

1993 REVIEW ■ PRO BOWL

PRO BOWL

In a Pro Bowl virtually devoid of offensive drama, the NFL can thank Andre Rison and his Falcon teammates for providing a few theatrics.

Rison had six catches for 86 yards, and his Atlanta teammate Bobby Hebert, a late substitute for injured Cowboy QB Troy Aikman, engineered two TD drives in the second half to lead the NFC past the AFC by a 17-3 score.

Rison was voted the game's Most Valuable Player. "It's the first time I've won the MVP of anything," Rison said. "It's especially great when you compete against such top-echelon athletes. This is the fourth year in a row I've been here, but this is the best."

After injuries sidelined Giant QB Phil Simms and Aikman, Hebert got his chance to play. He completed 4-of-6 passes for 68 yards, including a 15-yard TD pass to Viking WR Cris Carter 1:19 into the final quarter.

"That was a big play," said Hebert of the touchdown that gave the NFC its 14-point margin. "Cris Carter beat the coverage to get open and then get into the endzone."

That score was set up by a fumble recovery by Bear DE Richard Dent, who fell on the ball at the AFC 19 after the Vikings' John Randle stripped it away from Oiler QB Warren Moon. Moon had a poor game, completing 3-of-8 passes for 25 yards.

Ram rookie RB Jerome Bettis scored the game's only other touchdown on a four-yard run late in the third quarter. That capped a 48-yard drive which included a 32-yard pass from Hebert to Rison.

Seattle RB Chris Warren and Miami RB Keith Byars were the AFC's only offensive bright spots. Warren rushed for 64 yards on four carries, while Byars caught six passes for 53 yards.

Andre Rison

PRO BOWL ROSTERS

NATIONAL FOOTBALL CONFERENCE
OFFENSE
Quarterbacks — si-Troy Aikman, Dallas; Steve Young, San Francisco; i-Phil Simms, New York Giants; r-Brett Favre, Green Bay; r-Bobby Hebert, Atlanta.
Running backs — si-Emmitt Smith, Dallas; si-Barry Sanders, Detroit; Jerome Bettis, Los Angeles Rams; r-Rodney Hampton, New York Giants; r-Ricky Watters, San Francisco.
Fullback — Daryl Johnston, Dallas.
Wide receivers — s-Jerry Rice, San Francisco; s-Michael Irvin, Dallas; i-Sterling Sharpe, Green Bay; Andre Rison, Atlanta; r-Cris Carter, Minnesota.
Tight ends — s-Jay Novacek, Dallas; Brent Jones, San Francisco.
Offensive tackles — s-Erik Williams, Dallas; s-Harris Barton, San Francisco; i-John Elliott, New York Giants; r-Lomas Brown, Detroit.
Offensive guards — s-Nate Newton, Dallas; s-Randall McDaniel, Minnesota; Guy McIntyre, San Francisco.
Centers — si-Mark Stepnoski, Dallas; s-Jesse Sapolu; r-Bart Oates, New York Giants.

DEFENSE
Defensive ends — s-Reggie White, Green Bay; s-Richard Dent, Chicago; Chris Doleman, Minnesota.
Interior linemen — s-Sean Gilbert, Los Angeles Rams; s-John Randle, Minnesota; Russell Maryland, Dallas.
Outside linebackers — s-Rickey Jackson, New Orleans; s-Renaldo Turnbull, New Orleans; Pat Swilling, Detroit.
Inside linebackers — s-Hardy Nickerson, Tampa Bay; Ken Norton, Dallas.
Cornerbacks — s-Deion Sanders, Atlanta; s-Eric Allen, Philadelphia; Donnell Woolford, Chicago.
Safeties — s-Tim McDonald, San Francisco; s-Mark Carrier, Chicago; i-Thomas Everett, Dallas; LeRoy Butler, Green Bay.

SPECIALISTS
Punter — Rich Camarillo, Phoenix.
Placekicker — Norm Johnson, Atlanta.
Kick returner — Tyrone Hughes, New Orleans.
Special-teamer — Elbert Shelley, Atlanta

AMERICAN FOOTBALL CONFERENCE
OFFENSE
Quarterbacks — s-John Elway, Denver; i-Joe Montana, Kansas City; Warren Moon, Houston; r-Boomer Esiason, New York Jets.
Running backs — s-Thurman Thomas, Buffalo; s-Marcus Allen, Kansas City; i-Barry Foster, Pittsburgh; r-Chris Warren, Seattle.
Fullback — Keith Byars, Miami.
Wide receivers — s-Tim Brown, Los Angeles Raiders; si-Webster Slaughter, Houston; s-Anthony Miller, San Diego; i-Andre Reed, Buffalo; r-Irving Fryar, Miami; r-Haywood Jeffires, Houston.
Tight ends — s-Shannon Sharpe, Denver; i-Keith Jackson, Miami; Eric Green, Pittsburgh.
Offensive tackles — s-Richmond Webb, Miami; s-Howard Ballard, Buffalo; John Alt, Kansas City.
Offensive guards — s-Steve Wisniewski, Los Angeles Raiders; si-Mike Munchak, Houston; Keith Sims, Miami; r-Max Montoya, Los Angeles Raiders.
Centers — s-Bruce Matthews, Houston; Dermontti Dawson, Pittsburgh.

DEFENSE
Defensive ends — si-Bruce Smith, Buffalo; s-Neil Smith, Kansas City; Leslie O'Neal, San Diego; r-Sean Jones, Houston.
Interior linemen — s-Cortez Kennedy, Seattle; s-Ray Childress, Houston; Michael Dean Perry, Cleveland.
Outside linebackers — s-Derrick Thomas, Kansas City; s-Greg Lloyd, Pittsburgh; Cornelius Bennett, Buffalo.
Inside linebackers — s-Junior Seau, San Diego; Karl Mecklenburg, Denver.
Cornerbacks — s-Rod Woodson, Pittsburgh; s-Nate Odomes, Buffalo; Terry McDaniel, Los Angeles Raiders.
Safeties — s-Dennis Smith, Denver; s-Steve Atwater, Denver; Eugene Robinson, Seattle.

SPECIALISTS
Punter — Greg Montgomery, Houston.
Placekicker — Gary Anderson, Pittsburgh.
Kick returner — Eric Metcalf, Cleveland.
Special-teamer — Steve Tasker, Buffalo

s-starter; i-injured, did not play; r-inury replacement

ATLANTA FALCONS REVIEW

During the first five games of the season, the Falcons were going nowhere. Despite having made some aggressive moves during the offseason to upgrade its defense, Atlanta got off to an 0-5 start.

The Falcons needed a wake-up call. They needed a win. They needed something good to happen.

They needed CB Deion Sanders.

During the Falcons' awful 0-5 start, Sanders was completing his baseball season with the Atlanta Braves. When the baseball season ended, the Falcons' revival began.

On the day Sanders returned to the football field after the Braves' playoff loss in Philadelphia, he played for the Falcons in a Thursday-night victory over the Rams. Sanders wasn't used on kick returns in that game against the Rams, and his statistics weren't extraordinary, but his mere presence rejuvenated the Falcons.

"He brought a spark," said Falcon CB Darnell Walker, who had two interceptions and forced a fumble in that game. "Just playing with him is a motivator. I made a couple of plays, but he encouraged me, along with everybody else on the team."

Falcon QB Billy Joe Tolliver, who threw three TD passes in the win over the Rams, said of Sanders, "He's some athlete. Every time he's out (there), he elevates the play."

Sanders did more than provide a one-game spark. Despite the Falcons' 0-5 start, they rallied to a 6-5 record after Sanders' return. Despite missing the first five games of the season, Sanders led the NFC with seven interceptions. He also caught six passes, including a 70-yard TD reception against Dallas.

Former Phoenix coach Joe Bugel said, "I think he's the best football player in the National Football League, bar none."

Sanders did more than just post impressive statistics. More impressively, he helped his team gain confidence in itself.

"I just talk to my guys on the field, get them fired up, just try to make them believe in themselves," Sanders said. "If you don't believe in yourself, ain't nobody else will. I don't care what you do. I think that's all they needed to do. Just believe in themselves."

Once the team built its record to 6-7, it started to believe it might make the playoffs. That was before a late-season collapse in which the Falcons lost three straight games to teams with losing records — Washington, Cincinnati and Phoenix.

Playoff hopes were gone. So was coach Jerry Glanville. Two days after the regular season ended, Glanville was fired. The team's offensive coordinator, June Jones, was eventually hired as Glanville's replacement.

Jones inherited more than a one-man team. Although the Falcons' success was greatly tied to the return of Sanders last season, there were other members of the team who impressed in 1993.

As expected, the Falcon passing game was impressive. The team had three receivers with 70 or more catches: Andre Rison (86), Mike Pritchard (74) and Michael Haynes (72). This was in spite of the fact QB Bobby Hebert struggled with tendinitis in his throwing elbow, although the gutty quarterback still managed to throw for 2,978 yards and 24 touchdowns.

Unexpectedly, RB Erric Pegram enjoyed a breakthrough season. Pegram began the campaign as a backup to Eric Dickerson. Pegram ended the season ranked fourth in the NFL in rushing with 1,185 yards. Hebert's elbow problems gave Pegram his big opportunity. With a diminished passing attack, the Falcons began to use a tight end more often, and Pegram had 25 or more carries in six games.

PK Norm Johnson also had a big season, connecting on 26-of-27 field goals.

Despite all of those heroes on offense, the Falcons' record was an unimpressive 6-10. For the reason, look no further than the defense, which didn't get the job done. The Falcons' allowed a league-worst 385 points. They were also last in the NFL in average gain per pass play allowed, as well as average gain per defensive play allowed.

"I think the No. 1 thing as far as winning, we've got to get better on defense," said Jones.

1993 ROUNDUP

OFFENSIVE MVP: RB Erric Pegram ended the season ranked fourth in the NFL in rushing with 1,185 yards and three TD's on 292 carries.

DEFENSIVE MVP: CB Deion Sanders sparked the ailing Falcons when he arrived on the scene for the sixth game of the year. Sanders led the NFC with seven interceptions.

RESULTS
Pointspread Shown Refers To Atlanta

Date	Opponent	Spread	Score
Sept. 5	At Detroit	(+5.5)	13-30
Sept. 12	New Orleans	(+3.5)	31-34
Sept. 19	At San Francisco	(+13)	30-37
Sept. 27	Pittsburgh	(-3)	17-45
Oct. 3	At Chicago	(+6)	0-6
Oct. 14	L.A. Rams	(+2)	30-24
Oct. 24	At New Orleans	(+10.5)	26-15
Oct. 31	Tampa Bay	(-9.5)	24-31
Nov. 14	At L.A. Rams	(+4)	13-0
Nov. 21	Dallas	(+9.5)	27-14
Nov. 28	Cleveland	(-6.5)	17-14
Dec. 5	At Houston	(+7)	17-33
Dec. 11	San Francisco	(+8)	27-24
Dec. 19	At Washington	(-3.5)	17-30
Dec. 26	At Cincinnati	(-3.5)	17-21
Jan. 2	Phoenix	(-1.5)	10-27

1993 REVIEW ■ ATLANTA

GAME-BY-GAME STATISTICS

TEAM STATISTICS

OPPONENT	WK 1 DET.	WK 2 N.O.	WK 3 S.F.	WK 4 PITT.	WK 5 CHI.	WK 7 L.A.RM	WK 8 N.O.	WK 9 T.B.	WK 11 L.A.RM	WK 12 DALL.	WK 13 CLEV.	WK 14 HOU.	WK 15 S.F.	WK 16 WASH.	WK 17 CIN.	WK 18 PHX.	TOTALS
Score	13-30	31-34	30-37	17-45	0-6	30-24	26-15	24-31	13-0	27-14	17-14	17-33	27-24	17-30	17-21	10-27	
Total net yards	237	375	381	220	271	311	279	337	319	400	261	333	362	378	376	270	5110
Rushing yards	21	78	194	44	87	103	123	68	137	85	67	37	92	182	191	81	1590
Passing yards	216	297	187	176	184	208	156	269	182	315	194	296	270	196	185	189	3520
Rushing plays	8	20	29	17	23	28	39	15	34	34	24	12	25	35	39	13	395
Sacks allowed	6	4	2	3	3	1	1	1	1	0	2	3	0	4	7	2	40
Had intercepted	2	1	0	4	2	1	0	1	1	0	0	6	1	4	1	2	25
Fumbles lost	1	1	1	2	1	0	0	2	1	1	1	0	1	2	0	2	17
Yards penalized	34	60	5	50	73	5	39	91	55	40	45	88	80	80	15	78	838
Punts	8	6	2	3	7	4	3	4	6	2	6	3	4	4	7	3	72

OPPONENT STATISTICS

Time of possession	30:55	33:28	29:07	33:38	30:44	28:37	23:33	32:57	26:55	23:22	27:27	28:30	26:13	19:20	23:30	39:44	28:34
Total net yards	262	557	478	368	220	450	321	405	260	230	306	389	330	167	284	395	5422
Rushing yards	96	227	268	109	106	167	47	98	95	48	115	52	79	38	122	117	1784
Passing yards	166	330	210	259	114	283	274	307	165	182	190	337	251	129	162	278	3637
Rushing plays	35	31	33	34	30	30	12	34	20	13	29	23	19	10	24	34	420
Sacks allowed	2	2	0	0	1	2	1	2	6	2	0	1	3	0	2	0	26
Had intercepted	0	1	1	0	1	2	2	2	2	0	0	0	2	1	0	0	13
Fumbles lost	0	0	1	1	0	0	1	0	1	1	1	3	1	0	0	0	11
Yards penalized	20	82	65	88	49	50	72	70	58	51	20	71	30	0	25	123	874
Punts	6	4	0	4	6	2	4	5	8	6	5	1	4	7	8	4	74

INDIVIDUAL STATISTICS*

RUSHING

	WK 1	WK 2	WK 3	WK 4	WK 5	WK 7	WK 8	WK 9	WK 11	WK 12	WK 13	WK 14	WK 15	WK 16	WK 17	WK 18	TOTALS
Broussard			2-2-0						3-3-0								39-206-1
Dickerson	6-10-0	17-77-0		1-7-0	2-(3)-0		3-0-0		3-6-0	4-(3)-0	1-5-0		7-37-0	26-162-1	1-2-0		26-91-0
Hebert				3-0-0	2-4-0							1-10-0	6-18-0		1-9-0		24-49-0
Pegram		3-1-1	27-192-0	13-37-0	17-85-0	25-87-0	34-123-0	15-68-0	27-128-0	30-88-0	22-58-0	11-27-0	11-34-0	8-20-0	37-180-1	12-57-1	292-1185-3
Tolliver					2-1-0	3-16-0	1-7-0									1-24-0	7-48-0

PASSING***

Hebert		14-18-0 256-3	23-38-0 211-3	12-24-3 146-0	15-22-2 155-0		13-16-0 170-2	25-47-1 277-3	12-21-1 182-1	24-32-0 315-3	21-29-0 214-2	30-52-6 317-2	24-39-0 290-3	24-42-4 233-1	13-26-0 155-1	13-24-1 131-0	263-430-17 3052-24
Miller	26-50-2 260-1	6-15-1 85-0		0-1-0 0-0													32-66-3 345-1
Tolliver				5-13-2 66-0	8-13-0 77-0	18-34-1 218-3	0-2-0 0-0							0-1-0 0-0	3-5-1 52-0	5-8-1 66-0	39-76-5 479-3

RECEIVING

Dickerson	3-8-0	2-41-0			1-9-0												6-58-0
Haynes	4-32-0	7-182-2	6-55-0	5-43-0	6-56-0	2-15-0	4-47-1	7-49-0	1-11-0	6-61-0	4-47-0	8-55-0	5-40-1	5-63-0		2-22-0	72-778-4
Hill	3-17-0	2-11-0	3-25-0	2-40-0	3-40-0	1-4-0	1-27-0	1-17-0		4-42-0	1-10-0	4-32-0	2-39-0	2-13-0	2-30-0	4-41-0	34-384-0
Lyons					1-12-0	6-44-1	2-18-0	1-10-0		1-8-0	3-23-0		1-17-0				8-63-0
Mims				2-19-0										4-14-0	2-15-0	3-24-0	12-107-1
Pegram			1-5-0	1-0-0		6-79-0		1-9-0	3-19-0	3-27-0	2-11-0	6-94-0	2-19-0	8-92-1	1-1-0	4-36-0	33-302-0
Pritchard	10-97-0	4-29-1	6-43-0	3-43-0	4-23-0		1-10-0	4-45-1	3-32-0	6-71-2	4-32-1	6-60-1	6-57-0	3-35-0	5-66-0	4-59-0	74-736-7
Rison	6-106-1	5-65-0	7-71-3	4-50-0	7-76-0	3-71-2	5-61-1	11-147-2	5-120-1	3-36-0	5-78-1	6-76-1	6-107-2	3-35-0	6-84-1	4-59-1	86-1242-15
Sanders										1-70-1	2-13-0		1-7-0	2-16-0			6-106-1

* Doesn't include all players. ** Passing stats include completions, attempts, interceptions, gross yards gained and touchdowns.

PRO FOOTBALL WEEKLY 1994 ALMANAC

REVIEW: BUFFALO BILLS

The Buffalo Bills may not have proven themselves in the Super Bowl the last four years, but they have certainly proven to be resilient. No team in professional sports history had gotten to the championship level for four consecutive years without winning the big dance at least once.

Should the Bills be mocked or applauded for their accomplishments? That all depends on if the glass is seen as half-full or half-empty.

The optimist might say that the Bills are to be admired. In the 1993 season, they did not have Pro Bowl OT Will Wolford, ILB's Shane Conlan and Carlton Bailey and PR Clifford Hicks — all lost to free-agency — yet they still made it back to the Super Bowl.

In 1992 the Bills made it to the Super Bowl despite finishing in second place in the AFC East and coming from the wild-card position. In 1993 they went the more conventional route, winning their division and locking up home-field advantage in the process. It would be fair to say the Bills improved between the 1992 and '93 seasons.

A big reason for that improvement was the return to form of DE Bruce Smith, who led the team with 13.5 sacks, which tied for second in the league. Smith's quickness and variety of spin moves allowed other Buffalo defenders like DE Phil Hansen, LB's Marvcus Patton and Darryl Talley and S Henry Jones to make numerous big plays. The Bills finished the regular season at plus-12 on the turnover/takeaway table, and that defensive prowess played a big part in the Bills winning their last four games of the season.

Offensively, however, it seemed the Bills' once-powerful no-huddle machine was badly in need of a few new cogs. The Bills struggled to put points on the board — especially early in the season — and complaints were voiced.

QB Jim Kelly thought the Buffalo offense needed to go back to its peaceful days by speeding up the pace of the no-huddle. "We need to start making plays a little quicker," Kelly said. "The longer we wait, the more of a chance it gives the defense to make whatever adjustments are needed. The slower-paced offense is good in the second half when we have a lead, the faster-paced offense means we have an attack frame of mind."

Even with Kelly's backing, the Buffalo offense rarely was played at a frenetic pace. Many observers thought that was an impossibility because many of the key members on the team were getting older.

The key for the Bills during the 1993 season was their Week 16 confrontation with the Dolphins in Joe Robbie Stadium. In that game, the Bills' defense dominated, taking Miami out of the game with turnovers. They scored two defensive touchdowns and cruised to a 47-34 victory, leaving Miami defenseless and broken in its last two games.

In the postseason, the Bills gave signs that they might be able to exorcise their past Super Bowl demons. They overcame an 11-point, first-half deficit to beat the Raiders 29-23 before dismantling Joe Montana and the Chiefs 30-13. In the AFC championship game, RB Thurman Thomas was everywhere, ripping Kansas City for two touchdowns and almost single-handedly running out the clock in the fourth quarter.

The Super Bowl was a different story. While Buffalo showed none of the indecisiveness that marked the routs it suffered in defeats to the Redskins and Cowboys the previous two years, the '93 version of the team demonstrated it could not stand prosperity. Buffalo took a 13-6 lead over the Cowboys into the lockerroom, and instead of taking it to Dallas in the second half, it gave the game away. A Thomas fumble that was returned for a touchdown by Cowboy SS James Washington started the run, and, by the time it was all over, the Bills were outscored 24-0 in the second half in an eventual 30-13 defeat.

Did the fourth Super Bowl loss signal the end of the Bills' AFC dominance? Not according to beleaguered head coach Marv Levy.

"We're not going to break up the Bills," Levy said. "This team is not made up of quitters. We'll keep trying until we get it right."

1993 ROUNDUP

OFFENSIVE MVP: QB Jim Kelly's numbers weren't glittering, but he played the most cerebral season of his career.

DEFENSIVE MVP: DE Bruce Smith led the team in sacks with 13.5 and QB pressures with 24 in what was probably his best year ever.

RESULTS
Pointspread Shown Refers To Buffalo

Date	Opponent	Spread	Score
Sept. 5	New England	(-14.5)	38-14
Sept. 12	At Dallas	(+5)	13-10
Sept. 26	Miami	(-6)	13-22
Oct. 3	New York Giants	(-5.5)	17-14
Oct. 11	Houston	(-3.5)	35-7
Oct. 24	At New York Jets	(-2.5)	19-10
Nov. 1	Washington	(-9)	24-10
Nov. 7	At New England	(-10)	13-10*
Nov. 15	At Pittsburgh	(+3.5)	0-23
Nov. 21	Indianapolis	(-13)	23-9
Nov. 28	At Kansas City	(+3)	7-23
Dec. 5	L.A. Raiders	(-6.5)	24-25
Dec. 12	At Philadelphia	(-3.5)	10-7
Dec. 19	At Miami	(+2.5)	47-34
Dec. 26	New York Jets	(-7)	16-14
Jan. 2	At Indianapolis	(-11)	30-10
POSTSEASON			
Jan. 15	L.A. Raiders	(-6.5)	29-23
Jan. 23	Kansas City	(-3)	30-13
Jan. 30	Dallas (SB)	(+10.5)	13-30

* Overtime

1993 REVIEW ■ BUFFALO

GAME-BY-GAME STATISTICS

TEAM STATISTICS

OPPONENT	WK 1 N.E.	WK 2 DALL.	WK 4 MIA.	WK 5 N.Y.G.	WK 6 HOU.	WK 8 N.Y.J.	WK 9 WASH.	WK 10 N.E.	WK 11 PITT.	WK 12 IND.	WK 13 K.C.	WK 14 L.A.RD	WK 15 PHIL.	WK 16 MIA.	WK 17 N.Y.J.	WK 18 IND.	TOTALS
Score	38-14	13-10	13-22	17-14	35-7	19-10	24-10	13-10	0-23	23-9	7-23	24-25	10-7	47-34	16-14	30-10	
Total net yards	334	229	282	251	382	413	402	432	157	403	256	367	335	374	346	297	5260
Rushing yards	177	100	106	139	141	197	164	134	47	135	43	91	101	129	90	149	1943
Passing yards	157	129	176	112	241	216	238	298	110	268	213	276	234	245	256	148	3317
Rushing plays	42	38	22	35	46	45	42	37	14	38	18	24	29	44	36	40	550
Sacks allowed	1	4	4	5	2	1	0	2	0	1	4	1	3	0	0	1	31
Had intercepted	1	1	2	1	0	2	1	0	3	1	3	1	2	1	2	0	18
Fumbles lost	0	1	0	1	1	1	1	3	0	1	1	1	2	1	1	1	17
Yards penalized	35	20	28	51	35	58	59	20	32	45	64	23	40	45	45	30	630
Punts	4	7	5	7	6	1	3	5	8	4	7	5	3	3	2	4	74

OPPONENT STATISTICS

	WK 1	WK 2	WK 4	WK 5	WK 6	WK 8	WK 9	WK 10	WK 11	WK 12	WK 13	WK 14	WK 15	WK 16	WK 17	WK 18	TOTALS
Time of possession	33:13	33:09	39:21	34:16	27:52	22:44	29:52	38:39	44:51	29:59	34:34	38:00	30:59	25:06	30:10	32:19	32:30
Total net yards	268	393	412	299	329	237	309	284	400	365	314	399	368	423	352	402	5554
Rushing yards	133	103	137	146	84	78	140	187	227	113	106	138	70	23	120	116	1921
Passing yards	135	290	275	153	245	159	169	97	173	252	208	261	298	400	232	286	3633
Rushing plays	37	28	43	43	17	21	29	48	50	29	35	37	23	11	25	24	500
Sacks allowed	3	1	1	2	4	3	2	2	4	2	0	5	1	3	0	4	37
Had intercepted	1	2	1	3	4	2	4	1	0	1	1	0	0	3	0	0	23
Fumbles lost	2	2	1	1	1	1	1	3	0	0	1	0	4	2	1	4	24
Yards penalized	30	10	75	49	59	39	40	20	55	55	20	80	62	40	35	12	681
Punts	7	5	3	6	3	3	2	7	4	3	5	3	5	2	3	4	65

INDIVIDUAL STATISTICS*

RUSHING

	WK 1	WK 2	WK 4	WK 5	WK 6	WK 8	WK 9	WK 10	WK 11	WK 12	WK 13	WK 14	WK 15	WK 16	WK 17	WK 18	TOTALS
Brooks					1-8-0												3-30-0
Gardner	2-11-0	1-4-0			1-2-0	2-4-0	5-16-0	3-6-0				1-15-0	1-0-0	1-7-0	3-5-0	3-9-0	20-56-0
K. Davis	5-14-0	6-9-0	6-32-0	5-17-0	16-45-1	10-58-0	6-11-0	10-58-0	1-7-0	6-17-1	2-9-1	1-0-0	18-70-0	13-64-3	7-21-0	5-18-0	109-391-6
Kelly	3-15-0	3-(-1)-0	3-33-0	3-(-3)-0	1-0-0	4-14-0	3-8-0	4-17-0		2-1-0	1-9-0	3-2-0		1-(-2)-0	3-3-0	1-(-1)-0	36-102-0
Reed	1-15-0	1-9-0	1-(-5)-0	1-3-0	1-(-4)-0	1-4-0				1-(-2)-0				1-3-0		1-(-3)-0	9-21-0
Thomas	24-114-0	25-75-0	12-46-0	26-122-0	24-92-1	27-117-0	28-129-1	30-111-0	13-40-0	27-116-0	15-25-0	19-74-2	10-31-0	26-52-0	23-61-1	26-110-1	355-1315-6
Turner	4-11-0	2-4-0				1-0-0				1-5-0					3-16-0	11-36-0

PASSING**

	WK 1	WK 2	WK 4	WK 5	WK 6	WK 8	WK 9	WK 10	WK 11	WK 12	WK 13	WK 14	WK 15	WK 16	WK 17	WK 18	TOTALS
Kelly	13-22-1	16-27-1	20-39-2	14-25-1	15-25-0	22-35-2	18-24-1	29-46-0	7-19-0	19-27-1	23-36-3	20-30-1	17-27-2	20-30-1	20-31-2	15-27-0	288-470-18
Reich	167-4	155-1	199-1	142-1	247-3	224-0	317-1	93-0	274-2	214-0	276-1	210-0	245-1	256-0	125-1	3382-18
									4-9-0		5-6-0		6-10-0			1-1-0	16-26-0
									41-0		40-0		42-1			30-1	153-2

RECEIVING

	WK 1	WK 2	WK 4	WK 5	WK 6	WK 8	WK 9	WK 10	WK 11	WK 12	WK 13	WK 14	WK 15	WK 16	WK 17	WK 18	TOTALS
Beebe		3-26-0	1-24-0	1-22-0	3-61-1	4-58-0	2-13-0		2-33-0	3-42-0	1-9-0	4-115-1	2-23-0	3-49-1	1-8-0	3-34-0	31-504-3
Brooks	3-27-1	4-56-0	6-70-1	1-14-0	3-16-0	1-10-0	3-37-1	7-81-0		3-67-1	6-72-0	5-39-0	10-90-0	1-10-0	5-75-0	2-50-1	60-714-5
Copeland		2-23-1	2-41-0		3-28-0		2-18-0	2-66-0				3-29-0	1-60-0		1-5-0		13-242-0
Gardner		1-6-0			1-22-0												4-50-1
K. Davis			4-12-0			3-12-0	2-0-0	1-0-0		1-3-0			3-5-0		3-53-0	1-(-2)-0	21-95-0
McKeller										1-13-1				2-22-0			3-35-1
Metzelaars	3-27-0	3-26-0	2-9-0	6-44-1	4-85-2	2-21-0	2-13-0	10-74-1	1-4-0	4-37-0	10-98-0	4-76-0	5-59-1	7-65-0	4-35-0	5-21-1	68-609-4
Reed	6-110-3	1-10-0	2-9-0	3-41-0	1-35-0	5-56-0	7-159-1	3-56-0	4-72-0	4-64-0	4-28-0	1-6-0		3-65-0	3-51-0	4-51-0	52-854-6
Thomas	1-3-0	2-8-0	3-17-0	3-21-0		7-67-0	1-1-0	5-31-0		3-48-0	6-44-0	3-11-0	2-15-0	4-34-0	3-29-0	1-1-0	48-387-0

* Doesn't include all players. ** Passing stats include completions, attempts, interceptions, gross yards gained and touchdowns.

CHICAGO BEARS
REVIEW

In what was generally acknowledged as the first year of a two-year grace period, Dave Wannstedt exceeded expectations in his rookie campaign as the Bears' head coach after a highly successful stint as the Dallas Cowboys' defensive coordinator.

Thanks to a surprisingly effective defense patterned after the Dallas system, the Bears flirted with playoff status into mid-December.

Led by veteran DE Richard Dent and MLB Dante Jones, the Bears' leading sacker and tackler, respectively, and CB Donnell Woolford in the secondary, a unit that went from a No. 17 ranking in 1992 to the league's fourth-best raised eyebrows throughout the NFL, especially during a three-game stretch in November when it spearheaded an improbable, history-making three-game winning streak on the road in a 12-day span against San Diego, Kansas City and Detroit.

Bear opponents were held to an average of 12 points per game during this stretch, which was culminated by a superb defensive effort on Thanksgiving Day in Detroit — five sacks, two interceptions and a pair of fumble recoveries in a 10-6 victory.

The next week at home, the Bear defense remained in high gear, scoring three touchdowns in a 30-17 victory over Green Bay, and Wannstedt was looking like a solid Coach of the Year candidate.

Overshadowed up to that point in the season, however, was a powder-puff offense that put undue pressure on the defense and ultimately proved to be the Bears' undoing.

In order for the Bears to make it into the postseason, Wannstedt decided the best offensive plan of attack down the stretch would be a conservative approach totally devoid of risks.

Beginning with a lackluster effort in a 13-10 loss at Tampa one week after the Bears' impressive victory over the division-rival Packers, the Bear offense went steadily downhill, as the team suffered through a season-ending, four-game losing streak that emphatically knocked it out of playoff contention.

After falling on its face in Florida, the Bear offense fared no better at home vs. Denver the next week, dropping a 13-3 decision in which backup QB Peter Tom Willis suffered through an absolutely nightmarish outing.

Subbing for beleaguered starting QB Jim Harbaugh, whose bruised hand wouldn't have prohibited him from playing, Willis threw three interceptions and fumbled once. The Broncos, meanwhile, beat the one-dimensional Bears at their own game by avoiding turnovers and eating up the clock.

The season came to a merciful end two weeks later following a 20-6 loss on the road against a lowly Los Angeles Ram team that had lost 9-of-11 games going into its season finale.

Decimated by across-the-board personnel shortcomings that shattered preseason plans for a lively, Cowboy-style attack, the Bear offense finished the season dead-last in total yards per game, passing yards per game, percentage of quarterback sacks allowed, first downs per game and average gain per offensive play.

While Harbaugh was forced to endure a lion's share of the heat for the unit's total ineffectiveness, he was hardly the only player who had problems. Fanning the flames of offensive futility were a season-ending, career-threatening double knee injury to WR Wendell Davis in October, a disappointing effort by overweight free-agent acquisition FB Craig Heyward and the decline of RB Neal Anderson, who was eventually replaced in the starting lineup by Pittsburgh Steeler pickup Tim Worley.

The Bears did win two more games than in the previous season, though, and there was no denying the dramatic improvement in the morale of a team that appeared to be in disarray at the end of Mike Ditka's often-stormy, 11-year tenure as head coach.

"In the past when we hit a bad streak, we'd kind of turn in on ourselves and disintegrate as a team," said Bear DE Trace Armstrong, who cited confidence in his abilities by the new Bear coaching staff as one of the keys behind his improved performance in '93. "This staff has just not allowed that to happen."

1993 ROUNDUP

OFFENSIVE MVP: P Chris Gardocki was second in the NFL placing punts within the 20 and had the best difference between net and gross average (1.9 yards) in the league.

DEFENSIVE MVP: DE Richard Dent made things happen for other Bear players, thus helping the whole defense. He led the club with 12.5 sacks and had a slew of QB pressures.

RESULTS
Pointspread Shown Refers To Chicago

Date	Opponent	Spread	Score
Sept. 5	N.Y. Giants	(-1)	20-26
Sept. 12	At Minnesota	(+7)	7-10
Sept. 26	Tampa Bay	(-7)	47-17
Oct. 3	Atlanta	(-6)	6-0
Oct. 10	At Philadelphia	(+7)	17-6
Oct. 25	Minnesota	(-3.5)	12-19
Oct. 31	At Green Bay	(+5.5)	3-17
Nov. 7	L.A. Raiders	(+2.5)	14-16
Nov. 14	At San Diego	(+9)	16-13
Nov. 21	At Kansas City	(+10)	19-17
Nov. 25	At Detroit	(+7)	10-6
Dec. 5	Green Bay	(-2)	30-17
Dec. 12	At Tampa Bay	(-4.5)	10-13
Dec. 18	Denver	(+2)	3-13
Dec. 26	Detroit	(-3)	14-20
Jan. 2	At L.A. Rams	(-3)	6-20

1993 REVIEW — CHICAGO

GAME-BY-GAME STATISTICS

TEAM STATISTICS

OPPONENT	WK 1 N.Y.G.	WK 2 MINN.	WK 3 T.B.	WK 4 T.B.	WK 5 ATL.	WK 6 PHIL.	WK 7 MINN.	WK 8 G.B.	WK 9 LA.RD	WK 10 S.D.	WK 11 K.C.	WK 12 DET.	WK 13 G.B.	WK 14 T.B.	WK 15 DENV.	WK 16 DET.	WK 17 LA.RM	WK 18 TOTALS
Score	20-26	7-10	17-6	47-17	6-0	17-6	12-19	16-45-0	3-17	14-16	16-13	19-17	10-6	30-17	10-13	3-13	14-20	6-20
Total net yards	269	140	332	220	261	252	230	261	224	281	225	210	286	185	180	163	3719
Rushing yards	103	88	126	106	102	93	118	124	84	190	107	69	119	84	77	89	1679
Passing yards	166	52	206	114	159	159	112	137	140	91	118	141	167	101	103	74	2040
Rushing plays	26	22	38	30	41	21	34	36	26	42	35	23	28	26	32	16	476
Sacks allowed	4	4	3	1	1	9	7	2	2	0	4	1	1	4	2	3	47
Had intercepted	1	1	0	0	1	1	1	1	1	2	1	1	0	3	0	1	16
Fumbles lost	1	0	1	0	0	1	2	0	2	1	0	0	2	2	1	0	14
Yards penalized	88	20	69	49	20	55	40	50	10	55	15	15	40	25	7	29	587
Punts	5	8	4	6	7	6	4	6	4	3	5	4	5	5	3	5	80

OPPONENT STATISTICS

	WK 1	WK 2	WK 3	WK 4	WK 5	WK 6	WK 7	WK 8	WK 9	WK 10	WK 11	WK 12	WK 13	WK 14	WK 15	WK 16	WK 17	TOTALS
Time of possession	33:52	37:32	22:56	29:16	27:15	30:36	27:09	31:39	33:34	27:58	28:54	38:14	29:46	32:49	30:13	40:40	31:35
Total net yards	361	276	328	271	276	252	261	274	256	252	230	466	215	234	307	394	4653
Rushing yards	105	121	36	87	110	165	135	179	104	133	84	79	103	129	84	181	1835
Passing yards	256	155	292	184	166	87	126	95	152	119	146	387	112	105	223	213	2818
Rushing plays	28	37	18	23	23	34	27	40	32	29	23	29	29	33	26	47	478
Sacks allowed	4	4	2	4	3	1	2	2	3	5	5	2	3	0	0	0	46
Had intercepted	0	0	4	2	7	1	1	1	0	0	2	3	1	0	1	0	18
Fumbles lost	0	1	3	1	2	0	2	0	0	0	2	0	0	1	0	0	12
Yards penalized	45	30	61	73	50	95	25	86	24	69	40	71	64	105	20	30	783
Punts	4	6	5	7	6	8	4	6	5	6	4	2	5	5	2	3	78

INDIVIDUAL STATISTICS*

RUSHING

	WK 1	WK 2	WK 3	WK 4	WK 5	WK 6	WK 7	WK 8	WK 9	WK 10	WK 11	WK 12	WK 13	WK 14	WK 15	WK 16	WK 17	TOTALS
Anderson		13-60-0	23-104-1	24-84-0	20-24-0	16-45-0	19-61-0	28-75-1	7-32-0	17-42-1	15-68-0	9-15-0	8-28-1	1-0-0	2-3-0	3-8-0	202-646-4
Green		1-(-3)-0	6-1-0	3-10-0	7-35-1	5-25-0	1-30-0	4-35-0	4-3-0	1-10-0	2-8-0	1-5-0	1-5-0	1-5-0	15-29-0
Harbaugh	4-19-0	6-32-1	3-2-1	3-12-0	13-42-0	1-(-1)-0	11-26-0	4-14-0	1-1-0	7-61-0	2-(-7)-0	2-0-0	1-7-0	1-0-0	6-13-1	2-12-0	57-277-4
Heyward	13-51-0	1-0-0	3-9-0					11-33-0	11-59-1	6-18-0	5-11-0	1-15-0	1-4-0	3-6-0	3-13-0	68-206-0
Worley									11-33-0	11-59-1	8-32-0	11-49-0	18-80-0	20-72-0	24-61-1	7-51-0	110-437-2

PASSING**

	WK 1	WK 2	WK 3	WK 4	WK 5	WK 6	WK 7	WK 8	WK 9	WK 10	WK 11	WK 12	WK 13	WK 14	WK 15	WK 16	WK 17	TOTALS
Harbaugh	16-28-1 178-1	11-20-1 83-0	17-22-0 192-2	16-23-0 122-0	14-27-1 165-1	1-0-0	20-31-2 202-0	15-19-0 149-0	12-24-1 140-1	13-24-1 159-1	13-20-2 98-0	9-16-1 123-1	10-20-1 141-0	11-18-0 81-0	14-29-3 107-0	9-10-1 62-0	200-325-12 2002-7
Willis			1-1-0 29-0				0-1-1 0-0	3-32-0						11-18-0 86-0	14-29-3 120-0	4-11-1 33-0	30-60-5 268-0

RECEIVING

	WK 1	WK 2	WK 3	WK 4	WK 5	WK 6	WK 7	WK 8	WK 9	WK 10	WK 11	WK 12	WK 13	WK 14	WK 15	WK 16	WK 17	TOTALS
Anderson		3-11-0	1-35-0	5-6-0	9-60-0	4-12-0	3-22-0				2-5-0			1-8-0	31-160-0
Christian	1-6-0		1-8-0		2-17-0	1-25-0	2-40-0	1-5-0		1-3-0	4-40-0		3-17-0	16-160-0
Conway	2-21-0	1-14-0	5-49-0	1-10-0	6-69-0	1-7-0	2-50-1	1-4-0	1-15-0	1-11-0	1-9-0		19-231-2
Davis					2-22-0			3-13-0				1-2-0	12-132-0
Gedney		1-5-0		2-20-0	1-12-0	1-13-0	3-32-0	2-24-1	1-5-0	5-29-0	2-15-0		3-12-0	10-98-0
Green		1-8-0				1-7-0	2-24-1	2-21-0	1-4-0	1-6-0			1-4-0	13-63-0
Heyward	1-6-0	1-8-0				1-10-0	1-9-0		1-10-0	2-14-0	2-24-0		1-11-0	16-132-0
Jennings												3-38-0	2-24-0		1-11-0	14-150-0
Obee	3-26-1	3-45-0	4-55-0	4-51-0	2-43-0	3-46-0	2-28-1	2-21-0	1-42-1	4-73-0	3-33-0	2-24-0	4-35-0	26-351-3
Waddle	3-62-0	2-12-0	5-46-1				2-17-0	4-69-0	3-16-0	3-19-0	3-46-0	1-11-0	3-41-0	2-9-0	2-26-0	44-552-1
Wetnight		2-18-0	1-25-1										2-16-0	1-13-0	1-4-0	9-93-1

* Doesn't include all players. ** Passing stats include completions, attempts, interceptions, gross yards gained and touchdowns.

REVIEW: CINCINNATI BENGALS

After getting rid of virtually all of their high-priced veterans in 1993, a maneuver that left them without adequate talent and experience, the Bengals paid the price in the standings, tying a team mark for their worst record — 3-13.

In addition, the team lost a franchise-record 10 straight games and drew some of the smallest crowds ever at Riverfront Stadium.

"We've had a dismal year," said Bengal general manager Mike Brown shortly after the season ended. "The progress that we've made has been less than we would have wished."

The Bengals were especially bad on offense, scoring just 14 touchdowns the entire year, a total surpassed individually by Jerry Rice, Marcus Allen and Andre Rison. Their 16-game total of 187 points was a club-record low, as the offense never scored more than 21 points in a game and failed to produce a touchdown in six games.

The main problem was one of the league's worst offensive lines. The Bengal front wall shuffled personnel around a good part of the season and yielded a whopping 53 sacks. Making matters worse was an inexperienced quarterback, sophomore David Klingler, who continued to suffer growing pains.

Klingler had only two games in which he passed for 200 yards, and he threw only six TD passes all season, compared to nine interceptions. Most of the time, however, he was either lying flat on his back or running for his life.

Klingler didn't get much help from his receivers or running backs, either. Jeff Query and Carl Pickens, who combined for 10 TD's, had respectable-enough seasons, but the team got no productivity whatsoever from the third and fourth spots.

On the ground, the Bengals rushed for just 1,188 yards, not counting runs by quarterbacks. Emmitt Smith, Jerome Bettis and Thurman Thomas each had more rushing yardage. Leading rusher Harold Green, coming off a Pro Bowl season in which he rushed for 1,170 yards, seldom got decent running room and struggled all season, averaging a scant 2.7 yards per carry. An early-season contract squabble didn't help matters.

The Bengals managed to split their last six games, however, a stretch that began with a 16-10 upset victory over the playoff-bound Raiders that snapped their 10-game losing streak. Klingler, in particular, showed improvement down the stretch, as QB coach Ken Anderson took over the play-calling duties from offensive coordinator Mike Pope.

"I feel I played well at times, and I attribute that to the offensive line," said Klingler. "When they played well, I played well."

"We did what we felt we could do with the people we had," concluded Shula. "We need to get guys who can get it into the endzone. When we get the kind of people who can do those things, we'll take full advantage of it."

While the offense struggled in '93, Cincinnati's defense held up surprisingly well. Nine of the Bengals' 16 opponents scored 20 points or less, as young defenders such as FS Darryl Williams, CB's Mike Brim and Rod Jones, LB's James Francis and Alfred Williams and No. 1 pick DE John Copeland provided the foundation of a unit that improved to a middle-of-the pack ranking after being ranked third from the bottom the previous year. Improvement in the secondary was particularly noticeable, as the Bengals improved from 25th to second vs. the pass.

There were still significant problems on defense. The team had just 22 sacks, the second-lowest total in the league, and its run defense was ranked the second-worst.

In addition, the Bengals lost their defensive coordinator in mid-January when Ron Lynn resigned unexpectedly to take the same job with the Redskins. Interestingly, he was replaced by Larry Peccatiello, who had spent the last 13 years in Washington.

Bengal special-team play was encouraging for the most part. Rookie PK Doug Pelfrey converted 22-of-25 field goals, with seven of the kicks covering 45 yards or more, after missing four of his first six attempts. P Lee Johnson had a career-best 43.9-yard average and landed 24 punts inside the 20.

The Bengal return game, however, was virtually nonexistent.

1993 ROUNDUP

OFFENSIVE MVP: C Bruce Kozerski was a rock of consistency in a line laced with rookies and free agents.

DEFENSIVE MVP: FS Darryl Williams led the team in tackles with 123, recorded two sacks and netted a pair of interceptions.

RESULTS
Pointspread Shown Refers To Cincinnati

Date	Opponent	Spread	Score
Sept. 5	At Cleveland	(+7.5)	14-27
Sept. 12	Indianapolis	(+2.5)	6-9
Sept. 19	At Pittsburgh	(+9)	7-34
Sept. 26	Seattle	(+3)	10-19
Oct. 10	At Kansas City	(+14)	15-17
Oct. 17	Cleveland	(+5)	17-28
Oct. 24	At Houston	(+14)	12-28
Nov. 7	Pittsburgh	(+9.5)	16-24
Nov. 14	Houston	(+8.5)	3-38
Nov. 21	At New York Jets	(+16.5)	12-17
Nov. 28	L.A. Raiders	(+9)	16-10
Dec. 5	At San Francisco	(+23.5)	8-21
Dec. 12	At New England	(+6)	2-7
Dec. 19	L.A. Rams	(+2)	15-3
Dec. 26	Atlanta	(+3.5)	21-17
Jan. 2	At New Orleans	(+5.5)	13-20

* Overtime

1993 REVIEW ■ CINCINNATI

GAME-BY-GAME STATISTICS

TEAM STATISTICS

OPPONENT	WK 1 CLEV.	WK 2 IND.	WK 3 PITT.	WK 4 SEA.	WK 6 K.C.	WK 7 CLEV.	WK 8 HOU.	WK 10 PITT.	WK 11 HOU.	WK 12 N.Y.J.	WK 13 LA.RD	WK 14 S.F.	WK 15 N.E.	WK 16 LA.RM	WK 17 ATL.	WK 18 N.O.	TOTALS
Score	14-27	6-9	7-34	10-19	15-17	17-28	12-28	16-24	3-38	12-17	16-10	8-21	2-7	15-3	21-17	13-20	
Total net yards	227	269	170	354	277	194	346	191	165	226	269	339	160	393	284	188	4052
Rushing yards	55	128	44	30	115	34	97	103	102	50	131	144	102	170	122	84	1511
Passing yards	172	141	126	324	162	160	249	88	63	176	138	195	58	223	162	104	2541
Rushing plays	20	26	19	17	34	14	23	29	22	14	43	33	34	37	24	34	423
Sacks allowed	6	2	2	5	4	3	4	4	5	4	3	0	5	1	2	3	53
Had intercepted	2	1	1	1	1	0	0	0	0	2	0	1	0	1	0	0	11
Fumbles lost	1	0	0	2	1	1	2	0	2	0	0	0	0	0	0	1	9
Yards penalized	60	15	70	58	74	53	64	40	66	50	64	35	50	30	25	19	773
Punts	5	7	6	4	4	9	4	7	5	5	6	2	8	3	8	6	89

OPPONENT STATISTICS

	WK 1	WK 2	WK 3	WK 4	WK 6	WK 7	WK 8	WK 10	WK 11	WK 12	WK 13	WK 14	WK 15	WK 16	WK 17	WK 18	TOTALS
Time of possession	32:38	31:45	35:45	33:16	25:03	32:50	32:20	30:08	36:35	35:43	21:18	23:27	32:10	27:22	36:30	29:39	31:28
Total net yards	263	332	404	305	203	293	369	390	462	288	283	284	224	273	376	269	5018
Rushing yards	96	120	223	139	94	183	125	146	240	111	81	111	118	166	191	76	2220
Passing yards	167	212	181	166	109	110	244	244	222	177	202	173	106	107	185	193	2798
Rushing plays	30	29	36	35	28	42	25	33	37	39	16	26	44	32	39	30	521
Sacks allowed	2	1	1	0	3	2	1	0	1	2	4	1	2	0	2	0	22
Had intercepted	0	2	0	0	0	1	1	1	1	0	1	2	0	0	1	2	12
Fumbles lost	0	1	2	2	2	1	1	1	2	0	1	0	1	2	0	0	14
Yards penalized	35	15	57	21	25	51	40	45	30	50	21	51	43	35	15	30	564
Punts	6	4	2	6	4	7	4	6	2	5	4	3	6	5	7	3	74

INDIVIDUAL STATISTICS*

RUSHING

	WK 1	WK 2	WK 3	WK 4	WK 6	WK 7	WK 8	WK 10	WK 11	WK 12	WK 13	WK 14	WK 15	WK 16	WK 17	WK 18	TOTALS
Ball	1-0-0	1-3-0											1-(-)-0				8-37-1
Fenner	13-41-0	10-62-0	4-15-0	1-1-0	10-36-0	4-11-0	5-36-0	2-14-0		1-2-0	2-19-1	10-53-0	9-19-0	15-89-1	6-30-0	15-48-0	121-482-1
Green		12-25-0	12-16-0	13-16-0	22-68-0	8-12-0	13-47-0		1-0-0	3-7-0	16-34-0	19-60-0	21-45-0	18-76-0	15-56-0	16-24-0	215-589-0
Klingler	3-8-0	2-37-0	3-13-0	1-11-0	2-11-0	1-9-0		22-59-0	4-49-0	9-32-0	14-53-0	7-12-0	3-39-0	4-5-0	3-36-0	3-12-0	41-282-0
Miles	3-6-1	1-1-0					1-3-0		14-39-0	1-9-0	7-12-0	4-31-0					22-56-1
Schroeder				2-2-0		1-2-0	3-6-0	3-31-0	1-0-0		3-7-0						10-41-0

PASSING**

	WK 1	WK 2	WK 3	WK 4	WK 6	WK 7	WK 8	WK 10	WK 11	WK 12	WK 13	WK 14	WK 15	WK 16	WK 17	WK 18	TOTALS
Klingler	20-28-2 214-1	16-37-1 146-0	17-21-0 135-1	11-23-1 155-0	16-30-1 173-0	19-37-0 172-2	18-31-0 213-1	13-29-1 117-1	4-17-0 34-0	22-31-2 196-1	14-20-0 157-0	13-19-1 97-0	9-25-1 111-0	16-30-0 223-0	16-30-0 174-3	13-23-0 117-0	190-343-9 1957-6
Schroeder			1-5-1 3-0	14-22-0 183-1		19-37-0 172-2			4-11-0 46-0		10-24-0 98-0		21-45-0 111-0				79-159-2 832-5

RECEIVING

	WK 1	WK 2	WK 3	WK 4	WK 6	WK 7	WK 8	WK 10	WK 11	WK 12	WK 13	WK 14	WK 15	WK 16	WK 17	WK 18	TOTALS
Fenner	9-64-0	3-39-0	5-13-0	1-26-0	3-18-0	3-17-0	2-8-0			2-30-0	5-52-0	5-40-0	2-20-0	2-33-0	3-36-0	3-31-0	48-427-0
Frisch		2-5-0	1-3-0	1-12-0		1-0-0	1-11-0		1-8-0		2-9-0	2-13-0	1-9-0		1-12-0		6-43-0
Green	2-39-0	1-6-0	4-35-0	7-102-0		2-14-0	4-36-0	2-22-0		7-40-0		7-32-0		6-90-0	2-26-0	1-4-0	22-115-0
McGee	2-13-0						2-49-0			2-16-0	2-28-0	3-37-0	2-23-0			5-51-0	44-525-0
Miles									1-5-0			1-22-0					6-89-0
Pickens	1-5-1	4-41-0	5-57-1	5-81-1	3-33-0	6-67-1	7-127-0	2-22-0	1-11-0	2-39-0	5-52-0	3-36-0	2-17-0	5-74-0	6-71-2	1-11-0	43-565-6
Query	3-80-0	4-44-0		6-59-0	3-69-0	4-32-1	5-45-1	6-48-1	2-30-0	6-41-1	3-43-0				2-21-0	2-12-0	56-651-4
Rembert			2-27-0	4-50-0	2-24-0					2-14-0	1-14-0	2-15-0	3-29-0				8-101-0
Robinson															2-8-1		8-72-0
Thompson	2-9-0				1-8-0	6-36-0		1-1-0	2-22-0								19-113-1

* Doesn't include all players.   ** Passing stats include completions, attempts, interceptions, gross yards gained and touchdowns.

329

CLEVELAND BROWNS REVIEW

Nov. 8, 1993. A day that will forever live in infamy. Or at least it will be remembered for a long time to come by fans of the Browns.

It was the day coach Bill Belichick released long-time Cleveland starting quarterback and local hero Bernie Kosar. And, as it turned out, it was the end of a nice run and the beginning of a tumultuous remainder of the season.

The Browns entered the '93 campaign poised to win the division and make a run for the Super Bowl. According to some, it was the best Cleveland football team since the AFC championship squads of 1986 and '87.

The first three weeks of the regular season resulted in wins, including an impressive victory over the 49ers on Monday Night Football. Things were looking fine.

A few weeks later the Browns were one of the winningest teams in the league with a 5-2 mark. The following week the team lost to Denver 29-14, yet still remained atop the AFC Central at 5-3.

And then it all came crumbling down. After that loss, Belichick shocked the sports community by releasing Kosar, who had been with the Browns for nearly nine years. The coach, in his third year with the club, cited "diminishing skills" as the motive for the move.

"This is the most difficult decision I've ever made or been a part of," said Belichick after he cut Kosar. "Basically it came down to his production and a diminishing of his physical skills."

Kosar responded to the move by saying he knew he wasn't part of the Browns' future.

"I've known for a while that I don't really fit into their plans," said Kosar. "Bill has his way of doing things. That's been shown by the way they've been getting rid of the players who were here before he got here."

What made the move even more shocking was the fact that No. 2 QB Vinny Testaverde was out indefinitely with a separated shoulder, which meant the offense would be handed over to third-stringer Todd Philcox.

Six days after his release, Kosar found a new home with the Cowboys and actually had a hand in leading Dallas to victory. That same day the Browns were taken down by the Seahawks, 22-5 — a game in which Philcox performed miserably.

It certainly was the beginning of the end. The Browns lost their next three straight and fell to 5-6. This was all happening while the Oilers were cruising to the lead in the AFC Central.

When it was all over, the Browns had played their way out of the playoffs, losing six of their final eight contests to finish 7-9 and third in the division.

Despite the post-Kosar collapse, there were signs that the team may be headed for long-term offensive improvements.

Testaverde's numbers improved when he returned from the injury and actually finished ahead of Kosar in both passer rating (85.7 to 77.2) and average yards gained per attempt (7.81 to 5.85). Also, for the first time in his career, Testaverde threw more touchdown passes (14) than interceptions (nine). In addition, he set an NFL record for accuracy in the second-to-last game of the season against the Rams when he went 21-for-23.

The ball also found its way into the hands of all-purpose RB Eric Metcalf more often later in the season, primarily because Belichick gave play-calling control over to RB coach Steve Crosby.

Metcalf wound up being the NFL's most productive yardage gainer in '93, as he racked up 1,932 all-purpose yards.

Another disappointment the Browns had to deal with during the season was the dropoff of the defense, considered to be among the better units in the NFL before the start of the season.

Cleveland managed only 22 takeaways in '93, which was 11 less than Belichick's previous two seasons. Part of the reason for the decline was the controversial release of turnover-king LB David Brandon just a few weeks prior to Kosar's dismissal.

DLT Jerry Ball was another disappointment, as he was benched for the final three games because the coaching staff claimed his play had become ineffective due to his weight exceeding 300 pounds.

One of the more surprising things to come out of the season was the vote of confidence owner Art Modell gave to Belichick in the way of a two-year contract extension that will keep the coach with a 20-28 record and no playoff appearances paid through 1997.

1993 ROUNDUP

OFFENSIVE MVP: RB Eric Metcalf amassed 1,932 all-purpose yards to lead the NFL.
DEFENSIVE MVP: S Stevon Moore recorded 96 solo stops to lead the team, caused three fumbles and returned one for a TD.

RESULTS
Pointspread Shown Refers To Cleveland

Date	Opponent	Spread	Score
Sept. 5	Cincinnati	(-7.5)	27-14
Sept. 13	San Francisco	(+7)	23-13
Sept. 19	At L.A. Raiders	(+4.5)	19-16
Sept. 26	At Indianapolis	(-2.5)	10-23
Oct. 10	Miami	(+2)	14-24
Oct. 17	At Cincinnati	(-5)	28-17
Oct. 24	Pittsburgh	(+2.5)	28-23
Nov. 7	Denver	(-2.5)	14-29
Nov. 14	At Seattle	(+4)	5-22
Nov. 21	Houston	(+5.5)	20-27
Nov. 28	At Atlanta	(+6.5)	14-17
Dec. 5	New Orleans	(+3.5)	17-13
Dec. 12	At Houston	(+10)	17-19
Dec. 19	New England	(-6)	17-20
Dec. 26	At L.A. Rams	(-2)	42-14
Jan. 2	At Pittsburgh	(+5.5)	9-16

1993 REVIEW ■ CLEVELAND

GAME-BY-GAME STATISTICS

TEAM STATISTICS

OPPONENT	WK 1 CIN.	WK 2 S.F.	WK 3 L.A.RD	WK 4 IND.	WK 5 (Bye)	WK 6 MIA.	WK 7 CIN.	WK 8 PITT.	WK 10 DENV.	WK 11 SEA.	WK 12 HOU.	WK 13 ATL.	WK 14 N.O.	WK 15 HOU.	WK 16 N.E.	WK 17 L.A.RM	WK 18 PITT.	TOTALS
Score	27-14	23-13	19-16	10-23		14-24	28-17	28-23	14-29	5-22	20-27	14-17	17-13	24-27 (sic)	17-20	42-14	9-16	
Total net yards	263	304	316	253		202	293	245	266	232	349	306	314	410	377	315	295	4740
Rushing yards	96	128	113	100		90	183	98	75	175	49	115	131	105	80	102	61	1701
Passing yards	167	176	203	153		112	110	147	191	57	300	190	183	305	297	213	234	3038
Rushing plays	30	33	27	24		16	42	22	14	38	16	29	28	27	27	32	20	425
Sacks allowed	2	2	5	1		6	1	4	6	3	2	2	2	2	0	1	3	45
Had intercepted	0	0	0	1		1	1	0	0	2	4	0	2	2	2	0	0	19
Fumbles lost	0	0	0	1		1	1	1	0	5	1	1	2	1	0	0	2	17
Yards penalized	35	59	48	79		55	51	59	51	67	32	20	62	100	83	31	10	842
Punts	6	5	6	6		5	7	5	5	6	6	5	7	3	4	2	6	84

OPPONENT STATISTICS

Time of possession	27:22	26:07	31:28	30:23		32:35	27:10	36:29	37:30	26:53	33:14	32:33	30:31	24:53	29:12	26:31	34:32	30:28
Total net yards	227	396	156	357		338	194	440	392	223	384	261	127	257	323	382	320	4777
Rushing yards	55	130	71	97		70	34	92	159	119	202	67	79	128	120	95	135	1653
Passing yards	172	266	85	260		268	160	348	233	104	182	194	48	129	203	287	185	3124
Rushing plays	20	26	25	32		31	14	33	42	33	39	24	24	28	27	21	32	451
Sacks allowed	6	1	6	0		1	3	2	4	1	2	2	9	4	1	7	7	47
Had intercepted	2	3	0	0		1	0	1	0	0	2	4	0	1	1	2	0	13
Fumbles lost	1	1	0	0		0	1	1	1	0	0	0	0	0	1	0	0	9
Yards penalized	60	92	50	79		44	53	25	63	64	75	45	25	62	15	39	30	821
Punts	5	1	8	7		3	9	3	3	6	4	6	10	4	5	3	8	85

INDIVIDUAL STATISTICS*

RUSHING

	WK 1	WK 2	WK 3	WK 4		WK 6	WK 7	WK 8	WK 10	WK 11	WK 12	WK 13	WK 14	WK 15	WK 16	WK 17	WK 18	TOTALS
Baldwin	1-(-4)-0						6-35-0	2-13-0		6-19-0		1-(-2)-0					2-0-0	18-61-0
Hoard	8-27-0	3-6-0	2-(-4)-0	1-6-0				1-3-0	5-51-0	3-20-0	2-9-0		16-60-0	2-0-0		4-20-0	9-29-0	56-227-0
Kosar	1-(-1)-0	3-8-0	2-0-0	2-5-0				4-1-0	2-6-0					4-16-0	6-17-1			14-19-0
Mack														18-82-0	12-48-0	15-56-0	2-(-3)-0	10-33-1
Metcalf	4-14-0	12-71-0	7-(-2)-1	8-23-0		7-36-0	3-33-0	7-53-0	4-10-0	13-75-0		13-61-0	4-54-0			1-(-1)-0	2-0-0	129-611-1
Testaverde		13-41-0	2-15-0	1-13-0		3-37-0	7-2-0	1-9-0							1-(-1)-0			18-74-0
Vardell	16-60-1		14-104-0			6-17-0	25-98-0	7-19-0	3-8-0	15-61-0	13-48-0	13-52-0	8-17-0	3-7-0	14-33-0	6-10-2	4-29-0	171-644-3

PASSING**

Kosar	18-30-0 182-1	17-32-0 186-1	8-17-3 71-0	4-8-0 53-0		15-19-0 82-1		1-2-0 7-0	16-30-0 226-2									79-138-3 807-5
Philcox											22-47-4 316-2	14-26-0 207-1	7-15-1 91-1					52-108-7 699-4
Testaverde			10-22-1 159-1	9-16-1 127-1		6-13-1 44-0	11-24-1 127-3	9-14-0 167-2		9-20-2 85-0			9-20-1 92-1	19-37-2 319-2	21-31-2 297-2	21-23-2 216-2	15-30-0 249-0	130-230-9 1797-14

RECEIVING

Carrier	3-79-0	4-24-0	5-73-0	1-46-0		1-(-1)-0	3-55-0	2-20-0	1-12-0	1-3-0	7-123-1	3-47-1	4-62-0	3-45-1	4-81-0	3-41-0	4-18-0	43-746-3
Hoard		3-25-0	3-27-0	3-37-0		2-24-0		8-87-0	2-(-3)-0		1-2-0	1-38-0	6-65-2	2-19-0	1-17-0	2-12-0	2-22-0	35-351-0
Jackson	3-33-1	5-105-1	1-18-0	4-49-0		4-34-1	1-7-0	2-106-1	4-86-2		4-64-0	1-56-0	3-30-0	2-52-0	2-46-0	2-26-0	1-17-0	41-756-8
Kinchen	1-8-0	1-9-0	2-19-0	1-10-1		2-13-0	1-1-1				5-73-0	4-70-0		5-47-0	2-46-0	1-6-0	1-15-0	29-347-2
McCardell														2-55-0	4-51-2	4-72-2	3-56-0	13-234-4
Metcalf	9-60-0	4-23-0	2-26-0	2-12-0		9-66-0	1-28-1	3-18-0	3-41-0	2-(-1)-0	2-17-1	5-43-0	1-(-5)-0	5-101-1	8-81-0	8-57-0	1-2-0	63-539-2
Vardell	2-2-0		2-22-0	1-13-0		5-29-0						1-9-0	1-18-0		1-7-0		4-21-0	19-151-1

* Doesn't include all players. ** Passing stats include completions, attempts, interceptions, gross yards gained and touchdowns.

331

PRO FOOTBALL WEEKLY 1994 ALMANAC

REVIEW: DALLAS COWBOYS

Jimmy Johnson was not going to let it happen. He was simply not going to let the pressure of trying to repeat as NFL champions or the obstacles of holdouts, injuries and losing streaks get in his way.

Johnson did not fail. He poked, prodded and cajoled his Cowboys into winning the NFC East during the regular season, and he whipped them down the stretch in the postseason as they roared to another Super Bowl title by once again defeating the Bills on the last Sunday in January.

When the Cowboys won Super Bowl XXVII in Pasadena, they had just completed a dream season that saw everything go according to form. The 1993 season was one crisis after another, which may have made the second time around even more impressive than winning it the first time.

The Cowboys started the season shorthanded, as All-World RB Emmitt Smith and owner Jerry Jones were locked in a stubborn contract holdout. With Smith at home in Escambia, Fla., the Cowboys got bombed in their Monday-night season opener at Washington and followed that dismal performance with a loss at home to Buffalo. The 0-2 start forced Jones' hand, and Smith got a four-year, $13.6 million contract.

Immediately the Cowboy world brightened, as the team won its next seven games, including key victories over the 49ers and Giants. It appeared that Dallas was still the class of the league, and emerging with a victory in Super Bowl XXVIII was simply a matter of finishing out the schedule.

Nothing could have been further from the truth. In the win over the Giants, QB Troy Aikman went down with a hamstring injury that forced him out of the lineup for three games. Earlier in the season, MLB Ken Norton Jr. had torn his right biceps muscle but continued to play anyway. DE Charles Haley was an inconsistent factor in the lineup because of a bulging back disk. Even Smith showed he was not impervious after suffering knee and shoulder injuries.

The Dallas locomotive was temporarily derailed when the Cowboys were defeated by the Falcons and Dolphins. The loss to Miami, at a snowy Texas Stadium on Thanksgiving Day, was characterized by the bonehead play of the year. With the Cowboys leading 14-13 in the closing seconds, the Dolphins' Pete Stoyanovich had his attempt at a game-winning field goal blocked. As the ball skittered along the frozen carpet, Dallas DT Leon Lett went sliding after it, unaware of the rule that gave the Cowboys possession after the block — as long as they made no attempt to recover the ball. Lett's stumble led to a Miami recovery, and this time Stoyanovich was successful, and the Dolphins had an improbable win.

Johnson was desperate to get his team back in gear, and the Cowboys responded with a stabilizing 23-17 win over the Eagles. From there, the Cowboys won their remaining four regular-season games, including a 16-13 overtime thriller on the road against the Giants that gave Dallas the division title and the NFC's best record.

Smith suffered a shoulder separation in that game, but he refused to come out. "If we lost, it meant we had to play again next week in the wild-card game, and that's something I didn't want to do," Smith explained. "I knew that a victory meant we got a week off and home-field advantage."

Despite missing the first two games of the season and parts of two others, Smith won his third straight rushing title with 1,486 yards on 283 carries. Aikman also had a brilliant season, completing 271-of-392 passes for 3,100 yards with a 15-6 TD-interception ratio.

The Cowboys completed their improbable year by whipsawing through their postseason opponents. They defeated the Packers, 49ers and Bills by a combined score of 95-51. Their 30-13 triumph over Buffalo in the Super Bowl came after Dallas trailed 13-6 at halftime.

"Two Super Bowls back to back with basically the same group of players," crowed Jones. "I think this has to be one of the best teams the Cowboys ever had."

1993 ROUNDUP

OFFENSIVE MVP: RB Emmitt Smith was not only the NFL MVP but also the Super Bowl MVP. He won the rushing title for the third season in a row with 1,486 yards.

DEFENSIVE MVP: MLB Ken Norton was the heart and soul of the defense. He played injured the final three months, yet led the team in tackles (159) and tackles for loss (10).

RESULTS
Pointspread Shown Refers To Dallas

Date	Opponent	Spread	Score
Sept. 6	At Washington	(+2.5)	16-35
Sept. 12	Buffalo	(-5)	10-13
Sept. 19	At Phoenix	(-6.5)	17-10
Oct. 3	Green Bay	(-11)	36-14
Oct. 10	At Indianapolis	(-12)	27-3
Oct. 17	San Francisco	(-6.5)	26-17
Oct. 31	At Philadelphia	(-10)	23-10
Nov. 7	New York Giants	(-10.5)	31-9
Nov. 14	Phoenix	(-13)	20-15
Nov. 21	At Atlanta	(-9.5)	14-27
Nov. 25	Miami	(-10)	14-16
Dec. 6	Philadelphia	(-16.5)	23-17
Dec. 12	At Minnesota	(-7)	37-20
Dec. 18	At New York Jets	(-7)	28-7
Dec. 26	Washington	(-17)	38-3
Jan. 2	At New York Giants	(-6.5)	16-13*
POSTSEASON			
Jan. 16	Green Bay	(-14)	27-17
Jan. 23	San Francisco	(-3)	38-21
Jan. 30	Buffalo (SB)	(-10.5)	30-13

* Overtime

1993 REVIEW ■ DALLAS

GAME-BY-GAME STATISTICS

TEAM STATISTICS

OPPONENT	WK 1 WASH.	WK 2 BUFF.	WK 3 PHX.	WK 5 G.B.	WK 6 IND.	WK 7 S.F.	WK 9 PHIL.	WK 10 N.Y.G.	WK 11 PHX.	WK 12 ATL.	WK 13 MIA.	WK 14 PHIL.	WK 15 MINN.	WK 16 N.J.	WK 17 WASH.	WK 18 N.Y.G.	TOTALS
Score	16-35	10-13	17-10	36-14	27-3	26-17	23-10	31-9	20-15	14-27	14-16	23-17	37-20	28-7	38-3	16-13	
Total net yards	345	393	410	395	374	353	356	369	311	230	293	347	356	364	380	339	5615
Rushing yards	91	103	130	98	143	123	271	139	87	48	112	182	148	129	175	182	2161
Passing yards	254	290	280	297	231	230	85	230	224	182	181	165	208	235	205	157	3454
Rushing plays	21	28	33	30	35	34	39	32	34	13	28	29	35	30	32	36	489
Sacks allowed	2	1	1	2	2	2	2	2	0	0	0	0	0	3	2	4	29
Had intercepted	0	2	0	0	0	0	0	0	0	0	1	0	0	3	0	0	6
Fumbles lost	4	2	0	0	1	0	0	0	2	0	1	1	0	2	1	1	16
Yards penalized	64	10	59	23	24	64	41	66	42	51	46	53	64	37	78	22	744
Punts	3	5	3	1	4	2	3	3	5	6	3	4	1	3	2	5	56

OPPONENT STATISTICS

Time of possession	35:03	26:51	26:27	29:22	26:34	27:08	27:14	31:44	28:51	36:38	25:21	29:52	27:40	29:46	29:38	32:09	29:31
Total net yards	332	229	273	214	361	405	228	295	265	400	382	307	270	295	198	313	4767
Rushing yards	171	100	68	36	126	156	139	118	51	85	108	59	97	81	126	130	1651
Passing yards	161	129	205	178	235	249	89	177	214	315	274	248	173	214	72	183	3116
Rushing plays	35	38	19	18	25	24	30	28	20	34	20	18	24	27	28	35	423
Sacks allowed	0	4	2	1	1	4	2	5	0	0	2	1	3	2	4	4	34
Had intercepted	0	1	1	0	4	1	0	0	1	0	2	1	1	1	2	0	14
Fumbles lost	0	1	0	0	0	2	1	0	2	1	0	0	0	3	0	1	14
Yards penalized	45	20	15	70	30	60	57	20	40	40	25	30	60	24	68	49	653
Punts	5	7	4	5	3	2	5	7	7	2	5	6	3	6	7	6	78

INDIVIDUAL STATISTICS*

RUSHING

Aikman	2-14-0	3-21-0	3-(4)-0	3-5-0	2-7-0	3-16-0	6-9-0	2-17-0			1-1-0	1-(-1)-0		3-31-0	1-1-0	2-8-0	32-125-0
Coleman											10-57-0	3-7-0	10-33-1	2-7-0	6-19-1	2-6-0	33-129-2
E. Smith		28-45-2	8-45-0	13-71-1	25-104-1	27-92-1	30-237-1	24-117-2	24-80-1		16-51-0	23-172-0	19-104-1	20-91-0	21-153-1	32-168-0	283-1486-9
Gainer		4-21-0	3-9-0	2-(-1)-0													9-29-0
Johnston	2-2-0	1-4-0	2-5-0	2-11-0		5-15-0		3-7-0	1-4-0		1-3-0	2-4-1	1-1-1	2-4-1			24-74-3
K. Williams		1-5-1	1-9-0				2-14-0		1-(-2)-0				2-11-0	1-(-8)-0			7-26-2
Lassic	16-75-0	19-52-0	14-60-2	8-15-1	5-23-0		1-1-1	1-0-0	3-8-0	9-36-0							75-269-3

PASSING**

Aikman	17-29-0 267-2		21-27-0 281-0	18-23-0 317-1	21-28-0 245-1	21-35-0 243-1	9-19-0 96-0	11-13-0 162-2			28-43-1 181-1	17-24-0 178-1	19-29-0 208-1	21-27-3 252-2	16-20-0 193-2	24-30-0 180-1	271-392-6 3100-15
Kosar									13-21-0 199-1	22-39-0 186-2					1-3-0 25-0		36-63-0 410-3

RECEIVING

Coleman											1-10-0	2-11-0			1-3-0		4-24-0
E. Smith		3-13-0	1-3-0		4-39-0	5-30-0	6-43-0	4-102-0		4-9-0	9-46-0	4-26-0	5-26-0	2-11-0	3-18-0	10-61-1	57-414-1
Gainer		1-13-0	1-8-0		1-8-0					1-8-0							6-37-0
Harper	5-140-2		6-136-0	2-80-0	1-14-0	1-36-0	3-40-0	1-9-0	4-77-0		1-7-0	1-17-0	1-12-0	2-41-0	4-65-1	3-50-0	36-777-5
Irvin	7-88-0	8-115-0	5-74-0	7-155-1	7-112-0	12-168-1	3-74-0	3-74-0	4-63-0	1-5-0	3-31-0	6-90-1	8-125-1	6-91-2	5-53-1	6-47-0	88-1330-7
Johnston		4-24-0	6-49-0	2-19-0	5-37-1		2-14-0	3-18-0	2-24-0	4-30-0	11-75-0	2-25-0	2-12-0	2-8-0	2-11-0	6-47-0	50-372-1
K. Williams	1-1-0	1-5-0		1-4-0	1-0-0		1-1-1	1-1-1	1-9-0	2-30-1	2-8-1	2-9-0	1-4-0	6-70-0	2-11-0		20-151-2
Lassic	3-9-0	3-21-0								3-7-0							9-37-0
Novacek	3-31-0	8-106-0	2-11-0	6-59-0	3-35-0	1-5-0	2-16-0	2-17-0	3-17-1	2-19-0	1-4-0	2-9-0	2-29-0	3-31-0	2-46-0	4-19-0	44-445-1

*Doesn't include all players. **Passing stats include completions, attempts, interceptions, gross yards gained and touchdowns.

333

REVIEW: DENVER BRONCOS

In terms of playing with style, the Broncos were one of the most improved teams in the National Football League.

Jim Fassel introduced a "West Coast" offense in his first year as Denver's offensive coordinator, and it was particularly well-suited to the talents of QB John Elway. Instead of playing things close to the vest and then counting on Elway's heroics in the final two minutes, the new offense turned the star quarterback loose for 60 minutes each week.

As a result, Denver was the highest-scoring team in the AFC (23.3 points per game), Elway threw for a career-high 4,030 yards and TE Shannon Sharpe had a sensational season with 81 catches for 995 yards.

"When you look at John in the old offense, it was like hooking a plow to a racehorse," said Sharpe. "I mean, let the guy throw the football.

"That's what you pay him the big bucks for — to throw the ball, not hand it off. This year he got that opportunity, and look at his numbers!"

Elway got more than a new style of offense. He also found himself surrounded by new talent on offense.

The offseason acquisitions of Gary Zimmerman and Brian Habib solidified the offensive line. Elway said the offensive line was "playing as well as anybody's by the end of the year, especially in terms of pass protection. That was the big change we made this year — that and bringing in Jim Fassel to run the offense."

Another change was the offseason addition of RB Rod Bernstine. Until he was injured late in the season, Bernstine gave the Broncos a respectable running game. He gained 816 yards rushing and also caught passes for an additional 372 yards.

Change was everywhere, including the head coach. Gone was Dan Reeves, having been replaced by the more easy-going Wade Phillips.

"The most significant change that I see is direct player involvement in every decision that is made that affects players," said Bronco OLB Simon Fletcher of the different coaching style Phillips brought to the team. "Wade established a leadership committee, and most of the decisions that directly affect players are discussed with that committee representing the players on the team, and then a decision is reached."

For all the changes, though, there was little improvement where it counts the most — in the won-loss column.

Despite the fact that Elway's numbers skyrocketed, the team finished 9-8. The previous season Elway missed four games with an injured shoulder and performed in a more-limited scheme when healthy, yet the Broncos were 8-8.

That's not a very big improvement given all of the positive changes that were made.

The biggest problem for the Broncos could be found on defense. The secondary lacked speed. S's Dennis Smith and Steve Atwater were named to the Pro Bowl, but cornerback was a problem area.

Midway through the season, Phillips acknowledged the team's woes against the pass.

"The recurring thing is certainly giving up the big plays on defense," he said. "You can't say our running game is bad, or that our passing game is bad. We are stuffing the run, but they are killing us with the pass."

The Broncos ended the season ranked 27th in the NFL in passing yards allowed.

A bright spot on defense was the play of Fletcher. For the sixth consecutive season, he led the Broncos in sacks. He finished the 1993 season with 13.5 sacks and was named the team's defensive MVP. Yet, he still hasn't been named to a Pro Bowl in his career, despite the fact he has posted 11 or more sacks in each of the last five seasons.

Other than the defense's troubles against the pass, the Broncos' other problem was in the offense's passing game. Although Elway and Sharpe posted tremendous numbers, wide receiver was a trouble spot. Vance Johnson fractured his ankle during the middle portion of the season and never came back. Derek Russell sprained his ankle late in the season, knocking him out of the lineup down the stretch.

1993 ROUNDUP

OFFENSIVE MVP: QB John Elway still has a golden arm after 11 seasons. He had his best statistical year of his career and was fourth in NFL MVP voting.

DEFENSIVE MVP: OLB Simon Fletcher led the Broncos in sacks for the sixth-straight season. He had 13.5 in 1993.

RESULTS
Pointspread Shown Refers To Denver

Date	Opponent	Spread	Score
Sept. 5	At New York Jets	(-1.5)	26-20
Sept. 12	San Diego	(-3)	34-17
Sept. 20	At Kansas City	(+7)	7-15
Oct. 3	Indianapolis	(-7)	35-13
Oct. 10	At Green Bay	(+3)	27-30
Oct. 18	L.A. Raiders	(-6.5)	20-23
Oct. 31	Seattle	(-9)	28-17
Nov. 7	At Cleveland	(+2.5)	29-14
Nov. 14	Minnesota	(-6.5)	23-26
Nov. 21	Pittsburgh	(-3)	37-13
Nov. 28	At Seattle	(-3)	17-9
Dec. 5	At San Diego	(+3)	10-13
Dec. 12	Kansas City	(-2.5)	27-21
Dec. 18	At Chicago	(-2)	13-3
Dec. 26	Tampa Bay	(-13.5)	10-17
Jan. 2	At L.A. Raiders	(+3)	30-33*
POSTSEASON			
Jan. 9	At L.A. Raiders	(+1.5)	24-42

* Overtime

1993 REVIEW ■ DENVER

GAME-BY-GAME STATISTICS

TEAM STATISTICS

OPPONENT	WK 1 N.Y.J.	WK 2 S.D.	WK 3 K.C.	WK 5 IND.	WK 6 G.B.	WK 7 L.A.RD	WK 9 SEA.	WK 10 CLEV.	WK 11 MINN.	WK 12 PITT.	WK 13 SEA.	WK 14 S.D.	WK 15 K.C.	WK 16 CHI.	WK 17 T.B.	WK 18 L.A.RD	TOTALS
Score	26-20	34-17	7-15	35-13	27-30	20-23	28-17	29-14	23-26	37-13	17-9	10-13	27-21	13-3	10-17	30-33	
Time of possession	26:51	33:07	37:27	24:38	30:35	27:16	26:52	22:30	27:06	27:49	28:43	32:14	24:21	27:11	31:03	33:34	
Total net yards	422	390	414	271	299	308	287	266	429	356	288	298	311	185	236	398	5461
Rushing yards	71	68	160	111	64	53	103	75	71	101	127	95	77	84	65	94	1693
Passing yards	351	322	254	160	235	255	184	191	358	255	161	203	234	101	171	304	3768
Rushing plays	19	24	31	22	29	23	26	14	27	23	26	27	21	26	36	24	398
Sacks allowed	3	4	3	1	0	1	4	6	1	3	6	1	1	4	2	3	45
Had intercepted	1	1	0	2	3	1	2	0	1	1	1	0	1	3	0	1	18
Fumbles lost	2	1	1	0	1	1	0	0	2	2	1	1	1	2	0	1	13
Yards penalized	45	58	105	40	74	110	94	51	92	63	75	75	42	25	10	60	1019
Punts	2	6	6	4	3	5	3	5	5	3	12	6	4	5	8	4	81

OPPONENT STATISTICS

	WK 1	WK 2	WK 3	WK 5	WK 6	WK 7	WK 9	WK 10	WK 11	WK 12	WK 13	WK 14	WK 15	WK 16	WK 17	WK 18	TOTALS
Total net yards	353	342	335	454	388	253	326	392	343	364	307	224	340	234	335	471	5158
Rushing yards	99	58	35	196	55	132	87	159	93	107	101	86	136	129	110	110	1419
Passing yards	254	284	300	258	333	121	239	233	250	257	206	138	204	105	225	361	3739
Rushing plays	32	22	14	37	19	32	31	42	22	34	35	23	38	33	23	31	468
Sacks allowed	2	1	0	0	4	7	1	6	4	2	4	5	2	3	1	0	39
Had intercepted	0	1	1	0	1	1	1	0	1	0	1	1	2	3	1	0	10
Fumbles lost	1	1	2	2	1	1	1	3	3	0	1	1	0	1	3	0	18
Yards penalized	19	34	75	60	112	55	54	63	77	22	35	29	64	0	34	89	822
Punts	3	4	8	1	3	4	3	3	5	3	8	6	3	5	5	4	68

INDIVIDUAL STATISTICS*

RUSHING

	WK 1	WK 2	WK 3	WK 5	WK 6	WK 7	WK 9	WK 10	WK 11	WK 12	WK 13	WK 14	WK 15	WK 16	WK 17	WK 18	TOTALS
Bernstine	19-44-0	14-39-1	5-6-0	12-60-1	8-26-1	23-101-0	18-64-0	21-82-0	8-37-0	18-55-0	17-47-1	15-52-0	23-90-0	20-103-0	2-10-0		223-816-4
Delpino	2-(-2)-0	2-2-1	3-15-0	16-83-1	2-1-0	1-0-0	10-25-2	10-39-0	8-17-1	10-41-2	12-47-0	7-24-0	8-35-0	8-14-1	12-38-0	20-66-0	131-445-8
Elway	5-19-0	1-(-1)-0	1-0-0	4-30-0	5-27-0	2-8-0	3-(-2)-0	2-7-0	2-8-0	2-8-0	5-5-0	1-10-0	4-1-0	4-8-0	1-4-0	2-21-0	44-153-0
Milburn	5-38-0	3-15-0	5-14-0	4-19-0	4-1-0	5-23-0		5-25-0	4-30-0	2-1-0	1-2-0		3-10-0	1-4-0	4-31-0	6-17-0	52-230-0
Rivers	1-0-0	2-3-0		1-4-0						1-3-0					4-27-1	3-6-0	15-50-1

PASSING**

	WK 1	WK 2	WK 3	WK 5	WK 6	WK 7	WK 9	WK 10	WK 11	WK 12	WK 13	WK 14	WK 15	WK 16	WK 17	WK 18	TOTALS
Elway	20-29-0 269-2	24-34-1 294-2	28-45-1 300-1	20-30-0 230-2	33-59-1 367-1	16-30-1 188-2	23-36-1 255-2	17-23-0 244-3	30-40-1 290-2	18-25-0 276-1	20-37-1 226-1	14-32-1 171-0	20-30-2 221-3	14-24-0 113-0	26-41-0 225-0	25-36-0 361-3	348-551-10 4030-25

RECEIVING

	WK 1	WK 2	WK 3	WK 5	WK 6	WK 7	WK 9	WK 10	WK 11	WK 12	WK 13	WK 14	WK 15	WK 16	WK 17	WK 18	TOTALS
Bernstine	3-11-0	4-22-0	2-49-0	3-28-0	4-31-0		6-47-0	4-22-0	6-37-0	1-1-0	4-32-0	4-41-0	1-41-0	1-6-0	1-4-0		44-372-0
Delpino	1-5-0	2-2-1	1-1-0	2-11-0	1-4-0		4-34-0	1-25-0	1-9-0	1-2-0	4-37-0	2-23-0	1-6-0	2-17-0	3-15-0	3-18-0	26-195-0
Kimbrough				1-16-0		1-27-1							1-6-0		4-40-0		8-79-0
Marshall	6-76-1				2-25-0	1-3-0					1-3-0	3-44-0	4-48-0	4-24-0	2-49-0	5-64-0	28-360-2
Milburn	2-75-1	2-9-0	8-61-0	5-48-1	3-20-0	3-(4)-0	2-41-0	2-8-1	5-27-0	2-17-0	1-3-0			1-6-0	3-2-0	3-21-0	38-300-3
R. Johnson	4-70-0	1-18-0	1-2-1		1-9-0			1-11-0	2-12-0	1-31-0				1-13-0	2-8-0		21-245-1
Rivers	1-9-0	2-24-1	1-2-0										2-34-0				6-59-1
Russell	1-17-0	3-36-0	6-104-0	4-64-1	5-75-0	5-111-0	1-38-0	1-38-1	5-57-1	4-82-0	6-68-0	4-41-0	10-65-3		26-41-0	25-36-0	348-551-10
Sharpe	7-79-0	3-47-0	9-81-0	4-50-1	7-55-0	4-44-0	3-31-1	4-55-1	7-104-0	4-80-0	3-72-1	2-34-0		2-20-0	6-65-0	6-115-2	81-997-9
Taylor																1-28-0	1-28-0
Tillman	1-3-1		1-2-1	2-43-0		2-9-0		4-85-0	4-44-1	5-63-1	1-11-0		1-21-0	3-27-0	5-42-0	5-91-1	17-193-2
V. Johnson		2-57-0		10-148-1			7-64-1										36-517-5
Wyman												1-1-1					1-1-1

* Doesn't include all players. ** Passing stats include completions, attempts, interceptions, gross yards gained and touchdowns.

335

REVIEW: DETROIT LIONS

One wonders how far the Lions of 1993 could have gone had their season not been similar to a daytime soap opera.

The annual Detroit quarterback controversy played out weekly, with coach Wayne Fontes switching the designated starter depending on the date. In addition, a rash of injuries crippled the Lions throughout the season. And then there were rumblings of a coaching change. Fontes survived, but maybe only because he sacrificed offensive coordinator Dan Henning late in the year.

But, despite such a lack of smooth sailing, the Lions were able to finish atop the NFC Central Division with an overall record of 10-6 and earn a playoff berth for the second time in three years.

The postseason amounted to nothing more than an extra weekend in the Silverdome, however, as the Lions bowed out of the playoffs at the hands of division-rival Green Bay.

QB Rodney Peete was the first man to be designated the No. 1 gun by Fontes. He started the first three games and was less than consistent, and then he was demoted, despite taking the Lions to a 2-1 record.

Andre Ware, who had whined about not getting a fair chance to lead the Lions since his arrival in Detroit as a Heisman Trophy winner in 1990, was made the starter. Under Ware, the Lions were able to eke out a win against Phoenix, before falling to the NFC Central's weakest member, Tampa Bay.

That loss led to Fontes switching back to Peete. The move worked for a while, as the Lions patched together their longest string of victories of the season, winning their next four to move to 7-2.

Not a bad record at the midpoint of the season, considering the changes that were made, and all the injuries. Oh, the injuries. Pro Bowl OT Lomas Brown missed the first seven weeks with a severe ankle sprain. Pro Bowl LB Pat Swilling was hit doubly hard, having to suffer through the death of his father and then a severe ankle sprain. Pro Bowl FS Bennie Blades broke his ankle in the fourth game of the season and didn't see action the rest of the year. And yet another Pro Bowler, KR Mel Gray, sprained his ankle and missed four games near the middle of the season.

But all those ankle injuries were minor, compared to what was to come in the way of the injury bug. During a three-game losing streak that would drop Detroit to 7-5, RB Barry Sanders was lost for the rest of the regular season thanks to a sprained knee.

Facing the prospect of such a decent start fading to an ugly ending, Fontes made major moves. Henning was canned, and Dave Levy was moved from his assistant head coach position to offensive coordinator. Peete was again demoted, this time all the way to the No. 3 spot, and Erik Kramer was upped from No. 3 to No. 1.

"The bottom line is we couldn't score touchdowns and couldn't score points, so I decided to make the change," said Fontes after the shakedown.

All these changes, although appearing to be a desperation move by Fontes to stay employed, almost worked out brilliantly. With Levy calling the offense, the Lions opened it up more, and Kramer was successful in making big plays. And with Sanders on the sidelines, a couple of young running backs — Derrick Moore and Eric Lynch — proved to be saviors. The Lions went on to win three of their final four games, including a 30-20 victory against Green Bay to capture the division title in the season finale.

Unfortunately for the Lions, they had to face the Packers again the following week in the wild-card playoff game, which was won by Green Bay in the final minute of play.

Despite all the controversy, Fontes said he was proud of the work he and his team did in 1993.

"I think this season was the best job I've done here as an assistant or a head coach," said Fontes.

"I was able to hold this club together through some tough times," continued Fontes, who then added he received calls from general managers from around the league wondering how he accomplished what he did.

1993 ROUNDUP

OFFENSIVE MVP: RB Barry Sanders managed to gain 1,115 yards in only 12 games. He is only the third player in NFL history to rush for 1,000 yards in his first five seasons.

DEFENSIVE MVP: ILB Chris Spielman led the Lions in tackles for the sixth consecutive season with 148.

RESULTS
Pointspread Shown Refers To Detroit

Date	Opponent	Spread	Score
Sept. 5	Atlanta	(-5.5)	30-13
Sept. 12	At New England	(-7)	19-16*
Sept. 19	At New Orleans	(+6)	3-14
Sept. 26	Phoenix	(-5)	26-20
Oct. 3	At Tampa Bay	(-6)	10-27
Oct. 17	Seattle	(-5)	30-10
Oct. 24	At L.A. Rams	(+2.5)	16-13
Oct. 31	At Minnesota	(+4)	30-27
Nov. 7	Tampa Bay	(-12.5)	23-0
Nov. 21	At Green Bay (in Milw)	(+3.5)	17-26
Nov. 25	Chicago	(-7)	6-10
Dec. 5	Minnesota	(-3)	0-13
Dec. 12	At Phoenix	(+7.5)	21-14
Dec. 19	San Francisco	(+9)	17-55
Dec. 26	At Chicago	(+3)	20-14
Jan. 2	Green Bay	(+1)	30-20
POSTSEASON			
Jan. 8	Green Bay	(-1)	24-28

* Overtime

1993 REVIEW ■ DETROIT

GAME-BY-GAME STATISTICS

TEAM STATISTICS

OPPONENT	WK 1 ATL.	WK 2 N.E.	WK 3 N.O.	WK 4 PHX.	WK 5 T.B.	WK 7 SEA.	WK 8 L.A.RM	WK 9 MINN.	WK 10 T.B.	WK 12 G.B.	WK 13 CHI.	WK 14 MINN.	WK 15 PHX.	WK 16 S.F.	WK 17 CHI.	WK 18 G.B.	TOTALS
Score	30-13	19-16	3-14	26-20	10-27	30-10	16-13	30-27	23-0	17-26	6-10	0-13	21-14	17-55	20-14	30-20	
Total net yards	262	340	170	330	311	292	363	338	366	205	230	219	340	288	307	297	4658
Rushing yards	96	186	84	147	144	141	134	78	241	116	84	108	105	81	84	115	1944
Passing yards	166	154	86	183	167	151	229	260	125	89	146	111	235	207	223	182	2714
Rushing plays	35	44	21	26	26	32	34	23	43	25	23	27	23	18	26	30	456
Sacks allowed	2	0	3	5	3	2	4	4	0	2	5	5	0	0	1	0	46
Had intercepted	0	3	0	0	1	1	1	2	0	1	2	2	3	0	1	1	19
Fumbles lost	0	1	2	0	1	1	0	2	0	1	2	1	0	3	0	0	13
Yards penalized	20	57	35	30	10	65	40	63	55	26	40	64	40	45	20	55	665
Punts	6	2	7	4	6	6	3	4	4	5	5	6	6	3	2	6	72

	WK 1	WK 2	WK 3	WK 4	WK 5	WK 7	WK 8	WK 9	WK 10	WK 12	WK 13	WK 14	WK 15	WK 16	WK 17	WK 18	TOTALS
Time of possession	29:05	31:53	33:28	32:37	30:45	28:27	25:58	32:56	23:33	35:18	31:06	30:27	35:55	32:31	29:47	30:48	30:36
Total net yards	237	292	258	343	324	229	291	378	146	404	225	234	287	565	180	273	4666
Rushing yards	21	61	172	79	128	63	150	116	44	153	107	101	96	172	77	101	1641
Passing yards	216	231	86	264	196	166	141	262	102	251	118	133	191	393	103	172	3025
Rushing plays	8	23	35	25	31	20	30	30	14	41	35	26	25	37	32	22	434
Sacks allowed	6	2	2	4	3	3	3	1	3	1	4	3	4	0	2	2	43
Had intercepted	2	1	0	0	0	3	1	1	1	2	1	1	0	2	0	4	19
Fumbles lost	1	2	1	3	1	0	0	2	0	0	1	1	3	0	1	0	15
Yards penalized	34	30	25	30	55	60	21	21	35	30	15	34	33	50	7	20	500
Punts	8	5	7	5	6	7	4	5	8	3	5	6	5	0	3	4	81

INDIVIDUAL STATISTICS*

RUSHING

	WK 1	WK 2	WK 3	WK 4	WK 5	WK 7	WK 8	WK 9	WK 10	WK 12	WK 13	WK 14	WK 15	WK 16	WK 17	WK 18	TOTALS
D. Moore		4-18-0	1-(-1)-0	2-49-1	2-3-0	4-7-0	4-13-0	1-1-1	8-27-1	2-23-0	4-6-0	22-86-0	20-107-0	14-66-0	22-85-0	15-29-1	88-405-3
Lynch	4-14-0	8-20-0	3-8-0			4-26-0	4-30-0	8-13-0	3-20-1	4-3-0	3-15-0	4-16-0		1-7-0	30-115-2		53-207-2
Peete																	45-165-1
Sanders	26-90-1	32-148-0	16-76-0	23-90-0	22-130-1	22-101-0	26-91-1	14-64-0	29-187-0	17-75-0	16-63-0						243-1115-3

PASSING**

	WK 1	WK 2	WK 3	WK 4	WK 5	WK 7	WK 8	WK 9	WK 10	WK 12	WK 13	WK 14	WK 15	WK 16	WK 17	WK 18	TOTALS
Kramer					11-24-1 120-0								19-25-0 257-3	19-29-0 220-2	23-31-1 223-2	15-29-1 182-1	87-138-3 1002-8
Peete	11-20-0 178-1	16-25-3 175-0	12-17-0 99-0			14-26-1 157-2	15-25-1 249-0	20-28-2 273-1	16-22-0 134-0	13-25-1 100-2	22-34-2 167-0	18-30-4 138-0					157-252-14 1670-6
Ware			3-5-0 17-0	11-24-0 194-1	5-14-1 56-0							1-2-1 4-0					20-45-2 271-1

RECEIVING

	WK 1	WK 2	WK 3	WK 4	WK 5	WK 7	WK 8	WK 9	WK 10	WK 12	WK 13	WK 14	WK 15	WK 16	WK 17	WK 18	TOTALS
Campbell	1-4-0	2-11-0			2-17-0					1-12-0	1-11-0			6-67-1			7-55-0
D. Moore										2-8-0	2-5-0	6-43-0	7-54-0	2-21-0	1-11-0	1-11-0	23-177-1
Green	4-113-1	5-49-0	4-42-0	3-102-0	3-88-0	8-98-2	1-10-0	2-25-0	4-51-0	6-68-1	7-61-0	1-15-0	1-43-1	4-74-1	3-42-0	2-31-0	28-462-2
H. Moore				5-79-0	3-27-0		6-120-0	3-113-1				2-12-0	3-66-1		2-10-1	3-48-0	59-927-6
Hallock		2-34-0	1-6-0			1-5-0	1-24-0	2-17-0		1-1-1	1-5-0	1-5-0			3-16-0	1-8-1	8-88-2
Holman					3-17-0	2-23-0	1-25-0					4-36-0	4-60-1	2-15-0 1-7-0	3-16-0 7-46-0	5-29-0	25-244-2
Lynch	1-13-0							1-18-0	3-36-0	1-3-0	8-75-0				1-23-0		13-82-0
Matthews	3-21-1	4-51-1	2-26-0	1-9-1	1-6-0	2-24-1	2-45-1	3-47-0	5-40-0			5-31-0	4-34-0	1-13-0 3-23-0	7-46-0 6-75-1	3-55-0	11-171-0 49-496-2
Perriman	2-27-1	2-15-0	5-25-0	2-4-0	4-21-0		4-25-0	8-44-0	2-2-0	2-8-0	3-10-0						36-205-0
Sanders																	

* Doesn't include all players. ** Passing stats include completions, attempts, interceptions, gross yards gained and touchdowns.

337

REVIEW: GREEN BAY PACKERS

The fans in Title Town had something to feel good about in 1993 — a legitimate shot at the postseason.

The Packers were picked by many to win the NFC Central before the season began, a feat which would earn Green Bay its first playoff game since the strike season's Super Bowl Tournament of 1982. And if the team did not win the division outright, there was always the possibility of a wild-card berth.

In 1993 Green Bay went 9-7 overall, 4-4 in the division and 6-6 against NFC opponents. Those numbers matched the previous year's performance to a T. And it marked the first time the team has recorded back-to-back winning seasons since 1966-67.

But unlike '92, the Packers did get to play more than 16 games. With traditional conference powers like Washington, New Orleans and Philadelphia having off years, Green Bay pulled out the third wild-card spot.

Football has never been dead in Green Bay, considering the faithful line up every year in the bitter cold, almost content to be disappointed.

But in '93, there was a feeling of confidence among Packer fans that this was the year. With the addition of DE Reggie White, the presence of perennial Pro Bowl WR Sterling Sharpe and the expected maturity of QB Brett Favre, there was a feeling that the Packers were destined to do big things.

White helped a defensive unit that ranked 23rd in 1992 rise to second in the NFL in total defense.

Sharpe broke the NFL single-season reception record of 108, which he set in 1992, by hauling in 112 catches for 1,274 yards. He also led the team in touchdowns with 11.

And Favre's play can be interpreted in a couple of different ways. He was the guy who could almost single-handedly pull out a win, or throw the game away. In fact, it was his bad habit of letting the ball fly when it shouldn't that left many to wonder if Favre really was the man to bring glory back to Green Bay.

Despite throwing 24 interceptions in '93, Favre was still the man in the eyes of coach Mike Holmgren.

"Our football team will almost automatically take the next step with him," said Holmgren. "My thought is I've thrown so much at him in two years, sometimes you have to take two steps backward to take two steps forward. Perhaps that's what happened. To avoid some of the mistakes that took place, maybe he just has to calm down, to learn to throw the ball away."

Favre was blamed for the 30-20 loss to Detroit in the season finale because he was intercepted four times. That game cost the Pack the division title and home-field advantage for the playoffs.

The resilient Favre then came through six days later, lifting his team to a 28-24 victory over the Lions with a remarkable 40-yard TD pass to Sharpe with 55 seconds remaining.

It was the kind of pass that made folks cringe until they noticed that Sharpe was all alone in the endzone.

"I throw across my body 60 yards and it's a touchdown," Favre said. "Everybody says, 'That guy's great.' But if it gets picked, they say, 'What the hell's he doing?'"

The next hurdle, the divisional playoff game in Dallas, didn't end as nicely for the green and gold.

The Cowboys, who entered the contest as 14-point favorites, didn't exactly win easily, but they did prevail 27-17.

Still, the Packers made it to the next level, and believe they will continue to climb the ladder of NFL success.

"Hey, you've got to crawl before you can walk," said general manager Ron Wolf. "We feel we're just a couple of players away from being like them (the Cowboys)."

"History tells us that it wasn't time for this team," said Wolf. "Everybody anointed us as division champions, and really, we could have been. We had a pretty good run. It's a great steppingstone. We have an opportunity to do something special here."

Holmgren agrees good things are in store for the Packers.

"We're not going to start over," said Holmgren. "We're going to maintain what we have and get better."

1993 ROUNDUP

OFFENSIVE MVP: WR Sterling Sharpe had another phenomenal season with 112 receptions for 1,274 yards and 11 touchdowns. He had game-winning catches in three games.

DEFENSIVE MVP: DE Reggie White tied for the NFC lead with 13 sacks.

RESULTS
Pointspread Shown Refers To Green Bay

Date	Opponent	Spread	Score
Sept. 5	L.A. Rams (in Milw)	(-7)	36-6
Sept. 12	Philadelphia	(-3.5)	17-20
Sept. 26	At Minnesota	(+3)	13-15
Oct. 3	At Dallas	(+11)	14-36
Oct. 10	Denver	(-3)	30-27
Oct. 24	At Tampa Bay	(-5)	37-14
Oct. 31	Chicago	(-5.5)	17-3
Nov. 8	At Kansas City	(+3)	16-23
Nov. 14	At New Orleans	(+6.5)	19-17
Nov. 21	Detroit (in Milw)	(-3.5)	26-17
Nov. 28	Tampa Bay	(-12)	13-10
Dec. 5	At Chicago	(+2)	17-30
Dec. 12	At San Diego	(+3)	20-13
Dec. 19	Minnesota (in Milw)	(-6.5)	17-21
Dec. 26	L.A. Raiders	(-3)	28-0
Jan. 2	At Detroit	(-1)	20-30

POSTSEASON

| Jan. 8 | At Detroit | (+1) | 28-24 |
| Jan. 16 | At Dallas | (+14) | 17-27 |

1993 REVIEW ■ GREEN BAY

GAME-BY-GAME STATISTICS

TEAM STATISTICS

OPPONENT	WK 1 L.A.RM	WK 2 PHIL.	WK 4 MINN.	WK 5 DALL.	WK 6 DENV.	WK 8 T.B.	WK 9 CHI.	WK 10 K.C.	WK 11 N.O.	WK 12 DET.	WK 13 T.B.	WK 14 CHI.	WK 15 S.D.	WK 16 MINN.	WK 17 L.A.RD	WK 18 DET.	TOTALS
Score	36-6	17-20	13-15	14-36	30-27	37-14	17-3	16-23	19-17	26-17	13-10	17-30	20-13	17-21	28-0	20-30	
Total net yards	381	159	256	214	299	421	261	287	194	404	259	466	227	320	329	273	4750
Rushing yards	138	52	106	36	64	162	135	99	69	153	107	79	103	67	148	101	1619
Passing yards	243	107	150	178	235	259	126	188	125	251	152	387	124	253	181	172	3131
Rushing plays	36	20	23	18	29	34	27	24	21	41	30	29	39	19	37	22	449
Sacks allowed	3	1	0	1	0	2	2	4	6	1	2	2	2	1	2	2	31
Had intercepted	1	2	2	0	3	1	1	3	0	0	0	3	1	1	0	4	24
Fumbles lost	0	0	0	0	1	1	0	3	1	2	0	0	0	1	1	0	9
Yards penalized	71	25	50	70	74	72	25	68	33	30	55	71	25	35	10	20	734
Punts	3	4	5	5	3	5	4	2	5	3	9	2	6	5	9	4	74

OPPONENT STATISTICS

	WK 1	WK 2	WK 4	WK 5	WK 6	WK 8	WK 9	WK 10	WK 11	WK 12	WK 13	WK 14	WK 15	WK 16	WK 17	WK 18	TOTALS
Time of possession	23:51	38:21	31:45	30:38	29:25	22:03	32:51	30:28	33:24	24:42	23:58	21:46	29:21	35:52	28:18	29:12	
Total net yards	228	352	317	395	388	246	230	253	329	205	207	210	282	361	182	297	4482
Rushing yards	53	161	107	98	55	84	118	100	157	116	92	69	57	154	46	115	1582
Passing yards	175	191	210	297	333	162	112	153	172	89	115	141	225	207	136	182	2900
Rushing plays	19	39	29	30	19	20	34	26	35	25	22	23	17	38	18	30	424
Sacks allowed	0	3	2	2	4	2	7	4	5	5	3	1	3	0	8	0	46
Had intercepted	2	1	0	0	1	3	1	0	2	1	0	1	3	0	2	1	18
Fumbles lost	0	3	1	0	1	0	2	0	3	1	0	1	0	0	2	0	15
Yards penalized	13	19	25	23	112	45	40	116	42	26	39	15	55	73	14	55	712
Punts	5	1	3	1	3	8	4	2	3	5	10	4	5	7	9	6	79

INDIVIDUAL STATISTICS*

RUSHING

	WK 1	WK 2	WK 4	WK 5	WK 6	WK 8	WK 9	WK 10	WK 11	WK 12	WK 13	WK 14	WK 15	WK 16	WK 17	WK 18	TOTALS
Brooks												1-(-6)-0				1-2-0	3-17-0
E. Bennett	11-41-2	8-26-0	11-36-0	7-8-1	12-34-1	10-43-0	8-53-0	8-26-0	6-25-0	15-66-2	10-39-0	10-35-0	18-59-1	5-3-0	15-38-1	5-18-1	159-550-9
Favre	1-7-0	2-4-0	4-8-1	1-9-0	5-18-0	2-9-0	5-14-0	4-22-0	5-24-0	7-(-7)-0	4-25-0	3-30-0	4-7-0	5-24-0	1-9-0	5-13-0	58-216-1
Sharpe	1-3-0			1-(-4)-0	1-4-0	1-5-0											4-8-0
Stephens	17-75-0	9-22-0	8-62-0	5-0-0	9-14-1												48-173-1
Thompson	3-6-0			4-23-0	1-(-8)-0	21-105-0	14-68-1	12-51-0	9-20-0	18-73-0	16-43-0	13-27-0	17-37-1	9-40-0	21-101-1	11-68-0	169-654-3

PASSING**

	WK 1	WK 2	WK 4	WK 5	WK 6	WK 8	WK 9	WK 10	WK 11	WK 12	WK 13	WK 14	WK 15	WK 16	WK 17	WK 18	TOTALS
Favre	19-29-1 264-2	12-24-2 111-2	20-31-2 150-0	21-37-0 174-0	20-32-3 235-1	20-35-1 268-4	15-24-1 136-1	20-34-3 213-1	18-32-0 150-1	24-33-2 259-0	23-36-0 159-1	36-54-3 402-2	13-23-1 146-0	20-33-1 256-2	14-28-0 190-1	23-37-4 190-1	318-522-24 3303-19

RECEIVING

	WK 1	WK 2	WK 4	WK 5	WK 6	WK 8	WK 9	WK 10	WK 11	WK 12	WK 13	WK 14	WK 15	WK 16	WK 17	WK 18	TOTALS
Brooks												4-56-0		1-5-0		1-7-0	20-180-0
C. Harris			3-14-0	1-25-0	1-4-0	2-6-0	1-11-0		2-16-0	2-24-0	3-17-0						2-11-0
Chmura											1-6-0			1-5-0	1-6-0	1-7-0	2-13-0
Clayton	4-40-1		1-5-0	3-27-0	2-21-0	3-26-0	1-9-0	2-29-0	1-9-0	2-41-0	4-40-0	6-44-1	1-22-0	1-11-1		1-7-0	32-331-3
E. Bennett	1-8-0	2-2-0	6-49-0	8-61-0	2-12-0	2-7-0	2-13-0	3-21-0	1-(-4)-0	6-52-0	4-22-0	6-47-0	2-30-0	4-44-0	4-41-0	6-52-1	59-457-1
J. Harris	5-92-0	2-26-1	1-11-0	4-27-0	5-128-1	1-51-0	1-15-0	6-86-1	4-25-1			6-72-0	2-21-0	5-50-0			42-604-4
Lewis														1-4-0		1-17-0	2-21-0
Sharpe	7-120-1	7-72-1	5-46-0	4-34-0	10-70-0	10-147-4	7-75-1	7-76-0	6-79-0	7-75-0	6-43-1	10-114-1	7-65-0	6-106-1	7-119-1	6-33-0	112-1274-11
Stephens	2-4-0		2-18-0	1-9-0						2-5-0	2-5-0	2-49-0			1-0-0		5-31-0
Thompson				1-(-3)-0		3-32-0		1-0-0	3-18-0		3-26-0	2-20-0		2-36-0		3-23-0	18-129-0
West								1-(-4)-0	1-7-0				1-22-0		1-24-0	4-44-0	25-253-0
Wilson		1-11-0		1-11-0			1-7-0	1-5-0									2-18-0

* Doesn't include all players. ** Passing stats include completions, attempts, interceptions, gross yards gained and touchdowns.

HOUSTON OILERS

In the words of Jack Pardee, who went from being the head coach most likely to be fired in 1993 to many experts' choice as NFL Coach of the Year following his team's inspired turnaround, it was a season that had "the highest of highs and lowest of lows."

The highs for an Oiler unit, which was dubbed "Team Turmoil" for its stormy exploits on and off the field, came with an 11-game winning streak that led to a 12-4 record, an AFC Central Division title and a first-round bye in the playoffs.

The major spark in the longest winning streak in the NFL since 1972 — when the Dolphins went 17-0 — was provided by an improved defense devised by volatile coordinator Buddy Ryan that was tops against the run in the NFL and second only to Buffalo in takeaways with 43.

On offense, the key was RB Gary Brown, a seldom-used backup who shocked everyone when he took over for the injured Lorenzo White halfway through the season and proceeded to gain 1,002 yards behind an offensive line that steadily improved its run blocking as the season wore on.

But then there were the lows, enough of them to keep Team Turmoil in the national spotlight throughout most of the season:

■ On Oct. 17 OT David Williams decided to skip a road game at New England and remain home in Houston for the birth of his first child. When that decision cost him a $111,000 game check, Oiler management came under heavy fire in what became known as the "Babygate" incident.

Ironically, the Oilers' 28-14 victory over the Patriots in the game Williams missed ended up being the turning point of the season. The Oilers had gone to Foxboro with a 1-4 record and a three-game losing streak. Adding to the controversy surrounding the team was the fact veteran QB Warren Moon had been benched for the first time ever in favor of Cody Carlson. Carlson, however, suffered a first-half groin injury, and Moon looked good leading his team to victory in relief, thus ending a demotion that lasted less than two quarters.

■ Earlier that same week, team owner Bud Adams said Oiler players had too many outside activities, including charity work. Adams made the comments on a day when he asked the players to attend a Rotary Club luncheon.

■ On Dec. 14, DT Jeff Alm committed suicide, killing himself with a shotgun as he sat beside a freeway following an auto accident in which Alm was the driver and his best friend, a passenger, died. Both victims were legally drunk.

■ In the team's final regular-season game against the Jets on a Sunday night before a nationwide cable-TV audience, a season-long war of words between Ryan and offensive coordinator Kevin Gilbride came to a head when Ryan punched Gilbride over a turnover near the end of the first half. Ryan bad-mouthed Gilbride's run-and-shoot offense from the season's get-go, blaming it on more than one occasion for causing injuries to his defenders because of its inability to stay on the field and run out the clock.

"It's by far the strangest year I've ever been involved with," said Oiler WR Ernest Givins. "But it was also the most productive year."

The Oilers' productivity came to a crashing halt in the playoffs, however, courtesy of Joe Montana, one of the game's most celebrated signal-callers.

Within a 54-second span of the fourth quarter, Montana did what he does best by pulling the Kansas City Chiefs to a 28-20 victory that was punctuated by Chief TE Keith Cash's memorable bull's-eye on a Buddy Ryan poster after scoring K.C.'s first TD of the game.

The disappointment of the Oilers' seventh straight postseason failure without reaching the conference championship was too much for Oiler general manager Mike Holovak, who decided to retire and leave the job to assistant GM Floyd Reese.

One week later, Ryan caught the Oilers completely off guard by accepting the head-coaching job in Phoenix — a fitting capper to a wild and crazy season.

"We never did anything in a little way," Pardee said. "It seemed no matter what we did, it made national news."

1993 ROUNDUP

OFFENSIVE MVP: RB Gary Brown started only eight games but still rushed for 1,002 yards in the run-and-shoot offense.

DEFENSIVE MVP: CB Cris Dishman tied his career-best with six interceptions in 1993 and acted as a coach on the field.

RESULTS
Pointspread Shown Refers To Houston

Date	Opponent	Spread	Score
Sept. 5	At New Orleans	(+2.5)	21-33
Sept. 12	Kansas City	(-3.5)	30-0
Sept. 19	At San Diego	(+2.5)	17-18
Sept. 26	L.A. Rams	(-10.5)	13-28
Oct. 11	At Buffalo	(+3.5)	7-35
Oct. 17	At New England	(-6.5)	28-14
Oct. 24	Cincinnati	(-14)	28-12
Nov. 7	Seattle	(-9.5)	24-14
Nov. 14	At Cincinnati	(-8.5)	38-3
Nov. 21	At Cleveland	(-5.5)	27-20
Nov. 28	Pittsburgh	(-3)	23-3
Dec. 5	Atlanta	(-7)	33-17
Dec. 12	Cleveland	(-10)	19-17
Dec. 19	At Pittsburgh	(+4)	26-17
Dec. 25	At San Francisco	(+9)	10-7
Jan. 2	New York Jets	(-4)	24-0
POSTSEASON			
Jan. 16	Kansas City	(-7)	20-28

GAME-BY-GAME STATISTICS

TEAM STATISTICS

OPPONENT	WK 1 N.O.	WK 2 K.C.	WK 3 S.D.	WK 4 L.A.RM	WK 6 BUFF.	WK 7 N.E.	WK 8 CIN.	WK 10 SEA.	WK 11 CIN.	WK 13 PITT.	WK 14 ATL.	WK 15 CLEV.	WK 16 PITT.	WK 17 S.F.	WK 18 N.Y.J.	TOTALS
Score	21-33	30-0	17-18	13-28	7-35	28-14	28-12	24-14	38-3	23-3	33-17	19-17	26-17	10-7	24-0	14-41-2
Total net yards	405	247	295	370	329	246	369	458	462	391	389	257	383	311	363	5659
Rushing yards	70	57	71	82	84	104	125	111	240	125	52	128	117	116	108	1792
Passing yards	335	190	224	288	245	142	244	347	222	266	337	129	266	195	255	3867
Rushing plays	18	28	17	20	17	25	25	26	37	30	23	28	25	23	29	410
Sacks allowed	4	2	3	4	4	1	1	3	1	3	1	4	1	3	6	42
Had intercepted	1	1	4	2	4	0	1	2	2	2	0	1	0	3	1	25
Fumbles lost	4	1	1	0	3	0	1	0	2	0	3	0	2	0	1	20
Yards penalized	84	32	57	50	59	61	40	57	30	134	71	62	62	34	97	1005
Punts	2	3	5	2	3	6	3	3	2	5	1	4	4	4	4	56

OPPONENT STATISTICS

	WK 1	WK 2	WK 3	WK 4	WK 6	WK 7	WK 8	WK 10	WK 11	WK 13	WK 14	WK 15	WK 16	WK 17	WK 18	TOTALS
Time of possession	30:34	24:47	30:09	30:28	32:08	27:48	27:40	19:31	23:25	27:50	31:30	35:07	29:10	33:08	21:12	28:27
Total net yards	346	206	284	374	382	315	346	252	165	234	333	410	385	337	164	4882
Rushing yards	142	46	111	58	141	54	97	84	102	49	37	105	38	90	54	1273
Passing yards	204	160	173	316	241	261	249	168	63	300	296	305	347	247	110	3609
Rushing plays	30	18	29	32	46	19	23	21	22	16	12	27	18	23	17	370
Sacks allowed	2	4	1	0	2	5	4	2	5	6	3	2	6	2	6	52
Had intercepted	0	2	1	0	0	3	0	1	0	4	6	2	2	2	1	26
Fumbles lost	1	3	0	0	1	0	1	0	2	2	1	2	1	1	1	17
Yards penalized	61	62	20	25	35	48	64	43	66	88	88	100	32	5	17	786
Punts	2	6	6	5	6	3	4	5	5	6	3	3	7	4	7	78

INDIVIDUAL STATISTICS*

RUSHING

	WK 1	WK 2	WK 3	WK 4	WK 6	WK 7	WK 8	WK 10	WK 11	WK 13	WK 14	WK 15	WK 16	WK 17	WK 18	TOTALS
Carlson	2-9-1													3-(3)-0	4-11-0	14-41-2
G. Brown	1-2-0	2-(-4)-0	1-16-0		1-7-0	2-11-1	4-50-1	12-60-0	2-6-0	19-79-1	16-45-1	23-109-0	20-100-0	19-114-0	22-85-1	195-1002-6
Givins		2-13-0	3-8-0	1-8-0	3-37-0	3-(-1)-0	3-8-0	3-9-0	26-166-1	10-12-0	1-3-0	5-19-0	5-17-0			6-19-0
Moon	15-59-0	24-48-1	13-47-0	-19-74-0	12-38-0	20-94-0	17-63-1	11-42-0	7-57-0	1-34-0	5-4-0			1-5-0	1-3-0	48-145-1
Tillman																9-94-0
White																131-465-2

PASSING**

	WK 1	WK 2	WK 3	WK 4	WK 6	WK 7	WK 8	WK 10	WK 11	WK 13	WK 14	WK 15	WK 16	WK 17	WK 18	TOTALS
Carlson	6-13-0 128-0		4-6-0 43-0		9-15-1 95-0	6-9-0 46-0			0-6-2 0-0					3-3-0 46-0	23-38-1 247-2	51-90-4 605-2
Moon	21-32-1 241-1	22-35-1 204-1	19-37-4 199-1	19-42-2 310-1	16-25-3 177-1	16-21-0 102-2	24-34-1 253-2	36-55-2 369-2	23-31-0 225-4	21-34-1 295-1	24-42-0 342-1	13-28-1 155-1	19-38-0 268-1	11-26-3 158-1		303-520-21 3485-21

RECEIVING

	WK 1	WK 2	WK 3	WK 4	WK 6	WK 7	WK 8	WK 10	WK 11	WK 13	WK 14	WK 15	WK 16	WK 17	WK 18	TOTALS
Coleman						1-14-0	4-57-0	2-30-0						2-28-0		9-129-0
Duncan	4-90-0	4-29-1	3-54-0		2-31-0	4-26-0		5-49-0	1-3-1	4-22-0	3-28-0	1-2-0	3-27-0	2-37-0	5-50-0	41-456-3
G. Brown	7-78-0	4-50-0	4-34-0	3-107-1	2-24-1		1-7-0		1-9-0	2-10-0	2-41-0	1-2-0	4-80-1	1-20-0	7-43-1	21-240-2
Givins		2-29-0			5-60-0		4-38-0	8-78-1	5-47-0	5-86-0	5-89-0	5-54-0	5-71-0	4-35-1	3-63-1	68-887-4
Harris															1-3-0	4-53-1
Jeffires	7-85-1	4-41-0	3-34-0	3-34-0	5-45-0	7-47-0	7-68-1	7-47-0	7-81-3	7-139-1	2-23-0	3-37-0	2-10-0	3-30-0	1-12-0	66-753-6
R. Brown				1-26-0	2-34-0	1-4-0										2-30-0
Slaughter	4-85-0	6-74-0	7-60-1	6-83-0	2-34-0	9-57-2	4-34-0	9-135-1	8-77-0	3-38-0	8-108-1	2-47-0	1-21-0			77-904-5
Wellman						1-6-0	3-38-0	1-6-0				1-11-0	4-59-0	4-82-0	8-106-0	31-430-1
White	5-31-0	4-10-0	4-31-0	4-43-0	8-65-0	6-41-0	1-11-0	2-(-3)-0		5-40-0	4-53-0					34-229-0

* Doesn't include all players. ** Passing stats include completions, attempts, interceptions, gross yards gained and touchdowns.

1993 REVIEW ■ HOUSTON

PRO FOOTBALL WEEKLY 1994 ALMANAC

REVIEW: INDIANAPOLIS COLTS

Big things were expected from the Colts in 1993. After all, they finished the 1992 season with a 9-7 record. They were getting their star DT Steve Emtman back from a knee injury, and they had added a potential big-play maker in WR Sean Dawkins to their offense.

To put it kindly, things didn't go according to plan. The Colts basically stunk out the Hoosier Dome, as their offense was unproductive and their defense was unable to play well in clutch situations. The result: a 4-12 finish, which earned them last place in the AFC East.

The poor season left the club in a precarious position. After the season, owner Robert Irsay hired former Bear personnel boss Bill Tobin to run the show, thereby taking power away from his son, Jim. Tobin's first move was hiring *his* brother, Vince, to take over as defensive coordinator. While with the Bears, Vince Tobin was often rumored as a top candidate for head-coaching jobs around the NFL. As a result, his hiring means head coach Ted Marchibroda is on the firing line, unless he gets out of the gate strongly in 1994.

Despite a miserable 1993, Marchibroda tried to keep a positive frame of mind.

"To a large extent, our ball club played with a tremendous amount of intensity throughout the season," Marchibroda said. "Basically, it was a matter of not making the right play at the crucial moment or getting a penalty call at the wrong time. These are things that winning teams don't do. These are things that we did throughout the season."

The season had a dubious aura to it even before training camp got started. QB Jeff George said he no longer wanted to be a Colt, and that he wanted to be moved. He was unhappy, he said, with the way Colt fans treated him and his family. It wasn't a matter of salary or bonus, he just wanted to be liked.

The collective reaction of the city and the team was something like this: "Who does this guy think he is? Send the poor baby out of town."

Despite his bruised ego, the Colts did not trade George and his cannon arm until after the season. After slowly working his way back into his teammates' good graces, George played the majority of the season and completed 234-of-407 pass attempts for 2,526 yards. However, George threw only eight TD passes and six interceptions, as he was unable to make big plays when the Colts needed them. That led to season-end speculation that he might be traded before the start of 1994.

The Colts expected great production from Emtman, their second-year defensive tackle who was the overall No. 1 pick in the 1992 draft. However, after getting off to a solid start, Emtman's season ended in disaster when he tore the anterior cruciate ligament, medial collateral ligament and the patellar tendon of his right knee in a first-half play in Week Six against the Cowboys and missed the rest of the season. The morale level of the team sagged significantly after Emtman went down.

Emtman, whose rookie season was marred by an injury to his left knee, was distraught. "As soon as the injury happened, I knew it was a bad one," Emtman said. "Last year I felt a pop. This time, I felt three distinct pops right in a row.

"All I could think of was, 'not this again.' I knew it was over. I thought I was just about all the way back with the left knee, and I was looking forward to the expectations. But, boom, I'm back at the bottom again."

Not everything was bad news for the Colts. In addition to George's numbers, WR Reggie Langhorne had his best year in nine NFL seasons with 85 receptions for 1,038 yards and three TD's. DE Jon Hand contributed a top effort and recorded a team-leading 5.5 sacks. PK Dean Biasucci was once again at the top of his game, as he delivered 93 points. Rookie FB Roosevelt Potts had a great early season and showed signs of becoming a top player. He gained 711 yards on 179 carries, good for a 4.0-yards-per-carry average. WR Jessie Hester caught at least one pass in every game, extending his team record to 62 consecutive games with at least one reception.

But, on balance, the Colts were once again disappointing. Since relocating from Baltimore in 1984, the Colts' record is 59-100. They have had only three winning seasons and reached the playoffs just once.

1993 ROUNDUP

OFFENSIVE MVP: WR Reggie Langhorne, a nine-year veteran, snagged an AFC-high 85 receptions, which set a team record.

DEFENSIVE MVP: S Jason Besler was credited with 127 stops, the most by a Colt defensive back since 1984.

RESULTS
Pointspread Shown Refers To Indianapolis

Date	Opponent	Spread	Score
Sept. 5	Miami	(+6.5)	20-24
Sept. 12	At Cincinnati	(-2.5)	9-6
Sept. 26	Cleveland	(+2.5)	23-10
Oct. 3	At Denver	(+7)	13-35
Oct. 10	Dallas	(+12)	3-27
Oct. 24	At Miami	(+6.5)	27-41
Oct. 31	New England	(-6.5)	9-6
Nov. 7	At Washington	(+6.5)	24-30
Nov. 14	New York Jets	(+3.5)	17-31
Nov. 21	At Buffalo	(+13)	9-23
Nov. 29	San Diego	(0)	0-31
Dec. 5	At New York Jets	(+11)	9-6
Dec. 12	At New York Giants	(+12)	6-20
Dec. 19	Philadelphia	(+1.5)	10-20
Dec. 26	At New England	(+6)	0-38
Jan. 2	Buffalo	(+11)	10-30

342

1993 REVIEW ■ INDIANAPOLIS

GAME-BY-GAME STATISTICS

TEAM STATISTICS

OPPONENT	WK 1 MIA.	WK 2 CIN.	WK 4 CLEV.	WK 5 DENV.	WK 6 DALL.	WK 8 MIA.	WK 9 N.E.	WK 10 WASH.	WK 11 N.Y.J.	WK 12 BUFF.	WK 13 S.D.	WK 14 N.Y.J.	WK 15 N.Y.G.	WK 16 PHIL.	WK 17 N.E.	WK 18 BUFF.	TOTALS
Score	20-24	9-6	23-10	13-35	3-27	27-41	9-6	24-30	17-31	9-23	0-31	9-6	6-20	10-20	0-38	10-30	
Total net yards	274	332	357	271	361	322	268	405	215	365	262	169	305	261	136	402	4705
Rushing yards	42	120	97	111	126	88	89	49	92	113	55	67	55	31	37	116	1288
Passing yards	232	212	260	160	235	234	179	356	123	252	207	102	250	230	99	286	3417
Rushing plays	21	29	32	22	25	25	17	19	29	29	20	28	15	12	18	24	365
Sacks allowed	0	1	0	1	1	4	2	1	3	2	1	0	2	4	2	0	29
Had intercepted	1	2	0	2	4	3	0	1	0	1	0	1	0	0	0	0	15
Fumbles lost	2	1	0	0	1	1	0	2	1	1	2	1	0	3	1	4	20
Yards penalized	20	15	79	40	30	56	39	57	47	55	53	39	64	34	45	12	685
Punts	7	4	7	4	3	4	5	7	6	3	4	8	5	6	6	4	83

OPPONENT STATISTICS

	WK 1	WK 2	WK 4	WK 5	WK 6	WK 8	WK 9	WK 10	WK 11	WK 12	WK 13	WK 14	WK 15	WK 16	WK 17	WK 18	TOTALS
Time of possession	28:15	28:15	29:37	35:22	33:26	27:34	28:32	29:26	36:51	30:01	35:02	35:05	31:44	37:55	38:28	27:41	32:27
Total net yards	355	269	253	454	374	366	363	275	458	403	474	267	290	340	400	297	5638
Rushing yards	119	128	100	196	143	171	87	109	202	135	247	122	205	151	257	149	2521
Passing yards	236	141	153	258	231	195	276	166	256	268	227	145	85	189	143	148	3117
Rushing plays	28	26	24	37	35	33	25	28	38	38	44	39	43	39	58	40	575
Sacks allowed	0	2	5	1	2	1	1	4	0	1	0	0	0	3	0	1	21
Had intercepted	1	0	1	0	0	0	2	0	0	1	0	2	0	1	0	0	10
Fumbles lost	1	0	1	2	1	2	1	0	0	1	0	1	0	0	0	1	11
Yards penalized	35	15	79	60	24	37	25	40	22	45	45	35	49	45	24	30	610
Punts	8	7	6	1	4	1	3	8	6	4	4	6	5	6	2	4	71

INDIVIDUAL STATISTICS*

RUSHING

	WK 1	WK 2	WK 4	WK 5	WK 6	WK 8	WK 9	WK 10	WK 11	WK 12	WK 13	WK 14	WK 15	WK 16	WK 17	WK 18	TOTALS
Culver	1-1-0	3-18-0	2-(-1)-0	2-3-0	2-(-6)-0	6-8-2	2-5-0	1-5-0	5-16-1	6-28-0	8-18-0	13-25-0	4-17-0		8-15-0	3-3-0	65-150-3
George	18-39-0	16-64-0	9-29-1	11-67-0	3-15-0	3-28-0	4-(-2)-0		1-8-0	3-5-0	1-4-0	13-25-0	1-5-0	1-0-0		1-14-0	13-39-0
Johnson			17-64-0	9-41-0	18-113-0	15-54-0	23-86-0	15-33-0	6-16-0	18-67-0	2-(-1)-0	15-42-0	10-33-0	11-31-0	3-8-0	6-(-1)-0	95-331-1
Potts			1-6-0						6-23-0	1-7-0	9-34-0				7-14-0	14-100-0	179-711-0
Verdin						1-(-2)-0			1-29-0								3-33-0

PASSING**

George			7-110-0	3-8-1	27-44-3	18-26-0	37-59-1	14-27-0	21-41-1	17-28-0	11-24-0	22-38-0	21-39-0	13-25-0	30-48-1	234-407-7
Majkowski				27-0	260-2	200-0	376-3	144-1	262-0	209-0	102-0	254-0	252-1	110-0	330-1	2526-8
Trudeau	23-43-1	17-36-2	22-38-0	12-25-1	11-19-1						2-5-0						13-24-1
	232-1	218-0	260-0	138-1	96-0						9-0						105-0
					11-20-3												85-162-7
					144-0												992-2

RECEIVING

	WK 1	WK 2	WK 4	WK 5	WK 6	WK 8	WK 9	WK 10	WK 11	WK 12	WK 13	WK 14	WK 15	WK 16	WK 17	WK 18	TOTALS
Arbuckle					1-7-0	1-3-1								2-12-0		2-28-0	15-90-0
Cash	5-29-0	7-54-0	1-16-0	4-62-1	1-2-0	4-43-0	5-62-0	2-10-1	3-12-1	3-45-0	2-15-0	2-9-0	8-34-0	3-31-0	1-7-0	1-7-0	43-402-3
Cox	1-21-0	1-12-0	1-16-0					1-24-0			2-32-0	3-23-0	1-2-0	1-12-0			4-59-0
Culver	1-25-1			8-144-0	3-27-0		4-86-0			1-15-0	8-95-0	3-36-0	3-56-0	1-10-0	1-26-0	2-29-0	11-112-1
Dawkins	2-22-0	4-59-0	7-110-0	1-6-0	5-34-0	3-28-0	2-18-0	6-53-0	1-11-0	7-97-0	3-43-0		2-75-0	2-16-0	4-66-0	5-81-1	26-430-1
Hester	6-51-0	1-14-0	8-60-0	6-32-0	6-38-0	5-53-0	2-8-0	10-83-0	1-7-0	7-62-0	3-40-0	3-34-0	5-49-0	7-90-1	1-2-0	6-52-0	64-835-1
Johnson	8-84-0	4-79-0	3-47-0	1-14-0	1-15-0	9-97-1	1-6-0	12-203-1	8-112-0		7-62-0	3-34-0	5-49-0		4-44-0	9-61-0	55-443-0
Langhorne			2-11-0	3-51-0		2-9-0	4-20-0	5-27-0	1-6-0	6-53-0			3-38-0	7-90-1	4-45-0	9-61-0	85-1038-3
Potts										1-2-0	1-14-0			1-15-0	2-7-0	2-20-0	26-189-0

*Doesn't include all players. ** Passing stats include completions, attempts, interceptions, gross yards gained and touchdowns.

343

REVIEW: KANSAS CITY CHIEFS

A step in the right direction but still a step short.

The Chiefs advanced further into the playoffs than at any time since 1969 — the year they won their only Super Bowl — but despite winning their first division championship since 1971, they fell one giant step short of where they wanted to be.

"Playing for the conference championship was definitely a step," said Kansas City president/general manager Carl Peterson after the Chiefs' 30-13 loss in the AFC title game at Buffalo. "Winning two playoff games — one on the road — was significant. And you can look back and say we could've, would've, should've had one more victory, and we'd have had the homefield throughout the playoffs.

"But we're not in the Super Bowl."

They didn't get to the season's ultimate game, but it wasn't for a lack of tinkering.

After finishing the 1992 season ranked 25th in offense, the Chiefs made wholesale changes on offense for the '93 campaign. They brought in offensive coordinator Paul Hackett and the San Francisco offense. That done, they brought in legendary QB Joe Montana, around whom the offense was designed. For good measure, the Chiefs added RB Marcus Allen to the mix, finding that he had quite a bit of football left in him after languishing with the Raiders in previous years.

Despite missing five games with injuries and playing in only 38 of 64 quarters, Montana was the AFC's second-ranked quarterback, and he helped Kansas City average 302 yards per game in 1993 — 32 more than the previous year.

"It's just that he knows the offense so much better than the rest of us," said OG Dave Szott of Montana. "It gives everybody a little more confidence."

Allen said, "Perhaps subconsciously, some of us play harder. That's no knock against (backup and former starter) Dave Krieg. It's just that Joe knows the offense much better."

Although Montana did not get the Chiefs to the Super Bowl, he was magnificent in the playoffs. He rallied Kansas City from a 17-7 halftime deficit — with the help of a blocked punt by budding star TE Keith Cash — to a 27-24 overtime victory over Pittsburgh in the playoff opener at Arrowhead Stadium.

The next week against Houston, Montana completed 13-of-18 second-half passes for 212 yards and three touchdowns — two in the fourth quarter — to lead the Chiefs to a 29-20 upset in the Astrodome.

Montana was expected to play a big role in 1993. Allen, however, had rushed for 301 yards in 1992 and 287 in '91 for the Raiders. He was expected to be a backup to Harvey Williams. Instead, Allen enjoyed a Comeback of the Year season in '93 with the Chiefs, scoring an AFC-best 15 touchdowns.

"Marcus Allen looks like he's reborn," said Oiler CB Cris Dishman. "He's catching the ball well out of the backfield. He's running well.

"He's making a three-yard catch turn into a 30-yard gain. That's the old Allen that we've seen in the past when he used to play (on a regular basis) for the Raiders. He's running very smooth. He just looks reborn, like he's definitely got a new attitude."

Kansas City coach Marty Schottenheimer called Allen "the best short-yardage and goalline runner I've ever seen."

Chief DE Neil Smith said, "He gives all guys over 30 something to shoot for. He just keeps going."

The same could be said for Smith's sack total. It just kept going and going. It didn't stop until it reached an NFL-best 15. He also had two blocked field goals in a 17-14 win over the Chargers in a game that the Chiefs would have probably otherwise lost.

Kansas City had five players named to the Pro Bowl — Montana, Allen, Smith, LB-DE Derrick Thomas and OT John Alt.

"Derrick and Neil's abilities are well-documented, but I'm especially glad to see John Alt finally receive the recognition I believe he deserved as early as a few years ago," said Schottenheimer.

1993 ROUNDUP

OFFENSIVE MVP: QB Joe Montana made the new K.C. offense work, and he rallied his team against Houston in the AFC semifinals.

DEFENSIVE MVP: DE Neil Smith had 15 sacks to finish atop the NFL.

RESULTS
Pointspread Shown Refers To Kansas City

Date	Opponent	Spread	Score
Sept. 5	At Tampa Bay	(-7)	27-3
Sept. 12	At Houston	(+3.5)	0-30
Sept. 20	Denver	(-7)	15-7
Oct. 3	L.A. Raiders	(-9)	24-9
Oct. 10	Cincinnati	(-14)	17-15
Oct. 17	At San Diego	(-3.5)	17-14
Oct. 31	At Miami	(0)	10-30
Nov. 8	Green Bay	(-3)	23-16
Nov. 14	At L.A. Raiders	(+4)	31-20
Nov. 21	Chicago	(-10)	17-19
Nov. 28	Buffalo	(-3)	23-7
Dec. 5	At Seattle	(-6.5)	31-16
Dec. 12	At Denver	(+2.5)	21-27
Dec. 19	San Diego	(-8.5)	28-24
Dec. 26	At Minnesota	(-2.5)	10-30
Jan. 2	Seattle	(-7.5)	34-24

POSTSEASON

Jan. 8	Pittsburgh	(-7.5)	27-24*
Jan. 15	At Houston	(+7)	28-20
Jan. 23	At Buffalo	(+3)	13-30

* Overtime

1993 REVIEW ■ KANSAS CITY

GAME-BY-GAME STATISTICS

TEAM STATISTICS

OPPONENT	WK 1 T.B.	WK 2 HOU.	WK 3 DENV.	WK 5 L.A.RD	WK 6 CIN.	WK 7 S.D.	WK 9 MIA.	WK 10 G.B.	WK 11 L.A.RD	WK 12 CHI.	WK 13 BUFF.	WK 14 SEA.	WK 15 DENV.	WK 16 S.D.	WK 17 MINN.	WK 18 SEA.	TOTALS
Score	27-3	0-30	15-7	24-9	17-15	17-14	10-30	23-16	31-20	17-19	23-7	31-16	21-27	28-24	10-30	34-24	
Total net yards	400	206	414	242	203	347	305	253	338	252	314	337	311	321	220	372	4835
Rushing yards	122	46	160	115	94	83	99	100	164	133	106	106	77	104	37	109	1655
Passing yards	278	160	254	127	109	264	206	153	174	119	208	231	234	217	183	263	3180
Rushing plays	31	18	31	43	28	22	20	26	34	29	35	30	21	29	16	32	445
Sacks allowed	1	4	3	3	3	4	1	4	0	5	0	1	2	2	2	1	35
Had intercepted	0	2	0	0	0	1	0	0	0	1	1	0	0	1	2	1	10
Fumbles lost	3	3	1	0	2	0	3	0	1	0	1	0	1	2	1	1	18
Yards penalized	60	62	105	42	25	65	39	116	112	69	20	40	42	83	39	50	969
Punts	2	6	6	3	4	5	5	4	4	6	5	5	4	6	6	5	77

OPPONENT STATISTICS

	WK 1	WK 2	WK 3	WK 5	WK 6	WK 7	WK 9	WK 10	WK 11	WK 12	WK 13	WK 14	WK 15	WK 16	WK 17	WK 18	TOTALS
Time of possession	29:31	35:13	22:33	24:56	34:57	30:27	36:43	29:32	27:44	32:02	25:26	29:49	35:39	28:40	39:31	25:34	30:35
Total net yards	157	247	335	222	277	269	483	287	280	281	256	365	340	268	424	280	4771
Rushing yards	25	57	35	76	115	79	139	99	102	190	43	90	136	94	205	140	1625
Passing yards	132	190	300	146	162	190	344	188	178	91	213	275	204	174	219	140	3146
Rushing plays	20	28	14	20	34	26	40	24	25	42	18	24	38	28	46	25	452
Sacks allowed	1	2	0	6	4	3	0	4	1	1	4	3	2	3	0	1	34
Had intercepted	1	1	1	0	1	0	1	0	1	2	3	1	2	2	1	0	21
Fumbles lost	0	1	2	1	0	0	2	3	1	0	1	2	0	1	0	3	17
Yards penalized	57	32	75	168	74	75	26	68	60	55	64	35	64	45	61	49	1008
Punts	6	3	8	5	4	4	1	2	5	4	7	3	3	5	3	5	68

INDIVIDUAL STATISTICS*

RUSHING

	WK 1	WK 2	WK 3	WK 5	WK 6	WK 7	WK 9	WK 10	WK 11	WK 12	WK 13	WK 14	WK 15	WK 16	WK 17	WK 18	TOTALS
Allen	13-79-0	6-17-0	17-91-0	17-24-1	13-48-1	13-46-1	4-14-0	17-35-1	17-85-1	16-78-2	22-74-0	12-73-3	14-41-1	14-16-1	4-9-0	7-34-0	206-764-12
Anders	5-14-0	4-14-0	7-20-0	6-25-0	6-33-0	4-28-0	2-3-0	3-9-0	4-8-0	8-39-0	4-10-0	12-26-0	3-21-0	3-29-0	1-4-0	3-8-0	75-291-0
McNair				2-4-0		1-2-0	4-44-0	2-54-0	6-40-0	3-20-0	2-7-0		4-15-0	8-42-0	6-19-0	17-46-2	51-278-2
Montana	1-(-1)-0		3-25-0	2-9-0		3-(-2)-0					3-1-0	3-(-3)-0		4-17-0	1-2-0	1-1-0	25-64-0
Williams	11-28-0	5-12-0	4-24-0	13-56-0	3-9-0		6-20-0										42-149-0

PASSING**

	WK 1	WK 2	WK 3	WK 5	WK 6	WK 7	WK 9	WK 10	WK 11	WK 12	WK 13	WK 14	WK 15	WK 16	WK 17	WK 18	TOTALS
Krieg	4-5-0 38-0	15-27-2 175-0		5-9-0 77-0	10-20-0 140-1		12-19-0 126-1	17-30-0 170-0	12-27-0 178-3	14-28-1 157-0				4-4-0 53-1	6-9-0 68-1	6-11-0 56-0	105-189-3 1238-7
Montana	14-21-0 246-3		21-36-0 273-0	7-9-0 68-2		21-39-1 284-1	10-17-0 90-0				18-32-1 208-2	20-30-0 239-0	17-30-1 237-2	18-32-1 168-2	17-24-2 121-0	18-28-1 210-1	181-298-7 2144-13

RECEIVING

	WK 1	WK 2	WK 3	WK 5	WK 6	WK 7	WK 9	WK 10	WK 11	WK 12	WK 13	WK 14	WK 15	WK 16	WK 17	WK 18	TOTALS
Allen	1-12-1		1-10-0	1-8-0	1-9-0	3-30-1	5-36-0	2-15-0	1-4-0	1-11-0	2-28-1	4-26-0	1-0-0	5-20-0	3-15-0	3-14-0	34-238-3
Anders	3-32-1	2-14-0	4-30-0	1-9-0	4-70-0	3-14-0	2-25-0	2-19-0	1-15-1	1-6-0	1-5-0	4-16-0	3-17-0	4-30-0	4-23-0	1-1-0	40-326-1
Barnett	1-13-0	1-6-0	1-2-0	1-12-0	1-8-1	1-22-0	1-5-0		1-3-0		2-10-0		1-24-0	1-3-0	2-40-0	3-34-0	17-182-1
Birden	3-82-1	1-14-0	3-54-0	2-27-0	1-28-0	4-41-0	5-65-0	5-64-0		3-43-0	5-39-0	4-61-0	5-95-0	3-28-1	1-12-0	6-68-0	51-721-2
Cash			1-9-0			2-42-0	3-26-1	2-4-0	1-4-1	2-21-0	4-51-1			2-19-0	5-53-1	2-13-0	24-242-4
Davis	5-61-1	3-67-0	6-39-0	2-28-1	1-9-0	4-77-0	3-31-0	3-53-0	5-115-1	2-29-0	1-9-0	3-67-0	4-63-1	4-84-2	2-12-0	4-65-1	52-909-7
Dyal	1-7-0	3-31-1	2-14-0	1-31-0													7-83-0
F. Jones	1-14-0					2-34-0	1-21-0		1-6-0	3-29-0	1-16-0	3-46-0		1-8-0	2-12-0		9-111-0
H. Jones		1-13-0	1-8-0	1-5-0					1-10-0		2-50-0		1-0-0				7-91-0
Hayes	1-49-0	2-20-0	1-3-0	1-10-0	1-11-0	2-34-0	1-21-0	1-18-0	1-18-0	2-18-0	2-23-0		2-26-1	2-36-0	3-21-0	2-31-0	24-331-1
McNair						2-24-0		1-5-0	1-9-0				1-12-0	1-1-0	3-13-0	1-16-0	10-74-0

* Doesn't include all players. ** Passing stats include completions, attempts, interceptions, gross yards gained and touchdowns.

345

REVIEW: LOS ANGELES RAIDERS

Don't talk to the Raiders about moral victories. Don't expect the Raiders to be satisfied with mere progress.

Some might say the 1993 season was a job well done by the Raiders. After all, they went from a miserable 7-9 in 1992 to a spot in the second round of the AFC playoffs during the '93 campaign.

A job well done? More like a job unfinished to hear Raider MLB Joe Kelly talk after the team's 29-23 loss to the Bills during postseason play.

"We're a Super Bowl-caliber team," said Kelly. "It's the media and other people who felt we went further than they expected. We expected to go to the Super Bowl. No less. We're not satisfied because we went to (the second round). This don't mean nothing."

It meant something. It meant the Raiders came together after a '92 season that saw them fractured by dissension. It meant the team, by beating Denver 42-24 in a wild-card playoff, had earned its second postseason victory since '83.

The Raiders turned the corner by rebuilding through the free-agent market and the draft. They signed free-agent OLT Gerald Perry, QB Jeff Hostetler and Kelly to strengthen the team's weakest positions. All three had outstanding seasons.

In the draft the Raiders found Greg Robinson in the eighth round. He became the team's leading rusher with 591 yards in spite of a season-ending injury in early December. The Raiders also signed undrafted rookie James Jett, a speedy receiver who led the league in yards-per-catch average and was named to the All-Rookie team.

Of all the additions, Hostetler was the key. He provided leadership and stability, something the Raiders had lacked at quarterback for years.

"I think the guys here were just looking for someone to come in and play hard, be a leader by example," said Hostetler.

Hostetler also showed physical toughness, as he played through a number of injuries.

"He's a very tough, tough player," said Raider coach Art Shell. "This guy has taken some hits. The normal guy wouldn't get off the ground. He believes if he's able to walk, he thinks he's able to play. The team appreciates him."

Hostetler set club records for rushing TD's by a quarterback (five), consecutive completions in a game (15, Sept. 5 vs. Minnesota) and passing yards in a game (424, Oct. 31 vs. San Diego).

"He's not only very tough physically, but he's very bright with an excellent football IQ, and that's different from being smart," said Raider offensive coordinator Tom Walsh. "Some guys are smart without having that football IQ. He takes it with him on the field.

"He's a tremendous competitor who refuses to give up. He has a perfectionist mentality. He wants to be perfect. Although it can't always happen, he's working for that. I think that's great. He has a drive and a desire to excel."

The biggest beneficiary of Hostetler's arrival was WR Tim Brown. The two emerged as one of the NFL's more lethal receiver-quarterback combinations. Brown finished the season with 80 catches for 1,180 yards.

There were other standouts for the Raiders as well. OLG Steve Wisniewski had his fourth consecutive Pro Bowl season. PK Jeff Jaeger led the NFL in scoring and tied a league record with 35 field goals. Anthony Smith, Howie Long (who announced his retirement prior to the Super Bowl), Chester McGlockton, Greg Townsend and Nolan Harrison made up one of the league's best defensive fronts. Kelly and Winston Moss were steady linebackers, and CB Terry McDaniel earned his second consecutive Pro Bowl trip.

All was not perfect, however. The biggest problem was the Raider running game. Despite the surprising play of Robinson, the Raiders ranked 26th in the NFL in rushing yards and 27th in average gain per rushing attempt.

That said, however, it was a season in which the Raiders were headed in the right direction. They may not have been satisfied at getting knocked out of the playoffs, but the team mood at season's end was better than it was a year earlier.

"I think we turned the corner," said Shell. "I think we're headed for bigger and better things."

1993 ROUNDUP

OFFENSIVE MVP: QB Jeff Hostetler provided leadership and stability and set several team records, including most rushing touchdowns for a Raider quarterback with 5.

DEFENSIVE MVP: DT Chester McGlockton finished the season with six sacks, five batted passes and one interception.

RESULTS
Pointspread Shown Refers To L.A. Raiders

Date	Opponent	Spread	Score
Sept. 5	Minnesota	(+2.5)	24-7
Sept. 12	At Seattle	(-3)	17-13
Sept. 19	Cleveland	(-4.5)	16-19
Oct. 3	At Kansas City	(+9)	9-24
Oct. 10	New York Jets	(-2)	24-20
Oct. 18	At Denver	(+6.5)	23-20
Oct. 31	San Diego	(-4)	23-30
Nov. 7	At Chicago	(-2.5)	16-14
Nov. 14	Kansas City	(-4)	20-31
Nov. 21	At San Diego	(+3.5)	12-7
Nov. 28	At Cincinnati	(-9)	10-16
Dec. 5	At Buffalo	(+6.5)	25-24
Dec. 12	Seattle	(-8)	27-23
Dec. 19	Tampa Bay	(-9)	27-20
Dec. 26	At Green Bay	(+3)	0-28
Jan. 2	Denver	(-3)	33-30*
POSTSEASON			
Jan. 9	Denver	(-1.5)	42-24
Jan. 15	At Buffalo	(+6.5)	23-29

* Overtime

1993 REVIEW ■ L.A. RAIDERS

GAME-BY-GAME STATISTICS

TEAM STATISTICS

OPPONENT	WK 1 MINN.	WK 2 SEA.	WK 3 CLEV.	WK 5 K.C.	WK 6 N.Y.J.	WK 7 DENV.	WK 9 S.D.	WK 10 CHI.	WK 11 K.C.	WK 12 S.D.	WK 13 CIN.	WK 14 BUFF.	WK 15 SEA.	WK 16 T.B.	WK 17 G.B.	WK 18 DENV.	TOTALS
Score	24-7	17-13	16-19	9-24	24-20	23-20	23-30	16-14	20-31	12-7	10-16	25-24	27-23	27-20	0-28	33-30	
Total net yards	312	264	156	222	414	308	467	274	280	428	283	399	362	265	182	398	5014
Rushing yards	98	83	71	76	105	53	65	179	102	158	81	138	59	17	46	94	1425
Passing yards	214	181	85	146	309	255	402	95	178	270	202	261	303	248	136	304	3589
Rushing plays	35	28	25	20	30	23	22	40	25	44	16	37	23	18	24	433
Sacks allowed	1	3	6	6	0	2	3	2	1	0	4	5	2	3	8	3	49
Had intercepted	1	1	0	0	3	1	2	0	1	1	1	0	1	0	2	0	14
Fumbles lost	0	0	0	1	2	1	0	0	1	1	1	0	0	0	2	1	11
Yards penalized	85	40	50	168	94	110	72	86	60	68	21	80	68	102	14	60	1178
Punts	2	7	8	5	3	5	2	6	5	2	4	3	1	5	9	4	71

OPPONENT STATISTICS

Time of possession	20:25	28:05	28:32	35:04	32:33	32:44	29:34	28:21	32:16	18:12	38:42	22:00	30:24	32:50	31:42	33:36	29:26
Total net yards	205	232	316	242	286	253	336	261	338	154	269	367	303	366	329	471	4728
Rushing yards	58	112	113	115	96	132	177	124	164	59	131	91	134	101	148	110	1865
Passing yards	147	120	203	127	190	121	159	137	174	95	138	276	169	265	181	361	2863
Rushing plays	18	29	27	43	29	32	31	36	34	18	43	24	32	30	37	31	494
Sacks allowed	3	5	5	3	3	7	1	1	1	4	3	0	1	5	2	0	44
Had intercepted	2	2	4	0	1	1	0	0	0	1	0	1	0	1	0	0	14
Fumbles lost	1	1	0	0	1	1	0	0	0	0	0	1	0	2	1	0	9
Yards penalized	25	21	48	42	25	55	35	50	112	54	64	23	75	85	10	89	813
Punts	3	5	6	3	5	4	4	6	4	7	6	5	5	4	9	4	80

INDIVIDUAL STATISTICS*

RUSHING

Bell								1-1-0									
Evans				4-23-0	12-46-1	8-16-0					4-10-0	16-44-0	12-35-0	7-14-0	7-14-0		67-180-1
Hostetler	8-34-0	7-21-1			3-24-0		5-9-0	2-8-0		6-6-0	3-29-1	6-39-1	3-0-0	6-(-14)-1	4-4-0	2-26-0	14-51-0
Jordan					3-14-0	3-5-0	2-2-0						4-18-1	4-1-0	1-3-0	3-12-0	55-195-5
McCallum								9-50-1	6-15-1	6-4-0			2-15-0	6-16-1	5-23-0	5-6-0	12-33-0
Montgomery	4-15-0	1-(-6)-0	4-20-0	5-20-0	1-4-0	2-3-0	1-1-0	1-(-7)-0	1-(-7)-0	3-11-0						13-44-0	37-114-3
Robinson	15-25-1	17-54-0	18-59-0	10-29-0	10-17-0	9-27-0	13-53-0	12-70-0	17-90-0	21-89-0	5-22-0	9-56-0			1-2-0		37-106-0
S. Smith	8-24-0	3-14-0	2-2-0	1-4-0		1-2-0		15-51-0	1-4-0	6-17-0	4-20-0	5-12-0			1-6-0		156-591-1 47-156-0

PASSING**

Evans		2-2-0		15-26-0	14-22-1	0-1-0							3-5-1		11-20-1		45-76-3
		30-0		192-1	247-2	0-0							39-0		132-0		640-3
Hostetler	23-27-1	18-33-1	11-25-0		4-12-2	15-24-0	20-32-2	11-23-0	16-35-1	19-31-1	12-32-1	18-31-0	18-25-0	19-30-0	7-18-1	25-41-0	236-419-10
	225-1	195-1	94-1		62-0	264-2	424-2	108-0	187-1	270-0	220-0	289-1	278-1	260-1	56-0	310-3	3242-14

RECEIVING

Bell					5-66-0	6-116-0	5-156-2	2-20-0	3-36-0	5-52-0	1-15-0	3-38-0	3-27-0	1-13-0	1-2-0	2-16-0	11-111-0
Brown	4-41-1	9-97-1			2-20-0	1-10-0	2-25-0	6-61-0	6-69-1	3-46-0	5-71-0	10-183-1	4-45-0	4-44-0	7-80-0	11-173-2	80-1180-7
Horton	6-76-0	4-19-0			3-35-0	3-24-0	3-39-0		1-18-0	1-12-0		1-11-0	4-46-0	4-27-0	1-7-0	2-36-0	43-467-1
Ismail				4-75-1	4-86-1	1-74-1	3-88-0		1-12-0	7-138-0	2-17-0		4-71-0	3-49-0	2-13-0	3-48-0	26-353-1
Jett				3-74-0			2-63-0	1-4-0	1-6-0	2-13-0	4-117-0	1-10-0	1-56-1	1-23-0	3-41-0	33-771-3
Robinson	2-12-0		3-15-0	2-8-0	1-12-0							1-9-0					15-142-0
S. Smith	2-21-0		4-42-0	3-22-0				3-35-0				2-38-0			1-8-0		18-187-0
Wright	2-29-0	4-73-0	1-26-0		1-68-1	3-38-1		1-19-0	1-11-0	1-9-0			4-67-0	6-104-1		3-18-1	27-462-4

* Doesn't include all players. ** Passing stats include completions, attempts, interceptions, gross yards gained and touchdowns.

347

REVIEW: LOS ANGELES RAMS

The Rams of 1993 were appropriately situated. In a part of the country where earthquakes are a way of life, the Rams were just one more natural disaster.

Everywhere you looked, something was going wrong.

One starting cornerback left the team and it was learned he was the subject of a federal drug-trafficking investigation. The other starting cornerback suffered a season-ending knee injury during pregame warmups. The starting quarterback struggled so badly that he lost his job to a former ninth-round draft choice whose NFL game experience had consisted of just 26 plays. The head coach suffered through the first five-game losing streak of his 21-year NFL career. The numbers at the box office were distressing.

No, it wasn't an earthquake, but the damage was everywhere during a 5-11 season.

The Rams' collapse began when starting RCB Darryl Henley took a leave of absence from the team in mid-October. He was later indicted on federal drug-trafficking charges.

Starting LCB Todd Lyght suffered a season-ending knee injury during pregame warmups before the Rams played the Redskins Nov. 21. The Rams also lost pass-rushing DE Robert Young and backup CB Robert Bailey to season-ending knee injuries.

Then there was the collapse of QB Jim Everett. He probably set his bridge aflame when, after being yanked in the third quarter of a 16-13 loss to Detroit Oct. 24, he labeled the Rams' offensive game plan "obsolete" and angrily questioned coach Chuck Knox's faith in him.

Knox answered by starting T.J. Rubley the following week in San Francisco, ending Everett's streak of 87 consecutive starts, and the quarterback circus was open for business.

Rubley was clearly in over his head against the 49ers, and Knox went back to Everett the next game. But after Everett failed to lead the Rams to a score in 20 possessions, Knox went back to Rubley late in a 10-6 loss to Washington Nov. 21. Everett made a brief relief appearance two weeks later, but there was no salvaging this quarterback mess.

"I had not counted on that situation," said Knox. "It kind of blew up on us."

Everett finished the season with a 49.3 completion percentage — a career low — eight touchdown passes and 12 interceptions.

The numbers were just as bad at the box office. An average crowd of 45,401 came to see the Rams play in Anaheim in '93, the lowest average attendance since the club moved to Anaheim Stadium from the Los Angeles Coliseum in 1980. Three of their eight home games drew crowds of less than 40,000.

There were too many low points for the Rams to count in '93, but amid it all there were some rays of sunshine. The brightest reason for hope was the emergence of rookie RB Jerome Bettis and the vast improvement of second-year DT Sean Gilbert.

Bettis rushed for 1,429 yards, the seventh-highest total for a rookie in NFL history, and finished just 57 yards behind Dallas' Emmitt Smith in the race for the NFL rushing title. Not bad, considering Bettis was running behind a patchwork offensive line that was without former Pro Bowlers Tom Newberry and Jackie Slater much of the second half of the season.

"It's scary seeing him coming at you," said Phoenix CB Aeneas Williams of Bettis, who earned a spot in the Pro Bowl. "My eyes would get real big, and I'd try to grab ahold of him and hang on, then cry for help."

Bengal LB Ricardo McDonald said, "He can pound it inside and pound it outside. He's a fullback and a tailback mixed into one. He's like a runaway locomotive."

Gilbert teamed with former Redskin DE Fred Stokes to produce 20 sacks and became the Rams' first defensive player to reach the Pro Bowl since Kevin Greene in 1989.

These few bright spots weren't enough to outweigh all that went wrong for the Rams in '93.

"Please Georgia Sell The Team," one sideline banner said in an appeal to Rams' owner Georgia Frontiere at the season finale.

"They should just leave so we can use this nice stadium to attract a team that will actually win," said a bartender at a fan hangout.

By football standards, a natural disaster.

1993 ROUNDUP

OFFENSIVE MVP: RB Jerome Bettis was the second-leading rusher in the NFL and was named All-Pro as a rookie.

DEFENSIVE MVP: DT Sean Gilbert registered 10.5 sacks and went to the Pro Bowl.

RESULTS
Pointspread Shown Refers To L.A. Rams

Date	Opponent	Spread	Score
Sept. 5	At Green Bay (in Milw)	(+7)	6-36
Sept. 12	Pittsburgh	(+3.5)	27-0
Sept. 19	At New York Giants	(+6.5)	10-20
Sept. 26	At Houston	(+10.5)	28-13
Oct. 3	New Orleans	(+4)	6-37
Oct. 14	At Atlanta	(-2)	24-30
Oct. 24	Detroit	(-2.5)	13-16
Oct. 31	At San Francisco	(+13)	17-40
Nov. 14	Atlanta	(-4)	0-13
Nov. 21	Washington	(-2)	10-6
Nov. 28	San Francisco	(+14)	10-35
Dec. 5	At Phoenix	(+7)	10-38
Dec. 12	At New Orleans	(+14)	23-20
Dec. 19	At Cincinnati	(-2)	3-15
Dec. 26	Cleveland	(+2)	14-42
Jan. 2	Chicago	(+3)	20-6

# 1993 REVIEW ■ L.A. RAMS

GAME-BY-GAME STATISTICS

TEAM STATISTICS

OPPONENT	WK 1 G.B.	WK 2 PITT.	WK 3 N.Y.G.	WK 4 HOU.	WK 5 N.O.	WK 7 ATL.	WK 8 DET.	WK 9 S.F.	WK 11 ATL.	WK 12 WASH.	WK 13 S.F.	WK 14 PHX.	WK 15 N.O.	WK 16 CIN.	WK 17 CLEV.	WK 18 CHI.	TOTALS
Score	6-36	27-0	10-20	28-13	6-37	24-30	13-16	17-40	0-13	10-6	10-35	10-38	23-20	3-15	14-42	20-6	
Total net yards	228	314	171	374	256	450	291	220	260	282	300	303	306	273	382	394	4804
Rushing yards	53	99	45	58	127	167	150	110	95	89	161	152	266	166	95	181	2014
Passing yards	175	215	126	316	129	283	141	110	165	193	139	151	40	107	287	213	2790
Rushing plays	19	32	12	32	30	30	30	27	20	22	27	26	42	32	21	47	449
Sacks allowed	0	1	1	0	3	2	3	7	6	3	2	1	1	0	1	0	31
Had intercepted	2	2	2	0	2	2	1	2	2	0	0	1	0	0	2	0	19
Fumbles lost	0	0	1	0	3	1	1	1	1	1	0	0	1	2	0	0	11
Yards penalized	13	25	36	25	10	50	21	40	58	44	30	10	60	35	39	30	526
Punts	5	4	8	5	6	2	4	4	8	7	7	4	5	5	3	3	80

OPPONENT STATISTICS

	WK 1	WK 2	WK 3	WK 4	WK 5	WK 7	WK 8	WK 9	WK 11	WK 12	WK 13	WK 14	WK 15	WK 16	WK 17	WK 18	TOTALS
Time of possession	36:09	25:02	43:29	29:32	30:03	31:23	34:02	30:32	33:05	32:38	32:31	33:09	30:05	32:38	33:29	19:20	31:19
Total net yards	381	175	330	370	359	311	363	374	319	273	539	382	364	393	315	163	5411
Rushing yards	138	55	146	82	154	103	134	129	137	114	64	137	97	170	102	89	1851
Passing yards	243	120	184	288	205	208	229	245	182	159	475	245	267	223	213	74	3560
Rushing plays	36	19	47	20	32	28	34	33	34	29	25	35	24	37	32	16	481
Sacks allowed	3	5	5	4	0	1	4	0	0	3	4	1	0	1	1	3	35
Had intercepted	1	1	0	2	0	0	0	1	1	1	1	0	0	1	0	1	11
Fumbles lost	0	2	2	0	0	1	0	0	1	1	0	0	2	0	0	0	9
Yards penalized	71	38	28	50	40	55	40	50	55	15	30	10	20	30	31	29	542
Punts	3	6	5	2	3	4	3	3	6	6	3	2	2	3	2	5	58

INDIVIDUAL STATISTICS*

RUSHING

	WK 1	WK 2	WK 3	WK 4	WK 5	WK 7	WK 8	WK 9	WK 11	WK 12	WK 13	WK 14	WK 15	WK 16	WK 17	WK 18	TOTALS
Bettis	5-24-0	16-76-1	9-33-0	11-25-1	22-102-0	19-85-1	23-113-0	21-72-1	11-27-0	16-86-0	18-133-0	16-115-0	28-212-1	24-124-0	16-56-1	39-146-1	294-1429-7
Everett	1-(2)-0	3-(7)-0		6-8-0	2-2-0	3-12-0	1-4-0	1-4-0	3-21-0	1-3-0	6-22-0	1-3-0	6-36-0	2-18-0	3-31-0	3-16-0	20-41-0
Gary	13-31-0	14-30-1		15-25-0	4-13-0	5-41-0	2-8-0	1-4-0	3-16-0	1-(-1)-0			2-10-0	1-2-0	1-5-0	4-4-0	79-293-1
Lang									2-29-0	1-(-4)-0		6-4-0		5-22-0			9-29-0
Lester			3-12-0			2-28-0	1-1-0					2-21-0					11-74-0
Rubley							3-24-0	4-26-0		2-(-2)-0	3-6-0	1-9-0	6-8-0				29-102-0

PASSING**

Everett	17-41-2 175-0	21-34-2 221-1	11-28-2 135-1	19-28-0 316-3	10-25-1 126-0	17-35-2 294-2	2-9-1 12-0		20-41-2 203-0	12-20-0 102-0		6-13-0 68-1	5-13-0 47-1	11-24-0 107-0	24-32-2 294-1	18-28-0 213-1	135-274-12 1652-8
Rubley							12-17-0 151-2	15-26-2 158-1		5-6-0 112-1	13-28-1 167-1	5-15-1 89-0	2-22-1	2-18-0			108-189-6 1338-8

RECEIVING

Anderson	3-34-0		3-63-1	5-81-1	2-27-0	4-95-1			3-41-0	2-45-0	3-34-0	1-19-0			5-58-1	6-55-0	37-552-4
Bettis	1-6-0	1-(-4)-0	1-1-0	1-11-0		3-53-0	1-4-0	1-8-0	2-10-0	4-44-0	2-17-0	1-4-0	2-11-0		2-12-0	5-71-0	26-244-0
Carter	2-17-0	3-48-1			1-8-0		1-7-0		4-27-0	2-45-0			2-18-0	1-8-0	1-26-0	1-14-0	14-166-1
Drayton	2-45-0	9-127-0	2-26-0		2-32-0	6-62-0	2-35-0	3-17-0	1-5-0	1-25-1	3-6-0	2-12-1		2-8-0	3-49-0	5-49-1	27-319-4
Ellard	2-28-0			6-132-1	2-32-0		4-32-0	3-42-0	3-53-0	3-32-0	5-90-1	3-83-0	1-7-0	4-68-0	8-114-0	1-24-0	61-945-2
Gary	6-37-0	1-10-0	1-2-0	2-21-0	3-36-0	2-65-1	1-6-0	1-8-0	5-37-0	3-16-0	2-20-0	2-14-0	1-7-0	1-3-0			36-289-1
Jones							2-25-2								2-2-0		5-56-2
Kinchen					2-17-0	1-9-0	4-60-0	3-64-1	1-13-0								8-137-1
Lester		1-4-0	5-45-0	2-33-0	2-13-0	1-10-0	1-5-0	2-8-0	1-17-0	1-1-0	1-6-0	1-7-0	1-7-0		1-6-0		18-154-0
McNeal	1-8-0			2-36-1													8-75-1

* Doesn't include all players. ** Passing stats include completions, attempts, interceptions, gross yards gained and touchdowns.

REVIEW: MIAMI DOLPHINS

An adage that is usually applied to horse racing finds the winner's circle when assessing the 1993 Dolphins' season: "It's not where you start, it's where you finish."

The Dolphins were like an horse who moves four lengths into the lead at the half-mile pole and then runs out of gas, stumbling and snorting at the finish line. When watching that kind of horse from the stands, it looks like he's moving backward compared to the other horses on the track. That's just how the Dolphins looked compared to the other teams in the AFC.

The Dolphin season was loaded with promise, and the team began delivering on it bit by bit. After an early-season setback at home against the Jets, the Dolphins walked into Buffalo and smacked the Bills 22-13. A Monday-night win at home against the Redskins followed, and the Dolphins were cruising along with a 3-1 record.

A tough game in Cleveland followed. The Dolphins walked out of Cleveland Stadium with a 24-14 win, but they also walked out minus their quarterback. Dan Marino, the heretofore impervious one, tore his Achilles tendon on a seemingly innocuous play in the second quarter. Marino wasn't even touched as he attempted to move away from the pressure of the Cleveland defense. Blame his injury on the rock-hard dirt of Cleveland Stadium.

But before panic could set in, backup Scott Mitchell came in and didn't miss a beat. He rallied the Dolphins to victory over the Browns, and he led them to a win over the Colts and a rout of the Chiefs before head coach Don Shula's bid to become pro football's winningest coach failed against the Jets.

The next week, the Dolphins gave Shula the 325th victory of his career with a 19-14 triumph over the Eagles, but the game also marked another change at the QB spot. Mitchell went down with a separated shoulder. One week later the QB chores were in the hands of 38-year-old Steve DeBerg, the oldest player in the league.

DeBerg didn't perform badly, but it was clear that the Dolphin offense had lost the oomph it had under Marino and Mitchell. The running game, which had performed admirably in the first half of the season with rookie Terry Kirby and former Eagle Keith Byars providing the spark, fell completely off, and opponents started overplaying the pass. With DeBerg pulling the trigger, defenses knew he didn't have the arm strength to throw the deep out passes, so they concentrated on stopping passes over the middle. The results were a lot of turnovers, and the once-promising Dolphin season that peaked with a 9-2 record after a stunning 16-14 Thanksgiving Day upset at Dallas began a steep, harrowing descent that didn't end until New England QB Drew Bledsoe pulled the plug on the Miami season with a game-winning, overtime TD pass to Michael Timpson in the last game of the year.

The Dolphins' season-ending, five-game losing streak kept them out of the playoffs and gave Shula the most roller-coaster-like season of his 31-year career. The Dolphins became only the second team in league history to start the year with a 9-2 mark and not make the postseason (the 1976 Bengal team was the other).

Injuries were among the primary reasons for the Dolphins' collapse in the late going. CB Troy Vincent, S Louis Oliver and LB John Offerdahl were injured against the Cowboys, and backups Vestee Jackson, Stephen Braggs and Cliff Odom were unable to play at the predecessors' level. The Dolphin defense, which gave up 92.5 rushing yards per game in the first 11 games, allowed an average of 129.4 yards on the ground during the final five games.

Still, the Dolphins had some reasons to be happy about the 1993 season. Newly acquired Irving Fryar flourished in the Dolphin offense. He had the second 1,000-yard season of his career, and his blocking helped give the Dolphins the AFC's second-ranked offense.

The Dolphins also found themselves a very special special-teamer. Rookie O.J. McDuffie returned 38 punts 317 yards, and two of those returns went for touchdowns. McDuffie, Kirby and Fryar formed a very potent offensive nucleus and could be productive group of wide receivers for years to come.

1993 ROUNDUP

OFFENSIVE MVP: WR Irving Fryar had the second 1,000-yard season of his career, catching 64 passes for five touchdowns on the AFC's No. 2-ranked offense.

DEFENSIVE MVP: LB Bryan Cox led the team with 122 tackles and had five sacks.

RESULTS
Pointspread Shown Refers To Miami

Date	Opponent	Spread	Score
Sept. 5	At Indianapolis	(-6.5)	24-20
Sept. 12	New York Jets	(-9)	14-24
Sept. 26	At Buffalo	(+6)	22-13
Oct. 4	Washington	(-5.5)	17-10
Oct. 10	At Cleveland	(-2)	24-14
Oct. 24	Indianapolis	(-6.5)	41-27
Oct. 31	Kansas City	(0)	30-10
Nov. 7	At New York Jets	(-1.5)	10-27
Nov. 14	At Philadelphia	(-4.5)	19-14
Nov. 21	New England	(-7.5)	17-13
Nov. 25	At Dallas	(+10)	16-14
Dec. 5	New York Giants	(-3.5)	14-19
Dec. 13	Pittsburgh	(-3.5)	20-21
Dec. 19	Buffalo	(-2.5)	34-47
Dec. 27	At San Diego	(+1)	20-45
Jan. 2	At New England	(+1)	27-33*

* Overtime

1993 REVIEW ■ MIAMI

GAME-BY-GAME STATISTICS

TEAM STATISTICS

OPPONENT	WK 1 IND.	WK 2 N.Y.J.	WK 4 BUFF.	WK 5 WASH.	WK 6 CLEV.	WK 8 IND.	WK 9 K.C.	WK 10 N.Y.J.	WK 11 PHIL.	WK 12 N.E.	WK 13 DALL.	WK 14 N.Y.G.	WK 15 PITT.	WK 16 BUFF.	WK 17 S.D.	WK 18 N.E.	TOTALS
Score	24-20	14-24	22-13	17-10	24-14	41-27	30-10	10-27	19-14	17-13	16-14	14-19	20-21	34-47	20-45	27-33	
Total net yards	355	294	412	354	338	366	483	337	298	344	382	408	348	423	321	349	5812
Rushing yards	119	27	137	106	70	171	139	48	120	111	108	51	49	23	61	119	1459
Passing yards	236	267	275	248	268	195	344	289	178	233	274	357	299	400	260	230	4353
Rushing plays	28	14	43	27	31	33	40	18	38	24	20	20	17	11	25	30	419
Sacks allowed	0	4	1	1	1	1	0	1	1	3	2	3	5	3	0	4	30
Had intercepted	1	0	0	1	1	1	0	0	1	0	2	2	2	2	3	0	18
Fumbles lost	1	2	1	1	0	2	2	0	1	0	0	3	1	2	0	0	16
Yards penalized	35	19	75	96	44	37	26	35	35	50	25	81	3	40	20	40	661
Punts	8	4	3	5	3	1	1	4	7	5	3	6	3	2	2	4	58

OPPONENT STATISTICS

	WK 1	WK 2	WK 4	WK 5	WK 6	WK 8	WK 9	WK 10	WK 11	WK 12	WK 13	WK 14	WK 15	WK 16	WK 17	WK 18	TOTALS
Time of possession	31:45	38:08	20:39	30:47	27:25	32:26	23:17	36:53	29:57	31:07	34:39	31:40	32:47	34:54	30:47	31:39	
Total net yards	274	429	282	232	202	322	305	356	260	349	293	351	265	374	459	397	5150
Rushing yards	42	106	106	84	90	88	99	100	103	88	112	110	120	129	220	68	1665
Passing yards	232	323	176	148	112	234	206	256	157	261	181	241	145	245	239	329	3485
Rushing plays	21	38	22	23	16	25	20	36	27	24	28	29	38	44	37	32	460
Sacks allowed	0	0	4	2	4	4	1	0	4	2	0	3	2	0	1	0	29
Had intercepted	1	1	0	1	1	1	0	0	0	1	1	0	1	0	1	0	13
Fumbles lost	2	0	0	0	1	1	3	1	3	0	1	0	0	1	0	1	14
Yards penalized	20	73	28	57	55	56	39	15	28	15	46	58	56	45	25	34	650
Punts	7	4	5	6	5	4	5	4	7	3	6	6	7	3	2	2	76

INDIVIDUAL STATISTICS*

RUSHING

	WK 1	WK 2	WK 4	WK 5	WK 6	WK 8	WK 9	WK 10	WK 11	WK 12	WK 13	WK 14	WK 15	WK 16	WK 17	WK 18	TOTALS
Byars	6-43-0	2-5-0	8-24-0	2-7-0	8-26-0	3-5-0	4-27-0	1-5-0	6-12-0	1-(-1)-0	6-77-1	7-17-1	4-4-0	3-8-0	3-10-1		64-269-3
Higgs	14-76-0	10-23-0	22-77-0	7-9-1	5-12-0	17-114-0	17-42-0	10-30-0	22-68-1	19-108-0	8-17-0	7-17-0		5-13-0	5-10-0	18-77-1	186-693-3
Kirby	4-2-0	1-1-0	9-31-0	16-94-0	14-12-0	10-50-1	11-46-1	4-1-0	5-7-0	2-6-0	5-15-0	5-18-0	13-45-0	1-6-0	10-25-0	9-31-1	119-390-3
Mitchell			1-1-0		3-14-0	3-2-0	3-12-0	4-1-0	3-37-0					1-2-0	1-(-2)-0	3-11-0	21-89-0

PASSING**

	WK 1	WK 2	WK 4	WK 5	WK 6	WK 8	WK 9	WK 10	WK 11	WK 12	WK 13	WK 14	WK 15	WK 16	WK 17	WK 18	TOTALS
DeBerg										16-27-0 252-2	24-41-2 287-0	26-41-2 365-1	27-44-2 344-1	20-35-1 273-2			113-188-7 1521-6
Marino	22-40-1 236-3	19-29-0 286-2	20-32-1 282-1	16-30-1 253-1	14-19-0 161-1				8-17-1 150-1								91-150-3 1218-8
Mitchell					10-16-1 118-2	12-19-0 190-1	22-33-0 344-3	23-44-1 297-1						12-24-2 155-2	24-40-3 260-1	22-40-0 259-1	133-233-8 1773-12

RECEIVING

	WK 1	WK 2	WK 4	WK 5	WK 6	WK 8	WK 9	WK 10	WK 11	WK 12	WK 13	WK 14	WK 15	WK 16	WK 17	WK 18	TOTALS
Baty	1-1-1		1-0-0	1-9-0		1-32-0											5-78-1
Byars	3-19-0	2-11-0	5-52-0	1-12-0	5-51-0	2-22-0	6-57-1	2-19-0	1-12-0	5-48-1	7-80-0	6-65-0	5-57-0	2-11-0	5-64-1	1-26-0	61-613-3
Fryar	6-81-0	5-58-0	7-103-1	1-19-0	2-47-0	4-41-1	4-82-1	6-103-1	3-32-0	4-97-1	1-11-0	5-93-0	5-84-0	5-59-0	3-59-0	4-33-0	64-1010-5
Higgs	1-0-0	2-17-0		1-8-0		1-15-0			1-8-0			1-7-0	1-0-0	1-9-0		1-8-0	10-72-0
Ingram	3-22-0	2-37-1	1-26-0	3-36-0	4-39-1	5-62-0	4-103-1	4-58-0	2-95-0	5-99-0	3-85-0	3-61-0	3-32-0	6-80-2	3-26-0	5-61-1	44-707-6
K. Jackson	3-73-2	1-57-1		2-18-1	2-18-1	1-44-1	3-43-0	2-48-0	1-7-0		4-25-0	1-7-0	3-42-1	1-7-0	1-8-0	3-28-0	39-613-6
Kirby	4-29-0	4-23-0	6-91-0	3-36-0	7-61-0		2-18-0	4-28-0	2-19-1	5-99-0	7-76-0	8-95-0	7-107-0	9-148-1	7-74-0	3-20-0	75-874-3
Martin	1-11-0	2-57-0		4-110-1	2-36-1		4-103-1	2-26-0		1-5-0	2-31-1	2-10-0	1-4-0	3-38-0	2-10-0	1-24-0	20-347-3
McDuffie				2-23-0	2-27-0	1-15-0			1-11-0	1-3-0	2-10-0	1-13-0	2-18-0	3-41-0	2-18-0	1-18-0	19-197-0
Miller								2-15-0 2-15-0									2-15-0

*Doesn't include all players. ** Passing stats include completions, attempts, interceptions, gross yards gained and touchdowns.

351

REVIEW: MINNESOTA VIKINGS

The Vikings experienced a roller-coaster season that ended with QB Jim McMahon barely able to remember what hit him.

A relentless Giant defense that registered three sacks was responsible for giving McMahon a major-league headache in the 17-10 playoff loss that ended Minnesota's season.

The Vikings' top-ranked defense (sixth vs. the run) couldn't hold off an overpowering Giant ground game featuring Rodney Hampton, who gained 161 clock-consuming yards and scored a pair of touchdowns. Thus, a 10-3 Viking halftime lead fell by the wayside.

The Vikes had come on strong at season's end, winning their last three games to qualify for the playoffs as a 9-7 wild-card entry. But the loss to the Giants left a bad taste, accompanied by a lingering feeling of failure.

"It wasn't the type of year we wanted to have," said Tony Dungy, the coordinator of a talented defense that was particularly solid up front on the interior, thanks to DT's Henry Thomas and John Randle (21 sacks combined). "We just weren't consistent enough. We didn't grab it when it was in the grasp."

The Vikings were certainly a resilient lot, managing to survive a run of injuries that decimated their offensive backfield. The departures of three of their best offensive linemen (Kirk Lowdermilk and Brian Habib to free-agency and Gary Zimmerman to a holdout-forced trade) and a change in offensive coordinators (from Jack Burns to Brian Billick) after just two games hurt a lot.

Following an impressive 19-12, Monday-night victory in Chicago in which the defense authored nine sacks, the 4-2 Vikes had won two straight games and appeared ready to go on a big-time roll.

The next week on Halloween night, though, their season took a scary turn. As it would later in the playoffs, the Viking defense faltered late in a home game vs. the division-rival Lions, failing to hold a 27-13, fourth-quarter lead in a 30-27 defeat.

That loss to the Lions was the first of four defeats in a five-game span, a slump made even more painful by the fact the other three losses were to non-playoff teams San Diego, Tampa Bay and New Orleans.

"The two most disappointing games would have to be Detroit (the Halloween nightmare) and Tampa Bay (a 23-10 loss at Tampa Nov. 21)," said Viking head coach Dennis Green, who had led Minnesota to a division title and an 11-5 record in his rookie campaign the previous year.

"We didn't get two flat tires; two tires fell off the damn car. And it took us awhile to find them."

But the Vikings bounced back, charging into the playoffs by winning 4-of-5 games in December. They did so behind a revitalized McMahon, who had missed all of November with a shoulder injury and spent a good portion of the season embroiled in a QB controversy with Sean Salisbury, and Scottie Graham, a free agent signed off the team's practice squad who came out of nowhere to set team rushing records after replacing No. 1 pick Robert Smith, whose season ended with a Dec. 5 knee injury.

In addition to losing Smith, the Vikings were forced to go the entire season without Terry Allen, who rushed for 1,201 yards in 1992 but sustained a season-ending knee injury early in training camp.

In December, though, Graham was a revelation, gaining a team-record 305 yards on 63 carries in consecutive victories over Green Bay and Kansas City and averaging 97 yards per game in five starts, and the Vikings' patchwork offensive line came together, going 14 straight quarters without allowing a sack.

Yet, in the end, the '93 Vikings will be remembered more for their inconsistency on both offense and defense, as well as their second straight defeat in a postseason opener.

"I think you could say we had a gutty season, and I think we had some memorable games and showed a lot of courage to make a good run to the playoffs," said Green. "But I don't think you could call it a successful season."

"I don't think we played as well as the year before," added Dungy. "We gave up so many big plays."

1993 ROUNDUP

OFFENSIVE MVP: WR Cris Carter caught 86 passes for 1,071 yards and led the Vikings with nine touchdowns.

DEFENSIVE MVP: SS Vencie Glenn was the team's most consistent defender and produced the most big plays.

RESULTS
Pointspread Shown Refers To Minnesota

Date	Opponent	Spread	Score
Sept. 5	At L.A. Raiders	(-2.5)	7-24
Sept. 12	Chicago	(-7)	10-7
Sept. 26	Green Bay	(-3)	15-13
Oct. 3	At San Francisco	(+10)	19-38
Oct. 10	Tampa Bay	(-11)	15-0
Oct. 25	At Chicago	(+3.5)	19-12
Oct. 31	Detroit	(-4)	27-30
Nov. 7	San Diego	(-3.5)	17-30
Nov. 14	At Denver	(+6.5)	26-23
Nov. 21	At Tampa Bay	(-8)	10-23
Nov. 28	New Orleans	(-1)	14-17
Dec. 5	At Detroit	(+3)	13-0
Dec. 12	Dallas	(+7)	20-37
Dec. 19	At Green Bay (Milw)	(+6.5)	21-17
Dec. 26	Kansas City	(+2.5)	30-10
Dec. 31	At Washington	(-7)	14-9

POSTSEASON

| Jan. 9 | At N.Y. Giants | (+6) | 10-17 |

1993 REVIEW ■ MINNESOTA

GAME-BY-GAME STATISTICS

TEAM STATISTICS

OPPONENT	WK 1 L.A.RD	WK 2 CHI.	WK 4 G.B.	WK 5 S.F.	WK 6 T.B.	WK 8 CHI.	WK 9 DET.	WK 10 S.D.	WK 11 DENV.	WK 12 T.B.	WK 13 N.O.	WK 14 DET.	WK 15 DALL.	WK 16 G.B.	WK 17 K.C.	WK 18 WASH.	TOTALS
Score	7-24	10-7	15-13	19-38	15-0	19-12	27-30	17-30	26-23	10-23	14-17	13-0	20-37	21-17	30-10	14-9	
Total net yards	205	276	317	271	268	252	378	346	429	235	288	234	270	361	424	270	4824
Rushing yards	58	121	107	52	124	165	116	20	71	82	106	101	97	154	205	45	1624
Passing yards	147	155	210	219	144	87	262	326	358	153	182	133	173	207	219	225	3200
Rushing plays	18	37	29	15	33	34	30	13	27	18	32	26	24	38	46	27	447
Sacks allowed	3	4	2	3	5	1	1	3	1	2	4	3	3	0	0	0	35
Had intercepted	2	0	0	1	1	1	1	1	1	0	0	1	0	0	0	1	14
Fumbles lost	1	1	1	0	0	0	2	2	2	0	0	1	0	0	0	0	10
Yards penalized	25	30	25	74	65	95	21	24	92	62	35	34	60	73	61	30	806
Punts	3	6	3	9	7	8	5	5	5	7	7	6	3	7	3	6	90

OPPONENT STATISTICS

	WK 1	WK 2	WK 4	WK 5	WK 6	WK 8	WK 9	WK 10	WK 11	WK 12	WK 13	WK 14	WK 15	WK 16	WK 17	WK 18	TOTALS
Time of possession	39:35	22:28	28:15	29:03	23:55	29:24	27:04	34:49	32:54	38:36	29:52	29:33	32:20	24:08	20:29	30:06	29:28
Total net yards	312	140	256	254	169	252	338	411	343	300	254	219	356	320	220	263	4407
Rushing yards	98	88	106	50	59	93	78	148	93	100	154	108	148	67	37	110	1537
Passing yards	214	52	150	204	110	159	260	263	250	200	100	111	208	253	183	153	2870
Rushing plays	35	22	23	26	20	21	23	36	22	34	32	27	35	19	16	23	414
Sacks allowed	1	4	0	4	3	9	2	1	4	4	2	7	0	1	1	2	45
Had intercepted	1	1	2	1	4	2	2	0	1	0	5	0	0	0	2	0	24
Fumbles lost	0	0	0	0	1	1	0	1	3	0	1	0	0	1	1	0	10
Yards penalized	85	20	50	51	33	55	63	52	77	50	10	64	64	35	39	19	767
Punts	2	8	5	5	6	6	4	5	5	5	5	6	1	5	6	4	78

INDIVIDUAL STATISTICS*

RUSHING

	WK 1	WK 2	WK 4	WK 5	WK 6	WK 8	WK 9	WK 10	WK 11	WK 12	WK 13	WK 14	WK 15	WK 16	WK 17	WK 18	TOTALS
Craig	10-30-1	3-6-0						2-4-0	14-41-0	6-32-0	1-1-0		1-3-0	1-2-0			38-119-1
Evans	3-3-0	8-23-0	3-6-0		1-1-0	2-9-0											14-32-0
Graham	2-25-0	2-(2)-0	6-31-0	3-6-0	8-64-0	14-80-1	23-115-1	3-5-0	11-30-0			15-66-0 2-(2)-0	20-79-1 2-10-0	30-139-0 5-15-0	33-166-1 3-5-0	20-37-1 5-(2)-0	118-487-3 33-96-0
Smith											24-94-0	8-35-0					82-399-2
Word	2-6-0	24-94-0	19-65-0	12-46-0	20-53-1	17-78-0	5-8-0	8-11-1		10-36-0	6-10-0	1-2-0			9-25-0		142-458-2

PASSING**

	WK 1	WK 2	WK 4	WK 5	WK 6	WK 8	WK 9	WK 10	WK 11	WK 12	WK 13	WK 14	WK 15	WK 16	WK 17	WK 18	TOTALS
McMahon	15-27-2 161-0	23-29-0 173-1	18-35-0 217-0	25-45-1 223-2	15-25-1 157-0	14-27-1 90-0	4-5-0 33-0					15-32-0 145-0	13-18-1 117-0	22-31-0 207-3	17-25-1 219-2	19-32-1 225-1	200-331-8 1967-9
Salisbury				2-4-0 14-0	2-3-0 22-0		25-37-1 234-2	29-47-1 347-1	19-37-1 366-2	15-34-2 161-1	16-26-1 208-2		7-7-0 61-1				115-195-6 1413-9

RECEIVING

	WK 1	WK 2	WK 4	WK 5	WK 6	WK 8	WK 9	WK 10	WK 11	WK 12	WK 13	WK 14	WK 15	WK 16	WK 17	WK 18	TOTALS
A. Carter	2-32-0	6-40-0	2-23-0	1-3-0	2-37-0	5-31-0	8-86-1	10-164-1	4-111-0	9-104-1	3-50-1	4-58-0	3-28-1	3-26-0	5-88-2	6-62-1	60-774-5
C. Carter	7-74-0	8-52-1	4-44-0	5-70-1	5-57-0		9-88-1	6-75-0	6-134-1	2-10-0		2-9-0	6-70-0	6-106-2	7-113-0	7-113-0	86-1071-9
Graham	1-6-0	1-6-0	1-4-0	1-4-0				4-45-0	2-19-1	1-16-0		2-42-0		5-19-0	1-7-0	1-5-0	19-169-1
Ismail		1-6-0	3-45-0	5-65-0	1-2-0		1-4-0					1-4-0	1-(-2)-0	1-11-0	2-13-0	2-20-0	7-46-0
Jordan	3-27-0	2-11-0	3-31-0	7-49-0	3-37-0	3-28-0	5-57-0	5-26-0	6-85-0	3-31-0	1-37-0		3-27-0	1-6-1	3-20-0		19-212-1
Smith	1-1-0			4-16-0	3-16-0	3-8-0	4-20-0	2-12-0			1-59-1	3-14-0		5-29-0	4-58-0	2-14-0	56-542-1
Tennell				3-27-0	1-4-0	1-0-0		1-11-0			1-7-0	2-15-0	5-43-0		1-15-0		24-111-0 15-122-0
Tice			1-1-0	1-3-1	2-26-0		1-2-0		1-17-0			1-3-0	1-6-0			1-18-0	6-39-1
Word		5-58-0	1-10-0														9-105-0

* Doesn't include all players. ** Passing stats include completions, attempts, interceptions, gross yards gained and touchdowns.

REVIEW: NEW ENGLAND PATRIOTS

Hail the return of the conquering hero. The day the Patriots hired Bill Parcells to coach their franchise was the day many New England fans thought their long-suffering franchise finally turned it around.

"I'm not here to do anything but win football games," said Parcells, whose first NFL assistant-coaching job was with the Patriots in the mid-1970's. "I've never coached any game that I didn't try to win. I'm not very good at losing, and, in fact, I'm getting worse at it."

That's just the kind of talk that gets a team moving in the right direction, especially when it comes from the former coach of the two-time Super Bowl champion Giants.

Despite the brave talk, the season did not get off to a great start for the Patriots. The Patriots lost their first four games before eking out a win at Phoenix. Then the losing ways continued, as New England lost seven more in a row.

But a funny thing happened on the way to the losses. Instead of getting blown out, like they were in early losses to the Bills and Jets, the Patriots were giving everybody fits. A second meeting with Buffalo resulted in a three-point loss in overtime. A trip to Miami resulted in a narrow four-point defeat. Two weeks after that loss, the Patriots led the Steelers 14-10 with time for only one play on the game clock. Unfortunately for the Patriots, the Steelers scored on that play, and the result was nothing more than another mind-numbing defeat.

Nerves were frazzled, feelings were hurt and Parcells' players were on the edge. But instead of quitting on the season and cashing it in, the Patriots used that game as a springboard toward respectability. They defeated the Bengals at home the following week, and then closed the season with wins over Cleveland, Indianapolis and Miami.

The victory over the Dolphins in the season finale may have been the most dramatic game of the NFL season. The Patriots won 33-27 in overtime, as rookie QB Drew Bledsoe hit Michael Timpson with a perfect, over-the-shoulder, 48-yard TD pass in the extra session. The loss eliminated the Dolphins from playoff contention and left the Patriot players with a feeling of confidence about their future.

"One thing we were not going to do this season was give up," said Bledsoe. "We had a lot of tough games this season, a lot of games that could have gone our way if we had gotten a break or two. But the last four weeks of the season showed this team could play and that we have a great future in front of us."

Aside from the arrival of Bledsoe, the most significant New England development was the improvement of the offensive line, which happens to be a trademark of Parcells-coached teams. In 1992, that unit gave up 65 sacks and made every pass play a disaster waiting to happen. In 1993, it allowed only 23, the second-fewest in the league.

The Patriots went from the most penalty yards in the league, 1,051, to the fewest, 469. Another positive sign was that they rarely lost the ball on the ground. They lost only 10 fumbles for the season, better than all but three teams. For the first time since 1986, when they finished first in the AFC East, they outgained their opponents 316.6 yards per game to 299.8.

In rebuilding his team, Parcells took the long-term approach. He cut or traded players who may have helped him win more games in exchange for future stars he could develop.

This strategy began to pay off nicely toward the end of the year, as WR Vincent Brisby, WR Ray Crittenden, KR Ronnie Harris, OLB Chris Slade, SS Corwin Brown, CB Rod Smith, LB Dwayne Sabb, RB Kevin Turner and ILB Todd Collins made an impact.

With those young players and veterans such as OLT Bruce Armstrong, LB Vincent Brown and CB Maurice Hurst, Parcells was much happier with his combination of experience and youth than when he arrived in January of '93. The veteran leadership was also happy with the team's prospects.

"I told a lot of people about eight weeks ago that if the season had started over then, this team would make a run for the playoffs," Hurst said at the end of the year. "We played well over the last four weeks, and that means we have something to build on for the future."

1993 ROUNDUP

OFFENSIVE MVP: TE Ben Coates led the team in catches (53), yards (659) and TD's (eight).

DEFENSIVE MVP: LB Vincent Brown was in on 158 tackles, including 104 solo takedowns.

RESULTS
Pointspread Shown Refers To New England

Date	Opponent	Spread	Score
Sept. 5	At Buffalo	(+14.5)	14-38
Sept. 12	Detroit	(+7)	16-19*
Sept. 19	Seattle	(-2.5)	14-17
Sept. 26	At New York Jets	(+9.5)	7-45
Oct. 10	At Phoenix	(+10)	23-21
Oct. 17	Houston	(+6.5)	14-28
Oct. 24	At Seattle	(+9.5)	9-10
Oct. 31	At Indianapolis	(+6.5)	6-9
Nov. 7	Buffalo	(+10)	10-13*
Nov. 21	At Miami	(+7.5)	13-17
Nov. 28	New York Jets	(+4)	0-6
Dec. 5	At Pittsburgh	(+12)	14-17
Dec. 12	Cincinnati	(-6)	7-2
Dec. 19	At Cleveland	(+6)	20-17
Dec. 26	Indianapolis	(-6)	38-0
Jan. 2	Miami	(-1)	33-27*

* Overtime

1993 REVIEW ■ NEW ENGLAND

GAME-BY-GAME STATISTICS

TEAM STATISTICS

OPPONENT	WK 1 BUFF.	WK 2 DET.	WK 3 SEA.	WK 4 N.Y.J.	WK 6 PHX.	WK 7 HOU.	WK 8 SEA.	WK 9 IND.	WK 10 BUFF.	WK 12 MIA.	WK 13 N.Y.J.	WK 14 PITT.	WK 15 CIN.	WK 16 CLEV.	WK 17 IND.	WK 18 MIA.	TOTALS
Score	14-38	16-19	14-17	7-45	23-21	14-28	9-10	6-9	10-13	13-17	0-6	14-17	7-2	20-17	38-0	33-27	
Total net yards	268	292	276	211	432	315	295	363	284	349	289	217	224	323	400	397	5067
Rushing yards	133	61	51	31	151	54	166	87	187	88	155	53	118	120	257	68	1780
Passing yards	135	231	223	180	281	261	129	276	97	261	134	296	106	203	143	329	3285
Rushing plays	37	23	17	13	41	19	36	25	48	24	34	24	44	27	58	32	502
Sacks allowed	3	2	2	3	2	5	0	1	2	1	0	1	0	1	0	1	23
Had intercepted	1	1	1	2	1	3	2	2	1	1	5	5	0	0	0	1	24
Fumbles lost	2	2	1	2	0	0	0	0	1	1	1	1	0	0	0	1	10
Yards penalized	30	30	20	15	64	48	60	25	20	15	5	25	43	15	24	34	473
Punts	7	5	6	6	7	3	5	3	7	3	4	5	6	5	2	2	76

OPPONENT STATISTICS

	WK 1	WK 2	WK 3	WK 4	WK 6	WK 7	WK 8	WK 9	WK 10	WK 12	WK 13	WK 14	WK 15	WK 16	WK 17	WK 18	TOTALS
Time of possession	26:47	39:11	38:20	36:37	23:32	32:12	28:22	31:28	30:43	28:53	33:52	34:02	27:50	30:48	21:32	33:05	
Total net yards	334	340	334	388	311	246	261	268	432	344	294	217	160	377	136	349	4791
Rushing yards	177	186	209	167	124	104	67	89	134	111	120	125	102	80	37	119	1951
Passing yards	157	154	125	221	187	142	194	179	298	233	174	92	58	297	99	230	2840
Rushing plays	42	44	43	41	18	25	26	29	37	24	35	32	34	27	18	30	505
Sacks allowed	1	3	5	0	2	1	1	2	2	3	1	3	5	0	2	4	35
Had intercepted	1	3	2	0	2	0	1	2	0	0	0	0	1	2	0	0	13
Fumbles lost	0	1	1	0	1	0	0	0	3	1	0	0	0	1	1	0	9
Yards penalized	35	57	49	48	63	61	56	39	20	50	35	72	50	83	45	40	803
Punts	4	2	5	4	7	6	8	5	5	5	6	11	8	4	6	4	90

INDIVIDUAL STATISTICS*

RUSHING

	WK 1	WK 2	WK 3	WK 4	WK 6	WK 7	WK 8	WK 9	WK 10	WK 12	WK 13	WK 14	WK 15	WK 16	WK 17	WK 18	TOTALS
Bledsoe	3-6-0	3-10-0	1-1-0	1-1-0	1-0-0		1-0-0	1-1-0	5-14-0	1-12-0	5-4-0	5-(-1)-0	2-2-0	4-9-0	1-2-0	6-27-0	32-82-0
Croom	10-44-0	2-0-0	3-10-0		6-18-0				3-18-0	9-41-0			6-2-0	2-4-0	21-93-1	2-6-0	60-198-1
Gash			4-16-1	1-1-0	5-16-0				7-21-0	2-0-0			1-0-0	3-6-0	4-6-0	1-2-0	48-149-1
Russell	23-81-0	17-40-0	8-21-0	10-29-1	28-116-0	15-42-1	21-97-0	10-39-0	25-95-1	8-26-0	27-147-0	19-54-1	29-97-0	14-38-1	26-138-2	20-28-0	300-1088-7
Secules						2-6-0	2-11-0	2-16-0	2-0-0	2-11-0		3-69-0		1-6-0			8-33-0
Turner	1-2-0	1-11-0	1-3-0	1-4-0	1-1-0	2-6-0	12-58-0	3-9-0	6-23-0	4-9-0	1-4-0	2-33-0	5-17-0	4-63-0	5-16-0	3-5-0	50-231-0

PASSING**

	WK 1	WK 2	WK 3	WK 4	WK 6	WK 7	WK 8	WK 9	WK 10	WK 12	WK 13	WK 14	WK 15	WK 16	WK 17	WK 18	TOTALS
Bledsoe	14-30-1	28-49-1	20-44-2	19-42-2	8-17-0		15-30-2		8-16-0	23-42-1	10-18-1	18-48-5	11-22-0	19-47-1	9-11-0	27-43-1	214-429-15
	148-2	239-1	238-1	195-0	85-1		129-0		96-0	275-1	134-0	296-1	106-1	210-1	143-2	329-4	2494-15
Secules					12-20-1	23-40-3		23-37-2	2-7-1								75-134-9
					214-1	280-1		279-0	16-0								918-2

RECEIVING

	WK 1	WK 2	WK 3	WK 4	WK 6	WK 7	WK 8	WK 9	WK 10	WK 12	WK 13	WK 14	WK 15	WK 16	WK 17	WK 18	TOTALS
Brisby	1-16-0	5-52-1	3-39-0	2-15-0	3-65-0	3-36-0	2-18-0	2-39-0	6-86-0	2-43-0	2-43-0	2-28-0	6-77-0	1-2-0	6-69-1	45-626-2
Coates	1-54-1	6-39-0	4-47-1	1-6-0	4-24-2	3-68-0	3-10-0	6-108-0	3-22-0	3-32-0	2-20-0	3-33-1	3-21-1	3-36-0	21-93-1	2-6-0	53-659-8
Cook	2-17-0	2-9-0	1-4-0	3-32-0	3-26-0	2-13-0	2-10-0		2-11-0	2-11-0			1-6-0	1-7-0	4-6-0	6-95-2	22-154-1
Crittenden			5-68-0	1-44-0			1-26-0		1-40-1			3-69-0		1-6-0	1-1-1		16-293-1
Croom					1-8-0						1-7-0	2-33-0	2-16-0			1-14-0	8-92-0
Gash	3-20-0	1-1-0	1-8-0	1-6-0	2-20-0		2-19-0			3-17-0		2-14-0		1-14-0	1-7-0		14-93-0
McMurtry	3-21-1	6-68-0	4-49-0	2-28-0	2-28-0	3-28-0	3-28-0	2-18-0	2-18-0	1-14-0	1-14-0						22-241-1
Russell	4-20-0	4-58-0	1-0-0	2-0-0	1-77-0	1-4-0	3-28-0	1-26-0	2-18-0		2-6-0	1-4-0	1-1-0	1-11-0	2-44-0	1-14-0	26-247-0
Timpson		2-16-0	1-25-0	5-60-0	1-20-0		5-52-0	3-29-0	1-26-0	5-60-0	3-58-0	4-97-0	3-35-0	3-42-0	2-59-1	4-75-1	42-654-2
Turner		2-(-4)-0		2-4-0	2-23-0	5-65-1		6-78-0	2-7-0	3-29-0		1-3-0		3-17-1	3-32-0	8-61-0	39-333-2

* Doesn't include all players. ** Passing stats include completions, attempts, interceptions, gross yards gained and touchdowns.

REVIEW: NEW ORLEANS SAINTS

Rarely does a season that started with so much promise end with such despair.

The Saints started the season with five straight victories. They seemed to be climbing toward the very top of the NFL mountain. Then they lost their footing and went tumbling, unable to slow their negative momentum. When the Saints finally hit rock bottom, their record stood at 8-8.

When the dust cleared from this slide toward mediocrity, the Saints could only shake their heads and wonder what had happened.

"This isn't how any of us thought it would end up," said Saint FS Gene Atkins. "No one would have believed we'd end up .500 and out of the playoffs. Not just on the start of this season, but on how this team has played over the last couple of years."

New Orleans' OL Jim Dombrowski said, "I saw this team making the playoffs and playing much better than we have. Instead, it was a slow trickle of disaster. Never a flood you could dam up, just a dozen different trickles every week."

Reasons for the decline could be found in numerous areas of the team's roster.

For starters, QB Wade Wilson lived up to his reputation of being a hot-and-cold passer. When the Saints started out 5-0, Wilson threw only one interception. When the Saints went 3-8 the rest of the season, Wilson tossed 14 interceptions.

Injuries to the running game were also a problem. Vaughn Dunbar, the previous season's leading rusher, missed the season with a knee injury. Lorenzo Neal, a rookie fullback who in two games rushed for 175 yards on 21 carries, including a 74-yard touchdown, went on injured reserve Sept. 15. Rookie RB Derek Brown was a bright spot, rushing for 705 yards, but he sat out three games with an ankle injury.

In past seasons, the Saints may have been able to overcome health woes at running back and erratic play at quarterback, thanks to a dominating defense. But the defense that had been one of the league's finest from 1987 to '92 started to decline.

Individually, the loss of LB Pat Swilling to the Lions was offset by a Pro Bowl year from a younger Renaldo Turnbull.

Age and injuries, however, robbed the defense of its effectiveness.

NT Jim Wilks missed the first eight games with a torn tricep. LB Sam Mills missed seven weeks with a knee infection. SS Brett Maxie missed the season with a knee injury. DE Frank Warren missed five games with injuries before finally going on I.R. in December. DL Les Miller was out for four weeks, and CB Reggie Jones was put on I.R. with a knee injury Dec. 23.

The defense that had been so impenetrable in past seasons surrendered 343 points and ranked 22nd in the NFL. Just as disturbing was the inability of the defense to stop the run, which finished the season ranked 25th in rushing yards allowed per game.

The Saints' difficult season was felt off the field as well. General manager Jim Finks resigned due to illness.

Through all the disappointment, there were some positive aspects to the season. The play of Turnbull was much needed. Replacing a true star in Swilling, Turnbull finished the season with 13 sacks, which tied him for the NFC lead with the Packers' Reggie White.

The 1993 draft also appears to have helped the Saints add some young talent to the roster. No. 1 pick OT Willie Roaf had an excellent rookie season. He made steady progress, was very good in pass blocking and good on run blocking. His rookie year gave indications that he will be an outstanding NFL player.

Other rookies — TE Irv Smith, RB's Brown and Neal and Pro Bowl return specialist Tyrone Hughes — filled some holes for the Saints, although obviously not nearly enough to prevent the Saints from wasting their 5-0 start.

Indeed, when all was said and done, the team's inability to cash in on a 5-0 start is what defined the Saint season.

"I think there will be a lot of evaluations made and a lot of soul-searching done by everyone on this team," said Saint OT Richard Cooper. "It's the kind of season you'll wake up thinking about and wondering about for a long time."

1993 ROUNDUP

OFFENSIVE MVP: WR Eric Martin caught 66 passes for 950 yards to rank 10th in the NFC and scored three touchdowns.

DEFENSIVE MVP: LB Renaldo Turnbull recorded 13 sacks to finish in a first-place tie atop the NFC, in addition to forcing five fumbles.

RESULTS
Pointspread Shown Refers To New Orleans

Date	Opponent	Spread	Score
Sept. 5	Houston	(-2.5)	33-21
Sept. 12	At Atlanta	(-3.5)	34-31
Sept. 19	Detroit	(-6)	14-3
Sept. 26	San Francisco	(+1)	16-13
Oct. 3	At L.A. Rams	(-4)	37-6
Oct. 17	At Pittsburgh	(-2.5)	14-37
Oct. 24	Atlanta	(-10.5)	15-26
Oct. 31	At Phoenix	(-3)	20-17
Nov. 14	Green Bay	(-6.5)	17-19
Nov. 22	At San Francisco	(+9)	7-42
Nov. 28	At Minnesota	(+1)	17-14
Dec. 5	At Cleveland	(-3.5)	13-17
Dec. 12	L.A. Rams	(-14)	20-23
Dec. 20	New York Giants	(-2)	14-24
Dec. 26	At Philadelphia	(+3)	26-37
Jan. 2	Cincinnati	(-5.5)	20-13

1993 REVIEW ■ NEW ORLEANS

GAME-BY-GAME STATISTICS

TEAM STATISTICS

OPPONENT	WK 1 HOU.	WK 2 ATL.	WK 3 DET.	WK 4 S.F.	WK 5 L.A.RM	WK 7 PITT.	WK 8 ATL.	WK 9 PHX.	WK 11 G.B.	WK 12 S.F.	WK 13 MINN.	WK 14 CLEV.	WK 15 L.A.RM	WK 16 N.Y.G.	WK 17 PHIL.	WK 18 CIN.	TOTALS
Score	33-21	34-31	14-3	16-13	37-6	14-37	15-26	20-17	17-19	7-42	17-14	13-17	20-23	14-24	26-37	20-13	
Total net yards	346	557	258	264	359	264	321	272	329	261	254	127	364	304	158	269	4707
Rushing yards	142	227	172	103	154	49	47	96	157	119	154	79	97	11	83	76	1766
Passing yards	204	330	86	161	205	215	274	176	172	142	100	48	267	293	75	193	2941
Rushing plays	30	31	35	24	32	17	12	32	35	23	32	24	24	12	21	30	414
Sacks allowed	2	2	2	1	0	0	5	2	5	4	2	9	0	2	3	0	40
Had intercepted	0	1	0	0	0	3	2	1	2	4	2	0	1	2	2	1	21
Fumbles lost	1	0	1	0	1	2	0	1	3	0	1	0	2	0	1	0	13
Yards penalized	61	82	25	37	40	25	72	42	42	20	10	25	20	99	33	30	663
Punts	2	4	7	4	3	9	4	6	3	6	5	10	2	6	3	3	77
Time of possession	29:26	26:32	29:32	32:34	29:57	37:15	36:27	29:48	26:36	32:11	30:08	29:29	29:55	36:14	39:57	30:21	31:31

OPPONENT STATISTICS

Total net yards	405	375	170	339	256	393	279	143	194	455	288	314	306	277	314	188	4696
Rushing yards	70	78	84	176	127	201	123	89	69	219	106	131	266	133	134	84	2090
Passing yards	335	297	86	163	129	192	156	54	125	236	182	183	40	144	180	104	2606
Rushing plays	18	20	21	32	30	47	39	25	21	38	32	28	42	42	44	34	513
Sacks allowed	4	4	5	3	3	1	1	6	6	2	4	0	1	4	2	3	51
Had intercepted	1	1	0	1	2	1	0	1	0	0	1	0	1	0	0	1	10
Fumbles lost	4	1	2	1	1	2	0	0	1	0	0	2	1	1	1	1	20
Yards penalized	84	60	35	20	10	9	39	60	33	19	35	62	60	25	20	19	590
Punts	2	6	7	2	6	6	3	7	5	2	7	7	5	4	5	6	80

INDIVIDUAL STATISTICS*

RUSHING

Brown	12-52-1	18-82-0	25-125-0	21-88-1	14-57-0	10-7-0	9-20-0	14-32-0	21-106-0	5-27-0		13-47-0	5-16-1	6-9-0	13-62-0	12-38-0	180-705-2
Hilliard	2-3-1	3-6-0	4-16-0			1-5-0		5-25-0	2-15-0	1-0-0	3-7-0	8-30-0	4-(-1)-0	1-(-1)-0		10-26-0	50-165-2
McAfee	3-(-2)-0				7-25-0	1-5-0			9-22-0	7-33-0	21-70-0	1-2-0	13-53-0	2-1-1	8-21-1	4-16-0	51-160-1
Muster				2-7-0	6-19-0	2-5-0	1-0-0	7-23-1	9-22-0	6-38-0	3-7-0						64-214-3
Neal	13-89-0	8-86-1		1-8-0	3-0-0						4-44-0	2-0-0	2-29-0	1-(-4)-0			21-175-1
Wilson		3-51-0	2-12-0			3-27-0	1-20-0	6-16-0	3-14-0	1-11-0							32-228-0

PASSING**

M. Buck						10-11-0 164-2				10-15-1 122-1				11-21-2 148-1	1-7-0 14-0		32-54-3 448-4
Walsh															5-11-2 78-0	15-27-1 193-2	20-38-3 271-2
Wilson	16-25-0 206-0	22-34-1 341-3	11-22-0 99-2	18-32-0 170-0	15-25-0 205-2	6-23-3 85-0	27-45-2 277-1	16-27-1 186-1	20-29-2 197-2	6-15-3 46-0	13-20-2 111-0	15-29-0 119-1	25-43-1 267-0	11-19-0 148-0			221-388-15 2457-12

RECEIVING

Brown	3-28-0	3-36-0	1-6-0	3-16-0	2-26-1	1-9-0	1-2-0	3-19-0		1-2-0		4-35-1	8-97-0	2-14-0	1-2-0	1-12-0	21-170-1
E. Martin	7-111-0	4-91-0	2-27-1	4-44-0	1-30-0	5-75-0	3-29-0	3-53-0	7-70-0	1-12-0	5-61-0	3-16-0	6-53-0	6-80-0	1-15-0	5-120-1	66-950-3
Early	3-23-0	2-60-2	3-20-0	2-18-0	4-64-0	3-92-1	8-94-1	3-38-1	2-35-1	2-48-0		3-16-0	1-9-0	4-98-0	1-7-0	3-26-0	45-670-6
Hilliard		3-26-0	1-4-0	3-12-0	3-14-0		3-14-0	4-45-0		3-21-0	2-5-0	4-22-0	4-31-0	8-85-1	2-16-0		40-296-1
Muster				2-14-0			1-31-0	3-34-0	1-11-0				1-11-0	2-11-0		5-26-0	23-195-0
Small			2-19-0	2-26-0	1-13-0	4-34-1	5-55-0				1-6-0		1-19-0	1-15-0			16-164-1
Smith		1-1-1					1-23-0	1-5-0	3-23-0	1-19-0	4-45-0	2-21-0			1-52-0	1-9-1	16-180-2
Turner						1-6-0		1-11-0	1-11-0	5-47-1		4-47-0					12-163-1

* Doesn't include all players. ** Passing stats include completions, attempts, interceptions, gross yards gained and touchdowns.

REVIEW: NEW YORK GIANTS

The Giants were one of the league's biggest question marks going into the 1993 season. They had a new coach — former Bronco boss Dan Reeves — and two zombie-like seasons to overcome. Former coach Ray Handley had left this once-proud team in a somnambulant state, and it was up to Reeves to get the situation turned around.

Reeves demonstrated he still had the magic, as the Giants finished the season with an 11-5 record and returned to the playoffs. No longer lethargic and listless, Reeves had the Giants playing aggressive football for the first time since former head coach Bill Parcells had led them to the Super Bowl championship following the 1990 season.

What was the secret to Reeves' resuscitation of the Giants? The answer may have been provided even before the team reported to training camp. Reeves provided some needed discipline by saying that team rules applied to everyone, not just players whose names were not Lawrence Taylor.

Reeves sat down with "LT" and told him that he was still a valued member of the team, but that he needed him to take a leadership role and to follow team rules all the time — not just when he felt like it.

Did "LT" balk? Did he scream that he wasn't being respected? Nothing of the sort. Taylor embraced Reeves and provided the decisive leadership that had been lacking. Reeves also took a decisive step in naming Phil Simms as his starting quarterback over Jeff Hostetler, who left to take the No. 1 job with the Raiders. In training camp, Reeves released former Pro Bowl LB Pepper Johnson, who had questioned many of Reeves' decisions and was a divisive influence on the team.

Between Taylor, Reeves, Simms and RB Rodney Hampton, the Giants returned to prominence. They got out of the gate with a 5-1 mark, then stumbled after losses to the Jets and Cowboys. As the doubters were starting to surface, Reeves stuck to his combination of a strong running game and a powerful defense, which led to six straight wins and a position to control its own destiny.

The Giants were 11-4 and tied with the Cowboys going into their season finale at Giants Stadium. The Giants fell behind early but managed to send the game into overtime with a second-half rally. However, NFL MVP Emmitt Smith took over in the extra period, and the Giants were beaten by Eddie Murray's field goal.

That loss basically doomed the Giants' postseason hopes. While they won their wild-card game with the Vikings the following week, they had little left for their next matchup with the 49ers and were blown out of Candlestick Park 44-3. Reeves believed the last-second loss to the Cowboys and the hard-fought win over the Vikings left his team emotionally drained.

"The last part of the season probably took its toll," said Reeves, who was voted the NFL's Coach of the Year. "It was extremely difficult. Playing the wild-card game, then having a short week of practice and traveling cross country certainly didn't help."

Despite the season-ending obliteration, the Giants exceeded all expectations for the year. Simms came off two years of sitting on the bench to complete 247-of-400 passes for 3,038 yards with 15 TD's and nine interceptions. Hampton gave the Giants a powerful rushing attack, running for 1,077 yards and five touchdowns despite undergoing arthroscopic surgery after a Week Five loss to the Bills.

Defensively, the Giants got a lift from a pair of free-agent newcomers. ILB's Michael Brooks and Carlton Bailey played extremely well and were defensive mainstays. Bailey led the team with 136 tackles while DE Keith Hamilton led them in sacks with 11.5. CB Mark Collins had a team-leading four interceptions.

"We started at the bottom and continued to build all season," said Bailey. "We can keep our heads up. We were 12-6, and that's something we can feel good about."

1993 ROUNDUP

OFFENSIVE MVP: QB Phil Simms had a 61.8 completion percentage — the best of his career — and went to the Pro Bowl.

DEFENSIVE MVP: CB Mark Collins snagged four interceptions, led the team in passes defensed with 18 and had 71 tackles.

RESULTS

Pointspread Shown Refers To N.Y. Giants

Date	Opponent	Spread	Score
Sept. 5	At Chicago	(+1)	26-20
Sept. 12	Tampa Bay	(-10)	23-7
Sept. 19	L.A. Rams	(-6.5)	20-10
Oct. 3	At Buffalo	(+5.5)	14-17
Oct. 10	At Washington	(+3.5)	41-7
Oct. 17	Philadelphia	(-7.5)	21-10
Oct. 31	New York Jets	(-6)	6-10
Nov. 7	At Dallas	(+10.5)	9-31
Nov. 14	Washington	(-8)	20-6
Nov. 21	At Philadelphia	(-5)	7-3
Nov. 28	Phoenix	(-6.5)	19-17
Dec. 5	At Miami	(+3.5)	19-14
Dec. 12	Indianapolis	(-12)	20-6
Dec. 20	At New Orleans	(+2)	24-14
Dec. 26	At Phoenix	(-3)	6-17
Jan. 2	Dallas	(+6.5)	13-16*
POSTSEASON			
Jan. 9	Minnesota	(-7)	17-10
Jan. 15	At San Francisco	(+8.5)	3-44

* Overtime

1993 REVIEW ■ N.Y. GIANTS

GAME-BY-GAME STATISTICS

TEAM STATISTICS

OPPONENT	WK 1 CHI.	WK 2 T.B.	WK 3 L.A.RM	WK 5 BUFF.	WK 6 WASH.	WK 7 PHIL.	WK 9 N.Y.J.	WK 10 DALL.	WK 11 WASH.	WK 12 PHIL.	WK 13 PHX.	WK 14 MIA.	WK 15 IND.	WK 16 N.O.	WK 17 PHX.	WK 18 DALL.	TOTALS
Score	26-20	23-7	20-10	14-17	41-7	21-10	6-10	9-31	20-6	7-3	19-17	19-14	20-6	24-14	6-17	13-16	33-128-2
Total net yards	361	381	330	299	415	347	265	295	262	292	374	351	290	277	293	313	5145
Rushing yards	105	181	146	146	199	210	124	118	152	127	46	110	205	133	78	130	2210
Passing yards	256	200	184	153	216	137	141	177	110	165	328	241	85	144	215	183	2935
Rushing plays	28	41	47	43	47	31	32	28	38	33	17	29	43	42	26	35	560
Sacks allowed	4	1	5	2	1	1	1	5	3	2	1	3	0	4	3	4	40
Had intercepted	0	1	0	3	0	2	1	0	1	0	0	0	0	0	0	0	9
Fumbles lost	0	0	2	1	0	0	1	0	0	1	0	0	0	1	1	1	8
Yards penalized	45	25	28	49	15	19	34	20	50	40	65	58	49	25	25	49	596
Punts	4	3	5	6	2	5	2	5	5	7	5	6	5	4	6	6	78

OPPONENT STATISTICS

Time of possession	26:08	24:56	16:31	25:44	23:23	32:40	28:46	28:16	28:30	31:35	34:16	28:20	28:16	23:46	28:27	38:35	28:31
Total net yards	269	199	171	251	304	299	256	369	325	228	303	408	305	304	333	339	4663
Rushing yards	103	45	45	139	65	90	127	139	95	129	127	51	55	11	144	182	1547
Passing yards	166	154	126	112	239	209	129	230	230	99	176	357	250	293	189	157	3116
Rushing plays	26	19	12	35	12	25	37	32	25	29	32	20	15	12	28	36	395
Sacks allowed	4	3	1	5	3	3	0	2	1	4	3	3	2	2	1	4	41
Had intercepted	1	1	2	1	1	2	0	1	1	1	0	1	0	2	2	1	18
Fumbles lost	1	0	0	1	1	1	1	0	2	0	0	0	0	2	0	1	10
Yards penalized	88	11	36	51	60	58	37	66	25	35	40	81	64	99	47	22	820
Punts	5	6	8	7	2	5	3	3	4	8	6	3	5	6	4	5	80

INDIVIDUAL STATISTICS*

RUSHING

Bunch							3-10-0		5-31-0		1-0-0	2-5-0	3-13-1	7-29-0	1-1-0	1-1-1	33-128-2
Hampton	22-76-0	29-134-1	41-134-1	32-86-0	8-36-0	8-36-0	8-39-0	4-19-0	24-78-1	24-101-0	11-18-0	12-60-1	33-173-1	19-65-0	15-38-0	30-114-0	292-1077-5
Meggett	2-27-0	3-25-0	2-7-0	3-3-0	4-32-1	3-5-0		4-17-0	2-6-0	5-26-0	1-9-0	7-38-0		8-27-0	6-22-0	2-11-0	69-329-0
Rasheed				1-2-0	2-(2)-0			0-0-0					3-0-0	2-5-0			9-42-1
Simms	3-(2)-0	2-2-0	2-1-0	7-55-0	29-104-1	20-169-2	4-5-0	19-82-0	2-37-0	1-2-0	1-2-0	4-1-0	4-19-0	3-11-0	3-16-0	2-4-0	28-31-0
Tillman		4-9-0					17-70-0		7-37-0	2-5-0	3-17-0	4-6-0			1-1-0		120-585-3

PASSING**

Graham					0-1-0			6-15-0							2-6-0	8-22-0
					0-0			59-0							20-0	79-0
Simms	24-34-0	12-26-1	21-27-0	12-28-3	14-17-0	11-22-2	20-30-1	12-21-0	8-15-1	13-22-1	22-41-0	17-24-0	9-15-0	15-23-0	21-30-0	16-25-0	247-400-9
	277-2	204-1	217-0	160-2	182-3	148-1	142-0	155-0	100-0	187-1	337-1	257-1	85-1	166-2	214-0	207-0	3038-15

RECEIVING

Bunch	4-22-1		1-11-0				2-11-0	1-8-0			1-13-0	1-11-0	2-13-0	1-9-0			13-98-1
Calloway	1-24-0		1-21-0	2-12-1	2-24-2	1-14-0	1-6-0	4-87-0	2-37-1	1-7-0	6-83-0	3-58-0	2-30-1	1-27-0	6-69-0	6-58-0	35-513-3
Cross	2-23-0	2-50-1	1-12-0		1-9-0					3-41-0		2-34-1		3-26-1		3-31-0	21-272-5
De. Brown		1-2-0	2-13-0	2-16-0				1-12-0						1-6-0			7-56-0
Hampton	3-13-0	2-12-0	3-40-0		4-33-0	1-15-0		3-28-0	1-3-0	2-63-0		1-3-0		1-13-0	1-14-0	3-47-0	18-210-0
M. Jackson	4-73-1	1-26-0	5-58-0	1-2-1	2-23-1	5-43-0	6-76-0	3-34-0	5-61-0	5-61-1	7-113-0	3-29-0	2-26-0	5-44-1	6-63-0		58-708-4
McCaffrey	2-21-0	2-45-0	1-23-0	2-18-0	2-16-0	4-18-0	5-3-0	3-28-0	1-20-0	2-18-0	1-20-1		2-13-0	1-19-0	2-29-0	1-9-0	27-335-2
Meggett	1-9-0	1-(3)-0	1-(3)-0	2-37-0	2-16-0	4-18-0	5-3-0	4-19-0		2-60-0	3-28-0	4-24-0	2-13-0	2-22-0	7-65-0	1-21-0	38-319-0
Pierce	1-5-0			2-33-0	2-27-0		1-3-0					3-98-0				2-41-0	12-212-0
Sherrard	6-87-0	4-69-0	7-65-0	2-37-0	4-124-2	1-51-0											24-433-2

* Doesn't include all players. ** Passing stats include completions, attempts, interceptions, gross yards gained and touchdowns.

359

REVIEW: NEW YORK JETS

Every season the NFL has a team reminiscent of the classic horror story "Dr. Jekyll and Mr. Hyde," the tale of the scientist with dual personalities. By day, he was a researcher looking for medical miracles, and, by night, he prowled the streets of London looking for victims.

More often than not, the NFL's version of Jekyll and Hyde can be found prattling around New Jersey's Giants Stadium in Jet uniforms.

This is a team that goes to Miami and whips the Dolphins 24-14. The Dan Marino-led Dolphins. This is a team that whips Giants Stadium's other tenants, the Giants. This is a team that battles the Bills to near-victories on two occasions.

Yet, this is also a team that self-destructs in consecutive weeks against the Eagles and Raiders, loses at home to Indianapolis and completely disappears in the season finale at Houston. A win in that game would have given the Jets a slot in the playoffs, yet they merely showed up and allowed the Oilers to kick their butts all over the field.

As a result of that disastrous closing act, GM Dick Steinberg decided to fire his head coach, Bruce Coslet. Throughout the season, Coslet had been criticized for his less-than-imaginative play-calling. Steinberg wanted him to hire an offensive coordinator who would have some input in that area. Coslet refused to give up any of his control, and he was sent packing at the end of the season in favor of enthusiastic Pete Carroll, who had served as the team's defensive coordinator.

QB Boomer Esiason hoped to right the team's offensive ship after being acquired from the Bengals in the offseason. However, his season mirrored his team's lack of consistency. In some wins, Esiason was razor-sharp, as the Jets moved the ball downfield with ease and a certain style. At other times, the Jets' offensive ineptitude was laughable. Esiason's passer rating was 97.1, and he was among the league leaders after nine weeks. By the end of the year, that figure slipped to 84.5.

"This was a season of lost opportunities," Esiason said. "The Houston loss was the last one, and we'll remember it. But our playoff chances were lost with the Indianapolis, Philadelphia and Raider games. Instead of being a potential wild-card team, we could have been division champs. But that was obviously not the case."

It's interesting to note that Esiason is not the only Jet whose season contained more than its share of highs and lows. Second-year TE Johnny Mitchell opened a lot of eyes when he scored three TD's against Philadelphia in Week Five. Yet he also went weeks without making a significant contribution. WR Rob Moore was the Jets' primary go-to receiver, and he caught 64 passes for 843 yards. However, while it looked like he was ready to join the league's elite receivers in certain weeks, he was often injured and unable to contribute. Moore also scored only one touchdown in 1993.

The Jets were still an improved team in 1993. Their 8-8 record was significantly better than the 4-12 mark they put on the board in 1992. However, when you add an Esiason, a Ronnie Lott and a legitimate workhorse running back in former Cardinal Johnny Johnson, much more than .500 should be expected.

The Jets missed opportunities all season, and LB Mo Lewis was angry about letting those chances slip away. "You look at the games we should have won, and that overrides everything, and it hurts quite a bit," Lewis said. "We should have taken care of our destiny. We had it in our hands, and we should have gone out and taken care of business. We should have helped ourselves, but we didn't do that all season."

The Jets got a big boost last season from Johnson. The powerful ex-Cardinal established himself as the team's No. 1 running back by gaining 821 yards on 198 carries and scoring three touchdowns. He got some help from former No. 1 draft pick RB Blair Thomas, who overall failed once again to justify his once-lofty status.

Also, the Jet defense improved significantly. After finishing 16th in total defense in '93, it ranked No. 8 last year. Carroll's charges also rank third over the last three years in takeaways. If he can find a way to translate some of that improvement to the offensive side of the ball and get a better overall effort, the Jets may finally leave their Jekyll-and-Hyde personality behind.

1993 ROUNDUP

OFFENSIVE MVP: RB Johnny Johnson picked up 1,462 all-purpose yards, 28.1 percent of the total Jet offense.

DEFENSIVE MVP: DE Jeff Lageman collected 8.5 sacks one year after undergoing reconstructive knee surgery.

RESULTS
Pointspread Shown Refers To N.Y. Jets

Date	Opponent	Spread	Score
Sept. 5	Denver	(+1.5)	20-26
Sept. 12	At Miami	(+9)	24-14
Sept. 26	New England	(-9.5)	45-7
Oct. 3	Philadelphia	(-1)	30-35
Oct. 10	At L.A. Raiders	(+2)	20-24
Oct. 24	Buffalo	(+2.5)	10-19
Oct. 31	At New York Giants	(+6)	10-6
Nov. 7	Miami	(+1.5)	27-10
Nov. 14	At Indianapolis	(-3.5)	31-17
Nov. 21	Cincinnati	(-16.5)	17-12
Nov. 28	At New England	(-4)	6-0
Dec. 5	Indianapolis	(-11)	6-9
Dec. 11	At Washington	(-3)	3-0
Dec. 18	Dallas	(+7)	7-28
Dec. 26	At Buffalo	(+7)	14-16
Jan. 2	At Houston	(+4)	0-24

1993 REVIEW ■ N.Y. JETS

GAME-BY-GAME STATISTICS

TEAM STATISTICS

OPPONENT	WK 1 DENV.	WK 2 MIA.	WK 4 N.E.	WK 5 PHIL.	WK 6 L.A.RD	WK 8 BUFF.	WK 9 N.Y.G.	WK 10 MIA.	WK 11 IND.	WK 12 CIN.	WK 13 N.E.	WK 14 IND.	WK 15 WASH.	WK 16 DALL.	WK 17 BUFF.	WK 18 HOU.	TOTALS
Score	20-26	24-14	45-7	30-35	20-24	10-19	10-6	27-10	31-17	17-12	6-0	6-9	3-0	7-28	14-16	0-24	
Total net yards	422	429	388	412	286	237	256	356	458	288	294	267	308	295	352	164	5212
Rushing yards	71	106	167	115	96	78	127	100	202	111	120	122	210	81	120	54	1880
Passing yards	351	323	221	297	190	159	129	256	256	177	174	145	98	214	232	110	3332
Rushing plays	19	38	41	30	29	21	37	36	38	39	35	39	50	27	25	17	521
Sacks allowed	3	0	0	0	3	3	0	0	0	2	1	0	1	1	0	6	21
Had intercepted	1	1	0	2	1	0	0	0	1	0	1	2	0	1	0	1	12
Fumbles lost	2	0	0	1	1	2	1	1	0	0	1	1	3	1	1	1	16
Yards penalized	45	73	48	20	25	39	37	15	22	50	35	35	35	24	35	17	555
Punts	2	4	4	5	5	3	3	4	4	5	6	6	6	6	3	7	73

| Time of possession | 33:09 | 21:52 | 23:23 | 29:58 | 27:27 | 37:16 | 31:14 | 23:07 | 23:09 | 24:17 | 26:08 | 24:55 | 19:00 | 30:14 | 29:50 | 38:48 | 27:25 |

OPPONENT STATISTICS

Total net yards	353	294	211	301	414	413	265	337	215	226	289	169	150	364	346	363	4710
Rushing yards	99	27	31	110	105	197	124	48	92	50	155	67	39	129	90	108	1471
Passing yards	254	267	180	191	309	216	141	289	123	176	134	102	111	235	256	255	3239
Rushing plays	32	14	13	31	30	45	32	18	19	14	34	28	15	30	36	29	420
Sacks allowed	2	4	3	1	0	1	1	1	3	4	0	0	3	3	0	6	32
Had intercepted	0	0	2	1	3	2	1	1	0	2	1	1	0	3	2	1	19
Fumbles lost	1	2	1	1	2	2	1	1	1	0	1	1	0	3	1	1	18
Yards penalized	19	19	15	62	94	58	34	35	47	50	5	39	10	37	45	97	666
Punts	3	4	6	5	3	1	2	4	6	5	4	8	6	3	2	4	66

INDIVIDUAL STATISTICS*

RUSHING

B. Baxter	6-14-0	11-27-0	9-19-2	9-29-0	5-15-0	6-18-1	19-71-1	19-57-0	15-58-1	14-47-1	13-50-0	20-70-0	15-49-0	9-17-1	2-7-0	2-11-0	174-559-7
B. Thomas	9-44-0	10-29-0	10-44-0	7-33-0	5-13-1						5-22-0	10-31-0	1-3-0	1-5-0		1-(-3)-0	59-221-1
Chaffey		2-9-0	3-8-0		1-2-0	2-4-0	3-15-0	4-16-0	2-3-0	3-1-0	4-6-0	2-1-0	1-3-0	3-17-0	5-19-0	2-4-0	5-17-0
Esiason	1-0-0	7-10-1		5-17-0	1-2-0	11-49-0	11-26-0	12-24-0	21-141-1	12-43-1	13-42-0	6-26-0	32-155-0	12-42-0	16-94-0	12-42-0	198-821-3
J. Johnson	3-13-0	8-31-0	10-27-1	9-36-0	16-56-0	2-7-0	3-10-0			9-52-0				2-0-0	2-0-0		34-157-1
Murrell			8-52-1		2-10-0												45-118-1

PASSING**

Esiason	29-40-1	22-33-1	17-21-0	19-33-2	21-40-0	14-25-2	12-17-0	23-32-0	21-31-1	17-26-0	15-30-0	12-29-2	12-22-0	21-37-1	22-31-0	11-26-1	288-473-11
	371-2	323-2	215-1	297-4	216-0	189-0	129-0	256-3	256-2	192-0	182-0	145-0	105-0	194-0	232-2	119-0	3421-16
Nagle			1-1-0											3-9-0	2-4-0		6-14-0
			6-0											40-0	25-0		71-0

RECEIVING

B. Baxter	1-4-0	3-15-0	1-10-0	2-10-0	2-2-0		1-14-0	1-18-0	1-5-0			3-16-0		5-60-0	2-17-0	1-3-0	20-158-0
B. Thomas	3-9-0								5-48-2			3-96-0	1-0-0		3-18-1		7-25-0
Burkett	2-33-0	1-9-0	4-66-0	4-103-0	1-2-0	3-25-0	3-35-0	3-30-1	1-13-0	1-11-0			3-21-0	3-25-0		1-9-0	40-531-4
Carpenter	1-16-0	1-3-1												2-29-0		2-25-0	6-83-0
F. Baxter										2-45-0							3-48-1
J. Johnson	6-52-0	2-7-0	2-20-0	4-27-0	6-60-0	1-23-0	7-69-0	7-85-0	4-35-0	6-99-0	5-30-0		1-2-0	4-24-0	8-81-1	4-27-0	67-641-1
Mathis	4-74-0	1-46-0	4-55-0	7-93-0	7-146-3	3-43-0	1-14-0	4-38-2	3-58-0		1-10-0			1-11-0	2-25-0	4-38-0	24-352-0
Mitchell	3-43-1	4-64-0	2-52-0	7-146-3	1-4-0	2-26-0	1-11-0	7-82-0	6-89-0	7-47-0	4-81-0	1-10-0	1-2-0	2-16-0	6-78-0	1-42-0	39-630-6
Moore	9-140-1	6-124-0	4-40-0	1-4-0	3-54-0	1-22-0			1-8-0	1-6-0	3-16-0	2-20-0	7-82-0	7-69-0	1-13-0		64-843-1
Thornton			2-21-1	1-7-1	1-8-0			1-7-0									12-108-2

* Doesn't include all players. ** Passing stats include completions, attempts, interceptions, gross yards gained and touchdowns.

PRO FOOTBALL WEEKLY 1994 ALMANAC

REVIEW: PHILADELPHIA EAGLES

In Philadelphia, the 1993 Eagle season could be labeled the year of the doughnut. No, the Eagle players didn't put on tremendous weight because of their collective love of long johns and eclairs, but their season did resembl your local cop's favorite food. They were great in the beginning and end, but there was nothing in the middle.

The Eagles got out of the gate like they were prepared to wrest the division championship away from the Cowboys. Even though their premier player, DE Reggie White, had bolted to the Packers via free-agency, the Eagles had an unblemished 4-0 record. However, in the fourth game, a 35-30 triumph over the Jets, the worst kind of disaster hit the franchise.

Late in the second quarter, QB Randall Cunningham went down and out for the season with a broken leg. Cunningham had been the NFL's Player of the Month in September, and, once he was injured, the Eagle offense did not even operate at half-power.

After their fourth win, the Eagles didn't taste victory again until late November when Bubby Brister would finally hit his stride. Without Cunningham, the Eagle offense was limp, a handicap that was impossible to overcome. Also, the defense fell on hard times. It had been the cornerstone of the franchise for years, but it fell to 27th against the run and let seven NFC East running backs surpass the 100-yard mark.

After losing eight of nine games, the Eagles closed the year with a three-game winning streak, including a 37-34 triumph over the 49ers at San Francisco in the season finale. The strong finish enabled the Eagles to finish with an 8-8 record, and it gave head coach Rich Kotite something to hang his hat on.

"Our record is something very much to be proud of, after all the injuries," Kotite said. "We had the toughest schedule in the league, were in almost every game and we won four of our final six games.

"We came close so many times. We should have beaten Miami. We had a great chance to beat Buffalo, and we were in the games against Dallas. I think that is a valid measuring rod of how tough we played. But we still didn't make the playoffs, and that was our overall goal."

While Kotite was proud of his team's overall achievement, C David Alexander was more perplexed by what the team had done.

"It was like three different seasons," Alexander said. "There was the first when we were 4-0, then the second when we couldn't win a game and the third season, when we started getting some of our injured people back, and then we played pretty well."

The injuries Kotite and Alexander talked about were to stars (Cunningham and WR Fred Barnett), veterans (LB Byron Evans, OT Eric Floyd, OL Rob Selby and KR Jeff Sydner) and older players (Tim Harris and Keith Millard). The Eagles were the oldest team in the league, and it wasn't really surprising they were felled by what they considered more than their share of injuries.

There were some highlights during the '93 season. CB Eric Allen made six interceptions and returned an NFL-record four for touchdowns, including a remarkable 94-yarder against the Jets. The play came late in the game with the Jets threatening to put away the contest, and it featured several exhilarating moves by Allen that allowed him to break away from tacklers. Steve Sabol, president of NFL Films, said the play was the greatest interception return in NFL history. Other highlights included Herschel Walker picking up 1,356 total yards from scrimmage, the most by an Eagle since Mike Quick in 1983. James Lofton, a mid-year replacement for the injured Barnett, became the first NFL receiver to eclipse the 14,000-yard mark in receptions.

Brister set team records for fewest interceptions in a season and the best TD-interception ratio. He was the NFC's fourth-ranked passer, and he threw 14 touchdowns compared to just five interceptions.

Despite the team's overachievement, its mood at the end of the season was anything but optimistic. OLB Seth Joyner and DE Clyde Simmons were both free agents. This, just a year after White left the team.

1993 ROUNDUP

OFFENSIVE MVP: C Dave Alexander was one of only two Philadelphia offensive linemen to start all 16 games.

DEFENSIVE MVP: CB Eric Allen had six interceptions and tied an NFL record by returning four for touchdowns.

RESULTS
Pointspread Shown Refers To Philadelphia

Date	Opponent	Spread	Score
Sept. 5	Phoenix	(-6.5)	23-17
Sept. 12	At Green Bay	(+3.5)	20-17
Sept. 19	Washington	(-6.5)	34-31
Oct. 3	At New York Jets	(+1)	35-30
Oct. 10	Chicago	(-7)	6-17
Oct. 17	At New York Giants	(+7.5)	10-21
Oct. 31	Dallas	(+10)	10-23
Nov. 7	At Phoenix	(+2.5)	3-16
Nov. 14	Miami	(+4.5)	14-19
Nov. 21	New York Giants	(+5)	3-7
Nov. 28	At Washington	(+3)	17-14
Dec. 6	At Dallas	(+16.5)	17-23
Dec. 12	Buffalo	(+3.5)	7-10
Dec. 19	At Indianapolis	(-1.5)	20-10
Dec. 26	New Orleans	(-3)	37-26
Jan. 3	At San Francisco	(+12.5)	37-34*

* Overtime

362

1993 REVIEW ■ PHILADELPHIA

GAME-BY-GAME STATISTICS

TEAM STATISTICS

OPPONENT	WK 1 PHX.	WK 2 G.B.	WK 3 WASH.	WK 5 N.Y.J.	WK 6 CHI.	WK 7 N.Y.G.	WK 9 DALL.	WK 10 PHX.	WK 11 MIA.	WK 12 N.Y.G.	WK 13 WASH.	WK 14 DALL.	WK 15 BUFF.	WK 16 IND.	WK 17 N.O.	WK 18 S.F.	TOTALS
Score	23-17	20-17	34-31	35-30	6-17	10-21	10-23	3-16	14-19	3-7	17-14	17-23	7-10	20-10	37-26	37-34	
Total net yards	359	352	440	301	276	299	228	201	260	228	268	307	368	340	314	381	4922
Rushing yards	167	161	95	110	110	90	139	65	103	129	104	59	70	151	134	74	1761
Passing yards	192	191	345	191	166	209	89	136	157	99	164	248	298	189	180	307	3161
Rushing plays	38	39	22	31	23	25	30	17	27	29	29	18	23	39	44	23	457
Sacks allowed	0	3	4	1	7	3	2	1	4	4	1	0	1	3	2	3	42
Had intercepted	1	1	2	1	2	2	0	1	0	1	0	0	0	1	0	1	13
Fumbles lost	2	3	2	1	2	2	1	0	3	0	0	0	4	0	1	0	21
Yards penalized	75	19	76	62	50	58	57	60	28	35	10	30	62	45	20	83	770
Punts	5	1	5	1	6	5	5	4	7	8	6	6	5	6	5	4	83
Time of possession	25:22	21:39	29:58	30:02	32:45	27:20	32:46	38:59	30:03	28:25	29:48	30:08	29:01	22:05	20:03	42:25	29:26

OPPONENT STATISTICS

Total net yards	231	159	377	412	261	347	356	359	298	292	349	347	335	261	158	477	5019
Rushing yards	48	52	167	115	102	210	271	243	120	127	97	182	101	31	83	131	2080
Passing yards	183	107	210	297	159	137	85	116	178	165	252	165	234	230	75	346	2939
Rushing plays	19	20	31	30	41	31	39	46	38	33	21	29	29	12	21	27	467
Sacks allowed	1	1	2	0	1	1	2	0	1	2	5	4	3	4	3	5	36
Had intercepted	1	2	2	2	1	2	0	0	1	1	3	0	2	0	2	1	20
Fumbles lost	1	0	0	0	1	0	0	1	1	1	0	1	2	3	1	2	15
Yards penalized	35	25	35	20	20	19	41	20	35	40	69	53	40	34	33	91	610
Punts	7	4	6	5	7	5	3	2	7	7	4	4	3	6	3	2	75

INDIVIDUAL STATISTICS*

RUSHING

Cunningham	10-49-1	3-12-0	5-49-0	8-18-1	2-6-0	4-16-0						3-(-)-0	5-5-0		2-3-0		18-110-1
Hebron	10-66-1	9-32-0	7-19-0	1-9-0	1-1-0	3-9-0			12-61-0		11-41-1			8-24-0	13-46-0	13-51-0	84-297-3
Joseph	12-29-1	17-71-0	6-12-0	12-35-0		3-6-0	14-71-0	7-26-0	3-7-0	5-12-0		7-26-0	9-37-0	11-45-1	9-29-0		39-140-0
Sherman					15-89-0	15-58-0	15-65-0	8-39-0	12-35-0	14-80-0	9-45-0	8-34-0	9-28-0	18-79-0	16-56-0	9-25-0	115-406-2
Walker	6-23-0	10-46-0	4-15-0	6-29-1													174-746-1

PASSING**

Brister				11-16-0 120-2	18-33-2 209-1	2-3-0 15-0				9-20-0 94-0	19-31-0 170-1	27-45-1 248-2	28-48-0 299-1	21-39-1 217-1	20-30-0 195-3	26-43-1 350-3	181-308-5 1917-14
Cunningham	18-29-1 192-0	23-29-1 209-2	25-39-2 360-3	10-13-1 89-0			11-24-0 107-1										76-110-5 850-5
O'Brien						19-32-1 210-1		14-32-1 166-0	23-37-0 189-2	4-12-1 36-0							71-137-3 708-4

RECEIVING

Bailey	1-13-0	3-56-1	2-22-0	5-36-0	4-94-0	4-63-0	1-16-0	1-20-0		3-54-0	1-9-0	6-48-0	7-95-0	1-8-0	1-5-0	1-6-0	41-545-1
Barnett	7-76-0	3-25-0	4-26-0	3-43-0	3-18-0	5-69-1		4-48-0	2-19-0	1-22-0	1-6-0	7-53-2	1-19-0	2-16-0	2-18-1	2-25-0	17-170-0
Bavaro	3-40-0	5-56-1	1-12-0	4-60-1	1-17-0	1-9-0		1-9-0	1-11-0		1-2-1	2-18-0		1-12-0	3-14-0		43-481-6
Johnson	1-6-0	2-27-0	2-12-0	2-8-0		6-43-0		1-20-0	2-18-0				2-7-0	4-40-0	3-24-0	6-109-0	10-81-0
Lofton							4-57-0	2-35-0	2-18-0	5-20-0	10-103-0	1-5-0	11-109-0			1-32-0	29-291-1
Walker	3-15-0	3-11-0	5-87-0	1-5-0	4-22-0	2-15-0	3-14-1	3-24-0	7-44-0		4-32-0	5-63-0	3-40-1	6-29-0	4-32-1	7-75-1	13-167-0
Williams	2-11-0	2-12-0	8-181-3	2-16-1	4-44-1	3-26-0	1-8-0	2-9-0	8-72-2	2-22-0	1-11-0	4-44-0	1-4-0	6-105-1	3-21-0	5-63-1	75-610-3
Young					1-9-0										3-78-1	4-40-1	60-725-10 14-186-2

* Doesn't include all players. ** Passing stats include completions, attempts, interceptions, gross yards gained and touchdowns.

PHOENIX CARDINALS
REVIEW

The onus was on Joe Bugel from the start of training camp. He had gotten word from owner Bill Bidwill that if he wanted to remain the coach of the Cardinals in 1994, his team better win at least nine games. The critics were outraged that Bidwill would have the nerve to deliver such a public ultimatum, and toward the end of the season it looked like Bidwill might relent from his position because the Cardinals were beset by injuries throughout the season. But just when it looked like Bugel and his staff would escape, Bidwill fired the coach and decided to start over with that old owner-loving coach, Buddy Ryan.

Even though Bidwill parted company with his coach, the Cardinals were a much-improved team in 1993 — better than in any of their five previous seasons in Phoenix.

The Cardinals were 5-3 over the second half of the season. Only the 49ers and Cowboys rated ahead of them offensively, and those were the only two NFC teams to outscore Phoenix.

Defensively, the Cardinals gave up yards, but not a lot of points. Phoenix ranked 21st in yards allowed, but it had the conference's fourth-best scoring defense. It also held six opponents to 10 points or less, its best showing since 1936.

Offensively, the Cardinals had strength everywhere, including the backfield, where rookie RB Garrison Hearst was expected to become an impact player. The former Georgia star was lost with a knee injury in the second half of the season, but that didn't stop another rookie from shining. Unknown Ron Moore, a fourth-round draft pick from Pittsburg (Kan.) State, gave the Cardinals the punch in their ground game they were hoping to get from Hearst. Moore gained 1,018 yards on 263 carries and scored nine times.

"Was I surprised by what I did this year? No, not really," Moore said. "I believed in my ability all along. It was just a matter of getting the chance to play. It turned out pretty well. I really don't like to talk about what I do. I just like to go out and do it."

Since Moore was at camp all summer while Hearst was in the midst of a contract dispute, many of his teammates became big supporters of the relatively unheralded rookie.

"You can't help but appreciate a kid who comes in and keeps his mouth shut and goes out on the field and gives 110 percent," said standout OLT Luis Sharpe. "I mean, those are the type of football players that you hope you can build your team around. Very unselfish, very quiet, very good at what he does."

QB Steve Beuerlein, the Cardinals' top pickup in free-agency, did exactly what the Cardinals were hoping when they signed him. Beuerlein gave the Cardinals some consistency from the quarterback slot, and he took advantage of the top weapons they had in WR's Ricky Proehl, Randal Hill and Gary Clark. Beuerlein, despite missing time with injuries, completed 258-of-418 passes for 3,164 yards and 18 touchdowns along with 17 interceptions.

Beuerlein's numbers might have been even better if Clark, the former Redskin standout who came to the Cardinals through free-agency, wasn't plagued by nagging injuries throughout much of the season. Even with the injury difficulties, Clark managed to catch 63 passes during the season. If Clark can regain his health, the Cardinals appear to have a great chance at putting even more points on the board in 1994.

In addition to the Hearst, Beuerlein and Clark injuries, star DT Eric Swann went down with a torn knee ligament midway through the season. Swann was on his way to a potential Pro Bowl season when he got hurt, as many opposing offensive linemen described him as "unblockable" early in the year.

In the end, a gallant 7-9 finish was not enough to save Bugel. The game that hurt him the most was a Week 13, 19-17 loss to the Giants at Giants Stadium. In that contest, the Cardinals played aggressively and kept mistakes to a minimum. They took a 17-16 lead deep into the fourth quarter, but were done in by a last-minute Brad Daluiso 58-yard field goal into the wind. That game cost the Cardinals a .500 season — and probably cost their coach his job.

1993 ROUNDUP

OFFENSIVE MVP: RB Ron Moore took over as the team's top rusher, picking up 1,018 yards and nine touchdowns as a rookie.

DEFENSIVE MVP: LB Eric Hill came back from an early-season suspension to have the best season of his career and emerge as one of the best inside linebackers in the NFL.

RESULTS
Pointspread Shown Refers To Phoenix

Date	Opponent	Spread	Score
Sept. 5	At Philadelphia	(+6.5)	17-23
Sept. 12	At Washington	(+10)	17-10
Sept. 19	Dallas	(+6.5)	10-17
Sept. 26	At Detroit	(+5)	20-26
Oct. 10	New England	(-10)	21-23
Oct. 17	Washington	(+1.5)	36-6
Oct. 24	At San Francisco	(+10.5)	14-28
Oct. 31	New Orleans	(+3)	17-20
Nov. 7	Philadelphia	(-2.5)	16-3
Nov. 14	At Dallas	(+13)	15-20
Nov. 28	At New York Giants	(+6.5)	17-19
Dec. 5	L.A. Rams	(-7)	38-10
Dec. 12	Detroit	(-7.5)	14-21
Dec. 19	At Seattle	(+2.5)	30-27*
Dec. 26	New York Giants	(+3)	17-6
Jan. 2	At Atlanta	(+1.5)	27-10

* Overtime

1993 REVIEW ■ PHOENIX

GAME-BY-GAME STATISTICS

TEAM STATISTICS

OPPONENT	WK 1 PHIL.	WK 2 WASH.	WK 3 DALL.	WK 4 DET.	WK 6 N.E.	WK 7 WASH.	WK 8 S.F.	WK 9 N.O.	WK 10 PHIL.	WK 11 DALL.	WK 13 N.Y.G.	WK 14 L.A.RM	WK 15 DET.	WK 16 SEA.	WK 17 N.Y.G.	WK 18 ATL.	TOTALS
Score	17-23	17-10	10-17	20-26	21-23	36-6	14-28	17-20	16-3	15-20	17-19	38-10	14-21	30-27	17-6	27-10	
Total net yards	231	303	273	343	311	380	429	143	359	265	303	382	287	476	333	395	5213
Rushing yards	48	152	68	79	124	156	107	89	243	51	127	137	96	71	144	117	1809
Passing yards	183	151	205	264	187	224	322	54	116	214	176	245	191	405	189	278	3404
Rushing plays	19	39	19	25	18	34	24	25	46	20	32	35	25	29	28	34	452
Sacks allowed	1	1	2	4	2	3	1	6	1	1	1	0	4	3	1	0	33
Had intercepted	1	2	1	0	2	1	3	1	0	1	1	0	3	2	2	0	20
Fumbles lost	1	0	0	3	1	0	0	1	1	2	0	0	0	0	1	0	11
Yards penalized	35	20	15	30	63	15	40	60	20	40	40	10	33	53	47	123	644
Punts	7	3	4	5	7	4	4	2	2	7	6	2	5	2	4	4	73

OPPONENT STATISTICS

	WK 1	WK 2	WK 3	WK 4	WK 6	WK 7	WK 8	WK 9	WK 10	WK 11	WK 13	WK 14	WK 15	WK 16	WK 17	WK 18	TOTALS
Time of possession	34:38	24:06	33:33	27:23	36:28	26:48	31:05	30:12	21:01	31:09	25:44	26:51	24:05	27:52	31:33	20:16	28:25
Total net yards	359	233	410	330	432	246	428	272	201	311	374	303	340	365	293	270	5167
Rushing yards	167	58	130	147	151	138	144	96	65	87	46	152	105	212	78	81	1857
Passing yards	192	175	280	183	281	108	284	176	136	224	328	151	235	153	215	189	3310
Rushing plays	38	17	33	26	41	26	31	32	17	34	17	26	23	36	26	13	436
Sacks allowed	0	3	1	5	2	5	2	2	4	2	0	1	1	4	3	1	34
Had intercepted	1	1	0	0	0	1	0	1	1	0	0	1	1	0	0	2	9
Fumbles lost	2	1	0	0	0	3	1	1	0	2	0	1	2	1	1	2	17
Yards penalized	75	25	59	30	64	29	66	42	60	42	65	10	40	20	25	78	730
Punts	5	5	3	4	7	5	4	4	4	5	5	4	6	5	6	3	78

INDIVIDUAL STATISTICS*

RUSHING

	WK 1	WK 2	WK 3	WK 4	WK 6	WK 7	WK 8	WK 9	WK 10	WK 11	WK 13	WK 14	WK 15	WK 16	WK 17	WK 18	TOTALS
Bailey	2-6-0	4-19-0	7-34-0	1-2-0	7-40-0	4-45-1	6-31-0	3-15-0		8-31-0	3-22-0	2-(-2)-0	1-(-1)-0	2-7-0	2-1-0		49-253-1
Beuerlein		5-10-0	1-(-1)-0	3-13-0	1-3-0	3-1-(-1)-0	2-23-0			1-0-0		1-2-0	3-19-1	1-(-1)-0	2-2-0		22-45-0
Blount								1-1-0	1-7-0	2-3-0		2-12-0		1-6-0	1-6-0	1-13-0	5-28-1
Centers	7-3-0	22-76-0	9-31-0	15-45-0	10-81-0	13-28-1	15-47-0	6-59-0	20-72-0	36-160-0	11-52-0	29-126-4	20-61-1	24-62-0	23-135-2	32-96-0	25-152-0 76-264-1 263-1018-9
Hearst	9-39-0	8-47-1	2-4-0	6-19-0	1-3-0	13-80-1	1-6-0	20-72-0	36-160-0	9-17-0	17-53-0	1-(-1)-0	1-17-0	1-(-3)-0	1-8-0	8-47-0	
Moore						1-4-0	1-6-0		2-16-0								
Proehl																	

PASSING**

	WK 1	WK 2	WK 3	WK 4	WK 6	WK 7	WK 8	WK 9	WK 10	WK 11	WK 13	WK 14	WK 15	WK 16	WK 17	WK 18	TOTALS
Beuerlein	7-19-1	17-26-2	20-27-1	23-31-0	14-28-2	12-25-1	26-50-3	7-9-0			19-33-1	14-25-0	23-35-3	34-53-2	15-24-2	27-33-0	258-418-18
	93-0	164-0	218-1	288-2	196-3	250-1	334-2	52-0			193-2	250-1	219-0	431-3	198-0	278-3	3164-18
Chandler	8-20-0							7-17-1	10-20-0	27-46-1							52-103-2
	96-1							40-0	121-1	214-1							471-3

RECEIVING

	WK 1	WK 2	WK 3	WK 4	WK 6	WK 7	WK 8	WK 9	WK 10	WK 11	WK 13	WK 14	WK 15	WK 16	WK 17	WK 18	TOTALS
Bailey	2-35-0		2-8-0	1-9-0	1-7-0	1-12-0	4-50-0	4-6-0		6-34-0	2-16-0	2-11-0	3-22-0	6-53-0	2-10-0	1-3-0	32-243-0
Blount		3-1-0	2-14-0	3-38-0	2-13-0		6-43-0	2-21-0		7-59-1	4-25-0		9-77-0	6-61-1	5-84-0	2-14-0	5-36-0 66-603-3
Clark	3-49-1	6-93-0	4-43-0		2-20-0	3-1-(-1)-0		3-24-1	3-24-1	2-16-0	3-52-0	8-159-1	4-26-0	12-152-1	4-51-0	8-61-0 9-121-1	62-816-4
Edwards	5-59-0			2-39-0	1-55-0	2-67-0		1-21-0		2-20-0				1-12-0			13-326-1
Proehl	2-16-0	4-23-0	4-40-1	6-99-1	2-21-2	5-115-1	4-112-1	1-21-0	4-46-0	6-66-0	6-81-1	4-80-0	2-54-0	6-78-0	1-16-0	4-59-0	65-877-7
R. Hill	2-25-0	1-22-0	4-78-0	8-90-0	3-65-1	2-40-0	8-76-1	3-24-0	2-29-0	2-15-0	1-6-0		2-22-0	2-69-1	1-12-0	1-16-0 1-12-0	36-521-4
Reeves				2-8-1		2-16-0	4-53-0	2-8-0			1-7-0		1-5-0	1-6-0	2-25-0	4-59-0 4-59-0	9-67-1
Rolle			1-6-0		1-11-0			2-12-0	1-22-0	2-4-0	1-1-1		1-7-0			1-4-0	10-67-1

*Doesn't include all players. ** Passing stats include completions, attempts, interceptions, gross yards gained and touchdowns.

PRO FOOTBALL WEEKLY 1994 ALMANAC

REVIEW: PITTSBURGH STEELERS

In their second year under head coach Bill Cowher, the Steelers again made the playoffs. And there were times — like an eye-popping, Monday-night performance in a 23-0 slaughter of eventual Super Bowl participant Buffalo Nov. 15 — when Pittsburgh looked like the AFC's cream of the crop.

In the end, though, the cream got sour, mostly due to special-team breakdowns that resulted in the team's two most devastating defeats.

In the first one, the Steeler special teams failed miserably against Cleveland's Eric Metcalf, whose 91- and 75-yard punt-return touchdowns nailed the coffin in a 28-23 loss at Cleveland in late October.

In the second season-killer, a blocked punt set up the Chiefs' tying touchdown with 1:43 remaining in Kansas City's 27-24, overtime victory in the first round of the AFC playoffs.

The Steeler special teams allowed a league-high four TD's — three on punt returns and one on a kickoff return — and were ranked last in punt coverage. It came as no surprise when the Steelers fired special-team coach John Guy a few days after the playoff loss and quickly replaced him with Bobby April, Atlanta's special-team coach the previous three seasons.

But there were other factors besides faulty special teams which contributed to a 9-7 campaign that barely became a .500 season, counting the playoff loss. The biggest one was RB Barry Foster's season-ending ankle injury in the same game vs. Buffalo in which the Steelers put on a Super Bowl-caliber performance before a national TV audience.

Foster, who received a new contract early in the year along with star CB Rod Woodson, was coming off a team-record 1,690-yard season and was on a 1,300-yard pace when he went down for the count.

With Foster out of the lineup, the Steelers scored only eight touchdowns in the final seven regular-season games. Leroy Thompson was an adequate-enough replacement, finishing with a team-high 763 rushing yards, but the Steelers missed Foster's big-play ability, especially since the team's receivers were arguably the worst in the league.

Except for TE Eric Green (63 receptions for 942 yards and five TD's), Pittsburgh's pass catchers were particularly brutal the second half of the season, when they dropped pass after pass and ultimately cost WR coach Bob Harrison his job. Receivers dropped an average of five passes per game, and Jeff Graham, the leading pass catcher among wide receivers, didn't catch a TD pass all season.

The Steelers also had their share of attitude problems. Even though they showed spunk winning four in a row after a disappointing 0-2 start and registered their peak performance vs. Buffalo with a lopsided 400-157 advantage in yardage gained, there were a lot of unhappy players on the roster.

Included among them were TE Adrian Cooper, who claimed to be distracted all season by the lack of a 1994 contract; DE Donald Evans, who suggested management hurt the team down the stretch by not signing more veterans to new contracts, even after Foster and Woodson inked new deals; and Green, who, despite having his best season, spent much of it speculating that he'd be playing elsewhere in '94.

But there were still a lot of positive developments for the Steelers, most notably the continued development of QB Neil O'Donnell, who fought through season-long tendinitis in his throwing elbow to break Terry Bradshaw's single-season team records for attempts and completions, and a third-ranked defense led by Woodson and Pro Bowl LB Greg Lloyd that displayed flashes of Steel Curtain-like brilliance during a midseason stretch of six wins in seven games.

O'Donnell threw for 3,208 yards and 14 TD's despite his weak WR corps, and he threw for 286 yards and three TD's in the playoff loss. "I think he's a young guy on the rise," said offensive coordinator Ron Erhardt.

"We're going to take these last two experiences we've felt in January to get back," said Cowher.

"We're close, but we're not there yet."

1993 ROUNDUP

OFFENSIVE MVP: QB Neil O'Donnell threw for 3,208 yards and played in all 16 games.
DEFENSIVE MVP: CB Rod Woodson, who had eight interceptions for 138 yards, is considered by some the best defender in the league.

RESULTS
Pointspread Shown Refers To Pittsburgh

Date	Opponent	Spread	Score
Sept. 5	San Francisco	(+6.5)	13-24
Sept. 12	At L.A. Rams	(-3.5)	0-27
Sept. 19	Cincinnati	(-9)	34-7
Sept. 27	At Atlanta	(+3)	45-17
Oct. 10	San Diego	(-6)	16-3
Oct. 17	New Orleans	(+2.5)	37-14
Oct. 24	At Cleveland	(-2.5)	23-28
Nov. 7	At Cincinnati	(-9.5)	24-16
Nov. 15	Buffalo	(-3.5)	23-0
Nov. 21	At Denver	(+3)	13-37
Nov. 28	At Houston	(+3)	3-23
Dec. 5	New England	(-12)	17-14
Dec. 13	At Miami	(+3.5)	21-20
Dec. 19	Houston	(-4)	17-26
Dec. 26	At Seattle	(-3)	6-16
Jan. 2	Cleveland	(-5.5)	16-9
POSTSEASON			
Jan. 8	At Kansas City	(+7.5)	24-27*

*Overtime

1993 REVIEW ■ PITTSBURGH

GAME-BY-GAME STATISTICS

TEAM STATISTICS

OPPONENT	WK 1 S.F.	WK 2 L.A.RM	WK 3 CIN.	WK 4 ATL.	WK 6 S.D.	WK 7 N.O.	WK 8 CLEV.	WK 10 CIN.	WK 11 BUFF.	WK 12 DENV.	WK 13 HOU.	WK 14 N.E.	WK 15 MIA.	WK 16 HOU.	WK 17 SEA.	WK 18 CLEV.	TOTALS
Score	13-24	0-27	34-7	45-17	16-3	37-14	23-28	24-16	23-0	13-37	3-23	17-14	21-20	17-26	6-16	16-9	
Total net yards	211	175	404	368	304	393	440	390	400	356	234	217	265	385	380	320	5242
Rushing yards	102	55	223	109	148	201	92	146	227	101	65	125	120	38	116	135	2003
Passing yards	109	120	181	259	156	192	348	244	173	255	169	92	145	347	264	185	3239
Rushing plays	24	19	36	34	36	47	33	33	50	23	17	32	38	18	20	32	492
Sacks allowed	5	5	1	0	0	2	1	1	0	4	2	3	0	6	2	7	47
Had intercepted	2	1	0	0	0	0	1	1	0	1	2	0	0	2	1	0	12
Fumbles lost	1	2	1	1	0	2	1	1	0	2	2	0	0	1	1	0	15
Yards penalized	56	38	57	88	70	9	25	45	55	63	88	72	56	32	72	30	856
Punts	5	6	2	4	6	6	3	6	4	3	6	11	7	7	5	8	89

OPPONENT STATISTICS

	WK 1	WK 2	WK 3	WK 4	WK 6	WK 7	WK 8	WK 10	WK 11	WK 12	WK 13	WK 14	WK 15	WK 16	WK 17	WK 18	TOTALS
Time of possession	32:52	34:58	24:15	26:22	24:38	22:45	23:31	29:52	15:09	32:11	32:10	25:58	27:13	30:50	35:42	25:28	27:33
Total net yards	326	314	170	220	138	264	245	191	157	364	391	349	348	383	368	295	4523
Rushing yards	86	99	44	44	19	49	98	103	47	107	125	53	49	117	267	61	1368
Passing yards	240	215	126	176	119	215	147	88	110	257	266	296	299	266	101	234	3155
Rushing plays	32	32	19	17	20	17	22	29	14	34	30	24	17	25	45	20	397
Sacks allowed	1	1	2	3	1	5	4	4	3	2	0	0	5	1	5	3	43
Had intercepted	3	2	1	4	1	3	0	1	0	0	1	5	2	0	1	0	24
Fumbles lost	0	0	0	2	2	1	1	0	0	2	0	1	1	2	0	2	14
Yards penalized	55	25	70	50	15	25	59	40	32	22	134	25	3	62	20	10	647
Punts	3	4	6	3	7	9	5	7	8	3	5	5	3	4	4	6	82

INDIVIDUAL STATISTICS*

RUSHING

	WK 1	WK 2	WK 3	WK 4	WK 6	WK 7	WK 8	WK 10	WK 11	WK 12	WK 13	WK 14	WK 15	WK 16	WK 17	WK 18	TOTALS
Foster	17-80-1	15-50-0	23-103-0	20-65-3	23-110-0	21-75-1	28-87-2	25-120-1	5-23-0	3-17-0	1-7-0	10-43-0	6-21-0	2-5-1	4-17-0	4-48-0	177-713-8
Hoge	1-0-0	2-5-0			4-14-0	3-7-0	2-5-0	6-8-0	10-64-0	3-17-0	1-27-0		3-6-0	1-1-0	4-33-0	1-(-1)-0	52-253-1
O'Donnell	1-9-0	2-0-0		2-6-0	1-2-0	1-4-0	1-11-0	2-17-0	2-8-0	2-7-0		1-5-0	1-12-0	1-11-0		1-(-3)-0	25-109-0
Stone	2-14-0		2-65-1	2-10-0													12-121-1
Thompson	1-2-0		8-41-0	7-24-0	8-22-0	16-101-0		2-18-0	30-108-1	17-77-0	15-31-0	22-82-0	28-81-2	13-19-0	12-66-0	26-91-0	205-763-3

PASSING**

	WK 1	WK 2	WK 3	WK 4	WK 6	WK 7	WK 8	WK 10	WK 11	WK 12	WK 13	WK 14	WK 15	WK 16	WK 17	WK 18	TOTALS
O'Donnell	9-16-0	17-33-1	21-25-0	19-25-0	16-25-0	12-25-1	25-39-1	14-34-1	16-27-0	18-32-1	13-26-0	17-32-0	16-28-0	15-37-1	20-43-1	22-39-0	270-486-7
	92-0	169-0	189-3	259-2	156-0	137-1	355-0	244-2	212-1	197-0	153-0	115-2	163-1	256-1	285-0	226-1	3208-14
Tomczak	4-11-2					3-4-0				5-6-0	8-13-2		9-20-1				29-54-5
	46-0					66-1				81-1	61-0		144-0				398-2

RECEIVING

	WK 1	WK 2	WK 3	WK 4	WK 6	WK 7	WK 8	WK 10	WK 11	WK 12	WK 13	WK 14	WK 15	WK 16	WK 17	WK 18	TOTALS
Cooper				1-13-0		1-24-0			1-38-0								9-112-0
Davenport		1-13-0		1-19-0												1-9-0	4-51-0
Foster	6-30-0	2-23-0		2-24-0	4-24-0	3-35-1	3-40-0	3-35-0	5-23-0	1-9-0	1-3-0	1-6-0		2-6-0			27-217-1
Graham		1-(-4)-0	5-33-0	1-19-0	4-33-0		5-89-0	2-17-0	3-44-0	1-10-0	8-102-0	1-5-0		7-192-0	1-17-0	2-16-0	38-579-0
Green		3-35-0		2-28-0	5-81-0	3-52-1	6-108-0	3-91-1	6-69-1	7-99-0	3-15-0	1-7-0	3-37-0	6-92-1	7-119-0	6-65-1	63-942-5
Hastings	1-12-0		4-70-0											2-32-0			3-44-0
Hoge		1-9-0	3-20-0	3-33-0			4-43-0	1-9-1		3-0-0	1-5-0	8-51-2	3-20-1	2-25-0	1-5-0	4-36-0	33-247-4
Mills		4-63-0	1-3-1	2-34-0	1-9-0		1-8-0	3-55-0	2-16-0	3-35-0	6-86-0	1-13-0	1-12-0	2-39-0	2-13-0		29-386-1
Stone	3-52-0	2-21-0	2-28-1	4-68-1	1-8-0	3-53-0	5-54-0	2-37-0	2-29-0	2-48-0	1-3-0	1-13-0	5-33-0		4-100-0	4-40-0	41-587-2
Thigpen		1-4-0	1-18-1	1-7-1		1-16-0	1-13-0			2-57-1						2-39-0	9-154-3
Thompson	3-44-0	1-6-0	3-3-0	2-14-0	1-1-0	4-23-0			2-16-0	2-5-0	1-0-0	4-20-0	4-61-0	3-14-0	5-31-0	3-21-0	38-259-0

* Doesn't include all players. ** Passing stats include completions, attempts, interceptions, gross yards gained and touchdowns.

PRO FOOTBALL WEEKLY 1994 ALMANAC

REVIEW: SAN DIEGO CHARGERS

Is there a doctor in the house? Some teams spent the season in search of a starting quarterback. Others kept an eye out for an impact pass rusher. The Chargers spent the 1993 season looking for a good medical plan.

Injuries were the story of the season for San Diego. Early and often.

A preseason favorite to contend for a playoff spot, the Chargers seemed to fizzle even before they got started during a disappointing 8-8 campaign.

The medical nightmare began in an Aug. 28 exhibition game in San Francisco, the Chargers' last, when QB Stan Humphries bruised his right shoulder at the end of the first quarter. Though Humphries was forced from the game, nobody believed the injury was serious until he had trouble throwing the following week. And the next week. And the next week.

"He didn't have the zip on the ball you want," said Charger coach Bobby Ross. "It started to affect his timing. It started to affect his confidence. It started to affect his team's confidence, and those things started to build."

Ultimately, Humphries admitted the shoulder throbbed so badly he had trouble lifting his arm, and he struggled to deliver the ball on time to his receivers. That's when he gave way to backup John Friesz and missed six starts. The Chargers were 2-4 without Humphries.

Humphries' injury was merely the first of many. Pro Bowl CB Gill Byrd missed the season after he tore knee ligaments during training camp. TE Derrick Walker hurt his knee in training camp as well, but he played on before bowing out after 12 games.

OG Eric Moten suffered a severe knee injury and missed most of the season. LB Jerrol Williams, a $1.7 million free-agent addition, exited midway through the year with a shoulder injury. DE Burt Grossman's season ended after the 10th game with a shoulder injury. OG Joe Milinichik sprained both knees in the second game of the year, underwent knee surgery and finally called it quits after 13 games.

"There was never any kind of letup," said Ross, "and there was always something happening you had to be concerned about."

Even before the injury bug hit, the Chargers had been hurt by some key free-agent losses, including ORG David Richards, RB Rod Bernstine, CB Anthony Blaylock and LB Henry Rolling.

"I think that hurt us some," said Ross. "You have to understand that probably had as big an impact as anything. We ended up having eight players we lost through either free-agency or trading.

"We can't afford to lose eight and get back three. That's technically what did happen. Of the three that we got, two of them were injured most of the season (Williams and Milinichik). I don't think we ended up being equal in that area."

Despite a 2-4 start, the massive injuries and free-agent losses, the Chargers had managed to climb back to .500 at 4-4. With home games the next two weeks against the Bears and Raiders, the Chargers appeared ready to climb back into the playoff hunt.

Instead, the Chargers lost both of those games.

San Diego finished strong, scoring 45 and 32 points in its final two games. It won both of those contests, but all that did was salvage a .500 season instead of the playoff berth that had been anticipated before the year began.

After ranking fourth in total defense and sixth in total offense in 1992, the Chargers fell to 18th in defense and 14th in offense in '93.

Their sack total fell from an AFC-best 51 to 32, and they had the worst passing defense in the league.

There were some highlights. PK John Carney set a club record with 31 field goals and an NFL record by hitting 29 straight over two seasons. WR Anthony Miller had 84 catches for 1,162 yards. Rookie RB Natrone Means led the club with eight TD's. DE Leslie O'Neal led the team in sacks with 12. LB Junior Seau led the Chargers in tackles for a third straight year.

Still, once the year was over, the club could only wonder what happened to its lofty goals.

"We're all disappointed in the way it ended this year because, looking at our team, I believe it's good enough to be in the playoffs," said GM Bobby Beathard. "I think everybody does."

1993 ROUNDUP

OFFENSIVE MVP: WR Anthony Miller was the AFC's second-leading receiver with 84 receptions for 1,162 yards and seven TD's.

DEFENSIVE MVP: DE Leslie O'Neal was the team leader with 12 sacks and provided consistent pressure on quarterbacks.

RESULTS
Pointspread Shown Refers To San Diego

Date	Opponent	Spread	Score
Sept. 5	Seattle	(-11)	18-12
Sept. 12	At Denver	(+3)	17-34
Sept. 19	Houston	(-2.5)	18-17
Oct. 3	At Seattle	(-3.5)	14-31
Oct. 10	At Pittsburgh	(+6)	3-16
Oct. 17	Kansas City	(+3.5)	14-17
Oct. 31	At L.A. Raiders	(+4)	30-23
Nov. 7	At Minnesota	(+3.5)	30-17
Nov. 14	Chicago	(-9)	13-16
Nov. 21	L.A. Raiders	(-3.5)	7-12
Nov. 29	At Indianapolis	(E)	31-0
Dec. 5	Denver	(-3)	13-10
Dec. 12	Green Bay	(-3)	13-20
Dec. 19	At Kansas City	(+8.5)	24-28
Dec. 27	Miami	(-1)	45-20
Jan. 2	At Tampa Bay	(E)	32-17

1993 REVIEW ■ SAN DIEGO

GAME-BY-GAME STATISTICS

TEAM STATISTICS

OPPONENT	WK 1 SEA.	WK 2 DENV.	WK 3 HOU.	WK 5 SEA.	WK 6 PITT.	WK 7 K.C.	WK 9 L.A.RD	WK 10 MINN.	WK 11 CHI.	WK 12 L.A.RD	WK 13 IND.	WK 14 DENV.	WK 15 G.B.	WK 16 K.C.	WK 17 MIA.	WK 18 T.B.	TOTALS
Score	18-12	17-34	18-17	14-31	3-16	14-17	30-23	30-17	13-16	7-12	31-0	13-10	13-20	24-28	45-20	32-17	
Total net yards	269	390	284	315	138	269	336	411	256	154	474	298	282	268	459	364	4967
Rushing yards	160	68	111	94	19	79	177	148	104	59	247	95	57	94	220	92	1824
Passing yards	109	322	173	221	119	190	159	263	152	95	227	203	225	174	239	272	3143
Rushing plays	38	24	29	20	20	26	31	36	32	18	44	27	17	28	37	28	455
Sacks allowed	2	4	1	3	1	3	1	3	0	4	0	2	3	3	1	0	32
Had intercepted	2	1	1	2	1	1	0	0	0	1	0	0	3	2	0	0	14
Fumbles lost	0	1	0	0	2	1	0	1	0	0	0	0	0	1	0	0	5
Yards penalized	25	58	20	54	15	75	35	52	24	54	45	75	55	45	25	49	706
Punts	1	6	6	6	7	4	4	5	5	7	2	6	5	5	2	3	74

OPPONENT STATISTICS

	WK 1	WK 2	WK 3	WK 5	WK 6	WK 7	WK 9	WK 10	WK 11	WK 12	WK 13	WK 14	WK 15	WK 16	WK 17	WK 18	TOTALS
Time of possession	26:07	26:53	29:51	33:49	35:22	29:33	30:26	25:11	26:26	41:48	24:58	27:46	30:39	31:20	29:13	32:48	30:34
Total net yards	230	342	295	344	304	347	467	346	224	428	262	224	227	321	321	384	5066
Rushing yards	89	58	71	57	148	83	65	20	84	158	55	86	103	104	61	72	1314
Passing yards	141	284	224	287	156	264	402	326	140	270	207	138	124	217	260	312	3752
Rushing plays	21	22	17	31	36	22	22	13	26	44	20	23	39	29	25	23	413
Sacks allowed	4	1	3	2	0	4	3	3	1	0	1	5	2	2	1	0	32
Had intercepted	1	1	4	0	0	0	2	1	1	1	2	1	1	1	3	3	22
Fumbles lost	1	1	1	0	0	0	0	2	1	1	2	1	0	1	0	0	12
Yards penalized	40	34	57	18	70	65	72	24	10	68	53	29	25	83	20	56	724
Punts	5	4	5	7	6	5	2	5	3	2	4	6	6	6	2	4	72

INDIVIDUAL STATISTICS*

RUSHING

	WK 1	WK 2	WK 3	WK 5	WK 6	WK 7	WK 9	WK 10	WK 11	WK 12	WK 13	WK 14	WK 15	WK 16	WK 17	WK 18	TOTALS
Bieniemy	6-25-0	2-5-0		2-6-0		2-7-0					13-64-1	1-(-3)-0			7-31-0		33-135-1
Butts	15-87-0	8-4-0	16-66-0	11-62-1	9-8-0	11-38-0	11-64-1	12-10-1	10-27-0	10-36-0	13-80-1	11-58-0	9-30-0	15-61-0	11-63-0	13-52-0	185-746-4
Harmon	1-1-0	9-42-0	1-1-0	3-23-0	3-12-0		3-12-0	5-34-0	2-5-0	2-13-0	5-23-0	3-13-0	3-15-0	1-12-0	1-8-0	4-2-0	46-216-0
Humphries		1-4-0	1-5-0	1-(-1)-0							1-0-0	1-0-0				3-29-0	8-37-0
Jefferson	1-9-0			1-7-0			1-33-0					1-5-0		1-(-1)-0			5-53-0
Means	14-43-0	4-13-0	10-33-0	2-(-3)-0	5-6-0	12-34-1	14-68-0	17-105-1	18-69-0	4-10-0	10-74-0	10-22-1	5-12-0	10-22-1	18-118-3	7-19-1	160-645-8

PASSING**

	WK 1	WK 2	WK 3	WK 5	WK 6	WK 7	WK 9	WK 10	WK 11	WK 12	WK 13	WK 14	WK 15	WK 16	WK 17	WK 18	TOTALS
Friesz		3-6-0	8-15-0	9-14-0	15-26-1	18-35-1	13-25-0	20-32-0	19-37-0	3-8-0	1-1-0	11-58-0		19-38-2	0-1-0		128-238-4
		40-0	110-0	103-1	107-0	218-1	162-1	268-2	184-0	38-0	11-0	161-1					1402-6
Humphries	13-30-2	28-49-1	7-26-1	12-27-2	2-5-0					8-12-1	16-25-0	22-39-0	27-51-3	1-1-0	19-29-0	18-30-0	173-324-10
	123-0	298-2	73-0	141-0	20-0					84-1	216-2	221-0	257-1	28-1	248-3	272-2	1981-12

RECEIVING

	WK 1	WK 2	WK 3	WK 5	WK 6	WK 7	WK 9	WK 10	WK 11	WK 12	WK 13	WK 14	WK 15	WK 16	WK 17	WK 18	TOTALS
A. Miller	6-56-0	5-46-0	2-24-0	10-123-1	6-61-0	6-105-1	1-29-1	7-142-1	4-46-0	4-53-0	4-65-0	2-13-0	8-103-0	5-67-0	7-110-2	7-119-1	84-1162-7
Barnes		1-16-0	1-14-0		1-13-0		1-3-0	1-6-0			2-39-0	3-30-0		1-6-0	1-9-0	1-9-0	10-137-0
Butts	1-4-0	2-35-0	2-3-0		1-1-0	2-16-0	5-89-0	7-40-0	10-27-0	2-13-0	2-13-0		1-6-0				15-105-0
Harmon	2-14-0	10-81-0	4-30-0	4-56-0	4-15-0	2-35-0	5-89-0	7-40-0	6-43-0	1-12-0	2-11-0	3-26-0	3-42-0	5-53-1	6-77-1	4-41-0	73-671-2
Jefferson	1-14-0		1-16-0	2-8-0	1-7-0	1-22-0	2-23-0	1-18-1	4-45-0	1-12-0	3-64-1	4-46-0	3-42-0	2-16-0	3-27-0	3-47-0	30-391-2
Lewis		10-119-1	2-57-0	2-27-0	1-13-0	1-9-0	1-4-0	3-41-0		2-20-1	1-8-1	6-60-0	5-36-1	2-16-0	1-18-0	1-35-0	38-463-4
Means				2-18-0	1-4-0	4-20-0						2-15-0		1-2-0			10-59-0
Pupunu	1-28-0	1-5-0		1-12-0				1-21-0		2-20-0	2-20-0	1-20-0	2-22-0	6-48-0	1-7-0		13-142-0
Walker	2-7-0	2-36-1	3-39-0		2-13-0		2-14-0	1-6-0	3-25-0	1-5-0	1-7-0	1-11-0		1-3-1		2-21-1	21-212-1
Young						1-5-0											6-41-2

* Doesn't include all players.   ** Passing stats include completions, attempts, interceptions, gross yards gained and touchdowns.

PRO FOOTBALL WEEKLY 1994 ALMANAC

REVIEW: SAN FRANCISCO 49ERS

What have you done for me lately?

That pretty much summed up the attitude toward the 49ers this past season. For much of the season, all seemed to be going well for San Francisco.

Shaking off a 3-3 start, the 49ers finished the regular season at 10-6, giving them their 10th NFC West title in 13 years and extending their record string of seasons with at least 10 victories to 11.

The news continued to be good for the 49ers when they went out and mauled the Giants 44-3 in the playoffs.

Next up, though, were the Cowboys in the NFC championship game, and everything that San Francisco had accomplished all season went up in smoke.

The Cowboys, spurred by coach Jimmy Johnson's bold guarantee of victory, walked right up to the 49ers before the game and taunted them.

Then the Cowboys backed up their words with shocking conviction, outrunning, outhustling and outmuscling the 49ers in a 38-21 Dallas victory.

"I think I'd describe it like the playground when you were in grammar school," said 49er coach George Seifert. "The school bully called you out. And when all the kids said, 'Go fight him,' you do, and he kicks your ass. And so you're humiliated."

San Francisco QB Steve Young, who won his league-record third consecutive passing title, called the loss to the Cowboys "an emotional train wreck."

What have you done for me lately?

Not much, if the sole measuring stick is trips to the Super Bowl. The defeat to the Cowboys marked the third NFC championship game the 49ers lost in the past four seasons.

That, however, is a pretty demanding definition of success. Super Bowls became a level of expectation during the Joe Montana era, but the 49ers enjoyed a degree of success matched by few teams last season. Indeed, there were some very encouraging aspects to a 49er season that ended with their fifth trip to the conference finals in the last six years.

In training camp, offensive coordinator Mike Shanahan challenged the 49er offense to become one of the league's all-time best, and the 49ers gave it their best shot. During the regular season, they set a team record with 6,435 yards (402.2 per game) and finished with 473 points (29.6 per game), just two short of the franchise high.

As LB Lawrence Taylor of the Giants prepared for the playoff game against the 49ers, he could only shake his head in wonder at the weapons possessed by San Francisco.

"When you look at the film, they do everything well," said Taylor. "Steve (Young) throws the ball well. Jerry Rice and John Taylor are playing excellent ball. Now they have a very fine running game. Their tight ends play well. Their offensive line plays well."

Not that any of this came as a surprise.

"They have always had an awesome offense," Taylor said.

Young, hampered by a broken thumb he suffered in training camp, finished the season with a flourish. He extended his league record of consecutive seasons with a 100-plus passer rating to three and led the NFL with 29 TD passes.

As usual, Rice was Young's prime target. Rice caught 98 passes, two off his career high, for a league-best 1,503 yards — an NFL-record eighth consecutive 1,000-yard receiving season.

The running game was anchored by RB Ricky Watters, who rushed for 950 yards and averaged 4.6 yards per carry. A late-season knee injury kept him from cracking the 1,000-yard mark, but he returned to score a postseason-record five touchdowns vs. the Giants.

The offensive line was tremendous until the Dallas game, with OT Harris Barton, C Jesse Sapolu and OG Guy McIntyre earning Pro Bowl berths. OLT Steve Wallace had another stellar season.

Defensively, the bright spots were rookie DT Dana Stubblefield (10.5 sacks) and S's Merton Hanks and Tim McDonald.

1993 ROUNDUP

OFFENSIVE MVP'S: QB Steve Young and WR Jerry Rice were the leaders of the explosive 49er offense, which ranked No. 1 in the NFL.

DEFENSIVE MVP: DT Dana Stubblefield, a rookie, had 10.5 sacks and was the leading defensive lineman in tackles with 64.

RESULTS
Pointspread Shown Refers To San Francisco

Date	Opponent	Spread	Score
Sept. 5	At Pittsburgh	(-6.5)	24-13
Sept. 13	At Cleveland	(-7)	13-23
Sept. 19	Atlanta	(-13)	37-30
Sept. 26	At New Orleans	(-1)	13-16
Oct. 3	Minnesota	(-10)	38-19
Oct. 17	At Dallas	(+6.5)	17-26
Oct. 24	Phoenix	(-10.5)	28-14
Oct. 31	L.A. Rams	(-13)	40-17
Nov. 14	At Tampa Bay	(-16.5)	45-21
Nov. 22	New Orleans	(-9)	42-7
Nov. 28	At L.A. Rams	(-14)	35-10
Dec. 5	Cincinnati	(-23.5)	21-8
Dec. 11	At Atlanta	(-8)	24-27
Dec. 19	At Detroit	(-9)	55-17
Dec. 25	Houston	(-9)	7-10
Jan. 3	Philadelphia	(-12.5)	34-37*
POSTSEASON			
Jan. 15	N.Y. Giants	(-7.5)	44-3
Jan. 23	At Dallas	(+3)	21-38

* Overtime

1993 REVIEW ■ SAN FRANCISCO

GAME-BY-GAME STATISTICS

TEAM STATISTICS

OPPONENT	WK 1 PITT.	WK 2 CLEV.	WK 3 ATL.	WK 4 N.O.	WK 5 MINN.	WK 7 DALL.	WK 8 PHX.	WK 9 L.A.RM	WK 11 T.B.	WK 12 N.O.	WK 13 L.A.RM	WK 14 CIN.	WK 15 ATL.	WK 16 DET.	WK 17 HOU.	WK 18 PHIL.	TOTALS
Score	24-13	13-23	37-30	13-16	38-19	17-26	28-14	40-17	45-21	42-7	35-10	21-8	24-27	55-17	7-10	34-37	
Total net yards	326	396	478	339	254	405	428	374	448	455	539	284	330	565	337	477	6435
Rushing yards	86	130	268	176	50	156	144	129	124	219	64	111	79	172	90	131	2129
Passing yards	240	266	210	163	204	249	284	245	324	236	475	173	251	393	247	346	4306
Rushing plays	32	26	33	32	26	24	31	33	31	38	25	26	19	37	23	27	463
Sacks allowed	1	1	0	5	4	4	0	0	1	2	4	1	3	0	2	5	35
Had intercepted	3	3	1	1	1	0	0	0	0	0	1	2	2	0	2	1	17
Fumbles lost	0	1	1	1	1	2	0	1	0	1	0	0	2	0	1	2	13
Yards penalized	55	92	65	20	51	60	66	50	65	19	30	51	30	50	5	91	800
Punts	3	1	0	2	5	2	5	3	3	2	3	3	4	0	4	2	42

OPPONENT STATISTICS

	WK 1	WK 2	WK 3	WK 4	WK 5	WK 7	WK 8	WK 9	WK 11	WK 12	WK 13	WK 14	WK 15	WK 16	WK 17	WK 18	TOTALS
Time of possession	27:08	33:53	30:53	27:26	30:57	32:52	28:55	29:28	27:17	27:49	27:29	36:33	33:47	27:29	26:52	32:35	29:39
Total net yards	211	304	381	264	271	353	429	220	322	261	300	339	362	288	311	381	4997
Rushing yards	102	128	194	103	52	123	107	110	94	119	161	144	92	81	116	74	1800
Passing yards	109	176	187	161	219	230	322	110	228	142	139	195	270	207	195	307	3197
Rushing plays	24	33	29	24	15	34	24	27	21	23	27	33	25	18	23	23	403
Sacks allowed	5	2	2	1	3	3	2	7	3	4	2	0	4	2	3	3	44
Had intercepted	2	0	0	0	1	0	3	2	1	4	1	1	0	0	3	1	19
Fumbles lost	1	0	1	0	1	1	0	1	3	0	0	1	1	3	0	0	11
Yards penalized	56	59	5	37	74	64	40	40	41	20	30	35	80	45	34	83	743
Punts	5	5	2	4	9	2	4	4	3	6	7	2	4	3	4	4	68

INDIVIDUAL STATISTICS*

RUSHING

	WK 1	WK 2	WK 3	WK 4	WK 5	WK 7	WK 8	WK 9	WK 11	WK 12	WK 13	WK 14	WK 15	WK 16	WK 17	WK 18	TOTALS
Bono														3-(3)-0			3-(3)-0
Carter	1-(1)-0								3-(3)-0	3-9-0				1-50-1	1-1-0	3-11-1	12-14-1
Lee	9-19-0	1-3-0	3-4-0						4-9-0	3-5-0		2-(1)-0	13-55-0	18-66-0	16-65-1	4-17-0	10-72-1
Logan		6-33-1	5-57-0	2-26-1	1-0-0	8-67-0	6-12-1	7-16-2	3-10-0	5-10-0	3-12-0	2-4-0	1-3-0	7-13-2	1-4-0	5-15-0	72-230-1
Rathman	1-0-0				8-18-1				19-88-1	2-7-1	2-2-0	17-78-3	2-5-1			1-17-0	19-80-3
Watters	14-46-0	13-83-0	19-112-1	25-135-0	9-8-1	8-32-0	20-95-1	19-56-1	3-17-0	5-39-0	18-47-1	4-21-0	24-39-2	17-23-0	5-20-0	11-54-1	208-950-10
Young	7-22-0	4-13-0	10-50-0	5-15-0	3-27-0	4-40-0	5-37-0	6-61-0	3-34-1	14-21-0	2-3-0		3-16-1	3-19-0	2-12-0	2-12-0	69-407-2

PASSING

	WK 1	WK 2	WK 3	WK 4	WK 5	WK 7	WK 8	WK 9	WK 11	WK 12	WK 13	WK 14	WK 15	WK 16	WK 17	WK 18	TOTALS
Bono							2-5-0		14-0	3-4-0	2-5-0			3-5-0	11-13-0	18-29-1	39-61-1
Young	24-36-3	19-33-3	18-22-1	22-30-1	17-24-1	24-33-0	21-33-0	22-34-0	23-29-0	14-21-0	26-32-1	13-25-2	24-39-2	39-0	79-0	219-0	416-0
	240-3	274-0	210-3	194-0	224-1	267-1	247-2	245-1	311-4	205-3	462-4	179-0	268-1	17-23-0	15-29-2	15-19-0	314-462-16
														354-4	178-0	165-2	4023-29

RECEIVING

	WK 1	WK 2	WK 3	WK 4	WK 5	WK 7	WK 8	WK 9	WK 11	WK 12	WK 13	WK 14	WK 15	WK 16	WK 17	WK 18	TOTALS
Jones	6-50-1	2-35-0	3-55-1	5-51-0	8-68-0	7-68-1	6-72-0	1-9-0	2-17-0	4-53-0	4-53-0	4-51-0	3-28-0	3-51-0	3-17-0	7-57-0	68-735-3
Lee	1-4-0			5-23-0	3-15-0	4-33-0	3-27-0	1-8-0	3-32-0			3-8-1	6-50-1	5-45-0	5-60-0	16-115-2
Logan		2-30-0	5-57-0					4-34-0		5-39-0		1-9-0	2-28-0			1-9-0	37-348-0
Rathman	2-9-0			7-95-0	2-60-1	7-82-0	9-155-2		8-172-4	16-116-0	2-17-0	4-82-0	2-14-0	4-132-1	3-37-0	10-83-0	10-86-0
Rice	8-78-2	6-82-0	3-33-0	2-6-0	3-53-0	4-53-0	2-17-0	6-63-0	2-5-0	4-62-2	8-166-2		6-105-0	4-115-1	10-83-0	6-53-1	98-1503-15
Singleton			1-6-1							2-28-0							8-126-1
Taylor	4-48-0	4-71-0	3-32-0	2-8-0	1-28-0	2-31-0	2-17-0	4-90-1	4-51-0	6-90-1	6-150-1	1-15-0	3-48-0	4-115-1	3-40-0	3-61-1	56-940-5
Watters	1-4-0	4-47-0						5-35-0	5-35-0		5-82-1	2-26-0				2-13-0	31-326-1
Williams	1-15-0	1-9-0	2-21-1						1-6-0	2-14-0	1-11-0	2-15-0	4-23-0	1-8-0		1-10-0	16-132-1

*Doesn't include all players. ** Passing stats include completions, attempts, interceptions, gross yards gained and touchdowns.

REVIEW: SEATTLE SEAHAWKS

A 6-10 record and last-place finish in the AFC West may not sound like reason to bring out the champagne in celebration. But, for the Seahawks, it was cause for optimism.

After going 2-14 in 1992, last season marked significant progress for Seattle.

"This time last year, I was frustrated and just drained," said Seahawk coach Tom Flores after the end of this past season. "This year I'm drained but not frustrated."

To get an idea of Seattle's improvement, consider the lead paragraph of an *Associated Press* story 12 games into the season after the Seahawks' record fell to 5-7: "After back-to-back losses to Denver's John Elway and Kansas City's Joe Montana, Seattle's playoff hopes are virtually dead."

When a team goes 2-14 the season before, it is a major step forward when its playoff hopes aren't written off until after the 12th game of the season. In '92, the Seahawks never even had playoff hopes.

With that as background, it is easy to see why a 6-10 season is greeted with a positive outlook. Even better was the statistical growth of the offense. After scoring only 140 points in '92, the Seahawks upped that total to 280 in '93. Their turnover margin went from minus-9 in '92 to plus-6 in '93. The ground game went from an average of 99.8 yards in '92 to 125.9 yards in '93.

The biggest improvement in the offense was at quarterback, where rookie Rick Mirer's play provided a bright glimpse into the future. This was important to the Seahawks' growth, considering the instability at the position the previous season.

"He's a tough, tough kid," said Seahawk offensive coordinator Larry Kennan of Mirer. "The thing to remember about Rick, he is a rookie and he played beyond anybody's expectations."

Despite the fact that Mirer was sacked 47 times, blitzed, bent, folded and almost mutilated, he proved to be tougher than those trying to nail him. He completed 274-of-486 passes for 2,833 yards — all record numbers for a rookie. He also led all AFC quarterbacks with 343 rushing yards.

Although much of the credit for the offense's improvement goes to Mirer, he had some help. Newcomers to the team played an important role, especially WR Kelvin Martin, TE Ferrell Edmunds and C Ray Donaldson.

Martin, tired of being the No. 3 receiver in Dallas, caught 57 passes for a career-high 798 yards, led the team with five TD receptions and had five of the team's nine completions that went for at least 30 yards. Edmunds, pushed out in Miami when the Dolphins obtained Keith Jackson, combined with Paul Green to produce 47 receptions from the TE position. Even more important was Edmunds' role as a blocker in helping RB Chris Warren to a second straight 1,000-yard season. Donaldson, cut by the Colts, made every snap while anchoring a line that cut its sacks allowed considerably and opened holes so that three different backs (Warren, Jon Vaughn and John L. Williams) were able to string together consecutive 100-yard games to close the season.

Having WR Brian Blades for an entire season also helped. Blades played just five games in '92 after breaking his collarbone in the opener. In '93 he played with sore shoulders and ribs, but he still caught 80 passes to break Steve Largent's club single-season record.

The flip side of the improved play on offense came on defense. After being the only unit in the NFL to rank among the top 10 from 1990 to '92, the Seahawks plummeted from No. 9 to No. 23 over the last nine games of the season.

The pass defense finished 26th — allowing an average of 228.3 yards, compared to 166.3 the previous year. In '92 the Seahawks allowed seven pass plays of 40 yards or more in 16 games. In their first seven games in '93, they allowed one. But in the final nine games of the season, they were burned for seven 40-plus pass plays.

"Unacceptable. Totally unacceptable," said Seahawk Pro Bowl FS Eugene Robinson. "This is unfamiliar territory for me. We were in a funk. It was like, 'What's going on here?' That was not our defense."

Robinson was not the problem, as evidenced by his nine interceptions and 111 tackles. The two biggest problems were lack of a pass rush and injuries.

1993 ROUNDUP

OFFENSIVE MVP: QB Rick Mirer threw for 2,833 yards, and completed more passes than any other rookie quarterback before him.

DEFENSIVE MVP: FS Eugene Robinson tied for the league lead in interceptions with nine and led the team in tackles (111), passes defensed (15) and forced fumbles (three).

RESULTS
Pointspread Shown Refers To Seattle

Date	Opponent	Spread	Score
Sept. 5	At San Diego	(+11)	12-18
Sept. 12	L.A. Raiders	(+3)	13-17
Sept. 19	At New England	(+2.5)	17-14
Sept. 26	At Cincinnati	(-3)	19-10
Oct. 3	San Diego	(+3.5)	31-14
Oct. 17	At Detroit	(+5)	10-30
Oct. 24	New England	(-9.5)	10-9
Oct. 31	At Denver	(+9)	17-28
Nov. 7	At Houston	(+9.5)	14-24
Nov. 14	Cleveland	(-4)	22-5
Nov. 28	Denver	(+3)	9-17
Dec. 5	Kansas City	(+6.5)	16-31
Dec. 12	At L.A. Raiders	(+8)	23-27
Dec. 19	Phoenix	(-2.5)	27-30*
Dec. 26	Pittsburgh	(+3)	16-6
Jan. 2	At Kansas City	(+7.5)	24-34

* Overtime

1993 REVIEW ■ SEATTLE

GAME-BY-GAME STATISTICS

TEAM STATISTICS

OPPONENT	WK 1 S.D.	WK 2 L.A.RD	WK 3 N.E.	WK 4 CIN.	WK 5 S.D.	WK 7 DET.	WK 8 N.E.	WK 9 DENV.	WK 10 HOU.	WK 11 CLEV.	WK 13 DENV.	WK 14 K.C.	WK 15 L.A.RD	WK 16 PHX.	WK 17 PITT.	WK 18 K.C.	TOTALS
Score	12-18	13-17	17-14	19-10	31-14	10-30	10-9	17-28	14-24	22-5	9-17	16-31	23-27	27-30	16-6	24-34	
Total net yards	230	232	334	305	344	229	261	287	252	223	288	365	303	365	368	280	4666
Rushing yards	89	112	209	139	57	63	67	103	84	119	127	90	134	212	267	140	2012
Passing yards	141	120	125	166	287	166	194	184	168	104	161	275	169	153	101	140	2654
Rushing plays	21	29	43	35	31	20	26	26	21	33	26	24	32	36	45	25	473
Sacks allowed	4	5	5	2	2	3	1	4	2	2	6	3	1	2	5	1	48
Had intercepted	1	2	2	0	0	3	0	2	1	0	1	1	0	1	1	0	18
Fumbles lost	1	1	1	2	0	0	0	2	0	0	1	2	0	1	0	3	13
Yards penalized	40	21	49	21	18	60	56	94	43	64	75	35	75	20	20	49	740
Punts	5	5	5	6	7	7	8	3	5	6	12	3	5	5	4	5	91

OPPONENT STATISTICS

OPPONENT	WK 1	WK 2	WK 3	WK 4	WK 5	WK 7	WK 8	WK 9	WK 10	WK 11	WK 13	WK 14	WK 15	WK 16	WK 17	WK 18	TOTALS
Time of possession	33:53	31:55	21:40	26:44	26:11	31:33	31:38	33:08	40:29	33:07	31:17	30:11	29:36	38:53	24:18	34:26	31:30
Total net yards	269	264	276	354	315	292	295	326	458	232	307	337	362	476	380	372	5315
Rushing yards	160	83	51	30	94	141	166	87	111	175	101	106	59	71	116	109	1660
Passing yards	109	181	223	324	221	151	129	239	347	57	206	231	303	405	264	263	3653
Rushing plays	38	28	17	17	20	32	36	31	26	38	35	30	23	29	20	32	452
Sacks allowed	2	3	2	5	3	2	0	2	3	3	4	1	2	3	2	1	38
Had Intercepted	2	1	2	1	2	1	0	1	2	2	1	0	1	1	1	1	22
Fumbles lost	0	0	1	2	0	1	0	0	0	5	1	0	1	2	1	1	15
Yards penalized	25	40	20	58	54	65	60	54	57	67	35	40	68	53	72	50	818
Punts	1	7	6	4	6	6	5	3	3	6	8	5	1	2	5	5	73

INDIVIDUAL STATISTICS*

RUSHING

	WK 1	WK 2	WK 3	WK 4	WK 5	WK 7	WK 8	WK 9	WK 10	WK 11	WK 13	WK 14	WK 15	WK 16	WK 17	WK 18	TOTALS
Bates																1-6-0	2-12-0
Blades				1-26-0	1-6-0								1-7-0	2-13-0	1-6-0		5-52-0
C. Warren	12-38-0	20-76-1	36-174-1	19-75-0	23-32-1	15-37-0	12-26-0	13-54-1	24-112-0	19-95-0	18-59-1	21-73-1	27-168-1		4-44-0	4-30-0	273-1072-7
Johnson		1-5-0		1-5-0		1-3-0		2-(-3)-0	2-4-0		1-3-0						2-8-0
Mirer	3-36-0	5-27-0	2-21-0	9-17-0	3-15-1	3-10-0	7-12-0	5-23-0	5-44-1	2-22-0	3-18-0	2-19-0	9-52-1	5-18-1	26-131-0	4-30-0	68-343-3
Vaughn								2-4-0	1-3-0	1-5-0	1-4-0	1-4-0	1-2-0	2-13-0	14-86-0	4-2-0	36-153-0
Williams	6-15-0	2-2-0	3-11-0	5-21-0	3-5-0	2-19-0	7-29-0	9-43-2	2-7-0	6-5-0	4-14-0	3-8-0	1-2-0	2-13-0		16-102-1	82-371-3

PASSING**

	WK 1	...															TOTALS
Gelbaugh			3-5-1 39-0														3-5-1 39-0
Mirer	20-27-1 154-0	14-22-2 149-0	12-16-1 117-1	18-30-0 181-0	25-40-0 282-1	23-39-3 189-1	22-43-2 203-1	16-30-2 201-0	12-19-1 175-1	11-27-0 114-1	17-37-1 188-1	18-30-2 287-0	20-36-1 171-1	15-30-0 165-1	12-29-1 117-1	19-30-0 140-2	274-485-17 2833-12

RECEIVING

	WK 1	WK 2	WK 3	WK 4	WK 5	WK 7	WK 8	WK 9	WK 10	WK 11	WK 13	WK 14	WK 15	WK 16	WK 17	WK 18	TOTALS
Blades	5-54-0	2-18-0	6-50-1	5-64-0	10-132-1	3-28-0	9-70-1		5-44-0	2-22-0	3-35-0	7-134-0	5-47-0	2-31-0	4-60-0	5-69-0	80-945-3
C. Warren	4-13-0	4-61-0					3-11-0				1-3-0		3-11-0				15-99-0
D. Thomas	2-17-0	2-19-0				1-8-0	1-5-0	2-27-0			1-6-0		2-17-0			1-4-0	11-95-0
Edmunds	1-5-0		1-20-0	1-12-0	3-11-0	1-8-0	1-12-0	1-16-0	1-21-0	1-9-0	2-24-0	3-46-0	1-32-0	5-18-1	1-2-1	5-18-1	24-239-2
Green	3-21-0		1-8-0	1-0-0	4-29-0	1-17-0	2-23-0	1-14-0		1-12-0	2-8-0	1-9-0	2-11-0	2-14-0		2-10-0	36-153-0
Johnson											1-5-0			2-5-1		2-10-1	3-15-1
Martin	2-30-0	1-11-0	3-28-0	5-63-0	5-85-1	8-80-1	5-58-0	5-62-0	4-85-1	1-11-0	3-73-1	3-68-0	4-28-1	4-74-0	2-23-0	2-19-0	57-798-5
R. Thomas					1-12-0	1-8-0							1-6-0	2-25-0	2-16-0		7-67-0
Williams	3-14-0	5-40-0	4-50-0	6-38-0	3-30-0	9-48-0		5-62-0	2-5-0	6-60-1	4-34-0	4-30-0	2-19-0	3-16-0	3-16-0	1-4-0	58-450-1

* Doesn't include all players.   ** Passing stats include completions, attempts, interceptions, gross yards gained and touchdowns.

TAMPA BAY BUCCANEERS
REVIEW

True to form for a team that owns the NFL's worst record over the past 11 years, the Bucs ended up in the NFC Central cellar for the second time in three years, finishing with a 5-11 mark and, in the process, running their streak of seasons with six or fewer victories to 13.

There were enough encouraging signs in 1993, however, to convince head coach Sam Wyche the Bucs' fortunes are on the upswing.

"This is not a team that deteriorated as the season went on," said Wyche.

The Bucs started the season poorly, losing seven of their first nine games by 15 or more points. They were hurting also because of a prolonged contract impasse with durable OT Paul Gruber, who had been designated as the team's franchise player.

But, in their last seven games, the Bucs finished 3-4, with impressive victories over division rivals Minnesota and Chicago at home and Denver at Mile High Stadium, a place that traditionally makes life miserable for visitors.

The Bucs played the NFL's toughest schedule, facing off against foes with a combined record of 140-116 (.547), including 11 games against playoff teams. Three of their five wins came against postseason participants — Minnesota, Detroit and Denver.

In addition, they showed an ability to compete toe-to-toe in the revitalized NFC Central Division, defeating three opponents and finishing just 1:22 shy of a fourth win in a tightly contested, 13-10 defeat in Green Bay Nov. 28.

"Our division was the most improved in football with three playoff teams," said Wyche. "Yet, by the end of the season, I don't think our team was taking a back seat to any of them.

"We had a good year," Wyche concluded. "When your team gets better every week and is clearly better the second half than the first, you can make that statement."

Wyche was certainly not alone when it came to positive assessments of the Bucs down the stretch.

"Tampa Bay is the best 4-10 team in the league," said Bronco OG Brian Habib in advance of his team's upset loss to the Bucs late in the season. "On film, they don't look like a 4-10 team. They look like a team that has played a lot of tough, close games and has nothing to lose."

The major reasons for optimism were the development of young offensive players like QB Craig Erickson and WR's Courtney Hawkins and Horace Copeland, as well as the improved play of a defense that allowed a 362-yard average in its first nine games and just 283 yards per game in the last seven.

Erickson was ranked just 24th in the league overall (66.4 rating) and tied for second overall in most interceptions (21). Yet he became Tampa Bay's first 3,000-yard passer since 1989 and seemed to mature quickly down the stretch along with a WR corps that steadily improved, despite the absence most of the season of Lawrence Dawsey (knee injury), the Bucs' leading receiver the previous two years.

After a disappointing rookie campaign, Hawkins picked up the slack with a club-leading 62 receptions for 933 yards and five touchdowns. Copeland, a fourth-round draft pick out of Miami (Fla.), emerged as a big-play receiver, averaging 21.1 yards on 30 catches and scoring four TD's.

By far the biggest factor behind the defense's improvement was MLB Hardy Nickerson, a former Steeler who was arguably the top free-agent acquisition in 1993. Nickerson made a single-season team-record 214 tackles and led his team in tackles in every game in '93.

"I've been around a lot of Pro Bowl players in my career, and Hardy's contributions compared favorably with any of them," said Wyche. "He did it every single week of the season, and I believe he has had as big a positive impact on our team as Reggie White in Green Bay."

Another bright spot for the Bucs was special teams.

Rookie PK Michael Husted tied the team record for most 50-yard-plus field goals in a season (three) and notched 25 touchbacks. His 57-yarder on the road vs. the Raiders was the longest field goal in the NFC since 1991.

Dan Stryzinski was one of the NFL's best positional punters, posting a team-record 24 punts inside the 20, compared to just three touchbacks.

1993 ROUNDUP

OFFENSIVE MVP: WR Courtney Hawkins came on strong in the season's second half, finishing with nearly 1,000 receiving yards.

DEFENSIVE MVP: LB Hardy Nickerson set a single-season team record for tackles with 214, including at least 10 in 15 different games.

RESULTS
Pointspread Shown Refers To Tampa Bay

Date	Opponent	Spread	Score
Sept. 5	Kansas City	(+7)	3-27
Sept. 12	At New York Giants	(+10)	7-23
Sept. 26	At Chicago	(+7)	17-47
Oct. 3	Detroit	(+6)	27-10
Oct. 10	At Minnesota	(+11)	0-15
Oct. 24	Green Bay	(+5)	14-37
Oct. 31	At Atlanta	(+9.5)	31-24
Nov. 7	At Detroit	(+12.5)	0-23
Nov. 14	San Francisco	(+16.5)	21-45
Nov. 21	Minnesota	(+8)	23-10
Nov. 28	At Green Bay	(+12)	10-13
Dec. 5	Washington	(-2.5)	17-23
Dec. 12	Chicago	(+4.5)	13-10
Dec. 19	At L.A. Raiders	(+9)	20-27
Dec. 26	At Denver	(+13.5)	17-10
Jan. 2	San Diego	(E)	17-32

1993 REVIEW ■ TAMPA BAY

GAME-BY-GAME STATISTICS

TEAM STATISTICS

OPPONENT	WK 1 K.C.	WK 2 N.Y.G.	WK 4 CHI.	WK 5 DET.	WK 6 MINN.	WK 8 G.B.	WK 9 ATL.	WK 10 DET.	WK 11 S.F.	WK 12 MINN.	WK 13 G.B.	WK 14 WASH.	WK 15 CHI.	WK 16 L.A.RD	WK 17 DENV.	WK 18 S.D.	TOTALS
Score	3-27	7-23	17-47	27-10	0-15	14-37	31-24	0-23	21-45	23-10	10-13	17-23	13-10	20-27	17-10	17-32	
Total net yards	157	199	328	324	169	246	405	146	322	300	207	307	215	366	236	384	4311
Rushing yards	25	45	36	128	59	84	98	44	94	100	92	144	103	101	65	72	1290
Passing yards	132	154	292	196	110	162	307	102	228	200	115	163	112	265	171	312	3021
Rushing plays	20	19	18	31	20	20	34	14	21	34	22	31	29	30	36	23	402
Sacks allowed	1	3	2	3	2	2	2	3	3	4	3	0	3	5	2	0	39
Had intercepted	1	1	4	0	4	3	2	0	1	0	0	3	0	1	0	3	25
Fumbles lost	0	0	3	1	1	0	0	0	3	0	0	0	2	0	0	0	11
Yards penalized	57	11	61	55	33	45	70	35	41	50	39	53	64	85	10	56	765
Punts	6	6	5	6	6	8	5	8	3	5	10	5	5	4	8	4	94

OPPONENT STATISTICS

	WK 1	WK 2	WK 4	WK 5	WK 6	WK 8	WK 9	WK 10	WK 11	WK 12	WK 13	WK 14	WK 15	WK 16	WK 17	WK 18	TOTALS
Time of possession	30:29	35:04	37:04	29:15	36:05	37:57	27:03	36:27	32:43	21:24	36:02	28:48	30:14	27:10	28:57	27:12	31:22
Total net yards	400	381	332	311	268	421	337	366	448	235	259	238	286	265	335	364	5246
Rushing yards	122	181	126	144	124	162	68	241	124	82	107	175	119	17	110	92	1994
Passing yards	278	200	206	167	144	259	269	125	324	153	152	63	167	248	225	272	3252
Rushing plays	31	41	38	26	33	34	15	43	31	18	30	36	28	23	23	28	478
Sacks allowed	0	1	3	3	5	2	1	2	1	2	2	1	1	3	1	0	29
Had Intercepted	0	1	0	2	1	1	1	1	0	2	0	0	0	0	0	0	9
Fumbles lost	3	0	1	1	0	1	0	2	0	2	0	1	2	0	3	0	13
Yards penalized	60	25	69	10	65	72	91	55	65	62	55	59	40	102	34	49	913
Punts	2	3	4	4	7	5	4	8	3	7	9	6	5	5	5	3	76

INDIVIDUAL STATISTICS*

RUSHING

	WK 1	WK 2	WK 4	WK 5	WK 6	WK 8	WK 9	WK 10	WK 11	WK 12	WK 13	WK 14	WK 15	WK 16	WK 17	WK 18	TOTALS
Cobb	17-28-0	16-32-0	12-8-0	25-113-1	16-55-0	15-52-0	18-75-0	2-25-0	1-5-0	3-(-2)-0		15-59-0	19-68-0	22-59-2	25-42-0	21-67-0	221-658-3
Erickson			1-4-0	1-1-0	1-2-0	1-3-0	3-8-0	6-15-0	7-30-0			2-9-0	3-5-0	2-20-0	6-16-0		26-96-0
G. Anderson	3-(-3)-0		2-10-0		2-0-0	3-7-0	9-7-0	3-5-0	2-20-0	9-38-0	2-5-0	2-10-0	2-7-1	3-6-0		2-5-0	28-56-0
Royster			1-8-0	4-11-0	1-2-0		2-3-0		10-35-1	20-58-1	18-77-0	8-45-0	5-23-0	3-16-0	5-7-0		33-115-1
Workman		2-9-0						3-(-1)-0									78-284-2

PASSING**

	WK 1	WK 2	WK 4	WK 5	WK 6	WK 8	WK 9	WK 10	WK 11	WK 12	WK 13	WK 14	WK 15	WK 16	WK 17	WK 18	TOTALS
DeBerg	12-20-1 79-0		7-8-1 77-1			4-11-1 30-0											23-39-3 186-1
Erickson	8-15-0 61-0	16-28-1 174-1	13-32-2 240-1	14-25-0 210-2	12-29-4 122-0	8-20-2 151-2	18-28-2 318-4	13-26-1 122-0	17-27-1 239-2	19-32-0 239-0	12-35-0 144-1	15-34-3 163-1	12-21-1 128-0	21-34-0 295-0	14-30-1 176-2	21-41-3 272-2	233-457-21 3054-18
Weldon			0-1-1 0-0						2-5-0 15-0						4-5-0 40-0		3054-18 6-11-1 55-0

RECEIVING

	WK 1	WK 2	WK 4	WK 5	WK 6	WK 8	WK 9	WK 10	WK 11	WK 12	WK 13	WK 14	WK 15	WK 16	WK 17	WK 18	TOTALS
Armstrong	2-6-0	1-17-1					1-20-0			2-31-0							9-86-1
Copeland		4-70-0	2-22-0	1-49-0	2-9-0	2-93-2	2-104-2	1-23-0	3-71-0	2-35-0		1-8-0	3-32-0	5-74-0	1-21-0	7-101-0	30-633-4
Dawsey	1-10-0	1-1-0	9-101-0	1-22-0			5-51-0		4-31-1								15-203-0
G. Anderson	1-6-0								1-9-0			2-13-0		2-25-0		2-17-0	11-89-1
Hall	2-19-0	3-40-0		3-59-1	2-13-0	4-38-0	2-35-0	1-9-0		2-32-0	2-5-0	2-13-0	4-57-0	3-94-0	8-105-1	6-98-1	23-268-1
Hawkins	6-53-0	1-12-0	1-67-0	5-48-1	2-34-0	1-10-0	3-45-0	5-58-0	1-9-0	2-32-0	6-99-1	8-112-1		3-94-0		2-38-1	62-933-5
L. Thomas			2-78-1		1-18-0				1-12-0	1-23-0	1-20-0	1-17-0	1-20-0	1-19-0	1-9-0	3-34-0	8-186-2
Wilson	1-5-0			1-16-0	1-17-0	1-17-0	1-23-0	1-19-0	2-26-0						1-9-0		15-225-0
Workman		2-12-0	2-14-0	3-16-0	2-5-0	2-14-0	4-56-1	2-4-0	6-68-1	7-65-0	4-18-0	2-19-0	3-12-0	7-62-0	3-22-0	5-24-0	54-411-2

* Doesn't include all players. ** Passing stats include completions, attempts, interceptions, gross yards gained and touchdowns.

WASHINGTON REDSKINS

It was the worst of times and the worst of times for the Washington Redskins.

The season began with a thud when future Hall of Fame coach Joe Gibbs suddenly decided to retire. Owner Jack Kent Cooke thought he made a perfect replacement when he gave defensive coordinator Richie Petitbon the opportunity to lead the Skins, but it was just another example of the Peter Principle coming to fruition. By becoming head coach of the Redskins, one of the NFL's most glamorous positions, he had risen to his level of incompetence.

Believe it or not, the Redskin season started out on an incredibly high note. Facing the defending Super Bowl champion Cowboys in the Monday-night opener in RFK Stadium, the Redskins played spirited and cohesive football in registering a 35-16 upset.

But after that one superior performance, the Redskins were only a shell of the team they had been under Gibbs. Yes, there were injuries. All-Pro OLT Jim Lachey went down for the season with a knee injury in the first preseason game. ORG Mark Schlereth had a scary viral infection that left him with no feeling below his ankles. ORT Ed Simmons and C-OG Raleigh McKenzie played most of the season with injuries.

On the defensive side of the ball, DE's Charles Mann and Shane Collins were both troubled by leg injuries, while DT's Eric Williams and Bobby Wilson had hip and knee problems, respectively.

Besides the injury problems on both lines, QB Mark Rypien suffered a knee injury in the third week of the season. He was rushed back into action too quickly and remained primarily ineffective throughout the season. He completed only 166-of-319 passes for 1,514 yards with four TD's and 10 interceptions.

Rypien was the object of scorn from angry Redskin fans who were not used to seeing their team self-destruct. After beating the Cowboys, the Redskins lost six consecutive games before edging the hapless Colts 30-24 in early November.

How bad did things get in 1993? Consider these developments:

■ After beating the Cardinals in 19 of their previous 23 games, the Redskins were beaten twice by Phoenix. They were humiliated by a 36-6 margin in the Week Seven matchup in Phoenix.

■ They were beaten 41-7 at home by the Giants, their most lopsided loss at home since the Bears defeated them 73-0 in the 1940 NFL championship game.

■ The Redskins were beaten 10-6 by the Rams, a game in which the Skins could not even dent the endzone against one of the league's most permissive defenses.

There are other lowlights that one could point to, including a 3-0, Week 15 loss to the Jets and a 38-3 pounding by the Cowboys in Week 17 in which several members of the team appeared to be watching the clock from the midpoint of the second quarter. However, the most telling moment of the season came in Week 14, when the tradition-honored Redskins were made a 2.5-point underdog to the Tampa Bay Buccaneers. The *Buccaneers*.

With those humiliations staring him coldly in the face, Cooke decided that bringing back Petitbon would not be in the best interest of the team. Despite his genuinely warm feelings for Petitbon and his 15 years of service to the organization, Cooke pulled the plug shortly after the season ended and hired Cowboy assistant Norv Turner to revive the Redskins.

Turner will have some genuine talent on his roster. Rookie RB Reggie Brooks established himself as one of the game's top running backs by rushing for 1,063 yards, including an 88-yard TD burst against the Eagles. Also, rookie CB Tom Carter demonstrated great athletic talent with six interceptions.

Other than the performances of Brooks and Carter, there weren't many Redskin performers who gave the organization much to be proud of. Particularly depressing was the performance of the wide receivers. Ricky Sanders caught 58 passes for 638 yards and four TD's to lead the team, but he dropped several catchable passes. Former first-round pick Desmond Howard continued to be a disappointment, and Art Monk struggled all season to get open.

1993 ROUNDUP

OFFENSIVE MVP: RB Reggie Brooks gained 1,063 yards as a rookie and showed big-play ability, as he had the two longest TD runs from scrimmage in the league.

DEFENSIVE MVP: DT Tim Johnson was one of the few Washington linemen to stay healthy, and he had perhaps his best season.

RESULTS
Pointspread Shown Refers To Washington

Date	Opponent	Spread	Score
Sept. 6	Dallas	(-2.5)	35-16
Sept. 12	Phoenix	(-10)	10-17
Sept. 19	At Philadelphia	(+6.5)	31-34
Oct. 4	At Miami	(+5.5)	10-17
Oct. 10	New York Giants	(-3.5)	7-41
Oct. 17	At Phoenix	(-1.5)	6-36
Nov. 1	At Buffalo	(+9)	10-24
Nov. 7	Indianapolis	(-6.5)	30-24
Nov. 14	At New York Giants	(+8)	6-20
Nov. 21	At L.A. Rams	(+2)	6-10
Nov. 28	Philadelphia	(-3)	14-17
Dec. 5	At Tampa Bay	(+2.5)	23-17
Dec. 11	New York Jets	(+3)	0-3
Dec. 19	Atlanta	(+3.5)	30-17
Dec. 26	At Dallas	(+17)	3-38
Dec. 31	Minnesota	(+7)	9-14

1993 REVIEW — WASHINGTON

GAME-BY-GAME STATISTICS

TEAM STATISTICS

OPPONENT	WK 1 DALL.	WK 2 PHX.	WK 3 PHIL.	WK 5 MIA.	WK 6 N.Y.G.	WK 7 PHX.	WK 9 BUFF.	WK 10 IND.	WK 11 N.Y.G.	WK 12 L.A.RM	WK 13 PHIL.	WK 14 T.B.	WK 15 N.Y.J.	WK 16 ATL.	WK 17 DALL.	WK 18 MINN.	TOTALS
Score	35-16	10-17	31-34	10-17	7-41	6-36	10-24	30-24	6-20	6-10	14-17	23-17	0-3	30-17	3-38	9-14	
Total net yards	332	233	377	232	304	246	309	275	325	273	349	238	150	167	198	263	4271
Rushing yards	171	58	167	84	65	138	140	109	95	114	97	175	39	38	126	110	1726
Passing yards	161	175	210	148	239	108	169	166	230	159	252	63	111	129	72	153	2545
Rushing plays	35	17	31	23	12	26	29	28	25	29	21	36	15	19	28	23	397
Sacks allowed	0	3	2	2	3	5	2	4	1	3	3	1	3	1	4	2	40
Had intercepted	0	1	2	1	1	0	1	0	1	1	0	0	0	1	2	0	21
Fumbles lost	0	1	0	0	1	3	0	0	2	0	0	0	1	0	0	1	10
Yards penalized	45	25	35	57	60	29	40	40	25	15	69	59	10	0	68	19	596
Punts	5	5	6	6	2	5	2	8	4	6	4	6	6	7	7	4	83
Time of possession	24:57	35:54	30:02	29:13	36:37	33:12	30:08	30:34	31:30	27:22	30:12	31:12	41:00	40:40	30:22	29:54	32:26

OPPONENT STATISTICS

Total net yards	345	303	440	354	415	380	402	405	262	282	268	307	308	378	380	270	5499
Rushing yards	91	152	95	106	199	156	164	49	152	89	104	144	210	182	175	45	2113
Passing yards	254	151	345	248	216	224	238	356	110	193	164	163	98	196	205	225	3386
Rushing plays	21	39	22	27	47	34	42	17	38	22	29	31	50	35	32	27	513
Sacks allowed	2	1	4	1	3	3	0	2	1	3	3	0	1	0	7	2	31
Had intercepted	0	2	2	1	0	0	1	1	1	0	1	3	0	4	2	0	17
Fumbles lost	4	0	2	0	0	0	1	2	0	1	0	0	1	2	1	0	14
Yards penalized	64	20	76	96	15	15	59	57	50	44	10	53	35	80	78	30	782
Punts	3	3	5	5	2	4	3	7	5	7	6	5	6	4	2	6	73

INDIVIDUAL STATISTICS*

RUSHING

Brooks	11-53-0	5-21-0	22-154-1	11-28-0	3-13-0	6-33-0	24-117-1	21-105-0	22-91-0	22-87-0	11-43-0	20-128-1	9-28-0	4-9-0	18-85-0	14-68-0	223-1063-3
Byner	1-5-0	1-(-1)-0	1-7-0		2-23-0	1-(-2)-0	4-16-0	1-4-0	1-0-0		5-25-0	2-9-0	1-3-0	2-12-1	3-12-0	5-40-0	23-105-1
Ervins				3-11-0	3-20-0	17-98-0			2-4-0		4-25-0	5-15-0	2-9-0	10-16-0	4-7-0	3-4-0	50-201-0
Gannon	21-116-2	10-33-0	6-7-0	7-28-0	4-9-0	2-9-0		1-1-1		3-17-0	7-17-1	2-11-0	1-(-1)-0	1-0-0	1-3-0		92-92-1
Mitchell										4-9-0			2-0-0		2-19-0		63-246-3

PASSING**

Conklin		16-29-1 169-1	17-36-2 218-3	13-22-0 109-0				0-0-0 0-0									46-87-3 496-4
Gannon				5-12-1 49-1	5-8-2 40-0	1-1-0 12-0				24-39-1 170-0	20-31-2 279-2	9-16-1 71-0	7-15-0 62-0		3-3-0 21-0		74-125-7 704-3
Rypien	22-34-0 161-3	2-6-0 25-0			21-35-1 220-1	16-28-1 120-0	15-42-4 169-1	17-28-0 189-0	22-49-1 239-0				2-8-0 17-0	13-23-1 129-0	12-30-2 81-0	24-36-0 164-0	166-319-10 1514-5

RECEIVING

Brooks	5-30-0	2-20-0	1-9-0	1-5-0	3-40-0	1-7-0	3-17-0	1-43-0	1-8-0	5-41-0	3-34-0	1-17-0	1-9-0	4-9-0	2-4-0	3-7-0	21-186-0
Byner		2-22-0	1-8-0	1-7-0	6-72-1	3-37-0	1-20-0	1-6-0		2-10-0	1-15-0	2-4-0	1-4-0	2-12-1	1-8-0	6-30-0	27-194-0
Howard	1-6-0	1-10-0	6-93-1	5-36-0	1-14-0	2-5-0	2-38-0	1-6-0	2-33-0	2-25-0	1-14-0	2-18-0	1-14-0	3-44-0	2-19-0	6-68-0	23-286-0
Middleton	5-15-1	3-21-0	1-1-1		1-14-0	3-57-0	1-4-0	3-57-0	4-46-0	3-24-0	5-96-1	2-18-0	1-11-0	1-7-0		1-2-0	39-500-3
Mitchell	3-12-0	3-39-0	1-4-0	4-27-0	7-52-0	2-5-0	1-4-0	2-7-0		1-2-0	2-33-0	1-4-0			2-19-0		24-154-2
Monk	3-58-1	4-48-0	3-39-0	3-31-0	3-22-0	2-11-0	3-42-0	3-11-0	3-40-0	1-4-0	2-15-1	1-7-0	3-24-0	3-17-0	1-12-0	3-17-0	41-398-2
Sanders	5-40-1	5-56-1	2-42-1	4-52-1	2-22-0	2-8-0	4-37-0	3-34-0	8-91-0	8-57-0	2-15-0	1-11-0	3-67-0	2-41-0	3-28-0	4-37-0	58-638-4
Wycheck							1-11-0	4-31-0	3-14-0	2-7-0	2-34-0				4-16-0		16-113-0

* Doesn't include all players. ** Passing stats include completions, attempts, interceptions, gross yards gained and touchdowns.

377

PRO FOOTBALL WEEKLY 1994 ALMANAC

REVIEW: 1993 FINAL STANDINGS

AMERICAN FOOTBALL CONFERENCE

EAST	W	L	T	PCT.	PF	PA	HOME	AWAY	AFC	DIV.
BUFFALO	12	4	0	.750	329	242	6-2-0	6-2-0	8-4-0	7-1-0
MIAMI	9	7	0	.563	349	351	4-4-0	5-3-0	6-6-0	4-4-0
N.Y. JETS	8	8	0	.500	270	247	3-5-0	5-3-0	6-6-0	5-3-0
NEW ENGLAND	5	11	0	.313	238	286	3-5-0	2-6-0	4-10-0	2-6-0
INDIANAPOLIS	4	12	0	.250	189	378	2-6-0	2-6-0	4-8-0	2-6-0

CENTRAL	W	L	T	PCT.	PF	PA	HOME	AWAY	AFC	DIV.
HOUSTON	12	4	0	.750	368	238	7-1-0	5-3-0	10-2-0	6-0-0
PITTSBURGH	9	7	0	.563	308	281	6-2-0	3-5-0	7-5-0	3-3-0
CLEVELAND	7	9	0	.438	304	307	4-4-0	3-5-0	4-8-0	3-3-0
CINCINNATI	3	13	0	.188	187	319	3-5-0	0-8-0	1-11-0	0-6-0

WEST	W	L	T	PCT.	PF	PA	HOME	AWAY	AFC	DIV.
KANSAS CITY	11	5	0	.688	328	291	7-1-0	4-4-0	9-3-0	7-1-0
L.A. RAIDERS	10	6	0	.625	306	326	5-3-0	5-3-0	7-5-0	5-3-0
DENVER	9	7	0	.563	373	284	5-3-0	4-4-0	8-4-0	4-4-0
SAN DIEGO	8	8	0	.500	322	290	4-4-0	4-4-0	6-6-0	3-5-0
SEATTLE	6	10	0	.375	280	314	4-4-0	2-6-0	6-8-0	1-7-0

NATIONAL FOOTBALL CONFERENCE

EAST	W	L	T	PCT.	PF	PA	HOME	AWAY	NFC	DIV.
DALLAS	12	4	0	.750	376	229	6-2-0	6-2-0	10-2-0	7-1-0
N.Y. GIANTS	11	5	0	.688	288	205	6-2-0	5-3-0	9-3-0	5-3-0
PHILADELPHIA	8	8	0	.500	293	315	3-5-0	5-3-0	6-6-0	3-5-0
PHOENIX	7	9	0	.438	326	269	4-4-0	3-5-0	6-8-0	4-4-0
WASHINGTON	4	12	0	.250	230	345	3-5-0	1-7-0	3-9-0	1-7-0

CENTRAL	W	L	T	PCT.	PF	PA	HOME	AWAY	NFC	DIV.
DETROIT	10	6	0	.625	298	292	5-3-0	5-3-0	8-6-0	4-4-0
MINNESOTA	9	7	0	.563	277	290	4-4-0	5-3-0	7-5-0	6-2-0
GREEN BAY	9	7	0	.563	340	282	6-2-0	3-5-0	6-6-0	4-4-0
CHICAGO	7	9	0	.438	234	230	3-5-0	4-4-0	5-7-0	3-5-0
TAMPA BAY	5	11	0	.313	237	376	3-5-0	2-6-0	4-8-0	3-5-0

WEST	W	L	T	PCT.	PF	PA	HOME	AWAY	NFC	DIV.
SAN FRANCISCO	10	6	0	.625	473	295	6-2-0	4-4-0	8-4-0	4-2-0
NEW ORLEANS	8	8	0	.500	317	343	4-4-0	4-4-0	6-6-0	3-3-0
ATLANTA	6	10	0	.375	316	385	4-4-0	2-6-0	5-7-0	4-2-0
L.A. RAMS	5	11	0	.313	221	367	3-5-0	2-6-0	3-9-0	1-5-0

1993 FINAL STATISTICS

1993 REVIEW ■ INDIVIDUAL STATS

AFC PASSING

	Team	Att.	Comp.	Comp. Pct.	Yds.	TD	TD Pct.	Lg.	Int.	Int. Pct.	Avg. Gain	Rating
Elway	Denv.	551	348	63.2	4,030	25	4.5	63	10	1.8	7.31	92.8
Montana	K.C.	298	181	60.7	2,144	13	4.4	50	7	2.4	7.19	87.4
Testaverde	Clev.	230	130	56.5	1,797	14	6.1	62	9	3.9	7.81	85.7
Esiason	N.Y.J.	473	288	60.9	3,421	16	3.4	77	11	2.3	7.23	84.5
Mitchell	Mia.	233	133	57.1	1,773	12	5.2	77	8	3.4	7.61	84.2
Hostetler	L.A.Rd	419	236	56.3	3,242	14	3.3	74	10	2.4	7.74	82.5
Kelly	Buff.	470	288	61.3	3,382	18	3.8	65	18	3.8	7.20	79.9
O'Donnell	Pitt.	486	270	55.6	3,208	14	2.9	71	7	1.4	6.60	79.5
George	Ind.	407	234	57.5	2,526	8	2.0	72	6	1.5	6.21	76.3
DeBerg	Mia.	227	136	59.9	1,707	7	3.1	47	10	4.4	7.52	75.3
Moon	Hou.	520	303	58.3	3,485	21	4.0	80	21	4.0	6.70	75.2
Friesz	S.D.	238	128	53.8	1,402	6	2.5	66	4	1.7	5.89	72.8
Humphries	S.D.	324	173	53.4	1,981	12	3.7	48	10	3.1	6.11	71.5
Mirer	Sea.	486	274	56.4	2,833	12	2.5	53	17	3.5	5.83	67.0
Klingler	Cin.	343	190	55.4	1,935	6	1.8	51	9	2.6	5.64	66.6
Bledsoe	N.E.	429	214	49.9	2,494	15	3.5	54	15	3.5	5.81	65.0

NON-QUALIFIERS

	Team	Att.	Comp.	Comp. Pct.	Yds.	TD	TD Pct.	Lg.	Int.	Int. Pct.	Avg. Gain	Rating
Marshall	Denv.	1	1	100.0	30	1	100.0	30	0	0.0	30.00	158.3
Jackson	Clev.	1	1	100.0	25	0	0.0	25	0	0.0	25.00	118.8
Maddox	Denv.	1	1	100.0	1	1	100.0	1	0	0.0	1.00	118.8
Richardson	Hou.	4	3	75.0	55	0	0.0	34	0	0.0	13.75	116.7
McGwire	Sea.	5	3	50.0	24	1	50.0	17	0	0.0	4.80	111.7
Byars	Mia.	2	1	50.0	11	1	50.0	11	0	0.0	5.50	106.3
Reich	Buff.	26	16	61.5	153	2	7.7	30	0	0.0	5.88	103.5
Wilhelm	Cin.	6	4	66.7	63	0	0.0	27	0	0.0	10.50	101.4
Marino	Mia.	150	91	60.7	1,218	8	5.3	80	3	2.0	8.12	95.9
Evans	L.A.Rd	76	45	59.2	640	3	3.9	68	4	5.3	8.42	77.7
Krieg	K.C.	189	105	55.6	1,238	7	3.7	66	3	1.6	6.55	81.4
Kosar	Clev.	138	79	57.3	807	5	3.6	38	3	2.2	5.85	77.2
Schroeder	Cin.	159	78	49.1	832	5	3.1	37	2	1.3	5.23	70.0
Carlson	Hou.	90	51	56.7	605	2	2.2	47	4	4.4	6.72	66.2
Pederson	Mia.	8	4	50.0	41	0	0.0	12	0	0.0	5.13	65.1
Nagle	N.Y.J.	14	6	42.9	71	0	0.0	18	0	0.0	5.07	58.9
Trudeau	Ind.	162	85	52.5	992	2	1.2	68	7	4.3	6.12	57.4
Philcox	Clev.	108	52	48.1	699	4	3.7	56	7	6.5	6.46	54.5
Secules	N.E.	134	75	56.0	918	2	1.5	82	9	6.7	6.85	54.3
Tomczak	Pitt.	54	29	53.7	398	2	3.7	39	5	9.3	7.37	51.3
Majkowski	Ind.	24	13	54.2	105	0	0.0	17	1	4.2	4.38	48.1
Gelbaugh	Sea.	5	3	60.0	39	0	0.0	22	1	20.0	7.80	45.0
Blundin	K.C.	3	1	33.3	2	0	0.0	2	0	0.0	.67	42.4
Zolak	N.E.	2	0	0.0	0	0	0.0	0	0	0.0	0.00	39.6
Hoard	Clev.	1	0	0.0	0	0	0.0	0	0	0.0	0.00	39.6
Johnson	Cin.	1	0	0.0	0	0	0.0	0	0	0.0	0.00	39.6
Means	S.D.	1	0	0.0	0	0	0.0	0	0	0.0	0.00	39.6
Pickens	Cin.	1	0	0.0	0	0	0.0	0	0	0.0	0.00	39.6
Thomas	Buff.	1	0	0.0	0	0	0.0	0	0	0.0	0.00	39.6
Turner	N.E.	1	0	0.0	0	0	0.0	0	0	0.0	0.00	39.6
Tuten	Sea.	1	0	0.0	0	0	0.0	0	0	0.0	0.00	39.6
Williams	Sea.	1	0	0.0	0	0	0.0	0	0	0.0	0.00	39.6
Aguiar	N.Y.J.	2	0	0.0	0	0	0.0	0	1	50.0	0.00	0.0
Johnson	Ind.	1	0	0.0	0	0	0.0	0	1	100.0	0.00	0.0

AFC PUNTING

	Team	No.	Yds.	Lg.	Gross Avg.	TB	Ins. 20	Blk.	Ret.	Ret. Yds.	Net Avg.
Gr. Montgomery	Hou.	54	2,462	77	45.6	5	13	0	28	249	39.1
Tuten	Sea.	90	4,007	64	44.5	7	21	1	47	475	37.3
Rouen	Denv.	67	3,017	62	45.0	8	17	1	33	337	37.1
L. Johnson	Cin.	90	3,954	60	43.9	12	24	0	47	416	36.6
Mohr	Buff.	74	2,991	58	40.4	4	19	0	29	247	36.0
Stark	Ind.	83	3,595	65	43.3	13	18	0	41	352	35.9
Kidd	S.D.	57	2,431	67	42.6	7	16	0	28	243	35.9
Hansen	Clev.	82	3,632	72	44.3	10	15	2	49	438	35.6
Barker	K.C.	76	3,240	59	42.6	8	19	1	43	352	35.4
Gossett	L.A.Rd	71	2,971	61	41.8	9	19	0	35	301	35.1
Saxon	N.E.	73	3,096	59	42.4	7	25	3	34	313	34.8

Continued

PRO FOOTBALL WEEKLY 1994 ALMANAC

Continued

	Team	Att.	Yds.	Avg.	Lg.	TD				
Aguiar	N.Y.J.	73	2,806	71	38.4	7	21	0	26	156	34.4
Royals	Pitt.	89	3,781	61	42.5	3	28	0	50	678	34.2
Hatcher	Mia.	58	2,304	56	39.7	4	13	0	32	359	32.2

NON-QUALIFIERS

Sullivan	Hou.	15	614	50	40.9	1	4	0	6	33	37.4
Carney	S.D.	4	155	46	38.8	0	1	0	2	16	34.8

AFC RUSHING

	Team	Att.	Yds.	Avg.	Lg.	TD		Team	Att.	Yds.	Avg.	Lg.	TD
Thomas	Buff.	355	1,315	3.7	27	6	Humphries	S.D.	8	37	4.6	27	0
Russell	N.E.	300	1,088	3.6	21	7	Turner	Buff.	11	36	3.3	10	0
C. Warren	Sea.	273	1,072	3.9	45	7	F. Jones	K.C.	5	34	6.8	13	0
G. Brown	Hou.	195	1,002	5.1	26	6	Jordan	L.A.Rd	12	33	2.8	12	0
J. Johnson	N.Y.J.	198	821	4.2	57	3	Mack	Clev.	10	33	3.3	7	1
Bernstine	Denv.	223	816	3.7	24	4	Secules	N.E.	8	33	4.1	13	0
Allen	K.C.	206	764	3.7	39	12	Verdin	Ind.	3	33	11.0	29	0
Thompson	Pitt.	205	763	3.7	36	3	Brooks	Buff.	3	30	10.0	15	0
Butts	S.D.	185	746	4.0	27	4	E. Thompson	K.C.	11	28	2.6	14	0
Potts	Ind.	179	711	4.0	34	0	Carrier	Clev.	4	26	6.5	15	1
Foster	Pitt.	177	711	4.0	38	8	Krieg	K.C.	21	24	1.1	20	0
Higgs	Mia.	186	693	3.7	31	3	Reed	Buff.	9	21	2.3	15	0
Means	S.D.	160	645	4.0	65	8	Mathis	N.Y.J.	2	20	10.0	17	1
Vardell	Clev.	171	644	3.8	54	3	Kosar	Clev.	14	19	1.4	10	0
Metcalf	Clev.	129	611	4.7	55	1	Givins	Hou.	6	19	3.2	16	0
Robinson	L.A.Rd	156	591	3.8	16	1	Stephens	K.C.	6	18	3.0	7	0
Green	Cin.	215	589	2.7	25	0	Chaffey	N.Y.J.	5	17	3.4	7	0
B. Baxter	N.Y.J.	174	559	3.2	16	7	Parmalee	Mia.	4	16	4.0	12	0
Fenner	Cin.	121	482	4.0	26	1	Saxon	Mia.	5	13	2.6	9	0
White	Hou.	131	465	3.6	14	2	Query	Cin.	2	13	6.5	8	0
Delpino	Denv.	131	445	3.4	18	8	Mills	Pitt.	3	12	4.0	19	0
K. Davis	Buff.	109	391	3.6	19	6	Bates	Sea.	2	12	6.0	6	0
Kirby	Mia.	119	390	3.3	20	3	Stark	Ind.	1	11	11.0	11	0
Williams	Sea.	82	371	4.5	38	3	Maston	Hou.	1	10	10.0	10	0
Mirer	Sea.	68	343	5.0	33	3	Richardson	Hou.	2	9	4.5	11	0
Johnson	Ind.	95	331	3.5	14	1	Johnson	Sea.	2	8	4.0	5	0
Anders	K.C.	75	291	3.9	18	0	Brown	L.A.Rd	2	7	3.5	14	0
Klingler	Cin.	41	282	6.9	29	0	Cuthbert	Pitt.	1	7	7.0	7	0
McNair	K.C.	51	278	5.5	47	2	Toner	Ind.	2	6	3.0	6	0
Byars	Mia.	64	269	4.2	77	3	Wellman	Hou.	2	6	3.0	4	0
Hoge	Pitt.	51	249	4.9	30	1	Martin	Mia.	1	6	6.0	6	0
Turner	N.E.	50	231	4.6	49	0	Robinson	Cin.	1	6	6.0	6	0
Milburn	Denv.	52	231	4.4	26	0	Benjamin	Cin.	3	5	1.7	2	0
Hoard	Clev.	56	227	4.1	30	0	Majkowski	Ind.	2	4	2.0	4	0
B. Thomas	N.Y.J.	59	221	3.8	24	1	D. Thomas	Sea.	1	4	4.0	4	0
Harmon	S.D.	46	216	4.7	19	0	Friesz	S.D.	10	3	.3	2	0
Hostetler	L.A.Rd	55	202	3.6	19	5	Trudeau	Ind.	5	3	.6	2	0
Croom	N.E.	60	198	3.3	22	1	Philcox	Clev.	2	3	1.5	3	1
Bell	L.A.Rd	67	180	2.7	12	1	Barnett	K.C.	1	3	3.0	3	0
Murrell	N.Y.J.	34	157	4.6	37	1	Lewis	S.D.	3	2	.7	7	0
S. Smith	L.A.Rd	47	156	3.3	13	0	J. Jones	Clev.	2	2	1.0	1	1
Elway	Denv.	44	153	3.5	18	0	Saxon	N.E.	2	2	1.0	2	0
Vaughn	Sea.	36	153	4.3	37	0	Carter	K.C.	1	2	2.0	2	0
Culver	Ind.	65	150	2.3	9	3	Mayes	Sea.	1	2	2.0	2	0
Gash	N.E.	48	149	3.1	14	1	Coleman	Hou.	1	1	1.0	1	0
Williams	K.C.	42	149	3.6	19	0	Jackson	Clev.	1	1	1.0	1	0
Moon	Hou.	48	145	3.0	35	1	A. Miller	S.D.	1	0	0.0	0	0
Bieniemy	S.D.	33	135	4.1	12	1	Cash	K.C.	1	0	0.0	0	0
Stone	Pitt.	12	121	10.1	38	1	Hendrickson	S.D.	1	0	0.0	0	0
Esiason	N.Y.J.	45	118	2.6	17	1	Jett	L.A.Rd	1	0	0.0	0	0
McCallum	L.A.Rd	37	114	3.1	14	3	Martin	Sea.	1	0	0.0	0	0
O'Donnell	Pitt.	26	111	4.3	27	0	Rouen	Denv.	1	0	0.0	0	0
Montgomery	L.A.Rd	37	106	2.9	15	0	Woodson	Pitt.	1	0	0.0	0	0
Kelly	Buff.	36	102	2.8	17	0	Zolak	N.E.	1	0	0.0	0	0
Tillman	Hou.	9	94	10.4	34	0	Pederson	Mia.	2	-1	-.5	0	0
Mitchell	Mia.	21	89	4.2	32	0	Gelbaugh	Sea.	1	-1	-1.0	-1	0
Bledsoe	N.E.	32	82	2.6	15	0	McGwire	Sea.	1	-1	-1.0	-1	0
Testaverde	Clev.	18	74	4.1	14	0	Maddox	Denv.	2	-2	-1.0	-1	0
Montana	K.C.	25	64	2.6	17	0	Fina	Buff.	1	-2	-2.0	-2	0
Baldwin	Clev.	18	61	3.4	11	0	Crittenden	N.E.	1	-3	-3.0	-3	0
Miles	Cin.	22	56	2.6	15	1	Marino	Mia.	9	-4	-.4	4	1
Gardner	Buff.	20	56	2.8	8	0	Tomczak	Pitt.	5	-4	-.8	2	0
Jefferson	S.D.	5	53	10.6	33	0	DeBerg	Mia.	4	-4	-1.0	-1	0
Blades	Sea.	5	52	10.4	26	0	Fryar	Mia.	3	-4	-1.3	2	0
Evans	L.A.Rd	14	51	3.6	17	0	McDuffie	Mia.	1	-4	-4.0	-4	0
Rivers	Denv.	15	50	3.3	14	1	Ismail	L.A.Rd	4	-5	-1.3	10	0
Carlson	Hou.	14	41	2.9	10	2	Reich	Buff.	6	-6	-1.0	-1	0
Schroeder	Cin.	10	41	4.1	20	0	Moore	N.Y.J.	1	-6	-6.0	-6	0
George	Ind.	13	39	3.0	14	0	Gossett	L.A.Rd	1	-10	-10.0	-10	0
Ball	Cin.	8	37	4.6	18	1	Kidd	S.D.	3	-13	-4.3	2	1
							Aguiar	N.Y.J.	3	-27	-9.0	5	0

1993 REVIEW ■ INDIVIDUAL STATS

AFC RECEIVING

	Team	No.	Yds.	Avg.	Lg.	TD		Team	No.	Yds.	Avg.	Lg.	TD
Langhorne	Ind.	85	1,038	12.2	72	3	G. Brown	Hou.	21	240	11.4	38	2
A. Miller	S.D.	84	1,162	13.8	66	7	Walker	S.D.	21	212	10.1	25	1
Sharpe	Denv.	81	995	12.3	63	9	K. Davis	Buff.	21	95	4.5	28	0
Brown	L.A.Rd	80	1,180	14.8	71	7	Martin	Mia.	20	347	17.4	80	3
Blades	Sea.	80	945	11.8	41	3	R. Johnson	Denv.	20	243	12.2	38	1
Slaughter	Hou.	77	904	11.7	41	5	B. Baxter	N.Y.J.	20	158	7.9	24	0
Kirby	Mia.	75	874	11.7	47	3	McDuffie	Mia.	19	197	10.4	18	0
Harmon	S.D.	73	671	9.2	37	2	Vardell	Clev.	19	151	8.0	28	1
Givins	Hou.	68	887	13.0	80	4	S. Smith	L.A.Rd	18	187	10.4	22	0
Metzelaars	Buff.	68	609	9.0	51	4	Tillman	Denv.	17	193	11.4	30	2
J. Johnson	N.Y.J.	67	641	9.6	48	1	Barnett	K.C.	17	182	10.7	25	1
Jeffires	Hou.	66	753	11.4	66	6	Thompson	Cin.	17	87	5.1	10	1
Fryar	Mia.	64	1,010	15.8	65	5	Crittenden	N.E.	16	293	18.3	44	1
Moore	N.Y.J.	64	843	13.2	51	1	Robinson	L.A.Rd	15	142	9.5	58	0
Hesler	Ind.	64	835	13.1	58	1	Butts	S.D.	15	105	7.0	23	0
Green	Pitt.	63	942	15.0	71	5	C. Warren	Sea.	15	99	6.6	21	0
Metcalf	Clev.	63	539	8.6	49	2	Arbuckle	Ind.	15	90	6.0	23	0
Byars	Mia.	61	613	10.1	27	3	Gash	N.E.	14	93	6.8	15	0
Brooks	Buff.	60	714	11.9	32	5	Copeland	Buff.	13	242	18.6	60	0
Williams	Sea.	58	450	7.8	25	1	McCardell	Clev.	13	234	18.0	43	4
Martin	Sea.	57	798	14.0	53	5	Pupunu	S.D.	13	142	10.9	28	0
Query	Cin.	56	654	11.7	51	4	Thornton	N.Y.J.	12	108	9.0	22	2
Johnson	Ind.	55	443	8.1	36	0	Culver	Ind.	11	112	10.2	26	1
Coates	N.E.	53	659	12.4	54	8	Bell	L.A.Rd	11	111	10.1	18	0
Davis	K.C.	52	909	17.5	66	7	D. Thomas	Sea.	11	95	9.1	20	0
Reed	Buff.	52	854	16.4	65	6	Barnes	S.D.	10	137	13.7	21	0
Birden	K.C.	51	721	14.1	50	2	McNair	K.C.	10	74	7.4	24	0
Fenner	Cin.	48	427	8.9	40	0	Higgs	Mia.	10	72	7.2	15	0
Thomas	Buff.	48	387	8.1	37	0	Means	S.D.	10	59	5.9	11	0
Brisby	N.E.	45	626	13.9	39	2	Montgomery	L.A.Rd	10	43	4.3	9	0
Russell	Denv.	44	719	16.3	43	3	Thigpen	Pitt.	9	154	17.1	39	3
Ingram	Mia.	44	707	16.1	77	6	Coleman	Hou.	9	129	14.3	25	0
McGee	Cin.	44	525	11.9	37	0	Cooper	Pitt.	9	112	12.4	38	0
Bernstine	Denv.	44	372	8.5	41	0	F. Jones	K.C.	9	111	12.3	19	0
Carrier	Clev.	43	746	17.4	55	3	Rembert	Cin.	8	101	12.6	21	0
Pickens	Cin.	43	565	13.1	36	6	Croom	N.E.	8	92	11.5	21	0
Horton	L.A.Rd	43	467	10.9	32	1	Kimbrough	Denv.	8	79	9.9	16	0
Cash	Ind.	43	402	9.4	37	3	Robinson	Cin.	8	72	9.0	14	0
Timpson	N.E.	42	654	15.6	48	2	Gault	L.A.Rd	8	64	8.0	12	0
Jackson	Clev.	41	756	18.4	62	8	H. Jones	K.C.	7	91	13.0	22	0
Stone	Pitt.	41	587	14.3	44	2	Dyal	K.C.	7	83	11.9	31	0
Duncan	Hou.	41	456	11.1	47	3	R. Thomas	Sea.	7	67	9.6	16	0
Burkett	N.Y.J.	40	531	13.3	77	4	Williams	K.C.	7	42	6.0	14	0
Anders	K.C.	40	326	8.2	27	1	B. Thomas	N.Y.J.	7	25	3.6	7	0
Mitchell	N.Y.J.	39	630	16.2	65	6	Miles	Cin.	6	89	14.8	27	0
K. Jackson	Mia.	39	613	15.7	57	6	Carpenter	N.Y.J.	6	83	13.8	18	0
Turner	N.E.	39	333	8.5	26	2	Carroll	Cin.	6	81	13.5	28	0
Graham	Pitt.	38	579	15.2	51	0	Rivers	Denv.	6	59	9.8	17	1
Lewis	S.D.	38	463	12.2	47	4	Frisch	Cin.	6	43	7.2	12	0
Milburn	Denv.	38	300	7.9	50	3	Young	S.D.	6	41	6.8	12	2
Thompson	Pitt.	38	259	6.8	28	0	Baty	Mia.	5	78	15.6	32	1
V. Johnson	Denv.	36	517	14.4	56	5	Tillman	Clev.	5	68	13.6	18	1
Hoard	Clev.	35	351	10.0	41	0	Glover	L.A.Rd	5	55	13.8	26	1
Allen	K.C.	34	238	7.0	18	3	Wolfley	Clev.	5	25	5.0	9	1
White	Hou.	34	229	6.7	20	0	Murrell	N.Y.J.	5	12	2.4	8	0
Jett	L.A.Rd	33	771	23.4	74	3	Cox	Ind.	4	59	14.8	24	0
Hoge	Pitt.	33	247	7.5	18	4	Chaffey	N.Y.J.	4	55	13.8	20	1
Beebe	Buff.	31	504	16.3	65	3	Smith	Clev.	4	55	13.8	17	0
Wellman	Hou.	31	430	13.9	44	1	Harris	Hou.	4	53	13.3	17	1
Jefferson	S.D.	30	391	13.0	39	2	Davenport	Pitt.	4	51	12.8	19	0
Mills	Pitt.	29	386	13.3	30	1	Gardner	Buff.	4	50	12.5	22	1
Kinchen	Clev.	29	347	11.9	40	2	Jordan	L.A.Rd	4	42	10.5	33	0
Marshall	Denv.	28	360	12.9	40	2	Ball	Cin.	4	39	9.8	24	0
Wright	L.A.Rd	27	462	17.1	68	4	E. Thompson	K.C.	4	33	8.3	13	0
Foster	Pitt.	27	217	8.0	21	1	F. Baxter	N.Y.J.	3	48	16.0	25	1
Dawkins	Ind.	26	430	16.5	68	1	Hastings	Pitt.	3	44	14.7	18	0
Ismail	L.A.Rd	26	353	13.6	43	1	Rowe	Clev.	3	37	12.3	16	0
Russell	N.E.	26	245	9.3	69	0	McKeller	Buff.	3	35	11.7	13	1
Delpino	Denv.	26	195	7.5	25	0	Johnson	Sea.	3	15	5.0	8	1
Potts	Ind.	26	189	7.3	24	0	R. Brown	Hou.	2	30	15.0	26	0
Mathis	N.Y.J.	24	352	14.7	46	0	Tasker	Buff.	2	26	13.0	22	0
Hayes	K.C.	24	331	13.8	49	1	T. Brown	N.E.	2	22	11.0	14	0
Cash	K.C.	24	242	10.1	24	4	Verdin	Ind.	2	20	10.0	19	1
Edmunds	Sea.	24	239	10.0	32	2	Awalt	Buff.	2	19	9.5	10	0
Green	Sea.	23	178	7.7	20	1	Miller	Mia.	2	15	7.0	8	0
McMurtry	N.E.	22	241	11.0	20	1	Sadowski	N.Y.J.	2	14	7.0	11	0
Cook	N.E.	22	154	7.0	17	1	Thomason	Cin.	2	8	4.0	5	0
Green	Cin.	22	115	5.2	16	0	McCallum	L.A.Rd	2	5	2.5	3	0

Continued

381

PRO FOOTBALL WEEKLY 1994 ALMANAC

Continued

Taylor	Denv.	1	28	28.0	28	0
Banks	Mia.	1	26	26.0	26	0
Benjamin	Cin.	1	16	16.0	16	0
C. Williams	Clev.	1	14	14.0	14	0
Maston	Hou.	1	14	14.0	14	0
Norgard	Hou.	1	13	13.0	13	0
Jordan	Pitt.	1	12	12.0	12	0
M. Williams	Mia.	1	11	11.0	11	0
Stegall	Cin.	1	8	8.0	8	0
Bates	Sea.	1	6	6.0	6	0
Baldwin	Clev.	1	5	5.0	5	1
Toner	Ind.	1	5	5.0	5	0
Roberts	Sea.	1	4	4.0	4	0
Thomas	Sea.	1	4	4.0	4	0
Tillman	Hou.	1	4	4.0	4	1
Cuthbert	Pitt.	1	3	3.0	3	0
Drewrey	Hou.	1	3	3.0	3	0
Parmalee	Mia.	1	1	1.0	1	0
Valerio	K.C.	1	1	1.0	1	1
Wyman	Denv.	1	1	1.0	1	1
Bieniemy	S.D.	1	0	0.0	0	0
Esiason	N.Y.J.	1	-8	-8.0	-8	0

AFC SCORING

	Team	TD	XP/att.	FG/att.	Saf.	Pts.
Jaeger	L.A.Rd	0	27/29	35/44	0	132
Del Greco	Hou.	0	39/40	29/34	0	126
Carney	S.D.	0	31/33	31/40	0	124
Elam	Denv.	0	41/42	26/35	0	119
Anderson	Pitt.	0	32/32	28/30	0	116
Stoyanovich	Mia.	0	37/37	24/32	0	109
Lowery	K.C.	0	37/37	23/29	0	106
Christie	Buff.	0	36/37	23/32	0	105
Kasay	Sea.	0	29/29	23/28	0	98
Biasucci	Ind.	0	15/16	26/31	0	93
Allen	K.C.	15	0/0	0/0	0	90
Pelfrey	Cin.	0	13/16	24/31	0	85
Stover	Clev.	0	36/36	16/22	0	84
Blanchard	N.Y.J.	0	31/31	17/26	0	82
Bahr	N.E.	0	28/29	13/18	0	67
Sisson	N.E.	0	15/15	14/26	0	57
Foster	Pitt.	9	0/0	0/0	0	54
Sharpe	Denv.	9	0/0	0/0	0	54
Brown	L.A.Rd	8	0/0	0/0	0	48
Coates	N.E.	8	0/0	0/0	0	48
Delpino	Denv.	8	0/0	0/0	0	48
G. Brown	Hou.	8	0/0	0/0	0	48
Jackson	Clev.	8	0/0	0/0	0	48
Means	S.D.	8	0/0	0/0	0	48
A. Miller	S.D.	7	0/0	0/0	0	42
B. Baxter	N.Y.J.	7	0/0	0/0	0	42
C. Warren	Sea.	7	0/0	0/0	0	42
Davis	K.C.	7	0/0	0/0	0	42
Russell	N.E.	7	0/0	0/0	0	42
Byars	Mia.	6	0/0	0/0	0	36
Ingram	Mia.	6	0/0	0/0	0	36
Jeffires	Hou.	6	0/0	0/0	0	36
K. Davis	Buff.	6	0/0	0/0	0	36
K. Jackson	Mia.	6	0/0	0/0	0	36
Kirby	Mia.	6	0/0	0/0	0	36
Mitchell	N.Y.J.	6	0/0	0/0	0	36
Pickens	Cin.	6	0/0	0/0	0	36
Reed	Buff.	6	0/0	0/0	0	36
Thomas	Buff.	6	0/0	0/0	0	36
Brooks	Buff.	5	0/0	0/0	0	30
Carrier	Clev.	5	0/0	0/0	0	30
Culver	Ind.	5	0/0	0/0	0	30
Fryar	Mia.	5	0/0	0/0	0	30
Green	Pitt.	5	0/0	0/0	0	30
Hoge	Pitt.	5	0/0	0/0	0	30
Hostetler	L.A.Rd	5	0/0	0/0	0	30
Martin	Sea.	5	0/0	0/0	0	30
Metcalf	Clev.	5	0/0	0/0	0	30
Slaughter	Hou.	5	0/0	0/0	0	30
V. Johnson	Denv.	5	0/0	0/0	0	30
Bernstine	Denv.	4	0/0	0/0	0	24
Burkett	N.Y.J.	4	0/0	0/0	0	24
Butts	S.D.	4	0/0	0/0	0	24
Cash	K.C.	4	0/0	0/0	0	24
Givins	Hou.	4	0/0	0/0	0	24
J. Johnson	N.Y.J.	4	0/0	0/0	0	24
Lewis	S.D.	4	0/0	0/0	0	24
McCardell	Clev.	4	0/0	0/0	0	24
Metzelaars	Buff.	4	0/0	0/0	0	24
Query	Cin.	4	0/0	0/0	0	24
Russell	Denv.	4	0/0	0/0	0	24
Vardell	Clev.	4	0/0	0/0	0	24
Williams	Sea.	4	0/0	0/0	0	24
Wright	L.A.Rd	4	0/0	0/0	0	24
Beebe	Buff.	3	0/0	0/0	0	18
Blades	Sea.	3	0/0	0/0	0	18
Cash	Ind.	3	0/0	0/0	0	18
Duncan	Hou.	3	0/0	0/0	0	18
Higgs	Mia.	3	0/0	0/0	0	18
Jett	L.A.Rd	3	0/0	0/0	0	18
Langhorne	Ind.	3	0/0	0/0	0	18
Martin	Mia.	3	0/0	0/0	0	18
McCallum	L.A.Rd	3	0/0	0/0	0	18
Milburn	Denv.	3	0/0	0/0	0	18
Mirer	Sea.	3	0/0	0/0	0	18
Stone	Pitt.	3	0/0	0/0	0	18
Thigpen	Pitt.	3	0/0	0/0	0	18
Thompson	Pitt.	3	0/0	0/0	0	18
Rivers	Denv.	2	0/0	0/0	1	14
Birden	K.C.	2	0/0	0/0	0	12
Brisby	N.E.	2	0/0	0/0	0	12
Carlson	Hou.	2	0/0	0/0	0	12
Edmunds	Sea.	2	0/0	0/0	0	12
Harmon	S.D.	2	0/0	0/0	0	12
Jefferson	S.D.	2	0/0	0/0	0	12
Kinchen	Clev.	2	0/0	0/0	0	12
Marshall	Denv.	2	0/0	0/0	0	12
McDuffie	Mia.	2	0/0	0/0	0	12
McNair	K.C.	2	0/0	0/0	0	12
Thornton	N.Y.J.	2	0/0	0/0	0	12
Tillman	Denv.	2	0/0	0/0	0	12
Timpson	N.E.	2	0/0	0/0	0	12
Turner	N.E.	2	0/0	0/0	0	12
White	Hou.	2	0/0	0/0	0	12
Young	S.D.	2	0/0	0/0	0	12
Stephens	Sea.	1	0/0	0/0	2	10
Jones	Buff.	1	0/0	0/0	1	8
Anders	K.C.	1	0/0	0/0	0	6
B. Thomas	N.Y.J.	1	0/0	0/0	0	6
B. Washington	N.Y.J.	1	0/0	0/0	0	6
Baldwin	Clev.	1	0/0	0/0	0	6
Ball	Cin.	1	0/0	0/0	0	6
Barnett	K.C.	1	0/0	0/0	0	6
Baty	Mia.	1	0/0	0/0	0	6
Bell	L.A.Rd	1	0/0	0/0	0	6
Bieniemy	S.D.	1	0/0	0/0	0	6
Blackmon	Sea.	1	0/0	0/0	0	6
Brim	Cin.	1	0/0	0/0	0	6
Chaffey	N.Y.J.	1	0/0	0/0	0	6
Childress	Hou.	1	0/0	0/0	0	6
Cook	N.E.	1	0/0	0/0	0	6
Copeland	Buff.	1	0/0	0/0	0	6
Crittenden	N.E.	1	0/0	0/0	0	6
Croel	Denv.	1	0/0	0/0	0	6
Croom	N.E.	1	0/0	0/0	0	6
D. Williams	Cin.	1	0/0	0/0	0	6
Davidson	Pitt.	1	0/0	0/0	0	6
Dawkins	Ind.	1	0/0	0/0	0	6
Dishman	Hou.	1	0/0	0/0	0	6
Esiason	N.Y.J.	1	0/0	0/0	0	6
F. Baxter	N.Y.J.	1	0/0	0/0	0	6
Fenner	Cin.	1	0/0	0/0	0	6
Frank	S.D.	1	0/0	0/0	0	6
Gardner	Buff.	1	0/0	0/0	0	6
Gash	N.E.	1	0/0	0/0	0	6
Glover	L.A.Rd	1	0/0	0/0	0	6
Green	Sea.	1	0/0	0/0	0	6
Harris	Hou.	1	0/0	0/0	0	6

Continued

1993 REVIEW ■ INDIVIDUAL STATS

Continued

Hayes	K.C.	1	0/0	0/0	0	6
Herrod	Ind.	1	0/0	0/0	0	6
Hester	Ind.	1	0/0	0/0	0	6
Horton	L.A.Rd	1	0/0	0/0	0	6
Ismail	L.A.Rd	1	0/0	0/0	0	6
J. Jones	Clev.	1	0/0	0/0	0	6
Jackson	Hou.	1	0/0	0/0	0	6
Johnson	Ind.	1	0/0	0/0	0	6
Johnson	Sea.	1	0/0	0/0	0	6
Kidd	S.D.	1	0/0	0/0	0	6
Kirkland	Pitt.	1	0/0	0/0	0	6
Lewis	Hou.	1	0/0	0/0	0	6
Lewis	K.C.	1	0/0	0/0	0	6
Mack	Clev.	1	0/0	0/0	0	6
Marino	Mia.	1	0/0	0/0	0	6
Mathis	N.Y.J.	1	0/0	0/0	0	6
McDaniel	L.A.Rd	1	0/0	0/0	0	6
McKeller	Buff.	1	0/0	0/0	0	6
McMurtry	N.E.	1	0/0	0/0	0	6
Miles	Cin.	1	0/0	0/0	0	6
Mills	Pitt.	1	0/0	0/0	0	6
Moon	Hou.	1	0/0	0/0	0	6
Moore	Clev.	1	0/0	0/0	0	6
Moore	N.Y.J.	1	0/0	0/0	0	6
Murrell	N.Y.J.	1	0/0	0/0	0	6
Mustafaa	Clev.	1	0/0	0/0	0	6
Nash	Sea.	1	0/0	0/0	0	6
Odomes	Buff.	1	0/0	0/0	0	6
Oliver	Mia.	1	0/0	0/0	0	6
Orlando	Hou.	1	0/0	0/0	0	6
Philcox	Clev.	1	0/0	0/0	0	6
R. Johnson	Denv.	1	0/0	0/0	0	6
Robertson	Hou.	1	0/0	0/0	0	6
Robinson	L.A.Rd	1	0/0	0/0	0	6
Saleaumua	K.C.	1	0/0	0/0	0	6
Talley	Buff.	1	0/0	0/0	0	6
Thomas	K.C.	1	0/0	0/0	0	6
Thompson	Cin.	1	0/0	0/0	0	6
Tillman	Clev.	1	0/0	0/0	0	6
Tillman	Hou.	1	0/0	0/0	0	6
Valerio	K.C.	1	0/0	0/0	0	6
Verdin	Ind.	1	0/0	0/0	0	6
Walker	S.D.	1	0/0	0/0	0	6
Washington	Buff.	1	0/0	0/0	0	6
Wellman	Hou.	1	0/0	0/0	0	6
Wolfley	Clev.	1	0/0	0/0	0	6
Woodson	Pitt.	1	0/0	0/0	0	6
Wyman	Denv.	1	0/0	0/0	0	6
TEAM	Cin.	0	0/0	0/0	2	4
A. Williams	Cin.	0	0/0	0/0	1	2
Edwards	Sea.	0	0/0	0/0	1	2
Lathon	Hou.	0	0/0	0/0	1	2
M. Washington	N.Y.J.	0	0/0	0/0	1	2
Pleasant	Clev.	0	0/0	0/0	1	2
Riddick	Clev.	0	0/0	0/0	1	2
TEAM	Sea.	0	0/0	0/0	1	2

AFC INTERCEPTIONS

	Team	No.	Yds.	Lg.	TD
E. Robinson	Sea.	9	80	28	0
Odomes	Buff.	9	65	25	0
Woodson	Pitt.	8	138	63	1
Robertson	Hou.	7	137	69	0
Carrington	S.D.	7	104	28	0
B. Washington	N.Y.J.	6	128	62	1
Dishman	Hou.	6	74	30	0
Lewis	K.C.	6	61	24	0
McDaniel	L.A.Rd	5	87	36	1
Jackson	Hou.	5	54	22	1
Mincy	K.C.	5	44	20	0
Brown	Mia.	5	43	29	0
Turner	Clev.	5	25	19	0
Perry	Pitt.	4	61	30	0
Hunter	Sea.	4	54	34	0
Hurst	N.E.	4	53	24	0
Buchanan	Ind.	4	45	28	0
Lake	Pitt.	4	31	26	0
Frank	S.D.	3	119	102	1
Brim	Cin.	3	74	30	1
Talley	Buff.	3	74	61	1
Orlando	Hou.	3	68	38	1
Smith	Denv.	3	57	36	0
Johnson	Pitt.	3	51	26	0
Braxton	Denv.	3	37	25	0
Lott	N.Y.J.	3	35	29	0
Gray	Sea.	3	33	16	0
McDowell	Hou.	3	31	13	0
Baylor	Ind.	3	11	7	0
S. Jones	Clev.	3	0	0	0
Wren	N.E.	3	-7	2	0
D. Williams	Cin.	2	126	97	1
Jones	Buff.	2	92	85	1
Atwater	Denv.	2	81	68	0
Oliver	Mia.	2	60	56	1
Seau	S.D.	2	58	42	0
Anderson	L.A.Rd	2	52	27	0
Ross	K.C.	2	49	48	0
Hoskins	L.A.Rd	2	34	20	0
Darby	Buff.	2	32	32	0
Vincent	Mia.	2	29	23	0
Hasty	N.Y.J.	2	22	22	0
E. Thomas	N.Y.J.	2	20	20	0
White	Cin.	2	19	14	0
Bayless	K.C.	2	14	16	0
Pope	S.D.	2	14	12	0
Dronett	Denv.	2	13	7	0
Francis	Cin.	2	12	12	0
Jones	Pitt.	2	11	11	0
Williams	Buff.	2	11	6	0
Plummer	S.D.	2	7	6	0
Lang	Denv.	2	4	4	0
Lewis	N.Y.J.	2	4	3	0
Blackmon	Sea.	2	0	0	0
Green	Mia.	2	0	0	0
M. Patton	Buff.	2	0	0	0
Vanhorse	S.D.	2	0	0	0
Washington	L.A.Rd	2	0	0	0
Mustafaa	Clev.	1	97	97	1
Figures	Pitt.	1	78	78	0
Hilliard	Clev.	1	54	54	0
Lewis	Hou.	1	47	47	1
Barnett	N.E.	1	40	40	0
Herrod	Ind.	1	29	29	0
Washington	Buff.	1	27	27	1
Cox	Mia.	1	26	26	0
V. Brown	N.E.	1	24	24	0
Croel	Denv.	1	22	22	1
Speer	Clev.	1	22	22	0
Terry	K.C.	1	21	21	0
Marts	K.C.	1	20	20	0
McGlockton	L.A.Rd	1	19	19	0
Daniel	Ind.	1	17	17	0
Grant	Cin.	1	17	17	0
Hobley	Mia.	1	17	17	0
Hendrickson	S.D.	1	16	16	0
Lageman	N.Y.J.	1	15	15	0
Belser	Ind.	1	14	11	0
F. Robinson	Denv.	1	13	13	0
Nash	Sea.	1	13	13	1
Saleaumua	K.C.	1	13	13	0
Jefferson	Sea.	1	12	12	0
Henry	Pitt.	1	10	10	0
Matthews	Clev.	1	10	10	0
Wyman	Denv.	1	9	9	0
Collins	N.E.	1	8	8	0
Trapp	L.A.Rd	1	7	7	0
Davidson	Pitt.	1	6	6	0
Young	N.Y.J.	1	6	6	0
Bennett	Buff.	1	5	5	0
Porter	Sea.	1	4	4	0
Thompson	N.E.	1	4	4	0

Continued

PRO FOOTBALL WEEKLY 1994 ALMANAC

Continued					
Clifton	N.Y.J.	1	3	3	0
Gordon	S.D.	1	3	3	0
Smith	K.C.	1	3	3	0
Bishop	Hou.	1	1	1	0
B. Smith	Buff.	1	0	0	0
Bates	L.A.Rd	1	0	0	0
Bradford	Denv.	1	0	0	0
Carter	K.C.	1	0	0	0
Davis	S.D.	1	0	0	0
Dimry	Denv.	1	0	0	0

Hall	Denv.	1	0	0	0
Harper	Sea.	1	0	0	0
Houston	N.Y.J.	1	0	0	0
Jones	Cin.	1	0	0	0
Lambert	N.E.	1	0	0	0
M. Johnson	Clev.	1	0	0	0
Ray	N.E.	1	0	0	0
Taylor	K.C.	1	0	0	0
Tovar	Cin.	1	0	0	0
Richard	S.D.	1	-2	-2	0
Wheeler	Cin.	0	24	24	0

AFC KICKOFF RETURNS

	Team	No.	Yds.	Avg.	Lg.	TD
Ismail	L.A.Rd	25	605	24.2	66	0
McDuffie	Mia.	32	755	23.6	48	0
Ball	Cin.	23	501	21.8	45	0
Verdin	Ind.	50	1,050	21.0	38	0
Crittenden	N.E.	23	478	20.8	44	0
Lewis	S.D.	33	684	20.7	60	0
Bates	Sea.	30	603	20.1	46	0
Robinson	Cin.	30	567	18.9	42	0
Baldwin	Clev.	24	444	18.5	31	0
Copeland	Buff.	24	436	18.2	28	0
Murrell	N.Y.J.	23	342	14.9	23	0

NON-QUALIFIERS

	Team	No.	Yds.	Avg.	Lg.	TD
Anders	K.C.	1	47	47.0	47	0
McNair	K.C.	1	28	28.0	28	0
Gault	L.A.Rd	7	187	26.7	60	0
Thigpen	Pitt.	1	23	23.0	23	0
M. Williams	Mia.	8	180	22.5	39	0
Hoard	Clev.	13	286	22.0	39	0
Dickerson	K.C.	11	237	21.6	44	0
Kirby	Mia.	4	85	21.3	26	0
Metcalf	Clev.	15	318	21.2	47	0
A. Miller	S.D.	2	42	21.0	29	0
Mills	Hou.	11	230	20.9	37	0
Delpino	Denv.	7	146	20.9	49	0
Russell	Denv.	18	374	20.8	49	0
Lamb	Buff.	2	40	20.0	23	0
Woodson	Pitt.	15	294	19.6	44	0
Benjamin	Cin.	4	78	19.5	24	0
B. Thomas	N.Y.J.	2	39	19.5	28	0
Drewrey	Hou.	15	291	19.4	34	0
Thompson	Pitt.	4	77	19.3	27	0
Hughes	K.C.	14	266	19.0	30	0
W. Williams	Pitt.	1	19	19.0	19	0
Harmon	S.D.	1	18	18.0	18	0
Williams	K.C.	3	53	17.7	26	0
Stephens	K.C.	5	88	17.6	25	0
Vaughn	Sea.	16	280	17.5	31	0
F. Jones	K.C.	9	156	17.3	29	0
Milburn	Denv.	12	188	17.1	26	0
Culver	Ind.	3	51	17.0	20	0
Wright	L.A.Rd	10	167	16.7	28	0
Anderson	N.Y.J.	4	66	16.5	22	0
Miles	Cin.	4	65	16.3	24	0

	Team	No.	Yds.	Avg.	Lg.	TD
T. Brown	N.E.	15	243	16.2	29	0
Beebe	Buff.	10	160	16.0	22	0
Bieniemy	S.D.	7	110	15.7	18	0
Stone	Pitt.	11	168	15.3	30	0
Harris	N.E.	6	90	15.0	19	0
Hastings	Pitt.	12	177	14.8	22	0
Mathis	N.Y.J.	7	102	14.6	28	0
Vardell	Clev.	4	58	14.5	16	0
G. Brown	Hou.	2	29	14.5	16	0
Robinson	L.A.Rd	4	57	14.3	33	0
Prior	N.Y.J.	9	126	14.0	27	0
Smith	Clev.	1	13	13.0	13	0
Martin	Sea.	3	38	12.7	15	0
K. Davis	Buff.	8	100	12.5	18	0
Hendrickson	S.D.	2	25	12.5	13	0
Coleman	Hou.	3	37	12.3	16	0
McCallum	L.A.Rd	1	12	12.0	12	0
Miles	Sea.	1	12	12.0	12	0
Hoge	Pitt.	3	33	11.0	15	0
Means	S.D.	2	22	11.0	14	0
Miller	Mia.	2	22	11.0	16	0
Cash	Ind.	1	11	11.0	11	0
Ambrose	Ind.	1	10	10.0	10	0
Fryar	Mia.	1	10	10.0	10	0
Radecic	Ind.	1	10	10.0	10	0
Tuatagaloa	Sea.	1	10	10.0	10	0
Turner	Buff.	1	10	10.0	10	0
Peat	L.A.Rd	2	18	9.0	10	0
Meeks	Denv.	1	9	9.0	9	0
Cook	N.E.	1	8	8.0	8	0
K. Smith	L.A.Rd	2	15	7.5	8	0
Baty	Mia.	1	7	7.0	7	0
Saxon	Mia.	1	7	7.0	7	0
Cooper	Pitt.	1	2	2.0	2	0
Butcher	Ind.	2	2	1.0	2	0
Sabb	N.E.	2	0	0.0	0	0
Kinchen	Clev.	1	0	0.0	0	0
Marts	K.C.	1	0	0.0	0	0
R. Johnson	Denv.	1	0	0.0	0	0
Sadowski	N.Y.J.	1	0	0.0	0	0
Sharpe	Denv.	1	0	0.0	0	0
Smith	N.E.	1	0	0.0	0	0
Teeter	Hou.	1	0	0.0	0	0
Turk	L.A.Rd	1	0	0.0	0	0
Wren	N.E.	1	0	0.0	0	0
Vincent	Mia.	0	2	0.0	2	0

AFC PUNT RETURNS

	Team	No.	FC	Yds.	Avg.	Lg.	TD
Metcalf	Clev.	36	11	464	12.9	91	2
Gordon	S.D.	31	15	395	12.7	54	0
Brown	L.A.Rd	40	20	465	11.6	74	1
McDuffie	Mia.	28	22	317	11.3	72	2
Milburn	Denv.	40	11	425	10.6	54	0
Carter	K.C.	27	4	247	9.3	30	0
T. Brown	N.E.	25	9	224	9.0	19	0
Copeland	Buff.	31	7	274	8.8	47	1
Harris	N.E.	23	4	201	8.6	21	0
Martin	Sea.	32	15	270	8.4	33	0
Woodson	Pitt.	41	11	338	8.2	39	0
Robinson	Cin.	43	6	305	7.1	36	0
Drewrey	Hou.	41	19	275	6.9	18	0
Verdin	Ind.	30	17	173	5.8	24	0

NON-QUALIFIERS

	Team	No.	FC	Yds.	Avg.	Lg.	TD
Crittenden	N.E.	2	1	37	18.5	30	0
Hughes	K.C.	3	0	49	16.3	29	0
Carrier	Clev.	6	1	92	15.3	56	1
McCloughan	Sea.	1	0	10	10.0	10	0
Hicks	N.Y.J.	17	4	157	9.2	20	0
Birden	K.C.	5	3	43	8.6	12	0
Mathis	N.Y.J.	14	8	99	7.1	16	0
Lewis	S.D.	3	2	17	5.7	7	0
Mincy	K.C.	2	0	9	4.5	9	0
Pickens	Cin.	4	2	16	4.0	9	0
Figures	Pitt.	5	2	15	3.0	6	0

Continued

1993 REVIEW ■ INDIVIDUAL STATS

Continued							
Brooks	Buff.	1	0	3	3.0	3	0
Bradford	Denv.	1	0	0	0.0	0	0
Simmons	Cin.	1	0	0	0.0	0	0
Smith	N.E.	1	0	0	0.0	0	0
Tasker	Buff.	1	0	3	0.0	3	0
Turner	Cleve.	0	0	7	0.0	7	0
Vincent	Mia.	0	0	9	0.0	9	0

AFC FIELD-GOAL ACCURACY

	Team	1-19 Yds.	20-29 Yds.	30-39 Yds.	40-49 Yds.	50 or Longer	Total	Avg. Yds. Att.	Avg. Yds. Made	Avg. Yds. Miss	Lg.
Anderson	Pitt.	1-1 1.000	8-9 .889	14-14 1.000	5-6 .833	0-0 .000	28-30 .933	33.3	33.3	34.5	46
Del Greco	Hou.	0-0 .000	13-13 1.000	8-9 .889	4-7 .800	4-7 .571	29-34 .853	35.9	34.0	46.6	52
Biasucci	Ind.	1-1 1.000	14-14 1.000	7-8 .875	3-6 .500	1-2 .500	26-31 .839	33.3	30.8	46.2	53
Kasay	Sea.	1-1 1.000	5-5 1.000	10-11 .909	4-6 .667	3-5 .600	23-28 .821	37.9	36.1	46.2	55
Jaeger	L.A.Rd	0-0 .000	12-12 1.000	13-15 .867	6-10 .600	4-7 .571	35-44 .796	36.5	34.5	44.2	53
Lowery	K.C.	0-0 .000	8-8 1.000	7-9 .778	7-11 .636	1-1 1.000	23-29 .793	35.7	34.0	42.2	52
Carney	S.D.	1-1 1.000	7-7 1.000	14-17 .824	7-12 .583	2-3 .667	31-40 .775	37.4	35.8	42.7	51
Pelfrey	Cin.	0-0 .000	8-8 1.000	6-10 .600	8-10 .800	2-3 .667	24-31 .774	37.0	36.2	40.0	53
Stoyanovich	Mia.	2-2 1.000	9-10 .900	7-11 .636	4-7 .571	2-2 1.000	24-32 .750	33.2	31.7	37.6	52
Elam	Denv.	0-0 .000	11-12 .917	7-7 1.000	4-10 .455	4-6 .667	26-35 .743	37.1	35.2	42.4	54
Stover	Clev.	0-0 .000	4-4 1.000	5-6 .833	6-8 .750	1-4 .250	16-22 .727	39.9	36.4	49.2	53
Christie	Buff.	0-0 .000	4-5 .800	12-12 1.000	6-9 .667	1-6 .167	23-32 .719	39.4	36.6	46.7	59
Blanchard	N.Y.J.	1-1 1.000	7-8 .875	4-5 .800	5-10 .500	0-2 .000	17-26 .654	35.6	31.6	43.1	45
Sisson	N.E.	1-1 1.000	8-13 .615	3-4 .750	2-6 .333	0-2 .000	14-26 .539	33.1	28.8	38.2	40

NON-QUALIFIERS
| Bahr | N.E. | 1-1 1.000 | 1-1 1.000 | 3-3 1.000 | 0-0 .000 | 0-0 .000 | 5-5 1.000 | 28.8 | 28.8 | 0.0 | 37 |

AFC QUARTERBACK SACKS

	Team	Sacks
Smith	K.C.	15.0
B. Smith	Buff.	14.0
Fletcher	Denv.	13.5
S. Jones	Hou.	13.0
A. Smith	L.A.Rd	12.5
Greene	Pitt.	12.5
O'Neal	S.D.	12.0
Pleasant	Clev.	11.0
Cross	Mia.	10.5
Fuller	Hou.	10.0
Burnett	Clev.	9.0
Childress	Hou.	9.0
Mecklenburg	Denv.	9.0
Slade	N.E.	9.0
Lageman	N.Y.J.	8.5
Tippett	N.E.	8.5
Sinclair	Sea.	8.0
Thomas	K.C.	8.0
Townsend	L.A.Rd	7.5
Dronett	Denv.	7.0
McGlockton	L.A.Rd	7.0
Mims	S.D.	7.0
Evans	Pitt.	6.5
Kennedy	Sea.	6.5
Gl. Montgomery	Hou.	6.0
Lloyd	Pitt.	6.0
Long	L.A.Rd	6.0
Perry	Clev.	6.0
Coleman	Mia.	5.5
Hand	Ind.	5.5
J. Jones	Clev.	5.5
M. Washington	N.Y.J.	5.5
Matthews	Clev.	5.5
Bennett	Buff.	5.0
Cox	Mia.	5.0
Croel	Denv.	5.0
Lake	Pitt.	5.0
Stubbs	Cin.	5.0
Grossman	S.D.	4.5
Wright	Buff.	4.5
A. Williams	Cin.	4.0
Lewis	N.Y.J.	4.0
M. Johnson	Clev.	4.0
McCrary	Sea.	4.0
Bickett	Ind.	3.5
Hansen	Buff.	3.5
J. Robinson	Denv.	3.5
Jones	N.E.	3.5
Saleaumua	K.C.	3.5
Tuatagaloa	Sea.	3.5
Ball	Clev.	3.0
Brown	Pitt.	3.0
Copeland	Cin.	3.0
Edwards	Sea.	3.0
Harrison	L.A.Rd	3.0
Houston	N.Y.J.	3.0
Hunter	Mia.	3.0
Kragen	Denv.	3.0
Krumrie	Cin.	3.0
L. Williams	Hou.	3.0
Lee	S.D.	3.0
Pitts	N.E.	3.0
Davidson	Pitt.	2.5
Stephens	Sea.	2.5
Wooden	Sea.	2.5
Barnett	Buff.	2.0
Bruce	L.A.Rd	2.0
D. Williams	Cin.	2.0
E. Robinson	Sea.	2.0
Francis	Cin.	2.0
Herrod	Ind.	2.0
Jones	Buff.	2.0
Lathon	Hou.	2.0
Marshall	Hou.	2.0
Marshall	N.Y.J.	2.0
Marts	K.C.	2.0
Peguese	Ind.	2.0
Richard	S.D.	2.0
Sabb	N.E.	2.0
Talley	Buff.	2.0
Veasey	Mia.	2.0
Wallace	L.A.Rd	2.0
Williams	N.E.	2.0
Winter	S.D.	2.0
Woodson	Pitt.	2.0
Wyman	Denv.	2.0
Agnew	N.E.	1.5
Klingbeil	Mia.	1.5
McClendon	Ind.	1.5
Phillips	K.C.	1.5
R. Robinson	Sea.	1.5
Siragusa	Ind.	1.5
Steed	Pitt.	1.5
Alexander	Mia.	1.0
Anderson	L.A.Rd	1.0
Atwater	Denv.	1.0
B. Johnson	Clev.	1.0
Barrow	Hou.	1.0
Bayless	K.C.	1.0
Bishop	Hou.	1.0

Continued

Continued

Bowden	Hou.	1.0	Hurst	N.E.	1.0	TEAM	N.Y.J.	1.0
Broughton	L.A.Rd	1.0	Kelly	L.A.Rd	1.0	Teeter	Hou.	1.0
Bryant	Sea.	1.0	Kirkland	Pitt.	1.0	Terry	K.C.	1.0
Carrington	S.D.	1.0	Lott	N.Y.J.	1.0	Thompson	N.E.	1.0
Clancy	Ind.	1.0	M. Patton	Buff.	1.0	Turner	N.Y.J.	1.0
Clifton	N.Y.J.	1.0	McDonald	Cin.	1.0	V. Brown	N.E.	1.0
Collins	N.E.	1.0	McDowell	Hou.	1.0	Walls	Clev.	1.0
Coryatt	Ind.	1.0	Mersereau	N.Y.J.	1.0	Washington	L.A.Rd	1.0
D. Jones	N.Y.J.	1.0	Mickell	K.C.	1.0	Williams	Denv.	1.0
Emtman	Ind.	1.0	Newton	K.C.	1.0	Young	N.Y.J.	1.0
Footman	Clev.	1.0	Oshodin	Denv.	1.0	B. Thompson	K.C.	.5
Frase	N.Y.J.	1.0	P. Johnson	Clev.	1.0	Goad	N.E.	.5
Frier	Cin.	1.0	Parrella	Buff.	1.0	Griggs	Mia.	.5
G. Williams	Pitt.	1.0	Patton	Buff.	1.0	Lodish	Buff.	.5
Goganious	Buff.	1.0	Porter	Sea.	1.0	Nash	Sea.	.5
Gray	Sea.	1.0	Robinson	Hou.	1.0	Pope	S.D.	.5
Henry	Pitt.	1.0	Rodgers	Sea.	1.0	Ross	K.C.	.5
Hinkle	Cin.	1.0	Sims	Ind.	1.0	Washington	Buff.	.5
			Stargell	Ind.	1.0			

NFC PASSING

	Team	Att.	Comp.	Comp. Pct.	Yds.	TD	TD Pct.	Lg.	Int.	Int. Pct.	Avg. Gain	Rating
Young	S.F.	462	314	68.0	4,023	29	6.3	80	16	3.5	8.71	101.5
Aikman	Dall.	392	271	69.1	3,100	15	3.8	80	6	1.5	7.91	99.0
Simms	N.Y.G.	400	247	61.8	3,038	15	3.8	62	9	2.3	7.60	88.3
Brister	Phil.	309	181	58.6	1,905	14	4.5	58	5	1.6	6.17	84.9
Hebert	Atl.	430	263	61.2	2,978	24	5.6	98	17	4.0	6.93	84.0
Beuerlein	Phx.	418	258	61.7	3,164	18	4.3	65	17	4.1	7.57	82.5
McMahon	Minn.	331	200	60.4	1,968	9	2.7	58	8	2.4	5.95	76.2
Favre	G.B.	522	318	60.9	3,303	19	3.6	66	24	4.6	6.33	72.2
Harbaugh	Chi.	325	200	61.5	2,002	7	2.2	48	11	3.4	6.16	72.1
Wilson	N.O.	388	221	57.0	2,457	12	3.1	42	15	3.9	6.33	70.1
Erickson	T.B.	457	233	51.0	3,054	18	3.9	67	21	4.6	6.68	66.4
Peete	Det.	252	157	62.3	1,670	6	2.4	93	14	5.6	6.63	66.4
Everett	L.A.Rm	274	135	49.3	1,652	8	2.9	60	12	4.4	6.03	59.7
Rypien	Wash.	319	166	52.0	1,514	4	1.3	43	10	3.1	4.75	56.3

NON-QUALIFIERS

	Team	Att.	Comp.	Comp. Pct.	Yds.	TD	TD Pct.	Lg.	Int.	Int. Pct.	Avg. Gain	Rating
Meggett	N.Y.G.	2	2	100.0	63	2	100.0	42	0	0.0	31.50	158.3
Harper	Dall.	1	1	100.0	46	0	0.0	46	0	0.0	46.00	118.8
Taylor	S.F.	1	1	100.0	41	0	0.0	41	0	0.0	41.00	118.8
Gary	L.A.Rm	1	1	100.0	8	0	0.0	8	0	0.0	8.00	100.0
Barnhardt	N.O.	1	1	100.0	7	0	0.0	7	0	0.0	7.00	95.8
Kramer	Det.	138	87	63.0	1,002	8	5.8	48	3	2.2	7.26	95.1
Kosar	Dall.	63	36	57.1	410	3	4.8	86	0	0.0	6.51	92.7
Cunningham	Phil.	110	76	69.1	850	5	4.6	80	5	4.6	7.73	88.1
M. Buck	N.O.	54	32	59.3	448	4	7.4	63	3	5.6	8.30	87.6
Salisbury	Minn.	195	115	59.0	1,413	9	4.6	55	6	3.1	7.25	84.0
Rubley	L.A.Rm	189	108	57.1	1,338	8	4.2	54	6	3.2	7.08	80.1
Sharpe	G.B.	1	1	100.0	1	0	0.0	1	0	0.0	1.00	79.2
Bono	S.F.	61	39	63.9	416	0	0.0	33	1	1.6	6.82	76.9
Detmer	G.B.	5	3	60.0	26	0	0.0	25	0	0.0	5.20	73.8
Conklin	Wash.	87	46	52.9	496	4	4.6	34	3	3.5	5.70	70.9
O'Brien	Phil.	137	71	51.8	708	4	2.9	41	3	2.2	5.17	67.4
Chandler	Phx.	103	52	50.5	471	3	2.9	27	2	1.9	4.57	64.8
Walsh	N.O.	38	20	52.6	271	2	5.3	54	3	7.9	7.13	60.3
Gannon	Wash.	125	74	59.2	704	3	2.4	54	7	5.6	5.63	59.6
Mitchell	Wash.	2	1	50.0	50	0	0.0	50	1	50.0	25.00	56.3
Tolliver	Atl.	76	39	51.3	464	3	3.9	42	5	6.6	6.11	56.0
Garrett	Dall.	19	9	47.4	61	0	0.0	16	0	0.0	3.21	54.9
Ware	Det.	45	20	44.4	271	1	2.2	47	2	4.4	6.02	53.1
Miller	Atl.	66	32	48.5	345	1	1.5	32	3	4.5	5.23	50.4
Graham	N.Y.G.	22	8	36.4	79	0	0.0	18	0	0.0	3.59	47.3
Gardocki	Chi.	2	0	0.0	0	0	0.0	0	0	0.0	0.00	39.6
Anderson	Chi.	1	0	0.0	0	0	0.0	0	0	0.0	0.00	39.6
Moore	T.B.	1	0	0.0	0	0	0.0	0	0	0.0	0.00	39.6
Sanders	Atl.	1	0	0.0	0	0	0.0	0	0	0.0	0.00	39.6
Weldon	T.B.	11	6	54.5	55	0	0.0	20	1	9.1	5.00	30.5
Willis	Chi.	60	30	50.0	268	0	0.0	29	5	8.3	4.47	27.6
Pagel	L.A.Rm	9	3	33.3	23	0	0.0	10	1	11.1	2.56	2.8
Hearst	Phx.	1	0	0.0	0	0	0.0	0	1	100.0	0.00	0.0

1993 REVIEW ■ INDIVIDUAL STATS

NFC PUNTING

	Team	No.	Yds.	Lg.	Gross Avg.	TB	Ins. 20	Blk.	Ret.	Ret. Yds.	Net Avg.
Horan	N.Y.G.	44	1,882	60	42.8	1	13	0	25	107	39.9
Camarillo	Phx.	73	3,189	61	43.7	8	23	0	30	267	37.8
Jett	Dall.	56	2,342	59	41.8	3	22	0	32	169	37.7
Alexander	Atl.	72	3,114	75	43.3	3	21	0	41	350	37.6
Barnhardt	N.O.	77	3,356	58	43.6	6	26	0	36	348	37.5
Roby	Wash.	78	3,447	60	44.2	10	25	0	31	343	37.2
Arnold	Det.	72	3,207	68	44.5	9	15	0	45	377	36.8
Gardocki	Chi.	80	3,080	58	38.5	2	28	0	22	115	36.6
Wagner	G.B.	74	3,174	60	42.9	7	19	0	38	350	36.3
Newsome	Minn.	90	3,862	64	42.9	6	25	0	46	560	35.4
Feagles	Phil.	83	3,323	60	40.0	4	31	0	35	311	35.3
Stryzinski	T.B.	93	3,772	57	40.6	3	24	1	53	394	35.3
Wilmsmeyer	S.F.	42	1,718	61	40.9	5	11	0	15	171	34.5
Landeta	L.A.Rm	75	3,215	66	42.9	10	18	1	44	444	33.8

NON-QUALIFIERS

	Team	No.	Yds.	Lg.	Gross Avg.	TB	Ins. 20	Blk.	Ret.	Ret. Yds.	Net Avg.
Goodburn	Wash.	5	197	49	39.4	0	3	0	3	0	39.4
Bracken	L.A.Rm	17	651	51	38.3	0	3	0	8	86	33.2
McJulien	L.A.Rm	21	795	56	37.9	3	5	0	10	143	28.2

NFC RUSHING

	Team	Att.	Yds.	Avg.	Lg.	TD
E. Smith	Dall.	283	1,486	5.3	62	9
Bettis	L.A.Rm	294	1,429	4.9	71	7
Pegram	Atl.	292	1,185	4.1	29	3
Sanders	Det.	243	1,115	4.6	42	3
Hampton	N.Y.G.	292	1,077	3.7	20	5
Brooks	Wash.	223	1,063	4.8	85	3
Moore	Phx.	263	1,018	3.9	20	9
Watters	S.F.	208	950	4.6	39	10
Walker	Phil.	174	746	4.3	35	1
Brown	N.O.	180	705	3.9	60	2
Cobb	T.B.	221	658	3.0	16	3
Thompson	G.B.	169	654	3.9	60	3
Anderson	Chi.	202	646	3.2	45	4
Tillman	N.Y.G.	121	585	4.8	58	3
E. Bennett	G.B.	159	550	3.5	19	9
Graham	Minn.	118	487	4.1	31	3
Worley	Chi.	120	470	3.9	28	2
Word	Minn.	142	458	3.2	14	2
Young	S.F.	69	407	5.9	35	2
Sherman	Phil.	115	406	3.5	19	2
D. Moore	Det.	88	405	4.6	48	3
Smith	Minn.	82	399	4.9	26	2
Meggett	N.Y.G.	69	329	4.8	23	0
Hebron	Phx.	84	297	3.5	33	3
Gary	L.A.Rm	79	293	3.7	15	1
Workman	T.B.	78	284	3.6	21	2
Logan	S.F.	58	280	4.8	45	7
Harbaugh	Chi.	60	277	4.8	25	4
Lassic	Dall.	75	269	3.6	15	3
Hearst	Phx.	76	264	3.5	57	1
Bailey	Phx.	49	253	5.2	31	1
Mitchell	Wash.	63	246	3.9	29	3
Lee	S.F.	72	230	3.2	13	1
Wilson	N.O.	31	230	7.1	44	0
Favre	G.B.	58	216	3.5	27	1
Muster	N.O.	64	214	3.3	18	3
Lynch	Det.	53	207	3.9	15	2
Heyward	Chi.	68	206	3.0	11	0
Broussard	Atl.	39	206	5.3	26	1
Ervins	Wash.	50	201	4.0	18	0
Neal	N.O.	21	175	8.3	74	1
Stephens	G.B.	48	173	3.6	22	1
Hilliard	N.O.	50	165	3.3	16	2
Peete	Det.	45	165	3.7	28	1
McAfee	N.O.	51	160	3.1	27	1
Centers	Phx.	25	152	6.1	33	0
Joseph	Phil.	39	140	3.6	12	0
Coleman	Dall.	34	132	3.9	16	2
Bunch	N.Y.G.	33	128	3.0	13	2
Aikman	Dall.	32	125	4.0	20	0
Craig	Minn.	38	119	3.1	11	1
Royster	T.B.	33	115	3.5	19	1
Cunningham	Phil.	18	110	6.1	26	1
Byner	Wash.	23	105	4.6	16	1
Rubley	L.A.Rm	29	102	3.5	13	0
McMahon	Minn.	33	96	2.9	16	0
Erickson	T.B.	26	96	3.6	15	0
Dickerson	Atl.	26	91	3.5	10	0
Gannon	Wash.	21	88	4.2	12	1
Rathman	S.F.	19	80	4.2	19	3
Johnston	Dall.	24	74	3.1	11	3
Lester	L.A.Rm	11	74	6.7	26	0
Carter	S.F.	10	72	7.9	50	1
Ned	N.O.	9	71	7.9	35	1
Rice	S.F.	3	69	23.0	43	1
Anderson	Det.	28	56	2.0	13	0
Hebert	Atl.	24	49	2.0	14	0
Tolliver	Atl.	7	48	6.9	24	0
Proehl	Phx.	8	47	5.9	17	0
Beuerlein	Phx.	22	45	2.1	20	0
Conway	Chi.	5	44	8.8	18	0
Rasheed	N.Y.G.	9	42	4.7	23	1
Brister	Phil.	20	39	2.0	13	0
Everett	L.A.Rm	19	38	2.0	14	0
Copeland	T.B.	3	34	11.3	22	0
Evans	Minn.	14	32	2.3	5	0
Early	N.O.	2	32	16.0	26	0
Simms	N.Y.G.	28	31	1.1	9	0
Green	Chi.	15	29	1.9	10	0
Gainer	Dall.	9	29	3.2	8	0
Lang	L.A.Rm	9	29	3.2	28	0
Harris	T.B.	7	29	4.1	12	0
Blount	Phx.	5	28	5.6	7	1
K. Williams	Dall.	7	26	3.7	12	2
M. Jackson	N.Y.G.	3	25	8.3	20	0
Ware	Det.	7	23	3.3	8	0
Christian	Chi.	8	19	2.4	12	0
A. Carter	Minn.	7	19	2.7	9	0
Ellard	L.A.Rm	2	18	9.0	15	0
Barnhardt	N.O.	1	18	18.0	18	0
Walker	S.F.	5	17	3.4	11	0
O'Brien	Phil.	4	17	4.3	11	0
Brooks	G.B.	3	17	5.7	21	0
Howard	Wash.	2	17	8.5	9	0
Taylor	S.F.	2	17	8.5	12	0
Agee	Dall.	6	16	2.3	6	0
Perriman	Det.	4	16	4.0	16	0
Bono	S.F.	12	14	1.0	10	1
Ismail	Minn.	3	14	4.7	6	0
Lewis	Chi.	7	13	1.9	3	0
Miller	Atl.	2	11	5.5	6	0
Kinchen	L.A.Rm	2	10	5.0	8	0
R. White	L.A.Rm	2	10	5.0	5	0
Sharpe	G.B.	4	8	2.0	5	0

Continued

PRO FOOTBALL WEEKLY 1994 ALMANAC

Continued

Kosar	Dall.	9	7	1.3	4	0
Matthews	Det.	2	7	3.5	9	0
Wilson	T.B.	2	7	3.5	4	0
Drayton	L.A.Rm	1	7	7.0	7	0
Sanders	Wash.	1	7	7.0	7	0
Feagles	Phil.	2	6	3.0	6	0
Irvin	Dall.	2	6	3.0	9	0
McDowell	T.B.	2	6	3.0	3	0
Willis	Chi.	2	6	3.0	6	0
Kramer	Det.	10	5	.5	4	0
Armstrong	T.B.	2	5	2.5	4	0
Pritchard	Atl.	2	4	2.0	4	0
Jones	L.A.Rm	1	4	4.0	4	0
Wilson	G.B.	6	3	.5	5	0
Mims	Atl.	1	3	3.0	3	0
Rypien	Wash.	9	2	.2	5	3
Chandler	Phx.	3	2	.7	1	0
Novacek	Dall.	1	2	2.0	2	1
Richards	Det.	4	1	.3	1	0
Wilmsmeyer	S.F.	2	0	0.0	0	0
Camarillo	Phx.	1	0	0.0	0	0
M. Buck	N.O.	1	0	0.0	0	0
Roby	Wash.	1	0	0.0	0	0
TEAM	Atl.	1	0	0.0	0	0
Salisbury	Minn.	10	-1	-.1	6	0
Monk	Wash.	1	-1	-1.0	-1	0
Conklin	Wash.	2	-2	-1.0	-1	0
Detmer	G.B.	1	-2	-2.0	-2	0
Musgrave	S.F.	3	-3	-1.0	-1	0
Graham	N.Y.G.	2	-3	-1.5	-1	0
Walsh	N.O.	4	-4	-1.0	-1	0
Da. Brown	N.Y.G.	3	-4	-1.3	-1	0
Alexander	Atl.	2	-7	-3.5	0	0
Garrett	Dall.	8	-8	-1.0	0	0

NFC RECEIVING

	Team	No.	Yds.	Avg.	Lg.	TD
Sharpe	G.B.	112	1,274	11.4	54	11
Rice	S.F.	98	1,503	15.3	80	15
Irvin	Dall.	88	1,330	15.1	61	7
Rison	Atl.	86	1,242	14.4	53	15
C. Carter	Minn.	86	1,071	12.5	58	9
Walker	Phil.	75	610	8.1	55	3
Pritchard	Atl.	74	736	10.0	34	7
Haynes	Atl.	72	778	10.8	98	4
Jones	S.F.	68	735	10.8	29	3
E. Martin	N.O.	66	950	14.4	54	3
Centers	Phx.	66	603	9.1	29	3
Proehl	Phx.	65	877	13.5	51	7
Clark	Phx.	63	818	13.0	55	4
Hawkins	T.B.	62	933	15.1	67	5
Ellard	L.A.Rm	61	945	15.5	54	2
H. Moore	Det.	61	935	15.3	93	6
A. Carter	Minn.	60	774	12.9	39	5
Williams	Phil.	60	725	12.1	80	10
E. Bennett	G.B.	59	457	7.8	39	1
M. Jackson	N.Y.G.	58	708	12.2	40	4
Sanders	Wash.	58	638	11.0	50	4
E. Smith	Dall.	57	414	7.3	86	1
Taylor	S.F.	56	940	16.8	76	5
Jordan	Minn.	56	542	9.7	53	1
Workman	T.B.	54	411	7.6	42	2
Johnston	Dall.	50	372	7.4	20	1
Perriman	Det.	49	496	10.1	34	2
Early	N.O.	45	670	14.9	63	6
Waddle	Chi.	44	552	12.6	38	1
Novacek	Dall.	44	445	10.1	30	1
Bavaro	Phil.	43	481	11.3	27	6
J. Harris	G.B.	42	604	14.4	66	4
Bailey	Phil.	41	545	13.2	58	1
Monk	Wash.	41	398	9.7	29	2
Hilliard	N.O.	40	296	7.4	34	1
McGee	Wash.	39	500	12.8	54	3
Meggett	N.Y.G.	38	319	8.2	50	0
Anderson	L.A.Rm	37	552	14.9	56	4
Logan	S.F.	37	348	9.4	24	0
Harper	Dall.	36	777	21.6	80	5
Gary	L.A.Rm	36	289	8.0	60	1
Sanders	Det.	36	205	5.7	17	0
R. Hill	Phx.	35	519	14.8	58	4
Calloway	N.Y.G.	35	513	14.7	47	3
Hill	Atl.	34	384	11.3	30	0
Pegram	Atl.	33	302	9.2	30	0
Clayton	G.B.	32	331	10.3	32	3
Bailey	Phx.	32	243	7.6	30	0
Watters	S.F.	31	326	10.5	48	1
Anderson	Chi.	31	160	5.2	35	0
Copeland	T.B.	30	633	20.8	67	4
Joseph	Phil.	29	291	10.0	48	1
Green	Det.	28	462	16.5	47	2
McCaffrey	N.Y.G.	27	335	12.4	31	2
Drayton	L.A.Rm	27	319	11.8	27	4
Byner	Wash.	27	194	7.2	20	0
Obee	Chi.	26	351	13.5	48	3
Bettis	L.A.Rm	26	244	9.4	28	0
West	G.B.	25	253	10.1	24	0
Holman	Det.	25	244	9.8	28	2
Sherrard	N.Y.G.	24	433	18.0	55	2
Middleton	Wash.	24	154	6.4	18	2
Smith	Minn.	24	111	4.6	12	0
Howard	Wash.	23	286	12.4	27	0
Hall	T.B.	23	268	11.7	37	1
Muster	N.O.	23	195	8.5	31	0
Cross	N.Y.G.	21	272	13.0	32	5
Brooks	Wash.	21	186	8.9	43	0
Brown	N.O.	21	170	8.1	19	1
D. Moore	Det.	21	169	7.7	20	1
Brooks	G.B.	20	180	9.0	25	0
Mitchell	Wash.	20	157	7.9	18	0
K. Williams	Dall.	20	151	7.6	33	2
Conway	Chi.	19	231	12.2	38	2
Ismail	Minn.	19	212	11.2	37	1
Craig	Minn.	19	169	8.9	31	1
Hampton	N.Y.G.	18	210	11.7	62	0
Lester	L.A.Rm	18	154	8.6	21	0
Thompson	G.B.	18	129	7.2	34	0
Barnett	Phil.	17	170	10.0	21	0
Smith	N.O.	16	180	11.3	23	2
Small	N.O.	16	164	10.3	17	1
Christian	Chi.	16	160	10.0	36	0
Heyward	Chi.	16	132	8.3	20	0
Williams	S.F.	16	132	8.3	15	1
Ervins	Wash.	16	123	7.7	20	0
Lee	S.F.	16	115	7.2	22	2
Wycheck	Wash.	16	113	7.1	20	0
Wilson	T.B.	15	225	15.0	24	0
Dawsey	T.B.	15	203	13.5	24	0
Tennell	Minn.	15	122	8.1	17	0
Young	Phil.	14	186	13.3	49	2
Lofton	Phil.	14	167	11.9	32	0
Carter	L.A.Rm	14	166	11.9	38	1
Jennings	Chi.	14	150	10.7	29	0
Edwards	Phx.	13	326	25.1	65	1
Bunch	N.Y.G.	13	98	7.5	15	1
Lynch	Det.	13	82	6.3	11	0
Green	Chi.	13	63	4.9	9	0
Pierce	N.Y.G.	12	212	17.7	54	0
Turner	N.O.	12	163	13.6	52	1
Davis	Chi.	12	132	11.0	17	0
Mims	Atl.	12	107	8.9	19	1
Sherman	Phil.	12	78	6.5	21	0
Brenner	N.O.	11	171	15.6	27	1
Matthews	Det.	11	171	15.6	40	0
Anderson	Det.	11	89	8.1	28	1
Hebron	Phil.	11	82	7.5	12	0
Worley	Chi.	11	62	5.6	15	0
Gedney	Chi.	10	98	9.8	24	0
Rathman	S.F.	10	86	8.6	17	0
Johnson	Phil.	10	81	8.1	17	0
Rolle	Phx.	10	67	6.7	22	1
Word	Minn.	9	105	11.7	27	0

Continued

1993 REVIEW ■ INDIVIDUAL STATS

Continued												
Wetnight	Chi.	9	93	10.3	25	1	Lewis	Chi.	4	26	6.5	18	0
Armstrong	T.B.	9	86	9.6	29	1	Coleman	Dall.	4	24	6.0	10	0
Reeves	Phx.	9	67	7.4	18	1	Turner	S.F.	3	64	21.3	32	0
Cobb	T.B.	9	61	6.8	19	1	Ware	Phx.	3	45	15.0	27	0
Ned	N.O.	9	54	6.0	14	0	Carter	S.F.	3	40	13.3	14	0
Lassic	Dall.	9	37	4.1	9	0	Moore	Phx.	3	16	5.3	6	0
L. Thomas	T.B.	8	186	23.3	62	2	Banks	Chi.	2	45	19.0	26	0
Kinchen	L.A.Rm	8	137	17.1	35	1	Sydner	Phil.	2	42	21.0	31	0
Singleton	S.F.	8	126	15.8	33	1	LaChapelle	L.A.Rm	2	23	11.5	14	0
Newman	N.O.	8	121	15.1	32	1	Lewis	G.B.	2	21	10.5	17	0
Hallock	Det.	8	88	11.0	24	2	Johnson	Det.	2	18	9.0	9	0
McNeal	L.A.Rm	8	75	9.4	22	1	Wilson	G.B.	2	18	9.0	11	0
Lyons	Atl.	8	63	7.9	14	0	Clifton	Wash.	2	15	7.5	10	0
McDowell	T.B.	8	26	3.3	9	1	Chmura	G.B.	2	13	6.5	7	0
De. Brown	N.Y.G.	7	56	8.0	14	0	C. Harris	G.B.	2	11	5.5	6	0
Campbell	Det.	7	55	7.9	12	0	Young	S.F.	2	2	1.0	6	0
Graham	Minn.	7	46	6.6	11	0	Guliford	Minn.	1	45	45.0	45	0
Sanders	Atl.	6	106	17.7	70	1	T. Williams	Dall.	1	25	25.0	25	0
Dickerson	Atl.	6	58	9.7	30	0	Tillman	N.Y.G.	1	21	21.0	21	0
Whitaker	Chi.	6	53	8.8	18	0	Lofton	L.A.Rm	1	16	16.0	16	0
Dowdell	N.O.	6	46	7.7	11	1	Phillips	Atl.	1	15	15.0	15	0
Tice	Minn.	6	39	6.5	21	1	Thompson	Det.	1	15	15.0	15	0
Gainer	Dall.	6	37	6.2	8	0	Morgan	G.B.	1	8	8.0	8	0
Hearst	Phx.	6	18	3.0	9	0	Turner	Det.	1	7	7.0	7	0
Reed	Minn.	5	65	13.0	18	0	Crawford	N.Y.G.	1	6	6.0	6	0
Claiborne	T.B.	5	61	12.2	16	0	Lawrence	Phil.	1	5	5.0	5	0
Beach	S.F.	5	59	11.8	20	1	Broussard	Atl.	1	4	4.0	4	0
Jones	L.A.Rm	5	56	11.2	21	2	Price	Dall.	1	4	4.0	4	0
Blount	Phx.	5	36	7.2	9	0	Walker	S.F.	1	4	4.0	4	0
Stephens	G.B.	5	31	6.2	10	0	McAfee	N.O.	1	3	3.0	3	0
Royster	T.B.	5	18	3.6	10	0	Rasheed	N.Y.G.	1	3	3.0	3	0
Harris	T.B.	4	48	12.0	25	0	Elewonibi	Wash.	1	2	2.0	2	0
Moore	.B.	4	47	11.8	19	1	Galbraith	Dall.	1	1	1.0	1	1
Lang	L.A.Rm	4	45	11.3	21	0	Harbaugh	Chi.	1	1	1.0	1	0
Truitt	Minn.	4	40	10.0	13	0	Fralic	Det.	1	-4	-4.0	-4	0
Evans	Minn.	4	39	9.8	21	0	Simms	N.Y.G.	1	-6	-6.0	-6	0
							Hinton	Atl.	1	-8	-8.0	-8	0

NFC SCORING

	Team	TD	XP/att.	FG/att.	Saf.	Pts.						
Hanson	Det.	0	28/28	34/43	0	130	Allen	Phil.	4	0/0	0/0	0	24
Jacke	G.B.	0	35/35	31/37	0	128	Anderson	Chi.	4	0/0	0/0	0	24
Murray	Dall.	0	38/38	28/33	0	122	Anderson	L.A.Rm	4	0/0	0/0	0	24
Andersen	N.O.	0	33/33	28/35	0	117	Clark	Phx.	4	0/0	0/0	0	24
Johnson	Atl.	0	34/34	26/27	0	112	Cobb	T.B.	4	0/0	0/0	0	24
Cofer	S.F.	0	59/61	16/26	0	107	Copeland	T.B.	4	0/0	0/0	0	24
Reveiz	Minn.	0	27/28	26/35	0	105	D. Moore	Det.	4	0/0	0/0	0	24
Treadwell	N.Y.G.	0	28/29	25/31	0	103	Drayton	L.A.Rm	4	0/0	0/0	0	24
Butler	Chi.	0	21/22	27/36	0	102	Harbaugh	Chi.	4	0/0	0/0	0	24
G. Davis	Phx.	0	37/37	21/28	0	100	Haynes	Atl.	4	0/0	0/0	0	24
Rice	S.F.	16	0/0	0/0	0	96	J. Harris	G.B.	4	0/0	0/0	0	24
Rison	Atl.	15	0/0	0/0	0	90	Johnston	Dall.	4	0/0	0/0	0	24
Husted	T.B.	0	27/27	16/22	0	75	M. Jackson	N.Y.G.	4	0/0	0/0	0	24
Lohmiller	Wash.	0	24/26	16/28	0	72	R. Hill	Phx.	4	0/0	0/0	0	24
Zendejas	L.A.Rm	0	23/25	16/23	0	71	Sanders	Wash.	4	0/0	0/0	0	24
Sharpe	G.B.	11	0/0	0/0	0	66	Walker	Phil.	4	0/0	0/0	0	24
Watters	S.F.	11	0/0	0/0	0	66	Workman	T.B.	4	0/0	0/0	0	24
E. Bennett	G.B.	10	0/0	0/0	0	60	Brooks	Wash.	3	0/0	0/0	0	18
E. Smith	Dall.	10	0/0	0/0	0	60	Brown	N.O.	3	0/0	0/0	0	18
Williams	Phil.	10	0/0	0/0	0	60	Bunch	N.Y.G.	3	0/0	0/0	0	18
C. Carter	Minn.	9	0/0	0/0	0	54	Calloway	N.Y.G.	3	0/0	0/0	0	18
Moore	Phx.	9	0/0	0/0	0	54	Centers	Phx.	3	0/0	0/0	0	18
Bettis	L.A.Rm	7	0/0	0/0	0	42	Clayton	G.B.	3	0/0	0/0	0	18
Irvin	Dall.	7	0/0	0/0	0	42	E. Martin	N.O.	3	0/0	0/0	0	18
Logan	S.F.	7	0/0	0/0	0	42	Graham	Minn.	3	0/0	0/0	0	18
Pritchard	Atl.	7	0/0	0/0	0	42	Hebron	Phil.	3	0/0	0/0	0	18
Proehl	Phx.	7	0/0	0/0	0	42	Hilliard	N.O.	3	0/0	0/0	0	18
Ruzek	Phil.	0	12/15	9/11	0	39	Hughes	N.O.	3	0/0	0/0	0	18
Bavaro	Phil.	6	0/0	0/0	0	36	Jones	S.F.	3	0/0	0/0	0	18
Early	N.O.	6	0/0	0/0	0	36	Lassic	Dall.	3	0/0	0/0	0	18
H. Moore	Det.	6	0/0	0/0	0	36	Lee	S.F.	3	0/0	0/0	0	18
K. Williams	Dall.	6	0/0	0/0	0	36	McGee	Wash.	3	0/0	0/0	0	18
A. Carter	Minn.	5	0/0	0/0	0	30	Mitchell	Wash.	3	0/0	0/0	0	18
Cross	N.Y.G.	5	0/0	0/0	0	30	Muster	N.O.	3	0/0	0/0	0	18
Hampton	N.Y.G.	5	0/0	0/0	0	30	Obee	Chi.	3	0/0	0/0	0	18
Harper	Dall.	5	0/0	0/0	0	30	Pegram	Atl.	3	0/0	0/0	0	18
Hawkins	T.B.	5	0/0	0/0	0	30	Rathman	S.F.	3	0/0	0/0	0	18
Taylor	S.F.	5	0/0	0/0	0	30	Rypien	Wash.	3	0/0	0/0	0	18

Continued

PRO FOOTBALL WEEKLY 1994 ALMANAC

Continued

Sanders	Det.	3	0/0	0/0	0	18
Thompson	G.B.	3	0/0	0/0	0	18
Tillman	N.Y.G.	3	0/0	0/0	0	18
Bailey	Phx.	2	0/0	0/0	0	12
Baker	Chi.	2	0/0	0/0	0	12
Carter	S.F.	2	0/0	0/0	0	12
Clay	Det.	2	0/0	0/0	0	12
Coleman	Dall.	2	0/0	0/0	0	12
Conway	Chi.	2	0/0	0/0	0	12
Craig	Minn.	2	0/0	0/0	0	12
Davis	S.F.	2	0/0	0/0	0	12
Ellard	L.A.Rm	2	0/0	0/0	0	12
Gary	L.A.Rm	2	0/0	0/0	0	12
Green	Det.	2	0/0	0/0	0	12
Hallock	Det.	2	0/0	0/0	0	12
Holman	Det.	2	0/0	0/0	0	12
Jones	L.A.Rm	2	0/0	0/0	0	12
L. Thomas	T.B.	2	0/0	0/0	0	12
Lynch	Det.	2	0/0	0/0	0	12
McCaffrey	N.Y.G.	2	0/0	0/0	0	12
Middleton	Wash.	2	0/0	0/0	0	12
Monk	Wash.	2	0/0	0/0	0	12
Novacek	Dall.	2	0/0	0/0	0	12
Perriman	Det.	2	0/0	0/0	0	12
Sherman	Phil.	2	0/0	0/0	0	12
Sherrard	N.Y.G.	2	0/0	0/0	0	12
Smith	Minn.	2	0/0	0/0	0	12
Smith	N.O.	2	0/0	0/0	0	12
Williams	Phx.	2	0/0	0/0	0	12
Word	Minn.	2	0/0	0/0	0	12
Worley	Chi.	2	0/0	0/0	0	12
Young	Phil.	2	0/0	0/0	0	12
Young	S.F.	2	0/0	0/0	0	12
Coleman	Wash.	1	0/0	0/0	1	8
Elliott	Dall.	0	2/3	2/4	0	8
A. Johnson	Wash.	1	0/0	0/0	0	6
Anderson	Det.	1	0/0	0/0	0	6
Armstrong	T.B.	1	0/0	0/0	0	6
Bailey	Phil.	1	0/0	0/0	0	6
Beach	S.F.	1	0/0	0/0	0	6
Blount	Phx.	1	0/0	0/0	0	6
Bono	S.F.	1	0/0	0/0	0	6
Boykin	L.A.Rm	1	0/0	0/0	0	6
Brenner	N.O.	1	0/0	0/0	0	6
Brooks	G.B.	1	0/0	0/0	0	6
Broussard	Atl.	1	0/0	0/0	0	6
Butler	G.B.	1	0/0	0/0	0	6
Byner	Wash.	1	0/0	0/0	0	6
Carrier	Chi.	1	0/0	0/0	0	6
Carter	L.A.Rm	1	0/0	0/0	0	6
Clark	Atl.	1	0/0	0/0	0	6
Collins	N.Y.G.	1	0/0	0/0	0	6
Cunningham	Phil.	1	0/0	0/0	0	6
Dowdell	N.O.	1	0/0	0/0	0	6
Edwards	Phx.	1	0/0	0/0	0	6
Erickson	T.B.	1	0/0	0/0	0	6
Evans	Phil.	1	0/0	0/0	0	6
Favre	G.B.	1	0/0	0/0	0	6
Galbraith	Dall.	1	0/0	0/0	0	6
Gannon	Wash.	1	0/0	0/0	0	6
Gouveia	Wash.	1	0/0	0/0	0	6
Gray	Det.	1	0/0	0/0	0	6
Green	Wash.	1	0/0	0/0	0	6
Hall	T.B.	1	0/0	0/0	0	6
Hanks	S.F.	1	0/0	0/0	0	6
Hearst	Phx.	1	0/0	0/0	0	6
Ismail	Minn.	1	0/0	0/0	0	6
Jamison	Det.	1	0/0	0/0	0	6
Jones	Chi.	1	0/0	0/0	0	6
Jordan	Minn.	1	0/0	0/0	0	6
Joseph	Phil.	1	0/0	0/0	0	6
K. Smith	Dall.	1	0/0	0/0	0	6
Kinchen	L.A.Rm	1	0/0	0/0	0	6
Lincoln	Chi.	1	0/0	0/0	0	6
Lynch	Phx.	1	0/0	0/0	0	6
Mack	T.B.	1	0/0	0/0	0	6
McAfee	N.O.	1	0/0	0/0	0	6
McDowell	T.B.	1	0/0	0/0	0	6
McGriggs	Minn.	1	0/0	0/0	0	6
McGruder	S.F.	1	0/0	0/0	0	6
McMillan	Minn.	1	0/0	0/0	0	6
McNeal	L.A.Rm	1	0/0	0/0	0	6
Meggett	N.Y.G.	1	0/0	0/0	0	6
Mills	N.O.	1	0/0	0/0	0	6
Mims	Atl.	1	0/0	0/0	0	6
Moore	T.B.	1	0/0	0/0	0	6
Neal	N.O.	1	0/0	0/0	0	6
Ned	N.O.	1	0/0	0/0	0	6
Newman	N.O.	1	0/0	0/0	0	6
Peete	Det.	1	0/0	0/0	0	6
Rasheed	N.Y.G.	1	0/0	0/0	0	6
Reeves	Phx.	1	0/0	0/0	0	6
Rolle	Phx.	1	0/0	0/0	0	6
Royster	T.B.	1	0/0	0/0	0	6
Sanders	Atl.	1	0/0	0/0	0	6
Seals	T.B.	1	0/0	0/0	0	6
Simms	N.Y.G.	1	0/0	0/0	0	6
Singleton	S.F.	1	0/0	0/0	0	6
Small	N.O.	1	0/0	0/0	0	6
Stephens	G.B.	1	0/0	0/0	0	6
T. Smith	Atl.	1	0/0	0/0	0	6
Tamm	S.F.	1	0/0	0/0	0	6
Tice	Minn.	1	0/0	0/0	0	6
Turner	N.O.	1	0/0	0/0	0	6
Waddle	Chi.	1	0/0	0/0	0	6
Warren	N.O.	1	0/0	0/0	0	6
Wetnight	Chi.	1	0/0	0/0	0	6
Williams	S.F.	1	0/0	0/0	0	6
Daluiso	N.Y.G.	0	0/0	1/2	0	3
Flores	Phil.	0	0/0	0/0	1	2
Hamilton	N.Y.G.	0	0/0	0/0	1	2
Stowers	N.O.	0	0/0	0/0	1	2
Swann	Phx.	0	0/0	0/0	1	2
TEAM	G.B.	0	0/0	0/0	1	2
Thomas	Minn.	0	0/0	0/0	1	2
W. Thomas	Phil.	0	0/0	0/0	1	2

NFC INTERCEPTIONS

	Team	No.	Yds.	Lg.	TD
Sanders	Atl.	7	91	41	0
Allen	Phil.	6	201	94	4
Butler	G.B.	6	131	39	0
K. Smith	Dall.	6	56	32	1
Carter	Wash.	6	54	29	0
McGruder	S.F.	5	89	37	1
Glenn	Minn.	5	49	23	0
Carrier	Chi.	4	94	34	1
Collins	N.Y.G.	4	77	50	1
Jones	Chi.	4	52	22	0
Davis	S.F.	4	45	41	1
McMillan	Minn.	4	45	22	1
G. Jackson	N.Y.G.	4	32	29	0
Miano	Phil.	4	26	16	0
Green	Wash.	4	10	6	0
Del Rio	Minn.	4	3	3	0
Lincoln	Chi.	3	109	80	1
Hanks	S.F.	3	104	67	1
Atkins	N.O.	3	59	37	0
King	T.B.	3	29	28	0
McDonald	S.F.	3	23	21	0
Lee	Minn.	3	20	19	0
Swilling	Det.	3	16	14	0
Lynch	Phx.	3	13	13	0
Walker	Atl.	3	7	7	0
Griffin	S.F.	3	6	3	0
Williams	Phx.	2	87	46	1
Clark	Atl.	2	59	38	0
Jamison	Det.	2	48	35	1
Bailey	L.A.Rm	2	41	41	0
Holland	G.B.	2	41	30	0
W. Thomas	Phil.	2	39	21	0

Continued

1993 REVIEW ■ INDIVIDUAL STATS

Continued

	Team	No.	Yds.	Lg.	TD
Guyton	N.Y.G.	2	34	19	0
Taylor	N.O.	2	32	30	0
Buckley	G.B.	2	31	31	0
Crockett	Det.	2	31	31	0
Colon	Det.	2	28	27	0
V. Buck	N.O.	2	28	28	0
Coleman	Wash.	2	27	14	0
Scott	Minn.	2	26	26	0
Bates	Dall.	2	25	22	0
Everett	Dall.	2	25	17	0
McMillian	Phil.	2	25	17	0
Booty	Phx.	2	24	19	0
Rolling	L.A.Rm	2	21	12	0
Simmons	G.B.	2	21	19	0
McNeil	Det.	2	19	16	0
Miller	N.Y.G.	2	18	11	0
Woolford	Chi.	2	18	18	0
Raymond	N.Y.G.	2	11	11	0
McKyer	Det.	2	10	10	0
C. Jenkins	Minn.	2	7	4	0
Blaylock	Chi.	2	3	3	0
Terrell	L.A.Rm	2	1	1	0
Lyght	L.A.Rm	2	0	0	0
Spielman	Det.	2	-2	0	0
A. Johnson	Wash.	1	69	69	1
McGriggs	Minn.	1	63	63	1
Gouveia	Wash.	1	59	59	1
Washington	Dall.	1	38	24	0
Stewart	L.A.Rm	1	30	30	0
Conlan	L.A.Rm	1	28	28	0
Mack	T.B.	1	27	27	1
Norton	Dall.	1	25	25	0
Dent	Chi.	1	24	24	0
Teague	G.B.	1	22	22	0
Hager	Phil.	1	19	19	0
Edwards	Wash.	1	17	17	0
Jones	N.O.	1	12	12	0
Tate	N.Y.G.	1	12	12	0
Evans	Phil.	1	8	7	0
Paup	G.B.	1	8	8	0
Seals	T.B.	1	8	8	1
D. Anderson	T.B.	1	6	6	0
Homco	L.A.Rm	1	6	6	0
Joyner	Phil.	1	6	6	0
Nickerson	T.B.	1	6	6	0
A. Collins	Wash.	1	5	5	0
White	Det.	1	5	5	0
Reynolds	T.B.	1	3	3	0
Marion	Dall.	1	2	2	0
Turnbull	N.O.	1	2	2	0
Owens	Det.	1	1	1	0
Parker	Minn.	1	1	1	0
Prior	G.B.	1	1	1	0
Armstead	N.Y.G.	1	0	0	0
Beamon	N.Y.G.	1	0	0	0
Brock	G.B.	1	0	0	0
Campbell	N.Y.G.	1	0	0	0
Carter	T.B.	1	0	0	0
Cook	N.O.	1	0	0	0
Copeland	Wash.	1	0	0	0
Eaton	Atl.	1	0	0	0
Evans	G.B.	1	0	0	0
Gant	Dall.	1	0	0	0
Gibson	Det.	1	0	0	0
Hopkins	Phil.	1	0	0	0
Johnson	S.F.	1	0	0	0
Mangum	Chi.	1	0	0	0
McMichael	Chi.	1	0	0	0
Mitchell	G.B.	1	0	0	0
O. Smith	Phil.	1	0	0	0
Oldham	Phx.	1	0	0	0
Pearson	Minn.	1	0	0	0
Scroggins	Det.	1	0	0	0
Simmons	Phil.	1	0	0	0
Zordich	Phx.	1	0	0	0
Doleman	Minn.	1	-3	-3	0
Case	Atl.	0	3	3	0

NFC KICKOFF RETURNS

	Team	No.	Yds.	Avg.	Lg.	TD
Brooks	G.B.	23	611	26.6	95	1
Hughes	N.O.	30	753	25.1	99	1
T. Smith	Atl.	38	948	25.0	97	1
Gray	Det.	28	688	24.6	95	1
Bailey	Phx.	31	699	22.6	48	0
K. Williams	Dall.	31	689	22.2	49	0
Ismail	Minn.	42	902	21.5	47	0
Conway	Chi.	21	450	21.4	55	0
McAfee	N.O.	28	580	20.7	55	0
Mitchell	Wash.	33	678	20.6	68	0
Carter	S.F.	25	494	19.8	60	0
Wilson	T.B.	23	454	19.7	42	0
Sikahema	Phil.	30	579	19.3	35	0
Howard	Wash.	21	405	19.3	33	0
Meggett	N.Y.G.	24	403	16.8	35	0

NON-QUALIFIERS

	Team	No.	Yds.	Avg.	Lg.	TD
D. Moore	Det.	1	68	68.0	68	0
K. Smith	Dall.	1	33	33.0	33	0
C. Harris	G.B.	16	482	30.1	65	0
Bowles	Wash.	1	27	27.0	27	0
Montgomery	Atl.	2	53	26.5	33	0
Sanders	Atl.	7	169	24.1	31	0
Turner	Det.	15	330	22.0	46	0
Lynch	Det.	1	22	22.0	22	0
Mims	Atl.	1	22	22.0	22	0
Wilson	G.B.	9	197	21.9	37	0
Guliford	Minn.	5	101	20.2	29	0
Brown	N.O.	3	58	19.3	23	0
Thompson	G.B.	9	171	19.0	42	0
Phillips	Atl.	2	38	19.0	29	0
Griffith	L.A.Rm	8	169	18.8	29	0
Walker	Phil.	11	184	18.4	30	0
Blount	Phx.	8	163	18.1	27	0
Price	L.A.Rm	8	144	18.0	23	0
Worley	Chi.	6	121	18.0	26	0
Gant	Dall.	1	18	18.0	18	0
Lofton	Phx.	1	18	18.0	18	0
Obee	Chi.	9	159	17.7	34	0
Sydner	Phil.	9	158	17.6	36	0
Edwards	Phx.	3	51	17.0	20	0
Walker	S.F.	3	51	17.0	30	0
Clay	Det.	2	34	17.0	20	0
Hilliard	N.O.	1	17	17.0	17	0
Boykin	L.A.Rm	13	216	16.6	29	0
Lee	S.F.	10	160	16.0	28	0
Kinchen	L.A.Rm	6	96	16.0	22	0
Graham	Minn.	1	16	16.0	16	0
Pegram	Atl.	4	63	15.8	28	0
Green	Chi.	9	141	15.7	30	0
Anderson	Det.	15	232	15.5	24	0
Israel	L.A.Rm	5	92	15.3	23	0
R. White	L.A.Rm	8	122	15.3	35	0
Buck	Wash.	1	15	15.0	15	0
Calloway	N.Y.G.	6	89	14.8	21	0
Ervins	Wash.	2	29	14.5	18	0
Claiborne	T.B.	4	57	14.3	33	0
Smith	Minn.	3	41	13.7	16	0
Workman	T.B.	5	67	13.4	19	0
Royster	T.B.	8	102	12.8	26	0
Brooks	Wash.	1	12	12.0	12	0
Heyward	Chi.	1	12	12.0	12	0
R. Jones	Dall.	1	12	12.0	12	0
Sherman	Phil.	1	12	12.0	12	0
Hebron	Phil.	3	35	11.7	18	0
Jurkovic	G.B.	2	22	11.0	13	0
Craig	Minn.	1	11	11.0	11	0
Evans	Minn.	1	11	11.0	11	0
Hallock	Det.	1	11	11.0	11	0
Smith	Phx.	1	11	11.0	11	0
Turner	T.B.	6	61	10.2	19	0
Brandes	S.F.	1	10	10.0	10	0

Continued

PRO FOOTBALL WEEKLY 1994 ALMANAC

Continued

		No.	Yds.	Avg.	Lg.	TD
Moore	Phx.	1	9	9.0	9	0
Fontenot	Chi.	1	8	8.0	8	0
Cross	N.Y.G.	2	15	7.5	13	0
Hennings	Dall.	1	7	7.0	7	0
Johnson	Phil.	1	7	7.0	7	0
Ruether	Atl.	1	7	7.0	7	0
Ryan	Chi.	1	5	5.0	5	0
Del Rio	Minn.	1	4	4.0	4	0
A. Collins	Wash.	1	0	0.0	0	0
Chmura	G.B.	1	0	0.0	0	0
Gordon	Atl.	1	0	0.0	0	0
Jamison	Det.	1	0	0.0	0	0
Johnson	Chi.	1	0	0.0	0	0
Kelm	S.F.	1	0	0.0	0	0
Mangum	Chi.	1	0	0.0	0	0
McCaffrey	N.Y.G.	1	0	0.0	0	0
McMillian	Minn.	1	0	0.0	0	0
Rison	Atl.	1	0	0.0	0	0
Tennell	Minn.	1	0	0.0	0	0
Walls	S.F.	1	0	0.0	0	0
Dowdell	N.O.	0	52	0.0	52	0
O. Smith	Phil.	0	24	0.0	24	0
Novacek	Dall.	1	-1	-1.0	-1	0
Drayton	L.A.Rm	1	-15	-15.0	-15	0

NFC PUNT RETURNS

	Team	No.	FC	Yds.	Avg.	Lg.	TD
Hughes	N.O.	37	21	503	13.6	83	2
Carter	S.F.	34	20	411	12.1	72	1
K. Williams	Dall.	38	14	381	10.6	64	2
Meggett	N.Y.G.	32	20	331	10.3	75	1
Gray	Det.	23	14	197	8.6	35	0
Sikahema	Phil.	33	20	275	8.3	25	0
Obee	Chi.	35	20	289	8.3	28	0
Bailey	Phx.	35	5	282	8.2	58	1
T. Smith	Atl.	32	17	255	8.0	51	0
Guliford	Minn.	29	15	212	7.3	50	0
Mitchell	Wash.	29	7	193	6.7	48	0

NON-QUALIFIERS

Green	Wash.	1	1	27	27.0	24	0
Newman	N.O.	1	0	14	14.0	14	0
Prior	G.B.	17	3	194	11.4	24	0
Hawkins	T.B.	15	8	166	11.1	35	0
Sanders	Atl.	2	1	21	10.5	16	0
Blount	Phx.	9	3	90	10.0	25	0
Ellard	L.A.Rm	2	8	18	9.0	13	0
Turner	Det.	17	4	152	8.9	53	0
Brooks	G.B.	16	4	135	8.4	35	0
Henley	L.A.Rm	1	0	8	8.0	8	0
Parker	Minn.	9	6	64	7.1	20	0
Buckley	G.B.	11	5	76	6.9	39	0
Anderson	Det.	17	1	113	6.8	15	0
Howard	Wash.	4	0	25	6.3	13	0
Claiborne	T.B.	6	6	32	5.3	13	0
Buchanan	L.A.Rm	8	1	41	5.1	12	0
Carter	T.B.	5	0	24	4.8	12	0
Kinchen	L.A.Rm	7	4	32	4.6	8	0
Edwards	Phx.	3	3	12	4.0	11	0
Smith	Minn.	1	2	4	4.0	4	0
Price	L.A.Rm	1	2	3	3.0	3	0
Clark	Atl.	1	0	0	0.0	0	0
Kelm	S.F.	1	0	0	0.0	0	0
Mays	Wash.	1	0	0	0.0	0	0
Washington	Dall.	1	0	0	0.0	0	0
O. Smith	Phil.	0	0	9	0.0	9	0
Teague	G.B.	1	0	-1	-1.0	-1	0

NFC FIELD-GOAL ACCURACY

	Team	1-19 Yds.	20-29 Yds.	30-39 Yds.	40-49 Yds.	50 or Longer	Total	Avg. Yds. Att.	Avg. Yds. Made	Avg. Yds. Miss	Lg.
Johnson	Atl.	1-1 / 1.000	7-7 / 1.000	9-10 / .900	7-7 / 1.000	2-2 / 1.000	26-27 / .963	35.3	35.2	38.0	54
Treadwell	N.Y.G.	3-3 / 1.000	11-12 / .917	7-10 / .778	4-6 / .800	0-0 / .000	25-29 / .862	30.6	29.6	36.8	46
Murray	Dall.	4-4 / 1.000	4-4 / 1.000	9-12 / .750	8-8 / 1.000	3-5 / .600	28-33 / .849	36.5	35.5	42.0	52
Jacke	G.B.	1-1 / 1.000	12-12 / 1.000	6-10 / .600	6-7 / .857	6-7 / .857	31-37 / .838	35.4	34.8	38.5	54
Andersen	N.O.	2-2 / 1.000	7-7 / 1.000	7-7 / 1.000	11-14 / .786	1-5 / .200	28-35 / .800	38.7	36.5	47.7	56
Hanson	Det.	1-1 / 1.000	8-8 / 1.000	15-15 / 1.000	7-12 / .583	3-7 / .429	34-43 / .791	38.4	35.6	48.8	53
Butler	Chi.	0-0 / .000	7-8 / .875	12-13 / .923	3-7 / .429	5-8 / .625	27-36 / .750	38.1	36.5	42.9	55
G. Davis	Phx.	1-1 / 1.000	11-11 / 1.000	1-1 / 1.000	4-10 / .400	4-5 / .800	21-28 / .750	36.6	33.5	45.9	55
Reveiz	Minn.	4-4 / 1.000	12-12 / 1.000	6-6 / 1.000	3-7 / .429	1-6 / .167	26-35 / .743	34.7	29.4	50.0	51
Husted	T.B.	0-0 / .000	5-5 / 1.000	5-6 / .857	3-6 / .500	3-5 / .600	16-22 / .727	39.6	36.6	47.3	57
Zendejas	L.A.Rm	0-0 / .000	6-7 / .857	4-5 / .800	0-3 / .000	6-8 / .750	16-23 / .696	38.8	37.1	42.7	54
Cofer	S.F.	0-0 / .000	7-9 / .778	5-7 / .714	4-7 / .571	0-3 / .000	16-26 / .615	35.9	32.5	41.4	46
Lohmiller	Wash.	2-2 / 1.000	4-4 / 1.000	8-12 / .667	1-4 / .250	1-6 / .167	16-28 / .571	37.9	32.2	45.5	51

NON-QUALIFIERS

Ruzek	Phil.	0-0 / .000	4-4 / 1.000	3-4 / .750	1-1 / 1.000	0-0 / .000	8-9 / .889	30.4	30.4	31.0	46
Daluiso	N.Y.G.	0-0 / .000	0-0 / .000	0-0 / .000	0-0 / .000	1-3 / .500	1-2 / .500	52.0	54.0	50.0	54
Elliott	Dall.	0-0 / .000	1-1 / 1.000	0-1 / .000	1-2 / .500	0-0 / .000	2-4 / .500	36.0	32.5	39.5	43

1993 REVIEW ■ INDIVIDUAL STATS

NFC QUARTERBACK SACKS

	Team	Sacks						
Turnbull	N.O.	13.0	Geathers	Atl.	3.5	Banks	Wash.	1.0
White	G.B.	13.0	Howard	N.Y.G.	3.5	Boutte	L.A.Rm	1.0
Dent	Chi.	12.5	Swann	Phx.	3.5	Brooks	N.Y.G.	1.0
Doleman	Minn.	12.5	Bankston	Phx.	3.0	Butler	G.B.	1.0
Randle	Minn.	12.5	Booty	Phx.	3.0	Clay	Det.	1.0
Armstrong	Chi.	11.5	Dillard	N.Y.G.	3.0	Collins	N.Y.G.	1.0
Hamilton	N.Y.G.	11.5	Flores	Phil.	3.0	Colon	Det.	1.0
Harmon	Phil.	11.5	K. Wilson	S.F.	3.0	Cook	N.O.	1.0
Jackson	N.O.	11.5	Koonce	G.B.	3.0	Crockett	Det.	1.0
Paup	G.B.	11.0	M. Jones	Phx.	3.0	D. Smith	Dall.	1.0
Gilbert	L.A.Rm	10.5	Owens	Det.	3.0	D. Thomas	T.B.	1.0
Stubblefield	S.F.	10.5	Price	T.B.	3.0	E. Hill	Phx.	1.0
Harvey	Phx.	9.5	Robinson	L.A.Rm	3.0	Edwards	Dall.	1.0
Stokes	L.A.Rm	9.5	Romanowski	S.F.	3.0	Fagan	S.F.	1.0
Porcher	Det.	8.5	V. Buck	N.O.	3.0	Faulkner	Wash.	1.0
Seals	T.B.	8.5	Washington	S.F.	3.0	Fontenot	Chi.	1.0
Thomas	Minn.	8.5	Agee	Atl.	2.5	Gann	Atl.	1.0
Scroggins	Det.	8.0	C. Jenkins	Minn.	2.5	Gayle	Chi.	1.0
Tolbert	Dall.	8.0	Maryland	Dall.	2.5	George	Atl.	1.0
Young	L.A.Rm	7.0	Miller	N.O.	2.5	Gibson	Det.	1.0
Zorich	Chi.	7.0	Spellman	Chi.	2.5	Hager	Phil.	1.0
Holt	Atl.	6.5	Allen	Phil.	2.0	Henderson	L.A.Rm	1.0
Miller	N.Y.G.	6.5	Brock	G.B.	2.0	J. Johnson	Wash.	1.0
Nunn	Phx.	6.5	Casillas	Dall.	2.0	Jones	Chi.	1.0
Swilling	Det.	6.5	Cox	Chi.	2.0	Jones	N.O.	1.0
T. Bennett	G.B.	6.5	Gardner	Atl.	2.0	Jones	T.B.	1.0
W. Thomas	Phil.	6.5	Goff	N.O.	2.0	Kelly	S.F.	1.0
A. Collins	Wash.	6.0	Hayworth	Det.	2.0	Logan	Atl.	1.0
Barker	Minn.	6.0	Holland	G.B.	2.0	London	Det.	1.0
Coleman	Wash.	6.0	Jamison	Det.	2.0	Lynch	Phx.	1.0
Harrison	S.F.	6.0	Johnson	S.F.	2.0	Mann	Wash.	1.0
Jeffcoat	Dall.	6.0	Joyner	Phil.	2.0	Nickerson	T.B.	1.0
McMichael	Chi.	6.0	Mills	N.O.	2.0	Oldham	Phx.	1.0
Taylor	N.Y.G.	6.0	Norton	Dall.	2.0	Patterson	G.B.	1.0
Brown	S.F.	5.5	Roper	Dall.	2.0	Perry	Phil.	1.0
J. Jones	Dall.	5.5	Spindler	Det.	2.0	R. Davis	Phx.	1.0
Jurkovic	G.B.	5.5	Tuggle	Atl.	2.0	R. Harris	Minn.	1.0
Wilson	S.F.	5.5	Wheeler	T.B.	2.0	Reynolds	T.B.	1.0
Curry	T.B.	5.0	Williams	N.O.	2.0	Rocker	L.A.Rm	1.0
Dotson	T.B.	5.0	Wilson	Wash.	2.0	Sheppard	Minn.	1.0
Johnson	N.O.	5.0	Ahanotu	T.B.	1.5	Simmons	G.B.	1.0
Simmons	Phil.	5.0	Bailey	N.Y.G.	1.5	Smeenge	N.O.	1.0
W. Martin	N.O.	5.0	Case	Atl.	1.5	Stewart	L.A.Rm	1.0
Fox	N.Y.G.	4.5	Conner	Atl.	1.5	Strahan	N.Y.G.	1.0
Palmer	Wash.	4.5	Gouveia	Wash.	1.5	TEAM	Chi.	1.0
Haley	Dall.	4.0	McGhee	N.Y.G.	1.5	Warren	N.O.	1.0
Millard	Phil.	4.0	Roberts	S.F.	1.5	Woods	L.A.Rm	1.0
Noga	Wash.	4.0	Smith	S.F.	1.5	Del Rio	Minn.	.5
Pritchett	Det.	4.0	Stowe	Phx.	1.5	Simpson	Chi.	.5
T. Johnson	Wash.	4.0	White	Det.	1.5	Spielman	Det.	.5
C. Smith	Atl.	3.5	Atkins	N.O.	1.0	Thomas	S.F.	.5
			B. Thomas	T.B.	1.0			

PRO FOOTBALL WEEKLY 1994 ALMANAC

AFC TEAM STATISTICS

OFFENSE	BUFF	CIN	CLEV	DENV	HOU	IND	KC	LARD	MIA	NE	NYJ	PITT	SD	SEA
GAMES (W-L-T)	12-4-0	3-13-0	7-9-0	9-7-0	12-4-0	4-12-0	11-5-0	10-6-0	9-7-0	5-11-0	8-8-0	9-7-0	8-8-0	6-10-0
FIRST DOWNS	316	239	264	327	330	269	300	292	309	315	304	307	313	279
Rushing	117	89	91	105	101	71	94	95	85	116	106	116	120	114
Passing	176	133	152	187	208	180	180	168	207	169	173	180	171	144
Penalty	23	17	21	35	21	18	26	29	17	30	25	11	22	21
TOTAL YDS. GAINED	5260	4052	4740	5461	5658	4705	4835	5014	5812	5065	5212	5235	4967	4669
Avg. Per Game	328.8	253.3	296.3	341.3	353.6	294.1	302.2	313.4	363.3	316.6	325.8	327.2	310.4	291.8
RUSHING (NET)	1943	1511	1701	1693	1792	1288	1655	1425	1459	1780	1880	2003	1824	2015
Avg. Per Game	121.4	94.4	106.3	105.8	112.0	80.5	103.4	89.1	91.2	111.3	117.5	125.2	114.0	125.9
PASSING (NET)	3317	2541	3039	3768	3866	3417	3180	3589	4353	3285	3332	3232	3143	2654
Avg. Per Game	207.3	158.8	189.9	235.5	241.6	213.6	198.8	224.3	272.1	205.3	208.3	202.0	196.4	165.9
RUSHES	551	423	425	468	409	365	445	433	419	502	521	491	455	473
Avg. Yards	3.5	3.6	4.0	3.6	4.4	3.5	3.7	3.3	3.5	3.5	3.6	4.1	4.0	4.3
PASSES ATTEMPTED	497	510	478	553	614	594	490	495	581	566	489	540	563	498
Completed	304	272	262	350	357	332	287	281	342	289	294	299	301	280
Pct. Comp.	61.2	53.3	54.8	63.3	58.1	55.9	58.6	56.8	58.9	51.1	60.1	55.4	53.5	56.2
Tackled	31	53	45	39	43	29	35	50	30	23	21	48	32	48
Yards Lost	218	289	289	293	279	206	204	293	211	127	160	374	240	242
Had Intercepted	18	11	19	10	25	15	10	14	18	24	12	12	14	18
Yards Opp. Ret.	174	49	246	79	309	247	111	289	329	201	310	216	271	159
Opp. Tds On Int.	0	0	0	0	0	1	0	2	2	1	3	2	2	0
PUNTS	74	90	84	68	56	83	77	71	58	76	73	89	74	91
Gross Avg.	40.4	43.4	43.2	44.4	45.4	43.3	42.1	41.8	39.7	40.7	38.4	42.5	42.3	44.0
Touchbacks	4	12	10	8	7	13	8	9	4	7	7	3	7	7
Net Avg.	36.0	36.1	35.6	37.1	38.5	35.9	35.4	35.1	32.2	34.8	34.4	34.1	36.4	37.2
Blocked	0	0	2	1	0	0	0	0	0	3	0	0	0	1
PUNT RETURNS	33	48	42	41	41	30	37	40	28	51	31	46	34	33
Avg. Ret.	8.4	6.7	13.4	10.4	6.7	5.8	9.4	11.6	11.6	9.2	8.3	7.7	12.1	8.5
Ret. For Td	1	0	3	0	0	0	0	1	2	0	0	0	0	0
KICKOFF RETURNS	45	61	58	38	31	57	45	52	49	47	46	52	47	50
Avg. Ret.	16.6	19.9	19.1	18.9	18.9	19.7	19.4	20.7	21.8	17.4	14.7	16.9	19.2	18.6
Ret. For Td	0	0	0	0	0	0	0	0	0	0	0	0	0	0
PENALTIES	95	125	121	112	132	94	121	148	81	64	86	100	87	99
Yards	630	773	842	822	1005	685	969	1181	663	468	555	861	699	745
FUMBLES	26	24	27	29	37	34	28	23	30	30	38	27	13	25
Fumbles Lost	17	9	17	18	20	20	18	11	14	10	16	15	5	13
Opp. Fumbles	35	22	28	27	31	25	30	23	31	20	30	37	19	23
Opp. Fumbles Rec.	24	14	9	13	17	11	17	9	14	9	18	14	12	15
3RD DOWN ATTEMPTS	224	232	201	225	212	209	203	201	218	237	220	236	224	223
Converted to First Down	98	80	66	98	94	61	82	74	100	92	92	92	89	79
Third Down Efficiency	43.8	34.5	32.8	43.6	44.3	29.2	40.4	36.8	45.9	38.8	41.8	39.0	39.7	35.4
4TH DOWN ATTEMPTS	8	25	15	11	12	22	9	8	17	28	20	16	15	14
Converted to First Down	5	10	10	2	3	9	4	1	8	13	10	8	6	6
Fourth Down Efficiency	62.5	40.0	66.7	18.2	25.0	40.9	44.4	12.5	47.1	46.4	50.0	50.0	40.0	42.9
TOUCHDOWNS	37	16	36	42	40	16	37	29	40	26	31	32	33	29
Rushing	12	3	8	13	11	4	14	10	10	9	14	13	14	13
Passing	20	11	23	27	23	10	20	17	27	17	16	16	18	13
Returns	5	2	5	2	6	2	3	2	3	0	1	3	1	3
EXTRA POINTS ATT.	37	16	36	42	40	16	37	29	37	25	31	32	36	29
Extra Points	36	13	36	41	39	15	37	27	37	25	31	32	31	29
FG/FGA	23/32	24/31	16/22	26/35	29/34	26/31	23/29	35/44	24/32	19/31	17/26	28/30	31/40	23/28
Total Points	329	187	304	373	368	189	328	306	349	238	270	308	322	280

DEFENSE	BUFF	CIN	CLEV	DENV	HOU	IND	KC	LARD	MIA	NE	NYJ	PITT	SD	SEA
OPP. POINTS	242	319	307	284	238	378	291	326	351	286	247	281	290	314
OPP. FIRST DOWNS	331	306	290	280	289	334	300	302	332	269	266	267	299	322
Rushing	114	134	94	86	73	151	103	111	103	97	93	74	86	106
Passing	199	159	170	181	184	166	161	154	205	161	161	163	192	193
Penalty	18	13	26	13	32	17	36	37	24	11	12	30	21	23
OPP. YDS. GAINED	5554	5018	4778	5149	4874	5638	4771	4723	5150	4796	4712	4531	5066	5313
Avg. Per Game	347.1	313.6	298.6	321.8	304.6	352.4	298.2	295.2	321.9	299.8	294.5	283.2	316.6	332.1
RUSHING (NET)	1921	2220	1654	1418	1273	2521	1620	1865	1665	1951	1473	1368	1314	1660
Avg. Per Game	120.1	138.8	103.4	88.6	79.6	157.6	101.3	116.6	104.1	121.9	92.1	85.5	82.1	103.8
PASSING (NET)	3633	2798	3124	3731	3601	3117	3151	2858	3485	2845	3239	3163	3752	3653
Avg. Per Game	227.1	174.9	195.3	233.2	225.1	194.8	196.9	178.6	217.8	177.8	202.4	197.7	234.5	228.3
OPP. RUSHES	500	521	451	397	369	575	453	494	460	505	420	399	414	452
Avg. Yards	3.8	4.3	3.7	3.6	3.4	4.4	3.6	3.8	3.6	3.9	3.5	3.4	3.2	3.7
OPP. PASSES	582	457	541	562	582	454	525	457	572	474	497	521	556	595
Completed	323	251	306	314	302	270	312	258	350	280	296	277	329	333
Pct. Comp.	55.5	54.9	56.6	55.9	51.9	59.5	59.4	56.5	61.2	59.1	59.6	53.2	59.2	56.0
Tackled	37	22	48	46	52	21	35	45	29	34	32	42	32	38
Yards Lost	256	154	342	238	313	121	228	283	197	242	195	277	206	244
Intercepted By	23	12	13	18	26	10	21	14	13	19	24	22	22	22
Yards Ret.	306	272	208	236	412	116	225	199	175	122	233	386	319	196
Ret. for Td	3	2	1	1	3	0	1	1	0	1	0	1	1	1
OPP. PUNTS	65	74	85	81	78	71	68	80	76	90	66	82	72	73
Gross Avg.	41.8	42.2	42.4	43.7	43.7	40.2	44.6	42.1	41.3	41.2	43.3	44.0	42.1	42.4
Touchbacks	8	6	7	10	13	6	6	8	8	6	6	7	3	11
Net Avg.	35.1	36.2	34.1	36.0	36.8	36.1	37.8	34.3	34.9	34.7	37.6	38.0	35.5	35.6
Blocked	0	1	0	1	1	0	1	1	1	2	0	0	0	0
OPP. PUNT RET.	29	47	48	33	28	41	43	35	32	34	26	50	36	47
Avg. Ret.	8.5	8.9	9.1	10.2	8.9	8.6	8.2	8.6	11.2	9.2	6.0	13.7	8.2	10.2
OPP. KICKOFF RET.	43	38	46	63	60	37	49	45	62	44	47	54	64	52
Avg. Ret.	19.8	21.9	17.7	18.0	17.7	14.9	20.6	17.4	20.0	20.9	19.4	21.4	16.6	18.6
OPP. PENALTIES	102	74	106	128	104	91	129	104	93	112	88	76	95	110
Yards	681	560	831	1019	786	610	1008	803	650	808	654	647	724	818
OPP. 3RD DOWN ATT.	235	212	231	215	208	206	210	203	228	232	200	201	210	228
Converted To First Down	107	85	88	71	64	85	86	73	103	96	81	68	83	91
Third Down Efficiency	45.5	40.1	38.1	33.0	30.8	41.3	41.0	36.0	45.2	41.4	40.5	33.8	39.5	39.9
OPP. 4TH DOWN ATT.	18	11	12	17	25	12	13	9	10	13	19	13	8	13
Converted To First Down	6	7	6	8	12	8	3	5	3	5	9	4	4	6
Fourth Down Efficiency	33.3	63.6	50.0	47.1	48.0	66.7	23.1	55.6	30.0	38.5	47.4	40.0	50.0	46.2
OPP. TOUCHDOWNS	25	37	30	27	26	45	30	37	43	32	26	30	30	32
Rushing	7	15	9	6	9	20	11	17	12	9	8	6	10	12
Passing	18	20	19	21	16	22	18	17	26	15	15	18	17	16
Returns	0	2	2	0	1	3	1	3	5	2	3	5	3	4
OPP. EXTRA PTS. ATT.	24	37	30	29	26	45	29	37	42	32	26	30	30	30
Opp. Extra Points	23	37	30	27	25	43	27	37	40	32	26	29	30	30
OPP. FG/FGA	23/35	20/28	31/38	31/36	19/28	21/30	28/32	21/33	17/27	20/24	21/26	24/29	26/33	29/39

394

1993 REVIEW ■ TEAM STATISTICS

NFC TEAM STATISTICS

OFFENSE	ATL	CHI	DALL	DET	GB	LARM	MINN	NO	NYG	PHIL	PHX	SF	TB	WASH
GAMES (W-L-T)	6-10-0	7-9-0	12-4-0	10-6-0	9-7-0	5-11-0	9-7-0	8-8-0	11-5-0	8-8-0	7-9-0	10-6-0	5-11-0	4-12-0
FIRST DOWNS	292	226	322	248	282	279	283	264	300	302	295	372	241	255
Rushing	91	98	120	101	98	117	85	94	127	103	107	134	80	92
Passing	185	113	172	139	166	147	182	158	153	184	173	212	141	143
Penalty	16	15	30	8	18	15	16	12	20	15	5	26	20	20
TOTAL YDS. GAINED	5110	3717	5615	4658	4750	4804	4822	4707	5145	4922	5213	6435	4311	4271
Avg. Per Game	319.4	232.3	350.9	291.1	296.9	300.3	301.4	294.2	321.6	307.6	325.8	402.2	269.4	266.9
RUSHING (NET)	1590	1677	2161	1944	1619	2014	1623	1766	2210	1761	1809	2133	1290	1726
Avg. Per Game	99.4	104.8	135.1	121.5	101.2	125.9	101.4	110.4	138.1	110.1	113.1	133.3	80.6	107.9
PASSING (NET)	3520	2040	3454	2714	3131	2790	3199	2941	2935	3161	3404	4302	3021	2545
Avg. Per Game	220.0	127.5	215.9	169.6	195.7	174.4	199.9	183.8	183.4	197.6	212.8	268.9	188.8	159.1
RUSHES	395	477	490	456	448	449	447	414	560	456	452	463	402	396
Avg. Yards	4.0	3.5	4.4	4.3	3.6	4.5	3.6	4.3	3.9	3.9	4.0	4.6	3.2	4.4
PASSES ATTEMPTED	573	388	475	435	528	473	526	481	424	556	522	524	508	533
Completed	334	230	317	264	322	247	315	274	257	328	310	354	262	287
Pct. Comp.	58.3	59.3	66.7	60.7	61.0	52.2	59.9	57.0	60.6	59.0	59.4	67.6	51.6	53.8
Tackled	40	48	29	46	30	31	35	40	40	42	33	35	39	40
Yards Lost	267	230	163	229	199	231	181	242	245	302	231	178	274	219
Had Intercepted	25	16	6	19	24	19	14	21	9	13	20	17	25	21
Yards Opp. Ret.	345	105	47	177	437	347	166	444	175	107	143	157	280	209
Opp. Tds On Int.	2	1	0	1	3	2	3	6	1	0	0	0	1	2
PUNTS	72	80	56	72	74	80	90	77	78	83	73	42	94	83
Gross Avg.	43.3	38.5	41.8	44.5	42.9	40.9	42.8	43.6	41.9	40.0	43.7	40.9	40.1	43.9
Touchbacks	3	2	3	9	7	10	6	6	4	4	8	5	3	10
Net Avg.	37.6	36.6	37.7	36.8	36.3	31.7	35.3	37.7	37.8	35.3	37.8	34.5	35.3	37.4
Blocked	0	0	0	0	0	0	0	0	1	0	0	0	0	0
PUNT RETURNS	35	35	37	40	45	19	39	38	32	33	47	35	38	35
Avg. Ret.	7.9	8.3	10.3	8.4	9.0	5.4	7.2	13.6	10.3	8.6	8.3	11.7	8.2	7.0
Ret. For Td	0	0	2	0	0	0	0	2	1	0	1	1	0	0
KICKOFF RETURNS	55	45	36	52	60	49	55	62	32	53	45	41	58	59
Avg. Ret.	23.6	18.0	21.0	23.2	24.7	16.8	19.7	23.5	15.8	18.6	21.1	17.4	15.9	19.8
Ret. For Td	1	0	0	1	1	0	0	1	0	0	0	0	0	0
PENALTIES	111	68	94	93	85	71	109	81	90	101	77	95	89	90
Yards	838	587	744	665	734	526	806	663	586	758	644	800	765	596
FUMBLES	31	29	33	29	26	20	15	24	19	32	23	31	28	24
Fumbles Lost	17	14	16	13	10	11	10	13	8	21	11	13	11	10
Opp. Fumbles	25	24	22	34	33	26	22	30	27	33	27	20	27	25
Opp. Fumbles Rec.	11	12	14	16	15	9	10	20	10	15	17	11	13	14
3RD DOWN ATTEMPTS	208	211	198	211	218	201	212	203	221	222	220	186	213	213
Converted to First Down	79	73	83	74	81	79	72	72	90	91	103	89	74	74
Third Down Efficiency	38.0	34.6	41.9	35.1	37.2	39.3	34.0	35.5	40.7	41.0	46.8	47.8	34.7	34.7
4TH DOWN ATTEMPTS	18	13	12	12	16	11	7	11	11	16	13	16	12	16
Converted to First Down	10	4	7	5	9	5	4	7	5	7	7	10	3	5
Fourth Down Efficiency	55.6	30.8	58.3	41.7	56.3	45.5	57.1	63.6	45.5	43.8	53.8	62.5	25.0	31.3
TOUCHDOWNS	34	22	41	28	35	25	28	33	30	35	37	61	27	26
Rushing	4	10	20	9	14	8	8	10	11	8	12	27	6	11
Passing	28	7	18	15	19	16	18	18	17	22	21	29	19	11
Returns	2	5	3	4	2	1	2	5	2	5	4	5	2	4
EXTRA POINTS ATT.	34	22	41	28	36	25	28	33	30	33	37	61	27	26
Extra Points	34	21	40	28	35	23	27	33	28	30	37	59	27	24
FG/FGA	26/27	27/36	30/37	34/43	31/37	16/23	26/35	28/35	26/34	16/23	21/28	16/26	16/27	16/28
Total Points	316	234	376	298	340	221	277	317	288	293	326	473	237	230
DEFENSE	ATL	CHI	DALL	DET	GB	LARM	MINN	NO	NYG	PHIL	PHX	SF	TB	WASH
OPP. POINTS	385	230	229	292	282	367	290	343	205	315	269	295	376	345
OPP. FIRST DOWNS	278	290	297	279	261	304	259	273	268	271	278	297	280	304
Rushing	79	112	94	108	88	117	98	116	89	91	106	109	109	127
Passing	180	163	176	154	157	179	139	145	161	155	158	171	152	157
Penalty	19	15	27	17	16	8	22	12	18	25	14	17	19	20
OPP. YDS. GAINED	5421	4653	4767	4669	4482	5411	4404	4696	4663	5019	5167	4997	5246	5497
Avg. Per Game	338.8	290.8	297.9	291.8	280.1	338.2	275.3	293.5	291.4	313.7	322.9	312.3	327.9	343.6
RUSHING (NET)	1784	1835	1651	1649	1582	1851	1534	2090	1547	2080	1861	1800	1994	2111
Avg. Per Game	111.5	114.7	103.2	103.1	98.9	115.7	95.9	130.6	96.7	130.0	116.3	112.5	124.6	131.9
PASSING (NET)	3637	2818	3116	3020	2900	3560	2870	2606	3116	2939	3306	3197	3252	3386
Avg. Per Game	227.3	176.1	194.8	188.8	181.3	222.5	179.4	162.9	194.8	183.7	206.6	199.8	203.3	211.6
OPP. RUSHES	419	476	423	433	424	480	415	513	395	467	433	404	479	513
Avg. Yards	4.3	3.9	3.9	3.8	3.7	3.9	3.7	4.1	3.9	4.5	4.3	4.5	4.2	4.1
OPP. PASSES	505	504	555	514	529	488	478	444	514	463	495	564	503	483
Completed	308	306	334	309	290	299	310	259	298	251	281	314	300	291
Pct. Comp.	61.0	60.7	60.2	60.1	54.8	61.3	64.9	58.3	58.0	54.2	56.8	55.7	59.6	60.2
Tackled	27	46	34	43	46	35	45	51	41	36	34	44	29	31
Yards Lost	149	287	231	253	301	203	276	318	238	214	205	316	132	197
Intercepted By	13	18	14	19	18	11	24	10	18	20	9	19	9	17
Yards Ret.	160	300	171	156	255	127	211	133	184	323	124	267	79	241
Ret. for Td	0	2	1	1	0	0	2	0	1	4	1	3	2	2
OPP. PUNTS	74	78	78	81	79	58	78	80	80	75	78	68	76	73
Gross Avg.	40.9	41.4	41.3	43.1	40.2	42.3	42.4	42.3	40.3	41.8	42.7	43.8	43.3	41.1
Touchbacks	5	6	6	7	3	9	4	4	6	7	4	5	11	4
Net Avg.	35.9	36.2	34.8	37.3	34.3	37.4	37.8	34.8	34.7	36.2	36.7	36.2	36.3	36.6
Blocked	1	1	0	0	0	0	0	0	0	1	0	0	0	0
OPP. PUNT RET.	41	22	32	45	38	43	46	36	44	35	30	16	53	34
Avg. Ret.	8.5	5.2	5.3	8.4	9.1	12.4	12.2	9.3	5.6	8.9	8.9	10.7	7.4	10.1
OPP. KICKOFF RET.	55	53	66	30	70	47	58	40	29	53	51	62	28	36
Avg. Ret.	19.3	17.3	18.6	20.3	20.2	20.9	24.5	19.7	22.3	21.4	19.5	19.3	17.8	20.0
OPP. PENALTIES	100	91	88	75	86	80	97	87	98	86	95	99	126	100
Yards	878	783	653	500	712	532	767	590	820	615	730	743	913	783
OPP. 3RD DOWN ATT.	202	214	219	225	216	216	207	227	196	205	205	212	224	215
Converted To First Down	74	80	87	92	69	101	81	92	67	66	76	88	85	92
Third Down Efficiency	36.6	37.4	39.7	40.9	31.9	46.8	39.1	40.5	34.2	32.2	37.1	41.5	37.9	42.8
OPP. 4TH DOWN ATT.	16	15	17	11	18	17	6	16	23	19	5	20	16	15
Converted to First Down	6	6	6	7	3	10	3	9	12	15	1	9	5	5
Fourth Down Efficiency	37.5	40.0	35.3	63.6	16.7	58.8	50.0	56.3	52.2	78.9	20.0	45.0	31.3	33.3
OPP. TOUCHDOWNS	46	22	23	32	27	40	31	39	22	35	27	30	40	42
Rushing	14	9	7	12	6	18	14	7	7	11	13	6	15	14
Passing	27	12	14	19	16	17	11	22	13	22	14	23	22	24
Returns	5	1	2	1	5	5	6	10	2	2	0	1	3	4
OPP. EXTRA PTS. ATT.	46	21	23	32	27	40	32	39	22	34	27	29	40	42
Opp. Extra Points	45	20	23	31	27	38	30	35	22	34	27	29	38	40
OPP. FG/FGA	20/31	26/34	22/27	23/30	31/40	29/37	25/33	24/30	17/23	23/34	26/35	27/30	32/35	17/22

AFC TEAM RANKINGS

OFFENSE	BUF	CIN	CLE	DEN	HOU	IND	KC	LARD	MIA	NE	NYJ	PIT	SD	SEA
Total Yards/Game	6	27	20	5	3	22	16	13	2	12	9	7	14	23
Rushing Yards/Game	8	24	17	18	12	28	20	26	25	13	9	6	10	4
Avg. Gain/Rush	24	21	12	18	4	23	16	27	26	22	20	9	11	8
Passing Yards/Game	11	27	19	4	3	8	15	5	1	12	10	13	17	25
Avg. Gain/Pass Play	8	27	12	6	11	22	10	4	2	18	5	21	24	25
Pct. Had Intercepted	16	5	19	2	21	10	3	12	13	23	8	6	9	15
Pct. QB Sacks Allowed	8	26	22	15	14	3	16	25	4	1	2	21	6	24
First Downs/Game	5	27	22T	3	2	21	12T	15T	8	6	10	9	7	19T
Avg. Gain/Off. Play	16	27	13	6	4	19	14	7	3	23	9	17	20	24
3rd Down Efficiency	5	25	27	6	4	28	11	18	3	15	8	14	12	20
4th Down Efficiency	3T	21T	1	27	25T	20	16	28	12	13	10T	10T	21T	18
Punt Return Avg.	15	26	2	7	25	27	10	6	5	11	18	22	3	14
Kickoff Return Avg.	25	9	15	17	16	12	13	8	5	22	28	23	14	19
Gross Punting Avg.	23	8	11	3	1	9	16	18	26	22	28	14	15	4
Net Punting Avg.	15	14	17	9	1	16	18	22	27	23	25	26	12	8
Points/Game	7	28	15	3	4	27	8	14	5	22	21	13	10	19
Extra Point Pct.	16	28	1T	13	15	21	1T	23	1T	1T	1T	1T	27	1T
Field Goal Pct.	22	13	20T	18T	3	4	10	9	15T	27	25	2	12	6

DEFENSE	BUF	CIN	CLE	DEN	HOU	IND	KC	LARD	MIA	NE	NYJ	PIT	SD	SEA
Opp. Yards/Game	27	16	12	19	14	28	11	9	20	13	8	3	18	23
Opp. Rush Yds./Game	21	27	12	4	1	28	9	20	14	22	5	3	2	13
Avg. Gain/Rush	14	24	8	5	3	26	6	12	7	17	4	2	1	9
Opp. Pass Yds./Game	24	2	13	27	23	12	14	5	21	4	17	15	28	26
Avg. Gain/Pass Play	18	17	6	22	13	25	12	14	16	9	21	11	24	15
Pct. Intercepted By	7	19	22	16	3	26	5	17	23	18	8	2	6	9
QB Sack Pct.	21	27	6	9	5	28	17	2	26	14	18	10	24	20
Opp. 1st Downs/Game	26	24	15T	12T	14	28	20	21	27	6	3	4	19	25
Avg. Gain/Def. Play	17	19	3	21	13	25	6	11	12	10	18	7	20	14
3rd Down Efficiency	27	17	12	4	1	22	21	7	26	23	18	5	14	16
4th Down Efficiency	6T	25T	18T	15	17	27	3	22	4	10	16	11T	18T	14
Opp. Punt Return Avg.	9	13	17	22	15	11	6	12	25	19	4	28	7	23
Opp. Kickoff Ret. Avg.	16	26	5	8	6	1	21	4	17	23	13	24	2	10
Opp. Gross Punt Avg.	11	14	17	25	2	28	5	13	7	6	23	27	12	19
Opp. Net Punt Avg.	9	18	1	13	22	14	26	2	8	5	25	28	10	11
Opp. Points/Game	5	20	17	10	4	27	14	21	24	11	6	8	12T	18
Opp. Field Goal Pct.	4	8	22	25	6	7	26	2	1	24	20	23	18	11

MISCELLANEOUS	BUF	CIN	CLE	DEN	HOU	IND	KC	LARD	MIA	NE	NYJ	PIT	SD	SEA
Point Differential	5	25	16	4	3	28	9	18	15	22	12	11	10	21
Turnover Edge	2	8T	25T	11T	18T	25T	5T	18T	21T	24	7	3T	1	8T
Penalty Yards Edge	10	25	15	3	27	21	12	28	16	1	7	26	13	9
Punt Ret. Differential	16	22	4	13	23	24	9	7	12	14	8	27	5	21
KO Return Differential	22	20	11	13	12	1	17	5	9	23	26	25	7	15
Time of Possession	28	21	16	6	5	27	17	11	20	15	2	3	14	19

1993 REVIEW ■ TEAM STATISTICS

NFC TEAM RANKINGS

OFFENSE	ATL	CHI	DAL	DET	GB	LA	MIN	NO	NYG	PHI	PHX	SF	TB	WAS
Total Yards/Game	11	28	4	24	19	18	17	21	10	15	8	1	25	26
Rushing Yards/Game	23	19	2	7	22	5	21	14	1	15	11	3	27	16
Avg. Gain/Rush	10	25	3	7	19	2	17	6	14	15	13	1	28	5
Passing Yards/Game	6	28	7	24	18	23	14	21	22	16	9	2	20	26
Avg. Gain/Pass Play	13	26	3	16	17	19	14	15	7	23	9	1	20	28
Pct. Had Intercepted	24	22	1	26	27	20	11	25	4	7	17	14	28	18
Pct. QB Sacks Allowed	13	28	7	27	5	10	11	20	23	18	9	12	19	17
First Downs/Game	15T	28	4	25	18	19T	17	22T	12T	11	14	1	26	24
Avg. Gain/Off. Play	8	28	2	15	21	10	18	11	12	22	5	1	25	26
3rd Down Efficiency	16	24	7	21	17	13	26	19	10	9	2	1	22T	22T
4th Down Efficiency	8	24	5	19	7	14T	6	2	14T	17	9	3T	25T	23
Punt Return Avg.	21	19	9	16	12	28	23	1	8	13	17	4	20	24
Kickoff Return Avg.	2	20	7	4	1	24	11	3	27	18	6	21	26	10
Gross Punting Avg.	10	27	19	2	12	21	13	7	17	25	6	20	24	5
Net Punting Avg.	6	11	4	10	13	28	21	5	3	19	2	24	20	7
Points/Game	12	24	2	16	6	26	20	11	18	17	9	1	23	25
Extra Point Pct.	1T	20	14	1T	17	25	19	1T	22	26	1T	18	1T	24
Field Goal Pct.	1	15T	7	11	5	23T	18T	8	14	23T	15T	26	20T	28

DEFENSE	ATL	CHI	DAL	DET	GB	LA	MIN	NO	NYG	PHI	PHX	SF	TB	WAS
Opp. Yards/Game	25	4	10	6	2	24	1	7	5	17	21	15	22	26
Opp. Rush Yds./Game	15	17	11	10	8	18	6	25	7	24	19	16	23	26
Avg. Gain/Rush	23	15	18	13	11	16	10	20	19	27	25	28	22	21
Opp. Pass Yds./Game	25	3	10T	9	7	22	6	1	10T	8	19	16	18	20
Avg. Gain/Pass Play	28	2	5	7	1	27	8	4	10	19	23	3	20	26
Pct. Intercepted By	20	11	21	10	14	24	1	25	13	4	27	15	28	12
QB Sack Pct.	25	4	22	8	7	15	3	1	11	13	16	12	23	19
Opp. 1st Downs/Game	9T	15T	17T	11	2	22T	1	8	5	7	9T	17T	12T	22T
Avg. Gain/Def. Play	28	2	8	9	1	27	5	4	15	23	26	16	22	24
3rd Down Efficiency	8	10	15	20	2	28	13	19	6	3	9	24	11	25
4th Down Efficiency	9	11T	8	25T	1	24	18T	23	21	28	2	13	5	6T
Opp. Punt Return Avg.	10	1	2	8	18	27	26	20	3	14	16	24	5	21
Opp. Kickoff Ret. Avg.	12	3	9	20	19	22	28	15	27	25	14	11	7	18
Opp. Gross Punt Avg.	4	9	8	21	1	15	18	16	3	10	20	26	22	5
Opp. Net Punt Avg.	12	16	7	23	3	24	27	6	4	15	21	17	19	20
Opp. Points/Game	28	3	2	15	9	25	12T	22	1	19	7	16	26	23
Opp. Field Goal Pct.	3	13	21	14	16	17	12	19	9	5	10	27	28	15

MISCELLANEOUS	ATL	CHI	DAL	DET	GB	LA	MIN	NO	NYG	PHI	PHX	SF	TB	WAS
Point Differential	23	14	2	13	7	27	17	20	6	19	8	1	26	24
Turnover Edge	28	14T	8T	11T	17	23	5T	20	3T	13	21T	14T	25T	14T
Penalty Yards Edge	11	4	22	24	17	14	18	20	2	23	8	19	6	5
Punt Ret. Differential	20	6	1	15	17	28	26	3	2	18	19	10	11	25
KO Return Differential	3	14	8	6	2	24	27	4	28	21	10	18	19	16
Time of Possession	7	23	9	18	10	25	12	24	1	8	4	13	22	26

PRO FOOTBALL WEEKLY 1994 ALMANAC

OFFENSIVE TEAM EFFICIENCY

	OFF PLAYS	RUSH AVG	PASS AVG	OFF AVG
1. SAN FRANCISCO	1,022	4.61	7.70	6.30
2. DALLAS	994	4.41	6.85	5.65
3. MIAMI	1,030	3.48	7.12	5.64
4. HOUSTON	1,066	4.38	5.88	5.31
5. PHOENIX	1,007	4.00	6.13	5.18
6. DENVER	1,060	3.62	6.36	5.15
7. L.A. RAIDERS	978	3.29	6.59	5.13
8. ATLANTA	1,008	4.03	5.74	5.07
9. N.Y. JETS	1,031	3.61	6.53	5.06
10. L.A. RAMS	953	4.49	5.54	5.04
11. NEW ORLEANS	935	4.27	5.64	5.03
12. N.Y. GIANTS	1,024	3.95	6.33	5.02
13. CLEVELAND	948	4.00	5.81	5.00
14. KANSAS CITY	970	3.72	6.06	4.98
15. DETROIT	937	4.26	5.64	4.97
16. BUFFALO	1,079	3.53	6.28	4.87
17. PITTSBURGH	1,079	4.08	5.50	4.85
18. MINNESOTA	1,008	3.63	5.70	4.78
19. INDIANAPOLIS	988	3.53	5.48	4.76
20. SAN DIEGO	1,050	4.01	5.28	4.73
21. GREEN BAY	1,006	3.61	5.61	4.72
22. PHILADELPHIA	1,054	3.86	5.29	4.67
23. NEW ENGLAND	1,091	3.55	5.58	4.64
24. SEATTLE	1,019	4.26	4.86	4.58
25. TAMPA BAY	949	3.21	5.52	4.54
26. WASHINGTON	969	4.36	4.44	4.41
27. CINCINNATI	986	3.57	4.51	4.11
28. CHICAGO	913	3.52	4.68	4.07

DEFENSIVE TEAM EFFICIENCY

	DEF PLAYS	RUSH AVG	PASS AVG	DEF AVG
1. GREEN BAY	999	3.73	5.04	4.49
2. CHICAGO	1,026	3.86	5.12	4.54
3. CLEVELAND	1,040	3.67	5.30	4.59
4. NEW ORLEANS	1,008	4.07	5.26	4.66
5. MINNESOTA	938	3.70	5.49	4.70
6. KANSAS CITY	1,013	3.58	5.63	4.71
7. PITTSBURGH	962	3.43	5.62	4.71
8. DALLAS	1,012	3.90	5.29	4.71
9. DETROIT	990	3.81	5.42	4.72
10. NEW ENGLAND	1,013	3.86	5.60	4.73
11. L.A. RAIDERS	996	3.78	5.69	4.74
12. MIAMI	1,061	3.62	5.80	4.85
13. HOUSTON	1,003	3.45	5.68	4.86
14. SEATTLE	1,085	3.67	5.77	4.90
15. N.Y. GIANTS	950	3.92	5.61	4.91
16. SAN FRANCISCO	1,012	4.46	5.26	4.94
17. BUFFALO	1,119	3.84	5.87	4.96
18. N.Y. JETS	949	3.51	6.12	4.97
19. CINCINNATI	1,000	4.26	5.84	5.02
20. SAN DIEGO	1,002	3.17	6.38	5.06
21. DENVER	1,005	3.57	6.14	5.12
22. TAMPA BAY	1,011	4.16	6.11	5.19
23. PHILADELPHIA	966	4.45	5.89	5.20
24. WASHINGTON	1,027	4.12	6.59	5.35
25. INDIANAPOLIS	1,050	4.38	6.56	5.37
26. PHOENIX	962	4.30	6.25	5.37
27. L.A. RAMS	1,003	3.86	6.81	5.39
28. ATLANTA	951	4.26	6.84	5.70

TURNOVER TABLE

	TURNOVERS			TAKEAWAYS			
	FUMB LOST	INT THROWN	TOTAL	FUMB RECOV	INT MADE	TOTAL	TURNOVER DIFF
SAN DIEGO	5	14	19	12	22	34	+15
BUFFALO	17	18	35	24	23	47	+12
PITTSBURGH	15	12	27	14	24	38	+11
NEW YORK GIANTS	8	9	17	10	18	28	+11
KANSAS CITY	18	10	28	17	21	38	+10
MINNESOTA	10	14	24	10	24	34	+10
NEW YORK JETS	16	12	28	18	19	37	+9
CINCINNATI	9	11	20	14	12	26	+6
SEATTLE	13	18	31	15	22	37	+6
DALLAS	16	6	22	14	14	28	+6
DENVER	18	10	28	13	18	31	+3
DETROIT	13	19	32	16	19	35	+3
PHILADELPHIA	21	13	34	15	20	35	+1
CHICAGO	14	16	30	12	18	30	+0
SAN FRANCISCO	13	17	30	11	19	30	+0
WASHINGTON	10	21	31	14	17	31	+0
GREEN BAY	10	24	34	15	18	33	-1
HOUSTON	20	25	45	17	26	43	-2
L.A. RAIDERS	11	14	25	9	14	23	-2
NEW ORLEANS	13	21	34	20	10	30	-4
MIAMI	14	18	32	14	13	27	-5
PHOENIX	11	20	31	17	9	26	-5
L.A. RAMS	11	19	30	9	11	20	-10
NEW ENGLAND	10	24	34	9	13	22	-12
CLEVELAND	17	19	36	9	13	22	-14
INDIANAPOLIS	20	15	35	11	10	21	-14
TAMPA BAY	11	25	36	13	9	22	-14
ATLANTA	17	25	42	11	13	24	-18

REVIEW AWARDS

Offensive Player of the Year
EMMITT SMITH
Running back/Dallas Cowboys

Defensive Player of the Year
BRUCE SMITH
Defensive end/Buffalo Bills

Coach of the Year
DAN REEVES
New York Giants

Golden Toe Award
NORM JOHNSON
Placekicker/Atlanta Falcons

Comeback Player of the Year
MARCUS ALLEN
Running back/Kansas City Chiefs

Offensive Rookie of the Year
JEROME BETTIS
Running back/Los Angeles Rams

Defensive Rookie of the Year
DANA STUBBLEFIELD
Defensive tackle/San Francisco 49ers

Executive of the Year
GEORGE YOUNG
General manager/New York Giants

Assistant Coach of the Year
RAY RHODES
Defensive coordinator/Green Bay Packers

1993 ALL-NFL

OFFENSE
WIDE RECEIVERS
JERRY RICE/San Francisco
STERLING SHARPE/Green Bay
OFFENSIVE TACKLES
ERIK WILLIAMS/Dallas
HARRIS BARTON/San Francisco
OFFENSIVE GUARDS
RANDALL McDANIEL/Minnesota
STEVE WISNIEWSKI/L.A. Raiders
CENTER
BRUCE MATTHEWS/Houston
TIGHT END
SHANNON SHARPE/Green Bay
QUARTERBACK
STEVE YOUNG/San Francisco
RUNNING BACKS
EMMITT SMITH/Dallas
JEROME BETTIS/L.A. Rams

DEFENSE
DEFENSIVE ENDS
BRUCE SMITH/Buffalo
NEIL SMITH/Kansas City
DEFENSIVE TACKLES
CORTEZ KENNEDY/Seattle
JOHN RANDLE/Minnesota
OUTSIDE LINEBACKERS
GREG LLOYD/Pittsburgh
SETH JOYNER/Philadelphia
INSIDE LINEBACKERS
JUNIOR SEAU/San Diego
HARDY NICKERSON/Tampa Bay
CORNERBACKS
ROD WOODSON/Pittsburgh
DEION SANDERS/Atlanta
SAFETIES
LeROY BUTLER/Green Bay
EUGENE ROBINSON/Seattle

SPECIALISTS
PLACEKICKER
NORM JOHNSON/Atlanta
PUNTER
GREG MONTGOMERY/Houston
KICKOFF RETURNER
TYRONE HUGHES/New Orleans
PUNT RETURNER
ERIC METCALF/Cleveland
SPECIAL TEAMS
STEVE TASKER/Buffalo

1993 ALL-ROOKIE

OFFENSE
WIDE RECEIVERS
JAMES JETT/L.A. Raiders
VINCENT BRISBY/New England
OFFENSIVE TACKLES
WILLIE ROAF/New Orleans
BRAD HOPKINS/Houston
OFFENSIVE GUARDS
LINCOLN KENNEDY/Atlanta
WILL SHIELDS/Kansas City
CENTER
STEVE EVERITT/Cleveland
TIGHT END
TONY McGEE/Cincinnati
QUARTERBACK
RICK MIRER/Seattle
RUNNING BACKS
JEROME BETTIS/L.A. Rams*
REGGIE BROOKS/Washington

DEFENSE
DEFENSIVE ENDS
JOHN COPELAND/Cincinnati
ERIC CURRY/Tampa Bay
DEFENSIVE TACKLES
DANA STUBBLEFIELD/San Francisco
LEONARD RENFRO/Philadelphia
OUTSIDE LINEBACKERS
DARRIN SMITH/Dallas
WAYNE SIMMONS/Green Bay
INSIDE LINEBACKERS
CHAD BROWN/Pittsburgh
STEVE TOVAR/Cincinnati
CORNERBACKS
TOM CARTER/Washington
DARRIEN GORDON/San Diego
SAFETIES
GEORGE TEAGUE/Green Bay
ROGER HARPER/Atlanta

SPECIALISTS
PLACEKICKER
JASON ELAM/Denver
PUNTER
JOHN JETT/Dallas
KICKOFF RETURNER
TYRONE HUGHES/New Orleans*
PUNT RETURNER
TYRONE HUGHES/New Orleans
SPECIAL TEAMS
JESSIE ARMSTEAD/N.Y. Giants

*All-NFL selection

1993 REVIEW ■ AWARDS

1993 ALL-AFC

OFFENSE
WIDE RECEIVERS
TIM BROWN/L.A. Raiders
ANTHONY MILLER/San Diego
OFFENSIVE TACKLES
JOHN JACKSON/Pittsburgh
GARY ZIMMERMAN/Denver
OFFENSIVE GUARDS
STEVE WISNIEWSKI/L.A. Raiders*
MIKE MUNCHAK/Houston
CENTER
BRUCE MATTHEWS/Houston*
TIGHT END
SHANNON SHARPE/Denver*
QUARTERBACK
JOHN ELWAY/Denver
RUNNING BACKS
THURMAN THOMAS/Buffalo
MARCUS ALLEN/Kansas City

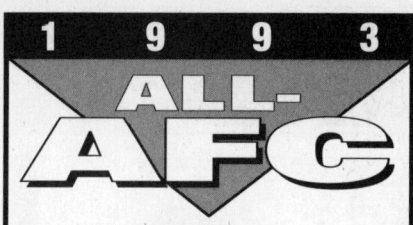

DEFENSE
DEFENSIVE ENDS
BRUCE SMITH/Buffalo*
NEIL SMITH/Kansas City*
DEFENSIVE TACKLES
CORTEZ KENNEDY/Seattle*
RAY CHILDRESS/Houston
OUTSIDE LINEBACKERS
GREG LLOYD/Pittsburgh*
DARRYL TALLEY/Buffalo
INSIDE LINEBACKERS
JUNIOR SEAU/San Diego*
VINCENT BROWN/New England
CORNERBACKS
ROD WOODSON/Pittsburgh*
TERRY McDANIEL/L.A. Raiders
SAFETIES
EUGENE ROBINSON/Seattle*
MARCUS ROBERTSON/Houston

SPECIALISTS
PLACEKICKER
GARY ANDERSON/Pittsburgh
PUNTER
GREG MONTGOMERY/Houston*
KICKOFF RETURNER
O.J. McDUFFIE/Miami
PUNT RETURNER
ERIC METCALF/Cleveland*
SPECIAL TEAMS
STEVE TASKER/Buffalo*

*All-NFL selection

1993 ALL-NFC

OFFENSE
WIDE RECEIVERS
JERRY RICE/San Francisco*
STERLING SHARPE/Green Bay*
OFFENSIVE TACKLES
ERIK WILLIAMS/Dallas*
HARRIS BARTON/San Francisco*
OFFENSIVE GUARDS
RANDALL McDANIEL/Minnesota*
NATE NEWTON/Dallas
CENTER
MARK STEPNOSKI/Dallas
TIGHT END
BRENT JONES/San Francisco
QUARTERBACK
STEVE YOUNG/San Francisco*
RUNNING BACKS
EMMITT SMITH/Dallas*
JEROME BETTIS/L.A. Rams*

DEFENSE
DEFENSIVE ENDS
REGGIE WHITE/Green Bay
RICHARD DENT/Chicago
DEFENSIVE TACKLES
JOHN RANDLE/Minnesota*
SEAN GILBERT/L.A. Rams
OUTSIDE LINEBACKERS
SETH JOYNER/Philadelphia
RICKEY JACKSON/New Orleans
INSIDE LINEBACKERS
HARDY NICKERSON/Tampa Bay*
MICHAEL BROOKS/N.Y. Giants
CORNERBACKS
DEION SANDERS/Atlanta*
ERIC ALLEN/Philadelphia
SAFETIES
LeROY BUTLER/Green Bay*
TIM McDONALD/San Francisco

SPECIALISTS
PLACEKICKER
NORM JOHNSON/Atlanta*
PUNTER
RICH CAMARILLO/Phoenix
KICKOFF RETURNER
TYRONE HUGHES/New Orleans*
PUNT RETURNER
TYRONE HUGHES/New Orleans
SPECIAL TEAMS
ELBERT SHELLEY/Atlanta

*All-NFL selection

PRO FOOTBALL WEEKLY 1994 ALMANAC

REVIEW: GOLDEN TOE AWARD

Atlanta PK Norm Johnson (right) received the Golden Toe Trophy from PFW publisher Hub Arkush

JOHNSON TOP NFL KICKER

In a season in which kicking excellence provided one of the major story lines, Atlanta PK Norm Johnson turned in a storybook season, one of the most flawless, in fact, in NFL history.

The 12-year veteran, originally signed by Seattle as a free agent out of UCLA in the strike-shortened season of 1982, was just one field goal short of perfection in '93, posting the second-most-accurate field-goal season ever by connecting on 26-of-27 three-pointers for a 96.2 percentage.

Johnson's 26 field goals tied a club single-season record, and his string of 21 straight field goals — which wasn't stopped until he missed a 37-yard attempt in the Week 15 game vs. San Francisco — was the longest ever to start a season. In addition, he was perfect on 34 extra points.

By virtue of sustaining one of the all-time great kicking grooves, Johnson beat out a talented collection of kickers in winning *Pro Football Weekly*'s Golden Toe Trophy, the NFL's most prestigious kicking honor.

Johnson was presented with the trophy in early March at the NFL Players Association banquet in Washington D.C. by PFW publisher/editor Hub Arkush. In addition, Johnson's name has been inscribed on a copy of the Golden Toe Trophy that is on display in the Pro Football Hall of Fame in Canton, Ohio.

Johnson, who was also selected to the Pro Bowl for a second time, became the second two-time winner in the Golden Toe Award's 23-year history. Washington PK Mark Moseley won it in 1977 and 1982.

Even on the day of his lone 1993 failure vs. the 49ers, Johnson bounced back in resounding fashion, making a 47-yard field goal with 2:12 remaining to tie the NFC West champs and hitting a 37-yarder with just 28 seconds remaining for a dramatic 27-24 upset triumph.

Heading into the Week 15 game vs. the 49ers, Johnson had kicked 26 straight field goals, including five in a row at the end of last season, and he was just three kicks shy of the NFL record of 29 consecutive field goals set earlier in the year by San Diego PK John Carney.

Johnson finished the season by making his final five field goals, including a 41-yarder the 16th week at Washington and a 49-yarder the 17th week at Cincinnati which made him 9-of-9 from 40 yards or longer.

SECTION III

Records, Honors and History

PRO FOOTBALL WEEKLY 1994 ALMANAC

RECORDS INDIVIDUAL

COACHING
Most seasons
- 40 George Halas, Chicago (1920-29, 1933-42, 1946-55, 1958-67)
- 33 Curly Lambeau, Green Bay (1921-49), Chicago Cardinals (1950-51), Washington (1952-53).
- 31 Don Shula, Baltimore (1963-69), Miami (1970-93)

Most games won, regular season
- 318 George Halas, Chicago (1920-29, 1933-42, 1946-55, 1958-67)
- 309 Don Shula, Baltimore (1963-69), Miami (1970-93)
- 250 Tom Landry, Dallas (1960-88)

Most games lost, regular season
- 162 Tom Landry, Dallas (1960-88)
- 148 George Halas, Chicago (1920-29, 1933-42, 1946-55, 1958-67)
- 143 Don Shula, Baltimore (1963-69), Miami (1970-93)

SERVICE
Most seasons
- 26 George Blanda, Chicago (1949), Baltimore (1950), Chicago (1950-58), Houston (1960-66), Oakland (1967-75)
- 21 Earl Morrall, San Francisco (1956), Pittsburgh (1957-58), Detroit (1958-64), N.Y. Giants (1965-67), Baltimore (1968-71), Miami (1972-76)
- 20 Jim Marshall, Cleveland (1960), Minnesota (1961-79)

Most seasons, one club
- 19 Jim Marshall, Minnesota (1961-79)
- 18 Jim Hart, St. Louis (1966-83)
     Jeff Van Note, Atlanta (1969-86)
     Pat Leahy, N.Y. Jets (1974-91)

Most games
- 340 George Blanda, Chicago (1949), Baltimore (1950), Chicago (1950-58), Houston (1960-66), Oakland (1967-75)
- 282 Jim Marshall, Cleveland (1960), Minnesota (1961-79)
- 263 Jan Stenerud, Kansas City (1967-79), Green Bay (1980-83), Minnesota (1984-85)

Consecutive games
- 282 Jim Marshall, Cleveland (1960), Minnesota (1961-79)
- 240 Mick Tingelhoff, Minnesota (1962-78)
- 234 Jim Bakken, St. Louis (1962-78)

SCORING
Points, career
- 2,002 George Blanda, Chicago (1949), Baltimore (1950), Chicago (1950-58), Houston (1960-66), Oakland (1967-75)
- 1,699 Jan Stenerud, Kansas City (1967-79), Green Bay (1980-83), Minnesota (1984-85)
- 1,473 Nick Lowery, New England (1978), Kansas City (1979-93)

Points, season
- 176 Paul Hornung, Green Bay (1960)
- 161 Mark Moseley, Washington (1983)
- 155 Gino Cappelletti, Boston (1964)

Points, game
- 40 Ernie Nevers, Chicago Cardinals (11/28/29)
- 36 Dub Jones, Cleveland (11/25/51)
     Gale Sayers, Chicago (12/12/65)

Points, seasons leading league
- 5 Don Hutson, Green Bay (1940-44)
    Gino Cappelletti, Boston (1961, 1963-66)

Most seasons, 100 or more points
- 11 Nick Lowery, Kansas City (1981, 1983-86, 1989-93)
- 8 Morten Andersen, New Orleans (1985-89, 1991-93)
- 7 Jan Stenerud, Kansas City (1967-71), Green Bay (1981, 1983)
     Gary Anderson, Pittsburgh (1983-85, 1988, 1991-93)

Consecutive games scoring
- 186 Jim Breech, Oakland (1979), Cincinnati (1980-92)
- 151 Fred Cox, Minnesota (1963-73)
- 133 Garo Yepremian, Miami (1970-78), New Orleans (1979)

Touchdowns, seasons leading league
- 8 Don Hutson, Green Bay (1935-38, 1941-44)
- 3 Jim Brown, Cleveland (1958-59, 1963)
    Lance Alworth, San Diego (1964-66)

Touchdowns, career
- 126 Jim Brown, Cleveland (1957-65)
- 125 Walter Payton, Chicago (1975-88)
- 124 Jerry Rice, San Francisco (1985-93)

Touchdowns, season
- 24 John Riggins, Washington (1983)
- 23 O.J. Simpson, Buffalo (1975)
    Jerry Rice, San Francisco (1987)

Touchdowns, game
- 6 Ernie Nevers, Chicago Cardinals (11/28/29)
    Dub Jones, Cleveland (11/25/51)
    Gale Sayers, Chicago (12/12/65)

Consecutive games scoring touchdowns
- 18 Lenny Moore, Baltimore (1963-65)
- 14 O.J. Simpson, Buffalo (1975)
- 13 John Riggins, Washington (1982-83)
    George Rogers, Washington (1985-86)
    Jerry Rice, San Francisco (1986-87)

Extra points, seasons leading league
- 8 George Blanda, Chicago (1956), Houston (1961-62), Oakland (1967-69, 1972, 1974)
- 4 Bob Waterfield, Cleveland (1945), L.A. Rams (1946, 1950, 1952)

Extra points, career
- 943 George Blanda, Chicago (1949), Baltimore (1950), Chicago (1950-58), Houston (1960-66), Oakland (1967-75)
- 641 Lou Groza, Cleveland (1950-59, 1961-67)
- 580 Jan Stenerud, Kansas City (1967-79), Green Bay (1980-83), Minnesota (1984-85)

Extra points, season
- 66 Uwe von Schamann, Miami (1984)
- 64 George Blanda, Houston (1961)
- 62 Mark Moseley, Washington (1983)

Extra points, game
- 9 Pat Harder, Chicago Cardinals (10/17/48)
    Bob Waterfield, L.A. Rams (10/22/50)
    Charlie Gogolak, Washington (11/27/66)

Extra-point percentage, career
- 99.43 Tommy Davis, San Francisco (1959-69)
- 99.18 Nick Lowery, New England (1978), Kansas City (1979-93)
- 98.97 Gary Anderson, Pittsburgh (1982-93)

Consecutive extra points
- 234 Tommy Davis, San Francisco (1959-65)
- 221 Jim Turner, N.Y. Jets (1967-70), Denver (1971-74)
- 202 Gary Anderson, Pittsburgh (1983-88)

Field goals, seasons leading league
- 5 Lou Groza, Cleveland (1950, 1952-54, 1957)

404

RECORDS ■ INDIVIDUAL

4   Jack Manders, Chicago (1933-34, 1936-37)
    Ward Cuff, N.Y. Giants (1938-39, 1943), Green Bay (1947)
    Mark Moseley, Washington (1976-77, 1979, 1982)

Field goals, career
373 Jan Stenerud, Kansas City (1967-79), Green Bay (1980-83), Minnesota (1984-85)
335 George Blanda, Chicago (1949), Baltimore (1950), Chicago (1950-58), Houston (1960-66), Oakland (1967-75)
329 Nick Lowery, New England (1979), Kansas City (1980-93)

Field goals, season
35 Ali Haji-Sheikh, N.Y. Giants (1983)
    Jeff Jaeger, L.A. Raiders (1993)
34 Jim Turner, N.Y. Jets (1968)
    Nick Lowery, Kansas City (1990)
    Jason Hanson, Detroit (1993)

Field goals, game
7   Jim Bakken, St. Louis (9/24/67)
    Rich Karlis, Minnesota (11/5/89, OT)

Field-goal percentage, career
80.05 Nick Lowery, New England (1978), Kansas City (1979-93)
79.62 Pete Stoyanovich, Miami (1989-93)
78.48 David Treadwell, Denver (1989-92), N.Y. Giants (1993)

Field-goal percentage, season
100.0 Tony Zendejas, L.A. Rams, 1991 (17-17)
96.3 Norm Johnson, Atlanta, 1993 (26-27)

Consecutive field goals
29 John Carney, San Diego (1992-93)
26 Norm Johnson, Atlanta (1992-93)
25 Morten Andersen, New Orleans (1992-93)

Longest field goal
63 Tom Dempsey, New Orleans (11/8/70)
60 Steve Cox, Cleveland (10/21/84)
    Morten Andersen, New Orleans (10/27/91)

Field goals, 50 yards or more, career
22 Morten Andersen, New Orleans (1982-93)
20 Nick Lowery, New England (1978), Kansas City (1979-93)
    Eddie Murray, Detroit (1980-91), Kansas City (1992), Tampa Bay (1992), Dallas (1993)

Safeties, career
4   Ted Hendricks, Baltimore (1969-73), Green Bay (1974), Oakland/L.A. Raiders (1975-83)
    Doug English, Detroit (1975-79, 1981-85)
3   By many players

Safeties, season
2   By many players

RUSHING

Yards, career
16,726 Walter Payton, Chicago (1975-87)
13,259 Eric Dickerson, L.A. Rams (1983-87), Indianapolis (1987-91), L.A. Raiders (1992), Atlanta (1993)
12,739 Tony Dorsett, Dallas (1977-87), Denver (1988)

Yards, season
2,105 Eric Dickerson, L.A. Rams (1984)
2,003 O.J. Simpson, Buffalo (1973)
1,934 Earl Campbell, Houston (1980)

Yards, game
275 Walter Payton, Chicago (11/20/77)
273 O.J. Simpson, Buffalo (11/25/76)
250 O.J. Simpson, Buffalo (9/16/73)

Yards, seasons leading league
8   Jim Brown, Cleveland (1957-61, 1963-65)
4   Steve Van Buren, Philadelphia (1945, 1947-49)
    O.J. Simpson, Buffalo (1972-73, 1975-76)
    Eric Dickerson, L.A. Rams (1983-84, 1986), Indianapolis (1988)

Seasons, 1,000 or more yards rushing
10 Walter Payton, Chicago (1976-81, 1983-86)

8   Franco Harris, Pittsburgh (1972, 1974-79, 1983)
    Tony Dorsett, Dallas (1977-81, 1983-85)

Most games, 100 or more yards rushing, career
77 Walter Payton, Chicago (1975-87)
64 Eric Dickerson, L.A. Rams (1983-87), Indianapolis (1987-91), L.A. Raiders (1992), Atlanta (1993)
58 Jim Brown, Cleveland (1957-65)

Most games, 100 or more yards rushing, season
12 Eric Dickerson, L.A. Rams (1984)
    Barry Foster, Pittsburgh (1992)
11 By four players

Longest run from scrimmage
99 Tony Dorsett, Dallas (1983)
97 Andy Uram, Green Bay (1939)
    Bob Gage, Pittsburgh (1949)

Attempts, career
3,838 Walter Payton, Chicago (1975-87)
2,996 Eric Dickerson, L.A. Rams (1983-87), Indianapolis (1987-91), L.A. Raiders (1992), Atlanta (1993)
2,949 Franco Harris, Pittsburgh (1972-83), Seattle (1984)

Attempts, season
407 James Wilder, Tampa Bay (1984)
404 Eric Dickerson, L.A. Rams (1986)
397 Gerald Riggs, Washington (1985)

Attempts, game
45 Jamie Morris, Washington (12/17/88, OT)
43 Butch Woolfolk, N.Y. Giants (11/20/83)
    James Wilder, Tampa Bay (9/30/84)

Attempts, seasons leading league
6   Jim Brown, Cleveland (1958-59, 1961, 1963-65)
4   Steve Van Buren, Philadelphia (1947-50)
    Walter Payton, Chicago (1976-79)

Highest average gain, career
(minimum 700 attempts)
5.22 Jim Brown, Cleveland (1957-65)
5.14 Mercury Morris, Miami (1969-75), San Diego (1976)
5.00 Gale Sayers, Chicago (1965-71)

Highest average gain, season
8.44 Beattie Feathers, Chicago (1934)
7.98 Randall Cunningham, Philadelphia (1990)
6.87 Bobby Douglass, Chicago (1972)

Highest average gain, game
(minimum 10 attempts)
17.09 Marion Motley, Cleveland (11/29/50)
16.70 Bill Grimes, Green Bay (1950)
16.57 Bobby Mitchell, Cleveland (1959)

Rushing touchdowns, career
110 Walter Payton, Chicago (1975-87)
106 Jim Brown, Cleveland (1957-65)
104 John Riggins, N.Y. Jets (1971-75), Washington (1976-79, 1981-85)

Rushing touchdowns, season
24 John Riggins, Washington (1983)
21 Joe Morris, N.Y. Giants (1985)
19 Jim Taylor, Green Bay (1962)
    Earl Campbell, Houston (1979)
    Chuck Muncie, San Diego (1981)

Rushing touchdowns, game
6   Ernie Nevers, Chicago Cardinals (11/28/29)
5   Jim Brown, Cleveland (11/1/59)
    Cookie Gilchrist, Buffalo (12/8/63)

Rushing touchdowns, most seasons leading league
5   Jim Brown, Cleveland (1957-59, 1963, 1965)
4   Steve Van Buren, Philadelphia (1945, 1947-49)

Consecutive games, rushing for a touchdown
13 John Riggins, Washington (1982-83)
    George Rogers, Washington (1985-86)
11 Lenny Moore, Baltimore (1963-64)
10 Greg Bell, L.A. Rams (1988-89)

PASSING

Most seasons leading league
6   Sammy Baugh, Washington (1937, 1940, 1943, 1945, 1947, 1949)

405

PRO FOOTBALL WEEKLY 1994 ALMANAC

    4   Len Dawson, Dallas Texans (1962), Kansas City (1964, 1966, 1968)
Roger Staubach, Dallas (1971, 1973, 1978-79)
Ken Anderson, Cincinnati (1974-75, 1981-82)

Pass rating, career
(minimum 1,500 attempts)
93.1 Steve Young, Tampa Bay (1985-86), San Francisco (1987-93)
92.7 Joe Montana, San Francisco (1979-90, 1992), Kansas City (1994)
88.1 Dan Marino, Miami (1983-93)

Pass rating, season
112.4 Joe Montana, San Francisco (1989)
110.4 Milt Plum, Cleveland (1960)
109.9 Sammy Baugh, Washington (1945)

Attempts, career
6,467 Fran Tarkenton, Minnesota (1961-66, 1972-78), N.Y. Giants (1967-71)
5,604 Dan Fouts, San Diego (1973-87)
5,434 Dan Marino, Miami (1983-93)

Attempts, season
655 Warren Moon, Houston (1991)
623 Dan Marino, Miami (1986)
609 Dan Fouts, San Diego (1981)

Attempts, game
68 George Blanda, Houston (11/11/64)
66 Chris Miller, Atlanta (12/24/89)
63 Rich Gannon, Minnesota (10/20/91, OT)

Attempts, most seasons leading league
4 Sammy Baugh, Washington (1937, 1943, 1947-48)
Johnny Unitas, Baltimore (1957, 1959-61)
George Blanda, Chicago (1953), Houston (1963-65)
Dan Marino, Miami (1984, 1986, 1988, 1992)

Completions, career
3,686 Fran Tarkenton, Minnesota (1961-66, 1972-78), N.Y. Giants (1967-71)
3,297 Dan Fouts, San Diego (1973-87)
3,219 Dan Marino, Miami (1983-93)

Completions, season
404 Warren Moon, Houston (1991)
378 Dan Marino, Miami (1986)
362 Dan Marino, Miami (1984)
      Warren Moon, Houston (1990)

Completions, game
42 Richard Todd, N.Y. Jets (9/21/80)
41 Warren Moon, Houston (11/10/91, OT)
40 Ken Anderson, Cincinnati (12/20/82)
     Phil Simms, N.Y. Giants (10/13/85)

Completions, seasons leading league
5 Sammy Baugh, Washington (1937, 1943, 1945, 1947-48)
   Dan Marino, Miami (1984-86, 1988, 1992)
4 George Blanda, Chicago (1953), Houston (1963-65)
   Sonny Jurgensen, Philadelphia (1961), Washington (1966-67, 1969)

Completion percentage, career
(minimum 1,500 attempts)
63.50 Joe Montana, San Francisco (1979-90, 1992), Kansas City (1994)
62.09 Steve Young, Tampa Bay (1985-86), San Francisco (1987-93)
62.03 Troy Aikman, Dallas (1989-93)

Completion percentage, season
70.55 Ken Anderson, Cincinnati (1982)
70.33 Sammy Baugh, Washington (1945)
70.21 Joe Montana, San Francisco (1989)

Completion percentage, game
91.30 Vinny Testaverde, Cleveland (12/26/93)
90.91 Ken Anderson, Cincinnati (11/10/74)
90.48 Lynn Dickey, Green Bay (12/13/81)

Completion percentage, seasons leading league
8 Len Dawson, Dallas Texans (1962), Kansas City (1964-69, 1975)

    7   Sammy Baugh, Washington (1940, 1942-43, 1945, 1947-49)
    5   Joe Montana, San Francisco (1980-81, 1985, 1987, 1989)

Yards gained, career
47,003 Fran Tarkenton, Minnesota (1961-66, 1972-78), N.Y. Giants (1967-71)
43,040 Dan Fouts, San Diego (1973-87)
40,720 Dan Marino, Miami (1983-93)

Yards gained, season
5,084 Dan Marino, Miami (1984)
4,802 Dan Fouts, San Diego (1981)
4,746 Dan Marino, Miami (1986)

Yards gained, game
554 Norm Van Brocklin, L.A. Rams (9/28/51)
527 Warren Moon, Houston (12/16/90)
521 Dan Marino, Miami (10/23/88)

Yards gained, most seasons leading league
5 Sonny Jurgensen, Philadelphia (1961-62), Washington (1966-67, 1969)
   Dan Marino, Miami (1984-86, 1988, 1992)
4 Sammy Baugh, Washington (1937, 1940, 1947-48)
   Johnny Unitas, Baltimore (1957, 1959-60, 1963)
   Dan Fouts, San Diego (1979-82)

Games, 300 or more yards passing, career
51 Dan Fouts, San Diego (1973-87)
44 Dan Marino, Miami (1983-93)
38 Warren Moon, Houston (1984-93)

Games, 300 or more yards passing, season
9 Dan Marino, Miami (1984)
   Warren Moon, Houston (1990)
8 Dan Fouts, San Diego (1980)

Longest completion
99 Shared by six players

Average gain, career
8.63 Otto Graham, Cleveland (1950-55)
8.42 Sid Luckman, Chicago (1939-50)
8.16 Norm Van Brocklin, L.A. Rams (1949-57), Philadelphia (1958-60)

Average gain, season
11.17 Tommy O'Connell, Cleveland (1957)
10.86 Sid Luckman, Chicago (1943)
10.55 Otto Graham, Cleveland (1953)

Average gain, game
18.58 Sammy Baugh, Washington (10/31/48)
18.50 Johnny Unitas, Baltimore (11/12/67)
17.71 Joe Namath, N.Y. Jets (9/24/72)

Average gain, most seasons leading league
7 Sid Luckman, Chicago (1939-43, 1946-47)
3 By four players

Touchdown passes, career
342 Fran Tarkenton, Minnesota (1961-66, 1972-78), N.Y. Giants (1967-71)
298 Dan Marino, Miami (1983-93)
290 Johnny Unitas, Baltimore (1956-72), San Diego (1973)

Touchdown passes, season
48 Dan Marino, Miami (1984)
44 Dan Marino, Miami (1986)
36 George Blanda, Houston (1961)
   Y.A. Tittle, N.Y. Giants (1963)

Touchdown passes, game
7 Sid Luckman, Chicago (11/14/43)
   Adrian Burk, Philadelphia (10/17/54)
   George Blanda, Houston (11/19/61)
   Y.A. Tittle, N.Y. Giants (10/28/62)
   Joe Kapp, Minnesota (9/28/69)

Touchdown passes, most seasons leading league
4 Johnny Unitas, Baltimore (1957-60)
   Len Dawson, Dallas Texans (1962), Kansas City (1963, 1965-66)
3 By four players

Touchdown passes, consecutive games
47 Johnny Unitas, Baltimore (1956-60)
30 Dan Marino, Miami (1985-87)

RECORDS ■ INDIVIDUAL

28 Dave Krieg, Seattle (1983-85)
Most interceptions, career
277 George Blanda, Chicago (1949), Baltimore (1950), Chicago (1950-58), Houston (1960-66), Oakland (1967-75)
268 John Hadl, San Diego (1962-72), L.A. Rams (1973-74), Green Bay (1974-75), Houston (1976-77)
266 Fran Tarkenton, Minnesota (1961-66, 1972-78), N.Y. Giants (1967-71)
Most interceptions, season
42 George Blanda, Houston (1962)
35 Vinny Testaverde, Tampa Bay (1988)
34 Frank Tripucka, Denver (1960)
Most interceptions, game
8   Jim Hardy, Chicago Cardinals (9/24/50)
7   By seven players
Most consecutive passes, none intercepted
308 Bernie Kosar, Cleveland (1990-91)
294 Bart Starr, Green Bay (1964-65)
233 Steve DeBerg, Kansas City (1990)
Lowest percentage passes intercepted, career
2.52 Bernie Kosar, Cleveland (1985-93), Dallas (1993)
2.65 Joe Montana, San Francisco (1979-90, 1992), Kansas City (1994)
2.72 Ken O'Brien, N.Y. Jets (1984-92), Philadelphia (1993)
Most times sacked, career
483 Fran Tarkenton, Minnesota (1961-66, 1972-78), N.Y. Giants (1967-71)
477 Phil Simms, N.Y. Giants (1979-81, 1983-93)
405 Craig Morton, Dallas (1965-74), N.Y. Giants (1974-76), Denver (1977-82)
Most times sacked, season
72 Randall Cunningham, Philadelphia (1986)
62 Ken O'Brien, N.Y. Jets (1985)
61 Neil Lomax, St. Louis (1985)
Most times sacked, game
12 Bert Jones, Baltimore (10/26/80)
    Warren Moon, Houston (9/29/85)
11 Shared by 13 players

RECEIVING

Receptions, seasons leading league
8   Don Hutson, Green Bay (1936-37, 1939, 1941-45)
5   Lionel Taylor, Denver (1960-63, 1965)
Receptions, career
888 Art Monk, Washington (1980-93)
819 Steve Largent, Seattle (1976-89)
764 James Lofton, Green Bay (1978-86), L.A. Raiders (1986-87), Buffalo (1989-92), L.A. Rams (1993), Philadelphia (1993)
Receptions, season
112 Sterling Sharpe, Green Bay (1993)
108 Sterling Sharpe, Green Bay (1992)
106 Art Monk, Washington (1984)
Receptions, game
18 Tom Fears, L.A. Rams (12/3/50)
17 Clark Gaines, N.Y. Jets (9/21/80)
16 Sonny Randle, St. Louis (11/4/62)
Receptions, most consecutive games
177 Steve Largent, Seattle (1977-89)
164 Art Monk, Washington (1983-93)
150 Ozzie Newsome, Cleveland (1979-89)
Yards gained, seasons leading league
7   Don Hutson, Green Bay (1936, 1938-39, 1941-44)
4   Jerry Rice, San Francisco (1986, 1989-90, 1993)
3   Raymond Berry, Baltimore (1957, 1959-60)
    Lance Alworth, San Diego (1965-66, 1968)
Yards gained, career
14,004 James Lofton, Green Bay (1978-86), L.A. Raiders, (1987-88), Buffalo (1989-92), L.A.

Rams (1993), Philadelphia (1993)
13,089 Steve Largent, Seattle (1976-89)
12,146 Charlie Joiner, Houston (1969-72), Cincinnati (1972-75), San Diego (1976-86)
Yards gained, season
1,746 Charley Hennigan, Houston (1961)
1,602 Lance Alworth, San Diego (1965)
1,570 Jerry Rice, San Francisco (1986)
Yards gained, game
336 Willie Anderson, L.A. Rams (11/26/89, OT)
309 Stephone Paige, Kansas City (12/22/85)
303 Jim Benton, Cleveland (11/22/45)
Most seasons, 1,000 or more yards receiving
8   Jerry Rice, San Francisco (1986-93)
    Steve Largent, Seattle (1978-81, 1983-86)
7   Lance Alworth, San Diego (1963-69)
Most games, 100 or more yards receiving
50 Don Maynard, N.Y. Giants (1958), N.Y. Jets (1960-72), St. Louis 1973)
44 Jerry Rice, San Francisco (1985-93)
43 James Lofton, Green Bay (1978-86), L.A. Raiders (1986-87), Buffalo (1989-92), L.A. Rams (1993), Philadelphia (1993)
Longest pass reception
99 Shared by six players
Average gain, career
22.26 Homer Jones, N.Y. Giants (1964-69), Cleveland (1970)
20.83 Buddy Dial, Pittsburgh (1959-63), Dallas (1964-66)
20.24 Harlon Hill, Chicago (1954-61), Pittsburgh (1962), Detroit (1962)
Average gain, season
32.58 Don Currivan, Boston (1947)
31.44 Bucky Pope, L.A. Rams (1964)
28.60 Bobby Duckworth, San Diego (1984)
Average gain, game
60.67 Bill Groman, Houston (11/20/60)
    Homer Jones, N.Y. Giants (12/12/65)
60.33 Don Currivan, Boston (11/30/47)
Touchdown receptions, seasons leading league
9   Don Hutson, Green Bay (1935-38, 1940-44)
6   Jerry Rice, San Francisco (1986-87, 1989-91, 1993)
3   Lance Alworth, San Diego (1964-66)
Touchdown receptions, career
118 Jerry Rice, San Francisco (1985-93)
100 Steve Largent, Seattle (1976-89)
99 Don Hutson, Green Bay (1935-45)
Touchdown receptions, season
22 Jerry Rice, San Francisco (1987)
18 Mark Clayton, Miami (1984)
17 Don Hutson, Green Bay (1942)
    Elroy "Crazylegs" Hirsch, L.A. Rams (1951)
    Bill Groman, Houston (1961)
    Jerry Rice, San Francisco (1989)
Touchdown receptions, game
5   Bob Shaw, Chicago Cardinals (10/2/50)
    Kellen Winslow, San Diego (11/22/81)
    Jerry Rice, San Francisco (10/14/80)
4   By many players
Consecutive games, touchdown receptions
13 Jerry Rice, San Francisco (1986-87)
11 Elroy "Crazylegs" Hirsch, L.A. Rams (1950-51)
    Buddy Dial, Pittsburgh (1959-60)

INTERCEPTIONS

Most interceptions by, seasons leading league
3   Everson Walls, Dallas (1981-82, 1985)
2   Shared by eight players
Interceptions, career
81 Paul Krause, Washington (1964-67), Minnesota (1968-79)
79 Emlen Tunnell, N.Y. Giants (1948-58), Green Bay (1959-61)
68 Dick "Night Train" Lane, L.A. Rams (1952-53),

407

PRO FOOTBALL WEEKLY 1994 ALMANAC

Chicago Cardinals (1954-59), Detroit (1960-65)

Most interceptions by, season
- 14 Dick "Night Train" Lane, L.A. Rams (1952)
- 13 Don Sandifer, Washington (1948)
  Orban "Spec" Sanders, N.Y. Yanks (1950)
  Lester Hayes, Oakland (1980)

Most interceptions by, game
- 4 By 17 players

Consecutive games, passes intercepted
- 8 Tom Morrow, Oakland (1962-63)
- 7 Paul Krause, Washington (1964)
  Larry Wilson, St. Louis (1966)
  Ben Davis, Cleveland (1968)

Interception yards gained, career
- 1,282 Emlen Tunnell, N.Y. Giants (1948-58), Green Bay (1959-61)
- 1,207 Dick "Night Train" Lane, L.A. Rams (1952-53), Chicago Cardinals (1954-59), Detroit (1960-65)
- 1,185 Paul Krause, Washington (1964-67), Minnesota (1968-79)

Interception yards gained, season
- 349 Charlie McNeil, San Diego (1961)
- 301 Don Doll, Detroit (1949)
- 298 Dick "Night Train" Lane, L.A. Rams (1952)

Interception yards gained, game
- 177 Charlie McNeil, San Diego (9/24/61)
- 170 Louis Oliver, Miami (10/4/92)
- 167 Dick Jauron, Detroit (10/18/73)

Longest interception return
- 103 Vencie Glenn, San Diego (11/29/87), TD
  Louis Oliver, Miami (10/4/92), TD
- 102 By six players

Interception touchdowns, career
- 9 Ken Houston, Houston (1967-72), Washington (1973-80)
- 7 Herb Adderley, Green Bay (1961-69), Dallas (1970-72)
  Erich Barnes, Chicago (1958-60), N.Y. Giants (1961-64), Cleveland (1965-70)
  Lem Barney, Detroit (1967-77)

Interception touchdowns, season
- 4 Ken Houston, Houston (1971)
  Jim Kearney, Kansas City (1972)
  Eric Allen, Philadelphia (1994)

Interception touchdowns, game
- 2 By 18 players

PUNTING

Punting average, seasons leading league
- 4 Sammy Baugh, Washington (1940-43)
  Jerrel Wilson, Kansas City (1965, 1968, 1972-73)

Most punts, career
- 1,154 Dave Jennings, N.Y. Giants (1974-84), N.Y. Jets (1985-87)
- 1,083 John James, Atlanta (1972-81), Detroit (1982), Houston (1982-84)
- 1,072 Jerrel Wilson, Kansas City (1963-77), New England (1978)

Most punts, season
- 114 Bob Parsons, Chicago (1981)
- 109 John James, Atlanta (1978)
- 108 John Teltschik, Philadelphia (1986)
  Rick Tuten, Seattle (1992)

Most punts, game
- 15 John Teltschik, Philadelphia (12/6/87, OT)
- 14 By five players

Longest punt
- 98 Steve O'Neal, N.Y. Jets (9/21/69)
- 94 Joe Lintzenich, Chicago (11/16/31)
- 93 Shawn McCarthy, New England (11/3/91)

Punting average, career
(minimum 300 punts)
- 45.10 Sammy Baugh, Washington (1937-52)
- 44.68 Tommy Davis, San Francisco (1959-69)
- 44.29 Yale Lary, Detroit (1952-53, 1959-69)

Punting average, season
- 51.40 Sammy Baugh, Washington (1940)
- 48.94 Yale Lary, Detroit (1963)
- 48.73 Sammy Baugh, Washington (1941)

Punting average, game
(minimum 4 punts)
- 61.75 Bob Cifers, Detroit (11/24/46)
- 61.60 Roy McKay, Green Bay (10/28/45)
- 59.40 Sammy Baugh, Washington (10/27/40)

Consecutive punts, none blocked
- 623 Dave Jennings, N.Y. Giants (1976-83)
- 619 Ray Guy, Oakland/L.A. Raiders (1979-86)
- 578 Bobby Walden, Minnesota (1964-67), Pittsburgh (1968-72)

Most punts blocked, career
- 14 Herman Weaver, Detroit (1970-76), Seattle (1977-80)
  Harry Newsome, Pittsburgh (1985-89), Minnesota (1990-93)

Most punts blocked, season
- 6 Harry Newsome, Pittsburgh (1988)
- 4 Bryan Wagner, Cleveland (1990)

PUNT RETURNS

Punt-return average, seasons leading league
- 3 Speedy Duncan, San Diego (1965-66), Washington (1971)
  Rick Upchurch, Denver (1976, 1978, 1982)

Most punt returns, career
- 292 Vai Sikahema, St. Louis (1986-87), Phoenix (1988-90), Green Bay (1991), Philadelphia (1992-93)
- 282 Billy Johnson, Houston (1974-80), Atlanta (1982-87), Washington (1988)
- 267 J.T. Smith, Washington (1978), Kansas City (1978-84), St. Louis (1985-87), Phoenix (1988-90)

Most punt returns, season
- 70 Danny Reece, Tampa Bay (1979)
- 62 Fulton Walker, Miami (1985), L.A. Raiders (1985)
- 58 By three players

Most punt returns, game
- 11 Eddie Brown, Washington (10/9/77)
- 10 Theo Bell, Pittsburgh (12/16/79)
  Mike Nelms, Washington (12/26/82)

Yards gained, seasons leading league
- 3 Alvin Haymond, Baltimore (1965-66), L.A. Rams (69)
- 2 By eight players

Punt-return yards, career
- 3,317 Billy Johnson, Houston (1974-80), Atlanta (1982-87), Washington (1988)
- 3,169 Vai Sikahema, St. Louis (1986-87), Phoenix (1988-90), Green Bay (1991), Philadelphia (1992-93)
- 3,008 Rick Upchurch, Denver (1975-83)

Punt-return yards, season
- 692 Fulton Walker, Miami (1985), L.A. Raiders (1985)
- 666 Greg Pruitt, L.A. Raiders (1983)
- 656 Louis Lipps, Pittsburgh (1984)

Punt-return yards, game
- 207 LeRoy Irvin, L.A. Rams (10/11/81)
- 205 George Atkinson, Oakland (9/15/68)
- 184 Tom Watkins, Detroit (10/6/63)

Longest punt return
- 98 Gil LeFebvre, Cincinnati (12/3/33), TD
  Charlie West, Minnesota (11/3/68), TD
  Dennis Morgan, Dallas (10/13/74), TD
  Terance Mathis, N.Y. Jets (11/4/90), TD

Punt-return average, career
- 12.78 George McAfee, Chicago (1940-41, 1945-50)
- 12.75 Jack Christiansen, Detroit (1951-58)

RECORDS ■ INDIVIDUAL

12.55 Claude Gibson, San Diego (1961-62), Oakland (1963-65)
Punt-return average, season
23.00 Herb Rich, Baltimore (1950)
21.47 Jack Christiansen, Detroit (1952)
21.28 Dick Christy, N.Y. Titans (1961)
Punt-return average, game
47.67 Chuck Latourette, St. Louis (9/29/68)
47.33 Johnny Roland, St. Louis (10/2/66)
45.67 Dick Christy, N.Y. Titans (9/24/61)
Punt-return touchdowns, career
8 Jack Christiansen, Detroit (1951-58)
  Rick Upchurch, Denver (1975-83)
6 Billy Johnson, Houston (1974-80), Atlanta (1982-87), Washington (1988)
5 Emlen Tunnell, N.Y. Giants (1948-58), Green Bay (1959-61)
Punt-return touchdowns, season
4 Jack Christiansen, Detroit (1951)
  Rick Upchurch, Denver (1976)
3 Emlen Tunnell, N.Y. Giants (1951)
  Billy Johnson, Houston (1975)
  LeRoy Irvin, L.A. Rams (1981)
Punt-return touchdowns, game
2 By seven players

KICKOFF RETURNS
Kickoff-return average, seasons leading league
3 Abe Woodson, San Francisco (1959, 1962-63)
2 Lynn Chandnois, Pittsburgh (1951-52)
  Bobby Jancik, Houston (1962-63)
  Travis Williams, Green Bay (1967), L.A. Rams (1971)
Most kickoff returns, career
275 Ron Smith, Chicago (1965, 1970-72), Atlanta (1966-67), L.A. Rams (1968-69), San Diego (1973), L.A. Raiders (1974)
264 Mel Gray, New Orleans (1986-88), Detroit (1989-93)
243 Bruce Harper, N.Y. Jets (1977-84)
Most kickoff returns, season
60 Drew Hill, L.A. Rams (1981)
55 Bruce Harper, N.Y. Jets (1978, 1979)
  David Turner, Cincinnati (1979)
  Stump Mitchell, St. Louis (1981)
Most kickoff returns, game
9 Noland Smith, Kansas City (11/23/67)
  Dino Hall, Cleveland (10/7/79)
  Paul Palmer, Kansas City (9/20/87)
Kickoff-return yards, career
6,922 Ron Smith, Chicago (1965, 1970-72), Atlanta (1966-67), L.A. Rams (1968-69), San Diego (1973), L.A. Raiders (1974)
6,374 Mel Gray, New Orleans (1986-88), Detroit (1989-93)
5,538 Abe Woodson, San Francisco (1958-64), St. Louis (1965-66)
Kickoff-return yards, season
1,345 Buster Rhymes, Minnesota (1985)
1,317 Bobby Jancik, Houston (1963)
1,314 Dave Hampton, Green Bay (1971)
Kickoff-return yards, game
294 Wally Triplett, Detroit (10/29/50)
247 Timmy Brown, Philadelphia (11/6/66)
244 Noland Smith, Kansas City (10/15/67)
Longest kickoff return
106 Al Carmichael, Green Bay (10/7/56)
  Noland Smith, Kansas City (12/17/67)
  Roy Green, St. Louis (10/21/79)
Kickoff-return average, career
30.56 Gale Sayers, Chicago (1965-71)
29.57 Lynn Chandnois, Pittsburgh (1950-56)
28.69 Abe Woodson, San Francisco (1958-64) St. Louis (1965-66)
Kickoff-return average, season
41.06 Travis Williams, Green Bay (1967)
37.69 Gale Sayers, Chicago (1967)
35.50 Ollie Matson, Chicago Cardinals (1959)
Kickoff-return average, game
73.50 Wally Triplett, Detroit (10/29/50)
67.33 Lenny Lyles, San Francisco (12/18/60)
65.33 Ken Hall, Houston (10/23/60)
Kickoff-return touchdowns, career
6 Ollie Matson, Chicago Cardinals (1952, 1954, 1958), L.A. Rams (1959-62), Detroit (1963), Philadelphia (1964)
  Gale Sayers, Chicago (1965-71)
  Travis Williams, Green Bay (1967-70), L.A. Rams (1971)
Kickoff-return touchdowns, season
4 Travis Williams, Green Bay (1967)
  Cecil Turner, Chicago (1970)
3 By five players
Kickoff-return touchdowns, game
2 Timmy Brown, Philadelphia (11/6/66)
  Travis Williams, Green Bay (11/12/67)
  Ron Brown, L.A. Raiders (11/24/85)

FUMBLES
Most fumbles, career
124 Dave Krieg, Seattle (1980-91), Kansas City (1992-93)
106 Dan Fouts, San Diego (1973-87)
105 Roman Gabriel, L.A. Rams (1962-72), Philadelphia (1973-77)
Most fumbles, season
18 Dave Krieg, Seattle (1989)
  Warren Moon, Houston (1990)
17 By three players
Most fumbles, game
7 Len Dawson, Kansas City (11/15/64)
6 Sam Etcheverry, St. Louis (9/17/61)
  Dave Krieg, Seattle (11/5/89)
Fumbles recovered, career
44 Warren Moon, Houston (1984-93)
43 Fran Tarkenton, Minnesota (1961-66, 1972-78), N.Y. Giants (1967-71)
Fumbles recovered, season
9 Don Hultz, Minnesota (1963)
  Dave Krieg, Seattle (1989)
Fumbles recovered, game
4 By five players
Opponents' fumbles recovered, career
29 Jim Marshall, Cleveland (1960), Minnesota (1961-79)
26 Rickey Jackson, New Orleans (1981-93)
25 Dick Butkus, Chicago (1965-73)
Opponents' fumbles recovered, season
9 Don Hultz, Minnesota (1963)
8 Joe Schmidt, Detroit (1955)
7 By four players
Fumble recovery touchdowns, career
4 Bill Thompson, Denver (1969-81)
  Jessie Tuggle, Atlanta (1987-93)
3 By 15 players

SACKS
Most sacks, career
137 Reggie White, Philadelphia (1985-92), Green Bay (1993)
132.5 Lawrence Taylor, N.Y. Giants (1982-93)
124.5 Richard Dent, Chicago (1983-93)
Most sacks, season
22 Mark Gastineau, N.Y. Jets (1984)
21 Reggie White, Philadelphia (1987)
  Chris Doleman, Minnesota (1989)
20.5 Lawrence Taylor, N.Y. Giants (1986)
Most sacks, game
7 Derrick Thomas, Kansas City (11/11/90)
6 Fred Dean, San Francisco (11/13/83)
5.5 William Gay, Detroit (9/4/83)

RECORDS TEAM

CHAMPIONSHIPS
Most seasons as league champion
- 11 Green Bay (1929-31, 1936, 1939, 1944, 1961-62, 1965-67)
- 9 Chicago Bears (1921, 1932-33, 1940-41, 1943, 1946, 1963, 1985)
- 6 N.Y. Giants (1927, 1934, 1938, 1956, 1986, 1990)

Most consecutive seasons as league champion
- 3 Green Bay (1929-31)
  Green Bay (1965-67)

GAMES WON
Most consecutive games won
- 17 Chicago Bears (1933-34)
- 16 Chicago Bears (1941-42)
  Miami (1971-73)
  Miami (1983-84)

Most consecutive games without defeat
- 25 Canton (1921-23)
- 24 Chicago Bears (1941-43)
- 23 Green Bay (1928-30)

Most games won, season
- 15 San Francisco (1984)
  Chicago (1985)
- 14 By 10 teams

Most consecutive games won, season
- 14 Miami (1972)
- 13 Chicago Bears (1934)
- 12 Minnesota (1969)
  Chicago (1985)

Most consecutive games won, start of season
- 14 Miami (1972)
- 13 Chicago Bears (1934)
- 12 Chicago (1985)

Most consecutive games without defeat, season
- 14 Miami (1972)
- 13 Chicago Bears (1926)
  Green Bay (1929)
  Chicago Bears (1934)
  Baltimore (1967)

Most consecutive home games won
- 27 Miami (1971-74)
- 20 Green Bay (1929-32)
- 18 Oakland (1968-70)
  Dallas (1979-81)

Most consecutive road games won
- 18 San Francisco (1988-90)
- 11 L.A. Chargers/San Diego (1960-61)
  San Francisco (1987-88)

GAMES LOST
Most consecutive games lost
- 26 Tampa Bay (1976-77)
- 19 Chicago Cardinals (1942-43, 1945)
  Oakland (1961-62)

Most consecutive games without victory
- 26 Tampa Bay (1976-77)
- 23 Rochester (1922-25)
  Washington (1960-61)

Most games lost, season
- 15 New Orleans (1980)
  Dallas (1989)
  New England (1990)
  Indianapolis (1991)

Most consecutive games lost, season
- 14 Tampa Bay (1976)
  New Orleans (1980)
  Baltimore (1981)
  New England (1990)

Most consecutive games lost, start of season
- 14 Tampa Bay (1976)
  New Orleans (1980)
- 13 Oakland (1962)
  Indianapolis (1986)

Most consecutive home games lost
- 14 Dallas (1988-89)
- 13 Houston (1972-73)
  Tampa Bay (1976-77)

Most consecutive road games lost
- 23 Houston (1981-84)
- 22 Buffalo (1983-86)
- 19 Tampa Bay (1983-85)
  Atlanta (1988-91)

POINTS
Most points, season
- 541 Washington (1983)
- 513 Houston (1961)
  Miami (1984)

Most points, game
- 72 Washington vs. N.Y. Giants (11/27/66)
- 70 L.A. Rams vs. Baltimore (10/22/50)
- 65 Chicago Cardinals vs. N.Y. Bulldogs (11/13/49)
  L.A. Rams vs. Detroit (10/29/50)

Most points, both teams, game
- 113 Washington (72) vs. N.Y. Giants (41), (11/27/66)
- 101 Oakland (52) vs. Houston (49), (12/22/63)
- 99 Seattle (51) vs. Kansas City (48), (11/27/83) OT

TOUCHDOWNS
Most seasons leading league, touchdowns
- 13 Chicago Bears (1932, 1934-35, 1939, 1941-44, 1946-48, 1956, 1965)
- 7 Dallas (1966, 1968, 1971, 1973, 1977-78, 1980)
- 6 Oakland (1967-69, 1972, 1974, 1977)
  San Diego (1963, 1965, 1979, 1981-82, 1985)

Most touchdowns, season
- 70 Miami (1984)
- 66 Houston (1961)
- 64 L.A. Rams (1950)

Most touchdowns, game
- 10 Philadelphia vs. Cincinnati (11/6/34)
  L.A. Rams vs. Baltimore (10/22/50)
  Washington vs. N.Y. Giants (11/27/66)

Most consecutive games scoring touchdowns
- 166 Cleveland (1957-69)
- 97 Oakland (1966-73)
- 96 Kansas City (1963-70)

POINTS AFTER TOUCHDOWN
Most points after touchdown, season
- 66 Miami (1984)
- 65 Houston (1961)
- 62 Washington (1983)

FIELD GOALS
Most field goals attempted, season
- 49 L.A. Rams (1966)
  Washington (1971)
- 48 Green Bay (1972)

Most field goals attempted, game
- 9 St. Louis vs. Pittsburgh (9/24/67)
- 8 Pittsburgh vs. St. Louis (12/2/62)

RECORDS ■ TEAM

    Detroit vs. Minnesota (11/13/66)
    N.Y. Jets vs. Buffalo (11/3/68)
Most field goals, season
 35 N.Y. Giants (1983)
    L.A. Raiders (1993)
 34 N.Y. Jets (1968)
    Kansas City (1990)
Most field goals, game
  7 St. Louis vs. Pittsburgh (9/24/67)
    Minnesota vs. L.A. Rams (11/5/89) OT
Most consecutive games scoring field goals
 31 Minnesota (1968-70)
 28 Washington (1988-90)
 22 San Francisco (1988-89)

FIRST DOWNS
Most first downs, season
387 Miami (1984)
380 San Diego (1985)
379 San Diego (1981)
Most first downs, game
 39 N.Y. Jets vs. Miami (11/27/88)
    Washington vs. Detroit (11/4/90) OT
 38 L.A. Rams vs. N.Y. Giants (11/13/66)
 37 Green Bay vs. Philadelphia (11/11/62)
Most first downs, rushing, season
181 New England (1978)
177 L.A. Rams (1973)
176 Chicago (1985)
Most first downs, rushing, game
 25 Philadelphia vs. Washington (12/2/51)
 23 St. Louis vs. New Orleans (10/5/80)
Most first downs, passing, season
259 San Diego (1985)
251 Houston (1990)
250 Miami (1986)
Most first downs, passing, game
 29 N.Y. Giants vs. Cincinnati (10/13/85)
 27 San Diego vs. Seattle (9/15/85)
 26 Miami vs. Cleveland (12/12/88)

NET YARDS GAINED RUSHING AND PASSING
Most yards gained, season
6,936 Miami (1984)
6,744 San Diego (1981)
6,535 San Diego (1985)
Most yards gained, game
735 L.A. Rams vs. N.Y. Yanks (9/28/51)
683 Pittsburgh vs. Chicago Cardinals (12/13/58)
682 Chicago Bears vs. N.Y. Giants (11/14/43)
Most yards gained, both teams, game
1,133 L.A. Rams vs. N.Y. Yanks (11/19/50)
1,102 San Diego vs. Cincinnati (12/20/82)
1,087 St. Louis vs. Philadelphia (12/16/62)

RUSHING
Most rushing attempts, season
681 Oakland (1977)
674 Chicago (1984)
671 New England (1978)
Most rushing attempts, game
 72 Chicago Bears vs. Brooklyn (10/20/35)
 70 Chicago Cardinals vs. Green Bay (12/5/48)
Most yards rushing, season
3,165 New England (1978)
3,088 Buffalo (1973)
2,986 Kansas City (1978)
Most yards gained rushing, game
426 Detroit vs. Pittsburgh (11/4/34)
423 N.Y. Giants vs. Baltimore (11/19/50)
420 Boston vs. N.Y. Giants (10/8/33)

Most touchdowns rushing, season
 36 Green Bay (1962)
 33 Pittsburgh (1976)
 30 Chicago Bears (1941)
    New England (1978)
    Washington (1983)
Most touchdowns rushing, game
  7 L.A. Rams vs. Atlanta (12/4/76)
  6 By many teams

PASSING
Most passes attempted, season
709 Minnesota (1981)
667 Houston (1991)
662 San Diego (1984)
Most passes attempted, game
 68 Houston vs. Buffalo (11/1/64)
 66 Atlanta vs. Detroit (12/24/89)
 65 San Diego vs. Kansas City (10/19/86)
Most passes completed, season
411 Houston (1991)
401 San Diego (1984)
399 Houston (1990)
Most passes completed, game
 42 N.Y. Jets vs. San Francisco (9/21/80)
 41 Houston vs. Dallas (11/10/91) OT
Most yards gained passing, season
5,018 Miami (1984)
4,870 San Diego (1985)
4,805 Houston (1990)
Most yards gained passing, game
554 L.A. Rams vs. N.Y. Yanks (9/28/51)
530 Minnesota vs. Baltimore (9/28/69)
521 Miami vs. N.Y. Jets (10/23/88)
Most yards gained passing, both teams, game
884 N.Y. Jets vs. Miami (9/21/86) OT
883 San Diego vs. Cincinnati (12/20/82)
849 Minnesota vs. Washington (11/2/86) OT
Most consecutive seasons leading league, fewest times sacked
  9 Miami (1982-90)
  3 St. Louis (1974-76)
  2 By many teams
Most times sacked, season
104 Philadelphia (1986)
 72 Philadelphia (1987)
 70 Atlanta (1968)
Fewest times sacked, season
  7 Miami (1988)
  8 San Francisco (1970)
    St. Louis (1975)
Most touchdowns passing, season
 49 Miami (1984)
 48 Houston (1961)
 46 Miami (1986)
Most touchdowns passing, game
  7 By seven teams
Most passes had intercepted, season
 48 Houston (1962)
 45 Denver (1961)
 41 Card-Pitt (1944)
Fewest passes had intercepted, season
  5 Cleveland (1960)
    Green Bay (1966)
    Kansas City (1990)
    N.Y. Giants (1990)
Most passes, intercepted, game
  9 Detroit vs. Green Bay (10/24/93)
    Pittsburgh vs. Philadelphia (12/12/65)

PUNTING
Most punts, season
114 Chicago (1981)
113 Boston (1934)
    Brooklyn (1934)
Fewest punts, season

23 San Diego (1982)
31 Cincinnati (1982)
32 Chicago Bears (1941)
Most punts, game
17 Chicago Bears vs. Green Bay (10/22/33)
Cincinnati vs. Pittsburgh (10/22/33)

PUNT RETURNS
Most punt returns, season
71 Pittsburgh (1976)
Tampa Bay (1979)
L.A. Raiders (1985)
Fewest punt returns, season
12 Baltimore (1981)
San Diego (1982)
Most punt returns, game
12 Philadelphia vs. Cleveland (12/3/50)
11 Chicago Bears vs. Chicago Cardinals (10/8/50)
Washington vs. Tampa Bay (10/9/77)
Most yards gained, punt returns, season
785 L.A. Raiders (1985)
781 Chicago Bears (1948)
774 Pittsburgh (1974)
Most yards gained, punt returns, game
231 Detroit vs. San Francisco (10/6/63)
225 Oakland vs. Buffalo (9/15/68)
219 L.A. Rams vs. Atlanta (10/11/81)
Highest average, punt returns, season
20.2 Chicago Bears (1941)
19.1 Chicago Cardinals (1948)
18.2 Chicago Cardinals (1949)
Most touchdowns, punt returns, season
5 Chicago Cardinals (1959)

KICKOFF RETURNS
Most kickoff returns, season
88 New Orleans (1980)
86 Minnesota (1984)
84 Baltimore (1981)
Most yards, kickoff returns, season
1,973 New Orleans (1980)
1,824 Houston (1963)
1,801 Denver (1963)
Most yards, kickoff returns, game
362 Detroit vs. L.A. Rams (10/29/50)
304 Chicago Bears vs. Green Bay (11/9/52)
295 Denver vs. Boston (10/4/64)
Highest average, kickoff returns, season
29.4 Chicago (1972)
28.9 Pittsburgh (1952)
28.2 Washington (1962)
Most touchdowns, kickoff returns, season
4 Green Bay (1967)
Chicago (1970)

FUMBLES
Most fumbles, season
56 Chicago Bears (1938)
San Francisco (1978)
54 Philadelphia (1946)
Fewest fumbles, season
8 Cleveland (1959)
11 Green Bay (1944)
Most fumbles lost, season
36 Chicago Cardinals (1959)
31 Green Bay (1952)
Fewest fumbles lost, season
3 Philadelphia (1938)
Minnesota (1980)
Most opponents' fumbles recovered, season
31 Minnesota (1963)
29 Cleveland (1951)
Most opponents' fumbles recovered, game
8 Washington vs. St. Louis (10/25/76)
Pittsburgh vs. Cleveland (12/23/90)

TURNOVERS
Most turnovers, season
63 San Francisco (1978)
58 Chicago Bears (1947)
Pittsburgh (1950)
N.Y. Giants (1983)
Fewest turnovers, season
12 Kansas City (1982)
14 N.Y. Giants (1943)
Cleveland (1959)
N.Y. Giants (1990)
Most turnovers, game
12 Detroit vs. Chicago Bears (11/22/42)
Chicago Cardinals vs. Philadelphia (9/24/50)
Pittsburgh vs. Philadelphia (12/12/65)

PENALTIES
Most seasons leading league, fewest penalties
13 Miami (1968, 1976-84, 1986, 1990-91)
9 Pittsburgh (1946-47, 1950-52, 1954, 1963, 1965, 1968)
6 Boston/New England (1962, 1964-65, 1973, 1987, 1989)
Most seasons leading league, most penalties
16 Chicago Bears (1941-44, 1946-49, 1951, 1959-61, 1963, 1965, 1968, 1976)
8 Oakland/L.A. Raiders (1963, 1966, 1968-69, 1975, 1982, 1984, 1991)
6 L.A. Rams (1950, 1952, 1962, 1969, 1978, 1980)
Fewest penalties, season
19 Detroit (1937)
21 Boston (1935)
24 Philadelphia (1936)
Most penalties, season
149 Houston (1989)
144 Buffalo (1983)
143 L.A. Raiders (1984)
Fewest penalties, game
0 By many teams
Most penalties, game
22 Brooklyn vs. Green Bay (9/17/44)
Chicago Bears vs. Philadelphia (11/26/44)

DEFENSE
SCORING
Most seasons leading league, fewest points allowed
9 Chicago Bears (1932, 1936-37, 1942, 1948, 1963, 1985-86, 1988)
N.Y. Giants (1935, 1938-39, 1941, 1944, 1958-59, 1961, 1990)
6 Cleveland (1951, 1953-57)
Fewest points allowed, season (since 1932)
44 Chicago Bears (1932)
54 Brooklyn (1933)
59 Detroit (1934)
Most points allowed, season
533 Baltimore (1981)
501 N.Y. Giants (1966)
487 New Orleans (1980)
Fewest touchdowns allowed, season (since 1932)
6 Chicago Bears (1932)
Brooklyn (1933)
7 Detroit (1934)
Most touchdowns allowed, season
68 Baltimore (1981)
66 N.Y. Giants (1966)
63 Baltimore (1950)

FIRST DOWNS
Fewest first downs allowed, season
77 Detroit (1935)
79 Boston (1935)

RECORDS ■ TEAM

82 Washington (1937)
Most first downs allowed, season
406 Baltimore (1981)
371 Seattle (1981)
366 Green Bay (1983)
Fewest first downs allowed, rushing, season
35 Chicago Bears (1942)
40 Green Bay (1940)
41 Brooklyn (1944)
Most first downs allowed, rushing, season
179 Detroit (1985)
178 New Orleans (1980)
175 Seattle (1981)
Fewest first downs allowed, passing, season
33 Chicago Bears (1943)
34 Pittsburgh (1941)
 Washington (1943)
Most first downs allowed, passing, season
218 San Diego (1985)
216 San Diego (1981)
 N.Y. Jets (1986)

NET YARDS ALLOWED RUSHING AND PASSING

Fewest yards allowed, season
1,539 Chicago Cardinals (1934)
1,703 Chicago Bears (1942)
1,789 Brooklyn (1933)
Most yards allowed, season
6,793 Baltimore (1981)
6,403 Green Bay (1983)
6,352 Minnesota (1984)

RUSHING

Fewest yards allowed, rushing, season
519 Chicago Bears (1942)
558 Philadelphia (1944)
762 Pittsburgh (1982)
Most yards allowed, rushing, season
3,228 Buffalo (1978)
3,106 New Orleans (1980)
3,010 Baltimore (1978)
Fewest touchdowns allowed, rushing, season
2 Detroit (1934)
 Dallas (1968)
 Minnesota (1971)
Most touchdowns allowed, rushing, season
36 Oakland (1961)
31 N.Y. Giants (1980)
 Tampa Bay (1986)

PASSING

Fewest yards allowed, passing, season
545 Philadelphia (1934)
558 Portsmouth (1933)
585 Chicago Cardinals (1934)
Most yards allowed, passing, season
4,389 N.Y. Jets (1986)
4,311 San Diego (1981)
4,239 San Diego (1985)
Fewest touchdowns allowed, passing, season
1 Portsmouth (1932)
 Philadelphia (1934)
Most touchdowns allowed, passing, season
40 Denver (1963)
38 St. Louis (1969)

SACKS

Most sacks, season
72 Chicago (1984)
71 Minnesota (1989)
70 Chicago (1987)
Fewest sacks, season
11 Baltimore (1982)

12 Buffalo (1982)
13 Baltimore (1981)
Most sacks, game
12 Dallas vs. Pittsburgh (11/20/66)
 St. Louis vs. Baltimore (10/26/80)
 Chicago vs. Detroit (12/16/84)
 Dallas vs. Houston (9/29/85)

INTERCEPTIONS

Most passes intercepted by, season
49 San Diego (1961)
42 Green Bay (1943)
41 N.Y. Giants (1951)
Fewest passes intercepted by, season
3 Houston (1982)
5 Baltimore (1982)
Most passes intercepted by, game
9 Green Bay vs. Detroit (10/24/43)
 Philadelphia vs. Pittsburgh (12/12/65)
Most consecutive games, one or more interceptions
46 L.A. Chargers/San Diego (1960-63)
37 Detroit (1960-63)
36 Boston (1944-47)
Most yards returning interceptions, season
929 San Diego (1961)
712 L.A. Rams (1952)
697 Seattle (1984)
Most yards returning interceptions, game
325 Seattle vs. Kansas City (11/4/84)
314 L.A. Rams vs. San Francisco (10/18/64)
245 Houston vs. N.Y. Jets (10/15/67)

PUNT RETURNS

Fewest opponents' punt returns, season
7 Washington (1962)
 San Diego (1982)
Most opponents' punt returns, season
71 Tampa Bay (1976, 1977)
69 N.Y. Giants (1953)
Fewest yards allowed, punt returns, season
22 Green Bay (1967)
34 Washington (1962)
Most yards allowed, punt returns, season
932 Green Bay (1949)
913 Boston (1947)
Most touchdowns allowed, punt returns, season
4 N.Y. Giants (1959)
 Atlanta (1992)

KICKOFF RETURNS

Fewest opponents' kickoff returns, season
10 Brooklyn (1943)
13 Denver (1992)
Most opponents' kickoff returns, season
91 Washington (1983)
89 New England (1980)
Fewest yards allowed, kickoff returns, season
225 Brooklyn (1943)
254 Denver (1992)
Most yards allowed, kickoff returns, season
2,045 Kansas City (1966)
1,827 Chicago (1985)
Most touchdowns allowed, kickoff returns, season
3 Minnesota (1963, 1970)
 Dallas (1966)
 Detroit (1980)
 Pittsburgh (1986)

TURNOVERS

Fewest opponents' turnovers, season
11 Baltimore (1982)
13 San Francisco (1982)
15 St. Louis (1982)

413

SUPER BOWL

INDIVIDUAL RECORDS
SERVICE
Most games
- 5 Marv Fleming, Green Bay, 1967-68; Miami, 1972-74
  Larry Cole, Dallas, 1971-72, 1976, 1978-79
  Cliff Harris, Dallas, 1971-72, 1976, 1978-79
  D.D. Lewis, Dallas, 1971-72, 1976, 1978-79
  Preston Pearson, Dallas, 1971-72, 1976, 1978-79
  Charlie Waters, Dallas, 1971-72, 1976, 1978-79
  Rayfield Wright, Dallas, 1971-72, 1976, 1978-79

Most games, coach
- 6 Don Shula, Balt., 1969; Mia., 1972-74, 1983, 1985
- 5 Tom Landry, Dallas, 1971-72, 1976, 1978-79
- 4 Bud Grant, Minnesota, 1970, 1974-75, 1977
  Chuck Noll, Pittsburgh, 1975-76, 1979-80

Most games, winning coach
- 4 Chuck Noll, Pittsburgh, 1975-76, 1979-80
- 3 Bill Walsh, San Francisco, 1982, 1985, 1989

Most games, losing coach
- 4 Bud Grant, Minnesota, 1970, 1974-75, 1977
  Don Shula, Balt., 1969; Mia., 1972, 1983, 1985
  Marv Levy, Buffalo, 1991-94

SCORING
POINTS
Most points, career
- 24 Franco Harris, Pittsburgh, 4 games (4-td)
  Jerry Rice, San Francisco, 2 games (4-td)
  Roger Craig, San Francisco, 3 games (4-td)
  Thurman Thomas, Buffalo, 4 games (4-td)
- 22 Ray Wersching, San Francisco, 2 games (7-pat, 3-fg)

Most points, game
- 18 Roger Craig, San Francisco vs. Miami, 1985 (3-td)
  Jerry Rice, San Francisco vs. Denver, 1990 (3-td)
- 15 Don Chandler, G.B. vs. Oak., 1968 (3-pat, 4-fg)

TOUCHDOWNS
Most touchdowns, career
- 4 Franco Harris, Pittsburgh, 4 games (4-r)
  Jerry Rice, San Francisco, 3 games (4-p)
  Roger Craig, San Francisco, 3 games (2-r, 2-p)
  Thurman Thomas, Buffalo, 4 games (4-r)

Most touchdowns, game
- 3 Roger Craig, San Francisco vs. Mia., 1985 (1-r, 2-p)
  Jerry Rice, San Francisco vs. Den., 1990 (3-p)
- 2 By many players

POINTS AFTER TOUCHDOWN
Most points after touchdown, career
- 9 Mike Cofer, San Francisco, 2 games (10 att)
- 8 Don Chandler, Green Bay, 2 games (8 att)
  Roy Gerela, Pittsburgh, 3 games (9 att)
  Chris Bahr, Oakland-L.A. Raiders (8 att)

Most points after touchdown, game
- 7 Mike Cofer, San Francisco vs. Denver, 1990 (8 att)
  Lin Elliott, Dallas vs. Buffalo, 1993 (7 att)

FIELD GOALS
Field goals attempted, career
- 7 Roy Gerela, Pittsburgh, 3 games
- 6 Jim Turner, N.Y. Jets-Denver, 2 games
  Rich Karlis, Denver, 2 games
- 5 Efren Herrera, Dallas, 1 game
  Ray Wersching, San Francisco, 2 games

Most field goals attempted, game
- 5 Jim Turner, N.Y. Jets vs. Baltimore, 1969
  Efren Herrera, Dallas vs. Denver, 1978

Most field goals, career
- 5 Ray Wersching, San Francisco, 2 games (5 att)
- 4 Don Chandler, Green Bay, 2 games (4 att)
  Jim Turner, N.Y. Jets-Denver, 2 games (6 att)
  Uwe von Schamann, Miami, 2 games (4 att)

Most field goals, game
- 4 Don Chandler, Green Bay vs. Oakland, 1968
  Ray Wersching, San Francisco vs. Cincinnati, 1982
- 3 Jim Turner, N.Y. Jets vs. Baltimore, 1969
  Jan Stenerud, Kansas City vs. Minnesota, 1970
  Uwe von Schamann, Miami vs. San Francisco, 1985
  Kevin Butler, Chicago vs. New England, 1986
  Jim Breech, Cincinnati vs. San Francisco, 1989

Longest field goal
- 54 Steve Christie, Buffalo vs. Dallas, 1994
- 48 Jan Stenerud, Kansas City vs. Minnesota, 1970
  Rich Karlis, Denver vs. N.Y. Giants, 1987

RUSHING
ATTEMPTS
Most attempts, career
- 101 Franco Harris, Pittsburgh, 4 games
- 64 John Riggins, Washington, 2 games
- 57 Larry Csonka, Miami, 3 games

Most attempts, game
- 38 John Riggins, Washington vs. Miami, 1983
- 34 Franco Harris, Pittsburgh vs. Minnesota, 1975
- 33 Larry Csonka, Miami vs. Minnesota, 1974

YARDS GAINED
Most yards gained, career
- 354 Franco Harris, Pittsburgh, 4 games
- 297 Larry Csonka, Miami, 3 games
- 230 John Riggins, Washington, 2 games

Most yards gained, game
- 204 Timmy Smith, Washington vs. Denver, 1988
- 191 Marcus Allen, L.A. Raiders vs. Washington, 1984
- 166 John Riggins, Washington vs. Miami, 1983

Longest run from scrimmage
- 74 Marcus Allen, L.A. Raiders vs. Washington, 1984
- 58 Tom Matte, Baltimore vs. N.Y. Jets, 1969
  Timmy Smith, Washington vs. Denver, 1988

AVERAGE GAIN
Highest average gain, career (20 attempts)
- 9.6 Marcus Allen, L.A. Raiders, 1 game (20-191)
- 9.3 Timmy Smith, Washington, 1 game (22-204)
- 5.3 Walt Garrison, Dallas, 2 games (26-139)

Highest average gain, game (10 attempts)
- 10.5 Tom Matte, Baltimore vs. N.Y. Jets, 1969 (11-116)
- 9.6 Marcus Allen, L.A. Rd. vs. Wash., 1984 (20-191)
- 9.3 Timmy Smith, Wash. vs. Denver, 1988 (22-204)

TOUCHDOWNS
Most touchdowns, career
- 4 Franco Harris, Pittsburgh, 4 games
  Thurman Thomas, Buffalo, 4 games

Most touchdowns, game
- 2 Elijah Pitts, Green Bay vs. Kansas City, 1967
  Larry Csonka, Miami vs. Minnesota, 1974
  Pete Banaszak, Oakland vs. Minnesota, 1977
  Franco Harris, Pittsburgh vs. L.A. Rams, 1980
  Marcus Allen, L.A. Raiders vs. Washington, 1984
  Jim McMahon, Chicago vs. New England, 1986
  Timmy Smith, Washington vs. Denver, 1988
  Tom Rathman, San Francisco vs. Denver, 1990
  Gerald Riggs, Washington vs. Buffalo, 1992

Emmitt Smith, Dallas vs. Buffalo, 1994

PASSING
ATTEMPTS
Most passes attempted, career
- 145 Jim Kelly, Buffalo, 4 games
- 122 Joe Montana, San Francisco, 4 games
- 98 Roger Staubach, Dallas, 4 games

Most passes attempted, game
- 58 Jim Kelly, Buffalo vs. Washington, 1992
- 50 Dan Marino, Miami vs. San Francisco, 1985

COMPLETIONS
Most passes completed, career
- 83 Joe Montana, San Francisco, 4 games
- 81 Jim Kelly, Buffalo, 4 games
- 61 Roger Staubach, Dallas, 4 games

Most passes completed, game
- 31 Jim Kelly, Buffalo vs. Dallas, 1994
- 29 Dan Marino, Miami vs. San Francisco, 1985
- 28 Jim Kelly, Buffalo vs. Washington, 1992

Most consecutive completions, game
- 13 Joe Montana, San Francisco vs. Denver, 1990
- 10 Phil Simms, N.Y. Giants vs. Denver, 1987

COMPLETION PERCENTAGE
Highest completion percentage, career (40 att.)
- 71.9 Troy Aikman, Dallas, 2 games (41-57)
- 68.0 Joe Montana, San Francisco, 4 games (83-122)
- 63.6 Len Dawson, Kansas City, 2 games (28-44)

Highest completion percentage, game (20 att.)
- 88.0 Phil Simms, N.Y. Giants vs. Denver, 1987 (22-25)
- 81.5 Joe Montana, San Francisco vs. Denver, 1990 (22-29)
- 73.5 Ken Anderson, Cincinnati vs. S.F., 1982 (25-34)

YARDS GAINED
Most yards gained, career
- 1142 Joe Montana, San Francisco, 4 games
- 932 Terry Bradshaw, Pittsburgh, 4 games
- 829 Jim Kelly, Buffalo, 4 games

Most yards gained, game
- 357 Joe Montana, San Francisco vs. Cincinnati, 1989
- 340 Doug Williams, Washington vs. Denver, 1988
- 331 Joe Montana, San Francisco vs. Miami, 1985

Longest pass completion
- 80 Jim Plunkett (to King), Oakland vs. Phil., 1981 (TD)
  Doug Williams (to Sanders), Washington vs. Denver, 1988 (TD)
- 76 David Woodley (to Cefalo), Miami vs. Washington, 1983 (TD)

AVERAGE GAIN
Highest average gain, career (40 attempts)
- 11.10 Terry Bradshaw, Pittsburgh, 4 games (84-932)
- 9.62 Bart Starr, Green Bay, 2 games (47-452)
- 9.41 Jim Plunkett, Oakland-L.A. Raiders, 2 games (46-433)

Highest average gain, game (20 attempts)
- 14.71 Terry Bradshaw, Pittsburgh vs. L.A. Rams, 1980 (21-309)
- 12.80 Jim McMahon, Chicago vs. N.E., 1986 (20-256)

TOUCHDOWNS
Most touchdown passes, career
- 11 Joe Montana, San Francisco, 4 games
- 9 Terry Bradshaw, Pittsburgh, 4 games
- 8 Roger Staubach, Dallas, 4 games

Most touchdown passes, game
- 5 Joe Montana, San Francisco vs. Denver, 1990
- 4 Troy Aikman, Dallas vs. Buffalo, 1993
  Terry Bradshaw, Pittsburgh vs. Dallas, 1979
  Doug Williams, Washington vs. Denver, 1988

HAD INTERCEPTED
Lowest percentage, passes had intercepted, career (40 attempts)
- 0.00 Joe Montana, San Francisco, 4 games (122-0)

RECORDS ■ SUPER BOWL

- Jim Plunkett, Oak.-L.A. Raiders, 2 games (46-0)
- 2.13 Bart Starr, Green Bay, 2 games (47-1)
- 4.08 Roger Staubach, Dallas, 4 games (98-4)

Most attempts without interception, game
- 36 Joe Montana, San Francisco vs. Cincinnati, 1989
- 35 Joe Montana, San Francisco vs. Miami, 1985
- 30 Troy Aikman, Dallas vs. Buffalo, 1993

Most passes had intercepted, career
- 7 Craig Morton, Dallas-Denver, 2 games
  Jim Kelly, Buffalo, 4 games
- 6 Fran Tarkenton, Minnesota, 3 games
- 4 By four players

Most passes had intercepted, game
- 4 Craig Morton, Denver vs. Dallas, 1978
- 4 Jim Kelly, Buffalo vs. Washington, 1992

PASS RECEIVING
RECEPTIONS
Most receptions, career
- 27 Andre Reed, Buffalo, 4 games
- 20 Roger Craig, San Francisco, 3 games
- 18 Jerry Rice, San Francisco, 2 games

Most receptions, game
- 11 Dan Ross, Cincinnati vs. San Francisco, 1982
- 11 Jerry Rice, San Francisco vs. Cincinnati, 1989
- 10 Tony Nathan, Miami vs. San Francisco, 1985

YARDS GAINED
Most yards gained, career
- 364 Lynn Swann, Pittsburgh, 4 games
- 363 Jerry Rice, San Francisco, 2 games
- 268 John Stallworth, Pittsburgh, 4 games

Most yards gained, game
- 215 Jerry Rice, San Francisco vs. Cincinnati, 1989
- 193 Ricky Sanders, Washington vs. Denver, 1988
- 161 Lynn Swann, Pittsburgh vs. Dallas, 1976

Longest reception
- 80 Kenny King (from Plunkett), Oakland vs. Philadelphia, 1981 (TD)
  Ricky Sanders (from Williams), Washington vs. Denver, 1988 (TD)
- 76 Jimmy Cefalo (from Woodley), Miami vs. Washington, 1983 (TD)

AVERAGE GAIN
Highest average gain, career (8 receptions)
- 24.4 John Stallworth, Pittsburgh, 4 games (11-268)
- 22.8 Lynn Swann, Pittsburgh, 4 games (16-364)
- 21.4 Ricky Sanders, Washington, 1 game (9-193)

Highest average gain, game (3 receptions)
- 40.33 John Stallworth, Pittsburgh vs. L.A. Rams, 1980 (3-121)
- 40.25 Lynn Swann, Pittsburgh vs. Dall., 1979 (4-161)
- 38.33 John Stallworth, Pitt. vs. Dallas, 1979 (3-115)

TOUCHDOWNS
Most touchdowns, career
- 4 Jerry Rice, San Francisco, 2 games
- 3 John Stallworth, Pittsburgh, 4 games
  Lynn Swann, Pittsburgh, 4 games
  Cliff Branch, Oakland-L.A. Raiders, 3 games

Most touchdowns, game
- 3 Jerry Rice, San Francisco vs. Denver, 1990
- 2 By eight players

INTERCEPTIONS BY
Most interceptions by, career
- 3 Chuck Howley, Dallas, 2 games
  Rod Martin, Oakland-L.A. Raiders, 2 games
- 2 By seven players

Most interceptions by, game
- 3 Rod Martin, Oakland vs. Philadelphia, 1981
- 2 Randy Beverly, N.Y. Jets vs. Baltimore, 1969
  Chuck Howley, Dallas vs. Baltimore, 1971
  Jake Scott, Miami vs. Washington, 1973

Barry Wilburn, Washington vs. Denver, 1988
Thomas Everett, Dallas vs. Buffalo, 1993

YARDS GAINED
Most yards gained, career
75 Willie Brown, Oakland, 2 games
63 Chuck Howley, Dallas, 2 games
     Jake Scott, Miami, 3 games
Most yards gained, game
75 Willie Brown, Oakland vs. Minnesota, 1977
63 Jake Scott, Miami vs. Washington, 1973
Longest return
75 Willie Brown, Oakland vs. Minnesota, 1977 (TD)
60 Herb Adderley, Green Bay vs. Oakland, 1968 (TD)
55 Jake Scott, Miami vs. Washington, 1973

TOUCHDOWNS
Most touchdowns, game
1 Herb Adderley, Green Bay vs. Oakland, 1968
   Willie Brown, Oakland vs. Minnesota, 1977
   Jack Squirek, L.A. Raiders vs. Washington, 1984
   Reggie Phillips, Chicago vs. New England, 1986

PUNTING
Most punts, career
17 Mike Eischeid, Oakland-Minnesota, 3 games
15 Larry Seiple, Miami, 3 games
14 Ron Widby, Dallas, 2 games
     Ray Guy, Oakland-L.A. Raiders, 3 games
Most punts, game
9 Ron Widby, Dallas vs. Baltimore, 1971
7 By seven players
Longest punt
63 Lee Johnson, Cincinnati vs. San Francisco, 1989
62 Rich Camarillo, New England vs. Chicago, 1986

AVERAGE YARDAGE
Highest average, punting, career (10 punts)
46.5 Jerrel Wilson, Kansas City, 2 games (11-511)
41.9 Ray Guy, Oak.-L.A. Raiders, 3 games, (14-587)
41.3 Larry Seiple, Miami, 3 games (15-620)
Highest average, punting, game (4 punts)
48.5 Jerrel Wilson, K.C. vs. Minn., 1970 (4-194)
46.3 Jim Miller, San Francisco vs. Cin., 1982 (4-185)
45.3 Jerrel Willson, Kansas City vs G.B., 1967 (7-317)

PUNT RETURNS
Most punt returns, career
6 Willie Wood, Green Bay, 2 games
   Jake Scott, Miami, 3 games
   Theo Bell, Pittsburgh, 2 games
   Mike Nelms, Washington, 1 game
   John Taylor, San Francisco, 2 games
Most punt returns, game
6 Mike Nelms, Washington vs. Miami, 1983
5 Willie Wood, Green Bay vs. Oakland, 1968
   Dana McLemore, San Francisco vs. Miami, 1985

YARDS GAINED
Most yards gained, career
94 John Taylor, San Francisco, 2 games
52 Mike Nelms, Washington, 1 game
51 Dana McLemore, San Francisco, 1 game
Most yards gained, game
56 John Taylor, San Francisco vs. Cincinnati, 1989
52 Mike Nelms, Washington vs. Miami, 1983
51 Dana McLemore, San Francisco vs. Miami, 1985
Longest return
45 John Taylor, San Francisco vs. Cincinnati, 1989
34 Darrell Green, Washington vs. L.A. Raiders, 1984
31 Willie Wood, Green Bay vs. Oakland, 1968

AVERAGE YARDAGE
Highest average, career (4 returns)
15.7 John Taylor, San Francisco, 2 games (6-94)

10.8 Neal Colzie, Oakland, 1 game (4-43)
10.2 Dana McLemore, San Francisco, 1 game (5-51)
Highest average, game (3 returns)
18.7 John Taylor, San Francisco vs. Cincinnati, 1989
11.6 Kelvin Martin, Buffalo vs. Dallas, 1993 (3-35)
11.3 Lynn Swann, Pittsburgh vs. Minn., 1975 (3-34)

KICKOFF RETURNS
Most kickoff returns, career
10 Ken Bell, Denver, 3 games
8 Larry Anderson, Pittsburgh, 2 games
    Fulton Walker, Miami, 2 games
Most kickoff returns, game
7 Stephen Starring, New England vs. Chicago, 1986
6 Darren Carrington, Denver vs. San Francisco, 1990

YARDS GAINED
Most yards gained, career
283 Fulton Walker, Miami, 2 games
207 Larry Anderson, Pittsburgh, 2 games
177 Ken Bell, Denver, 3 games
Most yards gained, game
190 Fulton Walker, Miami vs. Washington, 1983
162 Larry Anderson, Pittsburgh vs. L.A. Rams, 1980
153 Stephen Starring, New England vs. Chicago, 1986
Longest return
98 Fulton Walker, Miami vs. Washington, 1983 (TD)
93 Stanford Jennings, Cincinnati vs. San Francisco, 1989 (TD)

AVERAGE YARDAGE
Highest average, career (4 returns)
35.4 Fulton Walker, Miami, 2 games (8-283)
25.9 Larry Anderson, Pittsburgh, 2 games (8-207)
22.5 Jim Duncan, Baltimore, 1 game (4-90)
Highest average, game (3 returns)
47.5 Fulton Walker, Miami vs. Wash., 1983 (4-190)
32.4 Larry Anderson, Pittsburgh vs. L.A. Rams, 1980 (5-162)
31.3 Rick Upchurch, Denver vs. Dallas, 1978 (3-94)

TOUCHDOWNS
Most touchdowns, game
1 Fulton Walker, Miami vs. Washington, 1983
1 Stanford Jennings, Cincinnati vs. San Francisco, 1989

FUMBLES
Most fumbles, career
5 Roger Staubach, Dallas, 4 games
3 Franco Harris, Pittsburgh, 4 games
   Terry Bradshaw, Pittsburgh, 4 games
   Jim Kelly, Buffalo, 3 games
   Frank Reich, Buffalo, 1 game
Most fumbles, game
3 Roger Staubach, Dallas vs. Pittsburgh, 1976
   Jim Kelly, Buffalo vs. Washington, 1992
   Frank Reich, Buffalo vs. Dallas, 1993
2 Franco Harris, Pittsburgh vs. Minnesota, 1975
   Butch Johnson, Dallas vs. Denver, 1978
   Terry Bradshaw, Pittsburgh vs. Dallas

RECOVERIES
Most fumbles recovered, career
2 By 12 players
Most fumbles recovered, game
2 By six players

YARDS GAINED
Most yards gained, game
64 Leon Lett, Dallas vs. Buffalo, 1993 (opp)
49 Mike Bass, Washington vs. Miami, 1973 (opp)
37 Mike Hegman, Dallas vs. Pittsburgh, 1979 (opp)
Longest return
64 Leon Lett, Dallas vs. Buffalo, 1993

49 Mike Bass, Washington vs. Miami, 1973
37 Mike Hegman, Dallas vs. Pittsburgh, 1979 (TD)

TOUCHDOWNS
Most touchdowns, game
1 Mike Bass, Washington vs. Mia., 1973 (opp 49 yds)
Mike Hegman, Dallas vs. Pitt., 1979 (opp 37 yds)
Jimmie Jones, Dallas vs. Buffalo, 1993 (opp 2 yds)
Ken Norton, Dallas vs. Buffalo, 1993 (opp 9 yds)

TEAM RECORDS
GAMES, VICTORIES, DEFEATS
Most games
7 Dallas, 1971-72, 1976, 1978-79, 1993-94
5 Miami, 1972-74, 1983, 1985
Washington, 1973, 1983-84, 1988, 1992
Most consecutive games
4 Buffalo 1991-94
3 Miami, 1972-74
2 By seven teams
Most games won
4 Pittsburgh, 1975-76, 1979-80
San Francisco, 1982, 1985, 1989, 1990
3 Dallas, 1972, 1978, 1993-94
Oakland-L.A. Raiders, 1977, 1981, 1984
Washington, 1983, 1988, 1992
Most consecutive games won
2 Green Bay, 1967-68
Miami, 1973-74
Pittsburgh, 1975-76, 1979-80
San Francisco, 1989-90
Dallas, 1993-94
Most games lost
4 Minnesota, 1970, 1974-75, 1977
Denver, 1978, 1987-88, 1990
Buffalo, 1991-94
3 Dallas, 1971, 1976, 1979
Miami, 1972, 1983, 1985
Buffalo, 1991, 1992, 1993
Most consecutive games lost
4 Buffalo, 1991-94
2 Minnesota, 1974-75
Denver, 1987-88

SCORING
Most points, game
55 San Francisco vs. Denver, 1990
52 Dallas vs. Buffalo, 1993
46 Chicago vs. New England, 1986
Fewest points, game
3 Miami vs. Dallas, 1972
6 Minnesota vs. Pittsburgh, 1975
7 By four teams
Most points, both teams, game
69 Dallas (52) vs. Buffalo (17), 1993
66 Pittsburgh (35) vs. Dallas (31), 1979
65 San Francisco (55) vs. Denver (10), 1990
61 Washington (37) vs. Buffalo (24), 1992
59 N.Y. Giants (39) vs. Denver (20), 1987
Fewest points, both teams, game
21 Washington (7) vs. Miami (14), 1973
22 Minnesota (6) vs. Pittsburgh (16), 1975
23 Baltimore (7) vs. N.Y. Jets (16), 1969
Largest margin of victory, game
45 San Francisco vs. Denver, 1990 (55-10)
36 Chicago vs. New England, 1986 (46-10)
35 Dallas vs. Buffalo, 1993 (52-17)
Narrowest margin of victory, game
1 N.Y. Giants vs. Buffalo, 1991 (20-19)
3 Baltimore vs. Dallas, 1971 (16-13)
4 By three teams
Most points, each half
1st: 35 Washington vs. Denver, 1988
2nd: 30 N.Y. Giants vs. Denver, 1987

TOUCHDOWNS
Most touchdowns, game
8 San Francisco vs. Denver, 1990
7 Dallas vs. Buffalo, 1993
6 Washington vs. Denver, 1988
Fewest touchdowns, game
0 Miami vs. Dallas, 1972
1 In many games
Most touchdowns, both teams, game
9 Pittsburgh (5) vs. Dallas (4), 1979
San Francisco (8) vs. Denver (1), 1990
Dallas (7) vs. Buffalo (2), 1993
7 N.Y. Giants (5) vs. Denver (2), 1987
Washington (6) vs. Denver (1), 1988
Fewest touchdowns, both teams, game
2 Baltimore (1) vs. N.Y. Jets (1), 1969
3 In six games

POINTS AFTER TOUCHDOWN
Most points after touchdown, game
7 San Francisco vs. Denver, 1990
Dallas vs. Buffalo, 1993
6 Washington vs. Denver, 1988
Most points after touchdown, both teams, game
9 Pittsburgh (5) vs. Dallas (4), 1979
Dallas (7) vs. Buffalo (2), 1993
8 San Francisco (7) vs. Denver (1), 1990
Fewest points after touchdown, both teams, game
2 Baltimore (1) vs. N.Y. Jets (1), 1969
Baltimore (1) vs. Dallas (1), 1971
Minnesota (0) vs. Pittsburgh (2), 1975

FIELD GOALS
Most field goals attempted, game
5 N.Y. Jets vs. Baltimore, 1969
Dallas vs. Denver, 1978
4 Green Bay vs. Oakland, 1968
Pittsburgh vs. Dallas, 1976
San Francisco vs. Cincinnati, 1982
Denver vs. N.Y. Giants, 1987
San Francisco vs. Cincinnati, 1989
Most field goals attempted, both teams, game
7 N.Y. Jets (5) vs Baltimore (2), 1969
San Francisco (4) vs. Cincinnati (3), 1989
6 Dallas (5) vs. Denver (1), 1978
Fewest field goals attempted, both teams, game
1 Minnesota (0) vs. Miami (1), 1974
San Francisco (0) vs. Denver (1), 1990
2 Green Bay (0) vs. Kansas City (2), 1967
Miami (1) vs. Washington (1), 1973
Dallas (1) vs. Pittsburgh (1), 1979
Dallas (1) vs. Buffalo (1), 1993
Most field goals, game
4 Green Bay vs. Oakland, 1968
San Francisco vs. Cincinnati, 1982
3 N.Y. Jets vs. Baltimore, 1969
Kansas City vs. Minnesota, 1970
Miami vs. San Francisco, 1985
Chicago vs. New England, 1986
Cincinnati vs. San Francisco, 1989
Most field goals, both teams, game
5 Cincinnati (3) vs. San Francisco (2), 1989
Dallas (3) vs. Buffalo (2), 1994
4 Green Bay (4) vs. Oakland (0), 1968
San Francisco (4) vs. Cincinnati (0), 1982
Miami (3) vs. San Francisco (1), 1985
Chicago (3) vs. New England (1), 1986
N.Y. Giants (2) vs. Buffalo (2), 1991
Fewest field goals, both teams, game
0 Miami vs. Washington, 1973
Pittsburgh vs. Minnesota, 1975
1 Green Bay (0) vs. Kansas City (1), 1967
Minnesota (0) vs. Miami (1), 1974
Pittsburgh (0) vs. Dallas (1), 1979
Washington (0) vs. Denver (1), 1988
San Francisco (0) vs. Denver (1), 1990

PRO FOOTBALL WEEKLY 1994 ALMANAC

CHRONOLOGICAL LEADERS

SCORING

RECORD HOLDER	PTS	YEAR(S)
Career		
Paddy Driscoll, Cardinals, Bears	418	1920-29
Don Hutson, Packers	823	1935-45
Bobby Walston, Eagles	881	1951-62
Lou Groza, Browns	1,349	1950-67
George Blanda, Bears, others	2,002	1949-75
Season		
Paddy Driscoll, Bears	89	1926
Don Hutson, Packers	95	1941
Don Hutson, Packers	138	1942
Paul Hornung, Packers	176	1960

FIELD GOALS

RECORD HOLDER	FG'S	YEAR(S)
Career		
Jack Manders, Bears	40	1933-40
Bob Waterfield, Rams	60	1945-52
Gordy Soltau, 49ers	70	1950-58
Lou Groza, Browns	234	1950-67
George Blanda, Bears, others	335	1949-75
Jan Stenerud, Chiefs, others	373	1967-85
Season		
Jack Manders, Bears	10	1934
Lou Groza, Browns	13	1950
Bob Waterfield, Rams	13	1950
Lou Groza, Browns	19	1952
Lou Groza, Browns	23	1953
Gene Mingo, Broncos	27	1962
Pete Gogolak, Bills	28	1965
Bruce Gossett, Rams	28	1966
Jim Turner, Jets	34	1968
Ali Haji-Sheikh, Giants	35	1983

EXTRA POINTS

RECORD HOLDER	PAT'S	YEAR(S)
Career		
Bob Waterfield, Rams	315	1945-52
Sam Baker, Eagles, others	428	1953-69
Lou Groza, Browns	641	1950-67
George Blanda, Bears, others	943	1949-75
Season		
Benny Friedman, Giants	20	1929
Jack Manders, Bears	31	1934
Don Hutson, Packers	33	1942
Bob Snyder, Bears	39	1943
Pat Harder, Cardinals	53	1948
Bob Waterfield, Rams	54	1950
George Blanda, Oilers	64	1961
Uwe von Schamann, Dolphins	66	1984

RUSHING YARDAGE

RECORD HOLDER	YDS	YEAR(S)
Career		
Cliff Battles, Redskins	3,613	1932-37
Clarke Hinkle, Packers	3,850	1932-41
Steve Van Buren, Eagles	5,850	1944-51
Joe Perry, 49ers	9,723	1948-63
Jim Brown, Browns	12,312	1957-65
Walter Payton, Bears	16,726	1975-87
Season		
Cliff Battles, Boston Braves	576	1932
Jim Musick, Redskins	809	1933
Beattie Feathers, Bears	1,004	1934
Steve Van Buren, Eagles	1,008	1947
Steve Van Buren, Eagles	1,146	1949
Jim Brown, Browns	1,527	1958
Jim Brown, Browns	1,863	1963
O.J. Simpson, Bills	2,003	1973
Eric Dickerson, Rams	2,105	1984

RUSHING TOUCHDOWNS

RECORD HOLDER	TD'S	YEAR(S)
Career		
Ernie Nevers, Cardinals, others	37	1926-27 1929-31
Vern Lewellen, Packers	40	1924-32
Steve Van Buren, Eagles	69	1944-51
Joe Perry, 49ers*	71	1948-63
Jim Brown, Browns	106	1957-65
Walter Payton, Bears	110	1975-87
Season		
Ernie Nevers, Cardinals	12	1929
Steve Van Buren, Eagles	15	1945
Jim Brown, Browns	17	1958
Jim Taylor, Packers	19	1962
John Riggins, Redskins	24	1983

PASSING YARDAGE

RECORD HOLDER	YDS	YEAR(S)
Career		
Arnie Herber, Packers	7,943	1932-40
Sammy Baugh, Redskins	21,866	1937-52
Norm Van Brocklin, Rams, Eagles	23,611	1949-60
Bobby Layne, Lions, others	26,768	1948-62
Y.A. Tittle, 49ers, Giants	33,070	1948-64
Johnny Unitas, Colts, Chargers	40,239	1956-73
Fran Tarkenton, Vikings, Giants	47,003	1961-78
Season		
Arnie Herber, Packers	639	1932
Harry Newman, Giants	963	1933
Arnie Herber, Packers	1,239	1936
Davey O'Brien, Eagles	1,324	1939
Sammy Baugh, Redskins	1,367	1940
Cecil Isbell, Packers	1,479	1941
Cecil Isbell, Packers	2,021	1942
Sid Luckman, Bears	2,194	1943
Sammy Baugh, Redskins	2,938	1947
Johnny Unitas, Colts	3,099	1960
Sonny Jurgensen, Eagles	3,723	1961
Joe Namath, Jets	4,007	1967
Dan Fouts, Chargers	4,082	1979
Dan Fouts, Chargers	4,715	1980
Dan Fouts, Chargers	4,802	1981
Dan Marino, Dolphins	5,084	1984

PASSING COMPLETIONS

RECORD HOLDER	NO	YEAR(S)
Career		
Arnie Herber, Packers*	410	1932-40
Sammy Baugh, Redskins	1,693	1937-52
Bobby Layne, Lions, others	1,814	1948-62
Y.A. Tittle, 49ers, Giants	2,427	1948-64
Johnny Unitas, Colts, Chargers	2,830	1956-73
Fran Tarkenton, Vikings, Giants	3,686	1961-78

418

RECORDS ■ CHRONOLOGICAL

Season

Harry Newman, Giants	53	1933
Ed Danowski, Giants	57	1935
Arnie Herber, Packers	77	1936
Sammy Baugh, Redskins	81	1937
Parker Hall, Cleveland Rams	106	1939
Davey O'Brien, Eagles	124	1940
Cecil Isbell, Packers	146	1942
Sammy Baugh, Redskins	210	1947
Frank Tripucka, Broncos	248	1960
George Blanda, Oilers	262	1964
Sonny Jurgensen, Redskins	288	1967
Fran Tarkenton, Vikings	345	1978
Steve DeBerg, 49ers	347	1979
Dan Fouts, Chargers	348	1980
Dan Fouts, Chargers	360	1981
Dan Marino, Dolphins	362	1984
Dan Marino, Dolphins	378	1986
Warren Moon, Oilers	404	1991

PASSING TOUCHDOWNS

RECORD HOLDER	TD'S	YEAR(S)
Career		
Arnie Herber, Packers*	51	1932-40
Cecil Isbell, Packers*	59	1938-42
Sammy Baugh, Redskins	186	1937-52
Bobby Layne, Lions, others	196	1948-62
Y.A. Tittle, 49ers, Giants	242	1948-64
Johnny Unitas, Colts, Chargers	290	1956-73
Fran Tarkenton, Vikings, Giants	342	1961-78
Season		
Benny Friedman, Giants	19	1929
Cecil Isbell, Packers	24	1942
Sid Luckman, Bears	28	1943
Johnny Unitas, Colts	32	1959
George Blanda, Oilers	36	1961
Y.A. Tittle, Giants	36	1963
Dan Marino, Dolphins	48	1984

RECEIVING YARDAGE

RECORD HOLDER	YDS	YEAR(S)
Career		
Johnny Blood (McNally), Packers	2,755	1925-39
Don Hutson, Packers	7,991	1935-45
Billy Howton, Packers, others	8,459	1952-63
Raymond Berry, Colts	9,275	1955-67
Dan Maynard, Jets, others	11,834	1958-73
Charlie Joiner, Chargers, others	12,146	1969-86
Steve Largent, Seahawks	13,089	1976-89
James Lofton, Packers, others	14,004	1978-93
Season		
Paul Moss, Steelers	383	1933
Charley Malone, Redskins	433	1935
Don Hutson, Packers	526	1936
Gaynell Tinsley, Cardinals	675	1937
Don Hutson, Packers	846	1939
Don Hutson, Packers	1,211	1942
Elroy Hirsch, Rams	1,495	1951
Charley Hennigan, Oilers	1,746	1961

RECEPTIONS

RECORD HOLDER	NO	YEAR(S)
Career		
Johnny Blood (McNally), Packers	135	1925-39
Don Hutson, Packers	489	1935-45
Billy Howton, Packers, others	503	1952-63
Raymond Berry, Colts	631	1955-67
Don Maynard, Jets, others	633	1958-73
Charlie Taylor, Redskins	649	1964-77
Charlie Joiner, Chargers, others	750	1969-86

Steve Largent, Seahawks	819	1976-89
Art Monk, Redskins	888	1980-93

Season

Ray Flaherty, Giants	12	1932
Shipwreck Kelly, Brooklyn Dodgers	22	1933
Tod Goodwin, Giants	26	1935
Don Hutson, Packers	34	1936
Don Hutson, Packers	41	1937
Don Looney, Eagles	58	1940
Don Hutson, Packers	58	1941
Don Hutson, Packers	74	1942
Tom Fears, Rams	77	1949
Tom Fears, Rams	84	1950
Lionel Taylor, Broncos	92	1960
Lionel Taylor, Broncos	100	1961
Charley Hennigan, Oilers	101	1964
Art Monk, Redskins	106	1984
Sterling Sharpe, Packers	108	1992
Sterling Sharpe, Packers	112	1993

RECEIVING TOUCHDOWNS

RECORD HOLDER	TD'S	YEAR(S)
Career		
Don Hutson, Packers	99	1935-45
Steve Largent, Seahawks	100	1976-89
Jerry Rice, 49ers	118	1985-93
Season		
Bill Hewitt, Bears	5	1934
Don Hutson, Packers	7	1935
Don Hutson, Packers	9	1938
Don Hutson, Packers	10	1941
Don Hutson, Packers	17	1942
Elroy Hirsch, Rams	17	1951
Bill Groman, Oilers	17	1961
Mark Clayton, Dolphins	18	1984
Jerry Rice, 49ers	22	1987

INTERCEPTIONS

RECORD HOLDER	NO	YEAR(S)
Career		
Johnny Blood (McNally), Packers, others	31	1925-39
Irv Comp, Packers	33	1943-49
Frank Reagan, Giants, Eagles	35	1941-51
Don Doll, Lions, others	41	1949-54
Jack Christiansen, Lions	46	1951-58
Jack Butler, Steelers	52	1951-59
Bobby Dillon, Packers	52	1952-59
Emlen Tunnell, Giants, Packers	79	1948-61
Paul Krause, Vikings, Redskins	81	1964-79
Season		
Don Hutson, Packers	6	1940
Marshall Goldberg, Cardinals	7	1941
Art Jones, Steelers	7	1941
Bulldog Turner, Bears	8	1942
Sammy Baugh, Redskins	11	1943
Dan Sandifer, Redskins	13	1948
Spec Sanders. N.Y. Yankees	13	1950
Dick "Night Train" Lane, Rams	14	1952

* still active when his record was broken

NFL records did not become official until 1933.

RECORDS
TOP 20 LISTS

PRO FOOTBALL WEEKLY 1994 ALMANAC

POINTS SCORED

PLAYER	YRS	TD	FG	PAT	TOTAL
George Blanda	26	9	335	943	2,002
Jan Stenerud	19	0	373	580	1,699
Nick Lowery	15	0	329	486	1,473
Pat Leahy	18	0	304	558	1,470
Jim Turner	16	1	304	521	1,439
Mark Moseley	16	0	300	482	1,382
Jim Bakken	17	0	282	534	1,380
Fred Cox	15	0	282	519	1,365
Lou Groza	17	1	234	641	1,349
Eddie Murray	13	0	272	419	1,225
Chris Bahr	14	0	241	490	1,213
Jim Breech	13	0	224	486	1,158
Gary Anderson	10	0	257	355	1,147
Matt Bahr	14	0	234	430	1,132
Gino Cappelletti*	11	42	176	350	1,130
Ray Wersching	15	0	222	456	1,122
Don Cockroft	13	0	216	432	1,080
Garo Yepremian	14	0	210	444	1,074
Bruce Gossett	11	0	219	374	1,031
Sam Baker	15	2	179	428	977

*Cappelletti's total includes four two-point conversions

TOUCHDOWNS

PLAYER	YRS	RUSH	REC	RET	TOTAL
Jim Brown	9	106	20	0	126
Walter Payton	13	110	15	0	125
Jerry Rice	9	6	118	0	124
John Riggins	14	104	12	0	116
Lenny Moore	12	63	48	2	113
Marcus Allen	12	91	21	1	113
Don Hutson	11	3	99	3	105
Steve Largent	14	1	100	0	101
Franco Harris	13	91	9	0	100
Eric Dickerson	10	90	6	0	96
Jim Taylor	10	83	10	0	93
Tony Dorsett	12	77	13	1	91
Bobby Mitchell	11	18	65	8	91
Leroy Kelly	10	74	13	3	90
Charley Taylor	13	11	79	0	90
Don Maynard	15	0	88	0	88
Lance Alworth	11	2	85	0	87
Ottis Anderson	14	81	5	0	86
Paul Warfield	13	1	85	0	86
Tommy McDonald	12	0	84	1	85

RUSHING YARDAGE

PLAYER	YRS	ATT	YARDS	AVG	LG	TOTAL
Walter Payton	13	3,838	16,726	4.4	76	110
Eric Dickerson	10	2,970	13,168	4.4	85	90
Tony Dorsett	12	2,936	12,739	4.3	99	77
Jim Brown	9	2,359	12,312	5.2	80	106
Franco Harris	13	2,949	12,120	4.1	75	91
John Riggins	14	2,916	11,352	3.9	66	104
O.J. Simpson	11	2,404	11,236	4.7	94	61
Ottis Anderson	14	2,562	10,273	4.0	76	81
Earl Campbell	8	2,187	9,407	4.3	81	74
Marcus Allen	12	2,296	9,309	4.1	61	91
Jim Taylor	10	1,941	8,597	4.4	84	83
Joe Perry	14	1,737	8,378	4.8	78	53
Roger Craig	10	1,991	8,189	4.1	71	56
Gerald Riggs	10	1,989	8,188	4.1	58	69
Larry Csonka	11	1,891	8,081	4.3	54	64
Freeman McNeil	12	1,798	8,074	4.5	69	38
James Brooks	12	1,685	7,962	4.7	65	49
Mike Pruitt	11	1,844	7,378	4.0	77	51
Leroy Kelly	10	1,727	7,274	4.2	70	74
George Rogers	7	1,692	7,176	4.2	79	54

RUSHING TOUCHDOWNS

PLAYER	YEARS	TD
Walter Payton	14	110
Jimmy Brown	9	106
John Riggins	14	104
Franco Harris	13	91
Marcus Allen	12	91
Eric Dickerson	11	90
Jim Taylor	10	83
Ottis Anderson	14	81
Tony Dorsett	12	77
Pete Johnson	8	76
Leroy Kelly	10	74
Earl Campbell	8	74
Joe Perry	6	71
Chuck Muncie	9	71
Steve Van Buren	8	69
Gerald Riggs	10	69
Larry Csonka	11	64
Lenny Moore	12	63
O.J. Simpson	11	61
Curt Warner	8	56
Roger Craig	11	56

RECEPTIONS

PLAYER	YRS	REC	YARDS	AVG	LG	TD
Art Monk	14	888	12,026	13.5	79	65
Steve Largent	14	819	13,089	16.0	74	100
James Lofton	15	764	13,988	18.3	80	75
Charlie Joiner	18	750	12,146	16.2	87	65
Jerry Rice	9	708	11,776	16.6	96	118
Ozzie Newsome	13	662	7,980	12.1	74	47
Charley Taylor	13	649	9,110	14.0	88	79
Drew Hill	15	634	9,831	15.5	81	60
Don Maynard	15	633	11,834	18.7	87	88
Raymond Berry	13	631	9,275	14.7	70	68
Gary Clark	9	612	9,560	15.6	84	62
Harold Carmichael	14	590	8,985	15.2	85	79
Fred Biletnikoff	14	589	8,974	15.2	82	76
Mark Clayton	11	582	8,974	15.4	78	84
Harold Jackson	16	579	10,372	17.9	79	76
Lionel Taylor	10	567	7,195	12.7	80	45
Roger Craig	11	566	4,911	8.7	73	17
Wes Chandler	11	559	8,966	16.0	85	56
Roy Green	14	559	8,965	16.0	83	66
Stanley Morgan	14	557	10,716	19.2	76	72

RECEIVING TOUCHDOWNS

PLAYER	YEARS	TD
Jerry Rice	9	118
Don Hutson	11	100
Steve Largent	14	100
Don Maynard	15	88
Lance Alworth	11	85
Paul Warfield	13	85
Tommy McDonald	12	84
Art Powell	10	81
Mark Clayton	11	81
Charley Taylor	13	79
Harold Carmichael	14	79
Fred Biletnikoff	14	76
Harold Jackson	16	76
James Lofton	16	75
Nat Moore	13	74
Stanley Morgan	14	72
Bob Hayes	11	71
Wesley Walker	13	71
Gary Collins	10	70
Raymond Berry	13	68

RECORDS ■ TOP 20 LISTS

RECEIVING YARDAGE
PLAYER	YEARS	REC	YARDS
James Lofton	16	764	13,988
Steve Largent	14	819	13,089
Charlie Joiner	18	750	12,146
Art Monk	14	888	12,026
Don Maynard	15	633	11,834
Jerry Rice	8	708	11,776
Stanley Morgan	14	557	10,716
Harold Jackson	16	579	10,372
Lance Alworth	11	542	10,266
Drew Hill	15	634	9,831
Henry Ellard	11	593	9,761
Gary Clark	9	612	9,560
Raymond Berry	13	631	9,275
Charley Taylor	13	649	9,110
Harold Carmichael	14	590	8,985
Fred Biletnikoff	14	589	8,974
Mark Clayton	11	582	8,974
Wes Chandler	11	559	8,966
Roy Green	15	559	8,965
Mark Duper	12	511	8,869

PUNT-RETURN AVERAGE
PLAYER	YRS	NO	YARDS	AVG	LG	TD
George McAfee	8	112	1,431	12.8	74	2
Jack Christiansen	8	85	1,084	12.8	89	8
Claude Gibson	5	110	1,381	12.6	85	3
Bill Dudley	9	124	1,515	12.2	96	3
Rick Upchurch	9	248	3,008	12.1	92	8
Billy Johnson	14	282	3,317	11.8	87	6
Mack Herron	3	84	982	11.7	66	0
Billy Thompson	13	157	1,814	11.6	60	0
Mel Gray	8	160	1,851	11.6	80	3
Henry Ellard	10	135	1,527	11.3	83	4
Rodger Bird	3	94	1,063	11.3	78	0
Bosh Pritchard	6	85	1,072	11.3	81	2
Bobby Joe Edmonds	4	105	1,178	11.2	75	1
Terry Metcalf	6	84	936	11.1	69	1
Bob Hayes	11	104	1,158	11.1	90	3
Floyd Little	9	81	893	11.0	72	2
Louis Lipps	9	112	1,234	11.0	76	3
Vai Sikahema	8	292	3,169	10.9	87	4
Dave Meggett	5	176	1,907	10.8	76	4
Brian Mitchell	4	115	1,171	10.2	84	3

INTERCEPTIONS
PLAYER	YRS	NO	YARDS	AVG	LG	TD
Paul Krause	16	81	1,185	14.6	81	3
Emlen Tunnell	14	79	1,282	16.2	55	4
Dick (Night Train) Lane	14	68	1,207	17.8	80	5
Ronnie Lott	13	63	730	11.6	83	5
Ken Riley	16	65	596	9.2	66	5
Dick LeBeau	13	62	762	12.3	70	3
Dave Brown	15	62	698	11.3	90	5
Emmitt Thomas	13	58	937	16.2	73	5
Bobby Boyd	9	57	994	17.4	74	4
Johnny Robinson	12	57	741	13.0	57	1
Mel Blount	14	57	736	12.9	52	2
Everson Walls	13	57	504	8.8	40	1
Lem Barney	11	56	1,077	19.2	71	7
Pat Fischer	17	56	941	16.8	69	4
Willie Brown	16	54	472	8.7	45	2
Bobby Dillon	8	52	976	18.8	61	5
Jack Butler	9	52	826	15.9	52	4
Larry Wilson	13	52	800	15.4	96	5
Jim Patton	12	52	712	13.7	51	2
Mel Renfro	14	52	626	12.0	90	3

KICKOFF-RETURN AVERAGE
PLAYER	YRS	NO	YARDS	AVG	LG	TD
Gale Sayers	7	91	2,781	30.6	103	6
Lynn Chandnois	7	92	2,720	29.6	93	3
Abe Woodson	9	193	5,538	28.7	105	5
Claude "Buddy" Young	6	90	2,514	27.9	104	2
Travis Williams	5	102	2,801	27.5	105	6
Joe Arenas	7	139	3,798	27.3	96	1
Clarence Davis	8	79	2,140	27.1	76	0
Steve Van Buren	8	76	2,030	26.7	98	3
Lenny Lyles	12	81	2,161	26.7	103	3
Mercury Morris	8	111	2,947	26.5	105	3
Bobby Jancik	6	158	4,185	26.5	61	0
Mel Renfro	14	85	2,246	26.4	100	2
Bobby Mitchell	11	102	2,690	26.4	98	5
Ollie Matson	14	143	3,746	26.2	105	6
Alvin Haymond	10	170	4,438	26.1	98	2
Noland Smith	3	82	2,137	26.1	106	1
Al Nelson	9	101	2,625	26.0	70	0
Tim Brown	10	184	4,781	26.0	105	5
Vic Washington	6	129	3,341	25.9	98	1
Dave Hampton	8	113	2,923	25.9	101	3

GROSS PUNTING AVERAGE
PLAYER	YRS	NO	YARDS	AVG	LG	BLK
Sammy Baugh	16	338	15,245	45.1	85	9
Tommy Davis	11	511	22,833	44.7	82	2
Yale Lary	11	503	22,279	44.3	74	4
Rohn Stark	12	912	40,070	43.9	72	6
Horace Gillom	7	385	16,872	43.8	80	5
Jerry Norton	11	358	15,671	43.8	78	2
Don Chandler	12	660	28,678	43.5	90	4
Sean Landeta	9	568	24,631	43.4	71	4
Reggie Roby	11	633	27,483	43.4	77	3
Jerrel Wilson	16	1,072	46,139	43.0	72	12
Norm Van Brocklin	12	523	22,413	42.9	72	3
Rich Camarillo	13	854	36,615	42.9	76	5
Danny Villanueva	8	488	20,862	42.8	68	2
Tommy Barnhardt	7	387	16,562	42.8	65	2
Bobby Joe Green	14	970	41,317	42.6	75	3
Sam Baker	15	703	29,938	42.6	72	2
Ralf Mojsiejenko	7	413	17,533	42.5	74	5
Harry Newsome	9	683	29,032	42.5	84	14
Bob Waterfield	8	315	13,367	42.4	88	5
Ray Guy	14	1,049	44,493	42.4	74	3

FIELD-GOAL PERCENTAGE
PLAYER	YEARS	FG	FGA	PCT
Nick Lowery	16	329	411	80.05
Pete Stoyanovich	5	125	157	79.62
David Treadwell	5	124	158	79.48
Chris Jacke	5	116	148	78.38
Gary Anderson	12	285	364	78.30
Morten Andersen	12	274	350	78.29
Donald Igwebuike	6	108	143	75.52
Eddie Murray	14	277	367	75.48
Norm Johnson	12	222	300	74.00
Tony Zendejas	9	165	223	73.99
Raul Allegre	9	137	186	73.66
Paul McFadden	6	120	163	73.62
Fuad Reveiz	8	128	175	73.14
Kevin Butler	9	199	273	72.89
Mike Lansford	9	158	217	72.81
Chip Lohmiller	6	155	217	72.43
Roger Ruzek	7	120	166	72.29
Scott Norwood	7	133	184	72.28
Rich Karlis	9	172	239	71.96
Matt Bahr	15	250	348	71.84

… PRO FOOTBALL WEEKLY 1994 ALMANAC

COMBINED YARDS

PLAYER	YRS	TOTAL	RUSH	REC	INT RET	PUNT RET	KO RET	FUM RET
Walter Payton	13	21,803	16,726	4,538	0	0	539	0
Tony Dorsett	12	16,326	12,739	3,554	0	0	0	33
Jim Brown	9	15,459	12,312	2,499	0	0	648	0
Eric Dickerson	10	15,262	13,168	2,079	0	0	0	15
James Brooks	12	14,910	7,962	3,621	0	565	2,762	0
Franco Harris	13	14,622	12,120	2,287	0	0	233	-18
O.J. Simpson	11	14,368	11,236	2,142	0	0	990	0
James Lofton	16	14,261	246	13,988	0	0	0	27
Bobby Mitchell	11	14,078	2,735	7,954	0	699	2,960	0
Marcus Allen	12	13,799	9,309	4,496	0	0	0	-6
John Riggins	14	13,435	11,352	2,090	0	0	0	-7
Steve Largent	14	13,396	83	13,089	0	68	156	0
Ottis Anderson	14	13,364	10,273	3,062	0	0	0	29
Greg Pruitt	12	13,262	5,672	3,069	0	2,007	2,514	0
Roger Craig	11	13,232	8,189	4,911	0	0	32	0
Drew Hill	13	12,953	19	9,447	0	22	3,460	5
Ollie Matson	14	12,884	5,173	3,285	51	595	3,746	34
Timmy Brown	10	12,684	3,862	3,399	0	639	4,781	3
Lenny Moore	12	12,451	5,174	6,039	0	56	1,180	2
Don Maynard	15	12,379	70	11,834	0	132	343	0

PASSER RATING

PLAYER	YEARS	ATT.	COMP.	PCT COMP.	YARDS	TD	TD PCT.	INT	INT PCT	AVG GAIN	PASS RATING
Steve Young	9	1,968	1,222	62.1	15,900	105	5.3	58	2.9	8.08	93.1
Joe Montana	14	4,898	3,110	63.5	37,268	257	5.2	130	2.7	7.61	92.7
Dan Marino	11	5,434	3,219	59.2	40,720	298	5.9	168	3.1	7.49	88.1
Jim Kelly	8	3,494	2,112	60.4	26,413	179	5.1	126	3.6	7.56	85.9
Roger Staubach	11	2,958	1,685	57.0	22,700	153	5.2	109	3.7	7.67	83.4
Neil Lomax	8	3,153	1,817	57.6	22,771	136	4.3	90	2.9	7.22	82.7
Sonny Jurgensen	18	4,262	2,433	57.1	32,224	255	6.0	189	4.4	7.56	82.6
Len Dawson	19	3,741	2,136	57.1	28,711	239	6.4	183	4.9	7.67	82.6
Boomer Esiason	10	3,851	2,185	56.7	29,092	190	4.9	140	3.6	7.55	82.1
Dave Krieg	14	4,178	2,431	58.2	30,485	217	5.2	163	3.9	7.30	82.1
Ken Anderson	16	4,475	2,654	59.3	32,838	197	4.4	160	3.6	7.34	81.9
Bernie Kosar	9	3,213	1,889	58.8	22,314	119	3.7	81	2.5	6.94	81.9
Danny White	13	2,950	1,761	59.7	21,959	155	5.3	132	4.5	7.44	81.7
Ken O'Brien	10	3,602	2,110	58.6	25,094	128	3.6	98	2.7	6.97	80.7
Bart Starr	16	3,149	1,808	57.4	24,718	152	4.8	138	4.4	7.85	80.5
Fran Tarkenton	18	6,467	3,686	57.0	47,003	342	5.3	266	4.1	7.27	80.4
Mark Rypien	6	2,207	1,244	56.4	15,928	101	4.6	75	3.4	7.22	80.3
Randall Cunningham	9	2,751	1,540	56.0	19,043	131	4.8	87	3.2	6.92	80.3
Dan Fouts	15	5,604	3,297	58.8	43,040	254	4.5	242	4.3	7.68	80.2
Warren Moon	10	4,546	2,632	57.9	33,685	196	4.3	166	3.7	7.41	80.1

PASSING YARDS

PLAYER	YEARS	YDS
Fran Tarkenton	18	47,003
Dan Fouts	15	43,040
Dan Marino	11	40,720
Johnny Unitas	18	40,239
Joe Montana	14	37,268
Jim Hart	19	34,665
John Elway	11	34,246
Steve DeBerg	16	33,872
Warren Moon	10	33,685
John Hadl	16	33,513
Phil Simms	15	33,462
Y.A. Tittle	17	33,070
Ken Anderson	14	32,838
Sonny Jurgensen	18	32,224
John Brodie	17	31,548
Norm Snead	16	30,797
Dave Krieg	14	30,485
Joe Ferguson	17	29,816
Roman Gabriel	16	29,444
Len Dawson	19	28,711

PASSING TOUCHDOWNS

PLAYER	YEARS	YDS
Fran Tarkenton	18	342
Dan Marino	11	298
Johnny Unitas	18	290
Joe Montana	14	257
Sonny Jurgensen	18	255
Dan Fouts	15	254
John Hadl	16	244
Y.A. Tittle	17	242
Len Dawson	19	239
George Blanda	26	236
Dave Krieg	14	217
John Brodie	17	214
Terry Bradshaw	14	212
Jim Hart	19	209
Roman Gabriel	16	201
Ken Anderson	14	197
Bobby Layne	15	196
Joe Ferguson	17	196
Norm Snead	16	196
Ken Stabler	15	194

RECORDS ■ COACHING

COACHING

ACTIVE COACHES' CAREER RECORDS

			REG SEASON				POSTSEASON				CAREER			
COACH	TEAM(S)	YRS	W	L	T	PCT	W	L	T	PCT	W	L	T	PCT
Don Shula	Baltimore, Miami	31	309	143	6	.681	18	15	0	.545	327	158	6	.672
Chuck Knox	L.A. Rams, Buffalo, Seattle, L.A. Rams	21	182	135	1	.574	7	11	0	.389	189	146	1	.564
Dan Reeves	Denver, N.Y. Giants	13	121	78	1	.608	8	7	0	.533	129	85	1	.602
Marv Wyche	Kansas City, Buffalo	13	110	81	0	.576	10	6	0	.625	120	87	0	.580
Marty Schottenheimer	Cleveland, Kansas City	10	94	56	1	.626	5	8	0	.385	99	64	1	.607
Tom Flores	Oakland-L.A. Raiders, Seattle	11	91	77	0	.542	8	3	0	.727	99	80	0	.553
Bill Parcells	N.Y. Giants, New England	9	82	60	1	.577	8	3	0	.727	90	63	1	.588
Jack Pardee	Chicago, Washington, Houston	10	86	68	0	.558	1	5	0	.167	87	73	0	.544
Jim Mora	New Orleans	8	77	50	0	.606	0	4	0	.000	77	54	0	.588
Sam Wyche	Cincinnati, Tampa Bay	10	71	88	0	.447	3	2	0	.600	74	90	0	.451
George Seifert	San Francisco	5	62	18	0	.775	6	3	0	.667	68	21	0	.764
Ted Marchibroda	Baltimore, Indianapolis	7	54	52	0	.509	0	3	0	.000	54	55	0	.495
Jimmy Johnson	Dallas	5	44	36	0	.550	7	1	0	.875	51	37	0	.580
Art Shell	L.A. Raiders	5	45	31	0	.592	2	3	0	.400	47	34	0	.580
Buddy Ryan	Philadelphia, Arizona	5	43	35	1	.551	0	3	0	.000	43	38	1	.526
Wayne Fontes	Detroit	5	42	43	0	.494	1	2	0	.333	43	45	0	.489
Rich Kotite	Philadelphia	3	29	19	0	.604	1	1	0	.500	30	20	0	.600
Bill Belichick	Cleveland	3	20	28	0	.417	0	0	0	.000	20	28	0	.417
Bobby Ross	San Diego	2	19	13	0	.594	1	1	0	.500	20	14	0	.588
Bill Cowher	Pittsburgh	2	20	12	0	.625	0	2	0	.000	20	14	0	.588
Dennis Green	Minnesota	2	20	12	0	.625	0	2	0	.000	20	14	0	.588
Mike Holmgren	Green Bay	2	18	14	0	.563	1	1	0	.500	19	15	0	.559
Wade Phillips	New Orleans, Denver	2	10	10	0	.500	0	1	0	.000	10	11	0	.476
Dave Shula	Cincinnati	2	8	24	0	.250	0	0	0	.000	8	24	0	.250
Dave Wannstedt	Chicago	1	7	9	0	.438	0	0	0	.000	7	9	0	.438
Pete Carroll	N.Y. Jets	0	0	0	0	.000	0	0	0	.000	0	0	0	.000
June Jones	Atlanta	0	0	0	0	.000	0	0	0	.000	0	0	0	.000
Norv Turner	Washington	0	0	0	0	.000	0	0	0	.000	0	0	0	.000

COACHES WITH 100 CAREER VICTORIES

			REG SEASON				POSTSEASON				CAREER			
COACH	TEAM(S)	YRS	W	L	T	PCT	W	L	T	PCT	W	L	T	PCT
Don Shula	Baltimore, Miami	31	309	143	6	.681	18	15	0	.545	327	158	6	.672
George Halas	Chicago	40	318	148	31	.671	6	3	0	.667	324	151	31	.671
Tom Landry	Dallas	29	250	162	6	.605	20	16	0	.556	270	178	6	.601
Curly Lambeau	Green Bay, Chicago Cardinals, Washington	33	226	132	22	.624	3	2	0	.600	229	134	22	.623
Chuck Noll	Pittsburgh	23	193	148	1	.566	16	8	0	.667	209	156	1	.572
Chuck Knox	L.A. Rams, Buffalo, Seattle, L.A. Rams	21	182	135	1	.574	7	11	0	.389	189	146	1	.564
Paul Brown	Cleveland, Cincinnati	21	166	100	6	.621	4	8	0	.333	170	108	6	.609
Bud Grant	Minnesota	18	158	96	5	.620	10	12	0	.455	168	108	5	.607
Steve Owen	N.Y. Giants	23	151	100	17	.595	2	8	0	.200	153	108	17	.581
Joe Gibbs	Washington	12	124	60	0	.674	16	5	0	.762	140	65	0	.683
Hank Stram	Kansas City, New Orleans	17	131	97	10	.571	5	3	0	.625	136	100	10	.573
Weeb Ewbank	Baltimore, N.Y. Jets	20	130	129	7	.502	4	1	0	.800	134	130	7	.507
Dan Reeves	Denver, N.Y. Giants	13	121	78	1	.608	8	7	0	.533	129	85	1	.602
Sid Gillman	L.A. Rams, L.A.-San Diego, Houston	18	122	99	7	.550	1	5	0	.167	123	104	7	.541
Marv Levy	Kansas City, Buffalo	13	110	81	0	.576	10	6	0	.625	120	87	0	.580
George Allen	L.A. Rams, Washington	12	116	47	5	.705	2	7	0	.222	118	54	5	.681
Don Coryell	St. Louis, San Diego	14	111	83	1	.572	3	6	0	.333	114	89	1	.561
Mike Ditka	Chicago	11	106	62	0	.631	6	6	0	.500	112	68	0	.622
John Madden	Oakland	10	103	32	7	.750	9	7	0	.563	112	39	7	.731
Buddy Parker	Chicago Cardinals, Detroit, Pittsburgh	15	104	75	9	.577	3	1	0	.750	107	76	9	.581
Vince Lombardi	Green Bay, Washington	10	96	34	6	.728	9	1	0	.900	105	35	6	.740
Bill Walsh	San Francisco	10	92	59	1	.609	10	4	0	.714	102	63	1	.617

ANNUAL LEADERS

SCORERS

Year	Player, team	TD	FG	PAT	PTS
1932	Dutch Clark, Portsmouth	6	3	10	55
1933	Ken Strong, N.Y. Giants	6	5	13	64
	Glenn Presnell, Portsmouth	6	6	10	64
1934	Jack Manders, Chicago Bears	3	10	31	79
1935	Dutch Clark, Detroit	6	1	16	55
1936	Dutch Clark, Detroit	7	4	19	73
1937	Jack Manders, Chicago Bears	5	8	15	69
1938	Clarke Hinkle, Green Bay	7	3	7	58
1939	Andy Farkas, Washington	11	0	2	68
1940	Don Hutson, Green Bay	7	0	15	57
1941	Don Hutson, Green Bay	12	1	20	95
1942	Don Hutson, Green Bay	17	1	33	138
1943	Don Hutson, Green Bay	12	3	36	117
1944	Don Hutson, Green Bay	9	0	31	85
1945	Steve Van Buren, Philadelphia	18	0	2	110
1946	Ted Fritsch, Green Bay	10	9	13	100
1947	Pat Harder, Chicago Cardinals	7	7	39	102
1948	Pat Harder, Chicago Cardinals	6	7	53	110
1949	Pat Harder, Chicago Cardinals	8	3	45	102
	Gene Roberts, N.Y. Giants	17	0	0	102
1950	Doak Walker, Detroit	11	8	38	128
1951	Elroy Hirsch, Los Angeles	17	0	0	102
1952	Gordy Soltau, San Francisco	7	6	34	94
1953	Gordy Soltau, San Francisco	6	10	48	114
1954	Bobby Walston, Philadelphia	11	4	36	114
1955	Doak Walker, Detroit	7	9	27	96
1956	Bobby Layne, Detroit	5	12	33	99
1957	Sam Baker, Washington	1	14	29	77
	Lou Groza, Cleveland	0	15	32	77
1958	Jim Brown, Cleveland	18	0	0	108
1959	Paul Hornung, Green Bay	7	7	31	94
1960	Paul Hornung, Green Bay	15	15	41	176
	Gene Mingo, Denver, AFL	6	18	33	123
1961	Gino Cappelletti, Boston, AFL	8	17	48	147
	Paul Hornung, Green Bay	10	15	41	146
1962	Gene Mingo, Denver, AFL	4	27	32	137
	Jim Taylor, Green Bay	19	0	0	114
1963	Gino Cappelletti, Boston, AFL	2	22	35	113
	Don Chandler, N.Y. Giants	0	18	52	106
1964	Gino Cappelletti, Boston, AFL	7	25	36	155
	Lenny Moore, Baltimore	20	0	0	120
1965	Gale Sayers, Chicago	22	0	0	132
	Gino Cappelletti, Boston, AFL	9	17	27	132
1966	Gino Cappelletti, Boston, AFL	6	16	35	119
	Bruce Gossett, Los Angeles	0	28	29	113
1967	Jim Bakken, St. Louis	0	27	36	117
	George Blanda, Oakland, AFL	0	20	56	116
1968	Jim Turner, N.Y. Jets, AFL	0	34	43	145
	Leroy Kelly, Cleveland	20	0	0	120
1969	Jim Turner, N.Y. Jets, AFL	0	32	33	129
	Fred Cox, Minnesota	0	26	43	121
1970	Fred Cox, Minnesota	0	30	35	125
1971	Garo Yepremian, Miami	0	28	33	117
1972	Chester Marcol, Green Bay	0	33	29	128
1973	David Ray, Los Angeles	0	30	40	130
1974	Chester Marcol, Green Bay	0	25	19	94
1975	O.J. Simpson, Buffalo	23	0	0	138
1976	Toni Linhart, Baltimore	0	20	49	109
1977	Errol Mann, Oakland	0	20	39	99
1978	Frank Corral, Los Angeles	0	29	31	118
1979	John Smith, New England	0	23	46	115
1980	John Smith, New England	0	26	51	129

RECORDS ■ ANNUAL

Year	Player, team				
1981	Eddie Murray, Detroit	0	25	46	121
	Rafael Septien, Dallas	0	27	40	121
1982	Marcus Allen, L.A. Raiders	14	0	0	84
1983	Mark Moseley, Washington	0	33	62	161
1984	Ray Wersching, San Francisco	0	25	56	131
1985	Kevin Butler, Chicago	0	31	51	144
1986	Tony Franklin, New England	0	32	44	140
1987	Jerry Rice, San Francisco	23	0	0	138
1988	Scott Norwood, Buffalo	0	32	33	129
1989	Mike Cofer, San Francisco	0	29	49	136
1990	Nick Lowery, Kansas City	0	34	37	139
1991	Chip Lohmiller, Washington	0	31	56	149
1992	Pete Stoyanovich, Miami	0	30	34	124
1993	Jeff Jaeger, L.A. Raiders	0	35	27	132

TOUCHDOWNS

Year	Player, team	TD	Rush	Pass	Returns
1932	Dutch Clark, Portsmouth	6	3	3	0
	Red Grange, Chicago Bears	6	3	3	0
1933	Charlie Goldenberg, Green Bay	7	4	1	2
	Shipwreck Kelly, Brooklyn	7	2	3	2
	Kink Richards, N.Y. Giants	7	4	3	0
1934	Beattie Feathers, Chicago Bears	9	8	1	0
1935	Don Hutson, Green Bay	7	0	6	1
1936	Don Hutson, Green Bay	9	0	8	1
1937	Cliff Battles, Washington	7	5	1	1
	Clarke Hinkle, Green Bay	7	5	2	0
	Don Hutson, Green Bay	7	0	7	0
1938	Don Hutson, Green Bay	9	0	9	0
1939	Andrew Farkas, Washington	11	5	5	1
1940	John Drake, Cleveland	9	9	0	0
	Richard Todd, Washington	9	4	4	1
1941	Don Hutson, Green Bay	12	2	10	0
	George McAfee, Chicago Bears	12	6	3	3
1942	Don Hutson, Green Bay	17	0	17	0
1943	Don Hutson, Green Bay	12	0	11	1
	Bill Paschal, N.Y. Giants	12	10	2	0
1944	Don Hutson, Green Bay	9	0	9	0
	Bill Paschal, N.Y. Giants	9	9	0	0
1945	Steve Van Buren, Philadelphia	18	15	2	1
1946	Ted Fritsch, Green Bay	10	9	1	0
1947	Steve Van Buren, Philadelphia	14	13	0	1
1948	Mal Kutner, Chicago Cardinals	15	1	14	0
1949	Gene Roberts, N.Y. Giants	17	9	8	0
1950	Bob Shaw, Chicago Cardinals	12	0	12	0
1951	Elroy Hirsch, Los Angeles	17	0	17	0
1952	Cloyce Box, Detroit	15	0	15	0
1953	Joe Perry, San Francisco	13	10	3	0
1954	Harlon Hill, Chicago Bears	12	0	12	0
1955	Alan Ameche, Baltimore	9	9	0	0
	Harlon Hill, Chicago Bears	9	0	9	0
1956	Rick Casares, Chicago Bears	14	12	2	0
1957	Lenny Moore, Baltimore	11	3	7	1
1958	Jim Brown, Cleveland	18	17	1	0
1959	Raymond Berry, Baltimore	14	0	14	0
	Jim Brown, Cleveland	14	14	0	0
1960	Paul Hornung, Green Bay	15	13	2	0
	Sonny Randle, St. Louis	15	0	15	0
	Art Powell, N.Y. Titans, AFL	14	0	14	0
1961	Bill Groman, Houston, AFL	18	1	17	0
	Jim Taylor, Green Bay	16	15	1	0
1962	Abner Haynes, Dallas, AFL	19	13	6	0
	Jim Taylor, Green Bay	19	19	0	0
1963	Art Powell, Oakland, AFL	16	0	16	0
	Jim Brown, Cleveland	15	12	3	0
1964	Lenny Moore, Baltimore	20	16	3	1
	Lance Alworth, San Diego, AFL	15	2	13	0
1965	Gale Sayers, Chicago	22	14	6	2
	Lance Alworth, San Diego, AFL	14	0	14	0
	Don Maynard, N.Y. Jets, AFL	14	0	14	0

PRO FOOTBALL WEEKLY 1994 ALMANAC

Year	Player, team				
1966	Leroy Kelly, Cleveland	16	15	1	0
	Dan Reeves, Dallas	16	8	8	0
	Lance Alworth, San Diego	13	0	13	0
1967	Homer Jones, N.Y. Giants	14	1	13	0
	Emerson Boozer, N.Y. Jets, AFL	13	10	3	0
1968	Leroy Kelly, Cleveland	20	16	4	0
	Warren Wells, Oakland, AFL	12	1	11	0
1969	Warren Wells, Oakland, AFL	14	0	14	0
	Tom Matte, Baltimore	13	11	2	0
	Lance Rentzel, Dallas	13	0	12	1
1970	Dick Gordon, Chicago	13	0	13	0
	MacArthur Lane, St. Louis	13	11	2	0
1971	Duane Thomas, Dallas	13	11	2	0
1972	Emerson Boozer, N.Y. Jets	14	11	3	0
	Ron Johnson, N.Y. Giants	14	9	5	0
1973	Larry Brown, Washington	14	8	6	0
1974	Chuck Foreman, Minnesota	15	9	6	0
1975	O.J. Simpson, Buffalo	23	16	7	0
1976	Chuck Foreman, Minnesota	14	13	1	0
	Franco Harris, Pittsburgh	14	14	0	0
1977	Walter Payton, Chicago	16	14	2	0
1978	David Sims, Seattle	15	14	1	0
1979	Earl Campbell, Houston	19	19	0	0
1980	Billy Sims, Detroit	16	13	3	0
1981	Chuck Muncie, San Diego	19	19	0	0
1982	Marcus Allen, L.A. Raiders	14	11	3	0
1983	John Riggins, Washington	24	24	0	0
1984	Marcus Allen, L.A. Raiders	18	13	5	0
	Mark Clayton, Miami	18	0	18	0
1985	Joe Morris, N.Y. Giants	21	21	0	0
1986	George Rogers, Washington	18	18	0	0
1987	Jerry Rice, San Francisco	23	1	22	0
1988	Greg Bell, L.A. Rams	18	16	2	0
1989	Dalton Hilliard, New Orleans	18	13	5	0
1990	Barry Sanders, Detroit	16	13	3	0
1991	Barry Sanders, Detroit	17	16	1	0
1992	Emmitt Smith, Dallas	19	18	1	0
1993	Jerry Rice, San Francisco	16	15	1	0

RUSHING

Year	Player, team	Att.	Yards	Avg.	TD
1932	Cliff Battles, Boston	148	576	3.9	3
1933	Jim Musick, Boston	173	809	4.7	5
1934	Beattie Feathers, Chicago Bears	119	1,004	8.4	8
1935	Doug Russell, Chicago Cardinals	140	499	3.6	0
1936	Tuffy Leemans, N.Y. Giants	206	830	4.0	2
1937	Cliff Battles, Washington	216	874	4.0	5
1938	Byron "Whizzer" White, Pittsburgh	152	567	3.7	4
1939	Bill Osmanski, Chicago	121	699	5.8	7
1940	Byron "Whizzer" White, Detroit	146	514	3.5	5
1941	Pug Manders, Brooklyn	111	486	4.4	5
1942	Bill Dudley, Pittsburgh	162	696	4.3	5
1943	Bill Paschal, N.Y. Giants	147	572	3.9	10
1944	Bill Paschal, N.Y. Giants	196	737	3.8	9
1945	Steve Van Buren, Philadelphia	143	832	5.8	15
1946	Bill Dudley, Pittsburgh	146	604	4.1	3
1947	Steve Van Buren, Philadelphia	217	1,008	4.6	13
1948	Steve Van Buren, Philadelphia	201	945	4.7	10
1949	Steve Van Buren, Philadelphia	263	1,146	4.4	11
1950	Marion Motley, Cleveland	140	810	5.8	3
1951	Eddie Price, N.Y. Giants	271	971	3.6	7
1952	Dan Towler, Los Angeles	156	894	5.7	10
1953	Joe Perry, San Francisco	192	1,018	5.3	10
1954	Joe Perry, San Francisco	173	1,049	6.1	8
1955	Alan Ameche, Baltimore	213	961	4.5	9
1956	Rick Casares, Chicago Bears	234	1,126	4.8	12
1957	Jim Brown, Cleveland	202	942	4.7	9
1958	Jim Brown, Cleveland	257	1,527	5.9	17
1959	Jim Brown, Cleveland	290	1,329	4.6	14
1960	Jim Brown, Cleveland	215	1,257	5.8	9

	Player, team				
	Abner Haynes, Dallas, AFL	156	875	5.6	9
1961	Jim Brown, Cleveland	305	1,408	4.6	8
	Billy Cannon, Houston, AFL	200	948	4.7	6
1962	Jim Taylor, Green Bay	272	1,474	5.4	19
	Cookie Gilchrist, Buffalo, AFL	214	1,096	5.1	13
1963	Jim Brown, Cleveland	291	1,863	6.4	12
	Clem Daniels, Oakland, AFL	215	1,099	5.1	3
1964	Jim Brown, Cleveland	280	1,446	5.2	7
	Cookie Gilchrist, Buffalo, AFL	230	981	4.3	6
1965	Jim Brown, Cleveland	289	1,544	5.3	17
	Paul Lowe, San Diego, AFL	222	1,121	5.0	7
1966	Jim Nance, Boston, AFL	299	1,458	4.9	11
	Gale Sayers, Chicago	229	1,231	5.4	8
1967	Jim Nance, Boston, AFL	269	1,216	4.5	7
	Leroy Kelly, Cleveland	235	1,205	5.1	11
1968	Leroy Kelly, Cleveland	248	1,239	5.0	16
	Paul Robinson, Cincinnati, AFL	238	1,023	4.3	8
1969	Gale Sayers, Chicago	236	1,032	4.4	8
	Dick Post, San Diego, AFL	182	873	4.8	6
1970	Larry Brown, Washington	237	1,125	4.7	5
1971	Floyd Little, Denver	284	1,133	4.0	6
1972	O.J. Simpson, Buffalo	292	1,251	4.3	6
1973	O.J. Simpson, Buffalo	332	2.003	6.0	12
1974	Otis Armstrong, Denver	263	1,407	5.3	9
1975	O.J. Simpson, Buffalo	329	1,817	5.5	16
1976	O.J. Simpson, Buffalo	290	1,503	5.2	8
1977	Walter Payton, Chicago	339	1,852	5.5	14
1978	Earl Campbell, Houston	302	1,450	4.8	13
1979	Earl Campbell, Houston	368	1,697	4.6	19
1980	Earl Campbell, Houston	373	1,934	5.2	13
1981	George Rogers, New Orleans	378	1,674	4.4	13
1982	Freeman McNeil, N.Y. Jets	151	786	5.2	6
1983	Eric Dickerson, L.A. Rams	390	1,808	4.6	18
1984	Eric Dickerson, L.A. Rams	379	2,105	5.6	14
1985	Marcus Allen, L.A. Raiders	380	1,759	4.6	11
1986	Eric Dickerson, L.A. Rams	404	1,821	4.5	11
1987	Charles White, L.A. Rams	324	1,374	4.2	11
1988	Eric Dickerson, Indianapolis	388	1,659	4.3	14
1989	Christian Okoye, Kansas City	370	1,480	4.0	12
1990	Barry Sanders, Detroit	255	1,304	5.1	13
1991	Emmitt Smith, Dallas	365	1,563	4.3	12
1992	Emmitt Smith, Dallas	373	1,713	4.6	18
1993	Emmitt Smith, Dallas	283	1,486	5.3	9

PASSING

Year	Player, team	Att.	Cmp.	Yds.	TD	Int.
1932	Arnie Herber, Green Bay	101	37	639	9	9
1933	Harry Newman, N.Y. Giants	136	53	973	11	17
1934	Arnie Herber, Green Bay	115	42	799	8	12
1935	Ed Danowski, N.Y. Giants	113	57	794	10	9
1936	Arnie Herber, Green Bay	173	77	1,239	11	13
1937	Sammy Baugh, Washington	171	81	1,127	8	14
1938	Ed Danowski, N.Y. Giants	129	70	848	7	8
1939	Parker Hall, Cleveland	208	106	1,227	9	13
1940	Sammy Baugh, Washington	177	111	1,367	12	10
1941	Cecil Isbell, Green Bay	206	117	1,479	15	11
1942	Cecil Isbell, Green Bay	268	146	2,021	24	14
1943	Sammy Baugh, Washington	239	133	1,754	23	19
1944	Frank Filchock, Washington	147	84	1,139	13	9
1945	Sammy Baugh, Washington	182	128	1,669	11	4
	Sid Luckman, Chicago Bears	217	117	1,725	14	10
1946	Bob Waterfield, Los Angeles	251	127	1,747	18	17
1947	Sammy Baugh, Washington	354	210	2,938	25	15
1948	Tommy Thompson, Philadelphia	246	141	1,965	25	11
1949	Sammy Baugh, Washington	255	145	1,903	18	14
1950	Norm Van Brocklin, Los Angeles	233	127	2,061	18	14
1951	Bob Waterfield, Los Angeles	176	88	1,566	13	10
1952	Norm Van Brocklin, Los Angeles	205	113	1,736	14	17
1953	Otto Graham, Cleveland	258	167	2,722	11	9
1954	Norm Van Brocklin, Los Angeles	260	139	2,637	13	21

PRO FOOTBALL WEEKLY 1994 ALMANAC

Year	Player, team				
1955	Otto Graham, Cleveland	185	98	1,721	15	8
1956	Ed Brown, Chicago Bears	168	96	1,667	11	12
1957	Tommy O'Connell, Cleveland	110	63	1,229	9	8
1958	Eddie LeBaron, Washington	145	79	1,365	11	10
1959	Charlie Conerly, N.Y. Giants	194	113	1,706	14	4
1960	Jack Kemp, L.A. Chargers, AFL	406	211	3,018	20	25
	Milt Plum, Cleveland	250	151	2,297	21	5
1961	George Blanda, Houston, AFL	362	187	3,330	36	22
	Milt Plum, Cleveland	302	177	2,416	18	10
1962	Len Dawson, Dallas Texans, AFL	310	189	2,759	29	17
	Bart Starr, Green Bay	285	178	2,438	12	9
1963	Y. A. Tittle, N.Y. Giants	367	221	3,145	36	14
	Tobin Rote, San Diego, AFL	286	170	2,510	20	17
1964	Len Dawson, Kansas City, AFL	354	199	2,879	30	18
	Bart Starr, Green Bay	272	163	2,144	15	4
1965	John Hadl, San Diego, AFL	348	174	2,798	20	21
	Rudy Bukich, Chicago	312	176	2,641	20	9
1966	Len Dawson, Kansas City, AFL	284	159	2,527	26	10
	Bart Starr, Green Bay	251	156	2,257	14	3
1967	Sonny Jurgensen, Washington	508	288	3,747	31	16
	Daryle Lamonica, Oakland, AFL	425	220	3,228	30	20
1968	Earl Morrall, Baltimore	317	182	2,909	26	17
	Len Dawson, Kansas City, AFL	224	131	2,109	17	9
1969	Sonny Jurgensen, Washington	442	274	3,102	22	15
	Greg Cook, Cincinnati, AFL	197	106	1,854	15	11
1970	John Brodie, San Francisco	378	223	2,941	24	10
1971	Bob Griese, Miami	263	145	2,089	19	9
1972	Norm Snead, N. Y. Giants	325	196	2.307	17	12
1973	Roger Staubach, Dallas	286	179	2,428	23	15
1974	Ken Anderson, Cincinnati	328	213	2,667	18	10
1975	Ken Anderson, Cincinnati	377	228	3,169	21	11
1976	Ken Stabler, Oakland	291	194	2,737	27	17
1977	Bob Griese, Miami	307	180	2,252	22	13
1978	Roger Staubach, Dallas	413	231	3,190	25	16
1979	Roger Staubach, Dallas	461	267	3,586	27	11
1980	Brian Sipe, Cleveland	554	337	4,132	30	14
1981	Ken Anderson, Cincinnati	479	300	3,754	29	10
1982	Ken Anderson, Cincinnati	309	218	2,495	12	9
1983	Steve Bartkowski, Atlanta	432	274	3,167	22	5
1984	Dan Marino, Miami	564	362	5,084	48	17
1985	Ken O'Brien, N.Y. Jets	488	297	3,888	25	8
1986	Tommy Kramer, Minnesota	372	208	3,000	24	10
1987	Joe Montana, San Francisco	398	266	3,054	31	13
1988	Boomer Esiason, Cincinnati	388	223	3,572	28	14
1989	Joe Montana, San Francisco	386	271	3,521	26	8
1990	Jim Kelly, Buffalo	346	219	2,829	24	9
1991	Steve Young, San Francisco	279	180	2,517	17	8
1992	Steve Young, San Francisco	402	268	3,465	25	7
1993	Steve Young, San Francisco	462	314	4,023	29	16

PASS RECEIVING

Year	Player, team	No.	Yards	Avg.	TD
1932	Ray Flaherty, N.Y. Giants	21	350	16.7	3
1933	Shipwreck Kelly, Brooklyn	22	246	11.2	3
1934	Joe Carter, Phildelphia	16	238	14.9	4
	Red Badgro, N.Y. Giants	16	206	12.9	1
1935	Tod Goodwin, N.Y. Giants	26	432	16.6	4
1936	Don Hutson, Green Bay	34	536	15.8	8
1937	Don Hutson, Green Bay	41	552	13.5	7
1938	Gaynell Tinsley, Chicago Cardinals	41	516	12.6	1
1939	Don Hutson, Green Bay	34	846	24.9	6
1940	Don Looney, Philadelphia	58	707	12.2	4
1941	Don Hutson, Green Bay	58	738	12.7	10
1942	Don Hutson, Green Bay	74	1,211	16.4	17
1943	Don Hutson, Green Bay	47	776	16.5	11
1944	Don Hutson, Green Bay	58	866	14.9	9
1945	Don Hutson, Green Bay	47	834	17.7	9
1946	Jim Benton, Los Angeles	63	981	15.6	6
1947	Jim Keane, Chicago Bears	64	910	14.2	10
1948	Tom Fears, Los Angeles	51	698	13.7	4

Year	Player	Rec	Yds	Avg	TD
1949	Tom Fears, Los Angeles	77	1,013	13.2	9
1950	Tom Fears, Los Angeles	84	1,116	13.3	7
1951	Elroy Hirsch, Los Angeles	66	1,495	22.7	17
1952	Mac Speedie, Cleveland	62	911	14.7	5
1953	Pete Pihos, Philadelphia	63	1,049	16.7	10
1954	Pete Pihos, Philadelphia	60	872	14.5	10
	Billy Wilson, San Francisco	60	830	13.8	5
1955	Pete Pihos, Philadelphia	62	864	13.9	7
1956	Billy Wilson, San Francisco	60	889	14.8	5
1957	Billy Wilson, San Francisco	52	757	14.6	6
1958	Raymond Berry, Baltimore	56	794	14.2	9
	Pete Retzlaff, Philadelphia	56	766	13.7	2
1959	Raymond Berry, Baltimore	66	959	14.5	14
1960	Lionel Taylor, Denver, AFL	92	1,235	13.4	12
	Raymond Barry, Baltimore	74	1,298	17.5	10
1961	Lionel Taylor, Denver, AFL	100	1,176	11.8	4
	Jim "Red" Phillips, Los Angeles	78	1,092	14.0	5
1962	Lionel Taylor, Denver, AFL	77	908	11.8	4
	Bobby Mitchell, Washington	72	1,384	19.2	11
1963	Lionel Taylor, Denver, AFL	78	1,101	14.1	10
	Bobby Joe Conrad, St. Louis	73	967	13.2	10
1964	Charley Hennigan, Houston, AFL	101	1,546	15.3	8
	Johnny Morris, Chicago	93	1,200	12.9	10
1965	Lionel Taylor, Denver, AFL	85	1,131	13.3	6
	Dave Parks, San Francisco	80	1,344	16.8	12
1966	Lance Alworth, San Diego, AFL	73	1,383	18.9	13
	Charley Taylor, Washington	72	1,119	15.5	12
1967	George Sauer, N.Y. Jets, AFL	75	1,189	15.9	6
	Charley Taylor, Washington	70	990	14.1	9
1968	Clifton McNeil, San Francisco	71	994	14.0	7
	Lance Alworth, San Diego, AFL	68	1,312	19.3	10
1969	Dan Abramowicz, New Orleans	73	1,015	13.9	7
	Lance Alworth, San Diego, AFL	64	1,003	15.7	4
1970	Dick Gordon, Chicago	71	1,026	14.5	13
1971	Fred Biletnikoff, Oakland	61	929	15.2	9
1972	Harold Jackson, Philadelphia	62	1,048	16.9	4
1973	Harold Carmichael, Philadelphia	67	1,116	16.7	9
1974	Lydell Mitchell, Baltimore	72	544	7.6	2
1975	Chuck Foreman, Minnesota	73	691	9.5	9
1976	MacArthur Lane, Kansas City	66	686	10.4	1
1977	Lydell Mitchell, Baltimore	71	620	8.7	4
1978	Rickey Young, Minnesota	88	704	8.0	5
1979	Joe Washington, Baltimore	82	750	9.1	3
1980	Kellen Winslow, San Diego	89	1,290	14.5	9
1981	Kellen Winslow, San Diego	88	1,075	12.2	10
1982	Dwight Clark, San Francisco	60	913	15.2	5
1983	Todd Christensen, L.A. Raiders	92	1,247	13.6	12
1984	Art Monk, Washington	106	1,372	12.9	7
1985	Roger Craig, San Francisco	92	1,016	11.0	6
1986	Todd Christensen, L.A. Raiders	95	1,153	12.1	8
1987	J.T. Smith, St. Louis	91	1,117	12.3	8
1988	Al Toon, N.Y. Jets	93	1,067	11.5	5
1989	Sterling Sharpe, Green Bay	90	1,423	15.8	12
1990	Jerry Rice, San Francisco	100	1,502	15.0	13
1991	Haywood Jeffires, Houston	100	1,181	11.8	7
1992	Sterling Sharpe, Green Bay	108	1,461	13.5	13
1993	Sterling Sharpe, Green Bay	112	1,274	11.4	11

PRO FOOTBALL WEEKLY 1994 ALMANAC

HONORS HALL OF FAME

CLASS OF '94

TONY DORSETT
Running back

1977-87 Dallas Cowboys
1988 Denver Broncos

Dorsett was four-time All-American and the 1976 Heisman Trophy winner from the University of Pittsburgh. A first-round draft choice of the Cowboys in 1977, Dorsett rushed for more than 1,000 yards in eight of his first nine seasons, missing the mark only in the strike-shortened '82 season. He rushed for 12,739 yards, the third-highest total in NFL history, behind only Walter Payton (16,726) and Eric Dickerson (13,259). Dorsett is second in combined yards with 16,326, trailing only Payton's 21,803.

BUD GRANT
Head coach

1967-83, 1985 Minnesota Vikings

Grant's 18-year NFL coaching record was 168-108-5, including 10 postseason victories, for a .607 winning mark. His 168 coaching victories rank him eighth among all pro football coaches. From 1968 to '78, Grant's Vikings won 10 NFL and NFC Central Division championships, missing only in 1972. Grant's Minnesota teams appeared in four Super Bowls. Grant earlier coached 10 years in the CFL and had a record of 102-56-2 with four Grey Cup championships.

JIMMY JOHNSON
Cornerback

1961-76 San Francisco 49ers

Johnson was the first of three first-round draft choices of the 49ers in 1961. He was an outstanding track star at UCLA, and the 49ers tried him as a defensive back as a rookie, moved him to offense in his second season and then back to defense to stay in his third season. Recognized as one of the best man-to-man defenders of all time, Johnson's reputation was so great that opposing quarterbacks rarely threw to the player he was covering. Still, Johnson intercepted 47 passes and returned them 615 yards, both second-best in 49er history. A great all-around athlete, Johnson was named All-Pro four straight years and was selected to play in five Pro Bowls.

LEROY KELLY
Running back

1964-73 Cleveland Browns

Kelly was an eighth-round draft pick of the Browns in 1964. During his first two years, he was an understudy to superstar Jim Brown. When Brown retired following the '65 season, Kelly quickly filled the void. In each of the next three seasons, he rushed for more than 1,000 yards, winning All-NFL honors each year and being selected to three consecutive Pro Bowls. He led the NFL in rushing in 1967 and '68 and was named to three additional Pro Bowls following the '69, '70 and '71 seasons. A very durable runner, Kelly gained 12,329 combined net yards on rushes, receptions and returns. He missed only four games in his 10-year career.

JACKIE SMITH
Tight end

1963-77 St. Louis Cardinals
1978 Dallas Cowboys

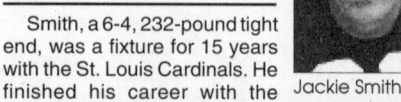

Smith, a 6-4, 232-pound tight end, was a fixture for 15 years with the St. Louis Cardinals. He finished his career with the Cowboys in 1978. At the time of his retirement, he ranked as the all-time leading receiver among tight ends with 480 receptions for 7,918 yards and 40 touchdowns. In addition, he ranked 11th among all receivers. Today, he is surpassed only by Roy Green among all Cardinal receivers. Smith played in five straight Pro Bowls from 1967 to '71.

RANDY WHITE
Defensive tackle

1975-88 Dallas Cowboys

White was the Cowboys' first pick and the second player taken in the 1975 draft. Originally tried at middle linebacker, White moved to the starting DRT position in his third season. For the remainder of his 14-year career, he was the anchor of the Cowboys' excellent defensive line. White was named the NFL Defensive Lineman of the Year in 1978, played in nine straight Pro Bowls from 1978 to '86 and was an All-Pro selection eight straight seasons, 1978 to '85. The co-MVP of Super Bowl XII, White recorded four sacks in three Super Bowl appearances.

HISTORY ■ HALL OF FAME

ROSTER OF MEMBERS

Herb Adderley — Cornerback, 1961-69 Green Bay, 1970-72 Dallas. College: Michigan State. Inducted: 1980.

Lance Alworth — Wide receiver, 1962-70 San Diego, 1971-72 Dallas. College: Arkansas. Inducted: 1978.

Doug Atkins — Defensive end, 1953-54 Cleveland, 1955-66 Chicago Bears, 1967-69 New Orleans. College: Tennessee. Inducted: 1982.

Red Badgro — End, 1927 New York Yankees, 1930-35 New York Giants, 1936 Brooklyn Dodgers. College: Southern Cal. Inducted: 1981.

Lem Barney — Cornerback, 1967-77 Detroit. College: Jackson State. Inducted: 1992.

Cliff Battles — Halfback, 1932 Boston Braves, 1933-36 Boston Redskins, 1937 Washington. College: West Virginia Wesleyan. Inducted: 1968.

Sammy Baugh — Quarterback, 1937-52 Washington. College: Texas Christian. Inducted: 1963.

Chuck Bednarik — Center-linebacker, 1949-62 Philadelphia. College: Pennsylvania. Inducted: 1967.

Bert Bell — Team owner, 1933-40 Philadelphia, 1941-42 Pittsburgh, 1943 Phil-Pitt, 1944-46 Pittsburgh. NFL commissioner, 1946-59. College: Pennsylvania. Inducted: 1963.

Bobby Bell — Linebacker, 1963-74 Kansas City. College: Minnesota. Inducted: 1983.

Raymond Berry — End, 1955-67 Baltimore. College: Southern Methodist. Inducted: 1973.

Charles W. Bidwill Sr. — Team owner, 1933-43 Chicago Cardinals, 1944 Card-Pitt, 1945-47 Chicago Cardinals. College: Loyola (Chicago). Inducted: 1967.

Fred Biletnikoff — Wide receiver, 1965-78 Oakland. College: Florida State. Inducted: 1988.

George Blanda — Quarterback-placekicker, 1949-58 Chicago, 1950 Baltimore, 1960-66 Houston, 1967-75 Oakland. College: Kentucky. Inducted: 1981.

Mel Blount — Cornerback, 1970-83 Pittsburgh. College: Southern University. Inducted: 1989.

Terry Bradshaw — Quarterback, 1970-83 Pittsburgh. College: Louisiana Tech. Inducted: 1989.

Jim Brown — Fullback, 1957-65 Cleveland. College: Syracuse. Inducted: 1971.

Paul Brown — Coach, 1946-62 Cleveland, 1968-75 Cincinnati. College: Miami (Ohio). Inducted: 1967.

Roosevelt Brown — Tackle, 1953-65 New York Giants. College: Morgan State. Inducted: 1975.

Willie Brown — Defensive back, 1963-66 Denver, 1967-78 Oakland. College: Grambling. Inducted: 1984.

Buck Buchanan — Defensive tackle, 1963-75 Kansas City. College: Grambling. Inducted: 1990.

Dick Butkus — Linebacker, 1965-73 Chicago. College: Illinois. Inducted: 1979.

Earl Campbell — Running back, 1978-84 Houston, 1984-85 New Orleans. College: Texas. Inducted: 1991.

Tony Canadeo — Halfback, 1941-44, 1946-52 Green Bay. College: Gonzaga. Inducted: 1974.

Joe Carr — NFL president, 1921-39. College: Did not attend. Inducted: 1963.

Guy Chamberlin — End, 1920 Decatur Staleys, 1921 Chicago Staleys. Player-coach, 1922-23 Canton Bulldogs, 1924 Cleveland Bulldogs, 1925-26 Frankford Yellow Jackets, 1927 Chicago Cardinals. College: Nebraska. Inducted: 1965.

Jack Christiansen — Defensive back, 1951-58 Detroit. College: Colorado State. Inducted: 1970.

Dutch Clark — Quarterback, 1931-32 Portsmouth Spartans, 1934-38 Detroit. College: Colorado College. Inducted: 1963.

George Connor — Tackle-linebacker, 1948-55 Chicago. College: Holy Cross, Notre Dame. Inducted: 1975.

Jimmy Conzelman — Quarterback, 1920 Decatur Staleys, 1921-22 Rock Island Independents, 1923-24 Milwaukee Badgers. Owner-coach, 1925-26 Detroit Panthers.

Player-coach, 1927-29; coach, 1930 Providence Steam Roller. Coach, 1940-42, 1946-48 Chicago Cardinals. College: Washington (Mo.), Missouri. Inducted: 1964.

Larry Csonka — Running back, 1968-74, 1979 Miami, 1976-78 New York Giants. College: Syracuse. Inducted: 1987.

Al Davis — Team owner, 1963-81 Oakland Raiders, 1982-94 Los Angeles Raiders. Commissioner, 1966, American Football League. Colleges: Wittenberg, Syracuse. Inducted: 1992.

Willie Davis — Defensive end, 1958-59 Cleveland, 1960-69 Green Bay. College: Grambling. Inducted: 1981.

Len Dawson — Quarterback, 1957-59 Pittsburgh, 1960-61 Cleveland, 1962 Dallas Texans, 1963-75 Kansas City. College: Purdue. Inducted: 1987.

Mike Ditka — Tight end, 1961-66 Chicago, 1967-68 Philadelphia, 1968-72 Dallas. Head coach, Chicago 1982-92. College: Pittsburgh. Inducted: 1988.

Art Donovan — Defensive tackle, 1950 Baltimore, 1951 New York Yanks, 1952 Dallas Texans, 1953-61 Baltimore. College: Boston College. Inducted: 1968.

Paddy Driscoll — Quarterback, 1920 Decatur Staleys, 1920-25 Chicago Cardinals, 1926-29 Chicago Bears. Coach, 1956-57 Chicago Bears. College: Northwestern. Inducted: 1965.

Bill Dudley — Halfback, 1942, 1945-46 Pittsburgh, 1947-49 Detroit, 1950-51, 1953 Washington. College: Virginia. Inducted: 1966.

Glen "Turk" Edwards — Tackle, 1932 Boston Braves, 1933-36 Boston Redskins, 1937-40 Washington. College: Washington State. Inducted: 1969.

Weeb Ewbank — Coach, 1954-62 Baltimore, 1963-73 New York Jets. College: Miami (Ohio). Inducted: 1978.

Tom Fears — End, 1948-56 Los Angeles. Colleges: Santa Clara, UCLA. Inducted: 1970.

Ray Flaherty — End, 1926 Los Angeles Wildcats, 1927-28 New York Yankees, 1928-29, 1931-35 New York Giants. Coach, 1936 Boston Redskins, 1937-42 Washington, 1946-48 New York Yankees, 1949 Chicago Hornets. College: Gonzaga. Inducted: 1976.

Len Ford — End, 1948-49 Los Angeles Dons, 1950-57 Cleveland Browns, 1958 Green Bay. College: Michigan. Inducted: 1976.

Dan Fortmann — Guard, 1936-43 Chicago Bears. College: Colgate. Inducted: 1965.

Dan Fouts — Quarterback, 1973-87 San Diego. College: Oregon. Inducted: 1993.

Frank Gatski — Center, 1946-56 Cleveland, 1957 Detroit. Colleges: Marshall, Auburn. Inducted: 1985.

Bill George — Linebacker, 1952-65 Chicago Bears, 1966 Los Angeles Rams. College: Illinois. Inducted: 1974.

Frank Gifford — Halfback-flanker, 1952-60, 1962-64 New York Giants. College: Southern Cal. Inducted: 1977.

Sid Gillman — Coach, 1955-59 Los Angeles Rams, 1960 Los Angeles Chargers, 1961-69 San Diego, 1973-74 Houston. College: Ohio State. Inducted: 1983.

Otto Graham — Quarterback, 1946-55 Cleveland. College: Northwestern. Inducted: 1965.

Harold "Red" Grange — Halfback, 1925 Chicago Bears, 1926-27 New York Yankees, 1929-34 Chicago Bears. College: Illinois. Inducted: 1963.

Joe Greene — Defensive tackle, 1969-81 Pittsburgh. College: North Texas State. Inducted: 1987.

Forrest Gregg — Offensive tackle, 1956, 1958-70 Green Bay, 1971 Dallas. College: Southern Methodist. Inducted: 1977.

Bob Griese — Quarterback, 1967-80 Miami. College: Purdue. Inducted: 1990.

Lou Groza — Tackle-placekicker, 1946-59, 1961-67 Cleveland. College: Ohio State. Inducted: 1974.

Joe Guyon — Halfback, 1920 Canton Bulldogs, 1921 Cleveland Indians, 1922-23 Oorang Indians, 1924 Rock Island Independents, 1924-25 Kansas City Cowboys, 1927 New York Giants. Colleges: Carlisle, Georgia Tech. Inducted: 1966.

George Halas — End-coach-owner, 1920 Decatur Staleys, 1921 Chicago Staleys, 1922-29 Chicago Bears. Coach-owner, 1933-42, 1946-55, 1958-67 Chicago Bears. Owner 1968-83 Chicago Bears. College: Illinois. Inducted: 1963.
Jack Ham — Linebacker, 1971-82 Pittsburgh. College: Penn State. Inducted: 1988.
John Hannah — Offensive guard, 1973-85 New England. College: Alabama. Inducted: 1991.
Franco Harris — Running back, 1972-83 Pittsburgh, 1984 Seattle. College: Penn State. Inducted: 1990.
Ed Healey — Tackle, 1920-22 Rock Island Independents, 1922-27 Chicago Bears. College: Dartmouth. Inducted: 1964.
Mel Hein — Center, 1931-45 New York Giants. College: Washington State. Inducted: 1963.
Ted Hendricks — Linebacker, 1969-73 Baltimore, 1974 Green Bay, 1975-81 Oakland, 1982-83 Los Angeles Raiders. College: Miami (Fla.). Inducted: 1990.
Wilbur "Pete" Henry — Tackle, 1920-23, 1925-26 Canton Bulldogs, 1927 New York Giants, 1927-28 Pottsville Maroons. College: Washington & Jefferson. Inducted: 1963.
Arnie Herber — Quarterback, 1930-40 Green Bay, 1944-45 New York Giants. Colleges: Wisconsin, Regis College. Inducted: 1966.
Bill Hewitt — End, 1932-36 Chicago Bears, 1937-39 Philadelphia, 1943 Phil-Pitt. College: Michigan. Inducted: 1971.
Clarke Hinkle — Fullback, 1932-41 Green Bay. College: Bucknell. Inducted: 1964.
Elroy "Crazylegs" Hirsch — Halfback-end, 1946-48 Chicago Rockets, 1949-57 Los Angeles Rams. Colleges: Wisconsin, Michigan. Inducted: 1968.
Paul Hornung — Halfback, 1957-62, 1964-66 Green Bay. College: Notre Dame. Inducted: 1986.
Ken Houston — Safety, 1967-72 Houston, 1973-80 Washington. College: Prairie View A&M. Inducted: 1986.
Cal Hubbard — Tackle, 1927-28 New York Giants, 1929-33, 1935 Green Bay, 1936 New York Giants, 1936 Pittsburgh Pirates. Colleges: Centenary, Geneva. Inducted: 1963.
Sam Huff — Linebacker, 1956-63 New York Giants, 1964-67, 1969 Washington. College: West Virginia. Inducted: 1982.
Lamar Hunt — Team owner, 1960-62 Dallas Texans, 1963-94 Kansas City. College: Southern Methodist. Inducted: 1972.
Don Hutson — End, 1935-45 Green Bay. College: Alabama. Inducted: 1963.
John Henry Johnson — Fullback, 1954-56 San Francisco, 1957-59 Detroit, 1960-65 Pittsburgh, 1966 Houston. Colleges: St. Mary's, Arizona State. Inducted: 1987.
David "Deacon" Jones — Defensive end, 1961-71 Los Angeles Rams, 1972-73 San Diego, 1974 Washington. College: Mississippi Vocational. Inducted: 1980.
Stan Jones — Offensive guard-defensive tackle, 1954-65 Chicago Bears, 1966 Washington. College: Maryland. Inducted: 1991.
Sonny Jurgensen — Quarterback, 1957-63 Philadelphia, 1964-74 Washington. College: Duke. Inducted: 1983.
Walt Kiesling — Guard, 1926-27 Duluth Eskimos, 1928 Pottsville Maroons, 1929-33 Chicago Cardinals, 1934 Chicago Bears, 1935-36 Green Bay, Chicago Bears, 1937-38 Pittsburgh Pirates. Coach, 1939-42 Pittsburgh Steelers. Co-coach, 1943 Phil-Pitt, 1944 Card-Pitt. Coach, 1954-56 Pittsburgh. College: St. Thomas. Inducted: 1966.
Frank "Bruiser" Kinard — Tackle, 1938-44 Brooklyn Dodgers-Tigers, 1946-47 New York Yankees. College: Mississippi. Inducted: 1971.
Earl "Curly" Lambeau — Coach, 1919-49 Green Bay, 1950-51 Chicago Cardinals, 1952-53 Washington. College: Notre Dame. Inducted: 1963.
Jack Lambert — Linebacker, 1974-84 Pittsburgh. College: Kent State. Inducted: 1990.
Tom Landry — Coach, 1960-88 Dallas. College: Texas. Inducted: 1990.
Dick "Night Train" Lane — Defensive back, 1952-53 Los Angeles Rams, 1954-59 Chicago Cardinals, 1960-65 Detroit. College: Scottsbluff Junior College. Inducted: 1974.
Jim Langer — Center, 1970-79 Miami, 1980-81 Minnesota. College: South Dakota State. Inducted: 1987.
Willie Lanier — Linebacker, 1967-77 Kansas City. College: Morgan State. Inducted: 1986.
Yale Lary — Defensive back-punter, 1952-53, 1956-64 Detroit. College: Texas A&M. Inducted: 1979.
Dante Lavelli — End, 1946-56 Cleveland. College: Ohio State. Inducted: 1975.
Bobby Layne — Quarterback, 1948 Chicago Bears, 1949 New York Bulldogs, 1950-58 Detroit, 1958-62 Pittsburgh. College: Texas. Inducted: 1967.
Alphonse "Tuffy" Leemans — Fullback, 1936-43 New York Giants. College: George Washington. Inducted: 1978.
Bob Lilly — Defensive tackle, 1961-74 Dallas. College: Texas Christian. Inducted: 1980.
Larry Little — Offensive guard, 1967-68 San Diego, 1969-80 Miami. College: Bethune-Cookman. Inducted: 1993.
Vince Lombardi — Coach, 1959-67 Green Bay, 1969 Washington. College: Fordham. Inducted: 1971.
Sid Luckman — Quarterback, 1939-50 Chicago Bears. College: Columbia. Inducted: 1965.
Roy "Link" Lyman — Tackle, 1922-23, 1925 Canton Bulldogs, 1924 Cleveland Bulldogs, 1925 Frankford Yellow Jackets, 1926-28, 1930-31, 1933-34 Chicago Bears. College: Nebraska. Inducted: 1964.
John Mackey — Tight end, 1963-71 Baltimore, 1972 San Diego. College: Syracuse. Inducted: 1992.
Tim Mara — Team owner, 1929-59 New York Giants. College: Did not attend. Inducted: 1963.
Gino Marchetti — Defensive end, 1952 Dallas Texans, 1953-64, 1966 Baltimore. College: San Francisco. Inducted: 1972.
George Preston Marshall — Team owner, 1932 Boston Braves, 1933-36 Boston Redskins, 1937-69 Washington. College: Randolph-Macon. Inducted: 1963.
Ollie Matson — Halfback, 1952, 1954-58 Chicago Cardinals, 1959-62 Los Angeles Rams, 1963 Detroit, 1964-66 Philadelphia. College: San Francisco. Inducted: 1972.
Don Maynard — End, 1958 New York Giants, 1960-62 New York Titans, 1963-72 New York Jets, 1973 St. Louis. College: Texas Western. Inducted: 1987.
George McAfee — Halfback, 1940-41, 1945-50 Chicago Bears. College: Duke. Inducted: 1966.
Mike McCormack — Tackle, 1951 New York Yanks, 1954-62 Cleveland. College: Kansas. Inducted: 1984.
Hugh McElhenny — Halfback, 1952-60 San Francisco, 1961-62 Minnesota, 1963 New York Giants, 1964 Detroit. College: Washington. Inducted: 1970.
Johnny Blood (McNally) — Halfback, 1925-26 Milwaukee Badgers, 1926-27 Duluth Eskimos, 1928 Pottsville Maroons, 1929-33, 1935-36 Green Bay, 1934 Pittsburgh Pirates. Player-coach, 1937-39 Pittsburgh Pirates. College: St. John's (Minn.). Inducted: 1963.
Mike Michalske — Guard, 1926-28 New York Yankees, 1929-35, 1937 Green Bay. College: Penn State. Inducted: 1964.
Wayne Millner — End, 1936 Boston Redskins, 1937-41, 1945 Washington. College: Notre Dame. Inducted: 1968.
Bobby Mitchell — Running back-wide receiver, 1958-61 Cleveland, 1962-68 Washington. College: Illinois. Inducted: 1983.
Ron Mix — Offensive tackle, 1960 Los Angeles Chargers, 1961-69 San Diego, 1971 Oakland. College: Southern Cal. Inducted: 1979.
Lenny Moore — Halfback-flanker, 1956-67 Baltimore. College: Penn State. Inducted: 1975.

HISTORY ■ HALL OF FAME

Marion Motley — Fullback, 1946-53 Cleveland, 1955 Pittsburgh. Colleges: South Carolina State, Nevada. Inducted: 1968.
George Musso — Guard-tackle, 1933-44 Chicago Bears. College: Millikin. Inducted: 1982.
Bronko Nagurski — Fullback-tackle, 1930-37, 1943 Chicago Bears. College: Minnesota. Inducted: 1963.
Joe Namath — Quarterback, 1965-76 New York Jets, 1977 Los Angeles. College: Alabama. Inducted: 1985.
Earle "Greasy" Neale — Coach, 1941-42, 1944-50 Philadelphia. Co-coach, 1943 Phil-Pitt. College: West Virginia Wesleyan. Inducted: 1969.
Ernie Nevers — Fullback, 1926-27 Duluth Eskimos, 1929-31 Chicago Cardinals. College: Stanford. Inducted: 1963.
Ray Nitschke — Linebacker, 1958-72 Green Bay. College: Illinois. Inducted: 1978.
Chuck Noll — Coach, 1969-91 Pittsburgh. College: Dayton. Inducted: 1993.
Leo Nomellini — Defensive tackle, 1950-63 San Francisco. College: Minnesota. Inducted: 1969.
Merlin Olsen — Defensive tackle, 1962-76 Los Angeles. College: Utah State. Inducted: 1982.
Jim Otto — Center, 1960-74 Oakland. College: Miami (Fla.). Inducted: 1980.
Steve Owen — Tackle, 1924-25 Kansas City Cowboys, 1926-30 New York Giants. Coach, 1931-53 New York Giants. College: Phillips. Inducted: 1966.
Alan Page — Defensive tackle, 1967-78 Minnesota, 1978-81 Chicago. College: Notre Dame. Inducted: 1988.
Clarence "Ace" Parker — Quarterback, 1937-41 Brooklyn Dodgers, 1945 Boston Yanks, 1946 New York Yankees. College: Duke. Inducted: 1972.
Jim Parker — Offensive guard-offensive tackle, 1957-67 Baltimore. College: Ohio State. Inducted: 1973.
Walter Payton — Running back, 1975-87 Chicago. College: Jackson State. Inducted: 1993.
Joe Perry — Fullback, 1948-60, 1963 San Francisco, 1961-62 Baltimore. College: Compton Junior College. Inducted: 1969.
Pete Pihos — End, 1947-55 Philadelphia. College: Indiana. Inducted: 1970.
Hugh "Shorty" Ray — Supervisor of officials, 1938-56. College: Illinois. Inducted: 1966.
Dan Reeves — Team owner, 1941-45 Cleveland Rams, 1946-71 Los Angeles Rams. College: Georgetown. Inducted: 1967.
John Riggins — Running back, 1971-75 New York Jets, 1976-79, 1981-85 Washington. College: Kansas. Inducted: 1992.
Jim Ringo — Center, 1953-63 Green Bay, 1964-67 Philadelphia. College: Syracuse. Inducted: 1981.
Andy Robustelli — Defensive end, 1951-55 Los Angeles Rams, 1956-64 New York Giants. College: Arnold College. Inducted: 1971.
Art Rooney — Team owner, 1933-40 Pittsburgh Pirates, 1941-42, 1945-88 Pittsburgh Steelers, 1943 Phil-Pitt, 1944 Card-Pitt. Colleges: Georgetown, Duquesne. Inducted: 1964.
Pete Rozelle — NFL commissioner, 1960-89. College: San Francisco. Inducted: 1985.
Bob St. Clair — Tackle, 1953-63 San Francisco. Colleges: San Francisco, Tulsa. Inducted: 1990.
Gale Sayers — Running back, 1965-71 Chicago. College: Kansas. Inducted: 1977.
Joe Schmidt — Linebacker, 1953-65 Detroit. College: Pittsburgh. Inducted: 1973.
Tex Schramm — General manager, 1947-57 Los Angeles Rams. President, gneral manager, 1960-88 Dallas Cowboys. College: Texas. Inducted: 1991.
Art Shell — Offensive tackle, 1968-81 Oakland, 1982 Los Angeles Raiders. College: Maryland State-Eastern Shore. Inducted: 1989.

O.J. Simpson — Running back, 1969-77 Buffalo. 1978-79 San Francisco. College: Southern Cal. Inducted: 1985.
Bart Starr — Quarterback, 1956-71 Green Bay. College: Alabama. Inducted: 1977.
Roger Staubach — Quarterback, 1969-79 Dallas. College: Navy. Inducted: 1985.
Ernie Stautner — Defensive tackle, 1950-63 Pittsburgh. College: Boston College. Inducted: 1969
Jan Stenerud — Placekicker, 1967-79 Kansas City, 1980-83 Green Bay, 1984-85 Minnesota. College: Montana State. Inducted: 1991.
Ken Strong — Halfback, 1929-32 Staten Island Stapletons, 1933-35, 1939, 1944-47 New York Giants, 1936-37 New York Yanks. College: New York University. Inducted: 1967.
Joe Stydahar — Tackle, 1936-42, 1945-46 Chicago Bears. College: West Virginia. Inducted: 1967.
Fran Tarkenton — 1961-66, 1972-78 Minnesota, 1967-71 New York Giants. College: Georgia. Inducted: 1986.
Charley Taylor — Wide receiver, 1964-75, 1977 Washington. College: Arizona State. Inducted: 1984.
Jim Taylor — Fullback, 1958-66 Green Bay, 1967 New Orleans. College: Louisiana State. Inducted: 1976.
Jim Thorpe — Halfback, 1915-17, 1919-20, 1926 Canton Bulldogs, 1921 Cleveland Indians, 1922-23 Oorang Indians, 1924 Rock Island Independents, 1925 New York Giants, 1928 Chicago Cardinals. College: Carlisle. Inducted: 1963.
Y.A. Tittle — Quarterback, 1948-50 Baltimore, 1951-60 San Francisco, 1961-64 New York Giants. College: Louisiana State. Inducted: 1971.
George Trafton — Center, 1920 Decatur Staleys, 1921 Chicago Staleys, 1922-32 Chicago Bears. College: Notre Dame. Inducted: 1964.
Charley Trippi — Halfback, 1947-55 Chicago Cardinals. College: Georgia. Inducted: 1968.
Emlen Tunnell — Safety, 1948-58 New York Giants, 1959-61 Green Bay. Colleges: Toledo, Iowa. Inducted: 1967.
Clyde "Bulldog" Turner — Center, 1940-52 Chicago Bears. College: Hardin-Simmons. Inducted: 1966.
Johnny Unitas — Quarterback, 1956-72 Baltimore, 1973 San Diego. College: Louisville. Inducted: 1979.
Gene Upshaw — Offensive guard, 1967-81 Oakland. College: Texas A&I. Inducted: 1987.
Norm Van Brocklin — Quarterback, 1949-57 Los Angeles, 1958-60 Philadelphia. College: Oregon. Inducted: 1971.
Steve Van Buren — Halfback, 1944-51 Philadelphia. College: Louisiana State. Inducted: 1965.
Doak Walker — Halfback, 1950-55 Detroit. College: Southern Methodist. Inducted: 1986.
Bill Walsh — Coach, 1979-88 San Francisco. College: San Jose State. Inducted: 1993.
Paul Warfield — Wide receiver, 1964-69, 1976-77 Cleveland, 1970-74 Miami. College: Ohio State. Inducted: 1983.
Bob Waterfield — Quarterback, 1945 Cleveland Rams, 1946-52 Los Angeles. College: UCLA. Inducted: 1965.
Arnie Weinmeister — Defensive tackle, 1948-49 New York Yankees, 1950-53 New York Giants. College: Washington. Inducted: 1984.
Bill Willis — Guard, 1946-53 Cleveland. College: Ohio State. Inducted: 1977.
Larry Wilson — Safety, 1960-72 St. Louis. College: Utah. Inducted: 1978.
Alex Wojciechowicz — Center, 1938-46 Detroit, 1946-50 Philadelphia. College: Fordham. Inducted: 1968.
Willie Wood — Safety, 1960-71 Green Bay. College: Southern Cal. Inducted: 1989.

PRO FOOTBALL WEEKLY 1994 ALMANAC

PAST PFW AWARDS

OFFENSIVE PLAYER OF THE YEAR

1993	Emmitt Smith, RB, Dallas
1992	Steve Young, QB, San Francisco
1991	Thurman Thomas, RB, Buffalo
1990	Randall Cunningham, QB, Philadelphia
1989	Joe Montana, QB, San Francisco
1988	Boomer Esiason, QB, Cincinnati
1987	Jerry Rice, WR, San Francisco
1986	Jerry Rice, WR, San Francisco
1985	No award
1984	Dan Marino, QB, Miami
1983	Joe Theismann, QB, Washington
1982	Dan Fouts, QB, San Diego
1981	Ken Anderson, QB, Cincinnati
1980	Brian Sipe, QB, Cleveland
1979	Earl Campbell, RB, Houston
1978	Earl Campbell, RB, Houston
1977	Walter Payton, RB, Chicago
1976	Ken Stabler, QB, Oakland
1975	Fran Tarkenton, QB, Minnesota
1974	Jim Hart, QB, St. Louis
1973	O.J. Simpson, RB, Buffalo
1972	Larry Brown, RB, Washington
1971	Otis Taylor, WR, Kansas City
1970	John Brodie, QB, San Francisco
1969	(NFL) Roman Gabriel, QB, L.A. Rams
	(AFL) Daryle Lamonica, QB, Oakland
1968	(NFL) Earl Morrall, QB, Baltimore
	(AFL) Joe Namath, QB, N.Y. Jets

DEFENSIVE PLAYER OF THE YEAR

1993	Bruce Smith, DE, Buffalo
1992	Cortez Kennedy, DT, Seattle
1991	Reggie White, DE, Philadelphia
1990	Bruce Smith, DE, Buffalo
1989	Keith Millard, DT, Minnesota
1988	Mike Singletary, LB, Chicago
1987	Reggie White, DE, Philadelphia
1986	Lawrence Taylor, LB, N.Y. Giants
1985	No award
1984	Kenny Easley, S, Seattle
1983	Bob Baumhower, NT, Miami
1982	Dan Hampton, DT, Chicago
1981	Joe Klecko, DE, N.Y. Jets
1980	Lester Hayes, CB, Oakland
1979	Lee Roy Selmon, DE, Tampa Bay
1978	Randy Gradishar, LB, Denver
1977	Harvey Martin, DE, Dallas
1976	Jack Lambert, LB, Pittsburgh
1975	Jack Ham, LB, Pittsburgh
1974	Joe Greene, DT, Pittsburgh
1973	Paul Smith, DT, Denver
	Alan Page, DT, Minnesota
1972	Joe Greene, DT, Pittsburgh
1971	Alan Page, DT, Minnesota
1970	Dick Butkus, LB, Chicago

COACH OF THE YEAR

1993	Dan Reeves, N.Y. Giants
1992	Bobby Ross, San Diego
1991	Wayne Fontes, Detroit
1990	Art Shell, L.A. Raiders
1989	George Seifert, San Francisco
1988	Mike Ditka, Chicago
1987	Jim Mora, New Orleans
1986	Bill Parcells, N.Y. Giants
1985	No award
1984	Dan Reeves, Denver
1983	Joe Gibbs, Washington
1982	Joe Gibbs, Washington
1981	Bill Walsh, San Francisco
1980	Chuck Knox, Buffalo
1979	Dick Vermeil, Philadelphia
1978	Walt Michaels, N.Y. Jets
1977	Red Miller, Denver
1976	Chuck Fairbanks, New England
1975	Ted Marchibroda, Baltimore
1974	Don Coryell, St. Louis
1973	Chuck Knox, L.A. Rams
1972	Don Shula, Miami
1971	George Allen, Washington
1970	Don Shula, Miami
1969	(NFL) Bud Grant, Minnesota
	(AFL) John Madden, Oakland
1968	(NFL) Don Shula, Baltimore
	(AFL) Hank Stram, Kansas City

OFFENSIVE ROOKIE OF THE YEAR

1993	Jerome Bettis, RB, L.A. Rams
1992	Jason Hanson, PK, Detroit
1991	Leonard Russell, RB, New England
1990	Emmitt Smith, RB, Dallas
1989	Barry Sanders, RB, Detroit
1988	John Stephens, RB, New England
	Ickey Woods, RB, Cincinnati
1987	Troy Stradford, RB, Miami
1986	Rueben Mayes, RB, New Orleans
1985	No award
1984	Louis Lipps, WR, Pittsburgh
1983	Eric Dickerson, RB, L.A. Rams
1982	Marcus Allen, RB, L.A. Raiders
1981	George Rogers, RB, New Orleans
1980	Billy Sims, RB, Detroit
1979	Ottis Anderson, RB, St. Louis
1978	Earl Campbell, RB, Houston
1977	Tony Dorsett, RB, Dallas
1976	Sammy White, WR, Minnesota
1975	Steve Bartkowski, QB, Atlanta
	Mike Thomas, RB, Washington
1974	Don Woods, RB, San Diego
1973	Chuck Foreman, RB, Minnesota
1972	Franco Harris, RB, Pittsburgh
1971	Jim Plunkett, QB, New England
1970	Dennis Shaw, QB, San Diego

1969 (NFL) Calvin Hill, RB, Dallas
(AFL) Greg Cook, QB, Cincinnati

DEFENSIVE ROOKIE OF THE YEAR

1993 Dana Stubblefield, DT, San Francisco
1992 Dale Carter, CB-PR, Kansas City
1991 Mike Croel, LB, Denver
1990 Mark Carrier, FS, Chicago
1989 Derrick Thomas, LB, Kansas City
1988 Erik McMillan, FS, N.Y. Jets
1987 Shane Conlan, LB, Buffalo
1986 John Offerdahl, LB, Miami
Leslie O'Neal, DE, San Diego
1985 No award
1984 Tom Flynn, S, Green Bay
1983 Vernon Maxwell, LB, Baltimore
1982 Chip Banks, LB, Cleveland
1981 Lawrence Taylor, LB, N.Y. Giants
1980 Buddy Curry, LB, Atlanta
1979 Jesse Baker, DE, Houston
1978 Al Baker, DE, Detroit
1977 A.J. Duhe, DE, Miami
1976 Mike Haynes, CB, New England
1975 Robert Brazile, LB, Houston
1974 Jack Lambert, LB, Pittsburgh
1973 Wally Chambers, DT, Chicago
1972 Sherman White, DE, Cincinnati
1971 Isiah Robertson, LB, L.A. Rams
1970 Bruce Taylor, CB, San Francisco
1969 (NFL) Joe Greene, DT, Pittsburgh
(AFL) James Marsalis, CB, Kansas City

COMEBACK PLAYER OF THE YEAR

1993 Marcus Allen, RB, Kansas City
1992 Randall Cunningham, QB, Philadelphia
1991 Jim McMahon, QB, Philadelphia
1990 Barry Word, RB, Kansas City
1989 Ottis Anderson, RB, N.Y. Giants
1988 Greg Bell, RB, L.A. Rams
1987 Charles White, RB, L.A. Rams
1986 Tommy Kramer, QB, Minnesota
Joe Montana, QB, San Francisco
1985 No award
1984 John Stallworth, WR, Pittsburgh
1983 Billy Johnson, WR-PR, Atlanta
1982 Lyle Alzado, DE, L.A. Raiders
1981 Ken Anderson, QB, Cincinnati
1980 Jim Plunkett, QB, Oakland
1979 Larry Csonka, RB, Miami
1978 John Riggins, RB, Washington
1977 Craig Morton, QB, Denver
1976 Greg Landry, QB, Detroit
1975 Dave Hampton, RB, Atlanta
1974 Joe Namath, QB, N.Y. Jets
1973 Roman Gabriel, QB, Philadelphia
1972 Earl Morrall, QB, Miami

GOLDEN TOE TROPHY

1993 Norm Johnson, PK, Atlanta
1992 Rich Camarillo, P, Phoenix
1991 Jeff Gossett, P, L.A. Raiders
1990 Nick Lowery, PK, Kansas City

1989 Eddie Murray, PK, Detroit
1988 Scott Norwood, PK, Buffalo
1987 Jim Arnold, P, Detroit
1986 Morten Andersen, PK, New Orleans
1985 No award
1984 Norm Johnson, PK, Seattle
1983 Ali Haji-Sheikh, PK, N.Y. Giants
1982 Mark Moseley, PK, Washington
1981 Rafael Septien, PK, Dallas
1980 Fred Steinfort, PK, Denver
1979 Bob Grupp, P, Kansas City
1978 Frank Corral, PK, L.A. Rams
1977 Mark Moseley, PK, Washington
1976 Toni Linhart, PK, Baltimore
1975 Ray Guy, P, Oakland
1974 Roy Gerela, PK, Pittsburgh
1973 David Ray, PK, L.A. Rams
1972 Don Cockroft, PK, Cleveland
1971 Garo Yepremian, PK, Miami

EXECUTIVE OF THE YEAR

1993 George Young, GM, N.Y. Giants

ASSISTANT COACH OF THE YEAR

1993 Ray Rhodes, def. coordinator, Green Bay

PRO FOOTBALL WEEKLY 1994 ALMANAC

LEAGUE CHAMPIONS
HISTORY

NATIONAL FOOTBALL LEAGUE

YEAR	LEAGUE CHAMPION
1920	Akron Pros
1921	Chicago Staleys
1922	Canton Bulldogs
1923	Canton Bulldogs
1924	Cleveland Bulldogs
1925	Chicago Cardinals
1926	Frankford Yellow Jackets
1927	New York Giants
1928	Providence Steam Roller
1929	Green Bay Packers
1930	Green Bay Packers
1931	Green Bay Packers
1932	Chicago Bears

YEAR	LEAGUE CHAMPION	RUNNER-UP	SCORE
1933	CHICAGO BEARS	New York Giants	23-21
1934	NEW YORK GIANTS	Chicago Bears	30-13
1935	DETROIT LIONS	New York Giants	26-7
1936	Green Bay Packers	Boston Redskins*	21-6
1937	Washington Redskins	CHICAGO BEARS	28-21
1938	NEW YORK GIANTS	Green Bay Packers	23-17
1939	GREEN BAY PACKERS	New York Giants	27-0
1940	Chicago Bears	WASHINGTON REDSKINS	73-0
1941	CHICAGO BEARS	New York Giants	37-9
1942	WASHINGTON REDSKINS	Chicago Bears	14-6
1943	CHICAGO BEARS	Washington Redskins	41-21
1944	Green Bay Packers	NEW YORK GIANTS	14-7
1945	CLEVELAND RAMS	Washington Redskins	15-14
1946	Chicago Bears	NEW YORK GIANTS	24-14
1947	CHICAGO CARDINALS	Philadelphia Eagles	28-21
1948	PHILADELPHIA EAGLES	Chicago Cardinals	7-0
1949	Philadelphia Eagles	LOS ANGELES RAMS	14-0
1950	CLEVELAND BROWNS	Los Angeles Rams	30-28
1951	LOS ANGELES RAMS	Cleveland Browns	24-17
1952	Detroit Lions	CLEVELAND BROWNS	17-7
1953	DETROIT LIONS	Cleveland Browns	17-16
1954	CLEVELAND BROWNS	Detroit Lions	56-10
1955	Cleveland Browns	LOS ANGELES RAMS	38-14
1956	NEW YORK GIANTS	Chicago Bears	47-7
1957	DETROIT LIONS	Cleveland Browns	59-14
1958	Baltimore Colts	NEW YORK GIANTS	23-17 (OT)
1959	BALTIMORE COLTS	New York Giants	31-16
1960	PHILADELPHIA EAGLES	Green Bay Packers	17-13
1961	GREEN BAY PACKERS	New York Giants	37-0
1962	Green Bay Packers	NEW YORK GIANTS	16-7
1963	CHICAGO BEARS	New York Giants	14-0
1964	CLEVELAND BROWNS	Baltimore Colts	27-0
1965	GREEN BAY PACKERS	Cleveland Browns	23-12
1966	Green Bay Packers	DALLAS COWBOYS	34-27
1967	GREEN BAY PACKERS	Dallas Cowboys	21-17
1968	Baltimore Colts	CLEVELAND BROWNS	34-0
1969	MINNESOTA VIKINGS	Cleveland Browns	27-7

HOME TEAM IN CAPS
* Game played in New York

HISTORY ■ LEAGUE CHAMPIONSHIPS

NATIONAL FOOTBALL CONFERENCE

YEAR	CONFERENCE CHAMPION	RUNNER-UP	SCORE
1970	Dallas Cowboys	SAN FRANCISCO 49ERS	17-10
1971	DALLAS COWBOYS	San Francisco 49ers	14-3
1972	WASHINGTON REDSKINS	Dallas Cowboys	26-3
1973	Minnesota Vikings	DALLAS COWBOYS	27-10
1974	MINNESOTA VIKINGS	Los Angeles Rams	14-10
1975	Dallas Cowboys	LOS ANGELES RAMS	37-7
1976	MINNESOTA VIKINGS	Los Angeles Rams	24-13
1977	DALLAS COWBOYS	Minnesota Vikings	23-6
1978	Dallas Cowboys	LOS ANGELES RAMS	28-0
1979	Los Angeles Rams	TAMPA BAY BUCCANEERS	9-0
1980	PHILADELPHIA EAGLES	Dallas Cowboys	20-7
1981	SAN FRANCISCO 49ERS	Dallas Cowboys	28-27
1982	WASHINGTON REDSKINS	Dallas Cowboys	31-17
1983	WASHINGTON REDSKINS	San Francisco 49ers	24-21
1984	SAN FRANCISCO 49ERS	Chicago Bears	23-0
1985	CHICAGO BEARS	Los Angeles Rams	24-0
1986	NEW YORK GIANTS	Washington Redskins	17-0
1987	WASHINGTON REDSKINS	Minnesota Vikings	17-10
1988	San Francisco 49ers	CHICAGO BEARS	28-3
1989	SAN FRANCISCO 49ERS	Los Angeles Rams	30-3
1990	New York Giants	SAN FRANCISCO 49ERS	15-13
1991	WASHINGTON REDSKINS	Detroit Lions	41-10
1992	Dallas Cowboys	SAN FRANCISCO 49ERS	30-20
1993	DALLAS COWBOYS	San Francisco 49ers	38-21

AMERICAN FOOTBALL LEAGUE

YEAR	LEAGUE CHAMPION	RUNNER-UP	SCORE
1960	HOUSTON OILERS	Los Angeles Chargers	24-16
1961	Houston Oilers	SAN DIEGO CHARGERS	10-3
1962	Dallas Texans	HOUSTON OILERS	20-17, OT
1963	SAN DIEGO CHARGERS	Boston Patriots	51-10
1964	BUFFALO BILLS	San Diego Chargers	20-7
1965	Buffalo Bills	SAN DIEGO CHARGERS	23-0
1966	Kansas City Chiefs	BUFFALO BILLS	31-7
1967	OAKLAND RAIDERS	Houston Oilers	40-7
1968	NEW YORK JETS	Oakland Raiders	27-23
1969	Kansas City Chiefs	OAKLAND RAIDERS	17-7

AMERICAN FOOTBALL CONFERENCE

YEAR	CONFERENCE CHAMPION	RUNNER-UP	SCORE
1970	BALTIMORE COLTS	Oakland Raiders	27-17
1971	MIAMI DOLPHINS	Baltimore Colts	21-0
1972	Miami Dolphins	PITTSBURGH STEELERS	21-17
1973	MIAMI DOLPHINS	Oakland Raiders	27-10
1974	Pittsburgh Steelers	OAKLAND RAIDERS	24-13
1975	PITTSBURGH STEELERS	Oakland Raiders	16-10
1976	OAKLAND RAIDERS	Pittsburgh Steelers	24-7
1977	DENVER BRONCOS	Oakland Raiders	20-17
1978	PITTSBURGH STEELERS	Houston Oilers	34-5
1979	PITTSBURGH STEELERS	Houston Oilers	27-13
1980	Oakland Raiders	SAN DIEGO CHARGERS	34-27
1981	CINCINNATI BENGALS	San Diego Chargers	27-7
1982	MIAMI DOLPHINS	New York Jets	14-0
1983	LOS ANGELES RAIDERS	Seattle Seahawks	30-14
1984	MIAMI DOLPHINS	Pittsburgh Steelers	45-28
1985	New England Patriots	MIAMI DOLPHINS	31-14
1986	Denver Broncos	CLEVELAND BROWNS	23-20, OT
1987	DENVER BRONCOS	Cleveland Browns	38-33
1988	CINCINNATI BENGALS	Buffalo Bills	21-10
1989	DENVER BRONCOS	Cleveland Browns	37-21
1990	BUFFALO BILLS	Los Angeles Raiders	51-3
1991	BUFFALO BILLS	Denver Broncos	10-7
1992	Buffalo Bills	MIAMI DOLPHINS	29-10
1993	BUFFALO BILLS	Kansas City Chiefs	30-13

HOME TEAM IN CAPS

PRO FOOTBALL WEEKLY 1994 ALMANAC

HISTORY: SUPER BOWL SUMMARIES

SUPER BOWL I
Los Angeles, Jan. 15, 1967
Kansas City (AFL)   0 10 0 0 — 10
Green Bay (NFL)   7   7 14 7 — 35
Scoring:
   Green Bay: McGee, 37 pass from Starr (Chandler kick)
   Kansas City: McClinton, 7 pass from Dawson (Mercer kick)
   Green Bay: Taylor, 14 run (Chandler kick)
   Kansas City: Mercer, 31 field goal
   Green Bay: Pitts, 5 run (Chandler kick)
   Green Bay: McGee, 13 pass from Starr (Chandler kick)
   Green Bay: Pitts, 1 run (Chandler kick)
Attendance: 61,946
Most Valuable Player: QB Bart Starr, Green Bay

SUPER BOWL II
Miami, Jan. 14, 1968
Green Bay (NFL)   3 13 10 7 — 33
Oakland (AFL)   0   7   0 7 — 14
Scoring:
   Green Bay: Chandler, 39 field goal
   Green Bay: Chandler, 20 field goal
   Green Bay: Dowler, 62 pass from Starr (Chandler kick)
   Oakland: Miller, 23 pass from Lamonica (Blanda kick)
   Green Bay: Chandler, 43 field goal
   Green Bay: Anderson, 2 run (Chandler kick)
   Green Bay: Chandler, 31 field goal
   Green Bay: Adderley, 60 interception return (Chandler kick)
   Oakland: Miller, 23 pass from Lamonica (Blanda kick)
Attendance: 75,546
Most Valuable Player: QB Bart Starr, Green Bay

SUPER BOWL III
Miami, Jan. 12, 1969
N.Y. Jets (AFL)   0 7 6 3 — 16
Baltimore (NFL) 0 0 0 7 — 7
Scoring:
   N.Y. Jets: Snell, 4 run (Turner kick)
   N.Y. Jets: Turner, 32 field goal
   N.Y. Jets: Turner, 30 field goal
   N.Y. Jets: Turner, 9 field goal
   Baltimore: Hill, 1 run (Michaels kick)
Attendance: 75,389
Most Valuable Player: QB Joe Namath, N.Y. Jets

SUPER BOWL IV
New Orleans, Jan. 11, 1970
Minnesota (NFL)   0   0 7 0 — 7
Kansas City (AFL) 3 13 7 0 — 23
Scoring:
   Kansas City: Stenerud, 48 field goal
   Kansas City: Stenerud, 32 field goal
   Kansas City: Stenerud, 25 field goal
   Kansas City: Garrett, 5 run (Stenerud kick)
   Minnesota: Osborn, 4 run (Cox kick)
   Kansas City: Taylor, 46 pass from Dawson (Stenerud kick)
Attendance: 80,562
Most Valuable Player: QB Len Dawson, Kansas City

SUPER BOWL V
Miami, Jan. 17, 1971
Baltimore   0   6 0 10 — 16
Dallas   3 10 0   0 — 13
Scoring:
   Dallas: Clark, 14 field goal
   Dallas: Clark, 30 field goal
   Baltimore: Mackey, 75 pass from Unitas (kick blocked)
   Dallas: Thomas, 7 pass from Morton (Clark kick)
   Baltimore: Nowatzke, 2 run (O'Brien kick)
   Baltimore: O'Brien, 32 field goal
Attendance: 79,204
Most Valuable Player: LB Chuck Howley, Dallas

SUPER BOWL VI
New Orleans, Jan. 16, 1972
Dallas   3 7 7 7 — 24
Miami   0 3 0 0 — 3
Scoring:
   Dallas: Clark, 9 field goal
   Dallas: Alworth, 7 pass from Staubach (Clark kick)
   Miami: Yepremian, 31 field goal
   Dallas: D. Thomas, 3 run (Clark kick)
   Dallas: Ditka, 7 pass from Staubach (Clark kick)
Attendance: 81,023
Most Valuable Player: QB Roger Staubach, Dallas

SUPER BOWL VII
Los Angeles, Jan. 14, 1973
Miami   7 7 0 0 — 14
Washington 0 0 0 7 — 7
Scoring:
   Miami: Twilley, 28 pass from Griese (Yepremian kick)
   Miami: Kiick, 1 run (Yepremian kick)
   Washington: Bass, 49 fumble recovery (Knight kick)
Attendance: 90,182
Most Valuable Player: S Jake Scott, Miami

SUPER BOWL VIII
Houston, Jan. 13, 1974
Minnesota   0 0 7 0 — 7
Miami   14 3 7 0 — 24
Scoring:
   Miami: Csonka, 5 run (Yepremian kick)
   Miami: Kiick, 1 run (Yepremian kick)
   Miami: Yepremian, 28 field goal
   Miami: Csonka, 2 run (Yepremian kick)
   Minnesota: Tarkenton, 4 run (Cox kick)
Attendance: 71,882
Most Valuable Player: RB Larry Csonka, Miami

HISTORY ■ SUPER BOWLS

SUPER BOWL IX
New Orleans, Jan. 12, 1975

| Pittsburgh | 0 | 2 | 7 | 7 | — | 16 |
| Minnesota | 0 | 0 | 0 | 6 | — | 6 |

Scoring:
  Pittsburgh: Safety, White downed Tarkenton in endzone
  Pittsburgh: Harris, 9 run (Gerela kick)
  Minnesota: T. Brown, recovered blocked punt in endzone (kick failed)
  Pittsburgh: L. Brown, 4 pass from Bradshaw (Gerela kick)
Attendance: 80,997
Most Valuable Player: RB Franco Harris, Pittsburgh

SUPER BOWL X
Miami, Jan. 18, 1976

| Dallas | 7 | 3 | 0 | 7 | — | 17 |
| Pittsburgh | 7 | 0 | 0 | 14 | — | 21 |

Scoring:
  Dallas: D. Pearson, 29 pass from Staubach (Fritsch kick)
  Pittsburgh: Grossman, 7 pass from Bradshaw (Gerela kick)
  Dallas: Fritsch, 36 field goal
  Pittsburgh: Safety, Harrison blocked Hoopes' punt through endzone
  Pittsburgh: Gerela, 36 field goal
  Pittsburgh: Gerela, 18 field goal
  Pittsburgh: Swann, 64 pass from Bradshaw (kick failed)
  Dallas: P. Howard, 34 pass from Staubach (Fritsch kick)
Attendance: 80,187
Most Valuable Player: WR Lynn Swann, Pittsburgh

SUPER BOWL XI
Pasadena, Calif., Jan. 20, 1977

| Oakland | 0 | 16 | 3 | 13 | — | 32 |
| Minnesota | 0 | 0 | 7 | 7 | — | 14 |

Scoring:
  Oakland: Mann, 24 field goal
  Oakland: Casper, 1 pass from Stabler (Mann kick)
  Oakland: Banaszak, 1 run (kick failed)
  Oakland: Mann, 40 field goal
  Minnesota: S. White, 8 pass from Tarkenton (Cox kick)
  Oakland: Banaszak, 2 run (Mann kick)
  Oakland: Brown, 75 interception return (kick failed)
  Minnesota: Voigt, 13 pass from Lee (Cox kick)
Attendance: 103,438
Most Valuable Player: WR Fred Biletnikoff, Oakland

SUPER BOWL XII
New Orleans, Jan. 15, 1978

| Dallas | 10 | 3 | 7 | 7 | — | 27 |
| Denver | 0 | 0 | 10 | 0 | — | 10 |

Scoring:
  Dallas: Dorsett, 3 run (Herrera kick)
  Dallas: Herrera, 35 field goal
  Dallas: Herrera, 43 field goal
  Denver: Turner, 47 field goal
  Dallas: Johnson, 45 pass from Staubach (Herrera kick)
  Denver: Lytle, 1 run (Turner kick)
  Dallas: Richards, 29 pass from Newhouse (Herrera kick)
Attendance: 75,583
Most Valuable Player: DT Randy White and DE Harvey Martin, Dallas (tie)

SUPER BOWL XIII
Miami, Jan. 21, 1979

| Pittsburgh | 7 | 14 | 0 | 14 | — | 35 |
| Dallas | 7 | 7 | 3 | 14 | — | 31 |

Scoring:
  Pittsburgh: Stallworth, 28 pass from Bradshaw (Gerela kick)
  Dallas: Hill, 39 pass from Staubach (Septien kick)
  Dallas: Hegman, 37 fumble recovery return (Septien kick)
  Pittsburgh: Stallworth, 75 pass from Bradshaw (Gerela kick)
  Pittsburgh: Bleier, 7 pass from Bradshaw (Gerela kick)
  Dallas: Septien, 27 field goal
  Pittsburgh: Harris, 22 run (Gerela kick)
  Pittsburgh: Swann, 18 pass from Bradshaw (Gerela kick)
  Dallas: DuPree, 7 pass from Staubach (Septien kick)
  Dallas: B. Johnson, 4 pass from Staubach (Septien kick)
Attendance: 79,484
Most Valuable Player: QB Terry Bradshaw, Pittsburgh

SUPER BOWL XIV
Pasadena, Calif., Jan. 20, 1980

| Los Angeles | 7 | 6 | 6 | 0 | — | 19 |
| Pittsburgh | 3 | 7 | 7 | 14 | — | 31 |

Scoring:
  Pittsburgh: Bahr, 41 field goal
  Los Angeles: Bryant, 1 run (Corral kick)
  Pittsburgh: Harris, 1 run (Bahr kick)
  Los Angeles: Corral, 31 field goal
  Los Angeles: Corral, 45 field goal
  Pittsburgh: Swann, 47 pass from Bradshaw (Bahr kick)
  Los Angeles: Smith, 24 pass from McCutcheon (kick failed)
  Pittsburgh: Stallworth, 73 pass from Bradshaw (Bahr kick)
  Pittsburgh: Harris, 1 run (Bahr kick)
Attendance: 103,985
Most Valuable Player: QB Terry Bradshaw, Pittsburgh

SUPER BOWL XV
New Orleans, Jan. 25, 1981

| Oakland | 14 | 0 | 10 | 3 | — | 27 |
| Philadelphia | 0 | 3 | 0 | 7 | — | 10 |

Scoring:
  Oakland: Branch, 2 pass from Plunkett (Bahr kick)
  Oakland: King, 80 pass from Plunkett (Bahr kick)
  Philadelphia: Franklin, 30 field goal
  Oakland: Branch, 29 pass from Plunkett (Bahr kick)
  Oakland: Bahr, 46 field goal
  Philadelphia: Krepfle, 8 pass from Jaworski (Franklin kick)
  Oakland: Bahr, 35 field goal
Attendance: 76,135
Most Valuable Player: QB Jim Plunkett, Oakland

SUPER BOWL XVI
Pontiac, Mich., Jan. 24, 1982

| San Francisco | 7 | 13 | 0 | 6 | — | 26 |
| Cincinnati | 0 | 0 | 7 | 14 | — | 21 |

Scoring:
   San Francisco: Montana, 1 run (Wersching kick)
   San Francisco: Cooper, 11 pass from Montana (Wersching kick)
   San Francisco: Wersching, 22 field goal
   San Francisco: Wersching, 26 field goal
   Cincinnati: Anderson, 5 run (Breech kick)
   Cincinnati: Ross, 4 pass from Anderson (Breech kick)
   San Francisco: Wersching, 40 field goal
   San Francisco: Wersching, 23 field goal
   Cincinnati: Ross, 3 pass from Anderson (Breech kick)
Attendance: 81,270
Most Valuable Player: QB Joe Montana, San Francisco

SUPER BOWL XVII
Pasadena, Calif., Jan. 30, 1983

| Miami | 7 | 10 | 0 | 0 | — | 17 |
| Washington | 0 | 10 | 3 | 14 | — | 27 |

Scoring:
   Miami: Cefalo, 76 pass from Woodley (von Schamann kick)
   Washington: Moseley, 31 field goal
   Miami: von Schamann, 20 field goal
   Washington: Garrett, 4 pass from Theismann (Moseley kick)
   Miami: Walker, 98 kickoff return (von Schamann kick)
   Washington: Moseley, 20 field goal
   Washington: Riggins, 43 run (Moseley kick)
   Washington: Brown, 6 pass from Theismann (Moseley kick)
Attendance: 103,667
Most Valuable Player: RB John Riggins, Washington

SUPER BOWL XVIII
Tampa, Fla., Jan. 22, 1984

| Washington | 0 | 3 | 6 | 0 | — | 9 |
| L.A. Raiders | 7 | 14 | 14 | 3 | — | 38 |

Scoring:
   L.A. Raiders: Jensen, recovered blocked punt in endzone (Bahr kick)
   L.A. Raiders: Branch, 12 pass from Plunkett (Bahr kick)
   Washington: Moseley, 24 field goal
   L.A. Raiders: Squirek, 5 interception return (Bahr kick)
   Washington: Riggins, 1 run (kick blocked)
   L.A. Raiders: Allen, 5 run (Bahr kick)
   L.A. Raiders: Allen, 74 run (Bahr kick)
   L.A. Raiders: Bahr, 21 field goal
Attendance: 72,920
Most Valuable Player: RB Marcus Allen, L.A. Raiders

SUPER BOWL XIX
Stanford, Calif., Jan. 20, 1985

| Miami | 10 | 6 | 0 | 0 | — | 16 |
| San Francisco | 7 | 21 | 10 | 0 | — | 38 |

Scoring:
   Miami: von Schamann, 37 field goal
   San Francisco: Monroe, 33 pass from Montana (Wersching kick)
   Miami: D. Johnson, 2 pass from Mariona (von Schamann kick)
   San Francisco: Craig, 8 pass from Montana (Wersching kick)
   San Francisco: Montana, 6 run (Wersching kick)
   San Francisco: Craig, 2 run (Wersching kick)
   Miami: von Schamann, 31 field goal
   Miami: von Schamann, 30 field goal
   San Francisco: Wersching, 27 field goal
   San Francisco: Craig, 16 pass from Montana (Wersching kick)
Attendance: 84,059
Most Valuable Player: QB Joe Montana, San Francisco

SUPER BOWL XX
New Orleans, Jan. 26, 1986

| Chicago | 13 | 10 | 21 | 2 | — | 46 |
| New England | 3 | 0 | 0 | 7 | — | 10 |

Scoring:
   New England: Franklin, 36 field goal
   Chicago: Butler, 28 field goal
   Chicago: Butler, 24 field goal
   Chicago: Suhey, 11 run (Butler kick)
   Chicago: McMahon, 2 run (Butler kick)
   Chicago: Butler, 24 field goal
   Chicago: Phillips, 28 interception return (Butler kick)
   Chicago: Perry, 1 run (Butler kick)
   New England: Fryar, 8 pass from Grogan (Franklin kick)
   Chicago: Safety, Waechter tackled Grogan in endzone
Attendance: 73,818
Most Valuable Player: DE Richard Dent, Chicago

SUPER BOWL XXI
Pasadena, Calif., Jan. 25, 1987

| Denver | 10 | 0 | 0 | 10 | — | 20 |
| N.Y. Giants | 7 | 2 | 17 | 13 | — | 39 |

Scoring:
   Denver: Karlis, 48 field goal
   N.Y. Giants: Mowatt, 6 pass from Simms (Allegre kick)
   Denver: Elway, 4 run (Karlis kick)
   N.Y. Giants: Safety, Martin tackled Elway in endzone
   N.Y. Giants: Bavaro, 13 pass from Simms (Allegre kick)
   N.Y. Giants: Allegre, 21 field goal
   N.Y. Giants: Morris, 1 run (Allegre kick)
   N.Y. Giants: McConkey, 6 pass from Simms (Allegre kick)
   Denver: Karlis, 28 field goal
   N.Y. Giants: Anderson, 2 run (kick failed)
   Denver: V. Johnson, 47 pass from Elway (Karlis kick)
Attendance: 73,818
Most Valuable Player: QB Phil Simms, N.Y. Giants

SUPER BOWL XXII
San Diego, Jan. 31, 1988

| Washington | 0 | 35 | 0 | 7 | — | 42 |
| Denver | 10 | 0 | 0 | 0 | — | 10 |

Scoring:
   Denver: Nattiel, 56 pass from Elway (Karlis kick)
   Denver: Karlis, 24 field goal

Washington: Sanders, 80 pass from Williams (Haji-Sheikh kick)
Washington: Clark, 27 pass from Williams (Haji-Sheikh kick)
Washington: Smith, 58 run (Haji-Sheikh kick)
Washington: Sanders, 50 pass from Williams (Haji-Sheikh kick)
Washington: Didier, 8 pass from Williams (Haji-Sheikh kick)
Washington: Smith, 4 run (Haji-Sheikh kick)
Attendance: 73,302
Most Valuable Player: QB Doug Williams, Washington

SUPER BOWL XXIII
Miami, Jan. 22, 1989

Cincinnati	0	3	10	3	—	16
San Francisco	3	0	3	14	—	20

Scoring:
San Francisco: Cofer, 41 field goal
Cincinnati: Breech, 34 field goal
Cincinnati: Breech, 43 field goal
San Francisco: Cofer, 32 field goal
Cincinnati: Jennings, 93 kickoff return (Breech kick)
San Francisco: Rice, 14 pass from Montana (Cofer kick)
Cincinnati: Breech, 40 field goal
San Francisco: Taylor, 10 pass from Montana (Cofer kick)
Attendance: 75,129
Most Valuable Player: WR Jerry Rice, San Francisco

SUPER BOWL XXIV
New Orleans, Jan. 28, 1990

San Francisco	13	14	14	14	—	55
Denver	3	0	7	0	—	10

Scoring:
San Francisco: Rice, 20 pass from Montana (Cofer kick)
Denver: Treadwell, 42 field goal
San Francisco: Jones, 7 pass from Montana (kick failed)
San Francisco: Rathman, 1 run (Cofer kick)
San Francisco: Rice, 38 pass from Montana (Cofer kick)
San Francisco: Rice, 28 pass from Montana (Cofer kick)
San Francisco: Taylor, 35 pass from Montana (Cofer kick)
Denver: Elway, 3 run (Treadwell kick)
San Francisco: Rathman, 3 run (Cofer kick)
San Francisco: Craig, 1 run (Cofer kick)
Attendance: 72,919
Most Valuable Player: QB Joe Montana, San Francisco

SUPER BOWL XXV
Tampa, Fla., Jan. 27, 1991

Buffalo	3	9	0	7	—	19
N.Y. Giants	3	7	7	3	—	20

Scoring:
N.Y. Giants: Bahr, 28 field goal
Buffalo: Norwood, 23 field goal
Buffalo: D. Smith, 1 run (Norwood kick)
Buffalo: Safety, B. Smith tackled Hostetler in endzone
N.Y. Giants: Baker, 14 pass from Hostetler (Bahr kick)
N.Y. Giants: Anderson, 1 run (Bahr kick)

HISTORY ■ SUPER BOWLS

Buffalo: Thomas, 31 run (Norwood kick)
N.Y. Giants: Bahr, 21 field goal
Attendance: 73,813
Most Valuable Player: RB Ottis Anderson, N.Y. Giants

SUPER BOWL XXVI
Minneapolis, Jan. 26, 1992

Washington	0	17	14	6	—	37
Buffalo	0	0	10	14	—	24

Scoring:
Washington: Lohmiller, 34 field goal
Washington: Byner, 10 pass from Rypien (Lohmiller kick)
Washington: Riggs, 1 run (Lohmiller kick)
Washington: Riggs, 2 run (Lohmiller kick)
Buffalo: Norwood, 21 field goal
Buffalo: Thomas, 1 run (Norwood kick)
Washington: Clark, 30 pass from Rypien (Lohmiller kick)
Washington: Lohmiller, 25 field goal
Washington: Lohmiller, 39 field goal
Buffalo: Metzelaars, 2 pass from Kelly (Norwood kick)
Buffalo: Beebe, 4 pass from Kelly (Norwood kick)
Attendance: 63,130
Most Valuable Player: QB Mark Rypien, Washington

SUPER BOWL XXVII
Pasadena, Calif., Jan. 31, 1993

Buffalo	7	3	7	0	—	17
Dallas	14	14	3	21	—	52

Scoring:
Buffalo: Thomas, 2 run (Christie kick)
Dallas: Novacek, 23 pass from Aikman (Elliott kick)
Dallas: J. Jones, 2 fumble recovery return (Elliott kick)
Buffalo: Christie, 21 field goal
Dallas: Irvin, 19 pass from Aikman (Elliott kick)
Dallas: Irvin, 18 pass from Aikman (Elliott kick)
Dallas: Elliott, 20 field goal
Buffalo: Beebe, 40 pass from Aikman (Christie kick)
Dallas: Harper, 45 pass from Aikman (Elliott kick)
Dallas: E. Smith, 10 run (Elliott kick)
Dallas: Norton, 9 fumble recovery return (Elliott kick)
Attendance: 98,374
Most Valuable Player: QB Troy Aikman, Dallas

SUPER BOWL XXVIII
Atlanta, Jan. 30, 1994

Dallas	6	0	14	10	—	30
Buffalo	3	10	0	0	—	13

Scoring:
Dallas: Murray, 41 field goal
Buffalo: Christie, 54 field goal
Dallas: Murray, 24 field goal
Buffalo: Thomas, 4 run (Christie kick)
Buffalo: Christie, 28 field goal
Dallas: Washington, 46 fumble recovery return (Murray kick)
Dallas: E. Smith, 15 run (Murray kick)
Dallas: E. Smith, 1 run (Murray kick)
Dallas: Murray, 20 field goal
Attendance: 72,817
Most Valuable Player: RB Emmitt Smith, Dallas

HISTORICAL HIGHLIGHTS

In 1994 the National Football League celebrates its 75th anniversary. Started in 1920 as the American Professional Football Association, it has never missed a season since, despite such obstacles as the Great Depression and World War II.

The league began with teams from the mining and mill towns of Ohio and Pennsylvania, along with a few from other Midwestern states. There are only two charter members still playing — the Bears, who were known as the Staleys in 1920 and were located in Decatur, Ill.; and the Cardinals, who were from Chicago then.

But, along the way, other teams from the big cities joined up, and another league, the American Football League, rose to challenge, and succeeded, forcing a merger that gave us the 28-team (and soon-to-be 30-team) National Football League of today.

Here is how it all came about.

1920 In Canton, Ohio, at a meeting in Ralph Hay's Hupmobile showroom, representatives from 10 cities meet to organize a professional football league. The result is the American Professional Football Association. Jim Thorpe, player-coach of the Canton Bulldogs, is named the league's first president.

1921 Joe Carr, manager of the Columbus (Ohio) Panhandles, is chosen to replace Thorpe as president of the league. ... The Green Bay Packers, managed and coached by their tailback, Curly Lambeau, join the league. ... The Decatur Staleys, run by George Halas and Dutch Sternaman, co-owners, co-coaches, and end and halfback, respectively, move to Chicago but do not change their name to the Bears until the following year.

1922 The APFA changes its name to the National Football League.

1925 In New York, Tim Mara purchases an NFL franchise and names his team the Giants. ... At the end of the season, the legendary Red Grange of the University of Illinois joins the Bears, and the team sets out on a cross-country barnstorming tour that draws hundreds of thousands of fans. It proves to be the first major step in popularizing the sport of professional football in America.

1926 The first American Football League is formed by C. C. Pyle, agent for Red Grange, when they cannot reach agreement with the Bears for Grange's services in the '26 season. Grange plays for the New York franchise, but the new league lasts only one season. ... Paddy Driscoll, tailback of the Chicago Bears, sets an NFL record when he scores 89 points in one season, a record that will stand for 15 years.

1927 The NFL, struggling financially, drops from a 22-team league to 12 teams.

1929 The NFL decides to increase the number of officials in a game to four, adding a "field judge" to the corps that previously consisted of referee, umpire and head linesman. ... Ernie Nevers of the Chicago Cardinals scores 40 points (six touchdowns and four extra points) in a game against the Chicago Bears, a record that has never been equaled. Nevers also sets a record with 12 rushing touchdowns, one that will stand until 1945. ... Benny Friedman of the Giants sets another record by throwing 19 touchdown passes, a mark that will last into the 1940's.

1930 The Portsmouth (Ohio) Spartans join the league, a franchise that later would be moved to Detroit in 1934 and renamed the Lions.

1931 The Green Bay Packers win their third consecutive NFL title, a feat that would not be accomplished again until the Packers repeat in the mid-1960's.

1932 Due to the Depression, the NFL is reduced to eight teams, the fewest ever in league history. ... A franchise for Boston is awarded to a syndicate headed by George Preston Marshall, and he names the team the Braves but changes it the following year to the Redskins. ... An unofficial championship game is played between the Bears (6-1-6) and the Spartans (6-1-4) indoors at the Chicago Stadium on an 80-yard field, which the Bears win 9-0.

1933 Three new franchises open. In Philadelphia, the Eagles are launched by joint owners Bert Bell and Lud Wray. In Pittsburgh, Art Rooney takes ownership of the Pirates, the name the team would play under until 1941, when it would be changed to Steelers. For the second time, Cincinnati fielded a team, this time called the Reds. ... At the urging of Bear owner George Halas and Redskin owner George Preston Marshall, the league is divided into two divisions, the East and the West, with a championship game between the two slated for the end of the season. ... The NFL adopts sweeping rule changes. Among them: The goalposts are moved from the endlines to the goallines; hashmarks are introduced and located 10 yards inbounds from each sideline; and passing from anywhere behind the line of scrimmage is made legal (previously a pass had to be thrown from at least five yards behind the line of scrimmage). ... Individual and team statistics are kept officially by the league for the first time.

1934 The first College All-Star Game is held at Soldier Field between the previous year's NFL champion (the Bears in 1933) and a team composed of the nation's top college players, a tradition that would start each preseason through 1976. The first game ends in a 0-0 tie. ... Beattie Feathers, a rookie halfback with the Bears, becomes the first player ever to rush for more than 1,000 yards in a season (1,004). His average of 9.9 yards per carry remains the all-time NFL high. ... Bear PK Jack Manders becomes the first player to kick more than 30 extra points in a season (31), a record that will not be surpassed for a decade. ... The Bears and the Giants play for the NFL title on an ice-covered field at the Polo Grounds, in what is to become the

HISTORY ■ HIGHLIGHTS

famous "Sneakers Championship" when the New Yorkers don basketball shoes in the second half and score 27 unanswered points for a come-from-behind, 30-13 win.

1936 The first draft of college players is held by the NFL. The first selection is Jay Berwanger, a halfback and Heisman Trophy winner out of the University of Chicago, by the Eagles, but he chooses not to play professional football. ... The passing combination of Green Bay's Arnie Herber and Don Hutson sets three NFL records. Herber becomes the first player to pass for more than 1,000 yards (1,239), and Hutson sets marks with 34 receptions for 526 yards.

1937 Cleveland is granted a franchise, and the team is named the Rams. ... George Preston Marshall moves his Redskins from Boston to Washington, D.C.

1938 The league institutes a 15-yard penalty for roughing the passer. ... After the season (Jan. 15, 1939), the first Pro Bowl game is played in Los Angeles, where the league-champion Giants defeat a team of NFL all-stars 13-10.

1939 Joe Carr, league president since 1921, dies and is replaced by Carl Storck. ... The first NFL game to be televised is played between the Brooklyn Dodgers and the Philadelphia Eagles at Ebbets Field; the Dodgers win 23-14. ... The Rams' Parker Hall becomes the first player to complete more than 100 passes in a season (106). ... For the first time in history, total gate attendance exceeds one million.

1940 Redskin QB Sammy Baugh becomes the first and only player in NFL history to average more than 50 yards on punts (51.4 on 35 punts). ... Eagle Don Looney is the first to catch more than 50 passes in a season (58). ... For the first time, an NFL game is broadcast on network radio — the NFL championship game between the Bears and the Redskins — with 120 stations tuned in and Red Barber announcing. ... In the most lopsided game in NFL regular-season or postseason history, the Bears defeat the Redskins 73-0 in Washington.

1941 Elmer Layden, one of Notre Dame's fabled Four Horsemen, takes over the league presidency from Carl Storck. ... The first NFL divisional playoff game is held when the Bears and Packers end the season with records of 10-1. The Bears take the NFL West crown with a 33-14 win.

1942 With Cecil Isbell passing and Don Hutson receiving, the two set seven NFL records for Green Bay. Isbell becomes the first to pass for more than 2,000 yards (2,021), and he adds marks of 146 completions and 24 touchdown passes. Hutson is the first to score more than 100 points in a season (138) and gain more than 1,000 yards on pass receptions (1,211). He also set records with 74 catches and 17 TD receptions. Hutson also set another NFL mark with 33 extra points.

1943 Because of the war, the Philadelphia and Pittsburgh franchises are allowed to merge, resulting in the Phil-Pitt Steagles, and the Cleveland Rams are allowed to suspend operations for one year. ... For the first time, the league allows free substitution, and platooning is initiated. ... Bear QB Sid Luckman sets a record by throwing seven touchdown passes against the Giants at the Polo

Clarke Hinkle led Green Bay to two titles in the 1930's

Grounds, a record that has since been equaled but never surpassed. Luckman also sets two other NFL marks by gaining 2,194 yards passing and throwing 28 TD passes. ... Redskin QB Sammy Baugh sets a league record by intercepting 11 passes while playing defensive back and also leads the league in pass completions (133) and punting (45.9-yard average).

1944 The Phil-Pitt merger ends, but the Steelers are allowed to merge with the Chicago Cardinals to form a team called Card-Pitt.

1946 The Rams are allowed to move the franchise from Cleveland to Los Angeles. ... The All-America Football Conference (AAFC) is founded by *Chicago Tribune* sports columnist Arch Ward, with franchises in eight cities to compete with the NFL. ... Bert Bell replaces Elmer Layden as commissioner of the NFL. ... For the first time since the early 1930's, black players are allowed to play in the NFL (and the new AAFC).

1947 New items: The bonus draft pick, selected by lottery drawing, is instituted; the roster limit is increased to 35; a sudden-death overtime for championship games is adopted; and a fifth official, the back judge, is added. ... Washington QB Sammy Baugh becomes the first player to complete more than 200 passes in a season (210). His 2,938 yards passing is another NFL standard that will last until 1960.

1948 Pat Harder of the Chicago Cardinals becomes the first player to kick more than 50 extra points in a season (53, 14 more than the previous record).

1949 For the first time in league history, two players rush for more then 1,000 yards in one season — Steve Van Buren of the Eagles (1,146) and Tony Canadeo of the Packers (1,052).

1950 The AAFC shuts down, but three teams are absorbed into the NFL: the Cleveland Browns, Baltimore Colts and San Francisco 49ers. With the addition of the new teams, the league is broken into two conferences instead of two divisions, the American with six teams and the National with seven. ... The Rams become the first team to televise all their games, home and away. ... After the season (Jan. 14, 1951) the first modern-day Pro Bowl game is held in Los Angeles, pitting all-star teams from each conference against each other.

1951 Ram QB Norm Van Brocklin passes for 554 yards in a game against the New York Yanks, an NFL record that has never been surpassed. ... For the first time the NFL championship game is televised coast-to-coast. The DuMont network pays $75,000 for the rights to broadcast the Cleveland Browns' 24-17 win over the Rams. ... Cleveland's Dub Jones ties the record for touchdowns in a game when he scores six against the Bears.

1952 Dallas is awarded an NFL franchise and fields a team called the Texans, which folds before the year is over, becoming the last NFL franchise to fail. ... Ram DB Dick "Night Train" Lane intercepts 14 passes, a record that has never been equaled.

1954 The battle for players between the NFL and the Canadian Football League begins.

1955 The NFL Players Association is formed.

1956 The league decrees that it is illegal to grab an opposing player's facemask. ... A single-game record attendance is set at the Los Angeles Coliseum when 102,368 pass through the gates to watch the Rams beat the 49ers 37-24.

1958 The bonus draft choice is eliminated. ... For the first time, NFL attendance exceeds three million, and average paid attendance tops 40,000. ... Jim Brown of Cleveland becomes the first player to rush for more than 1,500 yards in a season (1,527). ... The NFL has its first sudden-death championship game, with the Colts beating the Giants 23-17.

1960 Pete Rozelle is elected commissioner of the NFL. ... The Dallas Cowboys, owned by Clint Murchison and Bedford Wynne, join the NFL. ... The Cardinals relocate from Chicago to St. Louis. ... A new American Football League, founded by Lamar Hunt of Dallas, is launched with franchises in eight cities (Boston, Buffalo, Dallas, Denver, Houston, Los Angeles, New York and Oakland). ... Packer RB-PK Paul Hornung sets a still-unequaled record by scoring 176 points in a single season. ... Colt QB Johnny Unitas and Charger QB Jack Kemp become the first players to pass for more than 3,000 yards in a season (Unitas 3,099, Kemp 3,018).

1961 A franchise is awarded to the Minnesota Vikings. ... The Los Angeles Chargers of the AFL move to San Diego. ... Houston QB George Blanda throws 36 touchdown passes, a pro football record that will not be surpassed until 1984. ... Denver WR Lionel Taylor becomes the first player to catch 100 passes in a single season. ... Charley Hennigan of the Oilers gains more yards on pass receptions (1,746) than anyone in pro football history.

1963 Lamar Hunt's Dallas Texans of the AFL move to Kansas City and change their name to the Chiefs. ... Giant QB Y.A. Tittle tosses 36 TD passes, setting an NFL record. ... The AFL New York Titans change their name to the Jets. ... Packer Paul Hornung and Lion Alex Karras are suspended for gambling. ... The Pro Football Hall of Fame is dedicated in Canton, Ohio, with 17 charter members inducted.

1964 The NFL signs a two-year, $14.1 million contract with CBS, while the AFL gets a five-year deal with NBC for $36 million. ... Pete Gogolak joins the Buffalo Bills as pro football's first soccer-style kicker.

1965 The NFL adds a sixth official, the line judge. Chicago rookie Gale Sayers sets an NFL record of 22 touchdowns in a season and ties the single-game record of six TD's.

1966 The NFL and AFL agree to merge. Regular-season games will be played within each league, but a championship game between the two, later to be known as the Super Bowl, will be held at the end of the season. ... The Atlanta Falcons join the NFL, and the Miami Dolphins are enfranchised in the AFL. ... The first NFL-AFL championship game is held at the L.A. Coliseum, where the Packers defeat the Chiefs 35-10.

1967 The NFL divides into four divisions of four teams each. ... The New Orleans Saints are the newest expansion team to join the NFL. ...Jet QB Joe Namath becomes the first player to pass for more than 4,000 yards in a season (4,007). ...St. Louis PK Jim Bakken boots an NFL-record seven field goals in a game against the Steelers.

1968 The Cincinnati Bengals become a member of the AFL. ... The Houston Oilers become the first team to play their home games in a domed stadium, when they move to the Astrodome. ... The NFL-AFL championship game is officially named the Super Bowl.

1970 The NFL and AFL are formally merged into one league with a National Football Conference and American Football Conference under the umbrella title of the National Football League. The Steelers, Colts and Browns are moved to the AFC in the new alignment. ... A new system of playoffs is inaugurated with a wild-card playoff team added from each conference. ... Monday night football comes into existence, the contract being awarded to ABC. ... New Orleans PK Tom Dempsey kicks the longest field goal in NFL history, a 63-yarder against the Lions.

1971 The Boston Patriots move to Foxboro, Mass., and change their name to New England Patriots. ... George Blanda becomes pro football's all-time leading scorer, moving ahead of the 1,349 points scored by Cleveland's Lou Groza.

1972 The hashmarks are brought in to align with the goalposts. ... DB Jack Tatum of the Raiders returns a fumble 104 yards for a touchdown, erasing the record of 98 yards held by George Halas of the Bears since 1923. ... Ten NFL running backs rush for more than 1,000 yards, then a record.

1973 A new jersey-numbering system is adopted: 1-19 for quarterbacks and specialists; 20-49 for running backs and defensive backs; 50-59 for centers and linebackers; 60-79 for offensive and defensive linemen; 80-89 for wide receivers and tight ends. ... Ram DE Fred Dryer is credited with two safeties in a game against the Packers, a record that remains unsurpassed. ... Buffalo RB O.J. Simpson becomes the first player to rush for more than 2,000 yards in a season (2,003).

1974 The World Football League is launched to compete with the NFL with a total of 12 franchises. ... The NFL adopts a slew of new rules, among them: Kickoffs are moved from the 40-yard line back to the 35, goalposts are moved from the goallines back to the endlines, a missed field goal

HISTORY ■ HIGHLIGHTS

from outside the 20-yard line is brought back to the line of scrimmage, and a sudden-death overtime period (15 minutes) is instituted for all regular-season games.

1975 The "home-field advantage" in the playoffs is introduced, allowing the teams with the best records to host postseason games. ... The World Football League goes out of business.

1976 The Seattle Seahawks and Tampa Bay Buccaneers join the NFL, enlarging the NFL to 28 teams.

1977 Chicago RB Walter Payton sets a single-game rushing record when he gains 275 yards against the Vikings, a mark that still stands. ... NFL regular-season paid attendance exceeds 11 million for the first time.

1978 The NFL extends its season to 16 games. ... The playoff system is adjusted to allow for two wild-card teams from each conference. ... A seventh official, the side judge, is added. ... Minnesota QB Fran Tarkenton becomes the first player to complete more than 300 passes in a season (345).

1979 The "in-the-grasp" rule to help protect quarterbacks is instituted, and blocking below the waist on kickoffs, punts and field-goal attempts is prohibited. ... NFL regular-season attendance reaches 13.2 million.

1980 The Los Angeles Rams move to Anaheim, Calif. ... Jet QB Richard Todd completes the most passes in a single game in league history, 42 against the 49ers. ... The Oakland Raiders are the first wild-card team to win the Super Bowl, when they defeat the Eagles 27-10.

1982 The Oakland Raiders move to Los Angeles. ... NFL players go on strike after the second game of the regular season. Two months later the season resumes. A total of nine regular-season games are played and a special playoff tournament, involving the top eight teams from each conference, is devised.

1983 George Halas, long-time owner of the NFL charter-member Bears and the last survivor of the league founding meeting in Canton, Ohio, in 1920, dies at age 88. ... RB Tony Dorsett logs the longest run from scrimmage in the history of the NFL when he races 99 yards for a touchdown against the Vikings. ... Redskin RB John Riggins records the most rushing touchdowns ever in a season with 24. ... PK Ali Haji-Sheikh kicks more field goals (35) than any player in NFL history.

1984 The Baltimore Colts move to Indianapolis. ... The 49ers become the first team to win 15 games in the regular season. ... Miami QB Dan Marino is the first (and only) player to pass for more than 5,000 yards in a season (5,084). His 48 touchdown passes are also a record that still stands. ... RB Eric Dickerson of the Rams gains more yards rushing in a season than any player in the history of the league (2,105). ... Redskin WR Art Monk catches the most passes in NFL history (106). ... Miami's Uwe von Schamann sets the NFL record for extra points in a season (66).

1985 The Bears become the second team in NFL history to win 15 regular-season games, and the first to win back-to-back shutouts in the playoffs. ... Super Bowl XX, on Jan. 26, 1986, in which the Bears post the then-largest margin of victory

Walter Payton rushed for 275 yards in a 1977 game

in Super Bowl history, 46-10, becomes the most-watched television event in history with an estimated 127 million viewers.

1986 The use of instant replay — a reviewing official in the pressbox — is introduced. ... The NFL stages its first game in Europe, when the Bears and Cowboys meet in the preseason at Wembley Stadium in London (the Bears win 17-6).

1987 The regular season is reduced to 15 games because of a 24-day players' strike, with three games being played by replacement players. ... San Francisco WR Jerry Rice sets an NFL record for touchdown receptions in a season (22).

1988 The 45-second clock, the interval between plays from the time ball is signaled dead to the snap of the succeeding play, is instituted. ... The Cardinals move from St. Louis to Phoenix.

1989 Pete Rozelle announces his retirement as NFL commissioner. Paul Tagliabue is elected to replace him. ... The NFL's Plan B system of free-agency is introduced, and 229 unconditional free-agent players sign with new teams. ... Joe Montana of the 49ers produces the highest single-season passer rating in NFL history (112.4).

1990 College juniors become eligible for the NFL draft but must renounce their college football eligibility before entering the draft. ... A new playoff format includes an additional wild-card team from each conference. ... The 16-week schedule is revised to be played over 17 weeks, giving each team a bye week. ... Kansas City LB Derrick Thomas records the most sacks in a game ever (seven) against the Seahawks.

1991 The NFL launches the World League of American Football, the first sports league to operate on a weekly basis on two separate continents.

1992 Instant replay, after six years of operation, is voted out. ... Packer WR Sterling Sharpe sets the NFL mark for pass receptions in a season (108).

1993 The NFL owners and the players' union reach an agreement that revamps the entire free-agency system. A total of 120 players — many of them big-name stars — switch teams. ... The Carolina Panthers and Jacksonville Jaguars are awarded franchises under the NFL's expansion plan. ... Don Shula surpasses George Halas, who was credited with 324 victories, as the NFL's all-time winningest head coach. ... Packer WR Sterling Sharpe breaks his NFL record for receptions in a season (112).

1994 The NFL adopts the two-point conversion option.

PRO FOOTBALL WEEKLY 1994 ALMANAC

NFL DIRECTORY

National Football League
410 Park Avenue
New York, N.Y. 10022
Phone: (212) 758-1500 / Fax: (212) 826-3454

Commissioner: Paul Tagliabue
President: Neil Austrian
Executive vice president and league counsel: Jay Moyer
Vice president of communications and government affairs: Joe Browne
Vice president of broadcasting and productions: Val Pinchbeck Jr.
Vice president-business development: Roger Goodell
Chief financial officer: Tom Spock
Treasurer: Tom Sullivan
Executive director of special events: Jim Steeg
President of NFL Enterprises: Ron Bernard
Vice president of marketing and sales-NFL Enterprises: Tola Murphy-Baran
Vice president of worldwide distribution-NFL Enterprises: Bill Moses
Executive vice president for labor relations-chairman NFLMC: Harold Henderson
Vice president-general counsel: Dennis Curran
Vice president for operations and compliance: Peter Ruocco

ADMINISTRATION
Director of administration: John Buzzeo
Comptroller: Joe Siclare

BROADCASTING
Director of broadcasting services: Dick Maxwell
Director of broadcasting research: Joe Ferreira
Assistant director of broadcasting-productions: Nancy Behar

COMMUNICATIONS
Director of communications: Greg Aiello
Director of international public relations: Pete Abitante
Director of information, AFC: Leslie Hammond
Director of information, NFC: Reggie Roberts

INFORMATION PROCESSING
Director of systems and information processing: Mary Ollveti
Manager of information systems: Laurie Levy
Manager of software, systems and networking: Joe Manto
Manager of data-center services: Dave Port

LEGAL
Counsel operations-litigation: Jodi Balsam
Counsel broadcasting-corporate: Frank Hawkins

NFL ENTERPRISES
Director of broadcasting operations and technology: Michael Schlesier
Director of marketing: Philip Summers

OFFICIATING
Director of officiating: Jerry Seeman
Assistant director of officiating: Jack Reader
Supervisor of officials: Leo Miles
Supervisor of officials: Ron DeSouza

OPERATIONS
Director of club administration: Joe Ellis
Director of game operations: Jan Van Duser
Assistant director of game operations: Tim Davey

PLAYER EMPLOYMENT
Director of player personnel: Joel Bussert
Director of player programs: Lem Burnham
Director of compliance: Bill Duffy
Director of labor operations: Peter Hadhazy
Director of labor relations: Lal Heneghan
Labor-relations counsel: Belinda Lerner
Labor-relations counsel: Rapheal Prevot
Manager, player information and computer applications: Carol Constantine
Manager, player benefits: Valerie Cross

SECURITY
Director of security: Warren Welsh
Assistant director of security: Charles Jackson Jr.

SPECIAL EVENTS
Assistant director of operations: Ann Carroll
Assistant director of event planning: Sue Robichek

MISCELLANEOUS

TIE-BREAKING PROCEDURES

TO BREAK A TIE WITHIN A DIVISION

If, at the end of the regular season, two or more clubs in the same division finish with identical won-lost percentages, the following steps will be taken until a champion is determined.

Two clubs

1. Head-to-head (best won-lost percentage between the clubs).
2. Best won-lost percentage in games played within the division.
3. Best won-lost percentage in games played within the conference.
4. Best won-lost percentage in common games, if applicable.
5. Best net points in division games.
6. Best net points in all games.
7. Strength of schedule.
8. Best net touchdowns in all games.
9. Coin toss.

Three or more clubs

(Note: If one team wins multiple-team tie-breaker to advance to the playoff round, remaining teams revert to step 1 of applicable two-club format, i.e., either in division tie-breaker or wild-card tie-breaker. If two teams in a multiple-team tie possess superior marks in a tie-breaking step, these two teams revert to top of applicable two-club format to break tie. One team advances to playoff round, while other returns to original group and step 1 of applicable tie-breaker.)

1. Head-to-head (best won-lost percentage in games among the clubs).
2. Best won-lost percentage in games played within the division.
3. Best won-lost percentage in games played within the conference.
4. Best won-lost percentage in common games.
5. Best net points in division games.
6. Best net points in all games.
7. Strength of schedule.
8. Best net touchdowns in all games.
9. Coin toss.

TO BREAK A TIE FOR THE WILD-CARD TEAM

If it is necessary to break ties to determine the three wild-card clubs from each conference, the following steps will be taken.

1. If the tied clubs are from the same division, apply division tie-breaker.

2. If the tied clubs are from different divisions, apply the following steps.

Two clubs

1. Head-to-head, if applicable.
2. Best won-lost percentage in games played within the conference.
3. Best won-lost percentage in common games, minimum of four.
4. Best average net points in conference games.
5. Best net points in all games.
6. Strength of schedule.
7. Best net touchdowns in all games.
8. Coin toss.

Three or more clubs

(Note: If two clubs remain tied after third or other clubs are eliminated, tie-breaker reverts to step 1 of applicable two-club format.)

When the first wild-card team has been identified, the procedure is repeated to name the second wild card, i.e., eliminate all but the highest-ranked club in each division prior to proceeding to step 2, and repeated a third time, if necessary, to identify the third wild card. In situations where three or more teams from the same division are involved, the original seeding of the teams remains the same for subsequent applications of the tie-breaker if the top-ranked team in that division qualifies for a wild-card berth.

1. Apply division tie-breaker to eliminate all but highest-ranked club in each division prior to proceeding to step 2. The original seeding within a division upon application of the division tie-breaker remains the same for all subsequent applications of the procedure that are necessary to identify the three wild-card participants.
2. Head-to-head sweep (applicable only if one club has defeated each of the others, or if one club has lost to each of the others).
3. Best won-lost percentage in games played within the conference.
4. Best won-lost percentage in common games, minimum of four.
5. Best average net points in conference games.
6. Best net points in all games.
7. Strength of schedule.
8. Best net touchdowns in all games.
9. Coin toss.

PRO Football WEEKLY

THE BEST COVERAGE IN THE NFL.

For 27 years, Pro Football Weekly has been the largest and most complete newsmagazine devoted exclusively to professional football in the world. Its reputation as "The Authority On Professional Football" has been hard-earned and is widely accepted among hundreds of thousands of fans, as well as players, coaches and the powers-that-be in the National Football League.

In addition to this almanac, Pro Football Weekly publishes the following:

Pro Football Weekly — "The Best Coverage in the NFL." — is the industry's leading and most authoritative provider of game previews, reviews, analysis, predictions, inside information, award-winning columns, fascinating features, investigative reporting and complete team and individual statistics available anywhere.

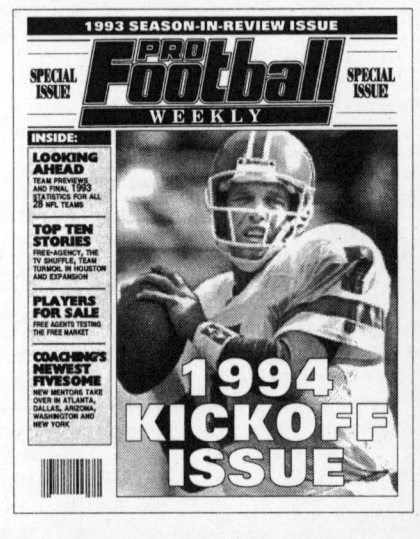

Preview '94 magazine — On sale now at newsstands across the country, this season primer for the pro football fan has team-by-team previews, playoff and Super Bowl predictions, fantasy-football specials and in-depth statistics and features. The perfect companion to the Pro Football Weekly 1994 Almanac.

Draft Preview book — The football season actually begins with the NFL draft, and this book, published annually in late March on an annual basis, contains scouting reports on the top 600 prospects, a mock draft and rankings of more than 800 players who will be eligible for the upcoming NFL college draft.

Pro Prospects Preview book — The first available guide detailing the following year's draft comes out before the start of each football season.

In addition, Pro Football Weekly has television and radio shows. "Pro Football Weekly on TV" is televised Saturdays on superstation WGN, and the radio show is syndicated in more than 200 cities across the country.

To learn more about Pro Football Weekly or to find out how to purchase these publications, call:

1-800-FOOTBALL
(1-800-366-8225)